THE
COMPLETE ENCYCLOPEDIA OF
WEAPONS
OF
WORLD WAR II

THE
COMPLETE ENCYCLOPEDIA OF
WEAPONS
OF
WORLD WAR II

General Editor
CHRIS BISHOP

PROSPERO
B·O·O·K·S
A DIVISION OF CHAPTERS INC.

Published by Prospero Books
a division of Chapters Inc.
90 Ronson Drive
Etobicoke
Ontario
Canada M9W 1C1

ISBN: 1-894102-22-3

Editorial and design by Brown Packaging Books Ltd
Bradley's Close
74-77 White Lion Street
London N1 9PF

Picture credits
TRH Pictures: 7, 9, 20, 31, 42, 52, 63, 73, 83, 93, 101, 111, 123,
136, 148, 159, 169, 179, 191, 203, 215, 225, 236, 249, 264, 275,
283, 293, 305, 318, 330, 340, 350, 361, 372, 383, 393, 404, 414,
424, 434, 443, 452, 462, 470, 478, 487, 497, 509, 519, 529, 540.

Printed in Singapore

Contents

Introduction	7
Axis Tanks	9
British and French Tanks	20
Soviet and American Tanks	31
Tank Destroyers	42
Special Purpose Tanks	52
Amphibious Vehicles	63
Allied and Axis Halftracks	73
Armoured Cars	83
Allied and Axis Trucks	93
Light Vehicles	101
Self-Propelled Guns	111
Heavy Artillery	123
Field Artillery	136
Heavy Anti-Aircraft Guns	148
Light Anti-Aircraft Guns	159
War Rockets	169
Anti-Tank Guns	179
Infantry Support Weapons	191
Infantry Anti-Tank Weapons	203
Allied and Axis Rifles	215
Allied and Axis Pistols	225
Allied and Axis Machine-Guns	236
Allied and Axis Sub-Machine Guns	249
Allied and Axis Flamethrowers	264
Allied Fighters	275
Axis Fighters	283
Heavy Bombers	293

Contents

Light and Medium Bombers	305	American Aircraft Carriers	470
Jet Aircraft	318	Allied and Axis Battleships	478
Axis Ground Attack Aircraft	330	Allied and Axis Cruisers	487
Allied Ground Attack Aircraft	340	Axis Destroyers	497
Night-Fighters	350	Escort Vessels	509
Allied and Axis Flying-Boats	361	Coastal Craft	519
Allied and Axis Seaplanes	372	Assault Ships	529
Anti-Shipping Aircraft	383	Glossary of Weapons	540
Carrier Aircraft	393		
Transport and Assault Aircraft	404		
Air-to-Ground Weapons	414		
Light Aircraft	424		
Axis Submarines	434		
Allied Submarines	443		
British Aircraft Carriers	452		
Japanese Aircraft Carriers	462		

Introduction

World War II affected virtually every corner of the globe. In the six years between 1939 and 1945, some 50 million people lost their lives, and very few who survived were not affected. It was the costliest and most widespread conflict the world has ever seen.

World War II was fought on land, sea and in the air with weapons which had first been used in the Great War of 1914–18. Ironically, an even greater conflict was to emerge from the burning embers of that "war to end all wars", and with it huge advances in weapons technology. The countries involved in World War II now had the means and the capability to fight each other in a more efficient – and more deadly – manner.

Yet only Great Britain, her Empire allies and Germany were involved during the whole period. For other nations the conflict was of a shorter duration. The USA and Japan, for example, were at war from December 1941 to August 1945 (and the USA was simultaneously at war with Germany, until Hitler's defeat in May 1945).

The situation was so complicated, the skeins of alliance and enmity so intertwined that it would take a very large chart indeed to describe them. Only one factor was more straightforward and common to all the countries involved: the nature of the weapons that the men (and sometimes women) used to fight their way to victory – or defeat.

There were differences in detail, of course: the German Panzerkampfwagen V 'Panther' tank was a very different vehicle from the American M4 Sherman, the Russian T-34, or the British Cromwell.

But essentially they were all much the same – armoured vehicles mounting powerful guns running on tracks. The small arms with which the various combatant nations equipped their armies were very different in detail too, but essentially they were all devices for launching projectiles at high speed.

In short, many would simply say that guns are guns, bombs are bombs, aircraft are aircraft, and so on. But there is certainly more to it than that, for the capacity to win or lose a war actually rested on these weapons' qualities, just as much as it did on the fighting skills of those who employed them and on the strategic sense of those who directed them in their use.

We cannot simply bundle these weapons together – not if we really want to understand why and how 20th century history unfolded the way it did.

The Complete Encyclopedia of Weapons of World War II makes a very important contribution to the subject – perhaps even a vital one – for it describes every major weapon and vehicle employed during the full period of the conflict, on land, sea and in the air, in enormous detail, both in textual and in graphic form. It also provides detailed specifications about the 'core' weapon or system and all its major variants. Thus it allows straightforward comparisons to be made accurately and effectively.

Its sheer comprehensiveness makes *The Complete Encyclopedia of Weapons of World War II* compelling reading. Clearly it will have considerable appeal to all manner of students of the period as the first – and probably the definitive – source of clear, concise information on the nature and history of different weapons, including specifications, capabilities

Introduction

and capacities, varying forms, the colour schemes in which they appeared and the manner in which they were employed.

The text and tables have been prepared by some of the foremost experts in the field, and this same team provided and approved specifications, plans and drawings and photographic reference material to assist the best graphic artists available to produce illustrations, the like of which, in terms of quality, precision and accuracy, are seldom seen outside offical circles.

The Complete Encyclopedia of Weapons of World War II covers the terrestrial equipment of all arms of service, from the infantryman's handgun, rifles and machine-guns, to the support weapons he used to take on tanks and subdue fortified defensive positions; from light armoured cars used for reconnaissance to heavy assault tanks and special-purpose armoured vehicles; from towed anti-tank guns to tank destroyers and from lightweight field artillery pieces to self-propelled guns and howitzers, not forgetting wheeled and tracked utility vehicles.

The war was also conducted at sea, and World War II saw warships of every calibre employed all over the globe, from the 70,000-tonne monster battleships to the diminutive motor gun-boats and motor torpedo-boats, and the best of these are described in detail. Pride of place, however, goes to the new breed of capital ships – the aircraft carriers, which were born in the inter-war period and which achieved maturity just as hostilities broke out. Alongside them space is also given to another new naval weapon: the submarine.

Here, too, are described the last of the old generation of capital ships – for which World War II was to be their swansong. The battleships of both sides were to become household names all over the world between 1939 and 1945, and here they are described and illustrated in full colour and in tremendous detail. Cruisers, destroyers and escorts, coastal craft

and assault ships also played vitally important parts, and they, too, are described, illustrated and documented here.

New weapons appeared throughout the war, but it was in the air that the real changes were rung. Until quite late in the 1930s, the world's air forces were equipped with biplanes with relatively low-powered engines, thus limiting their performance, endurance and load-carrying capacity. Germany, risen from the ashes of defeat in 1918 and plagued throughout the next decade by internal strife and near-revolution, was the first to recognize the potential for a new generation of all-metal aircraft, and soon produced such masterpieces as the Bf 109 interceptor/fighter, and the Dornier, Heinkel and Junkers medium bombers.

Britain followed suit, and began turning out long-range heavy bomber aircraft, such as the Lancaster, widely held to be the best of its type, while the USA – slow to get going initially – built up an aircraft industry second to none, which came to dominate the field by the end of the war, producing magnificent aircraft, such as the Mustangs and Thunderbolts, which doubled as both fighters and ground attack aircraft, and the redoubtable B-7 and B-29 Fortresses. The former USSR's powerful aviation industry also had its roots in World War II, and its products, as well as those of Japan, are also covered in great detail.

In all, *The Complete Encyclopedia of Weapons of World War II* is a unique and essential document, covering the equipment and weapons systems, which themselves dictated the nature of the most widespread, most expensive and most destructive conflict the world has ever seen. World War II quite literally altered the face of the planet and the nature of its peoples' lives, and its reverberations are still to be felt half a century later. Here, at least and at last, we have the means to understand how technological advances and fantastic leaps of imagination of this vitally important period manifested themselves in the tools with which the war was won – and lost.

Axis Tanks

By the end of World War I the tank was a familiar sight on the battlefield; it took the power of the German Blitzkrieg to convince conventional military strategists that the tank, and more importantly its method of use, can have a profound effect upon the outcome of a battle.

Although Italy and Japan produced significant numbers of tanks before and during World War II, it is the German tanks which are best known. At the outbreak of the war the Panzerkampfwagen (PzKpfw) I and PzKpfw II were the most common models, but within a few years these had been phased out of service and replaced by the PzKpfw III and PzKpfw IV. The latter had the distinction of remaining in production throughout the war. It was an excellent design that proved to be capable of being upgunned and up-armoured to meet the changing battlefield threat. The Panther and Tiger arrived on the scene towards the end of the war, but these could not be produced in anything like the required numbers as a result of shortages in materials and manpower and of the effectiveness of Allied bombing on German plants, even though many of these had been dispersed early in the war. The Panther and Tiger were rushed into production without proper trials, however, and many were lost during their initial deployments as a result of mechanical breakdown rather than direct enemy action. The Tiger was, in particular, a very heavy tank and lacked mobility on the battlefield. Its armour protection and guns

A German PzKpfw IV tank being held in reserve in anticipation of a call to action following the Allied landings at Normandy in June 1944. Note the side skirt.

were first class, and this tank proved a difficult one to destroy on both the Eastern and Western Fronts. Often four Shermans would be required to neutralize just one Tiger: two would try to draw its fire, often being knocked out in the process, while the others worked round its flanks and attacked it from its more vulnerable sides. Towards the end of World War II Germany turned its attention to producing more and more tank destroyers as by that time the German army was on the

defensive, and these vehicles were quicker, easier and cheaper to produce than tanks, such as the Panther and Tiger.

While some of the Italian tanks were fairly modern in 1939, by the early part of Italy's war they had become completely obsolete. The better armed and armoured P 40 heavy tank never entered service with the Italian army, although a few were taken over by the Germans.

Japan used tanks during the invasion of China before World

War II as well as during the Far Eastern campaigns from 1941. As few Allied AFVs were available at that time the Japanese vehicles were quite adequate, the more so as their primary role was infantry fire support rather than tank-against-tank operations.

Czech tanks are included, as many were subsequently taken over by the Germans during the invasion of France in 1940 and remained in production in Czechoslovakia after that country's occupation.

LT vz 35 light tank

In October 1934 the Czech army placed an order for two prototypes of a medium tank called the **S-11-a** (or **T-11**) which were completed in the following year. Army trials with these vehicles started in June 1935 and soon uncovered many faults as a result of the tank's rushed development. Without waiting for these faults to be corrected an order was placed for a first batch of 160 vehicles in October 1935, and the first five of these were delivered in the following year. So many faults were found with these vehicles that these were returned to Skoda for modifications. A further batch of 138 was ordered for the Czech army, which called it the **LT vz 35**, while Romania ordered 126 under the designation **R-2**. Gradually most of the faults were overcome and the vehicle gained a good reputation. The Germans took over the remaining vehicles under the designation **Panzerkampfwagen 35(t)**, and a further 219 were built specifically for the German army in the Skoda works. Such was the shortage of tanks in the German army at that time that the 6th Panzer Division was equipped with the PzKpfw 35(t) in time to take part in the invasion of France in 1940. These continued in service until 1942 when most of these were converted into other roles such as mortar tractors (German designation *Mörserzugmittel*), artillery tractors (German designation *Zugkraftwagen*) or maintenance vehicles with tank battalions. It is often not realized that Czechoslovakia was a leading exporter of armoured vehicles and artillery prime movers before World War II, with sales made to Austria, Bulgaria, Hungary, Latvia, Peru, Romania, Sweden, Switzerland and Turkey.

The hull of the LT vz 35 was of riveted construction that varied in thickness from 12 mm (0.47 in) to a maximum of 35 mm (1.38 in). The bow machine-gunner was seated at the front of the vehicle on the left and operated the 7.92-mm (0.31-in) ZB vz 35 or 37 machine-gun, with the driver to his right. The commander/gunner and loader/radio operator were seated in the two-man turret in the centre of the hull. Main armament consisted of a 37.2-mm Skoda vz 34 gun with a 7.92-mm (0.31-in) ZB 35 or 37 machine-gun mounted co-axially to the right. Totals of 72 rounds of 37 mm and 1,800 rounds of machine-gun ammunition were carried. The engine and transmission were at the rear of the hull, the transmission having one reverse and six forward gears. The suspension on each side consisted of eight small road wheels (two per bogie), with the drive sprocket at the rear, and idler at the front; there were four track-return rollers.

An unusual feature of the tank was that the transmission and steering were assisted by compressed air to reduce driver fatigue, so enabling the tank to travel long distances at high speed. Problems were encountered with these systems when the tanks were operated by the Germans on the Eastern Front because of the very low temperatures encountered.

Specification
LT vz 35
Crew: 4
Weight: 10500 kg (23,148 lb)
Dimensions: length 4.9 m (16 ft 1 in);

Czechoslovakia provided many of the tanks used by the Wehrmacht in the battle for France. The Pz 35(t) equipped the 6th Panzer Division in that campaign, and some tanks continued in service until 1942.

width 2.159 m (7 ft 1 in); height 2.209 m (7 ft 3 in)
Powerplant: one Skoda six-cylinder water-cooled petrol engine developing 120 hp (89 kW)
Performance: maximum road speed 40 km/h (25 mph); maximum range 193 km (120 miles); fording 0.8 m (3 ft 4 in); gradient 60 per cent; vertical obstacle 0.787 m (2 ft 7 in); trench 1.981 m (6 ft 6 in)

TNH P-S light tank

In 1937 the international situation was rapidly deteriorating, so the Czech army issued a requirement for a new light tank. This time the army was determined that the troubles encountered with the LT vz 35 light tank when it entered service, resulting from a lack of testing, would not be repeated. Skoda entered its S-11-a and S-11-b, while CKD entered an LT vz 35 with the engine and transmission of the TNH tank, the LTL, the **TNH P-S** (already produced for export) as well as a new medium tank called the V-8-H. During the extensive trials the TNH P-S was found to be the best design and on 1 July 1938 was adopted as the standard light tank of the Czech army under the designation **LT vz 38**, but none had entered service at the time of the German occupation in 1939. The vehicle remained in production for the German army between 1939 and 1942, more than 1,400 being built under the designation **Panzerkampfwagen 38(t) Ausf S** to **PzKpfw 38(t) Ausf G**. (*Ausführung* is the German word for model or mark.) The Germans also exported 69 vehicles to Slovakia, 102 to Hungary, 50 to Romania and 10 to Bulgaria. During the invasion of France the tank was used by the 7th and 8th Panzer Divisions, and continued in service as a light tank until 1941-2.

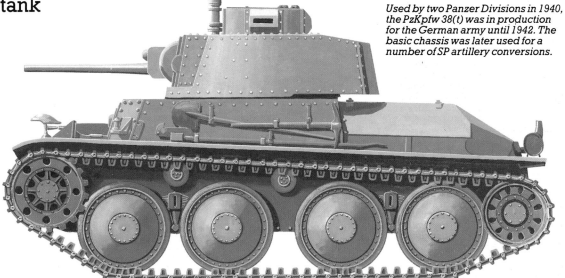

Used by two Panzer Divisions in 1940, the PzKpfw 38(t) was in production for the German army until 1942. The basic chassis was later used for a number of SP artillery conversions.

The hull and turret of the vehicle were of riveted construction, the top of the superstructure being bolted into position. Minimum armour thickness was 10 mm (0.4 in) and maximum thickness 25 mm (1 in), although from the Ausf E this was increased to 50 mm (1.96 in). The driver was seated at the front of the tank on the right, with the bow machine-gunner to his left and operating the 7.92-mm (0.31-in) MG 37(t) machine-gun. The two-man turret was in the centre of the hull and armed with a 37.2-mm Skoda A7 gun, which could fire both armour-piercing and HE rounds with an elevation of +12° and a depression of −6°. Mounted co-axial with and to the right of the main armament was another 7.92-mm (0.31-in) machine-gun. Totals of 90 rounds of 37-mm and 2,550-rounds of machine-gun ammunition were carried. The engine was at the rear of the hull and coupled to a transmission with one reverse and five forward gears. Suspension on each side consisted of four large rubber-tyred road wheels suspended in pairs on leaf springs, with the drive sprocket at the front and idler at the rear, and with two track-return rollers.

When outclassed as a tank the PzKpfw 38(t) was widely used as a reconnaissance vehicle, and the Germans even fitted some chassis with the turret of the SdKfz 222 light armoured car complete with its 20-mm cannon.

The chassis of the light tank was also used as the basis for a large number of vehicles including the **Marder** tank destroyer, which was fitted with a new superstructure armed with 75-mm (2.95-in) anti-tank gun, various self-propelled 15-cm (5.9-in) guns, a 20-mm self-propelled anti-aircraft gun, several types of weapons carriers and the **Hetzer** tank destroyer, to name just a few. The last was armed with a 75-mm (2.95-in) gun in a fully enclosed fighting compartment with limited traverse, and was considered by many to be one of the best vehicles of its type during World War II. A total of 2,584 was built between 1944 and 1945, and production continued after the war for the Czech army, a further 158 being sold to

Switzerland in 1946-7 under the designation **G-13**. These were finally withdrawn from service in the late 1960s.

Specification
TNH P-S
Crew: 4
Weight: 9700 kg (21,385 lb)
Dimensions: length 4.546 m (14 ft 11 in); width 2.133 m (7 ft 0 in); height 2.311 m (7 ft 7 in)
Powerplant: one Praga EPA six-cylinder water-cooled inline petrol engine developing 150 hp (112 kW)
Performance: maximum road speed 42 km/h (26 mph); maximum range 200 km (125 miles); fording 0.9 m (3 ft); gradient 60 per cent; vertical obstacle 0.787 m (2 ft 7 in); trench 1.879 m (6 ft 2 in)

A PzKpfw 38(t) during the invasion of France; the 7th and 8th Panzer Divisions used the tank. The commander of the 7th Division became well known later in the war – his name was Rommel.

Panzerkampfwagen I light tank

Above: Two PzKpfw Is and a heavier PzKpfw III in France in 1940. 523 of the little light tanks were used in the campaign, in spite of their unsuitability for combat.

In 1933 the German Army Weapons Department issued a requirement for a light armoured vehicle weighing about 5000 kg (11,025 lb) that could be used for training purposes, and five companies subsequentlay built prototype vehicles. After trials the Army Weapons Department accepted the Krupp design for further development, the design company being responsible for the chassis and Daimler-Benz for the superstructure. To conceal the real use of the vehicle the Army Weapons Department called the vehicle the **Landwirtschäftlicher Schlepper** (industrial tractor). The first batch of 150 vehicles was ordered from Henschel, and production commenced in July 1934 under the designation **PzKpfw I(MG) (SdKfz 101) Ausf A** and powered by a Krupp M 305 petrol engine developing only 57 hp (42 kW). There were problems with the engine, however, and the next-batch Ausf B had a more powerful engine which meant that the hull had to be longer and an additional roadwheel added on each side. This model was a little heavier, but its more powerful engine gave it a maximum road speed of 40 km/h (25 mph). This entered service in 1935 under the designation of the **PzKpfw 1(MG) (SdKfz 101) Ausf B.** Most of the vehicles were built by Henschel but Wegmann also became involved in the programme, peak production being achieved in 1935 when over 800 vehicles were completed.

The Panzerkampfwagen 1 was first used operationally in the Spanish Civil War, and at the start of the invasion of Poland in 1939 no less than 1,445 such vehicles were on strength. It had already been realized, however, that the vehicle was ill-suited for front-line use because of its lack of firepower and armour protection (7-13 mm/0.28-0.51 in), and in the invasion of France in 1940 only 523 were used, although many more were still in Germany and Poland. By the end of 1941 the PzKpfw I had been phased out of front-line service, although the **kleiner Panzerbefehlwagen I (SdKfz 265)** command

model remained in service longer.

Once the light tank was obsolete its chassis underwent conversion to other roles, and one of the first of these was the **Munitions-Schlepper** used to carry ammunition and other valuable cargoes. For the anti-tank role the chassis was fitted with captured Czech 47-mm anti-tank guns on top of the superstructure with limited traverse. These were used on both the Eastern and North African fronts, but soon became obsolete with the arrival of the more heavily armoured tanks on the battlefield. The largest conversion entailed the installation of a 15-cm (5.9-in) infantry gun in a new superstructure, but this really overloaded the chassis and less than 40 such conversions were made.

The turret was in the centre of the vehicle, offset to the right and armed with twin 7.92-mm (0.31-in) machine-guns, for which a total of 1,525 rounds of ammunition were carried. The driver was seated to the left of the turret.

Right: The PzKpfw I was heavily involved in the Polish campaign after its operational debut in the Spanish Civil War.

Specification
PzKpfw I Ausf B
Crew: 2
Weight: 6000 kg (13,230 lb)
Dimensions: length 4.42 m (14 ft 6 in); width 2.06 m (6 ft 9 in); height 1.72 m (5 ft 8 in)
Powerplant: one Maybach NL 38 TR six-cylinder petrol engine developing 100 hp (75 kW)
Performance: maximum road speed 40 km/h (25 mph); maximum road range 140 km (87 miles); fording 0.58 m (1 ft 11 in); gradient 60 per cent; vertical obstacle 0.36 m (1 ft 2 in); trench 1.4 m (4 ft 7 in)

Panzerkampfwagen II light tank

Despite being intended as a training machine, the PzKpfw II provided the majority of German Panzer strength during the invasions of Poland and France.

To bridge the gap until the arrival of the PzKpfw III and PzKpfw IV tanks, a decision was made in 1934 to order an interim model which became known as the **Panzerkampfwagen II**. Development contracts were awarded to Henschel, Krupp and MAN under the designation Industrial Tractor 100 (**LaS 100**) to conceal its true role. After evaluation of these prototypes the MAN model was selected for further development, MAN being responsible for the chassis and Daimler-Benz for the superstructure. Production was eventually undertaken also by Famo, MIAG and Wegmann, and the tank formed the backbone of the German armoured divisions during the invasion of France, about 1,000 being in front line service. The tank was also used in the invasion of the USSR in the following year although by that time it was obsolete, had inadequate armour protection and lacked firepower. It was in fact intended primarily as a training machine rather than for actual combat.

The first production **PzKpfw II Ausf A** vehicles were delivered in 1935, and were armed with a 20-mm cannon and 7.92-mm (0.31-in) co-axial machine-gun. There was a three-man crew, and combat weight was 7.2 tonnes. Tests with the early production models showed that the vehicle was under-powered with its 130-hp (97-kW) engine, so the **PzKpfw II Ausf B** was introduced with a 140-hp (104-kW) engine and other improvements (notably thicker frontal armour) which pushed up its weight to just under 8 tonnes. The **PzKpfw II Ausf C** was introduced in 1937, and had better armour protection. Additionally, the small bogie wheels were replaced by five independently-sprung bogies with leaf springs on each side, and this was to remain the basic suspension for all remaining production vehicles. In 1938 the **PzKpfw II Ausf D** and **PzKpfw II Ausf E** were introduced, with new torsion-bar suspension which gave them a much increased road speed of 55 km/h (34 mph), although cross-country speed was slower than that of the earlier models. The final production model of the series was the

PzKpfw II Ausf F, which appeared in 1940-1 and which was uparmoured to 35 mm (1.38 in) on the front and 20 mm (0.79 in) on the sides, this pushing up the total weight to just under 10 tonnes and consequently reducing the speed of the vehicle, which was felt to be acceptable because of the greater protection provided.

The hull and turret of the PzKpfw II was of welded steel construction, with the driver at the front, two-man turret in the centre offset to the left, and the engine at the rear. Armament consisted of a 20-mm cannon (for which 180 rounds were provided) on the left side of the turret, and a 7.92-mm (0.31-in) machine-gun (for which 1,425 rounds were carried) on the right of the turret.

The PzKpfw II was also used as the basis for a number of fast reconnaissance tanks called the **Luchs** (this name was subsequently adopted by the new West German Army in the 1970s for its 8×8 reconnaissance vehicle) but these and similar vehicles were not built in large numbers.

One of the more interesting vehicles was the special amphibious model developed for the invasion of England in 1940. This model was propelled in the water at a speed of 10 km/h (6 mph) by a propeller run off the main engine. A model with two flamethrowers was also produced as the **Flammpanzer II**; 100 of these were in service by 1942.

When the basic tank was obsolete

the chassis was quickly adopted for many other roles. One of the first of these was a self-propelled anti-tank gun using captured Soviet 76.2-mm (3-in) guns and called the **Marder I**. This was followed by a model called the **Marder II** with a 7.5-cm (2.95-in) German anti-tank gun, and some 1,200 of these were converted or built. The **Wespe** was a self-propelled gun fitted with a 10.5-cm howitzer and was produced in Poland until 1944.

Armed with a 20-mm cannon, some 1000 PzKpfw IIs were used during the Polish campaign.

Specification
PzKpfw II Ausf F
Crew: 3
Weight: 10000 kg (22,046 lb)
Dimensions: length 4.64 m (15 ft 3 in); width 2.30 m (7 ft 6.5 in); height 2.02 m (6 ft 7.5 in)
Powerplant: one Maybach six-cylinder petrol engine developing 140 hp (104 kW)
Performance: maximum road speed 55 km/h (34 mph); maximum road range 200 km (125 miles); fording 0.85 m (2 ft 10 in); gradient 50 per cent; vertical obstacle 0.42 m (1 ft 5 in); trench 1.75 m (5 ft 9 in)

Panzerkampfwagen III medium tank

It was envisaged in the mid-1930s that each German tank battalion would have three companies of relatively light medium tanks and one company of better armed and armoured medium tanks. The former eventually became the **Panzerkampfwagen III (PzkPfw III)** or **SdKfz 141**, while the latter became the **Panzerkampfwagen IV (PzKpfw IV)** which was to remain in production throughout World War II. In 1935 the Weapons Department issued contracts for the construction of prototype vehicles against the lighter concept to Daimler-Benz, Krupp, MAN and Rheinmetall-Borsig. At an early stage it was decided to arm the tank with a 37-mm gun which would fire the same ammunition as that used by the infantry anti-tank gun, but provision was made that the turret ring diameter

be large enough to permit the upgunning of the vehicle to 50 mm if this should be required. Following trials with the prototype vehicles the Daimler-Benz model was selected, although the first three production models, the **PzKpfw III Ausf A, PzKpfw III Ausf B** and **PzKpfw III Ausf C** were built only in small numbers, differing from each other mainly in suspension details. In September 1939 the vehicle was formally adopted for service, and mass production was soon under way. The

Continued on page 508

A Panzer III with accompanying infantry during 1942. By this time the German tanks had come up against the excellent Soviet T-34, and armour and armament were being increased.

PzKpfw III was first used in combat during the invasion of Poland. The next production models were the **PzKpfw III Ausf D** and **PzKpfw III Ausf F**, the former with thicker armour and a revised cupola, and the latter with an uprated engine and only six road wheels. In 1939 it was decided to push ahead with the 50-mm model and this entered production in 1940 under the designation **PzKpfw III Ausf F**. This was followed by the **PzKpfw III Ausf G** version with similar armament but more powerful engine. For operations in North Africa the vehicles were fitted with a tropical kit, while for the proposed invasion of England a special version for deep wading was developed. The latter were never used for their intended role but some were successfully used during the invasion of the USSR in 1941. The **PzKpfw Aus H** introduced wider tracks and a number of important improvements.

The 50-mm L/42 gun was inadequate to cope with the Soviet T-34 tank, so the longer-barrelled KwK 39 L/60 weapon was installed. This had a higher muzzle velocity, and vehicles fitted with the weapon were designated **PzKpfw III Ausf J**. Many vehicles were retrofitted with the 50-mm gun, and by early 1942 the 37-mm version had almost disappeared from front-line service. The next model was the **PzKpfw III Ausf L**, which had greater armour protection, pushing its weight up to just over 22 tonnes, almost 50 per cent more than the weight of the original prototype. The **PzKpfw III Ausf M** and **PzKpfw III Ausf N** were fitted with the 75-mm L/24 gun which had been installed in the

PzKpfw IV; a total of 64 rounds of ammunition were carried for this gun. Production of the PzKpfw III was finally completed in August 1943. The chassis was also used as the basis for the 75-mm assault gun (**Gepanzerte Selbstahrlafette für Sturmgeschutz 7.5 cm Kanone** or **SdKfz 142**), of which a few were used in the invasion of France in 1941; production of improved SP guns on PzKpfw III chassis continued until the end of World War II. Other variants included an armoured recovery vehicle, an armoured observation vehicle (**Panzerbeobachtungswagen**) and a command vehicle (**Panzerbefehlswagen III**). A total of 15,000 chassis was produced for both the tank and assault gun applications.

The layout of the PzKpfw III was

basically the same in all vehicles, with the driver at the front of the hull on the left and the machine-gunner/radio operator to his right. The three-man turret was in the centre of the hull, the commander having a cupola in the centre of the roof at the rear. The engine was at the rear of the hull, and the suspension, which was of the torsion-bar type from the PzKpfw III Ausf E, consisted on each side of six small road wheels, with the drive sprocket at the front and the idler at the rear; there were three track-return rollers.

Specification
PzKpfw III Ausf M
Crew: 5
Weight: 22300 kg (49,160 lb)

PzKpfw Ausf G, as used by the Afrika Korps. Tropicalized, and with a 50-mm gun, the German tank proved effective against the lighter British tanks, and was much more mobile than the heavy infantry tanks.

Dimensions: length (including armament) 6.41 m (21 ft 0 in); length (hull) 5.52 m (18 ft 1.5 in); width 2.95 m (9 ft 8 in); height 2.50 m (8 ft 2.5 in)
Powerplant: one Maybach HL 120 TRM 12-cylinder petrol engine developing 300 hp (224 kW)
Performance: maximum road speed 40 km/h (25 mph); maximum road range 175 km (110 miles); fording 0.8 m (2 ft 8 in); gradient 60 per cent; vertical obstacle 0.6 m (2 ft 0 in); trench 2.59 m (8 ft 6 in)

Panzerkampfwagen IV medium tank

The **Panzerkampfwagen IV** had the distinction of remaining in production throughout World War II, and formed the backbone of the German armoured divisions. In 1934 the Army Weapons Department drew up a requirement for a vehicle under the cover name of the medium tractor (**mitteren Traktor**) which was to equip the fourth tank company of each German tank battalion. Rheinmetall-Borsig built the VK 2001(Rh) while MAN proposed the VK 2002(MAN) and Krupp the **VK 2001(K)**. In the end Krupp took over total responsibility for the vehicle, which was also known as the **Bataillons Führerwagen** (battalion commander's vehicle). This entered production at the Krupp-Grusonwerke plant at Magdeburg as the PzKpfw IV

Ausf A, or **SdKfz 161**, as by this time all cover names had been dropped. This model was armed with a short-barrelled 75-mm (2.95-in) gun, co-axial 7.92-mm (0.31-in) machine-gun and a similar weapon in the bow. Turret traverse was powered and 122 rounds of 75-mm (2.95-in) and 3,000 rounds of machine-gun ammunition were carried. Maximum armour thickness was 20 mm (0.79 in) on the turret and 14.5 mm (0.57 in) on the hull. Only a few of these were built in 1936-7. The next model was the **PzKpfw IV Ausf B**, which had increased armour protection, more powerful engine and other

more minor improvements. Throughout the PzKpfw IV's long production life the basic chassis remained unchanged, but as the threat by enemy anti-tank weapons increased so more armour was added and new weapons were installed. (Other chassis often had to be phased out of production as they were incapable of being upgraded to take into account changes on the battlefield.) The final production model was the **PzKpfw IV Ausf J**, which appeared in March 1944. Total production of the PzKpfw IV amounted to about 9,000 vehicles.

Below: From 1943 the PzKpfw IV began to appear with the long-barrelled 7.5-cm KWK 40/L48 cannon, which made the tank able to give a good account of itself against almost any armoured opposition.

Above: Panzergrenadiers advance through cornfields in the 1942 German drive to the Caucasus, covered by a PzKpfw IV.

The chassis of the PzKpfw IV was also used for other, more specialized vehicles including the **Jagdpanzer IV** tank destroyer, self-propelled anti-aircraft gun systems of various types (including one with four 20-mm cannon and another with one 37-mm cannon), self-propelled guns, armoured recovery vehicles and bridgelayers to name but a few.

A typical PzKpfw IV was the **PzKpfw IV Ausf F2**, which had a hull and turret of all-welded steel armour construction, the former having a maximum thickness of 60 mm (2.36 in) and the latter of 50 mm (1.47 in). The driver was seated at the front of the hull on the left, with the bow machine-gunner/radio operator to his right. The commander, gunner and loader were seated in the turret in the centre of the hull, with an entrance hatch on each side of the turret and a cupola for the tank commander. The engine was at the rear of the hull and coupled to a manual transmission with six forward and one reverse gears. Main armament comprised a long barrelled 75-mm (2.95-in) KwK gun fitted with a muzzle brake and which could fire a variety of ammunition including HEAT, smoke, APCR, APCBC and high explosive, the last being used in the infantry support role. A 7.92-mm (0.31-in) MG34 machine-gun was mounted co-axial with and to the right of the main armament, while a similar weapon was mounted in the bow. Totals of 87 rounds of 75-mm (2.95-in) and 3,192 rounds of 7.92-mm (0.31-in) machine-gun ammunition were carried. Turret traverse was powered through 360°, though manual controls were provided for emergency use.

The additional armour and heavier armament pushed up the weight until in the final production version it reached 25 tonnes, but the PzKpfw IV still had a respectable power-to-weight ratio and therefore good mobility characteristics.

Specification
PzKpfw IV Ausf H
Crew: 5
Weight: 25000 kg (55,115 lb)
Dimensions: length (including armament) 7.02 m (23 ft 0 in); length (hull) 5.89 m (19 ft 4 in); width 3.29 m (10 ft 9.5 in); height 2.68 m (8 ft 9.5 in)
Powerplant: one Maybach HL 120 TRM 12-cylinder petrol engine developing 300 hp (224 kW)
Performance: maximum road speed 38 km/h (24 mph); maximum road range 200 km (125 miles); fording 1.0 m (3 ft 3 in); gradient 60 per cent; vertical obstacle 0.6 m (2 ft 0 in); trench 2.20 m (7 ft 3 in)

A PzKpfw IV is serviced in the field in the USSR. Visible is the short-barrelled 75-mm gun; this was soon found to be inadequate against Soviet tanks, and had to be replaced by a longer, higher-velocity gun.

Panzerkampfwagen V Panther heavy tank

In 1941 the most powerful tank in service with the German army was the

PzKpfw IV, infrequently a match for the new Soviet T-34 tank, which appeared in small numbers on the Eastern Front in that year. Work on a successor to the PzKpfw IV had started as far back as 1937, but progress had been slow because of changing requirements. In 1941 Henschel and Porsche had each completed prototypes of new tanks in the 30/35-tonne class designated the VK 3001(H) and VK 3001(P) respectively. These were not placed in production, and further development resulted in the Tiger (VK 4501). Late in 1941 a requirement was issued for a new tank with a long barrelled 75-mm (2.95-in) gun, well-sloped armour for maximum protection within the weight limit of the vehicle, and larger wheels for improved mobility. To meet this requirement Daimler-Benz submitted the VK 3002(DB) while MAN submitted the **VK 3002(MAN)**. The former design was a virtual copy of the T-34 but the MAN design was accepted. The first prototypes of the new tank, called the **Panzerkampfwagen V Panther (SdKfz 171)** were completed in September 1942, with the first production models coming from the MAN factory just two months later. At the same time Daimler-Benz started tooling up for production of the Panther, and in 1943 Henschel and Niedersachen were also brought into the programme together with hundreds of sub-contractors. It

Above: PzKpfw V Panther in its late-war form. Skirts have been added to offer some protection to the wheels, and spare track has been used as auxiliary armour. The tank is covered in special anti-magnetic paste as a protection against magnetic mines.

Right: Probably the finest German tank of the war, the Panther was hampered by its complexity. Some 4,800 were built, as compared to 11,000-plus T-34/85s built by the Soviets in 1944 alone!

was planned to produce 600 Panthers per month, but Allied bombing meant that maximum production ever achieved was about 330 vehicles per month. By early 1945 just over 4,800 Panthers had been built.

The Panther was rushed into production without proper trials, and numerous faults soon became apparent: indeed, in the type's early days more Panthers were lost to mechanical failure than to enemy action, and consequently the crew's confidence in the vehicle rapidly dwindled. The vehicle first saw action on the Eastern Front during July 1943 during the Kursk battles, and from then on it was used on all fronts. Once the mechanical problems had been overcome confidence in the tank soon built up again, and many consider the Panther to be the best all round German tank of World War II. In the immediate post-war period the French army used a number of Panther tanks until more modern tanks were available.

First production models were of the **PzKpfw V Ausf A** type, and were really pre-prodution vehicles; the **PzKpfw V Ausf B** and **PzKpfw V Ausf C** were never placed in production. Later models were the **PzKpfw V Ausf D** followed for some reason by another PzKpfw V Ausf A, which was widely used in Normandy, and finally by the **PzKpfw V Ausf G**. Variants of the Panther included an observation post vehicle (**Beobachtungspanzer Panther**), ARV, **Jagdpanther** tank destroyer, and command vehicle (**Befehlspanzer Panther**), while some were disguised to resemble M10 tank detroyers during the Battle of the Bulge.

Main armament of the Panther was a long barrelled 75-mm (2.95-in) gun for which 79 rounds of ammunition were carried. Mounted co-axial with the main armament was a 7.92-mm (0.31-in) MG34 machine-gun, while a similar weapon was mounted in the hull front and another on the turret roof for anti-aircraft defence.

Specification
PzKpfw V Panther Ausf A
Crew: 4
Weight: 45500 kg (100,310 lb)
Dimensions: length (including armament) 8.86 m (29 ft 0.75 in); length (hull) 6.88 m (22 ft 7 in); width 3.43 m (11 ft 3 in); height 3.10 m (10 ft 2 in)
Powerplant: one Maybach HL 230 P 30 12-cylinder diesel engine developing 700 hp (522 kW)
Performance: maximum road speed

German armour, committed piecemeal, could not stop the Allied invasion of Europe. Here a Panther burns after being hit by British anti-tank weapons.

46 km/h (29 mph); maximum road range 177 km (110 miles); fording 1.70 m (5 ft 7 in); gradient 60 per cent; vertical obstacle 0.91 m (3 ft 0 in); trench 1.91 m (6 ft 3 in)

Panzerkampfwagen VI Tiger heavy tank

With its thick armour and a version of the dreaded 88-mm AA/anti-tank gun, the PzKpfw VI Tiger was an outstandingly powerful design. It was not a particularly agile machine, but could command the battlefield.

As far back as 1938 it has been realized that the PzKpfw IV tank would have to be replaced by a more modern design some time in the future. Various prototypes were built by a number of German companies, but none was placed in production. In 1941 an order was placed with Henschel for a 36-ton tank called the VK 3601 which was required to have a maximum speed of 40 km/h (25 mph), good armour protection and a powerful gun. A prototype of this tank was built but further work was stopped as an order was placed in May 1941 for a 45-ton tank called the VK 4501. This was to be armed with a tank version of the dreaded 88-mm (3.46-in) AA/anti-tank gun, which had then become the scourge of European armies. It was required that the prototype be ready for testing on Hitler's next birthday, 20 April 1942. As time was short Henschel incorporated ideas from the VK 3601 and another tank called the VK 3001(H). The end product was the **VK 4501(H)**, the letter suffix standing for Henschel. Porsche also went ahead with its own design and built the **VK 4501(Porsche)** to meet the same requirement. Both prototypes were completed in time to be demonstrated on Hitler's birthday, and the Henschel design was selected for production in August 1942 under the designation **PzKpfw VI Tiger Ausf E (SdKfz 181)**.

The Tiger was in production from August 1942 to August 1944, a total of 1,350 vehicles being built. It was then succeeded in production by the Tiger II or King Tiger for which there is a separate entry. In case trials proved the VK 4501(H) a failure, a batch of 90 VK 4501(P) tanks was ordered, and these were subsequently completed as 88-mm (3.46-in) tank destroyers under the designation **Panzerjäger Tiger (P) Ferdinand (SdKfz 184)**. The vehicle was named after its designer, Dr Ferdinand Porsche.

There were three variants of the Ti-

ger, these being the Tiger command tank (**Befehlspanzer Tiger**) which was the basic gun tank with its main armament removed, but fitted with a winch but no crane, and the **Sturmtiger** which had a new superstructure fitted with a 38-cm (14.96-in) Type 61 rocket-launcher with limited traverse; only 10 of the last were built.

For its time the Tiger was an outstanding design with a powerful gun and good armour, but it was also too complicated and therefore difficult to produce. One of its major drawbacks was its overlapping wheel suspension which became clogged with mud and stones. On the Eastern Front this could be disastrous as during winter nights the mud froze and by the morning the tank had been immobilized, often at the exact time the Soviets would attack. When the vehicle travelled on roads a 51.5-cm (20.3-in) wide track was fitted, while a 71.5-cm (28.1-in) wide track was used for travel across country or in combat as this gave a lower ground pressure and so improved traction.

Main armament comprised an 88-mm (3.46-in) KwK 36 gun, with a 7.92-mm (0.31-in) MG 34 machine-gun co-axial with the main armament and a similar weapon ball-mounted in the hull front on the right. Totals of 84

rounds of 88-mm (3.46-in) and 5,850 rounds of machine-gun ammunition were carried.

The Tiger was first encountered in Tunisia by the British army and from then on appeared on all of the German fronts.

Specification
PzKpfw VI Tiger Ausf E
Crew: 5
Weight: 55000 kg (121,250 lb)
Dimensions: length (including armament) 8.24 m (27 ft 0 in); length (hull) 6.20 m (20 ft 4 in); width 3.73 m (12 ft 3 in); height 2.86 m (9 ft 3.25 in)

SS Tigers bivouac on the Brenner Pass, guarding the Italian border with Austria. By this time the Allies had landed in Italy and Mussolini had been overthrown.

Powerplant: one Maybach HL 230 P 45 12-cylinder petrol engine developing 700 hp (522 kW)
Performance: maximum road speed 38 km/h (24 mph); maximum range road 100 km (62 miles); fording 1.2 m (3 ft 11 in); gradient 60 per cent; vertical obstacle 0.79 m (2 ft 7 in); trench 1.8 m (5 ft 11 in)

Panzerkampfwagen VI Tiger II heavy tank

No sooner was the Tiger in production than the decision was taken to develop an even better armed and armoured version, especially to counter any vehicle that the Soviets could introduce in the future. Once again Henschel and Porsche were asked to prepare designs. Porsche first designed a tank based on the earlier VK 4501 design and armed with a 15-cm (5.9-in) gun. This was rejected in favour of a new design with a turret-mounted 88-mm (3.46-in) gun, which was soon cancelled as its electric transmission used too much copper, which at that time was in short supply. By this time the turrets were already in production and these were subsequently fitted to ear-

ly-production Henschel tanks. The **VK 4503(H)** Henschel design was completed in October 1943, somewhat later than anticipated as a decision was taken to incorporate components of the projected Panther II tank.

Production of the Tiger II, or **Panzer-kampfwagen VI Tiger II Ausf B (SdKfz 182)** to give its correct designation, got under way at Kassel in December 1943 alongside the Tiger, the first 50 production vehicles being completed with the Porsche turret. All subsequent tanks had the Henschel turret, and a total of 485 vehicles was built.

The Tiger II first saw action on the Eastern Front in May 1944 and on the Western Front in Normandy in August

of the same year, the Western Allies calling it the Royal Tiger or King Tiger while the Germans called it the **Königstiger** (King Tiger).

In many respects the Tiger II was similar in layout to the Panther tank, and was powered by the same engine as later production Panthers, resulting in a much lower power-to-weight ratio, and the tank was therefore much slower and less mobile than the Panther. While its armour gave almost complete protection against all of the guns fitted to Allied tanks, the Tiger II was unreliable and its bulk made it difficult to move about the battlefield and to conceal. Many were abandoned or destroyed by their crews when they ran out of fuel and no additional supplies were to hand.

The hull of the Tiger II was of all-welded construction with a maximum thickness of 150 mm (5.9 in) in the front of the hull. The driver was seated at the front on the left, with the bow machine-gunner/radio operator to his right. The turret was of welded construction with a maximum thickness of 100 mm (3.9 in) at the front, and accommodated the commander and gunner on the left with the loader on the right. The engine was at the hull rear. Main armament comprised a long-barrelled 88-mm (3.46-in) KwK 43 gun that could fire armour-piercing and HE ammunition,

the former having a much higher muzzle velocity than the equivalent round fired by the Tiger. A 7.92-mm (0.31-in) MG 34 was mounted co-axial with the main armament, and another weapon was mounted in the hull front. Totals of 84 rounds of 88-mm (3.46-in) and 5,850 rounds of 7.92-mm (0.31-in) machine-gun ammunition were carried.

The Tiger II chassis was also used as the basis for the **Jagdtiger B**, which was armed with a 128-mm (5.04-in) gun in a new superstructure with limited traverse; only 48 of these powerful tank destroyers had been built by the end of the war.

Specification
PzKpfw VI Tiger II Ausf B
Crew: 5
Weight: 69700 kg (153,660 lb)
Dimensions: length (including armament) 10.26 m (33 ft 8 in); length (hull) 7.26 m (23 ft 9.75 in); width 3.75 m (12 ft 3.5 in); height 3.09 m (10 ft 1.5 in)
Powerplant: one Maybach HL 230 P 30 12-cylinder petrol engine developing 700 hp (522 kW)
Performance: maximum road speed 38 km/h (24 mph); maximum road range 110 km (68 miles); fording 1.6 m (5 ft 3 in); gradient 60 per cent; vertical obstacle 0.85 m (2 ft 10 in); trench 2.50 m (8 ft 2 in)

Above: A Tiger II with Henschel turret passes American prisoners taken during the Ardennes offensive. Many of the tanks were abandoned as the attack failed for lack of petrol.

Right: A Königstiger with Porsche turret. Utilizing the latest in sloped armour and carrying a long-barrelled 88-mm high-velocity gun, the Tiger II was safe from almost any Allied tank at almost any range.

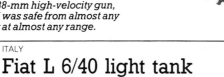

Fiat L 6/40 light tank

In the 1930s Fiat Ansaldo built an export tank based on the chassis of the L3 tankette, itself a development of the British Carden Lloyd Mark VI tankette. The first prototype was armed with twin machine-guns in the turret and a 37 mm gun in a sponson. This was followed by models with a turret-mounted 37-mm gun and a co-axial machine-gun, and another with twin turret-mounted 8-mm (0.315-in) machine-guns. The production version, designated **Carro Armato L 6/40**, was built from 1939 and armed with a Breda Model 35 20-mm cannon with a co-axial Breda Model 38 8-mm (0.315-in) machine gun. Totals of 296 rounds of 20-mm and 1,560 rounds of 8-mm (0.35-in) ammunition were carried. At the time of its introduction the L 6/40 was roughly equivalent to the German PzKpfw II, and was used by reconnaissance units and cavalry divisions. A total of 283 vehicles was built, and in addition to being used in Italy itself the

type was also used in North Africa and on the Russian front. The L 6/40 continued in service with the militia in post-war Italy, finally being phased out of service in the early 1950s.

The hull of the L 6/40 was of all-riveted construction varying in thickness from 6 mm (0.24 in) to 30 mm (1.26 in). The driver was seated at the front right, the turret was in the centre, and the engine at the rear. The turret was manually operated and could be traversed through 360°; its weapons could be elevated from −12° to +20°. The commander also acted as gunner and loader, and could enter the vehicle via the hatch in the turret roof or via a door in the right side of the hull. Suspension on each side consisted of two bogies each with two road wheels, with the drive sprocket at the front and idler at the rear; there were three track-return rollers.

There was also a flamethrower version of the L 6/40 in which the 20-mm

cannon was replaced by a flamethrower for which 200 litres (44 Imp gal) of flame liquid were carried. The command model had additional communications equipment and an open-topped turret. Some of the L 6/40s were completed as **Semovente L40 47/32** self-propelled anti-tank guns, which were essentially L 6/40 with the turret removed and a 47-mm anti-tank gun mounted in the hull front to the left of the driver. This had an elevation from

−12° to +20°, with a total traverse of 27°; 70 rounds of ammunition were carried. In addition to conversions from

Continued on page 518

A knocked-out L 6/40 light tank is inspected by Australians in the desert. In spite of being unsuitable for front-line service, the L 6/40 saw action in North Africa and the USSR as well as in Italy.

the L 6/40 tank about 300 vehicles were built from scratch and these saw service in Italy, North Africa and the USSR from 1941. A command version was also built on the same chassis and this had its armament replaced by an 8-mm (0.315-in) Breda machine-gun, which was made to look like the larger calibre gun to make detection of the vehicle more difficult.

Specification
Carro Armato L 6/40
Crew: 2
Weight: 6800 kg (14,991 lb)
Dimensions: length 3.78 m (12 ft 5 in); width 1.92 m (6 ft 4 in); height 2.03 m (6 ft 8 in)
Powerplant: one SPA 18D four-cylinder petrol engine developing 70 hp (52 kW)
Performance: maximum road speed 42 km/h (26 mph); maximum range 200 km (124 miles); fording 0.8 m (2 ft 8 in); gradient 60 per cent; vertical obstacle 0.7 m (2 ft 4 in); trench 1.7 m (5 ft 7 in)

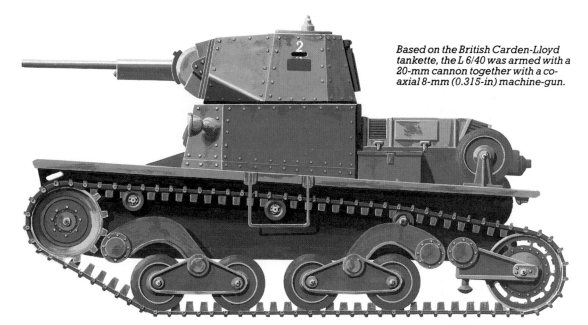

Based on the British Carden-Lloyd tankette, the L 6/40 was armed with a 20-mm cannon together with a co-axial 8-mm (0.315-in) machine-gun.

ITALY

Fiat M 11/39 and M 13/40 medium tanks

In 1937 the prototype of the **Carro Armato M 11/39** tank was built, with the suspension system of the L3 tankette but with six road wheels on each side. In layout this was similar to the American M3 Lee tank, but with a 37-mm (rather than 75-mm/2.95-in) gun in the right sponson, driver on the left, and in the centre of the hull a one-man turret armed with twin 8-mm (0.315-in) machine-guns. Further development resulted in a model with eight road wheels and this basic chassis was used for all subsequent Italian medium tanks. Only 100 M 11/39s were built as it was considered that the design was already obsolete, and in 1940 70 of these were sent to North Africa where many were captured or destroyed during the first battles with the British army.

Further development resulted in the **M 13/40** which had a similar chassis but a redesigned hull of riveted construction varying in thickness from 6 mm (0.24 in) to 42 mm (1.65 in). The driver was seated at the front of the hull on the left with the machine-gunner to his right; the latter operated the twin Modello 38 8-mm (0.315-in) machine-guns as well as the radios. The two-man turret was in the centre of the hull, with the commander/gunner on the right and the loader on the left, and with a two-piece hatch cover in the turret roof. Main armament comprised a 47-mm 32-calibre gun with an elevation of +20° and a depression of −10°; turret traverse was 360°. A Modello 38 8-mm (0.315-in) machine-gun was mounted co-axial with the main armament and a similar weapon was mounted on the turret roof for anti-aircraft defence. Totals of 104 rounds of 47-mm and 3,048 rounds of 8-mm (0.315-in) ammunition were carried. The engine was at the rear of the hull, its power being transmitted to the gearbox at the front of the hull via a propeller shaft. Suspension on each side consisted of four double-wheel articulated bogies mounted on two assemblies each carried on semi-elliptic leaf springs, with the idler at the rear; there were three track-return rollers.

The M 13/40 was built by Ansaldo-Fossati at the rate of about 60 to 70

vehicles per month, a total of 779 being produced. The tank was widely used in North Africa by the Italian army but was cramped, proved to be very unreliable in service and was prone to catching fire when hit by anti-tank projectiles.

Many vehicles were captured by the British army after being abandoned by their crews and subsequently issued to the British 6th Royal Tnk Regiment (RTR) and the Australian 6th Cavalry Regiment early in 1941 when tanks were in a very short supply on the Allied side. The Australian regiment had three squadrons of captured vehicles which they called Dingo, Rabbit, and Wombat. So that they were not engaged by Allied units, white kangaroos were painted on the sides, glacis and turret rear.

The **Semovente Comando M 40** command vehicle was basically the M 13/40 tank with its turret removed and fitted with additional communications equipment for use in the command role. Further development of the M 13/40 resulted in the M 14/41 and M 15/42, for which there is a separate entry.

Specification
Carro Armato M 13/40
Crew: 4
Weight: 14000 kg (30,865 lb)
Dimensions: length 4.92 m (16 ft 2 in); width 2.2 m (7 ft 3 in); height 2.38 m (7 ft 10 in)
Performance: one SPA TM40 eight-cylinder diesel engine developing 125 hp (93 kW)
Performance: maximum road speed 32 km/h (20 mph); maximum range 200 km (125 miles); fording 1.0 m (3 ft 3 in); gradient 70 per cent; vertical obstacle 0.8 m (2 ft 8 in); trench 2.1 m (6 ft 11 in)

Above: M 13/40s in the desert, 1941. These are the Semovente Comande version, without turrets and with additional radio gear. Many were abandoned by the Italians and taken over by the British.

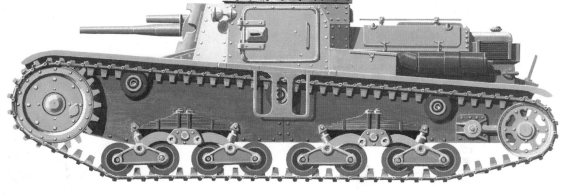

Below: With a 47-mm sponson-mounted main gun and twin 8-mm (0.315-in) machine-guns in the two-man turret, the M 11/39 was soon outclassed with the introduction of improved Allied tanks.

17

Fiat M 15/42 medium tank

The **Carro Armato M 14/41** was essentially the M 13/40 fitted with a more powerful diesel engine which was equipped with air filters designed to cope with the harsh conditions of the desert. Production amounted to just over 1,100 of these vehicles, which had a similar specification to the M 13/40 except for an increase in speed to 33 km/h (20 mph) and in weight to 14.5 tonnes. Further development resulted in the **Carro Armato M 15/42**, which entered service in early 1943. A total of 82 of these was built, most being issued to the Ariete Division which took part in the Italian attempt to deny Rome to the Germans in September 1943. Some of these vehicles were captured by the Germans and then used against the Allies.

The M 15/42 was slightly longer than the M 14/41 and distinguishable from it by the lack of a crew access door in the left side of the hull. It was driven by a more powerful engine which made it slightly faster, and had improved armour protection and other more minor modifications as a result of operator comments.

The hull of the M 15/42 was of all-riveted construction which varied in thickness from 42 mm (1.65 in) to 14 mm (0.55 in), with a maximum of 45 mm (1.77 in) on the turret front. The driver was seated at the front of the hull on the left, with the bow machine-gunner to his right, the latter operating the twin Breda Modello 38 8-mm (0.315-in) machine-guns as well as the radios. The turret was in the centre of the hull and armed with a 47-mm 40-calibre gun with an elevation of +20° and a depression of −10°; turret traverse, which was electric, was 360°. A Modello 38 8-mm (0.315-in) machine-gun was mounted co-axial with the main armament, and a similar weapon was mounted on the turret roof for anti-aircraft defence. Totals of 111 rounds of 47-mm and 2,640 rounds of

8-mm (0.315-in) ammunition were carried. Suspension on each side consisted of four double-wheel articulated bogies mounted in two assemblies each carried on semi-elliptical springs, with the drive sprocket at the front and the idler at the rear; there were three track-return rollers. The engine was at the rear of the hull and coupled to a manual gearbox with eight forward and two reverse gears.

By the time the M 15/42 had been introduced into service it was already obsolete, and design of another tank had been under way for several years. In 1942 the first prototypes of the **Carro Armato P 40** heavy tank were built. This was a major advance on the earlier Italian tanks and used a similar type of suspension to the M 15/42. The layout was also similar with the driver at the front, turret in the centre and engine at the rear. Armour protection was much improved and the hull and turret sides sloped to give maximum possible protection within the weight limit of 26 tonnes. The P 40 was powered by a V-12 petrol engine that developed 420 hp (313 kW) to give it a maximum road speed of 40 km/h (25 mph). Main armament comprised a 75-mm (2.95-in) 34-calibre gun with a co-axial Modello 38 8-mm (0.315-in) machine-gun. Totals of 75 rounds of 75-mm (2.95-in) and 600 rounds of machine-gun ammunition were carried. The P 40 was produced by Fiat in northern Italy, but none of these entered service with the Italian army and most were subsequently taken over by the German army, which ensured continued production for itself, some reports stating that over 50 vehicles were built for German use.

Specification
Carro Armato M 15/42
Crew: 4
Weight: 15500 kg (34,800 lb)
Dimensions: length 5.04 m (16 ft 7 in);

width 2.23 m (7 ft 4 in); height 2.39 m (7 ft 11 in)
Powerplant: one SPA 15 TB M42 eight-cylinder petrol engine developing 192 hp (143 kW)
Performance: maximum road speed 40 km/h (25 mph); maximum range 220 km (136 miles); fording 1.0 m (3 ft 3 in); gradient 60 per cent; vertical obstacle 0.8 m (2 ft 8 in); trench 2.10 m (6 ft 11 in)

A squadron of M 14/41 tanks in Cyrenaica in 1942. More than 1100 of these tanks, in effect tropicalized M 13/40s, were produced.

Another M 14/41, abandoned after the first battle of Alamein. The M 15/42 looked similar but had no side hatch. Only 82 were built.

Type 95 light tank

The **Type 95** light tank was developed to meet the requirements of the Japanese army in the early 1930s, the first two prototypes being completed in 1934 by Mitsubishi Heavy Industries. These were tested in China and Japan and the type was then standardized as the Type 95 light tank, the company calling the vehicle the **HA-GO** while the army called the vehicle the **KE-GO**. Over 1,100 Type 95s were built before production was completed in 1943, although some sources have stated that production continued until 1945.

The hull and turret of the Type 95 were of riveted construction and varied in thickness from 0.25 in (6 mm) to a maximum of 0.55 in (14 mm). The driver was seated at the front on the right with the bow machine-gunner to his left. The latter operated the Type 91 6.5-mm (0.255-in) weapon (with a traverse of 35° left and right), which was later replaced by the Type 97 7.7-mm (0.303-in) machine-gun. The turret was in the centre of the hull, offset slightly to the left and fitted with a Type 94 37-mm tank gun firing armour-piercing and HE ammunition. This gun was later replaced by the Type 98 gun of a similar calibre but with a higher muzzle velocity. There was no co-axial machine-gun, but another machine-

gun was mounted in the turret rear on the right side. Totals of 2,970 rounds of ammunition were carried for the two machine-guns and of 119 rounds for the main armament. A major drawback of this tank, like many French tanks of the period, was the fact that the tank commander also had to aim, load and fire the main armament in addition to carrying out his primary role of commanding the tank.

The Mitsubishi six-cylinder air-cooled diesel was mounted in the hull rear and coupled to a manual transmission with one reverse and four forward gears. Steering was of the clutch and brake type, and suspension of the bell crank type consisting of each side of

The Type 95 light tank had a 37-mm main gun and a hull-mounted 7.7-mm (0.303-in) machine-gun together with another 7.7-mm gun at the rear of the turret.

Type 95 tanks cross paddy fields while on exercise. The Type 95 suffered in its anti-infantry role, as the Japanese army did not come up against any armour of consequence until meeting the Marines in 1943.

four rubber-tyred road wheels, with the drive sprocket at the front and idler at the rear; there were two track-return rollers.

In those days no air-conditioning systems were available to keep the interior of the tank cooled so the walls of the crew compartment were lined with asbestos padding which in addition gave some protection to the crew from injury when travelling across

country.

In 1943 a few Type 95 light tanks were modified to carry the 57-mm gun as fitted to the Type 97 medium tank under the name **KE-RI**, but the variant was not very successful as the turret was too cramped. The **KE-NU** was the Type 95 with the complete turret of the Type 97 CHI-HA medium tank. The Type 95 was succeeded in production by the **Type 98 KE-NI** light tank, but only about 100 of these were built before production was completed in 1943 as the type was not considered a very satisfactory design. The **Type 2 KA-MI** amphibious tank used automotive components of the Type 95 light tank, and this was widely used in the early

Pacific campaigns of World War II. Japan also used tankettes on a large scale including the Types 92, 94 and 97, the last being the most common.

When used in China and during the early World War II campaigns against the Americans, the Type 95 proved a useful vehicle, but once confronted by American tanks and anti-tank guns it was outclassed.

Specification
Type 95
Crew: 4
Weight: 7400 kg (16,314 lb)
Dimensions: length 4.38 m (14 ft 4 in); width 2.057 m (6 ft 9 in); height 2.184 m (7 ft 2 in)

A Type 95 at speed, probably in Manchuria. Japan's conquests were aided considerably by the fact that none of her opponents possessed any significant amount of armour, nor any anti-tank capability.

Powerplant: one Mitsubishi NVD 6120 six-cylinder air-cooled diesel engine developing 120 hp (89 kW)
Performance: maximum road speed 45 km/h (28 mph); maximum range 250 km (156 miles); fording 1.0 m (3 ft 3 in); gradient 60 per cent; vertical obstacle 0.812 m (2 ft 8 in); trench 2.0 m (6 ft 7 in)

JAPAN
Type 97 medium tank

In the mid-1930s a requirement was issued for a new medium tank to replace the Type 89B medium tank which by then was rapidly becoming obsolete. As the Engineering Department and the General Staff could not agree on the better design, two prototypes were built. Mitsubishi built the design of the Engineering Department while Osaka Arsenal built the design of the General Staff. There was in fact little to choose between the two designs, although the Mitsubishi tank was heavier and driven by a more powerful engine. The Mitsubishi prototype was standardized as the **Type 97 CHI-HA** medium tank and some 3,000 vehicles were built before production was finally completed in the middle of World War II.

The hull and turret of the Type 97 medium tank were of riveted construction that varied in thickness from 8 mm (0.30 in) to 25 mm (0.98 mm). The driver was seated at the front of the hull on the right, with the 7.7-mm (0.303-in) Type 97 machine-gunner to his left. The two-man turret was in the centre of the hull, offset to the right, and could be traversed manually through 360°. Main armament consisted of a 57-mm Type 97 gun with an elevation of +11° and depression of −9°, and another 7.7-mm (0.303-in) machine-gun was located in the turret rear. Totals of 120 rounds of 57-mm (80 high explosive and 40 of armour-piercing) and 2,350 rounds of 7.7-mm (0.303-in) ammunition were carried.

The 12-cylinder air-cooled diesel

was mounted at the rear of the hull and transmitted power via a propeller shaft to the gearbox in the nose of the tank; the gearbox had four forward and one reverse gears. Steering was of the clutch and brake type, and suspension on each side consisted of six dual rubber-tyred road wheels, with the drive sprocket at the front and idler at the rear; there were three track-return rollers. The four central road wheels were paired and mounted on bell cranks resisted by armoured compression springs, while each end bogie was independently bell crank-mounted to the hull in a similar manner.

When first introduced into service the Type 97 was quite an advanced design apart from its main armament, which had a low muzzle velocity. A feature of most Japanese tanks of this period was that they were powered by diesel rather than petrol engines, which gave them a much increased operational range as well as reducing the ever-present risk of fire, the dread of any tank crew.

In 1942 the Type 97 medium tank (special) was introduced: this had a new turret armed with a 47-mm Type 97 gun that fired ammunition with a higher muzzle velocity and therefore improved penetration characteristics. This weapon used the same ammunition as Japanese anti-tank guns and therefore helped ammunition commonality in the front line.

The chassis of the Type 97 was also used as the basis for a number of other vehicles including a flail-equipped

mineclearing tank, self-propelled guns (including the 150-mm/5.9-in **Type 38 HO-RO**), self-propelled anti-aircraft guns (including 20-mm and 75-mm/2.95-in), an engineer tank, a recovery vehicle and an armoured bridgelayer. Most of these were built in such small numbers that they played little part in actual operations. The Type 97 was replaced in production by the **Type 1 CHI-HE** medium tank, followed by the **Type 3 CHI-NU**, of which only 60 were built by the end of the war. The last Japanese medium tanks were the Type 4 and Type 5, but neither of these well-armed vehicles saw combat.

Specification
Type 97
Crew: 4

Probably the best Japanese armoured vehicle to see any great amount of service, the Type 97 was a fairly advanced design that was handicapped by an inadequate gun.

Weight: 15000 kg (33,069 lb)
Dimensions: length 5.516 m (18 ft 1 in); width 2.33 m (7 ft 8 in); height 2.23 m (7 ft 4 in)
Powerplant: one Mitsubishi 12-cylinder air-cooled diesel engine developing 170 hp (127 kW)
Performance: maximum road speed 38 km/h (24 mph); maximum range 210 km (130 miles); fording 1.0 m (3 ft 3 in); gradient 57 per cent; vertical obstacle 0.812 m (2 ft 6 in); trench 2.514 m (8 ft 3 in)

British and French Tanks

Since the birth of the tank in 1916, the British have led the world in both the design and use of armoured forces, but by 1939 internal army politics and mistaken tactical doctrine had robbed Britain of this important and hard-won advantage.

French mechanized units parading with their Hotchkiss H35 tanks. A small, lightly armed vehicle with a crew of two, it saw service with the French in both cavalry and infantry-support roles.

The tanks discussed here are among some of the least successful of the World War II period. Some of them (such as the British Valentine, Matilda and Churchill) were eventually turned into good fighting machines, but – working in a rush and without a proper development base from which to work up their designs –

many British tank designers produced tanks that were no match for their counterparts in the German Panzer units. The reasons for this are described herein, but it is not all a sorry tale: despite their drawbacks, these tanks (both Infantry and Cruiser types) were at times all there was to hand and with them their crews and com-

manders learned the important lessons that were to produce the eventual Allied victory.

Some of the development and design results were remarkable. Working from a base where virtually no heavy engineering facilities existed, Australia was able to produce the Sentinel from scratch, and it was no fault of the

designers that their progeny was never to see action. The same can be said of the Canadians, who produced the Ram in a remarkably short time, again from scratch and with no tank production experience whatsoever. These two projects must rate among the more remarkable production feats of World War II, but today they are little known outside their home nations.

The tale of the Cruiser tanks produced by the United Kingdom has by now been often told but it still bears re-examination, showing as it does, how a doctrine accepted without proper investigation can affect the course of battles, even well past the point when the doctrine has been found wanting. British and Allied tank crews had to drive their charges into battle knowing that their main guns were too weak, their armoured protection too thin and their mechanical reliability all too suspect at a critical moment. But they went into battle all the same and often managed to defeat a better-armed and prepared enemy. Thus, while reading of the tanks onc must think of the men who manned and fought them, for tanks are but lumps of metal constructed in a certain fashion, and are nothing without men to drive and use them in combat.

Hotchkiss H-35 and H-39 light tanks

During the early 1930s the French army, in common with many other European armies, decided to re-equip its ageing tank parks with modern equipment. At that time the French followed the current practice of dividing tank functions into cavalry and infantry usage and one of the new tanks intended for cavalry use was a design known as the **Char Léger Hotchkiss H-35**. But although intended primarily for cavalry formation use, the H-35 was later adopted for infantry support as well, making it one of the more important of the French tanks of the day. The H-35 was a small vehicle with a crew of two, and it was lightly armed with only a 37-mm (1.46-in) short-barrelled gun and a single 7.5-mm (0.295-in) machine-gun. Armour was also light, ranging in the thickness from 12 mm (0.47 in) to 34 mm (1.34 in). It was also rather underpowered, and after about 400 H-35s had been produced from 1936 onwards the basic model was supplemented by the **Char Léger Hotchkiss H-39**, first produced during 1939. The production totals for the H-39 were much greater (eventually running to over 1,000 units), but in general French tank production was slow, being severely limited by a lack of mass production facilities, and was constantly beset by labour troubles, even after 1939.

The H-39 differed from the H-35 in having a 120- rather than 75-hp (89.5- rather than 56-kW) engine, and could be recognized by the raised rear decking, which on the H-39 was almost flat compared with the pronounced slope on the H-35. Also a new and longer 37-mm gun was fitted, but this was only marginally more powerful than the earlier weapon and soon proved to be virtually useless against most German tanks.

Both the H-35 and the H-39 were used in action in France in May 1940, and both were able to give a good account of themselves. However, their part in the fighting was more than diminished by their dismal tactical use. Instead of being used en masse (in the way that the Germans used their Panzer columns), the French tanks were scattered along the line in penny packets, assigned to local infantry support instead of being used as an effective anti-armour force and were able to make little impact. On occasion they

Fitted with the SA 38 37-mm L33, the H-39 had a respectable performance by 1930s standards. Its only major disadvantage was that the commander had to work the gun.

were able to surprise the Germans, but only in purely local actions, so many were either destroyed or captured by the advancing Germans. Always short of matériel, the Germans took many Hotchkiss tanks into their own service as the **PzKpfw 35-H 734(f)** and **PzKpfw 39-H 735(f)**, and these were used for some years by second-line and occupation units. Many of the H-35 and H-39 tanks later had their turrets removed and replaced by German anti-tank guns for use as mobile tank destroyers.

Not all the French tanks fell into German hands. Many were located in the French Middle East possessions and some were either taken over by the Free French or were used in action by the Vichy French during the campaign in Syria in 1941. Perhaps the Hotchkiss tanks with the most unusual travel tales were those taken by the Germans to the Soviet Union in 1941, when they were so short of tanks that even the captured French vehicles were found useful.

By 1945 there were few H-35s or H-39s left anywhere: the Middle East examples survived in small numbers, and post-war some were used to form part of the Israeli army tank arm, remaining in service as late as 1956.

Specification
Hotchkiss H-39
Crew: 2

Weight: 12.1 tonnes
Powerplant: one Hotchkiss 6-cylinder petrol engine developing 120 hp (89.5 kW)
Dimensions: length 4.22 m (13 ft 10 in); width 1.95 m (6 ft 4.8 in); height 2.15 m (7 ft 0.6 in)
Performance: maximum road speed 36 km/h (22.3 mph); maximum road range 120 km (74.5 miles); fording 0.85 m (2 ft 10 in); gradient 40°; vertical

H-35s, seen here on parade, equipped many French mechanized cavalry units. Although armed with the ineffectual SA 18 37-mm L21, they could still have performed effectively in the reconnaissance role but instead were deployed piecemeal to bolster the infantry.

obstacle 0.50 m (1 ft 8 in); trench 1.80 m (5 ft 11 in)

Renault R 35

The **Renault R 35** had its origins in a design known originally as the **Renault ZM**, produced in late 1934 in answer to a French army request for a new infantry support tank to supplement and eventually replace the ageing Renault FT 17 which dated back to World War I. Trials of the new tank started in early 1935, and in that same year the design was ordered into production without completion of the testing as Germany appeared to be in a mood for conflict. Before production got under way it was decided to increase the armour basis from 30 mm (1.18 in) to 40 mm (1.575 in).

The R 35 never entirely replaced the FT 17 in service, but by 1940 over 1,600 had been built and it was the most numerous French infantry tank in use. Its overall appearance was not unlike that of the FT 17, for it was a

small tank with a crew of only two. The design made much use of cast armour and the suspension followed the Renault practice of the day, being of the

Continued on page 1324

Two-man infantry support tanks in the Great War tradition, the R 35s were built in the belief that tank warfare had changed little since 1918.

type used on the Renault cavalry tank designs. The driver's position was forward, while the commander had to act as his own loader and gunner firing a 37-mm (1.456-in) short-barrelled gun and co-axial 7.5-mm (0.295-in) machine-gun mounted in a small cast turret. This turret was poorly equipped with vision devices and was so arranged that the commander had to spend much of his time in action standing on the hull floor. Out of action the rear of the turret opened as a flap on which the commander could sit.

For its day the R 35 was a sound enough vehicle, and was typical of contemporary French design. In 1940 a version with a revised suspension and known as the **AMX R 40** was introduced, and a few were produced before the Germans invaded in May 1940. The little R 35s soon proved to be no match for the German Panzers. For a start they were usually allocated in small numbers in direct support of infantry formations, and could thus be picked off piecemeal by the massed German tanks. Their gun proved virtually ineffective against even the lightest German tanks, though in return their 40-mm (1.575-in) armour was fairly effective against most of the German anti-tank guns. Thus the R 35s could contribute but little to the course of the campaign and many were either destroyed or simply abandoned by their crews in the disasters that overtook the French army as the Germans swept through France.

Large numbers of R 35s fell into German hands virtually intact. These were duly put to use by various garrison units in France while many eventually passed to driver and other tank training schools. With the invasion of the Soviet Union many R 35s were stripped of their turrets and used as artillery tractors or ammunition carriers. Later, many of the R 35s still in France had their turrets removed so that their hulls could be converted as the basis of several self-propelled artillery or anti-tank gun models, the turrets then being emplaced in concrete along the coastal defences of the Atlantic Wall.

Thus the R 35 passed into history, and despite its numbers its combat record was such that it proved to be of more use to the Germans than the French.

Specification
Renault R 35
Crew: 2
Weight: 10000 kg (22,046 lb)
Powerplant: one Renault 4-cylinder petrol engine developing 61 kW (82 bhp)
Dimensions: length 4.20 m (13 ft 9.25 in); width 1.85 m (6 ft 0.75 in); height 2.37 m (7 ft 9.25 in)
Performance: maximum speed 20 km/h (12.4 mph); range 140 km (87 miles); fording 0.8 m (2 ft 7 in); vertical obstacle 0.5 m (1 ft 7.7 in); trench 1.6 m (5 ft 3 in)

FRANCE

SOMUA S-35 medium tank

When the re-equipment of the French cavalry arm with tanks started during the mid-1930s several concerns became involved, among them a Schneider subsidiary in St Ouen and known as the Société d'Outillage Mécanique et d'Usinage d'Artillerie, better known as SOMUA. In 1935 this concern displayed a tank prototype that attracted immediate attention, and its very advanced design was quickly recognized by the award of a production order. One of the best if not the best AFV of its day, the type was known as the **SOMUA S-35** to most of Europe though to the French army it was the **Automitrailleuse de Combat (AMC) modele 1935 SOMUA**.

The S-35 had many features that were later to become commonplace. The hull and turret were both cast components at a time when most contemporary vehicles used riveted plates. The cast armour was not only well-shaped for extra protection but it was also much thicker (minimum of 20 mm/0.79 in and maximum of 55 mm/2.16 in) than the norm for the time. For all that it still had a good reserve of power provided by a V-8 petrol engine for lively battlefield performance, and a good operational radius of action was ensured by large internal fuel tanks. Radio was standard, at a time when hand signals between tanks were still common. To add to all these advantages the S-35 was armed with a powerful gun: the 47-mm (1.85-in) SA 35 was one of the most powerful weapons of the day and a gun that could still be regarded as a useful weapon in 1944. The secondary armament was a single 7.5-mm (0.295-in) co-axial machine-gun.

The S-35 was ordered into production but, as in nearly all other sectors of the French defence industry before 1939, this production was slow and beset by labour and other troubles. Only about 400 S-35s had been produced by the time the Germans invaded in May 1940, and of those only about 250 were in front-line service. But in action the S-35 gave a good account of itself though revealing a serious design defect when under fire: the upper and lower hull halves were joined by a ring of bolts along a horizontal join, and if an anti-tank projectile hit this join the two halves split apart with obvious dire results. But at the time this mattered less than the way in which the tanks had to be handled: the S-35 had a crew of three (driver, radio operator and commander), and it was the commander in his one-man turret who caused the problems, for this unfortunate had not only to keep an eye on the local tactical scene, but also to assimilate orders from the radio while loading and firing the gun. The tasks were too much for one man, so the full potential of the S-35 was rarely attained. As with other French tanks of the day the S-35s were split into small groups scattered long the French line and were called together on only a few occasions for worthwhile counterstrokes against the Panzer columns.

After the occupation of France the Germans took over as many S-35s as they could find for issue to occupation and training units under the designation **PzKpfw 35-S 739(f)**. Some were handed over to the Italian army, but many were still based in France when the Allies invaded in 1944 and S-35s were once more in action, this time in German hands. Any S-35s taken by the Allies were passed over to the Free French, who in their turn used them in the reduction of the beleaguered German garrisons locked up in their Atlantic sea-port strongholds.

Well protected and manoeuvrable, the SOMUA S-35 was undoubtedly the best Allied tank in 1940. It had a radio and its 47-mm gun could fire both armour-piercing shot and high explosive, an obvious requirement which had escaped British designers.

Specification
SOMUA S-35
Crew: 3
Weight: 19.5 tonnes
Powerplant: one SOMUA V-8 petrol engine developing 190 hp (141.7 kW)
Dimensions: length 5.38 m (17 ft 7.8 in); width 2.12 m (6 ft 11.5 in); height 2.62 m (8 ft 7 in)
Performance: maximum road speed 40 km/h (24.85 mph); maximum road range 230 km (143 miles); fording 1.00 m (3 ft 3 in); gradient 40°; vertical obstacle 0.76 m (2 ft 6 in); trench 2.13 m (7 ft)

In 1940 many SOMUAs were damaged and abandoned like the one seen here, but the vehicle was good enough for the Germans to use against the Allies four years later.

Below: Despite the weakness of having the commander operate the main armament, the S-35 was a fine tank.

Char B1-bis heavy tank

The series of tanks known as the **Char B** had a definite look of the 'Great War' era about them, and this is not surprising for their development can be traced back as far as 1921 and the aftermath of World War I. What was demanded at that time was a tank with a 75-mm (2.95-in) gun set in a hull-mounted embrasure, but it was not until about 1930 that the result of this request was finally built. This was the Char B heavy tank with a weight of about 25 tonnes, and prolonged development led in 1935 to the full production version, the **Char B1**.

The Char B1 was a powerful tank for the period as it had a turret-mounted 47-mm (1.85-in) gun and a 75-mm (2.95-in) gun set in the lower hull front. The limited traverse of this latter gun was partially offset by a complex steering system that allowed the vehicle to be rapidly pointed towards the correct target sector. Although its archaic appearance belied the fact, the Char B was full of very advanced design features that ranged from self-sealing fuel tanks to grouped lubrication for the many bearings; an electric starter was also provided and attention was given to internal fire protection. However, the crew of four men was scattered about the interior in a way that made internal communication difficult, and this led to many operational problems. The crew of the Char B1 had to be a highly-trained group of specialists to make the best of the vehicle's potential fighting value, and in 1940 these teams were few and far between.

The final production model was the **Char B1-bis** which had increased armour (maximum and minimum of 65 and 14 mm/2.56 and 0.55 in compared with the Char B1's 40 and 14 mm/1.57 and 0.55 in), a revised turret design and a more powerful engine. Later production models had an even more powerful aircraft engine and extra fuel capacity. Production of the Char B1-bis started in 1937, and by 1940 there were about 400 Char Bs of all types in service. By then the Char B1 and Char B1-bis were the most numerous and powerful of all the French heavy tanks, and the basic type was the main battle tank of the few French armoured formations.

The Germans had a great respect for the Char B1, for the 75-mm (2.95-in) gun was quite capable of knocking out even their PzKpfw IV, but they were considerably assisted during the May 1940 fighting by several factors. One was that the Char B1s were complex beasts and required a great deal of careful maintenance: many simply broke down en route to battle and were left for the Germans to take over undamaged. The type's combat potential was somewhat lessened by the need for a well-trained crew and by the usual drawback in French design and usage of the commander having to serve the gun as well as command the tank and crew. The final drawback for the French was that, as was the case with other tank formations, the Char B1 units were frequently broken up into small local-defence groups instead of being grouped to meet the German tank advances.

The Germans took over the Char B1-bis as the **PzKpfw B1-bis 740(f)** and used it for a variety of purposes. Some were passed intact to occupation units such as those in the Channel Islands, while others were converted for driver training or were altered to become self-propelled artillery carriages.

The Char B1 was easily able to deal with any German tank in existence, but abysmal handling rendered it largely ineffective.

Some were fitted with flamethrowers as the **PzKpfw Flamm(f)**. In 1944 a few were still around to pass once more into French army use but by 1945 only a handful were left.

Specification
Char B1-bis
Crew: 4
Weight: 31.5 tonnes
Powerplant: one Renault 6-cylinder petrol engine developing 307 hp (229 kW)
Dimensions: length 6.37 m (20 ft 10.8 in); width 2.50 m (8 ft 2.4 in); height 2.79 m (9 ft 1.8 in)
Performance: maximum road speed 28 km/h (17.4 mph); maximum road range 180 km (112 miles); fording not known; gradient 50 per cent; vertical obstacle 0.93 m (3 ft 1 in); trench 2.74 m (9 ft)

The 400 or so Char B1s possessed by the French army in 1940 were potentially a devastating striking force.

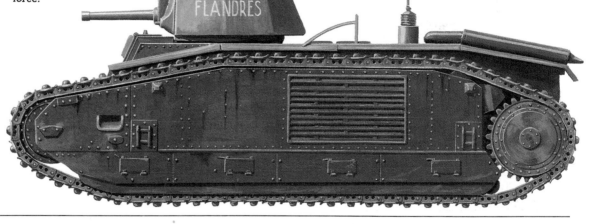

Vickers Light Tanks

The **Vickers Light Tanks** had their origins in a series of tankettes designed and produced by Carden-Loyd during the 1920s. The story of these little vehicles is outside the scope of this account but one of them, the **Carden-Loyd Mk VIII**, acted as the prototype for the **Vickers Light Tank Mk I**. Only a few of these innovative vehicles were produced and issued, but they provided a great deal of insight into what would be required for later models. The Mk I had a two-man crew and had a small turret for a 7.7-mm (0.303-in) machine-gun.

The Mk I led via the **Light Tank Mk IA** (better armour) to the **Light Tank Mk II** (improved turret and modified suspension) which appeared in 1930, and this formed the basis for later versions up to the **Light Tank Mk VI**. All these light tanks used a simple hull with riveted armour which was of the order of 10 to 15 mm (0.39 to 0.59 in) thick. From the **Light Tank Mk V** onwards the turret was enlarged to take

two men, making a three-man crew in all, and the same mark also saw the introduction of a 12.7-mm (0.5-in) machine-gun alongside the original 7.7-mm (0.303-in) weapon. Of course there were changes between all the various marks: for instance the **Light Tank Mk IV** was the first to use the armour as supporting plates for the chassis, rather than the other way round, and changes were made to the suspension to improve cross-country performance. With the Mk VI the light tanks came to the peak of their development and were agile vehicles capable of a nifty cross-country speed, and were up-armed to the point where the **Light Tank Mk VIc** had a 15-mm (0.59-in) heavy machine-gun in the turret. All manner of changes to items such as engine cooling and vision devices were also introduced on this late mark, and even the machine-gun was changed to the new Besa 7.92-mm (0.312-in) machine-gun of Czech origins.

The Vickers Light Tanks were

widely used throughout the 1930s and the early war years. Many of the early marks were used in India and for imperial policing duties, in which they proved ideal, but in action during the early campaigns of World War II they soon revealed themselves as being virtually useless. Their main drawback was their thin armour, which could be penetrated even by small-calibre armour-piercing projectiles, and their

Mounting a 0.50-in and later a 15-mm BESA machine-gun with a co-axial 7.92-mm machine-gun, the Vickers Light Tank was an adequate vehicle for armoured reconnaissance.

lack of a weapon heavier than a machine-gun. In France in 1940 they were frequently incorrectly deployed as combat tanks and suffered accordingly, for they were only reconnaissance vehicles. Their light armour and lack of an offensive weapon made them of little use for anything else, but in 1940 the lack of numbers of tanks on the ground often meant that they were rushed into action against the German Panzers with disastrous results.

The Light Tanks remained in use in the North African desert campaigns for some time until replacements came along. Back in the United Kingdom the later marks were often used for trials. One of them was an attempt to convert some of the otherwise wasted vehicles into anti-aircraft tanks, mounting either four 7.92-mm (0.312-in) or two 15-mm (0.59-in) machine-guns, but although some conversions were made they saw little use. Other attempts were made to fit a 2-pdr (40-mm/1.58-in) anti-tank gun in an enlarged turret, but that idea was not pursued.

Surprisingly enough, the Germans in France were happy to use any Light Tanks they could recover, not as battle tanks but as anti-tank gun carriers, but only small numbers are believed to have been so converted.

Specification
Light Tank Mk V
Crew: 3
Weight: 4877 kg (10,752 lb)
Powerplant: one Meadows ESTL 6-cylinder petrol engine delivering 66 kW (88 bhp)
Dimensions: length 3.96 m (13 ft); width 2.08 m (6 ft 10 in); height 2.235 m (7 ft 6 in)
Performance: maximum speed 51.5 km/h (32 mph); range 201 km (215 miles)

After suffering heavy losses in France when mistakenly used in close support of the infantry, the MK VI soldiered on in the Middle East and North Africa.

Light Tank Mk VII Tetrarch

The **Tetrarch** light tank started its life as the **Light Tank Mk VII**, and was a Vickers private-venture project to continue its line of light tank designs. That was in 1937, and the first prototype started its trials in 1938. These trials demonstrated that the new design, known at that time as the **Purdah**, lacked any of the attributes that would make it an outstanding weapon; but the type offered some potential, and it was decided to undertake further testing pending a possible production contract.

In its initial form the **Purdah**, later designated the **A17**, and later still the Tetrarch, differed from the earlier light tanks by having four large road wheels on each side. A two-man turret was centrally mounted, and this turret was large enough to mount a 2-pdr (40-mm/1.58-in) gun with co-axial 7.92-mm (0.312-in) machine-gun. Various alterations were demanded once the prototype had completed its initial trials, notably to engine cooling and for provision of more fuel tanks to improve range. Eventually the Tetrarch was put into production without any great enthusiasm, but it was at least something ready to hand at a period when the British army had few tanks of any kind to put into the field. Light tanks were recognized as a liability in action by 1941, however, so the few that were completed became surplus to requirements other than for limited operations such as the invasion of Madagascar in May 1942. Numbers of Tetrarchs were even handed over to the Soviet Union.

But the fortunes of the Tetrarch changed with the establishment of the airborne forces, and it was not long before the lightweight Tetrarch was accepted as the army's first airborne tank. A new glider, the General Aircraft Hamilcar, was designed and produced as the airborne carrier for the Tetrarch, but it was not until April 1944 that the first trial landings were made, some of them being spectacular in the extreme. For their new role the turrets were fitted with a 76.2-mm (3-in) infantry support howitzer, the vehicle being redesignated **Tetrarch ICS**.

The Tetrarchs went into action dur-

ing the Normandy landings of 6 June 1944 during the second airborne wave. Most of them landed near the River Orne, where their combat life was short. They were next used during the Rhine crossings on 24 March 1945, but only a few were used during that event as their numbers had been supplemented by the American M22 Locust. That marked the limits of the type's airborne operational career, but some were retained for a few years after the war until their Hamilcar gliders were withdrawn from service.

The basic design of the Tetrarch was used for a number of developments during the war years. One was the **Light Tank Mk VIII Harry Hopkins**, a number of which were produced but never used. The Harry Hopkins was

Above: Carried in a Hamilcar glider, the Tetrarch was used by British airborne forces during the Normandy landings. Hopelessly outclassed by German tanks, this Tetrarch has a Littlejohn adapter fitted to its 2-pdr gun to increase muzzle velocity and thus armour penetration.

Right: Originally a Vickers private venture, the Tetrarch was put into production despite lacking armour, effective armament or a properly defined purpose. It eventually saw limited action in Madagascar and the USSR before being adopted as Britain's first air-portable tank.

virtually a Tetrarch with thicker armour (6-38 mm/0.25-1.5 in rather than 4-15 mm/0.15-0.6 in) and many mechanical changes, but it also acted as the basis for yet another variant known as the **Alecto**. This was to have been an airborne or light self-propelled gun mounting a 95-mm (actually 94-mm/3.7-in) howitzer, but few of these were produced. Despite many plans to produce versions with 25-pdr or even 32-pdr guns, the only versions to be built were fitted with dozer blades for a possible airborne engineer role. In the event the Alectos ended up as hack tractors on Salisbury Plain.

Specification
Tetrarch
Crew: 3
Weight: 7620 kg (16,800 lb)
Powerplant: one Meadows 12-cylinder petrol engine delivering 123 kW (165 bhp)
Dimensions: length overall 4.305 m (14 ft 1.5 in); length of hull 4.115 m (13 ft 6 in); width 2.31 m (7 ft 7 in); height 2.121 m (6 ft 11.5 in)
Performance: maximum road speed 64 km/h (40 mph); maximum cross-country speed 45 km/h (28 mph); fording 0.914 m (3 ft); trench 1.524 m (5 ft)

Cruiser Tank Mk VI Crusader

The **Cruiser Tank Mk VI** that became known as the **Crusader** had its origins around the same time as the Covenanter, but was a Nuffield design and therefore used the Nuffield Liberty Mk III engine and a Nuffield gearbox. In overall appearance and layout the Crusader resembled the Covenanter, but there were several differences. One was that the Crusader had five road wheels on each side instead of the Covenanter's four.

The prototype was known as the **A15**. It had the unusual feature of two forward miniature turrets, one in front of the driver's hood and the other for a gunner seated in the front hull. Each of these turrets was fitted with a 7.92-mm (0.312-in) machine-gun, but after early trials the driver's gun and turret was eliminated. These early trials once more highlighted that engine cooling was inadequate and that the gear-change arrangements were unreliable. These problems, and others, took a long time to remedy and, indeed, many were still present when the Crusader was withdrawn from service.

The first production model was the **Crusader I**, which had a 2-pdr (40-mm/1.58-in) gun and armour with a 40-mm (1.58-in) basis. When Crusader Is entered service in 1941 they were already inadequate for combat, and as the new 6-pdr (57-mm/2.24-in) gun was still in short supply the armour alone was increased in thickness to a 50-mm (1.97-in) basis to produce the **Crusader II**, and it was not until the **Crusader III** that the 6-pdr gun was fitted. This turned out to be the main 'combat' version of the Crusader during the North African campaigns before it was replaced by the American M4 Sherman. In action the Crusader proved fast and nippy, but its armour proved to be too thin, and the Crusaders armed with 2-pdr guns were no match for their German counterparts. Their reliability problems did little for Crusaders' chances of survival under desert conditions, but gradual improvements were effected. The **Crusader IICS** was fitted with a 76.2-mm (3-in) howitzer.

Once they were no longer combat tanks the Crusaders were used for a variety of special purposes. Some were converted as anti-aircraft tanks

The Crusader III was the first British tank to be armed with an effective gun, the 6-pdr. Its other great strongpoint was its suspension, which was so tough that the theoretical maximum speed could often be exceeded.

mounting either a single 40-mm (1.58-in) Bofors gun (**Crusader III AA I**) or twin or triple 20-mm (0.787-in) cannon (**Crusader III AA II**). There was a **Crusader ARV** armoured recovery vehicle version without a turret (but with an 'A' frame jib) and another turretless version featured a dozer blade for combat engineering purposes (**Crusader Dozer**). Many Crusaders were fitted with an open box superstructure for use as high-speed artillery tractors (**Crusader Gun Tractor**), and were widely used in Europe during 1944 and 1945 to tow 17-pdr (76.2-mm/3-in) anti-tank guns. Many more were used for trials that ranged from engine installations via mine warfare devices to wading trials that led to the 'Duplex Drive' tanks.

The Crusader was one of the 'classic' British tanks of World War II, and had a dashing and attractive appearance that belied its lack of combat efficiency. Despite its low and aggressive silhouette it was outclassed as a battle tank on many occasions, but saw the war out in several special-purpose variants.

Two early model Crusaders are seen during Operation 'Crusader'. The battle demonstrated that gallantry alone is not a substitute for good equipment.

Specification
Crusader III
Crew: 3
Weight: 20067 kg (44,240 lb)
Powerplant: one Nuffield Liberty Mk III petrol engine developing 254 kW (340 bhp)
Dimensions: length 5.994 m (19 ft 8 in); width 2.64 m (8 ft 8 in); height 2.235 m (7 ft 4 in)
Performance: maximum road speed 43.4 km/h (27 mph); maximum cross-country speed 24 km/h (15 mph); range with extra fuel tank 204 km (127 miles); fording 0.99 m (3 ft 3 in); vertical obstacle 0.686 m (2 ft 3 in); trench 2.59 m (8 ft 6 in)

Cruiser Tank Mk VIII Cromwell

In the United Kingdom the differentiation between 'Cruiser' and 'Infantry' tanks persisted almost until the end of the war despite the fact that most other nations had never entertained the notion. It persisted even after the unfortunate experiences of the early 'Cruiser' designs had highlighted the drawbacks of producing a lightly armed and armoured main battle tank, and continued even when a replacement for the Crusader was being sought. The need for more armour and a bigger gun was finally realized (and a more powerful engine would be required) and in 1941 a new specification was issued. It was answered by two main entrants to the same basic **A27** design, one the A27L with a Liberty engine (this was to become the Centaur) and the other the A27M with a Rolls-Royce Meteor that was to become the **Cruiser Tank Mk VIII Cromwell**.

The first Cromwells were produced in January 1943. The first three marks (**Cromwell I** with one 6-pdr and two Besa machine-guns, **Cromwell II** with wider tracks and only one machine-gun, and **Cromwell III** produced by re-engining a Centaur I) all had as their main armament the 6-pdr (57-mm/2.244-in) gun, but by 1943 it had

A Cromwell roars through a village in Normandy, August 1944. Initially mounting a 6-pdr, by D-Day they were armed with a 75-mm gun which gave them a reasonable chance against German armour. The Cromwell entered service in 1943 and many crews were trained in it before the invasion. In the acid test of combat, the Cromwell itself did not let them down.

been decided that something heavier would be required and a new 75-mm (2.95-in) gun was demanded. For once things were able to move relatively swiftly on the production lines and the first 75-mm (2.95-in) **Cromwell Mk IV** tanks were issued to the armoured regiments in October 1943. Thereafter the 75-mm (2.95-in) gun remained the Cromwell's main gun until the **Cromwell Mk VIII**, which had a 95-mm (actually 94-mm/3.7-in) howitzer for close support.

Perhaps the main value of the Cromwell to the British armoured regiments during 1943 was as a training tank, for at last the troops had a tank that was something of a match for its German counterparts. There was better armour (8-76 mm/0.315-3 in) on the Cromwell than on any previous 'Cruiser' tank and the 75-mm (2.95-in) gun, which shared many components with the smaller 6-pdr, at last provided the British tankies with a viable weapon. But by the time they were ready for active service the Cromwells were in the process of being replaced by the readily-available M4 Sherman for purposes of standardization and logistic safety. But the Cromwell did see service. Many were used by the 7th Armoured Division in the campaigns that followed the Normandy landings. Here the excellent performance provided by the Meteor engine made the Cromwell a well-liked vehicle: it was fast and reliable, and the gun proved easy to lay and fire.

The Cromwell was but a stepping stone to the later Comet tank which was to emerge as perhaps the best all-round British tank of the war years. But the Cromwell was an important vehicle, not just as a combat tank but for several other roles. Some were used as mobile artillery observation posts (**Cromwell OP**) with their main gun removed and with extra radios installed. Others had their turrets entirely removed and replaced by all the various bits and pieces required for the Cromwell to be used as the **Cromwell ARV** armoured recovery vehicle. The Cromwell was also used as the basis for a heavily armoured assault

Above: Cromwell tanks move up to their start line for one of the breakout battles in Normandy, 1944. The price of attacking the well-sited German positions was often heavy, despite the improved quality of British armour.

Right: Although the majority of British tank units were equipped with the Sherman, the Cromwell was a successful design, doing much to restore the dreadful imbalance of quality between British and German armour.

tank that became known as the A33, which was ready by May 1944 but never got into production.

Specification
Cromwell IV
Crew: 5
Weight: 27942 kg (61,600 lb)
Powerplant: one Rolls-Royce Meteor V-12 petrol engine developing 570 bhp (425 kW)
Dimensions: length overall 6.42 m (21 ft 0.75 in); width 3.048 m (10 ft); height

2.51 m (8 ft 3 in)
Performance: maximum speed 61 km/h (38 mph); road range 278 km (173

miles); fording 1.219 m (4 ft); vertical obstacle 0.914 m (3 ft); trench 2.286 m (7 ft 6 in)

⬛ UK
Cruiser Tank Mk VIII Centaur

The **Cruiser Tank Mk VIII Centaur** was a contemporary of the Cromwell and was derived from the same general staff specification. But whereas the Cromwell was a Rolls-Royce Meteor-engined vehicle, the Centaur was a Leyland Motors project and was fitted with the Liberty engine. In many other respects the Centaur and the Cromwell were identical (apart from the engines, gearboxes and other transmission components) and some Centaurs were fitted with the Meteor engine at a later stage and redesignated Cromwells.

Leyland had already produced a 'Cruiser' tank design known as the **Cruiser Tank Mk VII Cavalier** which had proved to be a generally unsuccessful design as a result of poor performance, mechanical breakdowns and a short engine life. Leyland understandably used some features of the Cavalier on the Centaur but unfortunately it also carried over some of the earlier design's problems, for the Liberty engine was really too low-pow-

ered to provide the Centaur with the same performance as the Cromwell; nor was the engine life up to the standards of the Meteor's reliability.

The **Centaur I** was produced with the usual 6-pdr (57-mm/2.244-in) gun of the period, and the first examples were ready in June 1942. These early Centaurs were used only for training purposes, some with auxiliary fuel tanks mounted at the rear. The **Centaur III** was produced in small numbers only, but this mounted a 75-mm (2.95-in) main gun. Armour varied in thickness from 20 to 76 mm (0.8 to 3 in). The **Centaur IV** was the main 'combat' version of the series as it was specially produced for use by the Royal Marines Armoured Support Group during the D-Day landings in Normandy on 6 June 1944. These Mk IVs were fitted with 95-mm (actually 94-mm/3.7-in) close-support howitzers; 80 of them were issued, and these were intended to be used only in the initial stages of the amphibious assault. In fact most of them landed safely and performed so

well on the beaches and the area immediately inland that many were retained for some weeks afterwards for the slow and dangerous combat in the *bocage* country.

Thereafter the Centaurs were withdrawn from combat use and underwent the usual routine of conversion for other purposes. As usual the simplest conversion was to an artillery observation post (**Centaur OP**) while others simply had their turrets removed to act as **Centaur Kangaroo** armoured personnel carriers. The usual armoured recovery vehicle variant duly appeared as the **Centaur ARV** along with the **Centaur Dozer** turretless version fitted with a dozer blade for combat engineer duties. Two Centaur conversions that did mount guns were the two marks of **Centaur III/IV AAI** and **Centaur III/IV AAII** tanks. These had the same 20-mm anti-aircraft turrets as the earlier Crusader AA tanks, but the Centaur AA versions mounted 20-mm (0.787-in) Polsten cannon in place of the earlier Oerlikon cannon. Both of

these variants took part in the early stages of the Normandy campaign but were withdrawn once the anticipated threat of air attack did not materialize.

Specification
Centaur III
Crew: 5
Weight: 28849 kg (63,600 lb)
Powerplant: one Nuffield Liberty Mk V-12 petrol engine developing 295 kW (395 bhp)
Dimensions: length 6.35 m (20 ft 10 in); width 2.895 m (9 ft 6 in); height 2.489 m (8 ft 2 in)
Performance: maximum road speed 43.4 km/h (27 mph); maximum cross-country speed about 25.7 km/h (16 mph); range 265 km (165 miles); fording 0.914 m (3 ft); vertical obstacle 0.914 m (3 ft); trench 2.286 m (7 ft 6 in)

Cruiser Tank Challenger

The **Cruiser Tank Challenger** produced during World War II bore no resemblance to the mighty Challenger that is currently being issued to the British army, for the original Challenger was one of the British tank industry's least successful progeny. It was derived from a 1941 request to mount a heavy gun capable of tackling even the heaviest German tanks and the 17-pdr (76.2-mm/3-in) gun, then completing its development, was selected as a likely weapon. The A27 Cromwell/Centaur chassis seemed a suitable basic chassis and work began on adapting this for the heavy gun project.

The new gun would require two things. One was a much larger chassis to accommodate the weights involved and the other a larger turret ring to absorb the recoil forces. At that time all existing designs were too narrow to accommodate so large a turret ring, but by lengthening the existing Cromwell chassis and adding another road wheel the turret ring section could be widened to enable a larger ring to be installed. This formed the basis of what became known as the **A30**, and eventually the name Challenger was bestowed upon the vehicle.

The first pilot model was ready in March 1942 and like many hasty improvisations it showed up badly during its early trials. The extra weight of the rather high and awkward turret was not balanced by the lengthened suspension, which proved to be a source of many troubles, and the mounting of the heavy gun in the turret made traverse so slow that the original traverse mechanism had to be redesigned and replaced. The large size of the 17-pdr fixed ammunition meant that only a restricted number of rounds could be carried internally, and the hull machine-gun had to be removed to make more room, leaving only the co-axial 7.62-mm (0.3-in) gun. Perhaps the biggest problem was that the weight overall was such that the armour protection had to be reduced to bring weight down to a reasonable level. Armour varied from 20 to 102 mm (0.8 to 4 in) in thickness. Despite all these problems the Challenger was ordered into production purely on the strength of its powerful gun, which was at least something that could destroy any known German tank.

But the Challenger was slow to get into production for a variety of reasons. It was not until March 1944 that the first production examples were ready and by then it was too late for the Challenger to take part in the extensive waterproofing programme that would be required for the Normandy landings. Another blow to the Challenger programme was the fact that the M4 Sherman had been adapted to take the 17-pdr, and as the Firefly this conversion assumed many of the responsibilities intended for the Challenger during the early stages of the post-Normandy campaign. Thus the Challenger lan-

Arguably the ugliest tank design of the period, the Challenger was a stretched Cromwell armed with a 17-pdr, armour being reduced to keep weight down. Fortunately for British tank crews the Sherman Firefly was adopted instead.

guished while the Firefly fought its way across Europe.

But some Challengers did see service from late 1944 onwards. Numbers were issued to the reconnaissance regiments of the British armoured divisions to provide some extra fire support for the 75-mm (2.95-in) Cromwells which were by then the main equipment of these units. As soon as the war ended most Challengers were withdrawn. Some were sold overseas but the type rapidly vanished from the scene. The **Challenger II**, with a lower turret, was produced only in prototype form.

Specification
Challenger
Crew: 5
Weight: 33022 kg (72,800 lb)
Powerplant: one Rolls-Royce Meteor V-12 petrol engine developing 447 kW (600 bhp)
Dimensions: length overall 8.147 m (26 ft 8.75 in); width 2.90 m (9 ft 6.5 in); height 2.775 m (9 ft 1.25 in)
Performance: maximum speed 51.5 km/h (32 mph); range 193 km (120 miles); fording 1.37 m (4 ft 6 in) after preparation; vertical obstacle 0.914 m (3 ft); trench 2.59 m (8 ft 6 in)

Infantry Tank Mks I and II Matilda

A requirement for a British army 'Infantry' tank was first made in 1934 and the immediate result was the **All Infantry Tank Mk I**, later nicknamed **Matilda I**. This was a very simple and small tank with a two-man crew but with armour heavy enough to defeat any contemporary anti-tank gun. The small turret mounted a single 7.7-mm (0.303-in) Vickers machine-gun and the engine was a commercial Ford V-8 unit. Orders for 140 were issued in April 1937, but when the type was tried in combat in France in 1940 it revealed many shortcomings: it was too slow and underarmed for any form of armoured warfare, and the small numbers that remained in service after Dunkirk were used only for training.

The Matilda I was intended only as an interim type before the **A12 Infantry Tank Mk II** became available. This project began in 1936 and the first examples were completed in 1938. The Mk II, known later as Matilda II, was a much larger vehicle than the Matilda I with a four-man crew and a turret mounting a 2-pdr (40-mm/1.575-in) gun and liberal belts of cast armour (varying from 20 to 78 mm/0.8 to 3.1 in in thickness) capable of defeating all known anti-tank guns. The Matilda II was slow as it was intended for the direct support of infantry units, in which role speed was not essential. Overall it was a good-looking tank and it turned out to be far more reliable than many of its contemporaries. And despite the light gun carried it was found to be a good vehicle in combat. The **Matilda IIA** had a 7.92-mm (0.312-in) Besa

machine-gun instead of the Vickers gun.

The main combat period for the Matilda (the term Matilda II was dropped when the little Matilda I was withdrawn in 1940) was the early North African campaign, where the type's armour proved to be effective against any Italian or German anti-tank gun with the exception of the German '88'. The Matilda was one of the armoured mainstays of the British forces until El Alamein, after which its place was taken by better armed and faster designs. But the importance of the Matilda did not diminish, for it then entered a long career as a special-purpose tank.

One of the most important of these special purposes was as a flail tank for mine-clearing. Starting with the **Matilda Baron** and then the **Matilda Scorpion**, it was used extensively for this role, but Matildas were also used to push AMRA mine-clearing rollers. Another variant was the **Matilda CDL** (Canal Defence Light), which used a special turret with a powerful light source to create 'artificial moonlight'. Matildas were also fitted with dozer blades as the **Matilda Dozer** for combat engineering, and many were fitted with various flame-throwing devices as the **Matilda Frog**. There were many other special and demolition devices used with the Matilda, not all of them under British auspices for the Matilda became an important Australian tank as well. In fact Matilda gun tanks were used extensively by the Australian army in New Guinea and elsewhere until the war ended in 1945, and they devised several flame-throwing equipments. The Germans also used several captured Matildas to mount various anti-tank weapons of their own.

It is doubtful if a complete listing of all the many Matilda variants will ever be made, for numerous 'field modifications' and other unrecorded changes

The Matilda was the only British tank with enough armour to withstand German tank guns in the early years. After a brief moment of glory at Arras, it won its real reputation with the 8th Army in the desert.

were made to the basic design. But the Matilda accommodated them all and many old soldiers still look back on this tank with affection for, despite its slow speed and light armament, it was reliable and steady, and above all it had good armour.

Specification
Matilda II
Crew: 4˚
Weight: 26926 kg (59,360 lb)
Powerplant: two Leyland 6-cylinder petrol engines each developing 71 kW (95 bhp) or two AEC diesels each developing 65 kW (87 bhp)
Dimensions: length 5.613 m (18 ft 5 in); width 2.59 m (8 ft 6 in); height 2.51 m (8 ft 3 in)
Performance: maximum speed 24 km/h (15 mph); maximum cross-country speed 12.9 km/h (8 mph); road range 257 km (160 miles); vertical obstacle 0.609 m (2 ft); fording 0.914 m (3 ft); trench 2.133 m (7 ft)

A Matilda is seen in the desert in June 1941 during Operation 'Battleaxe', an unsuccessful attempt to relieve Tobruk which cost the 4th Armoured Brigade 64 of their Matildas. Tough but slow, the Matildas were cursed with the ineffectual 2-pdr as main armament.

Infantry Tank Mk III Valentine

In 1938 Vickers was invited to join in the production programme for the new Matilda II tank, but as the company already had a production line established to produce a heavy 'Cruiser' tank known as the A10, it was invited to produce a new infantry tank based upon the A10. Vickers duly made its plans and its A10-derived infantry tank was ordered into production in July 1939. Up to that date the army planners had some doubts as to the effectiveness of the Vickers submissions, resulting mainly in the retention of a small two-man turret which would limit possible armament increases, but by mid-1939 war was imminent and tanks were urgently required.

The new Vickers tank, soon known as the **Infantry Tank Mk III Valentine**, drew heavily on experience gained with the A10, but was much more heavily armoured 8-65 mm (0.3-2.55 in). As many of the A10's troubles had already been experienced their solutions were built into the Valentine, which proved to be a relatively trouble-free vehicle. Mass production began rapidly, and the first **Valentine I** examples were ready in late 1940. By 1941 the Valentine was an established type, and many were used as Cruiser tanks to overcome deficiencies.

The Valentine was undoubtedly one of the most important British tanks, but the main reason for this was quantity rather than quality. By early 1944, when production ceased, 8,275 had been made and during one period in 1943 one quarter of all British tank production was of Valentines. Valentines were also produced in Canada and by several other concerns in the United Kingdom apart from Vickers.

There were numerous variants on the Valentine. Gun tanks ran to 11 different marks with the main armament increasing from a 2-pdr (**Valentine I-VII**) via the 6-pdr (**Valentine VIII-X**) to a 75-mm (2.95-in) gun (**Valentine XI**), and there was even a self-propelled gun version mounting a 25-pdr field gun and known as the **Bishop**. Special-purpose Valentines ran the whole gamut from mobile bridges (**Valentine Bridgelayer**) to Canal Defence Lights (**Valentine CDL**) and from observation posts (**Valentine OP**) to mine-clearing devices (**Valentine Scorpion** and **Valentine AMRA**). The numbers of these variants were legion, many of them being one-off devices produced for trials or experimental purposes, typical of which were the early **Duplex Drive Valentine** vehicles used to test the DD system. Actually these tanks were so successful that the Valentine was at one time the standard DD tank. There were also **Valentine Flamethrower** tanks, and one attempt was made to produce a special tank-killer with a 6-pdr anti-tank gun behind a shield. That project came to nothing but the Valentine chassis was later used as the basis for the **Archer**, an open-topped vehicle with a 17-pdr gun pointing to the rear. This was used in Europe from 1944 onwards.

The basic Valentine tank was extensively modified throughout its operational career, but it remained throughout reliable and sturdy. The Valentine was one of the British army's most important tanks at one point. It was used by many Allied armies such as that of New Zealand, and many saw action in Burma. The bulk of the Canadian output was sent to the Soviet Union, where the type appears to have given good service. The Valentine did have its drawbacks, but overall its main contribution was that it was available in quantity at a time when it was most needed, and not many British tank designs could claim the same.

Specification
Valentine III/IV
Crew: 3
Weight: 17690 kg (39,000 lb)
Powerplant: one AEC diesel developing 98 kW (131 bhp) in Mk III or GMC diesel developing 103 kW (138 bhp) in Mk IV
Dimensions: length 5.41 m (17 ft 9 in); width 2.629 m (8 ft 7.5 in); height 2.273 m (7 ft 5.5 in)
Performance: maximum speed 24 km/h (15 mph); maximum cross-country speed 12.9 km/h (8 mph); road range 145 km (90 miles); vertical obstacle 0.838 m (2 ft 9 in); fording 0.914 m (3 ft); trench 2.286 m (7 ft 6 in)

An early model Valentine provides the focus of attention as Malta celebrates King George VI's birthday. The Valentine was one of the more successful pre-war designs, and saw service world-wide.

Mass-produced from 1940, the Valentine fought throughout the desert campaigns. Although slow like the Matilda, it was a sturdy vehicle and was able to be re-armed with better guns as the war progressed.

Infantry Tank Mk IV Churchill

UK

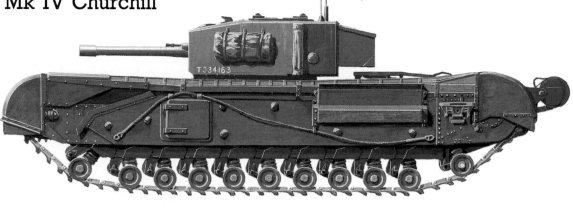

Even to provide a list of all the **Churchill** marks and variants would fill many pages, so this entry can provide only a brief outline of what was one of the most important British tanks of World War II. In production terms the Churchill came second to the Valentine, but in the scope of applications and variants it came second to none.

The Churchill was born in a specification known as the **A20** which was issued in September 1939 and envisaged a return to the trench fighting of World War I. Hence the A20 tank was a virtual update of the old World War I British 'lozenge' tanks, but experiences with the A20 prototype soon

Left: Churchills move up to the Normandy front line past a column of US M4 Shermans in early August 1944. Note how the crews have attached large sections of track to the front hull and the turret side as additional armour.

Above: The Churchill was essentially designed for a return to trench warfare. As such it was a classic infantry tank, slow but heavily armoured. Introduced in 1943, its chassis was subsequently used for a host of specialist vehicles.

showed that a lighter model would be required. Subsequently Vauxhall Motors took over a revised specification known as the **A22** and designed the **Infantry Tank Mk IV**, later named the Churchill.

Vauxhall had to work from scratch and yet came up with a well armoured tank with large overall tracks that gave the design an appearance not unlike that of World War I tanks. Unfortunately the early Churchill marks were so rushed into production that about the first 1,000 examples had to be extensively modified before they could even be issued to the troops. But they were produced at a period when invasion seemed imminent and even unreliable tanks were regarded as better than none. Later marks had these early troubles eliminated.

The armament of the Churchill followed the usual path from 2-pdr (**Churchill I-II**), via 6-pdr (**Churchill III-IV**) eventually to a 75-mm (2.95-in) gun in the **Churchill IV (NA 75)** and **Churchill VI-VII**. There were also CS (close support) variants with 76.2-mm (3-in) and eventually 95-mm (actually 94-mm/3.7-in) howitzers in the **Churchill V** and **Churchill VIII**. The Churchill I also had a hull-mounted 76.2-mm (3-in) howitzer. The turrets also changed from being cast items to being riveted or composite structures, and such refinements as track covers and engine cool-

ing improvements were added successively. In all there were 11 Churchill marks, the last three of them 'reworks' of earlier marks in order to update early models to Mk VII standard with the 75-mm (2.95-in) gun.

In action the heavy armour of the Churchill (16-102 mm/0.6-4 in in Mks I-VI and 25-152 mm/1-6 in in Mks VI-VIII) was a major asset despite the fact that the tank's first operational use was in the 1942 Dieppe landings, when many of the Churchills used proved unable to even reach the beach, let alone cross it. But in Tunisia they proved they could climb mountains and provide excellent support for armoured as well as infantry units, though they were often too slow to exploit local advantages.

It was as a special-purpose tank that the Churchill excelled. Many of these special variants became established as important vehicles in their own right, and included in this number were the **Churchill AVRE** (Armoured Vehicle Royal Engineers), the **Churchill Crocodile** flamethrower tank and the various **Churchill Bridgelayer** and **Churchill Ark** vehicles. Then there were the numerous Churchill mine-warfare variants from the **Churchill Plough** variants to the **Churchill Snake** with its Bangalore torpedoes. The Churchill lent itself to all manner of

modifications and was able to carry a wide assortment of odd gadgets such as wall demolition charges (**Churchill Light Carrot, Churchill Onion** and **Churchill Goat**) mine-clearing wheels (**Churchill AVRE/CIRD**), carpet-laying devices for use on boggy ground (**Churchill AVRE Carpetlayer**), armoured recovery vehicles (**Churchill ARV**), and so on.

The Churchill may have looked archaic, but it gave excellent service and many were still around in the mid-1950s in various guises, the last Churchill AVRE not being retired until 1965.

Specification
Churchill VII
Crew: 5
Weight: 40642 kg (89,600 lb)
Powerplant: one Bedford twin-six petrol engine developing 261 kW (350 bhp)
Dimensions: length 7.442 m (24 ft 5 in); width 2.438 m (8 ft); height 3.454 m (11 ft 4 in)
Performance: maximum speed 20 km/h (12.5 mph); maximum cross-country speed about 12.8 km/h (8 mph); range 144.8 km (90 miles); fording 1.016 m (3 ft 4 in); vertical obstacle 0.76 m (2 ft 6 in); trench 3.048 m (10 ft)

Cruiser Tank Sentinel AC1

AUSTRALIA

In 1939 Australia's armed forces had virtually no modern tanks and lacked almost any form of heavy engineering background to produce them; even an automobile industry was lacking. Nevertheless the Australian government realized that it was unlikely that any large amounts of heavy war matériel would be available to Australia from overseas, and so set to to produce its own. Among the requirements were tanks, and as there was no local expertise on the subject one engineer was sent to the United States and an experienced engineer was obtained from the United Kingdom.

With this experience to hand the Australian army staff issued a specification and Australian industry set to with a will. The first design, known as the **AC1 (Australian Cruiser 1)** was to have a 2-pdr (40-mm/1.57-in) gun and two

The outbreak of war found Australia with no modern tank force and little industrial infrastructure. The AC1 Sentinel was a home-grown tank developed at lightning speed to fight off the anticipated Japanese invasion.

7.7-mm (0.303-in) machine-guns, and it was decided to use as many components of the American M3 tank as possible. The powerplant was to comprise three Cadillac car engines joined together and extensive use was to be made of cast armour. A second model, to be known as the **AC2**, was mooted, but by late 1941 as the Japanese became increasingly aggressive in the Pacific, the AC2 was passed over in favour of the existing AC1, which had armour ranging from 25 mm (1 in) to 65 mm (2.55 in) in thickness.

The first AC1s were ready by January 1942 and were soon named **Sentinel**. The whole project from paperwork requests to hardware had taken only 22 months, which was a remarkable achievement since all the facilities to build the tank had to be developed even as the tanks were being built. But only a few AC1 tanks were produced as by 1942 it was realized that the 2-pdr gun would be too small to have any effect against other armour and anyway, the hurried design still had some 'bugs' that had to be modified out of the design. Most of these bugs were only minor, for the Sentinel turned out to be a remarkably sound

design capable of considerable stretch and modification. This was just as well, for the **Sentinel AC3** mounted a 25-pdr (87.6-mm/3.45-in) field gun barrel in the turret to overcome the shortcomings of the 2-pdr.

The 25-pdr was chosen as it was already in production locally, but it was realized that this gun would have only limited effect against armour and the **Sentinel AC4** with a 17-pdr (76.2-mm/3-in) anti-tank gun was proposed and a prototype was built. This was during mid-1943, and by then the background to the hurried introduction of the AC1 into service had receded. There was no longer the chance that the Japanese might invade the Australian mainland and anyway, M3s and M4s were pouring off the American production lines in such numbers that there would be more than enough to equip all the Allies, including Australia. Thus Sentinel production came to an abrupt halt in July 1943 in order to allow the diversion of industrial potential to more important priorities.

The Sentinel series was a remarkable one, not only from the industrial side but also from the design viewpoint. The use of an all-cast hull was

In spite of the speed with which it was produced, the AC1 Sentinel was a remarkably innovative design

way ahead of design practice elsewhere, and the ready acceptance of heavy guns like the 25-pdr and the 17-pdr was also way ahead of contemporary thought. But the Sentinel series had little impact at the time for the examples produced were used for training only.

**Specification
Sentinel AC1
Crew:** 5

featuring an all-cast hull and a heavy armament. This is the Mk IV, which mounted a 17-pdr gun.

Weight: 28450 kg (62,720 lb)
Powerplant: three Cadillac petrol engines combined to develop 246 kW (330 bhp)
Dimensions: length 6.325 m (20 ft 9 in); width 2.768 m (9 ft 1 in); height 2.56 m (8 ft 4.75 in)
Performance: maximum speed 48.2 km/h (30 mph); range 322 km (200 miles); trench 2.438 m (8 ft)

CANADA

Cruiser Tank Ram Mk I

When Canada entered World War II in 1939 it did not have any form of tank unit, and the first Canadian tank training and familiarization units had to be equipped with old World War I tanks from American sources. However, it was not long before the Canadian railway industry was asked by the UK if it could manufacture and supply Valentine infantry tanks, and this proved to be a major task for the Canadians who had to virtually build up a tank manufacturing capability from scratch. But the Valentines were 'Infantry' tanks and the new Canadian tank units would need 'Cruisers' for armoured combat. At that time there was little prospect of obtaining tanks from the United Kingdom and the United States was not involved in the war, so the only thing to do was design and build tanks in Canada.

But what tank? Again, at the time it seemed opportune to build the American M3 (then entering production for a British order) but this design, later known as the Grant/Lee, had the drawback of a sponson-mounted main gun at a time when it was appreciated that a turret-mounted gun was much more efficient. Thus the Canadians decided to adopt the main mechanical, hull and transmission components of the M3, but ally them to a new turret mounting a 75-mm (2.95-in) main gun. But there was no prospect of a 75-mm (2.95-in) gun at the time, so the readily-available (40-mm/1.58-in) weapon was chosen for initial installations, with the chance of fitting a larger gun later. This turned out to be the 6-pdr (57-mm/2.244-in) gun.

Building such a tank from scratch was a major achievement for Canadian industry, and the prototype was rolled out from the Montreal Locomotive Works in late June 1941. It was christened the **Cruiser Tank Ram Mk I**, and turned out to be a remarkably workmanlike design making much use of cast armour; the drive train and sus-

pension demonstrated its M3 origins. It was not long before the initial 2-pdr gun was replaced by a 6-pdr in the **Ram Mk II**, and production proper got under way by the end of 1941. The secondary armament was one co-axial and one hull-mounted 7.62-mm (0.3-in) machine-gun. Almost as soon as production commenced numerous design modifications were progressively introduced but none of these changes were fundamental as the Ram was a basically sound tank. Armour thickness ranged from 25 mm (1 in) to 89 mm (3.5 in).

All the output went to the new Canadian armoured regiments and many of these regiments, as they were formed, were sent to the United Kingdom. But the Ram was never to see action as a gun tank. By mid-1943 large numbers of M4 Shermans were pouring off American production lines and as this tank already had a 75-mm (2.95-in) gun it was decided to standardize on the M4 for all Canadian units. Thus the Rams were used for training only. As they were withdrawn many had their turrets removed to produce the **Ram Kangaroo**, which was a simple yet efficient armoured personnel carrier

widely used in the post-June 1944 campaigns. Some Rams had their guns removed and were used as artillery observation posts (**Ram Command/OP Tank**), while others were more extensively modified to become armoured recovery vehicles. Some were used for various experimental and trial purposes, such as the mounting of a 94-mm (3.7-in) anti-aircraft gun on top of the hull.

But the Ram's greatest contribution to the conflict was the adaptation of the basic Ram hull to take a 25-pdr artillery piece. The gun was placed in a simple open superstructure on top of the hull, and in this form the Ram became the **Sexton**. A total of 2,150 was produced for the Allied armies so the Ram production line made a definite contribution to the Allied victory.

**Specification
Ram Mk II
Crew:** 5
Weight: 29484 kg (65,000 lb)
Powerplant: one Continental R-975 radial petrol engine developing 298 kW (400 bhp)
Dimensions: length 5.79 m (19 ft 0 in); width 2.895 m (9 ft 6 in); height 2.667 m (8 ft 9 in)
Performance: maximum speed 40.2 km/h (25 mph); range 232 km (144 miles); vertical obstacle 0.61 m (2 ft); trench 2.26 m (7 ft 5 in)

Canada had no armoured forces in 1939 but decided to build her own tank to equip the expanding Canadian army. The Ram tank utilized the chassis of the American M3, but mounted its main armament in the turret rather than in a sponson as on the original US vehicle.

Soviet and American Tanks

Nowhere in the course of World War II was the industrial might of what were to become the Superpowers more evident than in the production of armoured vehicles. Manufacture of such war-winning weapons as the M4 Sherman and the Soviet T-34 was on a scale that the Axis could not hope to match.

The tanks described here include some of the best known examples which saw action in World War II. In these pages will be found the Sherman, the T-34, the Lee and the Grant, but also included are some slightly lesser known names. Few outside the former Soviet Union can be familiar with the little T-70 light tank, but in its day it was numerically an important part of the Red Army tank fleet, along with the almost equally unknown T-26.

The numbers and fame of the T-34 and the various Shermans have tended to obliterate the fact that between 1939 and 1945 there were many types of tank lurching around the battlefields. Despite the need for strict standardization to boost mass production totals, no combatant was able to say at any time that only one specific tank type would be produced. Constant supply and demand fluctuations prevented any such thing, although at one point the Soviets got very close to it with the T-34. Also, tanks were generally retained in service for as long as possible, sometimes until they had been outdated or rendered obsolete by events. Thus the M3 series of American light tanks continued to see action right through the war, long

The American M4 Sherman tank ranks as one of the most famous ever. This one is with General Leclerc's French Armoured Division a few weeks after the Allies had established their beachhead.

after there was no longer a place on the battlefield for their original services.

But if any of the tanks could be said to have overshadowed their fellows they were without doubt the Sherman and the T-34. Together these two examples made major contributions to the final Allied victory over Germany, and so ensured that their names were recorded in history. Both tanks had their faults. The T-34 was cramped inside and manufactured to a standard that was almost crude. The Sherman was high, lacked armour protection and was almost constantly undergunned. However, both types possessed the key attributes of mobility and availability, and in war these advantages can go far towards tipping the balance of fortune towards one side or another. By 1944 both the T-34 and the Sherman were instrumental in forcing the German army back towards the borders of its homeland, and for that alone they will always be remembered.

Light Tank M3

American light tank development can be traced back to the 1920s when several infantry-support light tanks were developed in small numbers. By the early 1930s these designs had evolved into the **Light Tank M2**, and there were a series of designs all using the M2 designation. For its day this series were quite well armed, with a 37-mm (1.46-in) main gun, but by 1940 the type was at best obsolescent and was used only for training after reaching its apogee with the **M2A4** model.

The events of 1940 in Europe were followed closely by the US Army, which realized that thicker armour would be required by its light tanks. This involved a better suspension to carry the extra weight and the result was the **Light Tank M3**, based generally on the M2A4. It was in full-scale production by 1941, and mass production of the **M3A1** really got under way once the USA had entered the war. Early versions used riveted construction, but welded turrets and eventually welded hulls were successively introduced, and there were also many detail design changes. By the time M3 production ceased 5,811 had been built. Basic armament of the M3A1 was one 37-mm (1.46-in) gun with a co-axial 7.62-mm (0.3-in) machine-gun, and four other 7.62-mm (0.3-in) machine-guns (one on the turret roof for AA defence, one in the hull front and two fixed in the sponsons for operation by the driver). Armour thickness ranged from 15 mm (0.59 in) to 43 mm (1.69 in).

The Light Tank M3 was used wherever the US Army was involved. It proved to be a thoroughly reliable vehicle and was greatly liked by its crews. Large numbers of M3s were passed to the USA's allies, and the largest recipient was the UK, where the M3 was known as the **Stuart**. To British eyes the Stuart was large for a light tank, but crews soon learned to appreciate the nippiness and reliability of the vehicle. One thing they did not particularly like was the fact that two main types of engine were fitted to different versions: the normal engine was a Continental 7-cylinder radial petrol engine (**Stuart I**), but in order to expedite production at a time of high demand the Guiberson T-1020 diesel engine was substituted (**Stuart II**). This sometimes caused logistic supply problems but it was a burden the Allies learned to survive. Major variants were the **M3A1** (**Stuart III** and **Stuart IV**

The Light Tank M3A1 was the main combat version of the M2/M3 light tank series in service when the United States entered the war in late 1941. It mounted a 37-mm (1.456-in) main gun, and there was provision for three machine-guns.

with petrol and diesel engines) fitted with a gyrostabilized gun, power-traverse turret and turret basket, and the product-improved **M3A3** (**Stuart V**) with a larger driving compartment, thicker armour and no sponson guns.

The 37-mm (1.46-in) gun was retained throughout the production life of the M3. By 1944 it had very little combat value, so many M3s and Stuarts serving with reconnaissance units had the turret removed to assist concealment. Extra machine-guns were carried instead. Many of these turretless M3s were employed as command vehicles by armoured formation commanders but these were not the only variations upon the M3 theme. The M3 was widely used for all manner of experiments that ranged from mine-clearing expedients to flame-throwers of several kinds. Some vehicles were used for carrying self-propelled artillery, but none were accepted for service. There was even an anti-aircraft version.

With the Allies the M3/Stuarts were used from the North African campaign onwards. Some were passed to the Red Army under Lend-Lease arrangements. The **Light Tank M5** was a development powered by twin Cadillac engines that was otherwise generally similar to the M3 series but was recognizable by the raised rear decking that accommodated the twin engines. In

British service the M5 was the **Stuart VI**, the same designation being used for the **M5A1** with an improved turret having a bulged rear for radio (as on the M3A3).

Specification
Light Tank M3A1
Crew: 4
Weight: in action 12.927 tonnes
Powerplant: one Continental W-970-9A 7-cylinder radial petrol engine developing 186.5 kW (250 hp)
Dimensions: length 4.54 m (14 ft 10.75 in); width 2.24 m (7 ft 4 in); height 2.30 m (7 ft 6.5 in)
Performance: maximum road speed 58 km/h (36 mph); maximum road

The M3 (and the M5) series were used by many Allied armies for reconnaissance. This example is seen negotiating an improvised German roadblock outside Harze in Belgium during the late summer of 1944

range 112.6 km (70 miles); fording 0.91 m (3 ft); gradient 60 per cent; vertical obstacle 0.61 m (2 ft); trench 1.83 m (6 ft)

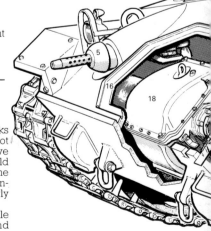

Light Tank M24 Chaffee

By 1942 it was evident that the day of the 37-mm (1.46-in) tank gun had passed, and requests were coming from the field for a light tank with a 75-mm (2.95-in) main gun. Attempts to fit such a gun into the Light Tank M5 were unsuccessful, so a new design was started by Cadillac. The first was ready by late 1943 and it carried over several features of the M5, including the twin engines, but the main change was to the turret and gun.

The new turret mounted the required 75-mm (2.95-in) gun, whose development was lengthy. Originally it had been the old French '75' field gun altered for use in tanks. Various efforts were made to lighten the gun to the extent that it could be mounted in B-25

bomber aircraft for anti-shipping use, and in this form the T13E1 was easily adapted as a light tank weapon.

The new light tank was initially known as the **T24** but when accepted for service it became the **Light Tank M24** and was later given the name **Chaffee**. It was not in full service until late 1944, and thus was able to take only a small part in the fighting in Europe during 1945. Perhaps its biggest contribution was not really felt until the war was over, for the M24 was designed to be only a part of what the designers called a 'combat team' of armoured vehicles. The idea was that a common chassis could be used to provide the basis for a whole family of armoured vehicles that included self-

propelled artillery, anti-aircraft tanks and so on. In fact this concept did not make the impression that it might have done as the war ended before it could be put into full effect, and indeed the M24 did not make its full combat impact until the Korean War of the early 1950s.

The M24 was a good-looking little tank, well armed for its size and weight, but the armour (minimum 12 mm/0.47 in and maximum 38 mm/1.5-in) had to be lighter than in heavier tanks to give the vehicle its agility. The M24 had a surprisingly large crew of five men (commander, gunner, loader, radio operator who sometimes acted as assistant driver, and driver). Apart from the main gun there were two 7.62-

mm (0.3-in) machine-guns (one co-axial with the main gun and one in the front hull) and a 12.7-mm (0.5-in) gun on the turret mounted on a pintle. To add to this array there was a 51-mm (2-in) smoke mortar. All this was a considerable armament for a vehicle with a tactical responsibility that was limited mainly to reconnaissance, but by the time the M24 entered service it was a luxury that the Americans could well afford.

As mentioned above, the M24 went on to make its greatest impact after 1945 and many nations retain the M24 to this day, several of them going to the trouble of re-engining the vehicles and updating their fire-control systems.

Specification
Light Tank M24
Crew: 5
Weight: in action 18.37 tonnes
Powerplant: two Cadillac Model 44T24 V-8 petrol engines developing 82 kW (110 hp) each
Dimensions: length, with gun 5.49 m (18 ft) and over hull 4.99 m (16 ft 4.5 in); width 2.95 m (9 ft 8 in); height 2.48 m (8 ft 1.5 in)

Performance: maximum road speed 56 km/h (35 mph); maximum road range 161 km (100 miles); fording 1.02 m (3 ft 4 in); gradient 60 per cent; vertical obstacle 0.91 m (3 ft); trench 2.44 m (8 ft)

Armed with a 75-mm (2.95-in) gun, the M24 was introduced into service during late 1944 and post-war it formed the basis for a new family of armoured vehicles.

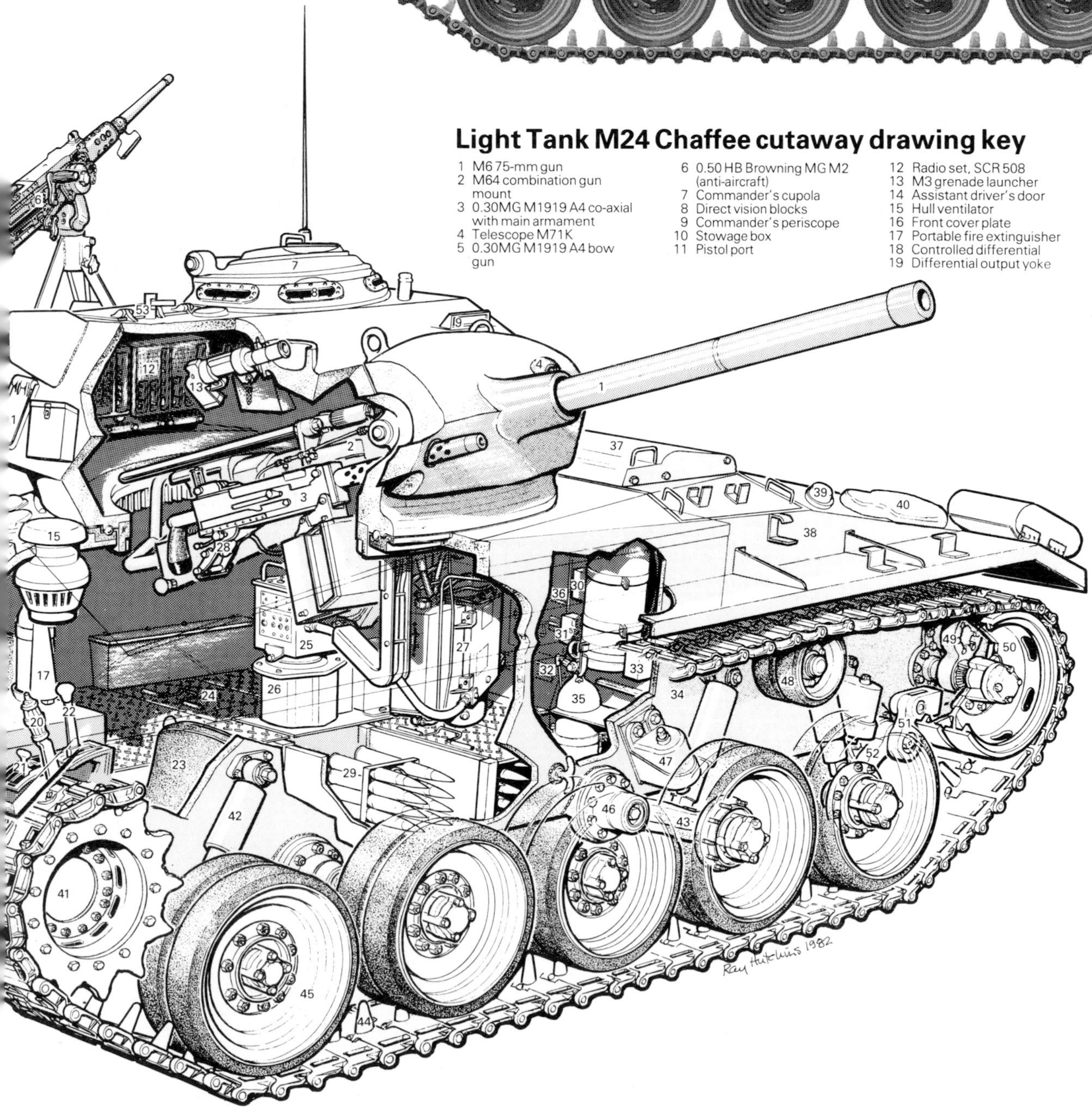

Light Tank M24 Chaffee cutaway drawing key

1 M6 75-mm gun
2 M64 combination gun mount
3 0.30MG M1919 A4 co-axial with main armament
4 Telescope M71K
5 0.30MG M1919 A4 bow gun
6 0.50 HB Browning MG M2 (anti-aircraft)
7 Commander's cupola
8 Direct vision blocks
9 Commander's periscope
10 Stowage box
11 Pistol port
12 Radio set, SCR 508
13 M3 grenade launcher
14 Assistant driver's door
15 Hull ventilator
16 Front cover plate
17 Portable fire extinguisher
18 Controlled differential
19 Differential output yoke
20 Driver's hand levers (steering brake)
21 Range selector/transmission lever
22 Hand lever transfer unit shift control
23 Driver's seat
24 Fire escape hatch door
25 Turret control box
26 Turret driving mechanism
27 Stabilizer and turret motor
28 Firing solenoid
29 Ammunition storage boxes
30 Left generator regulator
31 Left starter relay
32 Ventilating door
33 Master battery switch
34 Four 6-volt batteries
35 Fixed fire extinguisher
36 Radiator
37 Radiator air inlet grille
38 Two Cadillac 90 V-type 8-cylinder Model 44 T 24 engines
39 Fuel tank covers
40 Fuel compartment vents
41 Final drive sprocket
42 Shock absorber
43 Support arm
44 Track guide
45 Track wheel
46 Torsion bar
47 Bumper spring arm bracket
48 Track support roller
49 Compensating wheel and track wheel support linkage
50 Track compensating wheel
51 Compensating wheel link
52 Track wheel link
53 Loader's hatch

Medium Tank M3

When the Germans invaded France in May 1940 the consequent tank actions were closely observed by various US Army agencies. From their observations the Americans learned that the next generation of medium tanks had to have at least a 75-mm (2.95-in) gun as their main armament, but this presented them with problems as their next tank generation, already being produced in prototype form, was armed with only a 37-mm (1.46-in) gun of the type already seen to be obsolete.

The American answer was swift and drastic: they simply took their existing design and altered it to accommodate the required 75-mm (2.95-in) gun. The turret of the new design (the **Medium Tank M2**, destined never to see active service) could not take the larger gun so the weapon had to be situated in the hull. Consequently the revised tank design retained the 37-mm (1.46-in) gun turret, while the main armament was located in a sponson on the right-hand side of the hull. The 75-mm (2.95-in) gun was a revised version of the famous French '75' field piece as made in the USA, but new ammunition converted it into what was for the time a powerful tank weapon. Secondary armament comprised four 7.62-mm (0.3-in) machine-guns (one in the commander's cupola atop the 37-mm/1.46-in turret, one co-axial with the 37-mm/1.46-in gun, and two in the hull).

The new design became the **Medium Tank M3**, and was rushed into mass production in a factory meant for the earlier M2. Almost as soon as production started for the US Army, a British mission arrived in the United States on a purchasing trip to obtain tanks to replace those lost in France, and the M3 was high on its shopping list. They requested a few changes to suit their requirements, the most obvious of which were a revised turret rear outline to accommodate radio equipment and the absence of the cupola and this model was produced specifically for the British army. Once delivered the British knew the M3 as the **General Grant I** (or simply **Grant I**), and the first of them went into action at Gazala in May 1942 when they provided the Afrika Korps with a nasty fright as their arrival was entirely unexpected, their combination of armament and armour (12 mm/0.47 in minimum and 50 mm/1.97 in maximum) proving most useful.

The Grants were later joined in British service by the unmodified M3 which was then labelled the **General Lee I**. Further improvement led to the **M3A1** (**Lee II**) with welded construction, the uparmoured **M3A3** (**Lee IV**) with two General Motors 6-71 diesels

delivering 375 hp (280 kW), the **M3A4** (**Lee V**) with the Chrysler A-57 multi-bank engine delivering 370 hp (276 kW), and the **M3A5** based on the M3A3 but with a riveted hull. By the time production ended in December 1942 the total had reached 6,258 and the M3 was used in virtually every theatre of war in one form or another. Many were passed to the Red Army on a Lend-Lease arrangement.

The M3 turned out to be a reliable and hard-wearing vehicle, but its hull-located main gun was often a cause of tactical difficulties as its traverse was very limited. But it did provide the punch that Allied 'tankies' required at that time. Its tactical silhouette was really too high for comfort, but considering that the basic design was improvised and rushed into production, at a time when there were more questions being asked than answers provided, it turned out to be a remarkable effort. Many of the suspension and automotive features were later incorporated into other designs and continued to provide excellent service, but perhaps the main lesson to be learned from the M3 was the latent power of American industry that could churn out such a vehicle from scratch in such a short time.

As soon as the M4 entered service the M3s were usually withdrawn and converted to other roles such as armoured recovery vehicles, but in the Far East they remained in use until 1945 in both Grant and Lee forms.

Above: The M3 General Lee tank was a hasty design, but it had a powerful 75-mm gun which gave Allied tanks a parity with German tanks for the first time.

Specification
Medium Tank M3A2
Crew: 6
Weight: in action 27.24 tonnes
Powerplant: one Continental R-975-EC2 radial petrol engine developing 253.5 kW (340 hp)
Dimensions: length 5.64 m (18 ft 6 in); width 2.72 m (8 ft 11 in); height 3.12 m (10 ft 3 in)
Performance: maximum road speed 42 km/h (26 mph); maximum road

The M3 Grant was the 'British' version of the M3 Lee. The main change was to the turret profile, which had a rear overhang to house a radio set, and the silhouette was lowered by omitting the machine-gun cupola of the original turret.

range 193 km (120 miles); fording 1.02 m (3 ft 4 in); gradient 60 per cent; vertical obstacle 0.61 m (2 ft); trench 1.91 m (6 ft 3 in)

Medium Tank M4

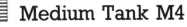

While the Medium Tank M3 was being rushed into production, a new design of medium tank with a turret-mounted 75-mm (2.95-in) main gun was being pushed through the drawing board stages. To save time this was to use the same basic hull and suspension as the M3, but the upper hull was revised to accommodate the gun turret. The first example of the new tank rolled out in September 1941 as the **Medium Tank T6** and proved to be a very good design. The upper hull was cast, and this not only provided added protec-

tion but speeded production, at that time a definite asset.

The new weapon was rushed into production as the **Medium Tank M4**, with a 75-mm (2.95-in) main gun and co-axial 7.62-mm (0.3-in) machine-gun, 7.62-mm (0.3-in) bow gun and 12.7-mm (0.5-in) gun for AA defence. This baseline model had minimum and maximum armour thicknesses of 15 mm (0.59 in) and 76 mm (2.99 in) respectively. It proved to be an excellent fighting platform and went on to be one of the war-winning weapons of the

Allies, being constructed in thousands. By the time the production lines stopped rolling in 1945 well over 40,000 had been made, and the type was built in a bewildering array of marks, sub-marks and variants of all kinds. There is no space in these pages even to attempt a complete listing of all the numerous versions, but suffice to say that once in service the M4 series was differently engined: up-gunned to even more powerful 75-mm (2.95-in), 76-mm (2.99-in) and 105-mm (4.13-in) main weapons; and developed into

numerous 'specials' such as engineer tanks, assault tanks, tank destroyers, flamethrowers, bridging tanks, recovery vehicles, rocket launchers, self-propelled artillery carriages, anti-mine vehicles and so on, which were produced from scratch or improvised in the field. Gradually the M4 series became the T-34 of the Western Allies.

The British army purchased large numbers of M4s or took them over as part of the Lend-Lease programme. To the British the M4 was the **General Sherman** (or simply **Sherman**) and they

The M4A3 was one of the most developed of all the Sherman variants used until 1945, as it had a 76-mm (2.99-in) gun and HVSS (horizontal volute spring suspension).

too added their variations to the long list of M4 specials: one of the best-known of these was the 1944 **Sherman Firefly**, which had a 17-pdr main gun. The first Shermans went into action with the British at El Alamein in October 1942. Thereafter the Sherman was the most numerous tank in British army service for the rest of World War II.

The main models of this seminally important armoured fighting vehicle were as follows: the M3 (**Sherman I**) already mentioned, engined with the 263-kW (353-hp) Wright Whirlwind or 298-kW (400-hp) Continental R-975 radial engines; the **M4A1** (**Sherman II**) with a fully cast rather than cast/welded hull, and alternatively engined with the 336-kW (450-hp) Caterpillar 9-cylinder diesel; the **M4A2** (**Sherman III**) with a welded hull and a 313-kW (420-hp) General Motors 6-71 twin-diesel powerplant; the **M4A3** (**Sherman IV**) with a 373-kW (500-hp) Ford GAA III engine and horizontal- rather than vertical-volute suspension; and the **M4A4** (**Sherman V**) with the 317-kW (425-hp) Chrysler five-bank engine. It is also worth noting that in British service the mark numbers were suffixed whenever the main armament was not the standard 75-mm (2.95-in) gun, A indicating a 76-mm (2.99-in)

gun, B a 105-mm (4.13-in) howitzer and C a 17-pdr anti-tank gun. The suffix W in US designations denoted the provision of wet ammunition stowage for reduced fire risk. Armour protection was also considerably developed in the lengthy production run, the M4A2 having a minimum and a maximum of 13 and 105 mm (0.51 and 4.13 in), equivalent figures for the M4A3 and M4A4 being 15 and 100 mm (0.59 and 3.94 in), and 20 and 85 mm (0.8 and 3.35 in) respectively.

It was the numerical superiority of the M4 that in the end made it a war-winner. The M4 had many drawbacks and was far from being the ideal battle

tank. It was often left behind in fire-power as the German tank guns increased in power and calibre, and the armour thicknesses and arrangement were frequently found wanting. Indeed many field improvizations had to be used to beef up the armour, these including the simple expedient of using stacked sandbags. The silhouette was too high for comfort and the interior arrangements far from perfect. Another problem frequently encountred was that with so many variants in use spares were often not available and engine interchangeability was frequently impossible, causing considerable logistical troubles.

Specification
Medium Tank M4A3
Crew: 5
Weight: in action 32.284 tonnes
Powerplant: one Ford GAA V-8 petrol engine developing 335.6 or 373 kW (450 or 500 hp)
Dimensions: length, with gun 7.52 m (24 ft 8 in), and over hull 6.27 m (20 ft 7 in); width 2.68 m (8 ft 9.5 in); height 3.43 m (11 ft 2.875 in)
Performance: maximum road speed 47 km/h (29 mph); maximum road range 161 km (100 miles); fording 0.91 m (3 ft); gradient 60 per cent; vertical obstacle 0.61 m (2 ft); trench 2.26 m (7 ft 5 in)

Heavy Tank M26 Pershing

The heavy tank did not have an easy time during World War II as far as the Americans were concerned. Early on they realized the operational need for a heavy tank but initially concentrated their considerable production potential on the medium tank, the M3 and M4 series in particular. A promising design, the **Heavy Tank M6**, came to nought as the result of this concentration of effort, but low-priority development facilities were thereafter accorded to the heavy tank. This requirement was emphasized when the German Panther and Tiger arrived on the battlefield, and the heavy tank was then given a greater degree of priority.

The first of the new generation of American heavy tanks was a trials model known as the **Medium Tank T20**. It had a 76-mm (2.99-in) gun and used a suspension very like that of the M4 medium tank, but progressive development led to a newer form of suspension of the torsion-bar type. The gun was also replaced by a new 90-mm (3.54-in) main gun in a revised turret, and after a further series of trials models culminating in the **Heavy Tank T26E3** (via the **Medium Tanks T22, T23, T25** and **T26**) was selected for production as the **Heavy Tank M26**. It was given the name **General Pershing** (or simply **Pershing**), but by the time the full series of trials on the new tank had been completed only a few were ready for action in World War II.

It was early 1945 before the first M26s arrived in Europe and of these only a relative handful saw any action there. More were sent to the Pacific theatre and there rather more were used in anger, but by the time they arrived on the scene there was little a

heavy tank could be called upon to perform.

Thus the M26 contributed little to World War II, but its design was the long-term result of the years of combat that had gone before. For perhaps the first time on an American tank adequate consideration was given to armour protection (a minimum of 12 mm/0.47 in and a maximum of 102 mm/4.02 in) and firepower. With the 90-mm (3.54-in) gun, originally intended for use as an anti-aircraft weapon, the M26 had armament that was the equal of any and the superior of most contemporary tanks. The secondary armament comprised the standard three machine-guns: one 12.7-mm (0.5-in) and two 7.62 (0.3-in) weapons. For all that the M26 still had a few design drawbacks: the turret shape was criticized for its shot-trap potential, and the retention of the bow machine-gun was

even then seen as something of an anachronism (later developments did away with it). In fact the M26 was only the start of a new generation of American tank design. After 1945 the M26 was progressively developed through various models including the M47 into the M48 Patton, which is still in widespread service with the US Army and also with other armies all over the world.

The M26 saw extensive action during the Korean War and was for long one of the main types fielded by the US Army in Europe as part of NATO. The M26 also spawned many variants and hybrids as post-war development continued.

Specification
Heavy Tank M26
Crew: 5
Weight: in action 41.73 tonnes

Powerplant: one Ford GAF V-8 petrol engine delivering 373 kW (500 hp)
Dimensions: length, with gun 8.79 m (28 ft 10 in) and over hull 6.51 m (21 ft 2 in); width 3.505 m (11 ft 6 in); height 2.77 m (9 ft 1 in)
Performance: maximum road speed 48 km/h (30 mph); maximum road range 148 km (92 miles); fording 1.22 m (4 ft); gradient 60 per cent; vertical obstacle 1.17 m (3 ft 10 in); trench 2.59 m (8 ft 6 in)

The M26 Pershing mounted a main 90-mm (3.54-in) gun and had a crew of five. It entered service in 1945, just too late to have any major impact on the fighting in Europe but in time to see action during the Okinawa campaign in the Pacific. It was the first of a series leading to the M60 of today.

T-40, T-60 and T-70 light tanks

During the 1920s and 1930s the tankette was a continuing attraction for the military mind and the tank designer, and the Soviet Union was no exception in this trend. By the late 1930s the Red Army had progressed through the stages where the one-man tankette had been tested and dropped and was in the usual stage where the tankette had developed into the two-man light tank. By the time the Germans attacked in 1940 the Red Army had invested fairly heavily in the light tank, and the models in service were the result of many years of development.

One of the main types in 1940 was the **T-40** amphibious light tank, armed with a 12.7-mm (0.5-in) machine-gun. It was the latest in a long line of models that could be traced back to the T-27 of the early 1930s. This had progressed through the T-33, the T-34 (not to be confused with the T-34 medium tank), the T-36, the T-37 and finally the T-38. Most of these lacked the amphibious capabilities of the T-40 which was placed in production in about 1940, so that by the time the invasion of 1941 started only a few (about 230) were ever completed. Many of the late-production **T-40** models (with streamlined nose and foldable trim vane) were converted into Katyusha rocket-launcher carriers and were never used as turreted tanks, whose normal armament was one 12.7-mm (0.5-in) and one 7.62-mm (0.3-in) machine-gun. Armour ranged from 6 to 13 mm (0.24 to 0.51 in) in thickness.

While the amphibious T-40 was being developed a non-amphibious version, known as the **T-40S**, was proposed. When the Germans invaded, the call was for many more tanks delivered as rapidly as possible, so the simpler T-40S was rushed into production and redesignated the **T-60** light tank. Unfortunately it was a bit of a horror in service and carried over the primary bad points of the T-40: it was too lightly armoured and, having only a 20-mm cannon plus a co-axial 7.62-mm (0.3-in) machine-gun as armament, was useless against other tanks. Also it was so underpowered that it could not keep up with the heavier T-34 tanks across country. T-60s were kept in production simply because they could be churned out quickly from relatively small and simple factories. They were powered by truck engines, many components being taken from the same source, and the slightly improved **T-60A** appeared in 1942 with slightly thicker frontal armour (35 mm/1.38 in instead of 25 mm/0.98 in) and solid instead of spoked wheels.

By late 1941 work was already under way on the T-60's successor. This was the **T-70**, whose first version used a twin-engine power train that could never have worked successfully in action and which was soon replaced by a revised arrangement. The T-70 was otherwise a considerable improvement over the T-40 and T-60. It had heavier armour (proof against 37-mm/1.46-in anti-tank guns) and the turret mounted a 45-mm (1.77-in) gun and 7.62-mm (0.3-in) machine-gun. This was still only of limited use against heavier tanks but was better than a mere machine-gun. The crew remained at two men, the commander having to act as his own gunner and loader in a fashion hardly conducive to effective operation of tank or units.

Production of the T-70 and thicker-armour **T-70A** ceased in October 1943, by which time 8,226 had been produced. In service the type proved remarkably unremarkable, and the vehicles appear to have been confined to the close support of infantry units and some limited reconnaissance tasks. By

Above: The T-70 light tank was a useful reconnaissance vehicle, but it had only a 45-mm (1.77-in) main gun and was thus of little use in combat against heavier German tanks. In action it proved to be adequate but unexceptional.

Right: The 20-mm gun armed T-60 light tank was not a great success in action, for it was too lightly armed and armoured and lacked power and mobility. It was kept in production simply to get some sort of vehicle to the Red Army following the disasters of the 1941 campaigns.

1943 the light tank was an anachronism, but the Soviets nonetheless went ahead with a replacement known as the T-80. Almost as soon as it went into production its true lack of value was finally realized and the production line was switched to manufacturing components for the SU-76 self-propelled gun.

Specification
T-40
Crew: 2
Weight: 5.9 tonnes
Powerplant: one GAZ-202 petrol engine delivering 52 kW (70 hp)
Dimensions: length 4.11 m (13 ft 5.9 in); width 2.33 m (7 ft 7.7 in); height 1.95 m (6 ft 4.8 in)
Performance: maximum road speed 44 km/h (27.3 mph); road range 360 km (223.7 miles); fording amphibious; gradient 34°; vertical obstacle 0.70 m (2 ft 3.75 in); trench 1.85 m (6 ft 1 in)

Specification
T-60
Crew: 2

Weight: 6.4 tonnes
Powerplant: one GAZ-203 petrol engine delivering 63 kW (85 hp)
Dimensions: length 4.11 m (13 ft 5.9 in); width 2.3 m (7 ft 6.5 in); height 1.74 m (5 ft 8.5 in)
Performance: maximum road speed 45 km/h (28 mph); road range 450 km (280 miles); fording not known; gradient 29°; vertical obstacle 0.54 m (1 ft 9.3 in); trench 1.85 m (6 ft 1 in)

Specification
T-70
Crew: 2
Weight: 9.2 tonnes
Powerplant: two GAZ-202 petrol engines delivering a total of 104 kW (140 hp)
Dimensions: length 4.29 m (14 ft 0.9 in); width 2.32 m (7 ft 7.3 in); height 2.04 m (6 ft 8.3 in)
Performance: maximum road speed 45 km/h (28 mph); road range 360 km (223.7 miles); fording not known; gradient 34°; vertical obstacle 0.70 m (2 ft 3.6 in); trench 3.12 m (10 ft 2.8 in)

T-26 light infantry tank

During the late 1920s Red Army planners inaugurated a programme to re-equip the tank elements of the Soviet armed forces. In common with many other nations they decided upon an infantry support tank for their non-cavalry units and after attempting to develop a new design of their own decided on the mass production of a British commercial model, the 6-ton Vickers Type E light tank. This was named the T-26 and the first examples of the British model arrived in the Soviet Union during 1930, being designated T-26A-1.

Soviet production of the T-26 started during 1931. The earliest models used a twin-turret arrangement mounting two machine-guns (two 7.62-mm/0.3-in weapons in the **T-26A-2**, and one 12.7-mm/0.5-in and one 7.62-mm/0.3-in gun in the **T-26A-3**), but some models had a machine-gun in one turret and a gun (27-mm in the **T.26A-4** and 37-mm **T-26A-5**); this arrangement did not survive for long and later **T-26B** models had a single turret mounting only a gun (37-mm in the **T-26B-1**, though a 45-mm gun was used later).

The early T-26 tanks were straightforward copies of the British original, and were simple, robust vehicles of mainly riveted construction. The first model was the **T-36 Model 1931** (T-26A), replaced by the **T-26 Model 1933** (T-26B) which had some design improvements. Before 1941 the Model 1933 was the most widely produced of all Soviet tanks, about 5,500 being built by the time production of that particular version ceased in 1936. A new model, the **T-26S Model 1937**, was then placed in production and this series had several changes compared with the earlier versions. The T-26S carried the 45-mm (1.77-in) main gun fitted to later versions of the Model 1933, but allied this to an improved turret design

and all-welded construction as introduced on the **T-26B-2**.

The welding was introduced following operational experiences in the border clashes with Japan that took place along the Mongolian and Manchurian boundaries in 1934 and 1935. Experience showed that a T-26 which encountered hostile fire was likely to have its rivets knocked out to fly around the interior. Welding was introduced with the later Model 1933 tanks but was standard on the T-26B-2.

Throughout their lives the T-26 tanks underwent many production and in-service changes, most of them aimed at improving armour protection (minimum of 6 mm/0.24 in and maximum of 25 mm/0.98 in) and armament. There were also many special versions. Perhaps the most numerous of these were the flame-throwing tanks prefixed by the designation OT. Again there were several of these, the earliest being the **OT-26** and the last the **OT-133**. Most of these had the flame-throwing projector in the turret and carried no main gun, but later models did carry a gun in addition to the projector. There were also bridge-carrying versions (the **ST-26**) and attempts were made to mount 76.2-mm (3-in) guns for increased infantry fire support. The type was also developed as a command vehicle, variants being the **T-26A-4(U)** and **T-26B-2(U)**.

Production of the T-26 series ceased entirely in 1941 when the Germans overran most of the production facilities. New production centres set up in the Soviet hinterlands launched the production of later tank designs, but by 1941 well over 12,000 T-26 tanks of all kinds had been made. Consequently

they were among the most numerous of the AFVs used during the early stages of the 'Great Patriotic War', and were also used in the 1939-1940 campaign in Finland. Some had been used during the Spanish Civil War.

After 1941 huge numbers of T-26 tanks were destroyed or passed into German hands. Many were later converted to artillery tractors or self-propelled gun carriers, usually by the Germans who always had a need for such vehicles.

Overall the T-26 was an unremarkable little tank that was unable to stand up to the demands of 1941, but it enabled the Soviet Union to establish its own mass production facilities and know-how, and these stood them in good stead after 1941.

Specification
T-26B
Crew: 3
Weight: 9.4 tonnes
Powerplant: one GAZ T-26 8-cylinder petrol engine developing 68 kW (91 hp)

Dimensions: length 4.88 m (16 ft); width 3.41 m (11 ft 2.25 in); height 2.41 m (7 ft 11 in)
Performance: maximum road speed 28 km/h (17.4 mph); maximum road range 175 km (108.7 miles); fording not known; gradient 40°; vertical obstacle 0.79 m (2 ft 7 in); trench 1.90 m (6 ft 2.8 in)

One of the many variants of the T-26 light infantry tank was the Model 1931, which had dual turrets, usually mounting two 7.62-mm (0.30-in) machine-guns, but sometimes having one of the machine-guns replaced by a 37-mm (1.46-in) short infantry support gun. The later T-26 Model 1933 had a single turret.

T-28 medium tank

The Soviet **T-28** medium tank was an indigenous design that entered production in Leningrad during 1933. It was greatly influenced by current trends shown in German and British (Vickers) experimental designs, and so featured the fashionable multi-turret layout. The T-28 had three, the main gun turret being partially flanked by two smaller ones armed with machine-guns, the driver's position being between the two auxiliary turrets.

The prototype T-28 had a 45-mm (1.77-in) main gun, but on T-28 and **T-28A** production models (the latter with thicker front armour) this was changed to a short 76.2-mm (3-in) gun, **T28B** production models after 1938 having a newer and longer 76.2-mm (3-in) gun with improved performance. The secondary armament was three 7.62-mm (0.3-in) machine-guns. Overall the T-28 was a large and slab-sided brute but the Soviet tank design teams were still in the process of learning their trade, and experience with the T-28 was later of great importance.

Construction of the original production model, the **T-28 Model 1934**, lasted until 1938 when the improved T-28B appeared with the new gun (see above), rudimentary gun stabilization and some engine modifications. This was the **T-28 Model 1938**, and manufacture of this version lasted until 1940, when production ceased in favour of later models. The armour of the different versions ranged from a minimum of 20 mm (0.79 in) to a maximum of 80 mm (3.15 in) in thickness.

There were several experimental versions of the T-28 including some self-propelled guns and specials such as bridging and assault engineering tanks. None of these experimentals got past the prototype stage, but experience with them was of great importance when later variations on production tanks were contemplated. In fact the T-28 was of more value as an educational tank than as a combat tank. Its service life was short, spanning only the years from 1939 to 1941. In 1939 it was used in action against the Finns during the 'Winter War'. In that short

conflict the T-28s fared badly as their crews found out the hard way that the vehicle's armour was too thin for safety and those tanks that survived underwent a hasty course of modifications to add extra armour (up to 80 mm/ 3.15 in). The modified T-28s were known as the **T-28E** (*ekanirovki*, or screened, i.e. uparmoured), but the crash programme proved to have been of doubtful effectiveness when the Germans invaded the Soviet Union in 1941. The T-28E was also known as the **T-28M** or **T-28 Model 1940**.

In 1941 the surviving T-28s demonstrated themselves to be of only limited combat value. Their large slab sides and stately performance made them easy prey for German anti-tank weapons. They also proved vulnerable to mines, and during the 'Winter War' of 1939-1940 some T-28s were modified to carry anti-mine rollers in front of the vehicle. These rollers were not a success, but again the experience gained with them proved to be of great value later. Thus the T-28 passed

from the scene, proving itself to belong to an earlier era of tank design.

Specification
T-28
Crew: 6
Weight: 28 tonnes
Powerplant: one M-17 V-12 petrol engine developing 373 kW (500 hp)
Dimensions: length 7.44 m (24 ft 4.8 in); width 2.81 m (9 ft 2.75 in); height 2.82 m (9 ft 3 in)
Performance: maximum road speed

The Soviet T-28 heavy tank weighed 28 tons but was termed a medium tank. It had a crew of six and had a short 76.2-mm (3-in) gun as its main armament, plus machine-guns in the two extra turrets mounted in front of the main turret. They were clumsy vehicles with armour that proved to be too thin once in action.

37 km/h (23 mph); maximum road range 220 km (136.7 miles); fording not known; gradient 43°; vertical obstacle 1.04 m (3 ft 5 in); trench 2.90 m (9 ft 6 in)

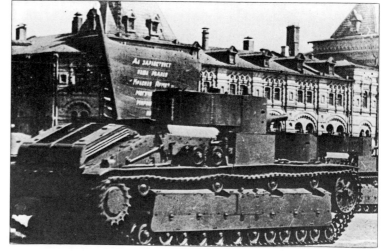

The T-28 medium tank was one of the least successful pre-war Soviet tank designs for in action in 1940 and 1941 it proved to be cumbersome, inadequately armoured and under-gunned. The main gun was a short 76.2-mm (3-in) weapon that was replaced in some cases by a longer-barrelled gun of the same calibre.

BT-7 fast tank

When the Red Army tank staff decided to modernize its tank fleet during the late 1920s it authorized the design bureaux to use whatever sources they liked to obtain the best ideas available. Accordingly many promising design concepts from all over the world were embraced, and among these were ideas of the American J. Walter Christie. His advanced suspension designs had little effect in his own country at that time, but the Soviets embraced his concepts willingly and took them over for their own further development. The Christie suspension was integrated into the BT series (*bystrochodya tank*, or fast tank).

The first Soviet BTs were copied exactly from a Christie prototype delivered to the Soviet union in 1930 and designated **BT-1**. The first Soviet model was the **BT-2**, and from 1931 onwards the BT series progressed through a series of design developments and improvements until the **BT-7** was produced in 1935. Like the earlier BT tanks the BT-7 was a fast and agile vehicle intended for Red Army cavalry units, and was powered by a converted aircraft engine. The suspension used the Christie torsion bars that allowed a large degree of flexibility at high speeds. The hull was all-welded and well shaped, but the main gun was only a 45-mm (1.77-in)

The BT-7 was introduced into service in 1935 and was produced in two main versions, both armed with a 45-mm (1.77-in) gun. Although fast and handy in action, the BT-7 proved to be too lightly armoured, but it led in time to the development of the T-34 series.

weapon, although this was still larger than that fitted on many contemporary equivalents. The secondary armament was two 7.62-mm (0.3-in) machine-guns, and armour varied from 10 to 22 mm (0.39 to 0.87 in).

The BT-7 proved to be very popular with its users. By the time it entered service (in its original **BT-7-1** form with a cylindrical turret, replaced by a conical turret in the **BT-7-2**) many of the automotive snags that had troubled some of the earlier BTs had been eliminated, and the BT-7 thus proved to be fairly reliable. Also, by the time it appeared there were many variants of the BTs: some were produced as flamethrower tanks, and there was a special **BT-7A** close-support version carrying a short 76.2-mm (3-in) main gun. Other experimentals included amphibious and bridging tanks, and variants with various tracks to improve terrain-crossing capabilities.

The BT-7 did have one major tactical disadvantage in that it was only lightly armoured. On the entire BT series armour protection had been sacrificed for speed and mobility, and once in action during 1939 the BTs, including the BT-7, proved to be surprisingly vulnerable to anti-tank weapons as small as anti-tank rifles. BT-5s had demonstrated this fact when small numbers were used during the Spanish Civil War, but even though the BT-7 had some armour increases this was still not enough, as revealed in Finland during 1939 and 1940. As a result the design of a successor to the BT series was undertaken and this led ultimately to the adoption of the T-34. Variants of the BT-7 were the **BT-7-1(U)** command tank and **BT-7M** (or **BT-8**) improved

model with full-width and well-sloped glacis plate plus a V-2 diesel engine.

Thus the BT-7 played its major part in World War II well before the Germans invaded the Soviet Union in 1941. Large numbers were still in service in 1941, but they fared badly against the advancing Panzers. Despite their mobility the Soviet tank formations were poorly handled and many tanks, including BT-7s, were lost simply because they broke down as the result of poor maintenance or poor training of their crews. It was an inauspicious beginning for the Red Army, but worse was soon to follow and the large fleet of BT-7s was virtually eliminated by the end of 1941.

Specification
BT-7
Crew: 3

The BT-2 was the first Soviet tank design to incorporate the Christie suspension, and led to a whole string of BT variants that were eventually developed into the T-34 series. The Christie suspension gave the BT-2 a good cross-country performance, as this photograph graphically demonstrates.

Weight: 14 tonnes
Powerplant: one M-17T V-12 petrol engine developing 373 kW (500 hp)
Dimensions: length 5.66 m (18 ft 6.8 in); width 2.29 m (7 ft 6 in); height 2.42 m (7 ft 11.3 in)
Performance: maximum road speed 86 km/h (53.4 mph); maximum road range 250 km (155 miles); fording 1.22 m (4 ft); gradient 32°; vertical obstacle 0.76 m (2 ft 6 in); trench 1.83 m (6 ft)

T-34 medium tank

It is now difficult to write of the **T-34** medium tank without using too many superlatives, for the T-34 has passed into the realms of legend. It was one of the main war-winning weapons of World War II, and it was produced in such vast numbers and in so many versions that entire books have been written on the subject without exhausting the possibilities of the vehicle and its exploits.

In simple terms the T-34 had its origins in the shortcomings of the BT-7 and its forebears. The first result of the BT series' up-dating were the designs known as the **A-20** and **A-30**, produced in 1938 as developments of the **BT-IS**, but passed over in favour of a heavier-gunned tank with increased armour and known as the **T-32**. In the T-32 can be seen most of the features of the later T-34. It had a well-shaped hull with sloped armour, and a cast and sloped turret which mounted a 76.2-mm (3-in) high-velocity gun. The Christie suspension, suitably beefed up, was carried over from the BT series, but the ability to run on wheels without tracks was abandoned.

Good as the T-32 was, a selection panel requested yet more armour and so the T-34 was born. It went into production in 1940 and mass production of the **T-34/76A** soon followed. When the Germans attacked the Soviet Union in 1941 the type was already well established, and its apperance came as a nasty shock to the Germans. The T-34's well-sloped and thick armour (minimum of 18 mm/0.71 in and maximum of 60 mm/2.36 in) was proof against most of their anti-tank weapons and the L/30 76.2-mm (3-in) gun, soon replaced in service by an even more powerful L/40 gun of the same calibre, was effective against most German Panzers. The secondary armament was two 7.62-mm (0.3-in) machine-guns.

From 1941 onwards the T-34 was developed into a long string of models, many of them with few external differences. Production demands resulted in many expediences, the finish of most T-34s being rough to an extreme, but the vehicles were still very effective fighting machines. Despite the disruption of the production lines during 1941, ever-increasing numbers poured off the extemporized lines, and all manner of time-saving production methods (ranging from automatic welding to leaving whole sections of surface unpainted) were used. The second production model was the **T-34/76B** with a rolled-plate turret.

In service the T-34 was used for every role, ranging from main battle tank to reconnaissance vehicle, and from engineering tank to recovery vehicle. It was converted into the simplest of armoured personnel carriers by simply carrying infantry on the hull over long distances; these 'tank descent' troops became the scourge of the Germans as they advanced westwards through the liberated Soviet Union and then Eastern Europe. Successively improved models of the T-34/76 were the **T-34/76C** with a larger turret containing twin roof hatches in place of the original single hatch; the **T-34/76D** with a hexagonal turret and wider mantlet, plus provision for jettisonable exterior fuel tanks; the **T-34/76E** with a cupola on the turret and of all-welded construction; and the **T-34/76F** identical to the T-34/76E apart from its cast rather than welded turret. (It should be noted

that the designations are Western, designed to provide a means of identification in the absence of Soviet information.) In time the 76.2-mm (3-in) gun was replaced by an 85-mm (3.34-in) gun using the turret taken from the KV-85 heavy tank. This variant became the **T-34/85**, which remains in service to this day in some parts of the world. Special assault gun versions using the 85-mm (3.34-in) gun and later the 100-mm (3.94-in) or 122-mm (4.8-in) artillery pieces were developed, and flame-throwing, tractor, engineer and mine-clearing versions were also produced.

But it was as a battle tank that the T-34 has its main claim to fame. Available in thousands, the T-34 assumed mastery of the battlefield, forcing the Germans back on the defensive and taking from them the tactical and strategic initiative thus winning the 'Great Patriotic War' for the Soviet Union. Post-war the T-34 and its successors went on to gain more laurels, but it was as a war-winner in World War II that the T-34 must best be remembered. It was a superb tank.

Specification
T-34/76A
Crew: 4
Weight: 26 tonnes
Powerplant: one V-2-34 V-12 diesel developing 373 kW (500 hp)
Dimensions: length 5.92 m (19 ft 5.1 in); width 3 m (9 ft 10 in); height 2.44 m (8 ft)
Performance: maximum road speed 55 km/h (34 mph); maximum road range 186 km (115 miles); fording 1.37 m (4 ft 6 in); gradient 35°; vertical obstacle 0.71 m (2 ft 4 in); trench 2.95 m (9 ft 8 in)

Above: The T-34 tank was a very advanced design for its time. This is a late production T-34/76 armed with a 76.2-mm (3-in) main gun, and well provided with sloping armour for added protection. The tank was produced in thousands and proved durable, mobile and highly effective in service.

Above: The commander of an early production T-34/76 tank looks out from his large one-piece hatch during Red Army exercises held during 1940, before the German invasion. At that time the T-34/76 was kept under security wraps and its appearance during the 1941 campaigns came as a nasty shock for the German Panzer troops.

Below: T-34s in East Prussia during the winter of 1944-5. By that time the main production version of the T-34 mounted an 85-mm (3.34-in) gun and was known as the T-34/85. This was an excellent tank that is still good enough to remain in service with many armies to this day – not bad for a vehicle introduced in 1944.

T-35 heavy tank

The **T-35** was one of the major disappointments for the Soviet tank designers before World War II. It had its origins in design studies that began in 1930, and the first prototype was rolled out in 1932. In appearance and in many other ways the T-35, via the T-28, was greatly influenced by the design of the British Vickers Independent, a tank that was produced as a one-off only and which featured in a notorious 'spy' court case of the period. The T-28 carried over from the Vickers design one major feature, namely the multi-turret concept.

Although there were changes between the various production batches, the tanks of the main batch (produced between 1935 and 1938) were longer than the originals. This increase in length made the T-35 an unwieldly beast to steer, and its ponderous weight did little to improve matters. The multi-turret approach to tank

weaponry also proved to be of doubtful value. Aiming and co-ordinating the fire of the five turrets proved very difficult, and the overall effectiveness of the armament was further limited by the relatively small calibre of the main gun. In fact the main gun and turret were exactly the same as those used on the lighter T-28 medium tank. Armour varied from 10 to 30 mm (0.39 to 1.18 in) in thickness.

Production of the T-35 was slow and limited compared with that of other Soviet tank programmes of the time.

The huge size of the T-35 can be readily appreciated in this shot of a damaged and captured example being put on show by German soldiers. The main turret had a 76.2-mm (3-in) gun with limited anti-armour performance, and two of the smaller turrets had 37-mm or 45-mm (1.45-in or 1.77-in) guns.

Only 61 were produced between 1933 and 1939, and all of these vehicles served with just one tank brigade stationed near Moscow. This was politically handy, for the T-35s featured regularly in the Red Square parades of the time and thus provided a false impression of Soviet tank strengths. The massive vehicles made a great impression as they rumbled past, but the service reality was considerably different.

When they had to go to war in 1941 only a relative handful actually saw action, for many were retained in Moscow for internal duties and for purely local defence. There appears to be no record of any T-35s going into action around Moscow, but the few used elsewhere to try to halt the German advances did not fare well. They were too lightly armed and their weight and bulk made them easy meat for the Panzers.

Specification
T-35
Crew: 11
Weight: 45 tonnes
Powerplant: one M-17M V-12 petrol engine developing 373 kW (500 hp)
Dimensions: length 9.72 m (31 ft 10.7 in); width 3.2 m (10 ft 6 in); height 3.43 m (11 ft 3 in)
Performance: maximum road speed 30 km/h (18.6 mph); maximum road range 150 km (93.2 miles); fording not known; gradient 20°; vertical obstacle 1.20 m (4 ft); trench 3.50 m (11 ft 6 in)

The T-35 heavy tank made an impressive showing on parade in Red Square, but in action they made little impact, with only about 60 built. Fire control of the five turrets was very difficult and the great length of the hull made it a cumbersome vehicle.

KV-1 heavy tank

By 1938 Soviet tank designers had realized that the T-35 heavy tank would need replacement and set about the design of its successor. Several design bureaux were involved and many proposed designs with multiple turrets, but by the time prototypes were produced most had just two turrets. This approach still did not appeal to one of the teams, which designed a heavy tank with only one turret and named it after Klimenti Voroshilov, who was defence commissar at the time. Known as the **KV-1**, the new design was far more mobile than the other submissions and was field-tested during the campaign in Finland in 1940. This first variant was armed with a short 76.2-mm (3-in) gun and three or four 7.62-mm (0.3-in) machine-guns, and armour up to 100-mm (3.94-in) thick was provided.

The KV-1 was ordered into production in two main forms: one was the **KV-1A** armed with a long 76.2-mm (3-in) gun, while the other version was the **KV-2**, a marriage of the KV-1 hull, chassis and suspension with a large slab-sided turret mounting a 152-mm (5.98-in) howitzer (originally a 122-mm/4.80-in howitzer). Thus the KV-2 did not lack in firepower, but the high turret was a ponderous load for the vehicle and the

KV-2 (and improved **KV-2B**) did not shine in action.

With the KV-1 the future for Soviet tank design was established for some time to come. The old multi-turret concept was finally set aside, and the KV-1 emerged as a formidable heavy tank that was to serve the Red Army for years. It was used often as an assault or break-through tank, forming the spearhead of many attacks, and as the war against Germany progressed the basic design was gradually improved.

High on the list of improvements were armour increases, achieved with the **KV-1B** that had an extra 25-35 mm (0.98-1.38 in) added to the hull front and sides. Other changes were made in the turret which progressed from being a mainly plated affair to a fully cast component, which on the **KV-1C** also gave an increase in protection. Much of the extra armour was simply bolted onto existing armour.

For its size the KV-1 was undergunned, but a scheme to increase the

The KV-1 heavy tank originally mounted a 76.2-mm (3-in) main gun on a chassis that was to be adapted for later models of Soviet heavy tanks. Several versions existed as progressive production changes were introduced to speed manufacture and improve protection for the crew of five.

armament to a 107-mm (4.2-in) weapon never came to anything other than trials. Instead the 76.2-mm (3-in) gun

was lengthened and the 152-mm (5.98-in) gun in its clumsy turret was withdrawn. After 1943 numbers of 85-mm (3.34-in) guns were fitted, and this model was known as the **KV-85**.

The KV-1 was a sound design, but had some serious automotive problems. On early models it was almost impossible to change gear because of clutch problems, and there were other transmission difficulties. Many of them were eventually eliminated but the numerous increases in armour protection were usually carried out with no increases in engine power, though the KV-1C had an extra 75 kW (100 hp), so many examples were quite unable to

A KV-1 rolls through snowy Moscow streets to the front in December 1941. The heavy tank had a 76-mm main gun (later to be replaced by an 85-mm weapon) and was used by the Red Army as a breakthrough tank where its lack of speed was not a handicap.

reach their expected performance. One solution attempted in a small number of **KV-1S** (*skorostnoy*, or fast) tanks was the omission of applique armour to reduce weight and so raise speed. One serious problem tactically was that the turret was so arranged internally that the tank commander had to

double as gun loader, a situation that often put him out of touch with the tactical situation for critical periods. Later versions had the usual angled armour of most other Soviet tank designs, and overall the KV-1 was a bit of a problem for German anti-tank units.

Specification
KV-85
Crew: 5
Weight: 43 tonnes
Powerplant: one V-2K V-12 diesel developing 448 kW (600 hp)
Dimensions: length 6.68 m (21 ft 11 in); width 3.32 m (10 ft 10.7 in); height

On the vast open spaces of the Russian plain, the lack of mobility inherent in the KV-1 was a definite handicap. In the campaigns of 1942 many KV-1s were lost due to mechanical failure. The tank was improved, however, and was to lead to the powerful Josef Stalin tanks.

2.71 m (8 ft 10.7 in)
Performance: maximum (rarely achieved) road speed 35 km/h (21.75 mph); maximum road range 150 km (93.2 miles); fording not known; vertical obstacle 1.20 m (3 ft 8 in); gradient 36°; vertical obstacle 1.20 m (3 ft 11.25 in); trench 2.59 m (8 ft 6 in)

IS-2 heavy tank
USSR

By the time 1943 was through the Red Army had gained the strategic initiative from the Germans and was starting the series of advances that took it to Berlin in 1945. Along the way the Soviets attempted to maintain an overall tank design supremacy over their enemies and on the whole succeeded. This was as true for the heavy tanks as it was for the T-34 series, and the KV-1 was progressively developed until by 1943 the KV-85 with its 85-mm (3.34-in) gun and reshaped turret was in service. But by gradually reworking the transmission, reshaping and redesigning the hull and suspension, a new lower and lighter tank design was evolved. The new design was named the **IS-1** (IS for Iosef Stalin).

The IS-1 retained the 85-mm (3.34-in) gun of the KV-85, and was in its earliest forms known as the **IS-85**, but it was felt that the new design could accommodate a more powerful weapon. Trials were carried out with a new 100-mm (3.94-in) gun (**IS-100** variant) and a long 122-mm (4.8-in) gun, the 100-mm (3.94-in) gun proving to be the better armour-penetration weapon. However, the 122-mm (4.8-in) gun was almost as effective and also had the explosive power to blow off an enemy tank turret even if it could not penetrate its armour. To cap things in the 122-mm (4.8-in) gun's favour, potential numbers were available while the 100-mm (3.94-in) gun was still not in full production.

So the IS tank was fitted with the long 122-mm (4.8-in) gun and this became the **IS-2**, which had a number of other improvements. The first examples appeared in 1944 and remained in production and service until the war ended. It was a massive vehicle, its size emphasized by the long gun barrel. The turret and hull were more than amply supplied with armour (max-

imum of 132 mm/5.2 in), but the Red Army tank crews placed greater importance on the tank-killing power of the 122-mm (4.8-in) gun. This gun had a slow rate of fire and used separate ammunition, which further slowed the loading time (the A-19 was originally designed as a naval gun), and the ammunition was so large that only 28 rounds could be carried inside the tank. The secondary armament comprised one 12.7-mm (0.5-in) and one 7.62-mm (0.3-in) machine-gun. Later versions introduced a modified fire-control system and a revised breech to increase the speed of loading. Other changes were introduced at the same time, but more were to come.

Good as the IS-2 was, it was felt that it could still be improved. The result was the **IS-3** which retained the 122-mm (4.8-in) gun but in a drastically revised well-rounded turret behind a new and heavily sloped bow shape combined

When the Red Army finally reached Berlin in May 1945 IS-2 tanks were at the head of the armoured forces; this example is seen near the Reichstag. Note the great length of the 122-mm (4.8-in) gun and the well-shaped turret and front glacis plate that could deflect armour-piercing projectiles.

with the usual armour. Only a few IS-3s were completed before the war ended, but the type went on to worry Western military thinkers for many years afterwards as it remained the most powerful tank in the world for well over a decade (it is still employed in some Soviet-influenced nations).

Specification
IS-2
Crew: 4
Weight: 46 tonnes
Powerplant: one V-2-IS (V-2K) V-12 diesel developing 447 kW (600 hp)
Dimensions: length 9.9 m (32 ft 5.8 in);

The IS-2 was introduced into service with the Red Army during 1944 and was the most powerful of all the Soviet heavy tanks. It mounted a long 122-mm (4.8-in) gun in a well-protected cast turret, and carried a crew of four. Ammunition stowage was limited to 28 rounds.

width 3.09 m (10 ft 1.6 in); height 2.73 m (8 ft 11.5 in)
Performance: maximum road speed 37 km/h (23 mph); maximum road range 240 km (149 miles); fording not known; gradient 36°; vertical obstacle 1.0 m (3 ft 3 in); trench 2.49 m (8 ft 2 in)

Tank Destroyers

Successful tank designs are the product of a careful compromise between firepower, protection and mobility. Nevertheless, during World War II many of the belligerent nations resorted to producing 'tank destroyers', vehicles which sacrificed armour, speed or flexibility to carry a much more powerful gun than contemporary tanks.

An M18 Hellcat of the US 3rd Army's 4th Armoured Division crossing the Moselle River, Germany, in November 1945. The M18 was very fast and excelled in its tank-destroying role.

The tank destroyer was very much a product of the military and economic developments peculiar to World War II. During the war years the tank destroyer flourished for various reasons which will be described in this study, but in the years that followed 1945, this type of tank all but vanished, and it is a rare thing to find in modern tank parks. The truth was (and still is) that the tank destroyer had severe limitations as a fighting vehicle, but that it was capable of carrying a large-calibre gun, one far heavier than the corresponding tank chassis of the time could ever carry and fire.

The tank destroyer and the tank were very different beasts. Although they often used identical chassis, and at times even looked alike, they were markedly dissimilar when it came to combat. The tanks, with their combination of firepower, mobility and protection, usually had the combat edge over the tank destroyer with its limited-traverse armament and relatively thin armoured protection, but to be set against this the tank destroyer usually had the more powerful gun and a low silhouette that gave it the edge in concealment. There was at one time the philosophy that as tanks were not expected to fight tanks, specialized tank destroyers would have to be used. This approach did not last long under the severe strictures of combat, where it was soon learned that the best way to defeat a tank was to use another tank. The tank destroyer could be used for this purpose but at a cost in weapon flexibility and all too often in protection for the crew.

Tank destroyers were also important during World War II for purely economic and production reasons. Among the types of tank destroyer and German Panzerjager (tank hunter) were some superb fighting vehicles such as the Hetzer, the M18 Hellcat and the superlative Jagdpanther, the latter of which would be a viable fighting machine today. But there were some dreadful lash-ups that were undergunned, lacked protection for their unfortunate crews and, in addition to these failings, were so underpowered they had difficulty in moving at combat speeds. Add to these lumbering monsters such as the Jagdtiger, and the scope of this study can be appreciated.

Panzerjäger I

When the first PzKpfw I (Panzerkampf-wagen I) light tanks were produced in 1934 it was intended that they would be used only as training vehicles, but in the event they had to be used as combat tanks during the early war years for the simple reason that larger and heavier tanks were not yet available in sufficient numbers. But the PzKpfw I had a crew of a mere two men, carried only a machine-gun armament, and was poorly protected by thin armour. By no stretch of the imagination was it a viable battle tank and most were phased out of use after the end of 1940 (but retained for the original training role). This left a number of spare tank chassis with no operational role, so the opportunity was taken to convert these vehicles into the first German self-propelled gun.

It had already been decided that some form of mobile anti-tank gun would be a great asset to the anti-tank units who would otherwise have to use towed guns. Thus the first example of this requirement was met by mounting a 3.7-cm (1.456-in) Pak 35/36 onto a turretless PzKpfw I. While this conversion showed promise it was not adopted because even by mid-1940 it was appreciated that the 37-mm gun lacked power to deal with future armour. Thus a Czech 47-mm (1.85-in) anti-tank gun was mounted instead, and this combination was adopted for service as the **Panzerjäger I für 4.7-cm Pak(t)**.

The Czech gun was a powerful, hard-hitting weapon that was well capable of penetrating most armour it was likely to encounter and Alkett AG produced a total of 132 conversions. The result was very much a first attempt, for all that was required was to remove the original turret, plate over the front of the turret ring and arrange a small working platform over the engine covers. The gun was mounted in a small

shield that was left open at the top and rear. The crew consisted of the driver, still using his original PzKpfw I position, and two men serving the gun. A total of 74 rounds could be carried as standard, although more could be added to this total. The chassis mainly used for the conversion was that of the PzKpfw I Ausf B.

The Panzerjäger Is served in North Africa and during the early stages of the campaigns in the Soviet Union. They proved to be powerful enough to defeat opposing tanks, but their overall lack of protection for the crew made them very vulnerable targets. Accordingly when better equipments became available they were withdrawn from front-line use and assigned to theatres where they could be used for policing rather than for combat duties. Among the locations so honoured were the Balkans, where the vehicles were used on anti-partisan operations. Units operating on the Eastern Front after about the end of 1942 frequently removed the guns and used the chassis for supply carrying, and some units replaced their Czech guns with captured ex-French 47-mm guns. Few Panzerjäger Is remained in use after mid-1944.

Specification
Panzerjäger I
Crew: 3
Weight: 6000 kg (13,228 lb)
Powerplant: one Maybach NL 38 6-cylinder petrol engine developing 74.6 kW (100 hp)
Dimensions: length overall 4.14 m (13 ft 7 in); width 2.013 m (6 ft 7.25 in); height 2.1 m (6 ft 10.7 in)
Performance: maximum road speed 40 km/h (24.8 mph); range 140 km (87 miles); gradient 57 per cent; vertical obstacle 0.37 m (14.6 in); trench 1.4 m (4 ft 7 in); fording 0.6 m (2 ft)

This SdKfz 101 Panzerjäger 1 was the first example captured by the Allies in North Africa and was subjected to a great deal of technical scrutiny. It mounted an ex-Czech 4.7-cm (1.85-in) anti-tank gun in an open mounting that used only a frontal shield for crew protection.

This photograph of a Panzerjäger I shows the extemporized nature of this early German conversion, made in an attempt to prolong the service life of the PzKpfw 1 light tank. The gun was powerful enough, but the mounting provided virtually no protection.

Marder II

As with the PzKpfw I, when the PzKpfw II entered service in 1935 it was meant to be used only as a training and development tank. In the event it had to be used as a combat tank from 1939 to 1942 simply because there were not enough combat tanks to replace the type, which acquitted itself well enough despite the fact that its main armament was limited to a 2-cm cannon: by 1941 the PzKpfw II was overdue for replacement as its armament was not able to penetrate other than soft-skin targets and the small turret ring could not accommodate a heavier weapon. However, the production line for the chassis was still in being and at the time it seemed to be too valuable to waste so the opportunity was taken to convert the PzKpfw II to a Panzerjäger.

The prototype of this new Panzerjäger was fitted with a 5-cm (1.97-in) anti-tank gun, but the full production version was fitted with a special version of the 7.5-cm (2.95-in) Pak 40 anti-tank gun known as the Pak 40/2. This powerful gun was the German army's standard anti-tank weapon and the incorporation of greater mobility added considerably to the gun's anti-armour potential. The gun was placed behind a 10-mm (0.39-in) thick armoured shield that sloped to the rear to provide the gun crew with adequate pro-

tection. To accommodate the weight of the gun the engine was moved to the rear of the hull and the engine covers were used as a working platform to serve the gun. The vehicle was known as the **Marder II** (Marder meaning marten) although other and more cumbersome designations (such as **7.5-cm Pak 40/2 auf Slf II**) were used on official documents.

The Marder II remained in production until 1944 and became one of the most widely used of all the many German self-propelled gun conversions. In production terms it was manufactured in greater numbers than any other weapon of its type, for 1,217 were made. The Marder II was certainly a handy and efficient weapon in combat for it was relatively small, had a good cross-country performance and the gun could knock out virtually any enemy tank other than super-heavy Soviet tanks such as the IS-2. Racks for 37 rounds were provided over the engine covers and there was also space for stowing 600 rounds for the machine-gun usually carried; this was a 7.92-mm (0.312-in) MG34 or MG42.

Most Marder II production was sent to the Eastern Front, but the Marder II was found wherever German troops were in action. By 1944 the type was out of production and the crew was

The SdKfz 131 Marder II mounted a 7.5-cm (2.95-in) Pak 40/2 and was one of the more important of the Panzerjäger conversions. Based on the PzKpfw II Ausf A, C or F, 1217 were produced to be used on all fronts. The crew was four, including the driver.

often reduced by one man to conserve manpower, but the development of the type did not cease. During the latter stages of the war some Marder IIs were equipped with infra-red searchlights for engaging targets at night and some of these equipments were used in action on the Eastern Front during the last stages of the war. By then such

novel equipment could have but little impact on the outcome of the war.

Specification
Marder II
Crew: 3 or 4
Weight: 11000 kg (24,251 lb)

A Marder II with the 7.5-cm (2.95-in) Pak 40/2 gun barrel clamps lowered. Although this vehicle was one of the more important (numerically) of the Panzerjäger, it was rather high and generally lacked protection.

Powerplant: one Maybach HL 62 petrol engine developing 104.4 kW (140 hp)
Dimensions: length 6.36 m (20 ft 10.4 in); width 2.28 m (7 ft 5.8 in); height 2.20 m (7 ft 2.6 in)

Performance: maximum road speed 40 km/h (24.8 mph); road range 190 km (118 miles); gradient 57 per cent; vertical obstacle 0.42 m (16.5 in); trench 1.8 m (5 ft 11 in); fording 0.9 m (35 in)

This profile of the Marder II shows the rather high mounting of the 7.5-cm (2.95-in) Pak 40/2, a special version of the standard German anti-tank gun of the late war years.

Marder III

There were two self-propelled guns that were known as the **Marder III**, and both used the same chassis, a derivation of the Skoda TNHP-S tank chassis. This tank had originally been produced by the Skoda factory at Pilsen for the Czech army, but with the annexation of the Czech state by Germany in 1939 the Skoda works continued production of tanks under the designation PzKpfw 38(t) for the German army. The Germans introduced many production and in-service changes to the original Skoda design, and by 1941 the PzKpfw 38(t) may be regarded as a German design, but the original turret was too small to carry weapons powerful enough to defeat enemy armour after 1941, and the chassis was then kept in production for a number of alternative purposes.

One of these purposes came to light in 1941. The appearance of tanks such as the Soviet T-34 meant for a while that the German army had no anti-tank gun powerful enough to knock them out and all manner of hasty improvisations were made to counter this state of affairs. One was to take the chassis of the PzKpfw 38(t) and mount on it a captured Soviet field gun, the 76.2-mm (3-in) Model 1936. This was a very good dual-purpose weapon that could be used as an anti-tank weapon, and the Germans even went to the length of converting some for use as specialized anti-tank guns. On the PzKpfw 38(t) the gun was mounted in a fixed shield and the conversion went into production in early 1942 as the Marder III, otherwise the **Panzerjäger 38(t) für 7.62-cm Pak 36(r)**. Some 344 of these conversions were made, and the Marder III was used not only on the Eastern Front but in North Africa and elsewhere. However, it was at the time regarded only as a stopgap until sufficient numbers of the German 7.5-cm (2.95-in) Pak 40 became available. When this happened during 1942 production of the Soviet-gunned Marder III ceased and that of the German-gunned version commenced. The gun/chassis combination was still called the Marder III, but had the designation **Panzerjäger 38(t) Ausf H für 7.5-cm Pak 40/3** and used a slightly differing gun shield and mounting from the earlier

model. The first of the Pak 40-armed Marder IIIs were rushed into action during the last stages of the Tunisian campaign where some were captured, providing Allied intelligence staffs with something to mull over. But their 'find' did not last for long, for the Marder III was soon to undergo another transformation.

Up to 1943 the various German self-propelled guns using the Skoda chassis used the PzKpfw 38(t) tank as a basis. However, with some early conversions (including the original Marder III) the vehicles were nose-heavy, which at times limited mobility. Using the original Czech design as a basis, German engineers now relocated the engine at the front of the chassis and moved the 'working platform' to the rear to produce a specialized self-propelled gun carrier. As soon as this became available Marder III production changed once more to the new **Panzerjäger 38(t) Ausf M für 7.5-cm Pak 40/3** configuration with the gun and its protection mounted at the rear of the vehicle. This provided a much better balanced vehicle and the new chassis was also used to mount a variety of other weapons. The late type of Marder III was manufactured by BMM of Prague, and when production ceased in May 1944 799 had been made. They were used on all fronts.

Specification
Panzerjäger 38(t) Ausf M
Crew: 4
Weight: 11000 kg (24,251 lb)
Powerplant: one Praga AC petrol engine developing 111.9 kW (150 hp)
Dimensions: length overall 4.65 m (15 ft 3.1 in); width 2.35 m (7 ft 8.5 in); height 2.48 m (8 ft 1.6 in)
Performance: maximum road speed 42 km/h (26 mph); road range 140 km (87 miles); gradient 57 per cent; vertical obstacle 0.84 m (33 in); trench 1.3 m (4 ft 3 in); fording 0.9 m (35 in)

This Marder III was captured in North Africa in April 1943 and mounted its 7.5-cm (2.95-in) Pak 40/3 in a central position. It was a very simple conversion of a Czech tank chassis but was effective enough.

The later Marder IIIs had the main gun position moved to the rear of the chassis and the engine to the front. This provided a better-balanced and more handy vehicle, and nearly 800 were produced, still using the basic components of the PzKpfw 38(t) tank.

Hetzer

Although tank-destroyer conversions of existing tank chassis to produce weapons such as the Marder III were moderately successful, the results were, in overall terms, high and clumsy vehicles that lacked finesse and showed every sign of the haste in which they had originally been produced. In contrast, the various Sturmgeschütz close-support artillery vehicles demonstrated on many occasions that they too could be used as tank destroyers, and thus in 1943 it was decided to produce a light Panzerjäger along Sturmgeschütz lines, the chassis of the PzKpfw 38(t) being taken as the basis.

The result was one of the best of all the German Panzerjäger: the Jagdpanzer 38(t) für 7.5-cm Pak 39, or Hetzer (baiter, as in bull-baiting). The Hetzer used the basic engine, suspension and running gear of the PzKpfw 38(t) allied to a new armoured hull that sloped inwards to provide extra protection for the crew of four. The armament was the usual 7.5-cm (2.95-in) Pak 39 modified for the vehicle, along with a roof-mounted machine-gun. Production of the new vehicle began in Prague at the end of 1943 and also involved were factories at Pilsen, Königgrätz, Böhm and Breslau. These factories were soon working flat out, for the Hetzer proved to be a very successful gun/chassis combination: it was small and low, yet it was well protected and had very good cross-country performance. The gun could knock out all but the very heaviest enemy tanks, yet the Hetzer itself was very difficult to knock out and in combat it was so small as to be virtually invisible to the enemy gunners. Calls for more and more came from the front line, to the extent that by late 1944 all available PzKpfw 38(t) production was diverted towards the Hetzer. Production continued until the factories were overrun in May 1944, by which time 1,577 had been built.

Several versions of the Hetzer were produced: one was a flamethrower, the Flammpanzer 38(t), and another a light recovery version, the Bergepanzer 38(t). But the Hetzer did not cease in 1945. It was not long before the Hetzer was placed back in production for the new Czech army. The Hetzer was even exported to Switzerland between 1947 and 1952, the Swiss army using these Hetzers until the 1970s.

The wartime Hetzers were used for a series of trials and various weapon mountings. At one point trials were carried out with guns connected directly to the front hull armour and with no recoil mechanism fitted to see if the concept would work (it did). One trial model was an assault howitzer mounting a 15-cm (5.9-in) infantry howitzer and there were several similar projects, but none reached the production stage for the assembly lines had to concentrate on churning out more and more basic Hetzers to meet demands.

The Hetzer is now regarded as one of the best of all the German Panzerjäger for it was a powerful little vehicle that was much more economical to produce and use than many of the larger vehicles. Despite being armed with only a 75-mm gun, it could knock out nearly every tank it was likely to find and yet it was little higher than a standing man.

Specification
Hetzer
Crew: 4
Weight: 14500 kg (31,967 lb)
Powerplant: one Praga AC/2800 petrol engine developing 111.9-119.3 kW (150-160 hp)
Dimensions: length overall 6.20 m (20 ft 4.1 in) and hull 4.80 m (15 ft 9 in); width

2.50 m (8 ft 2.4 in); height 2.10 m (6 ft 10.7 in)
Performance: maximum road speed 39 km/h (24.2 mph); road range 250 km (155 miles); gradient 75 per cent; vertical obstacle 0.65 m (25.6 in); trench 1.3 m (4 ft 3.2 in); fording 0.9 m (35 in)

This Jagdpanzer 38(t) Hetzer has a roof-mounted remote control machine-gun for local and self-protection. The small stand-off armour side plates are fitted with the large road wheels providing more side-on protection. Well over 1,500 of these vehicles were produced.

The low height of the Hetzer can be clearly appreciated. Note the well-shaped 'Saukopf' (pig's head) gun mantlet that provided extra head-on

protection and the lack of a muzzle brake, usually fitted to other German vehicles of this type.

Jagdpanzer IV

Combat experience gained during the 1942 campaigns indicated to German staff planners that the existing Sturmgeschütz close support artillery vehicles would have to be upgunned if they were to continue to be used as tank-destroyers, and the future standard weapon was selected as the long version of the 7.5-cm (2.95-in) tank gun fitted to the Panther tank. This gun was 70 calibres long (as opposed to the 49-calibre length of the tank and anti-tank versions of the Pak 40 family) and to house this gun in vehicles such as the Sturmgeschütz III would require considerable modifications. These modifications would take time so it was decided to adapt the larger PzKpfw IV tank chassis to act as a 'fail safe' model. Design work was soon under way on this new model, which emerged in 1943 as the Jagdpanzer IV Ausf F für 7.5-cm Pak 39 or Panzerjäger 39, but by the time the first examples were ready the long 7.5-cm guns were earmarked for the Panther tanks and so the first

examples had to be content with 48-calibre guns.

The first of these Jagdpanzer IVs appeared in October 1943. They consisted of the well-tried suspension and engine layout of the PzKpfw IV allied to a new armoured carapace with well-sloped sides. This hull was much lower

than the hull/turret combination of the tank, and mounted the gun in a well-protected mantlet on the front hull. The result was well-liked by the Panzerjäger crews, who appreciated the low silhouette and the well-protected hull, so the Jagdpanzer IV was soon in great demand. The gun was powerful

The Jagdpanzer IV (SdKfz 162) was a Panzerjäger version of the PzKpfw IV tank and housed its 7.5-cm (2.95-in) main gun in a superstructure formed from well-sloped armoured plates. This is an early example with the guns still retaining the muzzle brake, an item later omitted.

enough to tackle virtually any enemy tank, and in action the Jagdpanzer IV was soon knocking up appreciable 'kill' totals, especially on the Eastern Front where most were sent. The secondary armament of two 7.92-mm (0.312-in) MG34 or MG42 machine-guns also proved highly effective.

Many Panzer commanders considered that the Jagdpanzer IV was good enough in its original form to require no upgunning but Hitler insisted that the change to the long gun had to be made. Thus during 1944 some **Jagd-panzer IV mit 7.5-cm Stuk 42** equipments with the longer L/70 gun appeared, but the changeover on the production line took time, too much time for Hitler, who insisted that the changeover to the new gun had to be made even if it meant diverting all PzKpfw IV tank production to that end. Thus a third Jagdpanzer IV appeared, this time a hasty conversion of a basic PzKpfw IV hull to take a form of Jagd-panzer IV sloping carapace and mounting the 70-calibre gun. This conversion was known as the **Panzer IV/70 Zwischenlösung** (interim) and was in production by late 1944.

In service the 70-calibre gun Jagd-panzer IVs proved to be powerful tank killers, but the extra weight of the long gun made the vehicles nose-heavy to the extent that the front road wheels had to be ringed with steel instead of rubber to deal with the extra weight. The gun weight also reduced the overall performance of the vehicle, especially across rough terrain. But by late 1944 and early 1945 such drawbacks

simply had to be overlooked, for the Allies were at the gates of the Reich and anything that could be put into the field was used.

The Jagdpanzer IV proved to be a sound Panzerjäger that enabled the Germans to utilize existing production capacity and maintain the PzKpfw IV line in being when it would otherwise have been phased out. In service the Jagdpanzer IV was a popular vehicle and a powerful tank-killer.

Specification
Jagdpanzer IV mit 7.5-cm Stuk 42
Crew: 4
Weight: 25800 kg (56,879 lb)
Powerplant: one Maybach HL 120 petrol engine developing 197.6 kW (265 hp)
Dimensions: length overall 8.58 m (28 ft 1.8 in); width 2.93 m (9 ft 7.4 in); height overall 1.96 m (6 ft 5.2 in)
Performance: maximum road speed 35 km/h (22 mph); road range 214 km (133 miles); gradient 57 per cent; vertical obstacle 0.6 m (23.6 in); trench 2.3 m (7 ft 6.6 in); fording 1.2 m (3 ft 11 in)

This early production Jagdpanzer IV has the muzzle brake still fitted. Later versions used a much longer 7.5-cm (2.95-in) main gun, but this longer gun rather overloaded the chassis, and later versions also used side armour plates. This Panzerjäger was later considered to be one of the best of its type.

Nashorn

During the mid-war years the German army carried out a large number of hurried improvisations in order to get useful numbers of Panzerjäger into the field, and some of these improvisations fared better than others. One of these hasty measures was the adoption of the special weapon-carrier vehicle that had originally been produced to carry the large 15-cm (5.9-in) sFH 18 field howitzer and known as the Geschütz-wagen III/IV as it was based on the chassis of the PzKpfw IV but used some of the drive components of the PzKpfw III. Despite the great demand for the artillery version of this weapon carrier it was decided to adapt it to carry the large 8.8-cm (3.46-in) Pak 43 anti-tank gun as the **8.8-cm Pak 43/1 auf GW III/IV**. The first of these new Panzerjäger were issued during 1943, and the type went under two names: the official name was **Nashorn** (rhinoceros) but **Hornisse** (hornet) was also widely applied.

The Nashorn was very much one of the 'interim' Panzerjäger designs, for although the gun was mounted behind armour at the front and sides this armour was relatively thin, and the top and rear were open. The gun mounting itself was rather high, so the Nashorn had definite combat deficiencies, not the least of which was the problem of concealing the height and bulk of the vehicle on a battlefield. As the chassis had been intended as an artillery carrier the bulk problem was originally of little moment, but for a Panzerjäger of considerable importance, making the stalking of tank targets very difficult. Thus the Nashorn

was often used as a 'stand-off' weapon that was able to use the considerable power and long-range accuracy of its gun to pick off targets at ranges of 2000 m (2,187 yards) and more; most of the other Panzerjäger types fought at much closer combat ranges.

The Nashorn carried a crew of five with only the driver under complete armoured protection. The rest of the crew was carried in the open fighting compartment with only a canvas cover to protect it from the elements. Most of the 40 rounds carried were located in lockers along the sides of the open compartment and the gunner was equipped not only with the usual direct vision sighting devices but also with artillery dial sights for the occasions when the Pak 43 could be used as a long-range artillery weapon. During the latter stages of production the Pak 43 gun was replaced by the similar

8.8-cm Pak 43/41, a weapon introduced to speed up production of the Pak 43; although it was manufactured differently from the original it was identical as far as ballistics were concerned. The Nashorn carried a machine-gun for local defence and the crew was supposed to be issued with at least two sub-machine guns.

Most Nashorn production was centred at the Deutsche Eisenwerke, at Teplitz-Schönau and Duisburg, and by the time the last of the vehicles rolled off the lines during 1944 473 had been made. In combat the powerful gun made the Nashorn a potent vehicle/weapon combination, but it was really too high and bulky for the Panzerjäger role and only a shortage of anything better at the time maintained the type in production. As it was it was succeeded by the Jagdpanther.

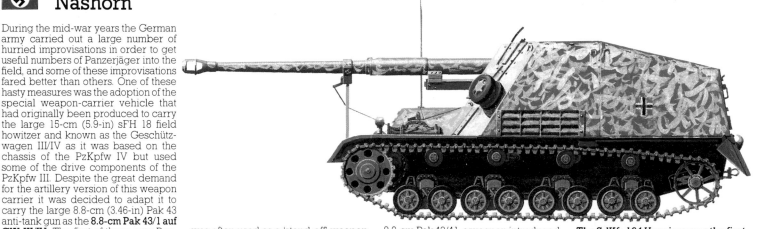

The SdKfz 164 Hornisse was the first Panzerjäger to mount the 8.8-cm (3.46-in) Pak 43/1, and used the same chassis as the Hummel.

Specification
Nashorn
Crew: 5
Weight: 24400 kg (53,793 lb)
Powerplant: one Maybach HL 120 petrol engine developing 197.6 kW (265 hp)
Dimensions: length overall 8.44 m (27 ft 8.3 in) and hull 5.80 m (19 ft 0.3 in); width 2.86 m (9 ft 4.6 in); height 2.65 m (8 ft 8.3 in)
Performance: maximum road speed 40 km/h (24.8 mph); range 210 km (130.5 miles); gradient 57 per cent; vertical obstacle 0.6 m (23.6 in); trench 2.3 m (7 ft 6.6 in); fording 0.8 m (2 ft 7.5 in)

Panzerjäger Tiger (P) Elefant

When the tank that was to become the Tiger was still in its planning stage two concerns, Henschel and Porsche, were in competition for the production contract. The Porsche entry was at one time the more favoured, mainly as a result of Professsor Porsche's influence with Hitler, but also because the design featured a radical approach by employing a petrol-electric drive with electric motors actually propelling the vehicle. However, the Porsche approach proved to be unreliable on test and the Henschel entry went on to become the PzKpfw VI Tiger.

But by the time the Henschel design was in production, Porsche drives and the hulls to put them in were also ready for production. It was then decided to place the Porsche design in production for use as a heavy tank-destroyer mounting the new 8.8-cm (3.46-in) Pak 43/2 anti-tank gun, a development of the earlier Flak 18-37 anti-aircraft gun series. (Actually the Pak 43 was virtually a new gun and fired more powerful ammunition than the earlier guns.) The gun would be placed in a large armoured superstructure with limited traverse, and 90 of these vehicles were produced to become the **Panzerjäger Tiger (P)**, later known as either **Ferdinand** or **Elefant**. The (P) denoted Porsche.

The Elefants were produced at the Nibelungwerke in something of a hurry during early 1943, the urgency being occasioned by the fact that Hitler demanded them to be ready for the opening of the main campaign of 1943, which was to commence against the Kursk salient on the Eastern Front; the new Panther tanks were also scheduled to make their combat debut in the same battle. Production delays and training the Panzertruppen to use their new charges delayed the start of the offensive until 5 July 1943.

By then the Red Army was more than ready for them. The defences of the Kursk salient were formidable and the delays had enabled the Red Army to add to their effectiveness in depth so that when the Germans attacked their efforts were of little avail. For the Elefants the Kursk battles were a dreadful baptism of fire. The Elefants were

Above: The Elefant used a complex twin-engine power pack driving an electric transmisison that did not work too well in service. It was heavy, slow and ponderous, making it more of a heavy assault gun than a Panzerjäger. Most were used in Russia but a few ended up in Italy in 1944.

organized in two battalions (*Abteilungen*) of Panzerregiment 654, and even before going into action their troubles began. The Elefants had been rushed into use before their many technical bugs had been entirely removed, and many broke down as soon as they started to move forward. Those that did make it to the Soviet lines were soon in trouble, for although the vehicles were fitted with the most powerful anti-tank guns then available they lacked any form of secondary armament for self-defence. Soviet tank-killer infantry squads swarmed all over them and placed charges that either blew off their tracks or otherwise disabled them. The Elefant crews had no way of defending themselves at all and those that could either withdrew or abandoned their vehicles and ran.

Some Elefants did survive Kursk and were later fitted with machine-guns to defend themselves, but the Elefant never recovered from its inauspicious debut. The few that were left were

withdrawn to other fronts such as Italy but even there their unreliability and lack of spares soon rendered them useless. Some were captured by the Allies in Italy.

Specification
Elefant
Crew: 6
Weight: 65000 kg (143,300 lb)
Powerplant: two Maybach HL 120 TRM V-12 petrol engines each developing 395.2 kW (530 hp) and driving a Porche/Siemens-Schuckert petrol-electric drive
Dimensions: length overall 8.128 m (26 ft 8 in); width 3.378 m (11 ft 1 in);

The Elefant was one of the failures of the German Panzerjäger designers, for despite its main 8.8-cm (3.46-in) gun it was too cumbersome and, more importantly, the first examples lacked any kind of self-defence armament. It was also too complicated and was generally unreliable.

height 2.997 m (9 ft 10 in)
Performance: maximum road speed 20.1 km/h (12.5 mph); road range 153 km (95 miles); gradient 40 per cent; vertical obstacle 0.8 m (31.5 in); trench 2.65 m (8 ft 8.3 in); fording 1.0 m (3 ft 3.4 in)

Jagdpanther

When the vehicle now known as the **Jagdpanther** was first produced in February 1944, it marked a definite shift away from a period where Panzerjäger were hasty conversions or improvisations to a point where the tank-destroyer became a purpose-built weapon of war. The Jagdpanther was first mooted in early 1943, at a time when tank destroyers were required in quantity, and by taking the best available tank chassis it was hoped that production totals would meet demand. Thus the Panther chassis was used virtually unaltered as the basis for the new Panzerjäger, and an 8.8-cm (3.46-in) Pak 43 anti-tank gun was mounted on a well-sloped armoured hull superstructure, with a 7.92-mm (0.312-in) MG34 or MG42 machine-gun for local defence. The prototype, then known as the **Panzerjäger Panther**, was demonstrated to Hitler in October 1943 and it was Hitler himself who decreed that the name should be changed to Jagdpanther.

The Jagdpanther was one of those vehicles where superlatives could be justifiably lavished, for it was a superb fighting vehicle and destined to be one of the most famous of all the many World War II armoured fighting vehicles. It was fast and well protected, and it mounted a potent gun, but not content with all that it had about it a definite aura that distinguished it from all its contemporaries. So well balanced was the design that it would not be too out of place in any tank park today, 40 years after it first appeared. The Jagdpanther could knock out virtually any enemy tank, including the heavy Soviet IS-2s, although for them a side shot was required for a certain kill. At times single Jagdpanthers or small groups of them could hold up Allied armoured advances for considerable periods. Fortunately for the Allies, production of the Jagdpanther never reached the planned rate of 150 per month. By the time the production facilities were overrun during April 1945 only 382 had been completed, a

fact for which Allied tank crews must have been very grateful. The main cause of these low production totals was the disruption and damage caused by Allied bomber raids on the two main centres of production, the MIAG plant at Braunschweig and the Brandenburg Eisenwerk Kirchmöser at Brandenburg. These disruptions led to their being several variations of Jagdpanther in use. Some had large bolted-on gun mantlets while others had much smaller mantlet collars. Late-production versions used guns built with the barrels in two parts to ease barrel changing when the bores became worn, and the stowage of tools and other bits and pieces on the outside also varied considerably.

The Jagdpanther had a crew of five and there was space inside the well-sloped and heavily-armoured superstructure for 60 rounds of ammunition. When the war ended plans had been made to produce a new version mounting a 12.8-cm (5.04-in) anti-tank gun, though in the event only a wooden

mock-up had been built. But even with the usual 8.8-cm gun the Jagdpanther was truly a formidable tank destroyer that was much feared and respected by Allied tank crews. Few other armoured fighting vehicles of World War II achieved its unique combination of power, lethality, mobility and protection.

Specification
Jagdpanther
Crew: 5
Weight: 46000 kg (101,411 lb)
Powerplant: one Maybach HL 230 petrol engine developing 447.4-522.0 kW (600-700 hp)
Dimensions: length overall 9.90 m (32 ft 5.8 in) and hull 6.87 m (22 ft 6.5 in); width 3.27 m (10 ft 8.7 in); height 2.715 m (8 ft 10.9 in)
Performance: maximum road speed 55 km/h (34.2 mph); road range 160 km (99.4 miles); gradient 70 per cent; vertical obstacle 0.9 m (35 in); trench 1.9 m (6 ft 3 in); fording 1.7 m (5 ft 7 in)

Jagdtiger

By 1943 it was an established German policy that as soon as any new tank design became available, a fixed-superstructure version mounting a limited-traverse gun would be produced. Thus when the massive Tiger II or Königstiger (King Tiger) appeared, a corresponding Panzerjäger was developed. An iron mock-up development model of this super-heavy tank destroyer appeared in October 1943, and production began during 1944 under the designation **Panzerjäger Tiger Ausf B**, more commonly known as the **Jagdtiger**.

With the Jagdtiger the Germans produced the heaviest and most powerful armoured vehicle of World War II. The Jagdtiger had an official weight of no less than 70000 kg (154,324 lb) but by the time extra combat equipment and a full load of ammunition plus the crew of six had been added the weight rose to around 76000 kg (167,551 lb). Much of this weight was attributable to the armour, which was no less than 250 mm (9.84 in) thick on the front plate of the superstructure. The main armament was originally a 12.8-cm (5.04-in) Pak 44 anti-tank gun, but this was later changed to the similar Pak 80 and at one time a shortage of these guns caused by Allied bomber raids meant that the much smaller 8.8-cm (3.46-in) Pak 43/3 had to be used. The 12.8-cm guns were the most powerful anti-tank weapons used by any side during World War II, and the large size of its ammunition meant that each Jagdtiger could carry only 38 or 40 rounds. The defensive armament was two 7.92-mm (0.312-in) machine-guns.

Without a doubt the Jagdtiger was a massive and powerful vehicle as far as weapon power and protection were concerned, but in respect of mobility it could be regarded only as ponderous. It was driven by the same engine as that used in the Jagdpanther, but this engine had to drive the much greater weight of the Jagdtiger and to do this had usually to be driven full out, considerably increasing the fuel consumption and reducing range. When moving across country the Jagdtiger had a speed of only 14.5 km/h (9 mph) and often less, and the maximum possible cross-country range was only 120 km (74.5 miles). This reduced the Jagdtiger from being a true Panzerjäger to a sort of mobile defensive pill-

box, but by the time the Jagdtiger was in service the Germans were fighting a defensive war so the lack of mobility was not so desperate as it once might have been.

The production line for the Jagdtiger was at the Nibelungwerk at St Valentin where total production ran to only 70 vehicles, as a result mainly of the disruption caused by Allied bombing, not only at the factories but in the raw material supply lines. By the time the war ended two types of Jagdtiger were to be encountered, one with Henschel suspension and later versions with an extra road axle and Porsche suspension. In both forms the Jagdtigers were ponderous to an extreme and although on paper they were the most heavily armed and protected of all the armoured fighting vehicles used during World War II (and for many years afterwards) they remained considerably underpowered, a fact that rendered them little more than mobile weapon platforms.

Above: Two types of suspension were used on the Jagdtiger. This example has the Henschel suspension; the other type used larger road wheels from Porsche. Based on the Tiger II tank chassis, only about 70 were produced, and it was the heaviest AFV to see service during World War II.

Specification
Jagdtiger
Crew: 6
Weight: 76000 kg (167,551 lb)
Powerplant: one Maybach HL 230 petrol engine developing 447.4-522.0 kW (600-700 hp)
Dimensions: length overall 10.654 m (34 ft 11.4 in); width 3.625 m (11 ft 10.7 in); height 2.945 m (9 ft 8 in)
Performance: maximum speed 34.6 km/h (21.5 mph); road range 170 km (105 miles); gradient 70 per cent; vertical obstacle 0.85 m (33.5 in); trench 3.0 m (9 ft 10 in); fording 1.65 m (5 ft 5 in)

The massive Jagdtiger with its 128-mm (5.04-in) gun was a powerful weapon, but it was underpowered and too heavy to be anything other than a purely defensive weapon. Not many were made before the war ended, but the 250-mm (9.84-in) frontal armour made it a difficult vehicle to knock out.

Semovente L.40 da 47/32

During World War II the Italians were never noted for dramatic innovations as far as armoured vehicle design was concerned. However, in one aspect they were abreast of tactical thinking elsewhere for they became interested in the tank-destroyer concept during the late 1930s. At that time they produced an intriguing design known as the **Semovente L.3 da 47/32** mounting a 47-mm (1.85-in) anti-tank gun with a barrel 32 calibres long (hence 47/32). The L.3 mounted the gun on an open

The Italian Semovente L.3 da 47/32 was an early attempt to mount an anti-tank gun on a light tank chassis, and was much used for trials and various gunnery tests. It generally lacked protection and was later replaced by better designs.

mounting at the front of a small and low chassis based on that of the L.3 tankette; a two-man crew was carried. This early project did not get far for there was virtually no protection for the crew and the idea attracted little attention.

When the Italians entered the war in 1941 they soon realized that their much-vaunted tank arm was seriously undergunned and lacked protection. This was particularlay true of their lighter tanks, in which the Italian treasury had invested to a considerable degree, especially the L.6 series that generally lacked protection and were armed only with a short 37-mm (1.456-in) gun of limited anti-armour capability. The main combat version, the L.6/40, soon proved to be of little combat value against the British armour then in use in North Africa and was obviously ripe for the usual limited-traverse anti-tank gun treatment. It was not long in coming when Fiat-SPA and Ansaldo combined to use the chassis for the basis of a tank destroyer.

The gun used for the new vehicle was the powerful 47-mm licence-built version of the Austrian Böhler dual-purpose anti-tank/infantry support gun, one of the hardest-hitting of all anti-armour weapons in its day. On the new **Semovente L.40 da 47/32** it was mounted in a simple box-like superstructure built directly onto the light tank chassis, and while this simple arrangement worked well enough the slab sides of the superstructure lacked the added protection that sloping sides would have provided. But it was better than nothing and went straight into service from 1942 onwards. In all about 280 were produced and in action they proved to be capable enough when dealing with the lighter British and other armour on the battlefields of North Africa. Ammunition stowage was 70 rounds.

When the Italians surrendered to the Allies in 1943 the Germans quickly took over as many Italian armoured vehicles and as much Italian equipment as they could. The Semovente L.40 da 47/32 was among this booty, and was quickly impressed as part of the equipment of German units fighting in Italy. However, the terrain of many of the Italian battlefields during the long slog north that lasted through 1944 and 1945 was such that armour could be used on few occasions, and the Semovente L.40s often had their anti-tank armament removed and were used instead as mobile command posts for senior commanders, with an armament of one 8-mm (0.315-in) Breda modello 38 machine-gun.

The Semovente L.40 da 47/32 may have been a simple conversion and it had little impact on enemy armour, but it did demonstrate that the Italians had absorbed the tank destroyer concept at an early stage of the war and used it as well as their limited production basis allowed.

Specification
Semovente L.40 da 47/32
Crew: 2
Weight: 6500 kg (14,330 lb)
Powerplant: one SPA 18D 4-cylinder petrol engine developing 50.7 kW (68 hp)
Dimensions: length 4.00 m (13 ft 1.5 in) and hull 3.782 m (12 ft 4.9 in); width 1.92 m (6 ft 3.6 in); height 1.63 m (5 ft 4.2 in)

The Semovente L.40 da 47/32 was used in some numbers by the Italian and later the German armies, and was a conversion of the L.6/40 light tank to take the powerful Italian 47-mm (1.85-in) anti-tank gun. Its box-like superstructure was later widely used to act as a mobile command post or ammunition carrier.

Performance: maximum road speed 42.3 km/h (26.3 mph); road range 200 km (124 miles); gradient 84 per cent; vertical obstacle 0.8 m (31.5 in); trench 1.7 m (5 ft 7 in); fording 0.8 m (31.5 in)

Semovente M.41M da 90/53

The Italians used the chassis of their M.13 tank as the basis for a number of self-propelled guns (Semovente), but most of them were built along the lines of the German Sturmgeschütz types and were intended for use as close-support assault artillery. At times they could be used against tanks with some degree of success, but that was not their primary function and the Italians produced only one really heavy type of tank destroyer. This was the **Semovente M.41M da 90/53**, which used the chassis of the M.14/41 tank, a development of the M.13 tank series.

The Semovente M.41M da 90/53 carried a powerful anti-armour weapon in the form of the cannone da 90/53 anti-aircraft gun, a long and very powerful weapon that had a performance very similar to that of the famous German 8.8-cm (3.46-in) Flak series. The gun's primary characteristics were denoted by the 90/53 designation, for it was a 90-mm (3.54-in) gun with a barrel 53 calibres long. To accommodate the gun mounting the engine was moved to the front of the chassis and the gun was mounted at the rear. In action two men sat on the gun mounting behind a gun shield; there was no other form of protection as the Italian approach was that such a powerful gun would not be used directly in the front line but would instead be used as a 'stand-off' weapon picking off tank targets at long ranges. No ammunition could be carried on the vehicle itself; 26 rounds were carried in a special conversion of the L.6 light tank that used a box-like superstructure very similar to that of the Semovente L.40 da 47/32, and another 40 rounds were carried in a trailer towed by the ammunition carrier. In action the long rounds were loaded into the gun breech by ammunition numbers standing on the ground behind the Semovente M.41.

After noting the power of the German 8.8-cm Flak series the Italians were quick to get their Semovente M.41M into production. The first example came off the Fiat, SPA and Ansaldo lines during 1941, but in the end only 48

were produced. The main reason for this small total was the lack of production potential within Italian industry and the ever-pressing requirements for the Cannone da 90/53 as an anti-aircraft gun. In the field the Semovente M.41M proved to be a powerful weapon, especially across the flat wastes of the North African deserts, but once that campaign ended so did the gun's career with the Italian army. Soon after the fall of Sicily and the invasion of the Italian mainland the Italians surrendered. The Germans had been expecting such a move and promptly took control of as much Italian war matériel as they could lay their hands on, and among the loot was a number of Semovente M.41Ms. The Germans soon had control of the gun's ammunition production facilities and thus the weapon ended up as part of the German army's inventory, with the type still in service in northern Italy when the war ended. By then there was little call for their tank-killing capabilities, for much of the Italian campaign took place over mountainous country where few tanks could move, so the Semovente M.41Ms were used mainly as long-range artillery.

Specification
Semovente M.41M da 90/53
Crew: (on gun) 2
Weight: 17000 kg (37,479 lb)
Powerplant: one SPA 15-TM-41 8-cylinder petrol engine developing 108.1 kW (145 hp)
Dimensions: length 5.205 m (17 ft 0.9 in); width 2.20 m (7 ft 2.6 in); height 2.15 m (7 ft 0.6 in)
Performance: maximum road speed 35.5 km/h (22 mph); road range 200 km (124 miles); vertical obstacle 0.9 m (35.4 in); trench 2.1 m (6 ft 10.7 in); fording 1.0 m (3 ft 3 in)

The Semovente M.41M da 90/53 was the most powerful of the Italian tank destroyers, and used the 90-mm (3.54-in) anti-aircraft gun mounted on an M.15/42 tank chassis.

A Semovente M.41M da 90/53 is examined by American troops after being knocked out in Sicily in 1943. To serve the gun, the crew had to stand behind the breech and only the driver had all-round armour. These guns were first used in North Africa in late 1943 and were much respected.

USA

3-in Gun Motor Carriage M10

During the late 1930s and early 1940s the US Army formulated a novel tactical doctrine, whereby fast-moving armoured formations were to be countered by a new tank destroyer force comprising towed and self-propelled high-velocity anti-tank guns. This tank destroyer force was to be used en masse and was to be armed with powerful guns, and one of the first operational results of this doctrine was the **Gun Carriage M10** self-propelled mounting armed with a 76.2 mm (3-in) gun known as the M7, a development of an anti-aircraft weapon. The secondary armament was one 12.7-mm (0.5-in) Browning machine-gun.

The M10 used the main chassis of the M4A2 medium tank (the Sherman) allied to a new thinly-armoured upper hull and an open-topped turret. The relatively thin armour of the hull was improved by the use of sloping armour plates to increase protection, and sloped armour was also used on the turret. Unlike many other tank destroyers of the time the M10 had a turret with 360° traverse, for although the M10 was intended for use as a tank destroyer it was seen by the US Army as a gun carrier and was not intended for close-order combat, hence the relatively thin armour. The gun was quite powerful for the period it was introduced. Production commenced during September 1942, and such was the potential of American industry that when production ceased in December 1942 4,993 had been produced.

The bulk of this total went to US Army tank destroyer battalions, and in early 1943 there were 106 active battalions. But as the war continued their number gradually decreased when it was realized that the tank destroyer concept as an arm separate from the rest of the American armoured forces was wrong and as it emerged that the best counter to a tank was another tank. But the tank destroyer force remained in being until the war ended, most of the battalions being used in Europe. By the end of the war many of the M10s and their associated equipments and towed guns were being

Above: The American M10 was designed to be the main weapon of the Tank Destroyer Command's mobile units, and mounted a 3-in (76.2-mm) gun in an open-topped turret. The armour protection was relatively thin, as the weight of better armour was sacrificed for all-round performance and speed once in action.

used more as assault forces than tank destroyers. The M10 was the primary equipment of these battalions and was used not only by the US Army but by the British (who knew the M10 as the **Wolverine**) and later by the French and Italian armies. In combat the M10 proved to be less than a complete success, for despite its thin armour it was a large and bulky vehicle and as time went on the gun lost much of its anti-armour effectiveness. But the M10s were still in use when the war ended. By then the British had re-gunned many of their M10s with 17-pdr guns and re-named the type **Achilles**. The M10 had in the meantime been joined by the **M10A1**, which was the same vehicle but using the chassis of the M4A3 medium tank with its different engine installation and some other changes.

The M10s were used in battalions, each with around 36 M10s and with strong reconnaissance and anti-

aircraft elements. By early 1945 most of the tank destroyer battalions were distributed among the more conventional armoured formations, and were then used exactly as other armoured formations and the exclusive tank destroyer concept died.

Specification
M10
Crew: 5
Weight: 29937 kg (66,000 lb)
Powerplant: two General Motors 6-cylinder diesel engines each developing 276.6 kW (375 hp)
Dimensions: length overall 6.83 m (22 ft 5 in); width 3.05 m (10 ft); height 2.57 m

Late in the war the M10 (left) was supplemented by the M36 (right), which used a 90-mm (3.54-in) gun, still in an open-topped turret. The M36 was designed as early as 1942 but took a long time to get into production, so that it was late 1944 before the first of them reached Europe. By then they were mainly used as assault guns.

(8 ft 5 in)

Performance: maximum road speed 51 km/h (32 mph); road range 322 km (200 miles); gradient 25°; vertical obstacle 0.46 m (18 in); trench 2.26 m (7 ft 5 in); fording 0.91 m (3 ft)

USA

3-in Gun Motor Carriage M18

Whereas the M10 was produced for the tank destroyer battalions by converting an existing tank chassis (the M4A2), the **Gun Motor Carriage M18** was designed from the outset for the tank destroyer role. Development began during 1942, and the first examples were ready during 1943.

In service the M18 proved to be one of the best examples of the American tank destroyer concept. It was much smaller than the M10 and weighed only about half as much, but it carried a more powerful gun and was much faster. Indeed, the M18 was the fastest tracked vehicle to be used in action during World War II. The gun was the 76.2-mm (3-in) M1A1 or M1A2, the latter having a muzzle brake. The M1A1 gun was a development of the gun used in the M10, but had a better all-round performance and it was mounted in an open-topped turret. In appearance the M18 resembled a tank, and it did indeed have a 360° traverse turret, but its armour protection was much less than would be ex-

pected in a tank and the M18 relied upon its mobility and striking power to defend itself. The engine was positioned to the rear of the hull and was a radial air-cooled petrol engine with aviation origins that was powerful enough to give the M18 a good power-to-weight ratio to provide the vehicle

with excellent acceleration and agility. Internal stowage was such that as well as carrying the crew of five men there was space for 45 76.2-mm rounds and a 12.7-mm (0.5-in) heavy machine-gun for local and anti-aircraft defence.

In service with the tank destroyer battalions the M18 was given the name

The M18 Hellcat had the distinction of being the fastest of all AFVs used during World War II. Armed with a long 76-mm (3-in) gun, it was an ideal tank-hunting vehicle, but as with other vehicles of its type it generally lacked armour and was fitted with an open-topped turret.

Hellcat. Despite their success in action the M18s were gradually switched from the tank destroyer battalions as the enthusiasm for the exclusive tank destroyer concept dwindled, and by 1945 many M18s were used by conventional armoured formations within the US Army. By then they were being used more and more as assault guns and conventional self-propelled artillery.

The production run of the M18 lasted from July 1943 to October 1944, when it was obvious that the war was not going to last much longer. Between those dates 2,507 M18s were produced, some being completed without turrets as the **M39** for use as high-speed troop or supply carriers. There was also a **T65 Flame Tank** based on the M18 with a much revised upper hull mounting a flame gun in front. The **T88 Howitzer Motor Carriage** was an attempt to mount a 105-mm (4.13-in) howitzer on the basic M18 and there were other

attempts to mount a 90-mm (3.54-in) gun and turret on the chassis. None of these versions got past the experimental stage, a fate shared by many other trial versions of the basic M18 including a mobile command post, a utility carrier and an amphibious variant.

Specification
M18
Crew: 5
Weight: 17036 kg (37,557 lb)
Powerplant: one Continental R-975 C1 radial petrol engine developing 253.5 kW (340 hp)
Dimensions: length overall 6.65 m (21 ft 10 in) and hull 5.44 m (17 ft 10 in); width 2.87 m (9 ft 5 in); height 2.58 m (8 ft 5.5 in)
Performance: maximum road speed 88.5 km/h (55 mph); road range 169 km (105 miles); gradient 60 per cent; vertical obstacle 0.91 m (36 in); trench 1.88 m (6 ft 2 in); fording 1.22 m (4 ft)

M18 Hellcats went out of production in October 1944 after 2,507 had been built. The M18 was the only vehicle specifically designed for the US Army's tank destroyer role, and was a most successful combat vehicle capable of tackling all but the very heaviest German tanks.

UK
Archer

Although the British army tended to lag behind the Germans in upgunning its tanks as World War II progressed, an early decision by British planners to make a quantum leap in anti-tank gun calibres from the 57 mm (2.244 in) of the 6-pdr to 76.2 mm (3 in) was a bold one, for it was made at a time when the 6-pdr was only just getting into production. It was realized that the new 76.2-mm gun, soon to be known as the 17-pdr, would be a very large and heavy weapon on its towed carriage, so it was decided to find some means of making it mobile. Ideally the 17-pdr was to be used as a tank gun, but the tanks large enough to carry such a large weapon were still a long way off (indeed had not even left the drawing boards) so a short-term alternative had to be found.

After investigating such in-production means as the Crusader tank chassis it was decided to mount the 17-pdr on the Valentine infantry tank chassis. The Valentine was in production and could be rapidly adapted for its new gun-carrying role by adding a sloping superstructure, open at the top, on the forward part of the hull. To ensure the gun/chassis combination would not be nose-heavy and unwieldy, it was decided to place the gun in a limited-traverse-mounting facing over the rear of the chassis. This vehicle was obviously meant to be a tank destroyer and it was placed in production in late 1943.

It was March 1943 before the first **SP 17-pdr Valentine** rolled off the production lines, the initial example of 800 that had been ordered. The troops looked at the new vehicle with some trepidation, for the idea of having a gun that faced to the rear only was against established practice. Drivers were also less than enchanted, for they were positioned at the centre front of the fighting compartment and the gun breech was directly behind their heads; on firing the breech block came to within a short distance of the back of the driver's head. The rest of the crew was made up of the gun layer, the commander and the loader. Protective fire could be supplied by one 7.7-mm (0.303-in) Bren gun.

It was October 1944 before the first of these Valentine/17-pdr combina-

tions reached the fighting in Europe. By then the type had become known as the **Archer**, and in action the Archer's tank-killing capabilities were soon demonstrated. The rearward-facing gun was soon seen to be no problem, but rather a virtue. The Archer was soon in use as an ambush weapon where its low silhouette made it easy to conceal in a hide. As enemy tanks approached a few shots could be fired to kill a tank and then the Archer was facing the right way to make a quick getaway before enemy retaliation arrived. The Archers were used by the anti-tank companies of the Royal Artillery, and they were definitely preferred to the weight and bulk of the towed 17-pdr guns used by the same companies.

The end of the war brought about a halt in Archer production at a point where 655 of the original order for 800 had been produced. The Archers went on to equip British army anti-tank units until the mid-1950s.

Specification
Archer
Crew: 4
Weight: 16257 kg (35,840 lb)
Powerplant: one General Motors 6-71 6-cylinder diesel developing 143.2 kW (192 hp)
Dimensions: length overall 6.68 m (21 ft 11 in) and hull 5.54 m (18 ft 6 in); width 2.76 m (9 ft 0.5 in); height 2.25 m (7 ft 4.5 in)
Performance: maximum road speed 32.2 km/h (20 mph); road range 225 km (140 miles); gradient 32°; vertical obstacle 0.84 m (33 in); trench 2.36 m (7 ft 9 in); fording 0.91 m (3 ft)

The British Archer was a conversion of the Valentine infantry tank to mount a 17-pdr (3-in/76.2-mm) anti-tank gun that fired over the rear hull.

The first of them were used in action in late 1944 and proved to be very useful weapons with a low silhouette. They were used by the Royal Artillery.

Although the rear-facing main gun of the Archer could have been a tactical liability, the users put it to advantage by using the Archers from an ambush position and then driving away after the action with the gun barrel still pointing to the rear.

Special Purpose Tanks

Modern armies can call upon a whole family of specialist armoured vehicles for combat engineering operations, but in World War II such vehicles were a novelty. Several nations developed tanks for roles, such as armoured recovery, but Britain led the way with a bewildering variety of tank conversions known as 'Funnies'.

A Churchill tank with a fascine attached to the front which could be used to lay a mat over soft ground – such as sand on the Normandy beaches – for other tracked vehicles to cross.

The contents of this section show something of an imbalance in comparison with the contents of other sections in this book, for they deal mainly with the many types of special purpose vehicles used by the British 79th Armoured Division. For once there is no preponderance of US designs because during World War II the Americans spent little of

their considerable potential on the types of vehicle included here. They concentrated on combat vehicles pure and simple, and from the factories of the United States poured streams of combat tanks and all manner of fighting vehicles.

But it was a different matter once these vehicles reached Europe. Once they had arrived

many of them were reworked for special purposes, which included developments ranging from armoured engineer vehicles to mine-clearing tanks of several types. The situation was different in Europe as far as the British were concerned: they had a special task to perform, namely the invasion of Europe in order to take on the German army on the

continent. The only way they could do that was by using special vehicles of all kinds: those which could clear battlefield obstacles, recover precious disabled vehicles and perform special tasks such as burning out stubborn strongpoints. The Germans and Americans did not bother to use specialist vehicles on such a large scale. Instead they decided to make do with what they had, and they often suffered accordingly. For the simple fact is that many of the special purpose vehicles included in this section actually saved lives. Combat engineers operating from inside the protection of an armoured vehicle were much safer in action than hapless soldiers attempting to work out in the open, while men using mine-clearing tanks of whatever type were safer than men using manual clearing methods.

However, not all special purpose vehicles fell into this category. Those described in this section include command vehicles, ammunition or cargo carriers, and even such oddities as the Rammtiger, which was supposed to knock down buildings in urban warfare. They are a motley bunch but full of interest and a subject worthy of study in its own right.

UK
Demolition charges

The demolition charges used by the British 'Funnies' were nearly all carried by Churchill AVREs, for the emplacing of these special powerful charges was one of the tasks for which the AVRE was intended. The charges themselves were special obstacle-demolishing packs of high explosive that had to be placed against the target, which might be anything from a sea or anti-tank wall to a blockhouse or an offending building. Sometimes the charges were large single chunks of explosive, and in others they were small charges set in a pattern and held in a steel frame. One thing all the various charges did have in common and that was odd and even bizarre names.

One of the more straightforward of these charge devices was the **Bangalore Torpedo**. These pipe charges were intended for mine- or barbed wire-clearing, but could be used for other purposes and on the AVRE they were held in front-mounted frames, also used for the **Jones Onion**. The Jones Onion first appeared in 1942 and was the codename given to a frame onto which various charges could be attached. The frame was carried on two arms, one on each side of the AVRE, and was held upright as the target was approached. Once in position the frame was released by pulling on a cable and two legs on the bottom of the frame were so arranged that the frame always fell against the target obstacle. The charges could then be fired electrically by a trailing cable after the AVRE had reversed away. The side-mounted arms could then be jettisoned if required.

Another device that appeared in 1942 was the **Carrot**. This was a much simpler device than the large Onion and consisted of a charge held in front

of the AVRE on a simple steel arm. The idea was that the AVRE simply moved up to the target and the charge was then ignited. The charges involved ranged in weight from 5.44 kg (12 lb) up to 11.34 kg (25 lb), the smaller charge rejoicing in the name of **Light Carrot**. The Carrot was used extensively for trials but was abandoned during late 1943 and was not used in action.

However, the **Goat** was used in action. This may be considered as a development of the Onion but it was much larger and involved the use of a frame 3.2 m (10 ft 6 in) wide and 1.98 m (6 ft 6 in) long. Onto this frame could be arranged up to 816 kg (1,800 lb) of ex-

plosive, and the whole device was carried on the AVRE by side arms. The Goat was so arranged that it could be pushed against the structure to be demolished and the frame would then automatically release in a vertical position. The AVRE would then reverse away leaving the charges in position to be fired either electrically or by means of a pull igniter. A close cousin of the Goat was the **Elevatable Goat**. This was intended for use against high obstacles such as anti-tank walls, and when fitted on the AVRE was carried on the nose of the hull rather like an assault bridge. The 'bridge' was in fact a frame on which linked charges were slung. The frame was placed against

The Jones Onion, seen here carried by a Churchill tank, was a demolition device carried on a steel frame that could be placed against an obstacle such as an anti-tank wall. The frame was then released to allow the tank to retire and detonate the charge.

the wall to be demolished and then released from the AVRE. Once in position another release cable allowed the linked charges to fall away from the frame. The top section of the frame was above the top of the wall, and this allowed the charges to fall onto each side of the wall, which could then be destroyed once the AVRE had moved away.

UK
Bangalore Torpedo tanks

The **Bangalore Torpedo** is an ancient combat engineering device that was revived during World War I for clearing barbed-wire entanglements. In its simplest form the Bangalore Torpedo is a metal tube filled with explosive and sealed at both ends. Most types have attachment points at each end to enable other torpedoes to be joined to make up extra lengths. The charges are set off either by a burning fuse or by some form of remote detonator. These torpedoes were soon in use by armoured combat engineers to clear paths through minefields, and simple delivery devices such as that fitted to the front of a Churchill AVRE were soon devised.

However the normal Bangalore Torpedo is only about 1.5 m (5 ft) long, and armoured engineers were often called upon to bridge minefields many metres deep. It would obviously save time and effort if longer torpedoes could be joined up to clear paths through deep minefields, and this course of action was followed to produce the 76.2-mm (3-in) **Snake**. On the Snake the lengths of explosive-filled

The Snake was a form of Bangalore Torpedo used to clear large minefields. Seen here carried on a Churchill, the Snake was assembled on the edge of a minefield, pushed across it by the tank and then detonated to clear a path.

tubing or pipe were 6.1 m (20 ft) long and could be joined together into lengths of up to 366 m (1,200 ft) to enable them to be pulled across a minefield and then detonated to clear a path up to 6.4 m (21 ft) wide. It was better if the Snake tubing could be pushed across a minefield, but when this happened the lengths involved were less. Only 122 m (400 ft) of Snake tubing could be pushed in front of a tank with any degree of control. The tanks involved with Snake were usually Shermans or Churchill AVREs, but the Royal Engineers did also have small numbers of a special vehicle. This was known as the **Snake Carrier**

and was a conversion of the Churchill Gun Carrier, a Churchill variant with a box superstructure that had been intended to mount a 76.2-mm gun for use as a tank destroyer. For a number of reasons the Churchill Gun Carrier was not accepted for service and the few vehicles involved carried Snake instead, on both sides of the box superstructure. The Gun Carrier moved the tubing to a point close to the target, and here the crew assembled the Snake, which was then pushed into position across the minefield and detonated. Although Snake was used for training and trials it was not used operationally.

The **Conger** was towed behind a

Churchill AVRE or a Sherman in an engineless Universal Carrier that carried a rocket, a length of hose and a tank of liquid explosive. The rocket carried the hose across the minefield, and when in place the hose was filled with the liquid explosive and detonated. The **Tapeworm** was another hose device that was carried in a trailer to the edge of a minefield where it was deposited. A tank with a CIRD (Canadian Indestructible Roller Device) then moved across the minefield and as it proceeded the tank pulled the explosive-filled hose across the minefield. When the full length of hose (457 m/500 yards) had been pulled

from the trailer the explosive was detonated to clear any mines that might have been missed by the rollers. The 15.2 m (50 ft) of hose nearest to the towing tank was filled with sand for safety purposes.

Perhaps the smallest of the Bangalore-type devices was the **Flying Bangalore**. This was used on Shermans fitted with CIRD rollers and was intended for barbed-wire clearing. Each of the CIRD arms carried a Bangalore Torpedo fitted with a rocket motor. The rockets carried the Bangalores across the wire and as they landed small grapnels held the torpedoes against the wire for exploding.

Mine-clearing flails

The notion of using chain flails to detonate mines in the path of a tank came from a South African engineer, Major A.S.J. du Toit. The idea was that a horizontally-mounted drum carried on arms in front of a tank would be rotated under power. As it turned it would beat the ground in front with chains that carried weights on their ends, and this beating would provide enough pressure to set off any mines underneath. Early trials proved the effectiveness of the idea, and the first sets of mine flails were fitted to Matilda tanks in North Africa during 1942.

These first flails were known as **Scorpion**, and on the **Matilda Scorpion** the flail drum was powered by an auxiliary engine mounted on the right-hand side of the tank. These Scorpions were used during the El Alamein battle in October 1942 and also during some later North African actions. They proved to be so effective that a more specialized version, known as the **Matilda Baron** was developed. On the Baron the turret was removed and the flail drum was powered by two auxiliary engines, one on each side. However the Scorpion concept offered more long-term promise as it could be fitted to several types of tank to produce, for example, the **Grant Scorpion** and the **Valentine Scorpion**. But before that could happen a great deal of further development work had to be carried out, for the early flails had demonstrated some unwelcome traits. Among these were uneven beating patterns that left unbeaten patches, and flail chains that either became tangled and useless or simply beat themselves to pieces. Another problem became apparent on uneven ground, where the flails were unable to beat into sudden dips.

The development work carried out in the UK resulted in a device known as the **Crab** which was usually fitted to Sherman tanks to produce the **Sherman Crab**. The Crab had 43 chains mounted on a drum powered by a take-off from the main engine and had such features as side-mounted wire-cutting discs to hack through barbed-wire entanglements, screens to shield the front of the tank from flying dust and debris and, later in the Crab's development, a device to follow ground contours and enable the flail drum to rise and fall accordingly. Crabs were used by the 79th Armoured Division and later a number were handed over to the US Army for use in North West Europe. The main advantages of the Crab system were that it was very

The Sherman Crab was the most widely-used mine flail tank of World War II. Although fitted to other types of tank, the Sherman was the preferred carrier. The odd-looking device at the hull rear is a station-keeping marker to guide other flail tanks.

effective in its own right, and also permitted the carrier to retain its turret and main gun, enabling it to be used as a gun tank if the occasion arose.

Needless to say there were many other experimental models of mine flails. One was the **Lobster**, a device that came chronologically before the Crab but was not accepted for service. The **Pram Scorpion** was an off-shoot of the Scorpion with the drum drive coming from gears on the front sprockets of the carrier tank. Again, it was passed over in favour of the Crab.

The Americans did not spend much development time on mine flails. Instead they concentrated on anti-mine rollers and when they did require flails, as they did when they encountered the large defensive mine belts along the German borders in the winter of 1944-5, they used numbers of

The Matilda Scorpion prototype shown here was an early attempt to produce a mine flail tank. The main flail drum was driven by two 22.4-kW (30-hp) Bedford engines, one each side of the hull, and the device was later fitted to Valentine and Grant tanks as well as the Matilda.

British Crabs which they redesignated the **Mine Exploder T4**.

UK
Churchill AVRE

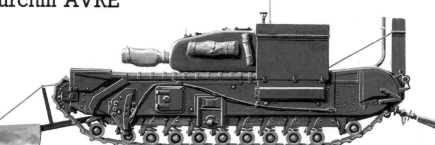

A Churchill AVRE is seen with deep wading gear over the side and rear engine air vents, and fitted with a Bullshorn anti-tank mine plough at the front and with a Porpoise skid trailer at the rear. These trailers could be used to carry a wide range of supplies such as fuel and ammunition.

One of the hard lessons learned during the Dieppe raid of 1942 was that the Canadian engineers were unable to proceed with their obstacle demolitions and general beach-clearing because of a complete lack of cover from enemy fire. In the period after the raid a Canadian engineer officer put forward the idea of using a tank converted to the combat engineer role that could carry engineers to the point at which they had to operate, and be capable of carrying a heavy demolition weapon. This would enable the combat engineers to operate from under armoured cover and would also enable them to operate in close co-operation with armoured formations.

The idea was accepted, and after some deliberation the Churchill tank was selected as the basic vehicle for conversion. The task consisted mainly of completely stripping out the interior of the Churchill tank and removing the main armament. The interior was completely rearranged to provide stowage for the various items combat engineers have to use, such as demolition explosives, special tools, mines etc. The main turret was retained but in place of the normal gun a special device known

as a Petard was fitted. This was a spigot mortar that fired a 290-mm (11.4-in) demolition charge known to the troops from its general shape as the 'Flying Dustbin'. The Petard projectile weighed 18.14 kg (40 lb) and could be fired to a range of 73 m (80 yards) to demolish structures such as pillboxes, bunkers and buildings. The Petard could be reloaded from within the vehicle.

The Churchill version was known as the **Churchill AVRE (Armoured Vehicle Royal Engineers)** and it quickly became the standard equipment of the armoured engineers attached to formations such as the 79th Armoured Division and the assault brigades, RE. As well as providing protection for combat engineers, the AVRE was soon in demand to carry all manner of special equipment.

The Churchill versions used for the AVRE were the Mk III and Mk IV. Many of the conversions were carried out using specially-produced kits, some by industry and some by REME workshops. The conversions included brackets and other attachment points around the hull to which items of specialized equipment could be fixed. A

hook at the rear was used to tow a special AVRE sledge for carrying combat stores.

The AVREs were first used on a large scale during the Normandy landings of June 1944, where they excelled themselves to such an extent that the AVRE has been with the Royal Engineers ever since, the current in-service version being the Centurion Mk V AVRE. The Churchill AVRE remained in service until the mid-1950s and even later with some units. They were used to lay fascines, lay mats across soft ground, demolish strongpoints with their Petard mortars, bring forward combat engineering stores, place heavy demolition charges and generally make themselves useful.

The Churchill AVRE Mark II featured a fixed turret mounting a dummy gun. It could carry a front-mounted dismountable jib crane or a rear jib with a higher lift capacity. There was also a powerful front-mounted winch that could be used in conjunction with the jibs, and an earth anchor was mounted at the rear.

Specification
Churchill AVRE
Crew: 6
Weight: 38 tons
Powerplant: one Bedford Twin-Six petrol engine developing 261 kW (350 hp)
Dimensions: length 7.67 m (25 ft 2 in); width 3.25 m (10 ft 8 in); height 2.79 m (9 ft 2 in)
Performance: maximum road speed

24.9 km/h (15.5 mph); maximum road range 193 km (120 miles)
Armament: one Petard mortar, and one 7.92-mm (0.312-in) Besa machine-gun

---

UK
Canal Defence Light

The device known under the cover name **Canal Defence Light** was one 'weapon' of World War II that was destined never to be used. In essence it was a simple idea, in which the normal gun turret of a tank was replaced with another housing an intense light to illuminate battlefields at night. All manner of tactical ploys were advocated for its use, ranging from simply blinding an enemy to providing general target illumination.

The idea of mounting powerful searchlights on tanks was first mooted during the mid-1930s by a group of interested civilians who 'sold' the idea to the War Office in 1937. The War Office carried out a series of development trials under conditions of great secrecy, and by late 1939 a turret was ready for production. The secrecy continued with the project being known as the Canal Defence Light, or **CDL**. The first turrets produced were for the Matilda II infantry tank, and all that the fitting of a CDL involved was the removal of the normal turret and its replacement by a new one, though changes had to be made to the Matilda's electrical systems as well. In the turret the searchlight was positioned behind a vertical slit in which was a shutter. In use the searchlight was switched on and the shutter was opened and closed very rapidly to provide a flickering impression to an observer in front. This flickering made the range of the CDL light difficult to

determine, and anyway the light was so powerful that it was difficult to look into the beam even at quite long ranges.

Some 300 CDL turrets were ordered to convert Matildas to the CDL role, and one brigade of **Matilda CDL** vehicles was based in the UK and another in North Africa. The military planners were determined to use the impact of the CDL units to the full and constantly awaited the chance to use them to maximum effect. That chance some-

how never came and the North African campaign was over before the CDLs could prove their worth. However the Normandy landings lay ahead, and it was planned to use the CDLs there. But at the same time it was felt that the CDL turrets should be placed on something rather more up-to-date than the slow and stately Matildas, so Grant tanks became the chosen carriers for the

The Grant CDL (Canal Defence Light) was a special vehicle mounting a turret in which was located a powerful searchlight that was supposed to dazzle an enemy during night operations or illuminate targets at night.

post-June 1944 campaigns. But once again the chance to use the **Grant CDL** in combat never arrived. Instead the CDLs were used for the relatively unexciting task of providing 'artificial moonlight' to illuminate the crossings of the Rhine and Elbe in early 1945.

Thus the CDL was carried throughout the war but never used. However, the idea certainly attracted attention. The US Army was most impressed by what it saw of the CDL at various demonstrations and decided to adopt the CDL for itself, and thus produced 355 CDL turrets for mounting on otherwise obsolete M3 Lee tanks. These were used to equip six tank battalions for special operations in Europe. The cover name **T10 Shop Tractor** was used for US CDL vehicles, but once again the CDL was destined not to be used in combat. As with the British the Amer-icans awaited the right moment to use their lights and the war ended before that could happen.

Specification
Matilda CDL
Crew: 3 or 4
Weight: 26 tons
Powerplant: two Leyland E148/E149 diesel engines each developing 70.8 kW (95 hp)
Dimensions: length 5.61 m (18 ft 5 in); width 2.59 m (8 ft 6 in); height 2.51 m (8 ft 3 in)
Performance: maximum road speed 24 km/h (15 mph); maximum road range 257 km (160 miles)
Armament: one 7.92-mm (0.312-in) Besa machine-gun

UK
ARK

The **ARK** bridging tanks were only one type of armoured bridging vehicles used by the Allies during World War II. The British army had for long had an interest in producing bridging tanks and actually produced its first such equipment during the latter stages of World War I. In the years just before World War II it carried out a great deal of experimental work and one of its main achievements was a scissors-type bridge carried on and laid by a Covenanter tank. However, during the early war years this work had to be put aside in favour of more pressing things until the 1942 Dieppe landing emphasized the need for armoured bridging vehicles, not only to cross wet or dry gaps, but to enable other vehicles to cross obstacles such as sea walls.

It was the 79th Armoured Division that produced the first ARK (**Armoured Ramp Carrier**) in late 1943. Known as the **ARK Mk I**, this was a conversion of a Churchill tank with the turret removed and a blanking plate (with an access hatch in the centre) welded over the turret aperture. Over the tracks were placed two timbered trackways carried on a new superstructure and in front, in line with the trackways, were two ramps, each 1.05 m (3 ft 5.25 in) long. At the rear were two more ramps, each 1.72 m (5 ft 8 in) long. In use the ARK I was driven up to an obstacle such as a sea wall and pushed up the obstacle as far as possible. The front and rear ramps were then lowered from their travelling positions and other vehicles could then use the ARK to cross the obstacle. The ARK could also be driven into a wet or dry obstacle to act as a bridge.

The ARK Mk I was soon supplemented by the **ARK Mk II**. Again this used a Churchill tank as the basis, and the same superstructure/ramp layout was used. But the Mk II used much longer ramps (3.8 m/12 ft 6 in) at both ends, and the right-hand set of trackways and ramps was half the width of the other (0.61 m/2 ft) as opposed to 1.213 m (4 ft). This enabled a much wider range of vehicles to use the ARK. In use the ramps were set up front and rear and held in the travelling position by cables and chains connected to front and rear kingposts. When the ARK came to a gap it drove into it and then released the cables to allow the ramps to drop. Other vehicles could then cross the ARK Bridge. The 8th Army in Italy produced its own ARK Mk IIs, but made them much simpler by omitting the trackways over the Churchill tank, the tank tracks and the top of the body being used as the roadway instead. These versions were known as the **ARK Mk II (Italian Pattern)**.

There were numerous variations on the basic ARK design. One was a raised ramp system carried on a Churchill and known as the **Churchill Great Eastern**, but that project was discontinued. Some Shermans were converted in Italy to what was roughly the equivalent of the ARK Mk II, but the numbers involved were not large.

Another system, known as the **Churchill Woodlark**, was generally similar to the ARK Mk II but went into action with the ramps closed down: they were meant to be opened up into position by the use of rockets on the end of each ramp and more rockets were used to soften the shock of the ramps hitting the ground. The type did not pass the trials stage.

No data can be provided regarding these Churchill conversions but a Churchill ARK Mk II had a crew of four men and weighed 38.5 tons. Most conversions were made using Churchill Mk IIIs and Mk IVs.

A Churchill ARK Mk I is shown with its approach ramp raised. These vehicles were supposed to be driven up against anti-tank walls as far as possible, to enable other vehicles to be driven up and over the roadway carried above their tracks.

Two ARK Mk IIs are used to allow other vehicles to cross a deep ravine. The first ARK was driven into the ravine and the second ARK was then driven onto it, after which its ramps were lowered to form a bridge. The ravine was formed by the River Senio in Italy, April 1945.

Fascine and mat-laying devices

The **fascine** is an item of combat engineering equipment that dates back to ancient times, and for armoured warfare the type was resurrected during World War I to be dropped by tanks taking part in the Battle of Cambrai. At that time they were used traditionally, being dropped into trenches to allow other tanks to cross, and they were used for the same purpose during World War II. The advantage of the fascine for the combat engineer is that he can make them on the spot when they are required. The usual method was to cut brushwood and tie it into large bundles 3.35 m (11 ft) long. These bundles were tied into rolls between 1.83 m (6 ft) and 2.44 m (8 ft) in diameter and pulled onto wooden or steel cradles on the front of the tank. They were then held in place by cables that could be released from within the carrier tank. The main disadvantage was that the fascines usually restricted the driver's vision so that a crew member had to position himself to give driving instructions. Attempts were made to use periscopes to overcome this drawback but in the end the solution was found by redesigning the form of fascine cradle.

A type of fascine could also be used to make an assault roadway over soft or rough ground. This was formed by rolling up lengths of chespaling joined together by wire, rather like a length of fencing. A Churchill AVRE would carry this roll into position, where one end of the roll could be placed under the front tracks. As the AVRE moved forward it unrolled the mat and rolled over it to allow other vehicles to use the rough roadway so formed. Rolls of up to 30.5 m (100 ft) could be laid using this method, and more durable roadways could be produced by using a similar arrangement involving logs tied together (**Log Carpet**).

These chespaling or log roadways were intended for heavy use, but for assault purposes hessian mats were also employed. These mats were carried in front of a Churchill AVRE on bobbins held by side arms or (on one model) above a **Churchill AVRE Carpetlayer** turret. There were two main types: the **Bobbin Carpet** unrolled a hessian mat reinforced by chespaling at intervals that was wide enough to cover the full width of a tank; the other was only wide enough to cover a track

Right: This post-war Churchill AVRE has an early Centurion-style turret equipped with smoke dischargers. The cargo remains much as it would have looked in 1944, or 1917 for that matter, and the restrictions the fascine places on the driver's field of vision are obvious.

width. Both were intended to cover wire obstacles to allow foot soldiers or wheeled vehicles to cross and the first of them was used during the Dieppe raid of 1942. On all types the bobbin could be jettisoned once it was empty or in an emergency.

Most of these fascine- or mat-laying devices were carried on Churchill AVREs, but Shermans were also used. In fact a special fascine carrier, known as the **Crib**, was developed for the Sherman. This was a special carrier frame that could be tilted forward to drop a fascine or a log mat. Some 'war weary' Shermans even had their turrets removed to allow them to be used as full-time fascine carriers.

It should be stressed that the mat-laying devices, both hessian or timber,

were meant for short-term use only. Prolonged use by heavy or tracked vehicles soon broke them up or simply tore them to pieces so they were usually used for assault purposes only or

during amphibious landings to cover soft ground. It was not until well after World War II that flexible metal roadways were developed to replace the earlier devices.

A Churchill AVRE carries a brushwood fascine at the front and tows another fascine on an AVRE skid trailer. The fascines were released from their carrier frame by a quick release device, and once in position could enable most tanks or tracked vehicles to cross with relative ease.

A Churchill AVRE operates a Carpet-Layer Type C, used to lay a continuous hessian mat over rough or soft ground to enable other wheeled or tracked vehicles to follow. These devices were used to cross the sand on some of the Normandy beaches on 6 June 1944.

To the front-line soldier every tank is a valuable asset and any damaged or disabled tank that can be got back into action is a viable weapon. Therefore the recovery of damaged or broken-down tanks from a battlefield is an important aspect of armoured warfare, but very often these recovery operations have to be undertaken under enemy fire. It therefore makes sense to provide the recovery crews with their own armoured vehicles and even more sense to provide these vehicles with mechanical handling devices, winches and other special recovery tools. Thus World War II saw the first large-scale use of recovery vehicles, and on the Allied side there were many different types.

Nearly all Allied **Armoured Recovery Vehicle (ARV)** types were conversions of existing tanks, usually models that were past their best and could be spared for the role. Nearly every type of Allied tank was used for the ARV role at some time or another but the main types involved on the British side were Crusader, Covenanter, Centaur, Cavalier, Cromwell, Ram and inevitably the Churchill. Most of these ARV conversions involved the removal of the turret (along with the main armament) and its replacement by either a fixed superstructure or an open compartment for the crew. Winches were installed and various forms of jib crane or sheerlegs were added. Many types also had the assistance of an earth spade to provide the winch with better purchase and thus extra pull. The British also made extensive use of turretless Shermans for the ARV role.

The American ARVs were generally more involved vehicles. They too were based on existing tank chassis, but the conversions were often carried out in factories rather than the base workshops of the other Allied armies (including the British) and thus more detail design care could be lavished upon the final product. A typical Amer-

ican product was the **Tank Recovery Vehicle M32**. On this the turret was fixed and a smoke-firing 81-mm (3.2-in) mortar was fitted. In the space normally taken up by the fighting compartment was placed a powerful 27216-kg (60,000-lb) capacity winch, and an A-frame jib was mounted on the forward hull. Extra stowage points for special equipment were added all over the hull. Several sub-variants of the M32 were produced. The M3 medium tank series was also used to produce the **Tank Recovery Vehicle M31** with a jib crane over the rear of the hull. The British also made their own conversion of the M3 Grant by removing all the armament and installing a winch in the main compartment.

The American ARVs were produced in large numbers, so large in fact that some of the M32s could be converted as artillery tractors. But one factor that both British and American ARVs had in common and that was that none of them matched the power of the German Bergepanther. The Bergepanther remained the most powerful ARV of World War II as far as operational models were concerned, but the Allied ARVs could still tackle most recovery tasks without difficulty, for they did not have to cope with the Tigers and Panthers of the German army.

Specification
Churchill ARV Mk II
Crew: 5 or 6
Weight: 40 tons
Powerplant: one Bedford Twin-Six petrol engine developing 261 kW (350 hp)
Dimensions: length 8.28 m (27 ft 2 in); width 3.35 m (11 ft); height 3.02 m (9 ft 11 in)
Performance: maximum road speed 24.9 km/h (15.5 mph); maximum road range 193 km (120 miles)
Armament: one or two machine-guns

A Churchill ARV (Armoured Recovery Vehicle) Mk I has its front jib erected and twin 7.7-mm (0.303-in) Bren machine-guns mounted in the hull. This vehicle had a crew of three and carried special tools and welding equiment for the recovery role. The vehicle was basically a turretless Churchill Mk IV.

A Cromwell ARV (Armoured Recovery Vehicle) is used to tow a captured German PzKPfw IV tank out of the way of other vehicles. The Cromwell ARV was a turretless conversion of an early mark of Cromwell tank that could be fitted with a jib crane and other gear.

An M32 Tank Recovery Vehicle rolls through a village in north west Europe, 1945. Based on the M4 tank hull, these vehicles were used from 1943 onwards and used a fixed superstructure in place of the M4 turret. A large winch was fitted along with other special recovery gear and tools.

A Sherman ARV Mk I tows a Sherman gun tank during the campaign in Normandy, June/July 1944. This ARV was a British conversion of a Sherman tank that involved removing the turret and fitting a front-mounted jib crane and other equipment.

Sherman BARV

UK/USA

By late 1943 plans for the amphibious landings in northern France had reached the stage where it was decided to have deep-wading recovery vehicles on hand at the beaches to assist any vehicles that got bogged or broken down while still in the water. It was decided to convert Churchill and Sherman tanks for the role but the Churchill conversion did not get past the prototype stage and all work concentrated on the Sherman.

The result was known as the **Sherman Beach Armoured Recovery Vehicle** (**Sherman BARV**). It was little more than an ordinary Sherman with the turret replaced by a tall superstructure. This superstructure was open at the top and had plates that sloped to a boat bow profile at the front. The turret opening was closed off and all air intakes and cowls were extended upwards. Waterproofing was extensive and a bilge pump was added to the hull.

The first BARV was ready for trials in December 1943 and these trials proved to be so successful that a request for 50 conversions (later increased to 66) was made immediately. By the time the D-Day landings were made in Normandy there were 52 BARVs ready to hand, and one of them was actually the first armoured vehicle to touch down on the beaches. They had plenty to do for the weather on D-Day was rough, to the extent that many armoured and other vehicles were swamped as they made their way from the landing craft to the safety of the beaches. The BARV was thus used as a towing vehicle to get them ashore. It could tow only, for in the haste to produce the BARVs it was decided to omit the usual winches. In their place some measure of assistance to stranded vehicles could be provided by nudging them with baulks of timber secured to the BARV nose. These nudgers could be used not only for vehicles but with small landing craft that got themselves stuck on the beaches.

The BARVs could operate in up to 3.05 m (10 ft) of water, depending on weather conditions, and often took on a nautical air enhanced by the use of lifelines fixed around the upper superstructure. Many BARV crews included a diver in their number and life jackets

The Sherman BARV featured a high box-type superstructure that allowed the BARV to be driven into deep water to recover stranded vehicles. At the front it mounted a nudging nose to push vehicles out of trouble, but failing that it could be used as a straightforward recovery tractor. It did not have a winch.

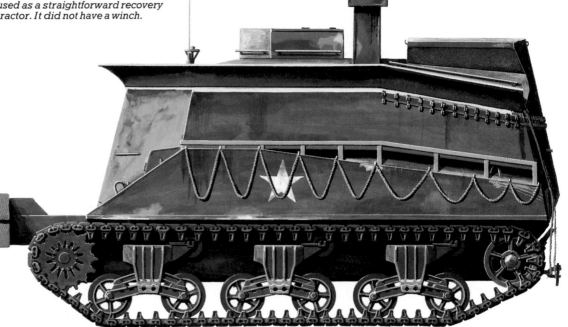

were frequently worn. The BARVs were a REME responsibility as they were primarily recovery vehicles. The REME even had a hand in their production, for this corps supervised BARV production in two small Ministry of Supply workshops.

The BARVs went on to a long postwar service career during which they acquired the name **Sea Lion**. They were eventually replaced by the Centurion BARV which closely followed the general outlines of the Sherman BARV. Over the years the Sherman BARVs were gradually updated with better radios and such refinements as ropes to soften the impact of their 'nudgers', but they never acquired winches or any form of earth spade to enable increased-capacity pulls to be made.

The Sherman BARV (Beach Armoured Recovery Vehicle) was developed during 1943 to tow bogged-down vehicles from deep water during amphibious operations. It was a tractor device only, and the crew usually included a trained diver to secure towing cables to stranded vehicles for towing.

Mine-clearing rollers

UK/USA/CANADA

The mine-clearing roller was one of the very first anti-land mine devices used with tanks and in theory rollers are among the simplest to use. They consist of a set of heavy rollers pushed ahead of the tank, their weight and pressure alone being sufficient to destroy the mines by setting them off in front of the tank. Translating this theory into practice should also have been simple but was not. The main problem was the weight and bulk of the rollers that had to be used: in order to make the rollers heavy enough they had also to be large, and this made them very difficult loads to handle using the average tank of the period. In fact some of them were so large and awkward to push that it sometimes took two tanks (the carrier tank plus another behind it to provide extra 'push') to move them forward. This two-tank arrangement was often necessary when rollers had

to be pushed over soft or rough ground.

The British were probably the first to develop anti-mine rollers, and experimented with them in the years before World War II fitted to vehicles such as the Covenanter. They knew their first models as the **Fowler Roller** or the **Anti-Mine Roller Attachment** (**AMRA**). From these were developed the **Anti-Mine Reconnaissance Castor Roller** (**AMRCR**) system that was fitted to Churchills and British Shermans. These rollers used leaf springs to keep

The Lulu roller device did not detonate mines by pressure, as the front rollers were only light wooden containers carrying electrical sensor devices to denote the presence of buried metal objects such as mines. Although it worked, the Lulu was too fragile for operational use.

the rollers in contact with the ground, but they were so cumbersome that they were not used operationally. A more successful design appeared in 1943 and was known as the **Canadian Indestructible Roller Device** (CIRD). This used two heavy armoured rollers mounted on side arms, and was so arranged that if a roller detonated a mine the resultant blast lifted the roller and a lever came into contact with the ground, the subsequent movement of the tank operating the lever to return the roller to the ground again for further use. CIRD was fitted to both Churchills and Shermans, but the system was not used in action.

The Americans also became involved with mine rollers and produced three main models. The first version was the **Mine Exploder T1** and was intended for use with M3 Lee tanks, but not many were made as these tanks had passed from front-line service by the time the rollers had been developed. From them evolved the **Mine Exploder T1E1** or **Earthworm**,

but again this was devised for use by one vehicle only, in this case the M32 Tank Recovery Vehicle. For use with the M4 Shermans came the **Mine Exploder T1E3** (later the **Mine Exploder M1**) which was generally known as the **Aunt Jemima**. This used two very large sets of roller discs mounted on side arms in front of the carrier, and the system was used in action despite its great bulk and awkwardness. It proved to be successful enough, and was even developed into an **M1A1** version which was even heavier.

The Americans developed a whole string of other types of mine roller, few of which got past the experimental stage. Perhaps the oddest of them was the **Mine Exploder T10** on which the rollers became the road wheels for an M4 tank body, complete with gun turret. Two rollers were mounted forward and another set of roller discs was at the rear with the tank body slung between them. This device got no further than trials, and neither did the series of vehicles known as the **Mine Resistant**

Vehicle T15. This was an M4 tank fitted with extra body and belly armour and intended to set off mines by simply driving over them, relying on its extra protection for survival. None of these vehicles was ready for use by the time the war ended, and work on the type then ceased.

Rollers were an apparently obvious solution to a minefield, but it proved exceedingly difficult to detonate enough mines by the rollers' weight alone. Solutions included rollers so heavy that it took several vehicles to move them, and plough and roller combinations.

Gun tractors

As a general rule most artillery tractors were specially developed for the task but some artillery weapons developed during the war years had to make do with what was to hand. In nearly every case this meant the conversion of an obsolete or obsolescent tracked vehicle, especially for the larger weapons. The use of tracked vehicles gave the gunners considerably more tactical mobility that could have been achieved by using wheeled tractors, but in general terms using tracked vehicles was expensive and it was a measure that was only bearable in wartime.

A typical use of an obsolete tank chassis can be seen with the British **Crusader Gun Tractor Mk I**. This was developed to tow the bulky 17-pdr anti-tank gun, and used the Crusader II tank chassis as the basis. Onto the chassis was built an open superstructure fitted out with seating for the gun crew and with ammunition lockers. These tractors were widely used by Royal Artillery anti-tank regiments serving with armoured divisions in Europe during 1944 and 1945, and proved to be well-liked and fast tractors capable of towing their 17-pdr guns almost anywhere. Some turretless Shermans were also used in this role.

The Crusader Gun Tractor was almost the only conversion of a tracked vehicle made by the British, but it was otherwise with the Americans. Their far more extensive automotive manufacturing resources enabled them to produce all manner of special artillery tractors, many of them based on existing vehicles. Typical of these was the **Full-track Prime Mover M34**, an odd vehicle, for it was an M32 Tank Recovery Vehicle stripped of its recovery kit and used as a tractor only. It was reserved for really large items of artillery such as the 240-mm (9.45-in) howitzer. Other attempts were made to convert old M2 Lee tanks for the tractor role, but they were not developed fully as special vehicles could be produced without difficulty.

There were two main types of tractor produced in the United States. One

was the **High-Speed Tractor M4** and the other the **High-Speed Tractor M5**. The M4 used components of the M2A1 Lee tank allied to a new box-type body that could house the crew and a quantity of ammunition. Compared to other types of tractor the gun crew could travel in comfort as the cab was weatherproof and fitted with such luxuries as heaters, and yet there was still plenty of room for stowage. The M5 tractor was smaller and used components from the M3 light tank series. The crew accommodation was more open than that of the M4 but the tractor still had plenty of space and was equipped with such handy items as winches. The

M4 was used to tow artillery up to 155 m (6.1 in) in calibre, and the M5 was used for artillery up to 203 mm (8 in) in calibre. Both types were produced in considerable numbers and many of both are in use to this day. Large numbers were handed out by the Americans to the Allied armed forces, and a few were used by the British before the war ended.

Specification
High-Speed Tractor M5
Crew: 9
Weight: 12837 kg (28,300 lb)
Powerplant: one Continental R-6572 petrol engine developing 175.2 kW

(235 hp)
Dimensions: length 4.85 m (15 ft 11 in); width 2.54 m (8 ft 4 in); height 2.64 m (8 ft 8 in)
Performance: maximum towing speed 56.3 km/h (35 mph); maximum road range 241 km (150 miles)
Armament: none

The M35 Full Track Prime Mover was a turretless conversion of the M10A1 tank destroyer for use as a tractor for heavy artillery. This example is towing the barrel of a 203-mm (8-in) Gun M1 towards Germany in February 1945; the Carriage M2 would have been towed separately.

Bergepanther

During the early war years the German army used the 18-tonne SdKfz 9/1 and 9/2 for recovering broken-down or damaged tanks, but with the arrival of the heavy tanks such as the Tiger and Panther these vehicles were no longer able to recover the weights involved. The only way they could be used effectively was in complicated tandem or other arrangements with one vehicle's crane acting in combination with the other, and it was not always possible to get two of these large halftracks to some locations, even supposing two were on hand. The only solution to the problem of large vehicle recovery was the development of a new heavy recovery vehicle. Some of the early Tiger units converted their machines to take winches in the turret in place of the main gun for recovery purposes, but this was a waste of a valuable gun tank and Tigers were always in short supply. In the end it was decided to use the Panther tank as the basis for the new vehicle.

The new vehicle became known as the **SdKfz 179 Bergepanther**, or **Bergepanzer Panther**. The first of these appeared during 1943, and they were conversions of early models of Panther gun tanks. On the conversion the turret and fighting compartments were completely removed and replaced by an open superstructure housing a large and powerful winch. To increase the 'pull' of this winch the vehicle had at the rear a large earth spade. In use this spade was lowered to the ground and the vehicle was reversed, the spade thus being dug down into the ground to

act as a stable anchor when the winch was in use with the cable running out over the vehicle rear. The combination of spade and winch enabled the Bergepanther to recover even the heaviest vehicles, and it also carried all manner of other recovery equipment, including a light crane jib on the left-hand side for use when carrying out running repairs.

It was spring 1944 before the first Bergepanthers reached the troops, the conversions being carried out by DE-MAG in Berlin. By the time the war ended 297 had been produced, but not all of them were fully equipped. For supply reasons some vehicles were issued without the rear-mounted spade which reduced them to little more than towing vehicles; they were of such limited utility that many of these incomplete vehicles had their winches removed to enable them to be employed as supply and ammunition carriers. The full standard Bergepanthers

proved to be invaluable and not surprisingly they were concentrated in Panther, Tiger and Königstiger formations. In service they had a crew of five, and most retained their front hull 7.92-mm (0.312-in) machine-gun. Many were also armed with a 2-cm cannon carried just forward of the open superstructure on a mount that allowed it to be used either in the anti-aircraft or ground target role.

When they were first introduced the Bergepanthers were well in advance of other contemporary recovery vehicles. Although it was a conversion of an existing tank, its combination of winch, earth spade and overall layout meant that it was quite simply the best recovery vehicle produced during World War II.

Specification
Bergepanther
Crew: 5
Weight: 42 tons

Powerplant: one Maybach HL210 P.30 petrol engine developing 478.7 kW (642 hp)
Dimensions: length 8.153 m (26 ft 9 in); width 3.276 m (10 ft 9 in); height 2.74 m (9 ft)
Performance: maximum road speed 32 km/h (20 mph); maximum road range 169 km (105 miles) maximum cross-country range 85 km (53 miles)
Armament: one 2-cm cannon and one 7.92-mm (0.312-in) machine-gun

The Bergepanther was the best-armoured recovery vehicle produced in World War II. Only 297 were completed by the end of the war, and they were generally concentrated in the heavy tank battalions.

The German Bergepanther was based on the Panther tank hull and suspension, and could be used for the recovery of even the heaviest German tanks. Shown here in its travelling configuration, the Bergepanther had a powerful winch in the hull interior and used a large earth anchor at the rear to improve winch pull.

Karl ammunition carriers

When the design teams that produced the massive Karl siege howitzer were drawing up their plans they at first overlooked one item: the massive short-barrelled howitzers they were producing were mounted on large tracked chassis to provide some measure of mobility (even though this mobility was strictly limited by the sizes and weights involved), but they forgot the matter of ammunition supply. This oversight was soon realized and plans were made to provide special ammunition carriers that could move to wherever the Karls might be emplaced, and these carriers had to be tracked as well. They also had to be large, for the Karls fired a huge concrete-busting projectile that weighed no less than 2170 kg (4,784 lb) and with a calibre of 60 cm (23.62 in); later versions had a calibre of 54 cm (21.26 in) and the projectile weighed 1250 kg (2,756 lb).

The vehicle selected to be the ammunition carrier for the Karls was the PzKpfw IV Ausf F. These vehicles were not conversions, but were built from new using the basic tank hull,

suspension and other components, though in place of the usual turret there was a platform that covered the entire top of the hull. At the front of the platform was a crane with a capacity of 3000 kg (6,614 lb), offset to the left and with the swivelling jib normally stowed

Above left: the Munitionpanzer IV Ausf F was used to carry the heavy projectiles for the 60-cm (23.62-in) Karl self-propelled mortar, and is seen here with its lifting jib raised ready for use. The jib could traverse through 360 degrees.

Above: A Munitionpanzer IV Ausf F is shown in its travelling configuration with the jib folded and with the shell lifting grab stowed on the front of the hull. Each of these ammunition carriers could carry three 60-cm (23.62-in) projectiles.

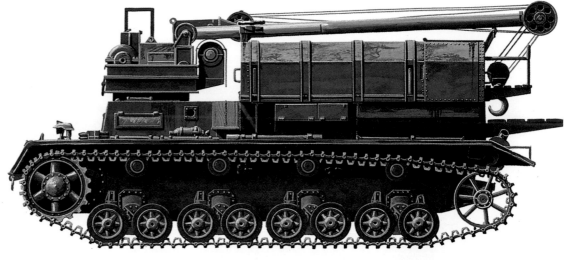

facing to the rear. The main platform was used as the carrying area for the projectiles, with space for two or three shells. Small metal side walls were fitted, but these were often removed in the field.

Much of the movement of the Karl equipments had to be carried out on railways, and the train that carried the components of Karl also had a couple of flat-cars to carry **Munitionpanzer** or **Munitionschlepper** ammunition carriers. Once close to the firing position the Karls were assembled and they moved off to the exact firing position. Projectiles for the weapons were taken from the train box-cars either by overhead gantry or by using the crane mounted on the carriers. The carriers then moved to the firing position and unloaded their projectiles by parking next to the Karl breech and lifting the ammunition directly to the breech loading tray with the crane. Special ammunition handling grabs were used on the crane itself. Once their load had been fired the carriers trundled off for more.

Not all Karl moves were made by rail. There was an arrangement whereby a Karl could be broken down into relatively small loads for road traction, but it was a long and arduous process to assemble the weapon on site. When this occurred the carriers were towed on special wheeled trailers towed by large halftracks. The usual allotment of carriers to a single Karl was two. Also included in each Karl 'train' were two trucks, two light staff cars and at least one 12-ton halftrack to carry the Karl crew.

The Karl howitzers were among the most specialized of all German artillery weapons. They were designed as fortification smashers, and during World War II were not much in demand. But they and their PzKpfw IV-based ammunition carriers did see use during the siege of Sevastopol, and in 1944 saw more action during the Battle of Warsaw against the unfortunate Polish home army.

Specification
Munitionpanzer
Crew: 4
Weight: 25 tonnes
Powerplant: one Maybach HL 120 TRM petrol engine developing 223.7 kW (300 hp)
Dimensions: length 5.41 m (17 ft 9 in); width 2.883 m (9 ft 5.5 in); height not

The Munitionpanzer IV Ausf F carried shells for the Karl self-propelled mortar on a platform over the hull. They were lifted onto the Karl loading tray by a front-mounted jib crane, seen here folded over the shell platform.

recorded
Performance: maximum road speed 39.9 km/h (24.8 mph); maximum road range 209 km (130 miles)
Armament: none

---

kleiner Panzerbefehlswagen

Once the German army had accepted the concept of the Panzer division with its large tank component it was appreciated that the large mass of tanks would carry with it considerable command and control problems. Tank formation commanders would have to move forward with the tanks and maintain contact with them at all times, and at first it seemed that the best way of doing this was to have the commanders travelling in tanks. But it was also appreciated that commanders would have to carry with them all manner of special equipment and extra personnel to transmit orders and generally assist the commander in his task. Thus some form of dedicated command tank would be needed.

In typically thorough style the German designers came up with an answer as early as 1938. They decided to convert the little PzKpfw I training tank for the command role, and the result was the **SdKfz 265 kleiner Panzerbefehlswagen** (small armoured command vehicle). The command vehicle was a relatively straightforward conversion of the basic tank in which the rotating tank turret was replaced by a box-like superstructure to provide extra internal space. The crew was increased from the two of the tank to three, in the form of the driver, the commander and a signaller/general assistant. The extra internal space was taken up with items such as a small table for the commander to work on, map display boards, stowage for more maps and other paperwork, and two radios, one for communicating with the tanks and the other to provide a link to higher command levels. These radios required the provision of extra dynamo capacity to power them and keep their associated batteries fully charged. For armament a 7.92-mm (0.312-in) MG34 machine-gun was mounted in the front plate.

There were three variations of this command vehicle, one with a small rotating turret set onto the superstructure. This latter feature was soon discontinued as it took up too much of the limited internal space and was soon found to be unnecessary. The other two variants differed only in detail. In all of them the small size of the vehicle inflicted space limitations, and with two men attempting to work within the close confines of the body things could get very cramped. But the concept worked very well and about 200 conversions from the PzKpfw I tank were made. The first of them saw action during the Polish campaign of 1939 and more were used in France during May and June 1940. Later they equipped the Afrika Korps. One of these North African campaign examples was captured by the British army and taken back to the United Kingdom. There it was closely examined by tank experts who produced a large report on the vehicle, which can now be seen in the Bovington Tank Museum.

Despite their relative success in the command role the little PzKpfw I tank conversions were really too small and cramped for efficiency and in time

The kleiner Panzerbefehlswagen was a command version of the PzKpfw I light tank. It had a crew of three and the fixed superstructure contained two radios, a map table and extra electrical equipment. The vehicles were widely used, as they allowed commanders to keep up with armoured formations.

Below: Just how cramped the PzKpfw I command tank was can be gauged from this photograph of the basic model PzKpfw I. About 200 conversions were made but they proved too small for the task, and they were replaced by modified versions of later tanks.

they were replaced by conversions of larger tank models.

Specification
kleiner Panzerbefehlswagen I
Crew: 3
Weight: 5.8 tons
Powerplant: one Maybach NL 38 TR petrol engine developing 74.6 kW

(100 hp)
Dimensions: length 4.445 m (14 ft 7 in); width 2.08 m (6 ft 9.9 in); height 1.72 m (5 ft 7.7 in)
Performance: maximum road speed 40 km/h (25 mph); maximum road range 290 km (180 miles)
Armament: one 7.92-mm (0.312-in) machine-gun

Amphibious Vehicles

Most of the Great Powers used amphibious vehicles during World War II. Some of these vehicles, such as the Soviets' pre-war amphibious light tanks, proved to be superfluous but others, like the DD Shermans and the DUKW, were of crucial importance.

The range of vehicles contained in this section is much wider than usual, simply because the range of amphibious vehicles used during World War II was very large. At the lower end of the range was the little German Schwimmwagen, while at the upper end of the scale the German LWS took some beating for sheer size even if the slab-sided American LVTs were far more numerous. Such a diversity of vehicles was a result of the many and various roles that amphibious vehicles needed to undertake. Some armed forces wanted them simply as personnel or supply carriers that could support amphibious operations, while other forces needed specialized reconnaissance vehicles that could cross water obstacles, and yet others required load carriers to transport supplies anywhere. They are all included in this section so it would be unfair to make comparisons between, say, the M29C Weasel and the Soviet T-38 amphibious light tank. The same disparities make comparisons between the DD Shermans and the Japanese Type 2 Ka-Mi impossible, because the DD Sherman was intended simply to accomplish a short journey from a vessel to a nearby shore where it immediately became a

American troops come ashore at Trinian in the Marianas Islands. These armoured amphibious landing vehicles served the Americans well in both Europe and the Pacific.

gun tank, while the Type 2 was more of a reconnaissance vehicle that was able to cross water obstacles.

Yet for all these differences the contents of this study include many of the most interesting vehicles used during World War II. Each of the types described here has some special design or other point in its favour, although a few

have more against than for them. Perhaps the most interesting of all, and not only because of its military importance, were the American LVTs. These vehicles were very much a compromise design to obtain the best possible performances overland and on water. The two are disparate requirements, but the LVTs achieved a good working

compromise and were thus able to carry amphibious warfare from the Rhine to the islands of the Pacific. Amphibious tanks were remarkable vehicles, but one can only wonder at how their crews had the courage to use their flimsy charges to approach a defended enemy shore and to drive them right at the muzzles of the defender's guns.

T-37

In 1931 the USSR purchased from Vickers Carden-Loyd of the UK a number of light tankettes. Among the purchases were a small number of Carden-Loyd A4E11 amphibious tanks, and these so impressed the Soviets that they decided to undertake local licence production in order to meet a Red Army requirement for light scouting tanks. However, it was not long before the Soviet design teams realized that the Carden-Loyd A4E11 did not meet all their requirements, and so they set about developing their own light amphibious tank based on the British design. This resulted in the **T-33**, which was subjected to some rigorous trials before it was deemed unsatisfactory. Further design work resulted in the **T-37** light amphibious tank.

By the time the T-37 was produced there was little left of the original British design other than the concept. The T-37 had a GAZ AA engine and the suspension was an improved version of that used on the French AMR light tank. Once again the first T-37s were subjected to a thorough testing programme, and as a result changes were introduced to the full production models, which first came off the lines in late 1933 and early 1934. The production T-37 was a small vehicle with a two-man crew, the commander in a turret offset to the right and the driver seated in the hull to the immediate left. Most of the buoyancy came from two pontoons on each side of the upper hull above the tracks, and at the rear there was the usual single propeller and a rudder. The T-37 was meant to be amphibious on inland waterways only. As it was designed as a light scouting or reconnaissance vehicle, the T-37 had only light armament, comprising a single 7.62-mm (0.3-in) air-cooled machine-gun.

Production of the T-37 continued until 1936, and during the production run several variants occurred. One was known as the **T-37TU** and had a prominent radio frame aerial around the upper hull; this was used only by commanders needing to maintain contact with rear command levels, while orders were transmitted to other tanks by signal flags. On some vehicles the usual riveted turret was replaced by a cast item. As was to be expected on such a small and light tank, armour was very thin, the maximum being only 9 mm (0.354 in) thick and the norm only 3 mm (0.118 in). This armour could not withstand even light anti-armour projectiles, but the T-37s were to be used as scouting vehicles only and were not intended for employment in a stand-up armoured fight. Nevertheless they were so used during the desperate days of 1941 and 1942 when the Soviet army had at times virtually nothing

Above: The tiny T-37 light amphibious tank was produced in several versions, but all were lightly armoured and had only two-man crews. They were in production from 1935 onwards, but few survived after the end of 1941 as they were too frail to stand up to prolonged combat.

with which to stem the advance of the German forces. By the end of 1942 the last of the T-37s had passed from use, though a few hulls were retained for use as light tractors.

Specification
T-37
Crew: 2
Weight: 3200 kg (7,055 lb)
Powerplant: one GAZ AA petrol engine developing 29.8 kW (40 hp)
Dimensions: length 3.75 m (12 ft 3.6 in); width 2.10 m (6 ft 10.7 in); height 1.82 m (5 ft 11.7 in)
Performance: maximum road speed 56.3 km/h (35 mph); maximum road range 185 km (115 miles)
Armament: one 7.62-mm (0.3-in) DT machine-gun

Disabled T-37 light amphibious tanks are seen in the snow of the Winter War against the Finns in 1939-1940. In this campaign the T-37s showed up badly, as they had only light armour. The front vehicle is a T-37(TU) command tank with the remains of an aerial showing.

T-37 light amphibious tanks on parade in the Soviet Union. The three leading tanks are T-37(TU) command tanks fitted with frame aerials and radios; most T-37s had to communicate with flag signals as the general issue of tank radios was not standard practice until after 1945.

T-38

Almost as soon as the first T-37 amphibious light tanks were rolling off the production lines a redesign was under way. A team based in Moscow virtually took apart the design of the T-37 and did whatever it could to improve and modernize it, for it was realized by 1934 that the basic T-37 design approach was already out of date. The result was known as the **T-38,** and although it looked very different to the T-37 was very little advanced over the original.

The T-38 was of the same general concept as the T-37 and the two-man crew was retained, but the turret position was switched to the left and the driver's position was also switched.

The T-38 was wider than the T-37 and had better floating characteristics. Carried over from the T-37 was the armament of a single 7.62-mm (0.3-in) DT machine-gun and the power train of the GAZ AA truck.

The first T-38 was built in 1936 and full production commenced in the following year. Manufacture continued until 1939, by which time about 1,300 had been completed. Some changes were introduced during the production run, the first of which was the **T-38-M1**, an attempt to introduce a new transmission system that in the end proved too complicated for mass production. Then came the **T-38-M2** which was accepted, for it used the power train and engine of the then-new GAZ-M1 truck. One field modification was the changing of the machine-gun for a 20-mm ShVAK cannon to produce more firepower.

When the T-38 went into action alongside the T-37 during the 1939-40 campaign in Finland, the weaknesses of the design became very apparent. The tank was quite simply too lightly protected, for even machine-gun projectiles could pierce the thin armour and knock out the vehicle. Despite attempts by their crews to keep out of the way and simply observe enemy positions, the T-37s and T-38s were shown to be too vulnerable on the battlefield; but they were not immediately withdrawn, for the simple reason that there was nothing to replace them at that time. Instead T-38s were still in use until 1942 to the detriment of their crews, who suffered heavy casualties as Soviet army commanders attempted to use them as light support tanks.

In an attempt to continue the use of the existing T-38 production facilities an effort was made to develop the T-38

by adding some extra armour but the result offered few advantages over the original and the project was terminated.

The T-38 did take part in some interesting experiments involving radio control. The idea was that T-26 light tanks packed with explosives should be directed towards bridges or other demolition targets and then exploded by radio command from a T-38. The T-38 was equipped with special radios for the purpose and was even given a new designation, **NII-20**. There are references to this demolition method being used during the Finnish campaign, but its success is not recorded.

Specification
T-38
Crew: 2
Weight: 3300 kg (7,275 lb)
Powerplant: one GAZ AA or GAZ M-1 petrol engine developing 29.8 kW (40 hp)
Dimensions: length 3.78 m (12 ft 4.8 in); width 3.33 m (10 ft 11.1 in); height 1.63 m (5 ft 4.2 in)

Performance: maximum road speed 40 km/h (24.9 mph); maximum road range 170 km (105.6 miles)
Armament: one 7.62-mm (0.3-in) DT machine-gun or one 20-mm ShVAK cannon

The T-38 (left) could easily be distinguished from the T-37: the turret was now mounted on the left hand side, and the driver's position moved to the right. It remained utterly inadequate as a combat vehicle.

USSR
T-40

Despite the lack of success of the T-37 and T-38 series, the planning authorities of the Red Army still considered there was a need for a light amphibious tank for reconnaissance purposes, and in 1938 a design team in Moscow was given the task of producing a replacement for the T-38. But for once an alternative to an amphibious vehicle was demanded, and it was decided to produce amphibious and non-amphibious versions of the same design: these were given the designations of **T-30A** (amphibious) and **T-30B** (non-amphibious).

The T-30A was completed during 1939 and the end of that year it had been accepted for Soviet army service as the **T-40**. In order to speed production the T-40 had been designed from the outset to include as many automobile and truck components as possible, but production was surprisingly slow, no doubt as a result of the low priority given to light tanks at that time. Compared to the earlier T-37 and T-38, the T-40 was an entirely new vehicle. The two-man crew was retained, but the small turret was now mounted in a more orthodox slightly offset position and mounted a 12.7-mm (0.5-in) DShK heavy machine-gun. (It had originally been suggested that a 20-mm cannon should be mounted.) The rear of the hull was rather bulky in order to provide the necessary flotation chambers. The original production versions had a blunt nose that did little for swimming characteristics, so this was later rounded off to a more streamlined outline in a version known as the **T-40A**. Propulsion in water was provided by a propeller at the rear, and there was a single rudder.

The main disadvantage of the T-40 continued to be the thin armour that had to be used. On the T-40 this was at best 14 mm (0.55-in), with the norm only 7 mm (0.275 in). By 1940 this was considered to be far too light, mainly as a result of operational experience gained during the fighting of the previous winter in Finland. It was decided that if the amphibious properties of the T-40 were dispensed with, more

The T-40 used as many automobile components as possible to speed production. It was armed with a 12.7-mm (0.50-in) machine-gun, although some mounted a 20-mm (0.787-in) cannon. Relatively few were produced.

armour could be carried and the resultant vehicle could be issued to armoured units where river crossings were an unlikely occurrence. A vehicle known as the **T-40S** was produced, but it emerged that this model would require far more production facilities than the original and it was bulkier as well, so that line of development was dropped. Instead it was decided to turn to the T-30B, the non-amphibious version of the prototypes produced in 1939. This was accepted for service as the **T-60**, which soon replaced the T-40 as the Soviet army's new light reconnaissance tank.

Thus the T-40 was not manufactured in very large numbers, and production ceased after only about 225 had been built (a trifling quantity by Soviet standards) and the Soviet light amphibious tank line came to an abrupt end.

Specification
T-40
Crew: 2
Weight: 5900 kg (13,007 lb)
Powerplant: one GAZ-202 petrol engine developing 52.2 kW (70 bhp)
Dimensions: length 4.11 m (13 ft 5.8 in); width 2.33 m (7 ft 7.7 in); height 1.95 m

(6 ft 4.8 in)
Performance: maximum road speed 44 km/h (27.3 mph); maximum road range 360 km (223.7 miles)
Armament: one 12.7-mm (0.5-in) DShK machine-gun

The T-40 was in small-scale service with reconnaissance units of cavalry and armoured formations in 1941, but was already being replaced by the slightly improved T-60.

Terrapin

UK

The **Terrapin** was the British equivalent of the American DUKW, and although it was never built in the numbers that the DUKW achieved it made a useful addition to the amphibious load-carrying fleet used by the British army in 1944-5.

The Terrapin was designed by Thornycroft, but production was carried out by Morris Commercial. About 500 were built, and the bulk of them were used by the 79th Armoured Division, first going into action during the autumn of 1944 when they were used to supplement DUKWs during operations to open up the water approaches to Antwerp. The Terrapin was a straightforward amphibious design but it had some odd features, some of which were not to its advantage. One concerned its two Ford V-8 petrol engines, each one driving the four wheels set along each side; with the Terrapin in the water, the engines each drove one of the two propellers at the rear. The snag with this arrangement turned out to be that if one of the engines stalled for any reason the other engine kept driving, causing the vehicle to go into a rapid turn which could cause alarm and damage to all concerned. Thus Terrapin drivers had to be specially alert to this hazard. The two engines were mounted almost centrally to spread wheel loadings, but this had the effect of dividing the cargo compartments into two halves. Thus although the Terrapin could carry more than the DUKW it could not carry the really large loads such as guns or large vehicles.

The overall performance of the Terrapin was not all that good. It was rather slow on land and in the water, and it was in the water that this performance really mattered. When fully loaded the Terrapin had only a limited

The Terrapin was powered by two Ford V-8 petrol engines and was driven in the water by two propellers at the rear. There were two cargo holds and the driver sat in the centre of the vehicle.

freeboard and it could be all too easily swamped in rough water. The top of the vehicle was completely open, but raised moulding boards around the holds could keep out the worst of the water. The driver was located roughly in the centre of the vehicle and his view to the front and rear was rather limited, meaning that other crew members had to give directions during tight landings or when travelling through restricted urban areas. The Terrapin was also a rather uncomfortable vehicle during bad weather conditions. Being seated in the open the driver and crew had to rough it, but an awning could be raised over the front compartment. This was meant to act as a spray shield in the water, but it could also double as weather protection; the

trouble was that it restricted even further the driver's forward view.

For all these drawbacks the Terrapin gave good service. Even before it was used operationally some of the drawbacks had been realized and Thornycroft was asked to produce a new design. This emerged as the **Terrapin Mk 2**, the original model thereupon becoming the **Terrapin Mk 1**. It had a large 'one-piece' hold, much better all-round performance and the driver positioned well forward under cover. The hull shape was improved to provide better seaworthiness and water manoeuvrability was much improved. But the Terrapin Mk 2 arrived on the scene too late: the war ended before it could be placed into production and the large numbers of DUKWs

to hand meant there was no point in developing it further, and with the end of the war the Terrapin Mk 1s were also withdrawn.

Specification
Terrapin Mk 1
Crew: 1+ at least 2
Weights: unloaded 6909 kg (15,232 lb); loaded 12015 kg (26,488 lb)
Powerplant: two Ford V-8 petrol engines each developing 63.4 kW (85 bhp)
Dimensions: length 7.01 m (23 ft); width 2.67 m (8 ft 9 in); height 2.92 m (9 ft 7 in)
Performance: maximum land speed 24.14 km/h (15 mph); maximum water speed 8 km/h (5 mph)
Armament: none

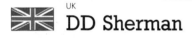

DD Sherman

UK

The **DD Sherman** was a British development that started during 1941. An engineer named Nicholas Straussler, who had been involved with armoured vehicles for some time, turned his attention to producing a method by which an ordinary tank could float in water during amphibious operations. Early experiments involved the Tetrarch light tank (Valentines were also used at a later date) but in the end it was decided to standardize the eventual results on the Sherman tank, then available in some numbers. To provide a cover, these floating tanks were named Duplex Drive (DD) Shermans.

The first DD Shermans were ready in 1943 and were converted by the addition of a collapsible fabric screen and 36 rubber air tubes or pillars. This screen/tube assembly was attached to a boat-shaped platform welded around the hull of the tank. The idea was that the pillars were inflated from two air cylinders carried on the tank, and as the inflation continued the pillars raised the screen to a point above the level of the turret. The screen was then locked into position by struts. All these operations could be carried out by the crew, and the whole operation could be carried out in 15 minutes aboard a tank landing craft. Once ready, the tank could be driven off the landing craft ramp into the water, where the tank would then float with

the turret at water level, about 0.914-m (3-ft) freeboard being provided by the screen. Drive in the water was provided by two small screw propellers at the rear. These were driven via a gearbox from the track drive, and steering was accomplished by swivelling the propellers. Extra steering could be carried out by the tank commander using a simple rudder and tiller arrangement behind the turret.

Forward progress in the water was slow, depending on the sea state, and the sea state also severely affected the ability of the DD tanks to float. Anything over sea state 5 was considered too risky, but at times this limitation

was disregarded, often with dire results. Once the DD Sherman was in about 1.5 m (5 ft) of water the screen could then be collapsed. It was here that the main advantage of the DD Sherman became apparent, for it was able to retain its main gun for immediate use after landing. The bow machine-gun could not be fitted to the DD Shermans but the main gun was often used to support 79th Armoured Division operations directly after landing on the beaches, especially during the D-Day landings of 6 June 1944.

The DD Sherman came as a great surprise to the Germans, for their own attempts to produce swimming tanks ended in relative failure during the early war years.

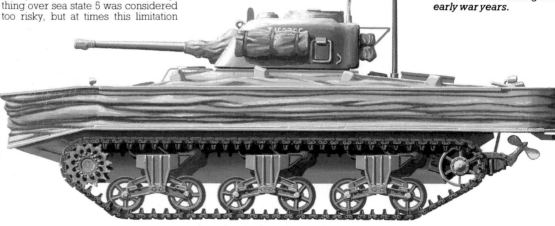

Once out of the water the twin propellers could be raised out of the way, and off the beaches the DD Shermans could be used in a normal combat role.

The DD Shermans were the only item of specialized amphibious warfare vehicles used by the US Army in June 1944, and the Americans even produced their own versions. During the Normandy landings the DD Shermans came as a nasty surprise for the German defenders as their own experiments with 'floating' tanks had proved unsuccessful and had been terminated some years earlier. The sight of DD Shermans clambering up the beaches was too much for some defenders who promptly made themselves scarce. In other locations the DD Shermans provided invaluable immediate fire support for units already in action on the beaches and in the immediate hinterland. DD Shermans were also used at the Rhine crossings and during some north Italian operations in 1944-5.

Below: The DD Sherman in the foreground is in the process of lowering its wading screen just after a river crossing. The wading screens were supported on columns of air contained in rubber tubes, and the soldier in the foreground is assisting their collapse.

Right: The twin propellers of this DD Sherman can be clearly seen under the wading screen, which is in the collapsed position. Only Shermans were used operationally with DD equipment from D-Day onwards until the crossing of the Elbe in 1945.

Above: DD Shermans are seen after crossing the River Elbe in the late stages of the war in Europe in 1945. The wading screens could remain attached to their parent tanks after use, as they did not hinder the tank's fighting efficiency.

USA
DUKW

The amphibious truck that became universally known as the **'Duck'** first appeared in 1942, and was a version of the standard GMC 6×6 truck fitted with a boat-like hull to provide buoyancy. It derived its name from the GMC model designation system – D showed that it was a 1942 model, U that it was amphibious, K indicated that it was an all-wheel-drive model, and W denoted twin rear axles. From this came **DUKW**, and this was soon shortened to 'Duck'.

The Duck was produced in large numbers. By the time the war ended 21,147 had been built, and the type was used not only by the US Army but also by the British army and many other Allied armed forces. Being based on a widely-used truck chassis it was a fairly simple amphibious vehicle to maintain and drive, and its performance was such that it could be driven over most types of country. In the water the Duck was moved by a single propeller at the rear driven from the main engine, and steering was carried out using a rudder behind the propeller; extra steering control could be achieved by using the front wheels. The driver was seated in front of the main cargo compartment, which was quite spacious and could just about carry loads such as light artillery weapons – it was even possible to fire some weapons such as the 25-pdr field guns during the 'run in' to a beach. The driver was seated behind a folding windscreen and a canvas cover could be erected over the cargo area. For driving over soft areas such as sand beaches the six wheels used a central tyre pressure-control system.

The Duck was meant for carrying supplies from ships over beaches, but it was used for many other purposes. One advantage was that it did not always have to unload its supplies directly on the beach: on many occasions it was able to drive its load well forward to where the freight was needed and then return. Many were used as troop transports and the number of special-purpose versions were legion. Some were fitted with special weapons, such as the 114.3-mm (4.5-in) rocket-firing version used in the Pacific and known as the **Scorpion**. Mention has been made of field guns firing from the cargo area, and some Ducks were armed with heavy machine-guns for self-defence or anti-aircraft use. A tow hook was fitted at the rear and some vehicles also had a

The main use of the DUKW was as a logistical stores carrier loading supplies from ships standing offshore. They could also carry overland to supply dumps. This DUKW is seen during a training operation in the pre D-Day period in 1944.

self-recovery winch. Twin bilge pumps were fitted as standard.

Many Ducks were sent to the USSR, and the type so impressed the Soviet army that the USSR produced its own copy, known as the **BAV-485**. This differed from the original by having a small loading ramp at the rear of the cargo area. Many of these BAV-485s are still in use by the Warsaw Pact nations, and the DUKW still serves on with a few Western armed forces. The British army did not pension off its Ducks until the late 1970s.

The Duck has been described as one of the war-winners for the Allies and certainly gave good service wherever it was used. It had some limitations in that the load-carrying

capacity was rather light and performance in rough water left something to be desired, but the Duck was a good sturdy vehicle that was well-liked by all who used it.

Specification: DUKW
Crew: 1+1

Weights: unloaded 6750 kg (14,880 lb); loaded 9097 kg (20,055 lb); payload 2347 kg (5,175 lb)
Powerplant: one GMC Model 270 engine developing 68.2 kW (91.5 bhp)
Dimensions: length 9.75 m (32 ft 0 in); width 2.51 m (8 ft 2.9 in); height 2.69 in (8 ft 10 in)

This DUKW has its canvas tilt raised over the load-carrying area and the driver's screen raised.

Performance: maximum land speed 80 km/h (50 mph); maximum water speed 9.7 km/h (6 mph)
Armament: see text

USA

LVT 2 and LVT 4

Developed from a civil design intended for use in the Florida swamps, the LVT-1 was not really suited for combat, being intended solely as a supply vehicle. The Pacific war was to prove the need for a more capable amphibious assault vehicle. This emerged as the **LVT 2**, which used a better all-round shape to improve water performance, though it was still a high and bulky vehicle. Another improvement was a new suspension and the track grousers were made better by the use of aluminium W-shaped shoes that were bolted onto the track and could thus be easily changed when worn or damaged. A definite logistic improvement was introduced by use of the engine, final drive and transmission from the M3 light tank. At the time the LVT 2 was being developed these components were readily available and made spare-part supply that much easier.

The steering system of the LVT 2 gave considerable trouble at first, for the brake drums operated in oil and prolonged use of the steering bars could result in the brakes seizing up on one side. Training and experience solved that problem.

On the LVT 2 the engine was mounted at the rear, which restricted the size of the cargo compartment. This was relatively easily designed out of the overall layout by moving the engine forward and mounting a ramp at the rear to ease loading and unloading. Thus the LVT 2 became the **LVT 4**, which was otherwise generally similar. Of all the LVT series the LVT 4 was produced in the largest numbers: 8,348 produced on five production lines; in contrast 2,963 LVT 2s were produced on six lines. There were some design differences between the LVT 2 and LVT 4: for instance, the driver's controls were rearranged on the LVT 4, but the main improvement was that all manner of loads could be carried on the LVT 4, ranging from a Jeep to a 105-mm (4.13-in) field howitzer.

Most LVT 2s and LVT 4s were armed with 12.7- or 7.62-mm (0.5- or 0.3-in) machine-guns on rails or pintles, but there were two versions of the LVT 2 that had heavier weapons. The **LVT(A) 1** was an LVT with an M3 light tank turret mounting a 37-mm gun; this was intended to supply fire support during the early phases of an amphibious landing during the interval immediately after reaching the beaches.

The gun proved to be too light for this role, so it was later supplanted by the short 75-mm (2.95-in) howitzer mounted in the turret of the M8 Howitzer Motor Carriage to produce the **LVT(A) 4**. On both of these gun vehicles the turrets were mounted towards the rear of the cargo area, which was covered in by armoured plate.

The ordinary LVT 2s and LVT 4s became the main load carriers of the early Pacific operations. The first LVTs were used in action at Guadalcanal,

and thereafter every island-hopping operation involved them. Some were used in Europe during the Scheldt and Rhine operations of 1944-5 and there were numerous odd 'one-off' attempts to mount various types of weapon in them, ranging from rocket batteries to light cannon. Flamethrowers were fitted in some numbers, but all these types of armament should not disguise the fact that the LVT 2 and LVT 4 were most often used to carry ashore the first waves of US Marines.

LVTs lumber ashore during a training exercise, with others following in a non-tactical line; in an assault the LVTs would land in waves side-by-side. The LVT on the right has shielded weapons that could be either machine-guns or flamethrowers.

The LVT 4 differed from the LVT 2 in having a loading ramp at the rear, which enabled it to carry large loads such as Jeeps and some light weapons. It carried machine-guns on pintles at the front and sides.

Specification
LVT 2
Crew: 2+7
Powerplant: one Continental W970-9A petrol engine developing 186.4 KW (250 hp)
Weights: unloaded 11000 kg (24,250 lb); loaded 13721 kg (30,250 lb)
Dimensions: length 7.975 m (21 ft 6 in); width 3.25 m (10 ft 8 in); height 2.5 m (8 ft 2.5 in)
Performance: maximum land speed 32 km/h (20 mph); maximum water speed 12 km/h (7.5 mph); road radius 241 km (150 miles); maximum water radius 161 km (100 miles)
Armament: one 12.7-mm (0.5-in) and one 7.62-mm (0.3-in) machine-guns

Right: The LVT(A) 1 was armed with the turret and 37-mm (1.45-in) gun of the M3 light tank to provide some measure of local fire support in the initial stages of an amphibious landing.

The British Army received a number of LVTs, and knew them as the Buffalo. Here a number are being prepared for the crossing of the River Elbe during the latter stages of the war in north west Europe; it was in these final river crossings that the Buffalo saw most use.

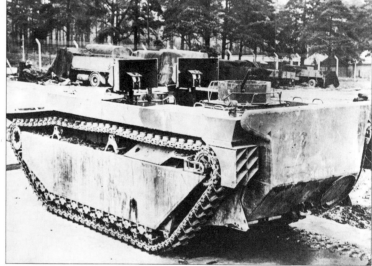

The LVT (F), commonly known as the Sea Serpent, was an LVT 4 converted by the British Army to mount two Wasp flamethrowers forward and a machine-gun aft. Despite the potential of this flame weapon the Sea Serpent was little used by the British.

USA
LVT 3

Compared with the earlier LVT 1 and LVT 2, the **LVT 3** (or **Bushmaster**) was an entirely new design. For a start it had two engines (Cadillac units), each mounted in a side sponson. This allowed an increase in size of the cargo-carrying area and enabled a loading ramp to be installed at the rear. The overall outline remained the same as on the earlier vehicles, but there were numerous changes. The track was entirely new, being rubber-bushed, and the width was reduced with no detriment to water propulsion which continued to be carried out using the tracks only.

The first LVT 3 appeared during 1945 and by the time production ended 2,692 had been produced. It went on to be the 'standard' post-war vehicle of its type but by 1945 the LVTs were used not only by the US Marines but by the US Army. This service had the usual doubts regarding the efficiency of LVTs, but after its initial misgivings came to value the type's

attributes just as much as did the US Marines (although the US Army used the LVT 4 mainly as a supply carrier). For a short while the LVT 3 was used by both the US Marines and the US Navy.

On the LVT 3 the driver and co-driver were located in a cab forward of the cargo area. Behind them was the gunner's firing step and by the time the LVT 3 arrived on the scene the armament of the LVTs had been increased from the initial single machine-gun to three: one 12.7-mm (0.5-in) heavy and two 7.62-mm (0.3-in) medium machine-guns. Along each side of the cargo area were the sponsons containing not only the engines but the hydramatic transmissions, bilge pumps and blowers to remove fumes. Some American references refer to these sponsons as pontoons, for they certainly added to the vehicle buoyancy. The rear ramp was raised and lowered by a hand-operated winch and had heavy rubber seals along the sides to keep out water.

Any water that did get in was drained through gratings in the cargo area deck to be dealt with by the bilge pumps.

The LVT 3 was armoured like the LVT 2 and LVT 4, but extra protection could be added by means of an armoured cab for the driver and co-driver and by the use of add-on panels of armour. (These armoured panels could also be added to the LVT 2). Extra shields were also available to protect the machine-guns and their gunners. Perhaps the most reassuring item of equipment carried was a wooden box in the driver's cab. This contained a quantity of rags, waste material and tapered wooden plugs of various sizes to stop any leaks caused by enemy action or otherwise induced. Other special-to-type equipment carried included signal lamps, a water tank and even some spare parts for on-the-spot repairs.

The LVT 3 represented the final wartime point in the line that could be

traced back to the Roebling tractors, but it was not the end of the line. During the post-war years the concept was developed still further and many of the present vehicles now in use can trace their origins to the LVTs.

Specification
LVT 3
Crew: 3
Weights: unloaded 12065 kg (26,600 lb); loaded 17509 kg (38,600 lb)
Powerplant: two Cadillac petrol engines developing a total of 164.1 kW (220 hp)
Dimensions: 7.95 m (26 ft 1 in); width 3.25 m (10 ft 8 in); height 3.023 m (9 ft 11 in)
Performance: maximum road speed 27.3 km/h (17 mph); maximum water speed 9.7 km/h (6 mph); road radius 241 km (150 miles); water radius 120.7 km (75 miles)
Armament: one 12.7-mm (0.5-in) and two 7.62-mm (0.3-in) machine-guns

M29C Weasel

In 1943 plans were made to invade German-held Norway, and it was appreciated that some form of snow-crossing cargo carrier would be required. After a series of trials a tracked vehicle known as the **T15 Weasel** was selected for service and this was later developed into the **T24**, still named Weasel and developed for use not only over snow but over mud, rough terrain and swamps. In time the T24 was standardized as the **M29 Cargo Carrier** and from this evolved the **M29C** amphibious light cargo carrier. The name Weasel was once more carried over, even though the official name **Ark** was promulgated.

The M29C was a simple conversion of the land-use M29. Changes were made to the flexible rubber tracks to enable them to provide propulsion in water, flotation chambers were provided at front and rear, and twin rudders were added for steering in water. The land M29 had already demonstrated its abilities to cross just about any type of terrain, including snow and rough stony ground, and the M29C retained all these qualities. In water it was somewhat slow and it could not operate in other than inland waterway conditions, so its use in surf or rough water was very limited. But when used correctly the M29C soon proved to be a valuable vehicle. Its uses were legion, especially during the many island-hopping campaigns in the Pacific theatre. Once ashore they were used to cross terrain that no other vehicle could attempt, and they carried men, supplies and even towed artillery using their rear-mounted towing pintle. Rice fields were no obstacle and the M29C was equally at home crossing sand dunes.

The M29C and the land-based M29 Weasels were used as ambulances on many occasions. Another use was for crossing minefields as the Weasel's ground pressure was very low, often too low to set off anti-tank mines. A technique was even evolved whereby

the Weasels could be controlled remotely using hand-operated cords, but this technique had its limitations. The Weasels were also very reliable: they rarely broke down and their track life was later found to be far in excess of anticipations.

The M29C was also used by signal units, for its ability to cross water and land impassable to other vehicles made it a very valuable wirelaying vehicle. But it was as a supply or personnel carrier that it was most useful. Although unarmoured, M29Cs were often used to carry armed troops across water obstacles and land them in front of an enemy position, other M29Cs then following up with ammunition and supplies.

By the time the war ended about 8,000 M29C Weasels had been produced, and orders for a further 10,000 were then cancelled. But the M29C concept had been well established by then and since 1945 many follow-on designs have been produced.

M29Cs were used by several of the Allied armies. The British army made use of a number during 1944 and 1945 and for a few years after that. Some European armies used them for years after the war, and numbers can still be found in civilian hands, hard at work over swampy terrain.

Specification
M29C
Crew: 1+3
Weights: unloaded 2195 kg (4,840 lb); loaded 2740 kg (6,040 lb); payload 390 kg (860 lb)
Powerplant: one Studebaker Model 6-170 petrol engine developing 55.9 kW (75 bhp)
Dimensions: length overall 4.794 m (15 ft 8.75 in); length over hull 4.4 m (14 ft 5.5 in); width 1.7 m (5 ft 7 in); height 1.797 m (5 ft 10.75 in)
Performance: maximum road speed 58.58 km/h (36.4 mph); maximum water speed about 6.4 km/h (4 mph)
Armament: none

American personnel undergo a rather bumpy ride in an M29C Weasel over swampy terrain. The rear-mounted rudders can be clearly seen, and these were lowered once the vehicle actually entered the water.

The M29C Studebaker Weasel was used as an amphibious cargo carrier, but could be used to carry personnel. Although small, it could carry useful loads over almost any type of terrain, and once in the water used its tracks to provide propulsion at slow but steady speed.

Type 2 Ka-Mi

The Japanese army produced an amphibious halftrack as early as 1930, and tested it extensively before deciding that it was too underpowered for full cross-country mobility and thus turning to other projects. However, the idea of an amphibious armoured vehicle of some kind was not entirely lost and some low-priority experimentation went on throughout the 1930s in an attempt to produce an amphibious vehicle for the Japanese navy. One of these projects was to add kapok-filled floats to a Type 95 Kyu-Go light tank, the tank/float combination being propelled by two outboard motors. The idea was to produce a tank-landing or river-crossing system only, but although the floats worked the combination was very difficult to steer and the project was abandoned at the trials stage.

But the idea of making the Type 95 Kyu-Go into an amphibious light tank did not disappear. Instead of the float devices it was decided to redesign the hull of the Type 95 and use steel pontoons fore and aft to provide buoyancy. The wheels, track, suspension and engine (along with many other components of the Type 95) were retained,

but the hull became a larger and bulkier shape. Large slabs of armour plate were used on the hull, which had in-built buoyancy chambers, and a redesigned turret carried a 37-mm anti-tank gun with a co-axial 7.7-mm (0.303-in) machine-gun. Special-to-role extras included a bilge pump, and drain holes were inserted into the road wheels. In the water the two steel pontoons were held in place by securing clamps, and once ashore the pontoons were discarded. Steering was

effected by rudders on the rear pontoon, controlled by cables from a steering wheel in the turret. As there was very little freeboard when floating a trunking arrangement was usually erected around the engine intake grills on the hull top.

The amphibious light tank was designated the **Amphibious Tank Type 2 Ka-Mi** and it went into production during 1942. Compared with the land-based light tanks it had several innovations, not the least of which was radio

The Type 2 Ka-Mi amphibious light tank was the most commonly-used of the Japanese swimming tanks. It had pontoon floats fore and aft to give most of the swimming buoyancy, and the bulky hull also had large buoyancy chambers to provide even more flotation once in the water.

and a telephone intercom system for all crew members. Compared with land-based tanks, the Type 2 also had an increase in crew numbers: the Type 95 Kyu-Go had a crew of only three, but the Type 2 could house five, mainly as a result of the increased internal volume of the hull. One of this increased crew was a mechanic who looked after the engine and the power transfer from the road wheels to the two propellers that drove the vehicle in water.

For its period the Type 2 Ka-Mi was a successful little amphibian, and was used operationally on several occasions by the Japanese navy. However, it suffered the fate of most Japanese armour, being used in dribs and drabs to provide purely local infantry support. By 1944 they were more often than not used simply as land-based pillboxes in attempts to defend islands against invasion, which was a waste of their amphibious potential. Their other problem was that there were never enough of them. Japanese industry could never produce enough to meet demands, and as every vehicle was virtually hand-built production was always slow. But for all that the Type 2 Ka-Mi was one of the best designs of its period.

Specification
Type 2 Ka-Mi
Crew: 5
Weights: with pontoons 11301 kg

(24,914 lb); without pontoons 9571 kg (21,100 lb)
Powerplant: one 6-cylinder air-cooled diesel developing 82 kW (110 hp)
Dimensions: length with pontoons 7.417 m (24 ft 4 in); length without pontoons 4.826 m (15 ft 10 in); width 2.79 m (9 ft 1.8 in); height 2.337 m (7 ft

8 in)
Performance: maximum land speed 37 km/h (23 mph); maximum water speed 9.65 km/h (6 mph); land radius 199.5 km (125 miles); water radius 149.6 km (93 miles)
Armament: one 37-mm gun and two 7.7-mm (0.303-in) machine-guns

This Type 2 Ka-Mi light amphibious tank has its forward pontoon float detached and resting on the ground, clearly showing the large size of this component. The truck is a 2-ton Nissan 180 cargo vehicle produced during the latter stages of the war in the Pacific.

GERMANY
Land-Wasser-Schlepper

In 1936 the German army general staff called upon Rheinmetall Borsig AG to develop a special tractor that could be used in amphibious operations. The idea was that the tractor could tow behind it a special trailer that could also float, capable of carrying vehicles or other cargo up to a weight of about 18000 kg (39,683 lb). Afloat the tractor would act as a tug for the floating trailer, but once ashore the tractor would have to pull the trailer to a point where it could be safely unloaded.

Rheinmetall undertook the project and produced the **Land-Wasser-Schlepper** (land-water tractor) or **LWS**. The LWS was very basically a motor tug fitted with tracks and was a large and awkward-looking machine that nevertheless turned out to be a remarkably workmanlike vehicle. The LWS had a flat bottom on each side of which were two long sets of tracks. On each side four sets of road wheels were suspended in pairs from leaf-spring suspensions. The LWS had a pronounced bow and on top was a cabin for the crew of three men and space for a further 20. What appeared to be a small funnel was in fact an air intake for the engine. At the rear, or stern, two large propellers were placed for water propulsion. To round off the nautical flavour of the LWS the sides of the crew cabin had portholes.

In contrast the floating trailer was a large slab-sided affair that, on land, moved on wheels located on one axle forward and two at the rear. At the rear a ramp could be folded down for loading, a typical load being an SdKfz 9 18-tonne halftrack whose crew transferred to the LWS for the water journey.

The LWS and trailer concept was

conducted through a series of trials with no great sense of urgency until the aftermath of May and June 1940 brought the prospect of 'Seelöwe' (Operation 'Sea Lion', the invasion of the UK) to the forefront. The LWS and trailer could no doubt have been used for such an operation but it was really intended for the calmer waters of inland water obstacles. Even so the LWS was pushed with a greater sense of urgency for a while, but the project never really got off the ground and by 1941 it had been abandoned.

One point that counted against the LWS was that it was unarmoured, and it was felt that armour would be needed for any operations likely to be undertaken. It was also felt that the floating trailer was a bit cumbersome so a new idea was taken up. The overall layout of the LWS was retained, but this time the trackwork and suspension of a PzKpfw IV tank was used to carry a lightly armoured floating chassis. Two of these vehicles, known as **Panzerfähre** or **PzF**, were supposed to carry a large pontoon between them with the tank or other load on it. Thus the PzF would have been a ferry rather than a tractor, but the whole project was abandoned during 1942 after two prototypes had been built and tested.

After 1945 the LWS was captured in

Germany and brought to the UK for a thorough technical evaluation by the British.

Specification
LWS
Crew: 3 + 20
Weight: 13000 kg (28,660 lb)
Powerplant: one Maybach HL 120 TRM V-12 engine developing 197.6 kW (265 hp)
Dimensions: length 8.60 m (28 ft 2.6 in); width 3.16 m (10 ft 4.4 in); height 3.13 m (10 ft 3.3 in)
Performance: maximum road speed 40 km/h (24.85 mph); maximum water speed unloaded 12.5 km/h (7.8 mph); road range 240 km (149 miles)
Armament: none

The German LWS was built to carry up to 20 men and a crew of 3, and it could also tow a floating trailer carrying a vehicle or some form of weapon.

Schwimmwagen

The term **Schwimmwagen** that is usually applied to the amphibious version of the military Volkswagen was not strictly correct, for the term merely means amphibious vehicle. The correct designation was **Schwimmfahiger Gelandeng Typ 166**, though the vehicle was usually just called the Schwimmwagen. It was originally developed during 1940 for use by airborne troops, and was supposed to have a good cross-country performance coupled with an amphibious capability. It was designed to make as much use of existing Kübelwagen (the military version of the Volkswagen) components as possible. In the end most of those built were used mainly on the Eastern Front, and the production reached a total of 14,625.

The Schwimmwagen was used to supplement the various types of motorcycle/sidecar combinations used by reconnaissance and other units. It was a small, sturdy little vehicle with a rather bulky body to provide flotation, and with a propeller at the rear for water propulsion. It could seat four men at a squeeze, especially if they carried all their equipment, for internal space was rather limited. The production line was at the Volkswagen plant at Wolfsburg, and it was often disrupted by Allied bombing raids before the line was closed during 1944, mainly as a result of raw material shortages.

But the German army demanded more and more of these vehicles during the early war years, for the Schwimmwagen was a handy little machine. Apart from its reconnaissance role, many were used by commanders of all types of unit who found them very useful for visiting scattered units, especially over the wide expanses of the Eastern Front. The vehicle was powered by a 1.3-litre petrol engine that was slightly more powerful than that of the Kübelwagen and which gave the Schwimmwagen a better all-

round performance. To make sure that none of the cross-country power was lost special all-terrain tyres were fitted.

The propeller used to drive the vehicle in water was located on a swinging arm at the rear. Before the vehicle entered the water this arm had to be lowered to align the screw with the drive chain, and once propeller drive had been selected the rest of the

transmission was isolated. Water steering was effected via the front wheels. Despite its handiness in water the Schwimmwagen proved to be equally at home in the desert wastes of North Africa, some ending in that theatre with the Deutsches Afrika Korps. Rommel made requests for more, but instead the bulk of the production went to the Eastern Front where the air-cooled engine and the

British troops maintain a captured German Schwimmwagen that has been pressed into Allied use as a runabout. They are working on the propeller unit that was lowered as the vehicle moved into the water. Note the overall chubby appearance of the design, produced by the use of flotation chambers.

presence of more water obstacles meant it could be used to better effect; Rommel instead got Kübelwagens. Many of the Eastern Front models were fitted with a special tank containing a very volatile fuel for starting under winter conditions.

The Schwimmwagen was an attractive little vehicle and many were used by the Allies, often as trophies but more usually for run-abouts by Allied commanders. Many still exist as collector's items.

Specification
Schwimmfahiger Gelandeng Typ 166
Crew: 1+3
Weights: unloaded 903.5 kg (1,992 lb); payload 434.5 kg (958 lb)
Powerplant: one VW 1.13 litre petrol engine developing 18.64 kW (25 hp)
Dimensions: length 3.825 m (12 ft 6.6 in); width 1.48 m (4 ft 10.3 in); height 1.615 m (5 ft 3.6 in)
Performance: maximum road speed 80 km/h (50 mph); maximum water speed 11 km/h (7 mph); range 400-450 km (250-280 miles)
Armament: none

Waffen SS soldiers from one of the SS Balkan units are about to board their Schwimmwagen during operations against partisans. During such operations the amphibious qualities of this vehicle could often be used to good advantage, as water obstacles were no problem.

Allied and Axis Halftracks

The need for the supporting arms to keep pace with the tanks was obvious to serious students of armoured warfare in the 1930s, but wheeled vehicles were roadbound and tracked support vehicles seemed an extravagance. Halftracks appeared to be the answer, and Germany and the USA built them by the thousand.

An American halftrack – the classic Half-Track Car M2 – loaded with jerry cans of fuel comes ashore to reinforce the Allied bridgehead.

Between 1939 and 1945 the mobility of the halftrack imparted to all arms the ability to move at a pace that had not been even contemplated in 1918. Halftracks of all kinds moved infantry, combat engineers, signallers and artillery around the battlefields of World War II at speeds not even the prophets of armoured warfare had envisaged. Instead of the long lines of marching infantry that advanced across the battlefields of 1918, the front-line soldier of 1945 moved in formations of halftracks carrying not only the vanguard of the infantry but also all the support arms.

The impact of the internal combustion engine on the battlefield is frequently quoted with reference to the tank, but it was soon learned that the tank by itself could not operate without support, of which the most important was that furnished by the infantry, followed by that of the engineers and artillery. With the latter two went all the other supply, command and communication functions, which had to have the mobility and speed of the tank. The halftrack was the best way of satisfying this operational requirement, and of all the nations involved in World War II the Soviet Union was alone in not producing

such vehicles. Even the British, with their penchant for the tracked Bren Gun and Universal Carriers, were pleased to receive American halftracks, and the Soviet Union also used many when it suited them to accept such machines. The French developed many models of halftracks but had little chance to use the type in combat in 1940, mainly as a result of the rapid acceptance of armoured warfare principles by their German opponents. It was the Germans who made the best

use of the halftrack's capabilities, and not even the massive output of the American arsenals can overshadow the impact that the German halftracks made at the time: even after a period of more than 40 years that impact still remains in the popular imagination. Thus, although the Americans produced more of their halftracks than can be easily appreciated, the main emphasis in this study is on the German halftracks, from the tiny Kettenrad to the mighty SdKfz 9.

But one factor must be borne in mind when reading this section; in cost terms, weight for weight the halftrack was, and still is, more expensive than the tank. The high degree of technology required to make the halftrack reliable is such that each example was an engineering achievement purchased at high cost in time and facilities. If only a small sector of that effort had been diverted to other weapons or equipment things might have been different for the German armed forces.

SdKfz 2 kleines Kettenrad

The **SdKfz 2 kleines Kettenrad** (SdKfz standing for *Sonderkraftwagen* or special vehicle, and *kleines Kettenrad* (meaning small wheel-track or half-track) was developed initially for use by the new German army and Luftwaffe airborne and paratroop units, and was supposed to be a very light type of artillery tractor. It was originally intended as a towing vehicle for the specialized 3.7-cm Pak 35/36 anti-tank gun developed for the airborne role, and also for the range of light recoilless guns that had also been developed for use by these specialized troops.

The first of these small tractors entered service in 1941. The initial service model was the **NSU-101**, a small but complex vehicle that could carry three men, including the driver who sat behind his steering bar close to the centre of the vehicle. The relatively long tracks took up much of the length of the vehicle on each side, and the engine was located under and behind the driver. Two men could sit at the rear, facing backwards, and the equipment to be towed was connected by a hitch at the rear. Apart from light artillery pieces the vehicle could also tow a specially-designed light trailer that could carry ammunition or fuel, and very often the seating for the two extra men was removed to make more room for cargo and supplies.

By the time the Kettenrad entered service its main intended use had passed with the mauling of the Luftwaffe airborne forces on Crete. Thereafter the German airborne formations fought as ground troops, and the need for light artillery tractors was no longer pressing. Accordingly the Kettenrad was used mainly as a supply vehicle for troops operating in areas where other supply vehicles could not move without difficulty. While the little Kettenrads could carry out supply missions over seemingly impassable tracts of mud or sand they could not carry very much, and their towing capacity was limited to 450 kg (992 lb). This was often a drawback compounded by the fact that relatively few Kettenrads were built, so the few that were available were usually reserved for really difficult missions. At one

Above: The little SdKfz 2 kleines Kettenrad was originally intended for use as a light artillery tractor by airborne units, but after Crete these vehicles were more often used as light forward area supply vehicles for use over difficult terrain. Three men could be carried.

point it was proposed that a larger version to be known as the **HK102** would be produced. This would have a larger 2-litre (122-cu in) engine (the original version had a 1.5-litre/91.55-cu in engine) that could power a larger vehicle capable of carrying five men or a correspondingly larger payload of supplies. It reached the design stage but got no further, since by 1944 it was finally appreciated that the Kettenrads were an expensive luxury that the German armed forces could no longer afford and the type went out of production.

Those Kettenrads in use in 1944 served up to the end, and there was even a specialized type for high speed cable-laying to link up command posts and forward positions. There were actually two variants of this cable-laying version, one for laying normal telephone cable (**SdKfz 2/1**) and the other for laying heavy-duty cable for large switchboards (**SdKfz 2/2**). Both mounted the cable drums above the centre of the vehicle on a steel

framework and a signaller guided the cable off the drums and onto the ground using a cable guide.

Specification
SdKfz 2
Crew: 3
Weights: 1200 kg (2,646 lb)
Powerplant: one Opel Olympia 38 petrol engine developing 26.8 kW (36 hp)
Dimensions: length 2.74 m (8 ft 11.9 in);

British soldiers try out a captured SdKfz 2 kleines Kettenrad. The driver sat in a well between the two tracks, with the engine just behind him.

width 1.0 m (3 ft 3.4 in); height 1.01 m (3 ft 3.8 in)
Performance: maximum road speed 80 km/h (49.7 mph)
Armament: none

SdKfz 10 leichter Zugkraftwagen 1t

From the mass and weight of the 18-tonne SdKfz 9 the numerical sequence changed back to the lightest of the artillery tractors, the **SdKfz 10 leichter Zugkraftwagen 1t**. This light tractor had its origins in a 1932 army requirement, and the development work was carried out by Demag of Wetter-Ruhr. The first prototype was completed during 1934 and in 1937 the production model (the **D 7**) emerged. This remained in production until 1944 with its basic form virtually unchanged, and later attempts to replace this model never did get very far since the original was deemed more than adequate for its role.

The task was to tow light infantry and other weapons, and to carry the weapon detachment of up to eight men. These weapons included the 3.7-cm (1.456-in) Pak 35/36 anti-tank gun, the 7.5-cm (2.95-in) leIG 18 infantry support gun, and the larger 15-cm (5.9-in) sIG 33 infantry gun. Other weapons towed included light anti-aircraft guns

and later in the war the 5-cm (1.97-in) Pak 38 and 7.5-cm Pak 40 anti-tank guns. The basic vehicle was also used as the basis for the armoured SdKfz 250 series. All in all the SdKfz 10 was a very popular little vehicle that remained in demand by all arms throughout the war. Production was carried out at two main centres, one of which was the Sauerwerke in Vienna, but by 1943 production concentrated at the other main centre (the Mechanische Werke at Cottbus) when the Vienna plant switched to other things. In German terms the production totals were large, more than 17,000 being completed.

By far the most numerous of this production total was the basic tractor but as usual this vehicle was used for other things. The first variants were produced as a reflection on the expected nature of the coming war for three variants, the **SdKfz 10/1**, **SdKfz 10/2** and **SdKfz 10/3** were all produced as chemical warfare vehicles: the first was a specially-equipped chemical recon-

SdKfz 10 leichter Zugkraftwagen 1t tractors are being used here in their intended role to tow 5-cm (1.97-in) Pak 38 anti-tank guns. The vehicles have their canvas covers stowed, and the gun crews' kit and equipment is stowed at the vehicle rear.

This SdKfZ 10/4, a variant of the basic 1-tonne tractor, is fitted with a 2-cm (0.79-in) Flak 30 complete with its curved shield and with the sides folded down for action. Some of these vehicles were fitted with armoured cabs to protect the driver. Extra ammunition was usually carried in a towed trailer.

naissance vehicle, while the second and third were decontamination vehicles carrying equipment-cleansing solutions in drums or a tank. Very few of these special vehicles appear to have been produced, and no records survive of any ever being encountered. It was different with SdKfz 10/4 and SdKfz 10/5, for these two vehicles were produced to mount single-barrel 2-cm light anti-aircraft guns: the SdKfz 10/4 carried the Flak 30 and the SdKfz 10/5 the faster-firing Flak 38 from 1939 onwards. These two vehicles were so arranged that their sides and rear could fold down to form a working platform for the gun crew, and many examples that operated in direct support of ground formations (as opposed to the vehicles used by the Luftwaffe) were fitted with extra armour over the driver's position.

As was usual at the time, there were unofficial modifications to the SdKfz 10 series to carry local 'field fit' weapons. A not uncommon weapon so fitted was the 3.7-cm Pak 35/36 anti-tank gun, which was usually mounted to fire forward while still fitted with its gun shield. A less common weapon was the later 5-cm Pak 38 carried in a similar manner, but these were less frequently encountered.

Specification
SdKfz 10
Crew: 8
Weight: 4900 kg (10,803 lb)
Powerplant: one Maybach HL 38 or 42 6-cylinder petrol engine developing 74.6 kW (100 hp)

The light SdKfz 10 could mount either the 2-cm (0.79-in) Flak 30 or the Flak 38. These guns could be used against ground targets if required, as seen here. This is an SdKfz 10/4 with a Flak 30 and with the sides folded down to provide a firing platform.

Dimensions: length 4.74 m (15 ft 6.6 in); width 1.83 m (6 ft); height 1.62 m (5 ft 3.8 in)
Performance: maximum road speed 65 km/h (40.4 mph); range 150 km (93 miles)
Armament: see text

 GERMANY

Maultier

The first winter of the war in the USSR (1941-2) demonstrated to the German army that most of its wheeled transport was completely unable to deal with the dreadful muddy conditions produced during the freeze-thaw weather that marked the beginning and end of the Russian winter. During these conditions it was only the halftracks that could make any headway, but to divert the precious halftracks from their operational purposes to carry out the mundane day-to-day supply functions was obviously uneconomic, so it was decided to produce low-cost halftrack trucks. This was done quite simply by taking Opel and Daimler-Benz trucks from the production lines and removing their rear axles. In their place went new driveshafts connected to tracked assemblies made from PzKpfw II running wheels and tracks. In itself this was a considerable economic advantage since the PzKpfw II was then going out of production and existing capacity could be retained, making the truck conversion an even more cost-effective venture.

The new halftrack trucks were provided with the name **Maultier** (mule). In the end the conversions used mainly Opel Typ S/SSM trucks, and in service they were generally a success although they tended to lack the overall mobility of the 'proper' halftracks. Not surprisingly, their use was confined to the Eastern Front, and the vehicles were used mainly for routine supply purposes.

Not content with a good thing, the Germans as ever were forced to employ the Maultiers for yet another purpose. The German Nebelwerfer (rocket) batteries had become an established part of the army artillery system

by late 1942, and it was decided that the Panzer formations should have their own dedicated rocket units. At that time most Nebelwerfer units used towed launchers, so in order to keep up with the Panzers a self-propelled version was required. The halftrack was the obvious choice as a starting point, but as none could be allocated the Maultier was pressed into use.

The basic truck was provided with a fully armoured cab, engine cover and hull. On the hull roof a 10-barrel launcher known as the 15-cm Panzerwerfer 42 was placed. This launcher had 270° of traverse and 80° of elevation, and it fired the 10 rockets in a ripple. The army ordered 3,000 of these conversions with the understanding that production would eventually switch to the sWS when production totals of the

latter allowed, which they never did (apart from a small batch of prototypes). The first of these Maultiers was used during 1943, and had a crew of three. The rockets were carried in the launcher, with reloads in compartments along each side of the lower hull. A machine-gun was usually carried. Some of these armoured Maultiers were produced without the launcher and were used to carry extra rockets for the launcher vehicles, and some of these were used by units other than the Nebelwerfer batteries as front-line ammunition supply vehicles, although their armour was proof only against small arms projectiles and shell splinters.

Specification
Maultier (rocket launcher)

The Maultier was a makeshift conversion of an Opel truck into a half-tracked truck for use as a supply vehicle in forward areas. The schwerer Wehrmachtschlepper was meant for this role, but could not be produced in sufficient numbers so the Maultier was produced.

Crew: 3
Weights: 7100 kg (15,653 lb)
Powerplant: one 3.6-litre 6-cylinder petrol engine
Dimensions: length 6.0 m (19 ft 8.2 in); width 2.2 m (7 ft 2.6 in); height 2.5 m (8 ft 6 in)
Performance: maximum road speed 38 km/h (30 mph)
Armament: see text

SdKfz 250 leichter Schützenpanzerwagen

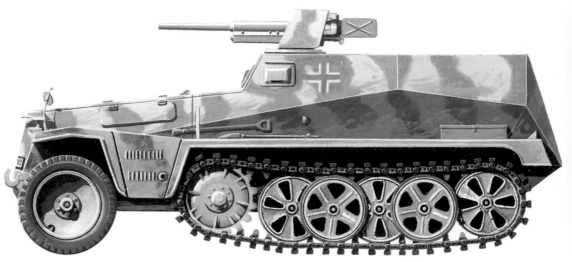

The vehicle that was to become the **SdKfz 250 leichter Schützenpanzerwagen** series had its origins in the same operational requirement produced during the mid-1930s that led to the SdKfz 251 series. It was intended that there would be both 1-tonne and 3-tonne halftracks to provide mobility for the infantry and other units operating with the Panzer divisions, and the 1-tonne model became the SdKfz 250.

The SdKfz 250 was first produced by Demag AG of Wetter in the Ruhr, although later other concerns were also involved in manufacture. The vehicle was based on the chassis of the **SdKfz 10 leichter Zugkraftwagen** 1-tonne vehicle, but featured an armoured hull with an open top to accommodate the crew of five men plus the driver. The first examples were produced during 1939, and the SdKfz 250 first went into action during the May 1940 campaign in France. Compared with its larger counterpart, the SdKfz 251, the SdKfz 250 halftrack was built and used on a much smaller scale but the type's production total was impressive enough (5,930 were made between 1942 and 1944) and by the time the war ended no less than 14 official variants had been produced (plus the usual crop of unofficial variants), and from 1943 onwards production modifications were introduced to the hull shape to assist manufacture while at the same time cutting down the amount of raw materials required. Armour thickness ranged from 6 to 14.5 mm (0.24 to 0.57 in).

The main run of SdKfz 250 vehicles commenced with the **SdKfz 250/1**, which had a crew of six men and carried two machine-guns. There followed a number of models equipped for either radio (**SdKfz 250/3**) or telephone (**SdKfz 250/2**) communications, and a variety of weapon-carrying variants. These were armed with all manner of weapons from an 8.1-cm (3.189-in) mortar (**SdKfz 250/7**) to a 2-cm anti-aircraft cannon (**SdKfz 250/9**). Perhaps the oddest of these weapon carriers was the **SdKfz 250/8**, which appeared to be rather overloaded with a short 7.5-cm (2.95-in) tank gun (from the early versions of the PzKpfw IV tank) allied with a co-axial/ranging 7.92-mm (0.312-in) MG34 or MG42 machine-gun. There were two variants that were allocated their own special designation numbers. One was the **SdKfz 252** which was supposed to be a special ammunition carrier towing a trailer; the reshaped and fully-enclosed interior was meant to carry ammunition for *Sturmgeschütz* (assault gun) batteries, but only a few were made before it was realized that the ordinary SdKfz 250 could carry out the role just as well and the SdKfz 252 was thus replaced by the **SdKfz 250/6** which could carry 70 7.5-cm rounds. The other special version was the **SdKfz 253** which acted as an observation post for the *Sturmgeschütz* batteries and was given a special radio 'fit'.

Other SdKfz 250 variants included the **SdKfz 250/9**, a special turreted version for the reconnaissance role; the **SdKfz 250/12** range-finding and artillery survey model; light anti-tank models armed with either a 37-mm (1.456-in) anti-tank gun (**SdKfz 250/10**) or a special 'taper-bore' 2.8-cm (1.1-in) heavy anti-tank rifle (**SdKfz 250/11**); and various types of command and communication models. Unofficial versions mounted a 2-cm anti-aircraft cannon, and there was at least one attempt to mount a 5-cm (1.97-in) anti-tank gun.

The SdKfz 250 series were popular little halftracks, and they remained in production right up till the end of the war. They were expensive to produce, but they were used on every front and in service proved reliable and sturdy.

The SdKfz 250/10 was armed with a 3.7-cm (1.456-in) Pak 35/36 anti-tank gun, and was just one of a long string of variants of this light armoured carrier. Other versions carried machine-guns and even 7.5-cm (2.95-in) assault howitzers (the SdKfz 250/8).

Specification
SdKfz 250
Crew: 6
Weight: 5380 kg (11,861 lb)
Powerplant: one Maybach HL 42 6-cylinder petrol engine developing 74.6 kW (100 hp)
Dimensions: length 4.56 m (14 ft 11.5 in); width 1.945 m (6 ft 4.6 in); height 1.98 m (6 ft 6 in)
Performance: maximum road speed 59.5 km/h (37 mph); road range 299 km (186 miles); gradient 24°; fording 0.75 m (29.5 in)
Armament: see text

SdKfz 11 leichter Zugkraftwagen 3t

The **SdKfz 11 leichter Zugkraftwagen 3t** series had a somewhat difficult early development life, for the first versions that appeared in early 1934 were produced by two firms, Hansa-Lloyd and Goliath who later combined to form Borgward AG. For various reasons development of these early vehicles passed to Hanomag of Hanover, which became responsible for the series from then onwards, and by 1939 the SdKfz 11 leichter Zugkraftwagen 3t was in full production.

The basic SdKfz 11 was intended for use primarily as an artillery tractor, and once in service it became a standard tractor with 10.5-cm (4.13-in) leFH 18 field howitzer batteries, and was later used to tow 7.5-cm (2.95-in) Pak 40 anti-tank guns. In fact the SdKfz 11 was so successful with the leFH 18 batteries that the larger SdKfz 6 which was also meant to tow these howitzers was phased out of production in favour of the lighter (and less expensive) tractor. The SdKfz 11 tractors were also used by the Luftwaffe to tow light flak weapons such as the 3.7-cm (1.456-in) Flak 36 and 37, and it was by the army's Nebelwerfer (literally smoke-thrower) batteries that the SdKfz 11 was mainly used.

Despite their name the Nebelwerfer units were primarily rocket troops firing their missiles to bolster artillery barrages. The SdKfz 11s used with these batteries not only towed various multi-barrel launchers but also carried spare rockets, launcher frames for the statically-emplaced launchers and crews to carry out the fire missions. Since the Nebelwerfer units were supposed to retain their smoke-producing skills for laying down smoke screens at times, some SdKfz 11s (the **SdKfz 11/1** and **SdKfz 11/4** models) were fitted with smoke-generating equipment but this could usually be removed for the more usual rocket-firing duties. These smoke-generating models had a crew of only two, compared with the nine that could be carried when the vehicle was used as a tractor.

Two variants, the **SdKfz 11/2** and **SdKfz 11/3**, were produced specifically for the chemical warfare decontamination role. These two vehicles could carry more equipment and decontaminants than the smaller SdkKfz 10 equivalents, and were intended for use with larger equipments such as tanks; but as with the smaller vehicles few appear to have been produced and no records have survived of any being encountered. No doubt they were converted to become normal tractors.

At one point several production centres were busy churning out SdKfz 11s and it was one halftrack that remained in production until the end although by then only one factory, Auto-Union at Chemnitz, was in full spate. The Borgward plant at Bremen was supposed to remain in production, but was damaged by bomber raids and could turn out components only. By then some changes had been made to simplify manufacture. The metal superstructures of the early models was replaced by wooden units, and to increase the operational radius of the new vehicles increased fuel capacity was introduced (the normal tankage being 110 litres/24.2 Imp gal). The need for these

An SdKfz 11 leichter Zugkraftwagen 3t of the Afrika Korps tows a 10.5-cm (4.13-in) leFH 18 field howitzer soon after the arrival of the Korps in North Africa in 1941 – hence the pith helmets (soon discarded). This tractor was developed by Hanomag and remained in production until 1944.

tractor vehicles by 1945 was such that many were in use towing far heavier artillery pieces (and other loads) than those for which they were intended, one example of which was the large 8.8-cm (3.46-in) Pak 43 and Pak 43/41 anti-tank guns.

The SdKfz 11 leichter Zugkraftwagen 3t was primarily used as a tractor for medium field artillery such as the 10.5-cm (4.13-in) howitzer and 7.5-cm (2.95-in) Pak 40 anti-tank gun. The SdKfz 11 was so successful that it largely superseded the bigger SdKfz 6.

GERMANY

SdKfz 251 mittlerer Schützenpanzerwagen

The **SdKfz 251 mittlerer Schützenpanzerwagen** series of halftracks had its origins in the same staff requirement as the SdKfz 250, but whereas the SdKfz 250 was a light 1-tonne vehicle the SdKfz 251 was classed as a medium (*mittlerer*) 3-tonne vehicle. The SdKfz 251 was a product of the Hanomag concern, based at Hanover, but the hull and superstructure were produced by Büssing-NAG. The basis of the SdKfz 251 was the **SdKfz 11 leichter Zugkraftwagen** 3-tonne artillery tractor halftrack, and the first production examples were issued to the 1st Panzer Division early in 1939.

The SdKfz 251 was primarily an armoured personnel carrier capable of carrying up to 12 men (a complete infantry section), and it was this **SdKfz 251/1** version that was produced in the greatest numbers. Armed with at least two machine-guns plus the carried crew weapons, the SdKfz 251/1 was a very useful fighting platform capable of keeping up with the fast-moving Panzer formations. No fewer than four differing hull versions were introduced, mainly as a result of the need to churn out more and more vehicles to meet the ever-expanding demand of front-line troops, but that was nothing compared to the number of variants produced for other roles. Armour varied in thickness from 6 to 14.5 mm (0.24 to 0.57 in).

There were no fewer than 22 of these special-purpose variants, plus the usual local and unofficial modifications. They ranged from weapon carriers of all kinds to ambulances, and in between came observation vehicles for various forms of artillery, command and communications versions (both radio and telephone), versions carrying infra-red searchlights or anti-aircraft weapons and even tank-killers mounting long 7.5-cm (2.95-in) anti-tank guns. The full listing is given elsewhere in this study, but perhaps the most powerful of the weapon carriers was a version of the basic SdKfz 251/1 known as the *'Stuka zum Fuss'* (divebomber on foot, or infantry Stuka). This was the personnel carrier with a tubular steel frame over the hull that carried three rocket-launcher frames on each side of the vehicle; 28-cm (11-in) or 32-cm (12.6-in) rockets were

The SdKfz 251/20 was known as 'Uhu' (owl) and carried an infra-red searchlight to illuminate targets for small groups of Panther tanks at night. These variants were produced late in the war and were used mainly on the Eastern Front.

mounted on these side frames while still in their carrying crates and fired at short ranges against fixed or area targets. They were powerful weapons, especially for street fighting, but other SdKfz 251 versions, such as the **SdKfz 251/9** armed with a short 7.5-cm tank gun, were far more accurate. There was even a flamethrower version (the **SdKfz 251/16**) and one model was a late-war low-level anti-aircraft defence expedient, the **SdKfz 251/21** mounting three 1.5-cm or 2-cm aircraft guns (the MG151) on a single mounting.

The SdKfz 251 in all its forms was produced in thousands and became a virtual 'trademark' of the Panzer formations. It was used on all fronts, usually in close co-operation with tanks, and although the early versions displayed some unfortunate reliability problems the type settled down to become a rugged and dependable vehicle in whatever role it was used.

The badge on the front of this SdKfz 251/9 denotes that it is part of the schwere Kanonenzug of the reconnaissance battalion of the 2nd Panzer Division. This is an early example of the mounting for the 7.5-cm (2.95-in) short assault gun used to provide local fire support; this vehicle is one of six in the company.

SdKfz 6 mittlerer Zugkraftwagen 5t

The SdKfz numbers allotted to the artillery halftracks used by the new German army during the early 1930s did not follow a logical sequence, and the **SdKfz 6 mittlerer Zugkraftwagen 5t** was a medium tractor. Development of this vehicle commenced during 1934, the early work being carried out by Büssing-NAG in Berlin. There were two main purposes: one was for the SdKfz 6 to act as the main tractor vehicle for the 10.5-cm (4.13-in) leFH 18 batteries, and the other was for the engineer units, where the tractor would be able to tow the heavy combat engineer equipment on trailers. In both cases the vehicle could carry up to 11 men, and more at a squeeze.

Production of the SdKfz 6 vehicles was carried out by Büssing-NAG and Daimler-Benz, but the numbers involved came to no more than about 737. The main reason for this was that the SdKfz 6 was rather an interim vehicle that fell between two stools: lighter vehicles could be used to tow the artillery pieces, and it was really too light for some of the heavier engineer equipment. It was also rather costly to produce, so by 1941 a decision was made to phase the vehicle from pro-

duction and replace it with the far less expensive sWS. Even so, it was late 1942 before production finally finished and the vehicles already produced continued in use right until the war ended, sometimes pulling artillery pieces far heavier than those for which the type had been designed.

Two versions of engine were produced for the SdKfz 6, the first developing 67.1 kW (90 hp) and the later version 74.6 kW (100 hp). Surprisingly enough, the SdKfz 6 differed only slightly during its service career. Most were produced as standard tractors with seating for the artillery detachment that could be covered by a canvas tilt, but there were also three weapon-carrier variants. The first was the **7.5-cm Slf L/40.8** and never really got past the prototype stage; it was an attempt to produce a mobile 7.5-cm (2.95-in) gun for use with cavalry units, and at least three prototypes were produced between 1934 and 1935. The type was never placed in production, but at least one was captured during the fighting in North Africa. Then there was the model known as the 'Diana' or **7.62-cm Pak 36(r) auf Panzerjäger Slf Zugkraftwagen 5t**, an attempt to mount

captured Soviet 76.2-mm (3-in) guns in a high armoured superstructure built onto the rear of an SdKfz 6. This superstructure was open and rather high and the gun was placed on the vehicle complete with its wheels and attenuated trails. The gun was the Soviet Model 1936 which was used as a dual anti-tank/field gun. Only nine were produced and again one was captured in North Africa by the Allies. The third SdKfz 6 weapon carrier was the **SdKfz 6/2**, which mounted a 3.7-cm (1.456-in) Flak 36 anti-aircraft gun on an open platform behind the driver's position; the sides folded down to act as a working platform for the gun crew. The first of these variants was produced during 1937 and most of them went to the Luftwaffe. They had a crew of seven and were widely used.

Specification
SdKfz 6
Crew: 11
Weights: 8700 kg (19,180 lb)
Powerplant: one Maybach NL 38 6-cylinder petrol engine developing 67.1 kW (90 hp)

First produced in 1937, the SdKfz 6 AA variant mounted a 3.7-cm (1.456-in) Flak 36 on an open platform. The presence of a crew member with rangefinder dates the picture as early in the war; later they were withdrawn to save manpower.

Dimensions: length 6.01 m (19 ft 8.6 in); width 2.20 m (7 ft 2.6 in); height 2.48 m (8 ft 1.6 in)
Performance: maximum road speed 50 km/h (31 mph)
Armament: see text

The Czech-built Praga SdKfz 6s featured longer track bogies than the Bussing-NAG models, and had different wings. They were powered by a Maybach HL54 TUKRM six-cylinder engine developing 86 kW (115 hp), giving a maximum road speed of 50 km/h (31 mph).

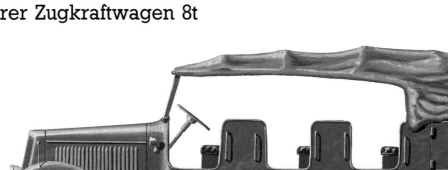

The SdKfz 6 was originally planned to tow the 10-5-cm (4.13-in) leFh 18 howitzer, but was phased out of production in 1942 as lighter tractors like the sWS were equally capable and the SdKfz 6 was too light for heavier loads. Three weapons-carrier versions were also produced.

SdKfz 7 mittlerer Zugkraftwagen 8t

The **SdKfz 7 mittlerer Zugkraftwagen 8t** had its origins in a series of Kraus-Maffei design projects that dated back as far as 1928, but it was not until an army staff requirement for an 8-tonne halftrack tractor was made in 1934 that development really got under way. Between 1934 and 1938 a number of trial versions were produced until the final version appeared in 1938 as the SdKfz 7 mittlerer Zugkraftwagen. This vehicle earned its primary fame as the main tractor for the well-known 8.8-cm (3.46-in) Flak 18, 36 and 37 guns, but it was also used as a tractor for many other artillery weapons including the 15-cm (5.9-in) sFH 18 and the 10.5-cm (4.13-in) K 18.

In its tractor form the SdKfz 7 could carry up to 12 men and their kit, and there was still space left for ammunition and/or other supplies. The gun detachment sat on open bench seats behind the driver, and could be covered by a canvas tilt to keep out some of the weather. The vehicle could tow

Famous as the main tractor for the 88-mm Flak 18, 36 and 37 guns, the SdKfz 7 also towed a wide variety of field artillery. Over 3,000 of these halftracks were in service by the end of 1942, and it was still in widespread use at the end of the war.

weights up to 8000 kg (17,637 lb), and most vehicles were fitted with a winch that could pull up to 3450 kg (7,606 lb). The SdKfz 7 proved to be a most useful vehicle and was widely admired. A captured example was copied in the United Kingdom by Bedford Motors with a view to manufacture for Allied use, and the Italian produced a near-copy known as the **Breda 61**. But the Germans carried on churning out as many as they could. By the end of 1942 there were 3,262 in service. Not all of these were tractors, for the load-carrying capacity of the SdKfz 7 was such that it also made an ideal weapon platform.

The first of these weapon carriers was the **SdKfz 7/1**, which mounted a 2-cm Flakvierling 38 four-gun anti-aircraft mounting on the open rear. On many of these vehicles the driver's position and the engine cover were provided with armoured protection. The SdKfz 7/1 was used extensively for the protection of columns in the field and the four cannon proved deadly to many Allied low-level fliers. This was not the only anti-aircraft version, for the **SdKfz 7/2** mounted a single 3.7-cm (1.456-in) Flak 36 anti-aircraft gun. An attempt was made to mount a 5-cm (1.97-in) Flak 41 on a SdKfz 7, but since

neither the gun nor the conversion was very successful no further work was carried out once trials had been completed. Some SdKfz 7s were also converted to mount single-barrel 2-cm cannon for anti-aircraft use.

Perhaps the oddest use for the SdKfz 7 was when existing vehicles were converted to accommodate armoured superstructures for use as observation and command posts for V-2 rocket batteries during 1944. The V-2 rockets were prone to explode on their launch stands as they were being fired so the armour protected the launch crews. How many of these **Fuerleitpanzer auf Zugkraftwagen 8t** conversions were made is uncertain.

Production of the SdKfz 7 series ceased during 1944, but by then numbers had been built by Krauss-Maffei in Munich, the Sauserwerke in Vienna and the Borgward works at Bremen. In the post-war years many were appropriated for Allied use, and the Czech army used numbers for some years.

Specification
SdKfz 7
Crew: 12
Weights: 11550 kg (25,463 lb)
Powerplant: one Maybach HL 62 6-

cylinder petrol engine developing 104.4 kW (140 hp)
Dimensions: length 6.85 m (20 ft 3 in); width 2.40 m (7 ft 10.5 in); height 2.62 m (8 ft 7.1 in)
Performance: maximum road speed 50 km/h (31 mph)
Armaments: see text

An SdKfz 7 mittlerer Zugkraftwagen 8t was captured in North Africa and was extensively tested back in the United Kingdom. It made such an impression that Bedford Motors built a direct copy, but this was not taken into British service. The Italians also built a copy known as the Breda 61.

 GERMANY

schwerer Wehrmachtsschlepper

By the end of 1941 experience in the field had demonstrated that the German halftrack fleet was in some need of revision. At the bottom end of the range the 1-tonne and 3-tonne cargo and supply/artillery tractors were well capable of carrying on as they were, but the medium to heavy range was proving more complex. It was decided that the 5-tonne range would be discontinued since the 8-tonne range would be required for heavy artillery and other purposes. Thus an interim between the 3-tonne and 8-tonne vehicles was sought, but it had to be a relatively low-cost solution for by 1941 the German war machine was being stretched, not in capacity alone but in the range of types of equipment required: a low cost halftrack was thus needed.

The design accepted was a Büssing-NAG offering, and eventually became known as the **schwerer Wehrmachtsschlepper** (sWS, or army heavy tractor). It was intended not so much for the Panzer or artillery formations but for infantry units, for which it would act as a general personnel carrier and supply vehicle. Accordingly it was virtually a half-tracked truck with virtually no armour in its cargo-carrying form and an open cab with a soft top for the driver and one passenger. In order to keep costs as low as possible the tracks did not use the time-consuming and expensive rubber capped tracks of front-line vehicles, but instead used single dry-pin all-steel tracks.

The sWS went into production at the Büssing-NAG plant in Berlin and also at the Ringhofer-Tatra plant in Czechoslovakia, but production was very slow. The sWS did not have a very high production priority and from time to time Bomber Command weighed in to disrupt things to an extent that in place of the expected 150 vehicles per month, from December 1943 (when production commenced) to Septem-

ber 1944 only 381 had been delivered. These serious shortcomings in production led to the hasty 'Maultier' improvisation, but sWS production limped on almost until the end of the war and some survived to serve the new Czech army for a number of years after the war.

The small numbers produced did not prevent the sWS from being subjected to the usual special-purpose variants. The basic truck model could be converted to act as a rudimentary front-line ambulance carrying stretchers under a canvas awning mounted on a frame. A special front-line supply version was fitted with an armoured cab and engine cover, and a similar arrangement was used for a projected version that would have carried a 3.7-cm Flak 43 anti-aircraft gun on a flatbed area at the rear; only a few of these **3.7-cm Flak 43 auf sWS** versions were produced. Another variant proposed but built in small numbers only was an armoured version with a hull over the rear. On the roof of this hull was placed a 10-barrel launcher for 15-cm (5.9-in) artillery rockets; 10 rockets were carried in the launcher tubes and more inside the hull. This **15-cm Panzerwerfer 42 (Zehuling) auf sWS** version was

to have had a crew of five, but it is doubtful if many actually reached the service stage.

Although few were actually produced when compared to the totals of other German halftracks, the sWS proved efficient enough in service, and was proportionately far more cost-effective than some other models.

Specification
sWS
Crew: 2
Weights: about 13500 kg (29,762 lb)
Powerplant: one Maybach HL 42 6-cylinder petrol engine developing 74.6 kW (100 hp)
Dimensions: length 6.68 m (21 ft 11 in); width 2.50 m (8 ft 2.4 in); height 2.83 m (9 ft 3.4 in)

During 1944 a number of Maultier trucks were fitted with armoured bodies onto which the 10-barrelled Panzerwerfer 42 was placed. Some 300 of these conversions were made, and were used to provide rocket artillery support for armoured formations. They had a crew of three and most of the conversions were made by Opel.

The schwerer Wehrmachtsschlepper was intended to be a low-cost general-purpose tractor to fulfil a number of roles. Production started during 1943 but always lagged behind demand, leading to the development of the Maultier. This version was fitted with an armoured cab as a forward supply vehicle.

Performance: maximum road speed 27 km/h (16.8 mph)
Armament: none

SdKfz 8 schwerer Zugkraftwagen 12t

As has already been mentioned, the SdKfz designation followed no logical sequence and the **SdKfz 8 schwerer Zugkraftwagen 12t** was actually the first of the German halftracks to be developed and produced. It consequently established many of the features and design details that were later to be used on other German halftrack designs. The line of development that led to the SdKfz 8 can be traced back to World War I, when Daimler-Benz was involved in some early halftrack design work, one result of which was an advanced vehicle known as the **Marienwagen**. After 1919 Daimler-Benz continued its development work, bringing out a series of vehicles, one of which attracted the attention of the Red Army (in 1931 there was even talk of a Soviet production order). This appears never to have come about, for instead the German army ordered a model known as the **Daimler-Benz DB S 7**. Later versions followed the general layout of this 1931 vehicle, but gradually more powerful engines were fitted until the series reached the **Daimler-Benz DB 10**.

The SdKfz 8 was designed as an artillery tractor, and an artillery tractor it remained throughout its service life. There was only one variation, a 1940 conversion of what was probably only one vehicle to mount an 8.8-cm (3.46-in) Flak 18. This was used in action in France in May 1940, and thereafter no

mention of this offshoot can be found. The SdKfz 8 remained in production until 1944 as an artillery tractor. Originally it was produced to tow two modernized ex-World War I artillery pieces, the 15-cm (5.9-in) K 16 and the 21-cm (8.27-in) lange Mörser, a stubby howitzer. As more modern equipment came into use the SdKfz 8 switched to towing weapons such as the heavy 8.8-cm Flak 41 and the even larger 17-cm (6.7-in) K 18 long-range gun. The SdKfz 8 was also used by the Luftwaffe to tow the ponderous 10.5-cm (4.13-in) Flak 38 and 39 anti-aircraft guns. At times these tractors were called upon to tow tank-carrying semi-trailers or other forms of heavy trailer, but usually the artillery batteries retained their vehicles jealously.

By late 1942 there were 1,615 SdKfz 8s in service. Production was concentrated at two main centres, the Daimler-Benz works at Berlin-Marienfelde and the Kruppwerke at Mülhausen. At one time some production work was also carried out the Skodawerke at Pilsen, and in the years after the war the new Czech army used a large number of SdKfz 8s, some of them lasting until well into the 1960s.

One variation of the SdKfz 8 was a vehicle known as the **HK 1601**. This differed from the normal Sdkfz 8 in many ways and was an attempt to combine the features of the large 18t halftracks and the SdKfz 8. The prototype

appeared in late 1941 and after three more had been built it was decided to produce a batch of another 30. These were apparently built and used on the Eastern Front. They had a cargo-type body to carry the crew of 13. Production of the SdKfz 8 ceased during 1944.

Specification
SdKfz 8
Crew: 13
Weight: 15000 kg (33,069 lb)
Powerplant: one Maybach HL 85 12-cylinder petrol engine developing 138.0 kW (185 hp)

A group of assorted British soldiers take advantage of a ride on a captured SdKfz 8 schwerer Zugkraftwagen 12t, somewhere in North Africa. The normal capacity of this vehicle was 13 men, but it has been exceeded here. This is the basic artillery tractor version of the SdKfz 8.

Dimensions: length 7.35 m (24 ft 1.4 in); width 2.50 m (8 ft 2.4 in); height 2.81 m (9 ft 2.6 in)
Performance: maximum road speed 51 km/h (31.7 mph)

SdKfz 9 schwerer Zugkraftwagen 18t

By far the largest of all the World War II halftracks was the mighty **SdKfz 9 schwerer Zugkraftwagen 18t**, a vehicle that had its origins in a requirement made during 1936 for a heavy recovery vehicle to support the Panzer formations and tow disabled tanks. The development contract was awarded to the Famo Fahrzeugwerke und Motorwerke AG at Breslau, which became the sole producer. The first example appeared in 1936: this was the **FM gr 1**, and later came two other models, the **FM gr 2** and **FM gr 3** which used larger and more powerful engines.

In the end both tractor and recovery versions of the SdKfz 9 were produced. The tractor version was the basic SdKfz 9, which was used to tow the German army's really heavy artillery weapons and some heavy engineer equipment including bridging (for which there was a tractor unit towing bridge units on special trailers and carrying 15 men). Among the heavy artillery towed by the SdKfz 9 were the 24-cm (9.45-in) K 3 (so large it had to be towed in five loads), the Krupp 21-cm (8.27-in) K 38, and the various Skoda heavy howitzers and guns. The Luftwaffe used a small number of tractors to tow the mobile versions of the superheavy 12.8-cm (5.04-in) Flak 40. An anti-aircraft gun was used on one weapon-carrier version of the SdKfz 9 which appeared in 1943. This variant carried a 8.8-cm (3.46-in) Flak 37, and the vehicle had an armoured cab. The sides of the rear firing platform could be folded down to act as a working platform for the gun crew, and there were small outrigger arms to stabilize the vehicle in action. Only one conversion was made.

The recovery versions appeared in two forms, the **SdKfz 9/1** and **SdKfz 9/2**.

The sdKfz 9/1 had a crane (*Drehkran*) with a 6000-kg (13,228-lb) lifting capacity, but this was insufficient for some lifting tasks and the SdKfz 9/2 was produced with a 10000-kg (22,046-lb) crane. Outrigger legs were fitted on the latter, and an extra jib was provided to suspend a counter-weight when really heavy loads were to be lifted. These vehicles were massive equipments, and although they were capable of dealing with tanks up to the size of the PzKpfw IV they could not handle the heavier Panthers and Tigers. Since the SdKfz 9 was the only recovery vehicle in use when these 'heavies' entered service, a way had to be found and the type was used in sections of three vehicles, at least two being needed to recover Tigers from some situations. In order to provide them with more traction some were fitted with a large earth spade at the

rear, but even so two vehicles still had to be used to drag a Tiger out of a ditch, and sometimes three to tow one in a disabled state. The only answer to that was to develop a heavy tracked recovery vehicle, which duly appeared as the Bergepanther.

Production of the SdKfz 9 ceased during 1944, by which time the last versions were powered by the same Maybach engines as those fitted to PzKpfw IV tanks. They were massive vehicles that were certainly impressive to look at, but one has to bear in mind that the basic tractor version cost 60,000 Reichsmarks: a Panther cost 117,100.

Specification
SdKfz 9
Crew: 9
Weight: 18000 kg (39,683 lb)

The SdKfz 9 schwere Zugkraftwagen 18t was the largest of the German halftracks and was used to tow heavy guns and similar equipment, mainly as a recovery vehicle, some being fitted with cranes and jibs for this role. This example is a heavy artillery tractor and could carry nine men.

Powerplant: one Maybach HL V-12 petrol engine developing 186.4 kW (250 hp)
Dimensions: length 8.25 m (27 ft 0.8 in); width 1.60 m (8 ft 6 in); height 2.76 m (9 ft 0.7 in)
Performance: maximum road speed 50 km/h (31 mph)
Armament: none

American halftracks

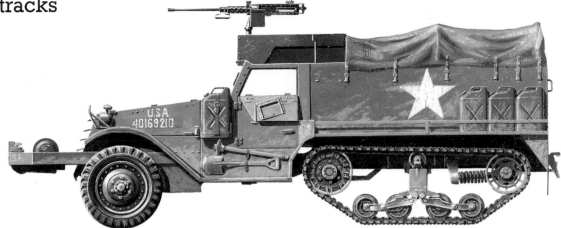

It is difficult to condense the entire story of the American halftrack into a few hundred words, for to even list the number of types would probably fill this study. The American halftrack development history started during the 1920s, when some Citröen-Kégresse halftracks were purchased, and subsequent trials led to a long series of development models before the hull of the White Scout Car M2 was allied with a Kégresse halftrack suspension and the 'classic' American halftrack emerged as the **Half-Track Car M2** that went into production in early 1941, the first examples reaching the troops in May of that year.

Thereafter the halftracks rolled off the assembly lines in their thousands. It would be easy to say that most of them were personnel carriers, but also included in the totals were mortar carriers, multiple gun motor carriages, gun motor carriages, trucks and a vast array of experimental types of all kinds. All manner of weapons were hung upon the basic halftrack chassis at one time or another but among those that were used in action were 57-mm (2.244-in) anti-tank guns, 75-mm (2.95-in) field guns and even 105-mm (4.13-in) howitzers. Anti-aircraft versions carried varying multiples of 12.7-mm (0.5-in) machine-guns, 20-mm cannon and 40-mm Bofors guns. Combat engineer equipment was another widely carried load (each model had racks along the sides to carry anti-tank mines).

It was the personnel carriers that were the most widely used, and in several versions. The early M2 was supplemented by the later **Half-Track Personnel Carrier M3** which could also be used as a communications vehicle, an artillery tow vehicle, and as an armoured ambulance. The even later **Half-Track Personnel Carrier M5** differed in production methods and there was also a **Half-Track Car M9**. Seating varied between models from 10 to 13, and there were various dispositions of machine-gun mountings. The usual arrangement was a 12.7-mm Browning at the front on a large ring mounting and a 7.62-mm (0.3-in) Browning on a pintle at the rear. To this could be added the weapons of the carried troops, and the picture of halftracks firing away as they went into action is complete. It now seems impossible to visualize troops operating in Europe in 1944 and 1945 without halftracks somewhere in the picture, for the Americans issued halftracks of all kinds to their Allies, including the British who started to use American halftracks even before the fighting in North Africa ended. Production of halftracks was some 41,170 units.

Above: The American M3 halftrack was such a widely used vehicle that it became a virtual trademark of the US Army and other Allied forces, including the Red Army. This M3 is complete with the canvas tilt, a forward-mounted winch and the 'pulpit' machine-gun mounting, here with a 0.50-in (12.7-mm) Browning.

After the war the halftrack story did not end, and even now is still not over for the halftrack in several forms is still a front-line vehicle for the Israel Defence Forces. Re-engined and refurbished for the umpteenth time, halftracks continue to be used by the mechanized formations of the Israeli army although most have now been relegated to the Reserve forces. Other armed forces still use halftracks, but now the most common use is as a recovery vehicle, a role that commenced during World War II with the Allied forces. It should not be forgotten that during World War II one of the halftrack user nations was the Soviet Union, for large numbers were shipped there from 1942 onwards. Rumour has it that some still survive with some of the smaller Warsaw Pact nations.

Specification
M3
Crew: 13
Weight: 9299 kg (20,500 lb)
Powerplant: one White 160AX 6-cylinder petrol engine developing 109.6 kW (147 hp)
Dimensions: length 6.18 m (20 ft 3.5 in); width 2.22 m (7 ft 3.5 in); height 2.26 m (7 ft 5 in)
Performance: maximum road speed 64.4 km/h (40 mph); range 282 km (175 miles); gradient 31°; fording 0.81 m (32 in)
Armament: one 12.7-mm (0.5-in) machine-gun and one 7.62-mm (0.3-in) machine-gun

An early shot of the M2 halftrack, taken when the US Army was still using the World War I helmets and equipment. This vehicle still has the original centre-mounted machine-gun mount for a 0.30-inch (7.62-mm) Browning machine-gun, and lacks the side racks for anti-tank mines that were often fitted to operational vehicles.

Unic Kégresse P 107

Some confusion still remains as to the actual manufacturer of the French halftrack known as the **P 107**. Some references state it was produced by the Unic concern while others refer to this vehicle as the Citröen-Kégresse P 107. The truth is that both companies produced the P 107, Citröen having what may now be described as the design parentage. Citröen employed Kégresse for some years after the engineer's return from Russia to France, and accordingly Citröen produced a long string of half-track designs using the Kégresse rubber-based track under the Citröen-Kégresse label. The P 107 was but one of these designs, and the first of this type appeared during the late 1930s. The P 107 went on to be among the more numerous of the many French halftracks.

The P 107 was produced in two forms. One was an artillery tractor for light field pieces and anti-tank guns. This version had a soft top covering the space for the crew of from five to seven men, and lockers at the rear for ammunition and other supplies. The second version, produced in smaller numbers, was an engineer tractor. This had an open cargo body behind the cab and was used to tow trailers carrying combat engineer equipment such as bridging pontoons. By 1939 both types were in French army service in some numbers. Both were sound and reliable vehicles and the demand for them was such that both Unic and Citröen had production lines devoted to them, hence the confusion in name.

The events of May 1940 caused a change of ownership for the P 107's. Large numbers of both types of vehicle fell into German hands and they had another change of name, this time to **leichter Zugkraftwagen U 304(f)**. Always short of halftracks, the German army took the type into immediate service and the French halftracks that had once towed French anti-tank guns were used to tow German weapons such as the 3.7-cm (1.456-in) Pak 35/36 anti-tank gun and later the hybrid 7.5-cm (2.95-in) Pak 97/38. But not content with this use the Germans decided to go one better. Deciding that the P 107 fell into the same category as the SdKfz 250 series, the Germans converted the French vehicles to become substitute **leichter Schützenpanzerwagen**. The French vehicles were stripped of their superstructures and fitted with armoured hulls almost exactly like those of the SdKfz 250 series and when completed they were used in exactly the same way as their German counterparts (apart from the fact that some were used as armoured ambulances). The one 'French' feature the Germans did not change was the forward-mounted roller under the nose of the vehicle. This was used to assist the vehicle in and out of ditches and similar obstacles and proved so useful it was not removed. Most of these conversions were retained for use in France by the units based there, and many were used during the fighting in Normandy in June 1944. Some of the original tractors were also encountered, so not all the P 107s underwent the armoured conversion.

Specification
P 107
Crew: 5-7
Weights: empty 2350 kg (5,181 lb); loaded 4050 kg (8,929 lb)
Powerplant: one 4-cylinder petrol

engine developing 41.0 kW (55 hp)
Dimensions: length 4.85 m (15 ft 10.9 in); width 1.80 m (5 ft 10.9 in); height 1.95 m (6 ft 4.8 in)
Performance: max road speed 45 km/h (28 mph); range 400 km (248.5 miles)
Armament: none

Above: this little Citroën-Kégresse five-seater was one of many French light halftracks that were used during the 1920s to develop the Kégresse rubber-based track. Many of these light halftracks were still in use in 1939, mainly as staff cars.

Soviet halftracks

For various reasons the Soviet Union did not make great use of halftracks during World War II other than employing American halftracks supplied to them under Lend-Lease. One of the main reasons for this was the relative cost in expense and production facilities that the halftrack demanded, and as the Soviet Union already had a large and productive full-tracked tractor industry geared to the requirements of the various agricultural Five-Year Plans, tracked tractors were frequently used for artillery when halftracks might otherwise have been considered.

This suggests that the Soviets were not interested in the halftrack concept; but they were. They recognized the strength of their mobility and handling advantages, and in 1931 considered the purchase of 12-tonne halftracks from Germany. At that time their interest was such that two indigenous designs were placed into limited production. These were the **YaSP** and the **Zis-33** trucks converted to the halftrack configuration, and later also used as artillery tractors. The YaSP was produced at Yaroslavl and was a Ya G-5 Komits truck fitted at the rear with a halftrack suspension (derived from the track system of the T-26 light tank) allied to a new drive shaft from the main engine at the front. The Zis-33 was a somewhat simpler vehicle that retained the main rear drive wheel allied to a halftrack suspension, and was built using the Zis-5 truck.

The relative success of these two design ventures engendered more during 1936. Most of these did not get very far. One was the **VM Pikap**, a version of the Zis-6 light truck. In 1937 more models appeared, most of them intended for the artillery tractor role. They included a 1¼-ton model (the **Vezdekhods Model B**), a 1½-ton model (the **BM**) and a 2-ton model (the **VZ**). As far as can be determined only the latter two models actually got to the production stage, and again they were halftrack conversions of existing trucks.

By the time 1941 came around the Soviet armed forces had few halftracks in service compared with the number of wheeled or fully-tracked vehicles. Many of what they did have were soon lost during the German advances of 1941, and all captured German halftracks were pressed into Soviet use. The Red Army soldiers soon learned how useful these were, and from 1942 onwards there was a deliberate programme to make use of even damaged German halftracks. Hulks were salvaged from battlefields and stripped of all useful items, especially the running wheel, tracks and drive components. These were taken to the GAZ plant in the Urals where they were allied with GAZ-63 trucks to form **GAZ-60** troop carriers. The GAZ-60 used all manner of German components, the most favoured being those from the SdKfz 251 series of vehicles. Few of these wartime expedient vehicles survived the war years.

One other known Soviet halftrack produced during 1942 was known as the **Zis-42**. It was a 2½-ton semi-tracked weapons carrier, but no other details have survived so it does not appear to have been produced in quantity.

Left: The Soviets made extensive use of US M3 halftracks supplied under Lend-Lease, modifying them for their own use. Here two M3s of the Red Army are seen fitted with 76.2-mm (3-in) guns as improvised tank destroyers, an arrangement the US army also experimented with.

Below: One of the most successful Soviet pre-war halftracks, the Zis-33 was built on a truck chassis. This vehicle is seen with a propaganda unit broadcasting news of Red Army victories in the south to German positions in the north.

The Soviets made great use of captured German halftrack components to construct hybrids like this GAZ truck.

Armoured Cars

Battles are often won as a result of a commander having more accurate information than his opponent. For a long time, such battlefield information was provided by the cavalry, but in the fast-moving mechanized war of 1939–45 it was the armoured car that operated on many fronts, ranging far ahead of its parent formations.

The armoured car today retains a niche in modern armoured warfare largely unchanged since the early days of World War II: its primary function was one of scouting and reconnaissance. The armoured car has this role because it is generally much faster and handier to employ than the more ponderous tank, though the armoured car does pay for these attributes by being relatively thinly armoured and lightly armed, if, indeed, it possesses any armament at all. In short, the armoured car has to rely on speed and manoeuvrability to survive. However, its reconnaissance role is a vital one as modern armoured and infantry formations cannot operate without knowing what is happening 'on the other side of the hill'.

By 1939 the armoured car had settled into an established form. It usually had a 4 x 4 drive configuration (although many larger designs had as many as eight wheels on four axles) and it was usually purpose-built. This did not prevent extemporized designs, such as the early South African Marmon Herringtons, from providing excellent service, but generally speaking most armoured cars were designed specifically for their job and were not the hurried conversions from

A German Panzerspähwagen or armoured car belonging to the 'Das Reich' Division of the Waffen-SS on the Eastern Front in the summer of 1941.

commercial chassis that were the general rule in World War I. The role of the armoured car had also been formalized, and by 1939 this car and the little scout cars were an integral part of the reconnaissance structure of virtually every type of operational structure from the German Panzer division to the ordinary infantry division.

It would be safe to say that the armoured car units had a relatively free and easy war. Their casualties were often heavy, but in general they enjoyed the benefits of

operating well away from the formal methods and organizational structure of the rest of their army, and they were thus able to employ their own initiative and tactics in a way that was impossible in most other units. They ranged far and wide, sometimes took part in spectacular raids and generally took the battle to the enemy, but in all armies their primary function was one of reconnaissance. The success of the armoured cars was not measured in casualties and combat but in

the quality and accuracy of the information and intelligence they were able to pass back to the rear. Their armament was primarily defensive, and although superlative fighting vehicles, such as the Puma and M8 Greyhound, were put in service, it should be borne in mind that perhaps the most successful of the vehicles described here was the little Daimler scout car, a vehicle type that survives to this day in the British Ferret reconnaissance vehicle.

Automitrailleuse Panhard et Levassor Type 178

The **Automitrailleuse Panhard et Levassor Type 178** armoured car was first produced in 1935, and was developed from a design known as the **TOE-M-32**, which was intended for use in the French North African colonies and mounted a short 37-mm turret gun. Panhard used this design as a basis for a new French army requirement but gave the new vehicle a 4×4 drive configuration and moved the engine to the rear of the vehicle. The result was the Panhard 178 and the armament varied from a single 25-mm cannon on some vehicles to two 7.5-mm (0.295-in) machine-guns on others, while some command vehicles had extra radios but no armament. The Panhard 178 was known also as the **Panhard Modèle 1935**.

The Panhard 178 was put into production for the French infantry and cavalry formation reconnaissance groups. Production was slow, but by 1940 there were appreciable numbers available for the fighting which followed the German invasion in May. Many of the Panhard 178s were in widely scattered units and were unable to take much part in the fighting that ensued, so many were seized intact by the victorious Germans. The Germans liked the sound design of the Panhard 178 and decided to take it into their own service as the **Panzerspähwagen P 204(f)**, some of them being rearmed with 37-mm anti-tank guns and/or German machine-guns. Some of these were retained for garrison use in France, but others were later sent to the USSR, where the type was used for behind-the-lines patrol duties against Soviet partisans. Some were even converted for railway use, having their conventional wheels changed to railway wheels, and many of these 'railway' conversions were fitted with extra radios and prominent frame aerials.

Perhaps the most unusual use of the Panhard 178s took place in 1941 and 1942, when 45 vehicles, hidden from the Germans by French cavalry units following the defeat of 1940, were pre-

pared by Resistance personnel for possible use against the Germans. These vehicles had no turrets, but these were manufactured under the nose of the Germans and fitted with 25-mm or 47-mm guns and/or machine-guns. The armoured cars were then secretly distributed throughout centres of resistance mainly in unoccupied France, where many were subsequently taken over by the German forces when they took over the unoccupied areas of France in November 1942.

After the Liberation the Panhard 178 was once more put into production during August 1944 at the Renault fac-

tory outside Paris. These new vehicles had a larger turret with a 47-mm gun, and were later known as the **Panhard 178B**. The new vehicles were issued to the new French cavalry units and were used for many years after 1945. Some saw action in Indo-China, and it was not until 1960 that the last of them was taken out of service.

Specification
Panhard 178
Crew: 4
Weight: (in action) 8.5 tonnes
Dimensions: length overall 4.79 m (15 ft 8½ in); width 2.01 m (6 ft 7¼ in); height 2.31 m (7 ft 7 in)

Two Automitrailleuse Panhard et Levassor Type 178s are seen here in German service following the fall of France in 1940. The Germans found them good enough for them to take into their own service, and many were used for anti-partisan operations in the USSR.

Powerplant: one 6.33-litre water-cooled petrol engine developing 105 bhp (78 kW)
Performance: maximum road speed 72 km/h (45 mph); road range 300 km (186 miles); fording 0.6 m (1 ft 11½ in); gradient 40°; vertical obstacle 0.3 m (11¾ in); trench 0.6 m (11¾ in)

schwerer Panzerspähwagen SdKfz 231

The **schwerer Panzerspähwagen SdKfz 231** 6×4 heavy armoured car had its origins at the Kazan test centre established in the Soviet Union during the 1920s. There the German automobile industry developed an 8×8 armoured car chassis that proved to be too expensive for further development, so a 6×4 chassis was tried instead. This model used a truck chassis as its basis, and originally this was a Daimler-Benz product but later Büssing-NAG and Magirus chassis and engines were employed. These chassis were fitted with suitable armoured hulls and turrets, and modifications were made to allow steering from either end of the hull. Early trials demonstrated the need for stronger front axles and revised radiators, and the resulting vehicle was issued to German army units during 1932. Production continued until 1935, by which time about 1,000 had been produced.

The 6×4 armoured cars were not a great success but they were produced at a time when the German army lacked experience in the use of armoured vehicles, and were thus invaluable as

training and preparation equipments. Using lorry chassis carrying armoured hulls that were really too heavy for their supporting structures, the six-wheeled armoured cars were under-powered and had only limited cross-

country capabilities. But when used on roads they were as good as anything else available, and they were used to good effect during the occupations of Austria and Czechoslovakia during 1938 and 1939, and were also used in

combat in Poland and France. Their very appearance had great propaganda impact, and they were accordingly given great media coverage at the time. After 1940 they gradually faded from front-line use and were relegated

Schwerer Panzerspähwagen SdKfz 231 armed with a 20-mm (0.787-in) cannon. This pre-war design used a truck chassis as its basis, but the overall weight made the vehicle unsuitable for prolonged cross-country use.

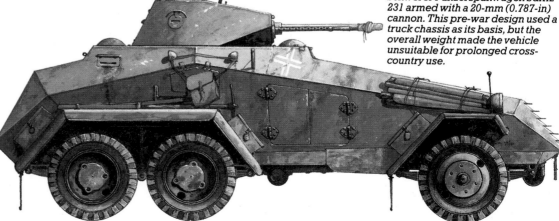

mainly to training roles.

Early examples of the six-wheeled armoured cars had provision for only one 7.92-mm (0.31-in) MG 34 machine-gun in the turret, but the version used mainly by the heavy platoons of the German army motorized units was the SdKfz 231. This had a turret mounting a 20-mm cannon, originally the KwK 30 but later the KwK 38 with a higher rate of fire. Mounted co-axially with this cannon was a 7.92-mm (0.31-in) MG 34, and there was provision for an anti-aircraft machine-gun on the turret roof. The SdKfz 231 was used as a tactical vehicle (undertaking a combat role in direct fire support of motorized infantry units mounted on trucks or later on halftracks), but at times it was also used in support of light reconnaissance units for Panzer formations. Another vehicle that was very similar to the SdKfz 231 was the **SdKfz 232**, which was basically a Sdkfz 231 fitted with a long-range radio set that required the fitting of a large and prominent frame aerial above the turret and over the hull rear, the turret acting as a support for the forward part of the aerial. Another similar vehicle was the **SdKfz 263**, which also had a large frame aerial, though on this vehicle the turret was fixed and had provision for a single machine-gun only. The SdKfz 263 was used as a command vehicle.

Specification
SdKfz 231
Crew: 4
Weight: (in action) 5.7 tonnes
Dimensions: length overall 5.57 m (18 ft 6¾ in); width 1.82 m (5 ft 11½ in); height 2.25 m (7 ft 4½ in)
Powerplant: one Daimler-Benz,

Büssing-NAG or Magirus water-cooled petrol engine developing between 60 and 80 bhp (45 and 60 kW)
Performance: maximum road speed 65 km/h (40 mph); maximum road range 250 km (150 miles); maximum cross-country range 200 km (125 miles); gradient 20°; fording 0.6 m (24 in)

Schwerer Panzerspähwagen SdKfz 232s seen during a pre-war parade in Berlin. These vehicles were equipped with a large and cumbersome radio antenna mounted over the turret which remained static while the turret rotated.

---

schwerer Panzerspähwagen SdKfz 231(8-Rad)

Almost as soon as the first six-wheeled armoured cars were issued to the expanding German army during the mid-1930s the German staff planners realized that they were not the vehicles that would be required in the long term as they were underpowered and lacked cross-country mobility. They requested an eight-wheeled armoured car with an engine to match, and decided to develop a Büssing-NAG 8×8 lorry chassis for use as an armoured car. Development began in full during 1935 and the first production examples were issued to the Army in 1937.

This 8×8 heavy armoured car was known as the **schwerer Panzer-spähwagen SdKfz 231**, and to avoid confusion with the six-wheeled armoured cars with the same designation the new series was always suffixed (8-Rad), and the troops knew the type as the Achtrad. When the new eight-wheelers appeared in service they were among the most advanced cross-country vehicles yet produced, but the high road-speed and mobility had been purchased only at a high price in chassis complexity, for the layout was highly complicated, expensive and slow to produce. The chassis had all-wheel drive and steering, and fully-independent suspension, and the vehicle was even able to travel across the thick mud of the Eastern Front. If the vehicle had one major fault other than its complexity it was that it was rather high and showed up prominently in combat.

The SdKfz 231 series remained in production until 1942, when it was phased out in favour of the SdKfz 234 series. By then 1,235 had been produced, and the type remained in widespread use throughout the war on all fronts. The type was particularly prominent in the North African campaigns.

The SdKfz 231(8-Rad) had a turret with a 20-mm KwK 30 or KwK 38 cannon with a co-axial 7.92-mm (0.31-in) MG 34 machine gun. The **SdKfz 232(8-Rad)** was the radio version with a prominent frame aerial, and the **SdKfz 263(8-Rad)** was a command version with a fixed superstructure in place of the rotating turret, and featuring a large frame aerial for the long-range radio equipments carried. The **SdKfz 233** had no direct six-wheeler equivalent, for it mounted a short 75-mm (2.95-in) tank gun (Stummelkanone) as used on early PzKpfw IV tanks. This gun was mounted in an open compartment formed by the removal of the normal turret and there was only a limited traverse for the gun. This vehicle had a crew of only three men, and was used to provide armoured reconnaissance units with improved offensive power.

The first SdKfz 233 was issued during late 1942 and proved to be highly effective, but there were times when the gun's limited traverse and lack of armour-piercing performance proved to be a liability. However, when pitted against the usual run-of-the-mill reconnaissance vehicles it was likely to encounter, the SdKfz 233 was very effective and often provided covering fire for other Achtrads.

Specification
SdKfz 231(8-Rad)
Crew: 4
Weight: (in action) 8.3 tonnes
Dimensions: length overall 5.85 m (19 ft 2 in); width 2.20 m (7 ft 2½ in); height 2.34 m (7 ft 8 in)
Powerplant: one Büssing-NAG L8V-Gs water-cooled petrol engine

This early example of a schwerer Panzerspähwagen 231 (8-Rad) is armed with a 20-mm (0.787-in) cannon and shows the distinctive spaced armoured stowage bin mounted on the front hull. The size and bulk of this vehicle in relation to the armament carried can be seen in this view; the complexity cannot.

developing 150 hp (112 kW)
Performance: maximum road speed 85 km/h (53 mph); maximum cross-country speed 30 km/h (19 mph); road radius of action 270 km (170 miles); cross-country radius of action 150 km (95 miles); fording 1.0 m (3 ft 3⅓ in); gradient 30°; vertical obstacle 0.5 m (1 ft 7¾ in); trench 1.25 m (4 ft 1¼ in)

leichter Panzerspähwagen SdKfz 222

When the Nazis came to power in Germany, the army was given a virtually free hand in selecting new equipment for the expanding German armed forces, and among the equipment requested was a new series of light armoured cars to be built on a standard chassis. The requirements laid down by the army were so demanding that commercial models could not be adapted to meet them, so an entirely new design was produced and in 1935 this was used as the basis for the **leichter Panzerspähwagen SdKfz 221** 4×4, a light three-man vehicle with a small turret mounting a single 7.92-mm (0.31-in) machine-gun. From this evolved the **SdKfz 222** armoured car with a slightly larger armoured turret with an open top and the potential to mount a slightly heavier armament. The first SdKfz 222 appeared in 1938 and thereafter was adopted as the standard German army armoured car for use by the new divisional reconnaissance units.

The SdKfz 222 was initially referred to as a Waffenwagen, or weapons vehicle, as it mounted a 20-mm KwK 30 cannon, a version of the standard anti-aircraft cannon adapted for use in armoured vehicles. Later the 20-mm KwK 38 was also used. Mounted alongside this cannon was a 7.92-mm (0.31-in) MG 34 machine-gun, and this combination left little room inside the turret for the commander/gunner and the radio operator, who were further restricted in action by the use of a wire screen over the top of the open turret to prevent hand grenades from being lobbed into the vehicle. The driver was situated centrally in the front of the hull, and the superstructure was made up from well-sloped armoured plates to provide extra protection. During the war the thickness of the front hull plates was increased from 14.5 mm (0.57 in) to 30 mm (1.18 in) and the 20-mm cannon mounting was adapted to provide more elevation for use against aircraft targets.

Once in widespread service the SdKfz 222 proved to be a reliable and popular little vehicle. It served well in France during 1940, often racing far ahead of the following Panzer columns, and in North Africa the type proved itself to be a very useful reconnaissance vehicle, although somewhat res-

tricted in its operational range by the amount of fuel that could be carried in the internal tanks. This restriction proved to be a problem during the invasion of the Soviet Union after 1941, to the extent that the SdKfz 222 was replaced by the SdKfz 250/9 halftrack mounting the same turret and used for the same role. In the west the SdKfz 222 continued in service until the end of the war, and in the Soviet Union the type was used for patrol duties in rear areas.

The SdKfz 221 and SdKfz 222 were not the only armoured cars of their line. There was also the **SdKfz 223**, which could be recognized by a large frame aerial over the rear of the vehicle hull as the vehicle was used as a command and communications centre and carried only a single machine-gun. The **SdKfz 260** was a long-range radio vehicle, used at higher command levels only, and the **SdKfz 261** was similar. The **SdKfz 247** was a personnel and stores carrier.

The SdKfz 222 was exported in some numbers to China before 1939, and once there was adapted to take a wide range of armament that ranged from heavy machine-guns to light anti-tank guns. Numbers of SdKfz 221s were also sent to China.

Specification
SdKfz 222
Crew: 3
Weight: (in action) 4.8 tonnes
Dimensions: length overall 4.80 m (14 ft 8½ in); width 1.95 m (6 ft 4¾ in); height 2.00 m (6 ft 6¾ in) with grenade screen
Powerplant: one Horch/Auto-Union V8-108 water-cooled petrol engine developing 81 hp (60 kW)
Performance: maximum road speed 80 km/h (50 mph); maximum cross country speed 40 km/h (25 mph); road radius of action 300 km (187 miles); cross-country radius of action 180 km (110 miles); gradient 20°; fording 0.6 m (24 in)

The leichte Panzerspähwagen SdKfz 222 is seen here in its usual form, armed with a 20-mm (0.787-in) cannon and MG 34 machine-gun. The wire mesh anti-grenade screen roof is in position. Note the tool and fuel-can stowage and the number of stowage boxes on the exterior, as the interior was rather cramped.

On the left is a SdKfz 223 light communications vehicle with its large and distinctive frame aerial; on the right is a SdKfz 250/3 half track, a type of vehicle that proved more suited to service in the USSR.

Light Armored Car M8

Armoured cars have long been a feature of the American armoured fighting vehicle scene, and in 1940 and 1941 the US Army was able to observe operational trends in Europe and so develop a new armoured car with a good performance, a 37-mm (1.45-in) gun, 6×6 drive, a low silhouette and light weight. In typical American fashion design submissions were requested from four manufacturers. One of the manufacturers, Ford, produced a design known as the **T22**, and this was later judged to be the best of all

The American Light Armored Car M8 was considered too light in armour by the British, but was otherwise widely used. The main gun was a 37-mm (1.46-in) gun with a 7.62-mm (0.30-in) machine-gun mounted co-axially. A common addition was a 12.7-mm (0.50-in) Browning mounted on the turret.

submissions and was ordered into production as the **Light Armored Car M8.**

The M8 subsequently became the most important of all the American armoured cars and by the time production was terminated in April 1945 no fewer than 11,667 had been produced. It was a superb fighting vehicle with an excellent cross-country performance, and an indication of its sound design can be seen in the fact that many were still in use with several armies until the mid-1970s. It was a low vehicle with a full 6×6 drive configuration, with the axles arranged as one forward and two to the rear. The wheels were normally well covered by mudguards, but these were sometimes removed in action. The crew of four had ample room inside the vehicle, and the main 37-mm (1.46-in) gun was mounted in a circular open turret. A 7.62-mm (0.3-in) Browning machine-gun was mounted co-axially, and there was a pintle for a 12.7 mm (0.5-in) Browning heavy machine-gun (for anti-aircraft use) on the turret rear.

A close cousin of the M8 was the **Armored Utility Car M20,** in which the turret was removed and the fighting compartment cut away to allow the interior to be used as a personnel or supplies carrier. A machine-gun could be mounted on a ring mount over the open area. In many way the M20 became as important as the M8 for it proved to be an invaluable run-about for any number of purposes, ranging from an observation or command post to an ammunition carrier for tank units.

The US Army employed the M8 and M20 widely from the time the first production examples left the production lines in March 1943. By November of that year over 1,000 had been delivered, and during 1943 the type was issued to British and Commonwealth formations. The British knew the M8 as the **Greyhound** but it proved to be too thinly armoured to suit British thinking, the thin belly armour proving too vulnerable to anti-tank mines. Operationally this shortcoming was overcome by lining the interior floor areas with sandbags. But these drawbacks were more than overcome by the fact that the M8 was available in large numbers and that it was able to cross almost any terrain. The 37-mm (1.46-in) main gun was well able to tackle almost any enemy reconnaissance vehicle the M8 was likely to encounter, and the vehicle's crew could defend the M8 against infantry with the two machine-guns. The M8 could be kept going under all circumstanes, but its

main attribute was that it nearly always seemed to be available when it was wanted.

An M8 in a typical reconnaissance situation during the Normandy fighting of 1944. The crew have stopped to observe some enemy movement or positions, and two men are observing through binoculars to obtain as comprehensive an assessment as possible.

Specification
Light Armored Car M8
Crew: 4
Weight: (in action) 7.94 tonnes
Dimensions: length 5.00 m (16 ft 5 in); width 2.54 m (8 ft 4 in); height 2.248 m (7 ft 4½ in)
Powerplant: one Hercules JXD 6-cylinder petrol engine developing 110 hp (82 kW)
Performance: maximum road speed 89 km/h (55 mph); maximum range 563 km (350 miles); fording 0.61 m (24 in); gradient 60%; vertical obstacle 0.3 m (12 in)

Light Armored Car T17E1 Staghound

Although the **Staghound** armoured car was an American product, it was not used by the American forces, all the output going to the British army and other Allied and Commonwealth forces. The design had its origins in a US Army requirement for a heavy armoured car which was not produced despite the building of prototypes since the requirement was changed to a call for a medium armoured car. Following the drawing up of a specification, which was much influenced by input from British experience in combat, two vehicles emerged, One was the **Light Armoured Car T17,** a 6×6 vehicle by Ford, and the other the **Light Armored Car T17E1** from Chevrolet.

Only relatively few of the 6×6 T17 armoured cars were produced, as by the time the type was ready for production the requirement for a large 6×6 vehicle appeared to have passed. However, the 4×4 T17E1 went into large-scale production even though the US Army no longer had any requirement for the design. The British Tank Mission asked for an initial batch of 300, but more orders followed and by the end of 1942 the first examples were coming off the production lines. After the perilous journey across the Atlantic the T17E1s were issued to British and Commonwealth units as the **Staghound Mk I.**

The Staghound emerged as a large and well-armoured vehicle with a turret mounting a 37-mm (1.46-in) gun and a co-axial 7.62-mm (0.3-in) Browning machine-gun. The vehicle looked good and in service proved to be easy to drive and maintain, and in addition was fast and had a good operational range. The type first went into action in Italy in 1943, where it proved well able to deal with the difficult conditions that prevailed. Thereafter the Staghound was issued to Canadian, New Zealand, Indian and Belgian units. The

A Staghound AA armoured car with twin 12.7 mm (0.50 in) machine-guns intended specifically for the defence of armoured units against low-flying aircraft.

Staghound had several unusual features for the day, not the least of which was the fully automatic hydraulic transmission. The vehicle had two engines mounted side-by-side at the rear, and the crew were well provided with periscopes. The turret was hydraulically traversed, and additional armament was provided by two more 7.62-mm (0.3-in) Browning machine-guns, one pintle-mounted for AA use and the other in the hull front.

Once the Staghound was in service several variations appeared. One was the fitting of a 76.2-mm (3-in) tank howitzer in place of the 37-mm (1.46-in) gun for use as a close-support weapon. The Americans had produced the **T17E3** version with a short 75-mm (2.95-in) howitzer in the turret, but with the introduction of the British version, known as the **Staghound Mk II,** this was not further developed. Another British innovation was the **Staghound Mk III,** a rather drastic conversion of the vehicle to accommodate a Crusader tank turret mounting a 75-mm (2.95-in) gun.

Small numbers of these were issued to the heavy troops of armoured car regiments during 1944. A production variant developed in the USA was the **Staghound AA (T17E2)** which had the usual turret replaced by a new power-operated turret mounting two 12.7-mm (0.5-in) Browning machine guns for anti-aircraft use. An order for 1,000 of these was placed, but production ceased in April 1944 after 789 had been built: by then the decline of the Luftwaffe was such that there no longer seemed to be any real need for the type.

There were numerous other conversions and local variations of the Staghound, ranging from mine-clearing experimental models pushing heavy rollers to the **Staghound Command,** a version with the turret removed and increased internal stowage for radios, plus a folding canvas tilt. Local modifications such as the provision of extra external stowage boxes were common, and extras such as smoke dischargers and machine-guns

were added for additional protection.

After 1945 the Staghound served on in the British army for several years, and the type was also passed to such nations as India, South Africa and Denmark (which used the Staghound Mk III for some years). The Staghound was a sturdy and well-liked armoured car that gave excellent service.

Specification
Staghound Mk I
Crew: 5
Weight: (in action) 13.92 tonnes
Dimensions: length 5.486 m (18 ft 0 in); width 2.69 m (8 ft 10 in); height 2.36 m (7 ft 9 in)
Powerplant: two GMC 270 6-cylinder petrol engines each developing 97 hp (72 kW)
Performance: maximum speed 89 km/h (55 mph); maximum range 724 km (450 miles); fording 0.8 m (2 ft 8 in); gradient 57%; vertical obstacle 0.533 m (1 ft 9 in)

Marmon Herrington Armoured Cars

Despite the fact that the vehicle construction industry in South Africa had never before produced any armoured vehicles, in 1938 the government of the day ordered the development of two types of armoured car. Work on these was slow until the outbreak of war in 1939 when, after a quick survey of possible alternatives, the experimental vehicles were ordered into production. Orders soon swelled to 1,000 and, despite the fact that no facilities existed for the large-scale production of such vehicles, within only a few months the first examples were appearing.

The South Africans produced their armoured cars by importing Ford truck chassis from Canada, four-wheel drive transmissions from Marmon Herrington in the USA and the armament from the United Kingdom. Local assembly and production was undertaken in local vehicle assembly plants and railway workshops, and the armour plate was produced at local steel mills. The first vehicles were known under the designation **South African Reconnaissance Vehicle Mk I**, and these had a long wheelbase and a 4×2 drive configuration. The **South African Reconnaissance Vehicle Mk II** had a shorter wheelbase and a full 4×4 drive. After early experience with the Mk Is against the Italians in East Africa, the South Africans thereafter confined the vehicles mainly to training purposes, but the Mk IIs went on to better things.

The Mk II, known to the British as the **Armoured Car, Marmon Herrington, Mk II**, was a fairly simple but effective conversion of the original truck chassis to take the new 4×4 transmission and a well-shaped armoured hull. The early versions had a turret on the roof mounting a Vickers 7.7-mm (0.303-in) machine-gun, another light machine-gun being located in the hull front, but once this combination had been tried in action it was changed to a Boys 13.97-mm (0.55-in) anti-tank rifle mounted alongside a 7.7-mm (0.303-in) machine-gun in the turret. The vehicle had a crew of four housed in the roomy hull, and the engine was a Ford V-8.

When they were first produced and issued to South African and British units in North Africa, the Marmon Herringtons were the only armoured cars available in any numbers and they formed the main equipments used by the reconnaissance units during the early Western Desert campaigns. They proved to be surprisingly effective vehicles, but their 12-mm (0.47-in) armour was often too thin to be of much use, and the armament was really too light. The troops in the field made their own changes to the armament and all manner of weapons sprouted from the

A typical Marmon Herrington Mk II armoured car in desert guise and armed in typical fashion with a Vickers water-cooled machine-gun, a Bren gun and a Boys 13.97-mm (0.55-in) anti-tank rifle. The extra spare wheel and sand channel stowage were other 'local' extras.

turrets or from the open hulls once the turrets had been removed. One of the more common weapon fits was a captured Italian 20-mm Breda cannon, but Italian and German 37-mm (1.45-in) and 45-mm (1.77-in) tank or anti-tank guns were also used. One vehicle mounted a British 2-pdr (40-mm) tank gun, and this became the preferred armament for later marks. The **Armoured Car, Marmon Herrington Mk III** was basically similar to the Mk II though based on slightly shorter chassis, and lacked the double rear doors of the Mk II.

The Mk IIs had a hard time during the desert campaigns, but they kept going and were well-liked and sturdy vehicles. Local modifications were many and varied, and ranged from command and repair vehicles to versions with as many as four Bren guns in a turret. Gradually they were supplemented and eventually replaced by more formal armoured car designs such as the Humber. Later marks of Marmon Herrington served in other theatres, some even falling into Japanese hands in the Far East, and the number of formal versions was later extended to eight, including the Mk IV inspired by the German eight-wheeler armoured cars, but after the Mk IV most remained as prototype vehicles only. The **Armoured Car, Marmon Herrington Mk IV** was a markedly different vehicle, being a monocoque design with rear engine. Weighing 6.4 tons, the Mk IV was armed with a 2-pdr

(40-mm) gun and co-axial 7.62-mm (0.3-in) Browning machine-gun. A variant was the **Mk IVF** with Canadian Ford rather than Marmon Herrington automotive components.

For a nation with limited production and development potential the Marmon Herrington armoured cars were an outstanding South African achievement.

Specification
Armoured Car, Marmon Herrington Mk II
Crew: 4
Weight: (in action) about 6 tonnes

This official photograph shows a Marmon Herrington Mk II armoured car in its original form with a Vickers 7.7-mm (0.303-in) machine-gun in the turret and another in a side-mounted mantlet. This latter weapon position was soon discarded and extra weapon positions were provided around the open turret.

Dimensions: not known
Powerplant: one Ford V-8 petrol engine
Performance: maximum speed 80.5 km/h; maximum range 322 km (200 miles)

Humber Armoured Cars

The Humber armoured cars were numerically the most important types produced in the United Kingdom, for production eventually reached a total of 5,400. The type had its origins in a pre-war Guy armoured car known as the **Tank, Light, Wheeled Mk I**, of which Guy produced 101 examples by October 1940. In that month it was realized that Guy's production facilities would be fully occupied producing light tanks, so production was switch-

ed to the Rootes Group and Karrier Motors Limited of Luton in particular. There the Guy design was rejigged for installation on a Karrier KT 4 artillery tractor chassis, Guy continuing to supply the armoured hulls and turrets. Although the new model was virtually identical to the original Guy design it was subsequently re-named the **Armoured Car, Humber Mk I**.

The Humber Mk I had a relatively short wheelbase, but it was never man-

oeuvrable and used a welded hull. The turret mounted two Besa machine-guns, a heavy 15-mm (0.59-in) and a lighter 7.92-mm (0.31-in) weapon. The type had a crew of three: a commander who acted as his own wireless operator, a gunner and the driver in the front hull. The first production batch ran to 500 vehicles before the **Armoured Car, Humber Mk II** introduced some improvements, mainly to the front hull which had a pronounced

slope. The **Armoured Car, Humber Mk III** had a larger turret that allowed a crew of four to be carried, while the **Armoured Car, Humber Mk IV** reverted to a crew of three as the turret housed an American 37-mm (1.45-in) gun. An odd feature of this vehicle was that the driver was provided with a lever which raised a hatch covering an aperture in the rear bulkhead for use as rear vision in an emergency.

The first Humber armoured cars

were used operationally in the North African desert from late 1941 onwards, while the Humber Mk IV did not see service until the early stages of the Italian campaign, but thereafter all four marks were used wherever British and Allied troops fought in Europe. A version was produced in Canada with some changes made to suit Canadian production methods. This was known as the **Armoured Car, General Motors Mk I, Fox I**, and the main change so far as the troops in the field were concerned was that the main armament was a 12.7 mm (0.5-in) Browning heavy machine-gun plus a 7.62 mm (0.3-in) Browning medium machine-gun. There was also an extensive conversion of the Humber Mk III as a special radio carrier known as a Rear Link vehicle. This had a fixed turret with a dummy gun. Another radio-carrying version was used as a mobile artillery observation post, and numbers of Canadian Foxes were converted for this role. A later addition to many Humber armoured cars was a special anti-aircraft mounting using Vickers 'K' machine-guns that could be fired from within the turret; this mounting could also be used with Bren Guns. Smoke dischargers were another operational addition. A more extreme conversion was made with the **Armoured Car, Humber, AA, Mk I**, which had four 7.92-mm (0.31-in) Besa machine-guns

in a special turret. These were introduced during 1943 at the rate of one troop of four cars for every armoured car regiment, but they were withdrawn during 1944 as there was no longer any need for them.

After 1945 many Humber armoured cars were sold or otherwise passed to other armies. Some were still giving good service to armies in the Far East as late as the early 1960s.

Specification
Armoured Car, Humber Mks I to IV
Crew: 3 (4 in Mk III)
Weight: (in action) 6.85 tonnes (Mk I) or 7.1 tonnes (Mks II to IV)
Dimensions: length 4.572 m (15 ft 0 in); width 2.184 m (7 ft 2 in); height 2.34 m (7 ft 10 in)
Powerplant: one Rootes 6-cylinder water-cooled petrol engine developing 90 bhp (67 kW)

A Humber Armoured Car Mk II, one of the few armoured vehicles to use the 15-mm (0.59-in) Besa heavy machine-gun as its main armament. Originally known as a wheeled tank, these vehicles gave sterling service in many theatres through the war.

Performance: maximum speed 72 km/h (45 mph); maximum range 402 km (250 miles)

Daimler Armoured Cars

When the BSA Scout Car was undergoing its initial trials, it was decided to use the basic design as the foundation for a new vehicle to be known as the **Tank, Light, Wheeled**. As with the Scout Car, Daimler took over the development of the project, and the result was a vehicle that outwardly resembled the little Scout Car but was nearly twice as heavy and had a two-man turret. Work started on the project in August 1939 and the first prototypes were running by the end of the year, although troubles soon arose as the extra weight of the turret and armour overloaded the transmission. It took some time before these problems were overcome, and it was not until April 1941 that the first production examples appeared. By then the vehicle was known as the **Armoured Car, Daimler Mk I**.

The Daimler Armoured Car was basically a Scout Car enlarged to accommodate a turret mounting a 2-pdr (40-mm) gun. The turret was the same as that designed for the Tetrarch light tank intended for use by airborne forces, but when this was placed on the Daimler it was the first such installation on a British armoured car. The turret also mounted a co-axial 7.92-mm (0.31-in) Besa machine-gun, and many vehicles also had smoke dischargers mounted on the sides of the turret. The four-wheel drive used double-coil springs on each wheel station although the early idea of using four-wheel steering was discarded as being too complex an idea without real operational benefit. One advanced feature was the use of Girling hydraulic disc brakes, well in advance of general use elsewhere. A fluid flywheel was used in place of the more usual clutch arrangement. A duplicate steering wheel and simple controls were pro-

Above: The Daimler armoured car was one of the best of all the British armoured cars, and the one that became the standard equipment for many reconnaissance regiments. Armed with a 40-mm (1.57-in) 2-pdr gun, it had limited combat capability but proved to be an excellent and reliable reconnaissance vehicle in all theatres.

Right: A Daimler armoured car in North Africa during November 1942 carries an unusual load of German prisoners-of-war. Note the North African additions of the front-mounted sand channel and the rack for extra fuel cans on the side, plus the kit stowage all over the vehicle.

vided for use by the commander in an emergency to drive to the rear. The commander also had to double as loader for the main gun.

The Daimler underwent surprisingly few changes once in service. An **Armoured Car, Daimler Mk II** version was later introduced with a new gun mounting, a slightly revised radiator arrangement and a new escape hatch through the engine compartment for the driver. There was also an experimental **Armoured Car, Daimler Mk I CS** which had a 76.2-mm (3-in) howitzer in place of the 2-pdr (40-mm) gun to provide close support fire with high explosive and smoke projectiles (the 2-pdr/40-mm gun could fire only armour-piercing projectiles), but only a few were produced. Another armament alteration was to a small number of operational Mk Is, which were fitted with the Littlejohn Adaptor, a squeeze-bore muzzle attachment that enabled the 2-pdr (40-mm) gun to fire small projectiles that could penetrate thicker armour than the normal-calibre projectile.

When the first Daimler Armoured Cars arrived in North Africa during 1941 and 1942 they were able to assume many of the operational roles of the Marmon-Herrington vehicles currently deployed in that theatre. They soon gained for themselves an

enviable reputation for good all-round performance and reliability which was to remain for many years. By the end of the war not all were still in use as armoured cars, some being employed as scout or command vehicles with their turrets removed, but this was only a temporary measure and turreted vehicles served for many years after 1945. Total production was 2,694.

Specification
Armoured Car, Daimler Mk I
Crew: 3
Weight: (in action) 7.5 tonnes
Dimensions: length 3.96 m (13 ft 0 in); width 2.44 m (8 ft 0 in); height 2.235 m (7 ft 4 in)
Powerplant: one Daimler 6-cylinder petrol engine developing 95 bhp (71 kW)
Performance: maximum speed 80.5 km/h (50 mph); maximum range 330 km (205 miles)

A British reconnaissance unit moves through the village of Gace in Northern France during August 1944. The turreted armoured cars are Daimlers and also visible are Daimler Scout Cars; the vehicle just visible on the left is a Humber Scout Car. The white star was the Allied recognition symbol of the period.

Daimler Scout Cars

During the late 1930s the British Army was converting to mechanized traction and forming its first armoured divisions. One of the requirements to equip the new formations was a small 4×4 scout car for general liaison and reconnaissance duties, and three companies produced prototypes for comparative trials. The three companies were BSA Cycles Ltd, Morris Commercial Cars Ltd and Alvis Limited. Of the three designs entered, the BSA submission emerged as the clear winner and a production contract was placed by the War Office in May 1939. A total of 172 examples was ordered as the **Car, Scout, Mk I**, and more orders followed later.

By the time the order was placed the BSA project had been taken over by Daimler, and the designation **Car, Scout, Daimler Mk I** was applied to the vehicle. But by the time the original order was placed the War Office had called for more all-round protection for the Scout Car, as in its original form it provided the two-man crew with frontal armour only. The resultant changes needed to provide the extra armour and a folding roof over the main crew compartment added enough weight to require an improved suspension and a more powerful engine, but once these changes had been incorporated in the **Daimler Mk IA**, the Daimler Scout Car remained virtually unaltered throughout its long service life. It was a simple enough design with a full 4×4 drive configuration and front-axle steering from the **Daimler Mk II** onwards. The engine was at the rear and the crew was seated side-by-side in an open compartment with only the folding roof for overhead cover. This roof was removed on the **Daimler Mk III** as experience showed that it was rarely used operationally. The only armament carried was a single 7.7-mm

Above: The little Daimler Scout Car was in production as World War II began and was still in production when it ended. Although only lightly armed it was quiet and nippy, and proved to be one of the best of all reconnaissance vehicles in use by any side throughout the war.

Right: These Daimler Scout cars are ready for the Tunis Victory Parade of May 1943. Behind them is a Daimler armoured car and a Humber Mk II; the aircraft is a French Caudron Goeland captured from the Luftwaffe. These vehicles were used on the occasion as escorts for some of the VIPs arriving for the parade.

(0.303-in) Bren Gun firing through a hatch in the front superstructure, although other arrangements such as anti-aircraft mountings were sometimes provided.

The Daimler Scout Car proved itself to be a very tough and reliable little vehicle. It had the unusual distinction of being one of the few World War II vehicles in service when the war started and still remaining in production as the war ended. It was used by all manner of units other than the re-connaissance units for which it was originally intended, for it was also used by artillery units as a mobile observation post and by Royal Engineer units for locating mine fields and bridging positions. Many staff officers used them as run-arounds and liaison vehicles, and they were often added to motorized infantry units for reconnaissance and liaison purposes. In all these roles the Daimlers ran for enormous distances without benefit of maintenance or care and still kept going when needed. They were used by many Commonwealth armies other than the British army, and many served on with several armed forces for many years after the war. Most of them left British army service in the mid-1950s, but a few served on for years afterwards. Many are now prized collector's pieces and it would not be surprising if a few were still kept operational by some of the smaller armies around the world.

Specification
Car, Scout, Daimler Mk I
Crew: 2
Weight: (in action) 3 tonnes
Dimensions: length 3.226 m (10 ft 5 in); width 1.715 m (5 ft 7½ in); height 1.50 m (4 ft 11 in)
Powerplant: one Daimler 6-cylinder petrol engine developing 55 bhp (41 kW)
Performance: maximum speed 88.5 km/h (55 mph); maximum range 322 km (200 miles)

AEC Armoured Cars

UK

The first AEC (Associated Engineering Company Ltd of Southall, London, a company that normally made London buses) armoured car was produced as a private venture based on information filtering back from the North African battlefields. What AEC had produced was virtually a wheeled tank, for the resultant vehicle was fairly large by contemporary standards and was equipped with armour nearly as thick as that used on the current 'cruiser' tanks. The basic chassis used for the AEC armoured cars was based on that used for the Matador artillery tractor, but by the time this had been revised for the armoured car role many changes had been introduced, including an engine set at a slight front-to-rear angle to enable the overall height of the vehicle to be lowered.

The first example was demonstrated in early 1941, and an order was placed in June of that year. The **Armoured Car, AEC Mk I** mounted a 2-pdr (40-mm) gun and co-axial 7.92-mm (0.31-in) Besa machine-gun in the same turret as that used on the Valentine infantry tank, but only 120 vehicles had been produced before calls came for something more powerful for use in North Africa. The result was a revision that introduced a new three-man turret mounting a 6-pdr gun with a calibre of 57 mm (2.244 in), but even this was not powerful enough for the troops in the field and the **Armoured Car, AEC Mk II** was replaced in production by the **Armoured Car, AEC MK III** with the same turret mounting the British-developed version of the American M3 75-mm (2.95-in) tank gun. This made the AEC Mk III a very powerful armoured car, and it was used as a fire-support vehicle for armoured car regiments until the end of the war, mainly in Italy.

The AEC vehicles had a conventional layout with the engine at the rear. Although the vehicle had a full 4×4 drive configuration, it was possible to alter this to a 4×2 form with the drive and steering on the front wheels, though this configuration was used only for road travel. The degree of protection for the crew was taken to the point where the driver had no direct vision devices when closed down; he had to rely on periscopes alone. With the hatch open the driver's seat could be raised to allow him to raise his head out of the hatch. The vehicle had a rather slab-sided appearance, largely as a result of the provision of large lockers between the front and rear mudguards, and on the Mk II revisions had to be made to the bluff front hull shape to improve obstacle crossing and to improve armour protection. The heavy turret of the Mks II and III was

One of the first AEC armoured cars to arrive in North Africa, this Mk I is recognizable by the ex-Valentine infantry tank turret and the 2-pdr gun. The bulk and height of these vehicles can be easily seen, but the vehicle appears to have few of the many extras which were fitted in the field to combat examples.

provided with electric power for traversing.

Production of all the AEC armoured car marks ceased after 629 had been produced. The vehicles were used in North Africa and Tunisia and thereafter in Italy. Some Mk IIIs were used in north west Europe until the end of the war, most of them in the heavy troops of armoured car regiments. A few were used for odd experiments such as pushing mine-clearing rollers, and at least one example was fitted with a special anti-aircraft turret mounting two 20-mm cannon.

In 1944 a batch of AEC armoured cars was sent into Yugoslavia for use by the partisans, but the activities of these vehicles have still to be fully uncovered. After 1945 numbers were issued to the newly re-formed Belgian reconnaissance regiments, and these vehicles served until at least 1950.

Specification
Armoured Car, AEC Mk I
Crew: 3
Weight: (in action) 11 tonnes
Dimensions: length overall 5.18 m (17 ft 0 in); width 2.70 m (8 ft 10½ in); height 2.55 m (8 ft 4½ in)
Powerplant: one AEC 6-cylinder diesel engine developing 105 bhp (78 kW)
Performance: maximum speed 58 km/h (36 mph); maximum range 402 km (250 miles)

Specification
Armoured Car, AEC Mk II and Mk III
Crew: 4
Weight: (in action) 12.7 tonnes
Dimensions: length overall (Mk II) 5.182 m (17 ft 10 in) or (Mk III) 5.613 m (18 ft 5 in); width 2.70 m (8 ft 10½ in); height 2.69 m (8 ft 10 in)
Powerplant: one AEC 6-cylinder diesel engine developing 155 bhp (116 kW)
Performance: maximum speed 66 km/h (41 mph); maximum range 402 km (250 miles)

An AEC Mk I armoured car proceeding through Aleppo, Syria during April 1943. This vehicle has an anti-aircraft Bren gun mounting on the turret and the driver's hatch is fully open. Behind are Marmon Herrington armoured cars, which were by then being phased out of service.

Autoblinda 40 and 41

The **Autoblinda 40** and **Autoblinda 41** armoured cars had their origins in a requirement for a high-performance car for use by the Italian colonial police in the new Italian colonies in Africa. The Italian cavalry branch had a requirement for a new armoured car at about the same time, so the two projects were merged to produce a new vehicle design that appeared in 1939. This new design had the engine at the rear and a turret (mounting a machine-gun) towards the front. There was another machine-gun in the hull rear and the vehicle could be driven from either the normal front position or another position in the hull rear. From this design evolved the Autoblinda 40, of which production began by the middle of 1940.

When the original production order was placed it was specified that a small number of Autoblinda 40s would be produced with a 20-mm cannon in place of the two 8-mm (0.315-in) turret machine-guns. This was achieved by using the turret of the L 6/40 light tank in place of the original turret, and with the appearance of this version known as the Autoblinda 41, it was realized that this vehicle/weapon combination was far more effective than the machine-gun version, and thereafter production centred on the Autoblinda 41. Relatively few Autoblinda 40s were produced, and many of these were later converted to the Autoblinda 41 configuration.

For its time the Autoblinda 41 was an advanced design and possessed good performance marred only by recur-

rent steering troubles that were never entirely eliminated. The main armament was a converted 20-mm Breda modello 35 anti-aircraft cannon, and this weapon was mounted co-axially with an 8-mm (0.315-in) Breda modello 38 air-cooled machine-gun specially designed for use in armoured vehicles. Another of these machine-guns was mounted at the hull rear. One vehicle in four had provision for an anti-aircraft machine-gun mounting on top of the turret. Special sand or normal road tyres could be fitted, and there was a kit available to convert the vehicle for use on railway tracks. This kit included railway wheels and extra lighting and signalling devices, along with a searchlight to be mounted on the turret. Autoblinda 41s fitted with these kits were used extensively for anti-partisan patrols in the Balkans.

The Autoblinda 40 and Autoblinda 41 were extensively used by Italian reconnaissance units in the Western Desert and Tunisia. At the end of September 1942 there were 298 Autoblinda 41s in use, and more were employed by the colonial police. Some development work was carried out on the basic design, which later led to the mounting of a 47-mm (1.85-in) gun in the turret (**AB 43**), while an open-hulled variant had a German 50-mm (1.97-in) tank gun but neither of these vehicles was placed in production. There was also an open-hulled variant that was produced in small numbers as a command vehicle or mobile observation post for artillery units.

Specification
Autoblinda 41
Crew: 4

The Autoblinda 41, one of the most numerous of the Italian armoured cars, is shown armed with a turret-mounted 20-mm cannon and a machine-gun at the hull rear.

Weight: (in action) 7.5 tonnes
Dimensions: length overall 5.20 m (17 ft 1½ in); width 1.92 m (6 ft 4¼ in); height 2.48 m (7 ft 11½ in)
Performance: one SAP Abm 1 6-cylinder water-cooled inline petrol engine developing 80 bhp (60 kW)
Performance: maximum road speed 78 km/h (49 mph); maximum cross-country speed 38 km/h (24 mph); maximum road range 400 km (248 miles); fording 0.7 m (28 in); gradient 40%; vertical obstacle 0.3 m (12 in)

BA-10

The first **BA-10** six-wheeled armoured car appeared in 1932. It was produced at the Gorki automobile plant, and was the logical outcome of a series of six-wheeled armoured cars that could be traced back to World War I, even though the configuration had been in abeyance for some years. The BA-10 was built on the chassis of the GAZ-AAA six-wheeled commercial truck, though the suspension was modified to assume the loads involved and some reinforcements were made to the chassis members. The layout of the BA-10 was orthodox, with the engine under an armoured cover at the front and the turret mounted at the rear over the twin rear axles. There were several variations in the armament carried, but the main armament was either a 37-mm (1.46-in) tank gun or a 12.7-mm (0.5-in) DShK heavy machine-gun. Later versions used a 45-mm (1.77-in) main gun.

Like other Soviet armoured fighting vehicles the BA-10 was a functional and hefty item of equipment. It had several typically Soviet design sub-features such as the ability to wear tracks or chains on the rear axles to assist traction in mud and snow, and the spare wheels were located so that they could turn when obstacles under the chassis were encountered, and thus take some of the load. There was a crew of four, one of whom attended to the 7.62-mm (0.3-in) machine-gun fitted into a mounting on the front superstructure to the right of the driver.

Later versions of the BA-10 are sometime known as the **BA-32**, and to confuse matters further one of these

The Soviet BA-10 armoured car looked as though it belonged to a previous era, but despite its weight and bulk it proved to be well suited to the distances and terrain of the Soviet Union. The large turret mounted a 37-mm (1.46-in) or 45-mm (1.77-in) main gun.

latter variants is sometimes known as the **BA-10M**. This first appeared in 1937 and used the turret of the T-26B light tank with its 45-mm (1.77-in) gun. This was not the only tank turret so used, for others known to have been fitted were the turret of the experimental T-30 light tank and that of the BT-3 tank. One odd variation of the BA-10 that appeared in 1932 was the **BAZ** amphibious vehicle, which used the basic BA-10 hull allied to a flotation body derived from contemporary German experimental vehicles. Only a few were produced.

When the Germans invaded the Soviet Union in 1941 the BA-10 and its later derivatives were in service in

some numbers with the Red Army, the number 1,200 often being quoted. However, the events of 1941 and 1942 decimated the numbers of BA-10s, and large numbers fell into German hands. The Germans found them to be serviceable vehicles, although they considered them not really modern or mobile enough for use with their Panzer units, and kept them for use with anti-partisan units both in the Soviet Union and in the Balkans. The Germans knew the BA-10 as the **Panzerspähwagen BAF 203(r)**; some of their reports mention the vehicle as a Ford.

After 1942 the Soviets started to phase out the use of heavy armoured cars such as the BA-10. Those that re-

mained were often relegated to the armoured personnel carrier role, having their turrets removed and the interiors stripped of all equipment other than the driver's seat and controls.

Specification
BA-10M
Crew: 4
Dimensions: length 4.70 m (15 ft 5 in); width 2.09 m (6 ft 10½ in); height 2.42 m (7 ft 11¼ in)
Powerplant: one GAZ-M-1 4-cylinder water-cooled petrol engine developing 85 hp (63 kW)
Performance: maximum speed 87 km/h (54 mph); maximum range 320 km (199 miles)

Allied and Axis Trucks

The sweeping strategic manoeuvres of armoured forces in World War II were made possible by large-scale mechanization of transport; without massive fleets of lorries, Blitzkrieg would not have been possible and the tempo of the conflict could not have been sustained.

Never had there previously been – and in all possibility will there ever be again – so mobile a war as was seen during World War II.

From the very outset, with the German Blitzkrieg on Poland, such warfare relied on mobility to push home the attack. During these early years much reliance was placed on the speed and efficiency of armoured thrusts backed by a mobile supply line. Unfortunately for the Germans, much of their supply line was still horsedrawn and the number of available motor transport vehicles was totally inadequate for the task. To compensate for this inadequacy, many civil trucks were conscripted into service along with the few surviving vehicles of the Polish army. In contrast with this, the British Expeditionary Force that landed in France in 1939 was a fully mechanized formation.

During the evacuation of Dunkirk very few vehicles could be rescued. They were thus captured (along with many different types of French trucks) by the Germans and pressed into service, leading to yet more spare parts problems. After this the German logistics department tried to rationalize matters in a standardization programme

Trucks were a logistical essential – overlooked as such by many – when the world's most mobile and mechanized war to date broke out in 1939. By D-Day the Allies had designed and built many new types of four-wheel-drive vehicles.

involving the Schell system, but even this never reached its target before the end of the war.

Perhaps the loss of about 90,000 vehicles in France was a blessing to the British military transport organization as it cleared all the 'dead wood', and thus paved the way for fresh ideas. The chronic shortage of transport forced a further temporary introduction of impressment until specific types of vehicles could be produced in greater numbers. The Commonwealth with its many assets was given

the orders to produce many of these urgently needed types. Canada made a contribution out of all proportion to the size of its small automotive industry with its series of all-wheel-drive tactical trucks ranging from 15-cwt 4 x 4 to 3-ton 6 x 6, produced with various types of cabs from 1940 to 1943. During the early period the Canadian chassis and cabs were built to Canadian designs but to British specifications. The early wooden bodies were later replaced by pressed steel bodies.

The invasion of Europe was soon in the minds of the Allied planners, and considerable thought was being given to supplying the vast armies that would make the attack across Europe into Germany. It would require a supply system of a magnitude never before envisaged, and the production of trucks would be at a premium for the next two to three years. The British truck industry thus began to produce its own four-wheel-drive vehicles, with such established names as Bedford, Ford, Karrier, Thornycroft and Albion being to the fore. Once the Allied assault had gained momentum the supply lines would soon be over-stretched, and to help overcome this problem heavier 10-ton trucks were also put into production. The biggest supplier of all military trucks during World War II was the USA, although it was slow at first to respond to the ever-growing transport need of its own army and the now famous Lend-Lease system to the UK. As the whole might of American industry turned on to a war footing, however, trucks were produced in countless thousands, ranging from the ¾-ton Dodge 4 x 4 to the massive Mack prime movers and Diamond T transporters.

Canadian and Australian trucks

To meet her urgent need for motor transport the UK turned to the Commonwealth for a degree of support, the major supplier to the UK from the Commonwealth being Canada. Canada herself, once on a war footing, had urgent need to supply her own armies with equipment as every transport vehicle then in service was of civil origin. During early 1937 Ford of Canada had been approached to produce 15-cwt trucks based on similar lines to those of British design. General Motors of Canada also participated. Ford's experimental vehicle was produced in no great haste at the Windsor plant, the pilot model being built up around a Ford V-8 chassis with wheels and tyres imported from England. When completed in 1937 the vehicle was tested at the then small army testing ground at Camp Petawawa, near Ottawa. On arrival it was discovered that the specification had changed to a four-wheel drive application. Nevertheless, the type gave a good account of itself, and the **Canadian Military Pattern Chassis** formed the basis of many 15-cwt and 8-cwt trucks. During early 1940 the standard pattern of Canadian truck began to emerge with four-wheel drive, and in July of 1940, after Dunkirk, the UK placed a preliminary order for 7,000 vehicles. By 1941 Canada was the Empire's main supplier of light and medium trucks. Standardization was again of the utmost importance within a range of trucks including 8-cwt, 15-cwt, 30-cwt, 3-ton 4×4, 3-ton 6×4 and 3-ton 6×6 vehicles. Various Canadian cabs were produced through the different stages of development: the number 11 cab was identifiable by the radiator externally mounted to the bonnet; the number 12 cab had the radiator mounted inside the bonnet; the number 13 cab was a complete revision in design to allow more cab interior space and better placing of the foot pedals, and also had a forward sloping windscreen; and the number 43 was basically a number 13 with a soft top.

The 3-ton 4×4 became the mainstay of Canadian production, and was a reliable vehicle produced by both Ford and Chevrolet. The body variations were enormous and can only be touched briefly within this text. All

Above: A 1940 Chevrolet WA is seen in the configuration developed by the LRDG for their operations in North Africa. The vehicle illustrated carries a Lewis gun behind the cab and a Browning .30 cal M1919 with AA barrel above the dashboard.

models were produced in the general-service role, some with timber and some with all-pressed-steel bodies, and other types included water and petrol tankers, mobile gun carriages, wireless house bodies, machinery vehicles (various types from 15-cwt mounted welding units to 6×6 fully-equipped workshops), office bodies, ambulances and other medical requirement vehicles, and breakdown and recovery vehicles. Canada also supplied many conventional types from all the large manufacturers, fitted with military tyres/wheels and bodies. Over 900,000 Canadian vehicles were produced within the five-year period.

The Australian commitment was not on so grand a scale, the majority of production trucks being in the light range. Most of the medium to heavy trucks were supplied in kit or chassis and cab form, usually from Canada, to which locally-built bodies were added. Some of the conventional trucks supplied were used in halftrack conversions, but this never progressed beyond the experimental stage. All Canadian Fords were reassembled

at the Ford subsidiary plant at Geelong, in Victoria state some 48 km (30 miles) west of Melbourne.

Specification
Ford F60
Powerplant: one 70.8-kW (95-bhp) Ford V-8 petrol engine
Dimensions: length 6.20 m (20 ft 4 in);

Two Chevrolet trucks pass through a rocky area of the desert carrying an interesting assortment of weapons, including a Boys Anti-Tank rifle.

width 2.29 m (7 ft 6 in); height 3.05 m (10 ft 0 in)
Performance: max speed 80 km/h (50 mph); range 270 km (168 miles)

Above: This Canadian-built Ford 3-ton truck is carrying a curious cargo of lighting equipment. Canadian Fords were also produced in Australia, the Ford subsidiary plant in Victoria State re-assembling vehicles for use in the Pacific theatre.

Below: The Chevrolet C60L GS truck became the mainstay of Canadian production and was built in a bewildering variety of different models including water and petrol tankers, ambulances and recovery vehicles.

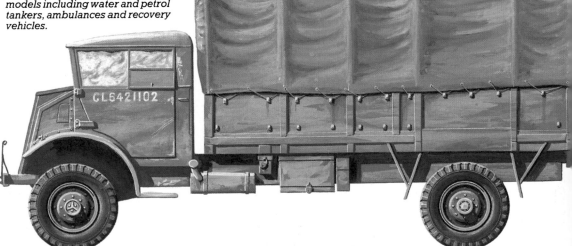

German light trucks

German light trucks before the outbreak of World War II were of commercial 4×2 design with only superstructure details to identify them as army vehicles.

The **Phaenomen Granit** had an air-cooled engine and was used in great numbers, most specifically in the ambulance role. Although the Granit was a useful vehicle for the transport of goods and supplies on hard roads, the type's cross country ability left much to be desired. A specification for a 6×4 truck was published and the response from the industry was immediate. Daimler-Benz had already built its **Daimler-Benz G3** 6×4 model from 1928, many for service with the German railways. Büssing-NAG of Braunschweig was also involved with its **Büssing-NAG G31**, in production from 1933 to 1935. Whilst all vehicles were fitted as standard with petrol engines, a few diesel engines were also fitted experimentally. Daimler-Benz, Buessing-NAG and Krupp produced chassis which were also used as the basis for armoured car bodies. Although a wide range of vehicle types were still in service during the invasion of Poland the Schell programme had introduced the idea of standard truck designs. For example the **Daimler-Benz 1500A** was built as the planned replacement for all current 2-ton payload types in service, many of which served in the German army for general-service use. Troop carrier versions were built on the lines of heavy cars with fold-down hoods.

Steyr of Austria built three basic types: a general-service truck, a heavy command car and a troop carrier, all powered by an air-cooled V-8 engine. Steyr also provided a 6×4 cargo **Steyr Model 640**, which was also produced in ambulance and command car variants. One of the most common types used during the early days of World War II was the **Krupp Kfz 81** 6×4, which was generally employed as an artillery tractor, a role in which it superseded the earlier **Kfz 69** purpose-built artillery tractor. The **Krupp Boxer**, as it became known, was powered by a 4-cylinder horizontally opposed engine and had all-round independent suspension.

Hungary built few vehicles: one 6×4 personnel carrier for 14 men was the **Botond**. In Czechoslovakia Tatra produced the **Tatra T92** 2-tonner powered by a V-8 engine; this model was first used by the Czech army, and later by the Germans. The **Praga RV** models were again 6×4 types, and were built as general-service trucks, wireless vehicles and command cars. The Schell programme was designed to make these 6×4 vehicles obsolete, but as production of Schell types could never keep up with demand, the older models soldiered on to the end of the war, some still being used immediately after the war in civilian hands.

Specification
Krupp Kfz 81
Powerplant: one 38.8-kW (52-bhp) Krupp M304 4-cylinder engine
Dimensions: length 4.95 m (16 ft 2.9 in), width 1.95 m (6 ft 4.8 in); height 2.30 m (7 ft 6.6 in)
Weight: 2600 kg (5,732 lb)

Below: The Krupp Kfz 81 (L2H43) had an air-cooled 'Boxer' engine and an all-independent suspension; it was used in a number of different roles, including prime mover for the 20-mm (0.78-in) anti-aircraft gun.

The Germans made extensive use of captured light trucks and vehicles manufactured in Hungary, Czechoslovakia and France. Their own models, like the Krupp L2H43 seen here, were similar to contemporary British six-wheelers.

Opel Blitz

By the late 1930s the German military inventory presented an enormous logistic problem, with over 100 different vehicle types in service.

A desperate programme to rationalize this situation was put in hand under the leadership of General von Schell, who was then director of mechanization. His aim was to cut down the vast number of types and bring in a degree of standardization which, when plans were finalized, allowed just 30 vehicle types.

In the 3-ton medium category Opel's design was the most successful. The **Opel Blitz** 4×2 was of a conventional layout and featured a pressed steel commercial type cab with wooden body. Under the so called Schell programme all 4×2 vehicles were designated **Typ S**. The 4×2 was produced in many different variants, for example general service, fuel tankers, house body etc. As the need for better cross-country performance became a premium it was decided by Opel to produce a four-wheel-drive 3-ton truck with the designation **Typ A** and based on the same basic vehicle design as the Typ S. The addition of a driven front axle gave tremendous advantages over the normal 4×2 truck, and the wheelbase for the 4×4 was shor-

Opel Blitzes of the Afrika Korps are seen on a busy road in Libya, 1941. For all his panache as a tank commander, Rommel consistently neglected the logistics of the Afrika Korps and imposed an impossible burden on his transport columns.

tened by 15 cm (5.9 in). A two-speed transfer box gave the vehicle a choice of 10 forward gears. During the production span from 1937 to 1944 some 70,000 Opel Blitz trucks were built, as well as over 25,000 'Allrad' (four wheel drive) models. By late 1944, however, manufacture was totally disrupted by Allied bombing and the Allied advance across Europe, making plans to produce vehicles in 1945 fruitless. The variations of body design were numerous, the most popular model being the house body. The Blitz's possibilities were endless, and the vehicles were used as field ambulances, mobile laboratories, laundries, mobile command posts, field caravans, radio vans, cipher offices, and mobile workshops to name just a few. The body was made of timber and compressed card to save valuable steel. Later during the war when raw materials were desperately short, the cabs were produced from wood and pressed card and termed *Ersatz* cabs. During the winter campaigns on the Eastern Front even the four-wheel-drive vehicles were almost brought to a standstill, and the Waffen-SS developed a unique three-quarter track vehicle from an Opel Typ A and obsolete PzKpfw I tank track assemb-

lies: the rear shaft was shortened and the driven axle was moved forward to line up with the sprockets, and because of its performance the **Maultier**, as the vehicle became known, was accepted for standard production. Similar conversions to Ford and Daimler-Benz vehicles were also carried out, but were not so numerous.

Specification
Opel Blitz
Powerplant: one 54.8-kW (73.5-bhp) Opel 6-cylinder petrol engine
Dimensions: length 6.02 m (19 ft 9 in); width 2.265 m (7 ft 5.2 in); height 2.175 m (7 ft 1.6 in)
Weights: chassis 2100 kg (4,630 lb); payload 3290 kg (7,253 lb)

Above: An Opel Blitz Kfz 31 ambulance model. The Germans also used heavy car chassis ambulances and captured some, like the Austin K2. It was also used to carry mobile operating theatres.

Performance: maximum speed 80 km/h (50 mph); range 410 km (255 miles)

German heavy trucks

Most German heavy trucks were basically civil-based vehicles or Typ S models under the Schell programme. The majority were 4×2 4½ to 6 tonners, such as the MAN ML4500 which was also built in Austria by OÄF. The **Mercedes-Benz L4500A** is a typical example of the type of German vehicle used by the Wehrmacht. Powered by a Daimler-Benz OM67/4 6-cylinder diesel engine, it formed part of the backbone of German army transport, and in one variant mobile anti-aircraft equipment was built on the Mercedes chassis in the form of a 37-mm Flak 41 gun.

An attempt was made to produce a tank transporter unit for use with PzKpfw I tanks, and a 4×4 version of the **Büssing-NAG** 6.5-ton lorry was used. Very little progress was made in this direction, and most tank haulage was carried out by the 6×4 **Faun L900D567** with a payload capacity of 8800 kg (19,400 lb). The German truck industry was never able to supply enough types to transport tanks, half-tracks with trailers eventually taking over this role.

With the German takeover of Czechoslovakia in 1938 many useful industries fell into German hands and were put to use supplying the German armed forces. In Kolin the excellent 6×6 **Tatra** 6.5-ton truck was produced with some outstanding features: they included a tubular frame and independent front and rear suspension, and power was supplied by a 12-cylinder air-cooled 157-kW (210-hp) engine. Skoda also supplied heavy trucks to the Germans, the **Skoda 6 ST6** 6×4

A Büssing-Nag 454 6½-ton 4×4 truck carries a PzKpfw I command tank in Afrika Korps colours. Only a small number of these vehicles were produced, the most widely used tank transporter being the Faun 6×4, which was capable of carrying the PzKpfw II.

Right: The control of far-flung armoured forces depended on a reliable network of radio communications, based on mobile radio stations mounted on heavy trucks. This vehicle is part of a German divisional headquarters outside Tobruk in 1941. Heavy trucks were mainly used for specialist tasks, general supplies being entrusted to lighter vehicles and the railways.

cargo truck generally being used in conjunction with four-wheel trailers. Skoda also produced one of the oddities of World War II, the 4×4 **Skoda 175** built as an artillery tractor for use in rough conditions on the Eastern Front. It featured huge steel wheels (1500×300 mm front and 1500×400 mm rear). Some of these production models were used in North West Europe.

Hanomag tractors were used to haul one or two laden trailers and were purpose-built for this role: the **Model SS100** was employed by the army and the Luftwaffe, the latter using the type to tow fuel bowsers. It was strictly a commercial type which was made available to the civil market. A larger but similar type was produced by Faun with a 13.54-litre engine, and this vehicle could be adapted to fit railway lines.

Overall the German transport system relied mainly on the railways, and on the road greater emphasis was placed on medium trucks.

Dimensions: length 10.40 m (34 ft 1.4 in); width 2.50 m (8 ft 2.4 in); height 2.60 m (8 ft 6.4 in)
Weight: 9200 kg (20,282 lb)

Specification
Faun L900D567
Powerplant: one 111.8-kW (150-bhp) Deutz F6M517 6-cylinder diesel engine

AEC Matador

The **AEC Matador** 4×4 tractor first appeared in 1939, and was built to a War Office specification to tow 4.5-in (114-mm), 5.5-in (140-mm) and 6-in (152-mm) howitzers. The requirement was for a four-wheel tractor with seating for the crew and ammunition stowage. The early production vehicles had a cab roof of different shape to that of later production trucks, the latter having a circular hatch for air observation; when not in use this was covered by a small canvas sheet. The basic design of the cab was very simple and robust, being built on a wooden frame with steel sheets. The body was of conventional timber construction with a drop tailboard and a side door for use by the gun crew. Special runners were fitted to the floor to allow shells to be moved to the rear tailgate for unloading. The Matador was powered by a 6-cylinder 7.58-litre AEC engine producing 71 kW (95 bhp), allowing a top speed of 58 km/h (36 mph). For pulling purposes (for example extracting guns from mud) a 7-ton winch was fitted with 76 m (250 ft) of wire rope. The Matador was used in most theatres of the war. In the desert it proved to be extremely popular with the gun crews for its reliability, and photographic evidence shows that some had the tops of the cabs cut down to door level. Matadors were also pressed into service in the desert to tow transporter trailers because of the lack of proper tractors for this purpose. Total production of Matadors was 8,612. The RAF was also a major user of this vehicle, 400 being supplied in various offerings. The **General Load Carrier** had a special all-steel body with drop down sides and tailgate to facilitate easy loading, and the support posts could also be removed. Special flat platform trucks were also supplied to transport heavy equipment such as dumpers and compressors. An armoured command post was also built on this chassis, called the **Dorchester**, in which accommodation was provided internally for high- or

An AEC Matador comes ashore from an American tank landing ship during the Allied amphibious operation at Salerno. Introduced as an artillery tractor in 1939, some of the 9,000 produced served for many years post-war, an indication of the soundness of the basic design.

low-powered radio transmitting and receiving equipment, and an external penthouse could be erected. As these vehicles were considered prime targets they were carefully disguised to look like general-service trucks.

Approximately 175 Matadors were built in 1942 as self-propelled gun carriages and comprised a 6-pdr anti-tank gun mounted in an armoured box. The cab and body were also armoured. Other variants included power equipment 20 kVA, power equipment 50 kVA, air-traffic control, and an experimental 25-pdr portée. The last did not progress beyond the prototype stage.

The last of the Matadors were auctioned off in the mid-1970s, this late disposal date proving the sound strength and reliability of these trucks.

Specification
AEC Matador
Powerplant: one 70.8-kW (95-bhp) AEC 6-cylinder diesel engine
Dimensions: length 6.32 m (20 ft 9 in); width 2.40 m (7 ft 10.5 in); height 3.10 m (10 ft 2 in)
Weights: unladen 7189 kg (15,848 lb) and laden 11024 kg (24,304 lb)
Performance: maximum speed 58 km/h (36 mph); radius 579 km (360 miles)

This AEC Matador has been fitted with the 'streamline' cab roof. Developed from a Hardy (AEC) design of the 1930s, the Matador was a medium artillery tractor used to move the 5.5-in (140-mm) medium gun.

Bedford QL

Bedford's involvement in four-wheel drive vehicles began in 1938, during the development stages of the square-nosed 15-cwt Bedford. It was suggested that the War Office be approached with permission to proceed with this design. Some degree of interest was expressed, but as no immediate requirement was envisaged the matter proceeded no further. Then Bedford decided to undertake private development on a low-priority basis with an eye to future military orders. After the outbreak of war the War Office issued orders for large quantities of 4×2 vehicles and also told Bedford to proceed with a prototype 4×4 3-ton general-service truck. In October 1939 a specification was approved, and on 1 February 1940 the first prototype was completed and was out on road tests. Within a month two more had joined it for extensive factory and military tests. The usual army tests were completed and the fitments for special tools installed, and drivers began training to operate this new truck. It had taken one year exactly from the first prototype to the first production vehicles, a commendable feat in a time of great stress and shortages. The **Bedford QL** was designed to use its four-

Used by the Army fire service, the Bedford QL fire tender was introduced in 1943 and saw service in north west Europe. It towed a trailer pump, and carried an integral water tank, hoses and PTO (power take-off) pump in the main body.

wheel drive on rough terrain, but could disengage the front drive for use on hard roads to ease the wear on tyres and gearbox, the change being effected by moving a lever on the secondary gearbox. Another feather in Bedford's cap (and a surprise one) was the lack of normal teething troubles during the QL's early use. It was only after about one year in service that the first sign of trouble occurred, and a rather peculiar one at that: a tendency for the vehicle to shudder when the brakes were applied slightly. These reports were followed up immediately, and it was found that only a small proportion of vehicles were showing this fault. After some time spent on investigation the fault was found to be simple, and the deep-treaded cross-country tyres were replaced by normal road tyres, whereupon the problem ceased.

The first production vehicle was the steel-bodied **QLD** issued to units of the Army Service Corps as a general carrier. From this model stemmed many variants, including the **QLT** 3-ton troop carrier with a modified and lengthened chassis to accommodate the extra long body to carry 29 troops and kit. The QLT was popularly known as the 'Drooper'. The **QLR** wireless house type was used by all arms of the signals. The truck featured an auxiliary generator, and other variants on this house type body were command, cipher office and mobile terminal carrier vehicles. A special requirement for use in the Western Desert was a

6-pdr portée, a vehicle designed to transport and fire a 6-pdr anti-tank gun from the body. It was necessary to modify the cab by cutting off the upper half and fitting a canvas top, and when this type became redundant the surviving vehicles were converted back to general-service types after being rebodied. The RAF was a major operator of the Bedford QL, many being used as fuel tankers with swinging booms to refuel aircraft. Two experimental vehicles that never progressed beyond the prototype stage were the **Giraffe** and **Bren**. The Giraffe was designed for amphibious landings: all the major components were

raised (along with the cab) on a special frame for deep wading. When fully elevated the vehicle's automotive parts were raised 2.13 m (7 ft) and the driver 3.05 m (10 ft). The vehicle was approved for production in the event that the waterproofing system then in use failed. The Bren was developed by the Ministry of Supply by taking a standard Bedford QLD and replacing the rear wheels with components from the Bren Gun Carrier, thus creating a half-track. The aim of this scheme was to reduce rubber wear. The vehicle was considered adequate during tests, but the shortage of rubber did not materialize and the project was dropped.

A Bedford QLB light AA (Bofors) tractor comes ashore from a 'Class 9' ferry during the 21st Army Group's Rhine crossing in March 1945. The QL saw service for many years after the war, finally retiring in the early 1960s.

Specification
Bedford QLD
Powerplant: one 53.7-kW (72-bhp) Bedford 6-cylinder petrol engine
Dimensions: length 5.99 m (19 ft 8 in); width 2.26 m (7 ft 5 in); height 3.0 m (9 ft 10 in)
Performance: maximum speed 61 km/h (38 mph); radius 370 km (230 miles)

Leyland Hippo

Designed as a heavy load carrier, the **Leyland Hippo** 6×4 10-ton truck entered military service in 1944 and eventually proved its worth hauling supplies during the closing stages of the Allied advance across North West Europe. The huge bodies on these trucks had a well-type floor incorporating the wheel arches, this giving a lower loading height, an important element in the war days as fork-lift trucks were few and much loading was accomplished by hand. Steel hoops and a canvas tilt gave weather protection to the stores carried. The **Hippo Mk 1** initial version was based on a pre-war commercial type with an open cab with canvas tilt and fixed windscreen, while the **Hippo Mk 2** had an all-steel cab. The Hippo Mk 2 had single rear wheels, whilst the **Hippo Mk 2A** had dual wheels fitted with 10-50-22 tyres. The difficulty experienced with the Mk 2A was the need to carry two spare wheels, one for the front and one for the rear. It is perhaps quite amazing to see these trucks still in service in the 1980s. Besides the general-service vehicle, many were fitted with large van type bodies, and several expandable body types were built, albeit of similar design. The side panels were split horizontally, the upper half being raised to form extra roof area and the lower half forming extra floor space to provide additional freedom around machinery. The vehicles could also be linked together to form a consolidated workshop area. Van bodies included an auto-processing type for developing photographs, an enlarging and rectifying type for exposing original film onto new film, a printing type

with a rotary offset printing machine, and a photo-mechanical type equipped with a rotary offset printer, work tables and plateracks. Entrance to all these bodies was through a single door in the rear. Because of the length of the body, the spare wheel had to be transferred from behind the cab and placed under the rear of the chassis.

A post-war fitting was the adoption of a 9092-litre (2,000-Imp gal) AVTUR refueller body and, with the rear body

removed, of a Coles Mk 7 or Neal Type QMC crane.

Specification
Leyland Hippo Mk 2 GS
Powerplant: one 74.6-kW (100-bhp) Leyland Type L 6-cylinder diesel engine
Dimensions: length 8.31 m (27 ft 3 in); width 2.46 m (8 ft 1 in); height 3.33 m (10 ft 11 in)

The 10-ton 6×4 format became widely used in the British army after the war. Manufacturers included Albion, Foden and Leyland. The Leyland Hippo, introduced in 1943, is seen here with WD pattern open cab and the GS body.

Weights: unladen 8941 kg (19,712 lb) and laden 19711 kg (43,456 lb)
Performance: radius 837 km (520 miles)

Italian trucks

Many of Italy's trucks were of old design, but during the build-up of the Italian armed forces before the outbreak of World War II some measure of standardization was achieved. The largest supplier of trucks to the Italian army was Fiat. Fiat vehicles equipped most of the transport units, vehicles like the **Fiat TL37** 4×4 light truck having large wheels and tyres to suit the terrain of Ethiopia and the Western Desert. The **OM Autocarretta 32** was a unique light truck, and was highly regarded by its crews, and even by British troops when examples were captured. The type was intended primarily for mountain operations, and featured a 4-cylinder air-cooled diesel engine and independent suspension front and rear. The gearbox was centrally mounted and drove both front and rear axles direct. The medium-truck range was dominated by the **Fiat 38R** 4×2 and the **Lancia 3 RO N** 6½-ton 4×2. The latter vehicle also formed the basis of a mobile anti-aircraft mount. To start these trucks a hand-cranked inertia start unit was placed forward of the crankshaft. The power unit was a Junkers two-stroke engine. The **Fiat 633 BM** was built on similar lines to the Lancia.

Most Italian tanks were of the lighter types, and could therefore be carried in the bodies of the Lancia, though a tank-transporter trailer could also be used. Two other widely used vehicles were the **Fiat 626BL** powered by a 46-

kW (62-bhp) engine, and the **Fiat 665NL**. The latter was quite advanced in truck body and cab design.

The Germans used large numbers of Italian vehicles, these seeing service on almost every German front. In Libya the British discovered that Italian diesel-engined trucks were of great value because of their lack of a car-

burettor, which had a tendency to clog up in dusty conditions.

Specification
OM Autocarretta
Powerplant: one 15.7-kW (21-bhp) OM Autocarretta 32 4-cylinder engine
Dimensions: length 3.80 m (12 ft 5.6 in); width 1.30 m (4 ft 3.2 in); height 2.15 m (7 ft 0.6 in)
Weight: 1615 kg (3,560 lb)

The Fiat/Spa Dovunque was built by the Spa factory, at that time under Fiat control. 'Dovunque' means cross-country (literally 'go anywhere').

A Fiat/Spa Model 38R 2½-ton 4×2 truck is seen in use as an artillery observation post in the pause after the end of Operation 'Crusader'.

A Lancia 3 RO N 6½-ton 4×4 AUP (Autocarro Unificate Pesante, or Standard Heavy Truck) is dug out of the sand in North Africa.

Dodge WC62

During 1941 the US logistic organization decided a vehicle was required to complement the ¾-ton Dodge T214 WC52 weapons carrier. The design was to include a larger payload area for stores or troops and the requirement called for a standardization of vehicle parts to be easily interchangeable. The front of the 6×6 **Dodge WC62** was typical Dodge, but the rear body was lengthened by 1.24 m (49 in) and a third axle was added.

The third axle allowed the doubling of payload compared with the ¾-ton Dodge. Other considerations besides interchangeability were envisaged during production, with the need for new military trucks increasing as the war drew on and it was decided that rather than design a specific new truck this type of adapted vehicle would en-

able the production lines to complete vehicles at a much faster rate. The two types used the same engine, clutch, transmission, front axle, steering gear, wheels, brakes, tyres, radiator, fan and belt, windshield, seats and electrical system. Basically designed as infantry carriers, these vehicles found their way into all arms of the American forces, including the Army Air Force. During stringent military tests the vehicle proved to have excellent stability as a result of its low centre of gravity and wide-tread tyres. Six-wheel drive and high ground clearance enabled

A WC62 towing an anti-tank gun (the M1 57-mm adaptation of the British 6-pdr) halts in front of Munich city hall as the 7th Army moves through the city in April 1945.

The ¾-ton Dodge T214 was elongated to produce the WC62, both shown here with French troops in the south of France in August 1944.

the vehicle to give a good account of itself over really rough terrain. Production of the personnel carriers continued throughout the war, many being distributed to other nations including the Free French, who were equipped almost entirely with American *matériel*. The majority of these vehicles were supplied with a complete canvas tilt, though a certain percentage was fitted with a pedestal gun mount on the passenger side of the cab to carry a 12.7-mm (0.5-in) machine-gun. Approximately 43,300 Dodge 6×6 trucks were produced between 1943 and 1945. Very few variants were developed on this chassis: one such was a scout car with an armoured shell fitted around the Dodge chassis and powerplant; another was the mounting of twin 12.7-mm (0.5-in) machine-guns (on a Gun Mount M33) on the rear body. This model was developed and tested in 1943, but no further progress was

made. The 6×6 saw extensive use post-war until the Korean War, after which the type became surplus as a result of wear and the introduction of new equipment. Today the WC62 is a much prized vehicle within the ranks

of vehicle preservation societies.

Specification
Dodge WC62
Powerplant: one 68.6-kW (92-bhp) Dodge 6-cylinder petrol engine

Dimensions: length 5.71 m (18 ft 8.75 in); width 1.91 m (6 ft 3.4 in); height 2.21 m (7 ft 3 in)
Performance: speed 80 km/h (50 mph); radius 386 km (240 miles)

USA

American medium trucks

When one thinks of US military medium trucks, the **GMC 2½-ton** 6×6 immediately springs to mind. However, this type is discussed overleaf and other types are treated here.

Semi-trailer tractors come into this category with designations from 2½-ton to 5-ton. These special-purpose vehicles were used to haul large trailers of all descriptions. The general-service bodies were used in great numbers during the advance across Europe, proving extremely useful in such organized deployments as the 'Red Ball Express' route. Starting with some of the less publicized vehicles, the **Autocar Model U4144T** 4×4 tractor was basically used in the USA, very few crossing the Atlantic and the US Army Air Force being a major user for the fuel bowser-towing role. Another early model, the **GMC AFKX-502-8E** COE tractor, was used to tow early horse box trailers for the cavalry. The GMC was powered by a 6-cylinder 91-kW (122-bhp) engine. Perhaps the two most popular and publicized tractors were the **Autocar Model U7144T** and the **Federal 94x93**, which were used in quite large numbers for haulage. The Autocar was used by artillery units to tow van bodies, fitted out with radio equipment mostly for use by anti-aircraft units. These trailers were designed to use a front dolly wheel for use as full towing trailer, though when the trailer was coupled to the tractor the dolly could be towed behind the whole assembly. Early vehicles had fixed steel cabs, these later being changed to soft tops in line with most other American-produced military transport vehicles. Many soft-top vehicles were fitted with a ring mount for a 12.7-mm (0.5-in) machine-gun. The

Federal model was used in the same basic way, the power unit for this type being the Hercules 6-cylinder RXC engine.

In the 4-ton cargo range the **FWD HARI** saw extensive service with American, British and Canadian forces. It was powered by a Waukesha GB2 6-cylinder engine. Many of the trucks were instrumental in hauling supplies along the Allied supply line from Persia to the USSR. One interesting deployment of the FWD in British service was its use to tow mobile smoke generators. The RAF used the truck as mobile power supply vehicles and as snow ploughs, the latter being fitted with a Bros rotary plough, for which the rear body was replaced by a large Climax R6 petrol engine unit. Transmission of power to the plough was twofold, first by V-belts to the rotary parts then through transmission shafts to the rotor assembly with a chain drive for final power to the rake.

Diamond T supplied a 6×6 medium truck, the **Diamond T 968**, this being one of the US Army's cargo trucks until the end of the war. Variants included tipper, map reproduction, wrecker and bitumen tank vehicles. A total of 10,551 was built, and a further 2,197 were supplied as long- and short-wheelbase vehicles (cab and chassis) for fitment of special engineering bodies. These were supplied to many other countries during and after World War II.

Specification
Diamond T 968
Powerplant: one 79-kW (106-bhp) Hercules RXC 6-cylinder petrol engine
Dimensions: length 6.82 m (22 ft 4.5 in); width 2.44 m (8.0 ft); height 3.01 m (9 ft 10.5 in)
Weights: unladen 8357 kg (18,424 lb) and laden 11939 kg (26,320 lb)

The attack transport William Tilghman *is loaded for the Allied armies in north west Europe. Visible are both major types of medium truck, including the cab-over-engine (COE) AFKWX 6×6, also made by GMC.*

Performance: maximum speed 64 km/h (40 mph); radius 266 km (165 miles)

Studebaker produced almost 200,000 2½-ton trucks, similar to the GMC 6×6, but more than half of that production went to the Soviet Union under Lend-Lease. Many were produced with the Studebaker commercial-type closed cab.

Light Vehicles

World War II saw much in the way of innovation, and one of the major changes involved the vastly increased mobility of armies. For the first time, whole formations were motorized, and supporting the fighting troops were a host of vehicles of many types.

In recent years a wealth of information has been published about armoured fighting vehicles, but relatively little has appeared on the ubiquitous 'B' vehicle, the unarmoured vehicle designed specifically for military use, without which modern armies would be unable to move. On the Allied side, there was almost total reliance upon US production: Britain had lost a major proportion of its 'B' vehicles with the retreat from Dunkirk; and the Soviet Union, in evacuating its industry to the east before the rapid German advance, had concentrated its industrial might upon AFV production, relying almost entirely upon US Lend-Lease vehicles for logistical and support functions.

All nations had gone to great efforts to achieve standardization and to reduce the variety of vehicle types to a minimum. In the Allies' case this was not difficult; the USA managed to restrict its unarmoured vehicle programme to a very limited number of types (six basic classes), and the fact that it was the principal contributor to Allied production facilitated widespread standardization with major advantages in maintenance and resupply. The Germans also had begun the war with a standardization

British SAS soldiers in an unarmoured but well-armed jeep on patrol in North Africa in early 1943. Jeeps were ideal for staging hit-and-run raids and reconnaissance missions.

programme, introducing the Einheit (standard) or 'E' vehicles, each class of which had several manufacturers producing models that were built to the same specification. Unfortunately for them, these vehicles suffered from severe mechanical reliability problems, were complex to service and maintain, and could not be easily mass-produced in the quantities required; so civilian models had to be adopted. As the Germans occupied country after country, they gathered more and more vehicles, and by the time the Soviet campaign was well under way there were some 1500 different types of unarmoured vehicle in German service. This made maintenance and resupply a nightmare, and contributed as a significant factor to the eventual German defeat. Towards the end of the war the Germans completed a new standardization programme (the Schell Programme) under which the famous Volkswagen Kubel and Opel-Blitz lorry bore most of the brunt of the requirements. By this time, however, it was far too late.

Kraftfahrzeug 2 (Stöwer 40)

During 1934 the Germans made the first attempts to create standardized (*Einheit*) vehicles for the Wehrmacht. Until this time vehicles employed for cross-country work had been based on commercial designs or were conversions of them. The new army motorization programme placed great emphasis upon the design of vehicles from not only technical but also operational considerations. A new system of Kfz (*Kraftfahrzeug*, or motor vehicle) numbers was introduced, whereby numbers were allotted to vehicles (irrespective of make or model) to denote their tactical or military function. With few exceptions, for the vehicles covered here these Kfz numbers were broken down into the following classes: 1 to 10 covered 1.Pkw (*leichter Personenkraftwagen*, or light personnel carrier); 11 to 20 covered m.Pkw (*mittlerer Personenkraftwagen*, or medium personnel carrier); and 21 to 30 covered s.Pkw (*schwerer Personenkraftwagen*, or heavy personnel carrier).

The 1.Pkw was a standard vehicle irrespective of its models or manufacturers, with the exception of the engine, which was always that of the manufacturer and commercially available. The engine was made by Stöwer, BMW and Hanomag from 1936 onwards. The Stöwer model (**Kraftfahrzeug 2**) used AW2 and R180W water-cooled 4-cylinder OHV petrol engines with dry-sump lubrication. The chassis was of normal type with a frame of rectangular section, side- and cross-members, and bracing to support the engine, transmission and body. The hood was hinged down the centre and fastened on each side by two clips. The chassis was used for the 4-seater light car (**Kfz 1**) and for a variety of other special-purpose vehicles.

Made from 1936, the Kfz 2 was a standard body design based on mechanical components of several manufacturers. The Stöwer 40 was a 4×4 design, and, as here, was often the basis for radio cars.

Specification
Kfz 2 (Stöwer 40)
Dimensions: length 3.58 m (11 ft 9 in); width 1.57 m (5 ft 2 in); height 1.78 m (5 ft 10 in); wheelbase 2.24 m (7 ft 4 in)
Weight: net 1815 kg (4,001 lb)
Powerplant: one Stöwer AW2 or R180W 4-cylinder OHV petrol engine developing 50 bhp (37.3 kW)
Transmission: five forward and one reverse gears
Tyres: 5.50×18 (metric)

A Luftwaffe Kfz 2 in the desert. The Junkers Ju 87 'Stukas' are just returning from a mission, as shown by their bombless condition.

Volkswagen Kübel

One of the most famous military cars of World War 2 was the **Volkswagen Kübel**, the German Jeep. During 1933 Hitler had instructed two car designers (Dr Porsche of Auto-Union and Werlin of Mercedes-Benz) to develop a 'people's car' (Volkswagen). The basic Volkswagen took shape on Porsche's drawing board as early as 1934. In 1936 the first design for a Volkswagen cross-country appeared, designated **Volkswagen Typ 62**. When the decision was reached that the only new personnel carrier to be employed by the Wehrmacht would be the Volkswagen, serving as the standard light passenger car for all arms, design changes were requested resulting in the **Typ 82**. During 1938 work was undertaken on the Volkswagen plant at Wolfsburg, and production began in March 1940.

The vehicle was designed for lightness and ease of manufacture. Built as cheaply as possible, it comprised components of simple design. Generally, the layout was very similar to that of the Jeep. The method of suspension, together with the use of a self-locking differential, gave it remarkably good cross-country performance. After initial problems, the 998-cc Volkswagen Typ 1 4-cylinder HIAR air-cooled engine soon became one of the most reliable powerplants ever. With its excellent automotive qualities and simple

maintenance level, the vehicle fully met the high demands of military use, especially in the desert and USSR. The military version had a touring body of sheet metal with a folding top. Four doors were provided, and weather protection was afforded by a folding canvas hood and side screens. The body panels were mostly of 18-gauge stampings. Tubular struts were used as the basic structural members of the body. The engine cylinders were of 'H' form and laid flat at the bottom of the car. The chassis consisted of a central welded-steel tube bifurcating at the rear to support the engine and trans-

mission, and the steel floor on each side of the central member supported the body. The front axle consisted of steel tube which housed the two torsion bars of the suspension. At each side of the differential were universal joints providing centres about which the two rear driving axles could articulate, and the rear wheels were stabilized laterally from the differential housing. The auxiliary gearboxes in each rear wheel brought the two half-shafts higher and so gave a greater ground clearance. There was independent suspension on all four wheels, and double-action hydraulic shock-

The ubiquitous Kübel (bucket) served wherever the German armies were. Allied/German production contrasts are underlined by the fact that only 55,000 of these handy vehicles were produced from 1940, as compared with 600,000-plus Jeeps produced from 1941-5.

absorbers controlled the movement of the rear springing. The steering gear and connectors were of conventional type. The brakes were mechanical, cable-operated, and had double lever action on the brake shoes. Transmission was through a single-plate clutch gearbox. An overdrive was incorporated in fourth gear. The fuel tank was located below the instrument panel, facing the front right-hand seat.

This vehicle was also designed with an enclosed body, designated **Typ 92**. All models built from March 1943 had a larger engine (1131-cc capacity). By the end of the war some 55,000 Typ 82s had been produced (production ceased in mid-1944). To accommodate the various bodies required, an order was issued on 2 August 1940 demanding widening of the chassis by between 6 and 8 cm (2.36 and 3.15 in) in what became the **Typ 86**. The normal Kübelwagen was not very successful in the desert and so the *Tropenfest* (tropical) version was developed with numerous changes including the use of larger sand tyres. Volkswagen Kübels used in Africa were often referred to as *Deutsches Kamel* (German camel). There were numerous special-purpose models of the Volkswagen Kübel, many of them adopted by the Wehrmacht.

Specification
Volkswagen Kübel
Dimensions: length 3.73 m (12 ft 3 in); width 1.60 m (5 ft 3 in); height 1.35 m (4 ft 5 in); wheelbase 2.39 m (7 ft 10 in)
Weight: net 635 kg (1,400 lb)
Powerplant: one Volkswagen Typ 1 4-cylinder HIAR 998-cc petrol engine developing 24 bhp (17.9 kW), or from March 1943 one Volkswagen 4-cylinder 1131-cc petrol engine developing 25 bhp (18.6 kW)
Transmission: limited-slip differential giving four forward and one reverse gears, with overdrive on fourth gear
Tyres: 5.25 × 16

Kübels were not at first successful in the desert, so a Tropenfest (tropical) version was developed. Changes were numerous, including the use of sand tyres, and the altered model came to be known as the 'German camel'.

Kraftfahrzeug 11 (Auto-Union/Horch Typ 830)

The Horch Typ 830 was one of many commercial designs fitted with military bodies in the 1930s. Originally used as a troop carrier and radio car, the vehicle saw action in most theatres.

Before the introduction of the standard (*Einheit*) vehicles, the German army made extensive use of commercial cars as a means of motorizing the various arms and services. The **Auto-Union/Horch Typ 830** was one of the many commercial passenger car chassis fitted with various military bodies between the late 1920s and early 1930s. V-8 powerplants with a capacity of 3, 3.2 and 3.5 litres were installed. Since only the rear wheels were driven, larger tyres and different rear-axle ratios helped to increase the types' cross-country performance. The vehicles saw action in most theatres of war, the majority of them fitted with open superstructures and used as prime movers for light infantry guns, as well as radio communications vehicles. The signal troops also used a variety of enclosed van-type bodies. The **Kfz 11** was a closed-bodied communications or radio vehicle based on this chassis with two seats and a boot. The closed body was often made of wood. Later production models were fitted with sheet-metal doors and removable side windows. Eventually production was discontinued in favour of the medium standard cross-country personnel carrier built from 1937 onwards by Horch and, after 1940, by Opel.

Specification
Kfz 11 (Auto-Union/Horch Typ 830)
Dimensions: length 4.80 m (15 ft 9 in); width 1.80 m (5 ft 11 in); height 1.85 m (6 ft 1 in); wheelbase 3.20 m (10 ft 6 in)
Weight: net 990 kg (2,183 lb)
Powerplant: one Horch V-8 2.98-litre petrol engine developing 70 bhp (52.2 kW)
Transmission: ZF Aphon with four forward and one reverse gears
Tyres: 6.0 × 18 (metric)

The Kfz 11 saw action in Poland as a personnel carrier. Infantry who were not lucky enough to get places in the cars or trucks had to make do with bicycles or their own two feet.

Kraftfahrzeug 15 (Mercedes-Benz 340)

The **Kfz 15 mittlerer geländegängiger Personenkraftwagen** (m.gl.Pkw, or medium cross-country personnel carrier) was used as a communications (*Fernsprech*) or radio (*Funk*) car. It had an open 4-seater body and a boot, and it was fitted with a towing hook. The vehicle was powered by a V-8 engine. Commercial chassis used for this role were: in 1933-8 the Horch 830 and 830B1, in 1937-9 the Wanderer W23S, and in 1938-40 the **Mercedes-Benz 340**.

The Mercedes-Benz 340, a larger version of the 320, was powered by a 3.5-litre engine and had a very long wheelbase, which tended to impair its cross-country performance. Like the Kfz 11 described above, production of this vehicle was discontinued in favour of the medium standard (*Einheit*) cross-country personnel carrier. This latter vehicle differed basically from the light model (described under Kfz 2, or Stöwer 40) in that the rear wheels were not steerable. As before, however, all-wheel-drive was used. The chassis was a conventional type used for staff cars, radio vehicles and other specialized types. Depending upon the manufacturer, the engine had a swept volume of between 2.9 and 3.5 litres. Horch engines were standard for most models, the few exceptions being equipped with an Opel type.

Specification
Kfz 15 (Mercedes-Benz 340)
Dimensions: length 4.44 m (14 ft 7 in); width 1.68 m (5 ft 6 in); height 1.73 m (5 ft 8 in); wheelbase 3.12 m (10 ft 3 in)
Weight: net 2405 kg (5,302 lb)
Powerplant: one Mercedes-Benz 6-cylinder petrol engine developing 90 bhp (67.1 kW)

Above: The Mercedes-Benz 340 was not the ideal vehicle upon which to base the Kfz 15 body, as the long wheelbase impaired cross-country ability in spite of four-wheel drive. Even so, many were used as radio cars, staff cars and other special types.

Right: The fall of Tobruk in June 1942 was a shock to the British, and soon the town square was filled with a motley collection of Afrika Korps vehicles, including this Mercedes 340 ambulance.

Transmission: four forward and one reverse gears
Tyres: 6.5×20 (metric)

Daimler-Benz G 5

During 1925-6 the first proposals were considered for the development of specialized vehicles for the Reichswehr (predecessor of the Wehrmacht). Among others, a requirement was laid down for a fully cross-country personnel carrier. This was to have six seats and use a six-wheeled chassis with more than one driven axle. The development of such a vehicle was taken up by the firms of Horch-Werk AG of Zwickau, Daimler-Benz AG of Stuttgart and Selve Automobilwerk AG of Hamelin, each of them supplying several models for trial purposes. The first Daimler-Benz model, designated **Daimler-Benz G 1**, several of which were produced between 1926-8, were powered by a 50-hp M03 6-cylinder engine. This had the drive taken to the four rear wheels. The unladen weight was 1200 kg (2,645 lb), and the payload was 1000 kg (2,205 lb). Daimler-Benz alone continued development of the three-axled personnel carrier. Between 1933 and 1934 it produced a small number of its **G 4** model. This was a vehicle widely known for its use by Hitler, although it was never suited to military usage. It had a poor cross-country performance and was too large, too heavy and too expensive. Between 1933 and 1934 57 were built and these were almost exclusively employed by high officials of the Nazi party and the general staff; one was modified as a communications vehicle for

use by Hitler during his field trips. With the development of the *Einheit* series of personnel carriers, Daimler-Benz, which appears to have been neglected in the share-out of production contracts for these vehicles, prepared a model of its own as a private venture. The **Daimler-Benz G 5** was basically orientated to the production model by Auto-Union AG. Between 1937 and 1941 378 were built, although only a few were actually adopted by the Wehrmacht. The vehicle had four-

wheel drive and steering. A few were fitted with elaborate superstructures for desert travel.

Specification
Daimler-Benz G 5
Dimensions: length 4.52 m (14 ft 10 in); width 1.70 m (5 ft 7 in); height 1.80 m (5 ft 11 in); wheelbase 2.79 m (9 ft 2 in)
Weight: net 1630 kg (3,593 lb)
Powerplant: one Mercedes-Benz 6-cylinder petrol engine developing 90 hp (67 kW)

A powerful vehicle, with four-wheel drive and four-wheel steering, the Daimler-Benz G 5 was designed as a private venture to meet the Wehrmacht Einheit specification. Few of the 378 built actually saw army service.

Transmission: five forward and one reverse gears
Tyres: 5.50×18 (metric)

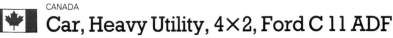

Car, Heavy Utility, 4×2, Ford C 11 ADF

The Ford C 11 ADF Heavy Utility Car was a commercial Canadian vehicle, based on the 1942 Ford Fordor Station Wagon, adopted for military use with only minimal changes. Canadian Ford produced the vehicle mainly for the British army, although several were used by the Canadian army. The type used extensively in the Western Desert and Italy by HQ staffs. The military version had right-hand drive (for the UK), heavy-duty tyres, black-out equipment, simplified and strengthened bumpers, internal rifle racks, a map-container, first-aid and medical kit, radio-interference suppression, fire-extinguishers, entrenching tools and other standard fittings, including a removable roof rack. In addition to the driver the all-steel body had seating for five passengers, two in front and three on the single bench-type rear seat. Access was via four doors. In addition there was a full-width rear door split horizontally and hinged top and bottom so that the lower portion formed a tailboard.

A similar vehicle, seating seven passengers and designated **Ford C 11 A 5**, was also used, this having lighter tyres and axles and making use of the luggage space for the additional two seats.

Another Ford Heavy Utility Car was essentially the same as the C 11 ADF but based on the 1941 production chassis. Weighing 91 kg (200 lb) more than

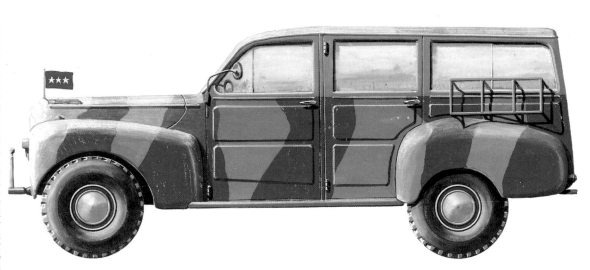

its predecessors, this variant had a slightly different estate car body and front radiator grill. Some of these vehicles had roof hatches added and jerry and water can racks fitted externally.

Specification
Car, Heavy Utility, 4×2, Ford C 11 ADF
Dimensions: length 4.93 m (16 ft 2 in);

width 2.01 m (6 ft 7 in); height 1.83 m (6 ft 0 in); wheelbase 2.90 m (9 ft 6 in)
Weight: net 1814 kg (4,000 lb)
Powerplant: one Ford mercury V-8 3.91-litre petrol engine developing 95 bhp (70.8 kW)
Transmission: three forward and one reverse gears
Tyres: 9,00×13 for C 11 ADF, and 6.00×13 for C 11 AS

Heavy utility cars were of two major types, those of military design and those converted from civilian models. The C 11 was developed from a commercial station wagon model, and was used extensively in the right-hand drive version by the British, in a variety of roles, and equipped HQ Staffs in Italy and the Desert.

Truck, ½-ton, 4×4, Weapons Carrier, Dodge T207-WC3

US Army ½-ton trucks were provided by a number of manufacturers including Dodge, Chevrolet, Diamond T, Ford, Marmon-Herrington and GMC. The ½-ton 4×4 vehicle was originally developed by the Marmon-Herrington Company of Indianapolis in July 1936. During the early stages of the war most of the ½-ton 4×2 vehicles were slightly modified civilian models and were retained for the home front. With the development of the war, standard tactical chassis began to be adopted to super-

sede these earlier models. As regards the **Truck, ½-ton 4×4**, Chrysler's Dodge Division began mass-production during 1939. The original **T202** series used many commercial components, and 4,640 of all types were manufactured by Dodge, most of them as command reconnaissance cars and light trucks. The **Truck, ½-ton, 4×4, Weapons Carrier, Dodge T207-WC3** was introduced in 1941, and replaced all previous models then in use. It became one of the basic trans-

portation means for all arms and services. The vehicle was open-topped with dismountable bows and a canvas tilt. As with most other Dodge trucks, a spare wheel was carried on the offside of the vehicle.

Specification
Truck, ½-ton, 4×4, Weapons Carrier, Dodge T207-WC3
Dimensions: length 4.60 m (15 ft 1 in); width 1.93 m (6 ft 4 in); height 2.24 m (7 ft 4 in); wheelbase 2.95 m (9 ft 8 in)
Weight: net 2014 kg (4,440 lb)
Powerplant: one Dodge 6-cylinder petrol engine developing 85 bhp (63.4 kW)
Transmission: four forward and one reverse gears
Tyres: 7.50×16

Truck, ½-ton, Ambulance, 4×4, Dodge T215-WC27

In the ½-ton range Dodge was the sole producer to US Army contracts. The first contract for 14,000 ½-ton 4×4 trucks was placed with Dodge in mid-1940. The basic chassis was a slight modification of the normal commercial vehicle to incorporate a new transfer gearbox and forward transmission to cater for the four-wheel drive requirement. The basic chassis was employed for numerous roles including command, command reconnaissance, radio, weapons carrier and **Truck, ½-ton, Ambulance, 4×4, Dodge T215-WC27.** Depending upon the role, they had the option of a fixed bodywork or open cab. The ambulance version had the former and the command, command reconnaissance, radio and weapons carrier versions, the latter. These earlier US military pattern 4×4 trucks were superseded in 1942 by a range of wider and more robust body types (¾-ton) with a lower silhouette and shorter wheelbase, also built by Dodge. By this time 82,000 ½-ton trucks had been built. These left-hand drive vehicles were built by the

Dodge trucks were adapted to serve as ambulances, with sheet steel bodies accommodating up to four stretcher cases. Early versions had enclosed cabs as shown, but later reverted to the open cab of the weapon carrier version.

A ½-ton Dodge 4×4, the T215 model, preceded the ¾-ton T214 in 1941. It was at this time that the Dodge

Dodge Brothers Corporation Division of the Chrysler Corporation of America and also, in a modified form, in Canada. The **International M-1-4** range was similar in layout but produced solely for the US Marine Corps and US Navy. A great number of these Dodge ½-ton trucks were supplied to the UK

division of Chrysler became the large-scale producer of such vehicles for the US forces.

Specification
Truck, ½-ton, Ambulance, 4×4, Dodge T215-WC27
Dimensions: length 4.67 m (15 ft 4 in); width 1.93 m (6 ft 4 in); height 2.13 m

and the USSR under the Lend-Lease programme.

(7 ft 0 in); wheelbase 2.95 m (9 ft 8 in)
Weight: net 2046 kg (4,510 lb)
Powerplant: one Dodge T215 6-cylinder petrol engine developing 92 bhp (68.6 kW)
Transmission: four forward and one reverse gears
Tyres: 7.50×16

The Dodge T215 WC 23 was a ½-ton command and reconnaissance vehicle of the same family as the T207. The 1941 pattern vehicles are identifiable from the heavier 1942 models by their sloping bonnet.

Truck, ¾-ton, 4×4, Command Reconnaissance, Dodge T214-WC56

Introduced during 1942, the **Dodge ¾-ton 4×4** range of light trucks superseded the original ½-ton 4×4 range. Both Ford and Dodge, previously the main suppliers of ½-ton 4×4 vehicles, each produced prototypes for US Army evaluation: these were slightly wider and lower than their predecessors, had larger wheels and tyres, and possessed stronger suspensions. The Dodge version was selected and officially introduced during June 1942 when production started into full swing. As with the ½-ton vehicles there were several special body types. The **Dodge T214** series comprised the **WC51** weapons carrier, **WC52** weapons carrier with winch, **WC53** general-purpose and field command vehicle, **WC54** ambulance, **WC55** 37-mm Gun Motor Carriage M6, **WC56** command reconnaissance vehicle, **WC57** command reconnaissance with winch, **WC58** radio vehicle, **WC59** light maintenance and installation vehicle, **WC60** emergency repair vehicle, **WC61** telephone maintenance and installation vehicle, and **WC64** ambulance. Generally, the vehicles in this series were referred to as 'Beeps' (contraction of Big Jeeps). The WC51 weapons carrier was used principally to transport personnel, weapons, tools and other equipment. It had an open body with a canvas tilt and canvas side-screens. The WC53 was fitted with a 'safari' type body with rear side doors, a map table, special seats and internal lighting. The WC56 command reconnaissance was the most common variant, and was used for reconnaissance and liaison, and as a staff car for high-ranking officers. It was fitted with map-boards and had a detachable canvas top and side-screens.

Powerplant: one Dodge T214 6-cylinder petrol engine developing 92 bhp (68.6 kW)
Transmission: four forward and one reverse gears
Tyres: 9.00×16

Above: Superseding the T207-WC3, the T214 range of trucks were ¾-ton vehicles. Introduced early in 1942, they were in full production by June. Used to transport personnel, weapons, tools and equipment, the T214 range were sometimes known as 'Beeps' (Big Jeeps).

Below: Dodge T214s can still be found in use in many parts of the world, a tribute to the vehicle's sturdy design. The command and reconnaissance version, the WC53, was used in much the same way as the Jeep.

Specification
Truck, ¾-ton, 4×4, Command Reconnaissance, Dodge T214-WC56
Dimensions: length 4.24 m (13 ft 11 in); width 1.99 m (6 ft 6.5 in); height 2.07 m (6 ft 9.5 in); wheelbase 2.49 m (8 ft 2 in)
Weight: net 2449 kg (5,400 lb)

Lorry, 8 cwt, 4×2, FFW, Humber

Just before the outbreak of war in 1939 the British army was in the process of intensive mechanization, and several classes of load capacity had been defined for 'B' vehicles. The second class was the 8-cwt truck which fulfilled such roles as the GS (General Service) and FFW (Fitted For Wireless). Such 8-cwt trucks with both 4×2 and 4×4 wheel arrangements were produced in considerable numbers from a period just before the war, but were eventually phased out of production in order to rationalize output and reduce the number of types in service. The 5-cwt and 15-cwt classes could carry out any duties that had been allocated to the 8-cwt class. These vehicles were manufactured by Ford, Morris and Humber. Similar in appearance, these vehicles had detachable well-type bodies with seating for three men (two facing offside and one nearside) and canvas tilts, though the wireless version had seating for two men only. Folding legs were fitted which enabled the body to be placed on the ground for use as a mobile command centre or wireless station. The **Humber 8-cwt Lorry** early production vehicles employed the chassis of the original 1939 Humber Snipe saloon with louvres in the bonnet sides. The **Lorry, 8-cwt, 4×4, FFW** incorporated the No. 11 wireless set, a map table and other fittings necessary for command operations. The wireless batteries could be recharged from a generator driven off the main engine. The GS model had the same body but lacked the radio equipment.

Specification
Lorry, 8 cwt, 4×2, FFW, Humber
Dimensions: length 4.44 m (14 ft 7 in); width 1.96 m (6 ft 5 in); height 1.89 m (6 ft 2.5 in); wheelbase 2.84 m (9 ft 4 in)
Weight: net 1769 kg (3,900 lb)
Powerplant: one Humber 6-cylinder petrol engine developing 85 bhp (63.4 kW)
Transmission: four forward and one reverse gears
Tyres: 9.00×13

Right: The Humber FFW (Fitted for Wireless) was an 8-cwt 4×2 truck with seating for two wireless operators in the body. The body was detachable for use on the ground as a wireless station or as a command centre.

The early production version of the Humber 8-cwt lorry was based on the chassis of the pre-war Humber Snipe saloon, and could be identified by the louvres in the bonnet sides. Later these were omitted, as shown here.

Car, Heavy Utility, 4×4 (FWD), Humber

Together with the Ford 4×2 Heavy Utility, the **Humber Heavy Utility Car** was the basic staff and command car of the British army during World War II at all levels of command. Nicknamed the **Humber 'Box'**, this was the only British-built four-wheel drive utility car, and production began during May 1941, continuing for the duration of the war. Employed on a very wide scale, this staff car remained in service until the late 1950s. The cab and body were integral and of all-steel construction, and later models were fitted with a sliding roof. The body was a six-seater with four individual seats and, at the rear, two tip-up occasional seats which could be folded down to leave the body clear for stowage: there was a folding map table behind the front seats. There were two hinged doors on each side with a full-width double door arrangement at the rear. The front mudguards, radiator grill and bonnet were identical to those of the Humber 8-cwt 4×4 chassis. In the Western Desert this vehicle was sometimes modified by replacement of the roof by a canvas folding tilt. Some vehicles,

A four-wheel-drive estate car, the Humber Heavy Utility was the basic staff and command car in British service, and remained so for some years after 1945. It was the only British vehicle of its type.

especially those used by high-ranking officers, were also fitted with a sliding roof.

Specification
Car, Heavy Utility, 4×4 (FWD), Humber
Dimensions: length 4.29 m (14 ft 1 in); width 1.88 m (6 ft 2 in); height 1.96 m (6 ft 5 in); wheelbase 2.84 m (9 ft 3.75 in)
Weight: net 2413 kg (5,320 lb)
Powerplant: one Humber 6-cylinder 1-L-W-F 4.08-litre petrol engine developing 85 bhp (63.4 kW)
Transmission: four forward and one reverse gear with auxiliary two-speed
Tyres: 9.25×16

Fitted with a folding map table, the Humber Heavy Utility was used mainly as a staff car. Some were given folding canvas tops for operations in North Africa. Staff officers occasionally had forward sliding roofs fitted.

Tractor, Artillery, 4×4, Morris C8

The Morris Company produced a whole range of vehicles for the British army, one of the most successful being the **Morris C8 Artillery Tractor** (popularly known as the **Quad**). Introduced in 1939, this vehicle had four-wheel drive and was equipped with a 4-ton winch driven from the transfer case. It had a distinctive beetle-shaped body and usually towed a limber and 18- or 25-pdr gun/howitzer. As far as the army was concerned the vehicles built for gun-towing had to have the same characteristics as the horse-drawn gun carriage team which they replaced, such as good cross-country performance, seating for the gun crew, and adequate stowage space for equipment and ammunition. They were always manned by artillerymen. In this vehicle there was accommodation for the driver, gun-crew commander and five men. The final model, introduced in 1944, was automotively identical but had a new body (no longer beetle-shaped) with an open top and canvas tarpaulin cover. This was introduced as a dual-purpose vehicle to tow the 17-pdr anti-tank gun or the 25-pdr gun/howitzer, and could now seat eight men including the driver. Two doors were provided on each side. At the rear of the body ammunition racks were installed to take all types of standard British artillery ammunition. This vehicle remained in service until the 1950s. The original vehicle was powered by a Morris 4-cylinder petrol engine and the gearbox had five forward and one reverse gear driving all four wheels. When the **C8 Mk III** version was introduced, however, four-wheel drive could be disengaged except in first gear and reverse.

Morris was one of the many suppliers of GS pattern trucks, and the C8 4×2 was one of the major types lost in numbers at Dunkirk. Some were used in the desert, however. The C8 was eventually upgraded to four-wheel drive.

Specification
Tractor, Artillery 4×4, Morris C8 Mk III
Dimensions: length 4.49 m (14 ft 8.75 in); width 2.21 m (7 ft 3 in); height 2.26 m (7 ft 5 in); wheelbase 2.51 m (8 ft 3 in)

Weight: net 3402 kg (7,500 lb)
Powerplant: one Morris 4-cylinder 3.5-litre petrol engine developing 70 bhp (52.2 kW)
Transmission: five forward and one reverse gears
Tyres: 10.5×16

Above: The C8 Artillery Tractors were originally four-wheel-drive versions of the C8 trucks. The Mk III, introduced in 1944-5, had a canvas top and square contour body.

Truck, 15 cwt, GS, 4×2, Bedford MWD

During 1935 the War Office carried out trials with new lorry models, and the Bedford Truck Division of Vauxhall Motors Ltd submitted various prototype vehicles. One of these was a modification of the commercial 2-ton lorry with rear-wheel drive. Following the trials the vehicle was fitted with a new radiator and larger tyres. After further trials in 1936 the chassis was modified to increase the ground clearance and a new engine cooling system was incorporated. In 1937 a special-to-type Bedford WD prototype was produced on this chassis, rated at 15-cwt payload capacity. The most noticeable feature was the flat full-width bonnet necessitated by the extra-large air-filter specified by the War Mechanisation Board. During 1938 a more powerful engine was used. An initial order for 2,000 **Bedford 15-cwt Truck** vehicles was placed in August 1939, the first 50 being constructed as special portée vehicles to carry the 2-pdr anti-tank gun. Originally, the vehicle had an open cab with folding windscreen and collapsible canvas tilt, but from 1943 an enclosed cab with side-doors, canvas top and perspex side screens was adopted. By the end of the war Bedford had produced a total of 250,000 vehicles, a large proportion of which were this model. The vehicle remained in service with the British army until the late 1950s. Although intended mainly

as a workhorse for the infantry, the Bedford 15-cwt GS eventually became used by all arms including the Royal Navy and the RAF.

Specification
Truck, 15 cwt, GS, 4×2, Bedford MWD
Dimensions: length 4.38 m (14 ft 4.5 in); width 1.99 m (6 ft 6.5 in); height 2.29 m (7 ft 6 in) with GS tilt and 1.93 m (6 ft 4 in) with GS tilt; wheelbase 2.51 m (8 ft 3 in)
Weight: net 2132 kg (4,700 lb)
Powerplant: one Bedford 6-cylinder OHV 3.5-litre petrol engine developing 72 bhp (53.7 kW)
Transmission: four forward and one reverse gears
Tyres: 9.00×16

The 15-cwt class of truck was most important to the British army, numbers in use rising from 15,000 in 1939 to 230,000 in 1945. The Bedford MWD with GS body is typical of a late-war 15-cwt 4×2 truck.

GAZ-67B light car

The **GAZ-67** (named for the Gorkiy Avtomobil Zavod, or Gorky Car Factory) was first manufactured in the Soviet Union during 1943 as a cross-country vehicle for the transportation of personnel and light equipment. It was obviously greatly influenced in design and construction by the US Bantam Jeep (the USSR received some 20,000 Jeeps during World War II under the Lend-Lease programme). In particular the body and headlamp arrangement were very similar to those of the Bantam. The vehicle was powered by the Soviet Ford (GAZ) Model A 4-cylinder side-valve engine, and the wheels, suspension and other automotive components were similar to those used on other GAZ cars, with the exception of the use of four-wheel drive. Suspension was through quarter-elliptic springs. The fuel tank was located below the dashboard. The vehicle was fitted out with four seats and was capable of speeds up to 90 km/h (56 mph). Compared with the US Jeep it had very poor acceleration. The **GAZ-67B** differed from the original GAZ-67 in that it had a longer wheelbase (1.85 m/6 ft 0.75 in as against 1.27 m/4 ft 2 in). This model saw extensive service in Indo-China (where the only existing specimen in the West was captured by the French) and Korea. Production ceased in 1953, the role being taken over by the GAZ-69A. This class of light vehicle has always been used as the workhorse of the airborne divisions.

Specification
GAZ-67B
Dimensions: length 3.34 m (10 ft 11.33 in); width 1.68 m (5 ft 6 in); height 1.70 m (5 ft 7 in); wheelbase 1.85 m (6 ft 0.75 in)

Above: First made in 1943 at Gorky, the GAZ-67 was influenced by early Jeeps (20,000 having been sent under Lend-Lease). Simple and rather crude, the GAZ-67 was nonetheless strong and a good off-road performer.

Right: The GAZ-67B saw extensive service in Korea, where this particular vehicle was captured, as well as being used in numbers during World War II. It was eventually replaced by the GAZ-69.

Weight: net 1220 kg (2,690 lb)
Powerplant: one GAZ-A 4-cylinder 3.28-litre petrol engine developing 54 bhp (40.3 kW)
Transmission: four forward and one reverse gears
Tyres: 6.50×16 or 7.00×16 (metric)

Autovettura Fiat 508 C.M.

Most light vehicles used by the Italian armed forces were of Fiat manufacture. Where the Germans had designed and produced several pseudo-military vehicles before the war, so had the Italians, the **Autovettura Fiat 508 C.M.** being one of them. The Italians referred to the type as a colonial vehicle, specially designed for use on rough terrain such as that encountered in Africa and Ethiopia. Also known as the **Fiat 1100 Torpedo Militare**, the Fiat 508 C.M. was the most prolific Italian military vehicle of World War II. Just before the war the Ispettorata della Motorizzazione (Inspectorate of Motorization) had requested development of a light, simple and robust vehicle capable of achieving high speeds on roads and reasonable performance cross country, with low production costs. As the result the Fiat Company developed the **Torpedo 508**, derived from a similar civilian model, from which it differed in an increase in ground clearance, a reduction in the gearbox ratios and a special military body. The vehicle was built in substantial numbers and in various versions between 1939 and 1945, one of which was a special colonial model adapted to avoid ingress of sand and sinking in soft terrain (**Modello 1100 Col.**).

Above: The Fiat 508 was developed from pre-war colonial designs, and like many Italian vehicles little was required to militarize a car designed for rough tracks in Libya and Eritrea.

Right: Based on the 'balilla' civilian model, the 508 C.M. was in production from 1939 to 1945. It was a simple vehicle, with reasonable cross-country performance and a high road speed.

Specification
Autovettura Fiat 508 C.M.
Dimensions: length 3.35 m (11 ft 0 in); width 1.37 m (4 ft 6 in); height 1.57 m (5 ft 2 in); wheelbase 2.26 m (7 ft 5 in)
Weight: net 1065 kg (2,348 lb)
Powerplant: one Fiat 108C 4-cylinder petrol engine developing 32 bhp (23.9 kW)
Transmission: four forward and one reverse gears
Tyres: 5.00×18 (metric)

Type 95 Scout Car (Kurogane Black Medal)

The **Type 95** was a lightweight reconnaissance vehicle developed after the Manchurian Incident, which had indicated a real need for such a vehicle. Some 4,800 examples were built by Kurogane with variations in bodywork. This was about the only native vehicle of its type used by the Imperial Japanese Army. Most others were of American origin or patterned on American designs. The air-cooled engine was ideal for operations in Manchuria and northern China, where there was often a lack of unpolluted water and frequently very low temperatures. Initial difficulties were experienced with the four-wheel drive and front universal joints, but these were eventually overcome. Special tyres, with heavy rubber treads, were provided for exceptionally difficult terrain. Power was supplied by a 4-stroke, 2-cylinder V-1-A-F 1399-cc air-cooled engine operating on petrol and developing a maximum of 33 bhp (24.6 KW). The engine had a compression ratio of 5:1 and a removable cylinder head. Ignition was provided by a high-tension magneto with a 12-volt generator for charging the battery; a 12-volt electric starter motor was used. Oil pressure was maintained by a gear-pressure feed pump, and a conventional fuel pump was used. There was a main fuel tank for 35 litres (7.7 Imp gal) and an auxiliary fuel tank of 4-litre (0.88-Imp gal) capacity. Fuel consumption was stated to be 4 litres (0.88 Imp gal) per hour. A dry single-plate clutch was used. The foot-brakes were mechanical contracting with an emergency mechanical expanding type.

Specification
Type 95 Scout Car
Dimensions: length 3.38 m (11 ft 1 in); width 1.52 m (5 ft 0 in); height 1.68 m (5 ft 6 in); wheelbase 3.84 m (12 ft 7 in)
Weight: net 1,100 kg (2,425 lb)
Powerplant: one 2-cylinder 4-stroke V-1-A-F petrol engine developing 33 bhp (24.6 kW)
Transmission: selective sliding type giving three forward and one reverse gears
Tyres: 18×6

The four-wheel-drive Type 95 Scout car was one of the few unarmoured vehicles used by the Imperial Japanese Army that was not based on an American original. The 'Black Medal' was made in closed cab and truck versions in addition to the more usual convertible.

Self-Propelled Guns

Once Germany had demonstrated the new pace of armoured warfare, most belligerent nations began to develop fully mechanized divisions. Field guns were mounted on tank chassis and a new generation of armoured fighting vehicles was born. Self-propelled guns became more important, and largely replaced towed artillery.

Self-propelled artillery was very much a product of the type of warfare that evolved during World War II: before 1939 self-propelled artillery scarcely existed (apart from a few trial weapons), but by 1943 it was used by all the combatant nations. The sudden rise of this new form of weapon can be attributed almost entirely to the impact of the battle tank on tactics, for warfare no longer took place at the speed of the marching soldier and the scouting horse, but at the speed of the tank. These swarmed all over Poland, France and eventually the Soviet Union, and the only way that the supporting arms, including the artillery, could keep up with them was to become equally mobile.

Many of the early self-propelled artillery platforms were simply conversions of existing tanks in order to mount artillery pieces, but the measure of conversion varied widely. Some were scarcely more than lash-ups to meet a hasty requirement or were built locally to suit a particular task. Others, however, were carefully designed from the outset and may be regarded as virtually new products. But two distinct trends can be discerned in the way self-propelled artillery was used in action. One school

Cossacks in German Waffen-SS service relax alongside a Sturmgeschütz III self-propelled gun, arguably the most famous of its type. The early versions had short-barrelled guns.

regarded mobile artillery as a simple adjunct to existing artillery doctrines, and this school designed and used the self-propelled platforms to deliver indirect supporting fire in the usual way. The other school regarded the mobile gun as a form of close-range direct-fire weapon to be used in close support of armour, and this

school was responsible for the assault gun. Today both types of weapon are extant, but in the West the modern accent is on the indirect-fire weapon and in the East it is on the close-support assault gun.

Only a selection of the many types of self-propelled artillery that proliferated between 1939 and 1945 can be found in this

section. While some important types have been omitted, some 'one-offs' have been included to demonstrate the variety of design concepts that were attempted. The number and approaches of the different designs were enormous before 1945, but only relatively few models actually found their way into action. Most of these are covered here.

sIG 33 auf Geschützwagen

The German infantry battalions each had a small artillery complement of four 7.5-cm (2.95-in) light howitzers and two 15-cm (5.9-in) infantry howitzers for their own local fire support. The 15-cm howitzer was known as the schwere Infantrie Geschütz 33 (sIG 33, or heavy infantry gun) and was a very useful and versatile weapon, but it was heavy and the only 'equipment' allocated to most infantry formations for the movement of the weapons were horse teams. Thus when an increasing degree of mechanization began to filter through the German army the sIG 33 was high on the list for consideration.

The first form of mobile sIG 33 was used during the French campaign of May 1940. It was one of the simplest and most basic of all the German self-propelled equipments, for it consisted of nothing more than a sIG 33 mounted complete with carriage and wheels on to a turretless PzKpfw I light tank as the **15-cm sIG 33 auf Geschützwagen I Ausf B**. Armoured shields were provided for the crew of four, and that was that. It was not a very satisfactory conversion as the centre of gravity was rather high and the chassis was overloaded. Moreover, the armour protection was not good, and so in 1942 the PzKpfw II was the subject for conversion. This **15-cm sIG 33 auf Geschützwagen II ausf C SdKfz 121** conversion had the howitzer mounted low in the chassis, and was so successful that during 1943 a version with a lengthened hull was produced as the **15-cm sIG 33 auf Fgst PzKpfw II (Sf) Verlänget**.

The ex-Czech PzKpfw 38(t) was also converted to act as a sIG 33 carrier. In 1942 the first of a series of vehicles known collectively as the **15-cm sIG 33 (Sf) auf PzKpfw 38(t) Bison SdKfz 138** were produced. The first series had the sIG 33 mounted forward on the hull top behind an open armoured superstructure, and this weapon/vehicle arrangement proved to be so successful that it was formalized in 1943 by the production of a new version. This was a factory-produced model rather than a conversion of existing tanks and had

One of the first German self-propelled conversions was the mounting of a 15-cm sIG 33 infantry howitzer onto the hull of a PzKpfw I light tank.

the vehicle engine mounted forward (instead of at the rear as originally located) this entailing the movement of the fighting compartment to the hull rear. This was the **SdKfz 138/1** (SdKfz for *Sonder Kraftfahrzeug*, or special vehicle) and it was this vehicle that was retained as the German army's standard sIG 33 carrier until the end of the war. The SdKfz 138/1 had a crew of four men including the driver, and 15 shells were carried on the vehicle. There was no room for more because the fighting compartment was rather restricted for space.

There was one other sIG 33 self-propelled version, this time on a PzKpfw III chassis. This **15-cm sIG 33 auf PzKpfw III** appeared in 1941 and used a large box superstructure on a PzKpfw III to house the sIG 33. This proved to be rather too much of a good thing, for the chassis was really too large for the weapon which could be easily carried by lighter vehicles. Thus production never got properly under way, being terminated after only 12 conversions had been made. These vehicles were used in action on the Eastern Front.

All the sIG 33 self-propelled equipments were used for their original role, i.e. the direct fire-support of infantry units in the field. Perhaps the most successful of these self-propelled carriages were the Bison and the later SdKfz 138/1. Over 370 of the vehicles were produced, and they were still in production in late 1944.

Specification
SdKfz 138/1
Type: self-propelled infantry-support howitzer
Crew: 4
Weight: 11500 kg (25,353 lb)
Powerplant: one Praga 6-cylinder

Taken from a German newsreel, this shot clearly shows how high and awkward the mounting of the 15-cm howitzer really was on the PzKpfw I chassis. The crew had only limited

petrol engine developing 111.9 kW (150 hp)
Dimensions: length 4.835 m (15 ft 10.4 in); width 2.15 m (7 ft 0.6 in); height 2.4 m (7 ft 10.5 in)

protection and stowage was minimal, but it provided the Germans with an indication of what would be required in future.

Performance: maximum road speed 35 km/h (21.75 mph); maximum road range 185 km (115 miles); fording 0.914 m (3 ft)
Armament: one 15-cm (5.9-in) howitzer

Wespe

Even as early as 1939 it was obvious that the days of the little PzKpfw II tank were numbered, for it lacked both armament and armour. However, it was in production and quite reliable, so when the need arose for self-propelled artillery the PzKpfw II was selected to be the carrier for the 10.5-cm (4.13-in) leFH 18 field howitzer. The conversion of the tank hull to carry the howitzer was quite straightforward, for the howitzer was mounted behind an open topped armoured shield towards the rear of the hull and the area where the turret had been was armoured over and the space used for ammunition stowage. Maximum armour thickness was 18 mm (0.7 in).

The result was the self-propelled howitzer known as the **Wespe** (wasp) though its full official designation was rather more cumbersome: **leFH 18/2 auf Fgst Kpfw II (Sf) SdKfz 124 Wespe**, but to everyone it was just the Wespe. It was a very popular little self-propelled weapon that soon gained for itself a reputation for reliability and mobility. The first of them were based

on the PzKpfw II Ausf F chassis and went into action on the Eastern Front during 1943. On this front they were used by the divisional artillery batteries of the Panzer and Panzergrenadier divisions. They were usually organized into batteries of six howitzers with up to five batteries to an *Abteilung* (battalion).

The Wespe was so successful in its artillery support role that Hitler himself made an order that all available PzKpfw II chassis production should be allocated to the Wespe alone, and the many other improvised weapons on the PzKpfw II chassis were dropped or their armament diverted to other chassis. The main Wespe construction centre was the Famo plant in Poland, and there production was so rapid that by mid-1944 682 examples had been built. Some time around that

The SdKfz 124 Wespe was a purpose-built carrier for a 105-mm howitzer based on the chassis of the PzKpfw II light tank. It was first used during 1942 and had a crew of five.

date manufacture of the Wespe ceased, but not before 158 had been completed without howitzers; these vehicles had the gap in the armour plate for the howitzer sealed off, the space behind the armour being used for resupply ammunition needed by batteries in the front line.

A typical Wespe went into action carrying its crew of five, including the driver, and 32 rounds of ammunition. A Wespe battery was completely mobile, although some of the vehicles were soft-skinned trucks for carrying ammunition and other supplies. The forward observers were usually carried in light armoured vehicles although some batteries used ex-Czech or captured French tanks for this purpose. Fire orders were relayed back to the battery by radio, and from the battery fire command post the orders were further relayed to the gun positions by land lines. The howitzer carried on the Wespe was the standard 10.5-cm leFH 18 as used by towed batteries (although most were

fitted with muzzle brakes) and so used the same ammunition. They also had the same range of 10675 m (11,675 yards).

Specification
Wespe
Type: self-propelled field howitzer
Crew: 5
Weight: 11000 kg (24,251 lb)
Powerplant: one Maybach 6-cylinder petrol engine developing 104.4 kW (140 hp)
Dimensions: length 4.81 m (15 ft 9.4 in); width 2.28 m (7 ft 5.75 in); height 2.3 m (7 ft 6.6 in)
Performance: maximum road speed 40 km/h (24.85 mph); road range 220 km (137 miles); fording 0.8 m (2 ft 7.5 in)
Armament: one 105-mm (4.13-in) howitzer and one 7.92-mm (0.31-in) MG34 machine-gun

This shot of a Wespe on the move shows that the top of the fighting compartment was open but protection was provided at the rear.

Note how small the vehicle actually was compared to the stature of the gun crew in the compartment.

GERMANY
Hummel

The self-propelled artillery vehicle that became known as the **Hummel** (bumble bee) was a hybrid combining components of the PzKpfw III and PzKpfw IV tanks into a new vehicle known as the **Geschützwagen III/IV.** The first of these hybrids was produced during 1941 and used a lengthened PzKpfw IV suspension and running gear combined with the final drive assemblies, track and transmission of the PzKpfw III. Onto this new hull was built an open superstructure formed with light armour plates, and two types of weapon were mounted. Vehicles intended for use as tank destroyers mounted a version of the 88-mm (3.46-in) anti-tank gun, but vehicles intended for use as self-propelled artillery mounted a special version of the 15-cm (5.9-in) FH 18 field howitzer.

The FH 18 vehicle was the **15-cm Panzerfeldhaubitze 18M auf GW III/IV SdKfz 165 Hummel,** and it formed the heavy field artillery element of the Panzer and Panzergrenadier divisions from 1942 onwards. The ordnance was known as the Panzerfeldhaubitz 18/1, and could fire a 43.5-kg (95.9-lb) projectile to a range of 13325 m (14,572 yards). The first howitzers produced for the self-propelled role were fitted with large muzzle brakes, but experience demonstrated that these were not really necessary and were accordingly left off later production versions. Maximum armour thickness was 50 mm (1.97 in).

The Hummel had a crew of five, including the driver who sat in an armoured position forward. The provision of an armoured compartment for the driver alone was considered a luxury in war-production terms, but instead of eliminating this feature the designers made the whole thing cheaper by enlarging the armoured position and employing more flat steel plates. Thus more internal space was provided for one of the crew members. The Hummel could carry only 18 rounds of ammunition so more had to be kept nearby and brought up when necessary. Trucks were often of little value for this task, so by late 1944 no less than 150 Hummels were produced

Above: The Hummel (bumble bee) was a purpose-built German vehicle that used components from both the PzKpfw III and IV. Used on all fronts, it was a successful weapon that remained in production until the war ended. It had a crew of five.

without the howitzer and the divided front armour plates replaced by a single plate. These vehicles were used as ammunition carriers for the Hummel batteries. By late 1944 no less than 666 Hummels had been produced and the type remained in production until the end of the war. They proved to be useful and popular weapons, and were used on all fronts. Special versions with wider tracks known as Ostkette were produced for use during the winter months on the Eastern Front, and the open superstructures were often covered with canvas tarpaulins to keep out the worst of the weather. The gun crew generally lived with the vehicle, so many Hummels were festooned not only with camouflage of all kinds but also with bed rolls, cooking pots and items of personal kit.

The Hummel was one of the Germans' best examples of purpose-built self-propelled artillery. It had plenty of

A battery of four Hummels stand ready for action on a Russian steppe in 1942. The closeness of the guns and the overall lack of concealment

room for the crews to serve the gun, and the carriage gave the howitzer the desired mobility to enable them to keep up with the Panzer divisions.

Specification
Hummel
Type: self-propelled howitzer
Crew: 5
Weight: 24000 kg (52,911 lb)

demonstrates that the Luftwaffe had air superiority at this time, otherwise the guns would have been much more dispersed and camouflaged.

Powerplant: one Maybach V-12 petrol engine developing 197.6 kW (265 hp)
Dimensions: length 7.17 m (23 ft 6.3 in); width 2.87 m (9 ft 5 in); height 2.81 m (9 ft 2.6 in)
Performance: maximum road speed 42 km/h (26.1 mph); road range 215 km (134 miles); fording 0.99 m (3 ft 3 in)
Armament: one 15-cm (5.9-in) howitzer and one 7.92-mm (0.13-in) machine-gun

The Waffentrager

The **Waffentrager** (literally weapons carrier) was a novel concept for the Germans when it was first mooted during 1942. The idea was that the Waffentrager was to be not so much a form of self-propelled artillery but a means of carrying an artillery piece in a turret into action, where it would be removed from the tank, emplaced, used in action, and picked up again when no longer required. The exact tactical requirement for this arrangement is still uncertain, for in 1942 the Panzer divisions were still dictating mobile warfare to all opponents and the need for a static artillery piece seems remote.

Be that as it may, a series of eight vehicles known generally as **Heuschrecke IVB** (locust) were produced during 1942. These vehicles were converted PzKpfw IV tanks with a gantry at the rear to lift off the turret mounting a 10.5-cm (4.13-in) light field howitzer. The turret could be emplaced on the ground for action or it could be towed behind the vehicle on wheels carried on the rear specifically for this purpose; this arrangement allowed the vehicle to be used as an ammunition carrier for the turret.

The eight vehicles produced were no doubt used in action, for one of them was captured and is now to be seen in the Imperial War Museum in London, but at the time no more were requested. But by 1944 things had changed somewhat. The German army was everywhere on the defensive and anything that could hold up the advancing Allies was investigated. The Waffentrager concept came within this category, and more designs were initiated. One was an interim design in which a normal field howitzer, a 10.5-cm leFH 18/40, was carried in an armoured superstructure on top of a modified Geschützwagen III/IV (normally used for the Hummel). The howitzer could be fired from the vehicle, but it was also designed to be removed from the carrier using a block and tackle and mounted on the ground as a normal field piece once the wheels and carriage trails had been fitted. This design did not get far for it was overtaken by a series of design

projects that were in turn overtaken by the end of the war.

These late-1944 and early-1945 Waffenträger all adopted the removable turret concept used in the 1942 Heuschrecke IVB. They had a variety of chassis, including both the modified PzKpfw IV and Geschützwagen III/IV. The artillery pieces involved ranged from 10.5-cm to 15-cm (5.9-in) howitzers. One that got as far as model form was to have carried either the 10.5-cm or 15-cm howitzer on a cruciform carriage that would have been used with the '43' series of weapons had they ever advanced further than the prototype stage. These howitzers were mounted in an open-backed turret, and could be fired from the carrier or from a ground mounting. They could also be towed behind the carrier on their field carriages. It was all rather complicated and overengineered as it involved the use of ramps and winches, and the concept was typical of many that never got to the hardware stage. But a few such equipments were built only to be overtaken by the end of the war, being broken up or scrapped in the post-war years.

Specification
Heuschrecke IVB
Type: self-propelled howitzer carrier
Crew: 5
Weight: 17000 kg (37,479 lb)
Powerplant: one Maybach petrol engine developing 140.2 kW (188 hp)
Dimensions: length 5.90 m (19 ft 4.3 in); width 2.87 m (9 ft 5 in); height 2.25 m (7 ft 4.6 in)
Performance: maximum road speed 45 km/h (28 mph); road range 250 km (155 miles)
Armament: one 10.5-cm (4.13-in) howitzer

This Heuschrecke prototype was one in which a 105-mm field howitzer was carried on a chassis produced from PzKpfw III and IV components in order for it to be lowered to the ground when at the firing position. The howitzer could be fired from the vehicle if required.

The Heuschrecke was one of a number of experimental German vehicles that were meant to carry an artillery piece to a firing site and then lower the piece to the ground for firing. The Heuschrecke was the only one of many similar designs to be produced in any numbers.

Karl series

The weapons known as **Karl** were originally devised as anti-concrete weapons for the demolition of the Maginot Line forts and other such fortified locations. They were produced during the 1930s following a great deal of mathematical and other theoretical studies carried out during the 1920s. Work on the actual hardware began during 1937, and the first equipment was ready by 1939.

The Karl series must be regarded as being the largest self-propelled artillery weapons ever produced. There were two versions. One was the **60-cm Mörser Gerät 040** which mounted a 60-cm (23.62-in) barrel and the other the **54-cm Mörser Gerät 041** which mounted a 54-cm (21.26-in) barrel. Both weapons fired special concrete-piercing projectiles. The range of the Gerät 040 was 4500 m (4,921 yards) and that of the Gerät 041 6240 m (6,824 yards). Both could penetrate between 2.5 and 3.5 m (8.2 and 11.5 ft) of concrete before detonating to produce maximum effect. These projectiles

were massive items. The 60-cm shell weighed no less than 2170 kg (4,784 lb), although a lighter version was also used. The 54-cm shell weighed 1250 kg (2,756 lb).

Both Karl weapons were massive, ponderous brutes. Although technically self-propelled, their mobility was limited by their sheer weight and bulk and the tracked carriages were meant for only the most local of moves. For long-distance travel they were carried slung between special railway trucks. Shorter moves were made by removing the barrel from the carriage and placing both the barrel and the carriage on separate special trailers towed by heavy tractors. Assembly

The Karl howitzers were intended to smash the Maginot Line forts, but were instead used against the Sevastopol defences and later against Warsaw in 1944. They fired special anti-concrete projectiles that exploded only when they had penetrated their targets.

and break-down was carried out using special mobile gantries. The whole process was difficult to an extreme, but the Karl weapons were not intended for mobile warfare. They were produced to reduce fortresses and that meant a long, planned approach to the firing site, a slow rate of fire (the best was one round every 10 minutes) and a steady withdrawal once the fortress had been reduced.

The Karls were too late for the Maginot Line, which fell along with the rest of France in 1940. Their first real engagement was the siege of Sevastopol in exactly their designed role. Following the successful end of that siege more Karls were used during the Warsaw uprising when they were used to demolish the centre of Warsaw and crush the Polish underground fighters.

By then it was 1944. Most of the early 60-cm barrels had then been replaced by 54-cm barrels, but Warsaw was their last period in action. The increasing mobile warfare of the last year of the war gave the Karls no chance to demonstrate their destructive powers,

and most were destroyed by their crews in the last stages of the war. Only a few of the special PzKpfw IV ammunition carriers produced to carry projectiles for the Karls survived for Allied intelligence staffs to examine. It is possible that one example of the Karl may survive as a museum piece in the Soviet Union, but that is all.

Specification
Gerät 041
Type: self-propelled siege howitzer
Crew: not recorded
Weight: 124000 kg (273,373 lb)
Powerplant: one V-12 petrol engine developing 894.8 kW (1,200 hp)
Dimensions: length of barrel 6.24 m (20 ft 5.7 in); length of carriage 11.15 m (36 ft 7 in); track 2.65 m (8 ft 8.3 in)
Performance: not recorded
Armament: one 54-cm (21.26-in) howitzer/mortar

The massive 60-cm and 54-cm Karl howitzers were really fortification-smashing equipments, and they had only limited tactical mobility. They *had to be carried to the firing positions by special trailers in pieces and assembled on site.*

GERMANY
Brummbär

Despite their overall success, the StuG III assault guns were considered by 1943 as being too lightly armoured for the assault role, and a new heavy assault vehicle was required. The existing 15-cm (5.9-in) sIG 33 self-propelled equipments lacked the armour protection required for the close-support role and so, with the PzKpfw IV tank gradually being replaced by the Panther and Tiger tanks, there was the chance to produce a purpose-built vehicle using the later versions of the PzKpfw IV as a basis.

The first examples of this new vehicle appeared during 1943 under the designation *Sturmpanzer IV Brummbär* (grizzly bear). The Brummbär used a box structure formed from sloping armour plates set over the front of a turretless PzKpfw IV, and mounted a specially developed howitzer in a ball mounting on the front plate. This howitzer was known as the Sturmhaubitze 43 and was a shortened version, only 12 calibres long, of the 15-cm sIG 33. Armour was provided all round (the frontal armour being 100 mm/2.54 in thick), so the crew of five men were well protected. Later stand-off side armour was added, and most vehicles acquired a coating of Zimmerit plaster paste to prevent magnetic charges being stuck on to the hull by close-in tank killer squads. A machine-gun was mounted on the hull front plate on late production models, earlier versions having lacked this self-defence weapon.

The roomy fighting compartment of the Brummbär could accommodate up to 38 rounds of 15-cm ammunition. The commander sat to the rear of the howitzer using a roof-mounted periscope to select targets. Two men served the gun and handled the ammunition, while another acted as the gun layer. The driver normally remained in his seat at the left front. Most targets were engaged with direct fire, but provision was made for indirect fire.

About 313 Brummbär vehicles were produced before the war ended, and most appear to have been used in direct support of Panzergrenadier and

infantry units. The vehicles moved forward with the first waves of attacking troops and provided fire to reduce strongpoints and smash bunkers. Infantry had to remain close to prevent enemy tank-killer squads from coming too close to the Brummbär vehicles, which were always vulnerable to close-range anti-tank weapons, especially as some of their side armour was as thin as 30 mm (1.18 in). Brummbär vehicles were generally used in ones and twos split up along an area of attack. As defensive weapons they were of less use, for the short howitzer had only a limited performance against armour as its prime mission was the delivery of blast effect HE projectiles. One factor that restricted the Brummbär's overall mobility was its weight, which gave the vehicle a rather poor ground-pressure 'footprint': it was nippy enough on roads, but across country it could get bogged down in soft ground.

The Brummbär was a well-liked vehicle that often provided exactly the degree of fire support required by infantry formations. On the debit side it was heavy, rather ponderous and the early examples lacked close-in protection. But they were well protected against most weapons and they carried a powerful howitzer.

Specification
Brummbär
Type: self-propelled heavy assault howitzer
Crew: 5
Weight: 28200 kg (62,170 lb)
Powerplant: one Maybach V-12 petrol engine developing 197.6 kW (265 hp)
Dimensions: length 5.93 m (19 ft 5.5 in); width 2.88 m (9 ft 5.4 in); height 2.52 m (8 ft 3.2 in)
Performance: maximum road speed 40 km/h (24.85 km/h); maximum road range 210 km (130 miles); fording 0.99 m (3 ft 3 in)
Armament: one 15-cm (5.9-in) howitzer and one or two 7.92-mm (0.31-in) machine-guns

Most German self-propelled equipments carried only light armour, so when a call was made for a special close-support assault gun *the result was the heavily-armoured Brummbär. The Brummbär was often used for street fighting, as this captured example shows.*

The Brummbär was normally used when infantry tank-killer squads were likely to be encountered. It was therefore liberally covered with a *plaster-like substance known as 'Zimmerit' that prevented magnetic charges from sticking to the hull.*

Sturmtiger

Stalingrad taught the German army many lessons, not least of which was that the Germans were ill-equipped for the art of close-quarter street fighting. In typical fashion they decided to meet any future urban warfare requirements by a form of overkill by using a super-heavy weapon that would do away with the need for house-to-house fighting by simply blowing away any defended houses or structures. This they decided to do with a land version of a naval weapon, the depth charge.

In 1943 the Germans produced a version of the Tiger tank known by several names including **38-cm Sturmmörser, Sturmpanzer VI** and **Sturmtiger**. Whatever the designation, the weapon was a Tiger tank with the turret replaced by a large box-shaped superstructure with a short barrel poking through the front sloped plate. This barrel was not a gun but a 38-cm (14.96-in) Raketenwerfer 61 rocket projector of an unusual type, for it fired a rocket-propelled depth charge that weighed no less than 345 kg (761 lb). As this projectile was based upon the design of a naval depth charge nearly all the weight was high explosive; the effect of this upon even the stoutest structure can well be imagined. The rockets had a maximum range of 5650 m (6,180 yards), and the projector barrel was so arranged that the rocket efflux gases were diverted forward to vent from venturi around the muzzle ring. The Sturmtiger was exceptionally well armoured, with 150 mm (5.9 in) at its front and between 80 and 85 mm (3.15 and 3.35 in) at the side.

The Sturmtiger had a crew of seven including the commander, a fire observer and the driver. The other four men served the rocket projector. Because of their massive size, only 12 projectiles could be carried inside the superstructure, with the possibility of one more inside the projector. Loading the rockets into the vehicle was helped by a small crane jib mounted on the superstructure rear, and a small hatch nearby allowed access to the interior. Once inside overhead rails assisted in the movement of the rockets to and from their racks along each side, and loading into the projector was carried out using a loading tray.

Although the Sturmtiger prototype was ready by late 1943, it was not until August 1944 that production of this massive vehicle got under way. Only about 10 were ever produced, and these were used in ones and twos on most fronts but in situations where their powerful armament was of little advantage. Consequently most were soon either knocked out in action or simply abandoned by their crews once their fuel allocation had been used.

Used as they were in isolation and in such areas as the North Italian campaign, the hulks fascinated the Allies who encountered them and many detailed intelligence reports were written on them. Most realized that the Sturmtiger was a highly specialized weapon that was simply pushed into the field during the latter stages of the war in the German effort to get any weapon into action. If the Sturmtigers had been used as intended for street fighting, they would have been formidable weapons. Instead, by the time they were ready the time of concentrated urban warfare had passed.

Above: This side shot of a Sturmtiger shows the large armoured superstructure, mounting the 38-cm (14.96-in) rocket projector with the roof-mounted crane needed to load the projectiles into the interior through a hatch at the rear.

Below: Largest of all the German close-support weapons was the Sturmtiger, carrying a 38-cm rocket projector that fired a form of naval depth charge to demolish buildings. This example has been captured by American troops.

Specification
Sturmtiger
Type: assault gun
Crew: 7
Weight: 65000 kg (143,300 lb)
Powerplant: one Maybach V-12 petrol engine developing 484.7 kW (650 hp)
Dimensions: length 6.28 m (20 ft 7.25 in); width 3.57 m (11 ft 8.6 in); height 2.85 m (9 ft 4.2 in)
Performance: maximum road speed 40 km/h (24.86 mph); road range 120 km (75 miles); fording 1.22 m (4 ft)
Armament: one 38-cm (14.96-in) rocket projector and one 7.92-mm (0.31-in) machine-gun

---

Sturmgeschütz III

Following from its experiences in World War I, the German army saw the need for an armoured mobile gun that could follow infantry attacks and provide fire support and the firepower to knock out strongpoints and bunkers. During the late 1930s such a gun was developed using the chassis, suspension and running gear of the PzKpfw III tank. This armoured gun was known as the **Sturmgeschütz III** though its formal designation was **Gepanzerte Selbstfahrlafette für Sturmgeschütz 7.5-cm Kanone SdKfz 142**, (assault gun model 3) and it had the usual upper hull and turret of the tank replaced by a thick carapace of armour with a short 75-mm (2.95-in) gun mounted in the front. This weapon was first issued for service in 1940 (**StuG III Ausf A**) and was soon followed by a whole series of vehicles that gradually incorporated overall and detail improvements, to the extent that when the war ended in 1945 many were still in service on all fronts. The 1941 models were the **StuG III Ausf B, C** and **D**, while the slightly improved **StuG III Ausf E** appeared in 1942.

The main change to the Sturmgeschütz III (or StuG III) series was a gradual programme of upgunning. The original short 75-mm gun was an L/24 weapon (i.e. the length of the barrel was 24 times the calibre) and had limitations against many targets except at short ranges. Thus it was replaced by longer guns with improved performance, first an L/43 (**StuG III Ausf F**) and then an L/48 gun (**StuG III Ausf G**). The latter gun also provided the StuG III series with an anti-tank capability, and this was in a way to the detriment of the original assault-support concept, for it was far easier to produce a StuG than it was a tank, so many StuG IIIs with L/48 guns were diverted to the Panzer divisions in place of battle tanks. Used as a tank-killer the StuG III had its moments, but it lacked traverse and adequate protection for the task. It had to be retained as such, however, for German industry simply could not supply enough tanks for the Panzer divisions.

As an assault gun the StuG III series was far more successful. Eventually the type was upgunned to the stage late in the war when many StuG IIIs were armed with the powerful 10.5-cm (4.13-in) Sturmhaubitze, a special assault howitzer produced for the **StuG III für 10.5-cm StuH 42**. The first of these was completed in 1943, but manufacture of this variant was initially slow. Instead the version with the 75-mm L/48 gun was rushed off the production lines for the Panzer divisions.

The StuG III had a crew of four and extra machine-guns were often carried behind a shield on the roof. The protective mantlet for the main gun underwent many changes before it ended up as a *Saukopf* (literally 'pig's head') mantlet which proved very good protection. More protection against short-range hollow-charge warheads was provided with the addition of *Schützen* (literally 'skirts') along both sides. These were simply sheets of stand-off armour to detonate the warheads before they hit the vehicle armour, and were used on many German tanks after 1943.

As a close-range assault support weapon the StuG III series was an excellent vehicle/weapon combination. It was also relatively cheap and easy to produce, and in war-time Germany that mattered a lot. Therefore the series was built in some numbers and numerically it was one of the most important German armoured vehicles.

Specification
StuG III Ausf E
Type: assault gun
Crew: 4
Weight: 23900 kg (52,690 lb)
Powerplant: one Maybach V-12 petrol engine developing 197.6 kW (265 hp)
Dimensions: length 6.77 m (22 ft 2.5 in); width 2.95 m (9 ft 8 in); height 2.16 m (7 ft 1 in)
Performance: maximum speed 40 km/h (24.85 mph); road range 165 km (102 miles); fording 0.8 m (2 ft 7.5 in)
Armament: one 75-mm (2.95-in) gun and two 7.92-mm (0.31-in) machine-guns

Type 4 HO-RO

The Japanese were behind in armoured warfare development throughout all their World War II campaigns. Their early military excursions into China and Manchuria misled them into disregarding the need for heavy armoured vehicles, and instead they concentrated on what were regarded elsewhere as light tanks and tankettes. This approach was supported by the state of Japanese industry, which was still in a relatively early state of industrial development and lacked large-scale production capability. Thus it was that the Japanese army fell way behind in the development of self-propelled artillery, and ultimately only a small number of equipments were produced.

One of these was the **Type 4 HO-RO**, a self-propelled howitzer that allied the Type 38 150-mm (5.9-in) howitzer with the Type 97 medium tank. The conversion to the self-propelled role was a straightforward design task in which the howitzer was mounted in a shield which provided forward and side armour protection while leaving the top and rear open; the side armour, it is worth noting, did not extend even to the rear of the fighting compartment. The howitzer dated from 1905 and was derived from a Krupp design. It fired a 35.9-kg (79.15-lb) projectile to a range of 5900 m (6,452 yards), but most of these weapons were so old and worn that they had been withdrawn from general use after about 1942. They had a slow rate of fire as a result of the type of breech mechanism employed, but they were apparently thought good enough for the self-propelled role.

The chassis used for the Type 4 was the Type 97 CHI-HA, a medium tank by Japanese standards and dating from 1937. It was a mobile enough vehicle, but showed a relative lack of development in its thin armour, which was only about 25 mm (1 in) thick on the gun shield frontal armour, and in its overall riveted construction. The use of rivets in tank construction had elsewhere long disappeared, but the Japanese had no option but to retain the method as they lacked any other form of construction capability.

They also lacked the ability to produce the Type 4 HO-RO in anything but small numbers. Even those were virtually hand-built, with few preten-

Above: The Type 97 mounted a short Type 38 howitzer with limited range, but the Japanese were never able to produce the numbers required and they were mainly used in ones and twos as local fire-support weapons.

sions to mass production. Even then the Japanese did not concentrate on the Type 4 HO-RO alone, for they also produced a version known as the **Type 2** mounting a 75-mm (2.95-in) gun and designed to double as a self-propelled artillery platform and a tank-killer. Again only small numbers were produced.

The Type 4 HO-RO vehicles appear not to have been organized into anything larger than four-howitzer batteries. No records survive of larger formations, and most accounts refer to these vehicles being captured or knocked out in ones or twos. Very often they were assigned for island defence in the amphibious campaign leading to the Japanese mainland, and only a few were captured intact.

Specification
Type 4 HO-RO
Type: self-propelled howitzer
Crew: 4 or 5
Weight: not recorded, but about 13600 kg (29,982 lb)
Powerplant: one V-12 diesel developing 126.8 kW (170 hp)
Dimensions: length 5.537 m (18 ft 2 in); width 2.286 m (7 ft 6 in); height to top of shield 1.549 m (5 ft 1 in)

The Type 97 had its 150-mm howitzer mounted in place of the turret normally carried. The howitzer was meant to be used as a form of mobile field artillery but was normally used as close support artillery.

Performance: maximum road speed 38 km/h (23.6 mph)

Armament: one 150 mm (5.9-in) howitzer

Semovente da 149/40

The Italian army was not far behind the Germans in realising the need for assault guns, and developed a string of vehicles that outwardly resembled the German StuG III. These Italian assault guns were produced in appreciable numbers, for they were better armoured and in relative terms quicker to produce than contemporary Italian tanks. But by the time significant numbers had been issued Italy was effectively out of the war, and most of these Italian assault guns fell into German hands.

The majority of Italian self-propelled weapons, known as *semovente*, mounted 75-mm (2.95-in) or 105-mm (4.13-in) guns and howitzers of varying lengths, but since these were direct-fire mounts the Italian artillery arm still required self-propelled artillery weapons to support the armoured formations. Accordingly Ansaldo di-

The long, lean lines of the Italian 149/40 can be seen at the Aberdeen Proving Grounds in Maryland, USA, still looking very serviceable as a modern artillery weapon despite the lack of crew protection and stowage on the vehicle for ammunition and other items.

verted some of its precious development facilities to design a powerful artillery weapon that could be carried on a trucked chassis. In the end Ansaldo plumped for an existing weapon, the long Canone da 149/40 modello 35, and decided to place it on a much-modified Carro Armato M.15/42 tank chassis. The selection of these two items of equipment was made in order to produce as good a carriage/weapon combination as possible, but the snag was that the Italian army was already

crying our for large numbers of both the gun and tank. Italian industry quite simply could not keep up with the existing demands and so the new self-propelled weapon, known as the **Semovente da 149/40**, got off to a shaky start.

The Semovente da 149/40 was a completely unprotected weapon as the long gun barrel was placed on an open mounting carried on the turretless tank chassis. The gun crew stood in the open to serve the gun, which had its trunnions mounted right to the rear to absorb some of the recoil forces produced on firing. It was late 1942 before the first prototype was ready for prolonged firing trials, but even before these were over unsuccessful attempts were being made to start production. Before the lines could start rolling the Italians surrendered to the Allies, and the Germans took over what was left of the Italian economy. Thus the Semovente da 149/40 prototype remained the sole example of what seemed to be a promising design. The gun of the Semovente da 149/40 was certainly a useful weapon: it could fire a 46-kg (101.4-lb) projectile to a range of 23700 m (25,919 yards), at which distance the lack of protection for the gun crew would have been of relatively little importance.

The prototype survived the war, and can now be seen at the Aberdeen Proving Grounds in the USA. It still looks a thoroughly modern piece of equipment that would not be too out of place in many modern gun parks.

Specification
Semovente da 149/40
Type: self-propelled gun
Crew: (on gun) 2
Weight: 24000 kg (52,911 lb)
Powerplant: one SPA petrol engine developing 186.4 kW (250 hp)
Dimensions: length 6.60 m (21 ft 7.8 in); width 3.00 m (9 ft 10 in); height 2.00 m (6 ft 6.7 in)
Performance: maximum road speed 35 km/h (21.75 mph)
Armament: one 149-mm (5.87-in) gun

USSR
SU-76

During the desperate days of 1941 the Red Army lost so much materiel that Soviet planners were forced to list mass production as their top priority, and in order to cut down the numbers of equipments being produced only a few types were selected for future use. One of these types was the superlative ZIS-3 76.2-mm (3-in) gun, which was not only an excellent field piece but at that period also a good anti-tank gun. Thus when it was decided to adopt the ZIS-3 in quantity the Red Army had a very good weapon for the future, especially when the chance arose to make the weapon a self-propelled one.

The events of 1941 had shown the Red Army that its light tanks were virtually useless, and the type was scheduled for withdrawal from production and service. A production line was in existence for the T-70 light tank, however, and it was decided to convert the T-70 to take the ZIS-76 gun as a highly mobile anti-tank weapon. Thus was born the **SU-76** (SU for *Samokhodnaya Ustanovka*, or self-propelled mounting). The conversion to take the 76.2-mm gun and 62 rounds of ammunition was a simple one, but the T-70 chassis had to be widened somewhat and an extra road wheel was added to take the extra weight. The first examples had the gun mounted centrally, but later models had the gun offset to the left. Maximum armour thickness was 25 mm (0.98 in).

It was late 1942 before the first SU-76s were produced, and it was mid-1943 before they were in Red Army service in any appreciable numbers. By that time the ZIS-3 gun had lost much of its edge against the ever-thickening German tank armour, and thus the Su-76 was gradually phased over to the direct fire-support of Red Army infantry formations. Some anti-tank capability was retained when new anti-armour ammunition was introduced, but by the end of the war the SU-76 was being phased out in favour of vehicles with larger-calibre guns. Many SU-76s were pressed into other roles by 1945. The usual process was to remove the gun and then use the vehicle as a supply and ammunition carrier, as an artillery tractor and as a light armoured recovery vehicle. Some were fitted with anti-aircraft cannon.

After 1945 there were still many SU-76s to hand, and the Soviets handed them on to many friendly nations including China and North Korea, with whom the type saw another bout of action during the Korean War that started in 1950. More went to some of the Warsaw Pact armed forces. It is doubtful that the new recipients welcomed the SU-76, for it was very much

The Soviet SU-76 was a wartime and rather rushed conversion of the T-70 light tank to carry a 76-mm field gun, and although it was produced in large numbers it was little liked by its crews, who called it the 'Bitch'.

a wartime expedient vehicle with no crew comforts whatsoever. Apart from a few examples that had an armoured roof, the crew compartment of the SU 76 was open to the elements and the driver had to sit next to the twin engines with no intervening bulkhead. The Red Army knew the SU-76 as the *Sukami* (bitch).

Thus the SU-76 started life as a mobile anti-tank weapon and ended up as an artillery support weapon. It was no doubt a very useful weapon in the latter role, but essentially it was a hasty expedient rushed into production at a time of desperate need. Surprisingly, the type may still be encountered in odd parts of the world.

Specification
SU-76
Type: self-propelled gun
Crew: 4
Weight: 10800 kg (23,810 kg)
Powerplant: two GAZ 6-cylinder petrol engines each developing 52.2 kW (70 hp)
Dimensions: length 4.88 m (16 ft 0.1 in); width 2.73 m (8ft 11.5 in); height 2.17 m (7 ft 1.4 in)
Performance: maximum road speed 45 km/h (28 mph); road range 450 km (280 miles); fording 0.89 m (2 ft 11 in)
Armament: one 76.2-mm (3-in) gun and one 7.62-mm (0.3-in) machine-gun

SU-76s wait to take part in one of the massive artillery actions that usually took place before any major Red Army action. The open structure of the SU-76 must have made life very uncomfortable for their crews under such conditions, as only tarpaulin covers were carried.

Red Army soldiers attack under the close supporting fire of SU-76 76-mm guns, providing a graphic example of what close-range artillery support means. By 1945 the SU-76 was used almost exclusively in this role after being used at one point as mobile field artillery.

ISU-122 and ISU-152

The first of the heavy Soviet self-propelled artillery carriages was the **SU-152**, which first appeared in 1943, just in time to take part in the tank battles at Kursk. It was built onto a KV-2 heavy tank chassis and was typical of later World War II designs in that the tank chassis was taken virtually unchanged and a large armoured box was built on to the front of the hull. The weapon was a 152-mm (6-in) M-1937 howitzer mounted in a large and heavy mantlet on the front superstructure plate and there were roof hatches, one of which had provision for mounting an anti-aircraft machine-gun. This first vehicle was intended for use as much as an anti-armour weapon as a heavy assault weapon, for the Red Army made no differentiation between anti-tank and other weapons when it came to tactics. The SU-152 relied upon sheer projectile weight and power to defeat enemy armour.

When the KV tank series was replaced in production by the IS series, these too were used for the SU self-propelled role. The conversion followed closely that of the original SU-152, and the IS-based conversion was originally known as the **ISU-152**. To the average observer the SU-152 and ISU-152 were visually identical, but the ISU-152 mounted a more modern howitzer known as the ML-20S (with 20 rounds), technically a gun-howitzer and a very powerful weapon, especially at the assault ranges favoured by Red Army tactics. The weapon was protected by an armoured box made up from sloping plates of thick armour, with hand rails around the edge of the roof for use by 'tank descent' infantry who used the vehicles to carry them into action. Maximum armour thickness was 75 mm (2.95 in).

The ISU-152 was joined by the **ISU-122**, a virtually identical vehicle carrying a powerful 122-mm (4.8-in) gun known as the M-1931/4 or A-19S (with 30 rounds), the ordnance being a modification of the then-standard 122-mm M-1931/37, though there was also another gun known as the D-25S which was ballistically identical to the A-19S but differed in the way it was constructed. Numerically the ISU-122 was less important than the ISU-152, but the 122-mm version was potentially the more powerful weapon as it fired a higher-velocity projectile than the heavier 152-mm weapon, which relied more upon shell weight for its effects.

During 1944 and 1945 the ISU-152 and ISU-122 were in the vanguard of the Red Army advances through Germany towards Berlin. Some of the first Red Army units entering Berlin were ISU-152 units, which used their howitzers to blast away strongpoints at close ranges and clear the way to the remains of the city centre.

If the ISU weapons had a fault it was that they lacked internal ammunition stowage space. Thus they had to have a virtual constant supply of ammunition brought foward by armoured carriers, which was often a hazardous undertaking. But the massive weapon carried by the ISU vehicles was considered to be of great value in the direct support of Red Army tank and motorized infantry divisions, and both types went on to be used for some years after the war.

ISU-152s were still in front-line service in 1956 when the Red Army ruthlessly crushed the Hungarian uprising. In the streets of Budapest the lack of traverse proved a serious disadvantage. The gun mechanism was never modernized; elevation and loading were done by hand.

The SU-122 was a conversion of the T-34 tank to accommodate a front-mounted 122-mm howitzer in a well-armoured and well-sloped superstructure. It was produced in large numbers for the close-support role, but could be used for 'stand-off' artillery fire.

An ISU-152 crosses a river during the latter stages of World War II. These vehicles appear to be carrying their crew members on the roof, but in action they would be carrying squads of 'tank descent' assault infantry instead. Note the size of the howitzer's muzzle brake.

Specification
ISU-122
Type: self-propelled assault gun
Crew: 5
Weight: 46430 kg (102,361 lb)
Powerplant: one V-12 diesel developing 387.8 kW (520 hp)
Dimensions: length overall 9.80 m (32 ft 1.8 in) and hull 6.805 m (22 ft 3.9 in); width 3.56 m (11 ft 8.2 in); height 2.52 m (8 ft 3.2 in)
Performance: maximum road speed 37 km/h (23 mph); road range 180 km (112 miles); fording 1.3 m (4 ft 3.2 in)
Armament: one 122-mm (4.8-in) gun and one 12.7-mm (0.5-in) machine-gun

The ISU-152 was a straightforward conversion of an IS-2 tank to carry a 152-mm howitzer as a powerful close-support artillery weapon; it was also a powerful tank killer. The howitzer was housed in a thick superstructure with dense frontal armour that made it a difficult vehicle to knock out.

119

Sexton

During early 1941 the British Purchasing Commission in Washington asked the Americans if the M7 Priest could be altered to allow it to carry the British 25-pdr (87.6-mm/3.45-in) gun-howitzer. While the British appreciated the amenities of the M7 Priest, it had the major disadvantage of mounting a 105-mm (4.13-in) howitzer that was not a standard British weapon calibre at that time. The Americans accordingly produced the M7 with the 25-pdr and named it the T51, but at the same time announced that there was no way that they could produce it in quantity as they had their production hands full already. The British accordingly looked around and noted that the Canadians had set up a production line for the Ram tank, a type that was soon to be replaced by the American M3 and M4. The Ram was accordingly altered to accommodate the 25-pdr, and thus was born the **Sexton**.

The Sexton used the overall layout of the M7 Priest, but many changes were introduced to suit British requirements. These included the movement of the driver's position to the right-hand side. The Sexton lacked the pronounced 'pulpit' of the M7, but the fighting compartment was left open with only a canvas cover to provide weather protection for the crew. The Sexton had a crew of six, and much of the interior was taken up with lockers for ammunition and some of the crew's personal kit; more stowage was provided in boxes at the rear. Maximum armour thickness was 32 mm (1.25 in).

The 25-pdr gun-howitzer was carried in a special cradle produced by the Canadians specifically for the Sexton. This allowed a traverse of 25° left and 40° right, which was very useful for the anti-tank role (18 AP rounds) but in the event the Sexton had little need of this facility. Instead it was used almost exclusively as a field artillery weapon (87HE and smoke rounds) supporting the armoured divisions in North West Europe from 1944 onwards. There were several variations, all of them incorporating the production changes progressively introduced on the lines of the Montreal Locomotive Works at Sorel. Production continued there until late 1945, by which time 2,150 Sextons had been manufactured.

The Sexton was a well-liked and re-

This Sexton is now a preserved 'runner' maintained by the Royal School of Artillery at Larkhill,

Wiltshire. It originally came from Portugal, where it was sent during the years after 1945.

liable gun and weapon combination that proved so successful that many are still in use in odd corners of the world to this day. The British army used the type until the late 1950s, and one is preserved as a museum piece at the Royal School of Artillery at Larkhill in Wiltshire.

There were a few in-service variants of the Sexton, some being converted to 'swim' for possible use on D-Day, but none appear to have been used in this role on the day. A more common conversion was the replacement of the gun-howitzer by extra map tables and radios in the **Sexton Gun**

Above: The Sexton mounted the British 25-pdr gun and was a well-liked and reliable vehicle that served on for many years after World War II with many armies. It is still used by India.

Position Officer command vehicle; there was usually one of these to a battery. In post-war years some Sextons were handed over to nations such as Italy who preferred the 105-mm (4.13-in) howitzer; in this instance the 25-pounders were replaced with German 105-mm howitzers.

Specification
Sexton
Type: self-propelled gun-howitzer
Crew: 6
Weight: 25855 kg (57,000 lb)
Powerplant: one Continental 9-cylinder radial piston engine developing 298.3 kW (400 hp)
Dimensions: length 6.12 m (20 ft 1 in); width 2.72 m (8 ft 11 in); height 2.44 m (8 ft 0 in)
Performance: maximum road speed 40.2 km/h (25 mph); road range 290 km (180 miles); fording 1.01 m (3 ft 4 in)
Armament: one 25-pdr gun-howitzer, two unmounted 7.7-mm (0.303-in) Bren Guns and (on some vehicles) one pintle-mounted 12.7-mm (0.5-in) Browning machine-gun

M7 Priest

Experience gained with 105-mm (4.13-in) howitzers mounted on halftracks enabled the US Army to decide that it would be better if the howitzer was mounted in a fully tracked carriage, and accordingly an M3 medium tank chassis was modified to take such a weapon. The M3 chassis was considerably reworked to provide an open-topped superstructure with the howitzer mounted in its front. The development vehicle was known as the T32, and following trials which added a machine-gun mounting to the right-hand side of the fighting compartment, the vehicle was adopted for service as the **Carriage, Motor, 105-mm Howitzer, M7**. Maximum armour thickness was 25.4 mm (1 in).

The first production examples were for the US Army, but many were soon diverted to the Lend-Lease programme for the Allies, among them the Brit-

The British gunners nicknamed the American M7 the 'Priest' after seeing the 'pulpit' that housed the 12.7-mm machine-gun for AA defence.

ish Army. The British soon named the M7 the **Priest**, legend having it that the prominent machine-gun mounting gave the impression of a pulpit. The British gunners adopted the M7 with alacrity, and the type first went into action with them at the 2nd Battle of El Alamein in October 1942. The British asked for 5,500 M7s to be produced for their use alone by the end of 1943, but this order was never completed in full. The figure nonetheless provides an indication of the success of the M7 with the British gunners. They appreciated the space and mobility of the carriage and also the extra space for personal stowage. The one snag was the howitzer, which was not a standard British Army type: thus ammunition (stowage was provided for 69 rounds on each vehicle) had to be supplied separately for the M7 batteries, which made for a considerable logistic complication. This was not resolved until the first Sextons with the 25-pdr weapons began to be issued in 1944. Until that time the British M7s were used all through the Italian campaign, and some were landed in Normandy in June 1944 though they were soon replaced by Sextons.

The M7 then began a new service

An M7 in action in the Ardennes, 1945, with the open fighting compartment covered by a tarpaulin to keep out the worst of the bitter weather. The tank obstacles behind the M7 are part of the infamous Siegfried Line defences that in the event were taken without too much trouble.

career in a revised form: the howitzers were removed and the hulls were used as armoured personnel carriers nicknamed Kangaroos. This soon became a normal fate for unwanted M7s, and the idea soon spread to Italy.

The US Army also made wide use of the M7, although production for the US Army was not a constant process. After 1942 M7 production proceeded in fits and starts. At one stage the original M3 chassis was replaced by the later M4A3 Sherman chassis, and these M7s were known by the designation **M7B1**.

After 1945 large numbers of M7s were handed over to other countries, and some remain in use to this day in such nations as Brazil and Turkey. The 105-mm howitzer is still a standard weapon all over the world, and thus the M7s continue to fire a 14.97-kg (33-lb) shell to a range of 11430 m (12,500

yards). Throughout their service life the M7s have always showed outstanding reliability, and have demonstrated their ability to cross all types of rough terrain.

Specification
M7
Type: self-propelled howitzer
Crew: 5
Weight: 22967 kg (50,634 lb)
Powerplant: one Continental 9-

cylinder radial piston engine developing 279.6 kW (375 hp)
Dimensions: length 6.02 m (19 ft 9 in); width 2.88 m (9 ft 5.25 in) height 2.54 m (8 ft 4 in)
Performance: maximum speed 41.8 km/h (26 mph); maximum road range 201 km (125 miles); fording 1.219 m (4 ft)
Armament: one 105-mm (4.13-in) howitzer and one 12.7-mm (0.5-in) machine-gun

---

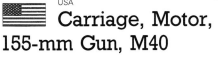

USA
Carriage, Motor, 155-mm Gun, M40

Although the M40 arrived on the scene later in the war, it was one of the best of all wartime self-propelled equipments and went on to a long post-war career. It used the chassis of the M4 tank as a basis.

The first 155-mm (6.1-in) self-propelled gun produced in quantity by the Americans during World War II was the **M12**, a design originally known as the **T6** and built on to a converted M3 medium tank chassis. Initially this weapon was not considered for service as it used an obsolescent World War I ordnance that had become available once the type's original carriages had become too worn for further use. However, once accepted for service, they gave good performance although it was agreed that a new ordnance was required if a long-term weapon was to be procured.

Starting in December 1943 a new weapon/carriage combination was initiated. The gun was the 155-mm M1A1 known as the 'Long Tom' (with 20 rounds) and the carriage was based on the chassis of the M4A3 medium tank, though much widened and fitted with the latest high volute suspension springing. The engine was moved from the rear to a new forward position, and to absorb some of the recoil forces a spade was added to the rear; this latter could be raised for travelling. A working platform under the breech was also provided. The gun had a range of 23514 m (25,715 yards) and fired a projectile weighing 43.1 kg (95 lb), which made it a very useful counterbattery and long-range bombardment weapon. Maximum armour thickness was 12.7 mm (0.5 in)

The development of this **Carriage, Motor, 155-mm Gun, M40** took rather longer than expected, so it was not until January 1945 that the first production examples rolled off the lines. They were rushed across the Atlantic in time to see the end of the war in Germany.

M40s took part in the bombardment of Köln and the short campaigning after this. Between January and May 1945 no less than 311 M40s were built, and production continued after the war. The M40 was to see its most concerted use during the Korean conflict, where it proved to be an excellent weapon/carriage combination.

On the M40 there was no protection for the crew as the type was designed for use so far behind the front line that none would be necessary. The M40 had a crew of eight, and there was provision on the carriage for their weapons and kit. The same carriage was also used to mount a 203-mm (8-in) howitzer, but this version (the **Carriage, Motor, 8-in Howitzer, M43**), was not used in great numbers; only 48 were built.

After 1945 M40s were distributed to many other armies. The British Army accepted a number and used them for

some years. More were used by nations such as France, with whom the type saw extensive service in Indo-China.

There was one variant of the M40, the **T30 Cargo Carrier**. As its designation implies, it could be used as a general supply carrier though its normal deployment was for the ammunition supply of M40 batteries. Not many were built as most of the manufacturing potential was concentrated on producing gun carriers.

One of the main claims to importance of the M40 was that it paved the way for the current generation of self-propelled weapons. It was produced at a time when nuclear warfare was just making its debut, and the need for protection against this new battle hazard was particularly noticeable on the M40 with its open fighting platform. The type was therefore used extensively for trials and experiments de-

signed to provide protection for the crew. The M40 proved beyond doubt that the only proper protection comes from an armoured turret, and most modern self-propelled weapons now use such an arrangement.

Specification
M40
Type: self-propelled gun
Crew: 8
Weight: 37195 kg (82,000 lb)
Powerplant: one Continental 9-cylinder radial piston engine developing 294.6 kW (395 hp)
Dimensions: length overall 9.04 m (29 ft 8 in) and hull only 6.65 m (21 ft 10 in); width 3.15 m (10 ft 4 in); height 2.84 m (9 ft 4 in)
Performance: maximum speed 38.6 km/h (24 mph); range 161 km (100 miles); fording 1.067 m (3 ft 6 in)
Armament: one 155-mm (6.1-in) gun

Bishop

The vehicle that became known as the **Bishop** was conceived at a time when 25-pdr batteries in the North African desert were perforce used as anti-tank weapons and were taking a terrible pounding as a result. It was decided to place the 25-pdr on a mobile carriage to increase protection for the gun crews, and it was soon clear that the Valentine infantry tank would make a good basis for such a conversion. Unfortunately the exact role of this gun/tank combination was uncertain from the start. The tank exponents saw it as a variant of the heavy-gun tank theme, while the gunners wanted a self-propelled carriage. These arguments were never really solved, and the result was something of a compromise even though the gunners won in the end.

The Valentine 25-pdr emerged as a straightforward conversion (officially the **Mounting, Valentine, 25-pdr Gun Mk I on Carrier, Valentine, 25-pdr Gun, Mk I**) the usual turret being replaced by a much larger turret mounting the 25-pdr. This new turret was fixed, and was a large slab-sided design too large for battlefield concealment and too small to allow much room inside for the gun crew. The turret design also had one major disadvantage for the gunners in that it restricted the elevation of the barrel and thus curtailed range to only 5852 (6,400 yards) which was a considerable reduction from the normal 12253 m (13,400 yards). The only way to increase this performance was the tedious and tactically-hampering construction of earth ramps up which the vehicle could be driven to increase the elevation angle. Traverse was also severely restricted, to a maximum of 4° to each side. Internal ammunition stowage was 32 rounds but more could be carried in a limber towed behind the vehicle. Armour varied in thickness from 8 mm (0.315 in) to 60 mm (2.36 in).

The 25-pdr Valentine went into action in North Africa during the latter stages of the campaign in that theatre, by which time the 25-pdr was no longer in use as an anti-tank gun, so the vehicles were used as self-propelled artillery with no distraction and the Royal Artillery learned a lot from their use. The type was eventually named Bishop, and it went on to be used in Sicily and Italy during the opening stages of that campaign. Throughout these campaigns the Bishop demonstrated all its several drawbacks, but also provided an indication of the potential of self-propelled artillery for it was the first British self-propelled weapon to see active service. The need for supporting logistics was more than emphasized, as was the need for improved radio links with forward observers.

The Bishop also demonstrated things to avoid in future designs. The most obvious one was for the gun to have its full range of movement if it was to be of any use; additionally, more room was needed to serve the gun, for the turret of the Bishop was cramped and ill-ventilated. More internal ammunition stowage was needed and the carrier had to be fast enough to keep up with tanks. Being an infantry tank, the Valentine chassis was too slow to keep up with the armoured formations.

All these things were put right when the gunners were issued numbers of M7 Priests. The gunners took to the Priest with a will, and before long the Bishops had been discarded. They may have been less than perfect, but they taught the gunners a lot and the Bishop has the distinction of being the British Army's first self-propelled artillery piece.

Above: A Bishop on the ranges with the gun detachment commander outside the fixed turret, as there was room for only two gunners inside. The fixed turret restricted the barrel elevation and thus range.

Above: This Bishop in 'factory' state clearly shows the high and bulky outline of the fixed turret mounting the 25-pdr gun. As this was a 'first attempt' design there was confusion as to whether the Bishop was a heavy gun tank or a self-propelled gun, but in the end the gunner's view prevailed.

Above: Ammunition stocktaking takes place on a Bishop with the projectiles laid out on the engine covers for counting. The Bishop could carry only 32 rounds internally, as space inside the fixed turret was cramped. The projectiles are 25-pdr HE shells, the normal round fired, although smoke could also be carried.

Below: The Bishop was an early British attempt to produce self-propelled artillery by placing a 25-pdr gun onto a Valentine tank chassis. The gun was mounted in a fixed turret with only limited elevation and the result was not a success, being replaced in service by the Priest as soon as possible.

Specification
Bishop
Type: self-propelled gun-howitzer
Crew: 4
Weight: 7911 kg (17,440 lb)
Powerplant: one AEC 6-cylinder diesel developing 97.7 kW (131 hp)
Dimensions: length 5.64 m (18 ft 6 in) width 2.77 m (9 ft 1 in); height 3.05 m (10 ft)
Performance: maximum road speed 24 km/h (15 mph); road range 177 km (110 miles); fording 0.91 m (3 ft)
Armament: one 25-pdr (87.6-mm/3.45-in) gun-howitzer

Heavy Artillery

The dramatic success of the German advance in 1940 seemed to herald a return to an era of mobile warfare, but the moment their advance into the Soviet Union became bogged down heavy artillery reappeared on the battlefield. The battles that were to decide the war, from North Africa to Berlin, were dominated by these monsters.

During World War II heavy artillery was as important a weapon as it had been in the past. Despite the overall impression given by much current military literature, the tank could not operate without the support and covering fire provided by heavy-calibre artillery of all types, and for all its many advantages the tank is of limited use against heavily protected strongpoints and defended localities. It is only heavy artillery that can be used to any effect against such targets and, while the same might be said of the bomber aircraft, the fact remains that only artillery can carry out its fire missions around the clock and under all weather conditions.

Thus heavy artillery was highly important during World War II. It was used on nearly all fronts and the weapons involved were many and varied. Not all of them can be mentioned here but an overall impression of the types of artillery involved has been provided. This section also includes some of the oddities of the artillery world, such as 'Little David' – even though this particular weapon did not see active service – and the massive German 35.5cm (14in) Haubitz M.1. Such items did exist during World War II and some were even used in action but, while their effect was

Poles of the 2nd Artillery Group, 2nd Polish Corps, man a heavy artillery piece bombarding German positions. No one was keener to liberate their homeland than the Poles.

no doubt devastating to the recipients, in the overall sense their impact was slight. Instead, attention should be given to weapons which were in the range from 150mm (5.9in) to 210mm (8.26in) in calibre, for it was with these weapons that the really hard heavy artillery work was accomplished. One has only to look at the power of the mas-

sive Red Army artillery battering ram to realize this fact: despite all its power this arm used nothing heavier than the Model 1931 203mm (8in) howitzer.

This section deals with the weapons that were used to reduce fortified areas, to lay down the counterbattery fire that silenced the enemy's field artillery batteries and to carry out the heavy and

long-range fire support without which the infantry and armoured formations of all combatants could neither move nor fight. Included here are the weapons that during World War II were the modern equivalents of the types of ordnance that were once 'the last argument of kings', but served instead on all sides of the most destructive war in history.

Skoda 149-mm vz 37 howitzer (K4)

By the early 1930s the Skoda works at Pilsen in Czechoslovakia were in a position to design, develop and produce entirely new artillery pieces that owed nothing to the old World War I weapons that had hitherto been the company's main output. By 1933 they had produced, among other things, an entirely new 149-mm (5.87-in) range of howitzers known as the 'K' series. The first of these, the **K1**, was produced in 1933 and the entire output of these **vz 33** weapons went for export to Turkey, Romania and Yugoslavia. The K1 was a thoroughly modern piece with a heavy split trail, and was designed for either horse or motorized traction. For the latter the piece could be towed as one load, but for the former the barrel could be removed for towing as a separate load.

Despite the success of the K1, the Czech army decided that the weapon did not meet its exact requirements and funded further development to the stage where a **K4** model met the specification. The K4 had much in common with the earlier K1, but had a shorter barrel and (as the Czech army was making considerable strides towards full mechanization) the need for removing the barrel for separate horse traction was no longer required. The K4 also used pneumatic wheels (the K1 had solid rubber-rimmed steel wheels) and some other modifications to suit it for the mechanized tractor-towing role.

With these changes the Czech army

decided to adopt the K4 as its standard heavy field howitzer to replace the large range of elderly weapons remaining from World War I. The K4 was given the army designation **15-cm hrubá houfnice vz 37**, vz 37 (vz for *vzor*, or model) denoting the equipment's year of acceptance for service. Skoda drew up production plans, but as always this took time and in the interim the Germans occupied the Czech Sudetenland. Plans for production became even more frantic, but with the Sudetenland line of defences in German hands Czechoslovakia was wide open to further German aggression and in 1939 they duly marched in to take over the rest of the country.

The Germans also secured the Skoda works at Pilsen, finding on the production lines the first of the full production vz 37 weapons. By that time only a few models had been produced, and these the German army tested on ranges back in the Reich, discovering that the vz 37 was a sound and serviceable howitzer with a good range of 15100 m (16,515 yards) and firing a very useful 42-kg (92.6-lb) projectile. The Germans decided to keep the vz 37 in production at Pilsen for their own requirements, and thus the vz 37 became the German army's **15-cm schwere Feldhaubitze 37(t)**, or 15-cm heavy field howitzer Model 1937 (Czech), the (t) denoting *tschechisch*, or Czech. With the German army the sFH 37(t) became a standard weapon of many divisions, forming part of the

divisional artillery equipment and even being used by some corps batteries. It was used during the French campaign of May and June 1940, and later in the invasion of the Soviet Union during 1941. Some were still in service in the Soviet Union as late as 1944, but by then many had been passed to the various Balkan forces under German control and operating within what is now Yugoslavia; the Slovak army was one such recipient.

Specification
SFH 37(t)
Calibre: 149.1 mm (5.87 in)
Length of piece: 3.60 m (11 ft 9.7 in)
Weight: travelling 5730 kg (12,632 lb)

The high water mark of German success in the late summer of 1942: elements of Army Group A penetrated over 300 km (200 miles) south-east of Stalingrad. Here a Czech-built vz 37 15-cm howitzer pounds Soviet positions in the foothills of the Caucasian mountain range.

and in action 5200 kg (11,464 lb)
Elevation: −5° to +70°
Traverse: 45°
Muzzle velocity: 580 m (1,903 ft) per second
Maximum range: 15100 m (16,515 yards)
Shell weight: 42 kg (92.6 lb)

Skoda 220-mm howitzer

Whereas the Skoda vz 37 howitzer was a completely new design, the slightly earlier **Skoda 220-mm howitzer** was very much a product that had its origins in earlier days. In the period up to 1918, when the Skoda works were the largest armament producers for the Austro-Hungarian empire, the Pilsen works had been only slightly behind the German Krupp concern in the manufacture of really heavy artillery, and the heavy Skoda howitzers were second to none in overall efficiency. Thus when the Skoda works started production again the 'classic' howitzer was one of its main products.

However, the accent was no longer on heavy calibres alone. Despite their dreadful efficiency in demolishing fortifications, such equipments were ponderous beasts to move and their rate of fire was extremely slow. They were also fearfully expensive, so when some of the new nations formed after the Treaty of Versailles started to arm themselves against a difficult future they still wanted heavy artillery, but not too heavy. An interim calibre of about 220 mm (8.66 in) was still about right for the destruction of heavy structures, but the howitzer itself need not be too ponderous. Skoda sensed the market and produced the required 220-mm design incorporating much of its considerable experience in such matters, and it was not long before customers arrived.

The first was Yugoslavia, formed from several of the pre-World War I Balkan states. The new nation decided it had much to fear from its neighbours, and thus was involved in numerous purchases of weapons of all kinds throughout Europe. Yugoslavia was a

good customer of Skoda, and in 1928 took delivery of a batch of 12 220-mm Skoda howitzers under the designation **M.28**. Another customer was Poland, which ordered no less than 27. These Polish howitzers featured prominently in many pre-war propaganda photographs of the Polish army, all with one feature in common: in all of these photographs the breech mechanism was obscured in some way, usually by a soldier, as part of the normal Polish security procedure in any artillery illustration intended for publication.

It did the Poles no good, for in 1939 the Germans invaded and captured or destroyed the entire Polish gun park. The unfortunate Yugoslavs followed just over a year later. Thus the Germans found themselves with a useful quantity of 220-mm howitzers, which promptly became part of the German army's inventory. There was not much of a role for such a relatively heavy piece in the German *Blitzkrieg* concept, so the captured howitzers were distributed mainly to garrison and static units in the occupied territories. Some of these were as distant as Norway, but in late 1941 a number of these howitzers were gathered together and added to the siege train that was sent to invest the fortress of Sevastopol in the Crimea. This was the last classic

Skoda produced some of the best heavy artillery pieces of World War I, and continued the tradition with the 220-mm howitzer, which was exported to both Poland and Yugoslavia. After the Germans invaded Eastern Europe they used the captured weapons against the fortress of Sevastopol.

investment of a fortress by the age-old method of assembling and using a siege train, and the fortress fell after the Skoda howitzers had played a useful part. Thereafter they were once more scattered and saw little use during the remainder of the conflict.

Specification
Skoda 220-mm howitzer
Calibre: 220 mm (8.66 in)
Length of piece: 4.34 m (14 ft 2.8 in)
Weight: travelling 22700 kg (50,045 lb) and in action 14700 kg (32,408 lb)
Elevation: +40° to +70°
Traverse: 350°
Muzzle velocity: 500 m (1,640 ft) per second
Maximum range: 14200 m (15,530 yards)
Shell weight: 128 kg (282.19 lb)

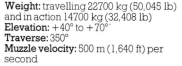

Obice da 210/22 modello 35

During the late 1930s the Italian army decided to attempt to replace the bulk of its heavy artillery park, which by that time resembled an oversize artillery museum. It selected two good and thoroughly modern designs, one a gun with a calibre of 149 mm (5.87 in) and the other a howitzer with a calibre of 210 mm (8.26 in). The howitzer was designed by an army organization known as the Servizio Tecnici Armi e Munizioni (STAM), but production was carried out by Ansaldo at Pozzuoli.

The howitzer was known as the **Obice da 210/22 modello 35**. Although shown in prototype form in 1935, it was not accepted for service until 1938 when a production order for no less than 346 was placed. The modello 35 was a very sound and modern design. It used a split-trail carriage with two road wheels on each side. When the howitzer went into action these wheels were raised off the ground and the weight was assumed by a firing platform under the main axle. The entire weapon could then be traversed easily through 360° once the stakes that anchored the trail spades to the ground had been raised.

The main problem for the Italians was that having designed a first-rate howitzer they could not produce it quickly enough. Despite the good intentions of the Italian army, it had to enter the war with its antique gun park still largely undisturbed by modern equipments, and by the autumn of 1942 the grand total of modello 35s was still only 20, five of them in Italy and the rest in action in the Soviet Union. Part of this state of affairs was due to the fact that despite the requirements of the Italian army, modello 35s were sold to Hungary as they came off the production line, no doubt in exchange for raw materials and food products. The Hungarians found it necessary to make their own carriage modifications to suit this **21-cm 39.M** to the rigours of their service and eventually set up their own **21-cm 40.M** and finally **21-cm 40a.M** production line in 1943.

In service the modello 35 was successful enough. It could be transported in two loads, but for prolonged moves it could be further broken down into four loads with an extra load for assembly equipment and accessories. The modello 35 attracted the attentions of the Germans, and when the Italians surrendered in September 1943 the Ansaldo concern was forced to continue production for German units based in Italy. Thus the modello 35 became the **21-cm Haubitze 520(i)** and was still in action with the Germans when the war ended.

After 1945 attempts were made by Ansaldo to sell the modello 35 on the home and export markets. There were no takers as the home market was sated with American equipment that was freely supplied to the Italian army and war-surplus equipment was widely available elsewhere.

Specification
Obice da 210/22
Calibre: 210 mm (8.26 in)
Length of piece: 5 m (16 ft 4.85 in)
Weight: travelling (two loads) 24030 kg (52,977 lb) and in action 15885 kg (35,020 lb)
Elevation: 0° to +70°
Traverse: 75°
Muzzle velocity: 560 m (1,837 ft) per second
Maximum range: 15407 m (16,850 yards)
Shell weight: 101 or 133 kg (222.7 or 293.2 lb)

Italy made extensive use of heavy artillery in World War I, but by the 1930s her big guns were looking decidedly obsolete and new weapons were ordered. The 210-mm howitzer pictured here was an excellent design, but Italian industry could not produce the guns with sufficient speed.

Most of Italy's 210-mm howitzers found their way into Hungarian hands for service on the Eastern Front. Those still in Italy at the time of the Italian surrender were promptly manned by Germans, and made their contribution to the tenacious defence of the peninsula until 1945.

8-in Howitzer M1

After the United States entered World War I in 1917, among the various types of heavy artillery its army received once US troops arrived in France was the British 8-in Howitzer Mks VII and VIII, which were incidentally being produced in the United States to a British order. The Americans took to this howitzer with a will, for they soon discovered that it was a very accurate weapon and in the years after 1918 set about producing their own version. This was under the aegis of an advisory body known as the Westervelt Board, which also recommended the introduction of the 155-mm Gun M1. The board also recommended that the 155-mm (6.1-in) gun and the 203-mm (8-in) howitzer should share the same carriage and thus the new howitzer used the same M1 carriage as the 155-mm Gun M1.

Despite the recommendations of the Westervelt Board, however, the development of the new howitzer was slow and erratic, and at times ceased altogether for years on end. Thus it was not until 1940 that the howitzer was standardized as the **8-in Howitzer M1**. The M1 owed much to its British origins but was longer, and as it used the M1 carriage it was even more accurate than its predecessor. However, it should not be thought that because the 8-in Howitzer M1 and the 155-mm Gun M1 shared the same carriage the two barrels were interchangeable. They were not, for to exchange the two barrels involved a great deal of workshop time and a great deal of trouble.

Once the Howitzer M1 had been introduced into service it soon became a very popular and powerful weapon. Because of its accuracy it could be used to bring down heavy fire on spot targets quite close to friendly troops and was frequently used thus in the

elimination of enemy strongpoints and bunkers. The shell fired by the M1 was initially a 90.7-kg (200-lb) high explosive shell also used by 203-mm (8-in) coast guns, but this was later replaced by a special high explosive shell known as the M106 which had the same weight as the earlier shell but

which could be fired to a range of 16596 m (18,150 yards). The M106 is still in service with the 8-in Howitzer M1, which in a post-war designation reshuffle was redesignated **M115**.

Like the 155-mm Gun M1 the 203-mm howitzer also went self-propelled, although the first version did not

Above: A good view of the interrupted-screw stepped-thread breech mechanism of an 8-in howitzer in action. Four crew members prepare to lift the 91-kg (200-lb) shell, the size of which gives some clue as to why the maximum rate of fire was one round per minute.

In addition to receiving the French 155-mm gun, the US Army in France received during 1918 the British 8-in howitzer, which was subsequently used as the basis for post-war US heavy gun design. The M1 howitzer resulted from years of intermittent, underfunded research and was not standardized until 1940. Once in action, however, it was an impressive piece; accurate and hard-hitting, it is still in service worldwide and was developed into a self-propelled gun, the M110.

The blast effect of an 8-in howitzer hits not just the ears but the whole body as the shock wave passes outwards. This is the first 8-in howitzer in action in Normandy, 1944, firing during the barrage the Americans organized to celebrate the Fourth of July.

appear until 1946. This was the M46 which used a much-modified M25 tank chassis as the carrier. Subsequent development along these lines has now led to the M110 series which originally used the 203-mm howitzer in a form virtually unchanged from its towed version but which has now been developed to the M110A2 which uses a much lengthened 203-mm howitzer barrel.

The towed 8-in Howitzer M115 is still in widespread service all over the world, and there are few signs that it is likely to be replaced in the near future. Thus the 203-mm howitzer can lay claim to being one of the longest-lived of all modern heavy artillery pieces: it can trace back its origins to World War I and is still in service.

Specification
8-in Howitzer M1
Calibre: 203 mm (8 in)
Length of piece: 5.324 m (17 ft 5.59 in)
Weight: travelling 14515 kg (32,000 lb) and in action 13471 kg (29,698 lb)
Elevation: −2° to +65°
Traverse: 60°
Muzzle velocity: 594 m (1,950 ft) per second
Maximum range: 16596 m (18,150 yards)
Shell weight: 90.7 kg (200 lb)

Right: Driving through the bitter December weather of 1944, these 8-in howitzers are travelling through Belgium to join the US First Army. Artillery was particularly effective in areas like the Ardennes, where roads were few and choke points obvious.

7.2-in Howitzers Marks I-V and 6

Between the wars the British army tended to neglect artillery; a number of programmes were initiated but came to naught, so when heavy artillery was required in 1940 all that there was to hand was a quantity of old World War I 203-mm (8-in) howitzers with ranges too short for current conditions. As a stopgap it was decided to reline the existing 203-mm barrels to a new calibre of 183 mm (7.2 in) and to develop a new range of ammunition. The original 203-mm carriages were to be retained, but the old traction engine wheels were replaced by new pneumatic balloon-tyred wheels on what became known as the **7.2-in Howitzer**.

The new ammunition provided the conversion with a useful increase in range, but when the weapon fired the full charge the recoil forces were too much for the carriage to absorb. Firing the 7.2-in howitzer on full charge was a risky business, for the whole equipment tended to rear up and jump backwards. Before the next round could be fired the howitzer had to be man-handled back into position and re-laid. Some of this unwanted motion could be partly overcome by placing behind each wheel wedge-shaped ramps up which the howitzer and carriage could climb, only to roll down again into roughly the original position, but sometimes even these ramps were insufficient and the howitzer would jump over them. But the conversion proved to be an excellent projectile-delivery system capable of good range and a high degree of accuracy, to the extent that the gunners in the field called for more.

In order to provide more, the number of 8-in howitzer conversions eventually ran to six marks depending on the original barrel and type of conversion; some of the 8-in barrels came from the United States. The first 7.2-in howitzers were used in action during the latter period of the war in North Africa (they were the howitzers mentioned in Spike Milligan's hilarious military memoirs) and in Tunisia, went

on to take part in the long slog north through Sicily and Italy; and were used following the Normandy landings.

But by 1944 numbers of 7.2-in barrels were being placed on imported American M1 carriages. These excellent carriages proved to be just as suitable for the 7.2-in howitzer as they were for the American 155-mm (6.1-in) gun and 203-mm howitzers, and the first combination of a 7.2-in barrel with the M1 carriage was the **7.2-in Howitzer Mk V**. Few, if any such combinations were made as it was obvious that the M1 carriage was capable of carrying more than the original conversion. Thus a much longer 7.2-in barrel was placed on the M1 carriage and this was the **7.2-in Howitzer Mk 6**. The longer barrel produced a considerable range increase to 17985 m (19,667 yards) and the carriage was much more stable than the old 203-mm carriage. As more M1 carriages became available they were used to mount the new Mk 6 barrels, and by the end of 1944 there were few of the original 8-in carriages left. With the increased stability came increased accuracy, and the Mk 6 howitzer gained an enviable reputation for good shooting, to the extent that they were retained for many years after the end of the war in 1945.

The 7.2-in howitzer could be as terrifying to its crew as to the target; seen here in action at Routot, France, in September 1944 the 10-ton gun

leaps into the air after firing at full charge. Surprisingly for such a makeshift design, the 7.2-in proved fairly efficient.

Specification
7.2-in Howitzer Mks I-V
Calibre: 183 mm (7.2 in)
Length of piece: 4.343 m (14 ft 3 in)
Weight: in action 10387 kg (22,900 lb)
Elevation: 0° to +45°
Traverse: 8°
Muzzle velocity: 518 m (1,700 ft) per second
Maximum range: 15453 m (16,900 yards)
Shell weight: 91.6 kg (202 lb)

Specification
7.2-in Howitzer Mk 6
Calibre: 183 mm (7.2 in)
Length of piece: 6.30 m (20 ft 8 in)
Weight: in action 13209 kg (29,120 lb)
Elevation: −2° to +65°
Traverse: 60°
Muzzle velocity: 497 m (1,630 ft) per second
Maximum range: 17984 m (19,667 yards)
Shell weight: 91.6 kg (202 lb)

The story of British heavy artillery after 1918 is the familiar one of inaction and neglect. When war broke out again, heavy guns had to be improvised by re-lining the old 8-in howitzers to a calibre of 7.2-in to give them a respectable range.

155-mm Gun M1

When the United States entered World War I in 1917 it was ill-equipped with heavy artillery, and consequently was issued with various Allied artillery models, including the French 155-mm (6.1-in) GPF (Grand Puissance Filloux). This gun was one of the best of its type at that time, but in the years after 1918 the American design teams sought to improve the overall efficiency of the gun and carriage by introducing a series of prototypes throughout the 1920s. Sometimes this programme stood in abeyance for years, but by the late 1930s the new design (very basically the original GPF barrel equipped to accommodate an Asbury breech mechanism) was standardized as the **155-mm Gun M1 on Carriage M1**, and production started at a steady pace at various American arsenals.

The M1 gun and carriage combination was very much an overall improvement on the old French GPF design, but introduced some new features. The barrel was 45 calibres long, and the carriage was of a heavy split-trail type carried on four double-tyred road wheels forward. This carriage

arrangement was such that in action the wheels were lifted to allow the carriage to rest on a forward firing platform that in use proved to be an excellent arrangement and very stable. This stability made the gun very accurate, and eventually the carriage was adopted by the British for use with their 7.2-in (183-mm) howitzer. For towing the trail legs were hitched up on to a limber device. There were two of these, the M2 and the M5, the latter having a rapid up-and-over lift arrangement that permitted quick use in action but which could also be dangerous to an untrained crew. For this reason the M2 limber was often preferred.

The M1 was gradually developed into an **M1A1** form and then into the **M2** in late 1944. These changes were mainly limited to production expedients and did not affect the gun's performance, which proved to be excellent: a 43.1-kg (95-lb) shell could be fired to a range of 23221 m (25,395 yards). The M1 soon became one of the standard heavy guns of the US Army and was often used for counter-

battery work. Numbers were issued to various allied nations, and the M1 was soon part of the British army gun park, which used the type in action in Europe from the Normandy landings onwards. The M1 also went self-propelled. This was carried out using a much-modified M4A3E8 Sherman tank chassis with the gun mounted in an open superstructure, and in this form the vehicle/gun combination was known as the M40. It was 1945 before the M40 actually got into production so its main career was post-war but it was widely used by many nations, again including the UK.

After 1945 the US Army underwent a period of internal reorganization and in the process the M1 and M2 guns became the **M59**. The post-war period also saw the end of the limber devices for the heavy tractors used to pull the guns all that was needed was to join the trails and connect them direct to the tractor towing eye, usually with chains. In this form the 155-mm (6.1-in) M59 serves on to this day with many armies around the world. It is still a good gun,

although now considered to be rather lacking in range and range flexibility as a result of the fixed charges used, and it is gradually being replaced by more modern designs. But it will still be some years before it is replaced in the armies of nations such as Austria, South Korea, Taiwan and Turkey.

Specification
155-mm Gun M1A1
Calibre: 155 mm (6.1 in)
Length of piece: 7.366 m (24 ft 2 in)
Weight: travelling 13880 kg (30,600 lb) and in action 12600 kg (27,778 lb)
Elevation: −2° to +65°
Traverse: 60°
Muzzle velocity: 853 m (2,800 ft) per second
Maximum range: 23221 m (25,395 yards)
Shell weight: 42 kg (92.6 lb)

240-mm Howitzer M1

The Westervelt Board of 1919 made many recommendations as to the future state of American artillery, too many in fact for the military funds available at the time. Thus some parts of the re-equipment programme had to be postponed following some preliminary design investigations that lasted until 1921. One part of these postponed projects concerned a common carriage that could mount either a 203-mm (8in) gun or a 240-mm (9.45-in) howitzer. At that time the 240-mm howitzer project could be dropped because the US Army was still trying to develop a 240-mm howitzer based on a French Schneider design, but that project was beset with problems and eventually came to nothing, only a few equipments being produced for training purposes.

But in 1939 things looked different, and the 203-mm gun/240-mm howitzer project was resurrected. The 203-mm gun took far longer to get into service than was at first envisaged, and it was not until 1944 that the first equipments were issued. But the 240-mm howitzer project was less problematical and was ready by May 1943. This **240-mm Howitzer M1** turned out to be a fairly massive piece of artillery using what was virtually an enlarged M1 carriage as used on the 155-mm (6.1-in) Gun M1. But the 240-mm howitzer carriage did not travel with the barrel fitted. Instead it travelled on a six-wheeled carriage and once on site its wheels were removed. The barrel was towed on a form of semi-trailer. At the chosen site the carriage had to be carefully emplaced and a pit was dug to permit barrel recoil at full 65° elevation. The barrel was then lifted into position, usually by a mobile crane that was also used to place the carriage into position and spread the trails. Emplacement of the 240-mm howitzer was thus no easy task, and sometimes took up to eight hours of arduous labour.

But once in place the howitzer proved to be a powerful weapon. It was first used extensively during the Italian campaign and afterwards in North West Europe whenever the fighting settled down behind static lines for any time. There was little call for the type to be employed whenever fighting was fluid as it took too long to emplace the weapons or get them out of action, but when they were used the heavy 163.3-kg (360-lb) high explosive shells were devastating weapons. The 240-mm howitzers were used by both the US and British armies, and they served on for many years after the war. A few attempts were made to place the 240-mm howitzer onto some form of self-propelled chassis but none of these projects got very far despite the advantages that self-propulsion would have given this heavy weapon. Instead attempts were made to simplify the assembly procedure or even allow the piece to travel in one load. Nothing came of these ideas and the 240-mm howitzer was gradually withdrawn from use during the late 1950s.

Today the only 240-mm Howitzer M1s still in use are those emplaced on the Chinese Nationalist-held islands off the coast of mainland China. There they act as heavy coast-defence weapons and are kept fully serviceable.

Weighing over 30 tons, the US 240-mm howitzer originated from a project begun after World War I, but little progress had been made before 1940, and America had been at war 18 months before the 240-mm weapon was ready. However, once in action it proved very useful against German emplacements in Italy and north west Europe.

Specification
240-mm Howitzer M1
Calibre: 240 mm (9.45 in)
Length of piece: 8.407 m (27 ft 7 in)
Weight: complete 29268 kg (64,525 lb)
Elevation: +15° to +65°
Traverse: 45°
Muzzle velocity: 701 m (2,300 ft) per second
Maximum range: 23093 m (25,255 yards)
Shell weight: 163.3 kg (360 lb)

A 240-mm howitzer prepared for action: it travelled on a six-wheel carriage, which was emplaced over a pit dug to absorb the recoil. The barrel was then lifted into place by a crane which was also used to spread the trails. Setting up the howitzer could take over eight hours.

'Little David'

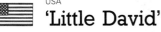

Despite the fact that many artillery pieces were much larger than the strange device known as 'Little David', the fact remains that this weapon still holds the record of having the largest calibre of any modern artillery piece at no less than 914 mm (36 in), and not even the largest German railway gun, the huge 80-cm K(E), got anywhere near that with its calibre of 800 mm (31.5 in).

Little David was one of the oddities of the artillery world. It had its origins in a device used to test aircraft bombs by firing them from converted large-calibre howitzers at chosen targets. Existing howitzers could not manage to fire the heavier bombs so a device known as the **Bomb Testing Device T1** was designed and produced. It performed well enough and gave somebody the idea of using the device as an artillery weapon proper. With the invasion of the mainland of Japan in prospect such a weapon would be ideal for demolishing the expected Japanese bunkers and strongpoints, so the project was given the go-ahead in March

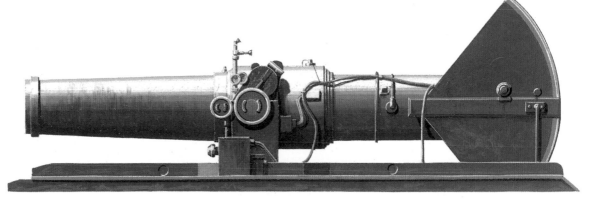

1944 and firing tests started later the same year.

Little David was little more than a large muzzle-loaded mortar with a rifled barrel. The barrel rested in a steel box buried in a deep pit which also contained the elevating gear and the six hydraulic jacks used to mount and remove the barrel. Some traverse was provided in the box mounting and the barrel was elevated and depress-ed using a geared quadrant on the breech end of the barrel. There was no recuperator mechanism, the barrel being simply pumped back into position after each firing. Loading was by a special crane which formed part of Little David's equipment train.

The projectile was of a unique form with a long tapered nose and a curved base. It weighed no less than 1678 kg (3,700 lb), of which 726 kg (1,600 lb)

The largest-calibre artillery piece of modern times, 'Little David' was originally a device for testing aircraft bombs by firing them at various targets. Someone suggested that it could be used as a gun proper, and with the invasion of Japan in prospect the US Army welcomed the idea of a monster howitzer to smash Japanese fortifications.

was explosive. Such a projectile would have had dreadful effects on any target, but Little David was never used in action. During its firing trials it was soon demonstrated that accuracy was poor, and the US Army was less than enchanted by the 12-hour emplacement time required every time the weapon was used. The war ended before the development trials were complete and the US Army promptly put the whole project 'on ice' before finally cancelling it during late 1946. Thus Little David never even left the Aberdeen Proving Grounds in Maryland where all its development and firing trials had been conducted, and the weapon promptly became a museum piece for the wonderment of all. Today it can still be seen there, forming part of the extensive ordnance museum that occupies much of the site open to the public. The weapon is still relatively complete. What appears to be a small metal shed is in fact the main mounting which was supposed to be

dug into a pit. The barrel rests on its transporter wheels ready to be towed in semi-trailer fashion by a heavy tractor, and one of the oddly-shaped shells is still to hand.

Specification
Little David
Calibre: 914 mm (36 in)
Length of piece: with elevating arc 8.534 m (28 ft 0 in)
Weight complete: 82808 kg (182,560 lb)
Elevation: +45° to +65°
Traverse: 26°
Muzzle velocity: not recorded
Maximum range: 8687 m (9,500 yards)
Shell weight: 1678 kg (3,700 lb)

Once the atomic bomb had saved the Allies from mounting a conventional invasion of Japan the fortress-crusher 'Little David' was without a role and the project cancelled.

USSR
Soviet 152-mm guns

When considering Soviet artillery development it is as well to remember that the Soviet artillery design teams rarely produced anything innovative. Instead they placed great emphasis upon a steady programme of development in which a new piece of ordnance was placed on an existing carriage, or in which a new carriage was allied to an existing gun or howitzer. Their continual aim was to produce an artillery piece that was as light as possible but firing as heavy a projectile as possible to as great a range as possible.

This was particularly true of the Soviet 152-mm (6-in) heavy guns. There were three main types of these, although others existed and the earliest of them could trace its origins back to 1910. Despite its age this weapon, designated the **152-mm Pushka obr. 1910g** was updated in 1930 to become the **152-mm Field Gun Model 1910/30**. In this form it was still in service when the Germans invaded in 1941. The Model 1910/30 was an unremarkable piece of artillery, so heavy that it had to be carried in two loads. This was considered to be too much of a disadvantage for modern use, and by 1941 the Model 1910/30 was being phased out of use. The Germans designated captured equipments **15.2-cm K 438(r)**.

In 1937 the Soviet design teams came up with a replacement. This was the **152-mm Gaubitsa-Pushka obr. 1937g (152-mm Gun-Howitzer Model 1937)** which emerged as a new and rather long gun barrel mounted on the carriage of an existing piece, the 122-mm (4.8-in) Field Gun Model 1931/37 (A-19). This combination was a gun-howitzer rather than a gun, and turned out to be a very versatile and powerful weapon, known to the Germans as the **15.2-cm K 433/1(r)** in captured service.

Seen here in German hands as a coastal defence piece, the Soviet 152-mm gun was a tough and reliable weapon and was produced in vast numbers. Massed batteries of heavy artillery played a vital role in driving the Germans back from Moscow to Berlin.

The 152-mm gun-howitzer M 1937 has a box section split trail carriage, and its double tyres were filled with sponge rubber. On the move, a two-wheeled limber is secured under the trails.

The Soviets wanted vast numbers, but the Artillery Plant Number 172 at Perm could not produce enough so another source of these gun-howitzers was sought. This turned out to be the same barrel as the Model 1937 but mounted on the carriage of an earlier 122-mm (4.8-in) field gun, the Model 1931. This combination was known for some reason as the **152-mm Gun-Howitzer Model 1910/34**, to the Soviets and as the **15.2-cm K 433/2(r)** to the Germans.

There was also one other Soviet 152-mm (6-in) field gun about which little is now known. This was apparently a long 152-mm naval barrel placed on the carriage of the 203-mm (8in) howitzers produced as a form of emergency design in 1941-2. Few details now exist.

These two major field guns designs, the Model 1937 and the Model 1910/34, formed the mainstay of the heavy field gun batteries of the Red Army throughout the war. Later development tended to concentrate on howitzers, but the field guns proved to be very useful weapons. They were often able to outrange their German counterparts and so impressed the German gunners that they used as many captured Soviet 152-mm guns as they could lay their hands on. Many of these captured weapons were used against their former owners and as many again were diverted to the Atlantic Wall defences.

Perhaps the best indication of how good the Model 1937 gun-howitzer was at the time it was introduced can

be seen by the fact that it is still in widespread service to this day. Now known as the **ML-20**, it remains in service with many Soviet-influenced armies throughout the world, from Cuba to China.

Specification
Model 1937
Calibre: 152.4 mm (6 in)
Length of piece: 4.925 m (16 ft 1.9 in)
Weight: travelling 7930 kg (17,483 lb) and in action 7128 kg (15,715 lb)
Elevation: −2° to +65°
Traverse: 58°
Muzzle velocity: 655 m (2,149 ft) per second
Maximum range: 17265 m (18,880 yards)
Shell weight: 43.5 kg (95.9 lb)

Soviet 152-mm howitzers

In 1941 the Red Army still had substantial numbers of short 152-mm (6-in) howitzers such as the **Field Howitzer Model 1909/30** and **Field Howitzer Model 1910/30**, but these were long in the tooth and despite an interim updating programme carried out after 1930 they lacked range. It was realized that these howitzers would have to be replaced and in 1938 the replacement appeared. For once this weapon was an all-new design combining a long 152-mm barrel with a sturdy and steady split-trail carriage. It went into production at two artillery factories, Artillery Plant Number 172 at Perm and Artillery Plant Number 235 at Volkinsk. The **Field Howitzer Model 1938**, later known as the **M-10**, turned out to be a great success and was widely used, later becoming one of the main types in Red Army service throughout the war.

The Red Army came to value the flexibility of the howitzer over the long-range capabilities of the gun to a great extent, and found during the early days of the war with the invading German army that the heavy 51.1-kg (112.6-lb) high explosive shell was also a powerful anti-tank weapon. This derived from the Red Army practice of using every available field piece as an anti-tank weapon, and was so successful that a special solid-shot projectile was introduced for use by the Model 1938. This weighed 40 kg (88.2 lb) and could

The Soviet Union not only produced some of the best artillery designs of World War II but also manufactured big guns in prodigious quantities. The 152-mm howitzer series was even used in the anti-tank role, for which it fired a 40-kg (88-lb) solid shot projectile.

knock out any known tank. The Germans also prized the Model 1938 highly, using as many as they could capture under the designation **15.2-cm sFH 443(r)**, either in the Soviet Union or as part of the Atlantic Wall defences. More turned up in Italy and France.

In their constant striving to make their progeny as light and efficient as possible, the Soviet artillery designers later converted the Model 1938 to be mounted on the carriage of the 122-mm (4.8 in) Model 1938 howitzer. A larger muzzle brake was fitted to reduce, at least in part, the recoil forces of the heavier barrel, and the new combination became the **152-mm Field Howitzer Model 1943**. As its designation implies this new howitzer/carriage combination was first produced in 1943 and soon replaced the earlier Model 1938 in production. It continued to fire the

same range of ammunition as the Model 1938 and the range capabilities remained the same. By 1945 it was in service with the Red Army in huge numbers and was later designated the **D-1**.

Post-war the Model 1938 and Model 1943 went on to serve in many more conflicts. Gradually the Model 1938 faded from use and is now known to be used only by Romania, but the Model 1943 is still very much in evidence. It is still in Red Army service; although now mainly with reserve units. It has been bestowed the accord of being thought fit to be copied by the Chinese army, which now has its own version, known as the **Type 54**. The Model 43 is used by nearly every nation that has come under Soviet influence, ranging from Czechoslovakia to Iraq and from Cuba to Vietnam. It has even turned up in

Ethiopia and Mozambique. There seems to be no sign of its ever passing away.

Specification
Model 1943
Calibre: 152.5 mm (6 in)
Length of piece: 4.207 m (13 ft 9.6 in)
Weight: travelling 3640 kg (8,025 lb) and in action 3600 kg (7,937 lb)
Elevation: −3° to +63.5°
Traverse: 35°
Muzzle velocity: 508 m (1,667 ft) per second
Maximum range: 12400 m (13,560 yards)
Shell weight: HE 51.1 kg (112.6 lb)

203-mm Howitzer Model 1931

The heaviest of the field-type weapons used by the Soviets between 1941 and 1945 was the **203-mm Howitzer Model 1931**, also known as the **B-4**. This was a powerful but heavy weapon that is now generally remembered as being one of the few artillery weapons to use a carriage that ran on caterpillar tracks. This was an outcome of the huge Soviet investment in tractor factories during the 1920s and 1930s, and the use of these tractor tracks was thus an obvious and economic measure for the Soviet carriage designers to take. The use of these tracks meant that the Model 1931 could traverse very bad or soft terrain where other weapons of similar weight could not venture.

This was an important point for the Model 1931, which was a heavy piece. It was so heavy that although most versions could be towed for short distances in two loads, long moves involved the breaking down of the weapon into as many as six separate

Above: The heaviest Soviet gun in field use during the war, the 203-mm Howitzer Model 1931 was mounted on converted agricultural tractor tracks widely available in the Soviet Union as a result of Stalin's lopsided industrialization programme. It fired a 100-kg (220-lb) shell to a maximum range of 18 km (11 miles).

The mighty 203-mm howitzer M1931 is still in service with some heavy artillery units of the Soviet army today, although it no longer uses its tracked chassis. The Germans were pleased to use any they captured, and fielded them not only in the Soviet Union but against the Allies in Italy and north west Europe.

loads. Some versions could move in five loads but there were about six different variants of the Model 1931. All of them used the tracked carriage but varied in the way they were towed. Movement of the Model 1931 involved the use of a limber onto which the split trails were lifted to be towed, usually by some form of heavy tracked tractor with (again) agricultural origins. Some of these limbers used tracks again but others had large single road wheels. Others had twin road wheels of smaller diameter.

To the soldier at the front all these variations made little difference as the howitzer itself remained much the same throughout its service life. It was rather a ponderous weapon to use in action, and the rate of fire was usually limited to one round every four minutes, although higher rates could be attained. It made a powerful barrage weapon but was also used for the demolition of heavy strongpoints, a heavy 100-kg (220.46-lb) high explosive shell being provided for the role. But essentially it was a weapon for static use as it was a ponderous beast, being limited on the move to a maximum speed of no more than 15 km/h (9.3 mph). Not sur-

prisingly, whenever mobile warfare was possible the Model 1931 was at a disadvantage and consequently many fell into German hands as they could not be moved quickly enough. The Germans were so short of heavy artillery that they used as many as they could, mainly in the Soviet Union but also in Italy and in North West Europe after 1944, under the designation 20.3-cm H 503(r).

After 1945 the Model 1931 appeared to fade from service but in recent years it has once more emerged. It is still part of the equipment of the current Red Army heavy artillery brigades and is still used for the destruction of strongpoints and any fortresses that might still be encountered. It has now lost the tracked travelling arrangements and has in their place a new wheeled road-wheel suspension with two wheels in tandem on each side. It is now very likely that this form of carriage allows the Model 1931 to be towed in one load, and it is also believed that this veteran will be replaced in the near future by a new 203-mm (8-in) howitzer on a self-propelled carriage.

Specification
Model 1931
Calibre: 203 mm (8 in)
Length of piece: 5.087 m (16 ft 8.3 in)
Weight: in action 17700 kg (39,022 lb)
Elevation: 0° to +60°
Traverse: 8°
Muzzle velocity: 607 m (1,991 ft) per second
Maximum range: 18025 m (19,712 yards)
Shell weight: 100 kg (220.46 lb)

Its tracks provided the 203-mm howitzer with unusual short-range mobility for such a heavy gun, although for long journeys it had to be broken down into several loads. Here the 203-mm howitzer ploughs its ponderous way through the snow to a new position, towed by a Stalin artillery tractor.

15-cm schwere Feldhaubitze 18

Shown here in an Eastern Front colour scheme, the 15-cm sFH 18 was a compromise between Krupp and Rheinmetall design and became the standard German heavy field ordnance of World War II.

Within Germany the two major artillery manufacturing concerns had been Krupp and Rheinmetall since the turn of the century. Both firms survived World War I intact, but with their usual markets shattered both decided to start again with new products. Thus for both the 1920s was a period of retrenchment and research so that by the time the Nazi party came to power in 1933 both were ready to supply their new customer. The new customer was shrewd enough to invite both parties to submit designs for every new artillery requirement made by the expanding German forces, and thus when a call was made for a new heavy field howitzer each company was ready with a suitable design.

The trouble for the army selectors was that the submissions were as good as each other. Thus the eventual equipment was a compromise, the Rheinmetall ordnance being placed on the Krupp carriage. This selection was made in 1933 and given the designation of **15-cm schwere Feldhaubitze 18 (15-cm sFH 18)**, although the actual calibre was 149 mm (5.87 in). The howitzer quickly became the standard German heavy field howitzer and it was churned out from numerous production lines all over Germany.

The first version of the sFH 18 was intended for horse traction and was towed in two loads, namely barrel and carriage. But before long a version intended to be towed by a halftrack tractor was produced, and this soon became the more common version. It proved to be a sound and sturdy howitzer and served well throughout all of Germany's World War II campaigns. Once the invasion of the Soviet Union was under way in 1941, however, it soon became apparent to the Germans that the piece was outranged by its Soviet 152-mm (6-in) equivalents. Various attempts were made to increase range, including two more powerful propellant charges to be added to the six already in use. These extra charges

worked to a limited extent but caused excessive barrel wear in the process and also overstrained the carriage recoil mechanism. To overcome the latter problem some howitzers were fitted with a muzzle brake to reduce recoil forces, but this modification was no great success and the idea was dropped; weapons so modified were designated **15-cm sFH 18(M)**.

As the war went on the sFH 18 was placed on a self-propelled carriage known as the Hummel (bumblebee), and thus formed part of the artillery component of a few Panzer divisions. Not all were used in the field role. Divisions that found themselves installed along the Atlantic Wall defences used their sFH 18s to bolster coastal defences, usually under German navy control. Some sFH 18s were handed out to some of Germany's allies, notably Italy (**obice da 149/28**) and, for a while, Finland (**m/40**).

The sFH 18 was still in use in very

large numbers when the war ended in 1945 and for a period the howitzers were used by many armies. Czechoslovakia used an updated version of the sFH 18 until quite recently, and the type was also used by the Portuguese army for a considerable period. Some still survive in parts of Central and South America, and the sFH 18 has surely been one of the soundest and sturdiest of all German artillery pieces.

Specification
15-cm sFH 18
Calibre: 149 mm (5.87 in)
Length of piece: 4.44 m (14 ft 6.8 in)

Weight: travelling 6304 kg (13,898 lb) and in action 5512 kg (12,152 lb)
Elevation: −3° to +45°
Traverse: 60°
Muzzle velocity: 520 m (1,706 ft) per second
Maximum range: 13325 m (14,570 yards)
Shell weight: 43.5 kg (95.9 lb)

This 15-cm sFH 18 is being towed into the cavernous mouth of an Me 323 transport by an Sdkfz 7 half track. The majority of German artillery was horse-drawn, but the 15-cm howitzer was modified early in the war to be towed by vehicles.

15-cm Kanone 18

When a German army requirement for a heavy gun to arm the new divisional artillery batteries was made in 1933, Rheinmetall was able to land the contract. Using the same carriage as that submitted for the 15-cm sFH 18 competition, Rheinmetall designed a long and good-looking gun with a range of no less than 24500 m (26,800 yards), which was well in excess of anything else available at the time. Production did not begin immediately for at the time priority was given to the sFH 18, so it was not until 1938 that the army got its first examples as the **15-cm Kanone 18 (15-cm K 18)**.

When the army began to receive the weapon it was very happy with the range and the projectiles, but was less than enchanted with some of the carriage features. One of these was the fact that as the gun was so long the gun and carriage could not be towed together except over very short distances. For any long move the barrel had to be withdrawn from the carriage and towed on its own special transporter carriage. The carriage itself was towed on its own wheels and a small limber axle carrying another two wheels. All this took time, an undesirable feature when getting the gun into and out of action, and this time was increased by another carriage feature, the use of a two-part turntable onto which the gun was lifted to provide 360° traverse. This too had to be got into and out of action, and the carriage was equipped with ramps and winches so that even when sectionalized for towing it made up into two heavy loads.

As if the time-consuming installation and removal drawbacks were not enough, the rate of fire of the K 18 was at best two rounds per minute. Not sur-

prisingly, the gunners asked for something better but in the interim the gun was in production and the gunners had to put up with things as they were. As things turned out, many of the K 18s were allocated to static coastal-defence batteries or garrison divisions where their relative lack of mobility was of small account. Not surprisingly, the coastal batteries soon found that the K 18 made a good coastal gun: its long range and the easily-traversed carriage made it ideal for the role, and it was not long before special marker projectiles using red dyes were produced specially for the marking and ranging of the guns.

Production of the K 18 ended well before the end of the war in favour of heavier weapons. But for the guns already in the field a range of ammuni-

tion in addition to the marker shells was made available. There was a special concrete-piercing shell with a much reduced explosive payload, and another was just the opposite, being a thin-walled shell with an increased explosive content for enhanced blast effect.

On paper the K 18 should have been one of Rheinmetall's better designs. It had an excellent range and fired a heavy projectile, but for the gunners who had to serve the thing it must have provided the source of a great deal of hard work. Gunners are always trained to get in and out of action as rapidly as possible, whatever weapon they are using, but the K 18 seems to have provided them with something that only hard work could turn into an acceptable battlefield weapon.

A 15-cm K 18 forms the centrepiece of a German artillery park captured by the British in Libya. This Rheinmetall design had an impressive range, but was dangerously time-consuming to deploy or withdraw.

Specification
15-cm K 18
Calibre: 149.1 mm (5.87 in)
Length of piece: 8.20 m (26 ft 10.8 in)
Weight: travelling 18700 kg (41,226 lb) and in action 12460 kg (27,470 lb)
Elevation: −2° to +43°
Traverse: on platform 360° and on carriage 11°
Muzzle velocity: 865 m (2,838 ft) per second
Maximum range: 24500 m (26,800 yards)
Shell weight: 43 kg (94.8 lb)

15-cm Kanone 39

The gun that became known to the Germans as the **15-cm Kanone 39 (15-cm K 39)** came to them via a roundabout route. The gun was originally designed and produced by Krupp of Essen for one of its traditional customers, Turkey, during the late 1930s. The gun was intended to be a dual field/coastal-defence gun and so used a combination of split-trail carriage allied with what was then an innovation, namely a portable turntable onto which the gun and carriage would be hoisted to provide 360° traverse, a feature very useful in a coastal-defence weapon. Two of the ordered batch had been delivered in 1939 when World War II broke out, and there was then no easy way of delivering any more to Turkey. With a war on its hands the German army decided it needed as many new field guns as possible and the design was taken into German service without modification as the 15 cm Kanone 39, and the type remained on the production lines at Essen for the German army alone.

Thus the German army found itself

The 15-cm Kanone 39 was a Krupp design commissioned by Turkey. Only two examples had been supplied when war broke out and the German army adopted it instead, along with large stocks of ammunition built to Turkish specifications.

with a large and useful gun that had to be transported in three loads: barrel, carriage and turntable. For most purposes the turntable was not really necessary and was only used when the gun was emplaced for coastal defence; the unit consisted of a central turntable onto which the carriage was placed, a series of outrigger struts and an outer traversing circle. The whole turntable was made of steel, and in use was anchored in place. The spread trails were secured to the outer traverse circle, and the whole gun and carriage could then be moved by using a hand crank arrangement. This platform attracted a great deal of attention from many other design teams, including the Americans who used it as the basis for the 'Kelly Mount' used with 155-mm (6.1-in) M1 guns.

The K 39 could fire conventional German ammunition, but when first introduced into service it came with sizable stocks of ammunition produced for Turkish use and to Turkish specifications. This involved a three-charge system and included a high explosive shell and a semi-armour-piercing projectile originally intended by the Turks to be used against warships. All this non-standard ammunition was gradually used up before the Germans switched to their normal ammunition types.

By that time the K 39 was no longer in use as one of the standard weapons of the German army. The full production run for the army was only about 40, and this was understandably thought to be too awkward a number for logistical comfort. Thus the K 39s were diverted to the training role and then to the Atlantic Wall defences, where they reverted to their intended purpose. On the static Atlantic Wall sites the turntables could be carefully emplaced to best effect and the guns could use their long range to good purpose.

Specification
15-cm K 39
Calibre: 149.1 mm (5.87 in)
Length of piece: 8.25 m (27 ft 0.8 in)
Weight: travelling 18282 kg (40,305 lb) and in action 12200 kg (26,896 lb)

Elevation: −4° to +45°
Traverse: on turntable 360° and on carriage 60°
Muzzle velocity: 865 m (2,838 ft) per second
Maximum range: 24700 m (27,010 yards)
Shell weight: 43 kg (94.8 lb)

A 15-cm K 39 lies abandoned on the frozen steppes, providing a subject of interest for the columns of Soviet troops marching westwards. The K 39 was eventually withdrawn to a training role for logistic reasons. Some were emplaced in the Atlantic Wall as a coastal defence gun.

17-cm Kanone 18 and 21-cm Mörser 18

When it came to artillery design in the years during both world wars, Krupp of Essen can be regarded as the virtual leaders. The company's sound approach, coupled with the thorough development of innovations, led to some of the most remarkable artillery pieces in use anywhere in their day, and one of these innovations featured on what were two of the most remarkable artillery pieces in service during World War II. This innovation was the 'double recoil' carriage on which the normal recoil forces were first taken up by the orthodox recoil mechanism close to the barrel and then by the carriage sliding inside rails set on the bulk of the travelling carriage. In this way all the recoil forces were absorbed with virtually no movement relative to the ground, and firing accuracy was thus enhanced. Further improvements were also ensured that the entire barrel and carriage could rest on a light firing platform that formed a pivot for easy and rapid traverse.

This double-action carriage was used mainly with two Krupp weapons. The smaller was the **17-cm Kanone 18** (actual calibre 172.5 mm/6.79 in) and the larger the **21-cm Mörser 18** (the Germans often followed the continental practice of calling heavy howitzers a mortar). These two weapons were first introduced in 17-cm (6.8-in) form in 1941 and in 21-cm (8.3-in) form in 1939. Both proved to be excellent weapons and demand was such that Krupp had to delegate extra production to Hanomag at Hannover. Of the two weapons priority was at first given to the **21-cm Mrs 18**, and a wide range of special projectiles was developed for this weapon, including concrete-piercing shells. But with the advent of the **17-cm K 18** it soon became apparent that the 17-cm shells were only marginally less effective than their 21-cm equivalents, and that the 17-cm gun had a much greater range (29600 m/32,370 yards as opposed to 16700 m/18,270 yards). Thus in 1942 priority was given to the 17-cm K 18, production of the 21-cm Mrs 18 ceasing.

But the 21-cm Mrs 18 remained in use until the end of the war, as did the 17-cm K 18 which continued to impress all who encountered it, either as recipients of the 68-kg (149.9-lb) shell or as gunners. In fact the Allies sometimes acted as gunners, for in 1944 some Allied batteries used captured 17-cm K 18s when ammunition supplies for their normal charges were disrupted by the long logistical train from Normandy to the German border. For all their weight and bulk, both the 17-cm (6.8-in) and 21-cm pieces were fairly easy to handle. A full 360° traverse could be made by only one man, and although both pieces had to be carried in two loads the carriage was well equipped with winches and ramps to make the process of removing the barrel from the carriage a fairly light and rapid task. For short distances both weapons could be towed in one load by a heavy halftrack tractor.

Specification
17-cm K 18
Calibre: 172.5 mm (6.79 in)
Length of piece: 8.529 m (27 ft 11.8 in)
Weight: travelling 23375 kg (51,533 lb) and in action 17520 kg (38,625 lb)
Elevation: 0° to +50°
Traverse: on platform 360° and on carriage 16°
Muzzle velocity: 925 m (3,035 ft) per second
Maximum range: 29600 m (32,370 yards)
Shell weight: HE 68 kg (149.9 lb)

21-cm Mrs 18
Calibre: 210.9 mm (8.3 in)
Length of piece: 6.51 m (21 ft 4.3 in)
Weight: travelling 22700 kg (50,045 lb) and in action 16700 kg (36,817 lb)
Elevation: 0° to +50°
Traverse: on platform 360° and on carriage 16°
Muzzle velocity: 565 m (1,854 ft) per second
Maximum range: 16700 m (18,270 yards)
Shell weight: HE 121 kg (266.8 lb)

A 21-cm Mörser 18, so called because the Germans referred to their heavy howitzers as mortars, used the same carriage as the 17-cm K 18.

As the 8th Army advanced deeper into Tunisia, this 17-cm K 18 was captured intact and used against its Afrika Korps former owners. Longer ranged than the 21-cm M 18, production facilities were devoted exclusively to the K 18 after 1942.

24-cm Kanone 3

During 1935 Rheinmetall began design work on a new heavy gun to meet a German army requirement for a long-range counterbattery gun firing a heavy projectile. The first example was produced during 1938, and a small batch was ordered soon after as the **24-cm Kanone 3 (24-cm K 3)**. The K 3 was a fairly massive piece of artillery that used the 'double recoil' carriage coupled to a firing table that could be easily traversed through 360°. The barrel could be elevated to 56° and thus fired in the upper register to ensure that plunging fire against fortifications and field works would make the shells as effective as possible.

The K 3 carriage was well endowed with all manner of technical novelties. In order to make the gun as mobile as possible the whole gun and carriage were broken down into six loads, and assembly on site was made as easy and rapid as possible by a number of built-in devices such as ramps and winches. Various safety measures were incorporated in case assembly was in some way incorrect; for instance, incorrect breech assembly left the gun unable to fire. Other safety measures ensured that if a winch cable broke the component involved could not move far enough to cause any damage. For all these measures it took some 25 men 90 minutes to get the gun into action. Once the gun was in action a generator, an integral part of the carriage, was kept running to provide power for the gun's services.

Not many K 3s were produced; most references mention eight or 10. They were all used operationally by one unit, schwere Artillerie Abteilung (mot) 83. This motorized artillery battalion had three batteries (each with two guns), and it was in action all over Europe from the USSR to Normandy.

The K 3 was the subject of much experimentation by German designers. Special barrels were produced in order to fire experimental projectiles with body splines that aligned with the barrel rifling as the projectile was rammed into the chamber. Other barrels fired projectiles fitted with sabots to increase range, and there was even a device fitted over the muzzle that 'squeezed' back skirts around special sub-calibre projectiles, again in an attempt to increase range. Some smooth-bore barrels were produced to fire the long-range Peenemünder Pfeilgeschosse (arrow shells).

By a quirk of production schedules the Rheinmetall-designed K 3 weapons were actually manufactured by Krupp of Essen. The Krupp engineers were not highly impressed by the engineering of the K 3 and decided they could do better, so producing their own version, the **24-cm K 4**. This was a very advanced design with the mounting carried on the move between two turretless Tiger tanks. There was even supposed to be a self-propelled version, but in 1943 the prototype was destroyed during an air raid on Essen and the whole project was terminated.

The K 3 was still in action when the war ended and at least one example fell into US Army hands. This was taken to the United States and underwent a great deal of investigation. Once the trials were over it went to Aberdeen Proving Grounds in Maryland, where it can still be seen.

Specification
24-cm K 3
Calibre: 238 mm (9.37 in)
Length of piece: 13.104 m (42 ft 11.9 in)
Weight: travelling (six loads) 84636 kg (186,590 lb) and in action 54000 kg (119,050 lb)

Elevation: −1° to +56°
Traverse: on turntable 360° and on carriage 6°
Muzzle velocity: 870 m (2,854 ft) per second
Maximum range: 37500 m (41,010 yards)
Shell weight: 152.3 kg (335.78 lb)

The 24-cm K 3 was a very long-range gun designed for counter-battery work as well as to pound fortifications to rubble. Only a handful were made, this one being captured by the US Army. Krupps produced a version which was carried by two turretless Tiger tanks.

35.5-cm Haubitze M.1

In 1935 the German army asked Rheinmetall to produce an enlarged version of its 24-cm K 3, and although the design of that gun was still at an early stage the Rheinmetall company went ahead and produced a new design with an actual calibre of 355.6 mm (14 in). The first example was produced ready to enter service in 1939, and emerged as a scaled-up version of the 24-cm (9.37-in) design. The new weapon was designated the **35.5-cm Haubitze M.1 (35.5-cm H M.1)** and incorporated many of the features of the 24-cm (9.37-in) design including the double-recoil carriage. The weapon was even carried in six loads, but an extra load had to be involved for the special gantry needed to assemble and disassemble the massive weapon. This gantry used electrical power from a generator carried on the same 18-tonne halftrack tractor that towed the disassembled gantry. Other 18-tonne halftracked tractors were also used to tow the other components; these were the cradle, top carriage, barrel, lower carriage, turntable and rear platform.

There appears to be no record of how long it took to get the H M.1 into action, but the time involved must have been considerable. It is known that the weapon was used by only one unit, namely 1 Batterie der Artillerie Abteilung (mot) 641. This motorized artillery battery was certainly involved in the siege of and assault on Sevastopol, but its exact whereabouts at other times are not certain.

In fact the H M.1 is something of a mystery weapon, and there are still a number of unknown facts regarding its service career. Even the exact number produced is uncertain. It is known that the weapon was manufactured at Rheinmetall's Dusseldorf factory, but the number completed varies from three to seven depending on the reference consulted. The projectiles fired included a high explosive shell weighing 575 kg (1,267.6 lb), and there was also a concrete-piercing shell that weighed 926 kg (2,041.5 lb). Four charges propelled these shells. It is known that it was possible to effect 360° traverse on the carriage platform by using power jacks.

For all its weight and bulk, the H M.1 had a range of only 20850 m (22,800 yards), so the efficiency of the weapon must have been questionable even at the time. Looking back it now seems doubtful that the considerable investment of money, manpower and equipment in a howitzer with such a limited range was generally not worth the efforts involved. But the H M.1 fired a shell that must have been devastating in effect when it landed on target. Even the strongest fortification would be hard put to remain operational after a few hits from such a shell, and this no doubt made the howitzer a viable weapon for the Germans. But the truth was that during World War II there were few such targets for the H M.1 to pulverize, and the only time that the howitzers were put to any great use was during the siege of Sevastopol. There are records of these howitzers firing 280 rounds, though they must have taken some time to accomplish this, for the rate of fire of the H M.1 was at best one round every four minutes.

The career of the monstrous 35.5-cm H M.1, seen here in action on the Eastern Front, is still shrouded in mystery. Several of them were used to pulverize the Soviet fortifications at Sevastopol.

Weight: travelling 123500 kg (272,271 lb) and in action 78000 kg (171,960 lb)
Elevation: +45° to +75°
Traverse: on platform 360° and on carriage 6°
Muzzle velocity: 570 m (1,870 ft) per second
Maximum range: 20850 m (22,800 yards)
Shell weight: HE 575 kg (1,267.6 lb) and anti-concrete 926 kg (2,041.5 lb)

Specification
35.5-cm H M.1
Calibre: 356.6 mm (14 in)
Length of piece: 10.265 m (33 ft 8.1 in)

Field Artillery

From the earliest days of gunpowder, artillery has often had a decisive impact upon the battlefield. The evolution of field artillery meant that armies could carry their own fire support with them, and by 1939 the field gun was an important weapon of all the major armies.

The German invasion forces in Norway in 1940. The horses are drawing a 105mm (4.13in) light howitzer or LeFH 18, a piece of field artillery that was overweight due to its solid construction.

Field artillery, whether in the form of guns or howitzers, plays the major part in providing fire support for other arms of the service to operate. Without the covering fire of field artillery, effective infantry and armoured operations would be all but impossible, while time and again throughout military history it has been demonstrated that

artillery fire support saves lives. It makes the enemy keep his head down as an attack goes in, it disrupts his supply lines and it destroys his installations and weapons.

By 1939 field artillery had grown into a well-established and well-organized arm in all major armies. Whatever its nationality, each army had ready for use a

well-exercised chain of artillery command and a well-tried chain of communications. Without these two essentials, field artillery could not, and still cannot even today, operate. Field artillery must have its orders carefully handed along a sensible command network and its orders must arrive at the correct place in as short a time as possible.

In all this interlocking system the guns and howitzers have only one part to play: they are but the delivery system for what is really the gunner's weapon, the projectile itself. The gun merely acts as the method of delivering that projectile, but this is often forgotten in the attraction that artillery has for so many. The guns of all nations are constantly cosseted and cleaned in a way no electronic black box can ever be, for each gun somehow acts as a gleaming example of a gunner's pride in his role and function: it is the guns that win battles, it is the guns that control the destinies of nations, and it is the guns upon which are lavished the care that would otherwise go to such equally intangible symbols as a regiment's colours.

Thus, the guns and howitzers discussed here are just a part of a much larger method of waging war. The selection contained in the following pages are merely an example. There were far more types and models of artillery pieces used during World War II than are shown in these pages, but the examples shown here are a good cross-section of the range of types used, from the ancient to the modern and from the little-used to those that were mass-produced.

Canon de 75 mle 1897

During World War I the French '75' or, more formally, the **Canon de 75 modèle 1897**, passed into French national legend as the gun that enabled the French to win the war. It was famous even before 1914 as what may now be regarded as the first of all modern field artillery designs: it coupled a highly efficient recoil mechanism with a rapid-action breech design and a carriage that enabled hitherto unheard-of rates of fire to be maintained. Before 1914 the 75 was a virtual state secret but once in action it more than proved its worth, to the extent that the French army depended on its high rate of fire to make up for deficiencies in the availability of heavier artillery weapons.

By 1939 the 75 was rather past its best, and was outranged by more modern field gun designs, but the French still had well over 4,500 of them in front-line use. Other nations also had the 75. The list of these nations was long for it included the USA (which was producing its own **75-mm M1897A2** and **75-mm M1897A4** versions), Poland (**armata polowa wz 97/17**), Portugal, many of the French colonies, some Baltic states, Greece, Romania, Ireland and many other nations. The 75 of 1918 was also very different from the 75 of 1939 in many cases. The Americans and Poles had introduced split trail carriages to the 75 in place of the original pole trail, and many nations (including the French) had introduced rubber-tyred wheels for motor traction in place of the original spoked wheels.

The 75 has also undergone some other changes in role. Before 1918 many 75 barrels had been placed on rudimentary anti-aircraft carriages, both static and mobile, and despite their limited value many were still around in 1939. The 75 has also undergone some adaptation as a form of tank weapon, but it was to be left to the Americans to make the full development of this possibility when they later adapted the type as the main gun for their M3 and M4 tank series. In France the 75 was updated to **Canon de 75 modèle 1897/33** standard with a new split trail carriage, but by 1939 there were few of these in service.

In the shambles of May and June 1940 huge numbers of 75s fell into the hands of the Germans, who were only too happy to use many of them for their own purposes as the **7.5-cm FK 231(f)** or, more commonly, as the **7.5-cm FK 97(f)**. At first many were issued to occupation garrisons and second-line formations, while others were later incorporated into the beach defences of the Atlantic Wall. Many more were stockpiled ready to be on hand when some use could be found for them. That came during 1941 when it was discovered the hard way that the armour of the T-34/76 Soviet tank was invulnerable to nearly all the German anti-tank weapons. As a hasty stopgap improvisation the stockpiled 75s were taken from the storerooms, fitted with strengthening bands around the barrel and placed on 5-cm Pak 38 anti-tank gun carriages. A muzzle brake was fitted and special armour-piercing (AP) ammunition was hastily produced. the results were rushed to the Eastern Front and there they proved just capable of tackling the Soviet tank armour. This rushed improvisation was known to the Germans as the **7.5-cm Pak 97/38** and was really too powerful for the

light anti-tank gun carriage, but it worked for the period until proper anti-tank guns arrived on the scene.

The 7.5 cm Pak 97/38 was not the only war-time development of the 75, for later the Americans developed the 75 to the stage where it could be carried in North American B-25 bombers as an anti-ship weapon.

After 1945 the 75 lingered on with many armies, and it would not be surprising if it is still in service here and there. In its day it was an excellent artillery piece that well deserved its famous reputation.

Specification
Canon de 75 modèle 1897
Calibre: 75 mm (2.95 in)
Length of piece: 2.72 m (107.08 in)
Weight: travelling 1970 kg (4,343 lb) and in action 1140 kg (2,514 lb)
Elevation: −11° to +18°
Traverse: 6°
Muzzle velocity: 575 m (1,886 ft) per second
Range: 11110 m (12,140 yards)
Shell weight: 6.195 kg (13.66 lb)

The Canon de 75 mle 1897 was still in widespread service in 1939; this example has been fitted with large pneumatic tyres for mechanized traction. Not all World War II examples were so fitted, but in any form the old 75 was still a viable field gun in 1939 and went on to serve with the Germans after 1940.

Right: French gunners after a range training session. These 75s have all been fitted with the large pneumatic tyres, but still retain the original 1897 carriage and shield. Note the lug under the muzzle that engaged with the recoil cylinder at full recoil.

Below: Not all the mle 1897 guns were fitted with tyres for pneumatic traction, as demonstrated by this example on tow behind a Citroen-Kegresse half-track.

Canon de 105 mle 1913 Schneider

The Canon de 105 mle 1913 had its origins in a Russian design, but it was a thoroughly modern weapon that was still good in 1939-45. Despite its age (1913) it was a good-looking gun with a good performance, and after 1940 it was pressed into service by the occupying German army.

In the first decade of this century the French Schneider concern took over the Russian Putilov armaments factory as part of a deliberate plan of commercial expansion. Putilov had for long been the main Russian armament concern, but during the early 1900s had been restricted in its expansionist ideas by the backwardness of the Russian commercial scene, so the infusion of French capital was a decided advantage.

Among the designs found on the Putilov drawing boards was an advanced design of 107-mm (4.21-in) field gun that appeared to offer considerable increase in range and efficiency over comparable models. Schneider eagerly developed the model and offered it to the French army, which was at first not interested as the 75 was all it required and there was no need for heavier weapons. But eventually the Schneider sales approach triumphed and in 1913 the Russian design was adopted by the French army as the **Canon de 105 modèle 1913 Schneider**, more usually known as the **L 13 S**. The events of 1914 rammed home to the French the fact that the 75 was not capable of supplying all the artillery fire support required, and that heavier guns would be necessary. Thus the L 13 S was placed in a higher priority bracket and large numbers began to roll off the Schneider production lines.

Between 1914 and 1918 the L 13 S provided sterling service. It was a handsome gun with a long barrel and a conventional box trail that provided enough elevation for the 15.74-kg (34.7-lb) shell to reach a range of 12000 m (13,130 yards). After 1918 the L 13 S became a French export as it was either sold or handed on to numerous armies under French influence. These nations included Belgium, Poland and Yugoslavia but it was in Italy that the L 13 S achieved its main market penetration. There the L 13 S became the **Cannone da 105/28**, and it remained one of the main field guns of the Italian forces until 1943. The Poles modified their L 13 S guns to take a new split trail design, and this **armata wz 29** was in service when the Germans attacked in 1939.

After 1940 the Germans found that the L 13 S was a viable weapon and out of the 854 still in French service in May 1940 they captured many that were still intact. Large numbers were handed over to various occupation units but it was not until 1941 that a real use was found for the bulk of the booty. When the Atlantic Wall was ready to be armed the L 13 S was decided upon as one of the primary weapons to be used. There were enough on hand to become a standard weapon, and there were stockpiles of ammunition ready for use. Thus the L 13 S became the German **10.5-cm K 331(f)** and was ready to play its most important part in World War II. Ex-Belgian guns were designated **10.5-cm K 333(b)**.

The Germans took the guns off their carriages and mounted them on special turntables protected by curved or angled armour shields. These were placed in bunkers all along the French and other coasts, and many of the bunkers can still be seen among the Atlantic sand dunes to this day. As a beach defence gun the L 13 S was more than suitable, and the bunkers were hard nuts to crack for any attacking force to crack. Fortunately the Normandy landings of June 1944 bypassed most of these bunkers. Not all the guns in these bunkers were directly ex-French; some found their way into the defences from as far away as Yugoslavia and Poland. Captured guns used by the Germans were the **10.5-cm K 338(i)** and **10.5-cm K 338 (j)** Italian and Yugoslav weapons, while unmodified and modified Polish weapons were the **10.5-cm K 13 (p)** and **10.5-cm K 29 (p)** respectively.

Specification
L 13 S
Calibre: 105 mm (4.134 in)
Length of piece: 2.987 m (117.6 in)
Weight: travelling 2650 kg (5,843 lb) and in action 2300 kg (5,070 lb)
Elevation: −0° to +37°
Traverse: 6°
Muzzle velocity: 550 m (1,805 ft) per second
Range: 12000 m (13,130 yards)
Shell weight: 15.74 kg (34.7 lb) for French guns and 16.24 kg (35.8 lb) for Italian guns

---

Canon de 105 court mle 1935 B

By the mid-1930s the French artillery park was beginning to take on the appearance of an antique supermarket. The vast bulk of the weapons in service were items retained from World War I, and if not already obsolete were at best obsolescent. Most of the weapons involved were 75s, which despite their one-time excellence had their limitations by the 1930s and were also unable to produce the plunging fire that was so often required when attacking fixed defences. Thus the need was forecast for a new field piece capable of easy transport for the support of mechanized forces, and two weapons were produced as the result of this forecast.

The first was a weapon known as the **Canon de 105 court modèle 1934 S**. It was a Schneider design which was entirely orthodox in design and appearance yet possessing a relatively short barrel. Although the mle 1934 was designated a gun, it had more in common with a howitzer. The mle 1934 was ordered into production, but only at a low priority as more was expected of a slightly better design.

The better design was a product of the state-run Atelier Bourges and appeared during 1935, hence the designation **Canon de 105 court Modèle 1935 B** (*court*, for short, and B for Bourges). The mle 1935 was a very advanced design for its day, and it too had a relatively short barrel, shorter in fact even than that of its Schneider equivalent. The carriage had a split trail which, when opened, also splayed the wheels outwards to improve crew protection. Once spread the trails were held in place with large spades that were pushed down into the ground through the trail extremities. The wheels could be either large steel items with solid rims or more modern designs with pneumatic tyres for towing by Laffly tractors. The rate of fire was about 15 rounds per minute, which was quite high for a weapon of its calibre.

The mle 1935 was ordered into production, but this was slow to the extent that although 610 were initially ordered this total was never reached. Instead production was terminated in 1940 in order to permit the churning out of more anti-tank guns, which were by then realized as having a higher operational priority. Thus there were only 232 mle 1935s in service when the Germans attacked in May 1940 (and only 144 of the Schneider mle 1934s). In action they proved to be excellent little field pieces, so much so that the Germans took over as many as they could. The Germans recognized the mle 1935 for what it was and gave it a howitzer designation as the **10.5-cm leFH 325(f)**. The weapons were used for training purposes and by various second-line occupation units. Some have been recorded as being incorporated into various coastal and beach defences. The mle 1934 became the **10.5-cm leFH 324(f)**.

Specification
Canon de 105 court mle 1935 B
Calibre: 105 mm (4.134 in)
Length of piece: 1.76 m (69.3 in)
Weight: travelling 1700 kg (3,748 lb) and in action 1627 kg (3,587 lb)
Elevation: −6° to +50°
Traverse: 58°
Muzzle velocity: 442 m (1450 ft) per second
Range: 10300 m (11,270 yards)
Shell weight: 15.7 kg (34.62 lb)

This photograph of a Canon de 105 mle 1935 B provides a good indication of how the steel carriage wheels were 'toed in' to provide extra protection for the carriage and gun crew.

105-mm Howitzer M2A1 – Carriage M2A2

The howitzer that was to become the 105-mm M2A1 was planned during 1919, but the first example was not ready until 1939. Thereafter it was produced in thousands and became the standard US Army field artillery howitzer. Rugged and basically simple, it was able to withstand all manner of use.

When the USA entered World War I in 1917 the US Army was poorly equipped with artillery and once in France was issued mainly with French or British equipments. The Americans decided to equip themselves properly with the French '75' and began production in the USA for their own use. Production was just getting under way when the war ended, leaving the US Army with a huge stockpile of 75s that was to last them until 1942. Thus when an investigating body met to report on the future equipments for the US Army the findings of their initial reports were not implemented.

The investigating body was the Westerveldt Board of 1919, and among its recommendations was the desirability of a 105-mm (4.13-in) howitzer. At the time little was done to put the suggestions into practice, so it was not until 1939 that the design of the proposed howitzer was completed. The weapon was placed into production the following year and thereafter the **105-mm Howitzer M2A1** poured off the American production lines in thousands.

The M2A1 was destined to become one of the most widely used of all American weapons in World War II. A measure of its success can be seen in the fact that it is still in widespread service in this decade, and even now some production batches are still run off.

The M2A1 was an orthodox piece of artillery with little of note in its overall design. The associated **Carriage M2A2** was a split-trail design with the gun assembly mounted in such a way that the centre of balance was just forward of the breech. The weapon was never intended for animal traction and so was fitted with rubber-tyred wheels from the outset. Overall the weapon was heavy for its calibre, but this meant that strength was so 'built-in' that the howitzer never seemed to wear out. The barrel and carriage could take enormously hard use and still keep firing.

The M2A1 was used in all theatres where the US forces fought, from Europe to the Pacific. Throughout the war years the basic design was the subject of numerous trials and improvements, and the ammunition underwent the same development process. By the time the war ended the range of ammunition fired by the M2A1 ranged from the usual HE through to propaganda-leaflet shells, various smoke marker shells and tear gas shells. Not all of the 105-mm (4.13-in) howitzers were towed. Some were placed on various self-propelled carriages, one of the most widely used being the M7, known to the British gunners who used it for a while as the 'Priest'. Later, Sherman tank chassis were used to mount the howitzer, and there was at least one attempt to mount the M2A1 on a half-track. Thus the M2A1 was able to provide fire support for armoured formations as well as infantry formations, and was among the first such weapons to provide mobile fire support, even though many others had undergone trials for the task.

Post-war the M2A1 was given a later form of designation (it is now the **M102**) and it is still a front-line weapon with the US Army and of the armies of many other nations. It is still used as a yardstick by which other artillery designs are measured.

Right: A 105-mm Howitzer M2A1 in action during the Korean War. Although taken in 1950, this photograph could be typical of many actions in which the howitzer was used in World War II. The M2A1 was eventually re-designated M102, and it is still in service with the US Army Reserve.

Below: 105 mm Howitzer M2A1s on a training range. In the foreground is a 37-mm (1.45-in) sub-calibre barrel that was used mounted over the barrel during training to decrease costs by firing smaller calibre and cheaper ammunition and to reduce wear and tear on the full-calibre howitzer barrels.

Specification
Howitzer M2A1
Calibre: 105 mm (4.134 in)
Length of piece: 2.574 m (101.35 in)
Weight: travelling and in action 1934 kg (4,260 lb)
Elevation: −5° to +65°
Traverse: 46°
Muzzle velocity: 472 m (1,550 ft) per second
Range: 11430 m (12,500 yards)
Shell weight: 14.97 kg (33 lb)

Cannone da 75/27 modello 06 and Cannone da 75/27 modello 11

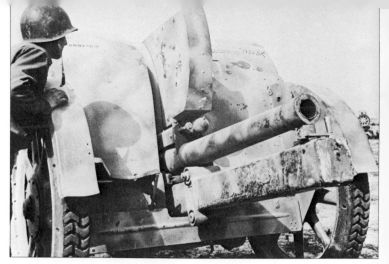

One of the most elderly of all field artillery pieces still in service during World War II was the Italian army's **Cannone da 75/27 modello 06** (gun of 75 mm, 27 calibres long, model 1906, in the standard way of interpreting Italian artillery designations). This was originally a German Krupp export model adopted by the Italian army in 1906 and retained thereafter until 1943.

The original Krupp designation was **M.06**, and the weapon was an entirely orthodox design with little of note other than a sound and sturdy construction. The carriage used a form of one-piece pole trail which restricted elevation and thus range, but for all that the 75/27 still had a useful range for a field gun. Not surprisingly, the original models had wooden spoked wheels for horse traction, but by 1940 some had been modified to take all-steel wheels and rubber tyres for powered traction, and it was this model that was most usually encountered outside the Italian mainland. The steel-wheeled gun was widely used throughout the North African and other Italian colonial campaigns, and was at one point issued to German field batteries in North Africa when their own equipment was not available. The Germans even supplied the 75/27 with their own designation,

An American soldier examines a captured Cannone da 75/27 modello 11. This had a barrel that elevated independently of its recoil mechanism.

7.5-cm FK 237(i). So widespread was the use of the 75/27 modello 06 in Italian service that there were even special versions produced for use in fixed fortifications.

The modello 06 was not the only 75/27 in Italian service. To confuse matters somewhat there was also a **Cannone da 75/27 modello 11.** This was another licence-built gun, this time from a French source, namely the Deport design centre. The 75/27 modello 11 had one unique feature, namely the original design of recoil and recuperator mechanism. On nearly all artillery pieces the recoil/recuperator mechanism is situated alongside the barrel, either above or below it and in some cases both. On the modello 11 the mechanism stayed in the horizontal position and the barrel elevated independently. The operation of the system was in no way impaired, but this feature did not catch on with other designers and soon fell into abeyance.

Nevertheless the modello 11 was still in widespread Italian service in

1940 and was used mainly in support of cavalry units, although some were issued to field batteries. As with the modello 06 some were modified to take steel wheels with rubber tyres for powered traction and some were also used by the Germans at one time or another as the **7.5-cm FK 244(i).**

Specification
Cannone da 75/27 modello 06
Calibre: 75 mm (2.95 in)
Length of piece: 2.25 m (88.6 in)
Weight: travelling 1080 kg (2,381 lb) and in action 1015 kg (2,238 lb)
Elevation: −10° to +16°
Traverse: 7°

Muzzle velocity: 502 m (1,647 ft) per second
Range: 10240 m (11,200 yards)
Shell weight: 6.35 kg (14 lb)

Specification
Cannone da 75/27 modello 11
Calibre: 75 mm (2.95 in)
Length of piece: 2.132 m (83.93 in)
Weight: travelling 1900 kg (4,190 lb) and in action 1076 kg (2,373 lb)
Elevation: −15° to +65°
Traverse: 52°
Muzzle velocity: 502 m (1,647 ft) per second
Range: 10240 m (11,200 yards)
Shell weight: 6.35 kg (14 lb)

Obice da 75/18 modello 35

Ever since the establishment of Italy as a nation, a certain sector of its armed forces has associated itself with the specialized art of mountain warfare. This has included the provision of special types of artillery adapted for the mountain role. Many of these mountain artillery pieces came from the Austrian firm of Skoda, and during World War I the Italians were happily firing Austrian mountain guns at their former suppliers.

By the 1930s much of this mountain artillery material was obsolescent and overdue for replacement. The Italian firm Ansaldo thus undertook to produce a new mountain howitzer design. By 1934 this had emerged as the **Obice da 75/18 modello 34**, a sound and thoroughly useful little howitzer that was intended for the mountain role and could thus be broken down into eight loads for transport. In the interests of standardization and logistics it was decided that the 75/18 was just what was required as the light howitzer component of the normal field batteries, and thus the weapon was ordered for them as well, but this time with a more orthodox carriage with no provision for being broken down into loads. This field version became the **Obice da 75/18 modello 35**.

The modello 35 was ordered into full-scale production but like its contemporary, the modello 37 gun, could not be produced in the numbers required. This was despite the fact that the carriage used by the modello 35 howitzer had many features in common with the later modello 37 gun, and the same barrel and recoil mechanism as that used for the mountain howitzer was carried over to the field howitzer design.

The supply situation was not eased in any way by the need for the Italians to sell the modello 35 abroad in order

to obtain foreign currency. In 1940 a sizable batch was sold to Portugal, and more went to some South American states to pay for raw materials. More production capacity was diverted to the production of versions for use on various forms of Italian *semovente* (self-propelled) carriages, but very few of these ever reached the troops. Those that did proved to be as efficient as any of the comparable German *Sturmgeschütze* (assault guns).

After 1943 the Germans took the modello 35 under their control as swiftly as they took over the rest of the available Italian gun parks, and the little howitzers took on a new guise as the **7.5-cm leFh 255(i).**

Italian gunners undergo training on an Obice da 75/18 modello 35. The box by the wheel contained the sights, not ammunition. That no firing was intended can be deduced by the fact that a dust cover is still in place over the muzzle. The small size of this howitzer can be clearly seen.

In contrast to many other Italian artillery pieces of World War II the Obice da 75/18 modello 35 was a very modern and handy little field piece. Designed by Ansaldo, it was the field howitzer version of a mountain howitzer design and thus lacked the ability to be broken down into several pack loads.

Specification
Obice da 75/18 modello 35
Calibre: 75 mm (2.95 in)
Length of piece: 1.557 m (61.3 in)
Weight: travelling 1850 kg (4,080 lb) and in action 1050 kg (2,315 lb)

Elevation: −10° to +45°
Traverse: 50°
Muzzle velocity: 425 m (1,395 ft) per second
Range: 9565 m (10,460 yards)
Shell weight: 6.4 kg (14.1 lb)

Cannone da 75/32 modello 37

When Italy emerged from World War I its economy, never particularly sound, was in no state to support a rearmament programme, and thus the weapons of World War I were bulked out by reparations from the Austro-Hungarian Empire, and the army was otherwise left to cope with what it already had. By the 1930s even the large numbers of weapons at hand were seen to be no real answer to more modern designs, so a programme of new weapon design was undertaken. The first weapons to be considered were those of the field artillery, and thus the first post-war artillery design to be introduced since 1918 was a field gun, the **Cannone da 75/32 modello 37**.

This new gun was an Ansaldo design. It was a good, sound and modern idea that was intended from the outset for powered traction, it had a long barrel fitted with a muzzle brake, and had a high enough muzzle velocity that it could be usefully employed on occasion as an anti-tank weapon. When the split trail was deployed it provided a traverse of 50°, which was no doubt useful in armoured warfare, but this was rather negated by the use of large trail spades that were hammered down into the ground through the trail legs, and thus a rapid change of traverse angle was not easy. Even with this slight disadvantage the modello 37 was a very useful field gun and the Italian gunners clamoured for as many as they could get.

Unfortunately they clamoured in vain, for Italian industry was in no position to provide the numbers required. There was quite simply no industrial potential to spare to produce the guns and all the raw materials, or at least the bulk of them, had to be imported. Thus gun production had to get under way at a time when all other arms of the Italian forces were in the process of re-armament; the air force was given a far higher degree of priority than the artillery, and the Italian navy was also absorbing a large proportion of the few available manufacturing and raw material resources. So demand for the modello 37 constantly exceeded supply, and by 1943 most of the Italian artillery park was still made up of weapons that dated from World War I or even earlier.

In 1943 the Italians changed sides. The Germans had already noted the finer points of the modello 37 and as the Italian nation withdrew from the Axis the Germans swiftly moved in to take over the Italian armoury, or at least as much of it as they could lay their hands on. In this grab for possession large numbers of modello 37s on the Italian mainland changed their designation to **7.5-cm FK 248(i)**. The Germans used their booty until the war ended, not only in Italy but also in the confused campaigns against Yugoslav partisan forces.

The Cannone da 75/32 modello 37 was another Ansaldo design, and was a good modern weapon that could stand comparison with any of its contemporaries. Its main fault for the Italian army was that there was never enough of them. After 1943 the Germans took over as many as they could find for their own use.

Specification
Cannone da 75/32 modello 37
Calibre: 75 mm (2.95 in)
Length of piece: 2.574 m (101.3 in)
Weight: travelling 1250 kg (2,756 lb) and in action 1200 kg (2,646 lb)
Elevation: −10° to +45°
Traverse: 50°
Muzzle velocity: 624 m (2,050 ft) per second
Range: 12500 m (13,675 yards)
Shell weight: 6.3 kg (13.9 lb)

Skoda 76.5-mm kanon vz 30 and 100-mm houfnice vz 30

When the Austro-Hungarian Empire vanished in the aftermath of World War I, the new state of Czechoslovakia was left with the huge Skoda arms manufacturing complex at Pilsen. Consequently the Czech state became a major supplier of all manner of arms to the Central European nations, but in the years after 1919 the arms market was still sated with the residue of World War I. The only way to break into the market was to offer something that was not already in the market and by 1928 the Skoda gun designers decided that they had found such a breakthrough.

What the Skoda designers discovered was that there was a definite market for a gun that could be all things to all men. Their suggestion was for a field gun with a high angle of barrel elevation that would enable it to be used as an anti-aircraft gun, or as an alternative act as a useful mountain gun. At that time the limitations imposed by the requirements of the anti-aircraft weapon were still not fully appreciated so the new Skoda proposal met with some interest. The new weapon was produced in two forms, one as a 75-mm (2.95-in) field gun/anti-aircraft gun and the other as a 100-mm (3.93-in) howitzer that could be used in a mountain role.

The first two weapons of this type were known as the **75-mm kanon vz 28** (*vzor*, or model) and **100-mm vz 28** as they were produced during 1928. Both types found ready markets in Yugoslavia and in Romania. Both weapons used a conventional enough carriage in appearance but what was not immediately obvious was that the barrel could be elevated to an angle of +80°. A firing table could be placed under the spoked wheel carriage enabling the barrel to be traversed rapidly in order to follow aerial targets. Needless to say the performance of the guns against aircraft targets was less than satisfactory for by the late 1920s it was formally being recognized that there was more to anti-aircraft firing than merely pointing a muzzle skywards; but as a field and mountain gun the vz 28 weapons were more than adequate and the anti-aircraft role was dropped. Instead the multi-role feature was emphasized by making the carriage easy to dismantle into three loads that could be carried on three horse-drawn carts for the mountain warfare role.

In 1930 the Czech army decided to adopt the two Skoda weapons as their vz 30 guns. The main change from the export models was that the calibre of the gun was altered to 76.5 mm (3.01 in) to suit the standard Czech calibre requirements, resulting in the **76.5-mm kanon vz 30**. The **100-mm houfnice vz 30** was fitted with a new pattern of rubber-tyred wheels and the result was a more than adequate field gun and howitzer combination to arm the field batteries of the Czech army.

These weapons never got a chance to prove their worth in Czech hands. The events of 1938 and 1939 meant that the Germans were able to take over the large Czech army gun parks and the assets of the Skoda complex at Pilsen without a shot being fired. All the Czech guns and the bulk of the various export models eventually found their way into German army service and Skoda was forced to supply

The Skoda 76.5 mm kanon vz 30 was an attempt to produce a field gun with enough barrel elevation for it to be used as an anti-aircraft gun. While it was a sound enough field gun, it proved to be of little use as an anti-aircraft weapon, but the type was used by the Czechoslovak and other armies.

ammunition, spares and even more guns for German army requirements. In German service the **7.65-cm FK 30(t)** guns and **10-cm leFH 30(t)** howitzers were used by all manner of units from front-line batteries to beach defence positions on the Atlantic Wall. They provided excellent service wherever they were, but not as anti-aircraft guns.

Specification
76.5-mm vz 30
Calibre: 76.5 mm (3.01 in)
Length of piece: 3.606 m (120.47 in)
Weight: travelling 2977 kg (6,564 lb) and in action 1816 kg (4,004 lb)
Elevation: −8° to +80°
Traverse: 8°
Muzzle velocity: 600 m (1,968 ft) per second
Range: 13505 m (14,770 yards)
Shell weight: 8 kg (17.64 lb)

Specification
100-mm vz 30
Calibre: 100 mm (3.93 in)
Length of piece: 2.5 m (98.4 in)
Weight: travelling 3077 kg (6,785 lb) and in action 1766 kg (3,894 lb)
Elevation: −8° to +80°
Traverse: 8°
Muzzle velocity: 430 m (1,410 ft) per second
Range: 16000 m (17,500 yards)
Shell weight: 16 kg (35.28 lb)

Skoda 100-mm houfnice vz 14 and houfnice vz 14/19

In the days of the Austro-Hungarian Empire the name of Skoda ranked only to that of Krupp in European armaments manufacture, and many of the old European nations armed themselves almost entirely with weapons produced at the massive Skoda works at Pilsen. By 1914 Skoda's designs were as good as any produced anywhere, and the range of weapon products was greater than most as Skoda also specialized in mountain guns. One of its products was a 100-mm (3.93-in) mountain howitzer mounted on a special carriage that could be broken down into loads for carrying over difficult terrain, and this weapon attracted the attention of many armies. Unfortunately they did not like the idea of the special carriage which was heavier than many would want for field artillery use so a new field carriage was produced. This was the **100-mm houfnice vz 14**.

The vz 14 was destined to be used mainly by the Italian army, which received large numbers in the upheavals of the break-up of the empire in 1918 and 1919. The type became a standard weapon for the Italians as the **Obice da 100/17 modello 14**, and was still in service in 1940 in large numbers. The numbers involved were so large that the Italians produced their own spare parts and ammunition. The type saw action in North Africa and served with Italian units on the Eastern Front alongside the Germans. But in 1943 the Italians withdrew from the conflict and their modello 14 howitzers were taken over by the German forces and remained in use until 1945 under the designation **10-cm leFH 315 (i)**, supplementing similar weapons taken over from the Austrians as the **10-cm leFH 14(ö)**. The type was also in service with the Polish and Romanian armies.

When Skoda resumed production for its new Czech owners the vz 14 was one of the first weapons placed back into production. However, the opportunity was taken to modernize the design, the main change being to the barrel length which was increased from 19 calibres (L/19) to 24 calibres (L/24), i.e. the length of the barrel was increased to 24 times that of the calibre (100 mm×24 for 2400 mm/7ft 10.5 in). This improved the range, and new ammunition was also introduced to provide the new design, soon known as the **100-mm houfnice vz 14/19**, with an improved all-round performance.

The vz 14/19 was soon in demand and numbers were exported to Greece, Hungary, Poland (**Haubica wz 1914/1919**) and Yugoslavia (**M.1914/19**). Italy also acquired the parts to modernize a proportion of its modello 14s and the Czech army also adopted the vz 14/19 as one of its standard field pieces. All in all the vz 14/19 became

one of the most important Central European field pieces, and by 1939 the howitzer was in service in numbers that ran into the thousands. It was a stout weapon with few design frills and it was capable of prolonged hard use. Many Italian examples were fitted with rubber-tyred wheels for motor traction (**Obice da 100/24**) but even after 1939 many examples retained their original spoked wheels and were pulled into action by horse teams.

After 1940 many vz 14/19s passed into German army service. The Czech army stocks had by then already passed into German hands as a result of the take-overs of 1938 and 1939 and the vz 14/19 was widely used during the French campaign of May-June 1940 as the **10-cm leFH 14/19(t)**. Many more were used during the initial stages of the invasion of the Soviet Union during 1941 but thereafter the vz 14/19s were gradually relegated to second-line use and many were incorporated into the Atlantic Wall defences where they remained until 1945. Examples taken

The Skoda 100-mm houfnice vz 14 was one of the better field weapons of the old Austro-Hungarian Empire during World War I, and went on to serve with many armies in World War II. By then it had been updated to the vz 14/19 standard by several modifications.

over from Greece were **10-cm leFH 318(g)**, those from Poland 10-cm **leFH 14/19(p)** and those from Yugoslavia 10-cm leFH 316(j).

Specification
100-mm vz 14/19
Calibre: 100 mm (3.93 in)
Length of piece: 2.40 m (94.5 in)
Weight: travelling 2025 kg (4,465 lb) and in action 1505 kg (3,318 lb)
Elevation: −7.5° to +48°
Traverse: 5.5°
Muzzle velocity: 415 m (1,362 ft) per second
Range: 9970 m (10,907 yards)
Shell weight: 14 kg (30.87 lb)

75-mm Field Gun Type 38 (Improved)

Field Gun Type 38 (Improved) was a title given by Western intelligence agencies to a field gun that was in widespread use with the Japanese field batteries between 1935 and 1945. The gun had its origins in a Krupp design that was obtained for licence production as far back as 1905. This was the original **Type 38**, and during World War I the Japanese had observed enough of artillery developments elsewhere to be able to make improvements to the original design.

Perhaps the most obvious of these Japanese innovations was the introduction of a form of box trail in place of the original Krupp pole trail. This innovation made possible extra elevation, and thus range was increased accordingly. Other alterations were made to alter the balance of the barrel on its cradle, and yet more minor changes were made to the recoil mechanism. Although the updated gun was given the full title Field Gun Type 38 (Improved) by the Allies, by 1941 few, if any, of the Type 38 guns had been left unmodified, so the extra terminology was superfluous.

Despite the changes introduced to the Type 38 by the Japanese, the overall design was unremarkable, and the overall performance was also unimpressive. Throughout its service life the gun was never adapted for vehicle traction, so horse or mule teams were used right up to 1945. In appearance

the gun was archaic, and it was indeed a design relic of a former era, maintained in service as the Japanese were never able to develop the industrial potential to produce artillery in the amounts required. Although much more modern and powerful field guns (with calibres of 75 mm/2.95 in and upwards) were produced right up to the beginning of World War II, they were never produced in numbers sufficient to permit the replacement of the Type 38. Thus Japanese gunners were saddled with obsolete guns in default of anything else.

During the initial stages of the Japanese war against the Chinese during the 1930s the Type 38 proved more

than adequate for all its required operational tasks, but once the Allies joined in the conflict after 1941 things were very different. Following initial easy successes, the Japanese gunners constantly found themselves outgunned by even small forces of Allied artillery, and in these circumstances the Type 38 did not shine. In fact the Type 38 became something of a liability for, being horse-drawn, it was easily rendered immobile by enemy action or terrain conditions and many precious Japanese guns were lost or knocked out simply because they could not be moved rapidly enough.

After 1945 quantities of Type 38 guns passed into the hands of various forces

The Japanese Field Gun Type 38 dated back to a Krupp design of 1905, but by World War II it had been modernized in several respects to obtain the (Improved) designation. It was an unremarkable gun, but the Japanese were so short of artillery production facilities that the type was kept in service until 1945.

in South East Asia, some official and some unofficial, and there were reports of the weapon being used against French forces in Indo-China during the late 1940s.

Specification
Field Gun Type 38 (Improved)
Calibre: 75 mm (2.95 in)
Length of piece: 2.286 m (90 in)
Weight: travelling 1910 kg (4,211 lb) and in action 1136 kg (2,504 lb)
Elevation: −8° to +43°
Traverse: 7°
Muzzle velocity: 603 m (1,978 ft) per second
Range: 11970 m (13,080 yards)
Shell weight: 6.025 kg (13.3 lb)

Ordnance, Q.F., 25-pdr

The British 25-pdr was one of the 'classic' field artillery weapons of World War II. It served in all theatres after 1940 and made its initial mark during the famous barrage at El Alamein. As well as being used as a field gun, it was at one time pressed into action as an anti-tank gun in the Western Desert.

The gun that was to become one of the most famous of all British artillery pieces had its origins in operational analysis after World War I that indicated that it would be possible to provide the Royal Artillery with a light field piece that could combine the attributes of a gun and a howitzer. Some development work on this concept was carried out in the 1920s and 1930s, but funds for the project were very limited and it was not until the mid-1930s that the go-ahead was given to develop the new weapon to replace the British Army's ageing stock of 18-pdr field guns and 114-mm (4.5-in) howitzers.

Since there were large stocks of the old 18-pdr guns still around in the 1930s the Treasury dictated that some way would have to be found to use them. From this came the **Ordnance, Q.F., 25-pdr Mk 1**, which was a new barrel placed on an 18-pdr carriage, and it was with this gun that the BEF went to war in 1939. The old carriages had been updated with new pneumatic wheels and other changes (some even had split trails), but the 25-pdr Mk 1 had little chance to shine before most of them were lost at Dunkirk.

By then the **25-pdr Mk 2 on Carriage 25-pdr Mk 1** was on the scene. This was a purpose-built weapon that was intended to be the full replacement for the old pieces, and was among the first examples of what can now be described as a gun-howitzer. It used an ammunition system with variable charges but could be used for lower-register firing with no loss in efficiency. The barrel itself was orthodox and

used a heavy vertical sliding breech mechanism, but the carriage had some unusual features. It was a humped box trail carried on a circular firing table that enabled one man to make large changes of traverse angle easily and quickly. The design was intended from the start for powered traction, the usual tractor being one of the large 'Quad' family.

Almost as soon as the first 25-pdr guns saw action in North Africa they were pressed into use as anti-tank guns. The little 2-pdr anti-tank gun proved to be useless against the Afrika Korps' tanks, and the 25-pdr had to be used as there was nothing else to hand. It was then that the circular firing table came into its own, for the guns could be rapidly moved from target to target, but the 25-pdr had to rely on shell power alone for its effects as there was no armour-piercing ammunition. Such a round was developed, but it entailed the use of an extra charge which in turn dicated the use of a muzzle brake, and in this form the 25-pdr was used

throughout the rest of World War II.

Some changes were made to the carriage design to suit local requirements. A narrower version was developed for jungle and airborne warfare (**25-pdr Mk 2 on Carriage 25-pdr Mk 2**) and a version with a hinged trail (**25-pdr Mk 2 on Carriage 25-pdr Mk 3**) was produced to increase elevation for hill warfare. The Australians produced a drastic revision for pack transport, and there was even a naval version mooted at one time. The 25-pdr went 'self-propelled' in the Canadian Sexton carriage and there were numerous trial and experimental versions, one classic expedient being the stopgap mounting of 17-pdr anti-tank barrels on 25-pdr carriages. Captured examples were designated **8.76-cm FK 280(e)** by the Germans.

The 25-pdr provided sterling service wherever it was used. It had a useful range, and the gun and carriage proved capable of absorbing all manner of punishment and hard use. It remained in service with numerous

armies for many years after 1945 and is still in service with many. The 25-pdr was one of those artillery pieces that will go down in history as a 'classic', and many gunners remember the weapon with what might almost be termed affection.

Specification
Ordnance, Q.F., 25-pdr Mk 2
Calibre: 87.6 mm (3.45 in)
Length of piece: 2.40 m (94.5 in)
Weight: travelling and in action 1800 kg (3,968 lb)
Elevation: −5° to +40°
Traverse: on carriage 8°
Muzzle velocity: 532 m (1,745 ft) per second
Range: 12253 m (13,400 yards)
Shell weight: 11.34 kg (25 lb)

25-pdrs on a training range are manned by Canadian gunners, the 25-pdr being the standard field gun for many Commonwealth armies. This photograph probably dates from mid-1943.

The 10.5-cm howitzer family

The 10.5-cm leFH 18 in its original form with no muzzle brake, pressed steel wheels of typical German form and the original heavy carriage. This was a Rheinmetall design that proved sound but too heavy for the mobile role intended, especially in the muddy conditions of the Russian front.

The 10.5-cm leFH 18(M) where the (M) of the Mundungbremse (muzzle brake) can clearly be seen. This allows the howitzer to fire a more powerful propellant charge and thus range was increased. Several designs of muzzle brake were used until one that allowed sub-calibre ammunition to be fired was devised.

The German army had chosen the calibre of 105 mm (4.134 in) for its standard field howitzers well before World War I, and then stuck with it. During World War I the standard field howitzer had been the **10.5-cm leFH 16** (*leichte FeldHaubitze*, or light field howitzer) which used the same carriage as the then-standard 7.7-cm FK 16. After 1918 numbers of these howitzers remained with the rump of the German army and were used to train the generation of gunners who were to be the battery commanders and NCOs of World War II.

The operational analysis carried out by German war planners during the 1920s indicated that in future conflicts a 105-mm (4.13-in) projectile would be far more effective than the 75-mm (2.95-in) equivalent for no great cost in delivery system weight, that is the artillery piece involved. Thus they plumped for a new 105-mm (4.13-in) howitzer, and design work started as early as 1928-9. Rheinmetall was the project leader, and the result of its efforts was ready for service in 1935.

The new weapon was the **10.5-cm leFH 18**, a conventional and sound howitzer with a useful projectile weight and adequate range. If there was a fault with the leFH 18 it was that it was so soundly constructed that it was rather heavy, but as motor traction was expected to provide the bulk of the pulling power that was no great disadvantage, at least in theory. The leFH 18 became a valuable export item, and numbers were sold to Spain, Hungary, Portugal and some South American nations; large numbers also came off the production lines to equip the expanding German forces.

As ever the gunners were soon asking for more range, and as a result an increased propellant charge was introduced for the leFH 18. This dictated the introduction of a muzzle brake which meant a change of designation to **10.5-cm leFH 18(M)**, the suffix denoting *Mundungbremse*, or muzzle brake. The introduction of this muzzle attachment meant that a special sabot sub-calibre 88-mm (3.46-in) projectile could not be fired until a new

revised design was introduced slightly later.

Thus the leFH 18 series went to war and proved itself efficient enough until the winter campaign in the Soviet Union took its toll in 1941-2. During the thaws involved in that campaign large numbers of 105-mm (4.13-in) howitzers were lost because the weights involved were too great for the available towing vehicles to drag weapons clear of the all-prevailing mud. Thus the overweight howitzers showed their disadvantage with a vengeance, and a hurried search for some form of alternative carriage then began.

The result was an unsatisfactory improvisation. The carriage of the 7.5-cm Pak 40 anti-tank gun was simply taken as the new mount for the leFH 18(M) gun, its associated cradle and the large shield. The result was slightly lighter than the original (but not by very much), and the improvised arrangement gave constant problems that were never properly eradicated. It was intended that the new howitzer/carriage combination, designated **10.5-cm leFH 18/40**, would become the standard field howitzer for all the German army, but this never happened and in 1945 even the old FH 16 was still in the line.

Specification
10.5-cm leFH 18/40
Calibre: 105 mm (4.134 in)
Length of piece: 3.31 m (130.23 in)
Weight: travelling and in action 1955 kg (4,310 lb)
Elevation: −5° to +42°
Traverse: 60°
Muzzle velocity: 540 m (1,770 ft) per second
Range: 12325 m (13,478 yards)
Shell weight: 14.81 kg (32.65 lb)

Above: Abandoned 10.5-cm leFH 18(M) howitzers in Normandy in June 1944. Note the obvious bulk and weight of the trail legs and spades that combined to make this howitzer too heavy for the mobile field role.

Below: 10.5-cm leFH 18s in action in France during May 1940 when these howitzers, towed into action by half-tracks, consistently outfought the more numerous French artillery units as they swept across France.

7.5-cm Feldkanone 16 nA and leichte Feldkanone 18

Almost as soon as the German army began to adopt new field guns in the late 19th century they adopted the calibre of 77 mm (3.03 in) as their standard field gun calibre. In 1896 they produced the **C/96** of this calibre, and in 1916 updated and revised the design to produce the **7.7-cm FK 16** (*Feld-Kanone*, or field gun, and 16 for 1916).

After 1918 there was a drastic rethink of German weapon practices, and among the changes that emerged from this study was the adoption of a new standard calibre of 75 mm (2.95 in); this calibre was (and still is) a standard field gun ammunition calibre, so the Germans were only following a well trodden path. The Versailles Treaty had left the rump of the German army with a stockpile of the old FK 16s, so in order to modernize these guns they were rebarrelled with new 75-mm (2.95-in) barrels. The guns were then known as the **7.5-cm FK 16 nA**, with the nA denoting *neuer Artillerie*, or new model.

The rebarrelled guns were issued during 1934, initially to horse-drawn batteries supporting cavalry units. The Germans continued to use horse cavalry units until 1945, but by then the FK 16 nA had fallen out of use for it was really a relic of a past era, and was as such too heavy and lacking in mobility for the cavalry role. Instead many were relegated to the training role or were issued to various second-line units. Large numbers were still in service when the war ended, and one fired its way into history when it held up an

Allied armoured formation for some time during the fighting near the Normandy beach-heads in June 1944. That particular gun was not destroyed until it had knocked out at least 10 Allied tanks.

Even while the rebarrelling of the old FK 16 carriages was under way a call for a new design of cavalry gun was put out. During 1930 and 1931 both Krupp and Rheinmetall produced designs, and although the Krupp design was finally chosen it was not until 1938 that the first examples were issued for service. The new design became the **7.5-cm leFK 18** (*leichte Feldkanone*, or light field gun), and it had such modern features as a split trail carriage to increase the on-carriage traverse (so useful for anti-armoured warfare) and a range of ammunition that included a hollow-charge warhead for use against tanks. The leFK 18 was judged to to be a great success. Its range was less than that of the weapon it was intended to replace, and the complex carriage made it an expensive and difficult item to produce. Consequently not many were produced and the emphasis for field artillery calibres changed to 105 mm (4.134 in). However, the leFK

18 was kept in production for export sales to gain influence and foreign currency. Some sales were made to various South American countries and in one of them (Brazil) the leFK 18 is still in limited use.

Specification
FK 16 nA
Calibre: 75 mm (2.95 in)
Length of piece: 2.70 m (106.3 in)
Weight: travelling 2415 kg (5,324 lb) and in action 1524 kg (3,360 lb)
Elevation: −9° to +44°
Traverse: 4°
Muzzle velocity: 662 m (2,172 ft) per second.
Range: 12875 m (14,080 yards)
Shell weight: 5.83 kg (12.85 lb)

Specification
leFK 18
Calibre: 75 mm (2.95 in)
Length of piece: 1.94 m (76.4 in)
Weight: travelling 1324 kg (2,919 lb) and in action 1120 kg (2,470 lb)
Elevation: −5° to +45°
Traverse: 30°
Muzzle velocity: 485 m (1,590 ft) per second
Range: 9425 m (10,310 yards)
Shell weight: 5.83 kg (12.85 lb)

10.5-cm Kanone 18 and 18/40

Among the post-war requirements for a new German artillery park to replace the lost relics of World War I was that for a new long-range gun for use by corps rather than field artillery batteries. This project was one of the very first put out to the underground German armaments industry, for by 1926 both Krupp and Rheinmetall had produced specimen designs and by 1930 both were ready with prototype hardware.

As it turned out the German army could not decide which design to approve; in the end it compromised by accepting the Rheinmetall barrel and the Krupp carriage. The Krupp carriage was destined to become one of the most widely used of all the German artillery carriages, for it was the same as that used on the larger 15-cm sFH 18 howitzer series. It was 1934 before the first guns actually reached the troops and for a while the new gun, known as the **10.5-cm K 18** (*Kanone*, or gun), was the standard weapon of the medium artillery batteries.

This state of affairs did not last long for the choice of 105-mm (4.134-in) calibre for a medium gun was to prove an unhappy one. In a nutshell the gun was too heavy for the weight of projectile fired. The larger 150-mm (actually 149 mm/5.87 in) howitzers fired a much more efficient projectile over almost the same range and at no great increase in weapon weight. There was also another snag: when the K 18 entered service it was at a time when the German army had yet to become even partially mechanized, so the guns had to be pulled by horse teams. The gun weighed too much for one horse team

to tackle, so the barrel and carriage had to be towed as separate loads, which was a bit much for a 105-mm (4.13-in) gun. Later on the introduction of half-tracked tractors enabled the piece to be towed in one load, but by then the K 18 was on a very low production priority.

In order to make the K 18 a more powerful weapon, the German staff planners called for an increase in range. There was no way to produce this increase without lengthening the length of the barrel from the original L/52 to L/60. The first of these improved models was ready in 1941 and was known as the **10.5-cm K 18/40**, but it

was not put into production until much later when the designation had been changed yet again to **10.5-cm sK 42** (*schwere Kanone*, or heavy gun). Very few were actually produced.

By 1941 the disadvantages of the K 18 and its later versions had been recognized, but there remained a role for them where their weight and bulk would be of a relatively minor disadvantage, namely coastal defence. Weapons for the Atlantic Wall, at that time still under construction, were in great demand and short supply, so the K 18 was assigned to that relatively static role. As a coastal defence weapon the piece had a considerable

A 10.5-cm K 18 stands in splendid isolation in the middle of an abandoned German field position in the Western Desert. In the background is one of the famous '88' Flak guns, giving an indication that the position was intended to be some form of strongpoint.

advantage in its long range, even if the projectile weight was still rather low. To enable it to be used to greater advantage when firing at marine targets a new range of ammunition was introduced, among which was a special sea marker shell for ranging purposes.

Calibre: 105 mm (4.134 in)
Length of piece: 5.46 m (214.96 in)
Weight: travelling 6434 kg (14,187 lb) and in action 5624 kg (12,400 lb)
Elevation: −0° to +48°
Traverse: 64°
Muzzle velocity: 835 m (2,740 ft) per second
Range: 19075 m (20,860 yards)
Shell weight: 15.14 kg (33.38 lb)

British infantry examine a 10.5-cm K 18; note the sheer size of this gun. In the foreground is a handspike used to move the trail legs either for a rapid change of traverse or to join them together for a move to a new position.

USSR

76.2-mm Field Gun Model 00/02 and 02/30

The family of field guns based on the old Russian 00/02 design are among that group of weapons which are little known or regarded but are yet among those which have provided excellent service over a long period. They are still hardly known outside the Soviet Union, but they were used throughout two world wars (and in a great number of other conflicts as well) and have all played their part in world history.

The original gun in the series was the Russian **76.2-mm Field Gun Model 00**, produced in 1900 by Putilov. The origins of the Model 00 may have been in a Krupp design, for the Russian weapon certainly had many of the current Krupp features, but by 1902 the full production model, the **Model 00/02** was being issued to the Tsarist armies. The type was used throughout the many large-scale campaigns on the Eastern Front in World War I, and throughout them all was used in an unspectacular but effective manner.

After the upheavals of 1918 the Model 00/02 was retained by the new Red Army but numbers were either sold or handed over to some of the new Baltic States and such nations under Soviet influence such as Finland. Poland also received a batch which they proceeded to convert from the original 76.2-mm (3-in) to 75-mm (2.95-in) calibre to match the rest of their French-supplied equipments. The Poles knew the gun as the **armata wz 02/26**, and it was still in service when Germany attacked in 1939, examples passing into German service being designated **7.5-cm FK 02/26(p)**.

In the Soviet Union the Red Army decided to modernize its large but elderly gun stocks and the Model 00/02

was an early candidate for the process. In 1930 most of the in-service guns were updated by the introduction of new ammunition, better propellants and in some cases new barrels. To confuse matters some guns retained their original L/30 barrels while others were fitted with entirely new L/40 barrels. Both of these modernized guns were then known as the **Model 02/30**, and became two of the standard Red Army artillery field pieces. Large numbers were in use when the Germans invaded in 1941, and the Germans in turn took over the types as two of their own standard field weapons (**7.62-cm FK 295/1(r)** for the L/30 and **7.62-cm FK 295/2(r)** for the L/40). The guns were later relegated to the usual round of second-line units and Atlantic Wall beach-defence purposes.

The Model 02/30 was not used only by the Red Army. Numbers found their way all over the world, especially in the years following 1945 when many started to appear in the Far East. Large numbers were handed over to the Communist Chinese, who used them both against their Nationalist foes and later against the United Nations forces in Korea. The type turned up again in the hands of the Viet Minh in Indo-China and it may be doubted if the last has yet been heard of this gun.

For all its longevity and variety of forms, the Model 00/02 and Model 03/30 were entirely orthodox guns in almost every way. Most never lost their original spoked wheels or their simple box trails, and the majority appear to have retained their gun shields throughout their service lives. They must have been produced in thousands, but perhaps the greatest

reasons for their longevity were their essential simplicity and design to meet the worst rigours of the Russian terrain and climate. Any weapon that could resist them could stand up to virtually anything.

Specification
Model 00/03 (L/30 type)
Calibre: 76.2 mm (3 in)
Length of piece: 2.286 m (90 in)
Weight: in action 1320 kg (2,910 lb)
Elevation: −5° to +37°
Traverse: 2.66°

Soviet field guns were captured in huge numbers during the early stages of the war in the east, and with Germany having a huge requirement for weapons both to continue the war and to control occupied territories many of these captured weapons were pressed into service. This 76.2-mm field gun is on the Atlantic Wall.

Muzzle velocity: 646 m (2,119 ft) per second
Range: 12400 m (13,565 yards)
Shell weight: 6.4 kg (14.11 lb)

USSR

76.2-mm Field Gun Model 1936

By the early 1930s the Red Army artillery staff was becoming aware that its stock of field pieces was falling behind those of the rest of Europe in power and efficiency, and so in the early 1930s the USSR began a programme for new weapons. One early attempt, made in 1933, was the placing of a new 76.2-mm (3-in) barrel on the carriage of a 107-mm (4-in) field gun, but this was intended only as a stopgap until

the introduction of what was intended to be one of the best all-round field guns in the world.

The new gun was introduced in 1936, and was thus known as the **76.2-mm Field Gun Model 1936**, usually known as the **76-36**. It was an excellent design that made quite an impression on artillery designers elsewhere when the details became known over the next few years. The 76-36 had a very

long and slender barrel mounted on a deceptively simple split-trail carriage that provided a wide angle of traverse. This wide angle had been deliberately designed into the weapon for even by that time (the early 1930s) the Red Army's anti-tank defence philosophy had been formulated to the extent where every gun and howitzer in the Soviet armoury had to have its own inherent anti-tank capability. Even

when firing a standard high explosive shell the 76-36 had a powerful anti-armour effect, and this factor was a constant benefit throughout the service life of the gun.

The 76-36 first saw active service in Finland in the Winter War of 1939-1940. It performed effectively enough in this campaign, but in its second major deployment it did not fare so well. The second campaign was the invasion of the Soviet Union by Germany, in which it was not so much that the 76-36s did not perform well but rather that they had little chance to do anything. The advancing German armies moved so fast that whole Soviet armies were cut off and destroyed. Huge numbers of 76-36s fell into German hands and, more disastrouslsy for the Soviets, the Germans also captured a great deal of the manufacturing plant that produced the guns. Thus almost the whole Red Army stock of 76-36 guns was lost within a very short time.

German artillery experts swarmed over the captured guns. They took measurements, carried out their own firing trials and came up with two suggestions. One was that the 76-36 should become a standard German field gun, 7.62-mm FK 296(r) as there was enough ammunition to hand to make them useful for some time, and long-term plans were laid to produce more ammunition in Germany. The second suggestion was also acted upon. That was to convert the 76-36 into a specialized anti-tank gun for use against even the most powerfully

armoured Soviet tanks, and this suggestion was also implemented. Large numbers of 76-36 guns were taken to Germany, and there modified to take new ammunition for the guns to become the **7.62-cm Pak 36(r)**, one of the best all-round anti-tank guns of World War II. The changes for the anti-tank role also involved some on-carriage changes (such as all the fire control wheels being used by the layer instead of the original two men) and a few other modifications.

Thus a Soviet field gun ended up being used just as much by the Germans as by the Red Army. With the disruption in production imposed by the German advances the 76-36 was never put back into full production, although spare parts were made in a few places for use on the few 76-36s remaining in Red Army hands. By 1944 the 76-36 was no longer a Red Army weapon, for they had by then a new gun in service.

Specification
Field Gun Model 1936
Calibre: 76.2 mm (3 in)
Length of piece: 3.895 m (153.3 in)

Weight: travelling 2400 kg (5,292 lb) and in action 1350 kg (2,977 lb)
Elevation: −5° to +75°
Traverse: 60°
Muzzle velocity: 706 m (2,316 ft) per second
Range: 13850 m (15,145 yards)
Shell weight: 6.4 kg (14.1 lb)

A long way from home for this 7.62-cm Model 1936 field gun, taken from the Eastern Front by the Germans in 1941 and converted for use as a very effective anti-tank gun in North Africa.

76.2-mm Field Gun Model 1942

The 76.2-mm Field Gun Model 1942 was produced in greater numbers than any other artillery weapon of World War II. Also known as the 76-42 or Zis-3, the Model 1942 was a very sound design with no frills and a good performance, as it fired a 6.21-kg (13.7-lb) shell to a range of 13215 m (14,450 yards).

With much of their artillery production facilities lost to the advancing German forces during 1941, the Soviet staff planners had some difficult decisions to make. Vast stockpiles of weapons of all kinds had been lost to the Germans and in order to make new weapons production capacity had to be hurriedly improvised in outlying areas where factories did not even exist. One factor in the Soviet's favour was that their weapon design bureaux were inherently conservative and made few innovations, depending rather on the gradual evolution of design and on the practice of using a new gun or carriage in conjunction with an existing carriage or gun.

This practice served the Soviets well after 1941, for in 1939 they had introduced a new gun known as the **76.2-mm Field Gun Model 1939, or 76-39**. This was introduced mainly because it was realized that good as the 76-36 was, it was really too bulky and a smaller design was thus desirable. The 76-39 used a shorter barrel on the carriage derived from that of the 76-36. When the Germans struck in 1941 they did not capture the main plant for 76-39 barrels, though they did take the carriage plant for the 76-36. Thus it was possible to use the barrel and recoil mechanism of the 76-39 on a new carriage to allow production to once more get under way. The result was the **76.2-mm Field Gun Model 1942**, later known as the **76-42 or Zis-3**.

The 76-42 was to achieve fame by being produced in greater numbers than any other gun during World War II. It was produced in its thousands, and if this had not been enough it turned out to be an excellent all-round weapon capable of being used not only as a field gun but an anti-tank gun,

a form of tank gun and a self-propelled gun. The new carriage was a very simple but sturdy affair using split pole trails and a simple flat shield. The gun assembly was modified to take a muzzle brake to reduce firing stresses and keep the carriage as light as possible and throughout the design process emphasis was given to ease of mass production. Once in action the 76-42 proved light and easy to handle, and it also had excellent range. To simplify the Red Army's logistic load the ammunition was ruthlessly standardized to the point where the 76-42 used the same types of ammunition as the 76.2-mm (3-in) guns carried by the T-34 tanks and many other similar guns. Only two basic types of projectile were used in World War II, namely HE and AP (though smoke was fired on occasion).

The 76-42 was produced in such large numbers that it remains in service with some nations to this day. Examples were encounterd in Korea and Indo-China, and the gun is still widely used in Africa and the Far East. The

A 76.2-mm Field Gun Model 1942, or Zis-3, in action in the ruins of the Tractor Works in Stalingrad during the ferocious fighting in the winter of 1942-3. Both sides discovered that this gun had a very good anti-tank capability.

76-42 has been widely issued to various guerrilla groups such as the PLO and SWAPO in South West Africa, and there seems to be no time limit on its active life.

Numerous attempts were made to mount the 76-42 on various self-propelled carriages but only one was ever produced in any quantity. This was the SU-76, another ex-Soviet weapon that is still in widespread service.

Specification
Field Gun Model 1942
Calibre: 76.2 mm (3 in)
Length of piece: 3.246 m (127.8 in)
Weight: travelling and in action 1120 kg (2,470 lb)
Elevation: −5° to +37°
Traverse: 54°
Muzzle velocity: 680 m (2,230 ft) per second
Range: 13215 m (14,450 yards)
Shell weight: 6.21 kg (13.7 lb)

Heavy Anti-Aircraft Guns

The dramatic rise in the power of aircraft between the wars saw many areas formerly safe from battle come under threat. While the major counter to high-altitude bombing was the defending fighter, ground forces also had a part to play, notably centred around the anti-aircraft gun.

The combatting of raiding bombers was the task of anti-aircraft guns, such as these Soviet 85mm (3.34in) examples, a design highly prized by the Germans who sent captured pieces to the Reich.

World War II was the scene of the last large-scale use of the heavy anti-aircraft gun – it was also its heyday. The weapon had been born during World War I, but by 1939 the heavy anti-aircraft gun was basically the same as that used in 1918, along with the fire-control systems which were hardly more advanced in 1939 than they had been in 1918. Although the guns appeared to be similar to the World War I weapons they had in fact been considerably advanced in performance: more powerful charges fired larger and more effective projectiles to greater heights than ever before and at much higher muzzle velocities. Their carriages had also been updated.

Here and there some leftovers from World War I had survived, especially among the French 75mm (2.95in) guns. But by 1939 many of the guns in service were no longer the hasty improvisations of 1918 and earlier, but purpose-designed and purpose-built weapons of considerable power. Upon them fell the brunt of the defence of cities and field armies against air attack, and the same guns defended the important centres of communication and pro-duction. At many and diverse locations these guns stood and waited for an enemy which often never arrived, but elsewhere the enemy came in droves and the heavy anti-aircraft guns were in action for as long as their crews could load them.

Among the guns discussed here is one that has by now become almost a legend, namely the German '88'. This famous gun earned its reputation outside its design spectrum as an anti-armour weapon, but all its details are provided here along with accounts of its use in action. Nevertheless, as will be seen, the '88' was not endowed with magical powers; nor did it have a specification that made it differ from many other weapons in this book. It was simply the way it was used that attracted so much notoriety. Many other guns could have been used in a similar way against armour but their owners were either not so inclined or not organized to use anti-aircraft guns against land targets. They were used instead for the role for which they were designed, namely the engagement of aircraft targets in defence of a locality or installation. Most of them were able to carry out this task more than adequately, and certainly as well as any German '88'.

Cannone da 75/46 C.A. modello 34

Between the two world wars the Italian armaments industry produced many good designs, but not many got to the hardware stage for the Italian economy was constrained, then as now, by an overall shortage of raw materials of every kind. Thus before any new weapon design was introduced into service it had to be vetted carefully to ensure that it was as good a design as possible to justify the expenditure involved. So when Ansaldo produced a new anti-aircraft gun in 1926 it was examined over a long period before production was authorized, and it was not until 1934 that the gun was actually in service.

The new gun was the **Cannone da 75/46 C.A. modello 34** (75/46 denoting the calibre of 75 mm and the barrel length of 46 calibres). In overall design the 75/46 was a sound though unremarkable effort that owed much to the influence of the contemporary Vickers designs produced in the United Kingdom. This was especially apparent in the carriage design, with a central pivot on which the gun saddle swivelled and a folding cruciform platform. On the move the platform legs were folded together, leaving the pivot resting on a two-wheeled carriage arrangement. When the equipment was ready for emplacement, the legs were swung forward and the wheels removed once the load had been taken by the centre of the carriage. The arrangement of the ordnance on the carriage was very simple and straightforward, and the fire-control instruments on the carriage were simple but adequate.

As always for the Italian armaments industry, the main problem with the 75/46 was one of production. Despite ever-increasing demands from the field, production was slow and erratic. Initially 240 equipments were ordered, but even by the end of 1942 only 226 had been delivered. Not all of these were used primarily as anti-aircraft guns, some being emplaced as dual-purpose anti-aircraft and coastal defence guns at selected points. This meant that many of the rather ancient AA weapons in use at the time had to be retained well past their planned replacement dates. Things were not helped greatly by the diversion of some finished barrels for use in *semovente* (tracked assault gun) mountings.

Despite this dispersion of effort, the 75/46 was spread as thinly as possible for home defence of the Italian mainland and the North African territories. When Italian army units moved to serve on the Eastern Front they took a further 54 guns with them, leaving even fewer to defend Italy. But even these guns were destined to follow a varied service career, for in 1943 after the Italian surrender the guns still around were taken over by German occupation forces. The 74/46 then became the **7.5-cm Flak 264/3(i)**, but the type was not used by the Germans outside Italy other than in some of their anti-Yugoslav partisan operations. Even this change of hands did not mark the end of the ownership list for the 75/46, for following the Allied invasion of the Italian mainland numbers were captured by the advancing Allied

This Cannone da 75/46 C.A. Modello 34 is in action against Allied aircraft flying over Libya. This Ansaldo gun was the standard Italian anti-aircraft gun; it was used on all the Italian fronts and was a good all-round performer, but could not be supplied in the quantities required.

armies and eventually used in a coastal defence role around such ports as Naples.

Specification
Cannone da 75/46 C.A. modello 1934
Calibre: 75 mm (2.95 in)
Weight: travelling 4405 kg (9,711 lb) and firing 3300 kg (7,275 lb)
Dimensions: length overall 7.4 m (24 ft 3 in); width 1.85 m (6 ft 0.8 in); height 2.15 m (7 ft 0.6 in); length of barrel 3.45 m (11 ft 3.8 in); length of rifling 2.844 m (9 ft 4 in)
Elevation: +90°/−2°
Traverse: 360°
Maximum effective ceiling: 8300 m (27,230 ft)
Shell weight: 6.5 kg (14.33 lb)
Muzzle velocity: 750 m (2,461 ft) per second

Cannone da 90/53

Of all the anti-aircraft guns in service with the Italian army from 1941 to 1943 none was better than the **Cannone da 90/53**. It was an excellent weapon that could stand comparison with any of its contemporaries, and it was a good, sound and modern design. It was another product of the Ansaldo design team and the first examples were produced during 1939. Production was authorized in three main versions.

The most numerous version of the 90/53 was supposed to be the **modello 41P** intended for static emplacement only; 1,087 examples of this version were ordered. A further 660 examples of the towed **modello 41C** were ordered, while another order was for a further 57 guns to be mounted on a variety of heavy trucks (**autocannoni da 90/53**). A later order requested yet another batch of barrels (30) for mounting on self-propelled tracked mountings.

Ordering these weapons was one thing, but producing them was quite another, and the final production figures never reached the original optimistic totals. By July 1943 only 539 weapons of all variants had been delivered, but by then the production line was in German hands and continued for German use alone. German formations in North Africa had already had the 90/53 in their service for some time, for they recognized it as a very good gun comparable with their own '88'. At first sight the 90/53 resembled the 8.8-cm (3.465-in) Flak 18 and Flak 37 weapons, but there were many differences and the similarities were only

superficial. The 90/53 had a pivot carriage mounted on a cruciform platform, but on the carriage itself the arrangement of the fire-control instruments was quite different from those of the German guns and the barrel was of one-piece construction instead of the multi-section arrangement of the later German guns.

The Italians used the 90/53 as a multipurpose weapon on occasion, but some were emplaced as dual-purpose anti-aircraft/coast defence weapons. At times they were used as long-range field guns and the performance of the gun was such that it could match the German '88' as an anti-armour weapon. Numbers were also diverted to the Italian navy. The Germans valued the 90/53 so highly that following the Italian surrender of 1943 they impressed as many 90/53s as they could find. Many of them were sent back to Germany for the defence of the Reich as the **9-cm Flak 41(i)** though the official designation was **9-cm Flak 309/1(i)**, and by December 1944 315 such equipments are mentioned in German records, though many of these would no doubt have been emplaced in Northern Italy. Numbers of 90/53s also fell into Allied hands during their advance north through Italy, and many of these were impressed for the coast defence role by British coastal batteries around the main captured ports.

Specification
Cannone da 90/53
Calibre: 90 mm (3.54 in)

Weight: travelling 8950 kg (19,731 lb) and firing 6240 kg (13,757 lb)
Dimensions: length 7.60 m (24 ft 11.2 in); width 2.30 m (7 ft 6.5 in); height 2.50 m (8 ft 2.4 in); length of barrel 4.736 m (15 ft 6.5 in); length of rifling 4.046 m (13 ft 3.3 in)
Elevation: +85°/−2°
Traverse: 360°
Maximum effective ceiling: 12000 m (39,370 ft)
Shell weight: 10.33 kg (22.77 lb)

This Cannone da 90/53 is rendered mobile by mounting on a Autocarro Pesante Lancio 3/RO heavy truck. The gun is seen here fitted with a protective shield for the gun crew in action, and very noticeable are the outriggers used to stabilize the gun when firing. Only a few of these combinations were made.

Muzzle velocity: 830 m (2,723 ft) per second

Type 88 75-mm anti-aircraft gun

The 75-mm (2.95-in) **Type 88 Mobile Field AA Gun** was a Japanese army weapon introduced into service in 1928. At that period the Type 88 was as good a gun as any in service, and was well capable of tackling the aerial targets then likely to be encountered. But it was soon overtaken by increases in aircraft performance, to the extent that it could at best be described as an efficient but indifferent performer.

The Type 88 design was chosen after an examination of other current and prospective anti-aircraft guns, and was an amalgam of some of the better points of several weapons. The barrel was a single-piece design with a sliding breech and mounted on the then-fashionable central pivot. The firing platform had five legs which folded fore and aft for transport, and to assist the overall balance on the move the barrel was partially retracted. In action each outrigger leg was supported on an adjustable foot for levelling and there was another adjustable foot under the central pivot. A central pair of wheels was used to tow the gun along roads, these being removed before firing.

Like so many other contemporary Japanese weapons, the Type 88 was difficult to produce as virtually everything on the gun had to be hand-made. It gradually became the standard Japanese army anti-aircraft gun and at one time or another was used by every army field formation, starting in China and Manchuria during the 1930s. It was also widely used during the early Japanese advances in the Pacific. However, once the Japanese mainland came increasingly under threat of air attack from 1943 onwards the Type 88s were gradually withdrawn from the more outlying island garrisons and sent to the home islands. Their places were taken by a motley array of diverse weapons, mainly ex-naval pieces dug into improvised land emplacements.

Back in Japan the Type 88 soon demonstrated that it suffered from a low maximum effective ceiling (the altitude to which the projectiles could be fired to engage an aircraft target for a useful amount of time). For the Type 88 this was about 7250 m (23,785 ft), and on many occasions Boeing B-29 bombers could operate at well above this altitude. But for the Japanese it was the Type 88 or nothing, for as always they lacked the large manufacturing base and design experience to produce anything better in the time available. Instead they had to impress all manner of modified naval guns for the home defence role and even resorted to the use of simple mortars for low-level defences in some areas.

The Type 88 is mentioned in some Allied intelligence reports as having an anti-armour role, but there appears to be little (if any) evidence of the Type 88 being used in this role. A special armour-piercing projectile known as the Type 95 was produced for use by the Type 88, but the usual high explosive projectile was the Type 90.

Specification
Type 88
Calibre: 75 mm (2.95 in)
Weight: travelling 2747 kg (6,056 lb) and firing 2443 kg (5,386 lb)
Dimensions: length travelling 4.542 m (14 ft 10.8 in); width 1.951 m (6 ft 4.8 in); height 2.019 m (6 ft 7.5 in); length of barrel 3.315 m (10 ft 10.5 in); length of rifling 2.578 m (8 ft 5.5 in)
Elevation: +85°/−0°
Traverse: 360°

Maximum effective ceiling: 7250 m (23,785 ft)
Shell weight: 6.58 kg (14.5 lb)
Muzzle velocity: 720 m (2,362 ft) per second

Above: The mount of a captured Type 88 75-mm gun is examined in the Pacific. Notice the five legs of the firing platform and the detached barrel at the bottom left of the photograph.

Left: An emplaced 75-mm (2.95-in) Type 88 anti-aircraft gun. This Japanese gun should not be confused with the German 88, for the Japanese Type 88 referred to the year of introduction according to the Japanese calendar and not to the calibre, as with the German gun; the two had very little in common.

The French 75-mm guns

When the problem of anti-aircraft defences arose during World War I the French army reacted in its usual manner, taking the ordnance of the famous '75', the mle 1897 field gun, and placing it onto a simple high-angle mounting. There were several of these mountings, one being a simple arrangement of the gun on a fixed turntable with the carriage knocked up from steel assemblies. This simple arrangement was the **Canon de 75 mm anti-aérien mle 1915**, but a better arrangement was produced by the **Canon de 75 mm anti-aérien mle 1913**, which was an early attempt to produce a self-propelled anti-aircraft gun by mounting a mle 1897 on a truck. Despite the early design date this turned out to be a remarkably good anti-aircraft weapon but it was not the only use of the mle 1897 for the role. There was also a **Canon de 75 mm contre aeronefs mle 1917** which was a towed piece but one in which all the fire-control instruments were mounted on the carriage; this was a Schneider design.

These three equipments were still in use in appreciable numbers in 1939 when World War II began for the simple reason that there appeared to be no real need to replace them; moreover, funds for new equipment for the French army were scant while the Maginot Line was being constructed. However, by the late 1920s it was appreciated that the old mle 1897 field gun was being rapidly outmoded as an anti-aircraft weapon and that higher-velocity weapons would soon be needed. Thus there started a desultory programme of re-equipping the many old batteries. Some of the first to be updated were the fixed batteries around such locations as Paris, where the old fixed mle 1915 equipments simply had their barrels replaced with a more powerful Schneider ordnance to produce the **Canon de 75 mm contre aeronefs mle 17/34**. This new barrel provided a much better performance with less time-of-flight and improved service ceiling. Similar barrels were placed on the old mle 1913 truck-mounted equipments and also on the almost-as-old mle 1917 equipments, but so slow was this gradual rebarrelling programme that many guns still had their original mle 1897 barrels in

The Canon de 75 mm mle 1936 was a Schneider design produced only in small numbers. This example was captured in North Africa from the Vichy French in 1943.

1940.

Some completely new equipments were produced during the 1930s. Using the new Schneider barrel a completely new anti-aircraft gun known as the **Canon de 75 mm contre aeronefs mle 1933** was produced during the mid-1930s. This was an odd-looking gun mounted in action on a cruciform platform with the barrel trunnions mounted well down the barrel near the breech; 192 equipments were in service in 1940. Another totally new Schneider weapon was produced in two forms as the **Canon de 75 mm contre aeronefs mle 1932** and **1936**, which differed only in detail. This was a thoroughly modern weapon designed from the outset for mobility. The mle 1932 had a crew of nine men and could fire up to 25 rounds per minute. On the road it could be towed at speeds of up to 40 km/h (24.85 mph).

When the Germans invaded in May 1940, the French army was thus still in a state of confusion regarding anti-aircraft guns. The planned programme of replacement of the old weapons was still far from complete, and many guns still had their obsolete mle 1897 barrels. There were really too many types of guns in service for logistical comfort but in the event the advances of May and June 1940 swept the French army away before the anti-aircraft guns could make any impact on the Luftwaffe. Huge amounts of French 75-mm (2.95-in) anti-aircraft equipment were captured by the Germans, who took over many for their own use – but not

the old mle 1897s, which were removed from their carriages and were later used as beach defence weapons in the Atlantic Wall. However, many of the more modern Schneider guns were still in German use in 1944. The designations were **7.5-cm FK 97(f)** for the 75-mm anti-aérien, **7.5-cm Flak M.17/34(f)** for the mle 17, **7.5-cm Flak M.33(f)** for the mle 1933, and **7.5-cm Flak M.36(f)** for the mle 36.

Specification
Canon de 75 mm contre aeronefs mle 1932
Calibre: 75 mm (2.95 in)
Weight: travelling 5300 kg (11,684 lb) and firing 3800 kg (8,377 lb)
Dimensions: length travelling 6.95 m (22 ft 9.6 in); width travelling 1.5 m (4 ft 11 in); length of barrel 4.05 m (13 ft 3.5 in); length of rifling 3.25 m (10 ft 8 in)
Elevation: +70°/−5°
Traverse: 360°
Maximum ceiling: 8000 m (26,245 ft)
Shell weight: 6.44 kg (14.2 lb)
Muzzle velocity: 700 m (2,297 ft) per second

The Germans were always short of anti-aircraft guns, and used as many ex-French guns as they could. This gun in German hands is a 75-mm mle 1933 formed by placing a modernized Schneider barrel onto a revised and updated World War I carriage. At one time the Germans had 160 of these in service.

Bofors 75-mm and 80-mm Model 1929 and Model 1930

The widely acknowledged success of the 40-mm Bofors gun has tended to overshadow the fact that the Swedish company of Bofors also made a larger and quite successful 75-mm (2.95-in) anti-aircraft gun. The Bofors concern has always been insistent that this gun was evolved by the company alone, but it cannot be overlooked that the design was being formulated at a time when Bofors was working in close association with the Krupp team resident in Sweden as a means to avoid the terms of the Versailles Treaty. It now seems almost certain that some form of cross-fertilization occurred between the two teams, for almost at the same instant the Krupp team produced a 75-mm (2.95-in) gun that led eventually to the famous German '88' and Bofors produced its 75-mm (2.95-in) **Model 1929**.

The Model 29 differed in many details from the Krupp 75-mm (2.95-in) design, but the two weapons had a very similar performance. Other similarities were that both used a cruciform carriage with a central traverse, and that both guns used barrels of similar length and construction. But whereas the Krupp gun was used in only limited numbers by the German navy and a few South American states, the Bofors model was adopted by the Swedish armed forces in two versions.

There were two main models of the Bofors gun, the Model 29 and **Model 30**. These differed only in detail, but to confuse matters both were produced for export in calibres of 75 mm and 80 mm (2.95 in and 3.15 in). Export versions were sold to Argentina, China, Finland, Greece, Hungary, Iran and Thailand, some in 75-mm (2.95-in) and

some in 80-mm (3.15-in) calibre. One of the largest customers was Hungary, which received 80 mm guns; these were used extensively during the period when the Hungarian army was allied with the Germans along the Eastern Front from 1941 to 1944, and more were retained for home defence. In Hungary the Model 29 was known as the **8-cm 29 M**. Another 80-mm (3.15-in) customer was the Dutch East Indies, but few of these weapons survived after 1942.

The Bofors gun was a sound but unspectacular performer. It used a cruciform firing platform that was lowered to the ground from two wheeled axles, which were then completely removed before firing. A horizontal breech block mechanism was fitted, and this was virtually the same as that used on the Krupp gun. However, the Bofors gun did have one thing that the Krupp design lacked, namely an overall simplicity of design: the Bofors gun had little of the complicated fire-control equipment that was used on the Krupp design and proved to be easy to operate, even in the hands of relatively untrained personnel. Thus when the Bofors gun was used in China it proved to be remarkably effective, and the type was chosen for its overall simple approach by such armed forces as those in the Dutch East Indies, which had to rely on a personnel force with few technical assets. Overall, the Bofors gun was a sound gun but one that was soon outperformed by later designs.

Specification
8-cm 29 M
Calibre: 80 mm (3.15 in)
Weight: travelling 4200 kg (9,259 lb) and firing 3300 kg (7,275 lb)
Dimensions: barrel length 4.0 m (13 ft 1.6 in)

Elevation: +80°/−3°
Traverse: 360°
Maximum effective ceiling: 10000 m (32,810 ft)
Shell weight: 8 kg (17.6 lb)
Muzzle velocity: 750 m (2,461 ft) per second

The Swedish Bofors Model 29 was sold to various countries in either 75-mm (2.95-in) and 80-mm (3.15-in) calibres. It was a sound design produced by Bofors when German designers were working in Sweden on the 88, and so there were many design features common to the two.

8.8-cm Flak 18 and Flak 37

The terms of the 1919 Versaille Treaty laid down strict guidelines as to what artillery production could be be carried out in Germany, so the largest German armaments company, Krupp of Essen, sent a team to Sweden to carry on research and development outside the imposed restrictions. Working with Bofors the Krupps team worked initially on a 75-mm (2.95-in) anti-aircraft gun using clandestine German army funds, but the army was not particularly happy with the result and asked for something heavier. The 'Swedish' Krupp team accordingly produced a new and advanced 88-mm (3.465-in) gun that by 1933 was in series production at Essen as the NSDAP came to power.

This new gun was the **8.8-cm Flak 18** (Flak standing for *Fliegerabwehr-kanone*, or anti-aircraft gun), and it was an immediate success. It was a long-barrelled gun mounted on a pivoted cruciform carriage which was in turn carried on the move by twin axles that allowed the gun to be rapidly placed into the firing position. The Flak 18 had a one-piece barrel but was later supplemented by an improved version, the **8.8-cm Flak 36**, which had a multi-section barrel on which only the worn part nearest the chamber needed to be changed after prolonged firing. Then came the **8.8-cm Flak 37**, which was a Flak 36 with a revised system of fire-control data transmission more suited to static use than field use. In practice the three models were interchangeable to a high degree, and it was not unusual to see a Flak 18 barrel on a Flak 37 carriage. Several changes were introduced to the weapons once they were in service, including a revised twin-axle carriage arrangement, and the 8.8-cm Flak series was adapted to be carried on a variety of self-propelled mountings, including railway flatcars.

The 8.8-cm Flak series became one of the most celebrated weapons in the entire German army, for it went on to be as famous as an anti-tank weapon as it was as an anti-aircraft gun: following the gun's 'blooding' in Spain during the Civil War and again in France in 1940, it was discovered that the high muzzle velocity coupled with an efficient and

heavy projectile made the weapon ideal as a 'tank killer'. This became very evident during the early North African and later Eastern Front campaigns, but the 8.8-cm Flak series was really too high and bulky for the anti-tank role and had to rely on its range and power rather than concealment in action.

As anti-aircraft guns the 8.8-cm Flak series was the mainstay of the German field armies and of the defence of the Reich under Luftwaffe control. The type was never replaced by later models as had been planned, and in August 1944 there were 10,704 of all three models in service. Production was undertaken at several centres, and a wide range of ammunition was produced for these weapons, including a high proportion of armour-piercing. By the end of the war versions for static

emplacement only were being produced, but by then the 8.8-cm Flak series had been used on self-propelled platforms, railway mountings, coastal defence locations, light shipping and in several experimental forms.

The 8.8-cm Flak guns were also used by the Italian army, and for a while in late 1944 the type was even used operationally by the US Army along the German borders when its own supply lines became overextended. Many were used by several armies post-war, and the Yugoslav army uses the 8.8-cm Flak as a coastal gun to this day.

Specification
8.8-cm Flak 18
Calibre: 88 mm (3.465 in)
Weight: travelling 6861 kg (15,126 lb)

This Flak 36 is seen in action during the Soviet campaign. After the tribulations of the bitter winter of 1941, the German army had become more familiar with sub-zero fighting, but 'General Winter' was still a potent contributor to the Soviet war effort.

and firing 5150 kg (11,354 lb)
Dimensions: length overall 7.62 m (25 ft 0 in); width 2.305 m (7 ft 6.75 in); height 2.418 m (7 ft 11.2 in); length of barrel 4.93 m (16 ft 2.1 in); length of rifling 4.124 m (13 ft 6.4 in)
Elevation: +85°/−3°
Traverse: 360°
Maximum ceiling: 8000 m (26,245 ft)
Shell weight: HE 9.24 kg (20.34 lb)
Muzzle velocity: 820 m (2,690 ft) per second

8.8-cm Flak 41

By 1939 it was obvious to the long-term German military planners that the expected increases in aircraft performance then on the way would render the existing 8.8-cm (3.465-in) and 10.5-cm (4.13-in) Flak weapons obsolete, so they initiated the development of a new 8.8-cm (3.465-in) weapon. Rheinmetall was given the contract for this new gun, and the company accordingly attempted to integrate into the design all the various lessons learned from the existing 8.8-cm Flak 18 and Flak 37 series. Thus the new weapon, known initially as the **Gerät 37**, was intended for use not only as an anti-aircraft gun but it also had to be suited for use as an anti-tank weapon and even a field or coastal artillery piece.

The result was that when development of the Gerät 37 was completed in 1941 a highly complicated weapon was presented to the troops. The Gerät 37 was adopted as the **8.8-cm Flak 41**, but service development took until 1943

for the design was full of 'bugs', some of which were never entirely eliminated. An example of this can be quoted as the ammunition, which in typical German style used a long and expensive cartridge case. These cases frequently jammed on extraction after firing, to the extent that special high-grade brass cases had to be manufactured specifically for some of the early examples. Both three- and four-section barrels were produced, and the weapon even had an automatic fuse setter on the loading mechanism. There were no fewer than three separate firing circuits, and a powered rammer was fitted.

The first production examples were sent to Tunisia during the latter stages of the North African campaign: here their technical troubles continued and they were given little chance to shine. Thereafter they were assigned to use within the borders of the Reich only, where they could be near the very

necessary workshop facilities that they constantly demanded. But it should not be thought that the Flak 41 was an unsuccessful weapon, for when it worked it was an excellent anti-aircraft gun. After the war it was generally regarded as the best of all the German anti-aircraft guns from a technical point of view, but one that required an inordinate amount of maintenance and repair time. When it did work properly it had a rate of fire of up to 25 rounds per minute and had a maximum effective ceiling of 14700 m (48,230 ft). It fired a different round from the other 8.8-cm (3.465-in) weapons.

Despite the technical promise of the Flak 41, the type was never produced in anything but limited numbers. It consumed a great deal of manufacturing potential and production was not assisted by the constant attention given by the Allied air forces to the weapon's main production centre at Düsseldorf. Further lengthy produc-

tion delays were imposed when an attempt was made to switch some production to the Skoda Werke at Pilsen, but for all their efforts the most the Germans could ever field was 318 and that was in January 1945.

Specification
8.8-cm Flak 41
Calibre: 88 mm (3.465 in)
Weight: travelling 11240 kg (24,780 lb) and firing 7840 kg (17,284 lb)
Dimensions: length overall 9.658 m (31 ft 8.2 in); width 2.4 m (7 ft 10.5 in); height 2.36 m (7 ft 8.9 in); length of barrel 6.548 m (21 ft 5.8 in); length of rifling 5.411 m (17 ft 9 in)
Elevation: +90°/−3°
Traverse: 360°
Maximum effective ceiling: 14700 m (48,230 ft)
Shell weight: HE 9.4 kg (20.7 lb)
Muzzle velocity: 1000 m (3,280 ft) per second

10.5-cm Flak 38 and Flak 39

As far back as 1933 the German military planners saw a need for an anti-aircraft gun heavier than the 8.8-cm (3.465-in) Flak series, and both Rheinmetall and Krupp were invited to submit designs for a 'shoot-off' contest for 10.5-cm (4.13-in) weapons held in 1935. Rheinmetall won the contract with its **Gerät 38**, which duly went into production as the **10.5-cm Flak 38**. This model had an electrical control system and a powered loading mechanism, but was soon replaced in production by the **10.5-cm Flak 39** with a revised electrical and fire-control data system.

Both 10.5-cm (4.13-in) Flak guns were intended for use by the German field armies, but in the event they were almost all employed in the home defence of the Reich. In appearance the Flak 38 and Flak 39 resembled scaled-up Flak 18 guns, but there were many detail differences and proportionally the Flak 38 and Flak 39 were much heavier and bulkier weapons. In overall terms the Flak 38 and Flak 39 were complex weapons and were made more complex to manufacture by the use of a sectional barrel (for rapid change of the worn portion only after firing) on the Flak 39. Unfortunately, in action they proved to be little better than the 8.8-cm (3.465-in) Flak series as far as overall performance was concerned, and at one point it was even intended to replace them in production by the 8.8-cm (3.465-in) Flak 41 though this never happened: production of the Flak 41 was so slow that the 10.5-cm (4.13-in) Flak guns were kept on the production lines. When the war ended there were still 1,850 in service, most of these within the borders of the Reich.

Although intended as a field weapon, the Flak 38 and Flak 39 were really too heavy for the role. They used a scaled-up version of the mobile twin-axle carriage of the 8.8-cm (3.465-in) Flak series, but even with the aid of integral winches and pulleys the guns

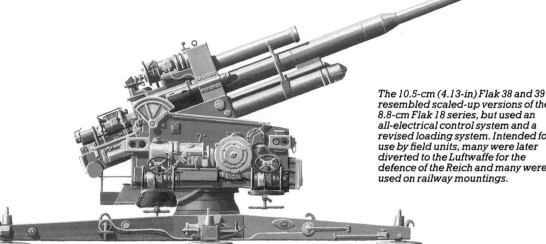

The 10.5-cm (4.13-in) Flak 38 and 39 resembled scaled-up versions of the 8.8-cm Flak 18 series, but used an all-electrical control system and a revised loading system. Intended for use by field units, many were later diverted to the Luftwaffe for the defence of the Reich and many were used on railway mountings.

were slow and awkward to emplace. Many were subsequently assigned to static emplacements, and 116 were mounted on special Flak railway trucks that rumbled around the Reich wherever they were needed. Each model needed a crew of a commander and nine men, though use of the manual loading system required a further two men.

The 10.5-cm (4.13-in) Flak series never acquired the fame of the 8.8-cm (3.465-in) Flak series, mainly because it was not widely used in the field and because its bulk and weight meant that it was only rarely used as an anti-armour weapon. Overall its performance was not as good as had been originally hoped, and despite a great deal of development work on a project known as the **10.5-cm Flak 40**, which was to have had a longer barrel to fire a heavier projectile, the 10.5-cm (4.13-in) Flak guns were never 'stretched' to the same extent as the other German Flak guns. Instead production went

steadily ahead at several centres until the war ended.

Specification
10.5-cm Flak 39
Calibre: 105 mm (4.13 in)
Weight: travelling 14600 kg (32,187 lb) and firing 10240 kg (22,575 lb)
Dimensions: length overall 10.31 m (33 ft 9.9 in); width 2.45 m (8 ft 0.5 in); height 2.9 m (9 ft 6 in); length of barrel 6.648 m (21 ft 9.7 in); length of rifling 5.531 m (18 ft 1.9 in)
Elevation: +85°/−3°
Traverse: 360°
Maximum ceiling: 12800 m (41,995 ft)
Shell weight: 15.1 kg (33.3 lb)
Muzzle velocity: 880 m (2,887 ft) per second

A 10.5-cm Flak 39 in action on a special railway truck mounting, here being used for harbour defence. These railway mountings were moved around the occupied territories and the Reich itself.

12.8-cm Flak 40

The idea of producing a German 128-mm (5.04-in) anti-aircraft gun was first mooted in 1936 when Rheinmetall was requested to produce a design known then as the **Gerät 40**. Progress on this design was not placed at a very high priority, so it was not until 1940 that the first prototype was ready. At that time it was intended that the Gerät 40 would be a weapon for the field army, but when the military saw the size and bulk

of the prototype they decided that the weapon would be produced for static use only. The weapon was ordered into production as the **12.8-cm Flak 40**.

By that time plans had already been made for a production-line mobile version, so the first six were produced on mobile carriages. The Flak 40 was so large that it proved impossible to carry the gun in one load over other than very short distances, so a two-load sys-

tem was initially employed. Even this proved to be too cumbersome, and was later revised to a single load once again. Later versions were produced for static use only, and such was the overall performance of the Flak 40 that it was carefully emplaced around some of the main production and population centres such as Berlin and Vienna. Special Flak towers were built in some locations to make best use of

these guns, and there was also a special railcar version to provide the guns with some sort of mobility.

Production of the static version began in 1942, but it was a costly and complex gun so by January 1945 there were only 570 in service, all of them based inside the borders of the Reich.

Soon after full-scale production began, the Flak 40 was joined by a twin version of the same gun known as the

Only six mobile versions of the 12.8-cm Flak 40 were produced before production was switched to static versions only. This gun is carried on a Sonderhanger 220 in one load, but some guns were carried as two loads.

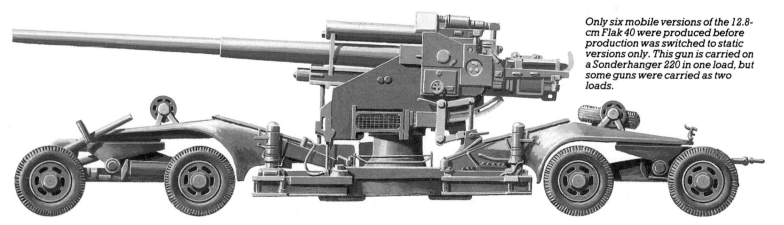

12.8-cm Flakzwilling 40. This consisted of two 12.8-cm (5.04-in) Flak guns mounted side-by-side on the same mounting and provided with 'mirror' loading arrangements. These powerful gun combinations were used only on special Flak towers around the main centres of population within the Reich, and were so costly and difficult to produce that there were never many of them; even by February 1945 there were only 33 in service. The Flakzwilling (*Zwilling*, or twin) was introduced as it was realized that ever heavier anti-aircraft guns would be needed to counter the increasing performance of Allied bombers, and despite strenuous efforts to develop guns with calibres of 150 mm (5.9 in) and even 240 mm (9.45 in), none got past the prototype stage at best and some failed to get even that far. Thus the twin arrangement of the Flakzwilling 40 was

an attempt to produce at least some form of increased firepower to counter the Allied heavy bombers, and in the event it turned out to be an excellent anti-aircraft weapon.

As the war ended the original mobile Flak 40s were still in use, many more were in use on special Flak trains. A new **12.8-cm Flak 45** gun was under development as the war ended, and this would have been an even more powerful weapon than the original. Only a single prototype was completed.

Specification
12.8-cm Flak 40
Calibre: 128 mm (5.04 in)
Weight: travelling (mobile) 27000 kg (59,524 kg), firing (mobile) 17000 kg (37,478 lb), and firing (static) 13000 kg (28,660 lb)
Dimensions: length overall 15 m (49 ft

2.6 in); height 3.965 m (13 ft); length of barrel 7.835 m (25 ft 8.5 in); length of rifling 6.478 m (21 ft 3 in)
Elevation: +87°/−3°
Traverse: 360°
Maximum effective ceiling: 14800 m (48,555 ft)
Shell weight: 26 kg (57.3 lb)
Muzzle velocity: 880 m (2,887 ft) per second

This photograph of 12.8-cm Flak 40s in the field was taken in 1940 in order to show the 'might' of the German army's anti-aircraft field defences. In fact only one battery was so used before all production of the gun was switched to the home defence of the Reich. This one battery was also moved out of the field.

Ordnance, QF, 3 in 20 cwt

The British 76.2-mm (3-in) anti-aircraft gun had the distinction of being one of the very first, if not the first gun to be designed specifically for the anti-aircraft role, the initial examples being in service as early as 1914. From that time the basic design was gradually modified and generally updated, and in 1940 there were still many in service as the **Ordnance, QF, 3 in 20 cwt**. The updating meant that the gun was still a viable weapon for its role, but its overall performance was such that it lacked the power of later designs and it was intended in 1939 that most of them would be replaced by more modern equipments (mainly the 94-mm/3.7-in weapon) by 1941.

In 1939 there were no fewer than eight marks of gun in service, some with sliding breech blocks, some with interrupted thread blocks, some with loose barrel liners, and so on. There was an equally formidable array of carriages in use as well: some of these had four wheels, others had but two and still more were statically emplaced in concrete. By 1940 nearly all in-service anti-aircraft (ack-ack) gunners had been trained on the 76.2-mm (3-in) gun for not only was it the standard weapon of the small regular forces but it was also the main equipment of the growing number of Territorial Army batteries that were formed during the late 1930s.

The gun was of simple design, being little more than a barrel and recuperator/recoil mechanism slung between two side mounting plates carried on a turntable. The turntable could be either mounted on a heavy cruciform firing platform or carried on a four-wheeled platform, the field army preferring the latter by 1939. The gun was the mainstay of the anti-aircraft batteries with the BEF, for although some batteries had been issued with the 94-mm (3.7-in) gun by 1940, they by far preferred the much lighter and handier 76.2-mm (3-in) gun with which they were familiar. However, the Dunkirk episode put paid to that source of dissent for most of the 76.2-mm (3-in) guns with the BEF were either destroyed or captured by the Germans (they later took over the type for their own use by units in France under the designation **7.5-cm Flak Vickers (e)**). There were few servicable 76.2-mm (3-in) guns left

The British 3-in (76.2-mm) was one of the first designed for anti-aircraft use during World War I and was still in widespread use in 1939-40. They had been progressively modernized, and many gunners preferred them to the new 3.7-in (94-mm) guns as they were so much handier. Many were lost at Dunkirk.

in the United Kingdom other than the few static installations, but gradually even they were soon phased out as front-line weapons and many of the mobile platform carriages were converted to rocket-launching platforms. About 100 platforms were eventually converted for this rocket role, and of the barrels removed some were used as the main armament for a tank destroyer using a Churchill tank chassis. That project eventually came to nothing, and mystery still surrounds a project to place 50 old 76.2-mm (3-in) guns onto surplus 17-pounder anti-tank gun carriages for home defence during 1944. There were few, if any, 76.2-mm (3-in) anti-aircraft guns left in service by 1945.

Specification
Ordnance, QF, 3 in 20 cwt (on four-wheel platform)
Calibre: 76.2 mm (3 in)
Weight: travelling and complete 7976 kg (17,584 lb)
Dimensions: length travelling 7.468 m (24 ft 6 in); width travelling 2.311 m (7 ft 7 in); height 2.794 m (9 ft 2 in); length of barrel 3.551 m (11 ft 7.8 in); length of rifling 2.977 m (9 ft 9.2 in)
Elevation: +90°/−10°
Traverse: 360°
Maximum ceiling: 7163 m (23,500 ft)
Shell weight: 7.26 kg (16 lb)
Muzzle velocity: 610 m (2,000 ft) per second

The usual model of the 3-in (76.2-mm) gun in use with the BEF in 1940 was this platform version, complete with twin axles. The platform used *outriggers when firing and the feet for these can be seen below the gun platform. The locker housed ready-use ammunition and the sights.*

Ordnance, QF, 3.7 in

Soon after World War I ended it was suggested that something heavier and more powerful than the existing 76.2-mm (3-in) anti-aircraft gun would be required by the UK to meet anticipated increases in aircraft performance, but at that time (1920) the report was simply shelved as there was then no prospect of any funding for even initial research into such a project. Instead it was not until 1936 that Vickers produced a prototype of a new gun with a calibre of 94 mm (3.7 in). The design was approved for production as the **Ordnance, QF, 3.7 in**, but initial progress towards this goal was so slow that it was not until 1938 that the pilot production models were issued for development trials.

The main reason for this slow progress was the gun's carriage. While the gun was a fairly straightforward but modern component, the carriage was complex to what seemed an extreme. The gun was intended for use in the field by the army and thus had to be fully mobile, but the final assembly was what can only be classed as 'semi-mobile'. The gun and its cradle and saddle rested on a large firing platform which in action rested on four outriggers. The front wheels were raised off the ground in action in order to provide some counter-balance for the weight of the gun mass, and the rear (towing end) axle was removed. Production of the carriage soon proved to be a time-consuming bottleneck, to the extent that production began of what was to be a purely static carriage for emplacement in concrete. As time went on the carriage was re-engineered to a more manageable form. Thus the first production carriage was the Mk I, the static carriage the Mk II and the final production version the Mk III; there were sub-marks of all of these.

When the equipment was first issued the gunners did not take kindly to it as they by far preferred the handier and familiar 76.2-mm (3-in) gun, but even they came to appreciate that the performance of the 94-mm (3.7-in) ordnance by far exceeded that of the older gun. In fact the 94-mm (3.7-in) had an excellent all-round performance even if emplacing and moving it was sometimes less than easy. As more equipments entered service they were gradually fitted with improved and centralized fire-control systems and such extras as power rammers and fuse setters. By 1941 the type formed the mainstay of the army's anti-aircraft defences, and went on through the rest of the war to prove itself to be an excellent weapon.

The 94-mm (3.7-in) gun was impressed into use as an anti-armour weapon in the Western Desert campaigns, but its weight and bulk made it less than effective in this role although it could still knock out any tank set against it. Instead it was retained for what it was best suited, the anti-aircraft role, and thus the 94-mm (3.7-in) never really got a chance to prove itself as the British equivalent of the German '88'. It was used on occasion as a long-range field piece and was even at one stage of the war used as a coastal defence gun. However, its use in this role was in the hands of the Germans, who had captured some of the type at Dunkirk. They appreciated the effectiveness of the weapon they termed the **9.4-cm Flak Vickers M.39(e)** so

Right: The static version of the British 3.7-in (94-mm) anti-aircraft gun was the Mk II, of which there were three slightly different versions. This version had a power rammer and had a characteristic counterbalance weight over the breech to compensate for the long barrel.

Below: A 3.7-in (94-mm) gun sited in a desert sangar formed by filling old Italian ammunition boxes with stones. The barrel is fitted with makeshift sights as the gun was no doubt operating away from its normal position.

much that they even went to the trouble of manufacturing their own ammunition for them for both the Flak and the coastal defence roles. In the latter they were particularly effective at Walcheren, where 94-mm (3.7-in) guns sank several Allied landing craft.

The gun soldiered on in British use until Anti-Aircraft Command was disbanded during the 1950s. Many were sold or handed over to other nations, and some still survive in use in such locations as South Africa and Burma.

Specification
Ordnance, QF, 3.7 in Mk III on Carriage Mk III
Calibre: 94 mm (3.7 in)
Weight: complete 9317 kg (20,541 lb)
Dimensions: length overall travelling 8.687 m (28 ft 6 in); width 2.438 m (8 ft); height 2.502 m (8 ft 2.5 in); length of barrel 4.7 m (15 ft 5 in); length of rifling 3.987 m (13 ft 0.95 in)
Elevation: +80°/−5°
Traverse: 360°
Maximum effective ceiling: 9754 m (32,000 ft)
Shell weight: HE 12.96 kg (28.56 lb)
Muzzle velocity: 792 m (2,600 ft) per second

A victory salute is fired in May 1945 by a complete battery of 12 3.7-in (94-mm) guns, probably on the Larkhill ranges on Salisbury Plain.

These guns were only just entering production when the war began, but they remained in British service until the late 1950s.

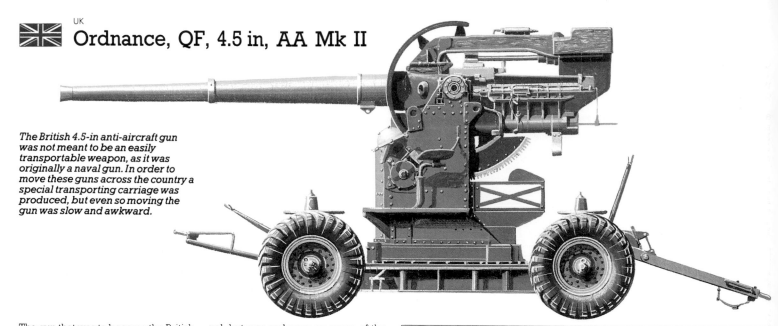

Ordnance, QF, 4.5 in, AA Mk II

The British 4.5-in anti-aircraft gun was not meant to be an easily transportable weapon, as it was originally a naval gun. In order to move these guns across the country a special transporting carriage was produced, but even so moving the gun was slow and awkward.

The gun that was to become the British army's 4.5-inch anti-aircraft gun had a rather muddled provenance, for it was actually a naval gun intended for use on board heavy vessels. It was undergoing acceptance trials in 1936 when it was decided that it would make an ideal anti-aircraft weapon for the army, and after some inter-service discussion the Admiralty agreed to divert some of its anticipated production to the army, but only on the understanding that the guns would be emplaced for the local defence of naval dockyards and other such installations. More muddle ensued when it was discovered by the army that the naval guns (actual calibre 113 mm/4.45 in) were intended for mounting in pairs. The army wanted single mountings, so time was lost while the necessary changes were made and tested.

When the type did eventually get into service (as the **Ordnance, QF, 4.5 in AA Mk II**) in time for the difficult days of 1940, it was emplaced as a static weapon only. Some measure of mobility could be provided by using a special heavy transporter trailer but such moves were difficult and lengthy, and required a great deal of preparation. Once emplaced, the guns demonstrated their naval origins by the retention of a turret-type mounting that rested on a base of heavy steel plate. The turret-type shelter over the gun had only limited protective value against steel splinters or falling shrap-

nel, but was welcome on some of the bleak gun-sites at which the weapons were located.

The gun had all the usual naval attributes, namely items such as a power rammer, a heavy counter-weight over the breech and a fuse setter on the loading tray. The ammunition handling equipment was very necessary, for each complete round weighed 38.98 kg (85.94 lb) and the movement of such weights over even a short period would soon have exhausted the ammunition handlers.

By 1941 the need to locate the guns around Admiralty-significant areas had been relaxed somewhat, allowing some of the guns to be relocated on stretches of coastline. There they could be used in a dual anti-aircraft/coastal defence role, but the numbers involved were never large as most of the guns remained in their static emplacements. These guns were issued with a special armour-piercing ammunition, but the projectiles generally fired were of the HE type, although there was a special but little-used shrapnel projectile intended for local defence against low-flying aircraft.

By 1944 it was intended that the gun should be phased out in favour of the more powerful 133-mm (5.25-in) weapon, but this never happened and some 113-mm (4.45-in) weapons were still in their static emplacements as late as 1951.

Specification
Ordnance, QF, 4.5 in, AA Mk II
Calibre: 113 mm (4.45 in)
Weight: emplaced 16841 kg (37,128 lb)
Dimensions: height of muzzle above ground emplaced (0° elevation) 2.438 m (8 ft) or (80° elevation) 7.163 m (23 ft 6 in); length of barrel 5.086 m (16 ft 8.25 in); length of rifling 4.341 m (14 ft 2.9 in)
Elevation: +80°/−0°

Originally produced as secondary armament for major warships, the 4.5-in retained some naval characteristics.

Traverse: 360°
Maximum ceiling: 12984 m (42,600 ft)
Shell weight: 24.7 kg (54.43 lb)
Muzzle velocity: 732 m (2,400 ft) per second

3-in Antiaircraft Gun M3

When the USA decided to adopt an anti-aircraft gun during World War I it saved a great deal of development time by taking a couple of 76.2-mm (3-in) coast defence guns and adapting them for the new task. Two main versions emerged from this operation, one a static gun and the other a mobile gun using a basic form of platform mounting. In time the mobile mounting was used as the basis for a more modern mobile equipment, and starting in the mid-1920s a great deal of experimental and development work was carried out, the original M1918 coastal defence guns still being used as the basis.

By the time that this development work had been completed, the original gun was virtually unrecognizable.

The rifling had been changed and practically every other item on the gun was altered to some degree as well. The main trouble was that the gun itself proved to be far too difficult to make and required a great deal of machining to very close tolerances. Some redesign resulted in the **3-in Antiaircraft gun M3**, which also had a semi-automatic breech block. It was this gun that was standardized for use with the new mobile platform, itself the result of a great deal of development. The original World War I platform had been very much a 'rushed' job, and as such left much to be desired in the eyes of the US Army, which sought an ideal solution. In time this emerged as the carriage known as the M2 or 'Spider Mount': this was a pedestal mounting

with a number of long outrigger legs over which a thick mesh platform was laid for the gun crew. The arrangement was certainly practical but the long outrigger legs, which folded upwards to the centre, took up a great deal of ground space.

By the mid-1930s it was obvious that the days of the M3 were coming to an end, and the basic design was once again revamped in an effort to secure better performance. An entirely new 90-mm (3.54-in) design was already on the way, however, and thus the revamped M3 did not prosper. Instead the existing equipments were gradually withdrawn from front-line use as the new 90-mm (3.54-in) guns appeared. This took time, and when the USA entered the war in 1941 the old M3 was

still in use in the Philippine Islands, where the weapons were used as long as the islands held out. Some lingered on for a while in other Pacific areas, and during early 1942 some were paraded through US west coast towns and cities in a programme to boost civilian morale. These west coast guns were culled mainly from training stocks, for by early 1942 the M3 was in use as a training gun only. Many of the gunners who subsequently went on to man the 90-mm (3.54-mm) guns started their service training using up the existing ammunition stocks for the M3 guns. Once this training role had been completed the old guns still found a use, for many were removed from their Spider Mountings and renovated for use as the barrels for the M5 anti-tank

gun. For this role the breech of the 105-mm (4.13-in) M2 howitzer was used, and thus the old anti-aircraft guns went on to a new service career.

At one point in the days immediately after Dunkirk there were plans to sell numbers of M3 guns to the United Kingdom to replenish AA guns lost at Dunkirk, but in the event none made the Atlantic crossing.

Specification
3-in Antiaircraft Gun M3 on Mount M2A2
Calibre: 76.2 mm (3 in)
Weight: complete 7620 kg (16,800 lb)
Dimensions: length travelling 7.62 m (25 ft 0 in); width 2.108 m (6 ft 11 in); height 2.87 m (9 ft 5 in); length of barrel 3.81 m (12 ft 6 in); length of rifling 3.196 m (10 ft 5.83 in)
Elevation: +80°/−1°
Traverse: 360°
Maximum ceiling: 9510 m (31,200 ft)
Shell weight: 5.8 kg (12.8 lb)
Muzzle velocity: HE 853 m (2,800 ft) per second

Left: The M3 was by 1941 largely relegated to home defence, as many of the guns dated back to World War I. Some did see action in the Far East during 1942, however.

Above: In 1941 the American 3-in (76.2-mm) gun was still in service in several forms. This static version was the 3-in Gun M4 on Mount M3, and was used in such locations as the Philippines and the Canal Zone.

USA

90-mm Gun M1

Once it was realized that the old 76.2-mm (3-in) anti-aircraft guns were coming to the end of their service life during the late 1930s, it was decided by the US Army to produce a weapon not only with a better performance but one capable of firing a heavier projectile. Since a 90-mm (3.54-in) projectile was considered the upper weight limit of what a soldier could handle manually this was fixed as the new calibre, and design work began in 1938. By 1940 the prototypes were approved for service

Right: The 90-mm Antiaircraft Gun M2 was a much revised version of the earlier M1 but used a new carriage with a turntable, a power rammer, fuse setter and other changes. This resulted in an excellent gun but one that was slow and expensive to produce.

use as the **90-mm Gun M1 on Antiaircraft Mount M1A1**, and production commenced with a high priority cachet.

The M1 was a handsome but a rather complex weapon which proved difficult to produce. The gun assembly itself was straightforward, but the carriage was another matter. It was designed to be towed on a single axle with two pneumatic tyres on each side,

This 90-mm M1 anti-aircraft gun is dug in to take part in beach defences. Other emplacements can be seen, including one at the left rear containing the battery's rangefinder and other fire control equipment. The mount is the M1A1; the later M2 mount used a turntable.

and in action it stood on a cruciform mounting with the crew standing around the gun on a folding platform. The problem was to get all this carriage and platform folded onto the single axle. The result can be described only as complicated.

Soon after the M1 gun was placed in production it was supplemented by the **M1A1**, which had provision for the fitting of a spring rammer. In practice this rammer proved to be more trouble than it was worth and was usually removed, but another change was on the way. In July 1941 it was decided that in future the 90-mm (3.54-in) gun and carriage would have to be capable of engaging sea and land targets as well. This meant a revision of the carriage as on the M1 carriage the gun could not

be depressed below 0°, and the opportunity was taken to incorporate a radical redesign. The M2 carriage had a totally different design with a low firing platform carried on four outrigger legs when firing. It was much handier and quicker to get into action, and some versions also had a small shield. The main change, however, was to the gun, which became the M2 in which the ammunition feed for a new fuse setter and rammer was added, this making fuse setting much more rapid and accurate, and also raising the rate of fire to a possible 27 rounds per minute. Yet more accuracy and lethality was added in late 1944 when the 90-mm (3.54-in) gun was used as

one of the first weapons on land to fire the new proximity-fused round, one of the most advanced weapon developments of the war years. Using this fuse one gunner managed to shoot down a Focke-Wulf Fw 190 fighter with a single shot as the unfortunate aircraft attempted to intervene in the Ardennes campaign. The 90-mm (3.54-in) gun and the proximity fuse were also instrumental in the defeat of the V-1 flying bombs over southern England.

The 90-mm (3.54-in) gun in all its forms was manufactured in large numbers. By August 1945 a total of 7,831 of all types had been produced. This included some guns intended for static mounting only, and some guns were

indeed used around the coasts of the continental USA in a dual anti-aircraft/coastal role.

The 90-mm (3.54-in) gun was also used in a purely coast defence mounting in a special armoured turret, and at one stage it was proposed that these turrets would even have their own automatic loaders, thus removing the need for men to crew them in action as they would be aimed and fired by remote control. The 90-mm (3.54-in) gun was also used in M36 tank destroyers mounted on Sherman chassis, and there were several advanced designs involved in the production of a towed 90-mm (3.54-in) anti-tank gun, but none of these saw service.

Specification
90-mm Gun M2 on Mount M2
Calibre: 90 mm (3.54 in)
Weight: complete 14651 kg (32,300 lb)
Dimensions: length travelling 9.021 m (29 ft 7.15 in); height 3.073 m (10 ft 1 in); wheelbase 4.166 m (13 ft 8 in); length of barrel 4.50 m (14 ft 9.2 in)
Elevation: +80°/−10°
Traverse: 360°
Maximum ceiling: 12040 m (39,500 ft)
Shell weight: 10.6 kg (23.4 lb)
Muzzle velocity: 823 m (2,700 ft) per second

The Soviet 85-mm guns

By the late 1930s the Soviet armed forces, in common with many other armed forces of the time, decided that the anticipated increases in aircraft performance over the next few years would soon render their current anti-aircraft weapons obsolete. Accordingly they set about looking for a more modern anti-aircraft gun with a better all-round performance, but, in typical Soviet fashion, instead of designing a new weapon they used an old design as the basis for a new weapon. They simply took the 76.2-mm (3-in) Model 1938 and enlarged it all round to become an 85-mm (3.346-in) gun. The new gun was designated the 85-mm **Anti-Aircraft Gun Model 1919**, and is sometimes known as the **KS-12**.

The Model 1939 was very similar to the 76.2-mm (3-in) Model 1938, but could be easily recognized by its multi-baffle muzzle brake, a feature lacked by the 76.2-mm (3-in) gun. A shield was an optional extra. Production of the Model 1939 was just getting under way at Kaliningrad, near Moscow, when the Germans invaded in 1941, so the entire plant was moved to the Urals for the rest of the war. Once back in production the Model 1939 became the standard heavy anti-aircraft gun of the Red Army, though it was replaced in production during 1944 by the more powerful **85-mm Anti-Aircraft Gun Model 1944** or **KS-18**. This was virtually the same weapon as the Model 1939, but could use a more powerful charge to boost all-round performance with the same projectile as that of the Model 1939.

Both the Model 1939 and the Model 1944 were designed from the outset to be used as anti-armour weapons in the same manner as the German '88'. They were so successful in this role that the Germans prized them as war booty and used any captured examples alongside their own 88s under the designations **8.5-cm Flak M.39(r)** and **8.5-cm Flak M.44(r)**. As with the Soviet 76.2-mm (3-in) guns, captured examples were also shipped back to the Reich, where they were rebored to the standard German 88 mm (3.465 in) once all captured ammunition stocks had been expended. Most of the guns used in this way by the Germans were Model 1939s, which became **8.5/8.8-cm Flak M.39(r)** guns.

The Model 1939 and the Model 1944 were both good anti-aircraft guns, and this is attested by the fact that many are still in active service to this day. Num-

bers are still in service with some of the Warsaw Pact nations (but not the Soviet Union itself) and they are likely to be encountered in countries as diverse as the Sudan and Vietnam. Large numbers were active during the Vietnam conflict against the US Air Force. These 'modern' guns now usually rely on some form of centralized fire-control system, usually radar-based, and the original on-carrier fire controls are now either removed or little used.

The 85-mm (3.346-in) gun itself was used as the basis for a number of other Soviet weapon projects. It was adopted to become the main armament of the SU-85 assault gun/tank destroyer, and was even adapted for use on a towed anti-tank gun mounting.

Specification
85-mm Anti-Aircraft Gun Model 1939
Calibre: 85 mm (3.346 in)
Weight: travelling 4220 kg (9,303 lb) and firing 3057 kg (6,739 lb)
Dimensions: length travelling 7.049 m (23 ft 1.5 in); width 2.15 m (7 ft 0.65 in); height 2.25 m (7 ft 4.6 in); length of barrel 4.693 m (15 ft 4.76 in); length of rifling 3.494 m (11 ft 5.54 in)
Elevation: +82°/−2°
Traverse: 360°
Maximum ceiling: 10500 m (34,450 ft)
Shell weight: 9.2 kg (20.29 lb)
Muzzle velocity: 800 m (2,625 ft) per second

The 85-mm anti-aircraft gun was developed from the successful 76.2-mm series, and proved highly effective in service. Much prized by the Germans, captured equipment was used alongside the famous '88'. Many were used in the defence of Germany from the Allied bombing campaign.

The Soviet 85-mm (3.346-in) Model 1939 was so good that some were still in use in Vietnam during the early 1970s. The gun was also known as the KS-12, and was much used by the Germans after 1941, many being rebored to take 88-mm (3.465-in) German ammunition.

Light Anti-Aircraft Guns

1939 saw tactical air power take its place as a significant factor in battle, its importance calling for newer, more effective methods to protect forces on the ground. High volumes of light anti-aircraft fire were seen to be the answer, with the Wehrmacht taking the lead.

In 1939 the light anti-aircraft gun was a relatively new concept. For the most part such weapons had calibres of between 20mm (0.787in) and 40mm (1.575in), and were all capable of putting into the air large volumes of automatic fire. They were mainly intended for the defence of an area of sky that extended to no more than 3000m (9843ft) at best, although they were usually employed against targets flying at altitudes much lower than that.

Most of the guns included in this study had a calibre of 20mm. This calibre had been established by the end of World War I as the optimum for a projectile that could carry a useful explosive payload and yet remain economic to fire automatically. However, after 1941 this calibre had to be revised upwards in size as aircraft targets increased in speed and in the degree of protection they carried. Some nations, such as Germany, had foreseen this trend and had equipped themselves accordingly with 37mm (1.457in) weapons; it is indicative that the best all-round weapon in this category in service during the war years was the Swedish Bofors gun with a calibre of 40mm (1.575in), one that is still in widespread use today. But the smaller-calibre weapons remained in use even

The operation to liberate Europe meant the building and maintenance of vast stockpiles in England ready to equip the troops once the battle began; these are 40mm (1.6in) Bofors Light AA guns.

though the only way that they could ensure a target 'kill' was to increase the number of projectiles actually hitting the target. Since to increase the rate of fire of most guns would mostly have entailed a major redesign, the only way to boost the weight of fire was to increase the number of barrels firing from one mounting at any one time. The best example of this

concept could be seen with the change of the single-barrelled 2cm Flak 38 to the four-barrelled 2cm Flakvierling 38, one of the German weapons most feared by Allied tactical flyers.

Not all the guns included in this section attained the fame of the German light Flak weapons. Some, such as the Schneider 37mm (1.457in) gun, were some-

what less than successful, but others, such as the Bofors gun, the Oerlikon cannon and the Soviet Model 1939, are assured of a place in artillery, if not world, history. They defended the ground forces against tactical attack aircraft and they defended home areas against more formal bomber forces in a war in which the aircraft became a dominant weapon.

Maxson Mount

One of the main American weapons produced as a counter to the low-flying aircraft was not of the same calibre as the other weapons in this study, for instead of using what are normally regarded as cannon calibres, the American solution used heavy machine-guns with a calibre of 12.7 mm (0.5 in). This was the **Maxson Mount**, which used a combination of four 12.7-mm Browning M2 heavy machine-guns on a single mounting with two guns on each side of a central pedestal-type housing. The proper service designation for this arrangement was **Multiple Caliber .50 Machine-Gun Carriage M51**.

The Maxson Mount was used on a variety of different carriages. One of the most common was a trailer towed by a light truck or even a Jeep. This trailer used twin axles, and in action legs could be lowered to the ground at each corner to provide increased stability when firing. The trailer also carried a number of batteries and a battery-charging set, for the Maxson Mount was electrically powered. The electrical supply was used for elevation and traverse, and the motors used were powerful enough to meet the most demanding calls made upon them by the gunner, who sat on the turret between the two pairs of machine-guns. The motors could move the guns from the horizontal to +60° in one second, and the turret could traverse at the same rate. In order to keep the two main batteries topped up at all times, they were normally kept on constant charge in action.

The combined fire of the four Browning machine-guns was sufficient to bring down any aircraft caught in their fire, despite the fact that the rounds carried no explosive payload. The guns were aimed using a naval reflector sight, but the tracer fired by the guns could also be used to assist aim and some gunners relied on the tracer alone to make fire control corrections.

The Maxson Mount was also used on halftracks as well as towed trailers. On both types of carriage the guns were supplied with 200 rounds each, fed into the guns from belts carried in enclosed chests mounted outboard of the guns. On some turrets the belts could be fed into the guns under electrical control but the normal gun action was more commonly used.

The Maxson Mounts were normally used to provide protection for convoys or mobile units against air attack, and after 1945 continued to serve with many armies. Many are still in use today, but recent years have seen a move away from the retention of the four machine-guns to a new configuration using two 20-mm cannon. Israel has adapted all the Maxson Mounts it has in service to this new form, and Brazil is another nation taking the same path. Israel continues to use its modernized Maxson Mounts on halftracks, but there is a towed version as well.

Specification
Maxson Mount
Calibre: 12.7 mm (0.5 in)
Length: (guns) 1.654 m (65.1 in)
Weight: in action 1087 kg (2,396 lb)
Elevation: −5° to +85°
Traverse: 360°
Muzzle velocity: 884 m (2,900 ft) per second
Maximum effective ceiling: about 1000 m (3,280 ft)
Rate of fire: (cyclic, all guns) 2,300 rpm

The crew of a Multiple Gun Motor Carriage M16 relax on stand-by close to the famous bridge at Remagen. The crew have toned down the appearance of the vehicle with hessian and a board over the tracks. Note the spare ammunition magazines.

A Maxson mount is dug in in the Solomons. The gun layout can be clearly seen, as can the box magazines that held up to 200 12.7-mm (0.50-in) rounds. The gunner was seated between the guns and used a reflector sight.

A Multiple Caliber .50 Machine-Gun Carriage M51 is seen in action at Hollandia on New Guinea against low-flying aircraft. This trailer-borne carriage was commonly known as the Maxson mount and the gunner's helmet can just be seen protruding from between the magazines.

USA

37-mm Antiaircraft Gun M1

The development work that led to the **37-mm Antiaircraft Gun M1 on Carriage M3** series started in 1921. It was yet another product of the fertile mind of John M. Browning, who continued to work on the gun until he died in 1926. Development of the project then lapsed until 1934, mainly as a result of defence spending cuts of the period. When work resumed it was not long before the gun was in production, not only for the US Army but for the US Navy (**37-mm AN-M4**) and US Army Air Corps (**37-mm Aircraft Automatic Gun M4** and **M10**) as well. Production started in 1940 under the auspices of the Colt Company, and to some the gun is still known as the **Colt 37 mm**.

The 37-mm (1.457-in) gun was an unremarkable design that performed well enough, but it was rather let down by its ammunition which proved to be underpowered and was thus of limited value against low and fast aircraft targets. Various production and carriage changes were introduced until the **M1A2** stage was reached, and at that point the British requested that the Americans should use some of their industrial potential to build Bofors guns for them. A quick perusal of the Bofors gun convinced the Americans that it was much better than their 37-mm design, and they promptly adopted the Bofors in its place. But it was some time before Bofors fabrication could get under way, so the M1A2 continued to roll off the Colt production lines.

Somewhere along the line combat analysis revealed that many anti-aircraft gunners were not using the gunsights to aim their weapons, but

It had been intended that the 37-mm (1.457-in) Antiaircraft Gun M1A2 was to be the standard US Army light anti-aircraft weapon, but the Bofors Gun took over that role. However, the M1A2 remained in production until there were enough Bofors Guns to hand.

were instead watching the tracer elements as they fired and correcting the aim onto the target by this means alone. While this was, and still is, a positive way to aim a gun, at calibres of 37 mm and above, it soon becomes an uneconomic practice on any scale. Accordingly a new **Combination Mount M54** was developed that carried two 12.7-mm (0.5-in) Browning heavy machine-guns, one on each side of the central 37-mm barrel. As the machine-guns were ballistically very similar to the main gun their tracer could be used as the aiming element and once on target the main gun could be fired. This worked out very well in practice. Most of these combination

mounts were used on halftracks or on board US Navy vessels right through and after the war, but there was a drawback as far as the original designers were concerned: far from using the two machine-guns as the aiming elements of the combination, many enthusiastic gunners continued to use all three weapons to fire tracer all the time, thereby negating the original intention.

During the war large numbers of M1A2 guns and combination mounts were delivered to the USSR as part of Lend-Lease. Many of these weapons never found their way back to the United States and still appear in odd corners of the world where Soviet influ-

ence is paramount. Some remain in service with Warsaw Pact militia forces, long after they have passed from use in the West.

Specification
M1A2 on Carriage M3A1
Calibre: 37 mm (1.457 in)
Length of piece: 1.986 m (78.2 in)
Weight: in action 2778 kg (6,124 lb)
Elevation: −5° to +90°
Traverse: 360°
Muzzle velocity: 853 m (2,800 ft) per second
Maximum ceiling: 5669 m (18,600 ft)
Rate of fire: (cyclic) 120 rpm
Projectile weight: 0.61 kg (1.34 lb)

SWITZERLAND

20-mm Oerlikon

The **20-mm Oerlikon** gun has a rather long history, stretching back as far as 1914 when it was produced by one Reinhold Becker in Germany. Versions of this gun were used during World War I as German air force weapons, but in 1919 Becker transferred his brainchild to Switzerland, where it was produced by a firm known as SEMAG until that concern was taken over by the Werkzeug Maschinenfabrik Oerlikon at Oerlikon, still in Switzerland. Under this new concern production of many types of Oerlikon gun expanded greatly (the original Becker weapon as the **Type F**, the SEMAG model as the **Type L** and its own version as the **Type S**), and the usual practice of licence production elsewhere soon followed. France was one early manufacturing location (**2-cm Mitrailleuse C.A. Oerlikon**), and Japan another (**Type 98**). Sales were made worldwide, and Oerlikon aircraft and anti-aircraft guns were a common sight in many nations.

The Oerlikon was a gas-operated gun with the mechanism action assisted by the large coil springs around the barrel that were a recognition feature of the weapon. After 1935 the Oerlikon was produced in the United Kingdom for the Royal Navy so that by 1939 there were considerable numbers of this **Gun, 20-mm, Oerlikon** in use. This was just as well, for by 1940 they were being pressed into service on land mountings of all kinds. Some of these British mountings were simple in the extreme but others such as the Haszard semi-mobile mount were

First introduced in its earliest form in 1914, the Oerlikon 20-mm saw its widest service as a naval weapon, as here, mounted on the escort carrier HMS Trumpeter on convoy duty in 1944.

much more 'formal'. Later in the war a triple-gun mounting with the three guns one over the other was placed into production and some of these types of mounts were later used on trucks.

The Swiss 20-mm (0.79-in) Oerlikon cannon was manufactured in the United Kingdom and many other countries, and was one of the most important weapons of its type in use during World War II. Although used mainly as a naval weapon, many were employed by land forces. This is the British HB Mk 1 mounting.

The Oerlikon normally used a 60-round drum magazine for the feed system, but a 20-round box magazine was used on some versions, including those used by the Germans, who knew the Oerlikon as the **2-cm Flak 28** or **Flak 29**, and some of their guns were later passed to the Italians (**Cannone-Mitragliera da 20 Oerlikon**). Over the Atlantic the Americans were producing Oerlikons by 1940 as the **20-mm Automatic Gun Mk IV**, originally for the Royal Navy but later for their own use, and the type was particularly useful in the Pacific against Japanese *kamikaze* attacks. Thus the Oerlikon gun was another of those weapons that started life in a neutral state but ended up being used by all sides, and some of the *kamikaze* aircraft that attacked US Navy shipping were shot down by Oerlikon guns carried on those same ships, firing back at aircraft that also carried Oerlikon guns. The same situation prevailed in Europe, for many Luftwaffe aircraft carried Oerlikon guns of one type or another.

Many of the guns used by the United Kingdom armed forces had their origins in Royal Navy models, but these were fairly easy to adapt to a number of land mountings. At sea most Oerlikons were used on simple pedestal mountings whatever navy happened to be using them. Many are still in use today (but only rarely on land) for they continue to be a popular naval weapon, which cannot be bad for a design that can trace its origins to 1914. Since then it is probable that more Oerlikon Guns have been produced than any other weapon of their type.

Specification
Automatic Gun Mk IV
Calibre: 20 mm (0.787 in)
Length of piece: 2.21 m (87 in)
Weight: (gun only) 66.68 kg (147 lb)
Elevation: −10° to +75°
Traverse: 360°
Muzzle velocity: 831 m (2,725 ft) per second
Maximum effective ceiling: 1097 m (3,600 ft)
Rate of fire: (cyclic) 465-480 rpm
Projectile weight: 0.119 kg (0.2625 lb)

Twin 20-mm Oerlikons are cleaned aboard the Indian Navy sloop HMIS Narabda late in the war. Still in service at sea after more than 70 years, the Oerlikon is now rarely encountered in towed form, although modern guns by the same firm are in wide use on land.

Polsten

In many ways the **Polsten** gun may be regarded as a Polish rather than a British weapon, but it was produced only in the United Kingdom. It had its origins in the fact that although the Oerlikon gun was a highly successful weapon it was difficult to manufacture and required a large number of machining processes. The Poles decided to make production easier: they took the basic design but introduced changes to make the weapon simpler. They were just about to complete the project when the Germans invaded Poland in September 1939. Subsequently the members of the design team fled to the UK, taking their drawings and experience with them and re-established the team there. They were joined by expatriate Czechs and some British designers and in time their results were placed in production in a weapon known as the Polsten ('Pol' after Poland and 'sten' after the British Sten Company, the same company that manufactured the cheap and cheerful Sten sub-machine gun).

The Polsten was a remarkable piece of design and production engineering. The Oerlikon gun used 250 components, but the Polsten reduced this to 119; the costs were considerably reduced as a result, falling from a nominal £320 for the original to between £60 and £70 for the Polsten. Not surprisingly, as soon as the Polsten was ready it was rushed into production. That was in March 1944 and thereafter production of the Oerlikon ceased in favour of the cheaper weapon.

Although the Polsten was cheaper and easier to make it was every bit as effective as the Oerlikon original. The Polsten could fit into any mounting intended for the Oerlikon, so it was used in a diversity of roles ranging from aircraft gun to tank co-axial weapon. On ground mountings it was used as an anti-aircraft gun on a Universal Mounting that could accommodate either an Oerlikon or a Polsten. The same mounting could also accommodate an American Hispano aircraft cannon, also in 20-mm (0.787-in) calibre.

One change that was introduced as standard on the Polsten was a new magazine. The old Oerlikon drum magazine proved to be unpopular in service as it was a bulky and awkward item and took some time to load properly. It was also very difficult to make and consumed a large number of machining operations. On the Polsten it was replaced by a vertical box magazine holding 30 rounds arranged in a 'double-stack' configuration that was not only easier to load but which was much easier to change on the gun. It was also far cheaper to make.

Above: Broken down into its operating position, a Polsten gun shows the sparse construction of this simplified, lightened version of the well-tried Oerlikon.

The Polsten never replaced the Oerlikon gun in service, for although the Oerlikon was expensive it was very robustly made and could last for a very long time. Instead the Polsten and the Oerlikon soldiered on side by side with the British army until both were withdrawn some time during the 1950s. Even now Polstens continue to appear at odd spots around the world, and as the ammunition for them and the Oerlikon is still in widespread production there is no reason why they should not continue to work on for many years to come.

Specification
Polsten (Universal Mounting)
Calibre: 20 mm (0.787 in)
Length of piece: 2.178 m (85.75 in)
Weight: (gun) 54.9 kg (121 lb)
Elevation: −5° to +85°
Traverse: 360°
Muzzle velocity: 831 m (2,725 ft) per second
Maximum effective ceiling: 2021 m (6,630 ft)
Rate of fire: (cyclic) 450 rpm
Projectile weight: 0.119 kg (0.2625 lb)

Right: A 20-mm (0.79-in) Polsten Mk 1 Gun on the Mounting, Universal Mk 1 (the wheel outline is diagramatic). The Polsten was a simplified Oerlikon Gun designed by a team of Polish engineers who fled from Poland to the United Kingdom in 1939.

Type 98 20-mm Machine Cannon

The **Army Type 98 20-mm Machine Cannon** was a Japanese army weapon introduced into service in 1938, and was designed from the outset as a dual-purpose weapon capable of use against aircraft and armoured ground targets. Thus it had a rather odd-looking carriage that added to its somewhat archaic appearance. This appearance was deceptive, for the Type 98 was a thoroughly modern weapon with good overall performance.

The carriage was rather high and mounted on two spoked wooden wheels that, were used to move the weapon, either as a towed unit behind a light truck or animal team, or by man-handling. Once in position the trail legs opened to form the rear components of a tripod with another outrigger leg forward. Once the tripod had been deployed the wheels were lifted off the ground to permit 360° traverse with the gunner/aimer behind the gun on a small seat. If required the entire weapon could be broken down into separate loads for animal or man-pack transport. It was possible to fire the gun direct from the wheels but since the weapon had a rather high centre of gravity it soon became unstable; moreover, it took only about three minutes to get the gun into action on its tripod with a two- or three-man crew.

The Type 98 was a very hard-hitting weapon. This was due mainly to its 20-mm (0.787-in) ammunition, which was similar to that fired from the Type 97 anti-tank rifle, though the Type 98 ammunition used a slightly longer and wider cartridge case. This cartridge enabled the Type 98 projectiles to penetrate 30 mm (1.18 in) of armour at a range of 247 m (270 yards), so the effect of the same projectile against a low-flying aircraft can well be imagined. According to many accounts the Type 98 was used more in the anti-aircraft than anti-tank role, despite the fact that its cyclic rate of fire was rather low (120 rounds per minute), decreased in service by the use of a box magazine holding 20 rounds in a vertical row.

A twin-barrelled version of the Type 98 was produced in small numbers, but this was not the only other 20-mm weapon used by the Japanese. By 1944 anti-aircraft guns were in great demand and all manner of odd weapons were impressed for the role. Surplus aircraft cannon were one source, and the Japanese navy often gave up precious weapons for extemporized mountings in the defence of strategic islands. Among these were 25-mm (0.98-in) cannon that were lifted direct with their original naval mountings into shore-located weapon pits in single-, double- and triple-barrelled mountings. These **Navy Type 96 25-mm Machine Cannon** weapons had a performance very similar to that of the Army Type 98 and were used by army personnel. To provide these navy weapons with mobility, some were mounted on simple sledges for towing across level ground.

Specification
Type 98

This Type 98 is emplaced for the anti-aircraft role and has the barrel at full elevation. The 20-round box magazine is fitted, and here the figure 11 points to a cocking handle.

Calibre: 20 mm (0.787 in)
Length of piece: 1.46 m (57.5 in)
Weight: in action 268.77 kg (593 lb)
Elevation: −10° to +85°
Traverse: 360°
Muzzle velocity: 830 m (2,723 ft) per second

Maximum effective ceiling: about 3650 m (11,975 ft)
Rate of fire: 120 rpm
Projectile weight: 0.136 kg (0.3 lb)

The seemingly high carriage is converted to a low and stable firing platform for the anti-aircraft role; note the combination of a muzzle brake with a rather short barrel.

20-mm Scotti

The Italian army had two standard 20-mm (0.787-in) anti-aircraft weapons in service during World War II. One was the Breda and the other the Scotti, or to give it its full Italian designation, the **Cannone-Mitragliera da 20/77 (Scotti)**, which was also known as the **Mitragliera Isotta Fraschini** from the production facility where it was manufactured; the name Scotti comes from Alfredo Scotti, the designer. The Scotti was first mooted in 1932, and the initial examples were produced in Switzerland at the Oerlikon works, which no doubt accounts for the use of a drum magazine very similar to that of the Oerlikon gun. This drum was later discarded in favour of 12-round trays.

Compared with the Breda the Scotti was a far simpler weapon. It resembled the Oerlikon gun in some respects, but used a different mechanism. It was much easier to manufacture than the Breda, but despite the use of a longer barrel the Scotti's overall performance appears to have been inferior to that of its contemporary. The same ammunition type (together with its super-sensitive fuse) appears to have been used, but the maximum effective ceiling was lower than that of the Breda, which indicates a different propellant charge. To balance this, against targets at low altitudes the rate of fire was slightly higher and for the benefit of the gun crew the Scotti was lighter than the other weapon.

The Scotti appears to have been used in smaller numbers than the Breda, but it was also used by other nations. Before 1940 many Scottis were sold to various South American nations, and it also appears that many made the long journey to China. After 1942 the ease of fabrication of the Scotti (compared with the more complicated Breda) led to an increase in Scotti production totals, but the type never seriously challenged the number of Bredas in service. Before 1943 many Scottis were used by German troops operating in North Africa as the **2-cm Scotti (i)**, and once the Italians had surrendered the Scotti became an established part of the German inventory for units based in Italy. It was certainly used by German units operating against the Yugoslav partisans and there seems to be enough evidence to state that after 1943 the guns were kept in production at the Isotta Fraschini facility in Turin for German use.

Two versions of the Scotti were produced. One was a semi-mobile version that could be carried on trucks and dismounted for use; once off the truck it could be manhandled on a twin-wheeled carriage, though in action the gun rested on a light flat tripod mounting. The other version was static, with the gun on a pedestal mounting. This latter version was used mostly on the Italian mainland, and after 1943 numbers of them were taken over by British troops for the local defence of coastal artillery positions. After 1945 the type was used for some years by the re-formed Italian army.

Specification
Scotti
Calibre: 20 mm (0.787 in)
Length of piece: 1.54 m (60.6 in)

Weight: in action 227.5 kg (502 lb)
Elevation: −10° to +85°
Traverse: 360°
Muzzle velocity: 830 m (2,723 ft) per second
Maximum effective ceiling: 2135 m (7,005 ft)
Rate of fire: (cyclic) 250 rpm
Projectile weight: 0.125 kg (0.276 lb)

The Cannone-Mitragliera de 20/77 (Scotti) was used alongside the Breda as the standard Italian army light anti-aircraft cannon. It was longer than the Breda and could use a 60-round drum magazine, but 12-round trays could also be used. Two types were produced, one static and the other for towing by light trucks.

20-mm Breda

One of the two standard Italian 20-mm (0.787-in) AA guns was the weapon known to the Italian army as the **Cannone-Mitragliera da 20/65 modello 35 (Breda)**. It was first manufactured in 1934 by the Società Italiana Ernesto Breda of Brescia, a company that was no stranger to weapon production but whose staple activity was building locomotives and trucks. The Breda gun was designed as a dual-purpose weapon for use against ground and aircraft targets, and was taken into service by the Italian army in 1935.

The 20-mm Breda gun was a very effective weapon, and was much used by the Italian army. It had a rather complicated twin-wheeled carriage that could be towed into action behind a truck, but it was light enough to be manhandled over considerable distances and it could even be broken down into four pack loads for man carriage or mule transport. In action the gun required a team of three men: the aimer sat on the gun and used a complex telescopic sight incorporating a predictor function. Ammunition was fed into the gun on 12-round trays, and the feed mechanism contained the odd Italian feature of placing the spent cartridge case back into the tray once it had been fired. Exactly what function this feature was supposed to impart is uncertain, but it appeared on several Italian automatic weapons and at least had the advantage of keeping the gun position tidy.

Against ground targets the gun fired armour-piercing rounds. Aircraft targets were engaged with a high explosive projectile that incorporated a very sensitive percussion fuse to operate against light aircraft structures. The projectile also had a self-destruct feature if it did not hit a target. The tripod platform of the gun provided a steady base for firing, and against aircraft the gun proved to be very successful. Against tanks it was less effective, but any weapons captured by the Allies during the North African campaigns were usually mounted on the light armoured cars of the day to provide them with more offensive capability than that provided by the usual machine-guns. The Germans also took over numbers of Breda guns for their

own use in North Africa under the designation **2-cm Breda (i)**, and the Italian surrender of 1943 meant that all guns on the Italian mainland immediately changed to German use. Much farther afield, some Breda guns were also used by various of the warring Chinese military factions.

Apart from the modello 35 there was also a **modello 39**. This was a much more complex weapon: it used the same gun as before, but allied to a static pedestal-type mounting on which the gun itself was suspended below curved arms that carried the sighting system. This version was usually retained for the defence of the Italian mainland.

Specification
Breda modello 1935
Calibre: 20 mm (0.787 in)
Length of piece: 1.30 m (51.2 in)
Weight: in action 307.35 kg (678 lb)
Elevation: −10° to +80°
Traverse: 360°
Muzzle velocity: 830-850 m (2,723-2,789 ft) per second
Maximum effective ceiling: 2500 m (8,202 ft)
Rate of fire: (cyclic) 200-220 rpm
Projectile weight: 0.135 kg (0.298 lb)

One very prominent feature of the 20-mm (0.79-in) Breda gun was the long sight arm arrangement, which was meant to keep the gun sight in front of the aimer's face at all angles of elevation. It worked very well, but was rather complex and heavy, and elsewhere much simpler design solutions were usually found.

Members of the Slovak division operating with the Wehrmacht are manning a 20-mm Breda. Following the Italian surrender, Germany commandeered much of the equipment of the Italian army, often giving it to their dwindling number of allies.

40-mm Bofors

The **40-mm Bofors** gun has by now passed virtually into legend as one of the most successful weapons of its type that has ever been produced, and it was used by nearly all protagonists during World War II, and a measure of its effectiveness can be seen by the fact that it is still in service to this day.

The 40-mm (1.575-in) Bofors gun had its origins in a 1928 request from the Swedish navy for AB Bofors to design a light anti-aircraft gun. The first weapon was manufactured in 1930 and was subsequently produced in single- and twin-gun mountings for the navy, and on a mobile ground mounting for the army. It was this latter version that became the most famous, for it was soon seen to be the best gun of its type available. It had a high muzzle velocity (making it an ideal anti-aircraft weapon), it fired a good-sized projectile with a worthwhile payload that could bring down virtually any aircraft that it hit, and the mounting and car-

riage were relatively light and handy to use in action. Within a few years orders were flooding into the AB Bofors factory at Karlskroga but, more importantly at the time, a number of foreign governments negotiated for licence production of the gun and its ammunition. These nations included Hungary, Poland, Finland, Greece, Norway and many other countries as well. Thus by 1939 the Bofors gun was in production all over Europe for many armies in a bewildering arrangement of cross-deals. For instance the United Kingdom took out a licence, but was in such a hurry to re-arm with the Bofors gun that it also purchased quantities from Poland and Hungary. France wanted to set up a line but purchased guns from Poland.

Some nations, such as Poland, incorporated their own modifications, contributing a lighter carriage (in the **40-mm armata przeciwlotnicza wz 36**) which was later adopted by the British.

Progressive developments to the carriage and sights were gradually introduced, and there were many and various models of naval mountings. Some of these variations are covered separately, though the gun itself changed but little. It used a robust clip-fed mechanism in which the sequence was automatic once the gunner had pressed the trigger. As he did so a round was rammed into the breech, the breech closed and the weapon fired, the spent case being ejected ready for another round to be fed, all in a sequence that continued as long as the trigger was pressed. If the barrel became overheated it could be rapidly changed.

After 1940 the main centres of Bofors production were the United Kingdom (**Gun, AA, Mk 1**) and the United States, where the original Swedish design was reproduced virtually unchanged as the **40-mm Gun M1**. On the German side production was continued at the

Kongsberg Arsenal in Norway for use by the German army and the Luftwaffe as the **4-cm Flak 28 (Bofors)**. In the Far East weapons captured in the Dutch East Indies were used by the Japanese. The Soviet Union received some numbers of Bofors from the Americans under Lend-Lease, so it can be seen that Bofors guns were in action on all fronts throughout the war.

Specification
Bofors gun
Calibre: 40 mm (1.575 in)
Length of piece: 2.25 m (88.6 in)
Weight: in action 2460 kg (5,423 lb)
Elevation: −5° to +90°
Traverse: 360°
Muzzle velocity: 854 m (2,802 ft) per second
Maximum ceiling: 7200 m (23,622 ft)
Rate of fire: (cyclic) 120 rpm
Shell weight: 0.89 kg (1.96 lb)

25-mm Hotchkiss

Between the world wars the French army retained great weapon stockpiles from World War I, and with them a military philosophy that dealt only in terms of World War I battles. Thus when it came to considerations of anti-aircraft weapons it was decided that an updated '75' (the famous 75-mm/2.95 in Model 1897) was all that was required, and that a new 12.7-mm (0.5-in) heavy machine-gun would suffice for low-level defences. The French armaments manufacturers, including Hotchkiss, thought otherwise and in 1932 brought out a new 25-mm (0.98-in) automatic weapon and presented it to the military authorities.

The response was negative. The staff planners saw no need for a weapon such as the **25-mm Hotchkiss** and were unwilling to consider the type. They did agree to carry out trials with the new gun, but that was all and by the mid-1930s it appeared that the project was defunct. Then came the Spanish Civil War, and French military observers on the spot soon noted that there most definitely existed a requirement for a weapon heavier than machine-guns to counter the activities of ground-attack aircraft. Thus there was a rushed order to Hotchkiss for large numbers of its 25-mm weapon. But this order was beset with uncer-

tainties regarding rates of fire, type of carriage and so on. It was late 1938 before the order was finally sorted out and by then things had got a bit out of hand, for Hotchkiss had already started production of a model for Romania and the French order meant changes to the design and the production line. But eventually the guns started to flow from the factory.

There were two types of 25-mm Hotchkiss. One was the **Mitrailleuse de 25mm sur affut universel Hotchkiss Modèle 1938**, which was a light weapon transported on a single-axle carriage; the other was the **Hotchkiss modèle 1939**, which was a heavier weapon intended for static use but capable of being moved if required. Both were basically simple and adequate weapons with a high rate of fire and good ammunition that was also intended for use against ground targets if the opportunity arose. Thus an armour-piercing projectile was available. A version for use by the French navy was produced using a pedestal mounting, and just before the Germans invaded France in May 1940 Hotchkiss produced a twin-barrelled variant known as the **Hotchkiss modèle 1940**, which did not get past the initial trials stage.

The main problem for the French army was that the Hotchkiss produc-

tion lines could not churn out the guns in sufficient numbers. Despite wartime urgency, the Hotchkiss works were beset by industrial troubles and other delays to the extent that when the Germans invaded France only just over 1,000 Hotchkiss guns were in service, which was way below the numbers required. In the event those that were produced mainly fell into the hands of the Germans. Some were retained by the Vichy French armed forces and some used by the Free French in the Middle East, but the bulk that survived May 1940 were impressed into German use and issued to various units based in France; some were later incorporated into the Atlantic Wall beach defences. The German designations were **2.5-cm Flak Hotchkiss 38** and **2.5-cm Flak Hotchkiss 39**.

There are two main models of the 25-mm (0.98-in) Hotchkiss cannon; this is the mle 38 ready for towing, but minus the usual muzzle flash-hider. Other versions used differing barrel and sighting arrangements.

Specification
Hotchkiss modèle 38
Calibre: 25 mm (0.98 in)
Length of piece: 1.50 m (59 in)
Weight: in action 850 kg (1,874 lb)
Elevation: −5° to +80°
Traverse: 360°
Muzzle velocity: 900 m (2,953 ft) per second
Maximum effective ceiling: 3000 m (9,843 ft)
Rate of fire: (cyclic) 350 rpm
Projectile weight: 0.29 kg (0.64 lb)

37-mm Schneider

The **37-mm Schneider** gun was produced initially during the early 1930s, and was at the time rejected by the French army which could then see no reason for obtaining such a weapon. A similar Hotchkiss proposal met with the same response. The Schneider concern decided to go ahead with development of the design under its own auspices, and in time these efforts were rewarded by a number of export orders from nations such as Romania. More were taken by the French navy, but the numbers involved were never large.

The Spanish Civil War changed French official thinking to a radical degree: it was now clear that the bulk of the anti-aircraft weapons used by the French armed forces were at best obsolescent or, in the case of low-level defence weapons, ineffective. Accordingly large production orders were placed for weapons initially to supplement and eventually to replace existing stocks. But in the case of the 37-mm guns the French staff planners were in something of a quandary, for they had nothing in what they came to regard as the medium-calibre bracket. At the bottom end 12.7-mm (0.5-in) and 25-mm (0.98-in) weapons were selected, and at the upper end of the weapon bracket the old '75s' (75-mm/ 2.95-in) weapons were being updated and new designs were in prospect: but there was nothing in the medium bracket and so a rushed procurement programme was established.

The Schneider 37-mm gun was an immediate candidate for selection, but at the same time it was appreciated that it was not a very satisfactory weapon. The gun itself had a rather short barrel (resulting in a lack of range and power) and the ammunition was also not particularly powerful. Moreover it was considered that the carriage was too heavy and awkward,

and took too long to get into action. Thus although the Schneider gun was ordered as the **Mitrailleur de 37 mm Schneider modèle 1930**, it was only ordered in parallel with the Swedish 40-mm (1.575-in) Bofors from Poland. An order for 700 Schneider guns was placed, with deliveries hopefully extending into 1941. In the event only some 20 had been produced by the time the Germans invaded; this handful was emplaced around Paris and thus never got a chance to take any part in the events of May and June 1940.

This delay in delivery was caused mainly by production and other troubles at the Schneider factories. The

37-mm gun was not easy to manufacture, and it took time to establish the production facilities. In fact things got so far behind schedule that by early 1940 the French army planners actually approached the United States and requested large numbers of Colt 37-mm anti-aircraft guns. Nothing came of this venture before the Germans invaded.

Thus the Schneider 37-mm gun faded from the scene. The numbers taken over by the Germans were too small to be considered for the usual inclusion in the German inventory, and by the time 1945 came around they had all apparently vanished into the scrap furnaces. Thus the Schneider gun may

be regarded as one of World War II's least successful weapons.

Specification
Schneider modèle 1930
Calibre: 37 mm (1.45 in)
Length of piece: not recorded
Weight: in action 1340 kg (2,954 lb)
Elevation: −0° to +80°
Traverse: 360°
Muzzle velocity: 800 m (2,625 ft) per second
Maximum effective ceiling: 3000 m (9,843 ft)
Rate of fire: (cyclic) 175 rpm
Projectile weight: about 0.55 kg (1.21 lb)

Only a few (some sources say 20) of the 37-mm (1.457-in) Schneider guns were produced for the French army, as the weapon was originally produced for export. It was passed over in favour of the Swedish Bofors Gun after 1938.

2-cm Flak 30

By the time the new German army was ready to re-arm during the early 1930s, the German armament manufacturers had built up a considerable degree of expertise in heavy automatic weapons. This was especially true of the giant Rheinmetall-Borsig concern, and accordingly it was given a contract to produce a light anti-aircraft gun with a calibre of 20 mm (0.787 in), and this was ready for service by 1935. Known as the **2-cm Flak 30**, the term Flak standing for *Fliegerabwehrkanone* (anti-aircraft gun), this light weapon was of the type often known as a cannon, and was the first of a series of weapons that were to become dreaded by low-flying Allied aircraft crews.

The Flak 30 was for its light calibre a rather complex weapon mounted on a carriage that could be towed on two wheels and in action rested on a ground platform. This platform provided a stable firing base with 360° traverse, and had a seat behind the gun for the firer who used, in the Flak 30's original form, a rather complicated form of reflector sight. These sights became even more complicated when simple predictor systems were built into it, and at one point the small sight had reached a state when it had to be driven by clockwork. In fact they got so complicated that the whole idea was dropped and later versions re-

The 2-cm (0.79-in) Flak 30 was a Rheinmetall-Borsig design that entered German army service in 1935. Seen here on its triangular firing platform, it was used on a number of self-propelled mountings.

verted to simple 'cartwheel and bead' iron sights. The gun had a crew of five, but in action was frequently managed by less, especially when the guns were located in static positions. Generally the number was at least four, and usually one man held and operated a stereoscopic rangefinder, though after 1944 this function was deleted as it was found to be operationally unnecessary.

Ammunition was fed into the gun in 20-round magazines, but for some never-fully determined reason the Flak 30 was prone to ammunition jams. Also, although it was perfectly adequate when first introduced, it was later discovered that its rate of fire was too slow to cope adequately with the increased aircraft speeds that prevailed after 1940. Consequently it was replaced on the production line by the later Flak 38, but those already in service were not replaced until they became worn out or were lost to enemy action.

In army light anti-aircraft

Abteilungen (battalions) there were usually three 2-cm batteries to one 3.7-cm (1.457-in) battery, but as the war continued there were many variations on this theme. The Flak 30 was used not only by the Germans. Before 1939 some were sold to the Netherlands and even to China. In Germany the Flak 30 was also used by the Luftwaffe for ground defences, and the German navy had many specialized naval mountings. Some saw service for the defence of armoured trains, and the weapon was one of those mounted on several types of halftracks or trucks for the defence of mobile formations and convoys. The Flak 30 was frequently

used in the ground target role, and there was even a special armour-piercing round for use against tanks.

Specification
Flak 30
Calibre: 20 mm (0.787 in)
Length of piece: 2.30 m (90.6 in)
Weight: in action 450 kg (992 lb)
Elevation: −12° to +90°
Traverse: 360°
Muzzle velocity: 900 m (2,953 ft) per second
Maximum effective ceiling: 2200 m (7,218 ft)
Rate of fire: (cyclic) 280 rmp
Projectile weight: 0.119 kg (0.262 lb)

2-cm Flak 38 and Flakvierling 38

By 1940 it was already appreciated that the low rate of fire of the 2-cm (0.787-in) Flak 30 was too low for future target speeds, so it was decided to increase the rate of fire in order to increase the possible numbers of projectiles hitting the target. It was also decided to redesign the gun to get rid of the inherent jamming problem. Rheinmetall-Borsig was not given the contract for this project. It went instead to Mauser, who came up with a new gun that was outwardly similar to the Flak 30 but internally much was changed to provide a cyclic rate of fire of 420 to 480 rounds per minute. The ammunition, feed system and most of the carriage remained much the same as before. So did the complicated sights which were later simplified, as on the Flak 30.

The **2-cm Flak 38**, as the Mauser design was known, entered service in late 1940 and eventually replaced the Flak 30 on the production lines. It served alongside the Flak 30 and was also used by the Luftwaffe and the German navy. There was even a special version for use by the German army's mountain units that could be broken down into pack loads. This used the same gun as the Flak 38, but the carriage was much smaller and lighter: it was known as the **2-cm Gebirgsflak 38** and was intended to be a dual-purpose weapon for use against ground targets as well as against aircraft.

By 1940 it was appreciated that aircraft targets were not only getting faster but also heavier and better protected against ground and air fire. Undertaken with typical German thoroughness, operational analysis revealed that although the high rate of fire of the Flak 38 was more likely to ensure a target hit, the low explosive payload of the projectile was unlikely to inflict enough damage to ensure a

The 2-cm (0.79-in) Flak 38 was a Mauser design introduced to overcome some of the drawbacks of the Flak 30, which included a slow rate of fire and various stoppages. It had a higher rate of fire but used the same carriage as the earlier weapon.

'kill'. The only easy and immediate way to remedy this was to increase the number of barrels firing from one mounting, and thus the **2-cm Flakvierling 38** was developed. This was simply a single Flak 38 carriage modified to accommodate four barrels capable of firing at once. This combination became a dreaded aircraft-killer that constantly drew a toll of low-flying Allied aircraft right until the end of the war. The first such equipments entered service in late 1940 and there were never enough of them. They were used by the German army, the Luftwaffe and the navy, and many self-propelled mountings were improvised or produced to make them more mobile. There was a special version for use on armoured trains and at one point there was even a radar-controlled version under development. The Flakvierling required a greater number of men to serve it in action (usually six or seven), but those

A British soldier examines a captured 2-cm (0.79-in) Flakvierling 38. The arrangement of the four barrels can be clearly seen, and the reflector sight is prominent. The curved box magazines can be seen protruding from the guns, and it was these magazines with their 20-round capacity that limited the fire rate of the guns.

For the Germans there were never enough of them and throughout the Reich many production facilities were devoted to manufacture of the guns, their carriages and ammunition. This last was produced in several forms including high explosive (HE), high explosive with tracer and various forms of armour-piercing.

Specification
Flak 38
Calibre: 20 mm (0.787 in)
Length of piece: 2.2525 m (88.7 in)
Weight: in action 420 kg (926 lb)
Elevation: −20° to +90°
Traverse: 360°
Muzzle velocity: 900 m (2,953 ft) per second
Maximum effective ceiling: 2200 m (7,218 ft)
Rate of fire: (cyclic) 420-480 rpm
Projectile weight: 0.119 kg (0.262 lb)

Specification
Flakvierling 38
Calibre: 20 mm (0.787 in)
Length of piece: 2.2525 m (88.7 in)
Weight: in action 1514 kg (3,338 lb)
Elevation: −10° to +100°
Traverse: 360°
Muzzle velocity: 900 m (2,953 ft) per second
Maximum effective ceiling: 2200 m (7,218 ft)
Rate of fire: (cyclic) 1,800 rpm
Projectile weight: 0.119 kg (0.262 lb)

A 2-cm (0.79-in) Flakvierling 38 is mounted on a SdKfz 7/1 half track with the crew ready for immediate action. This conversion was first produced during late 1941 and was widely used, not only against aircraft but also against tank targets. This vehicle had a crew of 10 men.

3.7-cm Flak 18, 36 and 37

When the **3.7-cm Flak 18** entered service in 1935 it was regarded by the German army and Luftwaffe as a medium-calibre anti-aircraft weapon. It had been developed in Switzerland by Rheinmetall to avoid the stipulations of the 1919 Versailles Treaty, and for a time was known as the **ST 10** or **Solothurn S10-100**. When it was first introduced the Flak 18 suffered from many teething troubles which were eventually ironed out, but even in its final form was not regarded as much of a success. In the weapon's original form, the gun and carriage were moved on a heavy and complex twin-axled arrangement, but getting in and out of action with this carriage was slow. Moreover, carriage traverse was slow and the gun mechanism was so prone to stoppages that crews had to be highly trained to cope with them. For all these drawbacks the 3.7-cm (1.457-in) Flak 18 was never replaced in service. Some examples were exported to China before 1939.

Manufacture of the original Flak 18 ceased in 1936, and in the same year production began of a new gun with the same calibre. This appeared to be the same design as before, but there were many changes, not the least of which was a new type of ammunition with only one driving band in place of the original two. The carriage was much altered to allow towing on a single axle only. Overall the new gun, known as the **3.7-cm Flak 36**, retained the same performance as the earlier weapon but was much handier to use in action. There was one further variant, the **3.7-cm Flak 37**, but this differed only in the type of sight fitted: this was a complex predictor-type sight powered by clockwork.

The Flak 36 and 37 were produced in large numbers, and by August 1944 the Luftwaffe alone had 4,211 in service. The German navy used various forms of the basic gun on special naval mountings, and there was a version for use on submarines. There were also several self-propelled types, some hastily mounted on trucks and converted tank chassis, and some on half-tracks. In action the usual number of men to each gun was seven, one of them operating a portable rangefinder, but after 1944 this crew member was withdrawn. Ammunition was fed

On the move, the 3.7-cm (1.457-in) Flak 36 was a compact load and used a two-wheeled carriage. The Flak 37 differed in using a more complex clockwork sighting system, but was otherwise identical to the Flak 36.

Below: The 3.7-cm (1.457-in) Flak series was used on numerous self-propelled mountings, one of which was nicknamed the 'Möbelwagen' (furniture van). It used a PzKfpw IV chassis with the gun mounted centrally and with sides that folded down to form a firing platform for the crew of seven (including the driver).

Right: A 3.7-cm (1.457-in) Flak 36 is in position as part of the Atlantic Wall coastal defences. This photograph was taken during 1940 or 1941, for the emplacement is still an earthwork (later it would be concrete) and the rangetaker is still included in the crew; later he would be removed to conserve manpower.

into the gun in linked six-round clips.

After about 1940 the Flak 18, 36 and 37 became the standard defence weapons against low-flying aircraft and were usually organized into nine- or 12-gun batteries. Many were statically emplaced on special flak towers that provided good all-round fire close to important target areas. Special flak trains that moved around the Reich to be in position wherever Allied air attacks were heaviest also carried numbers of Flak 36s or 37s. The type

was also used in the field as an anti-tank weapon on occasion and one weapon developed for use on the Eastern Front was a muzzle-loaded stick bomb that was fired against tanks using a special blank cartridge.

Production of the Flak 36 and 37 continued right up to the end of the war at three main centres (one in Czechoslovakia), but the Flak 36/37 was not an easy or cheap weapon to produce, a fact which led to the introduction of the Flak 43 guns.

Specification
Flak 36 and Flak 37
Calibre: 37 mm (1.457 in)
Length of piece: 3.626 m (142.75 in)
Weight: in action 1550 kg (3,417 lb)
Elevation: −8° to +85°
Traverse: 360°
Muzzle velocity: 820 m (2,690 ft) per second
Maximum effective ceiling: 4800 m (15,748 ft)
Rate of fire: (cyclic) 160 rpm
Projectile weight: 0.64 kg (1.41 lb)

3.7-cm Flak 43 and Flakzwilling 43

By 1942 the Allied air threat over all the various battlefields was reaching the point where there were never enough air defence weapons available. The 3.7-cm (1.457-in) guns were always in demand as they were the standard weapon against low-flying aircraft, and in 1942 Rheinmetall-Borsig was busy developing a gun to replace the existing costly and slow-to-make Flak 36/37 series. As ever, Rheinmetall-Borsig came up with a novelty, not in the gun or carriage design, but in the manner of manufacture: it decided to adopt methods already in use for small-arms production.

Rheinmetall-Borsig was in competition with Krupp for the new gun contract, and at one point the order was given to the Krupp gun, which used conventional production methods. But at the last moment the Krupp design developed weaknesses and Rheinmetall-Borsig got the award. This immediately resulted in the internal party and factional wrangling that often beset the German wartime industrial dream, so by the time Rheinmetall-Borsig was actually able to go ahead on a new production line well over a year had passed. Rheinmetall-Borsig was partially able to make up the leeway by the fact that its gun, known as the **3.7-cm Flak 43**, was produced with stampings, weldings and simply-fabricated components in the same way as sub-machine guns. The production time for a gun was cut by a factor of four, and the overall performance boosted by an increased rate of fire.

It was early 1944 before the first of the new guns was ready, and thereaf-

The German 3.7-cm (1.457-in) Flakzwilling 43 was an attempt to increase the firepower of the basic Flak 43 by adding an extra barrel, but relatively few were produced as the weapon was rather high and awkward to emplace.

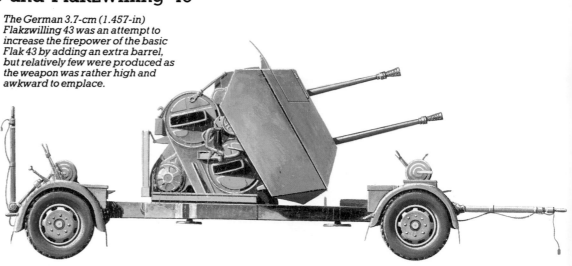

ter the type poured off the lines at Dürkopp. In service the Flak 43 proved very successful, but in the initial rush to get the new gun into production it had been decided to retain the original Flak 36/37 ammunition and barrel designs. Thus the Flak 43 was at a disadvantage from the start, for the increased speeds of low-flying aircraft and their increased degree of protection meant that a single strike from a Flak 43 did not always bring down the target aircraft. The only immediate answer to this was to multiply the number of barrels on a single carriage, and this led to the **3.7-cm Flakzwilling 43** with two barrels, one above the other, on a single mounting. This made a kill much more likely and the Flakzwilling

became preferred over the single-barrel version. In the event both were produced until the end of the war, and there were even plans for a four-barrel mounting at one stage. There was also a project on which the two barrels were mounted side-by-side.

The single- and twin-barrel Flak 43s were potent weapons, but the twin-barrelled version was something of an unwieldy brute to get in and out of action because of its general top-heaviness. Fortunately for Allied air crews, the number of Flak 43s was never enough to meet demands, especially regarding the Flakzwilling 43. By February 1945 there were 1,032 Flak 43s of both types in service, but of these only 280 were of the twin-

barrelled version. In action both types required six-man crews, and if a gun was to be maintained in action for any length of time more men were needed to supply ammunition to the gun.

Specification
Flak 43
Calibre: 37 mm (1.457 in)
Length of piece: 3.30 m (130 in)
Weight: in action 1392 kg (3,069 lb)
Elevation: −7.5° to +90°
Traverse: 360°
Muzzle velocity: 840 m (2,756 ft) per second
Maximum effective ceiling: 4800 m (15,748 ft)
Rate of fire: (cyclic) 250 rpm
Projectile weight: 0.64 kg (1.41 lb)

5-cm Flak 41

In World War II air warfare terms there was an altitude band that extended from approximately 1500 m (4,921 ft) to 3000 m (9,843 ft) that existing anti-aircraft guns could cover only with difficulty. Aircraft flying in this band were really too high or too low for small- or larger-calibre weapons. What was obviously required was an interim-calibre weapon that could deal with this problem but, as artillery designers in both the Allied and German camps were to discover, it was not an easy problem to solve.

The German solution to the interim-altitude band situation was a gun known as the **5-cm Flak 41**, and the best that can be said of it was that it was not a success. It was first produced in 1936, and was yet another Rheinmetall-Borsig design that was preferred over a Krupp submission. Development of the prototype was carried out with no sense of urgency, for it was 1940 before the production contract was awarded and in the event only 60 guns were completed. The first of them entered service in 1941 and the type's shortcomings soon became apparent. The main problem was the ammunition: despite its 50-mm (1.97-in) calibre, this was rather underpowered and on firing produced a prodigious amount of muzzle blast and flash that distracted the aimer, even in broad daylight. The carriage proved rather bulky and awkward to handle in action, and despite the characteristics of the expected targets the traversing mechanism was also rather underpowered

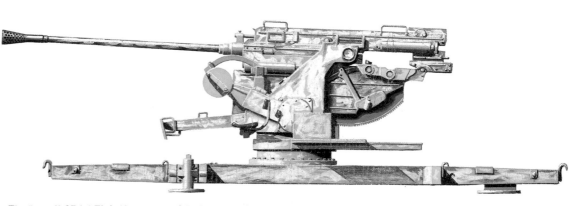

The 5-cm (1.97-in) Flak 41 was one of the least successful of all the German anti-aircraft guns, for it had excessive recoil and flash and the carriage traversed too slowly. Despite their shortcomings, 50 were used until the war ended.

and too slow to track fast targets.

Two versions of the Flak 41 were produced: a mobile one using two axles to carry the gun and carriage, and a static version for emplacing close to areas of high importance such as the Ruhr dams. Despite their overall lack of success the guns were kept in service until the war ended, but by then only 24 were left. During the war years some development work was carried out using the Flak 41s, not so much to improve the guns themselves but to determine the exact nature of the weapon that was to replace them. In time this turned out to be a design known as the **Gerät 56** (Gerät was a cover name, meaning equipment) but it was not finalized before the war en-

ded. One Flak 41 development was the formation of one battery operating under a single remote control.

In action the Flak 41 had a crew of seven men. Loading the ammunition was no easy task for it was fed into the gun in five-round clips that were somewhat difficult to handle. Though designed for use against aircraft targets, the Flak 41 was also provided with special armour-piercing projectiles for use against tanks, but this AP round appears to have been little used as the Flak 41 was one of the few German weapons that was not selected for mounting on a self-propelled carriage.

If the Germans were unsuccessful in their attempt to defend the interim-altitude band, it has to be stated that

the Allies were no more successful. Typical of their efforts was the British twin 6-pdr, a 57-mm (2.244-in) weapon that never got past the trials stage because of its indifferent performance.

Specification
Flak 41
Calibre: 50 mm (1.97 in)
Length of piece: 4.686 m (184.5 in)
Weight: in action 3100 kg (6,834 lb)
Elevation: −10° to +90°
Traverse: 360°
Muzzle velocity: 840 m (2,756 ft) per second
Maximum effective ceiling: 3050 m (10,007 ft)
Rate of fire: (cyclic) 180 rpm
Projectile weight: 2.2 kg (4.85 lb)

War Rockets

Used to attack strongpoints, lay smokescreens and simply to support the fire of conventional artillery, the rockets of World War II are most famous for their use in massive bombardments on the Eastern Front. Firing them in huge numbers would often more than compensate for their inaccuracy.

The war rocket is an old weapon that was resurrected during World War II to supplement existing attack and defence systems (artillery and anti-aircraft weapons). The rocket has much to offer the weapon designer as it is a relatively cheap and simple device that can be mass-produced with comparative ease, and when used *en masse* is capable of fearful devastation. But in the term *en masse* lies the main failing of the war rocket: it has to be used in great numbers to ensure that it will hit a precise target, for the rocket is inherently a projectile that will depart from a pre-selected trajectory with alarming ease and with little apparent reason. Set against this is the fact that it can carry a powerful payload for the costs involved, and so the arguments for and against such weapons continue.

The arguments for the rocket were in the ascendancy during World War II, nearly all the major protagonists making operational use of them to some degree. Mainly it was used to supplement existing weapons, but the Soviets discovered that the rocket could at times also be regarded as a weapon in its own right. Technologically, the Germans were the most advanced of all the World War II rocket users;

Mobile multiple-barrelled rocket launchers, such as this British 76.2mm (3in) anti-aircraft version, laid down huge blankets of fire; the most famous example of this weapon was the Soviet Katyusha.

however, they operated rockets as a supporting weapon to eke out artillery barrages, and only rarely attempted to deploy their rocket systems in the same offensive manner as the Red Army used its various Katyushas. The Katyushas were nearly always in the forefront of the offensive to oust the German invaders from the Soviet Union, and some of the Soviet rocket types used during those times are still in service all over the world. Indeed the Russian Army has maintained the multiple

rocket-launcher as an important item in its military inventory, and has improved the performance of the relevant rockets to an extraordinary degree. Only now are the Western nations beginning to relearn the importance of this weapon as a counter to massed armoured and infantry attacks.

Nevertheless, during World War II the rocket made a considerable impact on many ground campaigns. For example, the German Nebelwerfer units often tipped the balance in their favour

by their application of heavy barrage fire during several battles. British rocket batteries played their part in the defence of the nation. At lower tactical levels the various American M8 weapons were often used to devastating effect in the reduction of strongpoints and bunkers. Only the Japanese failed to use the rocket to its full effect. They did make some attempts in this direction, but for the Japanese the main problem was production, not tactics.

15-cm Wurfgranate 41

The 15-cm (5.9-in) German artillery rockets were the mainstay of the large number of German army Nebelwerfer (literally smoke-throwing) units, initially formed to produce smoke screens for various tactical uses but later diverted to use artillery rockets as well. The 15-cm (5.9-in) rockets were extensively tested by the Germans at Kummersdorf West during the late 1930s, and by 1941 the first were ready for issue to the troops.

The 15-cm (5.9-in) rockets were of two main types: the **15-cm Wurfgranate 41 Spreng** (high explosive) and **15-cm Wurfgranate 41 w Kh Nebel** (smoke). In appearance both were similar and had an unusual layout, in that the rocket venturi that produced the spin stabilization were located some two-thirds of the way along the rocket body with the main payload behind them. This ensured that when the main explosive payload detonated the remains of the rocket motor added to the overall destructive effects. In flight the rocket had a distinctive droning sound that gave rise to the Allied nickname 'Moaning Minnie'. Special versions were issued for arctic and tropical use.

The first launcher issued for use with these rockets was a single-rail device known as the 'Do-Gerät' (after the leader of the German rocket teams, General Dornberger). It was apparently intended for use by airborne units, but in the event was little used. Instead the main launcher for the 15-cm (5.9-in) rockets was the **15-cm Nebelwerfer 41**. This fired six rockets from tubular launchers carried on a converted 3.7-cm Pak 35/36 anti-tank gun carriage. The tubes were arranged in a rough circle and were fired electrically one at a time in a fixed sequence. The maximum range of these rockets was variable, but usually about 6900 m (7,545 yards), and they were normally fired en masse by batteries of 12 or more launchers. When so used the effects of such a bombardment could be devastating as the rockets could cover a considerable area of target terrain and the blast of their payloads was powerful.

On the move the Nebelwerfer 41s were usually towed by light halftracks that also carried extra ammunition and other equipment, but in 1942 a half-tracked launcher was issued. This was the **15-cm Panzerwerfer 42** which continued to use the 15-cm (5.9-in) rocket

Above: The 15-cm Panzerwerfer 42 was not only more mobile, but more survivable; rockets betrayed their position the moment they fired, so to avoid enemy artillery fire they needed to change position rapidly.

with the launcher tubes arranged in two horizontal rows of five on the top of an SdKfz 4/1 Maultier armoured halftrack. These vehicles were used to supply supporting fire for armoured operations. Up to 10 rockets could be carried ready for use in the launcher and a further 10 weapons inside the armoured body. Later in the war similar launchers were used on armoured schwere Wehrmachtschlepper (SWS) halftracks that were also used to tow more Nebelwerfer 41s. The SWS could carry up to 26 rockets inside its armoured hull.

The 15-cm (5.9-in) rockets were also used with the launchers intended for the 30-cm (11.8-in) rockets, with special rails for the smaller rockets fitted into the existing 30-cm (11.8-in) launcher rails.

Specification
15-cm Wurfgranate 41 Spreng
Dimensions: length 979 mm (38.55 in); diameter 158 mm (6.22 in)
Weights: overall 31.8 kg (70 lb);

The 15-cm rockets were among the earliest in widespread use by the German army, following an extensive pre-war test programme.

propellant 6.35 kg (14 lb); filling 2.5 kg (5.5 lb)
Performance: initial velocity 342 m (1,120 ft) per second; range 7055 m (7,715 yards)

Specification
15-cm Wurfgranate 41 w Kh Nebel

Originally fired from a 6-barrel mount converted from the Pak 35/36 gun carriage, by 1942 the 10-tube launcher had been developed.

Dimensions: length 1.02 m (40.16 in); diameter 158 mm (6.22 in)
Weights: overall 35.9 kg (79 lb); propellant 6.35 kg (14 lb); filling 3.86 kg (8.5 lb)
Performance: initial velocity 342 m (1,120 ft) per second; range 6905 m (7,550 yards)

21-cm Wurfgranate 42

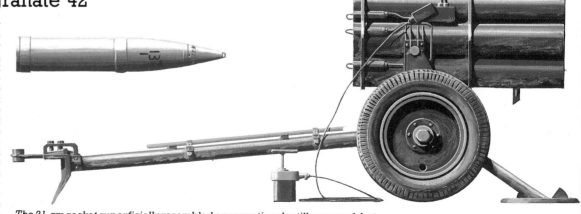

Following on from the success of their 15-cm (5.9-in) rockets, German designers decided to produce a larger rocket which by 1941 emerged as a 210-mm (8.27-in) design. At first sight this rocket, known as the **21-cm Wurfgranate 42 Spreng**, looked exactly like a conventional artillery projectile, but closer examination showed that the base had 22 angled venturi to impart the important spin stabilization. The long streamlined nose was also deceptive, for it was hollow and the warhead proper was located some distance from the tip. This rocket contained no less than 10.17 kg (22.4 lb) of high explosive, which on detonation produced a powerful blast effect. The weapon was so successful in this destructive role that only high explosive versions were produced.

The 21-cm rocket superficially resembled a conventional artillery round, but its streamlined nose was hollow and its base had 22 angled venturi to produce spin stabilization.

The 21-cm (8.27-in) rocket was used with only one type of projector, the **21-cm Nebelwerfer 42**. The first such equipment appeared in action in the Soviet Union during 1943 as it took some time to finalize the launcher design. Originally this was to have been a simple enlargement of the existing 15-cm (5.9-in) Nebelwerfer 41 complete with six launcher tubes, but the larger calibre gave rise to some imbalance problems when the launcher was being towed and fired, so the number of tubes was eventually reduced to five and that solved the problems. In all other respects the carriage was the same as the earlier design and was a modification of the 3.7-cm (1.456-in) Pak 35/36 anti-tank gun carriage. As with the 15-cm (5.9-in) rockets the firing of the 21-cm (8.27-in) weapon was by electrical means. Once the rockets had been loaded in their tubes the launcher crew withdrew to a safe distance (or even took cover), and on receipt of the firing order one of the crew operated a special switch-gear box and the full load of rockets were fired one at a time in a fixed sequence. The salvo firing of the rockets produced a considerable amount of smoke and dust that revealed the launcher and battery position to the enemy, and during their trajectory the rockets produced their characteristic moaning noise that made them so distinctive a weapon. This combination of smoke, dust and noise meant that the Nebelwerfer troops had to be experts at getting in and out of action quickly, for any firing of the large salvoes necessary to cover a target quickly produced counterbattery artillery or rocket fire that could neutralize the launcher units.

The 21-cm (8.27-in) rockets made a considerable impression on all who had to endure their effects, and the Americans in particular considered the rocket and launcher design to be so far in advance of anything they could produce that they took some examples back to the USA and copied them. The US version was the 210-mm (8.27-in) **T36**, which was used for a series of trials and research programmes that did nothing to produce an operational weapon but which added considerably to the Americans' knowledge of artillery rocket technology.

Specification
21-cm Wurfgranate 42 Spreng
Dimensions: length 1.25 m (49.21 in); body diameter 210 mm (8.27 in)
Weights: overall 109.55 kg (241.5 lb); propellant 18.27 kg (40.25 lb); explosive 10.17 kg (22.4 lb)
Performance: initial velocity 320 m (1,050 ft) per second; range about 7850 m (8,585 yards)

Entering service in 1943, the 21-cm Wurfgranate 42 was to have used the same carriage as the 15-cm rocket, but the number of tubes had to be reduced to five to compensate for the increased charge. The Americans were so impressed by the 21-cm weapon that they copied it.

GERMANY

28-cm and 32-cm Wurfkörper

The 28-cm (11-in) and 32-cm (12.6-in) rockets preceded the 15-cm (5.9-in) rockets in service with the German army, the first of them being issued for use during 1940. The two rockets shared the same rocket motor, but differed in their payload. Both were awkward and bulky rockets with a poor ballistic shape, but both had powerful payloads.

The smaller weapon was the **28-cm Wurfkörper Spreng**, which used a heavy high explosive warhead, while the larger weapon was the **32-cm Wurfkörper M Fl 50** with an incendiary warhead in heavy liquid form. Both had a range limitation of just over 2000 m (2,185 yards) and were highly inaccurate despite their spin stabilization, and were consequently used en masse whenever possible. Counterbalancing these disadvantages was the fact that both were devastating in their effects if they hit a target, and the high explosive rocket was highly regarded for use in urban fighting where houses or other structures had to be demolished.

Both rockets were issued to the troops in wooden carrying crates, or **Packkiste**. These crates doubled as launching frames and were fitted with simple forward supporting legs for rudimentary aiming purposes. In this form both rockets could be used by assault pioneers to demolish bunkers or strongpoints, but more often the rockets were used in batches of four resting on simple launcher frames known as the **schweres Wurfgerät 40** or **schweres Wurfgerät 41**, which differed from each other only in that the latter was tubular steel- rather than wooden-framed. Both could be used for pre-arranged barrages, as during the siege of Sevastopol in 1942. But this launching method was static, and to provide some form of mobility the **28/32-cm Nebelwerfer 41** was developed. This was a simple trailer with frames for six rockets in two superimposed rows of three, and after the 15-cm Nebelwerfer 41 this launcher was the most important early equipment of the Nebelwerfer units.

Another and still more mobile launcher for these rockets was the **schwerer Wurfrahmen 40**, in which six launcher frames were mounted on the sides of an SdKfz 251/1 half-track. The rockets were mounted on the side frames still in their carrying crates. Aiming was achieved by simply pointing the vehicle towards the target, and the rockets were then fired one at a time in a set sequence. This rocket/vehicle combination had several names but was often known as the 'Stuka-zu-Fuss' or 'heulende Kuh' (Foot Stuka or Howling Cow) and was often used to support Panzer operations, especially in the early days of the invasion of the Soviet Union. Later in the war other vehicles, usually captured French or other impressed vehicles, were used to bulk out the numbers of mobile launchers available. All manner of light armoured vehicles were used in this role, some carrying only four launchers. Many of these improvised launcher vehicles were used during the fighting in Normandy in 1944.

The short-ranged but powerful 28-cm and 32-cm rockets were among the first to be fitted to vehicles, in this case the ubiquitous SdKfz 251. This conversion was known as the 'Foot Stuka' or 'Howling Cow'.

Specification
28-cm Wurfkörper Spreng
Dimensions: length 1.19 m (46.85 in); body diameter 280 mm (11 in)
Weights: overall 82.2 kg (181 lb); propellant 6.6 kg (14.56 lb); filling 49.9 kg (110 lb)
Performance: range about 2138 m (2,337 yards)

Specification
32-cm Wurfkörper M Fl 50
Dimensions: length 1.289 m (50.75 in); body diameter 320 mm (12.6 in)
Weights: overall 79 kg (174 lb); propellant 6.6 kg (14.56 lb); filling 39.8 kg (87.7 lb)
Performance: range about 2028 m (2,217 yards)

30-cm Wurfkörper 42

Compared with 28-cm (11-in) and 32-cm (12.6-in) rockets which preceded it, the **30-cm Wurfkörper 42 Spreng** (also known as the **Wurfkörper Spreng 4491**) was a considerable improvement on the earlier designs when it appeared on the artillery scene during late 1942. Not only was it in aerodynamic terms a much smoother and cleaner design, but it had a much higher propellant/payload ratio than any other German artillery rocket. However, to the troops in the fields these technicalities were far less important than the fact that the more advanced type of propellant used with the new rocket produced far less smoke and exhaust trails than the other rockets, and was thus far less likely to give away the firing position. But for all this improvement the 30-cm (11.8-in) rocket did not have any marked range advantages over the existing rockets. It had a theoretical range of some 6000 m (6,560 yards), but practical ranges were of the order of 4550 m (4,975 yards).

The first launcher used with the new 30-cm (11.8-in) rockets was the **30-cm Nebelwerfer 42**. This was a simple conversion of the 28/32-cm Nebelwerfer 41 with the simple rail launching frames altered to accommodate the new rocket shape and size. But this simple conversion did not last long, for almost as it was issued a new programme of rationalization was drawn up and the special trailer of the Nebelwerfer 41 and 42 was eliminated. Instead a new trailer based on the carriage of the 5-cm (1.97-in) Pak 38 anti-tank gun was placed into production and the 30-cm (11.8-in) launcher frames were placed on this to produce the **30-cm**

Above: The 30-cm Wurfkörper 42 rocket was an improvement over its immediate predecessors, being much cleaner aerodynamically and leaving much less telltale smoke in its wake. Despite these advantages it could not be produced in sufficient quantity to supplant the earlier designs.

Raketenwerfer 56; to ensure that the new launcher could be used to the maximum each was provided with a set of launcher rail inserts to allow 15-cm (5.9-in) rockets to be fired if required. When not in use, these 15-cm (5.9-in) rails were stacked on top of the 30-cm (11.8-in) frames. Yet another rationalization was that the 30-cm (11.8-in) rockets could also be fired from the schwerer Wurfrahmen launcher frames of the SdKfz 251/1 half-track, originally intended for use by the 28-cm (11-in) and 32-cm (12.6-in) rockets. When launched from these frames, the 30-cm (11.8-in) rockets were fired from their carrying crates or Packkiste, and no doubt the 30-cm (11.8-in) rockets were used by assault pioneers for direct firing from their crates in the same manner as the earlier 28-cm (11-in) and 32-cm (12.6-in) weapons.

Despite its relative improvements over the earlier artillery rockets, the

A gunner places some rather optimistic camouflage over a 30-cm rocket launcher. Initially fired from modified 28/32 cm launchers, the 30-cm rocket was soon provided with its own carriage, based on that of the 5-cm Pak 38 anti-tank gun.

30-cm (11.8-in) rocket was not used in very great numbers. The earlier rockets remained in service right until the end of the war despite a late attempt to replace all existing weapons, including the 30-cm (11.8-in) type, by an entirely new 12-cm (4.72-in) spin-stabilized design. This decision was made too late in the war for anything actually to reach the troops, and it now appears doubtful if any 12-cm (4.72-in) rockets were ever made.

Specification
30-cm Wurfkörper 42
Dimensions: length 1.23 m (48.44 in); body diameter 300 mm (11.8 in)
Weights: overall 125.7 kg (277 lb); propellant 15 kg (33.07 lb); explosive 44.66 kg (98.46 lb)
Performance: initial velocity 230 m (754 ft) per second; range about 4550 m (4,975 yards)

Japanese rockets

The Japanese recognized the value of the artillery rocket to their under-armed forces and carried out considerable design and development work in order to provide a weapon that could make up for their lack of industrial capacity. Unfortunately for them their results were patchy and well behind the work carried out by the Allies. To add to the lack of Japanese success there were often development programmes carried out in opposition to each other, and typical of these were the projects to develop a 20-cm (7.87-in) rocket by both the army and the navy.

The **Army 20-cm Rocket** may be regarded as the better of the two projects. It was a spin-stabilized rocket using six base vents to impart propulsion and spin, and had an overall resemblance to an artillery projectile. To fire this rocket the army provided what appeared to be an oversize mortar known as the **Type 4 Rocket Launcher**. The rocket was inserted into the 'barrel' by raising part of the upper section of the barrel and part of the tube base was open. This launcher was supposed to deliver the rocket relatively accurately, but few equipments appear to have been issued and most of these were used for coastal defences.

The **Navy 20-cm Rocket** resembled the army weapon in many respects, but was intended for launching from troughs made from simple wooden planks, or in some cases more sophisticated metal troughs. At times the rockets were simply emplaced to be launched directly from holes dug in the ground. A more conventional launcher used in small numbers only was a simple barrel on a light artillery-type carriage.

These 20-cm (7.87-in) rockets formed the bulk of the Japanese rocket programmes but there were others. One was the **Type 10 Rocket Motor** which was a simple propulsion unit designed to push aircraft bombs along ramps or troughs to launch them. At least two versions of the Type 10 existed but they were very inaccurate and had a maximum range of only 1830 m (2,000 yards). The launchers used for these rocket motors were often improvised, and improvisation was also used in at least one case where the conventional fins of an aircraft 250-kg (551-lb) bomb were replaced by a large rocket motor for launching from a simple wooden trough. Some intelligence reports from the period (1945) speak of these launchers mounted on trucks, but no confirmation of these has been found.

The largest of all the Japanese rockets had a diameter of 447 mm (17.6 in), and this **44.7-cm Rocket** was a somewhat crude spin-stabilized design that was used in action on Iwo Jima and Luzon. It had a range of 1958 m (2,140 yards) at best, and was launched from short wooden racks or frames. It was wildly inaccurate, but it did have a warhead weighing 180.7 kg (398 lb).

By the time these rockets were used Japanese industrial capacity was in such a state that the conventional high explosive warheads for these rockets often had to be replaced by simple picric acid.

Specification
Army 20-cm Rocket
Dimensions: length 984 mm (38.75 in); diameter 202 mm (7.95 in)
Weights: overall 92.6 kg (44.95 lb); propellant not known; filling 16.2 kg (35.7 lb)
Performance: initial velocity not known; range not known

Japan undertook considerable development work on rockets, but lagged behind the other belligerent nations and produced few usable weapons. This 20-cm army rocket was one of the small number to see action.

Specification
Navy 20-cm Rocket
Dimensions: length 1.041 m (41 in); diameter 210 mm (8.27 in)
Weights: overall 90.12 kg (198.5 lb); propellant 8.3 kg (18.3 lb); filling 17.52 kg (38.6 lb)
Performance: initial velocity not known; range 1800 m (1,970 yards)

M-8 82-mm rocket

During the 1920s and 1930s the Soviet Union used a great deal of its research potential to determine exactly how propellants suitable for rockets could be mass produced. Even before 1918 the Russians had been great advocates of the war rocket, and after this the Soviets were determined to remain in the forefront of rocket technology despite the fact that they were hampered by a lack of industrial potential, which in turn led to their selection of the simpler and more easily produced fin-stabilized over the more accurate spin-stabilized rockets. One of their very first designs, produced during the late 1930s, was one of their most famous rockets, namely the 82-mm (3.23-in) **M-8**.

The M-8 rocket was an off-shoot of an aircraft rocket programme. The aircraft rocket was the RS-82, and such was the state of the Soviet rocket development programme that it actually entered service after the 132-mm (5.2-in) rocket. The M-8 was a small rocket with a maximum range of 5900 m (6,455 yards) that carried a fragmentation warhead. It was carried on and fired from a series of rails carried on 6×6 trucks, and these rail launchers were just one type of the series of weapons known as **Katyusha**. One of these multiple launchers was carried on a ZiS-6 6×6 truck. As this arrangement could carry and launch up to 36 M-8 rockets it was known as the **BM-8-36**, the BM denoting 'combat vehicle' as a cover name. It was not the only vehicle that fired the M-8 rocket, for

when sufficient US-supplied Lend-Lease trucks became available these too were used as M-8 launcher vehicles: typical of these was the Studebaker 6×6, which was large enough to take rails for 48 rockets and which thus became the **BM-8-48**. But being wheeled, these launchers could not always traverse the rough terrain of the Soviet Union or keep up with the tank units they were meant to support. At one point experiments were made to fit single-rail launchers to the sides of tank turrets, but they came to nothing. Instead numbers of the T-60 light tank, which had proved to be of little combat value in its designed role, were converted to take rails for 24 M-8 rockets and the type thus became known as the **BM-8-24**.

There were other launchers for the M-8 rocket, including a special eight-rocket frame intended for use by mountain troops. On all of the M-8 launchers the rockets were fired not in a massed salvo but in ripples under the control of an electrical rotary switch box.

The M-8 rockets had quite an effect on the recipient German troops who had to endure the high fragmentation warheads fired into them in large numbers. The Waffen SS was so impressed that it decided to copy the design direct (along with the launcher rails) as its own 'Himmlerorgel'. The M-8 rockets remained in service throughout the war, but following 1945 was gradually phased from use in favour of the heavier Soviet war rockets and in par-

Seen here mounted atop a T-70 light tank, the M-8 82-mm rocket had its origins in an aircraft rocket programme; it proved an enormous success and served throughout the war. The Waffen SS were so impressed that they copied it.

ticular the 132-mm (5.2-in) and 310-mm (12.2-in) rockets.

Specification
M-8
Dimensions: length 660 mm (26 in); body diameter 82 mm (3.23 in)
Weights: overall 8 kg (17.6 lb); propellant 1.2 kg (2.645 lb); explosive 0.5 kg (1.1 lb)
Performance: initial velocity 315 m (1,033 ft) per second; maximum range 5900 m (6,450 yards)

M-13 132-mm rocket

The most widely used of all the Soviet war rockets during World War II was the **M-13** 132-mm (5.2-in) weapon. It was designed during the late 1930s, and when the Germans invaded the Soviet Union in 1941 there were only a few production launchers and a small stock of rockets to hand. These were pressed into service as an emergency measure and first went into action on the Smolensk front in July 1941, when they caused near-panic among the hapless German troops. This is hardly surprising, for in a period of under 10 seconds a single M-13 battery could swamp a large area in high explosive to an extent hitherto unseen in warfare.

These first M-13 batteries were very much special units. The launchers for the M-13 fin-stabilized rockets were carried by ZiS-6 6×6 trucks with rails for 16 rockets. The rails were known as 'Flute' launchers to the Soviet troops as a result of their perforated appearance, but they soon gained the name Katyusha, and at one time were known as 'Kostikov guns' after their supposed designer. For security purposes the launchers were usually shrouded in tarpaulins when not in use, and the crews were culled from Communist party members in order to maintain tight security. But it was not long before the M-13 launchers were in widespread use and their secrets became common knowledge.

The basic M-13 rocket had a range of about 8000 to 8500 m (8,750 to 9,295 yards). The usual warhead was of the HE fragmentation type, and as always with fin-stabilized rockets accuracy was not of a high order. But as the M-13s were usually used in massed

Shunted off the road and abandoned, this is the most famous of the war rockets: the truck-mounted Katyusha. Because of the distinctive moaning sound the missiles made in flight, the Germans dubbed the weapon 'Stalin's organ'.

barrages this last mattered only little. Later versions of the M-13 used a form of efflux diversion to introduce more spin for increased accuracy, but this measure reduced the range slightly. As mentioned above, the first launcher type used 16 rails and was known as the **BM-13-16**, but when supplies of Lend-Lease trucks became available they too were used as Katyusha carriers. Several types of truck, including Studebakers, Fords, Chevrolets and Internationals were so used, along with STZ-5 artillery tractors and other vehicles. These BM-13-16 launchers had no traverse and only limited elevation, and were laid by pointing the carrier vehicle towards the target. Some carrier vehicles used steel shutters to protect the cab and crew during the launching sequence.

As the war progressed more types of M-13 warhead were introduced, including armour-piercing to break up tank formations, flare for night illumination, incendiary and signal. One variation was the **M-13-DD**, which used two

rocket motors burning together at launch to produce a possible range of 11800 m (12,905 yards), and this rocket was launched from the upper rails of the launcher only. The M-13-DD had the greatest range of all solid-propellant artillery rockets in World War II.

After 1945 the M-13 rocket batteries remained in Red Army use right up to 1980, when they were finally replaced

by later models. The M-13 is still in service with many countries, although modern trucks are now used as carriers in place of the old war-time models. In fact the development life of the basic M-13 is still not over, for the Chinese are now using the rocket as a form of minelet-laying device known as the **Type 74**.

Specification
M-13
Dimensions: length 1.41 m (55.9 in); body diameter 132 mm (5.2 in)
Weights: overall 42.5 kg (93.7 lb); propellant 7.2 kg (15.87 lb); explosive 4.9 kg (10.8 lb)
Performance: initial velocity 355 m (1,165 ft) per second; range 8500 m (9,295 yards)

The most widely used rocket of the war, the Russian M-13 132-mm weapon came as a disagreeable surprise to German troops on the Smolensk front in July 1941. It continued to serve in the Red Army until 1980 and still equips several Russian allies today.

USSR
M-30 and M-31 300-mm rockets

The **M-30** 300-mm (11.8-in) rocket was introduced during 1942 when it was appreciated that good as the M-8 and M-13 rockets were, a heavier explosive warhead would be an advantage. The M-30 used a modified M-13 rocket motor allied to a bulbous warhead which contained 28.9 kg (63.7 lb) of explosive, which more than met the requirement though the range was limited to no more than 2800 m (3,060 yards). The first M-30s were fired from their carrying crates with the aid of a frame known as **Rama**, which was a close copy of the German method of using the Packkiste for launching from the schwere Wurfgerät. These Ramas were cumbersome devices that were laborious to set up close to the front line, and were little liked by the Red Army troops. But they did like the M-30 rocket for its powerful effects, even going to the extent of using the M-30 for ambushes against tanks or for house-to-house fighting. When used in this role the M-30 was simply aimed at the target while still in its carrying crate and fired at very close range.

By the end of 1942 a newer type of 300-mm (11.8-in) rocket was ready and this was known as the **M-31** to differentiate it from the earlier model. The M-31 had an improved rocket motor that gave a range of 4300 m (4,705 yards). This rocket could be fired from the Rama frames in the same manner as the M-30, but later Ramas could take six M-31s or M-30s in place of the original four. By March 1944 the first mobile launchers for the M-31 appeared. These could carry up to 12 M-31s (the short range of the M-30 ruled out their use with the mobile launchers), and the type was thus known as the **BM-31-12**. Early versions

Entering service in 1942, the M-30 300-mm rocket carried almost six times as much explosive as the M-13, but its heavy payload reduced its range to under 3 km (1.8 miles). The first mobile launchers were introduced in 1944.

of this launcher were carried by the ZiS-6 6×6 truck, but most wartime production examples were carried on Lend-Lease Studebaker US-6 6×6 trucks. These American trucks were fitted with steel shutters over the cab windows for protection against blast when the rockets were fired.

After 1945 the M-31 rockets did not survive for many years as they were essentially short-range weapons, and as such often suffered from counterbattery fire. But the basic M-31 did undergo some developmenmt before it was dropped. There was an **M-31-UK** which used some of the efflux gases to impart a measure of spin for increased

stabilization and hence accuracy. Range was slightly reduced, but the M-31-UK could greatly decrease the area of ground covered by a battery and thus increase the amount of explosive falling upon a point target.

The M-30 and M-31 rockets were fitted only with HE warheads. They were undoubtedly powerful projectiles, but they lacked range and for much of the war their mobility was virtually nonexistent as they had to be fired from the static Rama frames. It was not until the later stages of the war that they were provided with mobility in the form of the BM-31-12, a tardiness for which the German troops on the Eastern Front were no doubt grateful.

Specification
M-30
Dimensions: length 1.20 m (47.24 in); body diameter 300 mm (11.8 in)
Weights: overall 72 kg (158.7 lb); propellant 7.2 kg (15.87 lb); explosive 28.9 kg (63.7 lb)
Performance: initial velocity not known

Specification
M-31
Dimensions: length 1.76 m (69.3 in); body diameter 300 mm (11.8 in)
Weights: overall 91.5 kg (201.7 lb); propellant 11.2 kg (24.7 kg); explosive 28.9 kg (63.7 lb)
Performance: initial velocity 255 m (836 ft) per second

Rocket, HE, 4.5-in, M8

When the USA entered the war in 1941, the US forces had no rockets at all in service or in prospect, but with typical energy the Americans used their considerable industrial potential and technical knowledge to remedy this deficit with great speed. In what seemed like no time at all they had erected huge facilities for producing rocket propellants of all kinds and were busy designing and producing rockets for all purposes. One of these rockets was a relatively straightforward fin-stabilized weapon known initially as the **T12** but later standardized as the **Rocket, HE, 4.5-in, M8**. This nose-fused 114.3-mm (4.5-in) rocket was destined to be fabricated in larger numbers than any other World War II artillery rocket, no fewer than 2,537,000 being produced by the time the war ended. The **M8A1** and **M8A2** were slight variations of the M8 and were used in the same manner: the former had a strengthened motor body and the latter had a smaller warhead with thicker walls. The **M8A3** was an M8A2 with modified fins.

Being only fin-stabilized, the M8 was inherently inaccurate and was accordingly used not for the engagement of point targets but for the saturation of large areas with fire. Thus it was used extensively for the mass bombardment of target areas before amphibious landings or as a supplement to massed artillery bombardments. Even at short ranges its accuracy was erratic, so nearly all the launchers used with the M8 were multiple types. Typical of these was the **T27 Multiple Rocket Launcher** which fired eight M8 rockets and was carried on the back of a GMC or Studebaker 2½-ton truck. There were several variations of this launcher, one (the **T27E2**) with capacity for up to 24 rockets. The **T34** or **Calliope** was a large launcher carried over the turret of an M4 Sherman

medium tank. The Calliope had no fewer than 60 launching tubes and was constructed from plywood as it was a one-shot weapon for use against strongpoints. After firing or in an emergency the whole device could be jettisoned. The **T44** was even larger than the Calliope as it had 120 launcher tubes, and was designed for installation in the cargo area of a DUKW or LVT amphibious vehicle. This was a simple area-saturation launcher as there was no method of varying elevation or traverse. A similar device known as the **Scorpion** but mounting 144 launchers was used on DUKWs in the Pacific theatre. The **T45** was a twin 14-barrel launcher that could be fitted to the sides of various vehicles, including light trucks. Yet another launcher that fired the M8 rocket was the **M12** which was a single-shot 'bunker-buster' along the lines of the British LILO.

Despite the large-scale use of the M8, its inaccuracy was such that it was considered inadequate as an artillery rocket. Using knowledge gained from trials with captured German rockets, the Americans developed a 114.3-mm (4.5-in) spin-stabilized rocket known as the **M16**, along with a multiple launcher known as the **T66** which could fire 24 rockets in two seconds. This combination arrived on the battlefronts somewhat late in the war and was used during only one engagement in Germany before the end of the war in Europe. It was not used in the Pacific theatre, but was retained on the books for some years after 1945.

Right: An unusual mounting for the M8 – a captured German half-track carries the 60-tube launcher more commonly fitted to tanks. A fin-stabilized projectile, the M8 was erratic in flight and needed to be fired in quantity to guarantee a hit.

When America entered the war the US Army had no rockets in service and none on the drawing board, but after a little experimentation the M8

4.5-in rocket was put into production and proved highly successful, over 2½ million being manufactured by 1945.

Specification
Rocket, HE, 4.5-in, M8
Dimensions: length 838 mm (33 in); body diameter 114.3 mm (4.5 in)
Weights: overall 17.5 kg (38.5 lb); propellant 2.16 kg (4.75 lb); explosive 1.95 kg (4.3 lb)
Performance: maximum velocity 259 m (850 ft) per second; maximum range 4205 m (4,600 yards)

Left: M4 Sherman tanks sport the T-34 60-tube launcher known as Calliope. The tubes were made of plywood and could only be used a few times before disintegrating, but the launcher provided tank units with awesome close-range firepower.

Above: A gunner checks the sights of the simple T-27 eight-tube launcher, generally fitted to GMC or Studebaker 2½-ton trucks. The M8 was also fired from massive 120- or even 140-round launchers fitted to DUKW amphibious vehicles for beach assault.

2-in Rocket

During the late 1930s the need for improved defence of the United Kingdom against air attack was finally appreciated, but at the time it was thought that to produce enough anti-aircraft guns to meet immediate needs would take too long . Thus the rocket was investigated to see if it could provide a cheap and easily-manufactured alternative to the gun, and among the first designs investigated was a type known as the **2-in Rocket**. As things turned out the later 76.2-mm (3-in) rocket was to prove more promising, but at the time the smaller rocket seemed quite encouraging and work went ahead on the design with some momentum.

The 51-mm (2-in) rocket was a simple device that used a propellant known as solventless cordite or SCRK. The overall simplicity of the weapon could be seen in the fact that the earliest designs used a direct-action wind vane on the nose to arm the fuse after firing, with a self-destruct timer to destroy the weapon after it had been in flight for 4.5 seconds, by which time it would have reached a maximum height of about 1370 m (4,500 ft).

In the event the 51-mm (2-in) rocket was used mainly to arm light naval vessels and some merchant shipping. There were many and various simple naval mountings such as the basic vertical launchers that were mounted on each side of the bridge on many light vessels. These were supposed to launch their rockets as a low-flying aircraft attacked the ship. As the rockets rose they were designed to carry aloft a length of light wire that would enmesh itself in the aircraft's propellers and bring it down. The system never worked and neither did many other similar and somewhat optimistic devices. There was a high explosive version that could carry a 0.25-kg (0.56-lb) warhead, but by the time this was

ready it was appreciated that the larger 76.2-mm (3-in) rocket was much better for this role and relatively few 51-mm (2-in) rockets were produced.

One naval mounting that was used on land was the one known as the **2-in Rocket Mounting Mk II, Pillar Box** mounting. This was used during the desperate days of 1940 and 1941 to provide at least a measure of coastal anti-aircraft defence, and could launch up to 20 rockets. The rockets were arranged in two vertical rows of five on each side of a central drum housing in which the aimer operated the simple controls. This drum housing gave the

Pillar Box mounting its name. The aimer could fire all 20 of the rockets in one salvo or two salvoes of 10 rockets using electrical ignition.

Other forms of land-mounted 51-mm (2-in) rocket launchers existed and were used but only in very small numbers as temporary defensive measures. The 51-mm (2-in) rocket was really too small and light to have any great destructive effect, but the lessons learned in the design and development of these early attempts at war rockets had a good effect on later designs.

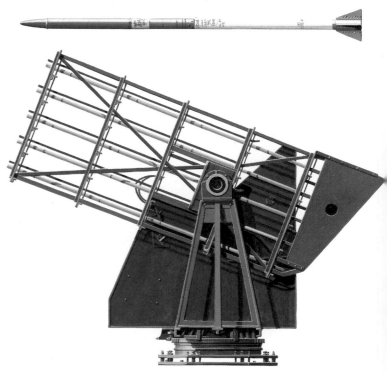

The 2-in rocket was an ingenious, if over-optimistic, anti-aircraft weapon, being designed to destroy low-flying aircraft by fouling their propellers with the long wire it left in its wake.

Specification
2-in Rocket
Dimensions: length 914.4 mm (36 in); body diameter 57 mm (2.25 in)
Weights: overall 4.88 kg (10.75 lb); warhead 0.25 kg (0.56 lb)
Performance: initial velocity 457 m (1,500 ft) per second

3-in Rocket

Design work on British artillery rockets started as early as 1934, though only on a low-priority basis, and by 1937 had reached the position where a **3-in Rocket** was proposed as an alternative to the anti-aircraft gun. Under strict security conditions, development of the new rocket went ahead with the cover name **UP** (unrotated projectile). Early firings were made at Aberporth in Wales, and by 1939 the final test firings were being made in Jamaica. These led to the establishment of the first operational battery near Cardiff in South Wales, where it was known as a 'Z' battery.

This first Z battery used a single-rail launcher known as the **Projector, 3-in, Mk 1**. It was a very simple, even crude device and it was produced for both the army and the Royal Navy, although in the event most of the Royal Navy's allocation went to the merchant navy. The rocket was a simple fin-stabilized tube containing a motor and the same SCRK cordite used on the 51-mm (2-in) rocket. These early designs were somewhat erratic in performance, and accuracy was such that huge salvoes had to be fired from all the projectors in a Z battery in order to have some chance of hitting an aircraft target. They did have their successes, but they were few and not improved until

Designed originally as an anti-aircraft system, the 3-in rocket achieved modest success as a ground weapon. However, it is better known as an air-to-ground weapon, fired from Hawker Typhoons over Normandy.

the **Projector, Rocket, 3-in, No. 2 Mk 1** came along. This used a two-rail launching system and was produced in some numbers, still firing the 76.2-mm (3-in) rocket but fitted with more sophisticated fusing systems including early attempts at proximity fusing and other electro-magnetic devices. Some of these No. 2 projectors saw action in North Africa, including port defence at Tobruk.

The next improvement in launching methods was the **Projector, Rocket, 3-in, No. 4 Mk 1** and **Mk 2**. This had no fewer than 36 launcher rails to fire nine rockets in a ripple sequence. This projector was mobile as it was carried on converted 76.2-mm (3-in) anti-aircraft platform trailers. Again some of these projectors were used in North Africa.

The largest of all the British 76.2-mm (3-in) rocket projectors was the **Projector, Rocket, 3-in, No. 6 Mk 1**, which could fire 20 rockets in four salvoes. This entered service in 1944 and was intended for use in static locations for home defence. By the time they were ready many were manned by Home Guard units as they were considered simple enough for relatively untrained users, especially when they were fired en masse by battery at easily-visible targets. In the event they were little used.

One unexpected offshoot from the anti-aircraft rocket programme was that the 76.2-mm (3-in) rocket was taken up as an aircraft weapon. Fired from short launcher rails it proved to be a devastating ground attack missile, especially against tanks, and during 1944 proved to be one of the most powerful of all anti-tank weapons when used by 'cab-rank' Hawker Typhoons over the Normandy battlefields. By the time the war ended the airborne 76.2-mm (3-in) rocket had reached a considerable state of design development and was even being used to sink U-boats.

Specification
3-in Rocket
Dimensions: length 1.93 m (76 in); body diameter 82.6 mm (3.25 in)
Weights: overall 24.5 kg (54 lb); propellant 5.76 kg (12.7 lb); warhead 1.94 kg (4.28 lb)
Performance: maximum velocity 457 m (1,500 ft) per second; service ceiling 6770 m (22,200 ft); horizontal range 3720 m (4,070 yards)

🇬🇧 UK
LILO

By 1944 the Allies were becoming accustomed to the Japanese tactic of using heavily-protected bunkers to delay Allied advances, not only on the Pacific Islands but also in the land warfare raging in South East Asia. The only effective way to demolish these formidable defensive works was by the use of heavy artillery at close ranges, but the Japanese did not always build their bunkers where such heavy weapons could get at them. The rocket was obviously a relatively portable method of dealing with such obstacles, and thus there emerged a programme known by the cover name **LILO**.

LILO was a very simple single-barrel launcher designed to fire a rocket at short range against bunker-type targets. It fired a projectile powered by the Motor, Rocket, 3-in, No. 7 Mark 1 to which two types of warhead could be fitted. Both were HE types, one weighing 17.8 kg (39.25 lb) complete and the other 35.5 kg (78.25 lb) complete. The idea was that the LILO projector could be carried to its firing location by one man, with another carrying a rocket on a suitable backpack. The projector was then set up as close to its intended target as possible and the rocket loaded into the launcher tube from the front. Open sights were used to aim the weapon, the back legs of the launcher being moved for changes in elevation. When all was ready the rocket was fired electrically, using a light 3.4-volt battery. The LILO rockets were capable of penetrating 3.05 m (10 ft) of earth plus a layer of logs, so they could normally penetrate any Japanese bunker. But the main problem was hitting the target: despite the fact that a degree of spin was imparted to the rocket as it was launched, the inherent inaccuracy of the rocket was such that to ensure a 95 per cent chance of hitting a point target distant only some 45 to 50 m (49 to 55 yards), five rockets had to be fired. This may sound uneconomic but the alternative was to bring up heavy artillery with all its attendant risks and labour.

The Americans also used a short-range rocket for the same purpose as LILO. Their device was known as the **M12 Rocket Launcher** which fired a 114.3-mm (4.5-in) rocket, and this resembled LILO in many ways apart from the fact that the first launcher tubes used were plastic and were discarded after firing. Such a system proved to be too wasteful, even for the US war economy, so a later version was developed as the **M12E1** which used a magnesium alloy tube that could be reloaded and reused. These projectors were used during the latter stages of the fighting on Okinawa when the Japanese defenders had to be blasted from their heavily-defended caves.

Specification
LILO rocket (9.53-kg/21-lb warhead)
Dimensions: length 1.238 m (48.75 in); body diameter 82.55 mm (3.25 in)
Weights: overall 17.8 kg (39.25 lb); propellant 1.93 kg (4.25 lb); explosive 1.8 kg (4 lb)
Performance: not stated

Specification
LILO rocket (27.2-kg/60-lb warhead)
Dimensions: length 1.321 m (52 in); body diameter 152 mm (6 in)
Weights: overall 35.5 kg (78.25 lb); propellant 1.93 kg (4.25 lb); explosive 6.24 kg (13.75 lb)
Performance: not stated

As the Allies drove the Japanese back towards their homeland, numerous expedients were tried to knock out the toughly-constructed bunkers that were the hallmark of Japanese positions. One such was LILO – a short-range single-shot 60-lb (27-kg) rocket.

Land Mattress

Although early development of the war rocket in the United Kingdom was initially to produce an anti-aircraft weapon, some consideration was also given to producing an artillery rocket. One early attempt at this was a design for a 127-mm (5-in) rocket which was rejected by the army but adopted by the Royal Navy for use in modified landing craft for the saturation of landing beaches and approaches by massed rocket fire. This eventually evolved as the 'Mattress', but range was limited. However, further trials revealed that the range could be improved by introducing, at launch, a degree of spin which would also improve accuracy, and this was simply achieved by using an aircraft 76.2-mm (3-in) rocket motor attached to a naval 13-kg (29-lb) warhead. This increased range to a possible 7315 m (8,000 yards), making the artillery rocket a viable proposition once more. Thus 'Mattress' became 'Land Mattress'.

The first army launchers for these new Land Mattress rockets had 32 barrels, but a later version had 30 barrels. Demonstrations of this launcher greatly impressed Canadian army staff officers, who requested a 12-launcher battery which in the event was ready for action on 1 November 1944. This battery went into action during the crossing of the River Scheldt and was a great success, to the extent that more were requested and produced. The Land Mattress launcher was limited in its elevation capabilities to between 23 and 45°, and this not only limited the maximum range to 7225 m (7,900 yards) but also limited the minimum range to 6125 m (6,700 yards). To reduce the minimum range possible, a

system of rotary spoilers over the rocket exhausts was formulated and put into use. The rotary spoiler disturbed the exhaust gases by closing off their efflux by varying amounts, and thus reducing the minimum range to 3565 m (3,900 yards).

For all the success of the Land Mattress, not many equipments were used in action before the war ended in Europe in May 1944. By that time many were only just emerging from the factories ready to be sent off to South East Asia, but their use there was very limited, as a result mainly of the weight and bulk of the projectors in the area's jungle conditions. A special 16-barrel version was accordingly developed for towing by a Jeep, but the war was over by the time it was ready for service.

In action, a single Land Mattress projector salvo could result in 50 per cent of the rockets falling in an area 215 m (235 yards) long by 219 m (240 yards) wide. The rockets were fired in ripples at 0.25-second intervals so that the entire salvo could be fired in 7.25 seconds. During the crossing of the Scheldt the first Land Mattress battery fired 1,146 rounds over a six-hour period. As each warhead payload weighed 3.18 kg (7 lb), the effects can well be imagined.

Specification
Land Mattress (rocket)
Dimensions: length 1.77 m (69.7 in)
Weights: overall 30.5 kg (67.25 lb); propellant 5 kg (11 lb); payload 3.18 kg (7 lb)
Performance: maximum velocity 335 m (1,100 ft) per second; maximum range 7225 m (7,900 yards)

Land Mattress was a curious hybrid – an army weapon constructed from an aircraft rocket motor and a 5-in naval warhead. Early models were severely restricted in performance since elevation was restricted between 23° and 45°.

Above: Loaded and ready to fire, the crews make their final checks before taking cover. Fired at a rate of four a second, half the rockets from a 32-round projector would hit a target zone 215 m (235 yards) long and 219 m (240 yards) wide.

Right: Land Mattress spent more time on the test range than in action. After much experimentation, minimum range was reduced and a light 16-round launcher was developed for jungle warfare.

Above: Loading 30.5-kg (67-lb) rockets into the 32-round launchers was an exhausting job, but to be effective rockets had to be fired in big volleys. The first Land Mattress battery fired over 1,000 rounds in six hours during the crossing of the Scheldt.

Anti-Tank Guns

The few years prior to and during World War II saw the anti-tank gun make a significant entry into the battlefield. Few realized that within a short time the recoilless rifle and guided missile would in turn come to the fore and the specialist anti-tank gun would virtually disappear.

The anti-tank gun was an important weapon during World War II, for it was the only one that could destroy a tank at ranges beyond those of the much smaller hand-held anti-tank weapons, such as the grenade or bazooka. When the war started the anti-tank gun was a small weapon, virtually a miniature version of larger field pieces. By 1945 the type had grown rapidly into large and heavy guns that sometimes dwarfed the field pieces. Their power had grown as well, for while the guns of 1939 were only able to punch their way through armour of about 25mm (1in) thickness, by 1945 they were required to have an effect on armour about 100mm (3.94in) in thickness, and to do so at ranges well in excess of those prevalent in 1939. At the beginning of the war 400m (440yd) was considered to be the top limit to an anti-tank gun's capabilities but by 1945 ranges of 2000m (2,190yd) or more were not uncommon.

Along with the increase in calibre, size, weight and performance went a corresponding escalation in projectile performance. The gun is really only the delivery system for the projectile, which is the anti-tank gunner's weapon, and the degree of development to which the anti-tank projectile was subjected to

Moving anti-tank guns around the battlefield was hard work. This 17-pounder belongs to the British Eighth Army in Italy and is being hauled into place to target enemy pillboxes.

between 1939 and 1945 can only be sketched in this section. Suffice it to say that the steel shot of 1939 had given way to the tungsten core of 1945, and even the very shape of the projectile had changed radically. The hollow- or shaped-charge projectile was also introduced to bring chemical energy into the gun-versus-armour conflict.

The war waged by the anti-tank gun was a specialized one

with a single objective: the destruction of tanks. The role of the anti-tank gunner was to serve the gun, to aim it and to fire it at the right moment, but with many of the guns mentioned here this was far from easy. All too often the target had to be allowed to approach very close, requiring of the gun crew nerve, courage and good training, so the role of the gunner must not be forgotten under the weights of fact and

detail. It is impossible to define exactly which gun was best at any period, for even the finest gun has to have a man or crew to use it, and on many occasions a good man or crew could provide results far better than those of others using theoretically better weapons. Thus a British 6-pounder could often have more influence on a battle than a German '88', for it was the man that mattered in the end, not the weapon.

Ordnance, Q.F., 2 pdr

The 2-pdr anti-tank gun (or more formally the **Ordnance, Q.F., 2 pdr**) is one of those unfortunate weapons that has been given a bad reputation for no real reason other than it had to be used at a time when it was no longer a viable weapon. In its day it was as good as, if not better, than any contemporary design, but the rapid increases in tank armour thicknesses during the late 1930s rendered it obsolete just at a time when it was being placed into widespread service.

The 2-pdr had its origins in a British staff requirement dated 1934. Much of the original development was carried out by Vickers-Armstrongs, and the first guns and carriages were produced for commercial sales. Some went to Spain, but the main recipient was the British army which received its first examples during 1938. Further development was required until the full army specification could be met and it was not until 1939 that the most commonly encountered carriage (the Carriage, 2 pdr, Mk III) was issued.

Compared with many other designs then in existence the 2-pdr was a complex piece of ordnance and it was almost twice as heavy as any other gun in its class. The main reason for this weight was the carriage which, in action, rested on a low tripod carriage that provided the gun with 360° traverse. A high shield was provided for the gun crew and there was provision for an ammunition chest to be carried on the back of the gun shield. The philosophy behind the design differed from contemporary thought as well. Many European armies intended the anti-tank gun to be used in a mobile attacking role, but the 2-pdr was intended for use in static defensive positions. The type was also manned by specialist anti-tank personnel from the Royal Artillery.

The events of 1940 showed the 2-pdr to be at best obsolescent, and the BEF had to leave the bulk of its 2-pdr guns behind at Dunkirk. The gun lacked the power to punch through the thick armour of most of the German tanks, and the effective range was too short for tactical comfort; the projectiles were too light to cause damage at ranges outside the machine-gun range of the target tanks, and many gun crews were thus decimated before they could fire a useful shot. But in the United Kingdom the production facilities to produce any modern form of anti-tank gun for the army that was almost devoid of any form of defence against tanks was quite simply not available. Industry had therefore to carry on producing the 2-pdr at a time when it was realized that it was no longer an effective weapon. The results of this had to be borne during the

Right: A drill-book photograph of a 2-pdr gun and crew in action with the gun about to be loaded. Note that the ammunition is being passed from a box to the rear as the box on the gun shield was for emergencies only.

North African campaigns of 1941 and 1942, when the 2-pdr proved to be almost useless against the Afrika Korps, to the extent that the 25-pdr field piece had to be used for anti-tank work in its place. All manner of remedies to make the 2-pdr more successful were tried, one measure being the placement of the gun on the back of an open truck to provide a mobile platform, and another the development of the Littlejohn Adaptor, a squeeze-bore device attached to the muzzle and firing special skirted projectiles to improve projectile performance. Neither of these measures saw much use, and after 1942 the 2-pdr was withdrawn from use and passed to infantry units for their anti-tank defences. The type did not remain in use for long in that role, but in the Far East the 2-pdr remained in service until 1945, for there the target tanks were lighter and the gun could still cope with them.

Specification
Ordnance, Q.F., 2 pdr
Calibre: 40 mm (1.575 in)
Length of piece: 2.0815 m (6 ft 9.9 in)
Length of rifling: 1.6723 m (5 ft 5.84 in)
Weight: complete 831.6 kg (1,848 lb)
Traverse: 360°
Elevation: −13° to +15°
Muzzle velocity: AP 792 m (2,626 ft) per second
Maximum effective range: 548 m (600 yards)
Projectile weight: 1.08 kg (2.375 lb)
Armour penetration: 53 mm (2.08 in) at 455 m (500 yards)

2-pdr gun crews undergo training during a chemical warfare exercise. The gun in the foreground shows the ammunition box carried on each

gun, but later marks were able to remove the road wheels to aid concealment.

A 2-pdr ready to be towed, usually by a small truck or Jeep. The 2-pdr was a rather complex little weapon with a tripod carriage and was too heavy for its tactical role when compared with other designs of the time. By 1941 it was rendered almost useless by increases in enemy tank armour, but was passed to infantry units for their anti-tank defences, and was used in the Far East.

 UK

Ordnance, Q.F., 6 pdr

British weapon planners had foreseen the need for an anti-tank gun more powerful than the 2-pdr as early as April 1938, but it took time to develop and then to produce the new gun. During late 1940 production was delayed as 2-pdr guns occupied the production lines, so that it was not until late 1941 that the new gun reached the troops. This new gun had a calibre of 57 mm (2.244 in) and fired a projectile weighing about 6 lb (2.72 kg) so the

new gun was known as the **6-pdr**.

By the time the 6-pdr reached the troops it was sorely needed, and once in action it proved to be effective against the enemy tanks then in use. Compared with the 2-pdr the 6-pdr was much more conventional, and used a split-trail carriage that gave a useful 90° traverse. There were two main variants, the **Ordnance, Q.F., 6 pdr Mk II** and **Ordnance, Q.F., Mk IV**; the **Ordnance, Q.F., 6 pdr Mk I** was

used for training only, and the Mks III and V were tank guns. The main difference between the Mks II and IV was barrel length, that of the Mk IV being slightly longer. Some slight carriage variations were produced but the most drastic was the Carriage, Q.F., 6 pdr, Mk III, which was developed for use by airborne units. This was narrower than the norm and the trail legs could be shortened for stowage in gliders; numbers of these special conversions

were used at Arnhem.

The 6-pdr provided some sterling service in North Africa, but once the Tiger tank appeared on the scene it was realized that the day of the 6-pdr was almost over, for the 2.85-kg (6.28-lb) projectile was unable to penetrate the thick frontal armour of the Tiger and only a lucky shot to the side could be effective. So the 6-pdr was gradually withdrawn from Royal Artillery use from 1943 onwards. They were issued

Although its operational career as a specialist anti-tank gun was relatively short (from 1941 to 1943 at the most), the 6-pdr went on to be a useful infantry anti-tank and support weapon. It was copied by the Americans as the 57-mm Antitank Gun M1 and was used by nearly all the Allied armies at some time or another.

instead to infantry anti-tank companies and with the infantry the 6-pdr saw out the war. Many were supplied to the Red Army.

The Soviets were not the only recipients of the 6-pdr, for the type was adopted by the Americans also. When the Americans realized that they too would need a heavier anti-tank gun than their 37-mm (1.46-in) M1 they saw that the easiest way to produce something was to copy the 6-pdr, and in early 1941 they obtained a set of drawings from the British and adapted them to suit their own production methods. The result was the **57-mm Antitank Gun M1**. At first the American carriage had a handwheel traverse in place of the shoulder pad of the British original, but in time the Americans adopted the shoulder pad also and in this form the M1A2 was used until the war ended in

1945. But it was as a weapon mounted on a self-propelled carriage that the American gun was most important. Large numbers of M1 guns were produced for mounting on half-tracks and in this form the American guns were widely used by the British army and many other Allied forces as well as by the US army.

The 6-pdr may have been outclassed by heavy tanks such as the Tiger, but against nearly all other German tanks it proved to be effective enough. It was also a relatively light and handy weapon and served on with many armies for long after 1945.

Specification
Ordnance, Q.F., 6 pdr, Mk IV
Calibre: 57 mm (2.244 in)
Length of piece: 2.565 m (6 ft 8.95 in)
Length of rifling: 2.392 m (7 ft 10.18 in)

Weight: complete 1112 kg (2,471 lb)
Traverse: 90°
Elevation: −5° to +15°
Muzzle velocity: 900 m (2,700 ft) per second
Projectile weight: 2.85 kg (6.28 lb)
Armour penetration: 68.6 mm (2.7 in) at 915 m (1,000 yards)

31 May 1942, and a truck-mounted 6-pdr goes into action near Tobruk. Within a month Rommel would have taken the town, and at the same time forced the 8th Army back towards Mersa Matruh and El Alamein.

UK
Ordnance, Q.F., 17 pdr

By 1941 the rapid increase in the armour protection of tanks was being forecast to the extent where it was realized that not even the 6-pdr would be able to cope. To deal with the expected armour increases it was decided to produce the next generation of anti-tank guns with a calibre of 3 in (76.2 mm) to fire a projectile weighing no less than 17 lb (7.65 kg). It was realized that the resultant gun would be a fair-sized piece of artillery but at the time there seemed to be no other option open, and the development of the gun proceeded with haste.

The first guns, soon known as the **Ordnance, Q.F., 17 pdr** or **17-pdr**, were made as early as August 1942 but these guns were prototypes only and getting the gun into full production took more time. This was to have dramatic results for from North Africa came news that the first consignment of Tiger tanks was expected in the theatre in the very near future. At that time some guns were ready but they had no carriages. To get some form of heavy anti-tank weapon into the hands of the troops it was decided to fly 100 guns to North

Africa, where they were hastily fitted onto 25-pdr field gun carriages to produce a hybrid known as the **17/25-pdr**. The conversions were made just in time, for a few weeks later the first Tigers appeared and the 17/25-pdr was on hand to tackle them. These 17/25-pdr guns served until 'proper' 17-pdr guns were to hand during the early stages of the Italian campaign in 1943.

When the 17-pdr guns arrived they were indeed a fair-sized weapon but the overall design was low and not too cumbersome. The carriage had long and angled split trails and a large double-thickness armoured shield was fitted. The gun was proportionately long, and was fitted with a muzzle brake and a large and heavy vertical block breech mechanism. To handle the gun a detachment of at least 7 men was required, and more were needed if any man-handling was necessary. But in mitigation of this factor the gun proved capable of firing a projectile that could penetrate any enemy tank at long ranges and the rate of fire was such that 10 rounds per minute were not uncommon.

By 1945 the 17-pdr was the standard anti-tank gun of the Royal Artillery anti-tank batteries and many had been handed on to Allied armed forces. The 17-pdr proved to be the last of the British Army's conventional anti-tank guns (a 32-pdr with a calibre of 94 mm/3.7 in was proposed but a 120-mm/4.72-in recoilless gun was selected instead), and many served on until the 1950s with the British army. The gun appears in the inventories of many current armed forces. Various types of 17-pdr tank guns were produced as well.

Specification
Ordnance, Q.F., 17 pdr
Calibre: 76.2 mm (3 in)
Length of piece: 4.4425 m (14 ft 6.96 in)
Length of rifling: 3.562 m (11 ft 8.25 in)
Weight: in action 2923 kg (6,444 lb)
Traverse: 60°
Elevation: −6° to +16.5°
Muzzle velocity: 950 m (2,900 ft) per second
Projectile weight: 7.65 kg (17 lb)

By September 1944 the 17-pdr had proved an extremely effective weapon, and in the 8th Army's assault on the Gothic line was well to the fore to deal with German heavy armour.

Armour penetration: 130 mm (5.12 in) at 915 m (1,000 yards)

First introduced into service in small numbers in late 1942, the 17-pdr went on to be one of the most

powerful of all the Allied anti-tank guns. Although rather heavy and awkward to move, the 17-pdr had a calibre of 3 in (76.2 mm) and could penetrate up to 130 mm of armour at about 1000 m (1094 yards). It was also used on occasion as a field gun firing high explosive shells.

Skoda 47-mm kanon P.U.V. vz 36 anti-tank gun

The Czech firm of Skoda, based at Pilsen, was one of the first European armaments manufacturers to turn its attention to the production of specialized anti-tank guns. All through the 1920s Skoda's technicians and designers carried out a long chain of experiments and design studies to formulate a viable anti-tank gun, and in 1934 the company produced a gun with a calibre of 37 mm (1.46 in). For various reasons this weapon was not widely adopted (it was generally felt that something heavier would be needed) and in 1936 there appeared the **Skoda 47-mm kanon P.U.V. vz 36** (vz for *vzor*, or model). The vz 36 had a calibre of 47 mm (1.85 in) and was immediately ordered into production by the Czech army.

In its day the vz 36 was one of the most powerful and hardest-hitting of all the contemporary European anti-tank guns. It fired a relatively heavy projectile, weighing 1.65 kg (3.6 lb), and this projectile could penetrate any tank then in service at ranges of up to 640 m (700 yards) at a time when most similar guns were confined to targets no more than 185 to 275 m (200 to 300 yards) distant. But despite this power the vz 36 appeared a rather clumsy design. It had anachronistic spoked wheels and a very long trail which split to form two legs when in the firing position. The crew was protected by a shield that had over the wheels flaps that were folded out in action, but an oddity was that the upper rim of the shield was finished off as an asymmetric curved line to aid concealment, the wavy line breaking up the outline. The gun had a prominent recoil cylinder over the barrel and another recognition feature was the unusual single-baffle muzzle brake.

Production for the Czech army proceeded at a high priority, and a few guns were exported to Yugoslavia at one point. In service the vz 36 was issued to the specialist anti-tank com-

An illustration from the Skoda brochure that advertised their 47-mm (1.85 mm) Model 1936 anti-tank gun for possible sales outside Czechoslovakia. The gun is here being towed by the gun crew using drag ropes.

panies of the Czech army, but was found to be a bit of a handful for the infantry anti-tank units, for whom a developed version of the earlier 37-mm (1.46-in) gun was placed in production. This became the **kanon P.U.V. vz 37**, and although this gun followed the same general lines as the larger 47-mm (1.85-in) model it was recognizable by the use of more modern steel wheels with rubber tyres.

The vz 36 was destined never to fire a shot for its Czech masters, for the Munich Agreement of 1938 allowed the Germans to take over the Czech Sudetenland defences without a shot being fired. This allowed the Germans to impress large numbers of a very special version of the vz 36 that had been developed for use in static fortifications, but large numbers of the wheeled vz 36 fell into German hands during the following year when Germany took over control of the rest of Czechoslovakia. The vz 36 then became the **4.7-cm Pak 36(t)** and was eagerly added to the German gun parks. The Czech gun became a virtual standard weapon with the German army and remained in use with some of their second-line units until the end of the war in 1945. It was mounted on several types of tracked chassis to become the armament of several German Panzerjäger (tank hunters) and proved itself to be a very viable anti-armour weapon. The vz 37s did not remain in German service long after 1941.

Specification
Kanon P.U.V. vz 36
Calibre: 47 mm (1.85 in)
Length of barrel: 2.04 m (6 ft 8 in)

German soldiers manhandle their 4.7-cm Pak 36(t) during training prior to the invasion of France in 1940. The soldiers are wearing drag-rope slings for towing the gun, and a full gun crew would be at least four men. A version of this gun was produced for use in fortifications.

Weight: travelling 605 kg (1,334 lb) and in action 590 kg (1,300 lb)
Traverse: 50°
Elevation: −8° to +26°
Muzzle velocity: AP 775 m (2,543 ft) per second
Maximum range: 4000 m (4,375 yards)
Projectile weight: AP 1.64 kg (3.6 lb) and HE 1.5 kg (3.3 lb)
Armour penetration: 51 mm (2 in) at 640 m (700 yards)

The Czech 47-mm Model 1936 looked archaic, mainly because of the small spoked wheels and the long trails, but the gun was one of the most powerful of its day. Many were taken over by the German army who used the type in large numbers, often mounted on special tank-destroyer self-propelled carriages.

3.7-cm Pak 35/36

The origins of the gun that was to become the **3.7-cm Pak 35/36** (Pak for *Panzerabwehrkanone*, or anti-tank gun) can be traced back to 1925 when Rheinmetall began actively to design and develop an anti-tank gun for the German army. Production began in 1928, and as the German army was at that time still largely horse-oriented the gun was fitted with spoked wheels

for horse traction. It was a very modern gun design for the period and used a well-sloped shield, tubular split-trail legs and a long slender barrel. At first production was relatively limited, but once the NSDAP came to power in 1933 production was greatly accelerated. In 1934 there appeared the first version with steel wheels and pneumatic tyres suitable for vehicle traction,

and the designation **3.7-cm Pak 35/36** was assigned in 1936.

It was in 1936 that the Pak 35/36 first saw action, during the Spanish Civil War where the little gun proved eminently suited against the relatively light armoured vehicles used during the conflict. It also proved successful in 1939 against the lightly-armed Poles, but in 1940 the Pak gun crews encoun-

tered the more heavily armoured French and British tanks and had the unfortunate experience of seeing their carefully-aimed armour-piercing projectiles bouncing off the hulls of attacking tanks. The truth was that by 1940 the Pak 35/36 had had its day. It was no longer powerful enough to penetrate the armour of the more modern tanks, and larger calibre weapons had to

ake its place. But these latter could not be produced quickly enough to prevent the 37-mm (1.46-in) guns from having to be rushed to action during the German invasion of the Soviet Union (Operation 'Barbarossa') in 1941; against the T-34/76 tank they again proved to be of no use at all. Some attempts were made to prolong the service life of the gun by firing large stick bombs that fitted over the muzzle but these weapons, although effective, were essentially close-range missiles of dubious combat worth. Consequently the Pak 35/36 was passed to second-line and garrison units, and to some training schools, so the type was still in limited service in 1945. Many carriages were later converted to take 75-mm (2.95-in) barrels to convert them to infantry support guns.

The Pak 35/36 was widely exported before 1939, and the design was copied in Japan as the **Type 97**. Other recipient nations were Italy (**Cannone contracarro da 37/45**), the Netherlands (**37-mm Rheinmetall**) and the Soviet Union, where the Pak 35/36 was known as the **M30**, was widely copied and formed the basis for a whole family of 37-mm (1.46-in) and 45-mm (1.77-in) anti-tank guns that served on for many years after 1945 (some were still in service in Soviet-influenced nations as late as the 1970s). The design was also copied in the United States to produce the **Antitank Gun M3**, although only the concept was copied as the M3 had many detail differences from the German original.

At one point the Germans produced a special version of the Pak 35/36 for paradropping.

Above: The original 3.7-cm Pak 35/36 produced during the late 1920s had spoked wheels for horse traction, but by the mid-1930s these had been replaced by steel disc wheels for motor traction. It was a light and low gun that was at first issued to all arms of the Wehrmacht.

Right: The German 3.7-cm Pak 35/36, seen here on exercises prior to 1939. The Pak 35/36 was a Rheinmetall design produced during the 1920s; at the time it had a great influence on anti-tank gun design elsewhere.

Specification
3.7-cm Pak 35/36
Calibre: 37 mm (1.46 in)
Length of gun: 1,665 m (5 ft 5.5 in)
Length of rifling: 1.308 m (4 ft 3.5in)
Weight: travelling 440 kg (970 lb) and in action 328 kg (723 lb)
Traverse: 59°
Elevation: −8° to +25°
Muzzle velocity: AP 760 m (2,495 ft) per second

Maximum range: 7000 m (7,655 yards)
Projectile weight: AP 0.354 kg (0.78 lb) or HE 0.625 kg (1.38 lb)
Armour penetration: 38 mm (1.48 in) at 30° at 365 m (400 yards)

5-cm Pak 38

It has been mentioned in the entry relating to the 3.7-cm Pak 35/36 that by 1940 the 37-mm anti-tank gun was of very limited value against the armour of tanks then in service. Fortunately for the German army this had been foreseen as early as 1937, and by 1938 Rheinmetall-Börsig had developed and produced a new gun with a calibre of 50 mm (1.97 in). By 1939 the gun was ready for production, but it was not until mid-summer 1940 that the first examples reached the troops. By then the new gun, designated the **5-cm Pak 38**, was too late to take much part in any European campaign and it was not until 1941 that the new gun was able to see action during a major campaign.

That campaign was the invasion of the Soviet Union, and by that time the new gun had been supplied with a new type of tungsten-cored ammunition known as AP40. This ammunition was developed from captured Czech and Polish ammunition, and was adopted because the dense tungsten core of the new projectiles offered a considerable increase in armour penetration. This was just as well, for when the Soviet T-34/76 appeared on the battlefields the Pak 38 firing AP40 ammunition proved to be the only gun/projectile combination capable of penetrating the Soviet tank's thick hide. But the numbers of Pak 38s in the field were limited, the gun could not be everywhere and it was some time before extemporized conversions of old French 75-mm (2.95-in) guns could be hurried up to fill the many gaps in the anti-tank defence lines. After that the 50-mm (1.97-in) gun proved good

Soviet troops examine a captured Pak 38 early in the war. With tungsten-cored shot, the 5-cm weapon was the only German anti-tank gun capable of knocking out the Soviet T-34 tank. The gun was easily handled due to extensive use of light alloys in the manufacture of the carriage.

The 5-cm Pak 38 was a light and low weapon that was easy to move and conceal. For manhandling it had a dolly wheel under the trail spades that was removed in action. In 1941 it was the only German anti-tank gun that could knock out the Soviet T-34, but it had to use tungsten-cored ammunition. It was still in use in 1945.

enough to remain in use for the rest of the war, although it was largely replaced by heavier-calibre weapons.

The Pak 38 was a well-designed gun with a curved shield, steel wheels and a tubular split-trail carriage that locked out the torsion bar suspension when the trail legs were spread. Light alloys were used throughout the construction of the carriage, which made it easy to handle, and a small dolly wheel was mounted under the trail legs for manhandling. The long barrel was fitted with a muzzle brake.

The Pak 38 was one of the German army's standard anti-tank guns and was further developed at one stage to take an automatic ammunition feed. This enabled it to be used as a heavy aircraft weapon, and at one point this was fitted to a variant of the Messerschmitt Me 262 jet fighter. Later this same weapon was further adapted to be used as a ground-mounted anti-aircraft gun but that was late in the war and none appear actually to have been produced. There was also a tank gun equivalent of the Pak 38 that was produced in a number of models, so many

Awaiting a Soviet tank assault, the dug-in Pak 38 presented a very small target. Superseded in production by the larger Pak 40 of 7.5-cm calibre, the Pak 38 remained in Wehrmacht service until the end of the war, remaining reasonably effective.

in fact that large numbers ended up as beach defence guns in the Atlantic Wall. The Pak 38 was also mounted on a number of tracked Panzerjäger carriages. At one point so many had been captured by the British army that they were reconditioned and stockpiled against some future contingency that never arose.

Specification
5-cm Pak 38
Calibre: 50 mm (1.97 in)
Length of piece: 3.187 m (10 ft 5.5 in)
Length of rifling: 2.381 m (7 ft 9.7 in)
Weight: travelling 1062 kg (2,341 lb) and in action 1000 kg (2,205 lb)
Traverse: 65°
Elevation: −8° to +27°
Muzzle velocity: AP 835 m (2,903 ft) per

second, AP40 1180 m (3,870 ft) per second and HE 550 m (1,805 ft) per second
Maximum range: HE 2650 m (2,900 yards)

Projectile weight: AP 2.06 kg (4.54 lb), AP40 0.925 kg (2.04 lb) and HE 1.82 kg (4 lb)
Armour penetration: AP40 101 mm (3.98 m) at 740 m (820 yards)

GERMANY

7.5-cm Pak 40

By 1939 intimations regarding the next generation of Soviet tanks were filtering back to the German war planner staffs in Berlin. Although the new 50-mm (1.97-in) Pak 38 gun had yet to reach the troops, it was felt that something heavier was going to be needed to counter the armour belts of the new Soviet tanks, and consequently Rheinmetall-Borsig was asked to produce a new design. In basic terms what Rheinmetall did was to scale up the Pak 38 design to the larger calibre of 75 mm (2.95 in). The result was adopted in 1940 as the **7.5-cm Pak 40**, but it was not until late in the following year that the first examples reached the hard-pressed troops on the Eastern Front.

In appearance the Pak 40 resembled its predecessor, but there were many differences apart from the scale. The basic layout of the 50-mm (1.97-in) gun was retained but this time the expected shortages of many raw materials and especially light alloys (which had been earmarked for the Luftwaffe production requirements) were becoming apparent, so the Pak 40 was constructed mainly from various forms of steel and was proportionately much heavier than the smaller gun. To simplify and speed production the shield was formed from flat instead of curved plates, and there were several other such alterations. The result was an excellent gun, well capable of tackling

virtually any Allied tank and encountered on all fronts.

The Pak 40 was destined to remain in production until the end of the war in 1945. It had a tank gun equivalent that was progressively developed, but the Pak 40 itself remained in service virtually unchanged. A version intended for use as an aircraft weapon was developed, and the carriage was even adapted at one stage to allow short 75-mm (2.95-in) barrels to be fitted to produce a form of infantry/anti-tank gun for use by infantry formations. The gun itself was even placed on a 105-mm (4.14-in) howitzer carriage to form a light field artillery piece, though another approach was to use the Pak 40 itself as a field gun, and by 1945 there were several artillery formations using this gun as the **7.5-cm FK 40** (FK for *Feldkanone*, or field gun).

But it was as an anti-tank gun that the Pak 40 was most important. Many German gunners rated it their best all-round weapon, and many Allied tank crews had occasion to agree with them. The Pak 40 fired a wide range of ammunition, varying from the straightforward solid armour-piercing shot to the tungsten-cored AP40. Also available were high explosive shells that carried enough payload to make the type a useful field artillery piece, and various forms of hollow-charge projectile. A measure of the efficiency of this gun can be seen in the range/armour

penetration figure that at 2000 m (2,190 yards) an AP40 projectile could penetrate no less than 98 mm (3.86 in) of armour plate; and at combat range of the order of 500 m (550 yards) this figure increased to 154 mm (6.06 in).

Specification
7.5 cm Pak 40
Calibre: 75 mm (2.95 in)
Length of piece: 3.7 m (12 ft 1.7 in)
Length of rifling: 2.461 m (8 ft)
Weight: travelling 1500 kg (3,307 lb)

and in action 1425 kg (3,141.5 lb)
Traverse: 45°
Elevation: −5° to +22°
Muzzle velocity: AP 750 m (2,460 ft) per second, AP40 930 m (3,050 ft) per second and HE 550 m (1,805 ft) per second
Maximum range: HE 7680 m (8,400 yards)
Projectile weight: AP 6.8 kg (15 lb), AP40 4.1 kg (9.04 lb) and HE 5.74 kg (12.65 lb)
Armour penetration: 98 mm (3.86 in) at 2000 m (2,190 yards)

Taper-bore anti-tank guns

The German taper-bore guns were an odd off-shoot from the main avenue of anti-tank development that, although successful, foundered for the simple fact that the German war economy could not afford the raw materials required to produce them. Three guns were produced and issued for service, and all relied on what is commonly known as the Gerlich principle. In simple terms this involved the use of a small projectile core made from tungsten, a hard and very dense metal ideal for punching a way through armour plating. In order to provide this tungsten core with the maximum punch the Gerlich system involved the use of guns with calibres that tapered downwards in size from the breech to the muzzle. The special projectiles involved used flanged or 'skirted' forms that allowed the flanges to fold back as the bore narrowed. This had the advantage of increasing the emergent velocity of the projectile, enabling it to travel farther and to hit the target harder. The principle was attractive to the German ordnance designers who adapted it for the anti-tank role, but the principle had some disadvantages: to ensure the maximum power of the gun expensive and relatively rare tungsten had to be used for the projectile core, and the guns themselves were costly to produce.

The first of the taper-bore guns to enter service was the **2.8-cm schwere Panzerbüchse 41 (2.8-cm sPzB 41)**, which was really little more than a heavy anti-tank rifle, with a bore that tapered from 28 mm (1.1 in) at the breech to 20 mm (0.787 in) at the muzzle. It used a light carriage, but an even lighter version of the carriage was produced for the German airborne formations. Both types were still in use at the end of the war.

Second of the taper-bore guns was the **4.2-cm leichte Panzerabwehrkanone 41 (4.2-cm lePak 41**, or light anti-tank gun 41). This used the carriage of the 3.7-cm Pak 35/36 but the ordnance was tapered from 40.3 mm (1.586 mm) at the start to 29.4 mm (1.157 in) at the muzzle. These guns were issued to German airborne units.

Largest of the trio was the **7.5-cm Pak 41**. This was a very powerful and advanced gun in which the bore decreased from 75 mm (2.95 in) to 55 mm (2.16 in). At one time this gun showed so much promise that it almost took over from the 7.5-cm Pak 40 as the standard German anti-tank gun, but despite having a better armour-piercing performance it was passed over because of the German tungsten shortage. Tungsten was normally used for the machine tools to produce more weapons, but the raw materials had to be brought into Germany by blockade runners and when these were repeatedly intercepted on the high seas the supplies dwindled. It was a choice between anti-tank guns and machine tools, and the result had to be the machine tools. Thus production of the taper-bore guns ceased. Only 150 Pak 41s were made, and once their

ammunition had been expended they passed from use. The same applied to the other two guns, though the sPzB 41 was still in use in 1945 as its small projectiles made few demands on available stocks.

Specification
2.8-cm sPzB 41
Starting calibre: 28 mm (1.1 in)
Emergent calibre: 20 mm (0.787 in)
Length of barrel: 1.7 m (5 ft 7 in)
Weight: in action 223 kg (492 lb)
Traverse: 90°
Elevation: −5° to +45°
Muzzle velocity: AP 1400 m (4,593 ft) per second
Projectile weight: AP 0.124 kg (0.27 lb)
Armour penetration: 56 mm (2.205 in) at 365 m (400 yards)

4.2-cm lePak 41
Starting calibre: 40.3 mm (1.586 in)
Emergent calibre: 29.4 mm (1.157 in)
Length of barrel: 2.25 m (7 ft 4.6 in)
Weight: in action 560 kg (1,234.5 lb)
Traverse: 60°
Elevation: −8° to +25°
Muzzle velocity: 1265 m (4,150 ft) per second
Projectile weight: AP 0.336 kg (0.74 lb)
Armour penetration: 72 mm (2.835 in) at 455 m (500 yards)

7.5-cm Pak 41
Starting calibre: 75 mm (2.95 in)
Emergent calibre: 55 mm (2.16 in)
Length of barrel: 4.32 m (14 ft 2 in)
Weight: in action 1390 kg (3,064 lb)
Traverse: 60°
Elevation: −10° to +18°
Muzzle velocity: AP 1230 m (4,035 ft) per second
Projectile weight: AP 2.5 kg (5.51 lb)
Armour penetration: 171 mm (6.73 in) at 455 m (500 yards)

Above: The 2.8-cm schwere Panzerbüchse 41 was the smallest of the German taper-bore guns, and was produced in two forms: one had large road wheels while a special airborne version, shown here, had small wheels and a light tubular alloy carriage. In this form it was used by Luftwaffe Fallschirmjäger units.

Below: A 2.8-cm schwere Panzerbüchse 41 is carried on a Kfz 15 light signals vehicle in order to provide a useful boost in firepower to a normally lightly-armed unit. The gun is carried complete with its light wheeled carriage, and could be easily lifted from the vehicle for more orthodox employment.

The 7.5-cm Pak 41 was the largest of the German taper-bore guns, but was prevented by the general tungsten shortage then prevalent in Germany from becoming the standard German army heavy anti-tank gun.

JAPAN

47-mm Anti-tank Gun Type 1

As with so many other weapons, Japan was short of anti-tank guns and had only a limited capacity to produce the numbers required. In 1934 it had introduced the 37-mm Gun Type 94 for use by infantry units, but realized even then that this gun would have only a limited performance, and it was therefore supplemented by the licence production of the 37-mm Anti-tank Gun Type 97, the origin of which was the German 3.7 cm Pak 35/36.

It was not until 1941 that a heavier gun was introduced in the form of the **47-mm Anti-tank Gun Type 1**. In overall design terms the Type 1 was entirely orthodox and used a split-trail carriage and a well-sloped shield. Compared with designs then being produced in Europe the Type 1 was not very powerful, but the Japanese considered it adequate as it had the advantage of a semi-automatic sliding breech carried over from the 37-mm (1.46-in) German gun, giving it a relatively high rate of fire; this was a possible 15 rounds a minute. As with many other Japanese weapons ease of handling was given high priority, and the Type 1 proved to be easy to handle in action and it was relatively light. In

combat this advantage was often squandered for as the Allies advanced these guns were often statically emplaced and were manned by crews who favoured death rather than capture.

Production of the Type 1 was never sufficient to meet the needs of hard-pressed Japanese army units as the Allies advanced on all fronts, and consequently the Japanese were forced to use all manner of anti-tank methods, ranging from pressing into use naval and anti-aircraft guns to the extreme of suicide attackers armed with pole charges and explosive blocks. By 1945 the use of such measures was becoming commonplace.

Despite the fact that the Japanese learned early on in the conflict that their small tanks were likely to be of very limited use against their Allied equivalents, they still diverted a proportion of the Type 1 gun production towards producing a tank gun for their Type 97 tank. The Type 1 was regarded as the standard Japanese anti-tank gun, and most of them were issued to regimental and divisional anti-tank battalions.

Specification
47-mm Anti-Tank Gun Type 1
Calibre: 47 mm (1.46 in)
Length of barrel: 2.527 m (8 ft 3.5 in)
Weight: in action 747 kg (1,660 lb)
Traverse: 60°
Elevation: −11° to +19°
Muzzle velocity: AP 824 m (2,700 ft) per second
Projectile weight: APHE 1.528 kg (3.37 lb) and APHE 1.4 kg (3.08 lb)
Armour penetration: 51 mm (2 in) at 915 m (1,000 yards)

The Japanese Anti-tank Gun Type 1 was the only indigenous Japanese weapon produced solely for the anti-tank role, and although it was effective enough against most light Allied armour it was never produced in significant enough numbers to make any overall impression. A tank gun version was produced and the Type 1 remained in production from 1941 until the war ended in 1945.

AUSTRIA

Böhler 4.7-cm anti-tank gun

The little **Böhler 4.7-cm** (1.85-in) anti-tank gun was first produced in 1935, and is thus sometimes known as the **Model 35**. It was first produced in Austria but its use soon spread outside that nation and licences to produce the gun were taken up by Italy. In fact the Italian production run reached the point where the Böhler gun became regarded almost as an indigenous Italian weapon, the **Cannone da 47/32 M35**.

The Böhler gun was a handy weapon that was soon diverted into other roles. It was widely issued as an infantry gun and as it could be rapidly broken down into a number of pack loads it was also employed as a mountain gun. But though as it turned out the Böhler was something of a multi-purpose weapon, it was not entirely successful in any of these extra roles. It did prove to be a fairly effective anti-tank gun, however, and was widely used during the early war years by a number of nations. Italy was the main user, but others were employed by the Netherlands (**Kanon van 4.7**), and Romania, and the type also turned up in the Soviet Union (in relatively small quantities) as the **M35B**. Some also found their way into German army service when Austria came under German domination after 1938, receiving the designation **4.7-cm Pak**.

There were several developments on the basic Böhler theme that issued from the company's Kapfenberg works. Although the basic gun remained unchanged, there were numerous variations on such things as types of carriage wheel, the width of the carriage axle and so on. Some models had muzzle brakes while others did not. All models had a feature whereby the wheels could be removed and the gun then rested on the trail legs and a small platform under the axle for firing. This gave the gun a lower silhouette for firing and concealment. The gun could fire both armour piercing and high explosive projectiles, the latter having a range of

Above: In action the Böhler anti-tank gun was often used with the wheels removed and with the forward part of the carriage resting on a firing platform. A periscope sight was used, even for anti-tank use, and no shield was usually fitted. The gun could be broken down into loads for pack transport on mules.

Right: Although the 47-mm Böhler was originally an Austrian weapon, it was licence-produced in Italy to such an extent that it was regarded as an Italian weapon. It was also a multi-role weapon that was used as an anti-tank gun, an infantry gun and a mountain gun.

7000 m (7,655 yards) to provide the gun with a useful infantry support role. As the armour thicknesses of tanks increased the Böhler increasingly assumed this infantry support role.

There was one odd side-line to the story of the Böhler that is still little known. In 1942 the Allied armies in North Africa were still relatively short of many weapons and the large numbers of captured Italian Böhler guns were a useful windfall. About 100 were refurbished at a Captured Weapons Depot in Alexandria and issued to various units for second-line service. But perhaps the oddest item in this story was that 96 were actually converted by the British for use by airborne forces: the fire-control system of the original gun was altered so that one man (instead of the original two) could lay the gun, and the carriage was modified to allow dropping by parachute; a rifle telescope for aiming and a shoulder pad from a 6-pdr gun were also added. These were, according to the records, issued for service where they proved 'very popular'. Unfortunately it has not yet been possible to trace the units involved, but these Böhler guns must

To the Italian army the 47-mm Böhler was known as the Cannone da 47/32 M35, and this example is seen in the infantry support role (the barrel is elevated for increased range) in North Africa. The firing platform for use when the wheels were removed can be seen over the axle. Many of these guns were used by the Germans later in the war, and some captured guns were used by the British.

have been the very first guns adopted for the airborne role.

Specification
Cannone da 47/32 M35
Calibre: 47 mm (1.85 in)
Length of barrel: 1.68 m (5 ft 6 in)
Length of bore: 1.525 m (5 ft)
Length of rifling: 1.33 m (4 ft 4.3 in)
Weight: travelling 315 kg (694.5 lb) and in action 277 kg (610.6 lb)
Traverse: 62°
Elevation: −15° to +56°
Muzzle velocity: AP 630 m (2,067 ft) per second and HE 250 m (820 ft) per second

Maximum range: HE 7000 m (7,655 yards)
Projectile weight: AP 1.44 kg (3.175 lb) and HE 2.37 kg (5.225 lb)
Armour penetration: 43 mm (1.7 in) at 500 m (550 yards)

Soviet 45-mm anti-tank guns

The Soviet Union purchased a batch of 37-mm (1.46-in) Rheinmetall anti-tank guns as early as 1930, and standardized the type as the M30 well before the German army adopted the identical model as the 3.7-cm Pak 35/36. The Soviets decided to licence-produce the 37-mm (1.46-in) gun, but in 1932 produced their own variant with a calibre of 45 mm (1.77 in). This was the **M1932**, and this could be identified by the wire-spoked wheels that were fitted to the otherwise unchanged Rheinmetall-based carriage. By 1940 there were large numbers of these guns in service with the Red Army and some had even been used in action on the Republican side during the Spanish Civil War.

In 1937 the slightly revised **Model 1937** appeared, and in the following year a tank gun variant, the **M1938**, was produced. These two guns first saw major action during the short but intense war with Finland during 1939 and 1940, but in many ways this war gave the Red Army the wrong impression of the effectiveness of their guns. The Finns had only small numbers of light armoured vehicles and the M1932 and M1937 proved quite effective against these. But when the Germans invaded the Soviet Union in 1941 the Red Army found out the hard way that its guns could not penetrate the armour of most German tanks. The only way the Red Army could stop the German attacks was to use massed artillery fire against the German forma-

Although considered by many to be too light for really effective anti-tank use by 1945, the little 45-mm (1.77-in) Model 1942 was still in large-scale Red Army service in that year and remained so for many years thereafter. This picture shows a Model 1942 in action in early 1945 on the final approaches to Danzig as the Red Army advanced westwards during the last winter of the war.

tions, and although there was an obvious need for heavier anti-tank guns Soviet war industry was in no position to produce any such new weapons. The huge German advances had overrun many of the Soviet military industrial centres, and it took time to set up new facilities deep in the hinterland of the Soviet Union.

When a new gun did appear it was nothing more than a lengthened version of the existing gun. The original M32 had a barrel that was about 46 calibres long (L/46) while the new gun had a barrel that was 66 calibres long. This extension of barrel length increased the muzzle velocity and provided the projectile with more penetrating power. The new and longer gun was produced some time during 1942 and was thus named the **M1942**, but it took time for appreciable numbers to reach the front line. In the meantime the M1938 tank gun was called upon partially to fill the gaps. Numbers of these tank guns were placed on simple improvised carriages and rushed into

action. These conversions were of limited value as they had only a small traverse arc, but they did work and as such were better than nothing.

When the M1942 did get into the front line it proved to be more effective than the earlier guns, but only marginally so, yet the Soviets continued to produce large numbers throughout the war. These M1942 guns had pressed steel wheels in place of the earlier wire-spoked units, and the trail legs were longer, but the Rheinmetall origins could still be seen. Although it would appear that the M1942 had only

a limited performance against the later tanks the type is still in service with some of the smaller Soviet-influenced armies around the world. Some were encountered during the Korean War and during some of the Middle East wars.

In 1941 the Soviet designers followed the increase in anti-tank calibres prevalent elsewhere. The first gun to be introduced had a calibre of 57 mm (2.24 in) and is known as the **M1941** and in 1944 a massive gun with a calibre of 100 m (3.94 in) was introduced as the **M1944**.

Specification
M1942
Calibre: 45 mm (1.77 in)
Length of barrel: 2.967 m (9 ft 8.8 in)
Weight: in action 570 kg (1,257 lb)
Traverse: 60°
Elevation: −8° to +25°
Muzzle velocity: 820 m (2,690 ft) per second
Projectile weight: 1.43 kg (3.151 lb)
Armour penetration: 95 mm (3.74 in) at 300 m (330 yards)

The 45-mm (1.77-in) Model 1942 was a scaled-up version of the earlier 37-mm (1.456-in) Model 1930. The Model 1930 was a licence-produced version of the German Pak 35/36 but the 45-mm Model 1942 had a proportionately much longer barrel and very often wire wheels in place of the original steel disc wheels.

Soviet 76.2-mm guns

One of the most widely used of the German heavy anti-tank guns was not originally a German weapon at all but a Soviet design. This hybrid weapon was originally designed as a field gun and was known as the 76.2-mm (3-in) **M1936**. It was the latest in a line of gun designs that stretched back many years, and the first of them were issued to the Red Army during 1939. The M1936 was a rather heavy gun for the field role and it possessed a long slender barrel mounted on a heavy but strong carriage that was ideally suited to the harsh conditions of the Soviet terrain.

In 1941 the lack of a suitable anti-tank gun other than the 45-mm (1.77-in) M1932 led to the simple expedient of using field guns for defence against tanks. In this role the M1936 proved itself to be an excellent anti-armour gun and, even firing high explosive shells, was powerful enough to inflict damage on German tanks of all kinds. This fact was duly noted by the Germans when they came to contemplate a use for the huge stockpiles of M1936 guns that they captured during 1941 and 1942. Many were simply turned around against their former owners, but large numbers were returned to Germany where they were reconditioned and altered to accommodate German ammunition. A muzzle brake

was added and the fire controls altered for the anti-tank role, the result being the **7.62-cm Pak 36(r)**, an excellent heavy anti-tank gun that was used on all fronts from North Africa to the Soviet Union.

Back in the Soviet Union, as early as 1939 a new field gun lighter than the M1936 was produced as the **M1939**. This was overall smaller than the M1936 with a shorter barrel. Again, many fell into German hands in 1941, and these were converted for German use, some as anti-tank guns. The Soviet designers produced other 76.2-mm (3-in) field guns in 1941 and at one desperate point were even placing 76.2-mm (3-in) tank guns on lash-up carriages in order to produce something to keep the advancing German forces at bay, but in 1942 came the first of what can be regarded as dual-purpose guns.

This was the 76.2-mm (3-in) **M1942**, or **ZiZ-2**, a handy and light field gun that could be readily used as an anti-tank gun if and when necessary. The M1942 had a light carriage that used split tubular trails, and the gun barrel was fitted with a muzzle brake. By the time it first appeared at the front, the Red Army was well versed in the art of using field artillery against attacking armoured vehicles and during many battles the Red Army relied on field

guns alone for defence. They simply turned their guns, of all calibres, against the target and started firing. The M1942 was ideal for this type of employment for it was well-balanced and handy. It was also very sturdy, and as it fired a shell weighing 6.21 kg (13.69 lb), it could pack a useful punch when fired against tanks. The M1942 turned out to be one of the best artillery pieces ever produced in the Soviet Union, where the type was churned out in thousands, and the type still remains a front-line equipment with many armies around the world. Between 1943 and 1945 the German also found any captured examples very useful indeed.

A Soviet 76.2-mm (3-in) Model 1936 field gun in service with the Germans in North Africa converted for the anti-tank role as the 7.62-cm Pak 36 (r). In this form the Soviet gun made an excellent specialist anti-tank gun and was considered by many to be one of the best all-round anti-tank guns in use anywhere during World War II.

Specification
7.62-cm Pak 36(r)
Calibre: 76.2 mm (3 in)
Length of piece: 4.179 m (13 ft 8.5 in)
Length of rifling: 2.93 m (9 ft 7.3 in)
Weight: in action 1730 kg (3,770 lb)
Traverse: 60°
Elevation: −6° to +25°
Muzzle velocity: AP40 990 m (3,250 ft) per second
Maximum range: HE 13580 m (14,585 yards)
Projectile weight: AP 7.54 kg (16.79 lb) and AP40 4.05 kg (8.9 lb)
Armour penetration: AP40 98 mm (3.86 in) at 500 m (545 yards)

The Soviet 76.2-mm (3-in) Model 1942 ZiZ-3 field gun was not intended primarily to be an anti-tank gun, but

on many occasions it was used as such and proved to be very effective. Firing mainly high explosive shells it was able to knock out nearly all contemporary tanks or at least inflict severe damage. The Model 1942 was used by the Germans as well as the Red Army.

37-mm Antitank Gun M3

When the US Army Ordnance Department decided to develop an anti-tank gun before 1939 it obtained an example of the German 3.7-mm Pak 35/36, and using this as a starting point proceeded to design a similar weapon, also in 37-mm (1.46-in) calibre. The result was outwardly different from the German original but was in fact closely influenced by it. The American gun was designated the **37-mm Antitank Gun M3**, but only a few had been made before it was decided to fit the gun with a muzzle brake, the change making the M3 the **M3A1**.

The muzzle brake was fitted in an attempt to reduce the recoil forces on the carriage, which was even lighter than the German original, but as it was soon discovered that the muzzle brake was unnecessary it was removed, though the guns were still produced with the fixtures on the muzzle for ease of production. The rest of the gun and carriage was quite unremarkable. The carriage used the usual split trails but the main carriage axle was rather wider than on other similar designs. A

small flat shield was provided for the gun crew and the breech mechanism was copied direct from the German gun and remained a vertical drop block.

By the time the M3A1 had been taken into service it was obsolete. By 1941 events elsewhere had demonstrated that something larger than 37 mm (1.46 in) would be required to penetrate the armoured hides of in-service enemy tanks and although the M3A1 was used in North Africa by the US Army the type was withdrawn there and replaced by heavier guns. But it was different in the Pacific theatre. There the expected enemy tanks were light (and in any event few and far between), so a place could be found for the M3A1 as an infantry support weapon. High explosive and canister rounds were developed for use during the various island-hopping campaigns and the armour-piercing projectiles were often called upon during 'bunker-busting' operations. The light weight and handiness of the gun proved to be highly effective dur-

Although the European war had shown it to be obsolete, the 37-mm M3 was still in US Army use at the Kasserine Pass in 1943, where its

inadequacy against the veteran Afrika Korps armour was disastrous. It was soon to be withdrawn from the European theatre.

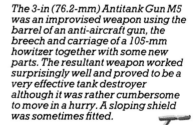

Although it appeared to be a very different weapon, the little 37-mm (1.456-in) Antitank Gun M3A1 was closely influenced by the German Rheinmetall 3.7-cm Pak 35/36. Although soon overtaken by armour increases in Europe, many were used as infantry support weapons in the Pacific and there was a widely used tank gun version.

ing these amphibious operations, so production continued specifically for the Pacific operations. By 1945 no fewer than 18,702 M3s had been produced. A tank gun version was also produced for use in American light tanks and armoured cars.

After 1945 many M3A1s were handed out to nations friendly to the Americans, and many are still in use in some Central and South American states. Numbers were also converted to become saluting guns with blank cartridges.

During World War II many attempts were made to turn the M3A1 into a self-propelled anti-tank weapon, but very few were ever used operationally for the simple reason that the gun lacked the power to tackle the tanks it was likely to encounter in the field. But as an infantry support gun it proved to be excellent.

Specification
37-mm Antitank Gun M3A1
Calibre: 37 mm (1.45 in)
Length of piece: 1.979 m (6 ft 10.5 in)
Weight: travelling 410.4 kg (912 lb)
Traverse: 60°

Elevation: −10° to +15°
Muzzle velocity: AP 885 m (2,900 ft) per second
Maximum effective range: 457 m (500 yards)
Projectile weight: 0.86 kg (1.92 lb)
Armour penetration: 25.4 mm (1 in) at 915 m (1,000 yards)

3-in Antitank Gun M5

When the US Army Ordnance Department decided during 1942 to produce a new heavy anti-tank gun it took a course of action that had already been taken elsewhere: it decided to combine existing weapon components to produce a new gun. The result was something of a 'dog's dinner'. The gun itself was taken from the 3-in (76.2-mm) Antiaircraft Gun M3 but the chamber had to be altered slightly to take different ammunition. The new gun was modified to take the breech mechanism of the 105-mm (4.13-in) Howitzer M2A1, then in full-scale production, and the same howitzer was used to supply the carriage and the recoil system. The new carriage became the Gun Carriage M1 and in this form the original straight shield of the 105-mm (4.13-in) howitzer was retained but in time the shield was modified to have

sloping shield plates and this became the M6.

The new gun became the **3-in Antitank Gun M5**, and it turned out to be a remarkably workmanlike-looking weapon. It was rather large and heavy for its role, but in this respect was no worse than many of its contemporaries and in action soon proved capable of being able to penetrate up to 84 mm (3.3 in) of sloping armour at ranges of almost 2000 m (2,190 yards). Not surprisingly the M5 proved to be a popular weapon with the anti-tank batteries of the US Army, and the type was used in all theatres of the war. Numerous types of armour-piercing ammunition were developed for the M5, but one of the more widely used was the capped armour-piercing (APC) projectile known as the M62. But the M5 did have a disadvantage and that was its weight.

Rapid movement of the M5 proved to be a major task, and a heavy 6×6 truck had to be used to tow the weapon although lighter tractors could be used on occasion.

The first M5s were issued for service in December 1941 but it took time for the weapon to be issued widely. The M5 was also in demand as the armament for a series of self-propelled tank destroyer projects, the most important of which turned out to be the **M10A1**, an open-topped M4 Sherman variant that mounted the M5 in a special turret. The importance of this demand can be seen as 2,500 M5s were completed for the anti-tank gun role but 6,824 guns for the M10A1.

Despite its success, once the war ended the M5 was gradually withdrawn from US Army service and passed to reserve units. It was overtaken

by newer and more technologically advanced forms of anti-tank weapon and few remained in use after 1950.

Specification
3-in Antitank Gun M5
Calibre: 76.2 mm (3 in)
Length of piece: 4.023 m (13 ft 2.4 in)
Weight: travelling 2632.5 kg (5,850 lb)
Traverse: 46°
Elevation: −5.5° to +30°
Muzzle velocity: AP 793 m (2,600 ft) per second, APC 853 m (2,800 ft) per second
Maximum effective range: 1830 m (2,000 yards)
Projectile weight: AP and APC 6.94 kg (15.43 lb)
Armour penetration: 84 mm (3.31 in) at 1830 m (2,000 yards)

The 3-in (76.2-mm) Antitank Gun M5 was an improvised weapon using the barrel of an anti-aircraft gun, the breech and carriage of a 105-mm howitzer together with some new parts. The resultant weapon worked surprisingly well and proved to be a very effective tank destroyer although it was rather cumbersome to move in a hurry. A sloping shield was sometimes fitted.

25-mm anti-tank guns

The first of two French 25-mm (0.98-in) anti-tank guns (in many references the correct term should be cannon instead of guns as the calibre of 25 mm is generally considered too light to apply to a gun) was the **Canon léger de 25 antichar SA-L mle 1934**. Produced by Hotchkiss et Cie, this weapon was based on the design of a gun originally intended for use in World War I tanks but too late for that conflict as its development was not completed until

1920. In 1932 Hotchkiss conceived the idea of placing the design on a light wheeled carriage in response to a French army requirement. The design was adopted in 1934 (hence the mle 1934 in the designation), and by 1939 there were well over 3,000 such equipments in service with the French army.

The other French 25-mm (0.98-in) gun was the **Canon léger de 25 antichar SA-L mle 1937**. This was a later arrival, designed and developed by the Atelier de Puteaux (APX), and first offered for service in 1937. It was not adopted for service until 1938 and the numbers produced for service never approached those of the mle 1934. In appearance the mle 1937 looked very similar to the mle 1934, but it was much lighter and had a slightly longer barrel. In fact the two guns were intended for different service roles: the mle 1934 was issued to nearly all French army armoured units and specialized anti-

tank units, while the mle 1937 was intended for use by the support companies of infantry battalions. The latter equipments were towed by horses, one horse pulling the gun towed behind a small limber vehicle, this carrying the ammunition and all the gun crew's kit and equipment. When the mle 1937 was towed in this fashion the cone-shaped muzzle brake was removed and stowed over the breech.

The mle 1934 was a serviceable

enough weapon, but its calibre was too small for the gun to be of much use against the German armour that swept across France in 1940. By that time the mle 1934 was also in use with the British army. In a show of Allied co-operation it had been decided that the BEF would use the mle 1934 as its anti-tank gun but this did not turn out well in practice. The BEF was the only all-mechanized formation in Europe at that time and when it tried to tow the mle 1934s behind its vehicles the guns very quickly proved to be too flimsy to withstand the hard knocks involved. Thus the BEF carried the guns on its vehicles and the mle 1934 became the first British portée guns. The mle 1937 fared even less well in service. It was even less stoutly built than the mle 1934 and ran into weakness problems even when confined to the horse-drawn

The Canon léger de 25 antichar SA-L mle 1934 was a light and handy weapon that proved to be virtually useless against even the lightest tank armour in 1940. This retouched picture is from a newspaper printed in late 1939.

role. But the main problem with both guns was that the round they fired was too small to make any sort of impact on attacking armour and their combat ranges were limited to something like 300 m (330 yards). Even in 1940 this was far too low for tactical comfort, but the French army had invested heavily in the 25-mm (0.98-in) guns, so all too often they were the only such weapons available.

In the 1940 campaign large numbers of these 25-mm (0.98-in) guns fell into

the hands of the Germans, who retained some for a while under the designations 2.5-cm Pak 112(f) and 2.5-cm Pak 113(f) to provide their occupation divisions with some form of anti-tank weapon. They do not appear to have been used long after 1942.

Specification
Canon léger de 25 antichar SA-L mle 1934
Calibre: 25 mm (0.98 in)
Length of barrel: 1.8 m (5 ft 10.8 in)
Weight: in action 496 kg (1,093.5 lb)
Traverse: 60°
Elevation: −5° to +21°
Muzzle velocity: 918 m (3,012 ft) per second
Maximum range: 1800 m (1,968 yards)
Projectile weight: (AP) 0.32 kg (0.7 lb)
Armour penetration: at 25° 40 mm (1.57 in) at 400 m (440 yards)

The little French 25-mm Hotchkiss guns, once issued to the BEF, proved light enough to be carried on 15 cwt trucks, which was just as well as they proved too flimsy for normal towing behind the truck. As such they were the first of the British Army's portée anti-tank guns.

Canon léger de 25 antichar SA-L mle 1937
Calibre: 25 mm (0.98 in)
Length of barrel: 1.925 m (6 ft 3.8 in)
Weight: in action 310 kg (683.5 lb)
Traverse: 37°
Elevation: −10° to +26°
Muzzle velocity: 900 m (2,953 ft) per second
Maximum range: 1800 m (1,968 yards)
Projectile weight: (AP) 0.32 kg (0.7 lb)
Armour penetration: at 25° 40 mm (1.57 in) at 400 m (440 yards)

FRANCE
Canon de 47 antichar SA mle 1937

The best of the French anti-tank guns was the **Canon de 46 antichar SA mle 1937**, a design that originated with the Atelier de Puteaux. It was developed in a great hurry and introduced into service once the French army had been provided with indications of the armour thickness of the German PzKpfw IV tank. Considering the rush with which the mle 1937 was developed it was an excellent anti-tank weapon and one of the best in service anywhere in 1939. The main trouble for the French army was that there were not enough of them to hand during the events of May 1940.

The mle 1937 was introduced into limited service in 1938, but the main production run was in 1939. The type was issued to French artillery batteries operating in support of army divisions and brigades, and was operated in batteries, each battery having six guns. The equipments were usually towed into action behind Somua half-tracks, and in action their low outlines made them easy to conceal. They were capable of penetrating the armour of any tank likely to be put into action against them. In appearance the mle 1937 looked powerful and low. The gun had a barrel nearly 2.5 m (8 ft 2 in) long, and the carriage used pressed steel wheels with solid rubber rims. On top of the shield there was the fashionable corrugated outline to break up the shape.

Along with production of the towed

anti-tank model of the mle 1937 went production of a very similar gun intended for use in the permanent fortifications of the Maginot Line. This version lacked the carriage of the towed version and instead was swung into its firing position (through specially constructed firing slits) suspended from overhead rails. In 1939 there appeared a slightly revised version of the mle 1937 known as the **Canon de 47 antichar SA mle 1937/39**, but the detailed differences between these two guns were slight. In 1940 there appeared the **Canon de 47 antichar SA mle 1939** and this was a quite different weapon. It used the gun of the mle 1937, but mounted on a new tripod carriage so arranged that once it was emplaced the gun could be swung through 360° to fire against targets appearing from any point of the compass. To emplace the gun a forward leg of the tripod was swung down, the trail legs were spread and the wheels were then raised to positions on each side of the shield. This futuristic concept was doomed never to see service, for the events of May 1940 intervened before production could start.

May and June 1940 saw the bulk of the French mle 1937s pass into German hands. The Germans regarded the mle 1937 very highly, for many of their tanks had suffered from the striking power of the gun, and after 1940 they used the mle 1937 widely as the **4.7-cm Pak 141(f)**; the gun was still in

service when the Allies landed in Normandy in June 1944. Before that the Germans had also used the mle 1937 to arm many of their early Panzerjäger (tank hunter) conversions produced by removing the turrets from captured French tanks and replacing them with anti-tank guns on open mountings.

Specification
Canon de 47 antichar SA mle 1937
Calibre: 47 mm (1.85 in)
Length of barrel: 2.49 m (8 ft 2 in)
Weight: travelling 1090 kg (2,403 lb) and in action 1050 kg (2,315 lb)
Traverse: 68°
Elevation: −13° to +16.5°

Muzzle velocity: 855 m (2,805 ft) per second
Maximum range: 6500 m (7,110 yards)
Projectile weight: 1.725 kg (3.8 lb)
Armour penetration: 80 mm (3.15 in) at 200 m (220 yards)

The Puteaux mle 1939 was a more involved development of the mle 1937 47-mm (1.85-in) anti-tank gun, which had a conventional wheeled carriage. The mle 1939 used a complex all-round-traverse carriage, although some were produced with normal wheeled carriages.

Infantry Support Weapons

In the mobile battlefields of World War II, infantry could not count on any artillery unit to be close enough to give support in case of trouble. One solution to the problem was to give the infantry their own artillery, but the most cost-effective method depended upon a weapon as old as gunpowder – the mortar.

Throughout World War II the standard infantry support weapon used in most armies was the mortar. Some armies tended to combine the light weight and plunging fire of the mortar with the more direct approach and heavier firepower of the infantry gun or howitzer, and there were even some infantry support weapons (such as the odd little Japanese Type 92 battalion gun) that could be said to combine the attributes of gun and mortar. One factor that will be seen to be important throughout this study is the number of really small calibre mortars that were used during World War II. These light-weight mortars were used right down to infantry squad level, enabling the squad to provide its own local fire support. This was a form of weapon that rose to prominence during World War II, for although the mortar was evolved during World War I it never reached the level of control that could extend right down to the individual squad. This concept has been maintained since 1945, and today provides the infantry with a powerful extension of its offensive and defensive range.

One weapon that rose to prominence during World War II but has faded out since is the infantry gun or howitzer. In the

These British SAS parachutists are firing their 3in (76.2mm) ML mortar in support of a partisan attack on German forces. The mortar remains an important and powerful infantry weapon today.

aftermath of World War I it seemed to be a good idea to many armies to provide their infantry units with integral artillery fire support. However, providing the infantry with special artillery weapons was rather extravagant in resources and manpower. The artillery piece has never been a true infantry weapon, for it is far too demanding in handling manpower, however small and light it is made. Even before the end of World War II the heavy mortar was replacing the infantry gun, and since 1945 the infantry gun has faded completely from the modern tactical scene. The mortar is now the dominant infantry support weapon, supplemented here and there by recoilless weapons and missiles, but infantry seem to prefer the mortar overall. The weapon was, and still is, portable, has range and firepower to a degree that the soldiers of World War I could not have imagined, and remains completely under the control of the infantry that it supports, just as it did during World War II.

Soviet light mortars

The Red Army used mortars of all kinds in great numbers throughout World War II. In general they were sound and reliable weapons that were usually much heavier than their counterparts elsewhere, but were correspondingly very robust.

During the 1930s the Soviet arms designers closely followed trends elsewhere, and thus developed several types of light infantry mortars with a calibre of 50 mm (1.97 in). After dealing for a short while with one design that could be used as a 37 mm (1.46 in) barrel for a weapon that could also be used as an entrenching tool, the main models settled down into a series that commenced with the **50-PM 38**, designated **5-cm Granatwerfer 205/1(r)** by the Germans. This was a conventional design that used gas vents at the base of the barrel to vary the range; the barrel was held in its bipod at either of two fixed angles. This model soon proved difficult to produce, so it was replaced by the **50-PM 39**, or **5-cm Granatwerfer 205/2(r)** to the Germans, which omitted the gas vent feature and used instead normal bipod elevation methods. While this model was effective enough, it was still thought to be too difficult to produce and was in its turn replaced by the **50-PM 40**. This was designed for mass production on a grand scale and the bipod legs and baseplate were simply pressed steel components. The bipod had a simple and novel method of barrel levelling and in service it proved reliable and useful, even though the range was somewhat restricted. There was one further model in this calibre, the **50-PM 41**, or **5-cm Granatwerfer 200(r)** to the Germans, that dispensed with a bipod and used instead a barrel yoke attached to a large baseplate. A gas venting system was also used, but not

many were made as production concentrated on the 50-PM 40. Many of the 50-PM 40s produced fell into German hands and they too used them on a large scale under the designation **5-cm Granatwerfer 205/3(r)**.

While the 50-mm mortars were used at company or squad level, the battalion mortars had a calibre of 82 mm (3.228 in). There were three models in this family, the **82-PM 36** which was a direct copy of the Brandt mle 27/31 and known to the Germans as the **8.2-cm Granatwerfer 274/1(r)**, the **82-PM 37** which was a revised model with recoil springs to reduce firing loads on the bipod and designated **8.2-cm Granatwerfer 274/2(r)** by the Germans, and the **82-PM 41**. The last was a much revised model that made extensive use of stampings to ease production, and was called the **8.2-cm Granatwerfer 274/3(r)** by the Germans. The short bipod was so arranged that wheels could be added to the ends for hand-towing, and this feature was taken one step further with the **82-PM 43**, which used an even simpler bipod to ease towing, one that is still in use today.

There remains one further 'light' mortar to mention. This was a specialized 107-mm (4.21-in) mountain warfare mortar known as the **107-PBHM 38**, or **10.7-cm Gebirgsgranatwerfer 328(r)** to the Germans. It was an enlarged version of the 82-PM 37, and was used with a light limber for horse traction. Alternatively the mortar could be broken down into loads for pack transport. Firing could be by the normal 'drop' method or by means of a trigger. This mountain version saw extensive use during World War II and it is still in use to this day, not only with the Soviet army but with many nations under Soviet influence.

The Soviet 82-PM 37 had a calibre of 82 mm (3.228 in) and was a close design relative of the French Brandt mortars. The Soviets introduced a circular baseplate and used recoil springs between the bipod and barrel to reduce recoil forces on the laying and sighting arrangements.

Specification
50-PM 40
Calibre: 50 mm (1.97 in)
Lengths: barrel 0.63 m (24.8 in); bore 0.533 m (20.98 in)
Weight: in action 9.3 kg (20.5 lb)
Elevation: 45° or 75° fixed
Traverse: 9° or 16°
Maximum range: 800 m (875 yards)
Bomb weight: 0.85 kg (1.874 lb)

82-PM 41
Calibre: 82 mm (3.228 in)
Lengths: barrel 1.32 m (51.97 in); bore 1.225 m (48.23 in)

Weight: in action 45 kg (99.2 lb)
Elevation: +45° to +85°
Traverse: 5° to 10° variable
Maximum range: 3100 m (3,390 yards)
Bomb weight: 3.4 kg (7.5 lb)

107-PBHM 38
Calibre: 107 mm (4.21 in)
Lengths: barrel 1.57 m (61.8 in); bore 1.4 m (55.12 in)
Weight: in action 170.7 kg (376 lb)
Elevation: +45° to +80°
Traverse: 6°
Maximum range: 6314 m (6,905 yards)
Bomb weight: 8 kg (17.64 lb)

120-HM 38

The Soviet **120-HM 38** is one of the success stories in mortar design, for it was first introduced into service in 1938 and it is still in widespread service to this day. It offered an excellent combination of bomb weight, mobility and range. When first introduced it was as a 120-mm (4.72-in) regimental mortar for producing fire support in place of artillery, and as World War II continued it was issued down to battalion level.

In design terms there was nothing really remarkable regarding the 120-HM 38. One feature that proved to be very useful was the large circular baseplate that allowed rapid changes in traverse without the usual need to dig out the baseplate and align it to the new direction of fire. The weapon was towed with the baseplate still attached with the weapon lying on a wheeled frame. A lunette was fitted into the muzzle and this was attached to the same limber as the 107-PBHM 38. Usually this limber incorporated an ammunition box holding 20 rounds, and the combination was towed either by a light vehicle or a team of horses. Getting the 120-HM 38 in and out of action was relatively rapid and easy, so after fire had been opened it was usually a simple matter to move off again before retaliatory fire started.

As the Germans moved across the USSR in 1941 and 1942 they were much

impressed by the firepower of the 120-HM 38. Being on the receiving end of the weapon's efficiency on many occasions, they had good reason to note the power of the bomb's warhead and they decided to adopt the design for themselves. In the short term they simply used as many captured examples as they could, under the designation **12-cm Granatwerfer 378(r)**, but they then went one better and copied the design exactly for production in Germany. This was known to them as the **12-cm Granatwerfer 42 (12-cm GrW 42)** and it was widely issued, even taking the place of infantry guns with some infantry formations. Thus the same weapon was in use on both sides during the fighting on the Eastern Front.

The usual bomb fired by the 120-HM 38 on both sides was the HE round, but smoke and chemical rounds were produced (although thankfully the latter were never used). The rate of fire could be as high as 10 rounds per minute, so a battery of four of these mor-

A Red Army mortar battery uses 120-HM 38s in action in the Caucasian hills during September 1942. The layer is using the mortar's simple sight to lay the mortar while the ammunition crew members stand by to load the heavy HE bombs.

tars could lay down considerable amounts of fire in a very short period. Over a period of action the baseplates did have a tendency to 'bed in', making relaying necessary, but this was partially eliminated by introduction of the **120-HM 43** which used a spring-loaded shock absorber on the barrel-bipod mounting. It is this version, which was otherwise unchanged from the original, that is most likely to be encountered today. Over the years some changes have been made to the ammunition, which now has a longer range than the wartime equivalent, and another change is that many modern versions are now carried on various types of self-propelled carriage.

Specification
120-HM 38
Calibre: 120 mm (4.72 in)
Lengths: barrel 1.862 m (73.3 in); bore 1.536 m (60.47 in)
Weight: in action 280.1 kg (617 lb)
Elevation: +45° to +80°
Traverse: 6°
Maximum range: 6000 m (6,562 yards)
Bomb weight: HE 16 kg (35.3 lb)

Left: The Soviet 120-HM 38 was one of the most successful mortar designs of World War II, and was even copied direct by the Germans for their own use. It combined heavy firepower and mobility and often replaced support artillery with some formations. It was simple and easy to use in action, and fired a heavy HE bomb.

Above: The 120-HM 38 is seen on its wheeled travelling carriage, from which the mortar could be rapidly and easily emplaced. The wheeled carriage was often coupled to a limber that carried some ammunition. So successful was this mortar design that it is still in production.

Ordnance, ML 2-inch Mortar

The first of the British 2-in (50.8-mm) mortars appeared in 1918, but it was not in service for long being rendered obsolete in 1919. It was not until the 1930s that the notion of reintroducing a light mortar for use at platoon or squad level was put forward, and as there was no 'history' of the development of such small mortars in the UK at that time it was decided to run a selection competition between the offerings from various armaments manufacturers. The result was a flood of models from a number of concerns, and after a series of trials one was selected.

The winner was a design from the Spanish manufacturer ECIA. In its original form this weapon was thought suitable for improvement, and the extra further work was carried out in the UK, leading to full production during 1938. The first production version was the **Ordnance, ML 2-inch Mortar Mk II** (ML for muzzle loading), but this was only the first of a long string of marks and sub-marks. In basic terms there were two types of 2-inch Mortar. One was the pure infantry version, which was a simple barrel with a small baseplate and a trigger mechanism to fire the bomb after loading. The second type was meant for use on Bren Gun or Universal Carriers and had a much larger baseplate and a more complicated aiming system. If required the carrier version could be dismounted for ground use and a handle was supplied for this purpose. However, between these two types there were at the least 14 different variants, with differences in barrel length, sighting arrangements and production variations. There were even special versions for use by the Indian Army and by airborne divisions.

To go with this array of weapon variations there was an equally daunting range of types of ammunition. The usual bomb fired by the 2-inch Mortar was HE, but smoke and flares were also fired, the latter being particularly useful for target illumination at night. Having a trigger firing mechanism the weapon could be used at angles close to the horizontal, a factor that was particularly useful in house-to-house combat. The bombs were normally carried in tubes, each holding three, and arranged in handy packs of three tubes. The normal 2-inch Mortar team consisted of two men, one carrying the mortar and the other carrying the ammunition.

The 2-inch Mortar is still around. The British army uses it for firing flares and other pyrotechnics pending the service debut of the new Light Mortar, and many other nations keep the weapon 'on the books'. These days the only version likely to be encountered is the infantry model with its small baseplate, the carrier version having long since passed away.

Specification
2-inch Mortar Mk II*
Calibre: 2 in (50.8 mm)
Lengths: barrel 0.665 m (26.2 in); bore 0.5065 m (19.94 in)
Weight: 4.1 kg (9 lb)
Maximum range: 457 m (500 yards)
Bomb weight: HE 1.02 kg (2.25 lb)

A 2-inch Mortar team of the Royal Scots Fusiliers in action during late June 1944 during an attack on Norrey-en-Bessin. The small size of the mortar means that most of it is hidden behind the mortar gunner, demonstrating how easy the mortar was to conceal and use in action at close ranges.

A drill book demonstration of the loading of a 2-inch Mortar. As the loader drops the bomb into the muzzle, he taps the firer on the back to order him to pull the trigger lever via a cord lanyard. The model is the Carrier version with the large baseplate.

Soldiers of the 1st Battalion, The Hampshire Regiment, in action in Sicily in 1943, using a 2-inch Mortar. The mortar gunner is operating the trigger lever at the base of the barrel to actually fire the bomb while his partner observes the fall of the bomb.

Ordnance, ML Mortar, 3 inch

The first 3-in (76.2-mm) mortar was the original Stokes Mortar that was first used in March 1917. This version remained in use for many years after World War I, and as funds for weapon development were sparse between the wars it remained in service virtually unchanged for some years. However there was some work carried out on the basic design to the point at which it was decided during the early 1930s that the **Ordnance, ML Mortar, 3 inch** would be the standard infantry support weapon. This was the **Mortar, 3 inch Mk II**, the weapon that was used by the army when World War II broke out in September 1939. This Mk II had numerous changes from the original World War I Mk I, especially in the ammunition which used many of the features of the French Brandt design innovations.

It was not long after the start of the war when it was noticed that although the Mk II was a sturdy and reliable weapon, it lacked the range of many of its contemporaries. The early versions had a range of only some 1463 m (1,600 yards), which compared badly with the 2400 m (2,625 yards) of its German equivalent, the 8-cm GrW 34. A long series of experiments and trials using new propellants increased this range to 2515 m (2,750 yards), which overcame many of the original drawbacks, but these new propellants took time to get into the hands of front-line troops, so at times many German and Italian mortars were used by British troops, especially during the North African campaigns.

Apart from the ammunition changes

other alterations were made to the basic design. Later marks were equipped with a new baseplate design and improved sighting arrangements, and there was even a special version (Mortar, 3 inch Mk V) developed for use in the Far East, but only 5,000 of them were made and some were used by the airborne divisions. The usual method of getting the weapon into action was pack carriage in three loads by men, but the mechanized battalions carried their weapons on specially-equipped Universal Carriers. On these the mortar was carried on the back of the vehicle ready to be assembled for normal ground use; it was not fired from the Carrier. The Carrier also had stowage for the ammunition. When dropped by parachute the barrel and bipod were dropped in one container. Another container carried the baseplate while yet another container held the ammunition.

The ammunition for the family was largely confined to HE and smoke, although other payloads such as illuminants were developed. By juggling with the propelling charge increments and barrel elevation angles it was possible to drop a bomb as close as 114 m (125 yards) away, a useful feature in close-quarter combat.

Somehow the weapon never achieved the respect that was given to its opponents, but once the original range shortcomings had been rectified it proved to be a sound enough weapon that remained in service with the British army until the 1960s. It is used by some of the smaller ex-Commonwealth armies.

The 3-inch Mortar was the standard infantry support weapon of the British and Commonwealth armies in World War II, but it generally lacked range compared to weapons in service elsewhere. During the war gradual ammunition changes improved the range, and the 3-inch Mortar was a handy and popular weapon in action.

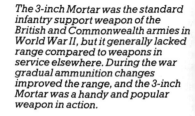

Specification
Mortar, 3-inch Mk II
Calibre: 3 in (76.2 mm)
Lengths: overall 1.295 m (51 in); barrel 1.19 m (46.85 in)

Weight: in action 57.2 kg (126 lb)
Elevation: +45° to +80°
Traverse: 11°
Maximum range: 2515 m (2,750 yards)
Bomb weight: HE 4.54 kg (10 lb)

Soldiers of the Black Watch are seen in action with their 3-inch Mortar near Herouvillette in Normandy during June 1944. The mortar is carefully emplaced in a purpose-dug pit, with adequate space for the mortar and crew and with camouflage netting handy for concealment.

A British 3-inch Mortar team provides fire support against German positions across the River Maas during the bitter weather of January 1945. This team appears to have a lengthy fire mission, judging from the pile of mortar bomb containers stacked ready to hand.

Ordnance, SB 4.2-inch Mortar

By 1941 it was noted by British army staff planners that there was a need for a mortar that could fire projectiles producing large amounts of tactical smoke for screening and other purposes; no doubt they had been influenced by the 10-cm Nebelwerfer mortars of the German Nebeltruppen. Accordingly a new design of 4.2-in (106.7 mm) heavy mortar was developed, but almost as soon as the first examples were ready for issue to Royal Engineer smoke production units the requirement was

changed to convert the new weapon into a heavy mortar firing conventional HE bombs for issue to Royal Artillery batteries. Thus the new mortar became the **Ordnance, SB 4.2-inch Mortar** (SB for smooth-bored).

The 4.2-inch Mortar was produced at a time when the British defence industry was fully stretched and production facilities of all kinds were in short supply. This was particularly noticeable in the production of the bombs, for the designers wanted them to have

forged bodies to reduce weight and to produce a better ballistic shape. At that time the required forging facilities were not available, so the bomb bodies had to be cast. This resulted in a maximum range of only 3018 m (3,300 yards) as opposed to the required 4023 m (4,400 yards). These bombs had to be used for they were all that could be made at the time pending the introduction of a new design with a streamlined body. Again, these had to be manufactured using cast iron but

they did manage a range of 3658 m (4,000 yards). By that time HE bombs were the main projectile used, but the original smoke function had not been entirely forgotten and some smoke bombs were produced.

The 4.2-inch Mortar was fairly hefty to move around, so the usual method of getting it into action was to tow it using a Jeep or other light vehicle. The base-plate and the barrel/bipod were so arranged that they could be easily lifted up onto a small wheeled mounting. Once on site they could be lowered from the mounting and the barrel and bipod quickly assembled. When carried on a Universal Carrier things were even simpler. The baseplate was simply dropped off the back, the barrel was inserted and the bipod shoved into place, and firing could start almost at once. Getting out of action was just as rapid. This led to the 4.2-inch Mortar being viewed with some suspicion by the troops that relied upon its firepower support. While they valued its supporting fire they knew that as soon as a 4.2-inch Mortar battery was brought into action nearby it would be off again before the incoming counterbattery fire from the enemy arrived. By that time the 4.2-inch Mortar battery would be some distance away, leaving the units close to their former position to receive the fire meant for the battery.

The 4.2-inch Mortars were widely used by the Royal Artillery, many field regiments having alternative gun or 4.2-inch Mortar complements. The 4.2-inch Mortar was used wherever British troops served from late 1942 onwards, and the weapon was still in use during the Korean War, in which it was used to tackle targets situated on reverse slopes behind hills or in valleys.

Specification
4.2-inch Mortar
Calibre: 106.7 mm (4.2 in)
Lengths: barrel 1.73 m (68.1 in); bore 1.565 m (61.6 in)
Weight: in action 599 kg (1,320 lb)
Elevation: +45° to +80°
Traverse: 10°
Maximum range: 3749 m (4,100 yards)
Bomb weight: 9.07 kg (20 lb)

A 4.2-inch Mortar fires on German positions in the foothills of Mount Etna in Sicily during 1943. The crew are protecting their ears against the considerable muzzle blast. The amount of dust stirred up could reveal a mortar position in action.

UK

95-mm Infantry Howitzer Mk II

At some point during 1942 a decision was made to produce a light howitzer for use by British infantry battalions but at that time the infantry themselves had not been consulted: perhaps the planners were influenced by the use of infantry artillery in nations such as Germany and the USA. In order to conserve production facilities it was decided that the new weapon would incorporate features from a number of existing weapons. The barrel was to be machined from a 94-mm (3.7-in) anti-aircraft gun liner, the breech mechanism would come from the 25-pdr field gun and the recoil system and cradle came from 6-pdr anti-tank gun components. To simplify matters the new weapon would fire the same ammunition as the old 3.7-inch Pack Howitzer and the close-support howitzers fitted in some tanks. The term **95-mm Infantry Howitzer** was applied to the project, 95 mm denoting the differences from other similar weapons.

The 95-mm Infantry Howitzer was not one of the success stories of World War II. The resultant amalgamation of components from various weapons allied to a new welded steel box carriage looked rather odd, and so it turned out to be once it was fired. The 6-pdr recoil system was simply not up to the task of absorbing the recoil loads and frequently broke. The wheel track also proved to be too narrow, leading to tow instability. Prolonged firing also showed that the overall construction of the weapon, designed for pack transport in 10 loads, was such that components could be shaken loose. No doubt more development could have eliminated many of these defects, but by the time they emerged the weapon was already in production.

It was at this point that the infantry were drawn into the programme. They quickly announced that they did not want the weapon. They had not been consulted at any stage and considered that they already had quite enough weapon types within their battalions, and there simply was not enough manpower to deal with a howitzer as well. This finally killed off the 95-mm Infantry Howitzer project altogether, and the majority of the numbers produced were never even issued. They were simply scrapped after the war and today only one remains.

Only two projectiles were produced for use with this weapon, HE and smoke. There were plans for an anti-tank HEAT projectile, but that was an offshoot of the 95-mm tank howitzer programme, and mention can be found of a flare shell. These projectiles were to be fired using a three-charge system.

The entire 95-mm Infantry Howitzer project now seems almost like a textbook example of how not to go about weapon design. No doubt the weapon could have been developed to the point of serviceability, but the recoil system was such a source of troubles that it now seems doubtful if it would ever have worked properly. Perhaps the biggest mistake in the entire project was going ahead with design and development without even troubling to find out if the intended operator really wanted the final product.

Specification
95-mm Infantry Howitzer
Calibre: 94 mm (3.7 in)
Lengths: barrel 1.88 m (74.05 in); bore 1.75 m (69 in)
Weight: in action 954.8 kg (2,105 lb)
Elevation: −5° to +30°
Traverse: 8°
Muzzle velocity: 330 m (1,083 ft) per second
Maximum range: 5486 m (6,000 yards)
Projectile weight: 11.34 kg (25 lb)

The experimental 95-mm (actually 3.7-in/94-mm) Infantry Howitzer undergoes troop trials in Italy in 1944. Formed from various parts of existing weapons, this infantry howitzer was not a great success and the infantry did not particularly want it, so the weapon was never accepted for full-scale service.

The British 3.7-in (94-mm) howitzer was meant to be a mountain weapon when it was first introduced during World War I, but was later used as a light pack howitzer in World War II.

45/5 modello 35 'Brixia'

To the little **45/5 modello 35 'Brixia'** must go the prize for being the most overdesigned and overengineered mortar of World War II. Quite why the designers of the modello 35 went to such lengths to introduce needless complexities to a light support mortar with a very limited performance and a relatively ineffective projectile is now difficult to fathom, but the result was issued to the Italian armed forces in large numbers.

In this weapon's designation the term 45/5 indicates the calibre of 45 mm (1.77 in) and the length of the barrel in calibres, i.e. 5×45 mm (actually it was marginally longer). Such a small calibre could encompass only a small bomb that weighed a mere 0.465 kg (1.025 lb), with a correspondingly small explosive payload. The barrel was breech-loaded: operating a lever opened the breech and closing it fed a propelling cartridge from a magazine holding 10 cartridges. A trigger was used to fire the bomb, and to vary the range a gas port was opened or closed to vent off some of the propellant gases. If this was not enough there were also complex

The Italian 45/5 modello 35 'Brixia' mortar was one of the most complicated mortar designs ever produced. It used a lever-operated breech mechanism and fired tiny 0.465-kg (1.025-lb) bombs.

elevation and traverse controls.

The barrel of the modello 35 was located in a folding frame arrangement that rested against a carrier's back using a cushion pad to ease the load against the body. In use this frame was unfolded in such a way that the firer could then sit astride the weapon if required. In action the modello 35 could manage a fire rate of up to about 10 rounds per minute, and in trained hands the weapon was quite accurate. But even when they landed right on target the small bombs were relatively ineffective, mainly as a result of the small payload that often resulted in

erratic and ineffective fragmentation.

The modello 35 was widely used by the Italian armed forces, mainly at platoon level. All Italian soldiers were trained in its use, some of them while still in one or other of the Italian youth movements, which were issued with an equally complex but even less effective version of the modello 35, this time in 35-mm (1.38-in) calibre. These weapons were meant only for training, usually firing inert bombs.

The Italians were not the only users of the modello 35. There were times during the North African campaigns when the Afrika Korps found itself using the things, usually for logistical reasons when serving alongside Italian formations. There was even an instruction manual written in German for this very purpose, the German designation of the weapon being **4.5-cm**

Granatwerfer 176(i).

It seems almost certain that the Italian soldiers found to their cost the limitations of the modello 35 and retained the weapon in service for the simple reason that there was little chance of Italian industry being able to produce anything better in the then foreseeable future. Having expended so much development time and production effort into getting the modello 35 into the hands of the troops, the limited ability of the Italian defence industries would have required too much time to design, develop and produce yet another weapon. So the Italian soldiers simply had to make do with what they were given; no doubt many of them thought it was not much.

Specification
45/5 modello 35
Calibre: 45 mm (1.77 in)
Lengths: barrel 0.26 m (10.2 in); bore 0.241 m (9.49 in)
Weight: in action 15.5 kg (34.17 lb)
Elevation: +10° to +90°
Traverse: 20°
Maximum range: 536 m (586 yards)
Bomb weight: 0.465 kg (1.025 lb)

5-cm leichte Granatwerfer 36

German weapon designers between the world wars were presented with virtually a clean slate on which to work as Germany gradually rearmed during the early 1930s. Thus when a requirement was issued for a light infantry mortar for issue at squad level, the designers at Rheinmetall-Borsig AG decided not to follow the usual barrel/baseplate/bipod form but instead evolved a design in which the barrel was permanently secured to the baseplate and the bipod was virtually eliminated in favour of a monopod device fixed to the baseplate. The result was a rather complex little weapon with a calibre of 50 mm (1.969 in) that was known as the **5-cm leichte Granatwerfer 36** or **leGrW 36** (light grenade-launcher model 1936) that was first issued for use during 1936.

The leGrW 36 was in many ways a prime example of the German's general love of gadgetry in weapons. It had all manner of them from the traverse controls built onto the baseplate to a very complicated but completely unnecessary telescopic sight. This sight was very much a designer's attempt to make the weapon as perfect as possible and ensure accuracy, but the ranges at which the little leGrW 36 was used were such that a simple line painted on the barrel was all that was needed and the sight soon went out of production during 1938.

The weapon could be carried by one man using a handle on the base of the barrel. For all its small size the leGrW 36 was rather heavy, weighing 14 kg (30.8 lb). Thus in action one man had to carry it, with another carrying the ammunition in a steel box. In action the baseplate was placed on the ground and all barrel adjustments

were made using coarse and fine control knobs. Firing was carried out using a trigger. Only HE bombs were fired.

While the designers felt rather proud of their achievement in the leGrW 36, the soldiers were not so enthusiastic. They felt that the leGrW 36, quite apart from the weight problem, was simply too complicated and the bomb not worth all the trouble involved. The bomb weighed only 0.9 kg (1.98 lb) and the maximum range was a mere 520 m (569 yards). On top of this the weapon took time to produce, and was costly in raw material terms and other resources. Such a situation could not last once the war was under way, and by 1941 the leGrW 36 was out of production. Those that had been manufacured were gradually withdrawn from front-line service in favour of something better, being passed on to second-line and garrison units. Many were used by units manning the Atlantic Wall as part of the beach defences. Some were passed on to the Italian army.

Overall the leGrW 36 was not one of the German weapon designers' best efforts. They allowed a small weapon to become far too complex and costly to justify the result, and the German army was astute enough to realize the fact and so went on to employ more useful weapons.

The 5-cm leGRW 36 was one of the standard German army light mortars of the early war years, but it was too complex and expensive for wartime production and its performance was not outstanding. Here one is being loaded while the layer adjusts the complicated fire controls on the heavy base plate and yoke.

Specification
leGrW 36
Calibre: 50 mm (1.969 in)
Lengths: barrel 0.465 m (18.3 in); bore 0.35 m (13.78 in)
Weight: in action 14 kg (30.8 lb)
Elevation: +42° to +90°
Traverse: 34°
Maximum range: 520 m (569 yards)
Bomb weight: 0.9 kg (1.98 lb)

8-cm schwere Granatwerfer 34

The German army's **8-cm schwere Granatwerfer 34** or **8-cm sGrW 34** (heavy grenade-launcher model 1934) gained for itself an enviable reputation among Allied front-line soldiers for its accuracy and rate of fire. The weapon was encountered everywhere the German army was in action, for the sGrW 34 was one of the German army's standard weapons in use from 1939 right through to the last days of World War II. It was a Rheinmetall-Börsig AG product, but was in truth a Germanic revision of the Brandt mle 27/31 and even used the same calibre of 81.4 mm (3.2 in).

Despite its reputation there was nothing remarkable regarding the design of the sGrW 34. Much of the respect it gained as a weapon should instead have gone to the thorough training and efficiency of the men who used it, for throughout the war the German mortar crews seemed always to have an edge over their rivals. They became experts at getting their sGrW 34s in and out of action rapidly and by careful use of plotting boards and other fire-control aids, they were able to obtain maximum accuracy from their fire.

The sGrW 34 was straightforward in design and very well made. It was consequently very robust and could be broken down into three loads for man-pack carrying; more men had to carry the ammunition. A special version existed for use from SdKfz 250/7 half-tracks. Several centres were concerned with production of the weapon, and even more were involved in making the ammunition for the range of bombs that could be fired from the sGrW 34 was wide. There were the usual HE and smoke bombs, but innovations included illuminating and target-marking bombs for use in association with ground-attack aircraft. There was even a special 'bouncing bomb' known as the 8-cm Wurfgranate 39 that was pushed back up into the air after it had struck the ground. This was done using a tiny rocket motor, and at a predetermined height the bomb exploded to scatter its fragments over a much wider area than would be the case with a conventional ground-detonated bomb. Again, this was a typical German weapon innovation that was really too expensive and unreliable for general use and the numbers produced were never large. One extra bonus for the sGrW 34 was that it could fire a wide range of captured ammunition, although usually with some loss in range performance.

For airborne use a special shortened version of the sGrW 34 was developed in 1940. This was the **kurzer Granatwerfer 42**, usually known as the **Stummelwerfer**. This was issued in quantity from about 1942 onwards, but saw little use by airborne forces and instead became a replacement for the little 5-cm leGrW 36. It fired the same ammunition variety as the sGrW 34 but the range was reduced by more than half.

The German 8-cm sGrW 34 was greatly respected by the Allies, who came to fear its accuracy and rapid rate of fire, but it was not an outstanding design and much of the praise it earned was mainly due to the careful and thorough training of the mortar crews.

Specification
sGrW 34
Calibre: 81.4 mm (3.2 in)
Lengths: barrel 1.143 m (45 in); bore 1.033 m (40.67 in)
Weight: in action 56.7 kg (125 lb)

Elevation: +40° to +90°
Traverse: 9° to 15° variable with elevation
Maximum range: 2400 m (2,625 yards)
Bomb weight: 3.5 kg (7.72 lb)

The shape of the 8-cm sGrW 34 bomb can be clearly seen here as it is held ready for loading into the muzzle. The bomb weighed 3.5 kg (7.72 lb) and used multiple tail fins to provide stability in flight. The layer is making fine traverse adjustments using the simple sight mounted on the bipod.

Right: A German army 8-cm sGrW 34 crew. The pear-shaped bomb is being introduced into the muzzle to fall down onto the fixed firing pin to fire the propelling charge and propel the bomb to a maximum range of 2400 m (2,625 yards).

Below: A propaganda photograph of an 8-cm sGrW 34 in action, clearly showing the elevation, traverse and levelling controls on the bipod. The crew member on the right is holding the bipod to provide an extra measure of stability on firing.

7.5-cm leichte Infantriegeschütz 18

One of the many tactical lessons learned by the German army during World War I was that each infantry battalion should have a measure of artillery support available to it at all times. This led to the introduction of light infantry guns to each infantry battalion, and it was appreciated that special light guns would be particularly useful for the role. Thus during the 1920s one of the first priorities of the then severely-restricted German weapons industry was the development of a light infantry gun, or leichte Infantriegeschütz. A 75-mm (2.95-in) design was produced by Rheinmetall-Börsig as early as 1927 and was issued for service in 1932. It was usually known as the **7.5-cm leIG 18**, or **7.5-cm leichte Infantriegeschütz 18**.

The first examples had wooden-spoked wheels, while later versions intended for use by motorized formations had metal disc wheels with rubber tyres. The leIG 18 had an unusual breech-loading mechanism: operating a lever opened not the breech but instead moved the entire barrel section upwards in a square slipper to expose the loading chamber. This system was yet another example of German design innovation simply for its own sake, for the mechanism offered no real advantage over conventional systems of the period, and has been used in no artillery design since. The rest of the gun was orthodox enough, and in action it proved to be sturdy and reliable although having only a limited range, as a result mainly of the short barrel. In common with most other artillery designs of the period, the leIG 18 was supposed to have an anti-tank capability using a hollow-charge warhead projectile, but this was not very effective and was little used.

There were two variants of the basic leIG 18. One was a version specially developed for use by mountain warfare units and known as the **leichte Gebirgs Infantriegeschütz 18** or **leGebIG 18** (light mountain infantry gun model 18). This was developed from 1935 onwards and was basically an ordinary leIG 18 that could be broken down into 10 loads for pack transport on mules or light vehicles. To save weight the ordinary box trail was replaced by tubular steel trail legs, and

the shield became an optional extra. The leGebIG 18 turned out to be heavier than the original but the pack load feature made it much more suitable for its intended role. It was meant to be a temporary measure for the mountain warfare units until purpose-built mountain guns could be developed and produced, but in the event those produced remained in service until the war ended.

There was also a special version of the leIG 18 developed for airborne forces and known as the **7.5-cm leIG 18F**, the F indicating *Fallschirmjäger*, or parachutist. This could also be broken down into loads, but this time only four for paradropping in special containers. This version had small metal wheels, no shield and tubular trail legs. Only six were produced as by the time they were ready their intended role had been assumed by the recoilless gun.

Specification
leIG 18
Calibre: 75 mm (2.95 in)
Lengths: gun overall 0.9 m (35.43 in); barrel 0.884 m (34.8 in)
Weight: in action 400 kg (882 lb)

A 7.5-cm leIG 18 is loaded, an unusual procedure where operation of the breech lever raised the rear end of the barrel upwards in a slipper to expose the chamber; the breech block remained fixed. This gun has spoked wheels for horse traction, while later models had metal wheels with rubber tyres.

Elevation: −10° to +73°
Traverse: 12°
Muzzle velocity: 210 m (689 ft) per second
Maximum range: 3550 m (3,882 yards)
Projectile weight: HE 5.45 kg or 6 kg (12 or 13.2 lb); hollow charge 3 kg (6.6 lb)

The crew of a 7.5-cm leIG 18 in training during early 1940. Note the relatively small size of the round being handed to the loader, and the way one crew member is kneeling on the end of the trail to provide extra weight for stability on firing.

15-cm schwere Infantriegeschütz 33

When the German army issued its infantry gun requirements during the early 1920s, two types of weapon were requested. One was to be a 75-mm (2.95-in) gun and the other a 15-cm (5.87-in) howitzer to act as a heavier counterpart to the light gun. Development of this heavy weapon commenced in 1927 at a leisurely pace, so that it was not finally approved for service until 1933. Even then it was 1936 before the first examples came off the production lines and they were then issued at the rate of two to each infantry battalion.

To confuse matters somewhat this 15-cm howitzer was actually designated as a gun, i.e. **15-cm schwere Infantriegeschütz 33** or **15-cm sIG 33** (15-cm heavy infantry gun model 1933). It was definitely a howitzer, however, with a short barrel set on a heavy box-trailed carriage. Early examples had pressed steel wheels with metal rims

for horse traction, but later examples intended for use with the motorized formations had wheels with rubber rims. Once again Rheinmetall-Börsig was responsible for the basic design (although production was carried out by several other manufacturers), and for once no gimmicks were introduced, the design of the sIG 33 being straightforward and orthodox. If anything it was too orthodox for the infantry gunners, for the adherence to standard design meant that the sIG 33 was really too heavy for the infantry role. It required a large horse team to drag the weapon, and once the sIG 33 was emplaced it was a slow and hard task to move it out. Some attempts were made before 1939 to lighten the heavy carriage by the use of light alloys, but these were in overall short supply and earmarked for the Luftwaffe so the heavy design had to be tolerated.

Throughout the war most sIG 33s

were towed by horse teams, although trucks or halftracks were used whenever possible. Even with a tractor it was still a job to handle the weapon in action, and it was not until the sIG 33 was placed upon a tracked self-propelled chassis that the weapon could give its full potential. It was then much more appreciated as a powerful support weapon firing a wide array of projectiles. Most of the tracked chassis used for the self-propelled role were old tank chassis that were no longer large or powerful enough for armoured warfare; in fact the very first attempt to mount a sIG 33 on a PzKpfw I hull resulted in the very first German self-propelled artillery weapon, and this was used during the 1940 campaign in France.

As with all other weapons of its era, the sIG 33 was supposed to have an anti-tank capability and was accordingly issued with hollow-charge pro-

jectiles. In use these proved to be less than fully effective, for even a normal 150-mm HE shell striking a tank could be effective and a lot less trouble to manufacture and issue. But for really strong targets the sIG 33 could fire a muzzle-loaded stick bomb known as a Stielgranate 42. This had only a short range and was guided by fins towards its target, which was usually a blockhouse, bunker or some other strongpoint.

Specification
sIG 33
Calibre: 149.1 mm (5.87 in)
Length: barrel 1.65 m (64.9 in)
Weight: in action 1750 kg (3,858 lb)
Elevation: 0° to +73°
Traverse: 11.5°
Muzzle velocity: 240 m (787 ft) per second
Maximum range: 4700 m (5,140 yards)
Projectile weight: HE 38 kg (83.8 lb)

Bofors 75-mm Model 1934

The **Bofors 75-mm Model 1934** was originally designed by AB Bofors as a mountain gun and was placed on the market in the 1920s. At that time the artillery markets around the world were awash with the surplus of World War I, but there was a small demand for specialized weapons and the Bofors 75-mm (2.95-in) gun fell into this category. As with all products from the Bofors plant at Karlskroga, the 75-mm gun was very well made from the finest materials, and used a sound and well considered design. And it was just what was required by one European nation, the Netherlands.

One would have thought that the last thing a nation as well endowed with flat terrain as the Netherlands would have wanted was a mountain gun, but the Dutch needed the gun not for service at home but away on the other side of the world in the Dutch East Indies. At that time the Netherlands maintained a sizeable force of troops in the islands that now make up much of Indonesia, and as the terrain is either very overgrown or mountainous some form of pack artillery was required. The Bofors gun was apparently just what was needed and a batch was duly acquired. The Bofors gun could be broken down into eight loads, carried in special harnesses by mules, but for normal towing a four-horse team was used with a further six mules carrying ammunition and other bits and pieces; the gunners themselves had to walk. These guns were still in use when World War II reached the Pacific, and with the Japanese invasion the guns had a brief period of action before fall-

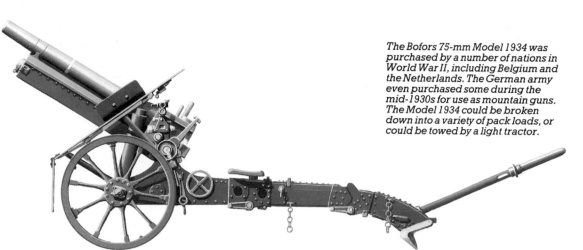

The Bofors 75-mm Model 1934 was purchased by a number of nations in World War II, including Belgium and the Netherlands. The German army even purchased some during the mid-1930s for use as mountain guns. The Model 1934 could be broken down into a variety of pack loads, or could be towed by a light tractor.

ing into Japanese hands. Their new masters used the guns for their own purposes until the ammunition stocks ran out, and by 1945 few were left.

Some of these Bofors 75-mm guns were sold to Turkey in the years leading up to World War II, but the main customer was another unlikely client for a mountain gun. This time the recipient was Belgium, for which a special version was produced as the **Canon de 75 modèle 1934**. This time the gun was for use by the Belgian troops based along the borders in the Ardennes region, but as this area was reasonably well provided with roads and tracks, there was no need for the full pack

transport facility. Instead the modèle 1934s were produced as 'one-piece' weapons with the only feature designed to save towing length being a section of the box trail that could be folded upwards on tow. Unlike the Dutch guns, the Belgian models were intended for towing by light tracked tractors and were delivered with rubber-tyred steel disc wheels.

The Belgian guns had little chance to shine, for when the Germans invaded in May 1940 they passed rapidly through the region where these guns were based. Thus the Bofors guns passed into German hands, but as the numbers involved were few the Ger-

mans made no use of this **7.5-cm Gebirgshaubitze 34** and the captured weapons were simply scrapped.

Specification
Model 34
Calibre: 75 mm (2.95 in)
Lengths: piece overall 1.8 m (70.87 in); barrel 1.583 m (62.32 in)
Weight: in action 928 kg (2,046 lb)
Elevation: −10° to +50°
Traverse: 8°
Muzzle velocity: 455 m (1,493 ft) per second
Maximum range: 9300 m (10,171 yards)
Projectile weight: 6.59 kg (14.53 lb)

The Netherlands army used their Bofors 75-mm Model 1934 howitzers in the Dutch East Indies, where they were carried into action in pack loads carried by mules. Note how brakes were applied to this carrier mule as it moved down a steep slope carrying the wheels and part of the carriage trails.

A Netherlands army Bofors 75-mm (2.95-in) Model 1934 howitzer is ready for action in the Dutch East Indies during 1941. The Japanese army overwhelmed this Dutch colony during early 1942 and took over many of these howitzers for their own local use until the war ended.

US mortars

The US Army mortar teams have always referred to their charges as 'cannon' and during World War II they had a lot of cannon to hand. Smallest of these was not an American but a French design as it was the **60-mm Mortar M2**, a direct licence-produced copy of a Brandt design. This became the standard US Army mortar for use down to company level, and for it American industry produced a wide range of ammunition including one odd projectile that was meant to illu-

minate low-flying enemy aircraft at night so that light anti-aircraft weapons could deal with them; the round had other uses as well.

From the M2 the Americans developed their **60-mm Mortar M19**, which can be regarded as the US equivalent of the British 2-inch Mortar, which it closely resembled. Not many M19s were produced, and of these most went to airborne formations.

The standard battalion mortar of the US Army was another Brandt licence-

built product, yet one more variation of the mle 27/31 design. The Americans produced their version as the **81-mm Mortar M1**, and with some slight alterations to suit local production methods it was manufactured throughout World War II. One odd American piece of equipment used with this weapon was a small hand cart onto which the mortar and its ammunition could be loaded. Two men were all that were required to tow this handy little carrier, known as the Hand Cart M6A1. Other carriers

included mules, for which a special harness set was devised, but perhaps the most universally used was the M21 halftrack carrier from which the M1 mortar could be fired without the need to dismount the weapon as was the case on such vehicles as the British Universal Carrier. Throughout its service life the M1 remained virtually unchanged. A special barrel extension tube was devised to increase range but it was little used, and a special shortened version, known as the **T27**

'Universal' and of which much was expected, was not accepted for service on a large scale.

Perhaps the best known of all World War II American mortars was the **4.2-inch Chemical Mortar**, the main reason for its fame probably being that it is still in service with the US Army. As with its British counterpart, it was devised to be a mortar firing smoke projectiles (hence the Chemical Mortar designation), but it was not long before it was realized that HE bombs would be very effective as well. It was a cumbersome and large weapon with a massive and heavy baseplate (that was later replaced by much lighter designs), and the barrel was rifled to fire bombs that closely resembled conventional artillery projectiles. The rifling made the 4.2-inch Chemical Mortar very accurate, and the projectiles were much heavier than their smooth-bore equivalents. In action they were often used as infantry support weapons, but many were issued to smoke screen units. The one major drawback to the 4.2-inch Chemical Mortar was its weight and bulk. It was not an easy weapon to deploy and to overcome this various self-propelled carriages were devised for it.

Specification
M2

Calibre: 60 mm (2.38 in)
Length: barrel 0.726 m (28.6 in)
Weight: in action 19.05 kg (42 lb)
Elevation: +40° to +85°
Traverse: 14°
Maximum range: 1815 m (1,985 yards)
Bomb weight: 1.36 kg (3 lb)

M1
Calibre: 81.4 mm (3.2 in)
Length: barrel 1.257 m (49.5 in)
Weight: in action 61.7 kg (136 lb)
Elevation: +40° to +85°
Traverse: 14°
Maximum range: 3008 m (3,290 yards)
Bomb weight: 3.12 kg (6.87 lb)

Above: A 4.2-in Chemical Mortar is seen in action on Arundel Island during the Solomons campaign. Note the stack of bombs for this mortar and how the shape resembles that of a conventional artillery projectile.

Chemical Mortar
Calibre: 106.7 mm (4.2 in)
Length: barrel 1.019 m (40.1 in)
Weight: in action 149.7 kg (330 lb)
Elevation: +45° to +59°
Traverse: 7°
Maximum range: 4023 m (4,400 yards)
Bomb weight: 14.5 kg (32 lb)

The American 60-mm Mortar M19 was a much simplified version of the 60-mm Mortar M2, and used a simple baseplate and no bipod. It was used mainly by American airborne forces and by a few infantry units, but its effective range was only about 320 m (350 yards) and it was not very accurate, being hand-held.

75-mm Pack Howitzer M1A1

In the aftermath of World War I the 1920 Westervelt Board recommended the design of a new 75-mm (2.95-in) light howitzer for use in mountain warfare and as a general-issue pack howitzer. This was one of the proposals that was actually pursued at the time, for by 1927 the **75-mm Pack Howitzer M1** had been standardized; some later production changes altered the designation to the **M1A1**. The howitzer was mounted on a carriage of ingenious design that could be easily broken down into six loads, and the box trail was perforated to save weight. The howitzer itself could be broken down for pack transport, and was so arranged that the barrel was held in a trough and kept in place by a cover along the top: this gave the weapon a distinctive appearance. Traverse was effected using a screw mechanism directly on the axle, so the cradle had to carry only the elevation mechanism.

The first M1A1s were mounted on the Carriage M1, which was intended for animal traction and so had wooden-spoked wheels. The introduction of mechanized traction led to the adoption of the Carriage M8, which used rubber-tyred metal wheels. This little howitzer became one of the first Allied airborne artillery weapons, for it was issued to nearly every Allied airborne formation, including the British airborne divisions. But it should not be thought that the M1 carriage went out of fashion: many were produced during World War II for issue to Allied armies such as the Chinese, who used the howitzer in some numbers.

On either carriage the little M1A1 was a popular and very useful weapon. It was a thoroughly modern design, and in action it was easy to serve and could be used to provide fire support at ranges up to 8925 m (9,760 yards). Despite its light weight some conver-

The 75-mm (2.95-in) Pack Howitzer M1A1 on Carriage M8 was one of the Allies' most successful light weapons of the type. It was a pack howitzer that could be readily adapted for paradropping, and was used by both British and American airborne units in 1944 and 1945. Some are still in use to this day.

sions to the self-propelled role were made (some being mounted on half-tracks) and it was just as successful in that role. One role for which the M1A1 was not much used appears to be mountain warfare. There were few campaigns where mountain warfare was necessary for the Allies, with the possible exception of that in Yugoslavia. There partisan troops were trained in the use of the M1A1 by British officers, and the partisans appear to have made good use of them during the latter stages of their war of self-liberation.

It was as one of the first Allied airborne artillery pieces that the M1A1 will probably be best remembered. It was used at Arnhem when some were landed from General Aircraft Hamilcar gliders, but the howitzer could also be broken down into nine loads for paradropping.

Not all M1A1s had such an adventurous life. Many were used simply as infantry support weapons or as pack artillery in the dense jungles of the Far East. The M1A1 was light enough to take part in the initial stages of amphibious assaults such as that on Walcheren in 1944, when howitzers meant

for mountain warfare were instead used in the flooded flatlands of the Scheldt estuary.

Specification
M1A1
Calibre: 75 mm (2.95 in)
Lengths: piece 1.321 m (52 in); barrel 1.194 m (47 in)
Weight: complete 587.9 kg (1,296 lb)
Elevation: −5° to +45°
Traverse: 6°

A US Army light howitzer battery trains with a 75-mm (2.95-in) Pack Howitzer, attired in an odd uniform intended for use by expeditionary forces in tropical climates. Dating from 1936, this howitzer has early-pattern M8 carriage spoked wheels.

Muzzle velocity: maximum 381 m (1,250 ft) per second
Maximum range: 8925 m (9,760 yards)
Projectile weight: 6.241 kg (13.76 lb)

50-mm light mortars

There were two main types of 50-mm (1.97-in) mortar in service with the Japanese army during World War II. Both of them could be regarded more as grenade-launchers than real mortars as they used projectiles that were little more than finned hand grenades, and they were mainly used as squad weapons for purely local support.

The first version to enter service was the **Type 10**, which entered service in 1921. It was a simple smooth-bore weapon that fired its grenade by means of a trigger mechanism. An adjustable gas vent was provided to give variations in range. The Type 10 originally fired HE grenades, but with the introduction of the later model it was used more and more to fire pyrotechnic grenades for target illumination and similar purposes. The main drawback of the Type 10 was its limited range, which was only some 160 m (175 yards), a factor that gave rise to development of the second weapon in this class, the **Type 89**.

By 1941 the Type 89 had all but replaced the Type 10 in service and differed from it in several respects, one being that the barrel was rifled instead of smooth-bored. The other main change was the elimination of the previous gas vent system in favour of a firing pin that could be moved up and down the barrel: the higher the firing pin was up the barrel the shorter the resultant range. The Type 89 mortar fired a new series of grenades to an effective range of 650 m (711 yards), which was a substantial increase over that possible with the Type 10. Grenades developed for the Type 89 included the usual HE, smoke, signalling and flares. Development of this weapon reached the point where a special version for use by airborne troops was produced. Normally both the Type 10 and Type 89 could be dismantled for carrying in a special leather case.

The main version encountered by the Allies was the Type 89. Somehow, the word spread among the Allies that these little mortars were 'knee' mortars and the name stuck. Exactly how many fractured thighs this completely misleading nickname caused among untrained users is now impossible to determine, but attempting to fire either of these mortars with the baseplate rest-

The Japanese 50-mm (1.97-in) Grenade Discharger Type 10 was first produced in 1921 and later replaced by the improved Type 89. With a limited range (160 m/175 yards), it remained a light and handy weapon that could fire a range of HE, smoke and flare grenades.

ing against a leg would result in immediate injury. The recoil of these little weapons was considerable and the baseplate had to be held against the ground or something really substantial. Aiming was rudimentary for there were no sights other than a line marked on the barrel, but in a short time almost any soldier could learn to use the weapon fairly effectively. The mortar was light and handy in action, but the grenade was somewhat on the light side. What really mattered was that any soldier could carry one slung

over a shoulder while still carrying a normal load and the resultant increase in squad firepower was appreciable, especially when using the longer-range Type 89.

Specification
Type 89
Calibre: 50 mm (1.97 in)
Lengths: overall 0.61 m (24 in); barrel 0.254 m (10 in)
Weight: 4.65 kg (10.25 lb)

How not to do it. For some reason the Americans decided that the small spade baseplate of the Japanese grenade dischargers enabled a soldier to fire them from the thigh or knee (hence 'knee mortars'), but anyone attempting this inevitably ended up with a broken leg, for the recoil forces were considerable.

Maximum range: 650 m (711 yards)
Grenade weight: 0.79 kg (1.74 lb)

70-mm Battalion Gun Type 92

The little **70-mm Battalion Gun Type 92** was one of the most successful infantry support weapons of World War II, despite its rather odd appearance. It was issued to every Japanese infantry battalion and could be used in several ways, as a battery weapon or, more frequently, as an individual weapon to produce harassing fire.

Despite its odd appearance the Type 92 was a thoroughly modern design. Much of the unusual appearance came from the use of a short barrel on a carriage travelling on large steel disc wheels. Normally the gun was towed by horses or mules, but in typical Japanese fashion there were various holes and brackets on the carriage through which long poles could be inserted to act as man-carrying handles for short moves. The shield could be removed to save weight when required, and the wheels were sup-

ported on cranked axles that could be turned through 180° to lower the silhouette of the gun when occasion demanded. Although it was a small weapon, the Type 92 required a crew of 10 men, most of these being used for manhandling or carrying the gun and acting as ammunition suppliers. In action the maximum number required was only five.

The Type 92 fired the usual HE projectiles along with smoke and shrapnel for close-range use against personnel in the open. There was also a rather

A team of Japanese Army gunners tows a Type 92 Battalion Gun over rough ground in the Aleutian Islands. The team are using special towing harnesses and are carrying wicker back-packs containing ammunition and spares for the gun. In action the gun weighed only 212.47 kg (468 lb).

ineffective armour-piercing projectile. The maximum range was rather short, being only some 2745 m (3,002 yards), and the effective range was only about half that, but as the Type 92 had only very simple sights and was rarely used against targets other than those clearly visible, this mattered but little in action. The Type 92 was certainly used well forward. Its direct or plunging fire could be very effective, in both defence and attack, and some Allied reports speak of the Type 92 being used in the same manner as a mortar. One operational method that was developed to a fine art by the Japanese for the Type 92 was harassing fire in jungle warfare. A small team would drag or carry the Type 92 forward, fire off a few rounds at a known target and then move hastily on to a new fire position or out of the area altogether. A single gun could keep large bodies of Allied soldiers awake and alert by such simple tactics.

Although labelled as a gun, the Type 89 used a variable propellant charge system and could be fired in the upper register (i.e. above an elevation angle of 45°) to drop projectiles onto targets as close as 100 m (109 yards) away. On target the HE projectiles were very destructive, and the shrapnel shell often proved to be very effective in breaking up massed infantry attacks such as those sometimes used by the

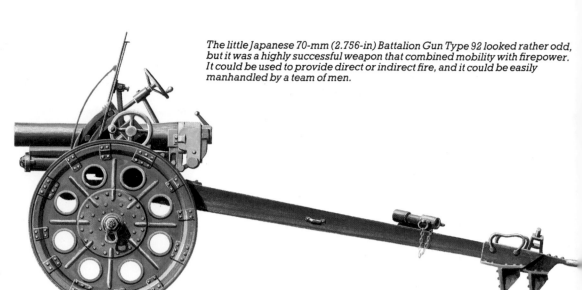

The little Japanese 70-mm (2.756-in) Battalion Gun Type 92 looked rather odd, but it was a highly successful weapon that combined mobility with firepower. It could be used to provide direct or indirect fire, and it could be easily manhandled by a team of men.

Chinese army. There was even a version of the Type 89 developed for use in some experimental tanks, but only a few of these (known as the **Type 94**) were actually produced.

The Type 92 was a small artillery piece but it often had an effect on its enemies that was quite out of proportion to its size, range and projectile weight. Many are still prized as museum pieces.

Specification
Type 92
Calibre: 70 mm (2.756 in)
Length: barrel 0.622 m (24.5 in)

Weight: in action 212.47 kg (468.4 lb)
Elevation: −10° to +50°
Traverse: 90°
Muzzle velocity: 198 m (650 ft) per second
Maximum range: about 2745 m (3,000 yards)
Projectile weight: HE 3.795 kg (8.37 lb)

FRANCE

Mortier Brandt de 81 mm modèle 27/31

Even though the Stokes Mortar of World War I established the overall design shape and form of the modern mortar, it was still a very rudimentary weapon. The Stokes Mortar was little more than a pipe supported on a simple frame and sitting on a base plate to take the recoil forces. The French Brandt company changed all that in the years after World War I by a careful redesign and drastic improvement in the type of bomb fired. At first sight the Brandt-inspired modifications were difficult to detect for the overall form of the Stokes design remained, but the improvements were there nevertheless. One of the first was that the new Brandt model, introduced as the **Mortier Brandt de 81 mm modèle 27** in 1927 and updated again in 1931 as the **modèle 27/31** to take advantage of ammunition improvements, was in the overall handiness of the weapon.

Setting up the original Stokes Mortar often took time, but the redesign of the Brandt bipod was such that it could be set up on any piece of ground: the levelling of the sights was easily carried out by the bipod leg design, on which only one leg needed to be adjusted. The sights were clamped to a position close to the muzzle, one that was convenient for the layer to peer through without having to stand over the weapon, and slight changes of traverse were easily made using a screw mechanism on the sight bracket. But the main changes came with the ammunition. The early grenades of the Stokes Mortar were replaced by well-shaped bombs that not only carried more explosive payload but had a much greater range. In fact Brandt produced a wide range of mortar bombs for its mle 26/31, but they fell into three main brackets. First there was one with an HE payload, and this

was used as the standard bomb. Then there was a bomb that was twice the weight of the standard, but which had a shorter range. The third type of bomb used was smoke. Within these three categories came numerous marks and sub-marks; for instance various coloured smokes were available.

The mle 27/31 greatly influenced mortar designs from the moment it was announced. Within a few years the mle 27/31 was being either licence-produced or simply plagiarized all over Europe and elsewhere. The mortar's calibre, 81.4 mm (3.2 in), became the virtual European calibre for infantry mortars and nearly every infantry mortar in use during World War II had some feature or other derived from the mle 27/81, and many were direct copies. This influence was wide enough to encompass the standard mortars of Germany, the USA, the Netherlands, China and even the USSR. All of these nations made their own alterations and innovations, but the resultant weapons were all basically the mle 27/31 at heart even if the mle 26/31 was in its turn derived from the Stokes Mortar.

The Brandt influence survives to this day, although the weapons of the current generation of 81-mm mortars outrange the mle 27/61 by a factor of nearly six. But the mle 27/31 was more than good enough to be used in its many forms throughout World War II and for years after it.

Specification
Mortier Brandt de 81 mm mle 27/31
Calibre: 81.4 mm (3.2 in)
Lengths: barrel 1.2675 m (49.9 in); bore 1.167 m (45.94 in)
Weights: in action 59.7 kg (131.6 lb); barrel 20.7 kg (45.6 lb); bipod 18.5 kg (40.8 lb); base plate 20.5 kg (45.2 lb)

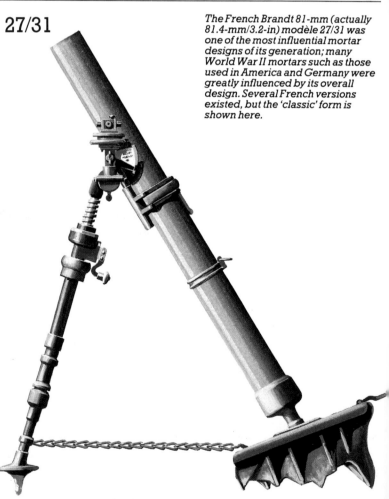

The French Brandt 81-mm (actually 81.4-mm/3.2-in) modèle 27/31 was one of the most influential mortar designs of its generation; many World War II mortars such as those used in America and Germany were greatly influenced by its overall design. Several French versions existed, but the 'classic' form is shown here.

Elevation: +45° to +80°
Traverse: 8° to 12° variable with elevation
Maximum range: standard bomb

1900 m (2,078 yards); heavy bomb 1000 m (1,094 yards)
Bomb weight: standard 3.25 kg (7.165 lb); heavy 6.9 kg (15.21 lb)

Infantry Anti-Tank Weapons

Modern infantry are equipped with man-portable anti-tank weapons capable of dealing with any armour at a respectable range. But in World War II anti-tank guns were bulky and scarce, and hand-held weapons were in their infancy. Nevertheless, these primitive short-range weapons began to evolve into a genuine defence against tanks.

Despite the success of the anti-tank gun during World War II, many tanks were destroyed in action by a diversity of other weapon types, often having little in common with each other except the fact that they had been developed to destroy enemy tanks. The range of these weapons was wide during World War II, varying from the bizarre Soviet dog mines to many variations of the hollow-charge warhead. As will be related, these varied in delivery method from being hand-thrown to rocket-propelled.

Nearly all the weapons described in this section were relatively short-range weapons. They therefore came into the domain of the foot soldier rather than the gunner, and it was the infantry which was the genre's main operator. This included the array of anti-tank rifles that were in service when World War II started, though few were still in use when 1945 came around. The anti-tank rifles were perhaps a minor class of their own, but it would be difficult to define weapons such as the Panzerfaust and Panzerwufmine in any category other than that of anti-tank weapon. In their day both were fearfully effective weapons, but today they have virtually passed from use (although relations of

British troops, including a two-man PIAT (Projector, Infantry Anti-Tank) team, taking cover in a roadside ditch in the Netherlands in early 1945, during the advance towards Germany.

the Panzerfaust can still be encountered). The anti-tank grenade has also virtually disappeared, and so too has the suicide tank killer made infamous by the Japanese in 1944 and 1945. But modern relatives of the bazooka and the Raketenpanzerbuchse can still be found in widespread use, and the Molotov cocktail is still a weapon favoured by many irregular armed forces, to say nothing of terrorists of every shade.

Being mostly close-range weapons, the anti-tank methods mentioned in this assessment became very personal weapons. None of them would have been of any use whatsoever without the application and determination of their users, and as always this is an important factor to be borne in mind when reading about them. It still evokes a considerable degree of admiration to consider how the British Home Guard trained to tackle the expected invading German tanks and even more to consider how the Soviet partisans risked their

lives to repel the German invaders. Consideration of the various forms of Japanese suicide methods may produce differing reactions, but the fact remains that the men who went out to destroy tanks and die in the process were essentially brave men, even if their psychology is still difficult to understand. All the weapons in these pages were essentially very personal ones, and perhaps even the Red Army soldiers grew attached to the dogs who carried their mines.

Bazooka

The American **bazooka** was one of the more original weapons of World War II and was founded on basic rocket research that had been conducted at Aberdeen Proving Ground, Maryland, since 1933. The active service development of the weapon began in earnest in early 1942 and the first of them went into action in North Africa in November 1942, although it was the following year before any were used against Axis armour. The full designation of the first model was **2.36-in Rocket Launcher, M1**. The rocket fired was the **M6A3** and the practice rocket was known as the **M7A3**.

The bazooka was a very simple weapon, being nothing more than a steel tube (open at both ends) through which the rocket was launched. A shoulder rest or wooden stock was provided along with two grips for aiming; the rear grip included the trigger group. The rocket was fired electrically and in low temperatures not all the propellant was consumed before the rocket left the launcher, allowing unburnt powder to be blasted into the firer's face. To prevent this it was possible to fit a small circular wire mesh screen just behind the muzzle. In practice the bazooka could be used at point targets up to 274 m (300 yards) away, but for most purposes range was confined to about 91 m (100 yards).

Soon after the M1 bazooka entered service it was replaced by the essentially similar **M1A1**. It was a popular weapon that could knock out any enemy tank and was normally served by a two-man team, one aiming and the other loading the rockets and connecting their electrical firing circuits. The bazooka soon found a great number of battlefield tasks other than use against tanks: it was very good at knocking out pillboxes of all kinds, and could even blast holes through barbed-wire obstacles; it could be used at area targets such as vehicle parks at ranges up to 594 m (650 yards), and at times was also used to clear combat lanes through minefields; and there are records of the bazooka being used against artillery pieces at close ranges.

But it was against tanks that the bazooka made its main mark, and it was seized upon by the Germans as the design basis for their Raketenpan-

Above: The American 2.36 in (60 mm) Rocket Launcher M1 was the first of the bazookas and was used by the Germans as the original for their RP series. The M1 used a 'one-piece' barrel that could not fold and early versions (shown here) used a wire mesh shield around the muzzle to protect against rocket blast.

Above: The rocket fired from the American bazookas was fin-stabilized and weighed 1.53 kg (3.4 lb). It had a maximum range of 640 m (700 yards), but was accurate only to ranges much shorter than that.

The original M1 bazooka is shown on the left and the M9 on the right. The M9 could be broken down into two halves, which greatly assisted carrying and stowage inside vehicles. By the time the war ended a version of the M9 was being produced in aluminium for lightness; this was the M18.

zerbüchse series after examples of the M1 had been captured in Tunisia in early 1943. Although the German counterparts were much larger in calibre, the Americans stuck to their 60-mm (2.36-in) calibre until after 1945. By then they had introduced a new model, the **M9** which differed from the M1 in being able to be broken down into two halves for ease of carrying. Smoke and incendiary rockets were de-

veloped and used before 1945, although much of their use was confined to the Pacific theatre. As the war ended the all-aluminium **M18** launchers were being introduced into service.

By the time the war ended no less than 476,628 bazookas of all types had been produced, along with 15,603,000 rockets of all kinds.

Specification
M1A1
Calibre: 60 mm (2.36 in)
Length: 1.384 m (4 ft 6.5 in)
Weights: launcher 6.01 kg (13.25 lb); rocket 1.54 kg (3.4 lb)
Range: maximum 594 m (650 yards)
Muzzle velocity: 82.3 m (270 ft) per second
Armour penetration: 119.4 mm (4.7 in) at 0°

Soviet anti-tank rifles

The Red Army used two types of anti-tank rifle during World War II, both of them very distinctive for they were long and powerful rifles that both fired the same 14.5-mm (0.57-in) ammunition. For some reason the Soviet armed forces had neglected the anti-tank rifle when other nations were just introducing the weapon, and only introduced the type into use at a time when other nations were busy discarding theirs. Set against that it must be said that the Soviet rifles were much more viable weapons than most in use at the time.

The more numerous of the Soviet anti-tank rifles was the **PTRD 1941**, a weapon produced by the Degtyarov design burea and introduced in mid-1941, just in time for the German invasion of the Soviet Union. The **PTRD-41** (as it was often known) was a very long weapon that was nearly all barrel and equipped with a semi-automatic breech mechanism. It could penetrate

up to 25 mm (0.98 in) of armour at 500 m (547 yards) and fired either steel or tungsten-cored projectiles. A large muzzle brake was fitted and a bipod under the barrel steadied the rifle in use.

The second anti-tank rifle was the **PTRS 1941** or **PTRS-41**, a product of the Simonov design bureau. Compared with the PTRD-41 it was a heavier and more complex weapon, but it fired the same ammunition and had an identical performance. The main change with the PTRS-41 was the use of a gas-operated mechanism and the addition of a five-round magazine. At the time these combined to make the PTRS-41 a more trouble-prone weapon than the

simpler and lighter PTRD-41. Further complexity was added by a feature that allowed the barrel to be removed from the weapon for ease in carrying.

Despite the fact that these two anti-tank rifles arrived in Red Army service at a time when their anti-armour capabilities were being reduced by a rapid increase in German tank armour thick-

The Soviet 14.5-mm (0.57-in) PTRS 1941 anti-tank rifle was a rather complex weapon with a semi-automatic gas-operated mechanism. It used a five-round magazine and was rather prone to jamming, so it was not as widely used as the simpler PTRD 1941.

The Soviet PTRD 1941 fired the same steel-cored ammunition as the more complex PTRS 1941. It fired single shots only, but used a semi-automatic breech. It was widely used by the Red Army and partisans, and even the Germans used captured examples to arm garrison units. It was used for many years after 1945.

nesses, they remained in service until well after 1945; indeed, some were encountered in use by the Communist Chinese during the Korean War. For several reasons the Red Army found the PTRD-41 and PTRS-41 to be very useful all-round weapons: they were still useful against soft-skin targets such as trucks, and in house-to-house fighting they were unhandy but very powerful weapons; despite their length and weight they were very useful partisan weapons that could be easily carried by two men; and when opportunity arose the Red Army even used these rifles against low-flying aircraft. Some light armoured cars carried these rifles as their main armament and Lend-Lease vehicles such as Universal Carriers often mounted one.

The Red Army was not the only World War II operator of these anti-tank rifles, for the Germans pressed into their own use any that they could capture during the early stages of their campaign against the Soviet Union: they knew the PTRD-41 as the **14.5-mm Panzerabwehrbüchse 783(r)** and the PTRS-41 as the **14.5-mm Panzerabwehrbüchse 784(r)**. Few of them remained in German front-line use after 1943.

Specification
PTRD-41
Calibre: 14.5 mm (0.57 in)

The Soviet 14.5-mm (0.57-in) PTRD 1941 anti-tank rifle has had a round loaded into the breech with the loader's left hand; a subsequent tap on the firer's helmet would then indicate that the rifle is ready to fire.

Lengths: overall 2.02 m (6 ft 7.5 in); barrel 1.35 m (4 ft 5.1 in)
Weight: 17.3 kg (38.14 lb)
Muzzle velocity: 1010 m (3,314 ft) per second
Armour penetration: 25 mm (0.98 in) at 500 m (547 yards)

PTRS-41
Calibre: 14.5 mm (0.57 in)
Lengths: overall 2.108 m (6 ft 11 in); barrel 1.216 m (3 ft 11.9 in)

Weight: 20.9 kg (46.1 lb)
Muzzle velocity: 1010 m (3,314 ft) per second
Armour penetration: 25 mm (0.98 in) at 500 m (547 yards)

Soviet dog mines

USSR

In common with many other European armies, the Red Army maintained a number of 'war dogs' for various military purposes such as sniffing out explosives or even delivering messages and medical supplies in front-line areas, but there can have been few roles more bizarre for dogs to play than the Soviet dog mines that were used for a short period during World War II. Exactly how the idea of using dogs as mobile anti-tank mines came about has yet to be determined, but the idea was simple and seemed to offer great things for the hard-pressed Soviet forces during 1942.

The basic idea of the dog mine was that the dogs were trained to dive under enemy tanks whenever they appeared. Each dog carried on its back a wooden box (or packets secured to its body by a harness) and from the top of the box (or packets) protruded a vertical wooden post. When this post was pushed backwards as the dog moved under the tank it detonated the explosives contained in the box (or packets) to the detriment of the tank and the unfortunate dog. Some accounts talk of wire sensors in place of the wooden post.

For all its simplicity the idea of the dog mines did not last very long. The Red Army soon discovered that there were two main disadvantages to the idea. One was that in order to train the dogs to dive under tanks they were

always given food under a tank. This was all very well, but to most dogs the familiar smells and sights under a Soviet tank were very different to those under German tanks. Thus in a battlefield situation once they were released with the explosives attached the dogs often tended to make for the familiar smells and sounds of Soviet tanks rather than the intended German tanks, with obvious results. The second snag was that the Germans soon learned of the Soviet *Hundminen* and spread the word through the efficient German military media machinery that all Soviet dogs likely to be encountered were rabid and were to be shot as soon as they were spotted. This alone caused the virtual disappearance of dogs all along the Eastern Front within a matter of days, making the further use of dog mines that much more unlikely. One other factor now seems obvious was that on any battlefield the noise and general chaos in progress would unhinge any normal dogs' behaviour, making them run amok in any direction other than to-

The Soviet dog mines seemed like a good idea when first mooted, but in use the dogs were easily distracted to friendly tanks, where their rod-operated explosive back-packs proved to be just as destructive as they would have been against German tanks.

wards tanks of any kind, and so hazardous to anyone in their vicinity.

The Soviet dog mines did have a few successes, but their period of 'action' was short once their two-edged nature became apparent. The idea was not used after 1942, but there were some reports of the Viet Minh attempting to use dog mines during the fighting in Indo-China during the late 1940s. Some reports on the Red Army after 1945 still contained references to the dog mines, no doubt just in case they were used again.

Raketenpanzerbüchse

In 1943 numbers of American 60-mm (2.36-in) M1 bazookas were captured in Tunisia and were rapidly examined by German technicians, who quickly appreciated that the simple and cheap construction of the rocket-launcher could be used to good advantage by the Germans themselves, and before very long the first German equivalents appeared. This German launcher fired a rocket very similar to that used on the Püppchen but was modified for electrical firing. This first German launcher was known as the **8.8-cm Raketenpanzerbüchse 43 (RPzB)** and was little more than a simple tube open at both ends, from which the rocket could be launched. The firer rested the 'pip' on his shoulder and operated a lever to power a small electrical generator. Releasing a trigger allowed the power so produced to be passed via wires to the rocket motor for firing. The weapon was completed by a simple sighting system.

The RPzB was an immediate success as an anti-tank weapon. Firing a larger rocket than the bazooka it had a better anti-armour capability, but the rocket was limited in range to about 150 m (164 yards). There was another disadvantage in that the rocket motor was still burning as it left the muzzle, so the user had to wear protective clothing and a gas mask to avoid being burnt. The rocket exhaust was dangerous for a distance up to 4 m (13.1 ft) to the rear of the tube on firing, and this exhaust could also kick up clouds of dust and debris to betray the firing position. This latter factor did little to endear the RPzB 43 to some users.

Further development produced the **RPzB 54**, which had a shield to protect the firer so that the protective clothing was no longer necessary, and the later **RPzB 54/1** fired a more developed rocket that required a shorter launching tube but which had a slightly increased range of 180 m (197 yards). The RPzB 54 and RPzB 54/1 replaced the earlier RPzB 43 in production, and the early models were passed to second-line and reserve formations.

These weapons soon became very widely distributed and used, to the extent that they were encountered on every front in large numbers. The later rockets could penetrate up to 160 mm (6.3 in) of tank armour, but they were esssentially close-range weapons that required careful handling in action; special care had to be taken regarding the dangerous effects of the backblast

British troops examine a captured 8.8-cm (3.46-in) RP 54 in Normandy, July 1944. The shield can be seen, as can the main lever for the electrical generator used for firing; this looks like a large trigger under the tube. The RP 54/1 was essentially similar but used a shorter launching tube.

The German RP43 was inspired by the American bazooka, but used a larger 8.8-cm (3.46-in) rocket. Sometimes known as Panzerschreck, this weapon had a range of 150 m (165 yards) and could knock out all Allied tanks.

An RP 54 about to be fired. The small shield was fitted to protect the firer from the back-blast of the rocket motor after firing; note that the loader behind is hiding his face for the same reason. The simple fixed foresight is just visible. Note also the webbing sling used for carrying.

Range: maximum 150 m (164 yards)

on firing. The usual crew for these weapons was two men, one aiming and the other loading the rockets and connecting the ignition wires to the launcher contacts. Tank targets often had to be 'stalked' for the crews to get within effective range, but if a hit was registered that tank was usually 'dead'. The only counter to the RPzB series was extra protection such as sandbags, track links or stand-off armour, along with the introduction of special tank-protection infantry squads that

travelled with the tanks.

The RPzB series had several nicknames, including **Ofenrohr** (oven chimney) and **Panzerschrek** (tank terror).

Specification
RPzB 43
Calibre: 88 mm (3.46 in)
Weights: launcher 9.2 kg (20.3 lb); rocket 3.27 kg (7.21 lb); warhead 0.65 kg (1.43 lb)
Length: 1.638 m (5 ft 4.5 in)

RPzB 54
Calibre: 88 mm (3.46 in)
Weights: with shield 11 kg (24.25 lb); rocket 3.25 kg (7.165 lb)
Length: 1.638 m (5 ft 4.5 in)
Range: maximum 150 m (164 yards)
Rate of fire: 4-5 rpm

Anti-tank grenades

The German army did not have any specialized hand-delivered anti-tank grenade other than the Panzerwurfmine, which came into a special category. Instead, when armour targets were contemplated it was a common practice to remove the throwing handles from a number of Stielgranate stick grenades and secure them with wire around the head of another Stielgranate complete with its handle. This combination of grenade warheads was known as a **geballte Ladung**, and could be used for a variety of purposes from demolishing strongpoints to disabling a tank.

For anti-tank use the Germans relied mainly on rifle grenades. The

chief type was fired from the standard Kar 98k service rifle muzzle using a device known as a Schiessbecker, which was a cup that could be secured to the muzzle using a lever locking device. This cup was grooved internally to correspond with grooves on the rifle grenade body so that on firing the grenade was given a twist to assist inflight stabilization. There were several anti-tank grenades that could be fired from this device, and these differed in size and the amount of explosive payload carried but all had a maximum range of about 200 m (219 yards). They were relatively ineffective against most tank armour after 1940 but were retained in service simply because they could not

be replaced immediately with anything better, and because they also had a secondary use against personnel targets. For maximum accuracy a complex little bubble sight on the rifle had to be used for aiming, and this sight alone was somewhat costly.

However, in complexity and cost this rifle grenade system paled when compared with what was almost certainly one of the most useless of the many gadgets delivered to front-line soldiers. This was the 27-mm (1.063-in) **Kampfpistole**, a device developed from a standard signal pistol to fire tiny grenades. Continued development had turned the signal pistol into a rifled weapon equipped with a complex

bubble sight and a folding butt together with a range of grenades that varied from the ordinary high explosive to grenades that produced whistling sounds to warn of gas attack. Among them was a hollow-charge grenade for use against armour, but this was only just over 51 mm (2 in) long and contained a miniscule charge of TNT. This grenade could be launched to a maximum range of 90 m (98 yards), but even if it hit a target it could produce little if any damage on even the lightest armoured target. But this weapon system, known as the **Sturmpistole** in its fully developed state, was issued to front-line troops.

Püppchen

Once the Germans had appreciated that the artillery projectile was not the most efficient manner of delivering hollow-charge warheads to an armoured target (it moved too fast for the hollow-charge to have full effect), they moved towards the rocket as a delivery system. They produced a small rocket with a calibre of 8.8 cm (3.46 in) with a hollow-charge warhead that was quite sufficient to penetrate any known armour on any Allied tank, and then set about producing a launching system.

At that stage of rocket development the German designers appear to have had little experience of what a rocket-launcher should be like, and in the end they developed what was to all intents and purposes a small artillery piece to 'fire' the rocket. This device was known as the **Püppchen** (dolly), or more formally as the **8.8-cm Raketenwerfer 43**, and it had all the

appearances of a small gun. There was a shield and the launcher was moved on wheels. Once in position the wheels could be removed to lower the silhouette and the weapon then rested on rockers. The rocket was even loaded using a conventional breech mechanism. Where the Püppchen differed from artillery pieces was that there was no recoil mechanism. The recoil forces produced by firing the rocket were absorbed by the mass of the carriage alone, and the aimer could point the launcher tube by using a twin-handled grip and looking along the barrel.

The Püppchen was introduced into service in 1943, and in use had a maximum range of about 700 m (766 yards), though for anti-tank use the maximum effective range was about 230 m (252 yards) as the sighting system was rather rudimentary and the time of flight of the rocket could be measured

in seconds. It was possible to fire up to 10 rockets per minute. Other design features of the Püppchen were that it could be broken down into seven loads for pack transport, and that skis could be used for movement over snow. There were even instructions printed on the inside of the shield for untrained personnel to use it on a battlefield.

The Püppchen did not last very long in production. Almost as soon at the first items had been issued American bazookas were being captured in Tunisia and examined by German technical personnel, who soon realized that the simple pipe was all that was needed to launch their 8.8-cm rocket and that the complexity of the Püppchen was unnecessary. Thus production ceased almost as soon as it started, and was then concentrated instead on the simple RPzB series. But those Püppchen equipments that had been made and

issued were not wasted. They were retained in use until the war ended, especially in Italy where a sizeable number were captured by the Allies and were subjected to close investigation by intelligence and technical staffs.

There were apparently intentions to mount modified Püppchen equipments on light armoured vehicles but none of these plans came to anything.

Specification
Püppchen
Calibre: 88 mm (3.46 in)
Lengths: overall 2.87 m (9 ft 5 in); barrel 1.60 m (5 ft 3 in)
Weights: travelling 146 kg (322 lb); in action 100 kg (220 lb); rocket 2.66 kg (5.86 lb)
Elevation: −18° to +15°
Traverse: 60°
Ranges: maximum 700 m (766 yards); anti-tank 230 m (252 yards)

A British soldier demonstrates a Püppchen captured in Tunisia in 1943, clearly showing its low silhouette. This rocket launcher had no recoil mechanism and used a simple breech, but compared with the RP 43 series it was much more complex and expensive to produce. The wheels could be removed if required.

The 8.8-cm (3.46-in) Raketenwerfer 43 or 'Püppchen' was a form of anti-tank rocket launcher that was superseded almost as soon as it entered service in 1943 by the RP 43 series firing a very similar rocket. The RP 43 could be produced far more cheaply and quickly than the Püppchen, here being examined by Americans.

Panzerwurfmine (L)

The **Panzerwurfmine (L)** was developed by the German army for use by special tank-killer infantry squads to provide them with a powerful standoff weapon that could be carried and used by one man. It was a specialized form of anti-tank grenade that used a hollow-charge warhead to defeat the target tank armour. To ensure that the warhead was actually facing the target armour when it struck the tank, the grenade was fitted with a finned tail for stabilization and guidance.

The Panzerwurfmine was thrown at its target in a special manner. The grenade warhead had behind it a steel body attached to a wooden handle. The user gripped this handle and held it behind his back with the warhead pointing vertically upwards. When ready the user swung his arm forward and released the handle. As soon as the grenade was in flight four canvas fins unfolded from the handle for guidance and stabilization, and the drogue effect of these fins maintained the warhead in its correct forward position

ready to have maximum effect as it struck. This sounds simple enough, but in practice the Panzerwurfmine was not an easy weapon to use effectively. For a start the maximum possible range was limited by the strength and ability of the thrower, and was usually no more than 30 m (32.8 yards) at best, and was frequently less. Accuracy could only be ensured by practice with special inert training versions.

But despite these disadvantages some of the special German anti-tank personnel greatly favoured the Panzerwurfmine. Compared with other close-in anti-tank weapons used by the Germans the Panzerwurfmine was relatively small, light and handy. It was also potent, for the warhead was made up of RDX and TNT in equal measures and weighed 0.52 kg (1.146 lb). Combined with the hollow-charge principle, this usually ensured penetration of even the thickest armour of nearly all Allied tanks. It also had the advantage of not requiring the user to approach the tank to place the grenade on the

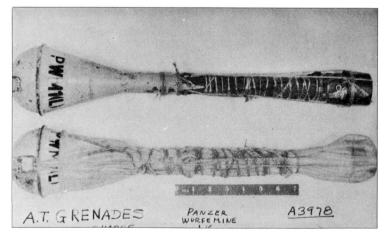

Two examples of the German Panzerwurfmine (L) are shown as they would have been issued, with their stabilizer tails wrapped in cord around the throwing handle. These grenades were not a general issue as they required some skill to use properly, and they were mainly issued to specialist close-in tank killer squads.

target, with all the attendant risks of such a tactic. Further safety was provided by the fact that the warhead was not fully fused until the grenade was in flight, for the act of throwing also armed the fuse.

Despite its success in German hands, the Panzerwurfmine was not copied closely by any of the Allies. Captured examples were used when they fell into Allied hands, especially by the Red Army, but the Americans often misused them for they at first thought that they were meant to be thrown in the same manner as an oversized dart; once the mistake had been discovered special intelligence bulletins were soon issued to correct this practice. After 1945 the principle was used for a while by various Warsaw Pact nations, and in recent years the Egyptians have seen fit to copy the Panzerwurfmine almost exactly as part of the output of their new indigenous armaments industry. They have discovered that this type of anti-tank weapon is exactly suited to their infantry anti-tank tactics, and their version is reported to be quite capable of 'killing' the most modern tanks.

Specification
Panzerwurfmine (L)
Body diameter: 114.3 mm (4.5 in)
Lengths: overall 533 mm (21 in); body 228.6 mm (9 in); fins 279.4 mm (11 in)

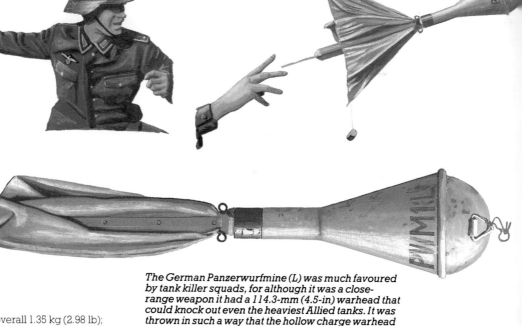

Weights: overall 1.35 kg (2.98 lb); warhead 0.52 kg (1.146 lb)

The German Panzerwurfmine (L) was much favoured by tank killer squads, for although it was a close-range weapon it had a 114.3-mm (4.5-in) warhead that could knock out even the heaviest Allied tanks. It was thrown in such a way that the hollow charge warhead was always in front to strike the tank armour first.

 GERMANY
Panzerfaust

When it first appeared in late 1942, the weapon that was soon known as **Panzerfaust** (tank devil) was unique. It was developed by HASAG (Hugo Schneider AG) at Leipzig to provide soldiers with a personal anti-tank weapon, and emerged as a form of recoilless gun that also incorporated some rocket principles. The Panzerfaust was meant to be cheap and simple, and was little more than a launching tube that projected a hollow-charge grenade. Simple firing and sighting facilities were provided, and that was it. The bulk of the propellant was contained in the launching tube, and in flight four spring steel fins sprang out from the projectile body to provide inflight stabilization.

The first Panzerfausts entered large-scale service in 1943, and this initial version was later known as the **Panzerfaust 30 (klein)**, the 30 referring to the 30-m (32.8-yard) range of the device. The suffix klein (small) was appended as it was not long before a larger-diameter projectile was introduced to provide an increased anti-armour penetration capability: this was then the **Panzerfaust 30**. The short range of these early models was often a great tactical disadvantage for the firer, who thus had to get dangerously close to the target tank. But the Panzerfaust worked and proved lethal to any tank likely to be hit. Aiming was a bit difficult as it relied on using a flip-up leaf sight that had to be aligned with a pip on the projectile body, and at the same time the launcher tube had to be carefully tucked under the arm to prevent the propellant exhaust from injuring the firer.

After the Panzerfaust 30 came the **Panzerfaust 60** and **Panzerfaust 100**, both with more range provided by more propellant, although the projectile remained the same. There were

The first model of Panzerfaust to enter service was the Panzerfaust 30, the number referring to the effective range in metres. By increasing the amount of propellant the range could be extended.

plans to introduce a **Panzerfaust 150** and even a **Panzerfaust 250**, but the end of the war prevented these versions ever getting past the testing stage.

The Panzerfaust projectile could penetrate up to 200 m (7.87 in) of armour set at an angle of 30°, while the smaller Panzerfaust 30 (klein) could penetrate 140 mm (5.51 in). Therefore any Allied tank was vulnerable to the Panzerfaust, and tank crews took to adding extra protection to their vehicles, this ranging from stand-off plates along the sides to piles of sandbags around the hulls and even lengths of spare track at all likely places. The Panzerfausts were produced in their tens of thousands right up until May 1945. They could be used only once, which was something of a liability for German raw material resources, so it was planned that the projected Panzerfaust 150 and Panzerfaust 250 would be reloadable to conserve metal stocks.

The Panzerfaust exactly suited the German defensive tactics of 1943-5, and Allied tank crews came to fear the weapon. Being available in huge numbers, at least one Panzerfaust was carried by almost every German vehicle,

Right: A drill book example of how to aim and fire a Panzerfaust 30 or 60. The weapon tube had to be held under the arm or over the shoulder to allow the propellant exhaust to vent to the rear safely, so the weapon was not meant to be used in enclosed areas.

and many of the hapless Volkssturm went into action with nothing else. If the Panzerfaust was aimed properly and used at the correct range, every German soldier could have at least one Allied tank destroyed to his credit, but the introduction of stand-off armour and infantry squads accompanying Allied tanks offset some of the worst the German infantry could do.

Specification
Panzerfaust 30 (klein)
Range: 30 m (32.8 yards)
Weights: total 1.475 kg (3.25 lb); projectile 0.68 kg (1.5 lb)
Projectile diameter: 100 mm (3.94 in)
Muzzle velocity: 30 m (98 ft) per second
Armour penetration: 140 mm (5.51 in)

Panzerfaust 30
Range: 30 m (32.8 yards)

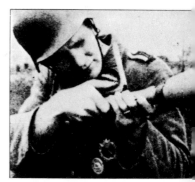

Weights: total 5.22 kg (11.5 lb); projectile 3 kg (6.6 lb)
Projectile diameter: 150 mm (5.91 in)
Muzzle velocity: 30 m (98 ft) per second
Armour penetration: 200 mm (7.87 in)

Panzerfaust 60
Range: 60 m (65.6 yards)
Weights: total 6.8 kg (15 lb); projectile 3 kg (6.6 lb)
Projectile diameter: 150 mm (5.91 in)
Muzzle velocity: 45 m (148 ft) per second
Armour penetration: 200 mm (7.87 in)

Anti-tank rifles

The German army used two main types of anti-tank rifle but, as will be related, they attempted to develop many more models. The first in-service weapon was the **7.92-mm Panzerbüchse 38**, an 0.312-in rifle produced by Rheinmetall-Borsig. This was a weapon that was both complex and expensive, for it resembled a miniature artillery piece so far as the breech mechanism was concerned. This featured a small sliding breech block and an automatic ejector for the spent cartridge case. About 1,600 of these anti-tank rifles were procured by the German army, but the type was not accepted as a full service-standard weapon although those that were produced were retained in service and were used during the early war years.

The standard German anti-tank rifle was the **7.92-mm Panzerbüchse 39**. This was a much simpler weapon than the Panzerbüchse 38 and was produced by the Gustloff-Werke of Suhl. This weapon still had a sliding breech block for the powerful cartridge, but the block was operated by pulling down the pistol grip. Like the earlier rifle it was a single-shot weapon and the stock could be folded to make carriage more handy. Extra ammunition could be carried on the weapon in small boxes secured on each side of the breech mechanism.

These two anti-tank rifles fired the same ammunition, which originally used a hard steel core. In 1939 numbers of Polish Marosczek anti-tank rifles were captured, and on examination it was found that the bullets fired by this very effective weapon had a tungsten core that gave much better armour penetration. The Germans seized upon this principle and adopted it to lengthen the service life of their own anti-tank rifles, which would otherwise have been rendered obsolete by increases in enemy tank armour.

The Germans developed a surprising number of follow-on designs in an effort to replace the Panzerbüchse 39. Various manufacturers produced a series of prototypes, all of them in 7.92-mm calibre, but none of them got past the prototype stage. There was even a programme to develop an anti-tank machine-gun known as the **MG 141**, but again that did not proceed far

The Panzerbüchse 39 is shown in the travelling position (below) and with the bipod lowered and stock extended ready for action (above). German anti-tank rifles were rendered obsolete by the increasing thickness of tank armour.

An Afrika Korps soldier is seen with a 7.92-mm (0.312-in) Panzerbüchse 39. This was a single-shot rifle that fired tungsten-cored projectiles. The projectile could penetrate 25 mm (0.5-in) of armour at 300 m (328 yards), making it unable to tackle any but the lightest tanks after 1940.

along its development path.

There was one further anti-tank rifle used by the Germans, but this was a Swiss product known as the **7.92-mm M SS 41**. This was produced by Waffenfabrik Solothurn in Switzerland to German specifications, but not many appear to have been made or delivered though some were used in North Africa. Solothurn was also responsible for the design and manufacture of a weapon more accurately described as an anti-tank cannon, for it was the **2-cm Panzerabwehrbüchse 785(s)**. This was a fairly bulky weapon that was towed on its own two-wheeled mounting, and again only a limited number were procured by the Germans. Others went to Italy, where the type was known as the **Fucile anticarro**. It was an automatic weapon that used five- or 10-round magazines, and was sometimes known as the **s18-1100**; some were used by the Netherlands during 1939 and 1940 as the **Geweer tp 18-1110**.

The German Granatbüchse 39 was a converted PzB 39 anti-tank rifle fitted with a 'Schiessbecher' grenade launcher cup on the muzzle. The grenades fired included small hollow-charge anti-tank grenades (see cross section) that were effective only against the very lightest armour at ranges up to 125 m (136 yards).

Specification
PzB 38
Calibre: 7.92 mm (0.312 in)
Lengths: overall with stock extended 1.615 m (63.58 in); barrel 1.085 m (42.72 in)
Weight: 16.2 kg (35.71 lb)
Muzzle velocity: 1210 m (3,970 ft) per second
Armour penetration: 25 mm (0.98 in) at 300 m (328 yards)

PzB 39
Calibre: 7.92 mm (0.312 in)
Lengths: overall with stock extended 1.62 m (63.78 in); barrel 1.085 m (42.72 in)
Weight: 12.6 kg (27.78 lb)
Muzzle velocity: 1265 m (4,150 ft) per second
Armour penetration: 25 mm (0.98 in) at 300 m (328 yards)

Suicide anti-tank methods

The users of Japanese lunge mines were often killed at the moment of explosion, but the lunge mine was not really a 'suicide weapon', for in theory the user had a good chance of surviving. The Japanese suicide anti-tank weapons were rather more extreme, for by 1944 it had become an accepted method of warfare that Japanese soldiers, sailors and airmen were called upon to commit suicide as a measure to destroy Allied equipment and personnel in an attempt to keep the Allies away from the Japanese home islands, together with their spiritual and material resources. The best known of these suicide measures was the *kamikaze* flying bomb, but there were others that are now less well known, including various forms of self-destruction involved in eliminating Allied tanks.

Perhaps the most extreme of these were the backpack human mines. This weapon was very simple to devise and devastating in use, for it consisted of little more than a canvas backpack loaded with about 9 kg (19.8 lb) of explosive to form a satchel charge. The user wore this charge and concealed himself until an Allied tank approached. He then ran forward to the tank and dived underneath it, at the same time pulling a length of cord that initiated a short delay to ensure the tank would be right over the charge before it exploded, destroying both tank and user. This tactic was hard to counter, for very often the user waited until the tank was really close before making his suicide rush, so protecting infantry had to be very quick to react if they were to prevent the attack. It was also very unnerving for Allied tank

crews. A variant on the satchel charge was a Type 93 anti-tank mine on a pole which was simply shoved under a track with dire results for both the track and the user.

A further modification on the suicide theme was encountered in some parts of Burma in 1945. Here there was no deliberate death rush, for the hapless anti-tank troops were concealed in foxholes either in the centre of roads or tracks, or at the sides of routes that Allied tanks were expected to use. There they remained until a tank approached, and once one was overhead or very close the idea was that it would be destroyed by the man in the foxhole setting off a charge: this might be a simple explosive device, or a form of mine, or sometimes even a small aircraft bomb. The charges were set off manually and deliberately by

the suicide candidate, who acted as little more than a human fuse. In practice this ploy did not work too well for the personnel in their foxholes were easily spotted by infantry and were killed before they could use their charges. Accounts exist of Allied personnel surrounding foxholes and their suicidal occupants without the Japanese making any attempts to injure the attackers with their charges: the philosophy appears to have been that such attackers were not tanks and the explosives had to be saved to use against tanks, not infantry. As these suicide anti-tank miners had no weapons other than their explosives they were killed in their foxholes to no benefit for the Japanese war effort.

Anti-tank Rifle Type 97

When it came to anti-tank rifles, the Japanese general staff decided to go one better than most contemporary designs and produce a rifle firing a powerful 20-mm (0.79-in) cartridge. This emerged as the **Anti-tank Rifle Type 97**, and while it was certainly a powerful weapon by the standards of the day it was also extremely heavy, weighing no less than 67.5 kg (148.8 lb) when being carried and 51.75 kg (114 lb) once emplaced. Much of this weight resulted from the adoption of a gas-operated mechanism which was locked by a tilting breech block. Ammunition was fed from an overhead seven-round box magazine.

Once emplaced the Type 97 used a bipod mounted just forward of the body and a monopod under the butt. Despite the ferocious recoil the weapon was intended to be directed and fired from the shoulder, which cannot have endeared the weapon to its users. Normally the Type 97 was carried on two special poles by two men, but more often four men were used. It was possible to fit a small shield for added protection and to this shield could be added a carrying bar that resembled bicycle handlebars, though this component was often omitted to reduce the weight of the weapon. Another one of these carrying bars could be added under the butt. In action the Type 97 was often difficult to spot as it was a long, low weapon.

During the early months of the Pacific campaign the Type 97 proved itself to be a useful weapon against the light tanks it was called upon to tackle but once larger and heavier tanks (such as the American M4 Sherman) appeared on the scene the Type 97 was no longer of much value. At best it could penetrate 30 mm (1.18 in) of case-hardened armour at 250 m (273

The Japanese Type 97 anti-tank rifle was a heavy weapon that weighed 51.75 kg in action, mainly due to the gas-operated semi-automatic mechanism. It had a calibre of 20 mm (0.787 in) and required a crew of two men to fire and four to carry it, using a system of frames.

yards), and against anything heavier it was of little use. But the Japanese did not phase out the Type 97 as they were far too short of modern weapons to let any be discarded. The Type 97 was retained, but no longer primarily for anti-armour use: instead many of those available were emplaced as anti-invasion weapons on the Pacific islands, where they were sometimes able to cause damage to landing craft and light amphibious landing vehicles. Some measure of anti-armour capability was retained by the fitting of special grenade launcher cups to some Type 97s. These launcher cups could be secured to the muzzle by means of a locking bar once the circular muzzle brake had been unscrewed. The idea was a copy of the German Schiessbecker grenade-launchers, and used very similar grenades. But the principle, although of some effectiveness, was more suited to orthodox service rifles than to the large and complex Type 97 so it was not used extensively.

Overall, the Type 97 was not used by the Japanese in any great numbers. The complexity of the weapon made it rather difficult and thus costly to produce, and after 1942 the operational

The 20-mm (0.787-in) Type 97 anti-tank rifle used a gas-operated mechanism, but the heavy recoil involved meant that a fully-automatic mode could be little used. Four men were needed to carry this rifle using special frames, and a shield was an optional extra. The box magazine held seven rounds.

requirement for it was limited.

The ammunition fired by the Type 97 was produced in several forms. Apart from the usual armour piercing round (with tracer) there was a high explosive projectile (with tracer and with an optional self-destruct), a high explosive incendiary and a practice

round. The armour-piercing projectile had a solid steel body, and there was also an incendiary projectile complete with a tracer element.

Specification
Anti-tank Rifle Type 97
Calibre: 20 mm (0.79 in)
Lengths: overall 2.095 m (6 ft 10.5 in); barrel 1.063 m (3 ft 5.9 in)
Weights: travelling 67.5 kg (148.8 lb); in action 51.75 kg (114.1 lb)
Muzzle velocity: 793 m (2,602 ft) per second

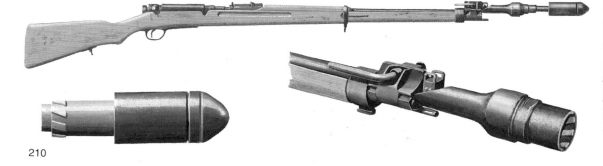

The Japanese Type 2 anti-tank grenade launchers could be fitted to the muzzle of all Japanese service rifles. They were direct copies of the German Gewehr Panzergranate and the grenades had calibres of 30 or 40 mm (1.18 or 1.57 in).

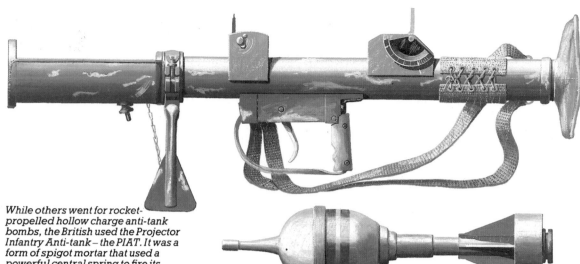

PIAT

UK

PIAT stood for **Projector, Infantry, Anti-Tank Mk 1**, and denoted a British anti-tank weapon that somehow bypassed the usual stringent weapon-selection procedures used by the War Office as it was a product of the unusual department known colloquially as 'Winston Churchill's Toy Shop'. It was designed to make use of the hollow-charge anti-armour effect and fired a useful grenade that could penetrate almost any contemporary tank's protection, and thus it came into the same general category as the American bazooka or the German Panzerfaust. However, the PIAT relied not upon chemical energy to deliver its grenade but coiled spring energy, for the weapon worked on the spigot mortar principle. Using this method the PIAT grenade was projected from an open trough and was supported for the initial part of its travel by a central spigot. Pulling the trigger released a powerful main spring and this spring enabled the spigot to strike the grenade's propelling charge to fire it from the trough. The propelling charge also recocked the main spring ready for another grenade to be loaded.

The PIAT was intended primarily as an anti-tank weapon, but it could also fire high explosive and smoke grenades, which made it much more versatile than many of its contemporaries. It was a very useful weapon in house-to-house and urban combat, for the forward monopod was capable of being extended to provide a fair degree of elevation for use in confined spaces.

The PIAT replaced the Boys anti-tank rifle as the infantry's standard anti-tank weapon, and it was issued widely throughout the British and some Commonwealth armies. However, it cannot be said to have been very popular for it was rather bulky and heavy and required a two-man team to handle it. The main point of unpopularity was the powerful mainspring. This generally required the efforts of two men to cock it. If a grenade failed to fire the weapon was all but uselesss, for recocking the PIAT when the enemy was nearby was a very risky business. But if it fired all was well and the grenade could knock out virtually any enemy tank. In fact the use of the PIAT spread outside the ranks of the infantry, for it was often the

main armament of light armoured vehicles such as the various Universal Carriers and some light armoured cars. There was also some limited use of the weapon on various carriers, which mounted up to 14 PIATs on a multiple mounting for use as a mobile mortar battery.

The PIAT served on for some years with the British army after World War II, but was replaced as soon as possible. Although it was an effective tank-killer it used a principle that was not adopted by any other designers. It did have the advantage that it could be produced in quantity and at a relatively low cost at a time when anti-tank weapons of any type were in great demand.

Specification
PIAT
Length: overall 0.99 m (3 ft 0 in)
Weights: launcher 14.51 kg (32 lb); grenade 1.36 kg (3 lb)
Muzzle velocity: 76-137 m (250-450 ft) per second
Ranges: combat 101 m (110 yards); maximum 338 m (370 yards)

While others went for rocket-propelled hollow charge anti-tank bombs, the British used the Projector Infantry Anti-tank – the PIAT. It was a form of spigot mortar that used a powerful central spring to fire its projectile from a front-mounted 'trough'. It was not a popular weapon, but it could kill tanks.

Above: The PIAT was the British Army's standard squad anti-tank weapon after 1941 and was carried and used by most combat arms and services. It was a rather hefty load to carry, but it could knock out most enemy tanks at close ranges and could fire HE and smoke bombs as well.

Below: Here the crew of a knocked-out British tank are covering their position armed with a PIAT until a recovery vehicle can arrive to retrieve the damaged vehicle. The men are from the 13/18th Hussars, and the location is near Mount Pincon, northern France, July 1944. Note the No. 4 rifle near the PIAT.

Northover Projector

In the aftermath of Dunkirk the British army was left with virtually no anti-tank weapons available in any quantity other than grenades and a few 2-pdr anti-tank guns. With invasion imminent there was a need for an easily-produced weapon that could be used to arm not only the army but the newly-formed Local Defence Volunteers, later to become the Home Guard. One of the weapons that was rushed into production was the Northover mortar, also known as the bottle mortar but later designated the **Northover Projector**. The Northover was typical of the British 'pipe guns' of the period, and was produced very quickly and cheaply indeed.

The Northover Projector was little more than a steel pipe with a rudimentary breech mechanism at one end. The ammunition consisted of orthodox hand and rifle grenades that were propelled from the muzzle by a small black-powder charge. Later the glass bottle No. 76 phosphorus grenade was fired, and this gave rise to the name bottle mortar. There was no recoil mechanism since all recoil forces were absorbed by the projector's four-legged mounting: the legs were simple tubes and were easily produced. The sights were very basic but were accurate enough up to about 91 m (100 yards), and the maximum range was about 274 m (300 yards).

The Northover Projector was a very rudimentary weapon and thankfully it never had to be used in action. During 1940 and for some time afterwards it was a standard Home Guard weapon, and it was also issued to many army units for a while to provide them with at least some form of anti-tank weapon. In practice the Northover was only as good as the projectiles it fired, and as these were orthodox hand or rifle grenades their efficiency against most tanks was doubtful. The use of the white phosphorus bottle grenades would no doubt have been more successful, but this was not a popular weapon with the projector crews for the simple reason that the glass bottles often broke inside the barrels as they were fired, with obvious and highly unfortunate results. The usual crew for a projector was two men, with possibly another in charge of the weapon and for designating targets. Many Home Guard units introduced their own local modifications to enable the Northover

to be moved around more easily. These included such measures as carrying the projector on simple hand-carts to mounting the projector barrels on motorcycle sidecars. There were even some mounted on simple artillery-type carriages. In order to make the normal four-legged carriage easier to handle, a lightened **Northover Projector Mk 2** version was introduced during 1941, but by that time the urgent need for pipe guns such as the Northover had begun to wane and relatively few of these carriages were produced.

Very few Northover Projectors appear to have survived the war years but from time to time the glass phosphorus grenades still emerge from their war-time hiding places.

Specification
Northover Projector
Calibre: 63.5 mm (2.5 in)
Weights: projector 27.2 kg (60 lb); mounting 33.6 kg (74 lb)
Range: effective 91 m (100 yards); maximum 274 m (300 yards)

The Northover Projector was a 1940s weapon produced to equip the Home Guard. It was supposed to be used as an anti-tank weapon to fire the No. 76 bottle grenade filled with phosphorus. There was no recoil mechanism as the frame carriage was supposed to absorb the recoil, and the propelling charge was black powder.

An enterprising Home Guard unit from Sussex mounted their Northover Projector on this small hand cart, and are seen optimistically using it as an anti-aircraft weapon, a role for which it was entirely unsuited. The range was far too short and the muzzle velocity of the glass grenade much too slow.

Boys anti-tank rifle

The **Rifle, Anti-tank, 0.55-in, Boys, Mk 1** was originally known as the **Stanchion Gun**, but the name was later changed to honour the name of its principle designer after he died just before the weapon entered service. It was designed to be the standard infantry anti-tank weapon of the British army, but it was soon overtaken by events and had only a short active career. The first of the type entered service during the late 1930s and by 1942 the weapon was obsolete, overtaken by rapid increases in enemy tank armour that the Boys rifle could no longer tackle.

The Boys anti-tank rifle had a calibre of 13.97 mm (0.55 in) and fired a powerful cartridge that could penetrate 21 mm (0.827 in) at 302 m (330 yards). The cartridge produced an equally powerful recoil, and this did

little to endear the weapon to its firer. To reduce this recoil somewhat the long slender barrel was fitted with a muzzle brake. Ammunition was fed into the bolt-action firing mechanism from an overhead five-round box magazine. Overall the Boys was rather long and heavy, which made it an awkward load to carry, so it was often mounted as the main weapon on board

A French officer is about to receive the hefty recoil from a Boys anti-tank rifle. The French army used a number of these rifles in 1940, provided by the British in exchange for a number of 25-mm (0.98-in) Hotchkiss anti-tank cannon. This example is the original Mk 1 with the monopod supporting leg.

Bren Gun or Universal Carriers. More were used as the main armament of some light armoured cars.

The first production Boys anti-tank rifles used a forward-mounted monopod combined with a handgrip under the butt plate. After Dunkirk various modifications were made to speed production, and among the measures taken was replacement of the forward monopod by a Bren Gun bipod and of the circular muzzle brake attachment by a new Solothurn muzzle brake with holes drilled along the sides; this latter was easier to produce than the original. In this form the Boys saw out its short service life, as by late 1940 it was regarded as being of only limited use as an anti-armour weapon. Eventually it was replaced by the PIAT, but before it finally departed it had a brief flurry of popularity during the Eritrean and Cyrenaica campaigns of 1940 and 1941. It was found to be a very effective anti-personnel weapon during these campaigns as it could be fired at rocks over or near a concealed enemy, the resultant rock splinters acting as effective anti-personnel fragments. The Boys also found its way into US Marine Corps hands during the Philippines campaign of early 1942, when some were used very sparingly against dug-in Japanese infantry positions. How these Boys rifles got to the Far East is not recorded. Some captured Boys anti-tank rifles were also used by the Germans for a short while after Dunkirk, but only in limited numbers; the type was known as the **13.9-mm Panzerabwehrbüchse 782(e)**.

In 1940 there were plans to produce a Mk 2 version of the Boys. This would have been a shortened and lightened version for use by airborne forces but it did not get very far before the project was terminated, no doubt because the shortened barrel would have produced an even more violent recoil.

Specification
Boys Mk 1
Calibre: 13.97 mm (0.55 in)
Lengths: overall 1.625 m (5 ft 4 in); barrel 0.914 m (36 ft 0 in)
Weight: 16.33 kg (36 lb)
Muzzle velocity: 991 m (3,250 ft) per second
Armour penetration: 21 mm (0.827 in) at 302 m (330 yards)

The two service versions of the Boys anti-tank rifle were the Mk 1 (above) and the generally simpler Mk 1* (below). The Mk 1* was introduced to speed production, and had a simpler muzzle brake and a Bren Gun bipod, plus some other slight changes.

An armourer services a Boys anti-tank rifle Mk 1, easily recognizable from its monopod and circular muzzle brake. These rifles were little used after 1941 as they could penetrate only the lightest enemy armour, yet they were awkward to carry and when fired had a recoil that was best described as fearful.

INTERNATIONAL
Molotov cocktail

The **Molotov cocktail** appears to have had its operational debut during the Spanish Civil War of 1936-9, when it was first used against Nationalist tanks by the Republican forces. From these beginnings the Molotov cocktail soon became used by most nations as it was an easy weapon to produce and use, by forces both regular and irregular.

The basic weapon known as the Molotov cocktail is simply a glass bottle containing petrol (or some other inflammable substance) with an oil-

The Molotov cocktail was an international weapon, and shown here from the left are examples from the Soviet Union, (the second an 'official' Red Army version), Britain (using a milk bottle), Japan and Finland. All use the same basic simple form, with petrol soaked rags to act as fuses for ignition.

soaked rag or something similar around the neck. This rag is ignited immediately before the weapon is thrown at a target, the breaking of the bottle as it hits its target allowing the contents to be ignited. It is all very simple, easily understood and easily used. The snag was that it was not very efficient. If the bottle smashes against the side armour or turret of a tank the results can be spectacular but not very harmful to the vehicle or its occupants. The only way to ensure damage is to detonate the bottle bomb over or near the engine louvres or perhaps the vision devices. It was also discovered early on that petrol alone was not a very efficient anti-armour weapon as it simply runs off the sides of a tank even as it was burning. In order to make the flame-producing mixture 'stick', the petrol had to be mixed with a thickening agent such as diesel or oil or in some cases various forms of latex. These niceties tended to move the Molotov cocktails out of the realms of the street fighter and into the domain of the regular soldier, and after 1939 the bottle grenade or bomb was used by many regular forces. The Finns were

British troops train with Molotov cocktails during 1940. The British Army referred to these weapons as 'bottle bombs' and even established production lines for them, often using milk bottles filled with petrol and phosphorus.

early exponents in their battles against the Soviet invaders of 1939-40, and after Dunkirk the petrol bomb was a weapon much used by British army units defending the United Kingdom. Later on, Soviet partisans made the Molotov cocktail their own particular weapon, but it was also used by regular Red Army forces. Many underground militias found the weapon easy to make and use.

An offshoot of the glass petrol bomb was the phosphorus grenade, used by several nations. This was designed as a smoke grenade, but the burning white phosphorus, which started to burn as soon as it was exposed to the air, also made it a very useful anti-personnel and anti-armour weapon. There were several of these types of grenade but typical was the British **Grenade, Self-Igniting, Phosphorus,**

No. 76. This was a glass milk bottle with a pressed-on cap (containing a mixture of phosphorus, water and benzine) and was intended primarily for the anti-tank role. It could be thrown at its target or launched from the Northover Projector, and contained a piece of smoked rubber that gradually dissolved in the mixture to make it 'stick' better to its target. Each No. 76 gre-

nade weighed about 0.535 kg (1.18 lb). It cannot be said that these phosphorus grenades were weapons popular with either the users or the recipients. They were the cause of frequent accidents in transit or use, and in the United Kingdom many were buried or hidden away when their fillings became unstable. Many are still discovered in their wartime caches to this day.

UK/USA/USSR
Anti-tank grenades

The British army used three types of anti-armour hand grenade. The first was the **Grenade, Hand, Anti-tank, No. 73**, known as the 'Thermos' bomb from its shape and size. It was a pure blast weapon which often had little effect on armour, so it was mainly used for demolition work. More common during the early war years was the infamous **Grenade, Hand, Anti-tank, No. 74 (ST)**, the 'Sticky bomb' which was coated in a gooey adhesive to make it stick to the side of a tank after landing. Normally the sticky surface was contained within two shell halves which were removed just before throwing. The No. 74 was a most unpopular weapon as the sticky substance tended to make it stick to anything, even before throwing, and the type was used as little as possible.

The best of the British anti-tank grenades was the **Grenade, Hand, Anti-tank, No. 75** otherwise known as the Hawkins Grenade. It was intended to be either thrown or laid as a mine to blow off a tank's tracks. It used a crush igniter fuse and about half of its weight of 1.02 kg (2.25 lb) was made up of the bursting charge. The type was often used in clusters for better effect, and the Germans captured so many of them before Dunkirk that they were later used as part of the minefields defending the Atlantic Wall with the designation Panzerabwehrmine 429/1(e).

The **Grenade, Rifle, Anti-tank, No. 68** was a rifle grenade fired from a muzzle cup fitted to the No. 1 Mk III rifle. It was withdrawn after 1941 as it was not much use against anything other than very light armour. It weighed 0.79 kg (1.75 lb) and could also be fired from the Northover Projector.

The American equivalent of the No. 68 was the **Antitank Rifle Grenade M9A1**, a much more successful grenade that could be fired from an M7 launcher fitted to the M1 Garand rifle or an M8 launcher fitted to an M1 Carbine. The M9A1 grenade weighed 0.59 kg (1.31 lb) and had an 0.113-kg (0.25-lb) warhead behind a thin steel

The American Anti-tank Rifle Grenade M9A1 could be fired from a muzzle attachment fitted to the M1 Garand rifle to a range of about 100 m (109 yards). Its hollow charge warhead could penetrate up to 101 mm (4 in) of armour. It could also be fired from the M1 carbine using the M8 launcher.

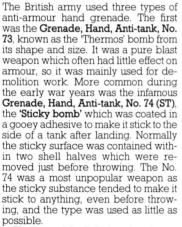

metal nose fitted with an impact fuse. Its capability against tanks was somewhat limited, but it was retained in service for some time as it was a very useful weapon against targets such as pillboxes. A ring tail was used for in-flight stabilization.

As with the anti-tank rifle, the Soviets tended to neglect the anti-tank grenade and had to rush something into service in rather a hurry in 1940. Their first attempt was the **RPG 1940**, which resembled a short stick grenade and relied mainly on blast for its effect; it was not a great success and was gradually replaced. The contemporary **VPGS 1940** was a rifle grenade which featured a long rod that fitted into the rifle barrel before firing. It too was no great success. The best of the wartime Soviet anti-tank grenades was the **RPG** introduced in 1943. This was a hand-thrown grenade which in some ways followed the example of the German Panzerwurfmine, but had a tail unit that trailed on two canvas strips to keep the warhead with its hollow charge pointed towards the target. The RPG weighed 1.247 kg (2.75 lb), and was thus quite a weight to throw, but it had a heavy explosive content and could be very effective. The RPG was retained in service for some years after 1945, and is still used by some Soviet-influenced armed forces.

Above: The RPG 1943 was the Soviet equivalent of the German Wurfmine, but it used a fabric strip stabilizer tail to keep the hollow charge warhead pointing towards the target tank when in flight. The tail was ejected from the throwing handle after the grenade had been thrown and after the arming pin had been removed.

Below: The Soviet RPG-6 was a late-war version of the RPG 1943. It used a revised warhead shape and four fabric tails to stabilize the warhead in flight. The revised warhead also had a good fragmentation effect, so it could be used as an anti-personnel weapon. It was used for many years after 1945.

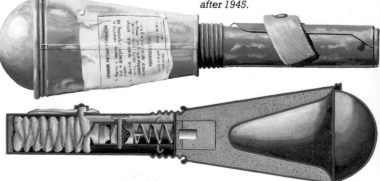

Allied and Axis Rifles

World War II saw the decline in importance of the infantryman as marksman and the first appearance of his replacement, the infantryman as firepower component. After an uncharacteristically tentative start, it was Germany that, as so often, led the way.

In any army the new soldier is always trained in the use of one basic form of service rifle, whatever his eventual trade may be. During World War II this was as true as it is now, but the rifle with which the individual soldier might be trained varied a great deal. Depending on the particular nation, the soldier might have been issued with a venerable antique while in others he might have received a shiny new model embodying all the latest technology, for the rifles used in World War II varied greatly.

At one end of the scale there were the old bolt-action rifles that had been in use since long before World War I; and at the other were the new self-loading or automatic rifles that eventually led to the first of what are now known as assault rifles. There were none of the latter in service when the war started in 1939, but as the war progressed the first operational models of such weapons appeared in service. These gave the infantryman a greatly increased firepower potential, but it was not until the true assault rifles (with their lower-powered cartridges) arrived from about 1943 onwards that the full quantum jump from the slow and steady single shots of the bolt-action rifle to the full

A US Marine dashes for cover carrying his .30in M1 Garand rifle, the standard infantry weapon for American soldiers during World War II. More than five million were made in total.

automatic fire of the assault rifle was fully appreciated. The bolt-action rifles were usually sound and reliable weapons, but they lacked the shock effect of an assault rifle fired in the fully automatic mode.

Thus World War II was a war of transition for the basic infantryman. When the war started, usually all he had to hand was a bolt-action rifle of a well-tried but frequently elderly pattern. By the time the war was over every soldier had at least a foretaste of what the future had in store in the form of the assault rifle. There were some odd digressions along the way, such as the underpowered US Carbine M1 and the ingenious but complex German FG 42. Some nations, such as the United Kingdom, did not make the transition and relied upon the Lee-Enfield bolt-action rifles throughout, but the move towards the self-loading or assault rifle was still there.

This section does not contain all the rifles used during World War II, but the weapons discussed are typical of the period. Millions of soldiers used them under all manner of conditions, and the survivors will remember them until their final days.

Gewehr 98 and Karabiner 98k

The 7.92-mm (0.312-in) **Gewehr 98** was the rifle with which the German army fought through World War I. It was a Mauser rifle first produced in 1898, but was based on a design dating back to 1888. In service the Mauser action proved sturdy and reliable, but in the years following 1918 the German army carried out a great deal of operational analysis that demonstrated that the Gewehr 98 was really too long and bulky for front-line use. As an immediate result the surviving Gewehr 98s underwent a modification programme that changed their designation to **Karabiner 98b**. *Karabiner* is the German for carbine, but there was nothing of the carbine in the Karabiner 98b, whose length was unchanged from that of the original Gewehr 98. The only changes were to the bolt handle, the sling swivels and the ability to use improved ammunition. To confuse matters further the original Gewehr 98 markings were retained.

The Karabiner 98b was still in service with the German army in 1939 (and remained so throughout the war), but by then the standard rifle was a slightly shorter version of the basic Mauser known as the **Karabiner 98k**. This was slightly shorter than the original Gewehr 98 but was still long for a carbine, despite the letter suffix 'k' standing for *kurz*, or short. This rifle was based on a commercial Mauser model known as the **Standard** and widely produced throughout the interwar years in countries such as Czechoslovakia, Belgium and even China. The German version was placed in production in 1935 and thereafter made in very large numbers. At first the standard of production was excellent, but once World War II had started the overall finish and standards fell to the extent that by the end of the war the wooden furniture was often laminated or of an inferior material, and such items as bayonet lugs were omitted. All manner of extras were evolved by the gadget-minded Germans for the Karabiner 98k, including grenade-launching devices, periscopic sights and folding butts for weapons used by airborne troops. There were also variations for sniper use, some with small telescopic sights mounted half way along the forestock and others with larger telescopes mounted over the bolt action.

Despite all the innovations by the Germans during World War II, the Karabiner 98k was still in production as the war ended, looking not all that different overall from the original

Gewehr 98, other than in the rough finish resulting from wartime shortages of labour and materials. By that time the Germans had to hand a whole array of Mauser rifles drawn from nearly all the armies of Europe, and most of them were used to equip one arm or another of the services by 1945. Some of these Mausers, most of which were very similar to the Gewehr 98 or Karabiner 98k, were kept in production on Czech and Belgian lines for German use after 1939-40. Away to the east the Chinese armies were mainly equipped with the Mauser Standard rifles that were virtually identical to the Karabiner 98k.

There will always be arguments as to whether or not the Mauser rifles were better service rifles than the Lee-Enfield, M1903 Springfield or the M1 Garand, but although the Mausers lacked some of the overall appeal of the Allied rifles they provided the German forces with long and reliable service. Few remain in use, but many are still prized as collector's pieces and many are retained for match rifle use.

Specification
Gewehr 98
Calibre: 7.92 mm (0.312 in)
Length: 1.25 m (49.2 in)
Length of barrel: 740 mm (29.1 in)
Weight: 4.2 kg (9.26 lb)
Muzzle velocity: 640 m (2,100 ft) per second
Magazine: 5-round box

Specification
Karabiner 98k
Calibre: 7.92 mm (0.312 in)
Length: 1.1075 m (43.6 in)
Length of barrel: 600 mm (23.6 in)
Weight: 3.9 kg (8.6 lb)
Muzzle velocity: 755 m (2,477 ft) per second
Magazine: 5-round box

The Karabiner 98k was a slightly shortened version of the Gewehr 98 which served Germany in World War I, and although supposedly a carbine the weapon was as long as many rifles of the period.

Wehrmacht soldiers train for combat, armed with Karabiner 98k rifles. The photograph was probably taken between the wars, as indicated by the old and new pattern helmets being worn at the same time.

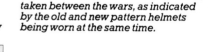

Left: Digging in during the early stages of the war. The length of the Mauser-designed 98k is obvious, making it difficult to handle in confined spaces. Given the short combat ranges typical of World War II, the long-range performance of the 98k was largely superfluous.

Gewehr 41(W) and Gewehr 43

The German army maintained an overall 'quality control' section that constantly sought ways in which the German forces could increase their efficiency, and by 1940 this section had discovered a need for some form of self-loading rifle to improve combat efficiency. A specification was duly issued to industry, and Walther and Mauser each put forward designs that proved to be remarkably similar. Both used a method of operation known as the 'Bang' system (after its Danish designer), in which gases trapped around the muzzle are used to drive back a piston to carry out the reloading cycle. Troop trials soon proved that the

Mauser design was unsuitable for service use and it was withdrawn, leaving the field free for the Walther design which became the 7.92-mm (0.312-in) **Gewehr 41(W)**.

Unfortunately for the Germans, once the Gewehr 41(W) reached front-line service, mainly on the Eastern Front, it proved to be somewhat less than a success. The Bang system proved to be too complex for reliable operation under service conditions and it was really too heavy for comfortable use, making the weapon generally unhandy. The Gewehr 41(W) also proved to be difficult to manufacture and, as if all this was not enough, in action the

weapon proved to be difficult and time-consuming to load. But for a while it was the only self-loading rifle the Germans had and it was kept in production to the extent of tens of thousands

Most of the Gewehr 41(W)s were used on the Eastern Front, and it was there that the Germans encountered the Soviet Tokarev automatic rifles. These used a gas-operated system that tapped off gases from the barrel to operate the mechanism, and once this system was investigated the Germans realized that they could adapt it to suit the Gewehr 41(W). The result was the **Gewehr 43**, which used the Tokarev

system virtually unchanged. Once the Gewehr 43 was in production, manufacture of the Gewehr 41(W) promptly ceased. The Gewehr 43 was much easier to make and it was soon being churned out in large numbers. Frontline troops greatly appreciated the ease with which it could be loaded compared with the earlier rifle and it was a popular weapon. All manner of production short-cuts were introduced into the design, including the use of wood laminates and even plastics for the furniture, and in 1944 an even simpler design known as the **Karabiner 43** was introduced, the *Karabiner* designation being adopted although the overall length was reduced by only some 50 mm (2 in).

Both the Gewehr 41(W) and the late Gewehr 43 used the standard German 7.92-mm (0.312-in) cartridge, and were in no way related to the assault rifle programme that involved the 7.92-mm *kurz* cartridge. The retention of the rifle cartridge enabled the Gewehr 43 to be used as a very effective sniper rifle, and all examples had a telescopic sight mount fitted as standard. The Gewehr 43 was so good in the sniper role that many were retained in Czech army service for many years after the war.

Specification
Gewehr 41(W)
Calibre: 7.92 mm (0.312 in)
Length: 1.124 m (44.25 in)
Length of barrel: 546 mm (21.5 in)
Weight: 5.03 kg (11.09 lb)
Muzzle velocity: 776 m (2,546 ft) per second

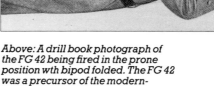

Magazine: 10-round box

Specification
Gewehr 43
Calibre: 7.92 mm (0.312 in)
Length: 1.117 m (44 in)

Length of barrel: 549 mm (21.61 in)
Weight: 4.4 kg (9.7 lb)
Muzzle velocity: 776 m (2,546 ft) per second
Magazine: 10-round box

Developed from the Gewehr 41(W) and influenced by the Tokarev, the Gewehr 43 was fitted with telescopic sights as standard, and was an excellent sniper's rifle.

Fallschirmjägergewehr 42

Above: A drill book photograph of the FG 42 being fired in the prone position wth bipod folded. The FG 42 was a precursor of the modern-concept assault rifle.

In the strange world of Nazi Germany internal strife and rivalry flourished (was even fostered), and in no sphere was this internal feuding more rife than between the German army and the Luftwaffe. By 1942 the Luftwaffe were encroaching on the preserves of the army to an alarming extent for no other reason than petty wrangling, and when the army decided to adopt a self-loading rifle the Luftwaffe decided that it too had to have such a weapon. Instead of following the path followed by the army with its adoption of the *kurz* round, the Lufwaffe decided instead to retain the standard 7.92-mm (0.312-in) rifle cartridge and asked Rheinmetall to design a weapon to arm the Luftwaffe parachute troops, the *Fallschirmjäger*.

Rheinmetall accordingly designed and produced one of the more remarkable small-arms designs of World War II. This was the 7.92-mm (0.312-in) **Fallschirmjägergewehr 42** or **FG 42**, a weapon that somehow managed to compress the action required to produce automatic fire into a volume little larger than that of a conventional bolt action. The FG 42 was certainly an eye-catching weapon, for the first examples had a sloping pistol grip, an oddly-shaped plastic butt and a prominent bipod on the forestock. To cap it all there was a large muzzle attachment and provision for mounting a spike bayonet. The ammunition feed was from a side-mounted box maga-

The FG 42, an early model of which is seen here, was an attempt to arm the German parachute forces with a rifle capable of providing full-power MG performance.

zine on the left, and the mechanism was gas-operated. All in all the FG 42 was a complex weapon, but was not innovative as it was an amalgam of several existing systems.

Needless to say the Luftwaffe took to the FG 42 avidly and asked for more. They did not get them, for it soon transpired that the novelties of the FG 42 had to be paid for in a very complex manufacturing process that consumed an inordinate amount of time and production facilities. Thus supply was slow and erratic, and in an attempt to speed production some simplifications were added. A simpler wooden butt was introduced and the pistol grip was replaced by a more orthodox component. The bipod was moved forward to the muzzle and other short-cuts were introduced. It was to no avail, for by the time the war ended only about 7,000 had been made. But it was after the war that the FG 42 made its biggest mark, for many of its design features were incorporated into later designs. Perhaps the most important of these was the gas-operated mechanism which could fire from a closed bolt position for single-shot fire and from an open bolt for automatic fire, all compressed into a relatively small space.

One thing that was not copied was the side-mounted magazine. This proved to be less than a success in action for not only did it snag on clothing or other items but it tended to unbalance the weapon when fired.

The FG 42 was a highly advanced design for its day and it incorporated many of the features now used on many modern assault rifles. Typical of these was the use of a 'straight line' layout from butt to muzzle and the gas-operated mechanism already mentioned. But for all this the FG 42 was too difficult to produce, and even by 1945 there were still some bugs that remained to be ironed out before the weapon was really problem-free. But for all that it was a truly remarkable design achievement.

Specification
FG 42
Calibre: 7.92 mm (0.312 in)
Length: 940 mm (37 in)
Length of barrel: 502 mm (19.76 in)
Weight: 4.53 kg (9.99 lb)
Muzzle velocity: 761 m (2,500 ft) per second
Magazine: 20-round box
Cyclic rate of fire: 750-800 rpm

First operational use of the FG 42 was in Skorzeny's daring commando raid to free Mussolini. Special camouflage smocks were worn for the raid, and the usual Fallschirmjäger helmets were worn.

Maschinenpistole 43 and Sturmgewehr 44

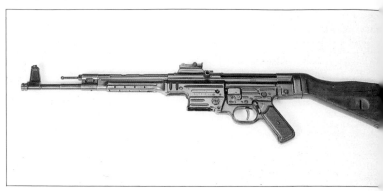

Despite the orders of Hitler, the German army was so determined to develop and use the assault rifle that had been developed by Louis Schmeisser to fire the new Polte *kurz* (short) 7.92-mm (0.312-in) cartridge that it hid the experimental work under a new name. Originally the new rifle/cartridge combination had been known as the **Maschinenkarabiner 42(H)** (the H was for Haenel), but to distract attention once Hitler'had issued his ill-advised order it was changed to **Maschinenpistole 43**, or **MP 43**. With the weapon in this form, the army went ahead from the development to the production stage, and the first examples were rushed to the Eastern Front where they soon proved to be invaluable.

The full development story of the MP 43 is provided elsewhere, but it must be stressed that the MP 43 was the first of what are today termed assault rifles. It could fire single shots for selective fire in defence, and yet was capable of producing automatic fire for shock effect in the attack or for close-quarter combat. It was able to do this by firing a relatively low-powered round that was adequate for most combat ranges but which could still be handled comfortably when the weapon was producing automatic fire. Tactically this had a tremendous effect on the way the infantry could fight, as they were no longer dependent on supporting fire from machine-guns, being able to take their own personal support fire with them. This enabled the German infantry to become a far more powerful force because of the quantum increase in firepower that units could produce compared with those equipped with conventional bolt-action rifles.

Once the importance of this firepower increase had been fully realized, the MP 43 became a priority weapon and urgent requests for more and more were made by the front-line troops. Initial supplies went mainly to elite units, but most went to the Eastern Front where they were most needed. Unusually for wartime Germany, prior-ity was given to production rather than development, and the only major change to the design was the **MP 43/1** which had fittings for a grenade-launching cup on the muzzle. In 1944 Hitler rescinded his opposition to the MP 43 and bestowed the more accurate designation of **Sturmgewehr 44 (StG 44)** upon the weapon, but there were few if any production alterations to the basic design.

Some accessories were produced for the MP 43 series. One was an infra-red night sight known as *Vampir*, but one of the oddest items ever to be produced for any weapon was the *Krummlauf* curved barrel that could direct bullets around corners. Apparently this device was developed to clear tank-killing infantry squads from armoured vehicles, but it was a bizarre device that never worked properly and yet managed to absorb a great deal of development potential at a time when that potential could have been directed towards more rewarding things. The curved barrels were intended to direct fire at angles of between 30° and 45°, and special periscopic mirror sights were devised to aim

The SS were among the first units to acquire the MP 43, and many were used in the battle of the Ardennes. First combat use was probably on the Eastern Front, however, where the weapon was an immediate success.

Developed to fire the lower-powered Kurz (short) 7.92-mm round, the MP 43 was the first of the modern assault rifles. The lower-powered round followed German combat analyses, which found that battles were usually fought at ranges which did not require high-power bullets.

their fire. Few were actually produced and even fewer were used operationally.

After the war large numbers of MP 43s were used by several nations such as Czechoslovakia, and were also used during some of the early Arab-Israeli conflicts. A few still turn up in the hands of 'freedom fighters' in Africa and elsewhere.

Specification
StG 44
Calibre: 7.92 mm (0.312 in)
Length: 940 mm (37 in)
Length of barrel: 419 mm (16.5 in)
Weight: 5.22 kg (11.5 lb)
Muzzle velocity: 650 m (2,132 ft) per second
Magazine: 30-round box
Cyclic rate of fire: 500 rpm

Tokarev rifles

The Soviets have developed over the years a considerable talent for small arms innovations, and accordingly they were early in the move towards self-loading rifles. The first of these was the **Avtomaticheskaia Vintovka Simonova** introduced in 1936 (and thus known also as the **AVS36**) and designed by one S. G. Simonov. Although many were made and issued for service, the AVS was not a great success for it produced a prodigious muzzle blast and recoil, and it was all too easy for dust and dirt to get into the rather complex mechanism. The AVS thus had but a short service life before it was replaced.

The **SVT38 (Samozariadnyia Vintovka Tokareva)** that in 1938 replaced the AVS was designed by F. V. Tokarev, and it was initially not much of an improvement on the AVS. It was a gas-operated weapon, like the AVS, but in order to keep the rifle as light as possible the mechanism was far too light for the stresses and strains of prolonged use. While the combination of a gas-operated system and a locking block cammed downwards into a recess in the receiver base proved basically sound, it gave rise to frequent troubles mainly because parts broke. Thus the SVT38 was removed from production during 1940 to be replaced by the

Above: The SVT 40 was an early Soviet self-loading rifle, usually issued to NCOs or marksmen. A most influential weapon, it was to lend features to the German MP 43, and was the start of a chain leading to the modern AK range.

Right: Marines of the Soviet Northern Fleet in defensive positions, probably on exercise near Murmansk. The nearest marine has a PPSh 41 sub-machine gun, the remainder being armed with SVT40 Tokarevs.

SVT40 in which the same basic mechanism was retained, but everything was made much more robust and the result was a much better weapon. However, the SVT40 suffered from the same problems as the AVS and the SVT38 in that the weapon had a fierce recoil and considerable muzzle blast. To off-set these effects at least partially, the SVT40 was fitted with a muzzle brake, initially with six ports but eventually with two. These muzzle brakes were of doubtful efficiency.

In order to get the best from the SVT40 the weapon was usually issued only to NCOs or carefully trained soldiers who could use their rapid fire potential to good effect. Some were fitted with telescopic sights for sniper use. A few weapons were converted to produce fully-automatic fire as the **AVT40**, but this conversion was not a great success and few were made. According to some accounts there was also a carbine version but this probably suffered excessively from the heavy recoil problem and again only a few were made.

When the Germans invaded the Soviet Union in 1941 they soon encountered the SVT38 and the SVT40. Any they could capture they promptly used under the designation **Selbst-ladegewehr 258(r)** and **Selbst-ladegewehr 259(r)**, but once the basic gas-operated mechanism was examined it was promptly copied and incorporated into the Gewehr 43.

Soviet production of the SVT40 continued almost until the end of the war. Although there were never enough produced to meet demands, the SVT40 had a considerable influence on future Soviet small-arms development for it initiated a series of automatic rifles that eventually culminated in the AK-47 series. It also made a considerable impact on Soviet infantry tactics for the SVT40 demonstrated the importance of increased firepower for the infantry, a factor later emphasized by the introduction of the German MP 43 on the Eastern Front.

Specification
SVT40
Calibre: 7.62 mm (0.3 in)
Length: 1.222 m (48.1 in)
Length of barrel 625 mm (24.6 in)
Weight: 3.89 kg (8.58 lb)
Muzzle velocity: 830 m (2,723 ft) per second
Magazine: 10-round box

Soviet Marines of the Baltic Fleet prepare for one of their many amphibious assaults on German *positions along the Baltic coast. Armament includes PPSh 41s, SVT40s and a Degtyayrov LMG.*

USSR
Mosin-Nagant rifles

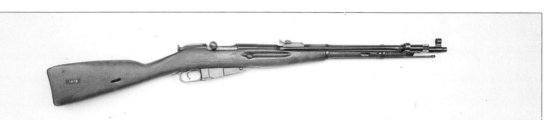

When the Russian army decided to adopt a magazine rifle to replace its Berdan rifles during the late 1880s, it opted for a weapon combining the best features of two designs, one by the Belgian Nagant brothers and the other a Russian design from a Captain Mosin. The result was the **Mosin-Nagant Model 1891** with which the Tsarist army fought its last battles up to 1917. The Model 1891 was then adopted by the new Red Army following the 1918 upsets, and it remained in use for many years thereafter.

The Model 1891 fired a 7.62-mm (0.3-in) cartridge and it was a sound but generally unremarkable design. The bolt action was rather complicated and the ammunition feed used a holding device that offered only one round under spring tension to the bolt for reloading. But for all this it was a sound enough weapon, although rather long. This was mainly to increase the reach of the rifle when fitted with the long socket bayonet, which was almost a permanent fixture once the user was in action. The bayonet had a cruciform point that was used to dismantle the weapon.

The original Model 1891s had their sights marked in arshins, an archaic Russian measurement equivalent to

A Red Army private at about the time of the Winter War with Finland in the winter of 1940. He is armed with the 1930 model of the Mosin-Nagant, a dragoon-length version of the rifle.

0.71 m (27.95 in), but after 1918 these sights were metricated. In 1930 there began a programme to modernize the old rifles, and all new rifles were produced in a new form. This new form was the **Model 1891/30**, which was slightly shorter than the original and had several design points introduced to ease production. It was the Model 1891/30 that was the main Red Army service rifle of World War II and the one used with telescopic sights as a sniper's rifle. Other 'extras' included a grenade-launching cup and a silencer.

The Mosin-Nagant weapons were also produced in carbine form for cavalry and other uses. The first of these was the **Model 1910**, followed much later by the **Model 1938** (the Model 1891/30 equivalent). In 1944 the **Model 1944** was introduced, but this was only a Model 1938 with a permanently fixed folding bayonet alongside the forestock.

The Mosin-Nagant rifles were also used by the Finns (**m/27** shortened Model 1891, **m/28/30** with altered sights, and re-stocked **m/39**), the Poles (**karabin wz 91/98/25**) and also by the Germans. The Germans captured piles of ex-Soviet rifles during 1941 and 1942, and many were issued by the Germans to their own second-line garrison and militia units. Most of these were Model 1891/30s redesignated **Gewehr 254(r)**, but by 1945 even Model 1891s were being issued to the hapless Volkssturm units under the designation **Gewehr 252(r)**. Many units

A Model 1938 Mosin-Nagant carbine. This model, like the 1930, was simplified for ease of manufacture, and was issued to the cavalry. A great many were captured by Germany in the early war years.

along the Atlantic Wall were issued with the Model 1891/30.

With the introduction of the automatic rifle in the post-war years the old Mosin-Nagant rifles were swiftly removed from Red Army use. Some were sold on the open market but most appear to have been stockpiled. Only the short and handy carbines now remain in service today, many in China and the Far East. Many still turn up in the hands of 'freedom fighters'.

Specification
Model 1891/30
Calibre: 7.62 mm (0.3 in)
Length: 1.232 m (48.5 in)
Length of barrel: 729 mm (28.7 in)
Weight: 4 kg (8.8 lb)
Muzzle velocity: 811 m (2,660 ft) per second
Magazine: 5-round box

Specification
Model 1938 carbine
Calibre: 7.62 mm (0.3 in)
Length: 1.016 m (40 in)
Length of barrel: 508 mm (20 in)
Weight: 3.47 kg (7.6 lb)
Muzzle velocity: 766 m (2,514 ft) per second
Magazine: 5-round box

Rifle No. 5 Mark I

By 1943 the British and Commonwealth armies were heavily involved in jungle warfare in Burma and other areas of the Far East, and for the conditions the existing No. 1 and No. 4 Lee-Enfield rifles proved to be too long and awkward in use. Some form of shortened No. 4 was requested, and by September 1944 approval was given for such a rifle to be introduced as the **Rifle No. 5 Mark I**. This was virtually a normal No. 4 Mark I with a much shortened barrel. The forestock was modified to accommodate the new shortened barrel, and the sights were modified to reflect the decreased range performance of the new barrel. There were two other modifications introduced as well, both of them associated with the short barrel: these were a conical muzzle attachment that was meant to act as a flash hider, and a rubber pad on the butt. Both had to be introduced as the shortening of the barrel gave rise to two unwanted side effects: the prodigious muzzle flash produced by firing a normal rifle cartridge in a short barrel, and the ferocious recoil produced by the same source.

In a normal long rifle barrel most of the flash produced on firing is contained within the barrel and so are some of the recoil forces. In a shortened barrel a good proportion of the propellant gases are still 'unused' as the bullet leaves the muzzle, hence the added recoil. The soldiers did not like it one bit but they had to admit that in jungle warfare the No. 5 Mark I was a much handier weapon to carry and use. They also welcomed the reintroduction of a blade-type bayonet that fitted onto a lug under the muzzle attachment. In fact, following on from the first production order for 100,000 rifles made in 1944 it was thought that the No. 5 Mark I would become the standard service rifle of the post-war years, despite all the recoil and flash problems. But this did not happen.

The No. 5 Mark I had one built-in problem, quite apart from the flash and recoil, and that problem was never eradicated. For a reason that was never discovered the weapon was inaccurate. Even after a long period of 'zeroing' the accuracy would gradually 'wander' and be lost. All manner of modifications to the stocking of the weapon was tried, but the inaccuracy was never eliminated and the true cause was never discovered. Thus the No. 5 was not accepted as the standard service rifle, the No. 4 Mark I being retained until the Belgian FN was adopted in the 1950s. Most of the No. 5s were retained for use by specialist units such as those operating in the Far East and Africa, and many are still in use in those areas by various armies.

Specification
Rifle No. 5 Mark I
Calibre: 0.303 in (7.7 mm)
Length: 1.003 m (39.5 in)
Length of barrel: 476 mm (18.75 in)
Weight: 3.25 kg (7.15 lb)
Muzzle velocity: about 730 m (2,400 ft) per second
Magazine: 10-round box

Developed specifically for jungle operations, the No. 5 rifle was not an unqualified success, having a vicious recoil. It saw action in Kenya and Malaya (shown here), as well as at the end of World War II.

De Lisle carbine

The **De Lisle** carbine was one of the more unusual weapons of World War II but very little has ever been written on the subject. The weapon was designed by one William Godfray De Lisle who was, in 1943, an engineer in the Ministry of Aircraft Production. During that period he patented a silencer for a 5.59-mm (0.22-in) rifle, and this attracted the attention of persons interested in producing silent weapons for use during the commando raids which were then being conducted around the coasts of occupied Europe.

Further development of the basic De Lisle silencer resulted in a drastic modification of a Lee-Enfield No. 1 Mark III rifle to accommodate the firing of an 0.45-in (11.43-mm) pistol cartridge. The basic bolt action was retained, but in place of the large box magazine a small magazine casing was substituted. Forward of the bolt action was the silencer itself, and this comprised a series of discs held within a tubular housing that allowed the gases produced on firing to 'swirl' around before they were discharged from ports around the muzzle. Firing the subsonic 0.45-in (11.43-mm) pistol cartridge with this silencer system produced very little noise at all, and even this sounded quite unlike a firearm being discharged. There was also no flash.

The first De Lisle carbines were produced in one of the tool rooms of the Ford works at Dagenham. From there the early prototypes were taken for field testing in commando raids along the north French coast. They proved themselves remarkably successful, and even these early weapons were used in what was to be their main operational role, a form of silent sniping to pick off sentries or other personnel during the early stages of a raid. As the De Lisle carbine fired a pistol cartridge its maximum effective range was limited to 250 m (275 yards), but this was usually more than enough for raids carried out on dark nights.

With trials successfully completed, a production order for 500 carbines was placed and this was later increased to 600. The 'production' programme of modifying the Lee-Enfield rifles was carried out by the Sterling Armament

Some folding stocked De Lisles (top) were used in the Far East, having been designed for paratroops. The early model (below) has been cut away to show the silencer mechanism.

Works, also in Dagenham, but when the programme got under way things had changed.

By the time the De Lisle carbines

were being produced it was mid-1944 and the invasion of Europe had taken place. With the Allies safely ashore there was far less need for a silenced commando weapon and the order was cancelled. By then about 130 had been completed and issued, but as they lacked a role in Europe most were sent to the Far East, where they were used by specialist units in Burma and elsewhere. Many were retained in the area after the war to see action once more during the Malayan Emergency. Some of these weapons did not have the solid butt of the earlier weapons, having instead a metal butt that folded under the weapon. This version had originally been produced for parachute troops, but only a small number was ever made.

Very few De Lisle carbines now exist, even in the most comprehensive small-arms collections. Most of them appear to have been destroyed during the post-war years, probably as the result of their potential as assassination weapons.

Specification
De Lisle carbine
Calibre: 11.43 mm (0.45 in)
Length: 895 mm (35.25 in)
Length of barrel: 184 mm (7.25 in)
Weight: 3.74 kg (8.25 lb)
Muzzle velocity: 253 m (830 ft) per second
Magazine: 7-round box

JAPAN

● Rifle Type 38

The **Rifle Type 38** was adopted for Imperial Japanese service in 1905 and was a development of two earlier rifles selected by a commission headed by one Colonel Arisaka, who gave his name to a whole family of Japanese service rifles. The Type 38 used a mixture of design points and principles taken from contemporary Mauser and Mannlicher designs, mixed with a few Japanese innovations. The result was a sound enough rifle that had a calibre of 6.5 mm (0.256 in). This relatively small calibre, coupled with a rather low-powered cartridge, produced a rifle with a small recoil that exactly suited the slight Japanese stature.

This fact was further aided by the Type 38 being a rather long rifle. When the rifle was used with a bayonet, as it usually was in action, this gave the Japanese soldier a considerable reach advantage for close-in warfare, but it also made the Type 38 a rather awkward rifle to handle. As well as being used by all the Japanese armed forces, the Type 38 was exported to such nations as Thailand, and was also used by several of the warring factions then prevalent in China. At one point during World War I the Type 38 was even purchased as a training weapon by the British army.

A shorter version, the **Carbine Type 38** was widely used, and there was a version with a folding butt for use by airborne troops. There was also a version of the Type 38 known as the **Sniper's Rifle Type 97** which, apart from provision for a telescopic sight, had a revised bolt handle.

During the 1930s the Japanese gradually adopted a new service cartridge of 7.7-mm (0.303-in) calibre, and the Type 38 was revised as the **Rifle Type 99**. The Type 99 had several new features, including a sight that was supposed to be effective for firing at aircraft, and a folding monopod to assist accuracy. A special paratroop model that could be broken down into two halves was devised but proved to be unreliable so it was replaced by a 'taken down' version known as the **Parachutist's Rifle Type 2**. Not many of these were made.

Once the Pacific war was under way in 1942 the production standards of Japanese rifles and carbines deteriorated rapidly; any items that could be left off were so, and simplifications were introduced onto the lines. But overall standards went down to the point where some of the late production examples were virtually lethal to the user, many of them being constructed from very low-quality raw materials, both wood and metal, for the simple reason that the Allied blockade and air raids prevented the use of anything better. By the end the arsenals were reduced to producing very simple single-shot weapons firing 8-mm (0.315-in) pistol cartridges, or even

black-powder weapons. There was even a proposal to use long bows and crossbows firing explosive arrows. It was all a long way from the days when the Type 38 was one of the most widely used service rifles in the Orient.

Specification
Rifle Type 38
Calibre: 6.5 mm (0.256 in)
Length: 1.275 m (50.2 in)
Length of barrel: 797.5 mm (31.4 in)
Weight: 4.2 kg (9.25 lb)
Muzzle velocity: 731 m (2,400 ft) per second
Magazine: 5-round box

The Type 99 was a monopod fitted version of the Type 38 employing the new 7.7-mm (0.303-in) calibre cartridge. The Japanese design utilized contemporary Mauser and Mannlicher features, and first appeared in 1905.

Japanese infantry assault the Yenanyaung oilfields in Burma. The great length of the Arisaka type rifle, especially with bayonet attached, is obvious. This made the weapon awkward to handle but gave the generally short-statured Japanese soldier an effective reach in close combat.

FRANCE
Lebel and Berthier rifles

In 1939 the French army was equipped with an almost bewildering array of rifles, for the French appear to have adopted a policy of never throwing anything away. Some of them could trace their origins back to the mle 1866 Chassepot rifle. One of them, the **Fusil Gras mle 1874**, was still only a single-shot weapon, but was still in use with some French second-line and colonial units in 1940 when the Germans invaded.

The original Lebel rifle, the **Fusil d'infanterie mle 1886**, was updated in 1893 to produce the **mle 1886/93**. It was with this Lebel rifle that the French army fought World War I, but another weapon also in use at that time was a Berthier carbine, the **Mousqueton mle 1890** (and similar **mle 1892**), a version of the original mle 1886 allied to a new Mannlicher magazine system. On the Berthier the magazine was of the orthodox box type loaded from a clip, but the Lebel system used a tubular magazine holding more rounds loaded one at a time. The first Berthier rifle was the **Fusil mle 1907**, but in 1915 this colonial-troop weapon was largely replaced by the **Fusil d'infanterie mle 07/15**. With the introduction of the mle 07/15 the older Lebel rifles gradually faded in importance as production concentrated on the Berthiers, but the Lebels were never replaced in service. They just soldiered on, and were still available in 1939.

A Muslim Spahi of the 1st Moroccan Spahi regiment of the Vichy colonial army is armed with the old Lebel rifle. Note the long bayonet in his belt.

The original Berthier magazine system held only three rounds, but it was soon realized that this was not enough and the **Fusil d'infanterie mle 1916** had a 5-round magazine. To complicate matters further there were carbine or other short versions of all the models mentioned above, and to complicate matters still further the French sold or gave away masses of all of these weapons in the inter-war years to many nations who promptly applied their own designations. Thus Lebel and Berthier rifles turned up not only in all the French colonies but in nations such as Greece, Yugoslavia, Romania and other Balkan states.

In 1934 the French decided to attempt to make some sense out of their varied rifle and carbine arsenal by adopting a new calibre. Up till then the normal French calibre had been 8 mm (0.315 in), but in 1934 they adopted a smaller calibre of 7.5 mm (0.295 in). That same year they started to modify the old Berthier rifles to the new calibre and at the same time fitted a new magazine (still holding only five rounds) and several other changes along with the new barrel. This 'new' version was the **Fusil d'infanterie mle 07/15 M34**, but the change-over programme went so slowly that in 1939 only a small proportion of the available stocks had been converted, ensuring that all the other models were still in use.

After the events of May and June 1940 the Germans found masses of all the various French rifles on their hands. Some they could use as they were, and many were issued to garrison and second-line formations. But

Some of the rifles in French reserve use in 1939 were obsolete 1886 models, unaltered from their introduction to service. They were outmoded within 10 years.

many others were stockpiled, to be dragged out in 1945 to arm Volkssturm and other such units. No doubt the Germans found that the array and variety of French rifle and carbine types were too much, even for their assorted stocks, but as they never had enough rifles to arm their ever-growing forces the French weapons were no doubt handy.

Few of the old French rifles are to be encountered today other than in the hands of museums and collectors. Most of them were museum pieces even in 1939 and only the general unpreparedness of France for war ensured that the relics were retained.

Specification
mle 1886/93
Calibre: 8 mm (0.315 in)
Length: 1.303 m (51.3 in)
Length of barrel: 798 mm (31.4 in)
Weight: 4.245 kg (9.35 lb)
Muzzle velocity: 725 m (2,380 ft) per second
Magazine capacity: 8-round tube

Specification
mle 1907/15 M34
Calibre; 7.5 mm (0.295 in)
Length: 1.084 m (42.7 in)
Length of barrel: 579 mm (22.8 in)
Weight: 3.56 kg (7.85 lb)
Muzzle velocity: 823 m (2,700 ft) per second
Magazine capacity: 5-round box

FRANCE
Fusil MAS36

In the period following World War I the French army decided to adopt a new standard service cartridge with a calibre of 7.5 mm (0.295 in). The new cartridge was adopted in 1924, but following some low-priority and therefore lengthy trials, it was found that the new cartridge was unsafe under certain circumstances and thus had to be modified in 1929. In that year the French decided to adopt a new rifle to fire the new round, but it was not until 1932 that a prototype was ready. Then followed a series of further trials that went on at a slow pace until 1936, when the new rifle was accepted for service.

The new rifle was the **Fusil MAS36** (MAS for Manufacture d'Armes de Saint-Etienne). This used a much-modified Mauser action which was so arranged that the bolt handle had to be angled forward quite sharply. The box magazine held only five rounds. The MAS36 had the odd distinction of being the last bolt-action service rifle to be adopted for military service anywhere (all later new weapons using some form of self-loading action) and in some other ways the MAS36 featured other anachronisms. In typical French style the weapon had no safety catch, and the overall appearance of the design belied its year of introduc-

tion, for it looked a much older design than it was.

Production of the new rifle was so slow that a modification programme to convert some of the old rifles for the new cartridge had to be undertaken. This lack of urgency was typical of the period for the nation seemed to suffer from an internal lethargy that could be traced back to the nation's exertions of World War I. Thus by 1939 only a relatively few French army units were equipped with the MAS36, and these were mainly front-line troops. The MAS36 could have had little effect on the events of May and June 1940, but many of the troops who left France at that time took their MAS36s with them and for a while it remained the favoured weapon of the Free French

forces in exile. The Germans also took over numbers of MAS36s and used them under the designation **Gewehr 242(f)** for their own garrison units based in occupied France.

One odd variation of the basic MAS36 was a version known as the **MAS36 CR39**. This was a short-barrelled version intended for paratroop use, and had an aluminium butt that could swivel forward alongside the butt to save stowage space. Only a relative few were ever made, and even fewer appear to have been issued for service use.

When the war ended the new French army once more took the MAS36 into use and retained it for many years, using it in action in North Africa and Indo-China. Many are still

The MAS 36 was the last bolt action rifle adopted by a major army anywhere. It was a fair weapon, but few saw service before 1939.

retained for use as ceremonial parade weapons and the type is still used by the forces and police authorities of many colonial or ex-colonial states.

Specification
MAS36
Calibre: 7.5 mm (0.295 in)
Length: 1.019 m (40.13 in)
Length of barrel: 574 mm (22.6 in)
Weight: 3.67 kg (8.09 lb)
Muzzle velocity: 823 m (2,700 ft) per second
Magazine: 5-round box

Rifle, Caliber .30, Model 1903

In 1903 the US Army decided to replace its existing Krag-Jorgensen rifles and adopted a rifle based on the Mauser system. This rifle, officially known as the **US Magazine Rifle, Caliber .30, Model of 1903** (or **M1903**) was first produced at the famous Springfield Arsenal and has thus become almost exclusively known as the **Springfield**. It was produced to be a form of universal weapon that could be used by both infantry and cavalry, and was thus much shorter than most contemporary rifles, but it was a well-balanced and attractive rifle that soon proved itself to be a fine service weapon with an accuracy that makes it a prized target rifle.

Almost as soon as the M1903 was placed in production the original blunt-nosed ammunition was replaced by newer 'pointed' ammunition that is now generally known as the .30-06 (thirty-ought six) as it was an 0.3-in (7.62-mm) round introduced in 1906. This remained the standard US service cartridge for many years and is still widely produced. The original M1903 served throughout World War I in US Army hands, and in 1929 the design was modified slightly by the introduction of a form of pistol grip to assist aiming, and this became the **M1903A1**. The **M1903A2** was produced as a sub-calibre weapon for inserting into the barrels of coastal guns and was used for low-cost training on these guns.

When the USA entered World War II in 1941 the new M1 Garand rifle was not available in the numbers required, so the M1903 was placed back into large-scale production, this time as the **M1903A3**. This version was modified to suit modern mass-production methods, but it was still a well-made rifle. Some parts were formed by using stampings instead of machined parts, but the main change was to the sights which were moved back from over the barrel to a position over the bolt action.

Above: A Mauser patterned rifle, the M1903 Springfield proved a fine weapon, serving into the Korean war. The sniper version had a Weaver telescopic sight, and the conventional 'iron' sights have been removed entirely.

Right: The accuracy of the M1903 made it a popular weapon with sharpshooters, and in positions where a single well-aimed shot can be decisive the small box magazine of five rounds was no handicap.

The only other version of the M1903 (apart from some special match rifle models) was the **M1903A4**. This was a special sniper's version fitted with a Weaver telescopic sight, and was specialized to the point where no conventional 'iron' sights were fitted. Numbers of the M1903A4 were still in service during the Korean War of the 1950s.

The M1903 was used by several Allied armies during World War II. Many of the US troops who landed in Normandy on D-Day in June 1944 were still equipped with the Springfields, but by then many had been passed on to various resistance units in France and elsewhere, and the M1903 was a virtual standard issue to the various 'island watchers' among the Pacific islands. In 1940 some were sent to the UK to equip Home Guard units, and the type was even placed back into production to a British order, only for the order to be taken over for the use of US forces.

The M1903 and its variants may still be encountered today with a few small armed forces around the world. But many are also retained as target or hunting rifles, for the M1903 Springfield is still regarded as one of the classic rifles of all time. It is still a rifle that a delight to handle and fire, and man are now owned by weapon collector for those reasons alone.

Specification
M1903A1
Calibre: 7.62 mm(0.3 in)
Length: 1.105 m (43.5 in)
Length of barrel: 610 mm (24 in)
Weight: 4.1 kg (9 lb)
Muzzle velocity: 855 m (2,805 ft) per second
Magazine: 5-round box

Rifle, Caliber .30, M1 (the Garand)

One of the main distinctions of the **Rifle, Caliber .30, M1**, almost universally known as the **Garand**, is that it was the first self-loading rifle to be accepted for military service. That acceptance happened during 1932, but there followed a distinct gap before the rifle entered service as it took some time to tool up for the complex production processes demanded by the design. The rifle was created by John C. Garand, who spent a great deal of time developing the design to the point that once in production it required very few alterations. Thus the last M1 looked very much like the first.

As already mentioned, the M1 was a complicated and expensive weapon to manufacture, and required a large number of machining operations on many of the components. But it was a strong design and proved to be sturdy in action, although this was balanced in part by the weapon being rather heavier than comparable bolt-action designs. The M1 was a gas-operated weapon.

When the USA entered World War II at the end of 1941, most of her regular forces were equipped with the M1, but the rapid increase of numbers of men in uniform meant that the old M1903 Springfield rifle had to be placed back

into production as a quick increase in the flow of M1s from the lines was virtually impossible, as a result largely of the tooling problems already mentioned. But gradually M1 production built up, and some 5,500,000 had been churned out by the end of the war; production was resumed during the Korean War of the early 1950s.

For the American forces the M1 Garand was a war-winner, whose strong construction earned the gratitude of many. But it did have one operational fault, namely its ammunition feed. Ammunition was fed into the rifle in eight-round clips, and the loading system was so arranged that it was possible to load only the full eight rounds or nothing. There was a further operational problem encountered when the last of the eight rounds was fired, for the empty clip was ejected from the receiver with a definite and pronounced sound that advertized to any nearby enemy that the firer's rifle was empty, sometimes with unfortunate results to the M1 user. This problem was not eliminated from the M1 until 1957, when the US Army introduced the M14 rifle which was virtually a reworked M1 Garand with an increased ammunition capacity.

Many sub-variants of the M1 were produced but few actually saw service

The Garand was the first self-loading rifle accepted as a standard military weapon. Strong and sturdy, the gas-operated M1 was rather heavier than the bolt action M1903 Springfield.

as the basic M1 proved to be more than adequate for most purposes. There were two special sniper versions, the **M1C** and the **M1D**, both produced during 1944 but never in any great numbers. Each had such extras as a muzzle flash cone and butt plates.

The M1 attracted the attention of the

USA's enemies to the extent that the Germans used as many as they could capture, with the designation **Selbstladegewehr 251(a)**, and the Japanese produced their own copy, the 7.7-mm (0.303-in) **Rifle Type 5**, but only prototypes had been completed by the time the war ended.

Post-war the M1 went on for many years as the standard US service rifle, and some are still issued to National Guard and other such units. Several nations continue to use the M1, and many designers have used the basic action as the basis for their own products: many of the modern Italian Beretta rifles use the Garand system as does the American 5.56-mm (0.22-in) Ruger Mini-14.

Specification
Rifle M1
Calibre: 7.62 mm (0.3 in)
Length: 1.107 m (43.6 in)
Length of barrel: 609 mm (24 in)
Weight: 4.313 kg (9.5 lb)
Muzzle velocity: 855 m (2,805 ft) per second
Magazine: 8-round box

Garand-armed infantrymen of the US 4th Armored Division are seen in action in the Ardennes during the drive to relieve Bastogne and the trapped 101st Airborne Division.

USA

Carbine, Caliber .30, M1, M1A1, M2 and M3

The traditional weapon for second-line troops and such specialists as machine-gunners has generally been the pistol, but when the US Army considered the equipment of such soldiers during 1940 they made a request for some form of carbine that could be easily stowed and handled. The result was a competition in which several manufacturers submitted their proposals, and the winner was a Winchester design that was adopted for service as the **Carbine, Caliber .30, M1**. The M1 used an unusual gas-operated system and was designed for use with a special cartridge that was intermediate between a pistol cartridge and a rifle cartridge in power.

From the start the Carbine M1 was an immediate success. It was light and easy to handle, to the extent that its use soon spread from the second-echelon troops who were supposed to be issued with the weapon to front-line troops such as officers and weapon teams. In order to speed its introduction into service the M1 was a single-shot weapon only, but there was a special variant with a folding stock known as the **M1A1**. This was produced for use by airborne units. When time

allowed later during the war the automatic fire feature was added. This version was known as the **M2**, and had a cyclic rate of fire of about 750 to 775 rounds per minute; the weapon used a curved box magazine holding 30 rounds that could also be used on the M1. The **M3** was a special night-fighting version with a large infra-red night sight, but only about 2,100 of these were made. The M3 proved to be the one version of the Carbine M1 series that was not produced in quantity, for by the time the war ended the production total had reached 6,332,000 of all versions, making the weapon the most prolific personal weapon of World War II.

For all its handiness, the Carbine M1 series had one major drawback, and that was the cartridge used. Being an intermediate-power cartridge it generally lacked power, even at close ranges. Being a carbine the M1 also lacked range, and was effective only to 100 m (110 yards) or so. But these drawbacks were more than countered by the overall handiness of the weapon. It was easy to stow in vehicles or aircraft, and the M1A1 with its folding butt was even smaller. It handled

well in action and was deemed good enough for German Army use as the **Selbstladekarabiner 455a** after enough had been captured during the latter stages of the war in Europe.

But for all its mass production and war-time success, the M1 is now little used by armed forces anywhere. Many police forces retain the type, mainly because of the low-power cartridge fired which is safer in police situations than more powerful rounds. Typical of these is the Royal Ulster Constabulary, which uses the Carbine M1 as a counter to the far more powerful Armalites of the IRA. Another part of the M1 story is the current lack of adoption of the M1's intermediate-power cartridge. During the war years these cartridges were churned out in millions but now the cartridge is little used and has not been adopted for any other major weapon system.

Originally produced by Winchester, the lightweight M1 carbine was eventually manufactured by more than 10 companies in numbers exceeding six million.

Specification
Carbine M1
Calibre: 7.62 mm (0.3 in)
Length: 904 mm (35.6 in)
Length of barrel: 457 mm (18 in)
Weight: 2.36 kg (5.2 lb)
Muzzle velocity: 600 m (1,970 ft) per second
Magazine: 15- or 30-round box

A Marine, member of a machine-gun crew, clutches his M1 carbine and the ammo for a Browning machine-gun while waiting for his partner to hurl a grenade.

Left: Front-line troops soon found that the easy handling M1 carbine was much less of a burden than a rifle when slogging through the surf or the jungle, and it began appearing with front-line Marine Corps units.

Allied and Axis Pistols

Pistols are very close to the heart of fighting soldiers, and in World War II one of the most prized trophies on the Allied side was a captured German or Italian pistol. Yet as a weapon of war the hand gun seems of very little value, so what is the explanation for the retention of the sidearm in the armies of the 20th century?

The pistol, be it a revolver or an automatic, has long had an attraction for the soldier. Quite apart from the intrinsic attraction of this weapon, the hand gun is very often a highly personal possession and one in which the soldier usually takes great pride. Even after a short time in service the soldier learns to appreciate the value of a hand gun to his well-being and his chances of survival, especially when he is carrying out an operational role where no other weapon is available.

This attraction is difficult for the layperson to appreciate, for even a limited firing of any service pistol will reveal that it is inaccurate, difficult to use effectively and possesses only a very limited range. It is somewhat tricky to reconcile these two completely accurate conclusions, but the plain fact is that the pistol was used on a scale during World War II that overshadowed its employment in any previous conflict. On all fronts demands for pistols, more pistols and still more pistols were made throughout the conflict, and as a result the range of models and types was immense, those mentioned in this section being only a general indication of some of the more important types.

A soldier of the Italian Alpini takes aim with a hand gun – the standard Italian service pistol, the 9mm Beretta modello 1934. Of excellent manufacture, it became a sought-after trophy of war.

Despite the many advances in pistol design and development made in the 20th century, it should be noted that the revolver was still in use between 1939 and 1945; and this remains true even to this day, for the automatic pistol has not been able fully to oust the strong and reliable revolver. But the automatic pistol was in widespread use during World War II all the same, employing a large number of operating systems and an equally diverse range of calibres, despite the fact that the 9mm Parabellum cartridge had emerged as the clear all-round leader. And quite apart from any other factors, an investigation of the pistol itself is rewarding for its revelation of the great degree of ingenuity that designers have been able to bring to pistol design. World War II brought with it innovations and oddities, but what may be regarded as antiques were still being used in the field during World War II. Examples of some of these will be found in this section; however, the reader is asked to use these entries only as a general guide.

Enfield No. 2 Mk 1 and Webley Mk 4

During World War I the standard British service revolver was one variant or other of the Webley 0.455-in (11.56-mm) pistol. These were very effective pistols, but their weight and bulk made them very difficult to handle correctly without a great deal of training and constant practice, two commodities that were in short supply at the time. After 1919 the British army decided that a smaller pistol firing a heavy 0.38-in (9.65-mm) bullet would be just as effective as the larger-calibre weapon but would be easier to handle and would require less training. So Webley and Scott, which up to that time had been pistol manufacturers of a virtually official status for the British armed forces, took its 0.455-in (11.56-mm) revolver, scaled it down and offered the result to the military.

To the chagrin of Webley and Scott, the military simply took the design, made a few minor alterations and then placed the result in production as an 'official' government design to be produced at the Royal Small Arms Factory at Enfield Lock in Middlesex. This procedure took time, for Webley and Scott offered its design in 1923 and Enfield Lock took over the design in 1926. Webley and Scott was somewhat nonplussed at the course of events but proceeded to make its 0.38-in (9.65-mm) revolver, known as the **Webley Mk 4**, all over the world with limited success.

The Enfield Lock product became the **Pistol, Revolver, No. 2 Mk 1** and was duly issued for service. Once in service it proved sound and effective enough, but mechanical progress meant that large numbers of these pistols were issued to tank crews and other mechanized personnel, who made the unfortunate discovery that the long hammer spur had a tendency to catch onto the many internal fittings of tanks and other vehicles with what could be nasty results. This led to a redesign in which the Enfield pistol had the hammer spur removed altogether and the trigger mechanism lightened to enable the weapon to be fired double-action only. This revolver became the **No. 2 Mk 1***, and existing Mk 1s were modified to the new standard. The double action made the pistol very difficult to use accurately at all except minimal range, but that did not seem to matter too much at the time.

Webley and Scott re-entered the scene during World War II, when supplies of the Enfield pistols were too slow to meet the ever-expanding demand. Thus the Webley Mk 4 was ordered to eke out supplies, and Webley and Scott went on to supply thousands of its design to the British army after all. Unfortunately, although the two pistols were virtually identical in appearance there were enough minor differences between them to prevent interchangeability of parts.

Both pistols saw extensive use between 1939 and 1945, and although the Enfield revolvers (there was a **No. 2**

The Webley Mk 4 revolver was used as the basis for the Enfield No. 2 Mk 1 but was passed over in favour of the government-sponsored development. In time the call for more revolvers was so great that the Mk 4 was placed in production for the British armed forces and used alongside the Enfield pistols.

Mk 1** which embodied wartime production expedients) were the official standard pistols, the Webley Mk 4 was just as widely used among British and Commonwealth armed forces. Both remained in service until the 1960s and both are still to be encountered as service pistols in various parts of the world.

Specification
Revolver No. 2 Mk 1*
Cartridge: 0.380 SAA ball (9.65 mm)
Length overall: 260 mm (10.25 in)
Length of barrel: 127 mm (5 in)
Weight: 0.767 (1.7 lb)
Muzzle velocity: 183 m (600 ft) per second
Chamber capacity: 6 rounds

Specification
Webley Mk 4
Cartridge: 0.380 SAA ball (9.65 mm)
Length overall: 267 mm (10.5 in)
Length of barrel: 127 mm (5 in)
Weight: 0.767 (1.7 lb)
Muzzle velocity: 183 m (600 ft) per second
Chamber capacity: 6 rounds

Above: The Enfield No. 2 Mk 1* revolver was the most widely used of all the British and Commonwealth armed forces. Firing a 0.38-in (9.65-mm) ball cartridge, it was an efficient combat pistol but lacked any finesse or frills; yet it was able to withstand the many knocks of service life.

Below: An airborne soldier stands guard on a house in Holland during Operation 'Market Garden'. The pistol is an Enfield No. 2 Mk 1* with the hammer removed to prevent snagging on clothing or within the close confines of vehicles or aircraft. They were issued to airborne soldiers such as glider pilots.

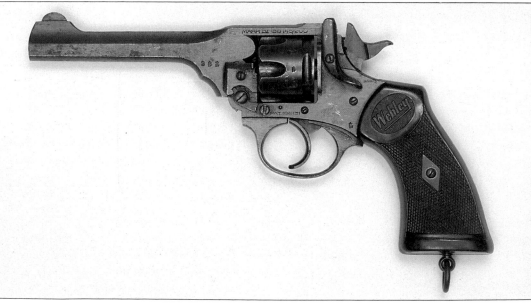

Tokarev TT-33

The first Tokarev automatic pistol to see extensive service was the **TT-30**, but not many of these pistols had been produced before a modified design known as the **TT-33** was introduced in 1933. This pistol was then adopted as the standard pistol of the Red Army to replace the Nagant revolvers that had served so well for many years. In the event the TT-33 never did replace the Nagant entirely until well after 1945, mainly because the revolver proved so reliable and sturdy under the rough active service conditions of the various fronts.

The TT-33 was basically a Soviet version of the Colt-Browning pistols, and used the swinging-link system of operation employed on the American M1911. However, the ever practical Soviet designers made several slight alterations that made the mechanism easier to produce and easier to maintain under field conditions, and production even went to the length of machining the vulnerable magazine feed lips into the main receiver to prevent damage and subsequent misfeeds. The result was a practical and sturdy weapon that was well able to absorb a surprising amount of hard use.

By 1945 the TT-33 had virtually replaced the Nagant revolver in service and as Soviet influence spread over Europe and elsewhere so did TT-33 production. Thus the TT-33 may be found in a variety of basically similar forms, one of which is the Chinese **Type 51**. The Poles also produced the TT-33 for their own use and for export to East Germany and to Czechoslovakia. The Yugoslavs still have the TT-33 in production and are still actively marketing the design as the **M65**. North Korea has its own variant in the form of the **M68**. The most drastic producer of the TT-33 is Hungary, which rejigged the design in several respects and recalibred it for the 9-mm Parabellum cartridge. The result was known as the **Tikagypt** and was exported to Egypt, where it is still used by the local police forces.

The Tokarev TT-33 was a sturdy and hard-wearing pistol that was used throughout World War II, but it never entirely replaced the Nagant.

Above: The Soviet Tokarev TT-33 in action in a well-posed propaganda photograph dating from about 1944. The officer is leading a section of assault infantry and has his pistol on the end of the usual lanyard. Snipers on all sides came to recognize these 'pistol wavers' as prime targets.

The TT-33 is now no longer used by the Soviet armed forces, who use the Markarov automatic pistol, but the TT-33 will be around for a long while yet. Despite the introduction of the Makarov many second-line and militia units within the Warsaw Pact are still issued with the TT-33 and as the type's overall standard of design and construction was sound there seems to be no reason why they should be replaced for many years.

Right: A Red Army military policeman, for whom the Tokarev TT-33 would have been the primary weapon. Military policemen of all nations still carry the pistol as the nature of their duties often precludes the use of any type of larger weapon, and they have no actual combat role.

Specification
TT-33
Cartridge: 7.62 mm Type P (M30)
Length overall: 196 mm (7.68 in)
Length of barrel: 116 mm (4.57 in)
Weight: 0.830 kg (1.83 lb)
Muzzle velocity: 420 m (1,380 ft) per second
Magazine: 8-round box

Pistole P 08 (Luger)

The pistol that is now generally, but misleadingly, known as the **Luger** had its design origins in a pistol design first produced in 1893 by one Hugo Borchardt. A George Luger further developed this design and produced the weapon that bears his name to this day. The first Lugers were manufactured in 7.65-mm (0.301-in) calibre and were adopted by the Swiss army in 1900. Thereafter the basic design was adopted by many nations and the type is still to be encountered, for by now well over two million have been produced by various manufacturers and at least 35 main variants are known to exist, together with a host of sub-variants.

The **Pistole P 08** was one of the main variants. It was taken into German army service in 1908 (hence the 08) and remained the standard German service pistol until the Walther P 38 was introduced in 1938. The main calibre encountered on the P 08 was 9 mm, and the 9-mm (0.354-in) Parabellum cartridge was developed for this pistol. However, 7.65-mm (0.301-in) versions were made as well. The P 08 is and probably always will be one of the 'classic' pistols, for it has an appearance and aura all of its own. It handles well, is easy to 'point' and is usually very well made. It has to be well made for it relies on a rather complicated action using an upwards-hingeing toggle locking device that will not operate correctly if the associated machined grooves are out of tolerance. In fact it is arguable that this action is undesirable in a service pistol for as it operates it allows the ingress of dust and debris to clog the mechanism. In practice this was often not the case for the pistol proved to be remarkably robust. It was only replaced in service and production for the simple fact that it was too demanding in production resources, took too long to produce and required too many matched spare parts. It was late 1942 before the last 'German' examples came off the production lines and it was never replaced by the P 38 in German service. Since 1945 it has reappeared commercially from time to time and will no doubt continue to be manufactured for years to come.

The standard P 08 had a barrel 103 mm (4.055 in) long, and earlier variants such as the **P 17 Artillerie** model with a 203 mm (8 in) or longer barrel and a snail-shaped magazine holding 32 rounds were no longer service weapons between 1939 and 1945. Lugers were among the most prized of all World War I and II trophies, and many still survive as collector's pieces.

Above: The Pistole P 08, commonly known as the Luger, was one of the classic pistol designs of all time. It still has a definite aesthetic appeal in the slope of the butt and the general appearance, and is a pleasant pistol to fire. However, it was expensive to produce and was destined to be replaced.

Right: The P 08 in service with a section of house-clearing infantry during the early stages of the advance into Russia during 1941. The soldier with the pistol is armed with Stielgranate 35 grenades and is festooned with ammunition belts for the section MG 34 machine-gun.

The type continues to attract the eye and attention of all pistol buffs throughout the world, and the P 08 was and still is a classic.

Specification
Pistole P 08
Cartridge: 9 mm Parabellum
Length overall: 222 mm (8.75 in)
Length of barrel: 103 mm (4.055 in)
Weight: 0.877 kg (1.92 lb)
Muzzle velocity: 381 m (1,250 ft) per second
Magazine: 8-round box

Below: A Stug 111 with a short 75-mm (2.95-in) gun supports advancing infantry during an attack on the Voronez front during January 1943. Although the pistol being carried by the soldier on the right is blurred, it appears to be a P 08.

Walther PP and PPK

The **Walther PP** was first produced in 1929 and was marketed as a police weapon (PP standing for Polizei Pistole), and during the 1930s it was adopted by uniformed police forces throughout Europe and elsewhere. It was a light and handy design with few frills and a clean outline but was intended for holster carriage. Plain clothes police were catered for by another model, the **Walter PPK** (K standing for *kurz*, or short). This was basically the PP reduced in overall size to enable it to be carried conveniently in a pocket or under a jacket.

Although intended as civilian police weapons, both the PP and the PPK were adopted as military police weapons and after 1939 both were kept in production for service use. Each model was widely used by the Luftwaffe, and was often carried by the many German police organizations. Both were also widely used by staff officers as personal weapons. Both types could also be encountered in a range of calibres, the two main calibres being 9 mm short and 7.65 mm, but versions were produced in 5.56 mm (0.22 LR) and 6.35 mm. All these variants operated on a straightforward blowback principle, and more than adequate safety arrangements were incorporated. One of these safeties was later widely copied, and involved placing a block in the way of the firing pin when it moved forward, this block only being removed when the trigger was given a definite pull. Another innovation was the provision of a signal pin above the hammer which protruded when a round was

actually in the chamber to provide a positive 'loaded' indication when necessary. This feature was omitted from wartime production, in which the general standard of finish was lower. Production resumed soon after 1945 in such countries as France and Turkey. Hungary also adopted the type for a while but production is now once more by the Walther concern at Ulm. Production is still mainly for police duties but purely commercial sales are common to pistol shooters who appreciate the many fine points of the basic design.

One small item of interest regarding the PP centres on the fact that it is now a little-known and rarely seen pistol used by the British armed forces as the

XL47E1. The weapon is used for undercover operations where civilian clothing has to be worn and it is often issued to soldiers of the Ulster Defence Regiment for personal protection when off duty.

The Walther PP pistol was, and still is, one of the best small pistol designs ever produced. In German service it was used by various police organizations and by Luftwaffe aircrew.

Specification
Walther PP
Cartridge: 9 mm short (0.38 ACP), 7.65 mm (0.32 ACP), 6.35 mm (0.25 ACP), 0.22 LR
Length overall: 173 mm (6.8 in)
Length of barrel: 99 mm (3.9 in)
Weight: 0.682 kg (1.5 lb)
Muzzle velocity: 290 m (950 ft) per second
Magazine: 8-round box

Specification
Walther PPK
Cartridge: 9 mm short (0.38 ACP), 7.65 mm (0.32 ACP), 6.35 mm (0.25 ACP), 0.22 LR
Length overall: 155 mm (6.1 in)
Length of barrel: 86 mm (3.39 in)
Weight: 0.568 kg (1.25 lb)
Muzzle velocity: 280 m (920 ft) per second
Magazine: 7-round box

Walther P 38

The **Walther P 38** was developed primarily to replace the P 08, which was an excellent weapon but expensive to produce. After the National Socialists came to power in Germany in 1933 they decided upon a deliberate programme of military expansion into which the old P 08 could not fit. What was wanted was a pistol that could be quickly and easily produced but one that embodied all the many and various design features such as a hand-cocked trigger and improved safeties that were then becoming more common. Walther eventually received the contract for this new pistol in 1938, but only after a long programme of development.

Walther Waffenfabrik produced its first original automatic pistol design back in 1908 and there followed a string of designs that culminated in the PP of 1929. The PP had many novel features but it was intended to be a police weapon and not a service pistol. Walther consequently developed a new weapon known as the **Armee Pistole** (or **AP**) which did not have the protruding hammer of the PP but was calibred for the 9-mm (0.354-in) Parabellum cartridge. From this came the **Heeres Pistole** (or **HP**) which had the overall appearance of the pistol that would become the P 38. But the German Army requested some small changes to facilitate rapid production. Walther obliged and the P 38 was taken into German service use, the HP being kept in production in its original form for commercial sales. In the event Walther was never able to meet de-

mand for the P 38 and the bulk of the HP production also went to the German armed forces.

The P 38 was (and still is) an excellent service pistol which was robust, accurate and hard wearing. Walther production versions, which were later supplemented by P 38s produced by Mauser and Spreewerke, were always very well finished with shiny black plastic grips and an overall matt black plating. The weapon could be stripped easily and was well equipped with safety devices, including the hammer safety carried over from the PP along

with the 'chamber loaded' indicator pin. It was a well-liked pistol and became a war trophy only slightly less prized than the Luger P 08.

In 1957 the P 38 was put back into production for the Bundeswehr, this time as the **Pistole 1** (or **P1**) with a dural slide in place of the original steel component. It is still in production and has been adopted by many nations.

Specification
Walter P 38
Cartridge: 9 mm Parabellum

Even today one of the best service pistols available, the Walther P 38 was developed to replace the P 08 Luger but by 1945 had only supplemented it. It had many advanced features including a double-action trigger mechanism.

Length overall: 219 mm (8.58 in)
Length of barrel: 124 mm (4.88 in)
Weight: 0.960 kg (2.12 lb)
Muzzle velocity: 350 m (1,150 ft) per second
Magazine: 8-round box

Pistole Automatique Browning modèle 1910

The **Pistole Automatique Browning modèle 1910** is something of an oddity among pistol designs, for although it has remained in production virtually nonstop since 1910, it has never been officially adopted as a service weapon. Despite this it has been used widely by many armed forces at one time or another and the basic design has been widely copied and/or plagiarized by other designers.

As the name implies, this automatic pistol was yet another product of the fertile mind of John Moses Browning. Nearly all the model 1910s have been produced at the Fabrique Nationale d'Armes de Guerre (commonly known simply as FN) at Liège in Belgium. The type is still in production in Belgium for commercial sales. The reason why this particular pistol should have achieved such longevity is now not easy to determine, but the overall design is clean enough, with the forward part of the receiver slide around the barrel having a tubular appearance. This results from the fact that the recoil spring is wrapped around the barrel itself instead of being situated under or over the barrel as in most other designs. This spring is held in place by a bayonet lug around the muzzle, providing the model 1910 with another recognition point. Grip and applied safeties are provided.

The model 1910 may be encountered in one of two calibres, either 7.65 mm or 9 mm short. Externally the

two variants are identical, and each uses a detachable seven-round box magazine. As with all other FN products the standard of manufacture and finish is excellent but copies made in such places as Spain lack this finish. The excellent finish was continued with one of the few large-scale production runs for the model 1910. This occurred after 1940 when the German forces occupying Belgium required large numbers of pistols. The model 1910 was kept in production to meet this demand, the bulk of the output

being issued to Luftwaffe aircrew who knew the type as the **Pistole P 621(b)**. Before that the model 1910 had been issued in small numbers to the Belgian armed forces, and many other nations obtained the type for small-scale use for their own military or police service. The numbers of model 1910s produced must by now be running into the hundreds of thousands.

Specification
Browning modèle 1910
Cartridge: 7.64 mm (0.32 ACP) or 9 mm

The Browning modèle 1910 was never officially adopted as a service pistol, but was nonetheless widely used and many of its design features were later incorporated in other pistol designs.

short (0.380 ACP)
Length overall: 152 mm (6 in)
Length of barrel: 89 mm (3.5 in)
Weight: 0.562 kg (1.24 lb)
Muzzle velocity: 299 m (980 ft) per second
Magazine: 7-round box

Pistole Automatique Browning, modèle à Grande Puissance (Browning HP)

The **Browning HP** may be regarded as one of the most successful pistol designs ever produced. Not only is it still in widespread service, in numbers that must surely exceed those of all other types combined, but it has also been produced at many locations in many countries. It was one of the last weapon designs produced by John Browning before he died in 1925, but it was not until 1935 that the HP was placed in production by FN at Liège. From this derives the name which is generally given as the HP (High Power) or **Pistole Automatique Browning GP 35** (Grand Puissance modèle 1935). Numerous versions may be encountered, but they all fire the standard 9-mm Parabellum cartridge. Versions exist with box fixed and adjustable rear sights, and some models were produced with a lug on the butt to enable a stock (usually the wooden holster) to be fitted, allowing the pistol to be fired as a form of carbine. Other versions exist with light alloy receiver slides to reduce weight.

One factor that is common to all the numerous Browning HP variants is strength and reliability. Another desirable feature that has often proved invaluable is the large-capacity box magazine in the butt, which can hold a useful 13 rounds. Despite this width the grip is not too much of a handful, although training and general familiarization are necessary to enable a firer to get the best out of the weapon. The weapon uses a recoil-operated mechanism powered by the blowback forces produced on firing and has an external hammer. In many ways the action can be regarded as the same as

that on the Colt M1911 (also a Browning design), but it was adapted to suit production and to take advantage of the experience gained in the design.

Within a few years of the start of production the Browning HP had been adopted as the service pistol of several nations including Belgium, Denmark, Lithuania and Romania. After 1940 production continued, but this time it was for the Germans who adopted the type as the standard pistol of the Waffen SS, although other arms of the German forces also used the weapon. To the Germans the Browning HP was known as the **Pistole P620(b)**. However, the Germans did not have the Browning

HP all to themselves, for a new production line was opened in Canada and from there the Browning HP was distributed to nearly all the Allied nations as the **Pistol, Browning, FN, 9-mm HP No. 1**, large numbers being sent to China to equip the nationalist forces. After 1945 the type was put back in production in Liège, and many nations now use the weapon as their standard pistol. Various commercial models have been developed, and the type has even been adapted to produce a target-shooting model. The British army still uses the Browning HP as the **Pistol, Automatic L9A1**.

The Browning GP 35 has been adopted by so many nations since its first appearance in 1935 that it must now be the most widely used of all pistols. It is remarkably robust, hard-hitting and reliable in use.

Specification
Browning GP 35
Cartridge: 9-mm Parabellum
Length overall: 196 mm (7.75 in)
Length of barrel: 112 mm (4.41 in)
Weight: 1.01 kg (2.23 lb)
Muzzle velocity: 354 m (1,160 ft) per second
Magazine: 13-round box

Liberator M1942

This very odd little pistol had its origins in the committee rooms of the US Army Joint Psychological Committee, who sold to the Office of Strategic Service the idea of a simple assassination weapon that could be used by anyone in occupied territory without the need for training or familiarization. The OSS took up the idea and the US Army Ordnance Department then set to and produced drawings. The Guide Lamp Division of the General Motors Corporation was given the task of producing the weapons, and the division took the credit for churning out no less than one million between June and August 1942.

The 11.43-mm (0.45-in) weapon was provided with the covername **Flare Pistol M1942**, but it was also known as the **Liberator** or the **OSS** pistol. It was a very simple, even crude device that could fire only a single shot. It was constructed almost entirely of metal stampings and the barrel was smoothbored. The action was just as simple as the rest of the design: a cocking piece was grasped and pulled to the rear; once back a turn locked it in place as a single M1911 automatic cartridge was loaded, and the cocking piece was then swung back for release as the trigger was pulled. To clear the spent cartridge the cocking piece was once more moved out of the way and the case was pushed out from the chamber by poking something suitable down the barrel from the muzzle.

Each pistol was packed into a clear plastic bag together with 10 rounds, and a set of instructions in comic strip form provided, without words, enough information for any person finding the package to use the pistol. There was space in the butt to carry five of the rounds provided but the pistol was virtually a one-shot weapon and had to be used at a minimal range to be effective. Exactly how effective it was is now difficult to say, for there seems to be no record of how these numerous pistols were ever employed or where they were distributed. It is known that some were parachuted into occupied Europe, but many more were used in the Far East and in China. The concept was certainly deemed good enough to be revived in 1964 when a much-modernized equivalent to the Liberator, known as the **'Deer Gun'**, was produced for possible use in Vietnam. In the event several thousands were made but were never issued, maybe because assassination weapons have a nasty tendency to be double-edged. Each Liberator pistol cost the American government just $2.40.

Specification
Liberator M1942
Cartridge: .45 ball M1911
Length overall: 140 mm (5.55 in)
Length of barrel: 102 mm (4 in)
Weight: 0.454 kg (1 lb)
Muzzle velocity: 336 m (1,100 ft) per second
Magazine: none, but space for five rounds in butt

The little Liberator M1942 was an assassination weapon pure and simple, and was produced as cheaply and easily as possible. The barrels were unrifled, there was no spent case ejector and the mechanism was crude to a degree. But they worked, and were used mainly in the Far East and in China.

Colt M1911 and M1911A1

The **Colt M1911** vies with the Browning HP as being one of the most successful pistol designs ever produced, for it has been manufactured in millions and is in widespread service all over the world some 70 years after it was first accepted for service in 1911. The design had its origins well before then, however, for the weapon was based on a **Colt Browning Model 1900** design. This weapon was taken as the basis for a new service pistol required by the US Army to fire a new 11.43-mm (0.45-in) cartridge deemed necessary, as the then-standard calibre of 9.65 mm (0.38 in) was considered by many to be too light to stop a charging enemy. The result was a series of trials in 1907, and in 1911 the **Pistol, Automatic, Caliber .45, M1911** was accepted. Production was at first slow, but by 1917 was well enough under way to equip in part the rapid expansion of the US Army for its new role in France.

As the result of that battle experience it was decided to make some production changes to the basic design and from these came the **M1911A1**. The changes were not extensive, and were confined to such items as the grip safety configuration, the hammer spur outline and the mainspring housing. Overall the design and operation changed only little. The basic method of operation remained the same, and this mechanism is one of the strongest ever made. Whereas many contemporary pistol designs employed a receiver stop to arrest the backwards progress of the receiver slide the M1911 had a locking system that also produced a more positive stop. The barrel had lugs machined into its outer surface that

fitted into corresponding lugs on the slide. When the pistol was fired the barrel and slide moved backwards a short distance with these lugs still engaged. At the end of this distance the barrel progress was arrested by a swinging link which swung round to pull the barrel lugs out of the receiver slide, which was then free to move farther and so eject the spent case and restart the loading cycle. This robust system, allied with a positive applied safety and a grip safety, make the M1911 and M1911A1 very safe weapons under service conditions. But the pistol is a bit of a handful to handle and fire correctly, and a good deal of training is required to use it to full effect.

The M1911 and M1911A1 have both been manufactured by numerous companies other than Colt Firearms and have been widely copied direct in many parts of the world, not always to very high levels of manufacture.

Specification
Colt M1911A1
Cartridge: .45 ball M1911
Length overall: 219 mm (8.6 in)

This pistol is the M1911 (the M1911A1 had several detail changes) and it is still the standard US Army service pistol after over 70 years in service. Firing a 0.45-in ball cartridge, it is still a powerful man-stopper, but is a bit of a handful to fire and requires training to use to its full potential.

Length of barrel: 128 mm (5.03 in)
Weight: 1.36 kg (3 lb)
Muzzle velocity: 252 m (825 ft) per second
Magazine: 7-round box

Smith & Wesson 0.38/200 Revolver

In 1940 the British army was in a desperate plight, with few men trained and even fewer weapons with which to arm them. Fortunately the United States, although not yet actually in the war, were at least sympathetic to the point where that nation would produce weapons for the British, and to British designs. The British planned huge increases in armed manpower levels and had to obtain weapons to match, and among these weapons were pistols. Smith & Wesson was willing to produce revolvers to a British specification, and the result was the pistol known either as the **Revolver .38/200** or the **Revolver No. 2 Cal.380**.

Whatever its designation, the pistol was a strictly orthodox design that was conventional in every respect. It was straightforward in design and operation, and embodied not only Smith & Wesson craftsmanship but British requirements, the resulting weapon being robust to an extreme. It was just as well, for the British pistol production lines were never able to catch up with demand and the British/American design more than filled the gap. These pistols were issued to all arms of the British forces, went to many Commonwealth forces as well, and were even handed out to various European resist-ance movements. Between 1940 and the time production ended in 1946 over 890,000 had been produced and issued. Many are still in service to this day, and it was well into the 1960s before some British units replaced them with the Browning HP.

The Revolver .38/200 fired a 200-grain bullet and used the classic Smith & Wesson chamber release to the left. Once the weapon was open, fired cartridge cases could be cleared with a sprung plunger rod. The trigger action could be either single- or double-action. The finish of the pistols was plain, and at times was neglected in order that the numbers required could be churned out. But the standard of manufacture never wavered: it was always good, and only the finest materials were used. Normally the pistol was carried in a closed leather or webbing holster which masked the hammer, so the snagging problem encountered with the Enfield revolver was not so acute, but a typical British touch was that the revolver was usually fitted to a waist or neck lanyard to prevent an enemy taking the pistol away from the firer at close quarters. The weapon appears never to have gone wrong, even when subjected to the worst possible treatment.

Below: A New Zealand officer armed with a Smith & Wesson 0.38/200 revolver during one of the campaigns in the desert. The revolver is being worn with the lanyard in the 'correct' position around the neck, but many preferred to wear it around the waist to prevent strangulation by an enemy in close-quarter combat.

Specification
0.38/200 Revolver
Cartridge: 0.380 SAA ball (9.65 mm)
Length overall: 257 mm (10.125 in)
Length of barrel: 127 mm (5 in)
Weight: 0.880 kg (1.94 lb)
Muzzle velocity: 198 m (650 ft) per second
Chamber capacity: 6 rounds

Above: A Canadian sergeant loads a Smith & Wesson 0.38/200 revolver. Empty cartridge cases were ejected by moving out the cylinder to the left and pressing a plunger normally under the barrel. All six spent cases were ejected together to allow each chamber to be reloaded one at a time, as seen here.

Below: The Smith & Wesson 0.38/200 revolver was an alliance of American workmanship and British combat experience that produced a robust and reliable pistol with no frills. Made from the very finest materials the finish was sometimes neglected to speed production, but manufacturing standards were never lowered.

Smith & Wesson M1917

During World War I the United Kingdom placed sizable orders in the United States for weapons of all types, and among these was one placed with Smith & Wesson of Springfield, Illinois, for the supply of military revolvers with a calibre of 11.56 mm (0.455 in), the then-standard British pistol cartridge. Large numbers of these were supplied, but after the USA had entered the war in 1917 it was realized that large numbers of pistols would be needed to arm the enlarged US Army, and that the output from the Colt M1911 production line would be insufficient to meet the requirements. As a direct result the Smith & Wesson contract was taken over for the American forces, only for a new problem to crop up once the pistol production had been adapted to the American 11.43-mm (0.45-in) calibre.

Nearly all pistol ammunition produced in 1917 was for the M1911 automatic pistol and was thus rimless. Using rimless ammunition in a revolver chamber posed several problems as revolver cartridges are normally rimmed. Hence a compromise solution was adopted in the form of three M1911 cartridges being held in 'half-moon' clips to keep the cartridges from slipping too far into the revolver chambers when loaded. After firing the spent cartridges could be ejected in the normal way together with their clips and the clips would be reused if necessary. This solution was taken into US Army service and the pistols subsequently saw service in France and elsewhere.

The **Revolver, Caliber .45, Smith & Wesson Hand Ejector, M1917**, as the pistol was subsequently designated,

was a large robust weapon that was completely orthodox in design, operation and construction, apart from the use of the three-round clips. The revolving chambers swung out to the left for loading and case ejection, and the action was either single or double. Like many other pistols of its type, the M1917 was extremely robust and had already been well accepted by the British army before the US Army took over the type. The British were to use it again in 1940 when large numbers were sent over for Home Guard and Royal Navy use.

Colt Firearms also produced a very similar revolver to the Smith & Wesson weapon, as the **Revolver, Caliber .45, Colt New Service, M1917**. Total production of both was over 300,000 and Brazil purchased a further 25,000 in 1938. Many US military police units were still using the type as late as 1945.

Specification
Smith & Wesson M1917
Cartridge: .45 ball M1911
Length overall: 274 mm (10.8 in)

When the United States entered the war in 1917 there were not enough pistols to arm the gathering throngs of recruits. The Smith & Wesson M1917 was rushed into production after being adapted to fire the standard 0.45-in cartridge and was produced in large numbers.

Length of barrel: 140 mm (5.5 in)
Weight: 1.02 kg (2.25 lb)
Muzzle velocity: 253 m (830 ft) per second
Chamber capacity: 6 rounds

Pistolet Radom wz.35

By the early 1930s the Polish army had a large number of pistol types in service, and wished to standardize on one particular type. Consequently an all-Polish design emerged and was put into production at the Fabryka Radom. This weapon became the standard Polish service pistol as the 9-mm **Pistolet Radom wz.35** (wz. stands for *wzor*, or model).

The Radom wz.35 was a combination of Browning and Colt design features with a few local Polish touches. In operation and use it was entirely conventional, but it lacked an applied safety and used only a grip safety, what appeared to be the applied safety catch on the left-hand side of the receiver being only a catch used when stripping the pistol. The ammunition used was the 9-mm Parabellum, but firing this rather powerful round from the Radom was no great problem as the bulk and weight of the pistol was such that the firing stresses were absorbed to a remarkable degree. This weight and bulk made the Radom a better-than-average service pistol as it was able to cope with all manner of hard use, a fact improved by the high standards of manufacture, materials and finish employed until 1939.

In 1939 the Germans overran Poland and took over the Radom arsenal complete with the pistol production line. Finding the Radom wz.35 a thoroughly serviceable weapon the Germans adopted the design as a service pistol and kept it in production for their own

use under the designation **Pistole P 35(p)**. However, the Germans' requirement for pistols was so great that to speed production they eliminated some small features and reduced the overall standard of finish to the extent that 'German' Radoms can be easily identified from the earlier 'Polish' versions by their appearance alone. The Germans kept the Radom in full-scale production until 1944 when the advancing Red Army destroyed the factory.

When the new Polish army was re-established after 1945 it adopted the Soviet TT33 as its new standard pistol and the Radom passed into history. Many are still around as collector's items, for the bulk of the German production went to the Waffen SS and was marked appropriately. Thus these pistols have an added collection value for many pistol buffs. Quite apart from this, the Radom wz.35 was one of the better service pistols of the war years and would continue to make a very serviceable sidearm to this day.

Specification
Radom wz.35
Cartridge: 9-mm Parabellum
Length overall: 197 mm (7.76 in)
Length of barrel: 121 mm (4.76 in)
Weight: 1.022 kg (2.25 lb)
Muzzle velocity: 351 m (1,150 ft) per second
Magazine: 8-round box

The Radom wz.35 was a sound and reliable pistol of entirely conventional design that was first produced in Poland in 1935. After 1939 it was produced in some numbers for the German forces and thus many now seen carry German markings. Featuring some of the best Colt and Browning features plus a few Polish touches, the Radom was an excellent service pistol.

Automaticky Pistole vz.38 (CZ 38)

By the time that the German army marched into Czechoslovakia in 1938 and 1939 the Czech nations had evolved into one of the most industrious and innovative armaments manufacturers in all Europe. Pistols were one of the many weapon types produced, mainly at the Ceska Zbrojovka (CZ) in Prague, and from there emanated a string of excellent designs that included the vz.22, 24, 27, and 30 (vz. stands for *vzor*, or model). These pistols all fired the 9-mm (0.354-in) short cartridge and had many features in common with the Walther pistols of the period, but in 1938 came a pistol that bore no relation to anything that had been produced before.

The new pistol was the **CZ 38** (otherwise known as the **Automaticky Pistole vz.38**), and by all accounts this was not one of the better service pistols of the time. It was a large automatic weapon using a simple blowback mechanism, but it fired the 9-mm (0.354-mm) short cartridge even though its size and weight could have accommodated a more powerful round. One feature that was unusual and outdated even at that time was that the trigger mechanism was double-action only (it could be fired only by using the trigger to cock and release the hammer) while most other actions of the time used an external hammer that could be cocked by hand. This double action required a long and heavy trigger pull, so accurate aiming of the weapon was very difficult. One good feature of the design was that the pistol could be stripped very easily, simply by releasing a catch to allow the barrel to be cleaned once the slide was clear.

Not many of these pistols were produced for the Czech army before the Germans moved in, but the type was kept in production for some time. To the Germans the CZ 38 was known as the 9 mm **Pistole P 39(t)**, but most of the production went to police forces and some second-line units. Few survived after 1945. It is one of the few pistol designs that has not contributed some points to later designs.

Specification
CZ 38
Cartridge: 9 mm short (0.380 ACP)
Length overall: 198 mm (7.8 in)
Length of barrel: 119 mm (4.69 in)
Weight: 0.909 kg (2 lb)
Muzzle velocity: 296 m (970 ft) per second
Magazine: 8-round box

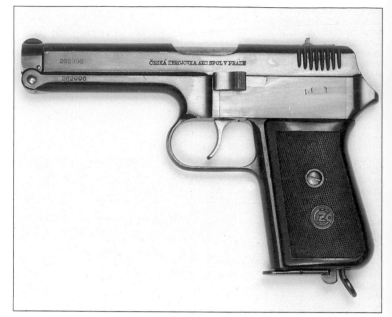

Generally regarded as a less than successful design, the Czech CZ 38 was a large and cumbersome 9-mm pistol. It could be stripped very easily but the stiff and slow double-action made accurate shooting difficul[t]

---

94 Shiki Kenju

In the 1930s the Japanese armed forces had in service a sound design of automatic pistol known to most Westerners as the 'Nambu' (8-mm Pistol Type 14), but following the large-scale Japanese incursions into China in the mid-1930s the demand for more pistols for the expanding Japanese forces could not be met. An easy solution appeared on the scene in the shape of an 8-mm (0.315-in) automatic pistol that had been commercially produced in 1934, but sales of this pistol had been few, as a result mainly of the odd and clumsy appearance of the weapon. The armed forces were then able to purchase existing stocks of these pistols and took over the production of more. The resultant weapons were initially issued to tank and air force personnel, but by the time production ended in 1945 (after more than over 70,000 had been made) its use had spread to other arms.

By all accounts this pistol, known as the **94 Shiki Kenju** (or **Pistol type 94**), was one of the worst service pistols ever produced: for a start the basic design was unsound in several respects, and then the overall appearance was wrong and the weapon handled badly, but allied to this was the fact that it was often unsafe. One reason for this last factor was that part of the trigger mechanism protruded from the left side of the frame, and if this was pushed when a round was in the chamber the pistol would fire. Another bad feature was the device to

ensure that only single shots would be fired each time the trigger was pulled, for this was so arranged that a cartridge could be fired before it was fully in the chamber. When these faults were allied to poor manufacture and poor quality materials the result was a weapon that was unsafe to an alarming degree. The problem for the Japanese personnel who had to use the gun was that production was often so rushed that the product was badly made, and troops had to use the Type 94 simply because Japanese industry could produce nothing better at that time. Examples have been found that still bear file or other machine tool marks on the outside, and the degree of 'slop' in the mechanisms of some should signify that the Type 94 is a pistol that should not be carried or fired: it is a collector's piece only.

The 94 Shiki Kenju was one of the worst pistol designs ever produced, for it was cumbersome, awkward to use and basically unsafe as the firing sear projected from the side and could be easily knocked to fire the pistol inadvertently. But it was all the Japanese had and it was kept in production until 1945.

Despite the fact that this Japanese captain is a tank officer, he is armed with a traditional sword as well as a Type 94 pistol. The sword must have been rather unwieldy in the confines of a tank turret.

Specification
Pistol Type 94
Cartridge: 8 mm Taisho 14
Length overall: 183 mm (7.2 in)
Length of barrel: 96 mm (3.78 in)
Weight: 0.688 kg (1.52 lb)
Muzzle velocity: 305 mm (1,000 ft) per second
Magazine: 6-round box

Pistola Automatica Glisenti modello 1910

The pistol that is now generally known as the **Pistola Automatica Glisenti modello 1910** was originally known as the **Brizia**, but the production and other patents were taken over by the Societa Siderugica Glisenti in the first decade of the 20th century. In 1910 this pistol was adopted by the Italian army as its standard service pistol, but for many years it managed only to supplement the earlier 10.35-mm modello 1889 revolver, and in fact this ancient pistol remained in production until the 1930s.

The Glisenti had several unusual features, and its mechanism was of a type little encountered in other designs. It used an operating system loosely described as a delayed blowback, in which the barrel and the receiver recoiled to the rear on firing. As it recoiled the action caused a rotary bolt to start to turn, and this rotation continued once the barrel had stopped moving after a distance of about 7 mm (0.276 in). The barrel was held in place by a rising wedge which was freed as the receiver moved forward again to chamber a fresh cartridge. All this movement had several effects: one was that while everything was moving the action was open and thus exposed to the ingress of debris such as sand (as in the North African deserts), and another was that the trigger pull was long and 'creepy', which made accurate fire that much more difficult. The action itself was made no more reliable by being constructed in such a way that the entire left side had no supporting frame and was held in

place by a screwed-on cover plate. In prolonged use this plate could come separated from the pistol, causing it to jam. Even when in place the action was generally 'sloppy' and the moving parts displayed an unpleasant amount of internal movement.

To overcome the worst of this action the Italians introduced a special cartridge for this pistol known as the 9-mm Glisenti. In appearance and dimensions it resembled the standard 9-mm Parabellum, but the propellant load

was reduced to produce less recoil and thus less internal stress. This cartridge was unique to the Glisenti, and if normal 9-mm ammunition was inadvertently loaded and fired the results could be disastrous to pistol and firer.

The Glisenti remained in production until the late 1920s but it was still in use in the Italian army until 1945. It is now a collector's piece only.

The Glisenti modello 1910 was an odd mixture of design innovations allied with a weak frame design.

Specification
Glisenti modello 1910
Cartridge: 9-mm Glisenti
Length overall: 210 mm (8.27 in)
Length of barrel: 102 mm (4.02 in)
Weight: 0.909 kg (2 lb)
Muzzle velocity: 320 m (1,050 ft) per second
Magazine: 7-round box

Pistola Automatica Beretta modello 1934

The little **Pistola Automatica Beretta modello 1934** is one of the joys of the pistol collector's world, for it is one of those pistols that has its own built-in attraction. It was adopted as the standard Italian army service pistol in 1934, but it was then only the latest step in a long series of automatic pistols that could be traced back as far as 1915. In that year numbers of a new pistol design were produced to meet the requirements of the expanding Italian army, and although the **Pistola Automatica Beretta modello 1915** was widely used it was never officially accepted as a service model. These original Beretta had a calibre of 7.65 mm, although a few were made in 9 mm short, the cartridge that was to be the ammunition for the later modello 1934.

After 1919 other Beretta pistols appeared, all of them following the basic Beretta design. By the time the modello 1934 appeared the 'classic' appearance had been well established with the snub outline and the front of the cutaway receiver wrapped around the forward part of the barrel to carry the fixed foresight. The short pistol grip held only seven rounds and thus to ensure a better grip the characteristic 'spur' was carried over from a design introduced back in 1919. The operation used by the mechanisms

Beretta automatics (right) were amongst the most sought after of war trophies. Although of excellent design, they were really too light to be effective service pistols, but as personal weapons to officers such as the colonel depicted (left), they were highly prized.

was a conventional blowback without frills or anything unusual, but although the receiver was held open once the magazine was empty it moved forward again as soon as the magazine was removed for reloading (most pistols of this type keep the receiver slide open until the magazine has been replaced). The modello 1934 did have an exposed hammer which was not affected by the safety once applied, so although the trigger was locked when the safety was applied the hammer could be cocked either by hand or by accident, an unfortunate feature in an otherwise sound design.

The modello 1934 was almost always produced to an excellent standard of manufacture and finish, and the type became a sought-after trophy of war. Virtually the entire production run was

taken for use by the Italian army, but there was a modello 1935 in 7.65 mm which was issued to the Italian air force and navy. Apart from its calibre this variant was identical to the modello 1934. The Germans used the type as the **Pistole P671(i)**. Despite its overall success the modello 1934 was technically underpowered, but it is still one of the most famous of all pistols used during World War II.

Specification
Beretta modello 1934
Cartridge: 9-mm short (0.380 ACP)
Length overall: 152 mm (6 in)
Length of barrel: 90 mm (3.4 in)
Weight: 0.568 kg (1.25 lb)
Muzzle velocity: 290 m (950 ft) per second
Magazine: 7-round box

Allied and Axis Machine-Guns

The machine-gun stood out from the weapons introduced during World War I. In fixed positions, in support of massed infantry, it largely dictated infantry tactics. Towards the end of the conflict, however, a new, more mobile kind of warfare emerged, and any future battles were to be very different.

British tank corps troops receiving instruction in how to handle their machine-gun; such 'grim reapers' could lay down devastating fields of fire.

During World War II the machine-gun never quite succeeded in regaining the influence over the battlefield that it managed to acquire during World War I. Generally speaking, tactics were more fluid and mobility was the key concept, but this did not mean that the machine-gun had no influence on tactics: it remained a dreadful killer, it could

still command ground, and it had been developed to still higher levels of technical perfection than its predecessors of World War I.

The machine-guns of 1939 to 1945 were still similar to those of World War I, but among the remaining relics of the earlier conflict there were many new designs. There was even a new type of machine-gun that had

grown out of the analysed results of World War I. In that conflict there had been two machine-gun types, the light machine-gun and the heavy machine-gun: the light machine-gun could be carried by one man, was located on a small bipod for aiming and firing, and usually carried the ammunition in some form of magazine; the heavy machine-gun was a team or squad

weapon capable of high and prolonged fire rates and was usually mounted on a heavy tripod; it was so heavy it was virtually static. From these two types of weapon the inter-war designers produced the general-purpose machine-gun, a machine-gun light enough to be carried by one man and used as an assault weapon but still capable of being mounted on a tripod and used to produce the fire power of a heavy machine-gun. The first design to combine these two possibly opposing requirements successfully was the German MG 34, but this was only the forerunner of many designs to come.

Apart from the MG 34 there were many other superb designs of machine-gun in use (and some very poor ones to balance them, the Breda modello 1930 perhaps being one of the worst); it remains as ever a paradox that the peak of human ingenuity should be devoted to the mechanized destruction of fellow humans. Thus the years 1939 to 1945 suffered from the excellence of the Bren Gun, the American M1919 series and the power of the 12.7mm (0.5in) Browning. But, from the design viewpoint perhaps the best design of all was the MG 34's successor, the magnificent MG 42.

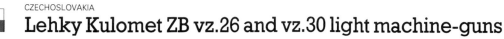

 CZECHOSLOVAKIA

Lehky Kulomet ZB vz.26 and vz.30 light machine-guns

When Czechoslovakia was established as a state after 1919 it contained within its borders a wide range of skills and talents, and among them was small arms expertise. In the early 1920s a company was established at Brno under the name of Ceskoslovenska Zbrojovka for the design and production of all types of small arms. An early product was a machine-gun known as the **Lehky Kulomet ZB vz.24** using a box magazine feed, but it remained a prototype only for an even better design was on the stocks. Using some details from the vz.24 the new design was designated the **Lehky Kulomet ZB vz.26.**

This light machine-gun was an immediate success and has remained one of the most inspirational of all such weapons ever since. The vz.26 was a gas-operated weapon with a long gas piston under the barrel and fed from an adjustable gas vent about half-way down the finned barrel. Gas operating on the piston pushed it to the rear and a simple arrangement of a hinged breech block on a ramp formed the locking and firing basis. Ammunition was fed downwards from a simple incline box magazine, and the overall design emphasized the virtues of easy stripping, maintenance and use in action. Barrel cooling was assisted by the use of prominent fins all along the barrel but a simple and rapid barrel change method was incorporated.

The vz.26 was adopted by the Czech army and soon became a great export success, being used by a whole string of nations that included China, Yugoslavia and Spain. The vz.26 was followed in production by a slightly improved model, the **Lehky Kulomet ZB vz.30**, but to the layman the two models were identical, the vz.30 differing only in the way it was manufactured and in some of the internal details. Like the vz.26, the vz.30 was also an export success, being sold to such countries as Iran and Romania. Many nations set up their own production lines under licence from ZB, and by 1939 the two designs were among the most numerous light machine-gun types in the world. When Germany started to take over most of Europe, starting with Czechoslovakia, the vz.26 and vz.30 became German weapons (**MG 26(t)** and **MG 30(t)**) and even remained in production at Brno for a while to satisfy the demands of the German forces. They were used all over the world and were even issued as standard German civil and military police machine-guns. Of all the nations involved in World War II none took to the type more avidly than China where production facilities were established. Perhaps the

Above: The Czech ZB vz.26, one of the most influential designs of its day and the forerunner of the British Bren gun; this example has its straight 20- or 30-round box magazine missing.

Right: Chinese Nationalist troops fighting under General Chian Kai Shek training with a ZB vz.26 light machine-gun.

most lasting influence the vz.26 and vz.30 had was on other designs; the Japanese copied them and so did the Spanish who produced a machine-gun known as the **FAO**. As is related elsewhere the vz.26 was the starting point for the British Bren, and the Yugoslavs produced their own variants.

If the Czech light machine-guns had any faults it was not in performance or handling but in production, for they were very expensive to make as many of the subassemblies had virtually to be machined and milled from solid metal. But this merely made them more robust and less prone to damage. They were, and still are, excellent light machine-guns.

Specification
ZB vz.26
Calibre: 7.92 mm (0.31 in)
Length: 1161 mm (45.71 in)
Length of barrel: 672 mm (26.46 in)
Weight: 9.65 kg (21.3 lb)
Muzzle velocity: 762 m (2,500 ft) per second
Rate of fire, cyclic: 500 rpm
Feed: 20- or 30-round box

Specification
ZB vz.30
Calibre: 7.92 mm (0.31 in)
Length: 1161 mm (45.71 in)

Length of barrel: 672 mm (26.46 in)
Weight: 10.04 kg (22.13 lb)
Muzzle velocity: 762 m (2,500 ft) per second
Rate of fire, cyclic: 500 rpm
Feed: 30-round box

Waffen SS troops firing a Czech ZB vz.30, a development of the ZB vz.26; the Germans knew this gun as the MG 30(t) and used it widely.

 ITALY

Breda machine-guns

During World War I the standard Italian machine-gun was the water-cooled Fiat modello 1914 and post-war this was modernized as the air-cooled Mitriaglice Fiat modello 1914/35. But it was still a heavy weapon, even in its new air-cooled form, and a newer design of light machine-gun was initiated. The new design was produced by Breda who used the experience gained by the production of earlier models in 1924, 1928 and 1929 to produce the **Fucile Mitriagliatori Breda modello 30.** This became the standard Italian army light machine-gun of World War II.

The modello 30 was one of those machine-gun designs that could at best be deemed unsatisfactory. In appearance it looked to be all odd shapes and projections and this was no doubt a hindrance to anyone who had to carry it, for these projections snagged on clothing and other equipment. But this was not all, for the Breda designers had tried to introduce a novel feed system using 20-round chargers which were rather flimsy and gave frequent trouble. These chargers were fed into a folding magazine that had a delicate hinge, and if this magazine or

the fitting was damaged the gun could not be used. To compound this problem, the extraction of the used cartridge cases was the weakest part of the whole gas-operated mechanism, and to make the gun work an internal oil pump was used to lubricate the used cases and thus assist extra extraction. While this system worked in theory the added oil soon picked up dust and other debris to clog the mechanism, and in North Africa sand was an ever-present threat. And as if this were not enough, the barrel-change method, although operable,

was rendered awkward by the fact that there was no barrel handle (and thus no carrying handle), so the operator had to use gloves. With no other type in production the modello 30 had to be tolerated, and there was even a later **modello 38** version in 7.35-mm (0.29-in) calibre.

The other two Breda machine-guns were at least better than the modello 30. One was the **Mitrigliera Breda RM modello 31**, produced for mounting on the light tanks operated by the Italian army. This had a calibre of 12.7 mm (0.5-in) and used a large curved vertic-

237

al box magazine that must have restricted the weapon's use in AFV interiors.

As a heavy machine-gun the company produced the **Mitragliace Breda modello 37**, and while this was overall a satisfactory weapon it did have an unusual feed feature: a flat 20-round feed tray which worked its way through the receiver to accept the spent cartridge cases. Exactly why this complex and quite unnecessary system was adopted is now impossible to ascertain, for the spent cases had to be removed from the tray before it could be reloaded with fresh rounds. The oil-pump extraction method was also used, rendering the modello 37 prone to the same debris clogging as the lighter modello 30. Thus the modello 37 was no more than adequate, even though the type became the standard Italian heavy machine-gun.

A version of the modello 37 for mounting in tanks was produced under the designation **Mitriaglice Breda modello 38**.

Specification
modello 30
Calibre: 6.5 mm (0.256 in)
Length: 1232 mm (48.5 in)
Length of barrel: 520 mm (20.47 in)

Weight: 10.32 kg (22.75 lb)
Muzzle velocity: 629 m (2,065 ft) per second
Rate of fire, cyclic: 450-500 rpm
Feed: 20-round charger

Specification
modello 37
Calibre: 8 mm (0.315 in)

Length: 1270 mm (50.0 in)
Length of barrel: 740 mm (29.13 in)
Weight: 19.3 kg (42.8 lb)
Weight of tripod: 18.7 kg (41.2 lb)
Muzzle velocity: 790 m (2,590 ft) per second
Rate of fire, cyclic: 450-500 rpm
Feed: 20-round tray

A Breda modello 30 6.5-mm (0.256-in) light machine-gun, one of the least successful machine-guns ever designed. For all its faults it served the Italians throughout the war.

Type 11 and Type 96 light machine-guns

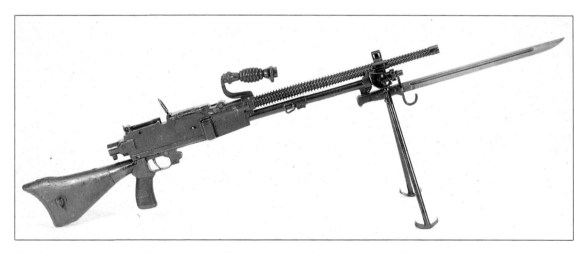

The Japanese heavy machine-guns used between 1941 and 1945 were both derivations of the French Hotchkiss machine-gun with only a few local changes. When it came to the lighter machine-guns the Japanese designed their own, the first of which was based on the same operating principles as the Hotchkiss but with the usual local variations.

The first of these was the 6.5-mm (0.256-in) **Light Machine-Gun Type 11**, which entered service in 1922 and remained in service until 1945. Its Hotchkiss origins were readily apparent in the heavily ribbed barrel and less obviously in the internal mechanisms. The design was credited to one General Kijiro Nambu and it was by the name of 'Nambu' that the type was known to the Allies. It was in its ammunition feed system that the Type 11 was unique, for it used a hopper system employed by no other machine-gun. The idea was that a small hopper on the left of the receiver could be kept filled with the rounds

fired by the rest of the Japanese infantry squad. The rounds could be fed into the hopper still in their five-round clips, thus rendering special magazines or ammunition belts unnecessary. But in practice this advantage was negated by the fact that the internal mechanism was so delicate and complex that firing the standard rifle round caused endless troubles. Thus special low-powered rounds had to be used and things were made no better by having to use a cartridge-lubrication system that attracted the usual dust and other debris to clog the works. The Type 11 was capable of automatic fire only, and when the weapon was fired the ammunition hopper tended to make the whole system unbalanced and awkward to fire. A special version, the **Tank Machine-Gun Type 91**, was produced for use in tanks, with a 50-round hopper.

The bad points of the Type 11 became very apparent after early combat experience in China during the 1930s, and in 1936 the first examples of

Above: The Japanese 6.5-mm (0.256-in) Type 96 light machine-gun was one of the few machine-guns ever equipped with a bayonet, and was a combination of Czech and French designs.

Right: Much of the fighting of the Pacific island war was between the Marines of the combatants. This Japanese Leading Seaman is a marine, and is carrying a Type 96 light machine-gun.

a new design known as **Light Machine-Gun Type 96** started to reach the troops. While the Type 96 was a definite improvement on the Type 11, it did not replace the earlier model in service, mainly as a result of the fact that Japanese industry could never produce enough weapons of any type to meet the demands of the armed forces. Overall the Type 96 used a mixture of the old Hotchkiss principles and some of the features of the Czech ZB vz.26 that the Japanese had encountered in China. One of these ex-Czech features was the overhead box magazine that replaced the hopper of the Type 11, but internally the cartridge-oiling system had to be retained along with the attendant clogging. But the Type 96 did have a quick barrel-change system and there was a choice of drum or telescopic rear sights. Once in production the telescopic sights soon became the exception, but a handy magazine-filling device was retained. One accessory that was unique to the Type 96 among all other machine-gun designs was that it had a muzzle attachment to take a bayonet.

Specification
Light Machine-Gun Type 11
Calibre: 6.5 mm (0.256 in)
Length: 1105 mm (43.5 in)
Length of barrel: 483 mm (19.0 in)
Weight: 10.2 kg (22.5 lb)
Muzzle velocity: 700 m (2,295 ft) per second
Rate of fire, cyclic: 500 rpm
Feed: 30-round hopper

Specification
Light Machine-Gun Type 96
Calibre: 6.5 mm (0.256 in)
Length: 1054 mm (41.5 in)
Length of barrel: 552 mm (21.75in)
Weight: 9.07 kg (20 lb)
Muzzle velocity: 730 m (2,395 ft) per second
Rate of fire, cyclic: 550 rpm
Feed: 30-round box

The Japanese Type 99 light machine-gun was a development of the earlier Type 96 calibred for a 7.7-mm (0.303-in) cartridge, but it retained a bayonet lug under the bipod hinge.

Browning Automatic Rifle

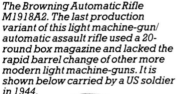

The Browning Automatic Rifle M1918A2. The last production variant of this light machine-gun/automatic assault rifle used a 20-round box magazine and lacked the rapid barrel change of other more modern light machine-guns. It is shown below carried by a US soldier in 1944.

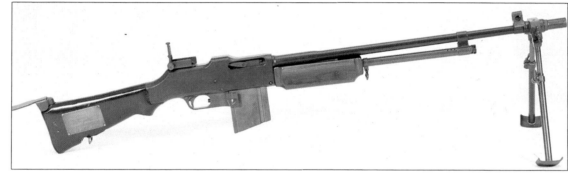

The **Browning Automatic Rifle**, or **BAR** as it is usually known, is one of those odd weapons that falls into no precise category. It may be regarded as a rather light machine-gun or as a rather heavy assault rifle, but in practice it was used as a form of light machine-gun.

As its name implies, the BAR was a product of John M. Browning's inventive mind, and Browning produced the first prototypes in 1917. When demonstrated they were immediately adopted for US Army service and were thus taken to France for active use during 1918. But the numbers involved at that time were not large, and the few used were employed as heavy rifles. This was not surprising as the first models, the **BAR M1918**, had no bipod and

could only be fired from the hip or shoulder. A bipod was not introduced until 1937 with the **BAR M1918A1** and the full and final production version, the **BAR M1918A2**, had a revised bipod and the facility for a stock rest to be added for added stability. It was the M1918A1 and M1918A2 that were to become the main American operational models, and they were issued to bolster squad fire power rather than as a squad support weapon.

The original M1918 did have a role to play in World War II, for it was sent over to the United Kingdom in 1940 to provide some form of weapon for the British Home Guard and some found their way into other second-line use. The later models were produced in thousands in the USA and once in service in large numbers they became the sort of weapon upon which soldiers came to rely. This is not to say that the BAR did not have faults, for the box magazine had a capacity of only 20 rounds, which was far too few for most infantry operations. Being something of an interim weapon type it had few tactical adherents in the theoretical field but the soldier swore by the BAR and always wanted more that could be produced. After 1945 the BAR was used again in Korea and was not finally replaced until 1957 by the US Army. Even today new versions intended to arm police forces are still available under the name **Monitor**.

One little-known facet of BAR production is the pre-1939 output of a variant designated **modèle 30** from the Fabrique Nationale (FN) plant at Liège in Belgium. From this factory emerged a string of BAR models in various calibres for the armies of Belgium itself, Sweden, some Baltic states and some Central and South American states, including Honduras. Many found their way to the Chinese army. Poland set up a national assembly line for the BAR but their calibre was 7.92 mm (0.31 in), whereas the bulk of the FN output was in 7.65 mm (0.301 in) to suit the domestic preferred calibre. Many of these Polish BARs ended up in Soviet army hands after 1939, and even the German army used the BAR after capture from a variety of sources. The Poles thought very highly of the BAR and went to the extent of mounting the weapon on specially produced and very complex and heavy tripods; there was also a special anti-aircraft version.

Specification
BAR M1918A2
Calibre: 7.62 mm (0.3 in)
Length: 1214 mm (47.8 in)
Length of barrel: 610 mm (24.0 in)
Weight: 8.8 kg (19.4 lb)
Muzzle velocity: 808 m (2,650 ft) per second
Rate of fire, cyclic: 500-600 rpm (fast rate) or 300-450 rpm (slow rate)
Feed: 20-round box

Browning M1919 machine-guns

The **Browning M1919** series differed from the earlier M1917 series in that the original water-cooled barrel was replaced by an air-cooled barrel. This air-cooled model was originally intended for use in the many tanks the United States was going to produce, but the end of World War I led to the tank contracts being cancelled along with those for the original M1919. But the air-cooled Browning was developed into the **M1919A1**, the **M1919A2** (for use by the US Cavalry) and then the **M1919A3**. The production totals for these early models were never very high, but with the **M1919A4** the totals soared. By 1945 the production total stood at 438,971 and more have been produced since then.

The M1919A4 was produced mainly for infantry use and it proved to be a first-class heavy machine-gun capable of pouring out masses of fire and absorbing all manner of abuse and punishment. As a partner for this infantry version, a special model for use on tanks was produced as the **M1919A5**. There was also a special US Air Force model, the **M2**, for use on both fixed wing and flexible installations, and the US Navy had its own range based on the M1919A4 and known as the **AN-M2**.

Among all these types and in such a long production run there were numerous minor and major modifications and production alterations, but the basic M1919 design was retained throughout. The basic M1919 used a fabric or metal-link belt feed. The normal mount was a tripod, and of these there were many designs ranging from normal infantry tripods to large and complex anti-aircraft mountings. There were ring- and gallows-type mountings for use on all sorts of trucks from jeeps to fuel tankers, and there were numerous special mountings for all manner of small craft.

Perhaps the strangest of the M1919 variants was the **M1919A6**. This was produced as a form of light machine-gun to bolster infantry squad power, which until the introduction of the M1919A6 had to depend on the fire-power of the BAR and the rifle. The M1919A6 was a 1943 innovation: it was basically the M1919A4 fitted with an awkward-looking shoulder stock, a bipod, a carrying handle and a lighter

Above: A Browning M1919A4 machine-gun on its normal tripod and clearly showing the perforated barrel cooling jacket and the square receiver; it was produced in huge numbers and the type is still in use all over the world.

A Long Range Desert Group Jeep armed with Vickers-Berthier G.O. machine-guns and with a Browning M1919A4 mounted at the front; this gun has every appearance of being adapted from an aircraft mounting.

barrel. The result was a rather heavy light machine-gun that at least had the advantage that it could be produced quickly on existing production lines. Disadvantages were the general awkwardness of the weapon and the need to wear a mitten to change the barrel when it got hot. For all that the M1919A6 was churned out in large numbers (43,479 by the time production ended), and the troops had to put up with it, for it was better in its role than the BAR.

If there was one overall asset that was enjoyed by all the versions of the M1919 series of machine-guns it was reliability, for the types would carry on working even in conditions in which other designs (other than perhaps the Vickers) would have given up. They all used the same basic recoil method: muzzle gases push back the entire barrel and breech mechanism until a bolt accelerator continues the rearward movement to a point at which springs

return the whole mechanism to restart the process.

The M1919 series (including the un-lovely M1919A6) is still in widespread use, although the M1919A6 is now used by only a few South American states.

Specification
M1919A4
Calibre: 7.62 mm (0.3 in)
Length: 1041 mm (41.0 in)
Length of barrel: 610 mm (24.0 in)
Weight: 14.06 kg (31 lb)
Muzzle velocity: 854 m (2,800 ft) per second
Rate of fire, cyclic: 400-500 rpm
Feed: 250-round belt

Specification
M1919A6
Calibre: 7.62 mm (0.3 in)
Length: 1346 mm (53.0 in)
Length of barrel: 610 mm (24.0 in)
Weight: 14.74 kg (32.5 lb)
Muzzle velocity: 854 m (2,800 ft) per second
Rate of fire, cyclic: 400-500 rpm
Feed: 250-round belt

Browning 12.7-mm (0.5-in) heavy machine-guns

Ever since the first Browning 12.7-mm (0.5-in) heavy machine-gun was produced in 1921 the type has been one of the most fearsome anti-personnel weapons likely to be encountered. The projectile fired by the type is a prodigious man-stopper, and the machine-gun can also be used as an armour-defeating weapon, especially when firing armour-piercing rounds. The round is really the heart of the gun, and early attempts by Browning to produce a heavy machine-gun all foundered on the lack of a suitable cartridge.

The classic Browning machine-gun on its usual tripod. It was first placed in production in 1921 and remains so, as it is one of the best anti-personnel weapons ever developed; it also has a very useful anti-armour capability.

It was not until the examination of a captured German 13-mm (0.51-in) round (used in the Mauser T-Gewehr anti-tank rifle) that the solution was found, and thereafter all was well. The basic cartridge has remained essentially unchanged, although there have been numerous alternative propellants and types of projectile.

From the original **Browning M1921** heavy machine-gun evolved a whole string of variants based on what was to become known as the **M2**. On all these variants the gun mechanism remained the same, being very similar to that used on the smaller M1917 machine-gun. Where the variants differed from each other was in the type of barrel fitted and the fixtures used for mounting the gun.

One of the most numerous of the M2s has been the **M2 HB**, the suffix denoting the use of a Heavy Barrel. The HB version can be used in all manner of installations and in the past has been employed as an infantry gun, as an anti-aircraft gun and even as a fixed or trainable aircraft gun. For infantry use the M2 HB is usually mounted on a heavy tripod, but it can also be used mounted on vehicle pintles, ring mountings and pivots. Other M2 types include versions with water-cooled barrels, which were usually employed as anti-aircraft weapons, especially on US Navy vessels where during World War II they were often fixed in multiple mountings for use against low-flying attack aircraft. Single water-cooled mountings were often used to provide anti-aircraft defence for shore installations. The main change between ground-based and aircraft versions was that the aircraft model had a barrel 914 mm (36 in) long whereas the ground version had a barrel 1143 mm (45 in) long. Apart from the barrel and some mounting fixtures, any part of the M1921 and M2 machine-guns can be interchanged.

More 12.7-mm (0.5-in) Browning machine-guns have been produced in the United States than any other design. To date the figures run into millions and the production run is still not complete, for during the late 1970s two American companies found it worthwhile to put the type back into production, and the same applied to the Belgian FN concern. Many more companies throughout the world find it profitable to provide spares and other such backing for the M2 series, and almost every year another ammunition producer introduces yet another type of cartridge for use with the weapon. Many dealers find it profitable just to sell or purchase such weapons alone, so there is no sign yet that demand for the gun is weakening in any way.

The M2 will be around for decades to come, and there is no sign of any replacement. It must rank as one of the most successful machine-gun designs ever produced.

This anti-aircraft mounting, known as the M45 Maxson Mount, used four heavy barrelled Browning M2s.

Specification
M2 HB
Calibre: 12.7 mm (0.5 in)
Length: 1654 mm (65.1 in)

Length of barrel: 1143 mm (45.0 in)
Weight: 38.1 kg (84 lb)
Weight of tripod: 19.96 kg (44 lb) for M3 type
Muzzle velocity: 884 m (2,900 ft) per second
Rate of fire, cyclic: 450-575 rpm
Feed: 110-round metal-link belt

Fusil Mitrailleur modèles 1924/29 and Mitrailleuse 1931 machine-guns

The French army was not slow to realize the impact of the light machine-gun on tactics during World War I, and soon after the Armistice spent considerable time and effort developing a national design suitable for extensive French deployment. Despite all the effort, the eventual result was a weapon with a mechanism based on that of the American Browning Automatic Rifle but altered in several ways to suit a new cartridge with a new calibre of 7.5 mm (0.295 in). The first production model was the **Fusil Mitrailleur modèle 1924** (Automatic Rifle M1924), which was manufactured at the large arsenal at Saint-Etienne. The design was clean and modern-looking, and used an overhead box magazine holding 25 or 26 rounds. A dual-trigger system was provided for single shots or full automatic fire.

Unfortunately neither the gun nor the cartridge was fully developed before the type was introduced into service, resulting in a series of internal barrel explosions and other shortcomings. The solution was to redesign the cartridge to make it slightly less powerful (becoming shorter in the process) and to beef up some of the weapon's parts. The result was the **Fusil Mitrailleur modèle 1924/29**, and it was this type that eventually became the standard French light machine-gun for much of the army in 1939. A range of mountings was devised for the weapon, and there was even a small monopod for mounting under the butt to make prolonged fire more accurate.

A special variant of the mle 1924/29 was produced, initially for use in the Maginot Line defences but eventually also for tanks and other AFVs. This was the **Mitrailleuse modèle 1931**, and at first sight it had little in common with the earlier model. The mle 1931 had a peculiarly-shaped butt and a prominent side-mounted drum magazine

holding no less than 150 rounds. Despite appearances the internal arrangements were the same as those of the mle 1924/29, even if the overall length and barrel length were increased. In static defences the increased weight was no handicap and the mle 1931 was produced in large numbers. In fact so many were produced that ultimately the model was used outside the concrete defences as an anti-aircraft weapon, often arranged in pairs on special or even improvised anti-aircraft mountings.

With the events of 1940 the mle 1924/29 and mle 1931 passed into German hands as the **Leichte MG 116(f)** and **Kpfw MG 331(f)** respectively. Only a relatively few remained in French hands in the Middle East and North Africa, and there they were used until 1945. After 1945 the type was once more put into production and it remained in service for many years, some examples ending up in the hands of the Viet Cong in the Far East. Postwar production involved only the mle 1924/29.

The German booty of 1940 meant that many mle 1924/29s and mle 1931 machine-guns were later incorporated into the defences of the Atlantic Wall, and the mle 1931 was especially favoured by the Germans as an anti-aircraft weapon. But for all this widespread use the mle 1924/29 and mle 1931 were never entirely trouble-free, and the cartridge they fired was generally deemed underpowered and lacking in range: maximum useful range was only 500 to 550 m (550 to 600 yards) instead of the 600+ m (655+ yards) of many contemporary designs.

Specification
Fusil Mitrailleur mle 1924/29
Calibre: 7.5 mm (0.295 in)
Length: 1007 mm (39.65 in)

A Chatellerault modèle 1924/29 light machine-gun, the standard French light machine-gun of 1940; it had a calibre of 7.5 mm (0.295 in) and used two triggers, one for automatic fire and the other for single shots.

Length of barrel: 500 mm (19.69 in)
Weight: 8.93 kg (19.7 lb)
Muzzle velocity: 820 m (2,690 ft) per second
Rate of fire, cyclic: 450-600 rpm
Feed: 25-round box

Specification
Mitrailleuse mle 1931
Calibre: 7.5 mm (0.295 in)
Length: 1030 mm (40.55 in)
Length of barrel: 600 mm (23.62 in)
Weight: 11.8 kg (26.0 lb)
Muzzle velocity: 850 m (2,790 ft) per second
Rate of fire, cyclic: 750 rpm
Feed: 150-round drum

How machine-guns work

The very first machine-guns operated on what was basically a recoil principle. The very simplest operated on the blow-back principle, in which the recoil forces attendant on firing a rifle-power cartridge impinge directly on a breech block and force it back, only the mass of the block and perhaps some springs preventing the block from moving back while the internal pressures in the barrel remain at a dangerously high level. The simplicity of this system is overcome by the weights and masses involved, so the blow-back principle is not widely used in machine-guns, especially where powerful cartridges such as those in the 12.7-mm (0.5-in) calibre category are concerned.

What is required is some form of system that can operate by using the considerable energy released when a cartridge is fired without any danger of these forces endangering the weapon or the firer. Thus the breech block and the barrel have to remain 'locked' during the short period that the projectile is pushed down the barrel by the rapid gas expansion of the detonated propellant charge. This locking is usually carried out by mechanical means, and until recently the number of principles employed was legion. Only in recent years has the modern rotary lock become established to the point of virtual exclusion of other systems. But during World War II the rotary lock was well in the future and several other locking systems were thus employed.

It would be difficult to mention all these locking systems in a few lines, but suffice to say they all operated using two methods of overall propulsion. One was the recoil system and the other the gas-operated system. The recoil system usually operates by using the gases produced at the muzzle to propel the entire barrel and the locked-on breech mechanism to the rear; at some point during this rearwards progress the barrel is held by a fixed stop, leaving the breech block to move even farther backwards, taking with it the spent cartridge case until a point is reached where compressed springs push the whole arrangement back to the start position, loading a new round on the way ready for the next firing cycle. On many designs once the barrel and breech were unlocked a mechanical device known as an accelerator ensured that the breech block (or bolt) moved to the rear at an increased rate. The recoil system could even be divided into short or long recoil systems.

The gas-operated system is generally much lighter than the recoil system as the individual parts are not so highly stressed as those on the recoil system and can thus be made smaller and simpler. Thus the gas-operated system was more usually found in World War II light machine-guns. The principle uses propellant gases tapped off from a point along the barrel through which they are diverted even while the projectile is still in the barrel. This is safe as the gases have to overcome the inertia of a gas piston, which eventually moves to the rear taking the breech block away from the fixed barrel. Again, accelerators may be used but the gas pressure usually provides all the propulsion required until a point is reached where the breech is far enough to the rear for the gases to be vented through open ports in the receiver. Springs then return the piston and the breech block to the start position, loading a new round on the way. Needless to say there are several variations on this principle but they all operate along the same general lines.

The locking devices involved in both recoil and gas-operated mechanisms were many and varied. Most relied on some form of ramp or roller to form an obstacle with sufficient mechanical advantage (at the precise point when the round was fired and pressures were at their highest) to prevent the breech from moving. Some, usually involving rollers and lugs, actually used the rearward-forcing gas pressures of the cartridge case to form the 'lock' at the instant of firing, while others used a simple wedge system. Some were very complex and some were simple to the point of absurdity, but generally speaking the simpler the system the more reliable it was in operation.

Quick release lever
The barrel was easy to change, by releasing the lever and drawing off by the carrying handle.

Gas tube and piston
The gas piston was made from high quality metals, as it had to bear the brunt of the gas operating system. As the firing gases came through the regulator they impinged directly onto the piston face, driving it to the rear. When the piston had been pushed back to the correct distance the gases were allowed to escape through vents in the side of the piston wall.

Gas regulator
The gas regulator has four positions, which allow the firing gases to escape through holes of four varying sizes into the gas piston cylinder.

Flash hider
At the end of the barrel the flash hider minimizes the amount of flame issuing from the weapon.

Propellant gases are drawn off through the regulator to act on a piston. This forces back the working parts, against the pressure of the return spring in the butt.

The hammer and bolt assembly, while withdrawing, extracts the empty cartridge case from the breech. Once clear it is ejected.

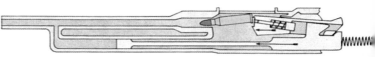

A fresh cartridge is fed from the magazine. The working parts are then moved back into position by the return spring in the butt.

The Bren gun is seen here in its original production form with a drum rearsight and adjustable bipod legs – later versions had these removed and replaced by simpler components.

Magazine *The magazine was curved to accommodate the rimmed 0.303-in cartridge and could hold up to 20 rounds.*

Hammer *The hammer actuator was a fixed post which struck the rear of the firing pin to allow it to strike the cartridge primer. The pin could not strike the primer until the round was properly chambered.*

Sights
Early models used drum sights with the rearsight on an arm, but later models used the simpler leaf sight.

Recoil spring
The main recoil spring was contained within the butt and was connected to the main moving parts by a steel rod which protruded into the receiver, so normally the recoil spring was neither touched nor seen when stripping. The rod was flexibly mounted to allow the piston group to be withdrawn for stripping.

Trigger *A fire selector lever close to the trigger had three positions; single shot, safe and automatic.*

UK
Bren light machine-gun

The **Bren Gun** was a development of the original Czech ZB vz.26 light machine-gun, but the development path was one that involved as much British as Czech expertise. During the 1920s the British army sought far and wide for a new type of light machine-gun to replace the generally unsatisfactory Lewis Gun, trying all manner of designs, most of which were found wanting in some way or other. By 1930 a series of trials commenced involving several designs, among them the vz.26 in the form of a slightly revised model, the ZB vz.27. The ZB vz.27 emerged as a clear winner from these trials but it was made in 7.92-mm (0.31-in) calibre only, and the British army wanted to retain its 7.7 mm (0.303-in) cartridge with its outdated cordite propellant and its awkward rimmed case.

Thus started a series of development models that involved the vz.27, the later vz.30 and eventually an interim model, the ZB vz.32. Then came the vz.33 and it was from this that the Royal Small Arms Factory at Enfield Lock evolved the prototype of what became the Bren Gun (Bren from the

BR of Brno, the place of origin, and EN from Enfield Lock). Tooling up at Enfield Lock resulted in the first production **Bren Gun Mk 1** being turned out in 1937, and thereafter the type remained in production at Enfield and elsewhere until well after 1945. By 1940 well over 30,000 Bren Guns had been produced and the type was well established in service, but the result of Dunkirk not only supplied the Germans with a useful stock of Bren Guns (**Leichte MG 138(e)**) and ammunition but also led to a great demand to re-equip the British army.

The original design was thus much modified to speed up production, and new lines were established. The original gas-operated mechanism of the

ZB design was retained and so was the breech locking system and the general appearance, but out went the rather complicated drum sights and extras such as the under-butt handle in the **Bren Gun Mk 2**. The bipod became much simpler but the curved box magazine of the 7.7-mm (0.303-in) Bren was carried over. In time more simplifications were made (**Bren Gun Mk 3** with a shorter barrel and **Bren Gun Mk 4** with a modified butt assembly), and there was even a reversion to the 7.92-mm (0.31-in) calibre when Brens were manufactured in Canada for the Chinese army.

The Bren Gun turned out to be a superb light machine-gun. It was robust, reliable, easy to handle and to maintain, and it was not too heavy for its role. It was also very accurate. In time a whole range of mountings and accessories was introduced, including some rather complex anti-aircraft mountings that included the Motley and the Gallows mountings. A 200-round drum was developed but little used, and various vehicle mountings were designed and introduced. The Bren Gun

outlived all these accessories, for after 1945 the type remained in service and the wartime 'extras' were phased out.

The Bren Gun on its basic bipod did linger on, however, and is still in British Army service as the **Bren Gun L4A2**. It now boasts a calibre of the standard NATO 7.62 mm (0.3 in) and the barrel is chrome-plated to reduce wear and the need to change barrels during prolonged fire using the simple barrel-change device. Today the type is still in army service with second-line and support arms and also with the Royal Navy, and there seems to be no replacement for the type in sight. It was and still is an excellent light machine-gun.

Specification
Bren Light Machine-Gun Mk 1
Calibre: 7.7 mm (0.303 in)
Length: 1156 mm (45.5 in)
Length of barrel: 635 mm (25.0 in)
Weight: 10.03 kg (22.12 lb)
Muzzle velocity: 744 m (2,440 ft) per second
Rate of fire, cyclic: 500 rpm
Feed: 20-round box magazine

Vickers machine-guns

The **Vickers machine-gun** range had its origins in the Maxim gun of the late 19th century, and was little changed from the original other than that the Maxim locking toggle design was inverted in the Vickers product. The **Vickers Machine-Gun Mk 1** had performed well in World War I, outperforming in many ways nearly all of its contemporaries. Consequently after 1918 the Vickers remained the standard heavy machine-gun of both the British army and many of the Commonwealth forces as well. Many were exported all over the world but many of these were ex-stock weapons as production was kept at a very low ebb at Vickers' main production plant at Crayford in Kent.

However, some innovations were introduced before 1939; the introduction of the tank in all its various forms had led to the design of Vickers machineguns to arm the new fighting machines, and by 1939 Vickers had in production two types of special tank machine-gun. These were in two calibres: the **Vickers Machine-Gun Mks 4B, 6, 6* and 7** being of 7.7-mm (0.303-in) calibre and the **Vickers Machine-Gun Mks 4 and 5** of the 12.7-mm (0.5-in) type firing a special cartridge. Both were produced for all types of tank initially, but the introduction of the air-cooled Besa machine-guns for the bulk of the heavier tanks meant that most of the Vickers tank machine-guns ended up either in the light tank series or in the infantry tank types, the Matilda 1 and 2. The 12.7-mm (0.5-in) machine-guns were also produced in a variety of forms for the Royal Navy as the **Vickers Machine-Gun Mk 3** with all manner of mountings for anti-aircraft defence of ships and shore installations. The ship installations included quadruple mountings, but the cartridge produced for the weapon was not a success and proved underpowered. Nevertheless, in the absence of an alternative the weapon was produced in some numbers, only later being replaced by 20-mm cannon and other such weapons.

Thus 1939 found the Vickers machine-gun in service still and in some numbers. By 1940 all manner of ancient models from stock were being used in all roles including emergency anti-aircraft mountings to bolster home defences and production was soon under way again in large quantities. Demand was so heavy (most of the British army's machine-gun stocks were lost before and during the Dunkirk episode) that production short-cuts were introduced, the most noticeable of which was the replacement of the corrugated barrel water jacket by a

simple smooth jacket. Later a new muzzle booster design was introduced and by 1943 the new Mark 8Z boat-tailed bullet was in widespread use to provide a useful effective range of no less than 4100 m (4,500 yards). This enabled the Vickers machine-gun to be used for the indirect fire role and a mortar sight was adapted for the role.

After the war the Vickers served on (and still does) with armies such as those of India and Pakistan. The British army ceased to use the type in 1968 but the Royal Marines continued to use theirs until well into the 1970s.

Specification
Vickers Machine-Gun Mk 1
Calibre: 7.7 mm (0.303 in)
Length: 1156 mm (45.5 in)
Length of barrel: 721 mm (28.4 in)
Weight of gun: 18.1 kg (40 lb) with water
Weight of tripod: 22 kg (48.5 lb)
Muzzle velocity: 744 m (2,440 ft) per second
Rate of fire, cyclic: 450-500 rpm
Feed: 250-round belt

Men of the Cheshire Regiment using their Vickers machine-guns on a range, in about 1940; note the water cans to retain evaporated steam from the barrel jacket.

A Vickers machine-gun in its late production form with no corrugations on the barrel jacket, the final form of the muzzle attachment and the indirect-fire sight in position.

The machine-gun seen here is not the usual 7.7-mm (0.303-in) version but a heavier 12.7-mm (0.5-in) version which was originally produced for use on light tanks; it is seen here in use on a Chevrolet truck belonging to the Long Range Desert Group.

Vickers-Berthier light machine-guns

Above: The Vickers-Berthier Mk 3B produced for the Indian Army, showing the overall clean lines and general resemblance to the Bren gun; the 30-round box magazine is not fitted.

Right: A patrol of the newly-formed SAS in North Africa in 1943; their jeeps are liberally armed with Vickers-Berthier G.O. guns and they have 96-round drum magazines.

The **Vickers-Berthier** series of light machine-guns originally evolved from a French design produced just before World War I. Despite some promising features the design was not adopted in useful numbers by any nation, but in 1925 the British Vickers company purchased licence rights on the type, mainly to keep its Crayford production lines in being with a new model to replace the Vickers machine-gun. After a series of British army trials the type was adopted by the Indian army as its standard light machine-gun and eventually a production line for this **Vickers-Berthier Light Machine-Gun Mk 3** was established at Ishapore.

In general appearance and design the Vickers-Berthier light machine-gun was similar to the Bren Gun, but internally and in detail there were many differences. Thus at times the Vickers-Berthier was often referred to by observers as the Bren. Apart from the large Indian Army contract the only other sales were to a few Baltic and South American states, and today the Vickers-Berthier is one of the least known of all World War II machine-guns. This is not because there was anything wrong with the type (it was a sound and reliable design) but because it had poor 'press' coverage and numerically was well outnumbered by the Bren Gun. But even today it remains in reserve use in India.

There was one Vickers-Berthier gun derivative that did, however, obtain a much better showing. This was a much-modified version of the basic design with a large drum magazine mounted above the receiver and a

spade grip fixed to the rear where the butt would normally have been. This was a special design intended for open cockpit aircraft, and was intended for use on a Scarff ring by the observer. Large numbers of this design were produced for the Royal Air Force, by whom it was known as the **Vickers G.O** (G.O. for gas operated) or **Vickers K** gun, but almost as soon as the type was introduced into service the open cockpit era came to a sudden close with the introduction of higher speed aircraft. The Vickers G.O. proved difficult to use in the close confines of aircraft turrets and impossible to use in wing installations, so it was placed almost immediately into store; some were used by the Fleet Air Arm on such aircraft as the Swordfish and thus remained in use until 1945 but their numbers were relatively few.

In 1940 many Vickers G.O. guns were taken out of store and widely used on various emergency mountings for anti-aircrft defences on airfields and other such installations. In North Africa the Vickers G.O. was avidly seized upon by the various irregular forces that sprang up for behind-the-lines operations, and the Vickers G.O. was thus used by such units as 'Popski's Private Army' on their heavily armed jeeps and trucks. The weapon proved ideal in the role and gave a good indication of how the original Vickers-Berthier machine-guns would have stood up under such conditions if they had been given the chance. The Vickers G.O. guns were used right until the end of the war in Italy and a few other theatres and they then passed right out of use, once more outnumbered by the more generally available Bren Guns.

This sepoy, carrying a Vickers-Berthier Mk 3, is dressed in standard issue khaki drill, with two large pouches for spare magazines. The Indian Army was the major user of the Vickers-Berthier gun.

Specification
Vickers-Berthier Light Machine-Gun Mk 3
Calibre: 7.7 mm (0.303 in)
Length: 1156 mm (45.5 in)
Length of barrel: 600 mm (23.6 in)
Weight: 11.1 kg (24.4 lb)
Muzzle velocity: 745 m (2,450 ft) per second
Rate of fire, cyclic: 450-600 rpm
Feed: 30-round box

Specification
Vickers G.O. Gun
Calibre: 7.7 mm (0.303 in)
Length: 1016 mm (40.0 in)
Length of barrel: 529 mm (20.83 in)
Weight: 9.5 kg (21 lb)
Muzzle velocity: 745 m (2,450 ft) per second
Rate of fire, cyclic: 1,000 rpm
Feed: 96-round drum

Maschinengewehr 34 general-purpose machine-gun

The terms of the Versailles Treaty of 1919 specifically prohibited (by means of a special clause) the development of any form of sustained-fire weapon by Germany, but this provision was circumvented by the arms concern

Rheinmetall-Borsig by the simple expedient of setting up a 'shadow' concern under its control over the border at Solothurn in Switzerland during the early 1920s. Research carried out into air-cooled machine-gun designs re-

sulted in a weapon that evolved into the **Solothurn Modell 1930**, an advanced design that introduced many of the features that were incorporated in later weapons. A few production orders were received, but it was felt

by the Germans that something better was required and thus the Modell 1929 had only a short production run before being used as the starting point for an aircraft machine-gun, the **Rheinmetall MG 15**. This long remained in production for the Luftwaffe.

From the Rheinmetall designs came what is still considered as one of the finest machine-gun designs ever produced, the **Maschinengewehr 34** or **MG 34**. Mauser designers at the Oberndorff plant used the Modell 1929 and the MG 15 as starting points for what was to be a new breed of machine-gun, the general-purpose machine-gun. This new type could be carried by an infantry squad and fired from a bipod or mounted on a heavier tripod for sustained fire over long periods. The mechanism was of the all-in-line type and the barrel had a quick-change facility for cooling. The feed was of two types, using either the saddle-drum magazine holding 75 rounds inherited from the MG 15 or a belt feed. To add to all this technical innovation the MG 34 had a high rate of fire and could thus be effective against low-flying aircraft.

The MG 34 was an immediate success and went straight into production for all the various arms and auxiliaries of the German armed forces (and even the police). Demand for the MG 34 remained high right until 1945, and consistently outstripped supply. The supply situation was not aided by the number of mounts and gadgets that were introduced to go with the weapon. These varied from heavy tripods and twin mountings to expensive and complex fortress and tank mountings. There was even a periscopic gadget to enable the weapon to fire from trenches. These accessories consumed a great deal of production potential to the detriment of gun production proper, but production of the MG 34 was in any case not aided by one fact and that was that the design was really too good for military use. It took too long to manufacture and involved too many complex and expensive machining processes. The result was a superb weapon, but actually using it was rather like using a Rolls-Royce car for ploughing a field – it was too good for the task. Thus the German forces found themselves using a weapon they could not afford in terms of production potential, while demands meant they had to keep production going until the end.

Variants of the basic model were the **MG 34m** with a heavier barrel jacket for use in AFVs, and the shorter **MG**

An MG 34 mounted for the heavy machine-gun role on a Lafette 34 tripod and complete with the indirect-fire sight; the pads on the front leg rested against the carrier's back when folded for transport.

34s and **MG 34/41** intended for use in the AA role and capable of automatic fire only. The overall length and barrel length of the two latter were about 1170 mm (46 in) and 560 mm (22 in) respectively.

Specification
MG 34
Calibre: 7.92 mm (0.31 in)
Length: 1219 mm (48.0 in)
Length of barrel: 627 mm (24.69 in)
Weight: 11.5 kg (25.4 lb) with bipod
Muzzle velocity: 755 m (2,475 ft) per second
Rate of fire, cyclic: 800-900 rpm
Feed: 50 round belt (five belt lengths), or 75-round saddle drum

An MG 34 advancing through the USSR with the man on the right carrying the folded Lafette 34, the man in the centre the MG 34 and the one on the right with a spare barrel slung across his back; the other man by the MG 34 carrier has an ammunition case.

Two Afrika Korps soldiers with an MG 34 in the heavy machine-gun role on a Lafette 34. By removing the indirect fire sights and trigger, the MG 34 quickly converts to an LMG.

Maschinengewehr 42 general-purpose machine-gun

Despite the overall excellence of the MG 34 it was really too good for its task in terms of cost and production requirements, so despite the establishment of a full production facility and constant demand, by 1940 the Mauser designers were looking for something simpler. With the production example of the 9-mm MP 40 sub-machine gun as an example in production simplicity and low cost, they decided to adopt new production methods using as few expensive machining processes as possible allied with new operating mechanisms. The new mechanisms came from a wide range of sources. Experience with the MG 34 had indicated how the feed could be revised, and designs captured when Poland was overrun appeared to promise a new and radical breech locking system. Other ideas came from Czechoslovakia, and the Mauser team also introduced its own ideas. From this wealth of innovation came a new design, the **MG 39/41**, and from a series of trials carried out with this design came the **Maschinengewehr 42** or **MG 42**, a design that must rank among the finest of its kind.

The MG 42 introduced mass-production techniques to the machine-gun on a large scale. Earlier designs had used some simple sheet metal stampings and production short-cuts (one example being the little-known French Darne light machine-gun), but the harsh environment that the machine-gun has to endure meant that few had any success. On the MG 42 that success was immediate. Sheet metal stampings were extensively used for the receiver and for the barrel housing which incorporated an ingenious barrel-change system. The latter was very necessary for the MG 42 had a prodigious rate of fire that sounded like tearing linoleum. This was produced by the locking mechanism employed, a mechanism that was developed from several sources and was both simple and reliable. The system involved the use of two locking rollers running up and down an internal ramp: in the forward position they locked the breech very effectively by mechanical advantage and then allowed the ramp to release the locking. On the ammunition feed an arm on the bolt was used to pull the ammunition belts across into the receiver in a simple and very effective fashion. Only the 50-round belt was used with the MG 42.

These design details merged to form a very effective general-purpose machine-gun and as is related elsewhere the type was attached to a wide range of mounts and other accessories. The MG 42's operational debut came in 1942, when it appeared in both the USSR and North Africa. Thereafter it was used on every front and in general, issue was made to front-line troops only, for though the MG 42 was intended to supplant the MG 34 it in fact only supplemented the earlier type.

Not content with producing one of the finest machine-gun designs ever produced, the Mauser design team tried to go one better and came up with the **MG 45** with an even higher rate of fire. The end of the war put paid to that design for the time being, but the MG 42 lives on with many armies.

An MG 42 for use in the light machine-gun role, with a bipod.

Above: An MG 42 mounted on the Lafette 42 for the heavy machine-gun role; this heavy tripod could be quickly adapted for the anti-aircraft fire role.

Right: MG 42 awaiting invasion as part of a fortified position on the Atlantic Wall, complete with ammunition belt loaded and spare barrel at the ready by the ammunition case.

Specification
MG 42
Calibre: 7.92 mm (0.31 in)
Length: 1220 mm (48.03 in)
Length of barrel: 533 mm (20.98 in)
Weight: 11.5 kg (25.4 lb) with bipod
Muzzle velocity: 755 m (2,475 ft) per second
Rate of fire, cyclic: up to 1,550 rpm
Feed: 50-round belt

DShK 1938, SG43 and other Soviet machine-guns

If there has ever been one factor differentiating Russian and Soviet machine-gun designs from those of other nations it was the simple factor of weight. For many years these machine-guns were built to such a standard of robustness that weight alone was used as a means of incorporating strength, the ultimate example being the old M1910 Maxim guns that almost resembled small artillery pieces with their wheeled and shielded carriages. Eventually this avoidable trait was recognized by the Red Army when mobility made its way into long-term planning and by the mid-1930s, when a new heavy machine-gun was required, emphasis being placed more on design than sheer mass for strength.

The new heavy machine-gun was intended to be in the same class as the 12.7-mm (0.5-in) Browning, but the Soviet equivalent turned out to be slightly lighter. It used a 12.7-mm (0.5-in) cartridge and was intended for a variety of roles. To the credit of the new design, the **DShK1938** (in full the *Krasnoi Pulemet Degtyereva-Shpagina obrazets 1938g*), has proved to be almost as successful as the Browning, for it is still in production, albeit in a post-war modified form as the **DShK1938/46**, and is still in widespread service.

If the DShK1938 was lighter as a gun than the Browning the same could not be said of the mount, for as an infantry gun the DshK1938 retained the old wheeled carriage of the M1910, but a special anti-aircraft tripod was introduced and is still in use. The type became a virtual fixture on most Soviet tanks from the JS-2 heavy tanks onwards, and the Czechs have produced a quadruple mounting with DShK1938s for anti-aircraft use. There was even a special version for use on armoured trains.

The smaller **SG43** was introduced during 1943 to replace earlier 7.62-mm (0.3-in) machine-guns, including the venerable M1910. During the initial phases of the German invasion of the USSR the Soviet forces lost huge amounts of material, including machine-guns, and if their new production facilities were to replace these losses they might as well be modern designs. Thus the *Stankovii Pulemet Goryunova obrazets 1943g* came into being. It was a gas-operated and air-cooled design that combined several operating principles (including the well-established Browning principles), but overall the design was original and soon proved to be sound. As the SG43 the design was issued in very large numbers and even today the basic weapon is still in widespread use, albeit in a much modified and upgraded form as the **SGM**.

Both the SG43 and the larger DShK1938 have the same basic operational: simplicity. Working parts have been kept to a minimum and very little routine maintenance apart from simple cleaning is required. Both designs can operate under extremes of temperature and they are most forgiving of dirt and dust in the works. In other words both suit exactly the type of environment in which they will be used.

Right: Similar in performance to the 12.7-mm (0.5-in) Browning, the DShK 38/46 is still in production and service.

Specification
DShK1938
Calibre: 12.7 mm (0.5 in)
Length: 1602 mm (63.1 in)
Length of barrel: 1002 mm (39.45 in)
Weight: 33.3 kg (73.5 lb)
Muzzle velocity: 843 m (2,765 ft) per second
Rate of fire, cyclic: 550-600 rpm
Feed: 50-round metal-link belt (five belts joined)

Specification
SG43
Calibre: 7.62 mm (0.3 in)
Length: 1120 mm (44.1 in)
Length of barrel: 719 mm (28.3 in)
Weight: 13.8 kg (30.4 lb)
Muzzle velocity: 863 m (2,830 ft) per second
Rate of fire, cyclic: 500-640 rpm
Feed: 50-round metal-link belt

The SG 43 was designed by P.M. Goryunov in 1942 to provide a wartime replacement for the elderly Maxim Model 1910, and even used the old Maxim's wheeled carriage.

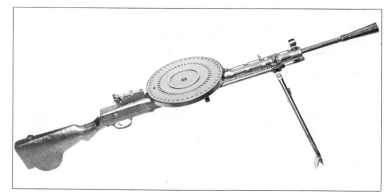

Above: The Degtyerev DP Model 1928 was a major Soviet light machine-gun during World War II. Simple and robust, the DP could stand rough treatment and extremes of weather. It can still be found in the hands of guerrilla groups all over the world.

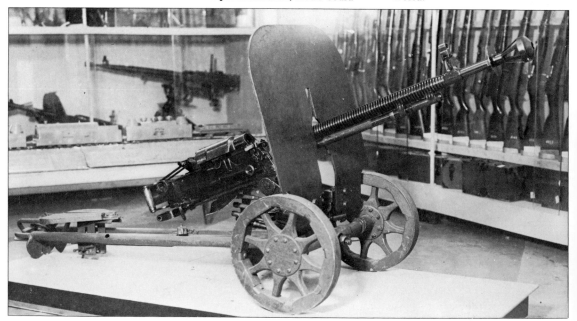

Allied and Axis Sub-Machine Guns

The sub-machine gun was born out of the trenches of World War I. In the confined close-quarter fighting troops began to feel the need for some form of compact automatic weapon that would be less awkward to handle than a bayonetted rifle. Faced with this demand, manufacturers came up with the sub-machine gun.

The Italians were the first to introduce what might be termed a sub-machine gun. This was the Villar-Perosa which, while often though to be the first sub-machine gun, was in many ways a blind alley, for the Villar-Perosa was used only as a light machine-gun. The first true example of what was to be termed the machine-pistol or sub-machine gun was in fact the German MP18. This appeared in front-line service in 1918 and still remains the best example of all the attributes of the sub-machine gun.

The MP18 used a pistol cartridge (a small, relatively low-powered charge firing a small but heavy bullet). If a hand-held weapon was to be used to fire fully automatically the round fired had to be light and the pistol cartridge was the obvious choice. The MP18 fired the 9mm Parabellum cartridge and in the years that followed this became an almost universal choice for most designs. Using a pistol cartridge also allowed the employment of an operating principle that had long been used on automatic pistols, the blow-back principle.

The blow-back principle is very simple. On the MP18 the magazine was fitted and the gun cocked by using a side-mounted lever in a slot. When the trigger was pulled it released the breech block to move

British troops wielding the American-designed .45in Thompson M1928 machine-gun, popularly known as the 'Tommy Gun'. These drum magazines carried 50 or 100 rounds but proved too troublesome in use so various box types replaced them.

forward under the energy from a large spring. As it moved forward the breech block picked up a cartridge from the feed, pushed it into the barrel chamber and once the round and breech block were in position the firing pin fired the cartridge. The recoil forces produced by the cartridge were initially overcome by the forward energy produced by the mass of the breech block and the spring, but the block remained in place long enough to 'lock' the system until the recoil forces were able to push back the breech block and

its spring to their original condition. If the trigger was still pulled, the cycle began again and went on until the trigger was released.

If this simple operating principle was ever abandoned, the result was usually less than satisfactory, for the mechanism would be over-complex and would have more pieces to break or jam. But if the operating system could be kept basic and light, and the MP18 was light enough to be carried and used by one man, the overall concept could be kept simple. At first this was not always realized as

gunsmiths lavished their considerable skills on many of the early sub-machine gun types. With the changing requirements of World War II it did not take long for the frills to be ditched in the rush to produce serviceable weapons. The resultant sub-machine guns were horrible to look at, the obvious examples being the British Sten and the American M3. But these types lent themselves to rapid and simple mass production. Welding took the place of machining from solid metal, pins took the place of time-consuming jointing methods, rivets took the place of screws and so on. At first the front-line soldiers looked askance at such products but they soon learned that they worked. Those crude weapons could produce as lethal a stream of lead as many of the more refined designs, they were easy to use, easy to maintain and their ammunition was usually easy to procure, often from the enemy.

The sub-machine gun is still with us now, in many refined forms; but close examination will usually reveal the shadow of the basic MP18 lurking in its interior. Designs such as the Sten, the M3, the German MP38 and the Soviet PPSh-41 all had their part to play during World War II, and their impact will be with us for years to come.

Owen Gun

It took some time and some fairly desperate measures before Lieutenant Evelyn Owen was able to persuade the Australian military authorities to adopt his design of sub-machine gun in 1940. At the time the Australian army had little or no interest in the weapon and by the time they realized the importance of the weapon they expected to receive all the Sten guns they required from the United Kingdom. It took some time before they appreciated the fact that they were going to receive no Sten guns as the British army wanted all that could be produced. So they decided after much procrastination to adopt the **Owen Gun**, but even then they were not sure in what calibre. Consequently the first trials batches were produced in four calibres before the universal 9-mm was adopted.

The Owen Gun can be easily recognized by the magazine, which points vertically upwards over the tubular gun body. This odd-seeming arrangement was apparently chosen for no other reason than that it worked, and it must be said that it worked very well to the extent that once the Australian soldiers got their hands on the type they preferred it to all others, and the Owen Gun was kept in service until well into the 1960s and its successor, the X-3, still retains the overhead magazine. The rest of the gun was fairly conventional and very robust to the point where it seemed to be able to take all manner of punishment and withstood being dropped in mud, dust, water and just about anything else. As production increased various changes were introduced to the design. The early fins around the barrel were removed and some changes were made to the butt, which could be found in versions with just a wire skeleton, an all-wood design, and one version that was half-outline and half wood. One feature of the Owen that was unique to it, apart from the overhead magazine, was that the barrel could be quickly removed for changing. Exactly why this feature was incorporated is uncertain, for it would have taken a long period of firing for the barrel to become unusably hot, but the feature was retained through the design life of the weapon. Another odd point regarding the Owen was that once in service they were often painted in camouflage

Above: The Owen sub-machine gun was a sturdy and reliable weapon that soon gained itself a high reputation. The example has a camouflage paint scheme.

Right: The Australian Owen sub-machine gun's most prominent recognition feature was the vertically-mounted box magazine. The example shown here is one of the early production models.

schemes to suit the local terrain. For the Australian army (and the Owen was used by no other forces) that meant the hot and sweaty jungles of New Guinea, where the Australian soldiers found the Owen ideal for the close-quarter combat that the jungles enforced. It was true that the Owen was rather heavier than most comparable models but the forward-mounted grip and the pistol grip made it easy to handle.

The top-mounted magazine had one slight disadvantage for the firer as the magazine position meant that the sights had to be off-set to the right side of the body, an awkward arrangement but one that mattered little once the weapon was used in action for, like most sub-machine guns, the Owen was almost always fired from the hip.

Production of the Owen ceased in 1945 but in 1952 many were virtually rebuilt and provision was made for a long bayonet to be fitted to the muzzle; some versions made in 1943 used a much shorter bayonet that fitted over the muzzle with an almost unique tubular mount but they were not widely issued.

Specification:
Calibre: 9 mm
Length: 813 mm (32 in)
Length of barrel: 250 mm (9.84 in)
Weight loaded: 4.815 kg (10.6 lb)
Magazine: 33-round vertical box
Rate of fire, cyclic: 700 rpm
Muzzle velocity: 420 m (1,380 ft) per second

ZK 383

The Czech **ZK 383** is one of those sub-machine guns that is now little known in the West for the simple reason that it was little used outside Eastern Europe and its combat use was mainly limited to the war against the Soviet Union. However, the ZK 383 was a very important weapon type for its time and it was considered good enough to stay in production from the late 1930s until 1948.

First designed during the early 1930s, the ZK 383 went into production

The Czech ZK 383 was very well made from machined parts and had such luxuries as a bipod and a variable rate of fire. There was even a quick-change barrel. The bulk of these weapons was later produced for the German Waffen SS, who found it a heavy but reliable weapon.

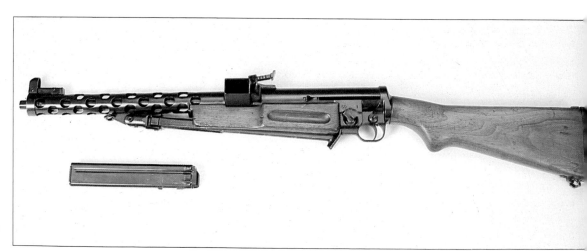

at the famous Czech Brno arms plant, known for the later introduction of what was to be the Bren gun. The ZK 383 was a relatively large and heavy weapon for the sub-machine gun class, a feature emphasized by uncommon application of a bipod under the barrel on some models. This bipod was the result of the Czech army's tactical philosophy, for it regarded the weapon as a form of light machine-gun, in direct contradiction of the usually accepted role of a close-quarter combat weapon. This odd approach was further emphasized by the use of what was one of the ZK 383's oddest features in the form of a capability for two rates of fire. The ZK 383 could fire at the rate of 500 or 700 rpm, the fire rate being altered by the addition or subtraction of a small 0.17-kg (0.37-lb) weight to the breech block – with the weight removed the breech block could move faster and thus the rate of fire could be increased. The slower rate of fire was used when the ZK 383 was used with its bipod as a light machine-gun, and the faster fire rate when the ZK was carried as an assault weapon.

But that was only the Czech army's point of view, and the feature does not appear to have been used much by the other customers for the weapon. The Bulgarian army adopted the type as their standard sub-machine gun (it used the ZK 383 until at least the early 1960s), but by far the largest number of ZK 383s were produced after 1939 for the German army. When they took over Czechoslovakia in 1939 the Germans found the ZK 383 production line still intact, and it was a sensible move as far as they were concerned to keep it intact for their own uses. The Brno factory was taken over for SS weapon production and thus the ZK 383 output was diverted to the Waffen SS, who used the weapon only on the Eastern Front. The Waffen SS examples were all known as the **vz 9** (vz for vzor, the Czech for model) and the Waffen SS found it effective enough for it to become one of their standard weapons. Numbers were kept in Czechoslovakia for use by the Czech civil police who had their own version, the **ZK 383P** which was produced without the bipod.

The only nations other than Czechoslovakia, Bulgaria and Germany that purchased the ZK 383 were Brazil and Venezuela, and even then the numbers involved were not large. Apart from the use in Eastern Europe the ZK 383 had few points to attract attention and in many ways it was too complicated for the role it was called upon to play. The Czech army's predilection for the design as a light machine-gun led to all manner of detail extras that the weapon did not need. The dual rate of fire feature has already been mentioned, as has the bipod, but the sub-machine gun does not really need a complex barrel-change mechanism, an all-machined mechanism made from the finest steels available or an angled breech block return spring angled into the butt. The ZK 383 had all these, making it a very reliable sound weapon but one that was really too complex for its role.

Specification:
Calibre: 9 mm
Length: 875 mm (34.45 in)
Length of barrel: 325 mm (12.8 in)
Weight loaded: 4.83 kg (10.65 lb)
Magazine: 30-round box
Rate of fire, cyclic: 500 or 700 rpm
Muzzle velocity: 365 m (1,200 ft) per second

FINLAND
Suomi m/1931

The **Suomi m/1931** is now little known but in its day it was one of the most sought-after and admired sub-machine guns produced anywhere. The design of this weapon went back to the early 1920s and was almost certainly influenced by some German weapon designers who used Finland as a means of escaping the turmoil and uproar of post-war Germany. Using the influence and advice of such Germans the Finns gradually produced a series of very sound and effective sub-machine guns that resulted in the m/1931.

As sub-machine gun designs go there is little remarkable with the m/1931, for it used a conventional blow-back action and an orthodox layout. Where it did score over many existing designs was that it was extremely well made, almost to the point of lavishness in the quality of material used and the excellence of the machining, and the other point was the feed systems employed. These feed systems used a number of magazines that were so effective that they were extensively copied later, even by the Soviets who normally preferred their home-produced designs. There were two main versions, one a 50-round vertical box magazine and the other a 71-round drum magazine. In the box magazine the normal lengthy bulk of 50 rounds of ammunition was overcome by having the magazine split into two vertical columns. Rounds were fed from one column and then the other. In action this feed system was much favoured as it enabled a soldier to carry into action far more ready rounds than would be possible with a conventional magazine (despite this there was a normal 30-round box magazine for the Suomi).

The m/1931 was produced for the Finnish army in some numbers and it proved itself in action during the 1940 Russian invasion of Finland. There were several export models of the m/1931, some of them with small bipods under the barrel or body, and these were purchased by Sweden and Switzerland, who both set up their own production lines, as did a company in Denmark. The type was adopted by the Polish police before 1939, and examples popped up during the Spanish Civil War on both sides. Since then the

Above: The Suomi m/1931 was one of the most well-manufactured sub-machine guns ever made, for practically every part was machined from solid metal.

Right: The Suomi m/1931 in action, fitted with the 71-round magazine. Unlike many other sub-machine guns the m/1931 had a long barrel that was accurate enough for aimed fire at most combat ranges.

m/1931 has kept appearing up all over the place whenever conflicts arise. It is still in limited service in Scandinavia to this day and this longevity can be explained by two simple factors. One is that the m/1931 is so well made that it just will not wear out. The same sound manufacture also explain the reliability, for the m/1931 is one of those weapons that will work under any conditions without ever seeming to go wrong, and as mentioned above the feed system for the ammunition is almost legendary in its reliability. These two factors alone explain the high regard shown to the m/1931 in the past, but there was another factor. When the m/1931 was produced no pains were spared on detail machining and such care was taken on this that the whole of the gun, the body and bolt included, were machined from the solid metal. Consequently the gun was, and still is, very accurate for its type. Most sub-machine gun types are accurate only to a few yards and most are almost useless at range over 50 m (55 yards). The m/1931 can be used accurately at ranges up to 300 m (330 yards). In relative numbers few were used during World War II but the influence of the design can be detected in many war-time models. The design was licence-produced in Switzerland for the Swiss army during 1943.

Specification:
Calibre: 9 mm
Length (butt extended): 870 mm (34.25 in)
Length of barrel: 314 mm (12.36 in)
Weight loaded (drum magazine): 7.04 kg (15.52 lb)
Magazine: 30- or 50-round box, or 71-round drum
Rate of fire, cyclic: 900 rpm
Muzzle velocity: 400 m (1,310 ft) per second

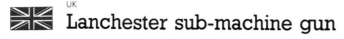

Lanchester sub-machine gun

In 1940, with the Dunkirk evacuation completed, the Royal Air Force decided to adopt some form of sub-machine gun for airfield defence. With no time to spare for the development of a new weapon it decided to adopt a direct copy of the German MP28, examples of which were to hand for the necessary copying. The period was so desperate that the Admiralty decided to join the RAF in adopting the new weapon; by a series of convoluted happenings the Admiralty alone actually took the resultant design into service.

The British MP28 copy was given the general designation **Lanchester** after one George Lanchester, who was charged with producing the weapon at the Sterling Armament Company at Dagenham, the same company that later went on to produce the Sterling sub-machine gun that is now the general standard weapon for so many armed forces. The Lanchester emerged as a sound, sturdy weapon that in many ways was ideal for the type of operations required of it by boarding and raiding parties. It was a very solid weapon, in many ways the complete opposite of its direct contemporary the Sten, for the Lanchester was a soundly engineered piece of weaponry with all the trimmings of a former era. Nothing was left off from the gunsmith's art. The Lanchester had a well-machined wooden butt and stock, the blow-back mechanism was very well made of the finest materials, the breech block well machined, and, to cap it all, the magazine housing was made from solid brass. A few typical British design details were added, such as a mounting on the muzzle for a long-bladed British bayonet (very useful in boarding party situations) and the rifling differed from the German original in details to accommodate the different types of ammunition the Lanchester had to use.

The magazine for the Lanchester was straight and carried a useful load of 50 rounds. Stripping was aided by a catch on top of the receiver and the very first models could fire either single-shot or automatic. That model was the **Lanchester Mk I** but on the Lan-

Above: Obviously based on the German MP28, the Lanchester was ideally suited to the rough-and-tumble of shipboard life. It had a one-piece wooden stock based on the outline of the Lee-Enfield No. 1 Mk 3 rifle and there was a bayonet lug under the muzzle. The brass magazine housing can be seen.

Right: Lanchesters in a typical naval environment as captured U-boat personnel are escorted ashore in a Canadian port – the blindfolds were a normal procedure. The Lanchesters are carried using Lee-Enfield rifle slings.

chester Mk I* this was changed to full automatic fire only, and many Mk Is were converted to Mk I* standard at RN workshops.

The Lanchester was an unashamed copy of a German design but it gave good service to the Royal Navy throughout the war and for many years after. Many old sailors still speak of the Lanchester with respect; not with affection, for it was a heavy weapon and it had one rather off-putting feature: if the butt was given a hard knock or jar while the gun was cocked and loaded it would fire. The last example left Royal Navy use during the 1960s and the type is now a collector's item.

Specification:
Calibre: 9 mm
Length: 851 mm (33.50 in)
Length of barrel: 203 mm (8.00 in)
Weight empty: 4.34 kg (9.57 lb)
Magazine: 50-round box
Rate of fire, cyclic: 600 rpm
Muzzle velocity: about 380 m (1,245 ft) per second

MAS Model 1938

Often quoted as the **MAS 38**, this French sub-machine gun was first produced at St Etienne in 1938, hence the model number. The MAS 38 was the outcome of a long period of development, and was the follow-on from a model produced in 1935. But it must be stated that the development period was well spent, for the MAS 38 proved to be a sound enough weapon well in advance of its period. There were some rather odd features about the MAS 38, however. One was that it was rather complicated and another that it fired a cartridge produced only in France. Both these features can be explained by the period when it was designed. At that time there appeared to be no reason to make the weapon as simple as possible for existing production methods seemed adequate to churn out the numbers required, and at the time such numbers were not very high. The calibre can be explained by the fact that it was available at the time and so the MAS 38 had a calibre of 7.65 mm and used a car-

tridge available only in France, the 7.65-mm Long. While this cartridge was accurate it was not very powerful, and had the disadvantage that no-one else was likely to adopt it once the 9-mm calibre had been universally

adopted.

The MAS 38 has a complex mechanism with a long bolt travel that was partially off-set by having the gun body sloping down into the solid wooden butt. The cocking handle was separate

The MAS Model 1938 was a sound, advanced weapon. Unfortunately for its future prospects, it fired an underpowered cartridge available only in France, and was complicated to manufacture.

from the bolt once firing started, a good feature but one which introduced complexity into the design and manufacture. Another good point was a flap over the magazine housing that closed as the magazine was withdrawn. While this kept out dust and dirt very few other designs had this feature and most of them managed to work perfectly well without it.

In fact the MAS 38 turned out to be rather too good for the customer, who at first decided that it did not want a sub-machine gun after all. The French army turned down the weapon when it was first offered, and the first production examples went to some of the more para-military members of one of the French police forces. When hostilities did start in 1939, the French army soon changed its mind and ordered large quantities, but the complex machining that went into the MAS 38 resulted in a slow rate of introduction into service, and the French army was driven to ordering numbers of Thompson sub-machine guns from the USA. These arrived too late to make any difference to the events of 1940 and the

French army capitulated. When the French forces rearmed under the Vichy regime the MAS 38 was kept in production, and in fact the weapon was kept in production until 1949, and it was used in the Indo-China War.

The MAS 38 never got the recognition it deserved. It was rather too complicated, fired an odd cartridge and it was never possible to produce it in

quantity when it was required. Consequently it is now little known outside France and few, if any, modern weapon designs owe anything to its influence. The only armies to use the MAS 38, other than some of the ex-French colonies, were the Germans who captured enough in 1940 to issue them to their garrison force stationed in France.

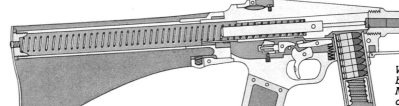

When seen in cutaway form the large breech block return spring of the MAS Model 1938 can be seen to occupy almost all the interior of the butt. While this design made for a compact weapon the manufacturing difficulties were compounded, and as can be seen the spring had to be 'angled' to enable the user to aim the weapon.

Specification:
Calibre: 7.65 mm
Length: 623 mm (24.53 in)
Length of barrel: 224 mm (8.82 in)
Weight loaded: 3.356 kg (7.40 lb)
Magazine: 32-round box
Rate of fire, cyclic: 600 rpm
Muzzle velocity: 350 m (1,150 ft) per second

✚ Steyr-Solothurn S1-100

Although the Steyr-Solothurn is described as a Swiss weapon, for it was mainly produced in Switzerland, it was originally an Austrian design produced by Steyr who took over the Swiss Solothurn concern to produce weapon designs at a time when they were forbidden to do so by the terms of the 1919 Versailles Treaty. Even then the design was originally German (actually a Rheinmetall product) but had been switched to Austria for full development during the 1920s.

In its full production form this sub-machine gun was known as the **Steyr-Solothurn S1-100** and by 1930 the design was being produced mainly for export purposes. As with so many other designs of the period, it was based on the general outlines and principles of the German MP18 but by the time the Swiss manufacturers had finished with their development the design had reached a high point of refinement and detail manufacture. The S1-100 was an excellent product that was robust, reliable and adaptable, for the export market meant that the model had to be produced in a whole host of calibres and a seemingly endless string of accessories and extras.

The S1-100 was produced in no less than three separate variations of the 9-mm calibre. Apart from the usual 9-mm Parabellum, the weapon was produced in 9-mm Mauser and 9-mm Steyr, the latter specially produced for the S1-100. Exports to China, Japan and South America were produced in 7.63-mm Mauser calibre, and the Portuguese purchased a large batch chambered for the 7.65-mm Parabellum cartridge. The extras were many and varied, with perhaps the most outlandish being a tripod to convert the weapon into what must have been a rather ineffective light machine-gun, though some of these were sold to China during the mid-1930s. There were also various forms of bayonet-securing devices and several barrel lengths were produced, some of them very long indeed for what were only pistol

cartridges. Another Steyr-Solothurn selling ploy was to present the S1-100 to a customer packed in individually-fitted chests containing not only the weapon but all manner of special magazines, special cleaning tools, spare parts, etc.

By the mid-1930s the S1-100 was the standard sub-machine gun of the Austrian army and police force, and when the Germans took over the state in 1938 they also took over the Austrian army armoury. Thus the S1-100 became the German **MP34(ö)**, which must have caused some confusion with the previously mentioned Bergmann MP 34. After a short period of front-line German service the confusion of no less than three types of 9-mm ammunition to be supplied for the type was too much even for the adaptable German army supply network and the MP34(ö) was relegated to German military police use; it was also retained by what was left of the Austrian police forces.

Today the S1-100 is still used in odd corners of the world, but only in very small numbers. Perhaps the most combat seen by the type was in China where at one point the S1-100 was in use by both the Chinese and Japanese armies. The latter even produced their

Above: The Steyr-Solothurn S1-100 was an Austrian version of the German MP18 produced during the 1920s and 1930s mainly for commercial sale on the export market. The type was well made and could be supplied with a range of accessories including tripods, bayonets and oversize magazines.

Right: The Steyr-Solothurn S1-100 is seen here in a drill-book position, mainly because the picture has been taken from a German manual produced for the type after the Germans had taken over Austria and its arsenal during 1938.

own copy at one point and used some of the design's features as the basis for their own 8-mm Type 100.

Specification:
S1-100 (9-mm Parabellum version)
Calibre: 9 mm
Length: 850 mm (33.46 in)
Length of barrel: 200 mm (7.87 in)
Weight loaded: 4.48 kg (9.88 kg)
Magazine: 32-round box
Rate of fire, cyclic: 500 rpm
Muzzle velocity: 418 m (1,370 ft) per second

Type 100

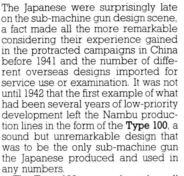

This Japanese private first class is armed with the Type 100 sub-machine gun. He is equipped for jungle fighting, typical of 1942.

The Japanese were surprisingly late on the sub-machine gun design scene, a fact made all the more remarkable considering their experience gained in the protracted campaigns in China before 1941 and the number of different overseas designs imported for service use or examination. It was not until 1942 that the first example of what had been several years of low-priority development left the Nambu production lines in the form of the **Type 100**, a sound but unremarkable design that was to be the only sub-machine gun the Japanese produced and used in any numbers.

The Type 100 was moderately well made but had several rather odd features. One was the use of a complex ammunition feed device that ensured that a round was fully chambered before the firing pin would operate. The exact purpose of this feature is rather uncertain (other than the safety aspect for the firer) for the cartridge used by all the Type 100 variants was the underpowered 8-mm Japanese pistol round, a rather weak and ineffective choice that was not aided by its being a bottle-shaped round that must have added its own feed complexities. The Type 100's barrel was chrome-plated to aid cleaning and reduce wear, and to add to such niceties the design had

complex sights and a curved magazine. Other oddities were the use of a complicated muzzle brake on some models and the use of a large bayonet-mounting lug under the barrel. Some versions also had a bipod.

There were three different versions of the Type 100. The first is described above. The second had a folding butt stock for use by paratroops: the stock was hinged just behind the gun body to fold along the side of the weapon. While this no doubt made the weapon handy for carrying and paradropping, it also weakened the weapon in combat situations and relatively few were made. The third version of the Type 100 appeared in 1944 at a time when demands for sub-machine guns were coming from all fronts. In order to speed up manufacture, the basic Type 100 was greatly simplified and in the result the design was lengthened slightly. The wooden stock was often left roughly finished and the rate of fire was increased from the early 450 rpm to 800 rpm. The sights were reduced to little more than aiming posts and the large muzzle lug for a bayonet was replaced by a simpler fitting. At the muzzle, the barrel protruded more from the perforated jacket and had a simple muzzle brake formed by two ports drilled in the barrel. Welding,

The Type 100 was not designed for ease of production and despite some production 'short cuts' such as spot welding and stampings there were never enough to meet demands.

often rough, was used wherever possible. The result was a much cruder weapon compared with the earlier version, but one that was sound enough for its purpose.

The main problem for the Japanese by 1944 lay not so much in the fact that the Type 100 was not good enough, but that the Japanese lacked the industrial capacity to turn out the huge numbers demanded. Consequently the Japanese troops had to fight their last-ditch defensive campaigns at a permanent disadvantage against the better-armed Allied troops.

Specification:
Type 100 (1944 version)
Calibre: 8 mm
Length: 900 mm (35.43 in)
Length of barrel: 230 mm (9.06 in)
Weight loaded: 4.4 kg (9.70 lb)
Magazine: 30-round curved box
Rate of fire, cyclic: 800 rpm
Muzzle velocity: 335 m (1,100 ft) per second

UD M'42

In accounts of the American sub-machine gun scene between 1939 and 1945 one weapon is often not mentioned at all, and that is the sub-machine gun known under a number of names but usually called the **UD M'42**. This weapon was designed in the days just prior to World War II as commercial venture in 9-mm calibre. was ordered under rather odd circumstances by an organization known as the United Defense Supply Corporation, a US government body that ordered all manner of items for use overseas, but the main point of its existence was that it was an American secret service 'front' for all forms of underground activities.

Exactly why the United Defense (hence UD) concern ordered the de-

sign that was produced by the Marlin Firearms Company is now not known, but the name 'Marlin' was subsequently often given to the weapon that became the UD M'42. The general impression given at the time was that the

weapons were to be shipped to Europe for use by some underground organizations working for the US in-

The UD M'42 was not accepted as an official US service weapon, but numbers were purchased for issue to some odd undercover and special mission units. It was a very well made and finished weapon and was popular with its users.

terest, but events in Europe overtook the scheme. Some UD M'42s were certainly sent to the Dutch East Indies before the Japanese invasion of the area, but they vanished without trace.

Most of the UD M'42 did find their way to Europe but in some very odd hands. Most were handed out to some of the numerous resistance and partisan groups that sprang up around and in the German- and Italian-occupied areas of the Mediterranean Sea. There

they took part in some very odd actions, the most famous of which was when British agents kidnapped a German general on Crete. Other actions were just as dramatic but often took place so far from the public gaze that today these actions and the part the UD M'42 took in them are virtually forgotten.

This is perhaps a pity for many weapon authorities now regard the UD M'42 as one of the finest sub-machine

gun types used in World War II. Being made on a commercial and not a military basis it was well machined and very strong. The action was smooth and the gun very accurate, and by all accounts it was a joy to handle. It could withstand all manner of ill-treatment (including immersion in mud and water) and still work.

After all these years it now seems very unlikely that the full service record of the UD M'42 will ever be told,

but at least the very existence of the weapon should be better known.

Specification:
Calibre: 9 mm
Length: 807 mm (31.75 in)
Length of barrel: 279 mm (11.00 in)
Weight loaded: 4.54 kg (10.00 lb)
Magazine: 20-round box
Rate of fire: 700 rpm
Muzzle velocity: 400 m (1,310 ft) per second

M3 and M3A1

By the beginning of 1941, although the United States was not yet directly involved in World War II, the American military authorities had acknowledged that the sub-machine gun had a definite role to perform on the modern battlefield. They already had to hand numbers of Thompson guns and more were on their way, but the appearance of the German MP38 and the British Sten indicated the production methods that could be employed in future mass-produced designs. Using an imported Sten, the US Army Ordnance Board initiated a design study to produce an American Sten-type weapon. The study was handed over to a team of specialists who included the same George Hyde who had developed the Hyde M2 and to executives from General Motors, to whom the mass-production aspects were entrusted. In a very short time they had designed a weapon and development models were produced for trials.

The first of these models was handed over for trials just before Pearl Harbor brought the United States into World War II. As a result the project got a higher priority and it was not long before the design was issued with the designation **M3**. The M3 was just as unpleasant-looking as the Sten. Construction was all-metal with most parts simple steel stampings welded into place. Only the barrel, breech block and parts of the trigger mechanism required any machining. A telescopic wire butt was fitted and the design was simple to the point that there was no safety system fitted and the gun could fire fully-automatic only. The main gun body was tubular and below it hung a long 30-round box magazine. An awkwardly placed and flimsy cocking handle was placed just forward of the trigger on the right-hand side, and the cartridge ejection port was under a hinged cover. The barrel screwed into the tubular body. Sights were very rudimentary and there were no luxuries such as sling swivels.

The M3 was rushed into production and once issued to the troops it soon ran into acceptance troubles. The very appearance of the weapon soon provided it with the nickname of 'Grease Gun' and it was regarded with about as much affection. But once in action it soon showed itself to be effective, but the rush into production on lines that were more used to producing motor car and lorry components led to all manner of in-service problems. The cocking handles broke off, the wire

Unpopular with its users in Europe, the 'Grease Gun' gained acceptance in the Pacific, where there was no alternative weapon.

stocks bent in use, some important parts of the mechanism broke because they were made of too soft a metal, and so on. Consequently the M3 received more than its fair share of in-service development and modification, but what was more important at the time, it rolled off the production lines in huge numbers for issue to the troops at the front.

The M3 never overcame the initial reception its appearance engendered. Whenever possible the troops in the front line opted for the Thompson M1 or used captured German MP38s and MP40s, but in the Pacific there was often no choice other than to use the M3 and when this happened the design often gained grudging acceptance. For some arms of the US forces the M3 became a virtual blanket issue. These arms included the drivers in the many transport units and tank crews. For both the M3 was easy to stow and easy to handle in close confines.

From the outset the M3 had been designed to have the capability of being rapidly converted to 9-mm calibre by simply changing the barrel, magazine and breech block. This facility was sometimes employed in Europe when the M3 was dropped to resistance forces. A silenced variant of the M3 was produced in small numbers.

Simple as the M3 was to produce it was decided in 1944 to make it even simpler. The result of combat experience allied with production know-how resulted in the **M3A1**, which followed the same general lines as the M3 but with some quite substantial changes. For the soldier the most important item was that the ejection cover was enlarged to the point where the full

The American M3 'Grease Gun' was the equivalent of the British Sten and the German MP40, for it was designed for mass production. It was a sound enough weapon but the American troops never really took to the type, preferring the Thompson.

breech block travel was exposed. This enabled the firer to place his finger into a recess in the block to pull the block to the rear for cocking, thus doing away with the awkward and flimsy cocking handle. A flash hider was added to the muzzle and some other minor changes were incorporated. The M3A1 was still in production when the war ended, by which time it had been decided to phase out the Thompson guns in favour of the M3 and M3A1.

Apart from the appearance problem, the M3 guns were not perfect weapons. They were rather prone to breakages, the ammunition feed was often far from perfect and the lack of a safety often gave rise to alarm. But it worked and it was available, and in war those two factors are more important than hankering after the something that might be better. Thus the M3 and M3A1 were used wherever the US Military went, and that was all over the world.

Specification: M3
Calibre: 0.45 in (11.43 mm) or 9 mm
Length, butt extended: 745 mm (29.33 in)
Length, butt retracted: 570 mm (22.44 in)
Weight loaded: 4.65 kg (10.25 lb)
Magazine: 30-round box
Rate of fire: 350-450 rpm
Muzzle velocity: 280 m (920 ft) per second

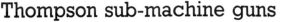

Thompson sub-machine guns

USA

The Cutt's Compensator was intended to divert some muzzle gases upwards to keep the muzzle down when firing, but was of limited value and complex to manufacture and so was left off on later models.

The M1928 could take many types of magazine. This is the 20-round box magazine but also produced were 18- and 30-round box magazines and 50- or 100-round drum magazines. The drum magazines proved troublesome in service so the box types were often preferred.

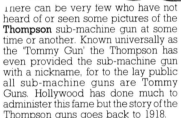

In close-range fighting such as street and house-to-house combat the sub-machine gun was the ideal weapon, and the robustness of the M1 and M1A1 variants of the Thompson added to the type's considerable popularity with the GIs.

There can be very few who have not heard of or seen some pictures of the **Thompson** sub-machine gun at some time or another. Known universally as the 'Tommy Gun' the Thompson has even provided the sub-machine gun with a nickname, for to the lay public all sub-machine guns are Tommy Guns. Hollywood has done much to administer this fame but the story of the Thompson guns goes back to 1918.

In that year the US Army was embroiled in the trench warfare of the Western Front, a need becoming apparent for some form of 'trench broom' to sweep the trenches clear of an enemy. Since this 'sweeping' had to be carried out at short ranges a powerful cartridge was not necessary and a pistol cartridge was all that was deemed necessary. The German army had drawn the same conclusions and produced the MP18, but on the American side one General John Thompson initiated the development of an automatic weapon using the standard 0.45-in pistol cartridge. The first examples used a belt feed but this was later changed to a two-hand weapon of the

type soon known as a sub-machine gun, and with a box magazine.

By the time the first examples were produced World War I was over and all development for the next two decades was carried out on a commercial basis. The Thompson Gun, as it was soon labelled, went through a long chain of different models. Military sales were few, other than small batches to the US Army and US Navy, but it was with the coming of Prohibition in the USA that the weapon gained its public notoriety. The gang warfare that mushroomed throughout the American underworld soon found the Thompson a most useful weapon, and when Hollywood started to make gangster films the gun became famous overnight. Gradually police forces started to purchase Thompson guns, and the type became more generally accepted. Even then, military sales were few until 1928 when the US forces started to purchase some large batches.

The **Thompson M1928** was a complex piece of gunsmithing with a complicated blow-back mechanism and a

choice of a large 50-round drum magazine and 20- or 30-round vertical box magazines. Just maintaining the M1928 was quite a task. There were many variations between different models, which did nothing to endear the type to the military supply systems, and it was not until 1940 that sales really started to build up.

In 1940 several European nations were clamouring for Thompson guns. The unexpected employment by the Germans of sub-machine guns on a large scale produced requests for similar weapons from all the European combatants, and the Thompson was

Above: In 1939 and 1940 the UK had to purchase large numbers of Thompson sub-machine guns. This soldier is holding an M1928 complete with the 50-round drum magazine, a device that soon proved to be too complex for service use and too noisy due to the 0.45 calibre rounds moving about inside. Consequently these were issued to either the Home Guard or second-line units.

Left: The Thompson M1928 was the 'classic' model of the famous Thompson sub-machine gun, the weapon that was used by gangsters and American soldiers alike. For all its notoriety it was not a great commercial success until 1940.

The original Thompson guns used a separate firing pin struck by a hammer, but this was really too complex for the task and later models used a fixed firing pin.

The M1928 originally had a 50-m (165-ft) open sight and a further long-range sight optimistically calibrated up to 550 m (1800 ft). The latter sight was of doubtful value.

e fire selector was on left of the trigger group d could be set for semiomatic single shot or automatic (600 or 725 n).

If required, the butt could be easily removed by unscrewing the two screws shown, but this was rarely utilized in action as the butt stabilized the aim and reduced firing vibrations. The butt contained an oiling bottle behind a butt trap.

the only example on offer. Large-scale production of the Thompson commenced for France, the UK and Yugoslavia, but these orders were overtaken by events as the Thompson was an awkward weapon to mass-produce because of the large number of complex machining processes involved.

In the event the French and other orders were diverted to the United Kingdom, where the M1928 was used until the Sten became available, and even then many were issed for Commando raids and the later jungle fighting in Burma. When the USA entered the war the US Army also de-

cided that it wanted sub-machine guns but the Thompson had to be redesigned to meet US Army requirements for mass production. After redesign the Thompson became a far simpler weapon with a straightforward blowback action with no frills and the old large, noisy and awkward drum magazine so beloved by Hollywood was replaced by the simple vertical box. The new design became the **M1** and a later version with some extra simplifications added became the **M1A1**.

The M1 still used a wooden stock, pistol grip and foregrip (this was later replaced by a straight foregrip), but the body was machined as were many other parts. In service the M1 proved to be a well-liked weapon that was usually preferred to the unlovely M3. Again, exactly how much of this preference was due to the Hollywood image is now almost impossible to determine, for compared with many of its contemporaries the M1 was heavy and not so easy to strip and maintain. This did not deter the M1928 and the M1 from being widely copied in many backyard workshops in the Far East where

the Thompson was regarded with great favour.

Over the years the Thompson underwent many changes and modifications. With time most of the more complex extras were removed. Out went the complex breech-locking mechanism, out went the Cutt's Compensator on the muzzle that was supposed to restrict the barrel 'climb' when firing, and out went the bulky drum magazine. The end result in the M1 form was a good sound weapon and one that is still as famous as it was in the days when the Tommy Gun was the symbol of the IRA and the Hollywood gangster era.

Specification:
Thompson M1
Calibre: 0.45 in (11.43 mm)
Length: 813 mm (32.00 in)
Length of barrel: 267 mm (10.50 in)
Weight loaded: 4.74 kg (10.45 lb)
Magazine: 20- or 30-round box
Rate of fire: 700 rpm
Muzzle velocity: 280 m (920 ft) per second

Above: A New Zealander armed with an M1928 during the Cassino campaign. This particular model is the M1928A1, a military version fitted with a horizontal foregrip in place of the original forward pistol grip. The M1928A1 also had some of the commercial refinements removed as well, and the 20- or 30-round box magazine was used instead of the larger drum magazine.

Right: The M1A1 was essentially the same weapon as the M1 but had a fixed firing pin and hammer, making the type a virtual blow-back design. It was the last production version of the famous Thompson family of weapons and retained the overall appearance and aura of the original.

Reising Model 50 and Model 55

The **Reising Model 50** and the later **Model 55** are two more examples of how things can go wrong when the basic blow-back action used on the sub-machine gun is ignored and replaced with something that seems to offer a better action. On the Reising Model 50, which was first produced in 1940, the basic action was altered so that instead of the breech block moving forward to the chamber when the trigger was pulled, the action operated when the bolt was forward with a round in the chamber. This action can work quite well but it needs a system of levers to operate the firing pin in the breech block and these levers have to disconnect once the breech block moves. This all adds complexity and cost and adds something to the system which can break.

Thus it was with the Reising Model 50. The design was the result of a commercial venture and was thus not so influenced by military considerations as would have been the case a few years later, but the Model 50 was a well-made design with an unusual system of cocking the weapon by means of a small catch sliding in a slot under the fore-stock. This left the top of the gun body free of many of the usual hazards such as the cocking slot that usually provides an ingress for dirt to clog the system. But on the Model 50 all that happened was that the dirt got into

the slot underneath and was difficult to clean out, thus providing one source of potential bother. From the outside the Model 50 looked a fairly simple weapon but the internal arrangements were complex to the point where there was too much to go wrong, hence there were more stoppages and general unreliability.

When the Reising Model 50 was first offered to the US forces the US Marine Corps was some way down the list of priorities, a position it was later dramatically to reverse, so in the absence of any other source of sub-machine guns it obtained numbers of the Model 50. Once the USMC had the Model 50 it soon found the weapon wanting and

obtained other weapon types. Some Model 50s were obtained by a British Purchasing Commission but few were involved and some others went to Canada. Yet more were sent to the Soviet Union and by 1945 the Model 50 was still in production and over 100,000 had been made, a modest enough total but well worthwhile as far as the manufacturers were concerned.

Some of this total was made up by the Model 55 which was the same as the Model 50 other than that the all-wood stock of the Model 50 was replaced by a folding wire butt for use by airborne and other such units. The Model 55 was no more successful than the Model 50.

The Reising Model 50 was one of the least successful of all American sub-machine guns to see service, for it employed a complex mechanism that allowed ingress of dirt and other debris to jam the weapon to an unacceptable extent.

Specification:
Model 50
Calibre: 0.45 in (11.43 mm)
Length: 857 mm (33.75 in)
Length of barrel: 279 mm (11.00 in)
Weight loaded: 3.7 kg (8.16 lb)
Magazine: 12- or 20-round box
Rate of fire, cyclic: 550 rpm
Muzzle velocity: 280 m (920 ft) per second

MP18 and MP28

Although it was preceded in the time scale by the Italian Villar Perosa, the **MP18** can be considered as the father of the modern sub-machine gun. In both the general concept, operating principle and all-round appearance the MP18 embodied all the features that have become commonplace, and even today many sub-machine gun designs are no more than gradual improvement results of the basic MP18.

The design of the MP18 began on a low priority in 1916 to provide front-line troops with some form of rapid-fire low-range weapon. The designer was the man whose name later came to be synonymous with the sub-machine gun, namely Hugo Schmeisser. It was not until 1918 that large numbers of the new weapon, known to the Germans as a *Maschinen-Pistole* (hence MP) or machine pistol were issued to the troops on the Western Front to be used in the gigantic offensives that were intended to win the war for the Germans. The offensives were unsuccessful, and the MP18 had little more than local impact, the lessons to be learned from the design being largely ignored outside Germany and the few troops who had come into contact with the weapons.

The MP18 was a simple blow-back weapon firing the classic 9-mm Parabellum round that was to become the prototype for nearly all weapons to come. Considering later designs the MP18 was very well made, with a solid wooden stock and a 32-round 'snail' magazine (intended originally for the famous Luger pistol) mounted in a housing on the left of the gun body. The barrel was covered by a prominent perforated jacket to aid barrel cooling after firing, and the weapon fired on full automatic only. In its intended role of trench fighting it was a great suc-

cess, but too many front-line commanders attempted to use it as a form of light machine-gun and were thus disappointed with the MP18's performance. Consequently the MP18 had a mixed reception other than with the storm-troopers in the front assault waves, who found it invaluable at close quarters.

When Germany was disarmed after 1919 the MP18 was passed to the German police in an attempt to keep the concept alive. Numbers were also handed over to the French army who used them (but so little) that they were still 'on the stocks' in 1939. In German police service they were modified during the 1920s to replace the Luger 'snail' magazine with a simple inline box magazine that again became the virtual prototype of what was to follow. In 1928 the MP18 was placed back into limited production in Germany, this time as the **MP28**, with new sights, a

single-shot fire feature, some small internal changes on the breech block and all manner of extras such as the mounting for a bayonet. The MP28 had the new box magazine as standard and the type was produced in Belgium, Spain and elsewhere for export all over the world, with China being one of the largest markets. Others went to South America and one batch, produced in the 7.65-mm calibre, was sold to Portugal.

By 1939 there were still appreciable numbers of MP18s and MP28s around, and the design went to war in Europe once again. By 1945 the weapons were still being encountered not only in the hands of the Germans but also in the hands of resistance forces and the many partisan forces.

Perhaps the greatest importance of the MP18 and the MP28 was not in their use as weapons, although they were successful enough in that, but in their

The German MP28 was a revised model of the original MP18. It retained the general outline of the MP18 but was able to fire either single shot or full automatic.

example for other designers to follow. With the MP18 the sub-machine gun design was virtually 'frozen' and the basic concept remains unchanged to this day.

Specification:
MP18
Calibre: 9 mm
Length: 815 mm (32.09 in)
Length of barrel: 200 mm (7.87 in)
Weight loaded: 5.245 kg (11.56 lb)
Magazine: 32-round 'snail', later 20- or 32-round box
Rate of fire, cyclic: 350-450 rpm
Muzzle velocity: 365 m (1,200 ft) per second

MP34 and MP35

At first sight the **MP34** and **MP35** appeared to be direct copies of the MP18 and MP28, but there were in reality many differences. Easily missed at first glance was that on the MP34 and MP35 the magazine protrudes from the right hand side of the gun body instead of on the left as with the MP18 and MP28. Another detail difference was the trigger mechanism, which on the MP34 and MP35 relied on a double-pressure system for control of rate of fire. A simple light pressure on the trigger produced single shots, while a full pressure on the trigger provided automatic fire.

The MP34 was designed by the Bergmann brothers, who almost undoubtedly used the MP18 as a basis on which to improve. As they had few facilities in Germany the brothers pro-

duced their first example in Denmark and only later was production switched to Germany. The first models were the MP34 but later improvements led to the MP35, which was produced in considerably greater numbers. At first production was slow, with sales being made to such nations as Ethiopia and Sweden, but with the Spanish Civil War sales really picked up to boost the company to a major position in the submachine gun market. The MP35 was produced in both long- and short-barrelled versions, and niceties such as bayonet attachments and even light bipods were introduced. One very noticeable point on the MP35 was the use of a rear-mounted bolt for cocking the weapon instead of the usual side-mounted cocking lever. This meant that the interior of the weapon body

along which the breech had to travel was kept clear of the dust and dirt that usually finds its way into open side-lever actions and the MP34 and MP35 were certainly reliable weapons, even if they were a little heavier than some of their rivals.

It was this reliability that brought the MP35 to the attention of what was to be the biggest customer for the weapon, namely the Waffen SS which was looking for its own weapons procurement separate from that of the German army, and after late 1940 all MP35 production went to the Waffen SS, continuing until the war ended in 1945. But MP34s and MP35s still cropped up elsewhere, and many can still be found in use with South American police forces, while small numbers can still be encountered in the Far East. The

reason for this longevity is quite simply that the MP34 and MP35 were very well manufactured, with nearly all parts machined from the solid metal. But in most countries today the MP35 is a much prized collector's piece as the bulk of the production carried the stamp of the Waffen SS.

Specification:
MP35
Calibre: 9 mm (plus many others in export models)
Length (standard model): 840 mm (33.07 in)
Length of barrel: 200 mm (7.87 in)
Weight loaded: 4.73 kg (10.43 lb)
Magazine: 24- or 32-round box
Rate of fire, cyclic: 650 rpm
Muzzle velocity: 365 m (1,200 ft) per second

MP38, MP38/40 and MP40

When the **MP38** was first produced in 1938 it revolutionized weapon design not by any particular feature of the design but by the method of manufacture employed. Gone was the accurate machine tooling of yesteryear, along with the finely-produced wooden fittings, and the standard of finish upon which gunsmiths so prided themselves. With the introduction of the MP38 came rough and simple metal stampings, die-cast parts, plastic instead of wood, and a finish that lacked any finesse or even plating of any kind. The MP38 looked what it was, a weapon mass-produced to meet a precise military need, namely a simple and cheap weapon that would work when called upon to fire, and nothing more. On the MP38 there was no wooden butt, just a bare folding heavy wire framework that folded under the body for use in close confines such as the back of a vehicle. The body was produced from simple sheet metal stampings that could be churned out in

any metal workshop anywhere and the breech block was provided with only a minimum of machining. Most of the outer surfaces were left in their bare-metal state and at the best they were painted. Despite all these apparently cheap and cost-cutting measures the MP38 had an immediate impact out of all proportion to its design attributes, for in the years after 1938 more and more weapons adopted similar mass-production techniques first introduced on the MP38.

The MP38 was quite orthodox so far as operation went. It had a conventionally-functioning blow-back bolt and the vertical magazine under the

Above: This MP38 was the original production version. Although the design was intended for mass production the receiver and many parts were machined – these were later replaced by the pressings and welds of the MP40.

Right: The MP40, as used by this corporal during the invasion of the USSR, was almost identical to the MP38 except that it was much simpler to manufacture.

body fed 9-mm Parabellum rounds into a conventional feed system. A cocking handle along the left-hand side of the body operated in an open slot but although dust and dirt could enter the internal workings the weapon could absorb an appreciable amount of foreign bodies before it jammed. Under the barrel muzzle there was an odd projection that was designed to catch on the edge of vehicles to act as a firing rest but the same item also acted as a muzzle cover to keep out dirt.

Once in action in 1939 one rather nasty habit of the MP38 came to light. The gun operated from the open-breech position (the bolt was cocked to the rear before the trigger could release it to fire) but if the gun was jarred or knocked the bolt jumped forward and started the firing cycle by itself. This nasty fault caused many casualties before it was modified out by the machining of a slot over the

Two German army Panzergrenadiers armed with MP40s occupying a shell hole on the outskirts of Stalingrad. As will be understood, the MP40 was at a slight disadvantage in such positions, for the long downward-pointing magazine was no assistance when firing over the lip of such a shell hole.

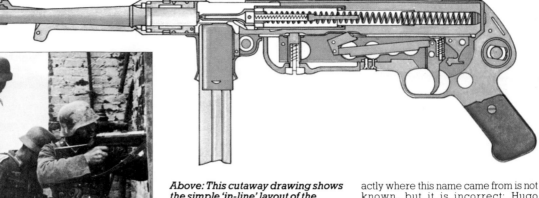

breech block 'home' position, through which a pin could engage and lock after being pushed through a hole on the other side of the body; it could be released when required for firing. With this modification fitted the MP38 became the **MP38/40**.

During 1940 the simple manufacture of the MP38 was taken one stage further with the introduction of even more metal stampings and even simpler manufacturing methods. The new version was called the **MP40**: to the soldier in the field it was little different from the MP38/40, but for the German economy it meant that the MP40 could be easily manufactured anywhere with sub-assemblies being produced in simple workshops and assembled only at central workshops. It was churned out in tens of thousands and in the field it proved a most popular and handy weapon with Allied troops using any examples they could find or capture. The MP38/40 was often used by resistance forces and partisans as well.

The only major change to the MP40 after 1940 was the introduction of a twin-magazine feature with the **MP40/2**. This was not a success and was little used. But the MP40 is still used today in odd corners of the world, especially by guerrilla forces.

One odd word about this weapon: It is often known as the 'Schmeisser'. Ex-

Above: This cutaway drawing shows the simple 'in-line' layout of the MP38. The compact design employs the blow-back principle, but the main return spring is housed in a telescopic tube that kept out dirt and foreign objects to ensure reliability. Note also the simple trigger mechanism.

Left: An MP40 in action during the Stalingrad fighting. Although many German propaganda photographs tend to give the impression that the MP38 and MP40 were in widespread use, their issue was largely restricted to front-line divisions only and the Panzergrenadiers in particular.

actly where this name came from is not known, but it is incorrect; Hugo Schmeisser had nothing to do with the design, which originated with the Erma concern.

Specification:
MP40
Calibre: 9 mm
Length, stock extended: 833 mm (32.80 in)
Length, stock folded: 630 mm (24.80 in)
Length of barrel: 251 mm (9.88 in)
Weight loaded: 4.7 kg (10.36 lb)
Magazine: 32-round box
Rate of fire, cyclic: 500 rpm
Muzzle velocity: 365 m (1,200 ft) per second

PPD-1934/38

The Soviet Union had enough troubles during the 1920s and 1930s without worrying too much about weapon design, but when things settled down enough for the re-equipment of the Red Army to be contemplated, sub-machine gun design was not very high on the list of priorities. Rather than make any innovations in sub-machine gun design the first Soviet sub-machine gun was a combination of existing designs. This was the **PPD-1934/38**.

When it was first produced in 1934, the weapon was a combination of features from the Finnish Suomi m/1931 and the German MP18 and MP28. It remained in production until 1940 by which time some modifications had been introduced to justify the use of the full designation of PPD-1934/38. There was nothing very remarkable about the PPD-1934/38. The mechanisms was almost the same as that used on the German sub-machine gun originals and, after a short attempt to produce a Soviet-designed component, the magazine was a direct take-off from the Suomi magazine. This was the Suomi 71-round drum magazine that was to become the virtual norm for later Soviet sub-machine guns, but there was also a curved 25-round box magazine issued on occasion. This box magazine had to be curved as the cartridge used for all the Soviet sub-machine guns was the 7.62-mm Tokarev (Type P) cartridge which had a bottle-necked shape and would not therefore lie completely flat for feeding from the magazine lips into the gun body.

There was one variant of the PPD-1934/38 that was placed in production in 1940. This was the **PPD-1940**, which was a general all-round improvement on the earlier design. It did have one very noticeable recognition feature in

that the drum magazine fitted up into the gun through a large slot in the stock. Very few other sub-machine gun designs used this magazine fixing system.

When the Germans and their allies invaded the USSR in 1941 the PPD-1934/38 and PPD-1940 were in relatively short supply among Red Army units and they had little impact on the course of events. Any the Germans captured they issued to their own second-line units, but the numbers involved were never very large. By the

end of 1941 even the PPD-1940 had passed out of production for the simple reason that the Germans had overrun the arsenals concerned and there was no time to set up the extensive machine-shops and production lines elsewhere. The Red Army had to resort to newer and more easily produced sub-machine gun models.

Specification:
PPD-1934/38
Calibre: 7.62 mm
Length: 780 mm (30.71 in)

The Soviet PPD-1934 introduced one feature later used on all Soviet sub-machine gun designs: the chromed barrel to reduce wear and ease cleaning.

Length of barrel: 269 mm (10.60 in)
Weight loaded: 5.69 kg (12.54 lb)
Magazine: 71-round drum or 25-round box
Rate of fire, cyclic: 800 rpm
Muzzle velocity: 488 m (1,600 ft) per second

PPSh-41

In many ways the **PPSh-41** was to the Red Army what the Sten was to the British and the MP40 to the Germans. It was the Soviet equivalent of the mass-produced sub-machine gun, using simple methods and a minimum of complicated machining operations. But unlike the Sten and the MP40 the PPSh-41 was the result of a more measured and involved development process than was possible with, say the British Sten and thus the end result was a much better all-round weapon.

The PPSh-41 was designed and developed starting in 1940 but it was not until early 1942, in the wake of the upheavals of the German invasion, that the first examples were issued to the Red Army on a large scale. As it had been designed from the outset for ease of production the PPSh-41 was churned out in the tens of thousands in all manner of workshops ranging from properly-equipped arsenals to shed workshops in rural areas. By 1945 it has been estimated that over five millions had been produced.

Considering that it was a mass-produced weapon, the PPSh-41 was a well-made design with a heavy solid wooden butt. It used the conventional blow-back system but it had a high rate of fire and to absorb the shock of the recoiling breech block a buffer of laminated leather or felt blocks was provided at the rear of the breech block travel. The gun body and the barrel jacket were simple shaped steel stampings and the muzzle had a downward sloping shape that doubled as a rudimentary muzzle brake and a device termed a compensator that was intended to reduce the amount of muzzle climb produced by the recoil forces when the gun was fired. The barrel was chrome-plated, a standard Soviet practice to ease cleaning and reduce barrel wear, but at one time the need for weapons was so great that the barrels were simply old Mosin-Nagant rifle barrels cut to size. The

Above: The PPSh-41 was one of the 'classic' Red Army weapons of World War II, and it was produced in millions. It was an emergency design born out of the disruption of the German invasion of 1941.

Right: Involvement in the fighting extended throughout the population, for during some of the many sieges, such as those at Leningrad, Sevastopol and Stalingrad, even the women and children took up weapons.

drum magazine used was the same as that used on the earlier Soviet sub-machine guns. Fire selection (single-shot or full automatic) was made by a simple lever just forward of the trigger. Construction of the PPSh-41 was welding, pins and seam stampings. The overall result was a tough, reliable weapon.

The PPSh-41 had to be tough, for once the Red Army started to receive the type in appreciable numbers it adopted the weapon in a way that no other army even attempted to consider. Quite simply the PPSh-41 was doled out to entire battalions and regiments to the virtual exclusion of any other type of weapon other than hand grenades. These units formed the vanguard of the shock assault units that were carried into the attack on the backs of T-34/76 tanks, from which they only descended for the attack or for food and rest. They carried only enough ammunition for their immediate needs, their general life standards were low, and their combat lives were very short. But in their thousands these hordes armed with the PPSh-41 swept across eastern Russia and across Europe, carrying all before them. They were a fearful force and their PPSh-41s became a virtual combat symbol of the Red Army.

Under such circumstances the PPSh-41 (known to their users as the Pah-Pah-Shah) received virtually no maintenance, or even cleaning. Under Eastern Front conditions it soon became apparent that the best way to keep the weapon going under dust or ice conditions was to keep it completely dry and free from any sort of oil, otherwise it clogged or froze.

So many PPSh-41s were produced that the type became a virtual standard weapon for the Germany Army as well as the Red Army, the Germans even

The German army was much impressed with the Soviet PPSh-41, and when supplies of their own MP40s were lacking they took to using large numbers of captured PPSh-41s. If Soviet 7.62-mm ammunition was in short supply the weapon could fire the German 7.63-mm Mauser pistol round, and by 1945 numbers of PPSh-41s were being adapted to fire German 9-mm ammunition.

going to the extent of recalibring some of their captured hoard to their own 9 mm. Partisans found the PPSh-41 an ideal weapon for their purposes, and after the war the type was used by virtually every nation that came within the Soviet sphere of influence. It still turns up in the hands of 'freedom fighters' all over the world and it will no doubt be around for a long time yet.

Specification:
Calibre: 7.62 mm
Length: 828 mm (32.60 in)
Length of barrel: 265 mm (10.43 in)
Weight loaded: 5.4 kg (11.90 lb)
Magazine: 71-round drum or 35-round box
Rate of fire, cyclic: 900 rpm
Muzzle velocity: 488 m (1,600 ft) per minute

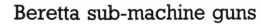

Beretta sub-machine guns

The first of the Beretta series was the **Beretta Model 1938A,** which was produced in Brescia. The first examples were produced in 1935 but it was not until 1938 that the first mass-produced examples appeared for issue to the Italian armed forces. The term 'mass production' is perhaps rather misleading for the Berettas, as although they were produced on normal production lines, the care and attention that went into each example was such that they can almost be regarded as handmade. In fact the Berettas are still regarded as some of the finest examples of the sub-machine gun that it is possible to obtain, and the early Model 1938As were destined to become among the most prized of all.

In design terms the Berettas had little enough of note. They had a well-finished wooden stock, a tubular body, a downwards-pointing box magazine and a perforated barrel jacket, some of them with provision for a folding bayonet at the muzzle. There was nothing really remarkable in these points, but what was very noticeable was the way in which the weapon was balanced and the way it handled in action. It turned out to be a truly remarkable sub-machine gun. The superb finish endeared it to all who used the type, and one result of the painstaking assembly and finishing was a weapon that proved reliable and accurate under all conditions. The ammunition feed proved to be exceptional, but only when the proper magazines were used. There were several sizes of magazines (holding 10, 20, 30 or 40 rounds) and these were issued together with a loading device. The rounds used on the early Berettas was a special high-velocity 9-mm cartridge but this was later changed to the universal 9-mm Parabellum.

There were several variations on the Model 1938A theme, one of which lacked the bayonet and some of the refinements as it was intended to be a special lightened model for use in desert regions. When Italy entered the war in 1941 some small revision of manufacturing methods was made, but the soldier at the front would be hard

The nature of the Italian Fascist state was such that by the time any youth entered the Army he was already well trained in the use of most of the weapons they would be issued with. This included the Beretta Model 1938, seen here carried by a Young Fascist being decorated by General Bastico.

Above: The Model 1938 was a sound and well-balanced weapon that was a joy to handle and use. No expense was spared in its manufacture, and consequently it was very reliable and accurate. This example is fitted with a 10-round magazine. Note the double-trigger arrangement and the well-finished wooden stock.

Right: Italian troops in Tunisia, their Beretta Model 1938s ready to hand. The weapon on the left is equipped with a 10-round magazine which was often employed when single-shot fire was required. The Model 1938 was very accurate and could be used in the manner of a rifle at combat ranges up to 300 m (985 ft).

put to recognize them, for the overall finish remained beautiful. Close examination revealed that the barrel jacket was altered to become a stamped and welded part but that was about the only concession to mass-production technology, and the Model 1938A retained its high reputation.

By 1944 the war situation had changed to the extent that Berettas were being produced for the German army, the Italians having surrendered in 1943. By then the basic design of the Model 1938A had been revised by the

The demands of war production meant that Beretta were unable to maintain their pre-war standards of excellence. Even so, the Model 38/42 was a much better weapon design than many of its contemporaries and retained many of the features of the pre-war model.

addition of simpler assembly and manufacturing methods to the point that it had become the **Model 38/42,** while an even later version was the **Model 1.** Relatively few of these two versions were produced and the bulk of them were produced after 1945. Both models were still easily recognizable as Berettas, and while they both retained the overall excellence they were generally simpler and lacked some of the finesse of the Model 1938A.

As mentioned above, by 1944 Berettas were being produced for the Germans. Earlier in the war the Germans had been happy to use numbers of the Model 1938A and the Romanians had purchased a number (they later purchased the Model 38/42 as well). After the Italian capitulation the Berettas became standard German weapons but were little used outside Italy. The Allies greatly prized the Berettas and used them in place of their own

weapons whenever they could capture sufficient numbers, but their use by the Allies was restricted to a great extent by a shortage of Beretta magazines. Apparently the sub-machine guns were often captured without their vital magazines, which was perhaps just as well for the Italians.

Specification:
Model 1938A
Calibre: 9 mm
Length: 946 mm (37.24 in)
Length of barrel: 315 mm (12.40 in)
Weight loaded: 4.97 kg (10.96 lb)
Magazine: 10-, 20-, 30- or 40-round box
Rate of fire, cyclic: 600 rpm
Muzzle velocity: 420 m (1,380 ft) per second

Sten sub-machine guns

After the Dunkirk evacuation of mid-1940 the British army had few weapons left. In an attempt to re-arm quickly the military authorities put out an urgent request for simple sub-machine guns that could be produced in quantity, and using the concept of the MP38 as an example the designers went to work. Within weeks the results were adopted. It was the product of two designers, Major R.V. Shepherd and H.J. Turpin who worked at the Enfield Lock Small Arms Factory, and from these three names came the universally-accepted name **Sten** for the new weapon.

The first result was the **Sten Mk I**, which must be regarded as one of the unloveliest weapon designs of all time. It was designed for production as quickly and cheaply as possible using simple tools and a minimum of time-consuming machining, so the Sten was made up from steel tubes, sheet stamping and easily produced parts all held together with welds, pins and bolts. The main body was a steel tube and the butt a steel framework. The barrel was a steel drawn tube with either two or six rifling grooves roughly carved. The magazine was again sheet steel and on the Sten Mk I the trigger mechanism was shrouded in a wooden stock. There was a small wooden foregrip and a rudimentary flash hider. It looked horrible and caused some very caustic comments when it was first issued, but it worked and the troops soon learned to accept it for what it was, a basic killing device produced in extreme circumstances.

The Sten Mk I was produced to the tune of about 100,000 examples all delivered within months. By 1941 the **Sten Mk II** was on the scene and this was even simpler than the Mk I. In time the Sten Mk II became regarded as the 'classic' Sten gun and it was an all-metal version. Gone was the wooden stock over the trigger mechanism, replaced by a simple sheet-metal box. The butt became a single tube with a flatt buttplate at its end. The barrel was redesigned to be unscrewed for changing and the magazine housing, with the box magazine protruding to the left, was designed to be a simple unit that could be rotated downwards once the magazine was removed to keep out dust and dirt. The butt could be easily removed for removing the breech block and spring for cleaning. By the time all these parts (barrel, magazine and butt) had been removed, the whole weapon occupied very little space and this turned out to be one of the Sten's great advantages. When the initial needs of the armed forces had been met, from several production lines, including those set up in Canada and New Zealand, the Sten was still produced in tens of thousands for paradrop into occupied Europe for use by resistance forces and partisans. There it found its own particular place in combat history, for the very simplicity of the Sten and the ease with which it could be broken down for hiding proved to be a major asset and the Germans came to fear the Sten and what it could do. The Germans learned, as did many others, that the bullet from a Sten was just as lethal as a bullet from something more fancy.

A silenced version of the Sten Mk II was produced in small numbers for Commando and raiding forces as the **Sten Mk IIS**, and then came the **Sten**

Above: The Sten Mk II was one of the most widely-used of all the Allied sub-machine guns. It looked crude but it worked, it could be stripped down for easy concealment, and it was available in quantity.

Right: The Sten was one of the first weapons issued to the newly-formed airborne troops of the British army, and this example is unusual in being fitted with a small spike bayonet.

Mk III. This was basically an even simpler version of the original Mk I as its barrel could not be removed and it was encased in a simple steel-tube barrel jacket. Again, tens of thousands were produced and were widely used.

The **Sten Mk IV** was a development model intended for parachute troops but it was not placed into production. By the time the **Sten Mk V** was on the scene things were going better for the Allies and the Mk V could be produced with rather more finesse. The Mk V was easily the best of the Stens for it was produced to much higher standards and even had such extras as a wooden butt, forestock and a fitting for a small bayonet. It had the foresight of the Lee-Enfield No. 4 rifle and the metal was even finished to a high degree, whereas the earlier marks had their metal left in a bare state with a minimum of fine finish. The Mk V was issued to the Airborne Forces in 1944, and after World War II it became the standard British army sub-machine gun.

The Sten was a crude weapon in nearly every way, but it worked and it

could be produced in large numbers at a time when it was desperately needed. In occupied Europe it was revealed as an ideal resistance weapon and all over the world underground forces have been busy copying the design almost direct. The Germans even produced their own copies in 1944 and 1945. It was one of the more remarkable weapons of World War II.

Right: Street fighting in the Mediterranean. This example has had a non-standard foregrip added to enhance handling.

Below: By the time the Sten Mk V was produced there was time for some finesse to be added to the basic design. While the original outline was retained a wooden butt and pistol grip and a No. 4 rifle foresight had been added.

Specification:
Sten Mk II
Calibre: 9 mm
Length: 762 mm (30.00 in)
Length of barrel: 197 mm (7.75 in)
Weight loaded: 3.7 kg (8.16 lb)
Magazine: 32-round box
Rate of fire, cyclic: 550 rpm
Muzzle velocity: 365 m (1,200 ft) per second

Allied and Axis Flamethrowers

Liquid fire was used in medieval times by the Byzantine navy, but its 20th-century use stems from flamethrowers introduced by Germany during World War I. By World War II such 'terror' weapons were in widespread service, adding new horror to the conflict.

A German Flammenwerfer being used to terrifying effect on an enemy-held position in Stalingrad. The flamethrower team was highly vulnerable and needed to be well protected.

Fire in all its guises has been an established weapon of war since ancient times, but when the flamethrower appeared in its modern form on the battlefields of World War I it seemed that a new aspect of its horrors had arrived. Despite the outcries of disgust that arose on all sides, the flamethrower quickly became an established military weapon and by World War II most armies either had the flamethrower in their armouries or were making active plans to place them there. These early World War II flamethrowers were very different beasts from those that came later in the war, for they were usually not much different from World War I models and in some cases, such as the several improvised designs rushed out in the UK during 1940, virtually identical. Flamethrower tanks had also been developed, although few armoured commanders knew how to use them to best effect when they first encountered them. The potential of the mobile and armoured flamethrower was enormous, as the British Wasp and Crocodile were to demonstrate during 1944 and 1945. Portable flamethrowers had many tactical uses as well, but generally speaking the portable equipments lacked the range and impact of their vehicle-borne counterparts.

Fire is a frightening weapon, for not only are its effects dreadful to bear and behold but it has a powerful effect on morale. Mankind has an instinctive dread of fire in all its forms and when it is used offensively in the form of the flamethrower, its impact on an enemy can be considerable. At times during World War II the mere sight of a flamethrower in action was enough to make the enemy break and run – often towards the flamethrower's operators in order to surrender. There are certain battlefield targets against which the flamethrower has no effect, but they are few and far between.

So why are they so little used today? That question is hard to answer, though the main reason seems to lie in the fact that flamethrowers are essentially short-range assault weapons best used in confined areas. Modern warfare is expected to involve mobile forces moving across open country, where flame weapons can be of only little use. This is a convenient assumption to make, but it may not be borne out in practice. If urban or close-quarter warfare is ever necessary in future, the flamethrower may well reappear. And if it ever does the contents of this study will provide an indication of what might be expected. Let us hope we never have to encounter them again.

German flamethrowers

The first time the German army used flamethrowers was in 1914, when some were used against the French during the Argonne fighting, but their first large-scale use was against the French (again), this time during the 1916 Verdun campaign. These early flamethrowers were large things that needed up to three men to handle them, but development led to a much lighter version that weighed 'only' 35.8 kg (79 lb). This was the **Flammenwerfer 35**, which was issued to the new German army during the 1930s. In design terms it owed much to the World War I equipment, and it remained in production in 1941.

The Flammenwerfer 35 was gradually supplemented by the **Flammenwerfer klein verbessert 40**, a much lighter 'lifebuoy' model that carried less inflammable fuel, but relatively few of these were produced as they were soon replaced by the **Flammenwerfer 41**, which reverted to the twin-tank arrangement. This remained the standard German flamethrower until 1945, though one important modification was introduced after the grim winter of 1941-2, when the intense cold prevented the normal flame ignition system from working. This system was replaced by a cartridge ignition device that was much more reliable at other temperatures as well. When full this version, which was otherwise identical to the 1941 model, weighed 18.14 kg (40 lb) and the range at best was 32 m (35 yards).

All these German equipments used the twin-tank operating process, one tank containing the inflammable liquid and the other a compressed gas for propulsion. They were all capable of producing multiple bursts but there

The Flammenwerfer 41, seen here resting on its side, used a hydrogen ignition system that proved to be too unreliable under the extreme winter conditions of the Eastern Front, so it was later replaced by a cartridge ignition system. The larger of the two tanks contained the fuel; the other nitrogen.

was one odd model produced for use by parachutists and assault troops. This was a single-shot model known as the **Einstoss Flammenwerfer tragbar** which fired a 1/2-second burst of fire to a range of about 27 m (30 yards). Not many were produced.

It should not be thought that the above were the only German flamethrower equipments, for in this field as in all others the Germans were liable to produce proliferations of models. For instance, in addition to the back-pack Flammenwerfer 35 mentioned above there was also a two-man version known as the **mittlerer Flammnwerfer**, which had its main fuel tank

carried on a small trolley. If this were not enough there was also a much larger model carried on a trailer towed behind a light vehicle: this carried enough fuel to produce flame for 24 seconds. Finally, for use in static situations there was a device known as the **Abwehrflammenwerfer 42**, a single-shot device to be buried into the ground with only the flame projector nozzle above ground and pointing towards a target area. This was set off by remote control as an enemy approached, and was the German variation of the old fougasse weapon used for many years in fortifications.

Needless to say, the Germans also

made as much use as possible of captured equipments.

Specification
Flammenwerfer 35
Weight: 35.8 kg (79 lb)
Fuel capacity: 11.8 litres (2.6 Imp gal)
Range: 25.6 to 30 m (28 to 33 yards)
Duration of fire: 10 seconds

The fearsome blast of a man-pack flamethrower is seen during a night attack at Stalingrad. Flamethrower operators had to be well protected by friendly infantry as they were vulnerable and highly conspicuous.

A Flammenwerfer 35 is seen in action against a concrete emplacement in Poland after the 1939 campaign. The Flammenwerfer 35 had a range of 25.6 to 30 m (28 to 33 yards) and carried enough fuel for 10 seconds of use, but it weighed 35.8 kg (79 lb) and so was often carried into action by two men.

A German assault pioneer team is seen with one member of the team carrying the weight and bulk of a Flammenwerfer 35. This equipment weighed 35.8 kg and was an awkward load for one man to carry, but the equipment remained in production until 1941. Its basic design dated from 1918.

GERMANY

German flamethrower tanks

Throughout World War II the Germans were not particularly energetic in the deployment of flamethrower tanks, even though they were fielding a light flamethrower tank at a time when no other nation was doing so. This was in 1941 when, following a period of trials, a PzKpfw I was converted to take a Flammenpanzer 40 flame projector in place of one of the machine-guns in the turret. This produced the **Flammpanzer I**, and the first of them were used in action by the Deutsches Afrika Korps in North Africa. This expedient was soon followed by another, this time the **Flammpanzer II** which was a conversion of the otherwise little-used PzKpfw II Ausf D or E. On this conversion two flame projectors were used, one on each side of the front hull. Each projector had a range of about 36.5 m (40 yards). Not many of these conversions were made, and most appear to have been used on the Eastern Front.

The most numerous conversions to the Flammpanzer role were made with the PzKpfw III Ausf H or M. At least 100 of these tanks were converted to take a flame projector in place of the main

gun, and there was capacity internally for 1000 litres (220 Imp gal) of fuel. These **Flammpanzer III** vehicles were very effective but do not appear to have been much used, mainly as a result of their inability to defend themselves against enemy tanks, for whenever they were used in action other 'gun' tanks had to be used to guard them.

Apart from the odd trials model, no PzKpfw IV was converted to the operational Flammpanzer role. Apparently there were plans to convert various marks of Panther and Tiger II to the flame role, but none appear to have seen fruition. Instead the little **Flammpanzer 38(t)** was placed into production during 1944 as the standard flame tank of the land forces. This small tank was well suited to the role as it used the low and easily concealed hull of the Hetzer tank destroyer. Once again the flame gun took the place of the main gun and some of the internal space was devoted to fuel for the projector.

A few captured tanks were used by the Germans for the flame role. One example was the large Char B, one of

the French tanks captured by the Germans in 1940, but once again the number involved was not great, probably about 10.

For much of the war the German army relied upon the SdKfz 251 half-track for the flamethrowing role. The version used was the **SDKfz 251/16 mittlerer Flammpanzerwagen**, first used during 1942. This carried two fuel

tanks, each containing 700 litres (154 Imp gal) of fuel, enough for 80 two-second bursts of flame. Each fuel tank supplied its own projector, one each side of the open vehicle rear; some had a third but smaller projector at the front, but on most vehicles this position was occupied by a machine-gun. The usual range of these projectors was about 35 m (38 yards).

A Flammpanzer III with a flame projector in place of the usual gun. These vehicles used later Panzer III chassis: a machine-gun was mounted co-axially and the fuel was carried internally in two tanks, enough for 70 to 80 two- to three-second bursts. The normal crew was three men.

Above: One of the forward-mounted flame projectors carried by the Flammpanzer II, which were mainly used on the Eastern Front although not many were actually produced. This projector is firing a rod of unlit fuel that could be ignited later when it lay on the ground.

Portable Flamethrower Types 93 and 100

If war-time propaganda photographs are to be believed, the Japanese army and marines made extensive use of flamethrowers during World War II. This impression came largely from a long series of 'official' photographs taken during Japan's protracted war against the Chinese, where weapons such as flamethrowers could have a morale effect that far outweighed their usefulness as combat weapons. Against the flimsy structures used as housing throughout mainland China flame weapons could gain impressive results, and accordingly the Japanese made much use of them.

At first the main version used by the Japanese was the **Portable Flamethrower Type 93**. This was first issued during 1933 and was an orthodox design that made much use of German experience in World War I. It used three cylinders on a rather awkward back-pack arrangement, two of the cylinders containing the fuel and the central (and smaller) cylinder containing the compressed gas. When the Type 93 was first issued this was compressed nitrogen, but this was soon changed to compressed air. From 1939 onwards a small petrol-driven air compressor was issued with each equipment. This was the Type 99 compressor and when not in use it was transported in a small wooden case.

For various reasons the flame projector of the Type 93 was considered to be unsatisfactory, and in 1940 it was changed to a new type. This was known as the **Portable Flamethrower Type 100**, but in every other aspect it

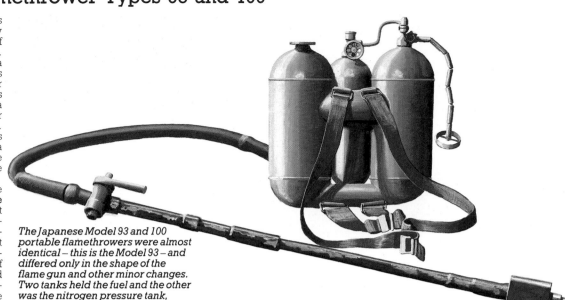

The Japanese Model 93 and 100 portable flamethrowers were almost identical – this is the Model 93 – and differed only in the shape of the flame gun and other minor changes. Two tanks held the fuel and the other was the nitrogen pressure tank, providing a flame jet duration of 10 to 12 seconds.

was identical to the Type 93. The new flame gun was shorter than the earlier model – 901 mm (35.5 in) as opposed to 1.197 m (47.125 in). The nozzle of the flame gun could also be easily changed on the Type 100, whereas on the Type 93 it was fixed.

Although the Japanese infantry made use of flamethrowers, the Japanese tank formations made only limited use of the weapon. Apparently only one attempt was made to produce flamethrower tanks and this was a small unit of specialized combat enineering tanks that were encountered on Luzon in 1944. These turretless tanks were fitted with obstacle-clearing equipment on the front hull and mounted a single flamethrower forward. Both internal and external fuel tanks were carried. The tank used as the basis appear to have been the Type 98 medium, whose only other armament was a single machine-gun.

Specification
Portable Flamethrower Type 100
Weight: 25 kg (55 lb)
Fuel capacity: 14.77 litres (3.25 Imp gal)
Range: about 22.9 to 27.4 m (25 to 30 yards)
Duration of fire: 10 to 12 seconds

Portable Flame-Thrower M1 and M1A1

When the US Army requested a new portable flamethrower in July 1940, the Chemical Warfare Service had absolutely no knowledge base upon which to work, and so had to start from scratch. Using a model known as the **Flame-Thrower E1**, gradual development reached the stage where the E1R1 was ready for troop trials, some of which were carried out under combat conditions in Papua. The E1R1 was far from perfect for it was easily broken and the controls were difficult to reach, but a more rugged version was accepted for service as the **Portable Flame-Thrower M1**. This M1 was much like the E1R1 in that it had two tanks, one for fuel and the other for compressed hydrogen.

The M1 went into production in March 1942, and the weapon was in action during the Guadacanal operations of January 1943. It proved to be something of a disappointment, for the M1 was prone to all manner of production faults, and these often meant that the weapon failed in action. The ignition circuit used electrical power supplied by batteries that often failed under active service conditions, and the tanks were liable to pin-hole corrosion spots that allowed pressure to escape. A special repair and inspection service had to be established to ensure a serviceable reservoir of M1s ready for action.

By June 1943 a new model was in use. This was the **M1A1**, of which 14,000 examples were produced. The M1A1 was an M1 modified to make use of the new thicker fuels produced by placing additives in the petrol-based

fuels previously employed. This thicker fuel gave better flame effects and a range of up to 45.7 m (50 yards) compared with the maximum of 27.4 m (30 yards) of the M1. Unfortunately the troublesome ignition system was not altered in any way and the previous problems persisted to the point where troops in action sometimes had to ignite the flame jets with matches or pieces of burning paper.

M1A1s were used in Italy and the Far East; their use in Europe after June 1944 appears to have been somewhat restricted once the Normandy campaign was over.

Specification
Portable Flame-Thrower M1A1
Weight: 31.8 kg (70 lb)
Fuel capacity: 18.2 litres (4 Imp gal)

The American M1 flamethrower was a development of the earlier E1R1 which, although technically an experimental model, was used in action in 1943. The M1 was used for the first time during the Guadalcanal campaign of June 1942, and used the old 'thin' type of fuel.

Range: 41 to 45.7 m (45 to 50 yards)
Duration of fire: 8 to 10 seconds

Portable Flame-Thrower M2-2

Above: In a typical flamethrower action the flame gun operator is given covering fire by an infantry team. The flame weapon is an M2-2, being used against a Japanese bunker to burn out the occupants, who were usually loth to surrender to anything but flamethrowers – and often not even then.

Left: The Portable Flame-Thrower M2-2 was produced by the Americans in greater numbers than any other type, and was first used on Guam in July 1944. It was to remain the standard American flame weapon for many years after 1945 and saw action in Korea. Its maximum range under good conditions was 36.5 m (40 yards).

By mid-1943 the Chemical Warfare Service had a much better idea of what kind of portable flamethrower the troops required and set about designing a new type. Based on an experimental design known as the **E3**, the **Portable Flame-Thrower M2-2** was evolved, and this featured several improvements over the old M1A1. The M2-2 continued to use the new thickened fuel but it was a much more rugged weapon carried on a back-pack frame (very similar to that used to carry ammunition) but the main improvement was to the ignition. This was changed to a new cartridge system using a revolver-type mechanism that

allowed up to six flame jet shots before new cartridges had to be inserted. It proved to be much more reliable than the old electrical methods.

The M2-2 was first used in action on Guam in July 1944 and by the time the war ended almost 25,000 had been produced, more than the totals of M1s and M1A1s combined. However, production was not easy and some troops in the Pacific theatre continued to use the old M1A1 until the war ended. It was March 1945 before the first M2-2s arrived in Italy.

M2-2s were used by armies other than that of the Americans. Some were passed to the Australian army, bring-

ing to a halt the development of an indigenous Australian flamethrower known as the Ferret.

Although the M2-2 was an improvement over the M1 and M1A1, the US Army still considered that it was not what was really wanted, and development continued to find a better and lighter weapon. Some work was carried out to evolve a single-shot flamethrower that could be discarded after use. A model that used a combustible powder to produce pressure to eject 9 litres (2 Imp gal) of thickened petrol-based fuel from a cylinder was under development as the war ended, but the project was terminated soon

afterwards. It would have had a range of 27.4 m (30 yards).

Specification
Portable Flame-Thrower M2-2
Weight: 28.1 to 32.7 kg (62 to 72 lb)
Fuel capacity: 18.2 litres (4 Imp gal)
Range: 22.9 to 36.5 m (25 to 40 yards)
Duration of fire: 8 to 9 seconds

In addition to their noise, flamethrowers had a powerful visual effect on morale, and the mere sight of their flame jet was often enough to make even the strongest men quail. This is an American M2-2 in action on Ie Shima in June 1945.

American tank flamethrowers

The first American tank flamethrower was produced in 1940, and this **Flame Projector E2** mounted in an M2 medium tank was demonstrated to US Army tank officers in mid-1940. They were not impressed and the project was allowed to lapse. It was not long before opinions changed, but by that time the Chemical Warfare Service designers had to start once again from the beginning and before long had a pump-operated **Flame Projector E3** mounted in the turret of an M3 Lee medium tank. The pump system tended to break up the fuel structure and so reduce flame performance and range, but when the pump was replaced by a compressed air system these drawbacks were eliminated.

At the same time as these experiments were under way, another programme to produce a service weapon rapidly was initiated under the **'Q'** (Quickie) designation. The British/Canadian Ronson flame system was obtained from Canada, but initial trials had to be conducted with the system mounted on the rear of a truck as no tanks were available. The 'Q' project continued until an installation to be fitted to the turret of the M5A1 light tank was developed, but the tanks into which this system was supposed to be installed were simply not forthcoming and the 'Q' project thus turned out to be anything but a quickie. In fact it was early 1945 before any of the 'Q' sys-

tems, by then known as the **M5-4**, were ready for service in the Far East. Four were used in the Philippines.

While all this development work was being conducted in the continental USA, troops in Hawaii were busy producing actual weapons. Using the Ronson flame projector as their basis, they mounted flame systems in place of the old turret guns on obsolete M3A1 light tanks which were renamed **Satan**. Once installed these Satan systems used compressed carbon dioxide as the propellant gas, and could fire thickened fuel to a range of 73 m (80 yards); each vehicle could carry 773 litres (170 Imp gal) of fuel. The initial 'production run' was for 24 Satans, and by June 1944 they were in action on Saipan.

The success of the Satan in action prompted commanders to request a similar installation in the M4 medium tank. Old 75-mm (2.95-in) tank gun barrels were used to mount the Ronson flame projectors and this new tank version, known officially as the **POA-CWS '75' H-1** (H denoting Hawaii), was used in action during the Ryukyus operation. The type was later used on Okinawa, in a special application to flame out defending Japanese from deep caves: several lengths of fire hose were connected together and taken deep in the caves, one end then being connected to the M4 flamethrower tank which pumped fuel along the hose to be

ignited at the other end by an operator using a portable flamethrower.

Both of these flame-producing systems mounted the flame projector in place of the main armament, a feature not greatly liked by the 'tankies', who wanted to retain some form of defensive armament. Attempts had already been made to mount a flame projector alongside the main gun on some M4 flame tanks and in the latter stages some M4s mounting 75-mm guns or 105-mm (4.134-in) howitzers also carried co-axial flamethrowers, but lack of spare parts prevented many conversions being made.

Other earlier attempts to mount portable flamethrowers that could fire through ports at the front of light tanks had been made but without much success, so in October 1943 the Chemical Warfare Service was asked to produce a flamethrower that could be mounted in place of the bow machine-gun on M3, M4 and M5 tanks, so that if required the machine-gun could be re-installed. Consequently 1,784 **M3-4-3** flamethrowers were produced for installing in M4 tanks and 300 **E5R2-M3** flamethrowers for use on M3 or M5 tanks. Many of these were used in Europe and in the Pacific theatre.

Many tank commanders did not like the idea of losing their bow machine-guns, so an alternative installation that could be mounted next to the commander's periscope on the turret top was

developed. One of these, the model **M3-4-E6R3**, was placed into production but was too late for war use.

Once again the troops stationed in Hawaii did not wait for weapons to arrive from the continental USA, and set about producing their own auxiliary flamethrowers. This time the M1A1 portable flamethrower was used as the basis for a projector that could be mounted in place of the bow machine-gun of an M4 medium tank. Some 176 of these conversions were made, and were on hand for the Okinawa and Iwo Jima campaigns, but they were not much used as the troops preferred the 'local' conversions with the turret-mounted systems on M4 medium tanks.

Mention must also be made of the installation of the 'Q' project M5-4 flamethrower in the LVT-4 amphibious carrier. Six of these were used on Peleliu, but the carrier proved to be rather unsatisfactory for flame operations. Although they were used very effectively, the LVT-4 was really too lightly armoured.

The Satan flamethrower was used on US Marine Corps M3A1 light tanks in place of the main turret gun. This example is in use on Saipan during July 1944, and the Satan was so successful that many more old M3A1 light tanks were converted to the flame warfare role.

Below: The Sherman Crocodile was a British development to use Shermans in the flame-throwing role, but only four were ever produced as US Army interest in the project waned almost as soon as it started. The flame gun was mounted to the right of the hull gunner's escape hatch.

ROKS-2 and ROKS-3

When the USSR entered the war in 1941, it had been developing flame weapons for some years, but at a relatively low priority. In 1941 it had a portable flamethrower type known as the **ROKS-2** (ranzewüj ognemjot K S-2). No details of the ROKS-1 have been discovered, but it is likely that this was a development model only. In design terms there was nothing really remarkable about the ROKS-2 apart from the attention paid to the appearance of the weapon. One of the tactical lessons learned during World War I regarding flamethrowers was that any soldier noticed by the enemy to be carrying a flame weapon immediately became the target of every weapon in sight, so if the appearance of the flamethrower could be altered in some way the user had a better chance of survival. Accordingly the Soviet designers went out of their way to make the ROKS-2 appear to be an ordinary infantry weapon. The main fuel tank was configured like a soldier's ordinary back-pack, and the flame projector was made to look like an ordinary rifle, and in fact the butt of the projector was taken from the standard Soviet Model 1891/30 rifle. The only noticeable flamethrower features were the small gas pressure bottle under the 'pack', the hose leading to the projector, and the rather prominent ignition device at the muzzle of the projector. On the battlefield these features would probably have merged into the general background.

After the German invasion of the USSR in 1941 most of the nation's industrial facilities were soon in a state of upheaval as factories were overrun or moved to the east. Flamethrower production was affected along with everything else, and in the struggle to meet the ever-increasing demands for weapons of all kinds the design niceties of the ROKS-2 had to be omitted. A new and simpler model known as the **ROKS-3** came into being, and this did away with the pack appearance and instead used two cylinders on a frame carried on the back. The flame projector still resembled a rifle, but it was much simpler and easier to make in quantity.

During their investigations into flame warfare the Soviets discovered how to make the thickened fuel that improved flame effects and range, and used this new fuel in both the ROKS-2 and ROKS-3. Using thickened fuel both equipments had a maximum possible range of 45.7 m (50 yards), though operational ranges were rather shorter.

The Soviets also produced static flamethrowers of the type meant to be buried in the ground with only the projector nozzle pointing towards the target area. The exact designation of these weapons is not known, but the Germans copied them to produce their own Abwehrflammenwerfer 42. The Soviets also developed a whole series of flamethrower tanks, starting with the T-26 of the early war years. The T-26 version was no great success but in 1941 the **ATO-41** flamethrower appeared. This was installed next to the main gun of the KV heavy tank to produce the **KV-8**, and when mounted in place of the bow machine-gun of a T-34/76 tank the vehicle became the **OT-34**. These early installations were not very successful, mainly because the internal fuel capacity was only 100 litres (22 Imp gal), which limited its

tactical usefulness, and there were also many technical drawbacks. Most of these were eliminated with the introduction of the **ATO-42** equipment, which could accommodate more fuel. A few of these improved equipments were installed in the KV-1S heavy tank to produce the **KV-8S**, but most of the ATO-42s were installed in place of the bow machine-gun of the T-34/85 which then became the **TO-34**. The ATO-42 could fire four or five flame bursts in 10 seconds, and the maximum range with thickened fuel was 120 m (131 yards). The Soviet flamethrower tanks were used in special three-company battalions.

Specification
ROKS-2
Weight: 22.7 kg (50 lb)
Fuel capacity: 9 litres (2 Imp gal)
Range: 36.5 to 45.7 m (40 to 50 yards)
Duration of fire: 6 to 8 seconds

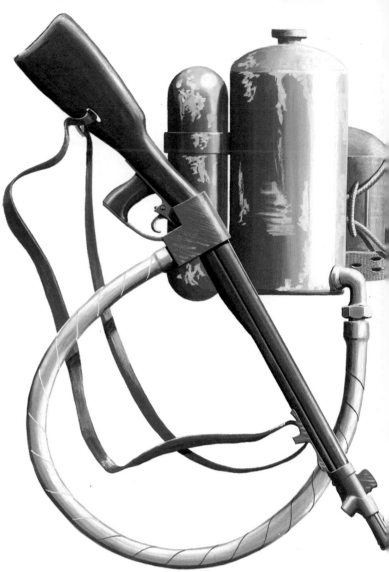

Right: The Soviet ROKS-2 was carried as a back pack with the cylinder tanks vertical. The flame gun was designed to resemble a rifle to conceal its function, as flamethrower operators usually attracted a great deal of enemy attention and fire. The large tank contained enough fuel for about eight seconds of use.

Below: Finnish troops surround a Soviet OT-26 flamethrower tank in 1941. This was a version of the twin-turret T-26 light infantry tank, with internal fuel tanks taking the place of one of the turrets and the other mounting a flame gun.

Ampulenjot 1941 System Kartukov

The weapon that was known as the **Ampulenjot 1941 System Kartukov** appears rarely in Western literature and it is still something of a mystery weapon. It was not a flamethrower in the usual sense used elsewhere in this study, but rather an incendiary projectile launcher. During World War II these were little used by any combatant, although there were plans to produce similar weapons in the UK during the dangerous days of 1940; the abortive Newton Mortar was one of these. The Kartukov gun appears to fall into exactly the same category, for it was produced in 1941 when the German army was rapidly overrunning most of the western areas of the USSR.

These western areas contained the vast bulk of the USSR's industrial potential. As many as possible of the machine tools and other raw materials of production were hurriedly uprooted and taken away to the east beyond the Urals. During this period of reorganization and confusion the Soviet Army was losing vast quantities of war weapons of every kind, and something had to be produced quickly to replace them. This was where the Kartukov gun came in, for it was a very simple weapon that could be produced with the absolute minimum of facilities and raw materials.

The Kartukov was what is now generally know as a 'pipe gun', i.e. it was simple length of steel pipe closed at one end and with a minimum of fire-control equipment. It would appear that the Kartukov gun was meant to be used at static locations, for the only

illustrations seen show the gun mounted on a simple yoke arrangement mounted on a steel post. There was no elevation or traverse controls other than two rudimentary handles, located behind the 'breech', with which the firer aimed the weapon. The breech itself was a very simple affair: when opened, the breech block moved back along a short slide to allow the charge to be inserted. It seems almost certain that the charge was only a small black-powder cartridge and that the projectile was loaded from the muzzle. To aim the weapon a fixed raised sight that aligned with a small 'pip' on the muzzle was used, holes in the raised sight being used to vary the range. Firing was by percussion. The projectile had a diameter of 127 mm (5 in) and was of a type once known during the Middle Ages as a 'carcass'. This was an incendiary device that burst into flames as it struck the target and spread flames or burning material in the general target area. Although it cannot be stated for a fact, it seems that the Kartukov gun used some form of phosphorus mixture allied to a thick oil-based fuel. The range at best was only about 250 m (274 yards).

The advancing Germans captured numbers of these Kartukov guns, and the only references now available regarding these weapons are to be found among German intelligence reports. Understandably enough the Germans did not have a very high opinion of them as weapons and they regarded them as 'primitive'.

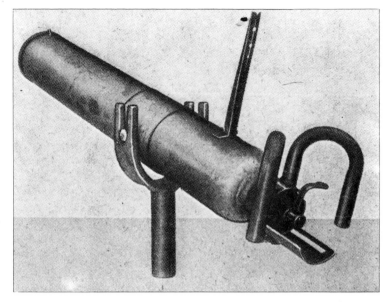

The Soviet Ampulenjot 1941 System Kartukov was a simple 'pipe' gun that used a small black powder charge to fire an incendiary 'carcass' projectile. It was an expedient defence weapon used for a short period in 1941. The maximum range was only 250 m (274 yards).

It would appear that by 1942 the Kartukov guns were no longer required and were scrapped.

Specification
Ampulenjot 1941 System Kartukov
Calibre: 127 mm (5 in)
Length: overall 1.02 m (40.16 in)

Weight: 26 kg (57.3 lb)
Elevation: 0 to + 12°
Traverse: 360°
Muzzle velocity: 50 m (164 ft) per second
Maximum range: 250 m (274 yards)
Projectile weight: 1.5 or 1.8 kg (3.3 or 3.97 lb)

Crocodile

The first general staff specification for a flamethrowing tank was put forward as early as 1938, although at that time there was no research department dealing specifically with flame warfare. Some desultory trials led to a number of experimental models, but nothing definite was achieved until a special Petroleum Warfare Department was established, and then some more definite work was commenced. The PWD concentrated on a type of projector that used compressed hydrogen to propel the flame fuel jet, and in time this led to the **Crocodile**.

The Churchill Crocodile was one of the most widely used of all the many Churchill tank variants, and towed a special trailer that carried both the flame fuel and the nitrogen gas cylinders. The flame gun was mounted in the hull front and the turret retained the main 75-mm (2.95-in) gun.

The Crocodile was meant to be used with the Churchill infantry tank, hence **Churchill Crocodile**. When it first appeared in 1942 a change of War Office policy meant that there was officially no longer a requirement for the flamethrower tank, but work nevertheless went ahead. It was just as well, for in April 1943 another policy change meant that the Crocodile was wanted once more and in August 1943 an order for 250 was placed, these vehicles being needed to equip units that would take part in the forthcoming Normandy landings.

The order was made despite the fact that no troop trials had taken place. Although the initial plan was that the Crocodiles were to be mounted on the Churchill Mk IV, most production weapons were installed in the Churchill Mk VII. The main part of the Crocodile was installed in a two-wheeled trailer towed behind the Churchill tank and connected to the tank via a universal joint through which the pressurized fuel had to pass. The projector itself was at the front of the tank, installed in place of the hull machine-gun. The Churchill's main 75-mm (2.95-in) gun and turret machine-gun were retained to enable the vehicle to be used as a normal gun tank if required. The trailer could be jettisoned when empty or if the occasion demanded. The trailer contained enough fuel and compressed gas to produce about 80 one-second flame bursts, and the usual

operational range was about 73 m (80 yards), although under favourable conditions 110-m (120-yard) range was possible.

The Churchill Crocodiles first went into action on D-Day, 6 June 1944. Thereafter they were used in all theatres of war and came to be very effective weapons that were greatly feared by the enemy. There were plans for Crocodiles to be used on Sherman tanks operated by the US Army and although some design work was carried out only six were built and of those only four were used in action by the Americans in Europe.

By the time the war ended 800 Churchill Crocodiles had been produced. The main British army user was the 79th Armoured Division, although other formations also had the type. Once the war was over most were withdrawn from use.

Lifebuoy

Development of what was to become officially known as the **Flame-Thrower, Portable, No. 2 Mk I**, began during 1941. It appears to have been influenced by the German Flammenwerfer 40, but the basic design of any portable flamethrower is fixed by physical constraints. This results from the fact that for a vessel that has to contain gas at high pressure the sphere is the best possible shape. On a flamethrower the fuel tank has to contain as much fuel as possible within as small a volume as can be managed. These design criteria virtually dictate the shape of the resultant equipment, i.e. a central sphere with a fuel tank having a circular cross-section wrapped around it. This produces the classic shape which gave the British equipment its **Lifebuoy** nickname, a name that stuck.

The first pilot model was ready by mid-1942 and a production order soon followed, despite the fact that the usual series of troop and other trials had not been completed. This was unfortunate, for after only a short time in service the Lifebuoy began to demonstrate a number of serious defects, many of them caused by hurried manufacture of the complex shape of the tanks. As always, ignition proved to be somewhat unreliable, and the position of the fuel valve under the tanks proved to be awkward to use in action. As a result the first production run of the Lifebuoy, the Mk I, was withdrawn and used for training only from mid-1943 onwards. It was not until the following year that the improved **Flame-Thrower, Portable, No. 2 Mk II** appeared. It was this version that the British army used until the war ended, and for many years after. In appearance there was little to differentiate the Mk I from the Mk II.

The Mk II was ready for service by June 1944, and was used during the Normandy landings and after them, including the campaigns in the Far East. However, the British army never was really enthusiastic regarding portable flamethrowers and decided that not many would be required. Production

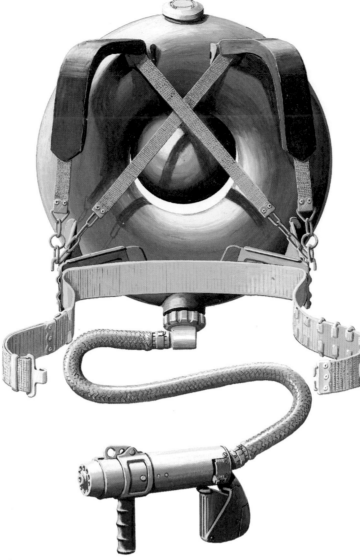

Above: The Mk I version of the Flame Thrower, Portable, No. 2 was usually known as the Lifebuoy from its shape, but it was not a great success and saw only limited operational use before being replaced in late 1943 by the Mk II.

Left: The Mk II version of the Lifebuoy became the standard British flamethrower from early 1944 onwards, but it was never a popular weapon and was used operationally only in limited numbers. Its shape was chosen to provide the maximum possible volume inside a pressure vessel.

The official solution was to produce a smaller device known as the **Ack-Pack** which weighed 21.8 kg (48 lb), not for use in Europe but for possible use in the Far East. In the event the Ack-Pack was given such a low development priority that it was not produced until after the war was over. So ended the rather unfortunate Lifebuoy project.

Specification
Lifebuoy
Weight: 29 kg (64 lb)
Fuel capacity: 18.2 litres (4 Imp gal)
Range: 27.4 to 36.5 m (30 to 40 yards)
Duration of fire: 10 seconds

of the Mk II ended as early as July 1944, after 7,500 had been made. Even the Mk II proved to be generally unreliable as it depended on a small battery to ignite the flame, and in the wet or

after even a short period of use the battery often failed. The old production problem of quality control was carried over as well, and as always the troops complained about the weight.

Wasp

The first British use of flamethrowers in connection with mobile warfare was during 1940, when the newly-established Petroleum Warfare Department developed a flame projector known as the **Ronson**. This had a relatively short range and was mounted on a Universal Carrier with the fuel and compressed gas tanks over the rear of the vehicle. For various reasons the British army decided not to proceed with the Ronson, requesting more range, but the Canadians persevered with the design, and later in the war it was adopted by the US Army, who called it the **Satan**.

By 1942 the PWD had developed the Ronson to the stage where ranges of 73 to 91.5 m (80 to 100 yards) were being reached, and this improved device was put into production as the **Wasp Mk I**. In September 1942 an order for 1,000 was placed and by November the following year all had been delivered. These Wasp Mk Is used a large projector gun that was routed over the top of the Carrier and connected to two fuel tanks inside the Carrier hull. However, these Mk Is were deemed unsuitable for service as by then a

Wasp Mk II had appeared with a much smaller and handier flame projector mounted at the front in place of the machine-gun otherwise carried. This new flame projector was a great advance over the previous design and gave a much better flame performance even though there was no improvement in range; the same type of projector was also used with the Churchill Crocodile. It was also easier to aim and much safer to use.

The Wasp Mk II first went into action during the Normandy fighting of July 1944. They were used mainly in support of infantry operations, whereas the Crocodile was used in conjunction with armoured formations. They were dreadfully effective weapons, and greatly feared by the unfortunate Germans who had to bear their effects, though for fear of these effects German infantry opposition very often ceased once the Wasps had arrived on the scene.

It was not long before the Wasp Mk IIs were joined by yet another Wasp variant, this time the **Wasp Mk IIC**, the suffix denoting Canada for the Canadians had also developed their own

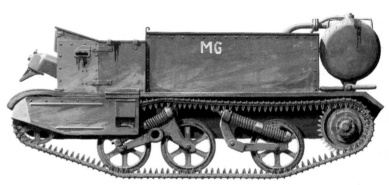

version of Wasp. They decided that to devote a Universal Carrier to the flamethrower role only was rather wasteful in vehicles and they redesigned the Wasp so that the Carrier could also function as a normal Carrier if it had to. Accordingly they moved the fuel tanks to a location outside the rear of the vehicle, and replaced the arrangement of two tanks with a single 341-litre (75-Imp gal) tank. This gave room inside the open hull for a third crew member, who could carry a light machine-gun. This gave the Wasp Mk

The Wasp Mk IIC was the Canadian version of the British Wasp, and carried its fuel in a single tank at the rear; the British Wasp Mk II had two internal tanks. The Wasp was a conversion of the Universal Carrier for the flame role first tested in 1943.

IIC much more tactical flexibility, and it gradually came to be the preferred type. In June 1944 all Wasp production was switched to the Mk IIC standard, and field conversions were also made, using the existing Mk II 272.7-litre (60-Imp gal) tanks. Operational experience demonstrated the need for more frontal armour, and many Wasp Mk IICs were fitted with plastic armour over the front hull plates.

Some Wasps were fitted with special smoke-producing equipment, and a few had wading screens installed for possible use during amphibious operations. The Canadians demonstrated their interest in flamethrower tanks by fitting Wasp equipments to old Ram tanks to produce the **Badger**. These conversions were carried out in the UK for the Canadian 1st Army. Early Badgers did not have turrets, though later versions did, the turretless versions being based on Ram Kangaroo personnel carriers. They were used by the Canadians from February 1945 onwards.

During early 1945 three Wasps and a quantity of their thickened fuel were sent to the USSR. What the Soviets made of them has not been recorded.

The Wasp Mk II differed from the earlier Mk I in having a much smaller flame projector mounted in the front hull. British Wasps had a crew of two while the Canadians had three, one of whom usually operated a machine-gun or light mortar.

Harvey flamethrower

In the grim period after the Dunkirk evacuation of 1940 it appeared to be very likely that the Germans would invade the UK. If they had actually done so things might well have been to their advantage, for the remains of the British army in the UK were few in number and ill-equipped with virtually every kind of military necessity. Even rifles were in short supply at one point, and items like flamethrowers were virtually nonexistent. However, it was decided to produce and issue whatever could be procured.

Fortunately for the British, things like flamethrowers were relatively easy to produce as long as nothing fancy was required. Thus the **Harvey** flamethrower was born by simply knocking together what was available and handing it over to the troops. The Harvey flamethrower was officially known as the **Flame-Thrower, Transportable, No. 1 Mk I**, but to the troops it was simply the 'Harvey'. In many ways it resembled the German *Flammenwerfer* of World War I but it was not intended that it should be used as a portable weapon. Instead it was taken to wherever it was to be set up and left for possible use. The 'Transportable' part of the designation was derived from the fact that it could be moved about on a two-wheeled carriage based on wheels taken from agricultural machinery production lines. The main fuel tank was an easily-manufactured pressure tank and the compressed air used by the weapon was contained in an ordinary commercial compressed air cylinder.

The flame projector was connected to the fuel tank by a 9.14-m (30-ft) hose, and the projector itself was a simple device held in position on a monopod. The idea was that the Harvey would be taken to a selected site and set up with the tanks under cover (probably behind a wall) and with the projector and hose near the target point, probably camouflaged in some fashion. When a potential target approached the flame was ignited as the fuel rushed through the projector under pressure.

The first Harveys were issued to regular troops defending the UK, but it was not long before the Home Guard got them as well. They were cumbersome things and were not greatly liked, but they worked after a fashion. Some of them even found their way to the Middle East where they were used not for flame work but for smoke production. They were never used operationally in a flame role.

This was the flame jet produced by the Harvey flamethrower, a static defensive device produced in 1940 mainly for the Home Guard. Although meant to be used in a static role, it could be moved on a simple two-wheeled carriage, but it was a cheap and crude weapon.

Specification
Harvey
Weight: not known
Fuel capacity: 127.3 litres (28 Imp gal)
Range: about 46 to 55 m (50 to 60 yards)
Duration of fire: 12 seconds

273

Lanciafiamme modello 35 e 40

As its designation implies the Italian **Lanciafiamme modello 35** entered service in 1935, just in time to make its operational debut during the Italian invasion of Abyssinia. There this flamethrower terrorized the hapless natives who had to endure its efficiency, and from this the weapon gained for itself a reputation for lethality within the Italian army.

From a design viewpoint there was nothing really remarkable about the modello 35. It was a relatively portable twin-cylinder back-pack equipment that used a rather cumbersome flame projector. This projector was fitted at the end with a large collar housing the flame ignition system. For various reasons this ignition system was not considered reliable enough, so it was modified to produce the **Lanciafiamme modello 40**. In general appearance and use the modello 40 was otherwise identical to the modello 35.

These flamethrowers were used by special troops known as Guastori, or assault pioneers. In action these flamethrower troops had to wear thick protective clothing and their faces were covered by normal service gas respirators. When so clothed their operational mobility and vision was restricted, so they were usually guarded by teams of supporting infantry. On the move their flamethrower equipments were usually carried on special brackets fitted to trucks or, if the formation was not mechanized, mules with special harnesses were employed. The fuel for the flamethrowers was carried in specially marked jerricans.

Both of these flamethrowers were used in some numbers by Italian troops operating in North Africa and by the hapless Italian troops who had to fight alongside the Germans on the Eastern Front. In both theatres of war the modello 35 and 40 worked well enough, but it was increasingly noticed that they lacked range compared with contemporary equivalents, and especially the later German designs. This did not stop the Germans from using them from time to time when it suited them.

Incidentally, the success of flamethrowers in Ethiopia moved the Italian army authorities to fit a special version of a lanciafiamme, much larger than the man-pack version, to the little L.3 tankette. As space within the low hull of this **L3-35Lf** vehicle was very limited the fuel was carried externally in a lightly armoured trailer, with a corrugated pipe passing the fuel to the projector from the trailer. There was also a version that dispensed with the trailer and carried a much smaller flat fuel tank over the top of the vehicle rear. Although much was made of these two flame-throwing tankettes

they appear to have been little used.

Specification
Lanciafiamme modello 35
Weight: 27 kg (59.5 lb)
Fuel capacity: 11.8 litres (2.6 Imp gal)
Range: about 22.8 m (25 yards)
Duration of fire: 20 seconds

Above: The flame projector of the L3 Lanciafiamme was mounted in place of the machine-gun carried on the L3/38 tankettes. These flamethrower tanks were of very limited tactical value as they were very lightly armoured and had a crew of only two.

Below: The L3 Lanciafiamme was the most widely used of the Italian flamethrower tanks. The fuel was carried in a trailer weighing 500 kg (1,102 lb), but some later models used a much smaller fuel tank mounted over the rear hull.

The Italian L3 Lanciafiamme carried its fuel in a trailer connected to the flame gun by a flexible hose. The propellant gas was contained in a cylinder on the rear of the chassis, but later versions carried both fuel and gas actually on the hull exterior. The L3 Lanciafiamme was the most widely used of the Italian mobile flamethrowers.

Allied Fighters

World War II saw a stunning evolution in the capability of the single-seat fighter aircraft. Few people observing the light, short-range aircraft of the first year of the war would have predicted the multitude of tasks to come its way in such a short time.

When devastating war once more burst on Europe in September 1939 the state of preparedness of the Allied air forces varied from the RAF's optimistic mediocrity to the downright ineptness of the French and Polish air forces, generally born of years of pacifism and parsimony. The monoplane fighter was in widespread use, albeit with little more than a couple of years' service behind it in most cases. Biplanes still served, if only to fill gaps yet to be occupied by more modern aircraft.

The finest Allied fighter in service in 1939, the immortal Supermarine Spitfire, served on only a handful of squadrons, was not regarded as fully operational, and demanded special servicing facilities at three or four nominated fighter bases. Yet within a year this aeroplane came to epitomize everything that was best in the RAF's fight against the Luftwaffe. Indeed it left its early partner, the Hawker Hurricane, far behind in the race to forge a weapon capable of matching Germany's great duo of fighters, the Messerschmitt Bf 109 and Focke-Wulf Fw 190. By 1941 RAF Fighter Command had adopted the Spitfire Mk VB, with its two 20mm cannon and four rifle-calibre machine-guns, as its standard equipment.

A group of USAAF long-range North American P-51 Mustang fighters – a superlative aircraft, believed by many to be the best of the war. It entered service in 1943 and achieved its 3347km (2080 mile) range by using wing drop tanks.

It was the shock introduction in 1941 by the Luftwaffe of the superb Fw 190, however, that fired the starting gun for the technological race to accelerate fighter development. The Spitfire Mk IX was rushed into service, as was the Hawker Typhoon, the latter still with many engine and airframe problems yet unresolved. US entry into the war at the end of 1941 did little to improve the fighter scene, neither the Bell P-39, Curtiss P-40 nor Republic P-43 being regarded as any match for the German

fighters. In due course, however, the marriage of the superlative Rolls-Royce Merlin to the North American P-51 Mustang produced the war's finest long-range single-seat fighter, entering service in late 1943.

On the Eastern Front, Germany's attack on the Soviet Union was accompanied by almost total destruction of the outdated indigenous equipment of the Red Air Force in 1941, a disastrous situation that was to some extent alleviated by the supply of Western aircraft to bolster

Soviet resistance in the air. In an amazingly short time, however, having moved the aircraft industry far to the East, the Soviets managed to introduce a number of promising new fighters, the Yakovlev Yak-3 and Lavochkin La-5 among them.

The last two years of the war found the Allies almost entirely re-equipped with fighters whose development had been undertaken wholly during the war, thereby drawing on combat experience. The Hawker Tempest joined the Typhoon (which nevertheless proved an excellent ground-attack weapon), while Griffon-powered Spitfires formed a large proportion of Fighter Command's air combat force. The USAAF was almost entirely equipped with the classic Lockheed P-38, P-47 and P-51 trio as well as late-series P-40s. In the Red Air Force the Lavochkin La-7 and Yakovlev Yak-9 were proving more than a match for the majority of Luftwaffe fighters, flown as they were by hastily trained young pilots, while in the Pacific the American and British fighters all but annihilated the air forces of Japan. In the field of jet fighters, where in airframes Germany unquestionably led the Allies, only the RAF managed to introduce very small numbers of early Gloster Meteors.

Lavochkin LaGG-3

Designed by a bureau headed by Semyon Lavochkin and including V. Gorbunov and M. Gudkov, the **Lavochkin LaGG-3** stemmed from the **LaGG-1**, whose prototype (the **I-22**) was first flown on 30 March 1940. These aircraft were unusual in retaining an all-wood structure; only the control surfaces (and later the landing flaps) were metal. This excellent little fighter was ordered into production in 1940 as the LaGG-1 with a 783-kW (1,050-hp) Klimov M-105 V-12 engine, but was too late to see service during the Winter War with Finland in 1939-40. With a top speed of 605 km/h (376 mph) and an armament of one 20-mm and two 12.7-mm (0.5-in) guns, the LaGG-1 was certainly one of the world's best fighters early in 1941, but pilots complained of poor climb performance and heavy controls, and a new version, the LaGG-3, was introduced by way of the **I-301** prototype after several hundred LaGG-1s had been delivered. At the time of the German attack two air regiments still flew the older aircraft, but within a year four regiments had received the LaGG-3, their task being to provide escort for the Ilyushin Il-2 close-support aircraft; they carried a variety of armament combinations, including wing attachments for six 8.2-cm (3.23-in) rockets or light bombs. The LaGG-3 featured a constant-speed propeller and improved rudder balancing, and was popular in service; it proved very robust and was capable of sustaining considerable battle damage. A better fighter was urgently needed, and the three designers each built new versions with the M-82 radial. In 1942 the liquid-cooled LaGG went out of production after about 6,528 had been built.

This LaGG-3 was flown by Captain G.A. Grigoryev in the winter of 1942/3, on the 6th Fighter Aviation Sector of the Central Front.

Specification
Lavochkin LaGG-3
Type: single-seat fighter
Powerplant: one 925-kW (1,240-hp) M-105PF V-12 piston engine
Performance: maximum speed 575 km/h (357 mph) at 5000 m (16,405 ft); initial climb rate 900 m (2,950 ft) per minute; service ceiling 9700 m (31,825 ft); range 650 km (404 miles)

Weights: empty 2620 kg (5,776 lb); maximum take-off 3300 kg (7,275 lb)
Dimensions: span 9.80 m (32 ft 1.75 in); length 8.81 m (28 ft 11 in); height 2.70 m (8 ft 10 in); wing area 17.51 m² (188.5 sq ft)
Armament: one 20-mm ShVAK hub-firing cannon and two 12.7-mm (0.5-in) UBS machine-guns or two 7.62-mm (0.3-in) ShKAS machine-guns, plus provision for six underwing 8.2-cm

LaGG-3s of the 9th IAP (Fighter Aviation Regiment) serving on the Black Sea. The LaGG did not fare well at the hands of the Luftwaffe, although this was more a reflection of respective pilot training than of any failure of the aircraft.

(3.23-in) rockets or four 50-kg (110-lb) bombs

Lavochkin La-5 and La-7

As the Soviet armies reeled back after the initial assault by Germany in the East during 1941, frantic demands were made for modern equipment to be supplied to the Soviet air force. In October 1941 Semyon Lavochkin started work on the **Lavochkin LaG-5** fighter with 1194-kW (1,600-hp) M-82 radial, passing on almost immediately to a development, the **La-5**, with cut-down rear fuselage which gave improved visibility for the pilot. The prototype completed its acceptance trials in May 1942 and entered production two months later; by the end of the year no fewer than 1,182 examples had been completed. In March 1943 the next and principal version, the **La-5FN**, entered production, a total of 21,975 aircraft including the later **La-7** being produced before the end of the war; the La-5FN featured the 1231-kW (1,650-hp) ASh-82FN engine, but its two 20-mm cannon were supplemented by four 8.2-cm (3.23-in) RS 82 rocket projectiles or two PTAB anti-tank weapons. A two-seat trainer version, the **La-5UTI**, was also produced. Later aircraft were armed with two 23-mm guns in place of the 20-mm weapons. In 1944 the La-7 appeared with an armament of three 20- or 23-mm cannon, an uprated ASh-82FN engine and a top speed of 680 km/h (423 mph). The first large-scale use of the La-5 was during the fighting around Stalingrad in November 1942; it was essentially a low/medium-altitude

fighter, and during the great armour battles at Kursk in July 1943 La-5s were employed in a tank-busting role, and after having discharged their hollow-charge missiles against ground targets they would climb to give fighter cover to the slower Ilyushin Il-2 support aircraft. The highest-scoring of all Allied fighter pilots of the war, Ivan Kozhedub, achieved all his 62 combat victories while flying La-5s, La-5FNs and La-7s between 26 March 1943 and 19 April 1945.

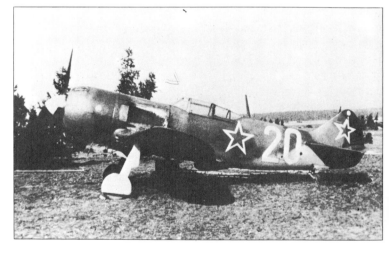

A refinement of the La-5, itself a development of the LaGG-3, the La-7 was to be the last of Lavochkin's mixed wood and metal construction fighters. By the time of its introduction to the battle in spring 1944, the Germans were in retreat all along the Eastern Front.

Ivan Kozhedub was the top-scoring Allied fighter pilot of the war. The La-7 shown is that in which he made the last of his 62 'kills', on 19 April 1945.

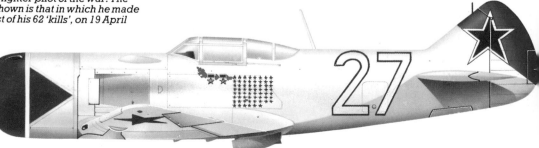

Kozhedub flew this La-5FN in the summer of 1944. The aircraft had been presented to the unit by the father of Hero of the Soviet Union Lieutenant-Colonel Konyev in memory of his son.

Specification
Lavochkin La-5FN
Type: single-seat fighter/fighter-bomber
Powerplant: one 1231-kW (1,650-hp) ASh-82FN radial piston engine
Performance: maximum speed 647 km/h (402 mph) at 5000 m (16,405 ft); climb to 5000 m (16,405 ft) in 5.0 minutes; service ceiling 11000 m (36,090 ft); range 765 km (475 miles)
Weights: empty 2605 kg (5,743 lb); normal take-off 3360 kg (7,408 lb)
Dimensions: span 9.80 m (32 ft 1.75 in); length 8.67 m (28 ft 5.3 in); height 2.54 m (8 ft 4 in); wing area 17.59 m² (189.3 sq ft)
Armament: two nose-mounted 20-mm ShVAK cannon (on later aircraft 23-mm NS cannon), plus provision for four 8.2-cm (3.23-in) RS-82 rockets or 150 kg (331 lb) of bombs

Semyon Lavochin's La-7 featured an uprated engine, giving it a top speed of 680 km/h (423 mph) and many minor improvements which made this aircraft one of the most effective of the war. Those made at the Moscow factory carried two cannon, whilst those built at Yaroslavl had three.

 USSR

Mikoyan-Gurevich MiG-3

Gaining a reputation as a 'hot ship' in the early years, the **Mikoyan-Gurevich MiG-3** was plagued by difficult handling and very poor armament, and although among the fastest of Soviet fighters of that period, it proved no match for the German Bf 109G or Fw 190. Flown in prototype form as the **I-61** in the spring of 1940, the initial design included the 895-kW (1,200-hp) Mikulin AM-35 V-12 engine, and this was retained in the production **MiG-1**, which started appearing in September 1940. Handicapped by the overall length of the engine, which resulted in poor pitch and directional stability, and armed with only three machine-guns, the MiG-1 suffered heavily in the opening months of Operation 'Barbarossa', and the MiG-3, delivered during the second half of 1941, proved little better with a 1007-kW (1,350-hp) AM-35A engine, which gave the fighter a top speed of 640 km/h (398 mph); introduced at the same time was a constant-speed propeller, increased wing dihedral and sliding cockpit canopy. Handling was only marginally improved, so the MiG-3 was transferred to attack bomber escort and close support duties; in 1942 two 12.7-mm (0.5-in) machine guns were added in underwing fairings by operational units, but gradually the aircraft was replaced by radial-engine fighters such as the La-5. Total production was 3,422, of which 100 were the earlier MiG-1.

Specification
Mikoyan-Gurevich MiG-3
Type: single-seat fighter
Powerplant: one 1007-kW (1,350-hp) Mikulin AM-35A V-12 piston engine
Performance: maximum speed 640 km/h (398 mph) at 7000 m (22,965 ft); initial climb rate 1200 m (3,935 ft) per minute; service ceiling 12000 m (39,370 ft); range 1250 km (777 miles)
Weights: empty 2595 kg (5,721 lb); maximum take-off 3350 kg (7,385 lb)
Dimensions: span 10.30 m (33 ft 9.5 in);

length 8.15 m (26 ft 9 in); height 2.67 m (8 ft 9 in); wing area 17.44 m² (187.7 sq ft)
Armament: one 12.7-mm (0.5-in) Beresin BS and two 7.62-mm (0.3-in) ShKAS nose-mounted machine-guns (later increased by two 12.7-mm/0.5-in underwing guns), plus provision for six 8.2-cm (3.23-in) underwing rockets or two 100-kg (220-lb) bombs

The MiG-3 had been designed for a high-altitude role but combats on the Eastern Front took place below 6000 m (19,685 ft), where the German Bf 109 had a distinct performance advantage. Consequently attrition was high, although many who were to become aces made their first 'kills' in the MiG fighter.

A MiG-3 of the 34 IAP operating from Vnukovko in the defence of Moscow in the winter of 1941/2. The aircraft is adorned with that most potent of Soviet slogans, 'For the Fatherland!'

Yakovlev Yak-1, Yak-3, Yak-7 and Yak-9

It is said that 37,000 Yakovlev fighters were produced during World War II, of which the vast majority were of the **Yakovlev Yak-9** that could outfight the German Bf 109G as early as the time of the Stalingrad campaign. Developed progressively from the **Yak-1** (which first flew in January 1940), through the **Yak-7B** which served from early 1942, the Yak-9 was first flown in its production form in the summer of that year, returning a speed of 600 km/h (373 mph). Numerous versions of this versatile fighter were developed, including the **Yak-9T** anti-tank fighter with 940-kW (1,260-hp) Klimov VK-105PF V-12 engine and 37-mm hub-firing cannon, the **Yak-9B** fighter-bomber with provision for 400 kg (882 lb) of bombs, the **Yak-9D** long-range fighter and the **Yak-9DD** very long-range escort fighter, the latter being flown as escort for USAAF bombers on shuttle raids between the UK and the Soviet Union late in the war. The **Yak-9U** fighter, with 1231-kW (1,650-hp) VK-107A engine and a top speed of 700 km/h (435 mph), was the final version to see combat during the war and represented the point at which Soviet technology may be said to have finally caught up with that of the West, and came to be much respected by the best Luftwaffe pilots in their final generation of Bf 109K and Fw 190D fighters. The **Yak-3** was perhaps the war's most manoeuvrable monoplane fighter, and entered service in 1944 as a lightened derivative of the Yak-1 series.

Right: The early production Yak-1 came to the front in large numbers in the early days of Barbarossa, and was disliked by some pilots who were used to the less advanced aerodynamics of the Polikarpov biplanes which had equipped many Soviet aviation regiments.

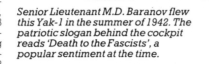

Senior Lieutenant M.D. Baranov flew this Yak-1 in the summer of 1942. The patriotic slogan behind the cockpit reads 'Death to the Fascists', a popular sentiment at the time.

By late 1944, the phenomenally agile Yak-3 was being replaced by improved models, but senior officers such as Major-General G.N. Zakharov of the 303 Fighter Aviation Division often kept them as personal mounts.

Above: Yak-9Ds of a Guards regiment operating in the Crimea. The nearest aircraft is the mount of Colonel Avdyeyev and bears the Order of the Red Banner. By the summer of 1944, when the photo was taken over Sevastopol, Soviet fighters were often superior.

Right: This Yak-1M was presented by the young Communists of Alma Alta and was flown by Sergei Lugansky, victor at the time over 32 enemies.

Specification
Yakovlev Yak-9U
Type: single-seat fighter
Powerplant: one 1231-kW (1,650-hp) VK-107A V-12 piston engine
Performance: maximum speed 700 km/h (435 mph) at 5000 m (16,405 ft); climb to 5000 m (16,405 ft) in 3.8 minutes; service ceiling 11900 m (39,040 ft); range 870 km (540 miles)
Weights: empty 2575 kg (5,677 lb); normal take-off 3098 kg (6,830 ft)
Dimensions: span 9.77 m (32 ft 0.6 in); length 8.55 m (28 ft 0.6 in); height 2.44 m (8 ft 0 in); wing area 17.25 m² (185.7 sq ft)
Armament: one 23-mm hub-firing VYa-23V cannon and two 12.7-mm (0.5-in) UBS machine-guns, plus provision for two 100-kg (220-lb) bombs

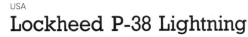

USA

Lockheed P-38 Lightning

Representing Lockheed's first fighter aircraft project, the twin-engine, twin-boom **Lockheed P-38 Lightning** was designed to meet a 1937 requirement for a high-altitude interceptor. First flown on 27 January 1939, the **XP-38** was followed by production **P-38**s with nose armament of one 37-mm and four 12.7-mm (0.5-in) guns and powered by Allison V-1710-27/29 engines; their top speed of 628 km/h (390 mph) was greater than any other twin-engine fighter in 1941. The first version to be considered fully operational was the **P-38D**, however, and this was reaching squadrons at the time of Pearl Harbor. The first of an order for 143 aircraft for the RAF arrived in the UK in December 1941, but after evaluation the Lightning was rejected (on account of a ban imposed on the export of turbochargers) and the contract cancelled. In the USAAF the P-38D was followed by the **P-38E**, in which the 37-mm cannon was replaced by a 20-mm weapon. The **P-38F**, with provision for up to a 907-kg (2,000-lb) bombload under the wings, was followed by the **P-38G** with minor equipment changes; the **P-38H** could carry up to 1452 kg (3,200 lb) of bombs. In the **P-38J** (of which 2,970 were produced) the radiators were located in deep 'chin' fairings immediately aft of the propellers; with maximum external fuel load this version had an endurance of about 12 hours, and it was in this model of the P-38 that America's top scoring fighter pilot of the war, Major Richard I. Bong, gained the majority of his 40 victories. The **P-38L** was the most-built version (a total of 3,923) and differed from the

P-38J only in having -111/113 engines in place of the -89/91s previously used. Photo-reconnaissance conversions, the **F-4** and **F-5**, were also widely used in Europe and the Far East. Production of all Lightnings totalled 9,394.

A P-38J of the 432nd Fighter Squadron based on New Guinea in late 1943. The 'J' models were the first to have relocated radiators and leading-edge tankage.

Specification
Lockheed P-38L Lightning
Type: single-seat fighter/fighter-bomber
Powerplant: two 1100-kW (1,475-hp) Allison V-1710-111/113 V-12 piston engines
Performance: maximum speed 666 km/h (414 mph) at 7620 m (25,000 ft); climb to 6095 m (20,000 ft) in 7.0 minutes; service ceiling 13410 m (44,000 ft); range 724 km (450 miles)
Weights: empty 5806 kg (12,800 lb); maximum take-off 9798 kg (21,600 lb)
Dimensions: span 15.85 m (52 ft 0 in); length 11.52 m (37 ft 10 in); height 2.99 m (9 ft 10 in); wing area 30.42 m² (327.5 sq ft)
Armament: one 20-mm and four 12.7-mm (0.5-in) guns in the nose, plus a bombload of up to two 726-kg (1,600-lb) bombs under the wings

Above: At the AAF Tactical Center in Orlando, Florida, technicians load a P-38 with bombs before a skip bombing run. With the retention of the full fighter nose armament of 20-mm and 12.7-mm guns, the P-38 could provide its own flak suppression at low level.

Below: The big Lockheed fighter saw service in a number of variants, the P-38M being a night fighter. This two-seat, radar-equipped model was used operationally in the Pacific during the latter stages of the war. It retained the full weapon fit of the day fighter versions.

USA

Bell P-39 Airacobra

The radical **Bell P-39 Airacobra** single-seat fighter was designed around the hub-firing 37-mm T-9 cannon which had given impressive demonstrations in 1935. The Allison V-12 engine was located amidships behind the cockpit, driving the propeller by an extension shaft, and nosewheel landing gear was adopted. The prototype **XP-39** was first flown in April 1939; production **P-39D** aircraft entered service with the USAAC in 1941 and first saw combat in the Pacific theatre in April 1942. P-39Ds also served with US forces in Europe but suffered heavily in action; they also flew with one RAF squadron (No. 601) but persistent problems caused them to be withdrawn after scarcely a single action. The Airacob-

ra flew with much better results with three USAAF groups based in North Africa from the end of 1942. The P-39D was followed by the **P-39F**, which introduced an Aeroproducts propeller in place of the former Curtiss type, the **P-39J** with V-1710-59 engine, the **P-39K** with -63 engine and Aeroproducts propeller, and the **P-39L** with -63 engine and Curtiss propeller. The **P-39M** introduced the -83 engine with large-diameter propeller. Final and most-built versions were the **P-39N** and **P-39Q** with -85 engine; production amounted to 2,095, bringing the total of all P-39s to 9,558. Of these, no fewer than 4,773 were shipped to the Soviet Union in response to Stalin's desperate appeals for military assistance.

A Bell P-39L Airacobra, operated by the 93rd FS, 81st FG in Tunisia in 1943. The P-39 proved no match for the agile Zero in the Pacific, but was reasonably effective in North Africa

Specification
Bell P-39N Airacobra
Type: single-seat fighter bomber
Powerplant: one 895-kW (1,200-hp)
Allison V-1710-85 V-12 piston engine
Performance: maximum speed 642
km/h (399 mph) at 2955 m (9,700 ft);
climb to 4570 m (15,000 ft) in 3.8
minutes; service ceiling 11735 m
(38,500 ft); range 1207 km (750 miles)
Weights: empty 2566 kg (5,657 lb);
maximum take-off 3720 kg (8,200 lb)
Dimensions: span 10.36 m (34 ft 0 in);
length 9.19 m (30 ft 2 in); height 3.78 m
(12 ft 5 in); wing area 19.79 m²
(213.0 sq ft)
Armament: one hub-firing 37-mm gun,
two 12.7-mm (0.5-in) machine-guns in
nose decking, and four 7.62-mm (0.3-
in) guns in the wings, plus provision for
one 227-kg (500-lb) bomb under the
fuselage

*Originally designed as an
interceptor, the Airacobra was used
also at low level, where its hub-
mounted 37-mm cannon was to
prove most effective in ground
attack. Soviet pilots, fighting at low
level, also achieved considerable
success in air combat.*

USA

Curtiss P-40 Warhawk

The USA's most important fighter at the
time of the Japanese attack on Pearl
Harbor, the **Curtiss P-40** continued to
give valuable service for the remainder of the war, though it never matched the excellence of the famous P-38/
P-47/P-51 trio. It had, after all, first
flown as the **X17Y** (later the **P-36** with
Pratt & Whitney R-1830 radial) and
been re-engined as the **XP-40** with supercharged Allison V-1710 V-12 engine in October 1938. Large orders followed, but most **P-40A** aircraft went to
the RAF (as the **Tomahawk Mk I**). The
P-40B followed with cockpit armour
and an armament of two 12.7-mm (0.5-
in) and four 7.62-mm (0.3-in) guns (the
Tomahawk Mk IIA in the RAF). The
P-40C (**Tomahawk Mk IIB**) featured
self-sealing fuel tanks. The **P-40D** intro-

duced a slightly shortened nose with
radiator moved forward and
deepened, this marked change in
appearance being identified by a
change of name to **Kittyhawk** in the
RAF (all P-40s in American service
being termed **Warhawk**); the P-40D
corresponded with the **Kittyhawk Mk I**
in RAF service. The first major USAAF
version was the **P-40E** (**Kittyhawk Mk
IA**), with six 12.7-mm (0.5-in) wing
guns, 2,320 being built. A Packard-
built Rolls-Royce Merlin powered the
P-40F (**Kittyhawk Mk II**). Most-
produced version was the **P-40N** (of
which 5,219 were built), this version
reverting to the Allison V-1710 engine
and featuring shackles for up to 680 kg
(1,500 lb) of bombs; in RAF service it
became the **Kittyhawk Mk IV**. The

majority of USAAF P-40s served in the
Pacific, although many served in the
Mediterranean theatre alongside the
Commonwealth Tomahawks and Kitty-
hawks. Total USAAF production was
12,014, 1,182 Tomahawks and 3,342 Kit-
tyhawks being built on British contracts.

Specification
**Curtiss P-40N-20 Warhawk (Kittyhawk
Mk IV)**
Type: single-seat fighter/fighter-
bomber
Powerplant: one 1015-kW (1,360-hp)
Allison V-1710-81 V-12 piston engine
Performance: maximum speed
609 km/h (378 mph) at 3200 m
(10,500 ft); climb to 4570 m (15,000 ft) in
6.7 minutes; service ceiling 11580 m

(38,000 ft); range 386 km (240 miles)
Weights: empty 2722 kg (6,000 lb);
maximum take-off 5171 kg (11,400 lb)
Dimensions: span 11.38 m (37 ft 4 in);
length 10.16 m (33 ft 4 in); height 3.76 m
(12 ft 4 in); wing area 21.92 m²
(236.0 sq ft)
Armament: six 12.7-mm (0.5-in)
machine-guns in the wings, plus a
bombload of up to three 227-kg
(500-lb) bombs

*The P-40E, seen here in 1942, was the
first to serve extensively with the
USAAF in Europe and North Africa.
Called Kittyhawk in RAF service and
Warhawk with the American forces,
the P-40 bore the brunt of the initial
fighting in the Pacific.*

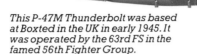

Republic P-47 Thunderbolt

Evolved from Major Alexander P. de Seversky's radial-powered **P-43**, the big **Republic P-47 Thunderbolt** was designed under the leadership of Alexander Kartveli to become one of America's three outstanding fighters of the war. First flown on 6 May 1941, the **XP-47B** was designed around the 1492-kW (2,000-hp) Pratt & Whitney R-2800 with exhaust-driven turbocharger in the rear fuselage; armament was eight 12.7-mm (0.5-in) machine-guns in the wings. 171 production **P-47B** fighters were built with minor improvements and a top speed of 691 km/h (429 mph), this version being brought to the UK in January 1943 by the 56th and 78th Fighter Groups; they were first flown in combat on 8 April that year, flying escort for B-17s. Early P-47s proved to possess poor climb and manoeuvrability, but were popular on account of their ability to survive heavy battle damage. A lengthened fuselage and provision for an under-fuselage drop tank identified the **P-47C**. The major version (of which no fewer than 12,60 were built) was the **P-47D** with water injection power boost, and cut-dow rear fuselage with 'bubble' hood on later sub-variants; P-47Ds served in the UK, the Mediterranean and the Fa East. In Burma 16 RAF squadrons flew the P-47B (as the **Thunderbolt Mk I** and P-47D (**Thunderbolt Mk II**), a tota of 826 being delivered. Developed a a result of demands for a 'sprint' version, the **P-47M** with improved turbo charger and a top speed of 762 km/h (473 mph) at 9755 m (32,000 ft) reached

This P-47M Thunderbolt was based at Boxted in the UK in early 1945. It was operated by the 63rd FS in the famed 56th Fighter Group.

Europe at the end of 1944, while the **P-47N** with blunt-tipped enlarged wing and increased fuel capacity was developed purely for service in the Pacific; a total of 1,816 was produced and these flew escort for B-29s in their raids on Japan in 1945. A total of 15,675 P-47s was produced.

Specification
Republic P-47D-25 (Thunderbolt Mk II)
Type: single-seat long-range fighter
Powerplant: one 1716-kW (2,300-hp) Pratt & Whitney R-2800-59 radial piston engine
Performance: maximum speed 689 km/h (428 mph) at 9145 m (30,000 ft); climb to 6095 m (20,000 ft) in 9.0 minutes; service ceiling 12800 m (42,000 ft); maximum range 2028 km (1,260 miles)
Weights: empty 4536 kg (10,000 lb); maximum take-off 8800 kg (19,400 lb)
Dimensions: span 12.43 m (40 ft 9½ in); length 11.01 m (36 ft 1¾ in); height 4.32 m (14 ft 2 in); wing area 27.87 m^2 (300.0 sq ft)
Armament: eight 12.7-mm (0.5-in) machine-guns in the wings, plus up to two 454-kg (1,000-lb) bombs

Fighters from the 82nd FS, 78th FG on the line after a mission over Germany in the autumn of 1944. Aircraft from this squadron claimed the first Me262 to be destroyed by the 8th Air Force on 29 August that year.

North American P-51 Mustang

One of the truly great fighters of the war, the **North American P-51 Mustang** was originally designed in 1940 to a British requirement. The prototype **NA-73** was first flown in October that year with a 820-kW (1,100-hp) Allison V-1710-F3F but, although two early aircraft were evaluated by the USAAF as **XP-51** aircraft, the type was not adopted by that air force. Most of the early aircraft were supplied to the RAF (620 aircraft as **Mustang Mk IA** and **Mustang Mk II**). Their outstanding low-level speed and range resulted in their assignment to the ground support (army co-operation) role. After the USA's entry into the war the USAAF adopted the aircraft, ordering 148 P-51s which had four 20-mm cannon (instead of four 0.5-in and four 0.3-in) wing bomb shackles in the attack category as the **A-36A**. The British in the meantime had re-engined four Mustangs with Rolls-Royce Merlins, and this expedient transformed the aircraft. In America the armament was reduced to four 12.7-mm (0.5-in) guns, all in the wings, and an 895-kW (1,200-hp) Allison V-1710-81 was used in the **P-51A**, 310 being ordered in 1942. So spectacular were the benefits of the Merlin that a Packard-built Merlin (as the V-1650) was used in the **P-51B**, of which

By the invasion of Normandy in June 1944, the Mustang was in extensive service with the USAAF. This P-51B operated out of Bottisham with the 374th FS, 361st FG, of the 8th Air Force over the invasion beaches.

1,988 were produced at Inglewood; 1,750 of the similar **P-51C** were built at Dallas, Texas. Later aircraft had the armament restored to six guns, while increased fuel capacity extended the range to a maximum of 3347 km (2,080 miles), enabling Mustangs to escort American bombers to Berlin. The **P-51D** featured a cut-down rear fuselage and 'tear-drop' canopy. The Merlin P-51 joined the RAF as the **Mustang Mk III** (P-51B and P-51C) and **Mustang Mk IV** (P-51D). Fastest of all versions was the lightened **P-51H** with a top speed of 784 km/h (487 mph), 555 being built

during the war. Total production of the P-51 was 15,586, including 7,956 P-51Ds and 1,337 generally similar **P-51K** fighters with an Aeroproducts propeller.

Specification
North American P-51D (Mustang Mk IV)
Type: single-seat long-range fighter
Powerplant: one 1112-kW (1,490-hp) Packard Rolls-Royce Merlin V-1650-7 V-12 piston engine
Performance: maximum speed 704 km/h (437 mph) at 7620 m (25,000 ft); climb to 9145 m (30,000 ft) in 13.0 minutes; service ceiling 12770 m (41,900 ft); maximum range 3347 km (2,080 miles)
Weights: empty 3232 kg (7,125 lb); maximum take-off 5262 kg (11,600 lb)
Dimensions: span 11.28 m (37 ft 0¼ in); length 9.85 m (32 ft 3¾ in); height 3.71 m (12 ft 2 in); wing area 21.65 m^2 (233.2 sq ft)
Armament: six 12.7-mm (0.5-in) machine-guns in the wings, plus provision for up to two 454-kg (1,000-lb) bombs or six 127-mm (5-in) rocket projectiles

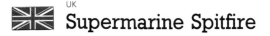

Supermarine Spitfire

Classic creation of designer R. J. Mitchell, the **Supermarine Spitfire** was the descendant of the race-winning Schneider Trophy seaplanes. First flown on 5 March 1936, the **Spitfire Mk I** with Merlin II engine and eight machine-guns entered RAF service in August 1938, this version being heavily committed to combat in the Battle of Britain. The **Spitfire Mk II** with Merlin XII followed in September 1940, the **Spitfire Mk IIB** being armed with two 20-mm guns and four machine-guns. The photo-reconnaissance **Spitfire Mk IV** was followed in March 1941 by the excellent **Spitfire Mk V** (of which 6,479 were produced) with 1074-kW (1,440-hp) Merlin 45; the **Spitfire Mk VC** fighter-bomber could carry one 227-kg (500-lb) or two 113-kg (250-lb) bombs. The **Spitfire Mk VB** remained the mainstay of Fighter Command between mid-1941 and mid-1942 when the **Spitfire Mk IX**, with 1238-kW (1,660-hp) Merlin 61 with two-stage, two-speed supercharger joined the RAF. The **Spitfire Mk VI** and **Spitfire Mk VII** were high-altitude fighters with extended wingtips, but the definitive **Spitfire Mk VIII** fighter and fighter-bomber was used principally in the Mediterranean and Far East, being fully tropicalized

The **Spitfire Mk X** and **Spitfire Mk XI** were unarmed photo-reconnaissance versions and the **Spitfire Mk XVI**, with a top speed of 652 km/h (405 mph) was produced in fighter and fighter-bomber versions. All the foregoing (of which 18,298 were built) were powered by the Rolls-Royce or Packard Merlin, and the first with 1294-kW (1,735-hp) Griffon IV was the **Spitfire Mk XII**, introduced in 1943 to counter the Fw 190 fighter-bomber. It was followed by the 1529-kW (2,050-hp) Griffon 65-powered **Spitfire Mk XIV** fighter and fighter-bomber. The fighter-reconnaissance **Spitfire Mk XVIII** was just joining the RAF at the end of the war and had a top speed of 712 km/h (442 mph). In the Fleet Air Arm **Seafire** variants also served in large numbers with both Merlin and Griffon engines. Total production of the Spitfire was 20,351, plus 2,334 Seafires.

Specification
Supermarine Spitfire Mk VB
Type: single-seat interceptor fighter
Powerplant: one 1074-kW (1,440-hp) Rolls-Royce Merlin 45/46/50 V-12 piston engine
Performance: maximum speed 602 km/h (374 mph) at 3960 m (13,000 ft); climb to 6095 m (20,000 ft) in 7.5 minutes; service ceiling 11280 m (37,000 ft); range on internal fuel 756 km (470 miles)
Weights: empty 2313 kg (5,100 lb); maximum take-off 3078 kg (6,785 lb)
Dimensions: span 11.23 m (36 ft 10 in); length 9.11 m (29 ft 11 in); height 3.48 m (11 ft 5 in); wing area 22.48 m^2 (242.0 sq ft)
Armament: two 20-mm cannon and four 7.7-mm (0.303-in) machine-guns in the wings

A Spitfire Mk VB of No. 306 (Polish) Squadron is depicted as it would have looked on Fighter Command's 'Rhubarb' sweeps over occupied France.

Two Spitfire Mk IXs are seen over Anzio in January 1944. The Mk IX was a hasty adaptation of the Mk V airframe to accept a Merlin 61 engine. Nevertheless, 5,665 were built, second in numbers only to the Mk V.

 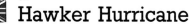

Hawker Hurricane

The first monoplane fighter and the first with a top speed of over 483 km/h (300 mph) to enter RAF service, the **Hawker Hurricane** was designed by Sydney Camm and first flown on 6 November 1935, joining the RAF in December 1937. The **Hurricane Mk I** with 768-kW (1,030-hp) Rolls-Royce Merlin II and an armament of eight 7.7-mm (0.303-in) machine-guns was Fighter Command's principal fighter in the Battle of Britain in 1940, and destroyed more enemy aircraft than all other defences combined. It was followed by the **Hurricane Mk IIA** with 955-kW (1,280-hp) Merlin XX before the end of 1940, the **Hurricane Mk IIB** with 12 machine-guns and the **Hurricane Mk IIC** with four 20-mm cannon during 1941. These versions were also able to carry up to two 227-kg (500-lb) bombs, drop tanks or other stores under the wings; they served as fighters, fighter-bombers, night-fighters, intruders and photo-reconnaissance aircraft on all fronts until 1943, and in the Far East until the end of the war. The **Hurricane**

Mk IID introduced the 40-mm anti-tank gun in 1942. Two of these weapons were carried under the wings, and this version was particularly successful in North Africa. The **Hurricane Mk IV** featured a 'universal wing' which allowed carriage of up to eight 27.2-kg (60-lb) rocket projectiles or any of the external stores carried by the Mk II. It is believed 14,231 Hurricanes were produced, including 1,451 built in Canada (**Hurricane Mks X, XI** and **XII**). This total, also included many **Sea Hurricane** models of which early versions

were catapulted from merchant ships and flown from converted merchant aircraft carriers, and later served aboard Royal Navy fleet carriers. Always regarded as somewhat slow among RAF fighters, the Hurricane was highly manoeuvrable and capable of withstanding considerable battle damage.

Specification
Hawker Hurricane Mk IIC
Type: single-seat fighter and fighter-bomber

In February 1938, Squadron Leader J. W. Gillan of No. 111 Squadron flew his then-brand-new Hurricane from Edinburgh to Northolt, averaging 657 km/h (408 mph) with a tail wind.

Powerplant: one 955-kW (1,280-hp) Rolls-Royce Merlin XX V-12 piston engine
Performance: maximum speed 541 km/h (336 mph) at 3810 m (12,500 ft); climb to 6095 m (20,000 ft) in 9.1 minutes; service ceiling 10850 m (35,600 ft); range on internal fuel

Axis Fighters

The superb fighter aircraft of Germany and Japan achieved substantial air superiority over the Allies, which greatly assisted the advance of their respective armies. By contrast, the Italians, short of first-class fighters, were rapidly outmatched.

The Luftwaffe had some superb fighter aircraft. The Messerschmitt Bf 110 (above), however, did not fare well against the RAF's Hurricanes and Spitfires and was reassigned to the fighter-bomber role; it later excelled as a night fighter.

The air forces of the three principal Axis partners, trained and equipped for wholly differing concepts of warfare, possessed fighter aircraft of widely varying qualities and capabilities at the start of World War II. Germany, whose Luftwaffe was intended mainly as a support arm of the Wehrmacht, possessed what was perhaps the world's finest fighter in 1939, the Messerschmitt Bf 109, albeit somewhat less well-armed than the Supermarine Spitfire. Moreover, it had gained a workout during the war in Spain, while the Spitfire was still hamstrung by tactical limitations. However, like the RAF's fighter, the Bf 109 underwent continuous development through World War II and remained the cornerstone of the Jagdverband (fighter arm) to the end.

Intended as a Bf 109 replacement, the Focke-Wulf Fw 190 entered service in 1941 and was roughly equivalent in concept to the RAF's Hawker Typhoon. It was infinitely superior in combat, yet was itself to become the Sturmjager (assault fighter) par excellence, being called on to take over from the highly vulnerable Junkers Ju 87 as the Wehrmacht reeled under the gigantic blows of the Red Army after Stalingrad.

Italy was particularly unfortunate during 1940 in not possessing aircraft engines comparable with the Rolls-Royce Merlin and Daimler-Benz DB 601, and had thus to make do with small air-cooled radials whose development potential was very limited, so that the early Regia Aeronautica fighters, such as the Fiat CR42 and G 50, were scarcely a match for the Hawker Hurricane and Curtiss P-40 Tomahawk against which they were ranged in Greece and the Western Desert. The Macchi C.202 was a marked improvement, but was itself two years too late to turn the tide in the Mediterranean.

In the Far East, Japan embarked on an intended two-year campaign, the basis of which was seaborne assault across the Pacific. Accordingly priority had been afforded to the development of the carrierborne fighter, of which the famous Mitsubishi A6M Zero was probably the best in the world in 1941. Even in 1943 it was capable of holding its own against Allied naval aircraft; but by then the fortunes of Japan were already on the decline and in 1944, as the Americans pushed back the enemy, there was no truly effective metropolitan-based interceptor available to combat the heavily armed and escorted Boeing B-29 bombers. Such an eventuality had never entered the Japanese war planners' minds.

Perhaps the most astonishing facet of the fighters' war was the superb quality of the German Jagdverband, with regard to the task for which it was originally intended: patrol in the skies over the battlefield. It was never envisaged that it would be employed for bomber escort (as in the Battle of Britain), or that it would be called on to defend the Reich against massed bombers. When misused, it suffered accordingly. Only by 'bolting on' special armament was the latter failing partly overcome.

A measure of the excellence of the German fighter pilot is afforded by the all-time highest scorer, Erich Hartmann: his ultimate tally of 352 accredited victories was achieved in three and a half years; of these, 260 were Allied fighters, and all were destroyed while flying the Bf 109. He himself was shot down only twice, and at the end of the war he was aged just 23.

By contrast the highest-scoring Allied pilot, a Soviet, reached a tally of 62, while the RAF's top score (gained by the South African, Pattle) was 41, a high proportion of them Italian biplanes.

Fiat CR.42 Falco

Often compared in concept and design with the Gloster Gladiator, against which it frequently fought in 1940-1, the **Fiat CR.42 Falco** (falcon) biplane did not first fly until 1939, however, and such an anachronism is difficult to understand. Employing the same Warren truss system of interplane struts as the 1933 **CR.32**, from which it was developed, Celestino Rosatelli's CR.42 was powered by a 626-kW (840-hp) Fiat A74 R1C 38 radial and had a top speed of 441 km/h (274 mph). By September 1939 the Falco equipped three *stormi* and, while the RAF was hurriedly reducing its Gladiator strength, the Regia Aeronautica was increasing its CR.42 inventory, so that when Italy entered the war in June 1940 there were 330 in service with four *stormi* in the Mediterranean plus two *squadriglie* in Italian East Africa. The Falco first saw combat in the brief French campaign, and later 50 aircraft accompanied the Corpo Aereo Italiano to bases in Belgium for attacks on southern England at the end of the Battle of Britain, suffering heavily to the guns of RAF Hurricanes. In the Middle East the Falco fared better, however, being more of a match for the widely-used Gladiator; during the Greek campaign one *gruppo* of three CR.42 *squadriglie* was committed and, except on a few occasions, acquitted itself well; but when Hawker Hurricanes eventually arrived the Italian biplane losses mounted steadily. In East Africa 51 crated CR.42s were received to supplement the 36 aircraft delivered to the 412ª and 413ª Squadriglie, but in due course they were destroyed in the air or on the ground, although they took a heavy toll of the antiquated aircraft of the RAF and SAAF. In the Western Desert CR.42 fighters were joined by the **CR.42AS** fighter-bomber version adapted to carry two 100-kg (220-lb) bombs, and these continued in service with the 5°, 15° and 50° Stormi Assalti until November 1942. A total of 1,781 CR.42s was built (some serving in Sweden and Hungary), but at the time of the Italian armistice in September 1943 only 64 remained serviceable.

Specification
Fiat CR.42 Falco

Spanish Civil War experience led the Italian air ministry to believe there was still a role for the biplane fighter, but the anachronistic CR.42 proved to be disagreeably vulnerable to enemy monoplanes.

CR.42s committed to the Battle of Britain suffered heavy casualties, but they enjoyed a brief period of success over Greece and Libya.

Type: single-seat fighter
Powerplant: one 626-kW (840-hp) Fiat A74 R1C 38 radial piston engine
Performance: maximum speed 441 km/h (274 mph) at 6000 m (19,685 ft); climb to 6000 m (19,685 ft) in 9.0 minutes; service ceiling 10100 m (33,136 ft); range 780 km (485 miles)
Weights: empty 1784 kg (3,933 lb); maximum take-off 2295 kg (5,060 lb)
Dimensions: span 9.70 m (31 ft 9.9 in); length 8.26 m (27 ft 1.2 in); height 3.05 m (10 ft 0.1 in); wing area 22.40 m² 241.1 sq ft
Armament: two 12.7-mm (0.5-in) Breda-SAFAT machine-guns in nose (some aircraft with two extra 12.7-mm/ 0.5-in machine-guns under lower wing), plus provision for two 100-kg (220-lb) bombs

Italy's CR.42s soldiered on through 1942 despite suffering mounting losses. The type was also exported to Belgium, where they were quickly destroyed during the German invasion, and to Hungary, which used them against Yugoslavia and in the 1941 Russian campaign.

Fiat G.50 Freccia

Representing the first design essay of the young technician Giuseppe Gabrielli with the Fiat company, the **Fiat G.50** fighter was designed in 1935-6 but, although a break from the traditional biplane formula, offered much less in operational potential than the contemporary Hawker Hurricane and Messerschmitt Bf 109. The prototype G.50 first flew on 26 February 1937 and was the first all-metal monoplane with constant-speed propeller and retractable landing gear to be evaluated by the Regia Aeronautica. Named **Freccia** (arrow), the G.50 was ordered into production with the CMASA company (a subsidiary of Fiat) and 12 of the first aircraft were sent to Spain for operational evaluation. Despite the superiority of the Macchi C.200, it was decided to go ahead and equip one *stormo* and one *gruppo* with the G.50, and an initial order for 200 aircraft was placed. In November 1939 the type was delivered to the 51° Stormo, and

soon afterwards to the 52° Stormo, and when Italy entered the war in the following June 118 Freccias were in service. In November 1940 48 G.50s of the 51° Stormo moved to Belgium to take part in the air attacks on the UK; however, they saw little action, being principally engaged in 'surveillance' duties. In September that year the prototype of a new version, the **G.50bis**, had flown, and with improved cockpit armour and increased fuel this entered production for eventual service with

five *gruppi* in North Africa. With a maximum speed of only 460 km/h (286 mph) and an armament of two machine-guns, the G.50 was hardly a match for RAF fighters in the Mediterranean, yet survived in service until July 1943. Production eventually reached 245 G.50 and 421 G.50bis fighters, and 108 of a dual-control two-seat trainer, the **G.50B**. G.50s were also supplied to the Croatian and Finnish air forces.

Specification
Fiat G.50 Freccia
Type: single-seat fighter

Powerplant: one 626-kW (840-hp) Fiat A74RC 38 radial piston engine
Performance: maximum speed 460 km/h (286 mph) at 4000 m (13,123 ft); climb to 4000 m (13,123 ft) in 4.6 minutes; service ceiling 10750 m (35,269 ft); range 580 km (360 miles)
Weights: empty 1965 kg (4,332 lb); maximum take-off 2400 kg (5,291 lb)
Dimensions: span 11.00 m (36 ft 1.1 in); length 7.80 m (25 ft 7.1 in); height 3.28 m (10 ft 9.1 in); wing area 18.25 m² (196.45 sq ft)
Armament: two nose-mounted 12.7-mm (0.5-in) Breda-SAFAT machine-guns

A Fiat G.50bis of 20 Gruppo, 51 Stormo based at Ursel, Belgium, in October 1940. Lack of range and poor armament severely restricted the type's participation in the Battle of Britain.

Fiat G.55 Centauro

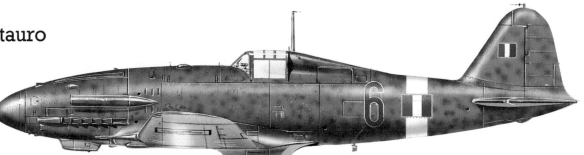

The Fiat G.55 Centauro (centaur) was an all-metal low-wing monoplane single-seat fighter designed by Giuseppe Gabrielli, and represented a great improvement by comparison with the previous Fiat monoplane fighter to go into production, the G.50. Great care was taken to blend an aerodynamically advanced airframe with a structure which was robust and would lend itself to mass production. Its configuration included fully-retractable landing gear and a raised cockpit providing an excellent view. Fast and maneouvrable, the type proved popular with its pilots.

The first of three prototypes was flown on 30 April 1942; the third (MM 493) was the only one to carry armament, comprising one engine-mounted cannon and four fuselage-mounted machine-guns. It was evaluated under operational conditions from March 1943, but by then the Italian air ministry had already decided on mass production of the G.55. However, only 16 **G.55/0** pre-production and 15 **G.55/I** initial production aircraft had been delivered to the Regia Aeronautica by September 1943, production thereafter being for

the Fascist air arm flying alongside the Luftwaffe. Before wartime production ended 274 more were completed and a further 37 were abandoned at an advanced construction stage.

Before the armistice of September 1943, G.55s had participated in the defence of Rome with the 353ª Squadriglia of the Regia Aeronautica. The post-armistice operations were mainly with the Fascist air arm's Squadriglia 'Montefusco', based at Venezia Reale, then with the three *squadriglie* which formed the 2° Gruppo Caccia Terrestre, but losses were heavy, as a result mainly of Allied attacks on the airfields. While the war was still in progress, Fiat flew two prototypes of the **G.56**, which was developed from the G.55 to accept the more powerful Daimler-Benz DB

The main users of the Fiat G.55 were the squadrons of the Fascist Air Arm. This example belonged to Squadriglia 'Montefusco'.

603A engine. Built during the spring of 1944, they incorporated minor structural changes and had the fuselage-mounted machine-guns deleted. The first prototype survived the war and was used subsequently by Fiat as a test-bed.

Specification
Fiat G.55/I
Type: single-seat fighter
Powerplant: one 1100-kW (1,475-hp) Fiat RA 1050 RC-58 Tifone (licence-built DB 605A) 12-cylinder inverted-Vee piston engine
Performance: maximum speed 630 km/h (391 mph); climb to 6000 m

(19,685 ft) in 7 minutes 12 seconds; service ceiling 12700 m (41,667 ft); range 1200 km (746 miles)
Weights: empty equipped 2630 kg (5,798 lb); maximum take-off 3718 kg (8,197 lb)
Dimensions: span 11.85 m (38 ft 10.5 in); length 9.37 m (30 ft 8.9 in); height 3.13 m (10 ft 3.2 in); wing area 21.11 m² (227.23 sq ft)
Armament: one 20-mm Mauser MG 151/20 engine-mounted cannon, two similar wing-mounted cannon, and two fuselage-mounted 12.7-mm (0.5-in) Breda-SAFAT machine-guns, plus provision for two 160-kg (353-lb) bombs on underwing racks

Macchi C.200 Saetta

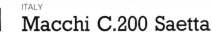

Handicapped by Italy's pre-war lack of a powerful engine suitable for fighters, Mario Castoldi's radial-powered **Fiat C.200** was so underpowered and undergunned that when it arrived in service in 1939 it was already outclassed by the Hawker Hurricane which had joined the RAF two years earlier. Indeed the first C.200 unit, the 4° Stormo, expressed a preference for the CR.42 and accordingly reverted to the biplane in 1940. First flown on 24 December 1937 by Giuseppe Burei, the C.200, named the **Saetta** (lightning), went on to equip the 1°, 2°, 3°, 4° (in mid-1941) and 54° Stormi, and the 8°, 12°, 13°, 21° and 22° Gruppi, a total of about 1,200 aircraft being produced by Macchi, Breda and SAI Ambrosini. On the date that Italy entered the war, 10 June 1940, two home-based *stormi* were combat-ready with the C.200, being first flown in action over Malta in September that year, and it was largely the losses suffered by the Italian fighter arm at this time and during the Greek campaign that prompted the Luftwaffe to deploy X Fliegerkorps in the Mediterranean to bolster the Regia Aeronautica's flagging resources. C.200s were heavily committed in North Africa, and were fairly evenly matched with the early Hurricane Mk Is, weighed down by tropical air filters, but the attrition suffered by all Italian air force units (principally through poor serviceability and air attacks on their airfields) quickly reduced the number of C.200s. Some 51 Saettas of the 22° Gruppo operated in the Odessa zone of the Eastern Front from August 1941 onwards, proving capable of

matching the older Soviet fighters in the early stages of that campaign. By the time of the Italian armistice in September 1943, however, the Regia Aeronautica's total inventory of serviceable C.200s stood at only 33.

Specification
Macchi C.200 Saetta (Breda-built Series 6)
Type: single-seat fighter/fighter-

The 649-kW (870-hp) engine was fitted to the Macchi C.200 against the wishes of the designer Castoldi, and handicapped the aircraft in action with more powerful opponents such as the Hurricane and Kittyhawk.

bomber
Powerplant: one 649-kW (870-hp) Fiat A 74 RC 38 radial piston engine
Performance: maximum speed 504 km/h (313 mph) at 4500 m (14,764 ft); climb to 4000 m (13,123 ft) in 4.55 minutes; service ceiling 8900 m (29,199 ft); range 570 km (354 miles)
Weights: empty 1960 kg (4,321 lb);

maximum take-off 2395 kg (5,280 lb)
Dimensions: span 10.58 m (34 ft 8.5 in); length 8.25 m (27 ft 0.8 in); height 3.05 m (10 ft 0.1 in); wing area 16.80 m² (180.8 sq ft)
Armament: two 12.7-mm (0.5-in) Breda-SAFAT machine-guns in nose, plus provision for two 150-kg (331-lb) bombs

The C.200 Saettas saw their first combat over Malta in 1940 and were subsequently deployed to North Africa, where they held their own against Hurricane Mk Is encumbered by tropical air filters. But their numbers were rapidly reduced by poor maintenance and British air attacks.

ITALY

Macchi C.202 Folgore

One of the best Italian fighters of the mid-war years, Mario Castoldi's **Macchi C.202 Folgore** (thunderbolt) was developed from the radial-engined C.200, but was powered by a Daimler-Benz DB 601 produced under licence as the Alfa Romeo RA 1000 RC 411. First flown by Carestiato on 10 August 1940, the **C.202 Series 1** production version entered service with the 1° Stormo at Udine in the summer of 1941, this unit arriving in Libya in the following November. The Folgore was a low-wing monoplane with inward-retracting landing gear and an armament of two 12.7-mm (0.5-in) Breda-SAFAT machine-guns in the nose; there was also provision for two 7.7-mm (0.303-in) guns in the wings. Engine production was slow and severely delayed the build-up of the Folgore in service.

The aircraft underwent very little change and development during its life span, and was produced in 11 series. It eventually served with 45 *Squadriglie* of the 1°, 2°, 3°, 4°, 51°, 52°, 53° and 54° Stormi in North Africa, Sicily, Italy, the Aegean and Russia. Production amounted to about 1,500, of which 392 were produced by the parent company and the remainder by Breda. In combat the Folgore proved to be well-matched with the Supermarine Spitfire Mk V in performance, but was badly undergunned and, although slightly superior to American fighters such as the Bell P-39 Airacobra, this armament deficiency prevented Folgore pilots from knocking down many Allied bombers.

Ultimate wartime development of the C.200/202 series of Italian fighters was the Daimler Benz-powered **C.205**; only 66 were in service by the time of Italy's withdrawal from the Axis. The **C.205V Veltro** (greyhound) would have been capable of meeting most Allied fighters on equal terms.

Macchi C.202 Serie III Folgore of 378ª Squadriglia, 155° Gruppo, 51° Stormo. The C.202 was the most effective of the Italian fighters but suffered from lack of armament.

The ultimate production Macchi fighter was the C.205 Veltro, exemplified here by an aircraft of 1ª Squadriglia, 1° Gruppo.

Specification
Macchi C.202 Series IX Folgore
Type: single-seat fighter
Powerplant: one 802-kW (1,075-hp) Alfa Romeo RA 1000 RC 411 12-cylinder inverted-Vee piston engine
Performance: maximum speed 600 km/h (373 mph) at 5600 m (18,373 ft); climb to 5000 m (16,404 ft) in 4.6 minutes; service ceiling 11500 m (37,730 ft); range 610 km (379 miles)
Weights: empty 2490 kg (5,490 lb); maximum take-off 2930 kg (6,460 lb)
Dimensions: span 10.58 m (34 ft 8.5 in); length 8.85 m (29 ft 0.4 in); height 3.50 m (11 ft 5.8 in); wing area 16.80 m² (180.8 sq ft)
Armament: two 12.7-mm (0.5-in) Breda-SAFAT machine-guns in the nose, plus provision for two 7.7-mm (0.303-in) guns in the wings

This C.202 was captured in Italy and transported to Wright-Patterson Field at Dayton, Ohio, for evaluation.

C.202s saw action in North Africa, Italy and on the Eastern Front.

ITALY

Reggiane Re.2000 series

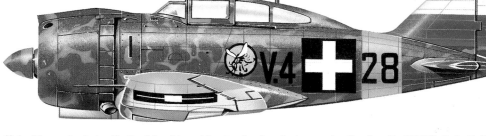

Officine Meccaniche Reggiane SA began development of a single-seat fighter which was based very closely on the US Seversky Aircraft Corporation's P-35 designed by Alexander Kartveli. Competitive evaluation against the Macchi MC.200 resulted in this latter aircraft being ordered into production for the Regia Aeronautica, although the **Reggiane Re.2000** had shown itself to be superior in manoeuvrability, even when flown against the Messerschmitt Bf 109E. The type was ordered by the Hungarian government, which also acquired a manufacturing licence. Re.2000s were supplied also to Sweden, being operated until 1945 by the Flygvapen under the designation **J 20**. And though rejected by the Regia Aeronautica, the Italian navy acquired 12 **Re.2000 Serie II** fighters especially strengthened for catapult launching, followed by 24 **Re.2000 Serie III** aircraft with increased fuel capacity for deployment as long-range fighters.

Installation of the Daimler-Benz DB 601A-1 engine led to the **Re.2001 Falco II**, first used operationally by the Regia Aeronautica over Malta in 1942. Luftwaffe priorities for DB 601 engines meant that the Re.2001 had to be powered by a licence-built version of this engine, the Alfa Romeo RA.1000 RC

41-1a Monsonie, but with the Macchi MC.202 having first call on production of these engines the manufacture of Re.2001s was limited to only 252.

About 50 **Re.2002 Ariete** (ram) fighter-bombers followed for service with the Regia Aeronautica, these being powered by the 876-kW (1,175-hp) Piaggio P.XIX RC 45 radial engine mounted in a slightly lengthened and strengthened fuselage. The type first saw operational service in 1942, suffering heavy losses while contesting the Allied landings on Sicily. Last of this related family of fighters, and one of the best produced in Italy during World War II, the **Re.2005 Sagittario** (archer) had the same general configuration as its predecessors. However, its design incorporated consider-

able structural redesign, and refined landing gear, and the type reverted to the inline engine. First flown in September 1942 with a Daimler-Benz DB 605A-1, the Re.2005 led to a production model, of which deliveries began in 1943, with a licence-built version of this engine, the Fiat RA.1050 RC 58 Tifone. Only 48 had been delivered before finalisation of the armistice with the Allies, these aircraft fighting in the defence of Naples, Rome and Sicily, the survivors battling above the crumbling ruins of Berlin.

Specification
Reggiane Re.2005 Sagittario
Type: single-seat fighter/fighter-bomber
Powerplant: one 1100-kW (1,475-hp)

Re.2000 Hejja I of 1./1 Szazad, Önallo Vadász Ostály (Independent Fighter Group) attached to the Hungarian army fighting in the USSR in 1942.

Fiat RA.1050 RC 58 Tifone 12-cylinder inverted Vee piston engine
Performance: maximum speed 630 km/h (391 mph) at 6950 m (22,802 ft); climb to 2000 m (6,562 ft) in 1.58 minutes; service ceiling 12190 m (39,993 ft); range 1265 km (786 miles)
Weights: empty 2600 kg (5,732 lb); maximum take-off 3560 kg (7,848 lb)
Dimensions: span 11.00 m (36 ft 1.1 in); length 8.73 m (28 ft 7.7 in); height 3.15 m (10 ft 4 in); wing area 20.40 m² (219.59 sq ft)

Reggiane Re.2001 of the 362ª Squadriglia, 22° Gruppo, 52° Stormo at Capodichino in May 1943. The DB 601 engine was licence-built by Alfa Romeo.

Armament: three 20-mm cannon and two 12.7-mm (0.5-in) machine-guns, all forward-firing, plus up to 630 kg (1,389 lb) of bombs when operated as a fighter-bomber

Focke-Wulf Fw 190

Proposed in 1937, as the Bf 109 was joining the Luftwaffe, Kurt Tank's **Focke-Wulf Fw 190** surprisingly featured a large air-cooled BMW radial engine. First flown on 1 June 1939, the prototype was followed by short- and long-span pre-production **Fw 190A-0** aircraft with BMW 801 14-cylinder radials. The long-span version was selected for production. **Fw 190A-1** fighters joined the Luftwaffe in mid-1941 and proved superior to the Spitfire Mk V. A-series variations included the **Fw 190A-3** with BMW 801D-2 and two 7.92-mm (0.31-in) and four 20-mm guns, the **Fw 190A-4** with water-methanol power-boosting (with fighter-bomber, bomber-destroyer and tropicalized sub-variants). The **Fw 190A-5** featured a slightly lengthened nose and sub-variants included versions with six 30-mm guns (A-5/U12) and torpedo-fighters (A-5/U14 and U15). The **Fw 190A-7** and **Fw 190A-8** entered production in December 1943 and featured increased armament and armour. The **Fw 190A-8/U1** was a two-seat conversion trainer. The next main production version, the **Fw 190D**, featured a lengthened nose and Junkers Jumo 213 liquid-cooled engine in an annular cowling. The **Fw 190D-9** was the main service version, which joined the Luftwaffe in the autumn of 1944, and was generally regarded as Germany's best wartime piston-engine fighter; with a top speed of 685 km/h (426 mph), it was armed with two cannon and two machine-guns, and was powered by a water-methanol boosted 1670-kW (2,240-hp) Jumo 213A engine. Other late versions included the **Fw 190F** and **Fw 190G** specialized ground-attack fighter-bombers capable of carrying up to 1800 kg (3,968 lb) of bombs.

A development of the Fw 190D was the long-span **Focke-Wulf Ta 152** with increased armament and boosted Jumo 213E/B (top speed 760 km/h; 472 mph at 12500 m/41,010 ft); a small number of **Ta 152H-1** fighters reached the Luftwaffe shortly before the end of the war.

Specification
Focke-Wulf 190A-8
Type: single-seat fighter
Powerplant: one 1566-kW (2,100-hp) BMW 801D-2 radial piston engine with water-methanol boosting
Performance: maximum speed 654 km/h (406 mph) at 6000 m

The Fw 190G-2 was a specialized ground attack version with wing racks for bombs or tanks, and an ETC 501 centreline rack for a 1800-kg (3,968-lb) bomb (in this case an SC 500 500-kg/1,102-lb bomb is carried). Strengthened landing gear was necessary for the heaviest load.

The Focke-Wulf Fw 190 was outnumbered on the Eastern Front by the Messerschmitt Bf 109G. This Fw 190A-5 flew with II/JG 54 'Grünherz' at Petseri in Estonia during 1944.

Above: Carrying 'Defence of the Reich' fuselage bands, this Fw 190A-9 flew with I/JG 6 at Delmenhorst in the winter of 1944-5.

Below: Fw 190D-9 ('Dora-9') of Stab/ JG 4, based at Babenhausen in early 1945 for the defence of the Reich.

(19,685 ft); initial climb rate 720 m (2,362 ft) per minute; service ceiling 11400 m (37,402 ft); normal range 805 km (500 miles)
Weights: empty 3170 kg (6,989 lb);

maximum take-off 4900 kg (10,803 lb)
Dimensions: span 10.50 m (34 ft 5.4 in); length 8.84 m (29 ft 0 in); height 3.96 m (13 ft 0 in); wing area 18.30 m² (196.99 sq ft)

Armament: two 7.92-mm (0.31-in) guns in nose and up to four 20-mm guns in wings, plus provision for wide range of underfuselage and underwing bombs, guns and rockets

Messerschmitt Bf 110

Germany's first essay in the twin-engined two-seat 'heavy fighter' (or *Zerstörer*, destroyer) category was the **Messerschmitt Bf 110**, conceived in 1934 and first flown on 12 May 1936; pre-production Bf 110A-0 fighters followed in 1937-8 with Junkers Jumo 210B engines. Production started with the **Bf 110B** in 1938 with Jumo 210Gs and forward armament of two 20-mm and four 7.92-mm (0.31-in) guns plus one 7.92-mm (0.31-in) gun in the rear cockpit. Daimler-Benz DB 601A-powered **Bf 110C** aircraft joined the Luftwaffe in 1939 in time for the attack on Poland, and were employed as fighters and fighter-bombers throughout 1940; the **Bf 110C-5** was a reconnaissance version.

The long-range **Bf 110D** entered service in 1940, and sub-variants were the first Bf 110s to be employed as night-fighters; there were also tropicalized and fighter-bomber versions. The **Bf 110E** fighter-bomber was powered by DB 601Ns and the **Bf 110F** by DB 601Es.

Despite its high top speed, the Bf 110 was quickly shown to be no match for opposing single-engine fighters, and from 1941 development was confined mainly to ground-attack and night-fighter versions. The **Bf 110F-4** introduced two 30-mm guns under the fuselage, and the **Bf 110F-4/U1** featured twin upward-firing 20-mm guns (*schräge Musik* installation). The **Bf**

This Bf 110E-1 was flown by an operational conversion unit (Ergänzungszerstörergruppe) from Deblin-Irena in Poland during 1942.

110G with DB 605Bs was produced in *Zerstörer*, fighter-bomber, reconnaissance and night-fighter versions, and sub-variants introduced the 37-mm gun under the fuselage. Radar-equipped Bf 110Gs formed the principal night-fighter equipment of the Luftwaffe between 1943 and 1945, as well as participating in the daylight air defence battles over Germany during this period.

Flown by Luftwaffe crews, several Bf 110D-3s of 4./ZG 76 supported Iraqi insurgent forces in May 1941. Tanks were carried for extra range.

Specification
Messerschmitt Bf 110C-4
Type: two-seat heavy fighter
Powerplant: two 820-kW (1,100-hp) Daimler-Benz DB 601A 12-cylinder inverted-Vee piston engines
Performance: maximum speed 560 km/h (348 mph) at 7000 m (22,966 ft); initial climb rate 660 m (2,165 ft) per minute; service ceiling 10000 m (32,808 ft); normal range 775 km (482 miles)

Weights: empty 5200 kg (11,464 lb); maximum take-off 6750 kg (14,881 lb)
Dimensions: span 16.27 m (53 ft 4.6 in); length 12.65 m (41 ft 6 in); height 3.50 m (11 ft 5.8 in); wing area 38.40 m^2 (413.3 sq ft)
Armament: two 20-mm MG FF cannon and four 7.92-mm (0.31-in) MG 17 guns in the nose, firing forward, and one 7.92-mm (0.31-in) MG 15 machine-gun on trainable mounting in the rear cockpit firing aft

Bf 110s were at their best operating at high altitude away from the restrictions of having to escort bombers.

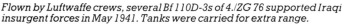

After the debacle over Britain, the Bf 110 was switched to other theatres such as the Mediterranean, where its heavy armament proved useful.

Kawanishi N1K1 Shiden

In 1941 Kawanishi was still engaged in design of an attractive float-equipped fighter, the **Kawanishi N1K1**, intended as a naval fighter to support an island-hopping conquest in the Pacific without dependence on carriers or shore bases; in due course 98 of these fighters (Allied reporting name **'Rex'**) were produced. However, while their design was still in progress Kawanishi undertook a wheel-landing gear version, designated the **N1K1-J Shiden** (violet lightning). The prototype of the new fighter was flown on 27 December 1942 powered by the new 18-cylinder Nakajima Homare radial. Production got under way in 1943 of the N1K1-J with Homare 21 radial and an armament of two 7.7-mm (0.303-in) nose guns and four 20-mm wing cannon (two of which were carried in underwing fairings). Despite being plagued by constant engine troubles and an inherently weak landing gear, the Shiden was an excellent aircraft in

combat, proving an equal match for the Grumman F6F Hellcat; given the reporting name **'George'** by the Allies, it was widely considered to be one of Japan's best wartime fighters. Three other main production versions were produced: the **N1K1-Ja** with nose guns deleted and all cannon mounted inside the wings; the **N1K1-Jb** with underwing racks for two 250-kg (551-lb) bombs; and the **N1K1-Jc** with racks for four 250-kg (551-lb) bombs. A new version, the **N1K2-J**, with improved landing gear, redesigned airframe structure and cleaner engine cowling, appeared during the last year of the war and proved even better than the N1K1; an instance occurred when a single Japanese pilot, Warrant Officer Kinsuke Muto, fought off 12 Hellcats, shooting down four. A total of 1,435 N1K Shiden landplane fighters was produced.

Specification
Kawanishi N1K1-J
Type: single-seat fighter
Powerplant: one 1484-kW (1,990-hp) Nakajima NK9H Homare 21 radial

piston engine
Performance: maximum speed 584 km/h (363 mph) at 5900 m (19,357 ft); climb to 6000 m (19,685 ft) in 7.8 minutes; service ceiling 12500 m (41,010 ft); range 1432 km (890 miles)
Weights: empty 2897 kg (6,387 lb); maximum take-off 4321 kg (9,526 lb)
Dimensions: span 12.00 m (39 ft 4.4 in); length 8.89 m (29 ft 2 in); height 4.06 m (13 ft 3.8 in); wing area 23.50 m^2 (252.95 sq ft)
Armament: two 7.7-mm (0.303-in) Type 97 machine-guns in nose and four wing-mounted 20-mm Type 99 cannon

Kawanishi N1K2-J Shiden of the 343rd Kokutai. The type gave a good account of itself despite niggling early problems.

Kawasaki Ki-61 Hien

Sometimes described as a cross between a Messerschmitt Bf 109 and a North American P-51 Mustang, the **Kawasaki Ki-61** certainly had the distinctive nose shape associated with an inverted V-12 inline engine, the Kawasaki Ha-40 being in effect a Daimler-Benz DB 601A built under licence. The Ki-61's designers, Takeo Doi and Shin Owada, had moreover worked under the German Richard Vogt. In December 1940 they were instructed to go ahead with the Ki-61, and one year later the prototype was flown. The first production **Ki-61-I** fighters were deployed operationally in April 1943 when the 68th and 78th Sentais arrived in New Guinea. Named **Hien** (swallow) in service (and codenamed 'Tony' by the Allies), the new aircraft proved popular with its pilots, being unusually well-armed and armoured, and the type was at least a match for opposing American fighters. Its armament (of four 12.7-mm/0.5-in machine-guns) proved inadequate to knock down enemy bombers, however, and the **Ki-61-I KAIc** was introduced with a pair of 20-mm cannon in the nose, these being replaced in a small number of **Ki-61-I KAId** fighters by two 30-mm cannon. The Ki-61-I and Ki-61-I KAI remained in production until 1945, but in 1944 they were joined in service by the **Ki-61-II** with more powerful Kawasaki Ha-140 engine (producing 1119-kW/1,500-hp); with a top speed of 610 km/h (379 mph) this would have been an excellent fighter but for constant engine problems; yet when fully serviceable the Ki-61-II was one of the few Japanese fighters fully able to combat the Boeing B-29 at its normal operating altitude, particularly when armed with four 20-mm cannon. Excluding prototypes and development aircraft, production totalled 1,380 Ki-61-Is, 1,274 Ki-61-I KAIs and 374 Ki-61-IIs.

The Ki-61 was one of few Japanese fighters that could really take on the B-29s at their operating altitude.

This Ki-61-I KAIc served with the 3rd Chutai, 19th Sentai flying from Okinawa during the American attack on that island.

Ki-61-I KAIc of the HQ Chutai, 244th Sentai, Chofu, Tokyo, flying interception sorties against the B-29.

Specification
Kawasaki Ki-61-I KAIc
Type: single-seat fighter
Powerplant: one 880-kW (1,180-hp) Kawasaki Ha-40 V-12 piston engine
Performance: maximum speed 590 km/h (367 mph) at 4260 m (13,976 ft); climb to 5000 m (16,404 ft) in 7.0 minutes; service ceiling 10000 m (32,808 ft); range 1800 km (1,118 miles)
Weights: empty 2630 kg (5,798 lb); normal loaded 3470 kg (7,650 lb)
Dimensions: span 12.00 m (39 ft 4.4 in); length 8.94 m (29 ft 4 in); height 3.70 m (12 ft 1.7 in); wing area 20.00 m² (215.3 sq ft)
Armament: two 20-mm Ho-5 cannon in nose and two 12.7-mm (0.5-in) Type 1 machine-guns in wings

Kawasaki Ki-100

The Kawasaki Ki-61-II with the company's Ha-140 engine was seen as an interim high-altitude interceptor to tackle the USAF's Boeing B-29s at their cruising altitude of some 9144 m (30,000 ft). However, development of the Ha-140 as a reliable powerplant was terminated finally when the Akashi factory where the engine was built was destroyed during an air raid. With the requirement becoming daily more urgent, Kawasaki was instructed to convert the 275 Ki-61-II airframes gathering dust in the Kagamigahara factory with alternative powerplant. No other similar engine was available and adaptation of the slender fuselage of the Ki-61 to allow installation of a large-diameter radial engine at first appeared impractical. However, Kawasaki's design team converted three airframes to serve as prototypes, installing a Mitsubishi Ha-112-II engine which had the same power output as the unreliable Ha-140. When the first of these was flown, on 1 February 1945, Kawasaki discovered that it had a first-class fighter, one that some commentators have described as Japan's premier fighter aircraft of the Pacific war. By the end of May 1945 all of the remaining 272 Ki-61 airframes had been converted to the new configuration, entering service as the Army Type 5 Fighter Model 1A, which was identified by the company as the **Kawasaki Ki-100-Ia**.

With the Ki-100 proving such a success, it was decided to initiate production of this aircraft, the resulting **Ki-100-Ib** differing only by having the cut-down rear fuselage and all-round-view canopy that had been designed for the proposed Ki-61-III. A total of 99 of this version was built before production was brought to an end by the growing weight of USAAF air attacks. A more effective version had been planned, to be powered by the Mitsubishi Ha-112-IIru engine which incorporated a turbocharger to improve high-altitude performance, but only three of these **Ki-100-II** prototypes had been built and flown by the end of the war.

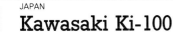

The Ki-100-Ib introduced a cut-down rear fuselage over the original Ki-61 shape, which improved pilot vision. This aircraft is from the 3rd Chutai, 59th Sentai.

Specification
Kawasaki Ki-100-Ia/b
Type: single-seat interceptor fighter
Powerplant: one 1119-kW (1,500-hp) Mitsubishi Ha-112-II 14-cylinder radial piston engine
Performance: maximum speed 590 km/h (367 mph) at 10000 m (32,810 ft); climb to 10000 m (32,810 ft) in 20 minutes; cruising speed 350 km/h (217 mph); service ceiling 10670 m (35,007 ft); range 2000 km (1,243 miles)
Weights: 2700 kg (5,952 lb); maximum take-off 3670 kg (8,091 lb)
Dimensions: span 12.00 m (39 ft 4.4 in); length 8.80 m (28 ft 10.5 in); height 3.75 m (12 ft 3.6 in); wing area 20.00 m² (215.3 sq ft)
Armament: two fuselage-mounted 12.7-mm (0.5-in) Ho-103 (Type 1) machine-guns and two wing-mounted 20-mm Ho-5 cannon, plus two drop-tanks or two 250-kg (551-lb) bombs

Mitsubishi J2M Raiden

Although designed to a 1939 requirement, at a time when Japanese war leaders scarcely imagined a situation requiring a home defence fighter, the **Mitsubishi J2M Raiden** (thunderbolt) only came into its own while defending the Japanese homeland against American raids in the last year of the war. The Japanese navy's emphasis upon speed and climb rate, rather than its customary demands for range and manoeuvrability, prompted the designer Jiro Hirikoshi to adopt a squat single-engine design with long-chord radial engine cowling, laminar-flow wings and high-raked, curved windscreen. First flight of the prototype **J2M1** took place on 20 March 1942, but the aircraft soon attracted criticism from navy pilots on numerous counts, not least that the view from the cockpit was inadequate. Modifications to rectify these shortcomings were delayed owing to Mitsubishi's preoccupation with the A6M. Production **J2M2** fighters left the factory slowly and entered service with the 381st Kokutai late in 1943,

and were followed by the **J2M3** with a stronger wing stressed to mount four 20-mm cannon. The heavier armament now restricted the performance of the Raiden to the extent that it no longer met the original demands, and the **J2M4** was an attempt to restore the performance by including a turbocharger. The final production variant, the **J2M5** (34 built), was powered by a 1357-kW (1,820-hp) Mitsubishi Kasei 26a radial. In all, 476 J2Ms were built. In acknowledgement of the fact that J2Ms could not combat the Boeing B-29s at their operating altitudes, some J2M3s were armed with two upward-firing 20-mm

cannon in addition to their wing guns. (The Allies selected the reporting name **'Jack'** for the J2M.)

Specification
Mitsubishi J2M3
Type: single-seat fighter
Powerplant: one 1342-kW (1,800-hp) Mitsubishi Kasei 23a radial piston engine
Performance: maximum speed 588 km/h (365 mph) at 5300 m (17,388 ft); climb to 10000 m (32,808 ft)

Conceived as a fast-climbing interceptor, the J2M suffered from reliability problems but scored well against the American bombers.

in 19.5 minutes; service ceiling 11700 m (38,386 ft); range 925 km (575 miles)
Weights: empty 2460 kg (5,423 lb); normal loaded 3435 kg (7,573 lb)
Dimensions: span 10.80 m (35 ft 5.2 in); length 9.95 m (32 ft 7.7 in); height 3.95 m (12 ft 11.5 in); wing area 20.05 m² (215.82 sq ft)
Armament: four wing-mounted 20-mm Type 99 cannon; some aircraft were also armed with two upward-firing 20-mm Type 99 cannon.

Nakajima Ki-27

Nakajima Ki-27 of the 3rd Chutai, 64th Sentai, based at Chiangmai in Thailand in March 1942. Ki-27s were quickly replaced by Ki-43s.

When in mid-1935 Kawasaki, Mitsubishi and Nakajima were instructed by the Imperial Japanese Army to build competitive prototypes of advanced fighter aircraft, Nakajima responded with a single-seat monoplane fighter derived from the company's Type P.E., which it had started to develop as a private venture. Service trials proved the Kawasaki Ki-28 to be fastest of the three contenders, but the **Nakajima Ki-27** was by far the most manoeuvrable and, on that basis, 10 pre-production examples were ordered for further service evaluation. Following further testing in late 1937 the type was ordered into production as the Army Type 97 Fighter Model A (**Nakajima Ki-27a**). Late production aircraft which introduced some refinements, including a further improved cockpit canopy, had the designation **Ki-27b**.

Nakajima could not have guessed that 3,399 aircraft would be built, by Nakajima (2,020) and Mansyu (1,379), before production came to a halt at the end of 1942, but the type's entry into service over northern China in March 1938 gave an immediate appreciation of its capability, the Ki-27s becoming masters of the airspace until confronted later by the faster Soviet Polikarpov I-16 fighters. At the beginning of the Pacific war the Ki-27s took part in the invasion of Burma, Malaya, the Netherlands East Indies and the Philippines. Allocated the Allied codename **'Nate'** (initially **'Abdul'** in the China-Burma-India theatre), the Ki-27 had

considerable success against the Allies in the initial stages before more modern fighters became available. When this occurred they were transferred for air defence of the home islands, remaining deployed in this capacity until 1943 when they became used increasingly as advanced trainers. As with many Japanese aircraft, their final use was in a *kamikaze* role.

Specification
Nakajima Ki-27a
Type: single-seat fighter
Powerplant: one 529-kW (710-hp) Nakajima Ha-1b 9-cylinder radial piston engine

Performance: maximum speed 470 km/h (292 mph) at 3500 m (11,483 ft); climb to 5000 m (16,404 ft) in 5.36 minutes; service ceiling 12250 m (40,190 ft); range 1710 km (1,063 miles)
Weights: empty 1110 kg (2,447 lb); maximum take-off 1790 kg (3,946 lb)
Dimensions: span 11.31 m (37 ft 1.3 in); length 7.53 m (24 ft 8.5 in); height 3.25 m (10 ft 8 in); wing area 18.55 m² (199.68 sq ft)

Seen in pre-war colours, this group of Ki-27s is typical of the aircraft which had performed so well against the Polikarpov fighters over China and Manchuria. The Ki-27 proved useful for training after replacement by more modern types.

Armament: two forward-firing 7.7-mm (0.303-in) Type 89 machine-guns

Nakajima Ki-43 Hayabusa

Ki-43-IIb of the 3rd Chutai, 25th Hiko Sentai, flying from Hankow, China, in January 1944. Even at this late date, the Ki-43 still formed the bulk of fighter assets on the China-Burma front.

With its relatively low-powered radial engine, two-blade propeller and twin rifle-calibre machine-gun armament, the **Nakajima Ki-43 Hayabusa** (peregrine falcon) was the most dangerously underestimated Japanese fighter of the early months of the Pacific war; yet, with its outstanding manoeuvrability, it gained complete mastery over Brewster Buffaloes and Hawker Hurricanes in Burma. It was the result of a 1937 design which emerged as a light-

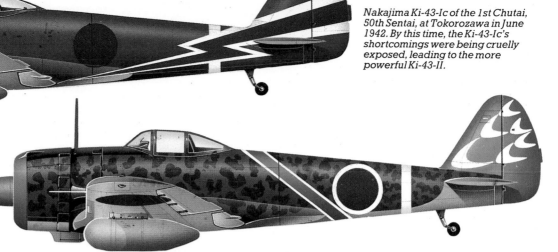

Nakajima Ki-43-Ic of the 1st Chutai, 50th Sentai, at Tokorozawa in June 1942. By this time, the Ki-43-Ic's shortcomings were being cruelly exposed, leading to the more powerful Ki-43-II.

This Hayabusa is a Ki-43-IIb of the Headquarters Chutai, 77th Sentai, in Burma.

weight fighter-bomber that required no more than its 709-kW (950-hp) to meet its speed demands. In common with other Japanese fighters of the time, however, its armament was puny by RAF standards, and it possessed neither armour nor self-sealing fuel tanks. As the Allied air forces pulled themselves together after the first shock of defeat, the Ki-43's weaknesses were discovered and increasing losses suffered, resulting in the introduction of the **Ki-43-II** (codenamed **'Oscar'** by the Allies), with pilot armour, rudimentary self-sealing fuel tanks and reflector gunsight; the engine was also changed to the 858-kW (1,150-hp) Nakajima Ha-115 radial which increased the top speed to 530 km/h (329 mph), roughly the same as that of the Hurricane Mk II. The **Ki-43-IIb** entered mass production in November 1942, first with Nakajima and six months later with Tachikawa. Final variant was the **Ki-43-III** with 917-

Right: A Ki-43-Ib of the 47th Independent Fighter Chutai at rest on a Japanese airfield. After service in all theatres throughout the war, the Ki-43 soldiered on against the Allies, but many were expended in kamikaze attacks.

kW (1,230-hp) engine and a top speed of 576 km/h (358 mph), but relatively few examples reached operational units. The Ki-43 was numerically the most important of all Japanese army air force aircraft, production totalling 5,886, plus 33 prototypes and trials aircraft.

Specification
Nakajima Ki-43-IIb
Type: single-seat fighter-bomber
Powerplant: one 858-kW (1,150-hp) Nakajima Ha-115 radial piston engine
Performance: maximum speed 530 km/h (329 mph) at 4000 m (13,123 ft); climb to 5000 m (16,404 ft) in

5.8 minutes; service ceiling 11200 m (36,745 ft); range 1760 km (1,094 miles)
Weights: empty 1910 kg (4,211 lb); maximum take-off 2925 kg (6,449 lb)
Dimensions: span 10.84 m (35 ft 6.8 in); length 8.92 m (29 ft 3.2 in); height

3.27 m (10 ft 8.7 in); wing area 21.40 m² (230.36 sq ft)
Armament: two 12.7-mm (0.5-in) Ho-103 machine-guns in wings, plus two 250-kg (551-lb) bombs carried under the wings

---

Nakajima Ki-44 Shoki

Of similar general configuration to the Ki-43, the **Nakajima Ki-44** prototypes incorporated the manoeuvring flaps that had been introduced on that aircraft, and carried an armament of two 7.7-mm (0.303-in) and two 12.7-mm (0.5-in) machine-guns. First flown in August 1940, the Ki-44 was involved in a series of comparative trials against Kawasaki's Ki-60 prototype, based on use of the Daimler-Benz DB 601 engine, and an imported Messerschmitt Bf 109E. The result of this evaluation, and extensive service trials, showed the Ki-44 to be good enough to enter production, and it was ordered under the designation Army Type 2 Single-seat Fighter Model 1A Shoki (demon), company designation **Ki-44-Ia**, which carried the same armament as the prototypes. A total of only 40 Ki-44-I aircraft was produced, including small numbers of the **Ki-44-Ib** armed with four 12.7-mm (0.5-in) machine-guns, and the similar **KI-44-Ic** with some minor refinements.

When introduced into service the high landing speeds and limited manoeuvrability of the **Shoki** made it unpopular with pilots, and very soon the **Ki-44-II** with a more powerful Nakajima Ha-109 engine was put into production. Only small numbers of the **Ki-44-IIa** were built, the variant being fol-

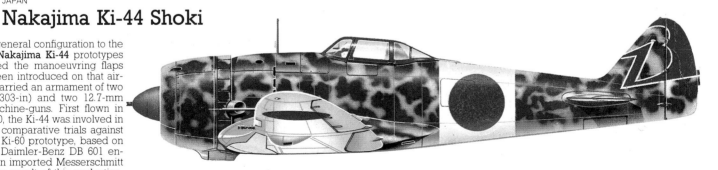

lowed by the major production **Ki-44-IIb**. The **Ki-44-IIc** introduced much heavier armament, comprising four 20-mm cannon or, alternatively, two 12.7-mm (0.5-in) machine-guns and two 40-mm cannon, and these proved to be very effective when deployed against Allied heavy bombers attacking Japan. Final production version was the **Ki-44-III** with a 1491-kW (2,000-hp) Nakajima Ha-145 radial engine, an increase in wing area and enlarged vertical tail surfaces.

This photograph of a Ki-44-IIb emphasizes the powerful lines of this interceptor. When armed with cannon, the Ki-44 proved very effective against the B-29 raids, as its high rate of climb enabled it to reach the bomber streams quickly.

This Ki-44-IIb was employed by the 23rd Sentai for home island defence in late 1944. Most home defence aircraft carried a white square around the Hinomaru.

Nakajima had built a total of 1,225 Ki-44s of all versions, including prototypes, and these were allocated the Allied codename 'Tojo'. They were deployed primarily in Japan, but were used also to provide an effective force of interceptors to protect vital targets, as in Sumatra where they defended the oil fields at Palembang.

Specification
Nakajima Ki-44-IIb
Type: single-seat interceptor fighter
Powerplant: one 1133-kW (1,520-hp) Nakajima Ha-109 14-cylinder radial piston engine
Performance: maximum speed 605 km/h (376 mph) at 5200 m (17,060 ft); climb to 5000 m (16,404 ft) in 4.28 minutes; service ceiling 11200 m (36,745 ft); maximum range 1700 km (1,056 miles)
Weights: empty 2105 kg (4,641 lb); maximum take-off 2993 kg (6,598 lb)

Dimensions: span 9.45 m (31 ft 0 in); length 8.79 m (28 ft 10.1 in); height 3.25 m (10 ft 8 in); wing area 15.00 m^2 (161.46 sq ft)
Armament: two fuselage-mounted and two wing-mounted 12.7-mm (0.5-in) Ho-103 machine-guns

Lacking the agility of other Japanese fighters, the Ki-44 followed a more Western approach, proving fast and stable with good climb and dive properties. This Ki-44-IIb flew from Canton in China with the 85th Sentai during 1944.

Nakajima Ki-84 Hayate

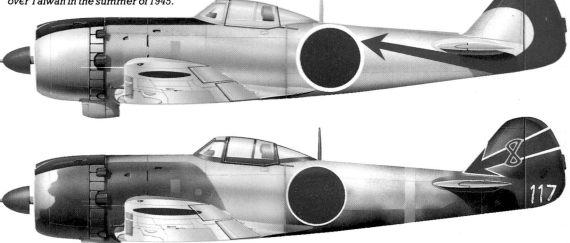

Above: One of the early Hayates, this Ki-84-Ia saw service with the 1st Chutai, 73rd Hiko-Sentai over the Philippines in late 1944.

Below: Ki-84-Ia of the Headquarters Chutai, 29th Hiko Sentai, operating over Taiwan in the summer of 1945.

Best of all Japanese fighters available in quantity during the last year of the war, the **Nakajima Ki-84 Hayate** (gale) not only possessed a reasonable performance but (unusual among Japanese aircraft) carried a powerful armament capable of knocking down the heavily armed and armoured American bombers. Not flown in prototype form until April 1943, the Ki-84 met with immediate approval by Japanese army air force pilots, but was subjected to lengthy service trials which undoubtedly delayed its introduction to combat operations. Production got under way at Nakajima's Ota plant in April 1944, pre-production aircraft having equipped the 22nd Sentai in China the previous month. Immediately afterwards 10 *sentais* of the **Ki-84-I**, codenamed '**Frank**' by the Allies, were deployed in the Philippines to confront the advancing American forces. In an effort to accelerate production of the excellent new fighter, Nakajima opened up a new line at its Otsonomiya plant, and as Boeing B-29 raids began to take their toll of Japanese cities a new 'bomber destroyer', the **Ki-84-Ic**, was produced with an armament of two nose-mounted 20-mm cannon and two wing-mounted 30-mm cannon. Some measure of the importance attached to the Ki-84 may be judged by the fact that in the last 17 months of war 3,382 aircraft were completed, this despite the tremendous havoc wrought by the B-29 raids and the fact that, owing to such damage at Musashi, Nakajima's engine plant had to be transferred elsewhere.

Specification
Nakajima Ki-84-Ia
Type: single-seat fighter and fighter-bomber
Powerplant: one 1342-kW (1,800-hp) Nakajima Ha-45 radial piston engine
Performance: maximum speed 631 km/h (392 mph) at 6120 m (20,079 ft); climb to 5000 m (16,404 ft) in 5.9 minutes; service ceiling 10500 m (34,449 ft); range 1695 km (1,053 miles)
Weights: empty 2660 kg (5,864 lb); maximum take-off 3890 kg (8,576 lb)
Dimensions: span 11.24 m (36 ft 10.5 in); length 9.92 m (32 ft 6.6 in); height 3.39 m (11 ft 1.5 in); wing area 21.00 m^2 (226.05 sq ft)
Armament: two nose-mounted 12.7-mm (0.5-in) Ho-103 machine-guns and two wing-mounted 20-mm Ho-5 cannon, plus two 250-kg (551-lb) bombs under the wings

Above: This Ki-84-Ia served with the 183rd Shimbutai (Special Attack Group) from Tatebayashi, Japan, during the last few days of the war.

The Ki-84 was a fine fighter which proved a handful for American pilots. Fortunately for them, the aircraft was not available in large numbers and these were overworked, resulting in maintenance and reliability problems.

Heavy Bombers

American general Billy Mitchell had predicted that large forces of heavy bombers could alone win a war. His ideas were slow in being transformed into aircraft, but eventually mighty new warplanes took to the skies. Great dramas unfolded as the enemies set out to destroy each other's homelands.

When Hitler embarked on his subjugation of Europe, the Luftwaffe's role was largely confined to providing air support for the German army, with little emphasis laid upon the use of strategic bombers, any plans for such a force having been abandoned in 1937. Thus at the outbreak of war in September 1939 the Luftwaffe's bombing arm comprised excellent medium bombers (the Dornier Do 17, Heinkel He 111 and Junkers Ju 88) which were regarded as adequate for the task of defeating Europe (which was expected to take no more than three years). With little to fear from opposing fighters, these aircraft also proved perfectly capable of carrying out daylight raids well beyond the advancing German armies.

The RAF, on the other hand, was steeped in the bomber tradition, recognizing the potential war-winning role of the bomber, and went to war with a trio of medium/heavy bombers (the Vickers Wellington, Armstrong Whitworth Whitley and Handley Page Hampden) in which a much greater emphasis had been laid on long range.

However, the manner in which the fortunes of war changed for Germany (starting with her inability to crush the British during the

Britain's RAF Bomber Command was equipped with an array of aircraft types during World War II – among them a trio of four-engine heavy bombers, one of which was this Short Stirling Mk III, seen here being readied for a mission.

summer of 1940) brought about a progressive reassessment of the Luftwaffe's capacity to carry the air war beyond the English Channel, tigether with the night Blitz of 1940–1, represented an unpremeditated use of its relatively small bombers for strategic purposes and, in view of Britain's wholly inadequate night defences, these achieved far more by night than had proved possible by day. But the proliferation of battlefronts in 1941 forced a dispersal of German bombers away from the Channel and, as a result

of growing demands for fighters and ground support aircraft, the Luftwaffe's bomber force henceforth declined both in strength and relative quality.

Meanwhile RAF Bomber Command was, in 1941, reaping the harvest from the strategic seeds sown in 1936 with the arrival on operations of the Short Stirling and Handley Page Halifax four-engine heavy bombers, later joined by the magnificent Avro Lancaster, all of which had been conceived as dedicated long-range strategic night heavy bombers.

Thereafter the strength of the British heavy bomber force increased steadily throughout the war. In 1942 Bomber Command was joined by the United States' mighty 8th Air Force, whose Boeing B-17s and Consolidated B-24s were to hit Germany by day in ever-growing strength in partnership with the RAF.

Thus by the time the Allies were ready to set foot in continental Europe in mid-1944 their day and night bomber fleets were capable of delivering devastating blows far beyond the ground battle, inflicting appalling damage on the enemy's ability to sustain his war machine. By contrast Germany, beset on all sides in the air and on the ground, had largely forsaken its bomber force, preferring to accord priority to the production of fighters with which to defend the Reich.

The fateful decision by Germany to abandon plans for a strategic bomber force long before the war, while fatally compromising the Luftwaffe's ability to strike at long range, was in all probability of little consequence in the end. Such a force, operating radially from within continental Europe, could never have matched the potential strength of the Allies' massive resources, dispersed as they were to strike diametrically across Festung Europa.

Armstrong Whitworth Whitley

It is unlikely that any other operational aeroplane of World War II came near to matching the austere, angular appearance of the **Armstrong Whitworth Whitley**, or to emulating its curious nose-down gait when flying 'straight and level'. Developed from the Armstrong Whitworth A.W.23 bomber/transport, the Whitley was designed to Specification B.3/34 and was first flown on 17 March 1936. That year it was selected to become the new Bomber Command's standard heavy bomber, replacing the Handley Page Heyford biplane. A total of 80 aircraft had been ordered, and these materialized as 34 **Whitley Mk I** bombers with two 682-kW (920-hp) Armstrong Siddeley Tiger IX radials, and 46 **Whitley Mk II** bombers with Tiger VIIIs. Early Whitley Mk Is possessed no dihedral on their outer wings. First squadron to receive Whitley Mk Is was No. 10 at Dishforth in March 1937.

The Whitley Mk I was already disappearing from front line service when war broke out (although the last examples did not leave No. 166 Squadron until April 1940). In the meantime the **Whitley Mk III** (also with Tiger VIIIs) had appeared; this version, of which 60 were produced, featured a retractable 'dustbin' ventral gun position. It served on Nos 7, 51, 58, 77, 97, 102 and 166 Squadrons, entering RAF service in August 1938. Also introduced that year was the **Whitley Mk IV** with 768-kW (1,030-hp) Rolls-Royce Merlin IV V-12 engines and the **Whitley Mk IVA** with 854-kW (1,145-hp) Merlin Xs; only 40 were produced, but they served to introduce a new power-operated four-gun Nash and Thompson tail turret (the 'dustbin' being abandoned).

The main production version was the **Whitley Mk V**, whose delivery started to Nos 77 and 78 Squadrons in September 1939, and of which 1,476 were built before June 1943, when production was halted. Also powered by Merlin Xs, the Whitley Mk V featured a 38-cm (15-in) longer fuselage and straight leading edges to the fins.

Although it was the Tiger-powered Mk III that performed almost all the early leaflet-dropping sorties of the first six months of the war (including the first sortie over Germany on the night of 3-4 September 1939 by 10 Whitleys of Nos 51 and 58 Squadrons), it was the Whitley Mk V that assumed the bombing role from March 1940 onwards; and on 11-12 May, immediately after the German attack in the West, Whitleys and Handley Page Hampdens dropped the first RAF bombs on the German mainland in an attack on railway targets near München Gladbach.

The following month Whitleys were the first RAF bombers to attack targets in Italy, flying from the UK and refuelling in the Channel Islands to attack Turin and Genoa. Though never to achieve fame for outstanding exploits, the immensely rugged Whitley gave yeoman service with Bomber Command despite being obviously slow and vulnerable in the face of fast improving enemy night defences. They were for instance among the aircraft that first raided Berlin on the night of 25-26 August 1940, and it was as the pilot of a Whitley during a raid on Cologne on 12-13 November that year that Leonard Cheshire (later Group Captain, VC) was awarded the DSO. Wing Commander P. C. Pickard (later to achieve fame as the Mosquito leader in the raid on Amiens gaol) led Whitleys of No. 51 Squadron in the airborne raid on the radar installation at Bruneval on 27-28 February 1942.

Whitleys flew their last raid with Bomber Command during an attack on Ostend on the night of 29-30 April 1942.

Specification
Armstrong Whitworth Whitley Mk V
Type: five-man bomber

Powerplant: two 854-kW (1,145-hp) Rolls-Royce Merlin X V-12 piston engines
Performance: maximum speed 370 km/h (230 mph) at 5000 m (16,400 ft); climb to 4570 m (15,000 ft) in 16 minutes; service ceiling 7925 m (26,000 ft); range 2415 km (1,500 miles) with normal tankage
Weights: empty 8777 kg (19,350 lb); maximum take-off 15196 kg (33,500 lb)
Dimensions: span 25.60 m (84 ft 0 in); length 21.11 m (69 ft 3 in); height 4.57 m (15 ft 0 in); wing area 105.63 m² (1,137.00 sq ft)
Armament: one 7.7-mm (0.303-in) machine-gun in the nose turret and four 7.7-mm (0.303-in) machine-guns in the tail turret, plus a maximum bomb-load of 3175 kg (7,000 lb)

Ground crew prepare a Whitley Mk V for operations in 1940. The aircraft flew from Dishforth and sports typical camouflage for the period. The Whitley Mk V was the mainstay of Bomber Command along with the Wellington until the arrival of the Halifax and Lancaster.

Avro 683 Lancaster

By cutting away the underfuselage and removing nose and dorsal turrets to save weight, the Lancaster B.Mk 1s (Special) of No. 617 Sqn at Waddington were able to carry the 22,000-lb (9979-kg) 'Grand Slam', first used to great effect on the Bielefeld Viaduct.

No one would dispute the statement that the **Avro Lancaster** was the finest British heavy bomber of World War II; indeed many would even argue that it was the finest heavy bomber serving on either side during the conflict, and it is therefore strange to recall that it had its genesis in the unsuccessful twin-engine Avro Manchester.

However, it is not entirely true to say that the Lancaster was virtually a four-engine Manchester, as four-engine installations in the basic airframe had been proposed before Manchester deliveries to the RAF began. But the prototype Lancaster was, in fact, a converted Manchester airframe with an enlarged wing outer panels and four 1,145-hp (854-kW) Rolls-Royce Merlin Xs. This prototype initially retained the Manchester's triple tail assembly, but was later modified to the twin fin and rudder assembly which became standard on production Lancasters.

The prototype flew on 9 January 1941 and later that month went to the Aeroplane and Armament Experimental Establishment, Boscombe Down, to begin intensive flying trials.

The new bomber was an immediate success, and large production orders were placed. Such was the speed of development in wartime that the first production Lancaster was flown in October 1941, a number of partially completed Manchester airframes being converted on the line to emerge as **Lancaster Mk I** (from 1942 redesignated **Lancaster B.Mk I**) aircraft.

Lancasters soon began to replace Manchesters, and such was the impetus of production that a shortage of Merlin engines was threatened. This was countered by licence-production by Packard in the USA of the Merlin not only for Lancasters but for other types. An additional insurance was effected in another way, the use of 1,735-hp (1294-kW) Bristol Hercules VI or XVI radial engines.

Meanwhile, the Merlin Lancasters were going from strength to strength. The prototype's engines gave way to 1,280-hp (954-kW) Merlin XXs and 22s, or 1,620-hp (1208-kW) Merlin 24s in production aircraft. Early thoughts of fitting a ventral turret were sadly discarded, and the Lancaster B.Mk I had three Frazer-Nash hydraulically-operated turrets with eight 7.7-mm (0.303-in) Browning machine-guns: two each in the nose and mid-upper dorsal positions and four in the tail turret. The bomb-bay, designed original-

Lancaster B.Mk I of No. 467 Sqn, Royal Australian Air Force, flying from Waddington. Now preserved at the RAF Museum, the aircraft flew 137 sorties and bore the inscription 'No enemy aircraft will fly over the Reich territory': Goering's inaccurate and ironic prophecy.

ly to carry 1814 kg (4,000 lb) of bombs, was enlarged progressively to carry bigger and bigger bombs: up to 3629 and 5443 kg (8,000 and 12,000 lb) and eventually to Barnes Wallis' enormous 9979-kg (22,000-lb) 'Grand Slam', the heaviest bomb carried by any aircraft in World War II.

The Lancaster's existence was not revealed to the public until 17 August of that year, when 12 aircraft from Nos 44 and 97 Squadrons carried out an unescorted daylight raid on Augsburg. Flown at low level, the raid inflicted considerable damage on a factory producing U-boat diesel engines, but the cost was high, seven aircraft being lost. Squadron Leaders Nettleton and Sherwood each received the Victoria Cross, the latter posthumously, for leading the operation, which perhaps confirmed to the Air Staff that unescorted daylight raids by heavy bombers were not a practicable proposition.

It would be true to say that development of the Lancaster went hand-in-hard with development of bombs. The early Lancasters carried their bomb loads in normal flush-fitting bomb bays, but as bombs got larger it became necessary, in order to be able to close the bomb doors, to make the bays deeper so that they protruded slightly below the fuselage line. Eventually, with other developments, the bomb doors were omitted altogether for certain specialist types of bomb.

The German battleship *Tirpitz* was attacked on several occasions by Lancasters until, on 12 November 1944, a combined force from Nos 9 and 617 Squadrons found the battleship in Tromso Fjord, Norway, and sank her with 5443-kg (12,000-lb) 'Tallboy' bombs, also designed by Barnes Wallis. The ultimate in conventional high explosive bombs was reached with the 9979-kg (22,000-lb) 'Grand Slam', a weapon designed to destroy concrete by exploding some way beneath the surface, so creating an earthquake effect. No. 617 Squadron first used the 'Grand Slam' operationally against the Bielefeld Viaduct on 14 March 1945, causing considerable destruction amongst its spans.

In spite of the other variants built from time to time, the Lancaster B.Mk I (**Lancaster B.Mk 1** from 1945) remained in production throughout the war, and the last was delivered by Armstrong Whitworth on 2 February 1946. Production had encompassed two Mk I prototypes, 3,425 Mk Is, 301 Mk IIs, 3,039 Mk IIIs, 180 Mk VIIs and

Lancaster Mk IIIs pour off the production line at A.V. Roe's Woodford factory. A total of 7,377 aircraft were built by a variety of manufacturers, and the sheer volume of this effort combined with the considerable qualities of the aircraft played a considerable part in the destruction of the Reich.

Right: A summer evening in 1943: briefing is over, pre-flight checks completed, the aircraft bombed-up; soon the calm of the dispersal area will be shattered by the sound of Merlins. The nightly raids were inevitably met by fierce AA and night fighters, and the nearest aircraft's seven missions are no small feat.

430 Mk Xs, a total of 7,377. These were built by Avro (3,673), Armstrong Whitworth (1,329), Austin Motors (330), Metropolitan Vickers (1,080), Vickers-Armstrongs (535) and Victory Aircraft (430). Some conversions between different mark numbers took place.

Statistics show that at least 59 Bomber Command squadrons operated Lancasters, which flew more than 156,000 sorties and dropped, in addition to 608,612 tons (618,350 tonnes) of high explosive bombs, more than 51 million incendiaries.

Specification
Avro Lancaster B.Mk I
Type: seven-seat heavy bomber
Powerplant: four 1223-kW (1,640-hp) Rolls-Royce Merlin XXIV V-12 piston engines
Performance: maximum speed 462 km/h (287 mph) at 3505 m (11,500 ft); cruising speed 338 km/h (210 mph) at 6096 m (20,000 ft); service ceiling 7470 m (24,500 ft); range 4070 km (2,530 miles) with 7,000-lb (3175-kg) bombload
Weights: empty 16738 kg (36,900 lb); maximum take-off 31751 kg (70,000 lb)
Dimensions: span 31.09 m (102 ft 0 in); length 21.18 m (69 ft 6 in); height 6.10 m (20 ft 0 in); wing area 120.49 m² (1,297.0 sq ft)
Armament: 7.7-mm (0.303-in) machine-guns (two each in nose and dorsal turrets, and four in tail turret), plus bomb load comprising one (9979-kg (22,000-lb) bomb or up to 6350 kg (14,000-lb) of smaller bombs.

Handley Page Halifax

Sporting the distinctive tail markings adopted by squadrons of Bomber Command's No. 4 Group, this Halifax Mk III of No. 466 Sqn, RAAF, was based at Leconfield in the mid-war years. The aircraft features the large H₂S radome under the rear fuselage.

Second only in importance to the Avro Lancaster in Bomber Command's great night offensive between 1941 and 1945, the four-engine **Handley Page Halifax** was originally designed around a pair of Vulture engines but, when first flown on 25 October 1939, the choice of four Merlins had been made. The first aircraft arrived in No. 35 Squadron in November 1940 and flew their first raid on 10-11 March 1941. Production was widely sub-

contracted and quickly accelerated, the Merlin X-powered **Halifax Mk I** with two-gun nose turret and no dorsal turret being followed by the **Halifax Mk IIA Series 1** with Merlin XXs and a two-gun dorsal turret. In the **Halifax Mk II Series 1A** a large transparent fairing improved the whole nose shape, this version also introducing a Defiant-type four-gun dorsal turret. The **Halifax Mk III** was powered by Bristol Hercules XVI radials, and later

examples introduced a wing span increased from 30.12 m (98 ft 10 in) to 31.75 m (104 ft 2 in). The **Halifax Mk V** with Dowty landing gear served with Coastal and Bomber Commands; the **Halifax Mk VI** with Hercules 100 engines and **Halifax Mk VII** with Hercules XVIs (both versions with increased fuel capacity) joined Bomber Command in 1944. Halifax Mks III, V and VII versions also served in paratrooping and glider towing roles with

the airborne forces (being the only aircraft to tow the big Hamilcar) and were joined by the **Halifax Mk VIII** just before the end of the war. Production totalled 6,176 Halifaxes, the bomber versions flying a total of 75,532 sorties and dropping 227,610 tons of bombs.

Specification
Handley Page Halifax Mk VI
Type: seven-crew night heavy bomber
Powerplant: four 1,800-hp (1343-kW) Bristol Hercules 100 radial piston engines
Performance: maximum speed 502 km/h (312 mph) at 6705 m (22,000 ft); climb to 6096 m (20,000 ft) in 50 minutes; service ceiling 7315 m (24,000 ft); range with 5897-kg (13,000-lb) bombload 2028 km (1,260 miles)
Weights: empty 17690 kg (39,000 lb); maximum take-off 30845 kg (68,000 lb)
Dimensions: span 31.75 m (104 ft 2 in); length 21.82 m (71 ft 7 in); height 6.32 m (20 ft 9 in); wing area 118.45 m² (1,275.0 sq ft)
Armament: one 7.7-mm (0.303-in) machine-gun in nose and four 7.7-mm (0.303-in) machine-guns in each of dorsal and tail turrets, plus a maximum bombload of 5897 kg (13,000 lb)

Two Merlin-powered Halifax Mk II Series 1 of No. 35 (Madras Presidency) Sqn, the first unit equipped with the type, are seen on air test during the winter of 1941. The dorsal turret created much drag and some later models had this removed.

Short Stirling

The **Short Stirling** was the first of RAF Bomber Command's trio of four-engine heavy bombers that mounted the great night offensive over Europe during the last four years of the war, and the only one conceived from the outset as a four-engine aircraft. Designed to a 1936 specification, the Stirling was initially flown as a half-scale prototype in 1938, this being followed by the full-size prototype which was destroyed on its first flight in May 1939. Production deliveries were first made to No. 7 Squadron in August 1940 (at the height of the Battle of Britain) and the **Stirling Mk I** flew its first operation on 10-11 February 1941. The type first bombed Berlin two months later. The Stirling Mk I of which 756 were produced, was powered by Hercules XI radials, but the **Stirling Mk II** with Wright Cyclones did not progress beyond the prototype stage. The **Stirling Mk III** was powered by Hercules XVIs and, with 875 built (plus many Mk Is converted) consti-

The Stirling was hampered throughout its bombing career by an inability to reach the optimum operating altitude of 6100 m (20,000 ft), due to too short a wingspan, and a bomb bay which could not be adapted to carry the ever-larger bombs being produced.

Stirling Mk I Series 1 bombers were delivered in January 1941 with no dorsal turret. These early deliveries were camouflaged in dark green and dark earth down the fuselage sides and were assigned to escorted daylight missions, in this instance with No. 7 Sqn.

tuted the main bomber variant; it also introduced the two-gun dorsal turret. Stirlings were the first operational aircraft to carry the original form of 'Oboe' navaid in 1941, and in August 1942 took part in the first Pathfinder operations. Two posthumous VCs were won by Stirling pilots (Flight Sergeant R. H. Middleton of No. 149 Squadron and Flight Sergeant A. L. Aaron of No. 218 Squadron), both during raids on northern Italy. By 1944 the Stirling Mk III was

obsolescent, and flew its last raid in September that year. The **Stirling Mk IV** (of which 577 were built) was a transport/glider tug without nose and dorsal turrets, and was widely used on operations by the airborne forces during the last year of the war. The **Stirling Mk V** transport (160 built), without armament, joined the RAF in January 1945. Stirling bombers equipped 15 squadrons.

Specification
Short Stirling Mk III
Type: seven- or eight-crew night heavy bomber
Powerplant: four 1,650-hp (1231-kW) Bristol Hercules XVI radial piston engines
Performance: maximum speed 435 km/h (270 mph) at 4420 m (14,500 ft); service ceiling 5180 m (17,000 ft); range with 6350-kg (14,000-lb) bombload 949 km (590 miles)

Weights: empty 19596 kg (43,200 lb); maximum take-off 31790 kg (70,000 lb)
Dimensions: span 30.20 m (99 ft 1 in); length 26.50 m (87 ft 3 in); height 6.93 m (22 ft 9 in); wing area 135.60 m² (1,460.0 sq ft)
Armament: two 7.7-mm (0.303-in) machine-guns in each of nose and dorsal turrets, and four 7.7-mm (0.303-in) guns in tail turret, plus a maximum bombload of 6350 kg (14,000 lb)

 UK
Vickers Wellington

No. 425 (Alouette) Sqn, RCAF flew Wellington Mk IIIs from Dishforth, and this aircraft was lost in a raid on Stuttgart. Bomber Command's Wellingtons flew their last mission in October 1943, but the type soldiered on in coastal and transport units until the war's end.

Employing the efficient geodetic lattice structure, the twin-engine **Vickers Wellington** continued in service with Bomber Command until 1943, far longer than its contemporaries, the Handley Page Hampden and Armstrong Whitworth Whitley. Designed to meet a 1932 requirement, the Wellington first flew on 15 June 1936 and in its **Wellington Mk I** form with Pegasus radials joined the RAF (No. 9 Squadron) in October 1938. The **Wellington Mk IA** (with Nash and Thompson nose and tail gun turrets) and the **Wellington Mk IC** (with lateral guns in place of the ventral turret) followed, together with the Merlin-powered **Wellington Mk II** and Hercules III- or XI-powered **Wellington Mk III**, and at the begining of the war six squadrons were flying the Wellington. Early daylight raids resulted in heavy losses owing to the Wellington's large defenceless arcs and in 1940 the aircraft joined the night bombing force. On 1 April 1941 a Wellington dropped the RAF's first 1814-kg (4,000-lb) bomb. Subsequent bomber versions included the Twin Wasp-powered **Wellington Mk IV**, and **Wellington Mk V** and **Mk VI** high-altitude aircraft with pressure cabins and Hercules or Merlin engines respectively; these latter versions did not see combat service. The **Wellington Mk X** with Hercules XVIIIs was the final bomber version, and the last raid by Bomber Command Wellingtons took place on 8-9 October 1943. In the meantime Wellingtons had been flying on maritime duties, the **Wellington DW. Mk I** with large mine-exploding hoops having operated in 1940 and Wellington Mk IC minelayers soon after this. Coastal Command versions included the **Wellington GR.Mk VIII** with Pegasus engines and ASV radar, the **Wellington GR.Mks XI, XII** and **XIV** with Hercules, Leigh Light and provision for

two torpedoes; the **Wellington T. Mks XVII** and **XVIII** were trainers, and many Mk Xs were converted to 'flying classrooms'. Wellingtons were also used as test-beds for early jet engines. The **Wellington C.Mks XV** and **XVI** were transport conversions of the Mk IC. A total of 11,461 aircraft was produced.

Specification
Vickers Wellington Mk III
Type: six-crew night medium bomber
Powerplant: two 1119-kW (1,500-hp) Bristol Hercules XI radial piston engines
Performance: maximum speed 411 km/h (255 mph) at 3810 m (12,500 ft); initial climb 283 m (930 ft) per minute; service ceiling 5790 m (19,000 ft); range with 2041-kg (4,500-lb) bombload 2478 km (1,540 miles)
Weights: empty 8605 kg (18,970 lb); maximum take-off 15422 kg (34,000 lb)
Dimensions: span 26.26 m (86 ft 2 in); length 19.68 m (64 ft 7 in); height 5 m (17 ft 5 in); wing area 78.04 m² (840.0 sq ft)
Armament: two 7.7-mm (0.303-in) machine-guns in nose turret, four 7.7-

mm (0.303-in) guns in tail turret, and two 7.7-mm (0.303-in) machine-guns in beam positions, plus a maximum bombload of 2041 kg (4,500 lb)

Armourers prepare the fuses of 500-lb (227-kg) bombs before moving the bomb train under the fuselage of a Wellington. The aircraft had a poor start on day missions, proving easy meat for German fighters, but found itself admirably suited for night ops, setting the trend for RAF bombing throughout the war.

Boeing B-17 Flying Fortress

This Boeing B-17G, A Bit o'Lace of the 711th BS, 447th BG was based at Rattlesden. Spectacular nose art became a speciality of the US Army Air Force, and art featuring the female form was invariably well executed. This contrasted with a virtual ban on nose art by RAF Bomber Command.

Pursuing an operational theory that high flying, heavily armed bombers were the surest means of striking strategic targets in daylight, the US Army Air Corps issued a requirement in 1934 for which the **Boeing Model 299 Flying Fortress** was designed and first flown on 28 July 1935. Twelve Y1B-17 (later **B-17**) service test aircraft entered service in 1937 and were followed by small numbers of **B-17B** and **B-17C** bombers in 1940-1, and by the **B-17D** in 1941. The **B-17E** introduced the enlarged vertical tail surfaces and tail gun position characteristic of all subsequent B-17s, as well as power-operated twin-gun turrets aft of the cockpit and below the centre fuselage. 512 B-17Es were produced, this version being the first US Army Air Force heavy bomber to see combat in Europe with the 8th Air Force. A total of 3,400 **B-17F** bombers, with enlarged one-piece nose transparency, was

produced during 1942-3, and these were followed by the principal variant, the **B-17G**, which, in reply to calls for improved nose armament to counter the Luftwaffe's head-on attacks, introduced the two-gun 'chin' turret; production totalled 8,680 B-17G aircraft by Boeing, Douglas and Lockheed-Vega. The Fortress was deployed principally in Europe during the war, with much smaller numbers operating in the Far East. The type carried out many epic raids, large formations of bombers, each bristling with heavy machine-guns and providing mutual protection against enemy fighters, pounding across the daylight skies over Hitler's Reich. In due course heavy losses forced the Americans to introduce escort fighters – the P-38, P-47 and P-51. One temporary expedient involved the use of a small number of B-17s modified as **YB-40** 'escort' aircraft, some aircraft carrying up to 30

machine-guns. Fortresses (B-17Cs, Fs and Gs) served in small numbers with RAF Bomber and Coastal Commands.

Specification
Boeing B-17G Flying Fortress
Type: 10-crew daylight medium/heavy bomber
Powerplant: four 895-kW (1,200-hp) Wright Cyclone R-1820-97 radial piston engines
Performance: maximum speed 462 km/h (287 mph) at 7620 m (25,000 ft); climb to 6096 m (20,000 ft) in 37 minutes; service ceiling 10850 m (35,600 ft); range with 2722-kg (6,000-lb) bombload 3220 km (2,000 miles)
Weights: empty 16391 kg (36,135 lb); maximum take-off 32660 kg (72,000 lb)
Dimensions: span 31.62 m (103 ft 9 in); length 22.78 m (74 ft 9 in); height 5.82 m (19 ft 1 in); wing area 131.92 m² (1,420.0 sq ft)
Armament: twin 12.7-mm (0.5-in) gun turrets under nose, aft of cockpit, under centre fuselage and in tail, and single-gun mountings in sides of nose, in radio operator's hatch and in waist (beam) positions, plus a maximum bombload of 7983 kg (17,600 lb)

Boeing B-17F Flying Fortress cutaway drawing key

1 Rudder construction
2 Rudder tab
3 Rudder tab actuation
4 Tail gunner's station
5 Gunsight
6 Twin 0.5-in (12.7-mm) machine guns
7 Tail cone
8 Tail gunner's seat
9 Ammunition troughs
10 Elevator trim tab
11 Starboard elevator
12 Tailplane structure
13 Tailplane front spar
14 Tailplane/fuselage attachment
15 Control cables
16 Elevator control mechanism
17 Rudder control linkage
18 Rudder post
19 Rudder centre hinge
20 Fin structure
21 Rudder upper hinge
22 Fin skinning
23 Aerial attachment
24 Aerials
25 Fin leading-edge de-icing boot
26 Port elevator
27 Port tailplane
28 Tailplane leading-edge de-icing boot
29 Dorsal fin structure
30 Fuselage frame
31 Tailwheel actuation
32 Toilet
33 Tailwheel (retracted) fairing
34 Fully-swivelling retractable tailwheel
35 Crew entry door
36 Control cables
37 Starboard waist hatch
38 Starboard waist 0.5-in (12.7-mm) machine gun
39 Gun support frame
40 Ammunition box
41 Ventral aerial
42 Waist gunners' positions
43 Port waist 0.5-in (12.7-mm) machine gun
44 Ceiling control cable runs
45 Dorsal aerial mast
46 Ball turret stanchion support
47 Ball turret stanchion
48 Ball turret actuation mechanism
49 Support frame
50 Ball turret roof
51 Twin 0-5-in (12.7-mm) machine guns

52 Ventral ball turret
53 Wingroot fillet
54 Bulkhead
55 Radio operator's compartment
56 Camera access hatch
57 Radio compartment windows (port and starboard)
58 Ammunition boxes
59 Single 0.5-in (12.7-mm) dorsal machine gun
60 Radio compartment roof glazing
61 Radio compartment/bomb-bay bulkhead
62 Fire extinguisher
63 Radio operator's station (port side)
64 Handrail links
65 Bulkhead step
66 Wing rear spar/fuselage attachment
67 Wingroot profile
68 Bomb-bay central catwalk
69 Vertical bomb stowage racks (starboard installation shown)
70 Horizontal bomb stowage (port side shown)
71 Dinghy stowage
72 Twin 0.5-in (12.7-mm) machine guns
73 Dorsal turret
74 Port wing flaps
75 Cooling air slots
76 Aileron tab (port only)
77 Port aileron
78 Port navigation light
79 Wing skinning
80 Wing leading-edge de-icing boot
81 Port landing light
82 Wing corrugated inner skin
83 Port out wing fuel tank (nine inter-rib cells)
84 No 1 engine nacelle
85 Cooling gills
86 Three-blade propellers
87 No 2 engine nacelle
88 Wing leading-edge de-icing boot
89 Port mid-wing (self-sealing) fuel tanks
90 Flight deck upper glazing
91 Flight deck/bomb-bay bulkhead
92 Oxygen cylinders
93 Co-pilot's seat
94 Co-pilot's control column
95 Headrest/armour
96 Compass installation
97 Pilot's seat

98 Windscreen
99 Central control console pedestal
100 Side windows
101 Navigation equipment
102 Navigator's compartment upper window (subsequently replaced by ceiling astrodome)
103 Navigator's table
104 Side gun mounting
105 Enlarged cheek windows (flush)
106 Ammunition box
107 Bombardier's panel
108 Norden bombsight installation
109 Plexiglas frameless nose-cone

110 Single 0.5-in (12.7-mm) nose machine gun
111 Optically-flat bomb-aiming panel
112 Pitot head fairing (port and starboard)
113 D/F loop bullet fairing
114 Port mainwheel
115 Flight deck underfloor control linkage
116 Wingroot/fuselage fairing
117 Wing front spar/fuselage attachment
118 Battery access panels (wingroot leading edge)
119 No 3 engine nacelle spar bulkhead
120 Intercooler pressure duct
121 Mainwheel well
122 Oil tank (nacelle inboard wall)
123 Nacelle structure
124 Exhaust
125 Retracted mainwheel (semi-recessed)
126 Firewall
127 Cooling gills
128 Exhaust collector ring assembly
129 Three-blade propellers
130 Undercarriage retraction struts
131 Starboard mainwheel
132 Axle
133 Mainwheel oleo leg
134 Propeller reduction gear casing
135 1,200 hp Wright R-1820-65 radial engine

136 Exhaust collector ring
137 Engine upper bearers
138 Firewall
139 Engine lower bearers
140 Intercooler assembly
141 Oil tank (nacelle outboard wall)
142 Supercharger
143 Intake
144 Supercharger waste-gate
145 Starboard landing light
146 Supercharger intake
147 Intercooler intake
148 Ducting
149 No 4 engine nacelle spar bulkhead
150 Oil radiator intake
151 Main spar web structure

152 Mid-wing fuel tank rib cut-outs
153 Auxiliary mid spar
154 Rear spar
155 Landing flap profile
156 Cooling air slots
157 Starboard outer wing fuel tank (nine inter-rib cells)
158 Flap structure
159 Starboard aileron
160 Outboard wing ribs
161 Spar assembly
162 Wing leading-edge de-icing boot
163 Aileron control linkage
164 Wing corrugated inner skin
165 Wingtip structure
166 Starboard navigation light

B-17 Flying Fortress in Action

One of the most famous bombers of all time, the Boeing B-17 was so impressive when the prototype appeared in July 1935 that it was dubbed 'the Flying Fortress'. The name stuck and became a registered trademark. The US Army Air Corps had merely asked for a 'multi-engine' bomber, to carry a 2,000-lb (907-kg) bombload. Rival companies built twin-engine machines, but Boeing went for four engines to get more speed and altitude. Eventually the first B-17 was delivered on 1 March 1937, with a crew of eight distributed around the tube-like fuselage, five of them each manning a defensive machine-gun. Amidships was a short but deep bomb bay housing up to 2177 kg (4,800 lb) of bombs, with a catwalk down the centre.

By 1940 the production model was the B-17C, with 1,200-hp (895-kW) turbosupercharged Cyclone engines giving a maximum speed of 515 km/h (320 mph), much faster than later models. In 1941 the RAF was given 20 because the US Army wanted to see how this model, with more guns, self-sealing tanks and armour, performed in combat. The result was a disaster, nine being destroyed in a few weeks, but a lot of the trouble was bad luck and bad management. Enough was learned, however, for Boeing to redesign the B-17 and the resulting B-17E flew on 5 September 1941.

The B-17E had a giant dorsal fin, giving better bombing accuracy at high altitudes, and a

An unusually clean B-17G is marshalled to a halt on delivery to a unit in England. Such pristine condition would not be long-lived; nose art and battle damage would soon make the aircraft look more businesslike.

larger tailplane. There were many internal changes, but the main difference was in radically better defensive firepower, with 10 12.7-mm (0.5-in) Brownings and two or three of 7.62-mm (0.3-in) calibre. The small guns were manually aimed from the nose, while the big weapons were in a two-gun power-driven dorsal turret, a twin manual installation in the roof of the radio compartment, two manual waist positions, a manual tail turret (filling what was previously a blind spot) and under the fuselage a powered ball turret whose occupant had to be small. In the event of a belly landing the ball turret had to be vacated, and if the door jammed the whole turret had to be severed from the aircraft by a special spanner carried on board, the occupant then escaping as it fell. On at least one occasion it was found the special tool was not on board, and the operations officer of an 8th Air Force bomb group took off in another B-17 and passed the implement across trailing on a long piece of string.

In April 1942 the B-17F introduced many improvements including a frameless Plexiglas nose which in later versions had two 12.7-mm (0.5-in) guns in left and right cheek mountings. Hundreds of B-17Fs formed the backbone of the growing might of the 8th Air Force, which from August 1942 operated over Germany and other European countries. After much action the Luftwaffe decided head-on attacks were especially effective and to counter these the main change in the B-17G was to add a chin turret with two more guns, making a total of 13, all of 12.7-mm (0.5-in) calibre (only one gun was fitted in the roof of the radio compartment, making the odd number, and later this was often omitted). The B-17G was the final mainstream variant, and 8,680 were built, the last 7,000 or so being unpainted instead of olive-drab.

Consolidated B-24 Liberator

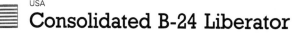

One of the last B-24s to get into action, this B-24J-190 was given a particularly flamboyant paint job by the 43rd Bomb Group operating against the Japanese mainland from Ie Shima in the spring of 1945. The dorsal turret was omitted, reflecting the approach of victory.

Used as an electronic warfare aircraft, this Liberator B.Mk IV flew with No. 223 Sqn, RAF. Flying in ahead of bombing formations, these aircraft jammed German ground and night fighter radars.

The RAF flew several hundred Liberators in India, where they were the major weapon used to bomb Japanese targets in Burma and China.

Produced in larger numbers than any other American aircraft during the war (and any other four-engine aircraft in history) the **Consolidated B-24 Liberator** did not enter the design stage until 1939, and the prototype **XB-24** was flown on 29 December that year. Minor development batches followed in 1940 before the first major production version, the **B-24D**, appeared late in 1941. A policy decision to concentrate B-24s primarily in the Pacific theatre (where the type's long range was used to good effect) resulted in most of the 2,738 B-24Ds being deployed against Japan, but the 8th and 9th Air Forces in Europe and North Africa also received the aircraft, one of their outstanding raids being the attack on the Ploesti oil refineries on 1 August 1943. A total of 791 **B-24E** bombers with changed propellers was produced before pro-

duction switched to the **B-24G**, of which 430 were built. This version introduced a two-gun nose turret to counter German head-on fighter attacks and was followed by 3,100 **B-24H** aircraft with various makes of nose turret. Major production version was the **B-24J**, of which 6,678 were built, incorporating a Motor Products nose turret, new-type autopilot and bombsight. The **B-24L** (1,667 built) featured two manually operated tail guns in a Consolidated turret, and the **B-24M** (2,593 built) introduced a Motor Products two-gun tail turret. This huge manufacturing effort (which produced a total of 18,313 aircraft in five and a half years) involved Consolidated, Douglas, Ford and North American plants, the total including many aircraft for the RAF (in which Liberators served with 42 squadrons) and US Navy (with

whom Liberators served under the designation **PB4Y**) and also the 25-passenger **C-87** version, of which 282 were produced.

Specification
Consolidated B-24J Liberator
Type: eight/ten-crew daylight medium/heavy bomber
Powerplant: four 1,200-hp (895-kW) Pratt & Whitney R-1830-65 radial piston engines
Performance: maximum speed 467 km/h (290 mph) at 7620 m (25,000 ft); climb to 6096 m (20,000 ft) in 25 minutes; service ceiling 8535 m (28,000 ft); range 3220 km (2,000 miles) with a 3992-kg (8,800 lb) bombload
Weights: empty 16556 kg (36,500 lb); maximum take-off 29484 kg (65,000 lb)
Dimensions: span 33.53 m (110 ft 0 in); length 20.47 m (67 ft 2 in); height 5.49 m

(18 ft 0 in); wing area 97.36 m² (1,048.0 sq ft)
Armament: two-gun turrets in nose, tail, upper fuselage aft of cockpit and under centre fuselage, and single manual guns in waist (beam) positions for a total of 10 12.7-mm (0.5-in) machine-guns, plus a normal bombload of 3992 kg (8,800 lb)

Formation flying is an art in itself, and formating a heavy aircraft while joining up in formations of 40 or more, often in partial cloud, took concentration. The Americans used brightly coloured 'assembly ships', usually with polka dots to facilitate the forming of combat boxes. Such gaudy aircraft did not fly on missions but returned to base when the formation had set course.

Boeing B-29 Superfortress

A feature of the B-29's gun armament was the use of remotely controlled turrets, periscopically sighted by gunners located within the fuselage. The aircraft illustrated, carrying BTO (bombing through overcast) radar, was based on Tinian for the final raids on Japan.

Design of the **Boeing B-29 Superfortress** heavy bomber started in 1940 to meet a US Army Air Corps requirement for a 'Hemisphere Defense Weapon', an aircraft capable of carrying 907 kg (2,000 lb) of bombs for 8582 km (5,333 miles) at 644 km/h (400 mph); only after the Japanese attack on Pearl Harbor put an end to the USA's isolationism was the project given top priority, and the first **XB-29** was flown on 21 September 1942. The very big four-engine mid-wing bomber had by then been ordered in large numbers and in 1943 the decision was taken to deploy the B-29 only against Japan, concentrating the new bombers in the XX Bomber Command on bases in India and China. The first **YB-29** service test aircraft were delivered to the 58th Bomb Wing in July 1943 and were followed by **B-29-BW** production bom-

bers three months later. Production was concentrated at Boeing, Wichita (BW), Bell, Marietta (BA), Martin, Omaha (MO), and a new Boeing-run factory at Renton (BN). Four groups of B-29s moved to India early in 1944, making their first raid on Bangkok on 5 June, and on the Japanese mainland 10 days later. For the first nine months the B-29s were principally employed in high-level daylight raids, but on 9 March 1945, when operations were run primarily from five vast bases in the Marianas islands, they switched to low-level night attacks with devastating incendiary raids on Japanese cities (the first of which on Tokyo caused 80,000 deaths). Two other main versions of the B-29 appeared during the war, the **B-29A-BN** with four-gun forward upper turret and increased wing span, and the **B-29B-BA** with reduced

gun armament and increased bomb-load. The B-29-45-MOs *Enola Gay* and *Bock's Car* of the 393rd Bomb Squadron dropped the atomic bombs 'Little Boy' and 'Fat Man' on Hiroshima and Nagasaki on 6 and 9 August 1945 respectively, bringing the war to an end. Total B-29 production was 3,970.

Specification
Boeing B-29A Superfortress
Type: 10-crew heavy strategic bomber
Powerplant: four 1641-kW (2,200-hp) Wright R-3350-57 radial piston engines
Performance: maximum speed 576 km/h (358 mph) at 7620 m (25,000 ft); climb to 6095 m (20,000 ft) in 38 minutes; service ceiling 9695 m (31,800 ft); range 6598 km (4,100 miles)
Weights: empty 32369 kg (71,360 lb); maximum take-off 64003 kg

(141,100 lb)
Dimensions: span 43.36 m (142 ft 3 in); length 30.18 m (99 ft 0 in); height 9.01 m (29 ft 7 in); wing area 161.27 m² (1,736.0 sq ft)
Armament: four-gun turret over nose, two-gun turrets under nose, under and over rear fuselage, all with guns of 12.7-mm (0.5-in) calibre, and one 20-mm and two 12.7-mm (0.5-in) guns in tail, plus a bombload of up to 9072 kg (20,000 lb)

The mighty Superfortress. One of the most remarkable achievements of the war was the design, development and production of this bomber in the space of four years. All B-29s were assigned to the assault on Japan, the two aircraft here – YB-29s – being flown by the 58th Bomb Wing (Very Heavy).

Mitsubishi G4M 'Betty'

Identified by its dihedral tailplane, the Mitsubishi G4M3 'Betty' was produced in limited numbers during the last two years of the war. The main improvement over previous models was increased protection for the crew. The aircraft portrayed flew with the Yokosuka Kokutai, Atsugi during the last days of the war.

Codenamed **'Betty'** by the Allies, the **Mitsubishi G4M** long-range medium bomber remained in service with the Japanese navy from the first to the last day of the war: it took part in the attack that sank the British warships HMS *Prince of Wales* and HMS *Repulse* in December 1941, and it carried the Japanese surrender delegation on 19

August 1945. Designed to a 1937 requirement for a long-range bomber, the **G4M1** prototype made its first flight on 23 October 1939, and during trials recorded an extraordinary performance of a 444-km/h (276-mph) top speed and 5555-km (3,450-mile) range, albeit without bombload. The first production G4M1s (**Navy Type 1 Attack**

Bomber Model 11) were initially deployed against China in mid-1941 but on the eve of the attack on Malaya the bombers moved to Indo-China and within a week had successfully attacked the *Prince of Wales* and *Repulse*. When Allied fighter opposition eventually increased to effective proportions, the G4M1 was seen to be very

vulnerable, possessing little armour protection for crew and fuel tanks, and it was in a pair of G4M1s that Admiral Yamamoto and his staff were travelling when shot down by P-38s over Bougainville on 18 April 1943. Little improvement had been secured in the **Navy Type 1 Attack Bomber Model 22** with revised powerplant. The **G4M2** was therefore introduced with increased armament, increased fuel and 1,800-hp (1343-kW) Mitsubishi Kasei radials, and this version (**Navy Type 1 Attack Bomber Model 22A** and **Model 22B**) remained in production until the end of the war in steadily improved **Navy Type 1 Attack Bomber Model 24** variants. A further improved version, the **G4M3**, with increased crew protection, was also produced in small numbers as the **Navy Type 1 Attack Bomber Model 34**. Production amounted to 1,200 G4M1s, 1,154 G4M2s and 60 G4M3s.

Specification
Mitsubishi G4M2 'Betty'
Type: seven-crew land-based naval bomber

Powerplant: two 1,800-hp (1343-kW) Mitsubishi MK4P Kasei 21 radial piston engines
Performance: maximum speed 438 km/h (272 mph) at 4600 m (15,090 ft); climb to 8000 m (26,245 ft) in 32.4 minutes; service ceiling 8950 m (29,365 ft); range 6059 km (3,765 miles)
Weights: empty 8160 kg (17,990 lb); normal loaded 12500 kg (27,558 lb)
Dimensions: span 25.00 m (82 ft 0¼ in);

length 20.00 m (67 ft 7⅜ in); height 6.00 m (19 ft 8¼ in); wing area 78.125 m² (840.93 sq ft)
Armament: two 7.7-mm (0.303-in) Type 92 machine-guns in nose, one 7.7-mm (0.303-in) Type 92 machine-gun in dorsal turret, one 20-mm Type 99 cannon in dorsal turret and one 20-mm Type 99 in tail, plus 1000 kg (2,205 lb) of bombs or one 800-kg (1,764-lb) torpedo

---

USSR
Ilyushin Il-4

The Ilyushin Il-4 was roughly in the same class as the Heinkel He 111 and first saw service in the Winter War with Finland. It was the first Soviet bomber to raid Berlin, and served until the last few months of the war, when it was relegated to glider towing.

One of the great bombers of the war, the **Ilyushin Il-4** has not unnaturally been overshadowed in Western thinking by the great British and American aircraft, yet well over 5,000 Il-4s were produced between 1937 and 1944, the vast majority in the last three years. The original prototype of this low-wing twin-engine bomber, designated the **TsKB-26**, flew in 1935, was developed through the **TsKB-30**, and entered production in 1937 as the **DB-3B** (DB being a Soviet contraction denoting long-range bomber). Early examples were powered by 765-hp (571-kW) M-85 engines, but these were replaced by 960-hp (716-kW) M-86s in 1938. Although a tough and relatively simple design, the aircraft suffered from a poor defensive

armament of single nose, dorsal and ventral 7.62-mm (0.3-in) guns, and lost heavily to such aircraft as the Bristol Bulldog, Gloster Gladiator and Fokker D.XXI during the Winter War against Finland in 1939-40. In 1939 a modified version with lengthened nose and more armour (the **DB-3F**) appeared, and in 1940, in conformity with changed Russian practice, the designation became Il-4 (denoting the designer, Sergei Ilyushin). Soon after the German attack on the USSR opened in 1941 it was decided to withdraw Il-4 production to newly opening plants in Siberia, at the same time replacing a large proportion of the metal structure by less strategically critical wood. Il-4s also entered service with

Soviet Naval Aviation, and it was a naval-manned force of these bombers that first raided Berlin from the east on 8 August 1941. Thereafter the Il-4 paid frequent visits to the German capital and other targets in Eastern Europe. In 1944 production ended, although the Il-4 served until the end of the war and afterwards. Apart from increasing the calibre of its guns and giving it a torpedo-carrying ability, the Il-4 remained virtually unchanged between 1941 and 1944.

Specification
Ilyushin Il-4
Type: four-crew bomber/torpedo-bomber

Powerplant: two 1,100-hp (821-kW) M-88B radial piston engines
Performance: maximum speed 410 km/h (255 mph) at 4725 m (15,500 ft); initial climb rate 270 m (886 ft) per minute; service ceiling 10000 m (32,810 ft); range with bombload 2600 km (1,616 miles)
Weights: empty 6000 kg (13,228 lb); maximum take-off 10000 kg (22,046 lb)
Dimensions: span 21.44 m (70 ft 4¼ in); length 14.80 m (48 ft 6½ in); height 4.10 m (13 ft 5½ in); wing area 66.7 m² (718.0 sq ft)
Armament: single 12.7-mm (0.5-in) UBT machine-guns in nose, dorsal turret and ventral positions, plus a maximum bombload of 1000 kg (2,205 lb) or three 500 kg (1,102 lb) torpedoes

---

GERMANY
Heinkel He 111

Longest-serving medium bomber of the Luftwaffe, the **Heinkel He 111** stemmed from a design by Siegfried and Walter Günther for a dual-purpose commercial transport/bomber produced in 1934 and flown on 24 February 1935. Early versions featured a conventional stepped windscreen and

elliptical wing leading edge, and a bomber version with these features, the **He 111B-1**, served with the Legion Condor in the Spanish Civil War. The first production version with straight wing leading edge was the **He 111F**, and the **He 111P** incorporated a fully-glazed asymmetric nose without external windscreen step. He 111Ps with DB 601Aa engines were delivered to the Luftwaffe in 1939 before production switched to the most widely-used variant, the **He 111H** with Junkers Jumo 211 engines; sub-variants of this series formed the backbone of the Luftwaffe's bomber force between 1940 and 1943;

Among the bomber units switched from the night assault on Britain to the Eastern Front in 1941 was KG 55 'Greif' (Griffon Wing), one of whose Heinkel He 111Hs is seen here being armed with an externally carried bomb prior to a raid.

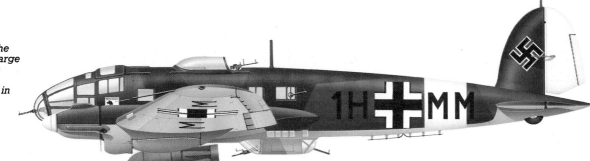

From mid-1940 onwards, with the arrival in service of bombs too large to be carried internally, He 111s frequently carried their loads externally. A Heinkel He 111H-6 in the markings of KG 26 is shown.

they took part in numerous raids in the Battle of Britain and were flown by the pathfinder unit, KGr 100. The first version to carry torpedoes was the **He 111H-6**, followed by the **He 111H-15**; the **He 111H-8** was fitted with a large and cumbersome balloon cable fender; the **He 111H-11/R2** was a glider tug for the Go 242, while pathfinder versions with special radio were the **He 111H-14** and **He 111H-18**; the **He 111H-16** featured increased gun armament, and the **He 111H-20** included 16-

paratroop transport, night bomber and glider tug sub-variants. The **He 111H-22** carried a single Fi 103 flying bomb and was used against the UK late in 1944. The most extraordinary of all was the **He 111Z** (Zwilling, or Twin) which consisted of two He 111Hs joined together with a new wing and fifth engine; it was used mainly to tow the huge Me 321 Gigant gliders. A total of about 7,300 He 111s was built.

Specification
Heinkel He 111H-16
Type: five-crew medium bomber
Powerplant: two 1,350-hp (1007-kW) Junkers Jumo 211F inverted V-12 piston engines
Performance: maximum speed 436 km/h (271 mph) at 6000 m (19,685 ft); climb to 6000 m (19,685 ft) in 42 minutes; service ceiling 6700 m (21,980 ft); range 1950 km (1,212 miles)
Weights: empty 8680 kg (19,136 lb); maximum take-off 14000 kg (30,865 lb)

Dimensions: span 22.60 m (74 ft 1¾ in); length 16.40 m (53 ft 9½ in); height 3.40 m (13 ft 1¼ in); wing area 86.50 m² (931.07 sq ft)
Armament: one 20-mm MG FF cannon in nose, one 13-mm (0.51-in) MG 131 gun in dorsal position, two 7.92-mm (0.31-in) MG 15 guns in rear of ventral gondola and two 7.92-mm (0.31-in) MG 81 guns in each of two beam positions, plus a bombload of 2000 kg (4,409 lb) internally and 2000 kg (4,409 lb) externally

Heinkel He 177 Greif

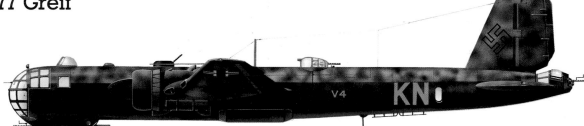

Heinkel He 177A-5 of II Gruppe, Kampfgeschwader 1 'Hindenburg' based at Prowehren, East Prussia, mid-1944. KG 1 assembled about 90 of these bombers for attacks on Soviet communications and military installations, but unreliability dogged operations.

After the scrapping of German plans for a strategic bombing force in 1936, the Luftwaffe abandoned plans to develop a heavy bomber until in 1938 the RLM approached the Heinkel company with a requirement for such an aircraft, resulting in the **Heinkel He 177 Greif** (Griffon), a four-engine mid-wing aircraft in which the 1,000-hp (746-kW) DB 601 engines were coupled in pairs (termed DB 606s) to drive single propellers. The first aircraft, the **He 177 V1**, was flown on 19 November 1939. Continuing engine overheating problems as well as persistent structural failures delayed production, the first **He 177A-1** not reaching I/KG 40 for operational trials until July 1942; in the course of these He 177s took part in raids on the UK, but generally they proved disappointing in service. Several sub-variants of the **He 177A-3** were produced, including the **He 177A-3/R3** which could carry three Hs 293 anti-shipping missiles, the **He 177A-3/R5** with 75-mm gun in the ventral gondola and the **He 177A-3/R7** torpedo-bomber. He 177A-3s were used by KGr 2 to fly supply missions to the beleaguered German forces at Stalingrad in January 1943. The **He 177A-5** incorporated a stronger wing to carry heavier external loads, and a small number were converted to the Zerstörer role with 33 upward-firing rocket tubes in the space normally occupied by the bomb bays. Small numbers of He 177A-5s returned to the night attack on the UK early in 1944; this version proved to be the last to serve with the

Luftwaffe (bombers being afforded low priority during the last year of the war), but many interesting projects continued to be pursued, including one involving the conversion of **He 177 V38** as a carrier of Germany's atomic bomb, which in the event did not materialize. About 1,160 production and 30 prototype He 177s were built.

Specification
Heinkel He 177A-5/R2 Greif
Type: six-crew heavy bomber
Powerplant: two 2,950-hp (2200-kW) Daimler-Benz DB610A-1/B-1 paired inverted V-12 piston engines
Performance: maximum speed 488 km/h (303 mph) at 6000 m (19,685 ft); initial climb rate 190 m

(623 ft) per minute; service ceiling 8000 m (26,245 ft); range with two Hs 293 weapons 5500 km (3,418 miles)
Weights: empty 16900 kg (37,257 lb); maximum take-off 31000 kg (68,342 lb)
Dimensions: span 31.44 m (103 ft 1¾ in); length 20.40 m (66 ft 11¼ in); height 6.40 m (20 ft 11¾ in); wing area 102.00 m² (1,098.0 sq ft)
Armament: one 7.92 (0.31-in) MG 81 gun in nose, one 13-mm (0.51-in) MG 131 gun in forward dorsal turret, one 13-mm (0.51-in) MG 131 gun in rear dorsal turret, one 13-mm (0.51-in) MG 131 gun in rear of ventral gondola, one 20-mm MG FF cannon in front of ventral gondola and one 20-mm MG FF in tail, plus a maximum internal bombload of 6000 kg (13,228 lb) or two Hs 293 missiles

Dornier Do 217

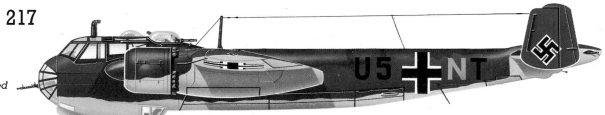

In 1941 KG 2 re-equipped with Do 217Es; this Do 217 E-2 carries the codes of 9.Staffel. This version introduced an electrically operated dorsal turret with a single 13-mm machine-gun.

In the normal process of design evolution it was recognised that, culminating from a design compromise, the Dornier Do 17 could at best represent a stopgap for three or four years in Luftwaffe service, and in 1937, as that aircraft was entering operational units, the manufacturer proposed a slightly larger and dedicated development, the **Dornier Do 217**.

Powered by 1,075-hp (802-kW) DB 601A engines, the prototype **Do 217 V1**

was flown in August 1938 but at once showed that many of the excellent handling qualities of the earlier aircraft had disappeared; indeed, the prototype soon crashed. Several further prototypes followed with various modifications, including enlarged tail surfaces to overcome directional instability, but none received altogether favourable response from Luftwaffe pilots.

Eventual recourse was made to

greatly increased engine power, and after limited production of the **Do 217A** reconnaissance aircraft and **Do 217C** bomber, a standard for full production settled upon the **Do 217E**, powered by two 1,550-hp (1156-kW) BMW 801MA radials. Pre-production **Do 217E-O** aircraft appeared in 1940, and service **Do 217E-1** bombers early in 1941; the latter carried a bombload of 2000 kg (4,409 lb), a crew of four or five, and a defensive armament of five MG 15

machine-guns and a 15-mm MG 151 cannon.

First to receive the Do 217E bomber, in March 1941, was II/KG 40 for anti-shipping duties over the Atlantic, followed by all three *Gruppen* of KG 2. A large number of sub-variants and *Rüstsätze* (field conversion kits) existed, including provision to carry two Henschel Hs 293 missiles, increased armour protection and armament progressively increased to seven MG 15s and a

20-mm cannon. The **Do 217E-2**, for example, introduced an electrically operated dorsal turret mounting a single 13-mm (0.51-in) MG 131 heavy machine-gun. Dornier Do 217Es of KG 2 constituted a large part of the Luftwaffe bomber force sent against British towns and cities in the so-called 'Baedeker raids' of April and May 1942.

During the autumn of that year a new version, the **Do 217K**, joined KG 2; powered by 1,700-hp (1268-kW) BMW 801D radials, this version was in effect a more powerful counterpart of the Do

217E series and could accommodate all the *Rüstsätze* previously applied; it also eliminated the windscreen 'step' by introducing a completely new and bulbous nose profile. Produced almost simultaneously was the **Do 217M**, which was similar to the Do 217K series but with 1,750-hp (1306-kW) Daimler-Benz DB 603A liquid-cooled inverted V-12 engines.

These two versions continued in service up to the end of the war, frequently being employed to deliver such weapons as the Hs 293A and Fritz-X

both against ships and key land targets. However, no more than 1,730 Do 217s of all versions were produced, of which almost half were reconnaissance aircraft and night-fighters.

Specification
Dornier Do 217M-1
Type: four-seat bomber
Powerplant: two 1,750-hp (1306-kW) Daimler-Benz DB 603A inverted V-12 piston engines
Performance: maximum speed 600 km/h (348 mph) at 5700 m

(18,700 ft); initial climb rate 210 m (690 ft) per minute; service ceiling 9500 m (31,180 ft); range 2500 km (1,555 miles)
Weights: empty 9065 kg (19,985 lb); maximum take-off 16700 kg (36,817 lb)
Dimensions: span 19.00 m (62 ft 4 in); length 17.00 m (55 ft 9¼ in); height 4.96 m (16 ft 3½ in); wing area 57.00 m² (613.54 sq ft)
Armament: eight 7.92-mm (0.31-in) MG 81 and two 13-mm (0.51-in) MG 131 machine-guns, plus up to 4000 kg (8,818 lb) of bombs

---

GERMANY
Junkers Ju 88 (bomber versions)

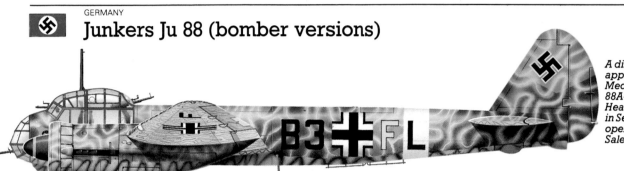

A disruptive white streaking was applied over the standard splinter Mediterranean camouflage of this Ju 88A-4 of I/KG 54 'Totenkopf, (Death's Head Wing) based at Bergamo, Italy, in September 1943 during operations against the Allies at Salerno.

In terms of versatility and long service the **Junkers Ju 88** bomber matched the outstanding record of the Messerschmitt Bf 109 fighter. Conceived as a high-speed medium bomber in 1936, the first prototype **Ju 88 V1** was flown by Flugkapitän Kindermann at Dessau on 21 December the same year. The three-seat all-metal aircraft was originally powered by two 1,000-hp (746-kW) Daimler-Benz DB 600A V-12 engines in annular cowlings. Nine further prototypes followed before construction of 10 pre-production **Ju 88A-O** aircraft was started in 1939, by which time the nose and cabin had been revised to accommodate a four-man crew. Dive brakes were now fitted under the outer wings to enable dive attacks to be made, and external bomb racks under the inner wings increased the bomb load from 500 kg (1,102 lb), carried internally, to a total of 1500 kg (3,307 lb).

Production **Ju 88A-1** bombers were joining the Luftwaffe at the outbreak of war, and about 60 aircraft had been completed by the end of 1939. The Ju 88 test unit commanded by Hauptmann Pohl, Erprobungskommando 88, was redesignated I/KG 25 in August 1939,

and the following month became I/KG 30, carrying out its first operation with an attack on British warships in the Firth of Forth on 26 September. A further raid on the same target followed on 16 October, when two Ju 88s were shot down by Supermarine Spitfires.

By the time of the German invasion of Norway seven *Gruppen* of LG 1, KG 30 and KG 51, together with Aufklärungsgruppe 122, had been equipped or were re-equipping with Ju 88As, production of which was nearing 300 a month. New bomber variants included the **Ju 88A-2** with rocket-assisted take-off gear, the **Ju 88 A-4** with increased wing span, strengthened landing gear and 1,340-hp (1000-kW) Junkers Jumo 211J-1 or J-2 engines, and the generally similar **Ju 88 A-5**. All these versions appeared during 1940, the Ju 88A taking a prominent part in the summer Battle of Britain and winter Blitz with 17 *Gruppen*, of which 14 were *Kampfgruppen*. By reason of their relatively high speed, the Ju 88As proved the most difficult of the German bombers to destroy, and carried out a number of very successful attacks.

The Ju 88A series remained the principal bomber version, later sub-

variants including the **Ju 88A-6** with balloon cable fender, the **Ju 88A-6/U** three-seat long-range maritime bomber with FuG 200 *Hohentwiel* search radar, the **Ju 88A-9, Ju 88A-10** and **Ju 88A-11** which were tropicalized versions of the Ju 88A-1, Ju 88A-5 and Ju 88A-4 respectively, the **Ju 88A-14** anti-shipping strike bomber, the **Ju 88A-15** with bulged bomb bay capable of enclosing 3000 kg (6614 lb) of bombs, and the **Ju 88A-17** torpedo-bomber.

Ju 88As saw considerable action in the Balkans and Mediterranean, and of course on the Eastern Front. Perhaps their most outstanding service was however with III/KG 26 and KG 30 when based in northern Norway for operations against the Allied North Cape convoys in 1941-2; in all, the 120 Ju 88As involved are estimated to have sunk 27 merchant ships and seven naval vessels. Ju 88As of LG 1 operated with similar success against the Malta convoys during the summer of 1942.

Towards the end of the war many redundant Ju 88As were converted to become the unmanned, explosive-filled component of the *Mistel* composite aircraft weapon that was used with some success in the last desperate months of the Third Reich.

Specification
Junkers Ju 88A-4
Type: four-seat medium/dive bomber
Powerplant: two 1,340-hp (1000-kw) Junkers Jumo 211J-1 or 211J-2 inverted V-12 piston engines
Performance: maximum speed 450 km/h (280 mph) at 6000 m (19,685 ft); climb to 5400 m (17,715 ft) in 23 minutes; service ceiling 8200 m (26,900 ft); range 2730 km (1,696 miles)
Weights: empty 9860 kg (21,737 lb); maximum take-off 14000 kg (30,865 lb)
Dimensions: span 20.00 m (65 ft 7½ in); length 14.40 m (47 ft 2⅔ in); height 4.85 m (15 ft 11 in); wing area 54.50 m² (586.63 sq ft)
Armament: up to seven 7.92-mm (0.31-in) MG15 or MG81 machine-guns, plus a maximum internal and external bombload of 3600 kg (7,935 lb)

The Ju 88 served in the bomber role throughout the war and in every theatre. This Ju 88A is seen in the North African desert (note the white theatre band on the rear fuselage) with a pair of 250 kg (551 lb) bombs under the wings, inboard of the engine nacelles.

Light and Medium Bombers

The light/medium bomber was an ill-defined classification, and many types can lay claim to having performed this role. Here, the aircraft typifying this role are described, along with their phenomenal development and exploits during the course of the war.

The light and medium bombers of World War II were sandwiched between the glamorous day and night fighters on the one hand, and the strategic heavy bombers – such as the Boeing B-17, Consolidated B-24, Avro Lancaster and Handley Page Halifax – on the other. For a multitude of reasons the Japanese, Germans and Italians failed to introduce an efficient four-engine long-range heavy into service: the Heinkel He 177A-5 did become operational, but was in service with only a few Gruppen, and such was the nature of its maintenance and unreliability that its contribution to the Axis effort was minimal. The Axis nations therefore opted for a selection of light and medium bombers, restricted their use to tactical and naval work, and could never mount anything suggestive of a damaging campaign of bombing of strategic concept. Nevertheless much of the triumphal gain that fell to the Axis in the first half of World War II was born on the wings of the light bomber: for the Luftwaffe, the fabulous Junkers Ju 88 was the workhorse of 1939–45; and for the Regia Aeronautica, the 'evil hunchback' Savoia-Marchetti S.M.79 and the graceful CANT Z.1007; and for the Japanese, the Mitsubishi G3M2 'Nell' and G4M1 'Betty' of the Imperial Navy's land-based flotillas,

The wooden de Havilland DH 98 Mosquito was a legendary medium bomber which went into service in an extraordinary variety of configurations, including night fighter and reconnaissance.

and the Kawasaki Ki-48 'Lily' and Mitsubishi Ki-21 'Sally' of the Imperial Army's regiments. These represented the striking force of the Axis powers and, in their heyday before the advent of Allied air superiority, they were formidable.

The relative importance of tactical needs over those of a strategic nature dictated that the Soviet air forces (V-VS) would place much reliance on intermediate-range light bombers: the four-engine Tupolev TB-3 and Petlyakov Pe-8 served well, but only in small

numbers. The best Soviet bomber of 1941-4 was the Petlyakov Pe-2; it was replaced by the Tupolev Tu-2 in 1944. The Americans had the immediate advantage of having a wide selection of very powerful air-cooled radial engines when they went to war in 1941. Also they gained pre-knowledge of actual operations from their British ally. The light bombers produced for the US Army and US Navy – the North American B-25 Mitchell, the Martin B-26 Marauder, the Douglas A-20 Havoc,

the Lockheed POB-1 and PV-1 and others – served not only in the US forces but with a host of grateful Allies. All were universally efficient: there was not a failure among them. The Mitchell got the headlines in the papers for its daring low-level work in the Pacific theatre. For the British, the best was undoubtedly the extraordinary de Havilland Mosquito bomber series which defied logical design practice. But over Germany nothing could catch them, and a legend was born.

Bristol Blenheim

Flying for the first time on 12 April 1935 the **Bristol Type 142** was a twin-engine high-speed transport designed at the request of the press baron, Lord Rothermere. So startling was the performance that the Type 142, and later the **Type 142M**, were adopted for development as a light bomber under the Air Ministry Specification B.28/35. The result was the **Bristol Blenheim Mk I**, which was ordered straight from the drawing board. The first examples went to No. 114 Squadron at Wyton in March 1937. At the time of the Munich Crisis in September 1938 the Blenheim Mk I equipped 16 squadrons in Nos 1, 2 and 5 (Bomber) Groups of Bomber Command. As early as January 1938 the Blenheim Mk I entered service with No. 30 Squadron at Habbaniya, Iraq, while other Blenheim Mk Is were posted to AHQ India early in the following year. The Blenheim Mk I was powered by two 840-hp (626-kW) Bristol Mercury VIII radial engines. The light armament consisted of one 7.7-mm (0.303-in) machine-gun in the wing, and one manually-operated 707-mm (0.3-in) Vickers K gun in a dorsal turret; 454 kg (1,000 lb) of bombs could be carried. A total of 1,365 Blenheim Mk I bombers were produced by Bristol, Avro and Rootes: 45 were made under licence by the Finnish VLT company, and the Ikarus firm of Yugoslavia made 16. With its characteristic short-nosed glazed canopy the Blenheim Mk I saw service with the RAF in Greece, Malaya and North Africa.

Engines of increased power and a longer, scalloped, nose characterized the main production variant, the **Blenheim Mk IV**, of which 3,286 were produced. Powered by two 920-hp (686-kW) Bristol Mercury XV radials, the Blenheim Mk IV equipped seven squadrons in No. 2 (Bomber) Group at the outbreak of war in September 1939: armament was increased by the installation of two 7.7-mm (0.303-in) guns in a Bristol B.I. Mk IV dorsal tur-

ret, while a rearward-firing twin-gun turret could be installed under the nose section, sighted by a periscope. The Blenheim Mk IV scored a number of 'firsts' in World War II. On 3 September Blenheim Mk IV (N6215) of No. 139 Squadron, under Flying Officer A. McPherson, became the first RAF aircraft to enter German airspace and photograph the fleet units off Wilhelmshaven. On the following day Blenheim Mk IVs of Nos 107 and 110 Squadrons made the first offensive attack by Bomber Command. The RAF's first U-boat kill was made on 11 March 1940, by a Blenheim Mk IV of No. 82 Squadron flown by Squadron Leader M.V. Delap. Blenheim Mk IVs saw extensive service over France, off Norway, over Germany, Greece, Crete, North Africa, India, Malaya and Sumatra until August 1942 when they

were phased out. Finland and Greece operated Blenheim Mk IVs, as did Canada where it was known as the **Bolingbroke**. The **Blenheim Mk V** (945 built) appeared in late 1942, powered by two 950-hp (708-kW) Mercury 25 or 30 engines, and saw service in North Africa and Tunisia, and in the Far East. Underpowered and poorly armed, the Blenheim lost more crews than any other RAF type.

Specification
Bristol Blenheim B.Mk IV
Type: three-seat light bomber
Powerplant: two 920-hp (686-kW) Bristol Mercury XV radial piston engines
Performance: maximum speed 428 km/h (266 mph) at 3595 m (11,800 ft); cruising speed 318 km/h (198 mph); service ceiling 8310 m

Bristol Blenheim Mk I of No. 114 Sqn, RAF, serving at Larissa, Greece in 1941. The Middle East was a major theatre for the Blenheim, where its ability to absorb battle damage helped it to several successes in the early years of the war.

(27,260 ft); maximum range 2340 km (1,460 miles)
Weights: empty 4445 kg (9,790 lb); maximum take-off 6537 kg (14,400 lb)
Dimensions: span 17.17 m (56 ft 4 in); length 12.98 m (42 ft 7 in); height 2.99 m (9 ft 10 in); wing area 43.57 m² (469 sq ft)
Armament: up to five 7.7-mm (0.303-in) machine-guns (one fixed in wing, two in dorsal turret, and two optional rear-firing), plus a normal bombload of 454 kg (1,000 lb)

The crew of a Bristol Blenheim Mk IV board their aircraft prior to a raid. The Blenheim was the premier light bomber of the RAF in 1939, and continued to serve until the more potent Mosquito arrived in large-scale service. Those serving overseas continued to see action until late 1942.

Handley Page Hampden

As early as 1932, in answer to the Air Ministry specification B.9/32, a team at the Handley Page concern under G.R. Volkert designed the **Handley Page HP.52**, a slim twin-engine aircraft featuring a boom-type fuselage of very narrow width and considerable depth. Powered by two Bristol Pegasus PE.55(a) engines, the HP.52 flew for the first time on 21 June 1935 with Major J.L.H.B. Cordes at the controls. The first production HP.52, now known to the Royal Air Force as the **Handley Page Hampden Mk I**, flew its initial trials flight on 24 June 1938 following the issue of promising orders. The first example to serve with the RAF was passed to the Central Flying School at Upavon, and by December 1938 Nos 49, 50 and 83 Squadrons of RAF

Bomber Command were in the process of re-equipment. On the outbreak of war Hampden Mk I bombers were in service with Nos 44, 49, 50, 61, 83, 106, 144 and 185 Squadrons based in Lincolnshire and Huntingdonshire under No. 5 (Bomber) Group. The Scampton-

based No. 83 Squadron sent an armed reconnaissance to the Schillig Roads on 3 September 1939, but fog forced an early return to base. In common with other RAF bombers of the period, the Hampden Mk I was grossly under-armed: defensive gunnery was limited to only three 7.7-mm (0.303-in) hand-

Handley Page Hampden Mk I of No. 106 Sqn based at Finningley, Yorkshire in the spring of 1940. The yellow roundel has been painted out in the interests of camouflage. During this time, No. 106 Sqn flew intensive sorties against Germany, incurring heavy losses in the process.

held Vickers K guns. Operating within a few miles of the German coast in broad daylight soon brought repercussions. On 29 September Nos 61 and 144 Squadrons were operating over the German Bight when their Hampdens were bounced by a mixed formation of cannon-firing Messerschmitt Bf 109Es and Bf 110Cs from Jever and Nordholz: in a running battle five Hampdens were shot down. Some time later the Vickers Wellington Mk Is of Bomber Command encountered similar experiences, and the RAF was forced to commit its bomber force to nocturnal operations. On night missions the sturdy Hampden Mk I, with its respectable bombload, performed very well. The first German land base to be attacked, Hörnum near Sylt (Westerland), was raided by Hampdens on 19/20 March 1940. The type made the first attack on the industrial Ruhr in the company of Wellingtons on 11/12 May, and it took part in the first RAF bomber mission to Berlin on the night of 25/26 August 1940. Two Victoria Crosses went to crews of Hampdens: the first to Flight Lieutenant R. A. B. Learoyd (No. 49 Sqn) for action against the Dortmund-Ems canal on 12/13 August 1940, and the second to Sergeant John Hannah (No. 83 Sqn) for putting out a fire over Antwerp on 15/16 September 1940.

Total production numbered 1,532. Hampden Mk Is were built by Handley Page (500), English Electric (770), and

the Canadian CAA (160); 141 Hampden Mk Is were converted to Hampden TB.Mk I torpedo-bombers, which served with Nos 144, 455 and 408 Squadrons in Coastal Command from bases in Scotland and the northern USSR during 1942; two **Hampden Mk II** aircraft with 1,100-hp (820-kW) Wright Cyclones were produced. The 1,000-hp (745-kW) Napier Dagger VIII engine was installed in the Hampden's cousin, the **Hereford**: 100 were built, saw no action, and nine were converted to Hampden Mk Is. The Hampden was phased out of Bomber Command's first-line units by August 1942, but the Hampden TB.Mk I continued in service until December 1943.

Specification
Handley Page Hampden Mk I
Type: four-seat medium bomber
Powerplant: two 980-hp (731-kW) Bristol Pegasus XVIII radial piston engines
Performance: maximum speed 426 km/h (265 mph) at 4725 m (15,500 ft); cruising speed 269 km/h (167 mph); climb to 4570 m (15,000 ft) in 18 minutes 55 seconds; service ceiling 6920 m (22,700 ft); maximum range 3200 km (1,990 miles)
Weights: empty 5343 kg (11,780 lb); maximum take-off 9526 kg (21,000 lb)
Dimensions: span 21.08 m (69 ft 2 in); length 16.33 m (53 ft 7 in); height 4.49 m (14 ft 9 in); wing area 62.06 m²

The Hampden did not have any power-operated gun turrets, and so with only hand-held guns for tail defence it was particularly vulnerable in the presence of fighters. This is a Hampden Mk I with Bristol Pegasus engines.

(669 sq ft)
Armament: initially single 7.7-mm (0.303-in) Browning and Vickers K guns in nose (fixed), nose cupola and rear dorsal and ventral stations, after January 1940 upgunned by twin 7.7-mm (0.303-in) Vickers K guns in ventral and dorsal stations, plus a bombload of 1814 kg (4,000 lb)

---

de Havilland Mosquito
UK

In October 1938 the design team under Geoffrey de Havilland, with R.E. Bishop and C.C. Walker, started work on a light bomber constructed entirely of wood to offset the demand for strategically vital materials that war would inevitably bring. After a 1940 order of 50, built to Specification B.1/40, the first prototype **de Havilland Mosquito** flew on 25 November 1940, powered by two 1,460-hp (1089-kW) Merlin 21s. It displayed the most outstanding performance from the very start, being faster than the RAF's contemporary interceptor fighters. Of the initial production batch 10 were converted to de Havilland **Mosquito B.Mk IV Series I** light bombers with glazed nose and internal bomb bays: the first of these, W4072, flew for the first time on 8 September 1941. The main production version was the **Mosquito B.Mk IV Series II** which had Merlin 21, 23 or 25 engines in lengthened nacelles. No. 105 Squadron, then based at Marham in No. 2 (Bomber) Group, received its first Mosquito B.Mk IVs in the spring of 1942. Its first mission was to Köln on 31 May 1942, the morning after the 'One Thousand Bomber' raid. Crews learned to use the Mosquito's speed as the primary method of evading enemy fighters, for the type was entirely unarmed. Low-altitude missions with shallow-dive approaches to the target soon proved to be the Mosquito bomber's forte by day, and one of No. 105 Squadron's first major attacks was a daring low-level strike on the Gestapo headquarters in Oslo. Such was the demand for Mosquitoes as reconnaissance and night-fighter aircraft that bomber units were slow in formation: by the autumn of 1942, No. 139 Squadron was working up on Mosquito B.Mk IVs. Both Nos 105 and 139 Squad-

ML963 was a Mosquito B.Mk XVI built at Hatfield in 1944 and seen serving with No. 571 Sqn at Oakington in Cambridgeshire. The Mk XVI was a development of the Mk IX with pressurized cockpit and extra fuel. The enlarged bomb bay enabled a 1814-kg (4,000-lb) bomb to be carried.

One of a small batch of Hatfield-built B.Mk IX high-altitude bombers, which set up a fantastic record of night missions with No. 105 Sqn. Ten aircraft reached 100 missions and two reached 200. The aircraft carries standard Bomber Command night camouflage.

rons were over Berlin on the morning of 30 January 1943, and caused fury and consternation during a series of speeches by Nazi leaders who were celebrating an anniversary of the Führer's appointment as Chancellor of the Third Reich. Reconnaissance and bomber Mosquitoes roamed over Germany and the occupied territories at will during 1943-4. The specialist Jagdgruppen Nrn 25 and 50 were formed in the Luftwaffe in 1943 with souped-up Messerschmitt Bf 109G-6 fighters, but gained no success. In Bomber Command 54 Mosquito B.Mk IVs were

modified with bulged bomb bays to carry a single 1814-kg (4,000-lb) HC bomb, and these served in the Fast Night Striking Force equipped with Oboe Mk I-III. Canada built the **Mosquito B.Mk VII** with 1,418-hp (1057-kW) Packard Merlin 31s. Fifty-four **Mosquito B.Mk IX** aircraft with extra bombload and Merlin 72 engines were produced. The most efficient was the **Mosquito B.Mk XVI** with a pressurized cabin, comprehensive navigational equipment and a bulged bomb bay. Canada's de Havilland subsidiary also produced the **Mosquito B.Mk XX** and

Mosquito B.Mk 25 before the war's end. Production totalled 7,785.

Specification
de Havilland Mosquito B.Mk XVI
Type: two-seat medium bomber
Powerplant: two 1,680-hp (1253-kW) Rolls-Royce Merlin 72 V-12 piston engines
Performance: maximum speed 656 km/h (408 mph) at 7925 m (26,000 ft); cruising speed 394 km/h (245 mph); initial climb rate 853 m (2,800 ft) per minute; service ceiling 11280 m (37,000 ft); maximum range

2389 km (1,485 miles)
Weights: empty 6638 kg (14,635 lb);
maximum take-off 10433 kg (23,000 lb)
Dimensions: span.16.51 m (54 ft 2 in);
length 12.47 m (40 ft 11 in); height 3.81 m

(12 ft 6 in); wing area 42.18 m² (454 sq ft)
Armament: four 227-kg (500-lb) bombs internally and two more under wings, or one 1814-kg (4,000-lb) bomb

Flying with No. 139 Sqn from Marham in the early summer of 1943, this Mosquito B.Mk IV Srs II shows the potent lines of the marque. No. 139 Sqn took its Mosquitoes to Wyton

in June that year on Pathfinder duties, flying 'spoof' attacks and conducting radar dislocation raids using 'Window' (chaff).

FRANCE

Breguet 693

The **Breguet 690** was designed in response to a 1934 French air ministry specification calling for a twin-engined three-seat fighter. Several manufacturers submitted proposals, and the contest was won by the Potez 630. The Breguet proposal had been heavier and more powerful than the other submissions, its designers believing it to be a more versatile, multi-role aeroplane. Design of the Breguet 690 was started in 1935 and a prototype was completed in 1937, first flying on 23 March 1938. The aircraft was found to have a performance superior to that of the Potez 630, and Breguet received a contract to supply 100 aircraft, configured as light attack bombers.

The resulting **Breguet 691** was a clean-looking cantilever mid-wing monoplane of all-metal construction, with two wing-mounted engines and a short fuselage nose reminiscent of that of the Bristol Beaufighter. Aft of the wing, however, the fuselage tapered to a tailplane with twin endplate fins and rudders. Conversion from Bre.690 to Bre.691 was relatively simple, the main change being deletion of the navigator's position to provide a small bomb bay. Experience with the Bre.691 proved the Hispano-Suiza powerplants to be unreliable, and the **Bre.693.01** was introduced with two Gnome-Rhône 14M-6/7 engines after only 78 Bre.691s had been built. Two hundred and thirty four examples of

Right: This Breguet Bre.695 was on the strength of the 1ere Escadrille of GBA I/51. The Bre.695 was powered by the Pratt & Whitney Twin Wasp Junior engine, but it was severely outclassed by the German fighters it encountered.

Above: Formerly of GBA I/51 of the Armée de l'Air, this Breguet Bre.693 is pictured after being transferred to the Regia Aeronautica in 1943. The red of the French roundels were retained, with the Italian fasces replacing the blue.

the Bre.693 were built, later examples having two extra 7.5-mm (0.3-in) machine-guns, one installed in the tail of each engine nacelle, to improve self-defence.

Foreign interest in the Bre.690 series was cut short by the German invasion of France and the single **Bre.694.01** built, intended as a three-seat reconnaissance aircraft, was delivered directly to the Aéronavale. The Bre.694 was generally similar to the original Bre.690 with no bomb bay and a navigator's compartment, but with Gnome-Rhône 14M-4/5 engines.

The **Bre.695** was virtually identical to the Bre.693 but with Pratt & Whitney SB4G Twin Wasp Junior engines. It was felt desirable to design a version of the aircraft using foreign engines in case the supply of French powerplants was disrupted by enemy action. Fifty Bre.695s were built, being delivered to Groupe 18 in June 1940.

The **Bre.696** and **697** were built only as prototypes and were respectively a two-seat light bomber and a two-seat heavy destroyer. The Breguet 693 proved extremely vulnerable and almost half were lost to enemy action.

Specification
Breguet 693
Type: two-seat light attack bomber
Powerplant: two 700-hp (522-kW) Gnome-Rhône 14M-6/7 radial piston engines
Performance: maximum speed 490 km/h (304 mph) at 5000 m (16,400 ft); maximum cruising speed 400 km/h (248 mph) at 4000 m (13,125 ft); maximum range 1350 km (839 miles)
Weights: empty 3010 kg (6,636 lb); maximum take-off 4900 kg (10,803 lb)
Dimensions: span 15.37 m (50 ft 5 in);

length 9.67 m (31 ft 8¾ in); height 3.19 m (10 ft 5¾ in); wing area 29.20 m² (32 sq ft)
Armament: one 20-mm Hispano-Suiza cannon and two 7.5-mm Darne machine-guns firing forward, plus one similar gun on pivoted mount in rear cockpit, one fixed 7.5-mm gun firing obliquely aft from ventral position and (late models) two 7.5-mm guns, one in each engine nacelle firing aft, and up to 400 kg (882 lb) of bombs.

Martin Model 187 Baltimore

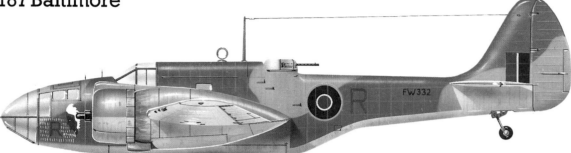

A powerful and much modified version of the Martin Maryland light bomber, the **Martin Model 187 Baltimore** was produced specifically to RAF orders, the first of 50 **Baltimore Mk I** aircraft (AG685) was shipped to the UK in October 1941 to commence trials at Burtonwood, near Liverpool. The first 150 Baltimore Mk I and **Baltimore Mk II** bombers were delivered without power-operated dorsal turrets, the single 7.7-mm (0.303-in) Vickers K machine-gun in the Baltimore Mk I's dorsal position being replaced by a twin mount in the Baltimore Mk II. Because of the shortage of RAF medium and light bombers in RAF Middle East Command, the first Baltimores were delivered to No. 223 Squadron based at Shandur, Egypt, in January 1942, and were initially used for conversion training. The next squadron to re-equip was No. 55, which took its new **Baltimore Mk III** bombers into action during the Battle of Gazala and the fall of Tobruk in May 1942: a power-operated Boulton-Paul turret was installed in this version with either two or four 7.7-mm (0.303-in) Browning machine-guns. Both Nos 55 and 223 Squadrons continued to operate over Cyrenaica, being based under No. 211 Wing at Amiriya along with the Douglas Boston Mk IIIs of Nos 12 and 24 (SAAF) Squadrons as part of the Desert Air Force's light bomber force. Baltimores were issued to No. 21 (SAAF) Squadron and No. 1437 Flight, and for maritime reconnaissance duties to No. 69 Squadron and No. 203 Squadron. Operations by day and by night were mounted against Benghazi and Tobruk, against military camps of the Afrika Korps and on many desert airfields.

After the 2nd Battle of El Alamein Baltimores continued to operate over Libya and Tunisia, before turning to the pre-invasion bombing offensive on Luftwaffe airfields in Sicily, Pantellaria and Sardinia. The type proved to be sturdy and easy to handle. In 1943, the RAF took charge of the first **Baltimore Mk IIIA** aircraft on Lend-Lease and produced to an USAAF order for the **A-30**: the main difference was the inclusion of a Martin 250CE turret with twin 12.7-mm (0.5-in) Brownings in place of the Boulton-Paul turret. The **Baltimore Mk IV** (**A-30A**) was similar to the Baltimore Mk IIIA, while the final version, the **Baltimore Mk V**, had uprated Wright GR-2600 engines, and wing-mounted 12.7-mm (0.5-in) guns. Baltimores served with the RAF over Sicily and Italy until May 1945, with the Free French air force and the Italian co-belligerent air forces, while a num-

ber were sent to Turkey under Lend-Lease. Production totalled 1,575, the last being FW880 (a Baltimore Mk V) that was issued to the RAF in May 1944.

Specification
Martin Baltimore Mk III
Type: four-seat light/medium bomber
Powerplant: two 1,660-hp (1238-kW) Wright Cyclone GR-2600-19 radial piston engines
Performance: maximum speed 486 km/h (302 mph) at 3355 m (11,000 ft); climb to 4570 m (15,000 ft) in 12 minutes 0 seconds; service ceiling

7315 m (24,000 ft); normal range 1530 km (950 miles)
Weights: empty 6895 kg (15,200 lb); maximum take-off 10433 kg (23,000 lb)
Dimensions: span 18.69 m (61 ft 4 in); length 14.77 m (48 ft 5¾ in) height 5.41 m (17 ft 9 in); wing area 50.03 m² (538.5 sq ft)
Armament: four 7.7-mm (0.303-in) wing-mounted Browning machine-guns, two (or four) 7.7-mm (0.303-in) Brownings in dorsal turret and two 7.7-mm (0.303-in) Brownings in ventral position, plus a maximum bombload of 907 kg (2,000 lb)

An ex-USAAF Martin A-30A-10-MA Baltimore Mk V of No. 232 Wing, North-west African Tactical Air Force; comprising Nos 55 and 223 Sqns, the wing flew the Baltimore Mk V during the Italian campaign of 1944.

Among the first batch of Baltimores to arrive was AG697, a Mk I. As it was pictured here it had been updated to Mk II standard with twin dorsal guns. The subsequent aircraft featured Boulton-Paul power-operated four-gun turrets as the Baltimore Mk III.

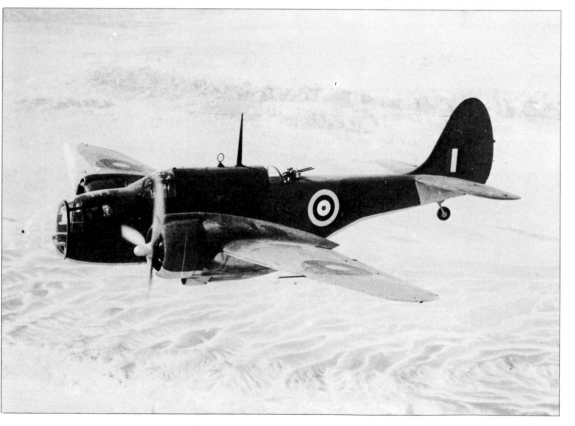

Martin B-26 Marauder

High wing-loadings, break-neck landing speeds and malicious single-engine flying characteristics nearly put paid to the career of the **Martin B-26 Marauder** in October 1942 when a US Army Air Force committee was called in to investigate its future. However, certain improvements were made and the B-26 went on to become one of the USAAF's medium bomber stalwarts. In the competition for medium and light bombers for the US Army Air Corps of January 1939, the Glenn L. Martin Company was awarded a contract for 200 B-26 aircraft. Going all out for speed, designer Peyton M. Magruder produced an aircraft with torpedo-like fuselage, two huge engines, tricycle landing gear and stubby wings. Powered by two Pratt & Whitney R-2800-5 engines the prototype B-26 first flew on 25 November 1940, by which time orders for 1,131 **B-26A** and **B-26B** bombers had been received. The first B-26s and B-26As were passed to the US 22nd Bombardment Group at Langley Field in February 1941. With the outbreak of war the 22nd BG was the only unit with B-26s and, after service at Muroc, California, the group was sent to Brisbane, Australia, to operate against the Japanese in the South West Pacific Area: the 22nd BG made its first raid on Rabaul on 5 April 1942, in addition to frequent attacks on Lae, Salamaua, and Buna. In the epic Battle of Midway four B-26As with torpedoes attacked the Japanese fleet, flown by pilots drawn from the 22nd and 38th Groups. The B-25 Mitchell was more successful than the B-26 in this theatre, and by

Though frequently criticized on account of its tricky handling qualities, the B-26 packed a heavy punch and was widely used by the USAAF in Europe. This B-26B of the 598th Bomb Sqn, 397th Bomb Wing, pictured during the invasion of Normandy, displays an impressive tally on the nose.

Marauders served on only two RAF squadrons, both in the Mediterranean; the short-span Marauder Mk I shown here flew with

No. 14 Sqn in North Africa from August 1942 to September 1944. Later, the long-span Marauder Mk III served with No. 39 Sqn.

early 1943 the 22nd BG had been re-equipped. The B-26B came into the war in May 1942, powered by R-2800-5, R-2800-41 or R-2800-43 engines, without the spinners of the B-26A, with extra armour and guns, and with enlarged wing span on the 642nd and following production aircraft. Martin's Omaha subsidiary made the **B-26C**, which was identical with the increased-span B-26B.

The B-26 saw service in the Aleutians in 1942, and in the Western Desert under RAF Middle East Command as the **Marauder Mk I** (B-26A), **Marauder Mk IA** (B-26B), and **Marauder Mk II** (B-26C), No. 14 Squadron being the first recipient. The type was used by the Free French Air Force, the SAAF, and as **AT-23A and JM-1** target tugs by the US Army and US Navy. Four groups of the US 8th Air Force arrived in England in March 1943, flew low-level attacks over

heavily defended targets and paid the price: on 17 May 1943 the 322nd BG was wiped out on the Ijmuiden strike. Adopting medium-level pattern bombing, the B-26B and B-26C (with the US VIII Air Support Command, and later the US 9th Air Force) were the backbone of the Allied medium bomber forces to the end of the war in Europe. Total production was 4,708.

Specification
Martin B-26B Marauder
Type: seven-seat medium bomber
Powerplant: two 2,000-hp (1491-kW) Pratt & Whitney R-2800-41 radial piston engines
Performance: maximum speed 510 km/h (317 mph) at 4420 m (14,500 ft); cruising speed 418 km/h (260 mph); climb to 4570 m (15,000 ft) in 12 minutes 0 seconds; service ceiling 7165 m (23,500 ft); range 1850 km (1,150 miles)

A Martin B-26B-40 of the 444th Sqn, 320th BG based at Decimomannu, Sardinia, in 1944. The Marauder was widely used in Italy, its high speed and agility suiting it to penetrating heavy defences. The original aircraft letter shows through the hastily-applied olive-drab finish.

Weights: empty 10152 kg (22,380 lb); maximum take-off 15513 kg (34,200 lb)
Dimensions: span 19.81 m (65 ft 0 in); length 17.75 m (58 ft 3 in); height 6.04 m (19 ft 10 in); wing area 55.93 m^2 (602 sq ft)
Armament: two 7.7-mm (0.3-in) Browning machine-guns (one each in nose and ventral stations) or two 12.7-mm (0.5-in) M2 machine-guns in beam positions instead of ventral gun, and four 12.7-mm (0.5-in) guns (two each in dorsal turret and in tail station), plus a maximum bombload of 2359 kg (5,200 lb)

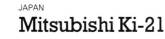

Mitsubishi Ki-21

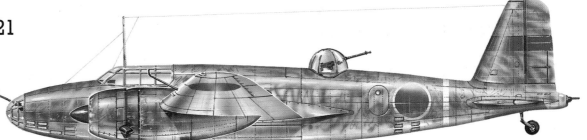

The **Mitsubishi Ki-21 (Army Type 97 Heavy Bomber)** was produced by engineers Nakata and Ozawa in response to an operational specification issued by the Air Headquarters (Daihonei) of the JAAF on 15 February 1936. The first of two prototypes flew on 18 December 1936, the first production model being the **Mitsubishi Ki-21-Ia (Army Type 97 Model 1A)**. Because of production bottlenecks it was not until the end of 1939 that Ki-21-Ia bombers equipped the first JAAF unit, the 60th Hikosentai (air regiment) based in China, in totality; the next unit to be equipped was the 61st Sentai. Early lessons learned from China demonstrated lack of firepower and protection, and the **Ki-21-Ib** and **Ki-21-Ic** subvariants had extra armour, additional 7.7-mm (0.3-in) Type 89 machine-guns, more fuel and larger bomb-bays. The engines were 850-hp (634-kW) Nakajima Ha-5 KAI radials. By the time of the outbreak of war in December 1941, the majority of the Mitsubishi Ki-21-Ia, Ki-21-Ib and Ki-21-Ic bombers had been relegated to second-line duties, or to service as operational bomber trainers. First-line bomber *sentais* had by now received the more powerful **Ki-21-II**, with 1,500-hp (1119-kW) Mitsubishi Ha-101 engines in modified cowlings: production models in ser-

vice in 1941 were the **Ki-21-IIa (Army Type 97 Heavy Bomber Model 2A)**, and the **Ki-21-IIb** which had a pedal-operated dorsal turret with one 12.7-mm (0.5-in) Type 1 heavy machine-gun. Three *sentais* remained in Japan, Korea and in Manchuria when the Japanese high command went to war in South East Asia. For operations over the Philippines the JAAF's 5th Air Group, based in Formosa, mustered the 14th and 62nd Hikosentais; these went into action early on the morning of 8 December 1941 striking at Aparri, Tuguegarao, Vigan and other targets in Luzon. Mitsubishi Ki-21s of the 3rd Air Group, based in French Indo-China, were earmarked for bombing strikes against Siam (Thailand) and Malaya: units were the 12th, 60th and 98th Hikosentais. These smashed RAF and RAAF facilities at Alor Star, Sungei Patani and Butterworth, being

escorted by Nakajima Ki-27 and Ki-43 fighters. In the flush of Japanese victory in 1941-2 the Mitsubishi Ki-21, code-named 'Sally', performed well; only over Rangoon over December 1941 and January 1942 did the Ki-21s suffer heavy casualties. The Ki-21-IIb was the final model to enter service, which was seen on all fronts in the Pacific and Far East theatres. Some 2,064 Ki-21s were built.

Specification
Mitsubishi Ki-21-IIb
Type: five-seat medium bomber
Powerplant: two 1,500-hp (1119-kW) Mitsubishi Ha-101 (Army Type 100) radial piston engines
Performance: maximum speed 486 km/h (302 mph) at 4720 m (15,485 ft); cruising speed 380 km/h (236 mph); climb to 6000 m (19,685 ft) in 13 minutes 13 seconds; service ceiling

Mitsubishi Ki-21-IIb of the Imperial Japanese Army. This type was virtually obsolescent at the outbreak of the Pacific war but it soldiered on until 1945, scoring many notable successes before finally ending its active life on kamikaze attacks.

10000 m (32,810 ft); maximum range 2700 km (1,680 miles)
Weights: empty 6070 kg (13,382 lb); maximum take-off 10610 kg (23,391 lb)
Dimensions: span 22.50 m (73 ft 9¾ in); length 16.00 m (52 ft 6 in); height 4.85 m (15 ft 11 in); wing area 69.6 m² (749.16 sq ft)
Armament: five single manually-operated 7.7-mm Type 89 machine-guns (in nose, tail, ventral and two beam stations) and one 12.7-mm (0.5-in) Type 1 machine-gun (in dorsal position), plus a maximum bombload of 1000 kg (2,205 lb)

Nakajima Ki-49 Donryu

The **Nakajima Ki-49 Donryu** (storm dragon) was designed early in 1938 to replace the JAAF's successful Mitsubishi Ki-21 heavy bomber which, in fact, was only just entering service with *sentais* based in China and Manchuria. Later code-named 'Helen', the Nakajima Ki-49 was a workmanlike design but was destined to be just not good enough for the conditions prevailing over the various fronts in 1942, when the initial production **Ki-49-I (Army Type 100 Heavy Bomber Model 1)** started operations with the 61st Hikosentai in China. Production was preceded by the flight of the first prototype in August 1939, powered by two 950-hp (708-kW) Nakajima Ha-5 KAI radials: the more powerful 1,250-hp (932-kW) Ha-41 radial engines were installed in pre-production versions, and in the Ki-49-I bomber. In appearance the 'Helen' was deceptive in size, for it appeared to be a comparatively large aircraft because of its proportions: actually, its dimensions were similar to those of the Lockheed Hudson. However, a crew of seven or eight was crammed into the narrow fuselage. In the spring of 1942 the usual steps were taken to increase performance, protection and defensive firepower. The **Nakajima Ki-49-IIa (Army Type 100 Heavy Bomber Model 2A)**, the first of the new series, was powered by two Nakajima Ha-109 radial engines with increased ratings. The aircraft was fast, well protected by 5-mm (0.2-in) armour plating and rubberized fuel cells, and heavily armed. The **Ki-49-IIb** was upgunned with 12.7-mm (0.5-in) Ho-103 machine-guns. Both the Ki-49-IIa and Ki-49-IIb were in action with the 7th and 61st Sentais based in China in the summer of 1942, and made many attacks on Chungking and air bases of General C.L. Chennault's China Air Task Force. 'Helen' bombers equipped the 12th

Sentai, based at Medan and Sabang (Sumatra) under the 3rd Air Army, and these attacked objectives in Burma and eastern India, joining Ki-21s on some occasions in raids on Calcutta. In 1943 the Ki-61s of the 7th and 61st Sentais, now operating from Timor, attacked Darwin to face strong reaction by the Supermarine Spitfire Mk VCs of No. 1 Fighter Wing. Units equipped with Ki-49s suffered most in New Guinea, where 4th Air Army came under constant attack on its airfields at Wewak, But and Dagua after August 1943, when the RAAF and the US 5th Air Force went onto the offensive. Six **Ki-49-III** bombers, powered by very potent 2,420-hp (1805-kW) engines, were built as prototypes. Other variants produced in experimental form were the **Ki-58** escort fighter, and the **Ki-80** escort bomber. Total production amounted to 819 aircraft. After action in the Philippines in 1944, Ki-49s were used with increasing frequency on suicide missions.

Specification
Nakajima Ki-49-IIa Donryu
Type: seven/eight-seat medium bomber
Powerplant: two 1,450-hp (1081-kW) Nakajima Ha-109 (Army Type 2) radial piston engines
Performance: maximum speed 492 km/h (306 mph) at 5000 m (16,405 ft); cruising speed 350 km/h (217 mph); climb to 5000 m (16,405 ft) in

13 minutes 39 seconds; service ceiling 9300 m (30,510 ft); maximum range 2950 km (1,835 miles)
Weights: empty 6530 kg (14,396 lb); maximum take-off 11400 kg (25,133 lb)
Dimensions: span 20.42 m (67 ft 0 in); length 16.50 m (54 ft 1½ in); height 4.25 m (13 ft 11¼ in); wing area 69.05 m² (743.24 sq ft)
Armament: five single manually-operated 7.7-mm (0.303-in) Type 89 machine-guns (in nose, tail, ventral and two beam stations) and one flexible 20-mm Ho-1 cannon in dorsal turret, plus a maximum bombload of 1000 kg (2,205 lb)

A Ki-49-IIa of the 3rd Chutai, 95th Sentai, operating in north east China during September 1944. The 'palm-frond' camouflage was applied in the field.

Despite its Japanese designation of 'heavy bomber', the Nakajima Ki-49 had a maximum bombload of only 1000 kg (2,205 lb). It saw much action but suffered at the hands of Allied fighters due to lack of performance.

Mitsubishi Ki-67 Hiryu

Fortunately for the Allies in the latter stages of the Pacific war, comparatively few of the formidable **Mitsubishi Ki-67 Hiryu** (flying dragon) medium bombers and torpedo-bombers, code-named **'Peggy'** by air intelligence, were encountered in action. Production was limited and got off to a late start in the war, and by the time of its service debut in 1944 the Ki-67's potency was negated both by Allied fighter superiority and by the poor quality of the JAAF and JNAF crews which operated it. To take the place of the Mitsubishi Ki-21 'Sally' and the Nakajima Ki-49 'Helen', the Air Office (Koku Hombu) issued specifications for a new bomber to the Mitsubishi concern in November 1940. The work was led by Chief Engineer Ozawa on an aircraft based on the beautiful Japanese lines and powered by the new generation of powerful Ha-100 double-row 18-cylinder radial engines. Three prototypes of the **Ki-67-I** were completed between December 1942 and March 1943, the first making its initial flight on 27 December 1942. The Ki-67-I proved to be fast (though not as fast as originally specified), and extremely manoeuvrable with loops and barrel-rolls being carried out with ease in an unloaded configuration. Although adopted for service as the **Army Type 4 Heavy Bomber**, such was the promise of the Ki-67-I that even the Imperial Japanese Navy was impressed, and made early representations to Mitsubishi. On 5 January 1943 Mitsubishi received an order to convert 100 Ki-49s as torpedo-bombers, with internal racks capable of handling the standard 450-mm (17.7-in) Navy Type 91 Model II aerial torpedo: these saw service with the 762nd Kokutai (air group) from the autumn of 1944 onwards. The Ki-67-I was issued in small numbers to the veteran 7th, 14th, 16th, 61st, 62nd, 74th, 98th and 110th Hikosentais (air regiments) and saw limited action over Chi-

na, Biak and Sansapor in north western New Guinea, and Sumatra in the summer of 1944. The type was recognized as such for the first time by the Allies in October 1944, during the US 3rd Fleet's attacks on Formosa and the Ryukyus where the Hiryu served in the 8th Hikoshidan (air division) based on Formosa under navy control. Thereafter Ki-67-Is were encountered over the Philippines, off Iwo Jima, in the strikes on the US 20th Air Force's bases on Saipan and Tinian, and in the Okinawa campaign where it was used as a suicide aircraft. For suicide missions the JAAF used modified Peggys known as the **Ki-61-I KAI** with armament removed and a solid nose packed with explosive. Only two of the more powerful **Ki-67-II** variant were made, production of army and navy Ki-67-Is amounting to 696. It was the best Japanese medium bomber of World War II.

Specification
Mitsubishi Ki-67-I Hiryu
Type: six/eight-seat medium bomber and torpedo-bomber
Powerplant: 1,900-hp (1417-kW) Mitsubishi Ha-104 (Army Type 4) radial piston engines
Performance: maximum speed 537 km/h (334 mph) at 6000 m (19,685 ft); cruising speed 400 km/h (249 mph); climb to 6000 m (19,685 ft) in 14 minutes 30 seconds; service ceiling

9470 m (31,070 ft); maximum range 3800 km (2,360 miles)
Weights: empty 8649 kg (19,068 kg) maximum take-off 13765 kg (30,346 lb)
Dimensions: span 22.50 m (73 ft 9¾ in); length 18.70 m (61 ft 4¼ in); height 7.70 m (25 ft 3¼ in); wing area 65.85 m² (708.86 sq ft)
Armament: four 12.7-mm (0.5-in) Type 1 machine-guns (one each in nose, two beam blisters, and tail turret) and one 20-mm Ho-5 cannon in dorsal turret, plus a maximum bombload of 800 kg (1,765 lb), or one Type 91 or Type 94 torpedo

Mitsubishi Ki-67-I of the Imperial Japanese Army. During the closing months of the war, these aircraft had their noses packed with explosives for use as kamikaze aircraft.

Built along classic Japanese lines, the Ki-67 was an impressive aircraft but its service was limited due to its late arrival in the war. Armament consisted of four machine-guns and a 20-mm cannon.

CANT Z.1007 Airone

Along with the Savoia-Marchetti S.M.79, the **CANT Z.1007 Airone** (heron) series of bombers served as the backbone of the Regia Aeronautica's conventional and torpedo strike forces in World War II. Under the aegis of the firm of CANT (Cantieri Riuniti dell' Adriatico), Ingeniere Filippo Zappata began design studies of the CANT Z.1007 and Z.1011 in 1935: both were powered by 625-kW (840-hp) Isotta-Fraschini Asso XI RC.15 engines, for which the former had three and the latter two. The relatively low power ratings of this engine forced the Regia Aeronautica to order the tri-motor CANT Z.1007 for production, the first prototype flying in March 1937. The aircraft was constructed entirely of wood, save for the usual metal ancillaries and nacelle cladding. The first examples had two-bladed wooden propellers, but all later versions adopted the three-bladed metal Alfa Romeo types. In 1938, as a means to better load and performance, the **CANT Z.1007bis** entered production, having three 745-kW (1,000-hp) Piaggio B.XIbis RC.40 radial engines as standard. The CANT Z.1007bis was the major production model, and featured revised armament, engine cowlings and dimensions. A single fin and rud-

Above: This CANT Z.1007bis served with 230ª Squadriglia, 95° Gruppo, 35° Stormo in Greece, February 1941. Known as the Airone (heron), the type was built in both single- and twin-finned versions.

Right: Owing to its weak gun defence and poor performance, the CANT Z.1007 was a sitting duck for Allied fighters, but the type served until late 1943 in the Mediterranean and on the Russian front.

der was used on the Z.1007 Serie I-III, with a twin fin-rudder format being adopted on the Z.1007 Serie IV-IX sub-types.

When Italy entered the war on 10 June 1940 the Regia Aeronautica had

87 CANT Z.1007 and Z.1007bis bombers in commission, of which 38 were serviceable. These served with the 16° and 47° Stormi da Bombardamento Terrestre stationed at Vicenza and Ghedi in northern Italy. These units saw first action against Greek forces in October 1940, before turning their energies to anti-shipping strikes off Crete and North Africa, and on medium-level day and night bombing raids on Malta. Subsequently the type was employed by the 8°, 9°, 27°, 30° Stormi, and by the 41°, 51°, 59°, 87°, 90°, 95° and 107° Gruppi BT plus two *squadriglie*. During the climax of the

Malta battles in May 1942, CANT Z.1007s took heavy casualties from the RAF's newly-arrived Supermarine Spitfire Mk VC fighters; similar losses were experienced during the epic 'Harpoon' and 'Pedesta' convoy battles of the summer. Dwindling numbers were on hand to attempt to counter the Allied landings in Sicily in July 1943, and by the time of the armistice in September only a few were still available, these continuing to fight both with the RSI (Fascist regime) and the Italian co-belligerent air forces. Thirty-five CANT Z.1007ters were produced; production of the CANT Z.107bis and

Z.1007ter (Piaggio P.XIX engines) amounted to 526.

Specification
CANT Z.1007bis Alcione
Type: five-seat medium bomber
Powerplant: three 1,000-hp (745-kW) Piaggio P.XI RC.40 radial piston engines
Performance: maximum speed 455 km/h (283 mph) at 4600 m (15,090 ft); cruising speed 338 km/h (210 mph); climb to 6000 m (19,685 ft) in 16 minutes 8 seconds; service ceiling 7500 m (24,605 ft); normal range 1795 km (1,115 miles)

Weights: empty 9396 kg (20,715 lb); maximum take-off 13621 kg (30,029 lb)
Dimensions: span 24.80 m (81 ft 4½ in); length 18.35 m (60 ft 2½ in); height 5.22 m (17 ft 1½ in); wing area 70.0 m² (753.47 sq ft)
Armament: two 12.7-mm (0.5-in) Breda-SAFAT or Scotti machine-guns (one each in dorsal turret and ventral step) and two 7.7-mm (0.303-in) Breda-SAFAT guns in beam positions, plus a maximum bombload of 1200 kg (2,646 lb) or two 450-mm (17.7-in) torpedoes

---

Fiat B.R.20 Cicogna

A well designed and sturdy medium bomber, the **Fiat B.R.20 Cicogna** (stork) series fell nevertheless into that category which was nearing obsolescence by the outbreak of World War II. Designed by Ingeniere Celestino Rosatelli, and owing much of its parentage to the sleek Fiat APR.2 commercial transport, the Fiat B.R.20 prototype flew first on 10 February 1936. The first unit of the Regia Aeronautica to receive B.R.20s was the 13° Stormo BT stationed at Lonate Pozzolo: the 7° Stormo BT, also at Lonate, received Fiat B.R.20s in February 1937. Powered by two 1,000-hp (745-kW) Fiat A.80 RC.41 radial engines, the B.R.20 possessed a maximum speed of 430 km/h (267 mph) at 4000 m (13,125 ft), and was armed with two 7.7-mm (0.303-in) and one 12.7-mm (0.5-in) machine-guns. Elements of the 7° and 13° Stormi BT were despatched to Spain in May 1937 for combat experience, while other B.R.20s were exported to Japan, and saw service with indifferent results in China and Manchuria as the JAAF's **Army Type 1 Model 100 Heavy bomber**. Modified nose contours, increased armour protection and revised armament featured in the **B.R.20M**, of which 264 were ultimately produced. When Italy declared war on 10 June 1940 the Regia Aeronautica had 162 Fiat B.R.20s and B.R.20Ms in commission with the 7°, 13°, 18° and 43° Stormi BT. The first bombing mission was made on 13 June when 19 B.R.20Ms of the 13° Stormo BT attacked installations at Hyères and Fayence in southern France. A detachment of 80 B.R.20Ms of the 13° and 43° Stormi BT were sent to the Belgian airfields of Chieveres and Melsbroeck in late September 1940 to assist the Luftwaffe in its bombing campaign against Eng-

Above: An early BR.20M belonging to the 277ª Squadriglia, 116° Gruppo, 37° Stormo based at Grottaglie, south Italy late in 1940. The unit served over the Greco-Albanian front during the invasion of Greece.

Right: The Fiat BR.20 was an unimaginative design with no better than mediocre performance. It was widely used early in the war on account of its useful bomb load, but lack of defensive armament made it extremely vulnerable.

land. As part of the Corpo Aereo Italiano the B.R.20Ms suffered losses as a result of crew failings and fighter attacks. The campaign in Greece saw the 116° Gruppo (37° Stormo) in action from bases in Albania, followed by action over Crete, and on a day and night attacks against Malta. In the USSR B.R.20Ms of the 38ª and 116ª Squadriglie operated from August 1942 in the southern sector.

Fifteen of the improved **B.R.20bis** model were produced. These were powered by two 1,250-hp (932-kW) Fiat A.82 RC.42S engines, had additional 7.7-mm (0.303-in) machine-guns

and a power-operated dorsal turret. Early in 1943 the B.R.20M bomber had been withdrawn from active service with the Regia Aeronautica, units being re-equipped either with CANT Z.1007s or with Savoia-Marchetti S.M.79s. Production totalled 602 of all marks.

Specification
Fiat B.R.20M Cicogna
Type: five-seat medium bomber
Powerplant: two 1,000-hp (745-kW) Fiat A.80 RC.41 radial piston engines
Performance: maximum speed 440 km/h (273 mph) at sea level;

cruising speed 340 km/h (211 mph); climb to 6000 m (19,685 ft) in 25 minutes 0 seconds; service ceiling 8000 m (26,245 ft); maximum range 2750 km (1,709 miles)
Weights: empty 6500 kg (14,330 lb); maximum take-off 10100 kg (22,270 lb)
Dimensions: span 21.56 m (70 ft 8¾ in); length 16.68 m (54 ft 8 in); height 4.75 m (15 ft 7 in); wing area 74.00 m² (796.5 sq ft)
Armament: three 12.7-mm (0.5-in) Breda-SAFAT machine-guns (in nose, dorsal turret and ventral gun stations), plus a maximum bombload of 1600 kg (3,528 lb)

Dornier Do 17 and Do 215

Much propaganda value was gained by the Luftwaffe during the years before World War II by the emphasis of speed on selected aircraft. The truth was that most were stripped-down quasi-commercial transports or mail carriers, and their record-breaking performance bore little resemblance to that of service versions.

Ordered in quantity production, the Dornier **Do 17E-1** bomber and the **Do 17F-1** reconnaissance aircraft saw service in the formative years of the Luftwaffe. The outbreak of war saw these models superseded by the primary version, the **Do 17Z-1** and **Do 17Z-2**

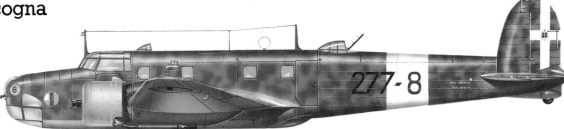

bombers, and the lighter **Do 17M-1** reconnaissance version, the last equipping many *Fernaufklärungsgruppen* by September 1939. The Dornier Do

Dornier Do 17Z-2 of 10.(Kroat)/KG 3 deployed on the central sector of the Eastern Front in December 1941. KG 2 and KG 3 continued to operate the

Do 17Z until late 1942, but the type had been largely withdrawn from front-line service by early 1941.

Above: These two Dornier Do 17Zs of KG 2 are seen during the campaign against the Low Countries. The type faired well in these early battles, but when more professional defence was encountered, such as that over England in 1940, the aircraft was found to be lacking and was soon relegated to less dangerous roles.

17Z bombers equipped nine *Kampf-gruppen* on the outbreak of war: I and II/KG 2 at Liegnitz; II and III/KG 3 at Heiligenbeil; I and III/KG 76 at Wels and Wiener-Neustadt; and I-III/KG 77 at Prague-Kbely, Olmütz and Brünn, numbering about 370 in total. Elements of these units provided much of the Luftwaffe's striking force when Poland was invaded on 1 September. Although not conspicuously fast, the Dornier Do 17Z could be handled much like a fighter, being very light on the controls: structurally it was tough, and it soon surprised its opponents by being able to evade attacks by wheeling into a wing-over and plummeting down in a dive often in excess of 610 km/h (380 mph). In Poland Do 17Z-1s and Do 17Z-2s made many very low-level strikes on airfields and military installations.

Gradually superseded by the Junkers Ju 88A, the Dornier Do 17Z-2 (the variant built in the largest numbers) saw extensive service with Kampfgeschwader Nrn 2, 3 and 76 during the assault on the West in May 1940, in attacks on shipping off Dunkirk, during the massive raids of the summer of 1940 against England, and in the nocturnal *Blitz* of the autumn and winter of 1940. By the time of the Balkans campaign in April 1941, Do 17Z-2s served only with KG 2 and III/KG 3, but continued in service in the fighting over Greece and Crete during the summer,

After serving with great success in the Spanish Civil War, the next action for the Dornier Do 17 was during the attack on Poland in 1939, where this example is seen. Operating virtually unopposed, the Do 17s made many devastating low-level attacks on military installations.

before taking part in the Soviet campaign. Export versions saw service with the air forces of Finland and Yugoslavia. By November 1942 the type had been withdrawn from first-line units. Limited service was seen by the **Do 215B** series, which were powered by two 1,075-hp (802-kW) Daimler-Benz DB 601A-1 inverted V-12 engines: built primarily for export, 112 Do 215Bs were produced, including small numbers of **Do 215B-4** reconnaissance-bombers. Total production of Dornier Do 17Zs amounted to around 1,200.

Specification
Dornier Do 17Z-2
Type: five-seat medium bomber
Powerplant: two 1,000 hp (745 kW) Bramo Fafnir 323P radial piston engines
Performance: maximum speed 410 km/h (255 mph) at 4000 m (13,125 ft); cruising speed 270 km/h (168 mph); service ceiling 8200 m (26,905 ft); maximum range 1500 km (932 miles)
Weights: empty 5200 kg (11,465 lb); maximum take-off 8590 kg (18,940 lb)
Dimensions: span 18.00 m (59 ft 0½ in); length 15.80 m (51 ft 9¾ in); height

Dornier Do 17Z-2 of Stab III Gruppe, KG 3 based at Heiligenbeil in East Prussia during September 1939. Such aircraft were heavily committed to the assault on Poland alongside the Junkers Ju 87 dive-bombers.

4.60 m (15 ft 1 in); wing area 55.00 m² (592.01 sq ft)
Armament: four (later up to eight) 7.92-mm (0.31-in) MG 15 machine-guns in windscreen, nose, beam, ventral and dorsal stations, plus a bombload of 1,000 kg (2,205 lb)

Tupolev SB-2

The two **ANT-40** light bomber prototypes of Andrei N. Tupolev's design bureau were years ahead of their time when they first flew in October 1934: the all-metal construction, enclosed cockpit and retractable landing gear were then comparatively novel features. Indeed the ANT-40's maximum speed of 325 km/h (202 mph) at operating height was faster than the biplane interceptor fighters that equipped most of the peacetime air forces. The initial production version as selected for export and service with the V-VS was based on the second prototype, and was known as the **Tupolev SB-2** (*skorostnoi bombardirovshchik*, or fast bomber); the engines were two 830-hp (619-kW) licence-built Hispano-Suiza 12Ybr engines, termed M-100 by Soviet industry, and initially these were fitted with two-bladed fixed-pitch propellers. The first SB-2s were passed to the V-VS's bomber aviation regiments in February 1936, and in October of that year the first of 210 were transferred with Soviet crews to Spain to fight on the side of the Republican air force against the insurgent Nationalists. Over Spain the performance of the SB-2 caused considerable concern to the Nationalist fighter units which were equipped with Heinkel He 51 and Fiat CR.32 biplanes, and the urgent call went out for fighters of better speed and climb properties. At this time SB-2s were passed to the Chinese Nationalist air force to fight aganst the Japanese, and to Czechoslovakia, where the type went into licensed manufacture as the **B.71** bomber. In general the SB-2 performed well until faced with sterner fighter opposition, which occurred over Spain in 1938 and in particular over Finland during the Winter War of 1939-40, when many were shot down. Steps were taken to improve performance by installing the 860-hp (641-kW) M-100A engine with variable-pitch propellers. Increased fuel capacity and two 960-hp (716-kW) M-103 engines were installed in the **Tupolev SB-2bis**, the performance of which was improved by three-bladed VISh-22 propellers. In addition to the **PS-40** and **PS-41** transport versions the **SB-RK** (Arkhangelskii **Ar-2**) was a modified SB-2bis dive-bomber with reduced wing area and powered by two supercharged M-105R engines.

The SB-2's record as a day bomber came to an abrupt end during the fierce fighting following the German invasion of the USSR on 22 June 1941. Those that were not destroyed on the ground ventured into the air on numerous and gallantly-flown missions over the front line, and paid a heavy price to the Luftwaffe's Messerschmitt Bf 109F fighters. Thereafter the SB-2 and SB-2bis bombers were relegated to night work with the V-VS and the Soviet naval air arm. Production amounted to 6,967 of all marks.

Specification
Type: three-seat light/medium bomber
Powerplant: two 830-hp (619-kW) M-

A Tupolev SB-2 in landing configuration, displaying the broad wing and tail surfaces which characterized the type. The SB-2 had earlier fought in the Spanish Civil War, but it was outclassed during World War II, falling in enormous numbers.

Late production Tupolev SB-2bis with faired-over dorsal position. The type had a useful bombload of 1000 kg (2,205 lb).

Tupolev SB-2bis with dorsal turret and hand-held machine-gun in the ventral position.

The Tupolev SB-2 was painfully undergunned, and fell in large numbers over Finland and the Eastern Front.

100 V-12 piston engines
Performance: maximum speed 410 km/h (255 mph) at 4000 m (13,125 ft); service ceiling 8500 m (27,885 ft); normal range 1200 km (746 miles)

Weight: loaded 5732 kg (12,636 lb)
Dimensions: span 20.33 m (66 ft 8½ in); length 12.27 m (40 ft 3¼ in); height 3.25 m (10 ft 8 in); wing area 51.95 m² (559.2 sq ft)
Armament: two 7.62-mm (0.3-in)

ShKAS machine-guns in nose turret, one 7.62-mm (0.3-in) ShKAS in dorsal station (or turret), and one 7.62-mm (0.3-in) ShKAS in ventral position, plus a maximum bombload of 1000 kg (2,205 lb)

Petlyakov Pe-2

Arriving in small numbers in the ranks of the V-VS to witness the mass devastation of the summer of 1941, the **Petlyakov Pe-2** was destined to become the best Soviet light bomber of World War II. The aircraft was derived from V.M. Petlyakov's **VI-100** pressurized high-altitude twin-engined interceptor, which displayed a phenomenal top speed of 623 km/h (387 mph) at 10000 m (32,810 ft), had a crew of two and was powered by 1,100-hp (820-kW) M-105R V-12 engines. The VI-100 first flew on 7 May 1939. With the approach of war in Europe the V-VS made urgent requests for dive-bomber aircraft, and to this end the design bureau adapted the VI-100 fighter by removing the TK-3 high-altitude turbo-chargers, fitting standard M-105R engines, lattice type dive-brakes, and giving the tailplane pronounced dihedral to increase stability. Two prototype **PB-100** (*pikiruyushchii bombardirovshchik*, or dive-bomber) aircraft were built with these items installed in addition to an extensively glazed nose and defensive armament. This type became the Petlyakov Pe-2 light bomber and dive-bomber. The crew of three (pilot, bombardier and air-gunner) sat under a long glazed canopy with 9-mm (0.35-in) armour protection. Initial armament consisted of two fixed 7.62-mm (0.3-in) ShKAS guns in the nose, one in the dorsal station, and a fourth in the ventral aimed by a 120° vision periscope. The M-105R engines drove three-bladed VISh-61 propellers. The aircraft proved to be fast, highly manoeuvrable, but was quite demanding to novice pilots under asymmetric conditions. By the time of the German invasion in June 1941 some 458 Pe-2s had been produced from the factories, but it is suspected that deliveries to service units was tardy. Certainly, even

Above: Petlyakov Pe-2 of the V-VS. The Pe-2 was referred to often as the 'Russian Mosquito' due to its versatility of roles, and its ability to carry them all out excellently.

Below: Many Soviet aircraft carried legends, often as they were 'gift' aircraft from collectives and organizations.

by September 1941 the numbers of Pe-2s in front-line units were few: Colonel General I.S. Konev's Western Front had only five in commission with which to stem the German assault on Moscow, and the establishment of Pe-2s with the Bryansk and Kalinin Fronts was even lower. Although limited in numbers, Pe-2s contributed to the victories of the Soviet winter offensive of 1941-2, and were seen in increasing numbers during the defensive battles at Leningrad, Kharkov, Rostov, and in the Stalingrad campaign. Late in 1942 came the improved **Pe-2FT** with 1,260-hp (940-kW) Klimov M-105PF engines, and a 12.7-mm (0.5-in) UBT machine-gun in a dorsal turret. The **Pe-2I** and **Pe-2M** were fighter-bombers, powered by 1,620-hp (1,208-kW) VK-107A engines. The reconnaissance version was the **Pe-2R**, whilst a dual-control trainer was termed the **Pe-2UT**. The aircraft saw distinguished service in every major Soviet campaign from 1941 to 1945, including operations in Manchuria against the Japanese in September 1945. A total of 11,427 Pe-2s and Pe-3s (the fighter version) was produced.

Specification
Petlyakov Pe-2
Type: three-seat light/medium bomber and dive-bomber
Powerplant: two 1,100-hp (820-kW) Klimov M-105R V-12 piston engines
Performance: maximum speed 540 km/h (336 mph) at 5000 m (16,405 ft); cruising speed 428 km/h (266 mph); climb to 5000 m (16,405 ft) in 7 minutes 0 seconds; service ceiling 8800 m (28,870 ft); normal range 1500 km (932 miles)

Weights: empty 5876 kg (12,943 lb); maximum take-off 8496 kg (18,730 lb)
Dimensions: span 17.16 m (56 ft 3½ in); length 12.66 m (41 ft 6½ in); height 4.0 m (13 ft 1½ in); wing area 40.50 m² (436 sq ft)
Armament: two fixed 7.62-mm (0.3-in) ShKAS machine-guns or one 7.62-mm ShKAS and one 12.7-mm (0.5-in) Beresin UBT machine-gun in nose, and single 7.62-mm (0.3-in) ShKAS or 12.7-mm (0.5-in) UBT machine-guns in dorsal and in ventral stations, plus a maximum bombload of 1200 kg (2,646 lb)

High-level bombing was never a forte of the Soviet air forces, and in the bombing role the Pe-2 was confined largely to medium-level and dive-bombing, proving to be a fast and elusive target.

Tupolev Tu-2

The origin of the **Tupolev Tu-2** lay in the **ANT-58**, **ANT-59** and **ANT-60** light bomber prototypes that came from the design bureau of Andrei N. Tupolev during 1938-40: powered by two 1,400-hp (1044-kW) Mikulin AM-37 V-12 engines, the ANT-58 made its first flight on 29 January 1941 with M.P. Vasyakin at the controls. The ANT-60 was re-engined with the big and powerful 1,480-hp (1104-kW) M-82 radials because of the relative unreliability of the AM-37s. The result was the definitive Tu-2 bomber that was to see service with the V-VS during the last year of World War II and well into the 1950s. Soviet industry was still in a state of upheaval following the terrible years of 1941-2, when the German army struck deep into Belorussia and the Ukraine. The Tu-2 was too complicated an aircraft for the conditions prevailing, and after many months in which the Tu-2 was modified and simplified for the mass production lines, the **Tu-2S** (*Seriinyi*, or series) appeared, flying for the first time on 26 August 1943. A small number of Tu-2s had previously been passed to front-line regiments in September 1942, where their performance, armament and bombload had received general enthusiasm.

By January 1944 the first production Tu-2 and Tu-2S bombers had been passed to the regiments of the V-VS, but it was not until June of that year that Tu-2s saw action on a large scale. The sector was the Karelian (Finnish) front in the north where the V-VS forces, under the overall command of General A.A. Novikov, numbered 757 aircraft of the 13th VA (Air Army), the V-VS KBF (Red Banner Baltic Fleet) and the 2nd GV IAK (guards fighter corps). Of the 249 Tu-2 and Petlyakov Pe-2 light bombers in the Soviet order of battle, many came under Colonel I.P. Skok's 334th Bomber Air Division which subsequently received a citation for its work. Reconnaissance work was now being carried out by **Tu-2D** and **Tu-2R** aircraft with modified mainplanes, nose glazing, and capacity for vertical and oblique cameras. Wartime production of the Tupolev Tu-2 and its sub-types amounted to 1,111. As a bomber it did not come into its own until the autumn of 1944. However, as German resistance stiffened on nearing the eastern borders of the Reich V-VS bombers,

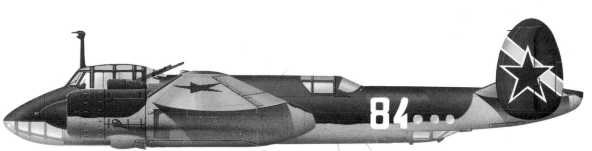

Many wartime Tupolev Tu-2s had their numbers hand painted. This Tu-2S served on the Kalinin front.

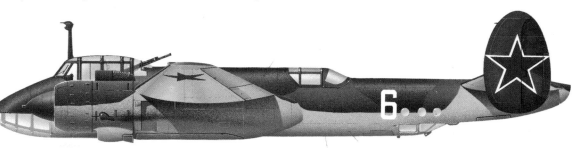

The Tupolev Tu-2S carried two wing root cannon and three machine-guns mounted in the rear cockpit and the dorsal and ventral positions.

This Tupolev Tu-2S was delivered to the V-VS in the summer of 1944 and wears the standard camouflage of that period.

including Tupolev Tu-2s, were called up to attack strongpoints at Kustrin, Königsberg and other fortified ports and cities. September 1945 saw many Tu-2s in action against the Japanese Kwantung Army in Manchuria before the final surrender.

Specification
Tupolev Tu-2S
Type: four-seat medium bomber
Powerplant: two 1,850-hp (1,380-kW) Shvetsov ASh-82FN radial piston engines

Performance: maximum speed 547 km/h (340 mph) at 5400 m (17,715 ft); cruising speed 442 km/h (275 mph); climb to 5000 m (16,405 ft) in 9 minutes 30 seconds; service ceiling 9500 m (31,170 ft); normal range 2000 km (1,243 miles)
Weights: empty 8260 kg (18,200 lb); normal take-off 12800 kg (28,219 lb)
Dimensions: span 18.86 m (61 ft 10½ in); length 13.80 m (45 ft 3½ in); height 4.56 m (14 ft 11 in); wing area 48.80 m² (525.3 sq ft)
Armament: two 20-mm ShVAK cannon

in wing roots and three 12.7-mm (0.5-in) UBT machine-guns (one each in both dorsal positions and ventral station), plus a maximum bombload of 3000 kg (6,614 lb)

Andrei Tupolev was commanded by Stalin to produce a better bomber than the Junkers Ju 88, and the resulting Tu-2 proved to be one of the finest wartime aircraft. This is a Tu-2S with broadened ailerons.

Jet Aircraft

Whilst piston-engined aircraft fought out World War II, aircraft and engine designers were hard at work to harness the new jet and rocket propulsion and to perfect its use for fighting aircraft. The results of their labours were varied, but the technological advances were great.

Although combat by jet-propelled aircraft during World War II was limited to the final year of the conflict, and then undertaken only by German (and to a much lesser extent British) aircraft, the knowledge that jet reaction was potentially the most efficient of all aircraft propulsion systems had existed for some 15 years beforehand. In Germany exploitation of this knowledge had shown greatest promise, through the efforts of F. W. Sander and Fritz von Opel with solid-fuel rocket power, Paul Schmidt with pulse jets and Dr Hans von Ohain with the gas turbine, all of whom had either achieved limited jet reaction-powered flight or were on the threshold of doing so when war broke out in September 1939. In the UK work had progressed under the leadership of Frank Whittle, but with very little commercial support. Elsewhere in the world there was even less interest in jet propulsion.

Germany was the first to fly an air-breathing jet aircraft, the Heinkel He 178, which took to the air under its own power for the first time on 27 August 1939. Next to fly a 'jet' was Italy with its crude ducted fan-jet Caproni-Campini N1, which flew in August 1940. While the Italian effort proved to be dead-ended, the

Although jet development was well underway when World War II broke out, jet aircraft were hardly to feature in the conflict. Germany led the way with Britain following; this reconnaissance version Arado Ar 234B was just one of several designs.

Germans moved steadily forward towards operational realism as other manufacturers were encouraged into the jet propulsion field by the development of viable powerplants produced, notably, by Heinkel and Junkers.

Meanwhile in the UK Frank Whittle, with increasing practical assistance and eventual domination by Rolls-Royce, Rover, de Havilland and others, succeeded in producing a gas turbine which, as the Power Jets W.1, first flew in the Gloster E.28/39 in May 1941. But the two-year lead gained by

Germany proved unassailable and, despite the demise of the Heinkel He 280 as a potential combat aircraft, enabled the Luftwaffe to achieve operational status with its Messerschmitt Me 262 during the summer of 1944, narrowly predating the first RAF Gloster Meteors. Moreover the rocket-powered Me 163 proved to be the fastest of any combat aircraft produced during the war.

The build-up of German Me 262s (as well as He 162s and Arado Ar 234s) far outstripped the tentative introduction of the

British Meteor, all reliance on operational jet engine development being placed on the Rolls-Royce Welland (a direct development of the Whittle engine). The USA, on the other hand, scarcely achieved any progress in the field until 1941 when Whittle technology was provided by the UK, only managing to fly the Bell P-59 Airacomet and Lockheed P-80 Shooting Star, neither of which was operational during World War II.

Japan, like Germany, frantically sought to combat the growing menace to its homeland from the US's air onslaught and received technical assistance from Germany. It managed to fly a twin-jet fighter, the Nakajima Kikka (modelled on the Me 262), before the end of the war and also the rocket-powered Yokosuka Ohka suicide aircraft.

Nevertheless, despite growing awareness in the UK and USA of the enormous potential of the jet engine, the Allies were astounded to discover the advances made by Germany when they examined the spoils of war in 1945. But much of the technology had already disappeared eastwards, and it was here that the wartime momentum gained by the Soviet Union was able to accommodate these great technical strides into its post-war plans for world military superiority.

Arado Ar 234

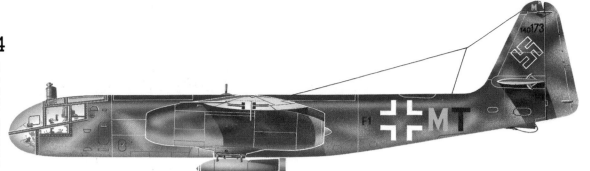

The world's first turbojet-powered bomber, the **Arado Ar 234 Blitz** (lightning) was originally conceived as a twin-jet high-speed reconnaissance aircraft late in 1940. Delayed by slow delivery of the Junkers 004B, the **Ar 234 V1** prototype was not first flown until 15 June 1943; this aircraft featured an auxiliary trolley, which was jettisoned on take-off, in place of conventional landing gear. Further prototypes followed, including the **Ar 234 V6** and **Ar 234 V8** which were powered by four 800-kg (1,764-lb) thrust BMW 003A-1 turbojets.

When production finally started, it was of the twin-jet **Ar 234B** which featured conventional nosewheel landing gear, the mainwheels retracting into a slightly widened centre fuselage. The **Ar 234B-1** was an unarmed reconnaissance aircraft which first served with 1 Versuchsverband Oberbefehlshaber der Luftwaffe late in 1944, and soon after with Sonderkommando Hecht and Sperling. These units were replaced in 1945 by 1 (F) 33, 1 (F) 100 and 1 (F) 123, and many reconnaissance sorties were flown over the UK. The bomber version was the **Ar 234B-2**, which could carry a bombload of 2000 kg (4,409 lb), and other variants included the **Ar 234B-2/b** reconnaissance aircraft, the **Ar 234B-2/1** pathfinder and **Ar 234B-2/r** long-range bomber. Ar 234B-2 bombers joined KG 76 in January 1945 and carried out a number of daring and hazardous raids before the end of the war. A small number of Ar 234s was also employed as night-fighters with Kommando Bonow, but the four-jet **Ar 234C**, although just beginning to appear at the end of the war, failed to reach squadron service. Many other advanced projects were in hand when hostilities ceased.

Able to carry a bombload of 2000 kg (4,409 lb), the Arado Ar 234B-2 went into service with KG 76 in January 1945. Based at Rheine and Achmer, these made many accurate strikes.

Specification
Ar 234B-2
Type: single-seat tactical light bomber
Powerplant: two 800-kg (1,764-lb) thrust BMW 003A-1 turbojets
Performance: maximum speed 742 km/h (461 mph) at 6000 m (19,685 ft); climb to 6000 m (19,685 ft) in 12.8 minutes' service ceiling 10000 m (32,810 ft); range 1630 km (1,013 miles)
Weights: empty 5200 kg (11,464 lb); maximum take-off 9800 kg (21,605 lb)
Dimensions: span 14.44 m (46 ft 3½ in); length 12.64 m (41 ft 5½ in); height 4.29 m (14 ft 1½ in); wing area 27.3 m (284.17 sq ft)
Armament: bombload of up to 2000 kg (4,409 lb); some aircraft carried two rear-firing 20-mm guns

The Ar 234B proved of immense interest to the Allies and intact examples underwent rigorous testing in Britain and America. This is an Ar 234B-1 reconnaissance version, with no hardpoints.

Bachem Ba 349 Natter

The Bachem Ba 349 Natter was a somewhat desperate attempt to stem the Allied bombing campaign. Launching vertically, the Natter climbed quickly on its rocket motor, attacked the bombers with rockets and then pilot and aircraft returned separately to earth by parachute.

Among the ingenious expedients borne of desperation in Germany at the end of the war was the **Bachem Ba 349 Natter** (viper), a semi-expendable, vertically-launched, piloted missile. Designed under the leadership of Erich Bachem, the small aircraft was constructed mainly of bonded and screwed wooden components, and was powered by an internal Walter 109-509A-2 liquid fuel rocket (of the same type as in the Messerschmitt Me 163); for take-off boost four solid fuel Schmidding rockets provided a total thrust of 4800 kg (10,582 lb) for 10 seconds before being jettisoned. It was intended to launch the Natter on approach of Allied bombers, the pilot selecting his target and then launching his weapon load of 24 7.3-cm (2.87-in) Föhn unguided rockets. He would then jettison the nose section of the aircraft and deploy his own parachute. The remainder of the aircraft would also descend by parachute for recovery and re-use. Gliding trials started in October 1944, followed in February 1945 by the first unmanned vertical

launches. However, during the first piloted launch the same month, the cockpit canopy failed and the pilot, Lothar Siebert, was killed. About 20 Ba 349s were completed, and 10 were deployed at Kirchheim, but before any Allied bombers could be intercepted the sites were overrun by advancing American forces.

Specification
Type: single-seat expendable interceptor

Powerplant: one 1700-kg (3,748-lb) thrust Walter 109-509A-2 liquid-fuel rocket motor (of 70 seconds' power duration) and four 1200-kg (2,646-lb) thrust Schmidding 109-533 solid-fuel jettisonable booster rockets (of 10 seconds' power duration)
Performance: maximum speed 800 km/h (497 mph) at sea level; initial climb rate 11140 m (36,550 ft) per minute; service ceiling 14000 m (45,930 ft); radius of action 40 km (24.8 miles)
Weight: loaded at launch 2200 kg (4,850 lb)
Dimensions: span 3.60 m (11 ft 9¾ in); length 6.10 m (20 ft 0 in); wing area 2.75 m² (29.6 sq ft)
Armament: 24 Föhn 7.3-cm (2.87-in) unguided rocket projectiles in nose

Fieseler Fi 103R

One of the many macabre projects being studied as Germany approached defeat at the end of the war involved the use of the **Fieseler Fi 103R**, a manned version of the Argus pulsejet-powered Fieseler Fi 103 flying bomb. Mass production of these weapons had been achieved by mid-1944 for the campaign against southern England when proposals were made to launch a manned bomb from beneath a carrier aircraft. The intention was that, after release, the flying bomb would be piloted towards a target and put into a dive before the pilot baled out at the last moment. Pilot survival was rated as being most unlikely as a result of the canopy fouling the pulsejet inlet immediately aft of the cockpit, yet the Germans steadfastly claimed a subtle distinction between their *Selbstopfermänner* (self-sacrifice men)

and the Japanese *Kamikaze* pilots who were sealed into their cockpits before take-off. A total of about 175 piloted Fi 103Rs (*Reichenberg* being the operational codename covering the project) were completed: the **R-I**, **R-II** and **R-III** were test and training versions, and the **R-IV** was intended for operational use. Testing was undertaken by Rechlin pilots but after two had crashed development flying was taken over by DFS test pilots Hanna Reitsch and Heinz Kensche. Handling in the air was fairly straightforward but landing was extremely tricky owing to the rudimentary control provided and the very high landing speed. Although some 70 volunteer pilots were selected for training the plan came to naught simply owing to the German

The Fi 103 (V1) is well known in its unpiloted form, but the piloted version, the Reichenberg, was more obscure. Intended for accurate attacks against shipping, the pilot was supposed to bale out after he had aimed at the target. In practice this would have been unlikely.

Fieseler Fi 103R Reichenberg IV.

high command's refusal to take the Reichenberg project seriously.

Specification
Fi 103R-IV
Type: single-seat flying bomb

Powerplant: one 350-kg (772-lb) thrust Argus 109-014 pulsejet
Performance: maximum powered level speed 650 km/h (404 mph) at sea level; endurance (limited by pulsejet life) 20 minutes

Weight: at launch 2180 kg (4,806 lb)
Dimensions: span 5.715 m (18 ft 9 in); length 8.00 m (26 ft 3 in); maximum fuselage diameter 0.838 m (2 ft 9 in)
Warhead: 850 kg (1,874 lb)

GERMANY

Heinkel He 162 Salamander

Despite all that Germany could do to press the Messerschmitt Me 163 and Me 262 into service in the latter half of 1944, it became all too clear that both aircraft demanded production skills, materials and flying experience beyond the resources of the nation, and thus were inadequate to stem the tide of Allied air attack. Accordingly, as the RLM underwent its final reorganization, proposals were studied for the mass production of a relatively simple, lightweight jet interceptor which demanded the minimum of strategic materials, engineering skill and pilot training. Within five weeks the design of the **Heinkel He 162** had been accepted and dozens of component subcontracts organized, it being intended to reach a production of 2,000 aircraft per month by May 1945. The first prototype He 162 was flown on 6 December 1944, but by the following month severe lateral instability had been disclosed, resulting in the wing tips being sharply angled down. The aircraft was a small shoulder-wing monoplane with the turbojet mounted on top of the fuselage amidships, nose-wheel landing gear and twin fins and rudders. In February a score of further prototypes flew, together with the first production examples. The first operational unit, I/JG 1, under Oberst Herbert Ihlefeldt, flew **He 162A-1** production aircraft at Parchim but, despite a prodigious effort and the completion of some 275 aircraft, the swift advance by the Allied armies prevented the little fighter from taking any significant part in the air fighting at the end of the war.

Specification
Type: single-seat interceptor fighter
Powerplant: one 800-kg (1,764-lb) thrust BMW 109-003E turbojet
Performance: maximum speed 835 km/h (519 mph) at 6000 m (19,685 ft); initial climb rate 1290 m (4,230 ft) per minute; service ceiling about 11000 m (36,090 ft); maximum range 1000 km (621 miles)
Weights: empty 1750 kg (3,858 lb);

Despite its hurried development, the ingenious Heinkel He 162 would have proved an effective fighter in experienced hands, but there was insufficient time to train men of the calibre required by the Luftwaffe.

Above: Several Heinkel He 162s were captured by the Allies and extensively tested after the war. This He 162A-2 was serving with II Gruppe, Jagdgeschwader 1 at Leck when it was captured on 8 May 1945. It has since been restored and is on display at RAF St Athan.

maximum take-off 2700 kg (5,952 lb)
Dimensions: span 7.20 m (23 ft 7½ in); length 9.05 m (29 ft 8½ in); height 2.55 m (8 ft 4⅜ in); wing area 11.15 m² (120.0 sq ft)
Armament: two 30-mm MK 108 or two 20-mm MG 151 cannon in nose

Right: The He 162 suffered from all the symptoms of 1945 Germany – lack of fuel, poor materials, inexperienced workmen and pilots, and hasty design and development. Attempts to overcome these problems were swamped by the Allied advance.

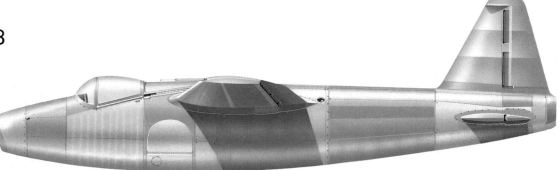

GERMANY
Heinkel He 178

The world's first aircraft to fly solely powered by a turbojet was the German **Heinkel He 178**, which was flown by Flugkapitän Erich Warsitz at Marienehe on 27 August 1939, one week before the outbreak of World War II. The first step in the development of this aeroplane was taken in March 1936 when Ernst Heinkel engaged the services of the German gas turbine pioneer Dr Hans Pabst von Ohain and his assistant Max Hahn. The first demonstration turbojet, the HeS 1, was bench running by September 1937, and a development of this engine, the HeS 3, was flight tested suspended beneath a Heinkel He 118 in 1938. By 1939, it had been decided to instal a new version, the HeS 3b, in a special aircraft, the He 178, which commenced building that year; it was a shoulder-wing aircraft with wings made largely of wood but with a semi-monocoque metal fuselage. Tailwheel landing gear was incorporated, and the engine drew its air from an inlet in the nose and exhausted through a long jet pipe which extended to the extreme tail. The 178 was damaged on its first flight when the engine ingested a bird which caused it to flame out, but the aircraft made a safe landing. It was later flown with a 590-kg (1,301-lb) thrust HeS 6 engine, but a number of airframe defects limited the speed to about 600 km/h (373 mph). The He 178 was later moved to the Berlin Air Museum where it was destroyed in 1943 during an Allied air raid.

Specification
He 178 (initial powerplant)
Type: single-seat research aircraft

The first flight by a jet-powered aircraft occurred on 27 August 1939 when this He 178 flew from Marienehe, near Rostock. Despite their superior engine, it was two years before the British matched this feat.

Powerplant: one 500-kg (1,102-lb) thrust Heinkel HeS 3b centrifugal-flow turbojet
Performance: (estimated) maximum speed 580 km/h (360 mph) at sea level; landing speed 165 km/h (103 mph)

Weights: empty 1590 kg (3,505 lb); maximum 1990 kg (4,387 lb)
Dimensions: 7.10 m (23 ft 3½ in); length 7.51 m (24 ft 6½ in); height 2.10 m (6 ft 10⅝ in); wing area 7.90 m² (85.04 sq ft)
Armament: none

Only one He 178 was built, and was an extremely clean design for its day, with fully retracting and faired-in undercarriage. Maximum speed was 580 km/h (360 mph).

GERMANY
Heinkel He 280

Designed from the outset as a fighter, the He 280 was plagued with development problems and was abandoned in favour of the Messerschmitt Me 262.

The world's first turbojet aircraft designed from the outset as a potential fighter, the **Heinkel He 280** made its first flight on 2 August 1941 (19 months before the first Gloster Meteor). Design of the He 280, which started before the end of 1939, included a low wing with twin underslung turbojets, tricycle landing gear and twin fins and rudders. Despite the obvious need for low-diameter engines, Dr von Ohain succeeded in developing the centrifugal-flow HeS 8 (or 109-001) to produce 700-kg (1,543-lb) thrust, and a pair of these engines powered the **He 280 V1** on its first flight (the engines being left uncowled on this occasion). A total of nine prototypes flew, including the **He 280 V2** and **He 280 V3** with HeS 8 engines (the former also being re-engined with Jumo 109-004s), the **He 280 V4** with BMW 109-003s and later with six Argus 109-014 pulsejets, the **He 280 V5** first with HeS 8s and later with 109-003s, the **He 280 V6** (as well as the V5) with three MG 151 20-mm cannon, the **He 280 V7** with 109-004s (and later tested as a high-speed glider for aerodynamic research), the **He 280 V8** with 109-004s and a V-type tail unit, and the **He 280 V9** with 109-003s.

After several flights towed behind a pair of Bf 110s, the He 280V-1 made its first powered flight on 2 April 1941 and is seen here landing back at Marienehe. For this first flight the engines were kept uncovered, as during test runs fuel had gathered in the cowlings.

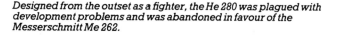

Although production of the He 280 was planned, recurring complaints (which included structural weakness in the tail, together with tail flutter, and inadequate fuel and armament provision) caused the design to be abandoned in favour of the Messerschmitt Me 262. It was, incidentally, from the He 280 V1 that the first-ever bale-out using an ejector seat was made when Argus test pilot Schenk abandoned the aircraft when his controls locked from icing-up.

Specification
He 280 V5
Type: single-seat prototype interceptor fighter

Powerplant: two 750-kg (1,653-lb) thrust HeS 8A (109-001A) turbojets
Performance: maximum short-burst speed 900 km/h (559 mph) at 6000 m (19,685 ft); initial climb rate 1145 m (3,755 ft) per minute; estimated service ceiling 11500 m (37,730 ft); range 650 km (404 miles)
Weights: empty 3215 kg (7,088 lb);

maximum take-off 4310 kg (9,502 lb)
Dimensions: span 12.20 m (40 ft 0 in); length 10.40 m (34 ft 1½ in); height 3.06 m (10 ft 0½ in); wing area 21.50 m² (231.5 sq ft)
Armament: three nose-mounted 20-mm MG 151 cannon (intended later to be increased to six)

Henschel Hs 132

During the last half of 1943 experience showed that losses during conventional dive-bombing with the venerable Junkers Ju 87 were becoming prohibitive without heavy fighter escort, particularly in the face of ever-growing Soviet air presence on the Eastern Front. The Henschel company, with considerable experience in producing ground-support aircraft, put forward late in 1944 proposals for an essentially simple single-jet attack bomber with a BMW 109-003E-2 turbojet mounted above the fuselage. In essence the aircraft resembled the Heinkel He 162 with twin fins and rudders, although the sharply tapered wing was mounted at mid-fuselage depth; more significant, the pilot occupied a prone position in the extreme nose so as to withstand the likely 12g forces expected to accompany shallow dive recovery. Simplified construction with widespread use of wood in the structure was welcomed by the RLM and three prototypes were ordered, and commenced building in March 1945. Only the **Henschel Hs 132 V1** had been completed (but not flown) by the war's end, and all three aircraft were taken over by the Soviet forces in their advance from the east. The first aircraft was to have carried a single 500-kg (1,102-lb) bomb recessed into the underfuselage; the second, with 900-kg (1,984-lb) thrust engine combined this load with two nose-mounted 20-mm MG 151 cannon; and the third, with 1300-kg (2,866-lb) thrust Heinkel-Hirth 109-011A turbojet would carry a 1000-kg (2,205-lb) bomb, two 30-mm MK 103 and two 20-mm MG 151 guns. It was intended that the PC 1000RS Pol rocket-assisted armour-piercing bomb would be used for battlefield support attacks.

Specification
Hs 132 V1
Type: single-seat dive bomber
Powerplant: one 800-kg (1,764-lb) thrust BMW 109-003E-2 turbojet
Performance: maximum speed 780 km/h (485 mph) at 6000 m (19,685 ft); service ceiling 10250 m (33,630 ft); range 680 km (423 miles)
Weights: maximum take-off 3400 kg (7,496 lb)
Dimensions: span 7.20 m (23 ft 7½ in); length 8.90 m (29 ft 2½ in); wing area 14.82 m² (159.4 sq ft)
Armament: one 500 kg (1,102-lb) bomb under the fuselage

Although it never flew, the Henschel Hs 132 was a most interesting concept. With a configuration resembling the Heinkel He 162, the most striking feature of the aircraft was the prone pilot position, incorporated to enable the pilot to withstand the expected 12g when the aircraft pulled out from its dive after releasing the bomb.

Horton Ho IX (Gotha Go 229)

The Horten Ho IX V2 was the only aircraft of this series to achieve powered flight. Its career ended abruptly following an engine failure.

The **Horton Ho IX** twin-jet tailless fighter-bomber, of which two prototypes were flown before the end of the war, was of extremely advanced design, which benefited from considerable experience gained by the brothers Reimar and Walter Horten in the development of flying-wing aircraft, of which the majority were gliders. Designed by Sonderkommando 9, starting in 1942, the first prototype **Ho IX V1** was found to be unable to accommodate the two intended BMW 109-003-1 turbojets owing to an unforeseen increase in engine diameter, and it was therefore flown as a glider at Oranienburg during the summer of 1944. The redesigned **Ho IX V2** was fitted with two Junkers 109-004B-1 turbojets and flown successfully at Oranienburg, demonstrating speeds of up to 960 km/h (597 mph) before it was destroyed while making a single-engine landing. Such promise encouraged the RLM to instruct Gothaer Waggonfabrik to assume development of the design, and a third prototype, the **Go 229 V3**, was produced with 1000-kg (2,205-lb) thrust Jumo 109-004C turbojets, but was prevented from flying by the end of hostilities in May 1945. Work had also started on the two-seat **Go 229 V4** and **Go 229 V5** night-fighter prototypes, the **Go 229 V6** armament test prototype, and the **Go 229 V7** two-seat trainer. No progress had been made on 20 pre-production Go 229A-0 fighter-bombers, on order at the end of the war, that were intended to carry two 1000-kg (2,205-lb) bombs and four 30-mm MK 103 cannon.

Specification
Go 229A-0
Type: single-seat fighter-bomber
Powerplant: two 1000-kg (2,205-lb) thrust Junkers Jumo 109-004C turbojets
Performance: maximum speed 1000 km/h (621 mph) at 6100 m (20,015 ft); landing speed 130 km/h (81 mph)
Weight: maximum take-off 8500 kg (18,739 lb)
Dimensions: span 16.78 m (55 ft 0⅝ in); length 7.47 m (24 ft 6⅛ in); wing area 51.5 m² (554.36 sq ft)
Armament: four 30-mm MK 103 cannon and up to 2000 kg (4,409 lb) of bombs

 GERMANY

Junkers Ju 287

The revolutionary **Junkers Ju 287** was the outcome of development of a bomber project being studied by Dipl.Ing. Hans Wocke at Junkers in June 1943 at a time when fast bombers still enjoyed priority in Luftwaffe planning. Instead of employing a 'conventional' swept-back wing (advocated as early as 1935 by Prof. A. Busemann) Wocke suggested using a swept-forward wing in which the high-speed benefits of reduced thickness-chord would be more readily achieved, at the same time reducing low-speed instability. To speed manufacture of the prototype, the **Ju 287 V1** featured an extraordinary mixture of existing components, including the fuselage of a Heinkel He 177, Ju 388 tail unit, Ju 352 mainwheels and the nosewheels of captured Consolidated B-24 Liberators. Design of the aircraft was directed by Dipl.Ing. Ernst Zindel and, powered by four Jumo 109-004B-1 turbojets, this was flown by Flugkapitän Siegfried Holzbauer at Brandis on 16 August 1944; the prototype required take-off assistance in the form of a jettisonable Walter 109-501 rocket under each turbojet. A total of 17 flights was made before priority for jet bombers was abandoned at about this time. For some reason, never satisfactorily explained, the RLM returned to a bombing philosophy in March 1945 and ordered the Ju 287 into production. Construction of two further prototypes, the **Ju 287 V2** with six jet engines and the **Ju 287 V3** returning to four more powerful turbojets, commenced but neither was flown before the end of the war. The entire programme was then transferred to Podberezhnye in the USSR, together with many of its associated technicians, and flight trials continued there until about 1948.

Specification
Ju 287 V1
Type: prototype high-speed heavy bomber
Powerplant: four 900-kg (1,984-lb) thrust Junkers Jumo 109-004B-1 turbojets
Performance: maximum speed 559 km/h (347 mph) at 6000 m (19,685 ft); service ceiling 10800 m (35,435 ft); maximum range 1500 km (930 miles)
Weights: empty 12510 kg (27,579 lb); maximum take-off 20000 kg (44,092 lb)
Dimensions: span 20.11 m (65 ft 11¾ in); length 18.30 m (60 ft 0½ in); wing area 58.30 m² (627.3 sq ft)
Armament: (V3) bombload of up to 4000 kg (8,818 lb) and gun armament in tail barbette

The most futuristic of all jets to fly during the war, the Ju 287V-1 was the only example built by Junkers. The second prototype was completed by the Russians after the war, flying with six engines.

 GERMANY

Messerschmitt Me 262

The **Messerschmitt Me 262** was one of the first turbojet-powered aircraft to achieve combat status, and was the result of pre-war research with gas turbines in Germany. Design of the aircraft started in 1938 and prototype airframes were ready in 1941 but, as the Junkers jet engines were not then ready, the first flight on 18 April was made using a single Jumo 210G piston engine; it was not until 18 July 1942 that the **Me 262 V3** first made an all-jet flight powered by two 840-kg (1,852-lb) thrust Junkers 109-004A-0 turbojets. Early prototypes featured tailwheel landing gear, but when production started in 1944 a tricycle arrangement had been standardized. As Hitler persisted in demanding development of the Me 262 as a bomber for reprisal raids on the UK, development of the fighter was badly delayed and it was not until late in 1944 that the aircraft entered Luftwaffe service. The **Me 262A-1a Schwalbe** (swallow) fighter was armed with four 30-mm guns in the nose and joined Kommando Nowotny in October; it was followed by the **Me 262A-1a/U1** with two additional 20-mm guns, the **Me 262A-1a/U2** bad-weather fighter and the **Me 262A-1a/U3** unarmed reconnaissance aircraft. The **Me 262A-2a Sturmvogel** (stormy petrel) bomber could carry up to 500 kg (1,102 lb) of bombs in addition to the four 30-mm guns, and a two-seat version (with prone bomb-aimer), the **Me 262A-2a/U2**, was also produced. Before the end of the war Me 262s were being flown with some success against Allied bombers both as day and night fighters (the latter were radar-equipped **Me 262B-1a/U1** aircraft), and air-to-air rockets were being developed. Dogged by difficulties brought on by Allied raids on factories and airfields, the Luftwaffe's jet fighter units nevertheless posed a formidable threat to Allied air superiority during the last few months of the war.

This bomb-carrying Me 262A-2a/U1 flew with Erprobungskommando Schenk, an experimental detachment from KG 51 to investigate the operational use of this fine jet.

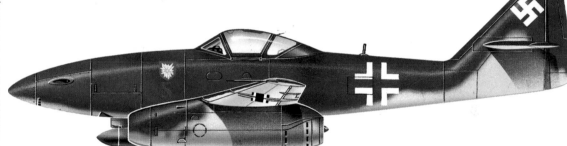

Specification
Me 262A-1a
Type: single-seat interceptor fighter
Powerplant: two 900-kg (1,984-lb) thrust Junkers Jumo 109-004B-4 turbojets
Performance: maximum speed 870 km/h (541 mph) at 7000 m (26,965 ft); initial climb rate 1200 m (3,937 ft) per minute; service ceiling 11000 m (36,090 ft); normal range 845 km (525 miles)
Weights: empty 4000 kg (8,818 lb); maximum take-off 6775 kg (14,936 lb)
Dimensions: span 12.50 m (41 ft 0⅛ in); length 10.61 m (34 ft 9½ in); height 3.83 m (12 ft 6¾ in); wing area 21.68 m² (233.3 sq ft)
Armament: four MK 108 30-mm cannon in nose

Featuring a tailwheel, the Me 262V-2 became the second Me 262 to fly solely on turbojet power, the first prototype having a piston engine as well as the jets mounted in the nose.

323

Messerschmitt Me 163 Komet

The **Messerschmitt Me 163 Komet** (comet) rocket interceptor stemmed from prolonged research by Dr Alexander Lippisch over 15 years before the war. The prototype was initially test flown as a glider during the spring of 1941 before being fitted with a Walter RII-203 rocket using *T-Stoff* and *Z-Stoff* propellants. Powered flights by the **Me 163 V1** started in the late summer of 1941, and on 2 October the aircraft reached 1004.5 km/h (623.8 mph); two months later the **Me 163B Komet** was ordered into production.

Production Me 163Bs were powered by Walter 109-509A rocket motors using *T-Stoff* (hydrogen peroxide) and *C-Stoff* (hydrazine hydrate, methyl alcohol and water) to give a thrust of 1700 kg (3,748 lb). Early **Me 163B-0** aircraft were armed with a pair of 20-mm guns, but **Me 163B-1** fighters carried two 30-mm weapons. The aircraft possessed no conventional landing gear, but took off from a trolley which was jettisoned immediately after take-off.

Introduction to Luftwaffe service was a protracted and hazardous process owing to difficulties in handling the fuels and a number of fatal accidents, and only very experienced pilots were selected. Production **Me 163B-1a** fighters equipped I/JG 400 at Brandis, near Leipzig, in June 1944 and first intercepted B-17 Fortress daylight bombers on 16 August that year. All manner of difficulties faced the pilots, apart from the hazards already mentioned, and it was found difficult to aim and fire the guns with the result that upward-firing 50-mm shells and underwing rockets came to be developed.

Although some 300 Me 163Bs were produced (as well as a few **Me 163C** aircraft with increased fuel) and JG 400's other two *Gruppen* re-equipped by the end of 1944, only nine confirmed air victories were achieved by the *Geschwader*.

Above: The badge of this Me 163B-1 of JG 400 bears the legend 'Wie ein Floh, aber Oho!' (Only a flea, but oh-oh!). The concept of this tiny fighter was sound, but the practice proved difficult, and only nine victories were confirmed.

Below: The Me 163B-1 suffered the same problems as other German jets during the last few months of the war and did not change history. The prominent 'T' and 'C' stencils indicated fuelling points for the two liquid fuels, accidental contact between which would result in catastrophe.

Specification
Me 163B-1a Komet
Type: single-seat interceptor fighter
Powerplant: one 1700-kg (3,748-lb) thrust Walter 109-509A-2 rocket motor
Performance: maximum speed 960 km/h (596 mph) at 3000 m (9,845 ft); initial climb rate 3600 m (11,810 ft) per minute; service ceiling 12100 m (39,700 ft); normal range 80 km (50 miles)
Weights: empty 1905 kg (4,200 lb); maximum take-off 4110 kg (9,061 lb)
Dimensions: span 9.33 m (30 ft 7¼ in); length 5.69 m (18 ft 8 in); height 2.76 m (9 ft 0½ in); wing area 19.62 m² (211.2 sq ft)
Armament: two 30-mm MK 108 cannon

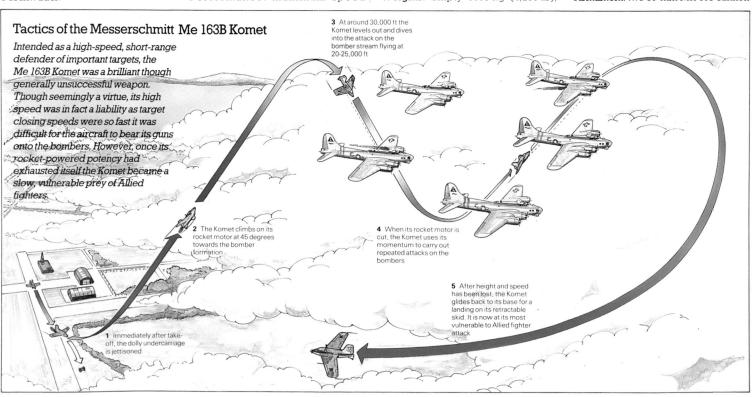

Tactics of the Messerschmitt Me 163B Komet

Intended as a high-speed, short-range defender of important targets, the Me 163B Komet was a brilliant though generally unsuccessful weapon. Though seemingly a virtue, its high speed was in fact a liability as target closing speeds were so fast it was difficult for the aircraft to bear its guns onto the bombers. However, once its rocket-powered potency had exhausted itself the Komet became a slow, vulnerable prey of Allied fighters.

3 At around 30,000 ft the Komet levels out and dives into the attack on the bomber stream flying at 20-25,000 ft

2 The Komet climbs on its rocket motor at 45 degrees towards the bomber formation

4 When its rocket motor is cut, the Komet uses its momentum to carry out repeated attacks on the bombers

5 After height and speed has been lost, the Komet glides back to its base for a landing on its retractable skid. It is now at its most vulnerable to Allied fighter attack

1 Immediately after take-off, the dolly undercarriage is jettisoned

Caproni-Campini N1 (CC.2)

It is perhaps surprising at first sight that, having been the second nation to fly an air-breathing jet-propelled aeroplane, Italy did not feature among the leading nations in this field of technology. But in truth the **Caproni-Campini N1** was no more than an ingenious freak which employed a conventional piston engine to drive a variable-pitch ducted-fan compressor with rudimentary afterburning. As such it did nothing to further gas turbine research, and was to all intents and purposes a technical dead-end. The engineer Secondo Campini had created a company in 1931 to pursue research into reaction propulsion and in 1939 persuaded Caproni to build an aircraft to accommodate the fruits of this work, namely the adaptation of an Isotta-Fraschini radial engine driving a ducted-fan compressor; the compressed air was exhausted through a variable-area nozzle in the aircraft's extreme tail, and additional fuel could be ignited in the tailpipe to increase thrust. The two-seat low-wing N1 (sometimes referred to as the **CC.2**) was first flown at Taliedo on 28 August 1940 by Mario de Bernadi. A number of set-piece demonstration flights was undertaken, including one of 270 km (168 miles) from Taliedo to Guidonia at an average speed of 209 km/h (130 mph), but it was clear from the outset that use of a three-stage fan-compressor driven by a piston engine would limit further development, and

With a maximum speed of only 375 km/h (233 mph), the N1 served only to prove its propulsion concept was possible. The design limitations meant that development would be fruitless, and as Italy's war effort gained momentum, thoughts turned to more immediate problems.

the experiment was abandoned early in 1942 when Italy was faced with sterner priorities. The N1 survives today in the Museo della Scienza Technica at Milan as a monument to ingenuity if not sophisticated technology.

The Caproni-Campini N1 used an ingenious way of propelling itself. The piston engine inside the fuselage drove a ducted fan and fuel was bled and ignited in the compressed air emitted through the tailpipe.

Specification
Type: two-seat research aircraft
Powerplant: one 900-hp (671-kW) Isotta-Fraschini radial piston engine driving a three-stage ducted-fan compressor
Performance: maximum speed 375 km/h (233 mph)
Weights: empty 3640 kg (8,025 lb); maximum take-off 4195 kg (9,248 lb)
Dimensions: span 15.85 m (52 ft 0 in); length 13.10 m (43 ft 0 in); wing area 36.00 m² (387.51 sq ft)
Armament: none

Nakajima Kikka

Encouraged by enthusiastic reports of the German Messerschmitt Me 262 from the Japanese air attaché in Berlin, the Japanese naval staff instructed Nakajima to develop a single-seat attack bomber based on the Me 262, capable of a speed of 690 km/h (430 mph) and able to carry a small bombload. Design started in September 1944 under the direction of Kazuo Ohno and Kenichi Matsumur, and the resulting aircraft resembled the German design although somewhat smaller owing to the very low power available from the early Japanese jet engines. Initially the first prototype **Nakajima Kikka** (orange blossom) was fitted with a pair of 200-kg (440-lb) thrust Tsu-11 ducted-flow engines, but these were quickly replaced by 340-kg (750-lb) thrust Ne-12 turbojets. These also proved inadequate and for the first flight two 475-kg (1,047-lb) thrust Ne-20 axial-flow turbojets were fitted; however, it was still necessary to employ an auxiliary rocket for assisted take-off. The Kikka was first flown on 7

Based on the Me 262, the Kikka had less power and had to be built smaller. Even then it had too little power and needed rockets to get it off the ground. Only one example flew before the programme was abandoned due to the impending Japanese defeat.

August 1945 at Kisarazu Naval Air Base by Lieutenant Commander Sasumu Tanaoka; the second flight ended in damage when Tanaoka abandoned the take-off owing to the ATO rockets being incorrectly mounted. A second prototype was then nearing completion and manufacture of 18 further aircraft had started when, on 15 August, the entire programme was abandoned. Production, which included versions for training, reconnaissance and air combat, had also been planned.

Specification
Kikka (1st prototype)
Type: single-seat attack bomber
Powerplant: two 475-kg (1,047-lb) thrust Ne-20 axial-flow turbojets
Performance: maximum speed 697 km/h (433 mph) at 10000 m (32,810 ft); climb to 10000 m (32,810 ft) in 26 minutes; service ceiling 12000 m (39,370 ft); range 940 km (586 miles)
Weights: empty 2300 kg (5,071 lb); maximum take-off 4080 kg (8,995 lb)
Dimensions: span 10.00 m (32 ft 9¾ in); length 8.125 m (26 ft 7⅛ in); height 2.95 m (9 ft 8⅛ in); wing area 13.2 m² (142.08 sq ft)
Armament: one 500-kg (1,102-lb) or one 800-kg (1,764-lb) bomb; fighter version proposed with two 30-mm Type 5 cannon in nose

Yokosuka MXY7 Ohka

It was during the summer of 1944 when, faced with overwhelming and fast-increasing Allied strength in the Pacific theatre, the Japanese naval staff first seriously entertained the concept of employing suicide tactics to defeat enemy attacks, and it was Ensign Mitsuo Ohta who first produced a rough design for a piloted flying bomb, a design which was assigned to Yokosuka for detailed completion. The resulting device was a small, mainly wooden aircraft with three solid-propellant rockets in the rear fuselage and a 1200-kg (2,646-lb) explosive warhead in the nose. Carried aloft in the bomb bay of a modified Mitsubishi G4M bomber and flown towards the target area, the **Yokosuka MXY7 Ohka** (cherry blossom) bomb would be released, its rockets fired and then flown directly to impact on a selected target; the pilot was sealed into his cockpit before take-off. Initial powered flights started at Sagami in October 1944, followed by unmanned, powered flights the next month. Production was put in hand,

and a total of 755 Ohkas was built before March 1945 when production ended. The weapon was first employed by the 721st Kokutai on 21 March 1945, but the carrier aircraft were intercepted and forced to release their flying bombs too early. On 1 April the US battleship *West Virginia* and three transport vessels were hit and damaged by Ohkas. Limited success attended other suicide attacks by Ohkas, but the transport aircraft proved fatally vulnerable in the presence of powerful American defences and the Japanese suicide tactic was never a serious threat to Allied operations in the Pacific, for all its macabre implications.

Specification
Ohka Model 11
Type: single-seat suicide aircraft
Powerplant: three solid-fuel Type 4 Mark 1 Model 20 rockets with total thrust of 800 kg (1,764 lb)
Performance: maximum level speed

Powered by three rockets in the tail, the Ohka was a piloted bomb released from its mother aircraft when near the target. The pilot was

650 km/h (403 mph); terminal diving speed 927 km/h (576 mph); range 37 km (23 miles)
Weights: empty 440 kg (970 lb); maximum take-off 2140 kg (4,718 lb)

sealed into his cockpit before the flight, so once released he had only one hope: to cause maximum damage to his target.

Dimensions: span 5.12 m (16 ft 9½ in); length 6.07 m (19 ft 10¾ in); height 1.16 m (3 ft 9⅝ in); wing area 6.0 ^{2} (64.6 sq ft)
Warhead: 1200 kg (2,646 lb)

---

de Havilland Vampire

The first production Vampire made its first flight in April 1945, but production examples such as this F.Mk 1 did not reach the RAF until 1946.

Among the earliest British gas turbines destined for flight was the Halford H.1, designed by Major F.B. Halford and manufactured by de Havilland. In response to Air Ministry Specification E.6/41 the de Havilland company decided to employ this engine in a radical little fighter prototype initially known as the **Spidercrab**. In an effort to avoid thrust losses through long intake and exhaust ducts the engine intakes were located in the wing roots and the fuselage terminated immediately aft of the engine jet pipe, the aircraft's tail being carried on slender twin booms. The result was an extremely neat and compact design, and the first flight of the prototype, made by Geoffrey de Havilland Jr, took place at Hatfield in Hertfordshire on 20 September 1943, just 16 months after the start of design, the aircraft (LZ548/G) featuring pointed fins. Two further prototypes (LZ551/G and MP838/G) quickly joined the flight programme, the latter carrying the planned armament of four

20-mm Hispano cannon under the nose. The name was changed to **Vampire** and on 13 May 1944 a contract for 120 production examples of the **Vampire F.Mk I** (later increased to 300) was placed for manufacture by the English Electric Company, Preston. The first production aircraft (TG274/G), with square-cut fins and Goblin turbojet (as the Halford engine was named) was flown at Samlesbury on 20 April 1945, becoming the first British fighter with a speed of over 805 km/h (500 mph). Pre-service and handling trials occupied the remainder of 1945, however, and the Vampire saw no operational

service during the war, entering RAF Fighter Command in the summer of 1946.

Specification
Type: single-seat interceptor fighter
Powerplant: one 1225-kg (2,700-lb) thrust de Havilland Goblin centrifugal-flow turbojet
Performance: maximum speed 824 km/h (512 mph) at 10365 m (34,000 ft); initial climb 1235 m (4,050 ft) per minute; service ceiling 12620 m (41,400 ft); range 1190 km (740 miles)
Weights: empty 2803 kg (6,180 lb); maximum take-off 4627 kg (10,200 lb)

Dimensions: span 12.19 m (40 ft 0 in); length 9.37 m (30 ft 9 in); height 2.69 m (8 ft 10 in); wing area 24.71 m² (266.0 sq ft)
Armament: four 20-mm Hispano cannon under the nose

TG 278 was the fifth production Vampire F.Mk 1, all of which were built by English Electric to relieve de Havilland. The first 40 aircraft had Goblin I engines and carried an armament of four 20-mm cannon in the nose. Later versions had pressurized cockpits with bubble canopies.

Gloster E.28/39

Assured of a place in aviation history, the **Gloster E.28/39** was the first British jet aircraft to fly. Although its design was based on possible fighter requirements (with weight and space allowance for an armament of four rifle-calibre machine-guns), the small low-wing aircraft was strictly a research vehicle intended to prove the flight characteristics of the pioneering Whittle W.1 reverse-flow gas turbine with centrifugal compressor. It was an attractive aircraft with nosewheel landing gear and nose inlet for the midships-mounted turbojet, which exhausted through the extreme rear fuselage. Specification E.28/39 was issued to the Gloster Aircraft Company on 3 February 1940; the first prototype underwent taxiing trials at Hucclecote in April 1941 and on 15 May that year was first flown by P.E.G. Sayer from Cranwell with a 390-kg (860-lb) thrust W.1 engine. On 4 February 1942 the aircraft was flown with a 526-kg (1,160-lb) thrust W.1A; on 30 July 1942, while flying with a 692-kg (1,526-lb) thrust Rover W.2B engine, the aircraft entered an inverted spin with jammed ailerons, forcing the RAE pilot to bale out. A second prototype had joined the test programme, and was powered by a 771-kg (1,700-lb) thrust Power Jets W.2/500 turbojet, later boosted to 798-kg (1,760-lb) thrust, and it was with this engine that the aircraft survived to be put on permanent exhibition in the South Kensington Science Museum.

Specification

Type: single-seat research aircraft
Powerplant: one 798-kg (1,760-lb) thrust Power Jets W.2/500 turbojet
Performance: maximum speed 750 km/h (466 mph) at 3050 m (10,000 ft); service ceiling 9753 m (32,000 ft)
Weights: empty 1309 kg (2,886 lb); maximum take-off 1700 kg (3,748 lb)
Dimensions: span 8.84 m (29 ft 0 in); length 7.72 m (25 ft 3¾ in); height 2.82 m (9 ft 3 in); wing area 13.61 m² (146.5 sq ft)
Armament: none

Two Gloster E.28/39s were built; one was lost in an accident and the other survived to be displayed in the Science Museum in London. It was fitted with provision for armament but remained as a research aircraft throughout its flying career.

Gloster Meteor

The **Gloster Meteor** was the only Allied jet aircraft to reach combat status during the war, and indeed survived in service with the RAF as a fighter for some 15 years afterwards. Designed by George Carter to Air Ministry Specification F.9/40, the aircraft employed twin engines owing to the low power available from turbojets early in the 1940s. Eight prototypes were built: the first had Rover W.2B engines, the second Power Jets W.2/500s, the third Metrovick F.2 axial-flow turbojets, the fourth W.2B/23 engines, the fifth Halford/de Havilland H.1s, the sixth (prototype **Meteor Mk II**) DH Goblin engines, the seventh also Goblins but with modified fin and rudder, and the eighth Rolls-Royce W.2B/37 Derwent Is. Although the first prototype was completed first and underwent taxiing trials in July 1942 at Newmarket, it was the fifth aircraft that was first flown on 5 March 1943 at Cranwell. The first production batch comprised 20 **Meteor Mk I** aircraft with Rolls-Royce W.2B/23 Welland I reverse-flow turbojets with centrifugal-flow compressors; roughly half of these were delivered to No. 616 Squadron at Culmhead in July 1944, and the squadron then moved to Manston where it flew operational sorties against the flying bombs being launched against southern England; the first such weapon was destroyed on 4 August. The squadron later moved to Belgium where it was joined by No. 504 Squadron with **Meteor Mk III** aircraft, also with Welland engines, but fitted with sliding hoods. One of the production Meteor Mk Is was shipped to the USA in exchange for a Bell YP-59A for evaluation purposes. Another was the world's first turboprop-powered aircraft, being fitted with two Rolls-Royce Trents, although this aircraft was not flown until two weeks after the end of the war.

Specification
Meteor F.Mk I
Type: single-seat interceptor fighter
Powerplant: two 771-kg (1,700-lb) thrust Rolls-Royce Welland I turbojets
Performance: maximum speed 668 km/h (415 mph) at 3050 m (10,000 ft); service ceiling 12190 m (40,000 ft)
Weights: empty 3692 kg (8,140 lb); maximum take-off 6257 kg (13,795 lb)
Dimensions: span 13.11 m (43 ft 0 in); length 12.57 m (41 ft 3 in); height 3.96 m (13 ft 0 in); wing area 34.74 m² (374.0 sq ft)
Armament: four nose-mounted 20-mm Hispano cannon (provision for six)

EE211/G was the second production Meteor, an F.Mk 1. Armed with four 20-mm cannon and powered by two Welland I turbojets, it could reach a speed of 668 km/h (415 mph). Meteors provided good training for American bomber crews now faced with attacks from Me 262s.

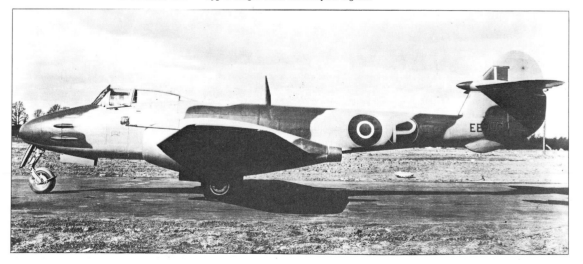

Bell P-59 Airacomet

In the almost total absence of work on gas turbines for aircraft in the USA before 1941, the UK undertook to supply the General Electric Company (which had worked on industrial turbines for many years) with details of Frank Whittle's progress to date. On account of the Bell Aircraft Corporation's proximity to General Electric's engine plant, that company was selected to develop a fighter around the USA's first turbojet on 5 September 1941. With a Whittle-type General Electric 1-A turbojet on each side of the fuselage beneath the wing roots, the **Bell Model 27** was designated the **XP-59A**, the first of three being flown by Robert M. Stanley at Muroc Dry Lake on 1 October 1942. Named **Airacomet**, 13 development **YP-59A** aircraft followed during 1943-4 with the more powerful General Electric I-16 (J31) turbojet, and these were used primarily to provide basic flight data on turbojets. Production orders for 20 **P-59A** aircraft with J31-GE-3 engines and 80 **P-59B** aircraft with J31-GE-5 engines were awarded but, as a result of successful development of the Lockheed P-80 Shooting Star the last 50 of the latter were cancelled as superfluous. All production had been completed by the end of the war and many of the aircraft were issued to a special USAAF unit, the 412th Fighter Group, for use as drones or drone controllers, some aircraft having a second open cockpit in the nose for an observer. No P-59 ever achieved operational status, being found to lack adequate performance, although a single YP-59A was shipped to the UK for evaluation at the Royal Aircraft Establishment and the Aeroplane & Armament Experimental Establishment late in 1943.

Specification
P-59B Airacomet
Type: single-seat interceptor fighter
Powerplant: two 907-kg (2,000-lb) thrust General Electric J31-GE-5 turbojets

Performance: maximum speed 658 km/h (409 mph) at 10670 m (35,000 ft); climb to 3050 m (10,000 ft) in 3 minutes 20 seconds; service ceiling 14040 m (46,200 ft); range 644 km (400 miles)
Weights: empty 3704 kg (8,165 lb);

maximum take-off 6214 kg (13,700 lb)
Dimensions: span 13.87 m (45 ft 6 in); length 11.62 m (38 ft 1½ in); height 3.66 m (12 ft 0 in); wing area 35.84 m² (385.8 sq ft)
Armament: one 20-mm M4 cannon and three 12.7-mm (0.5-in) machine-guns in the nose

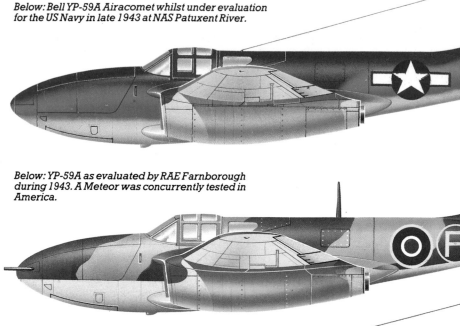

Below: Bell YP-59A Airacomet whilst under evaluation for the US Navy in late 1943 at NAS Patuxent River.

Below: YP-59A as evaluated by RAE Farnborough during 1943. A Meteor was concurrently tested in America.

Below: P-59B-1 with redesigned fin under test in May 1945.

Below: The first three prototypes (XP-59A) featured a flush canopy – later models having a stepped canopy. The P-59 was ordered in production but the P-80 was preferred, and the Airacomet never saw service, lacking adequate performance.

Lockheed P-80 Shooting Star

The second American jet fighter to fly during the war was the **Lockheed P-80 Shooting Star**, two development examples of which reached the Italian war zone just before VE-day, but failed to fly an operational sortie. Designed under the leadership of Clarence L. Johnson around the British Halford (de Havilland) H.1 turbojet of 1361-kg (3,000-lb) thrust, the first prototype **XP-80** was flown at Muroc Dry Lake by Milo Burcham on 8 January 1944, only 143 days after the start of the project. The next two prototypes were designated **XP-80A** and were powered by the Allison-developed General Electric J33 engine of 1814-kg (4,000-lb) thrust, the first being flown by Tony Le Vier on 10 June 1944. With low-set equitapered laminar-flow wings and engine air intakes set into the fuselage just forward of the wing roots, this version had a top speed of 898 km/h (558 mph) at sea level. Thirteen development **YP-80A** aircraft for service trials, with J33-GE-9 or J33-GE-11 engines and an armament of six machine-guns in the nose, started delivery to test establishments in October 1944 and it was aircraft of this type that arrived in Italy in May 1945. Production deliveries of the **P-80A** did not start until December that year, however, four months too late to see action against the Japanese. Subsequently the P-80 gave long and valuable service in the post-war USAF (particularly in the Korean War of 1950-3).

Specification

P-80A Shooting Star
Type: single-seat interceptor fighter
Powerplant: one 1814-kg (4,000-lb) thrust General Electric J33-A-11 turbojet
Performance: maximum speed 933 km/h (580 mph) at 8535 m (28,000 ft); initial climb rate 1395 m (4,580 ft) per minute; service ceiling 13715 m (45,000 ft); range 870 km (540 miles)
Weights: empty 3593 kg (7,920 lb); maximum take-off 6577 kg (14,500 lb)
Dimensions: span 12.17 m (39 ft 11 in); length 10.52 m (34 ft 6 in); height 3.45 m (11 ft 4 in); wing area 22.11 m² (238.0 sq ft)
Armament: six 12.7 mm (0.5-in) machine-guns in the nose

The P-80 was powered by a J33 engine which replaced the British Halford H.1. Through its developments it became the most successful first-generation jet, leading to the T-33 trainer and the F-94 Starfire. This is a P-80A-1-LO serving with the 412th Fighter Group in 1946.

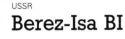
USSR

Berez-Isa BI

Under the direction of Prof. Viktor Bolkhovitinov, with detail design by Aleksandr Bereznyak and Aleksei Isayev (accounting for the BI of the designation), the **Berez-Isa BI** was the first liquid rocket-engined fighter flown in the USSR. A low-wing monoplane, the BI had a Dushkin D-1A rocket engine in the tail, and this was highly temperamental, its volatile fuel mixture of kerosene and nitric acid being not only dangerous to handle, but also causing corrosion of tanks and fuel lines. The BI was flown initially as a glider on 10 September 1941, the first significant powered flight of 3 minutes 9 seconds, being made by the third prototype on 15 May 1942. Work on 50 pre-production aircraft was started, but halted when a prototype dived into the ground on 27 March 1943 during a low-level high-speed run, killing its pilot. The endurance of the BI was inadequate for operational use, but a two-chamber engine developed by Dushkin to overcome this deficiency, with low (cruising) and high (combat) thrust settings was almost double the weight and considered unsuitable. Wind tunnel testing that followed the fatal crash revealed a stability problem that could not be resolved and further development was abandoned. Before this, however, the seventh prototype with a more powerful engine had demonstrated a rate of climb of 4980 m (16,340 ft) per minute.

Specification

Powerplant: one 1000-kg (2,205-lb) thrust Dushkin D-1A rocket engine
Performance: (estimated) maximum speed 1000 km/h (621 mph) at 5000 m (16,405 ft); climb to 10000 m (32,810 ft) in 59 seconds; endurance 8 to 15 minutes
Weights: empty 958 kg (2,112 lb); maximum take-off 1683 kg (3,710 lb)
Dimensions: span 6.48 m (21 ft 3 in); length 6.40 m (21 ft 0 in); wing area 7.00 m² (75.35 sq ft)
Armament: two nose-mounted 20-mm ShVAK cannon

The third prototype Berez-Isa (Bolkhovitinov) BI seen taking off on its first powered flight. Performance in terms of speed and rate of climb were phenomenal, but the aerodynamics showed insoluble stability problems and the project was abandoned.

Below: The BI first appeared as a glider for testing purposes before having its rocket motor installed.

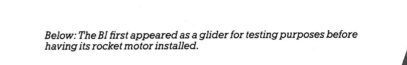

Above: The third prototype BI was fitted with retractable skis which could be interchanged with wheels depending on the ground conditions. Armament was two 20-mm cannon.

Axis Ground Attack Aircraft

Ground attack aircraft played a vital role in the victorious German campaigns of 1939-41. The German army's Blitzkrieg doctrine involved close integration of tactical air power and mechanized army units. This combination of Panzer mobility and airborne artillery firepower seemed to be unstoppable.

The Focke Wolfe FW 190, one of Germany's leading ground attack aircraft. This one, loaded and ready for action, has been abandoned at an aerodrome by retreating Axis forces in Italy.

One of the most significant aspects of the history of land warfare in Europe during World War II was the inexorable change in the relative air power of the Axis and Allies over the battlefields. When the war started the German army was the principal weapon of aggression, to which all else played a supporting role; its tactic was the Blitzkrieg – the smashing of all opposition by assault troops with fast-moving armour continuously supported by tactical aircraft. So long as the

Luftwaffe possessed air superiority over the ground battle, the German army held the initiative. This had been the pervading doctrine that dictated the swift expansion of Germany's armed forces after the Nazis had taken power in 1933.

By contrast the Allies had almost totally ignored air support of their armies, other than to provide very limited tactical reconnaissance. This proved a major cause of one defeat after another during the first two years

of the war as Poland, Denmark, Norway, the Netherlands, Belgium, France, Yugoslavia, Greece and Crete fell to the smashing blows of Blitzkrieg.

Inevitably, the mounting losses suffered by the Luftwaffe on the Eastern Front and in the Mediterranean (as Allied strength increased everywhere) deprived the Luftwaffe of air superiority over the land battle. The traditional weapon of the Blitzkrieg, the notorious Stuka (the Junkers Ju 87), could no longer attack at

will, being faced by formidable fighter opposition almost everywhere. Yet in the absence of a more advanced replacement for the Stuka, the Germans were forced to persevere with this weapon, and as a result suffered catastrophic losses. Such efforts as they were able to extemporize tended to be set-piece expedients, planned and executed by the Luftwaffe, rather than continuous support that could be called up by ground forces in a moment of emergency – and immediately appreciated by the hard-pressed soldier below. Once the German army no longer saw friendly aircraft continuously flying overhead, the Blitzkrieg was impossible.

No other Axis air force had been as closely integrated with its own land forces as had the Luftwaffe. The Allies were quick to appreciate the paramount importance of assuming air superiority over the ground battle, so much so that, after the pendulum of fortune swung back following the battles at Stalingrad and El Alamein, the British, Soviet and American armies were afforded powerful and continuous air support. The Luftwaffe no longer had it in its power to dispute Allied superiority in the skies over the German army.

Mitsubishi Ki-30

In May 1936 the Imperial Japanese Army issued its specification for a light bomber required to supersede the Mitsubishi Ki-2 and Kawasaki Ki-3 then in service. The **Mitsubishi Ki-30** prototype that resulted was of cantilever mid-wing monoplane configuration with fixed tailwheel landing gear, the main units faired and spatted, and powered by a 615-kW (825-hp) Mitsubishi Ha-6 radial engine. Flown for the first time on 28 February 1937 this aircraft performed well, but it was decided to fly a second prototype with the more powerful Nakajima Ha-5 KAI radial engine. This aircraft showed some slight improvement in performance but, in any case, exceeded the army's original specification, so there was no hesitation in ordering 16 service trials aircraft. These were delivered in January 1938 and, two months later, the Ki-39 was ordered into production.

First used operationally in China during 1938, the Ki-30s proved to be most effective, for in that theatre they had the benefit of fighter escort. The situation was very much the same at the beginning of the Pacific war, but as soon as the Allies were in a position to confront unescorted Ki-30s with fighter aircraft they immediately began to suffer heavy losses and were soon relegated to second-line use. The Allied codename 'Ann' was allocated to the Ki-30, but few were seen operationally after the opening phases of the war. A total of 704 had been built when pro-

duction ended in 1941, 68 manufactured by the First Army Air Arsenal at Tachikawa, and many of these ended their days in a *kamikaze* role during the closing stages of the war.

Specification
Type: two-seat light bomber
Powerplant: one 708-kW (950-hp) Nakajima Ha-5 KAI radial piston engine
Performance: maximum peed 423 km/h (263 mph) at 4000 m (13,125 ft); cruising speed 380 km/h (236 mph); service ceiling 8570 m (28,115 ft); range 1700 km (1,056 miles)
Weights: empty 2230 kg (4,916 lb); maximum take-off 3220 kg (7,099 lb)
Dimensions: span 14.55 m (47 ft 8.8 in); length 10.35 m (33 ft 11.5 in); height 3.65 m (11 ft 11.7 in); wing area 30.58 m² (329.17 sq ft)

Above: A Mitsubishi Ki-30 of the 2nd Chutai, 10th Hikosentai, in 1942. A two-seater light bomber, code-named 'Ann' by Allied forces, the Ki-30 enjoyed some success over China but proved hopelessly vulnerable to hostile fighter aircraft unless closely escorted.

Armament: one wing-mounted 7.7-mm (0.303-in) machine-gun and one gun of the same calibre on trainable mount in rear cockpit, plus a maximum bombload of 400 kg (882 lb)

Above: By the time production ended in 1941 over 700 Ki-30s had been produced and the type had largely been relegated to second-line use.

Mitsubishi Ki-51

To meet an Imperial Japanese Army specification of December 1937 for a ground-attack aircraft, which it was suggested could be a development of the Ki-30 light bomber, Mitsubishi produced two prototypes under the designation **Mitsubishi Ki-51**. Of similar external appearance to the Ki-30, the new design was generally of smaller dimensions, had a revised and simplified cockpit that put the two-man crew more closely together and, because the bomb bay was not required, the monoplane wing was moved from a mid- to low-wing configuration. Powerplant chosen was the Mitsubishi Ha-26-II radial engine.

Tested during the summer of 1939, the two prototypes were followed by 11 service trials aircraft, these being completed before the end of the year. They differed from the prototypes by incorporating a number of modifications, but most important were the introduction of fixed leading-edge slots to improve slow-speed handling and armour plate beneath the engine and crew positions. In addition to the standard production aircraft, there were attempts to develop dedicated reconnaissance versions, initially by the conversion of one Ki-51 service trials aircraft which had the rear cockpit redesigned to accommodate reconnaissance cameras. Test and evaluation of this aircraft, redesignated Ki-51a, brought a realization that the standard Ki-51 could be modified to have provisions for the installation of reconnaissance cameras, and this change was made on the production line. Subsequently, three Ki-71 tactical reconnaissance prototypes were developed from the Ki-51, introducing the 1119-

kW (1,500-hp) Mitsubishi Ha-112-II engine, retractable landing gear, two wing-mounted 20-mm cannon and other refinements, but no production examples were built.

Allocated the Allied codename 'Sonia', the Ki-51 was used initially in operations against China, and was deployed against the Allies until the end of the Pacific war. In more intensely contested areas the fairly slow Ki-51s were easy prey for Allied fighters, but in secondary theatres, where an ability to operate from rough and short fields was valuable, these aircraft gave essential close support in countless operations. In the closing stages of the war they were used in *kamikaze* attacks.

Specification
Mitsubishi Ki-51
Type: two-seat ground-attack/reconnaissance aircraft
Powerplant: one 701-kW (940-hp) Mitsubishi Ha-26-II radial piston engine
Performance: maximum speed 425 km/h (264 mph) at 3000 m (9,845 ft); service ceiling 8270 m (27,130 ft); range 1060 km (659 miles)
Weights: empty 1873 kg (4,129 lb); maximum take-off 2920 kg (6,437 lb)
Dimensions: span 12.10 m (39 ft 8.4 in);

length 9.20 m (30 ft 2.2 in); height 2.73 m (8 ft 11.5 in); wing area 24.02 m² (258.56 sq ft)
Armament: two wing-mounted 7.7-mm (0.303-in) machine-guns (early production) or two wing-mounted 12.7-mm (0.5-in) guns (late production), and one 7.7-mm (0.303-in) gun on trainable mount in rear cockpit, plus a bombload of 200 kg (441 lb) increasing to 250 kg (551 lb) in *kamikaze* role

Slow and vulnerable, the Mitsubishi Ki-51 nevertheless served throughout the war, mainly in secondary theatres, where its rough landing capability was a valuable asset.

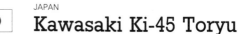

JAPAN

Kawasaki Ki-45 Toryu

In early 1937 Kawasaki was instructed by the Imperial Japanese army to initiate the design and development of a twin-engine fighter that would be suitable for long-range operations over the Pacific. The concept derived from army interest in developments taking place in other countries, and particularly in the Messerschmitt Bf 110. The first **Kawasaki Ki-45 Toryu** (dragon killer) prototype flew in 1939, a cantilever mid-wing monoplane with retractable tailwheel landing gear. A slender fuselage provided enclosed accommodation for two in tandem. Problems followed with the engine installation, and it was not until September 1941 that the **Ki-45 KAIa** entered production. Armament of this initial series version comprised one forward-firing 20-mm cannon, two 12.7-mm (0.5-in) machine-guns in the nose, and a 7.92-mm (0.31-in) machine-gun on a flexible mount in the rear cockpit; there was also provision to carry two drop tanks or two 250-kg (551-lb) bombs on underwing racks. The type entered service in August 1942 but was first used in combat during October 1942, soon being allocated the Allied codename 'Nick'. The Ki-45 KAIa was joined by a new version developed especially for the ground-attack/anti-shipping role, the **Ki-45 KAIb**. Stan-

The Kawasaki Ki-45 KAIc was the night-fighter variant of this highly successful twin-engined fighter-bomber. Carrying one forward-firing and two obliquely-mounted upward-firing cannon, this is a machine belonging to the 1st Chutai, 53rd Sentai, based at Matsudo in early 1945.

dard armament comprised one 20-mm cannon in the nose, a forward-firing 37-mm cannon in the fuselage, and one rear-firing 7.92-mm (0.31-in) machine-gun, plus the underwing provision for drop tanks or bombs; a number of alternative weapon installations were tried experimentally, including the use of a 75-mm (2.95-in) cannon for attacks on shipping.

The Ki-45 KAIa was, for its day, heavily armed and proved effective against the USAF's Consolidiated B-24 Liberators and, when these bombers were used more extensively for night operations, the Ki-45 was adapted to attack them. Thus the night-fighting capability of the type was discovered, leading to development of the Ki-45 KAIc night-fighter, which proved to be

one of the most successful Japanese aircraft in this category. Ki-45 Toryus remained in service until the end of the Pacific war, production totalling 1,701 including prototypes, being used for the defence of Tokyo, and in the Manchuria, Burma and Sumatra areas of operations.

Specification
Kawasaki Ki-45 KAIc
Type: two-seat night-fighter
Powerplant: two 805-kW (1,080-hp) Mitsubishi Ha-102 radial piston engines
Performance: maximum speed 545 km/h (339 mph) at 7000 m (22,965 ft); climb to 5000 m (16,405 ft) in 6 minutes 7 seconds; service ceiling 10000 m (32,810 ft); range 2000 km

(1,243 miles)
Weights: empty 4000 kg (8,818 lb); maximum take-off 5500 kg (12,125 lb)
Dimensions: span 15.05 m (49 ft 4.5 in); length 11.00 m (36 ft 1.1 in); height 3.70 m (12 ft 1.7 in); wing area 32.00 m² (344.46 sq ft)
Armament: cannon and machine-guns as listed in text; all versions had provision for two drop tanks or two 250-kg (551-lb) bombs on underwing racks

Heavily armed by Japanese standards, the Kawasaki Ki-45 was developed as a long-range fighter. It doubled as a ground attack aircraft, one model being fitted with an experimental 75-mm (2.95-in) mount for the anti-shipping role.

JAPAN

Kawasaki Ki-48

Imperial Japanese Army aircraft confronted by the Soviet-built Tupolev SB-2 bomber, providing support for the Chinese during 1937, were rudely surprised by its capability, its maximum speed being such that Japanese army fighter aircraft were virtually unable to incercept it. Almost at once the army instructed Kawasaki to begin the design of a twin-engine light bomber of even better capability, specifying a maximum speed of about 485 km/h (301 mph). Work on what was to become known as the **Kawasaki Ki-48** began in January 1938, the result being a cantilever mid-wing monoplane with conventional tail unit, retractable tailwheel landing gear and, in the type's

In 1937 the Japanese encountered the Tupolev SB-2 in Chinese hands, and were very impressed as the Soviet aircraft could outpace Japanese fighters. The Ki-48 was Japan's reply: a light bomber of similar appearance.

prototype form, two 708-kW (950-hp) Nakajima Ha-25 radial engines mounted in nacelles at the wing leading edges. The fuselage provided accommodation for a crew of four (the bombardier, navigator and radio-operator each doubling as gunners) and incorporated an internal bomb bay.

Ki-48s entered service in the summer of 1940, becoming operational in China during the autumn of that year. In China their speed gave the Ki-48s almost complete immunity from enemy defences, but their deployment against Allied aircraft at the be-

ginning of the Pacific war revealed that their superior performance was illusory. Codenamed 'Lily' by the Allies, this initial production version had a number of deficiencies for the different kind of operations then required, and it was fortunate for the Japanese army that an improved version was already under development. This had the company designation **Ki-48-II** and differed from the earlier model by introducing a slightly lengthened fuselage, protected fuel tanks, armour protection for the crew, increased bomb-load and more powerful Nakajima Ha-115 engines.

Unfortunately for the Japanese army, when the Ki-48-II was introduced into operational service its speed was still too low and its defensive armament inadequate. Attempts to increase armament merely upped the overall weight and speed suffered proportionately: it was clear by the summer of 1944 that the day of the Ki-48 had passed, and in October it was declared obsolescent.

Specification
Kawasaki Ki-48-IIb
Type: four-seat light/dive-bomber
Powerplant: two 858-kW (1,150-hp)

Nakajima Ha-115 radial piston engines
Performance: maximum speed 505 km/h (314 mph) at 5600 m (18,375 ft); service ceiling 10100 m (33,135 ft); maximum range 2400 km (1,491 miles)
Weights: empty 4550 kg (10,031 lb); maximum take-off 6750 kg (14,881 lb)
Dimensions: span 17.45 m (57 ft 3 in); length 12.75 m (41 ft 10 in); height 3.80 m (12 ft 5.6 in); wing area 40.00 m² (430.57 sq ft)
Armament: three 7.7-mm (0.303-in) machine-guns on trainable mounts in nose, dorsal and ventral positions, plus up to 800 kg (1,764 lb) of bombs

---

JAPAN

Kawasaki Ki-102

Derived from the Ki-96 twin-engine single-seat fighter, development of which was abandoned after three prototypes had been completed, the **Kawasaki Ki-102b** was intended as a two-seat attack fighter for primary deployment in the close-support role. Some assemblies of the Ki-96 prototypes were incorporated into the three Ki-102 prototypes, the first of which was completed in March 1944. A cantilever mid-wing monoplane with a conventional tail unit, retractable tail-wheel landing gear and two Mitsubishi Ha-112-II radial engines, the Ki-102 accommodated its two-man crew in separate enclosed cockpits in tandem. Completion of the prototypes was followed by the construction of 20 pre-production aircraft and in October 1944 the type was ordered into production. With the Imperial Japanese Army still anxious to procure a twin-engine high-altitude fighter, Kawasaki modified six of the preproduction Ki-102s to serve as prototypes of such an interceptor. This differed from the attack fighter by having improved two-seat accommodation, a revised tail unit and Mitsubishi Ha-112-IIru engines with turbochargers. Successful testing of this version in mid-1944 resulted in a high-priority production order, but problems with the turbocharged engine resulted in only about 15 being

delivered to the army before the war ended. The design had also been revised to produce a night-fighter version under the designation Ki-102c, but there was only time to complete two examples. These had increased wing span, a lengthened fuselage, redesigned tail surfaces, primitive AI radar, and armament comprising two 30-mm Ho-105 cannon in the underfuselage and two 20-mm Ho-5 cannon mounted obliquely in the fuselage to fire forward and upward. Ki-102b aircraft, which were allocated the Allied code-name 'Randy', saw comparatively little service, some being used in action over Okinawa, but the majority were

held in reserve in Japan.

Specification
Kawasaki Ki-102b
Type: twin-engine ground-attack aircraft
Powerplant: two 1119-kW (1,500-hp) Mitsubishi Ha-112-II radial piston engines
Performance: maximum speed 580 km/h (360 mph) at 6000 m (19,685 ft); service ceiling 11000 m (36,090 ft); range 2000 km (1,243 miles)
Weights: empty 4950 kg (10,913 lb); maximum take-off 7300 kg (16094 lb)
Dimensions: span 15.57 m (51 ft 1 in); length 11.45 m (37 ft 6.8 in); height

3.70 m (12 ft 1.7 in); wing area 34.00 m² (365.98 sq ft)
Armament: one 57-mm Ho-401 cannon in the nose, two 20-mm Ho-5 cannon in the underfuselage, and one 12.7-mm (0.5-in) machine-gun on a flexible mounting in the rear cockpit, plus two 200-litre (44-Imp gal) drop tanks or two 250-kg (551-lb) bombs carried on underwing racks

The Ki-102b in its ground attack form entered service around November 1944, a few seeing action at Okinawa but the majority being retained to defend the homeland from the expected invasion.

ITALY

Caproni Bergamaschi Ca 306/Ca 309/310/314

At the 1935 Milan Exhibition there appeared the prototype of the **Caproni Bergamaschi Ca 306 Borea** (north wind), a six-passenger low-wing transport. Although built only in small numbers, the Borea was important as the progenitor of a range of light twin-engine aircraft manufactured for a wide variety of roles. The first of these was the aptly-named **Ca-309 Ghibli** (desert wind), 78 of which were built for use in Libya. The military versions were used as light transports or reconnaissance bombers with a lengthened glazed nose, bomb racks, cameras, and with armament comprising three 7.7-mm (0.303-in) machine-guns. Another model featured a fixed forward firing 20-mm cannon. Seven squadrons equipped with Ghiblis were operational when Italy entered the war in 1940.

Developed in parallel with the Ghibli, the **Ca 310 Libeccio** (south west wind) was structurally similar to the earlier machine, but was provided with retractable landing gear and po-

A Caproni Ca 310 Libeccio (south west wind), is seen in Norwegian service based at Sola airfield near Stavanger. Other countries to acquire the Ca 310 included Peru and Yugoslavia.

wered by two 350-kW (470-hp) Piaggio P.VII C.35 radial engines. Export deliveries went to Norway, Peru and Yugoslavia, and this last nation also acquired 12 more under the designation **Ca 310bis**; this variant differed primarily by having an unstepped extensively-glazed nose.

The prototype of the Ca 310bis served as a development aircraft for

the following **Ca 311**. As built they were similar to the Ca 310bis, but most were later modified by the introduction of a stepped windscreen, then being redesignated **Ca 311M**. Defensive armament of this version comprised a Caproni Lanciani turret with a single 7.7-mm (0.303-in) machine-gun, complemented by one machine-gun in the port wing root and another firing aft

through a ventral hatch. A modified Ca 310 with two Isotta-Fraschini Asso 120 IRCC 40 engines served as the **Ca 313** prototype, first flown on 22 December 1939, but France had already confirmed an order for 200 of these aircraft on 1 October, followed closely by British and Swedish orders for 300 and 64 respectively. However, Italy's entry into the war prevented delivery of any of the British machines and France received only five **Ca 313F** models, the remainder being diverted to the Regia Aeronautica.

Most extensively built version was the **Ca 314**. Variants included the **Ca 314A** or **Ca 314-SC** (Scorta), a convoy escort/maritime patrol aircraft, the **Ca 314B** or **Ca 314-RA** (Ricognizione Aerosiluranti) torpedo-bomber and the ground-attack **Ca 314C**.

Specification
Caproni Ca 314A
Type: convoy escort and maritime patrol aircraft
Powerplant: two 544-kW (730-hp) Isotta-Fraschini Delta RC.35 12-cylinder inverted-Vee piston engines
Performance: maximum speed 395 km/h (245 mph) at 4000 m (13,125 ft); cruising speed 320 km/h (199 mph) at 4200 m (13,780 ft); service ceiling 6400 m (21000 ft); maximum range 1690 km (1,050 miles)
Weights: empty 4560 kg (10,053 lb); maximum take-off 6620 kg (14,595 lb)
Dimensions: span 16.65 m (54 ft 7.5 in);

length 11.80 m (38 ft 8.6 in); height 3.70 m (12 ft 1.7 in); wing area 39.20 m² (421.96 sq ft)
Armament: two 12.7-mm (0.5-in) machine-guns in the wing roots and one 7.7-mm (0.303-in) gun in a dorsal turret, plus a bombload of 500 kg (1,102 lb)

This Caproni Ca 310M of the 8ª Escuadrilla, Grupo 18, Agrupacion Espanola (the Nationalist air force), operated in Spain during late 1938.

The Caproni Ca 314 was the last and most widely built of the series, and was used in maritime roles as well as for ground attack.

ITALY

Breda Ba.65

Intended as an *aeroplano di combattimento*, capable of fulfilling the roles of intereceptor fighter, light bomber, or reconnaissance/attack aircraft as required, the prototype **Breda Ba.65** made its initial flight in September 1935. Experience in Spain indicated that the Ba.65 was suited only to the attack role, and the type served thenceforth with most of the eight *squadriglie* attached to the two Regia Aeronautica assault *stormi* (wings), the 5° and 50°. A second series of 137 aircraft was built by Breda (80) and Caproni-Vizzola (57), before production ended in July 1939. They differed from the first production batch by having Fiat A.80 engines. Six Fiat-powered Ba.65s and four more of the Gnome-Rhône-powered version were sent to the Aviazione Legionaria in Spain in 1938.

Following Italy's entry into World War II in June 1940, Ba.65s were involved in the fighting in North Africa against the British. They had a low serviceability rate in desert conditions and put up an unimpressive performance. The last serviceable aircraft was lost during the British offensive in Cyrenaica in February 1941.

A large number of the Ba.65s serving with Italian units were of two-seat configuration, with an observer/gunner in an open cockpit above the trailing edge of the wing. A smaller number of the type had a Breda L type turret, but in either case the observer/gunner operated a single 7.7-mm (0.303-in) machine-gun. While offensive armament could theoretically comprise up to 1000 kg (2,205 lb) of bombs, the load usually carried was up to 300 kg (661 lb) in the fuselage bomb bay or, alternatively, up to 200 kg (441 lb) on underwing racks.

Exports included 25 Fiat-powered Ba.65s to Iraq in 1938, two of them dual-control trainers and the remainder with Breda L turrets; 20 Ba.65s with Piaggio P.XI C.40 engines to Chile later in the same year, 17 of them single-seaters and three dual-control trainers; and 10 Fiat-powered two-seaters with Breda L turrets to Portugal in

This Breda Ba.65 was flown by the Aviazione Legionaria on the Nationalist side during the Spanish Civil War.

Spanish experience showed the Ba.65 to be suitable for ground attack only, although 25 two-seaters were sold to Iraq, where they served in No. 5 (Fighter) Squadron.

November 1939. A single Fiat-powered production aircraft was tested with an American Pratt & Whitney R-1830 engine in June 1937 in anticipation of an order from the Chinese Nationalist government, but this failed to materialize. The Iraqi Ba.65s saw limited action against the British during the 1941 insurrection in that country.

Specification
Breda 65/A.80 (single-seat version)
Type: ground-attack aircraft
Powerplant: one 746-kW (1,000-hp) Fiat A.80RC.41 radial piston engine
Performance: maximum level speed 430 km/h (267 mph); maximum level speed, two-seat version 410 km/h (255 mph); service ceiling 6300 m (20,670 ft); range 550 km (342 miles)
Weights: empty equipped 2400 kg (5,291 lb); maximum take-off 2950 kg (6,504 lb)
Dimensions: span 12.10 m (39 ft 8.4 in);

length 9.30 m (30 ft 6.1 in); height 3.20 m (10 ft 6 in); wing area 23.50 m² (252.96 sq ft)
Armament: two 12.7-mm (0.5-in) and two 7.7-mm (0.303-in) Breda-SAFAT fixed forward-firing machine-guns in wings, plus up to 300 kg (661 lb) of bombs in fuselage bomb-bay and up to

The Breda Ba.65 served with most of the eight squadrons of the two Regia Aeronautica assault Stormi (wings). These are from the original batch of 81 aircraft.

200 kg (441 lb) of bombs on underwing racks (usually alternatively)

Breda Ba.88 Lince

A propaganda triumph when its appearance was trumpeted by Mussolini's Facist regime in 1936, the **Breda Ba.88 Lince** (lynx) was a sleek all-metal shoulder-wing monoplane. In April 1937 it established two world speed-over-distance records. Regarded as an *aeroplano di combattimento*, suitable for attack, long-range reconnaissance or bombing operations, the Ba.88 then had its military equipment and weapons installed. Immediately, performance and flight characteristics fell off dramatically, but by then production orders were already being executed.

On 16 June 1940, just after Italy's declaration of war on France and her allies, the Ba.88 had its first taste of action. Twelve aircraft from the Regia Aeronautica's 19° Gruppo Autonomo made bombing and machine-gun attacks on the principal airfields of Corsica; three days later nine Ba.88s made a repeat attack. Analysis of these operations showed that the Ba.88 had only limited value, and any remaining doubts were settled when Ba.88s of the 7° Gruppo Autonomo joined action in Libya against the British. Fitted with sand filters, the engines overheated and failed to deliver their designed power. Attacks on targets at Sidi Barrani had to be aborted in September 1940, the aircraft failing to gain sufficient altitude or maintain formation, and reaching a speed less than half that claimed by the manufacturers.

By mid-November 1940 most surviving Ba.88s had been stripped of useful equipment and were scattered around operational airfields as decoys for attacking British aircraft.

Three Ba.88s were modified by the Agusta plant in 1942 to serve as ground-attack aircraft. Wing span was increased by 2.00 m (6 ft 6.75 in) to alleviate wing loading problems, their

A Breda Ba.88 of 7° Gruppo, 5° Stormo, based at Castel Benito in Libya.

engines were replaced by Fiat A.74s, nose armament was increased to four 12.7-mm (0.5-in) machine-guns, and dive brakes were installed. These Breda Ba.88Ms were delivered to the 103° Gruppo Autonomo Tuffatori (independent dive-bombing group) at Lonate Pozzolo on 7 September 1943. They were flight-tested by Luftwaffe pilots, but that was the last heard of the Breda Ba.88 which represented, perhaps, the most remarkable failure of any operational aircraft to see service in World War II.

Specification
Breda Ba.88
Type: fighter-bomber/reconnaissance aircraft
Powerplant: two 746-kW (1,000-hp) Piaggio P.XI RC.40 radial piston engines
Performance: maximum speed 490 km/h (304 mph); service ceiling 8000 m (26,245 ft); range 1640 km (1,019 miles)
Weights: empty 4650 kg (10,251 lb); maximum take-off 6750 kg (14,881 lb)
Dimensions: span 15.60 m (51 ft 2.2 in); length 10.79 m (35 ft 4.8 in); height 3.10 m (10 ft 2 in); wing area 33.34 m² (358.88 sq ft)
Armament: three fixed forward-firing 12.7-mm (0.5-in) Breda-SAFAT machine-guns in nose and one 7.7-mm (0.303-in) Breda-SAFAT machine-gun

In spite of its sleek, powerful appearance, the Ba.88 was somewhat less than successful, since the excellent prototype performance declined dramatically once in operational trim. Indeed, so bad was the Lince's combat performance that within five months from the start of the war survivors of the initial batch of 80 were gutted and used as ground decoys on airfields.

on trainable mounting in rear cockpit, plus up to 1000 kg (2,204 lb) of bombs in fuselage bomb-bay or, alternatively, three 200-kg (441-lb) bombs carried semi-exposed in individual recesses in the fuselage belly

---

Junkers Ju 87

Forever deprecated as a Nazi terror weapon, the **Junkers Ju 87** (widely referred to as the Stuka – a contraction of the word *Sturzkampfflugzeug*) was nevertheless an imaginative weapon of considerable accuracy when operating in skies clear of enemy fighters. Conceived as a form of support artillery for the Wehrmacht's Blitzkrieg tactics, the Ju 87 was first flown in 1935, a small number of Ju 87A-1s and Ju 87B-1s being flown by the Legion Condor in Spain in 1938-9. To support the invasion of Poland the Luftwaffe fielded all five *Stukageschwader* thus far equipped with Ju 87s, and it was in this campaign that, with little effective opposition in the air, the Stuka's legend was born. With sirens screaming, the cranked-wing dive-bombers wrought havoc among Poland's helpless troops and civilians, effectively destroying the country's lines of communications, bridges, railways and airfields. During the difficult Norwegian campaign the Ju 87R with underwing fuel tanks was introduced to cope with the great distances involved, and in the Battle of Britain this version and the Ju 87B were heavily committed until withdrawn temporarily as a result of losses suffered at the hands of British fighter pilots. At the end of 1941 the **Ju 87D**, a much cleaned-up version with an uprated Jumo 211, entered service on the

Russian front, and appeared in North Africa the following year. The **Ju 87G**, a specialist anti-tank aircraft, featured a pair of 37-mm guns under the wings and achieved spectacular success, particularly in the East. Unquestionably the greatest exponent of the Stuka was Hans-Ulrich Rudel whose personal tally of a battleship, cruiser and a destroyer sunk, and 519 tanks destroyed, far exceeded any other. Total Ju 87 production was said to be 5,709.

Specification
Junkers Ju 87D-1
Type: two-seat dive-bomber/assault aircraft
Powerplant: one 1044-kW (1,400-hp) Junkers Jumo 211J-1 inverted-Vee piston engine
Performance: maximum speed 410 km/h (255 mph) at 3840 m (12,600 ft); cruising speed 320 km/h (199 mph) at 5090 m (16,700 ft); service ceiling 7290 m (23,915 ft); maximum range 1535 km (954 miles)
Weights: empty equipped 3900 kg (8,598 lb); maximum take-off 6600 kg (14,551 lb)
Dimensions: span 13.80 m (45 ft 3.3 in); length 11.50 m (37 ft 8.75 in); height 3.90 m (12 ft 9.5 in); wing area 31.90 m²

The Stuka established its reputation in the hands of the Condor Legion in Spain. Here a formation of Ju 87B-1s approaches its target.

(343.38 sq ft)
Armament: two 7.92-mm (0.31-in) forward-firing MG 17 machine-guns in wings and twin 7.92-mm (0.31-in) MG 81Z machine-guns in rear cockpit, plus a maximum bombload of one 1800-kg (3,968-lb) bomb beneath fuselage, or various alternative loads beneath fuselage and wings, including anti-personnel bombs

Junkers Ju 88P

Although the **Junkers Ju 88** was originally intended to perform the dual roles of level and dive bombing, the early versions were seldom employed in the ground-support role in the same manner as the Ju 87 dive-bomber, being largely confined to level bombing attacks for which its excellent performance rendered it ideally suited. It was not until 1942, with the increasing ferocity of fighting on the Eastern Front, that attention focussed on a dedicated ground-attack version, the **Ju 88P**. The prototype **Ju 88P V1**, modified from a standard Ju 88A-4, featured a single 75-mm (2.95-in) KwK 39 gun housed in a large fairing under the fuselage, and during trials against captured T-34 tanks at Rechlin in 1943 promising results were obtained. A small number of **Ju 88P-1** aircraft followed, featuring the 'solid' nose of the C-series *Zerstörer*, armour protection for the engines and the more suitable semi-automatic PAK 40L 75-mm anti-tank gun; production amounted to about 40 aircraft, these being distributed between the Versuchskommando für Panzerbekämpfung, the Panzerjägerstaffel 92 and 6./KG 3 for operational trials and development of tactics as train-busters, this role becoming increasingly important on the Eastern Front.

The Ju 88P-1 proved both cumbersome and vulnerable, and was soon followed by the **Ju 88P-2** with a large fairing offset to port under the fuselage mounting a pair of 37-mm BK 3.7 cannon. The higher muzzle velocity proved more effective against Soviet armour and also prompted the air-

craft's use by Erprobungskommando 25 as a bomber-destroyer; the aircraft had lost the necessary manoeuvrability for air combat, however. The **Ju 88P-3**, with further increased armour protection for the crew, was delivered to one *Staffel* in each of the Nachtschlachtgruppen (night ground-attack groups) 1, 2, 4, 8 and 9 for combat use on the Eastern Front, in northern Norway (NSGr 8) and Italy (NSGr 9). Some success was achieved by these units, but in an effort to improve the aircraft's performance the **Ju 88P-4** was introduced with a much smaller gun fairing mounting a single 50-mm BK5 gun, and at least one Ju 88P-4 was equipped with a 6.5-cm RZ 65 solid-fuel rocket-launcher with a 22-round magazine. The Ju 88P-4 was also planned to mount an 88-mm Düka 8.8 U-boat gun as well as various types of flame-thrower; none of these reached operational units, however, and by the time that NSGr 2 was moved to the West late in 1944 few, if any, Ju 88Ps remained in service.

Specification
Junkers Ju 88P-3
Type: three-crew ground attack aircraft
Powerplant: 999-kW (1,340-hp) Junkers Jumo 211J-2 inverted V-12 piston engines
Performance: maximum speed 360 km/h (224 mph) at 1600 m (5,250 ft); climb to 2700 m (8,860 ft) in 10.6 minutes; service ceiling about 5500 m (18,045 ft); normal range 1580 km (982 miles)
Weights: empty about 11080 kg (24,427 lb); maximum take-off about 12670 kg (27,932 lb)
Dimensions: span 20.00 m (65 ft 7.5 in); length 14.85 m (48 ft 8.5 in); height 4.85 m (15 ft 11 in); wing area 54.56 m² (587.30 sq ft)
Armament: two 37-mm BK Flak 18 cannon in a fairing under the front fuselage, and up to six 7.92-mm (0.31-in) MG 17 machine-guns on trainable mountings in the cockpit

The Junkers Ju 88P-3 featured increased armour protection for the crew and it packed a devastating punch of twin 37-mm cannon in the ventral fairing. It was delivered to five Nachtschlachtgruppen.

Focke-Wulf Fw 190

A cantilever low-wing monoplane of stressed-skin construction, the prototype **Focke-Wulf Fw 190** was rolled out in May 1939 and the first flight took place on 1 June 1939. A second aircraft, the Fw 190 V2, flew in October 1939, armed with two 13-mm (0.51-in) MG 131 and two 7.92-mm (0.31-in) MG 17 machine-guns. Initial production version was the Fw 190A-1 which, flown by 6./JG 26, first clashed with RAF Supermarine Spitfires on 27 September 1941. Fighter-bomber versions included the **Fw 190A-5/U6** and the long-range **Fw 190A-5/U8**, and the **Fw 190A-5/U11** close-support aircraft carried a 30-mm MK 103 cannon beneath each wing. The **Fw 190A-5/U14** and **Fw 190A-5/U15** were both torpedo-bomber variants, able to carry an LT F5b and LT 950 torpedo respectively, and a 30-mm MK 108 cannon mounted in the outboard wing position was standard for the **Fw 190A-5/U16**.

In late 1943 several Fw 190A-7s were modified by the installation of Junkers Jumo 213A V-12 engines to serve as **Fw 190D-0** prototypes. Thus was derived the **Fw 190D-9** production version, known popularly as the 'longnose 190' or 'Dora 9'. A 300-litre (66-Imp gal) drop tank or a 250-kg (551-lb) bomb could be carried on each underwing rack. Variants included the **Fw 190D-12**, which was essentially a ground-attack aircraft with additional

The Fw 190 was modified to produce a series of highly successful fighter-bombers. This taxiing Fw 190A-5/U8 carries a crew member to give guidance to the pilot inside.

The Focke-Wulf Fw 190A-5/U8 was the long-range fighter bomber variant of the Fw 190A-5 introduced in early 1943. Engine overheating, which had been a problem with previous models, had been overcome by the introduction of a new mounting which positioned the engine further forward.

armour protection for the engine, and armed with two MG 151/20s in the wings and a single Mk 108 cannon firing through the spinner. However, the Fw 190D had been preceded into service by the **Fw 190F-1**, a specialized ground-attack version which was introduced in early 1943; generally similar to the Fw 190A-4, it differed by having additional armour protection for the cockpit and powerplant, the outboard 20-mm cannon deleted, and an ETC 501 bomb rack installed beneath the fuselage. The **Fw 190F-2** introduced a bubble canopy, and the **Fw 190F-3** could carry a 250-kg (551-lb) bomb beneath the fuselage and, in the **Fw 190F-3/R1** and **Fw 190F-3/R3** versions, four ETC 50 underwing bomb racks or two similarly-located 30-mm MK 103 cannon. The **Fw 190F-8/U2** and the **Fw 190F-8/U3** were fitted with the TSA bomb sight for anti-shipping strikes with, respectively, a 700-kg (1,543-lb) BT 700 or a 1400-kg (3,086-lb) BT 1400 weapon. Alphabetically the

last of the Fw 190s, and a specialized ground-attack version like the F-series which it preceded into service, the **Fw 190G-1** fighter-bomber was derived from the Fw 190A-5, but carried a 1800-kg (3,968-lb) bomb which necessitated the introduction of strengthened landing gear; wing-mounted armament was reduced to two MG 151/20 cannon, and the Junkers-designed wing racks accommodated two 300-litre (66-Imp gal) drop tanks.

Specification
Focke-Wulf Fw 190D-9
Type: single-seat fighter-bomber
Powerplant: one 1324-kW (1,776-hp) Junkers Jumo 213A-1 inverted-Vee piston engine
Performance: maximum speed 685 km/h (426 mph) at 6600 m (21,655 ft); climb to 6000 m (19,685 ft) in 7 minutes 6 seconds; service ceiling 12000 m (39,370 ft); range 835 km (519 miles)
Weights: empty 3490 kg (7,694 lb);

maximum take-off 4840 kg (10,670 lb)
Dimensions: span 10.50 m (34 ft 5.4 in); length 10.20 m (33 ft 5.6 in); height 3.35 m (11 ft 0 in); wing area 18.30 m² (196.99 sq ft)
Armament: two 13-mm (0.51-in) MG 131 machine-guns and two 20-mm MG

Two Fw 190F-8s set off on a bombing mission in the USSR in 1944 carrying 250-kg bombs.

151 cannon, plus one 500-kg (1,102-lb) SC500 bomb

GERMANY
Henschel Hs 123

Designed to an official requirement for a dive-bomber, issued in 1933, the **Henschel Hs 123** single-bay sesquiplane was of all-metal construction, with fabric covering used only for the rear portions of the wings and the control surfaces. Powered by a 485-kW (650-hp) BMW 132A-3 radial engine, the prototype flew in 1938 and quickly established its superiority over the rival Fieseler Fi 98. The third prototype was the first to be armed, carrying two fixed forward-firing 7.92-mm (0.31-in) MG 17 machine-guns in the fuselage top decking. The first three aircraft were flown to Rechlin for testing in August 1935, in the course of which activity two of them were destroyed when their wings came off in dives. A fourth prototype tested successfully the structural changes introduced to overcome this problem and initial production orders were placed for the **Hs 123A-1**, which retained the blistered cowling of the second and third prototypes, rather than the NACA cowling of the first. Power was provided by the BMW 132Dc radial engine and, in addition to the two fixed MG 17 machine-guns, a mounting for a 250-kg (551-lb) bomb or an external fuel tank was included beneath the fuselage, and four 50-kg (110-lb) bombs could be carried on underwing racks. The Hs 123 was built at Henschel's Schönefeld and Johannisthal factories in Berlin, but although the company built two prototypes of an improved **Hs 123B** version with the 716-kW (960-hp) BMW 132K engine, the second having two additional MG 17 machine-guns and an enclosed cockpit, the Luftwaffe expressed its satisfaction with the Junkers Ju 87 and production ended. The Hs 123A first entered service with 1./StG 162 in the autumn of 1936, although its career as a front-line dive-bomber was short-lived because the Junkers Ju 87A Stuka began to replace it in 1937. Five 123As were supplied to the Legion Condor in Spain in December 1936; the type also saw operational service as a close support aircraft in Poland during the closing months of 1939 and in the campaigns in France and Belgium during the spring of 1940. It was withdrawn finally in 1944.

Above: The Henschel Hs 123 dive bomber entered service in 1936, but was soon overshadowed by the Ju 87 Stuka, which joined the Luftwaffe the following year. Tested in Spain, it saw operational service in Poland and in the campaign in the West in 1940.

Above: An Hs 123A of 7. Staffel, Stukageschwader 165 'Immelmann' in 1937. Plans for an Hs 123B with increased armament and enclosed cockpit were cancelled after the Ju 87 was introduced.

Specification
Henschel Hs 123a-1
Type: dive-bomber/close-support aircraft
Powerplant: one 656-kW (880-hp) BMW 132Dc radial piston engine
Performance: maximum speed 340 km/h (211 mph) at 1200 m (3,935 ft); cruising speed 315 km/h (196 mph) at 2000 m (6,560 ft); service ceiling 9000 m (29,530 ft); range 855 km (531 miles)

Weights: empty 1500 kg (3,307 lb); maximum take-off 2215 kg (4,883 lb)
Dimensions: span, upper 10.50 m (34 ft 5.4 in) and lower 8.00 m (26 ft 3 in); length 8.33 m (27 ft 4 in); height 3.20 m (10 ft 6 in); wing area 24.85 m² (267.49 sq ft)
Armament: two fixed forward-firing 7.92-mm (0.31-in) MG 17 machine-guns, plus provision for 450 kg (992 lb) of bombs

Three Henschel Hs 123s pose for the camera in pre-war colours. Production ceased after only one year.

Henschel Hs 129

Henschel was one of four companies (the others being Focke-Wulf, Gotha and Hamburger Flugzeugbau) to which, in April 1937, the Reichsluftfahrtministerium issued a specification for a twin-engine ground-attack aircraft. It was required to carry at least two 20-mm MG FF cannon and to have extensive armour plating protection for crew and engines. The two designs for which development contracts were awarded on 1 October 1937 were the Focke-Wulf Fw 189C and Henschel Hs 129. The latter was a Friedrich Nicolaus design with a light alloy stressed-skin fuselage of triangular section. It contained a small cockpit with a restricted view, necessitating the removal of some instruments to the inboard sides of the engine cowlings. The windscreen was made of 75-mm (2.95-in) armoured glass and the nose section was manufactured from armour plating. Nose armament comprised two 20-mm MG FF cannon and two 7.92-mm (0.31-in) MG 17 machine-guns. Although the Henschel aircraft was considered to be underpowered and to have too small a cockpit, the company was awarded a contract for eight pre-production aircraft, two of which were converted at Schönefeld to accept Gnome-Rhône 14M 4/5 radial engines. It was with this powerplant that 10 Hs 129B-0 development aircraft were delivered from December 1941; armament comprised two 20-mm MG 151/20 cannon and two 7.92-mm (0.31-in) MG 17 machine-guns. The production Hs 192B-1 series became operational on the Eastern Front, where the type was to be used most widely, although it served also in North Africa, Italy, and in France after the D-Day landings.

By the end of 1942 the growing capability of Soviet tank battalions made it essential to develop a version of the Hs 129 with greater fire-power, leading to the Hs 129B-2 series which was introduced into service in the early part of 1943. They included the Hs 129B-2/R1 which carried two 20-mm MG 151/20 cannon and two 13-mm (0.51-in) machine-guns; and the Hs 129B-2/R3 with the two MG 13s deleted but equipped with a 37-mm BK 3.7 gun. Final production variant was the Hs 129B-3 of which approximately 25 were built and which carried an electro-pneumatically operated 75-mm BK gun.

Specification
Henschel Hs 129B-1/R2
Type: single-seat ground-attack aircraft
Powerplant: two 522-kW (700-hp) Gnome-Rhône 14M radial piston engines
Performance: maximum speed 407 km/h (253 mph) at 3830 m

The Henschel Hs 129 was designed to a 1937 specification for an armoured, twin-engined ground attack aircraft. Far superior to Allied equivalents, it showed how much importance the Germans attached to close air support.

(12,565 ft); service ceiling 9000 m (29,525 ft); range 560 km (348 miles)
Weights: empty 3810 kg (8,400 lb); maximum take-off 5110 kg (11,266 lb)
Dimensions: span 14.20 m (46 ft 7.1 in); length 9.75 m (31 ft 11.9 in); height

3.25 m (10 ft 8 in); wing area 29.00 m² (312.16 sq ft)
Armament: two 20-mm MG 151/20 cannon, two 7.92-mm (0.31-in) MG 17 machine-guns and one 30-mm Mk 101 cannon

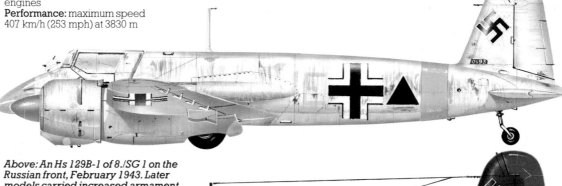

Above: An Hs 129B-1 of 8./SG 1 on the Russian front, February 1943. Later models carried increased armament to deal with heavily-armoured Soviet tanks.

Twenty-five Henschel Hs 129s mounted a 75-mm (2.95-in) gun capable of destroying even the most well-protected enemy AFVs.

Messerschmitt Bf 110

Like so many German aircraft which underwent adaptation for service in operational roles other than those for which they were originally intended, the **Messerschmitt Bf 110 Zerstörer** (destroyer, or heavy fighter) had proved unsuitable in the role of day bomber escort when confronted by modern interceptor single-seat fighters, but came to be widely used in the ground attack/fighter-bomber role. During the Battle of Britain Bf 110Cs and Ds of V(Z)/LG 1, II/ZG 26 'Horst Wesel', I/ZG 76, and 1. and 2./ErpGr 210 carried out numerous fighter-bomber attacks, the latter *Staffeln* being components of a *Gruppe* specifically created to introduce fighter-bombing/pathfinding tactics to the Luftwaffe under Hauptmann Walter Rubensdörffer (who was killed following a raid on Croydon on 15 August 1940).

The first dedicated fighter-bomber version of the Bf 110, after the Bf 110C-4B and D-2 sub-series adaptations, was the **Bf 110E** series, and this version equipped the two ground-attack units deployed in the East when Operation 'Barbarossa' was launched against the

USSR on 22 June 1941. These were Zerstörergeschwader 26 'Horst Wessel' and Schnellkampfgeschwader (fast bomber wing) 210, the latter having been created out of ErpGr 210, expanded to *Geschwader* proportions and equipped with Bf 110E-1 aircraft following the failure of the Me 210 to meet operational demands. These were soon joined by Bf 110E-equipped

Above: the Messerschmitt Bf 110G-2 was widely used in the ground attack role. This is an aircraft of II/ZG 1 over Italy in 1943.

Right: A close-up of the BK 37-mm (1.45-in) anti-tank gun fitted to some Bf 110G-2s. No heavier weapons were introduced, as the Bf 110s were diverted to the night-fighter role.

Staffeln of 11/ZG 1, and were heavily committed during the early fast-advancing offensives, attacking Soviet aircraft on their airfields as well as soft-skinned transport vehicles with deluges of fragmentation bombs.

The E-series was joined early in 1942 by sub-variants of the DB 605B-powered **Bf 110G-series**. The **Bf 110G-2** was widely used in the ground attack/anti-tank role, the R1, R2 and R3 *Rustsatz* field kit introducing 37-mm Flak 18 and 30-mm MK 108 cannon to the Bf 110's armament. Towards the end of 1942, however, these guns began to fail to penetrate Soviet tank armour, particularly in the case of the arrival of the T-34 tank, and much less reliance came to be placed on the *Zerstörergruppen* in the ground attack function. In any case almost all Bf 110 production was by then being distributed among night-fighter units for the defence of Germany against the growing offensive by RAF Bomber Command. Only in the closing weeks of the war, when the Allies were jamming the night-fighters into helplessness, were the surviving Bf 110s ordered to pursue night ground-attacks against the advancing Allied armies, but by then the RAF de Havilland Mosquitoes ruled the night skies over Germany.

A Messerschmitt Bf 110E of 8./ZG 26 based at Berca, North Africa, in September 1942. It is armed with the powerful MK 101 30-mm cannon, for use in the tank-busting role.

Specification
Messerschmitt Bf 110C-4/B
Type: two-seat ground attack fighter-bomber
Powerplant: two 895-kW (1,200-hp) Daimler-Benz DB 601N inverted V-12 piston engines
Performance: maximum speed 473 km/h (294 mph) at sea level; climb to 1650 m (5,415 ft) in 3.8 minutes; service ceiling 8300 m (27,230 ft); normal range about 790 m (490 miles)

Weights: empty 5200 kg (11,464 lb); maximum take-off 6910 kg (15,234 lb)
Dimensions: span 16.28 m (53 ft 4.75 in); length 12.10 m (39 ft 8.5 in); height 3.51 m (11 ft 6 in); wing area 38.37 m² (413.0 sq ft)
Armament: two 20-mm MG FF cannon and four 7.92-mm MG 17 machine-guns in the nose and twin 7.92-mm MG 81 guns in the rear cockpit, plus racks for two 250-kg (551-lb) bombs under the wing roots

Messerschmitt Me 210 and Me 410

The Germans pinned high hopes on the **Messerschmitt Me 210**, which first flew on 2 September 1939, as an ultimate replacement for the Bf 110. However, after the prototype (with twin fins and rudders, like the Bf 110) displayed chronic instability and later crashed during flutter trials (even after resort to a large single fin and rudder), development was slow. It was not until the end of 1940 that a few preproduction aircraft were delivered to Erprobungsgruppe 210, the unit that had been formed to introduce the aircraft into operational service before the Battle of Britain. The principal ground attack variants were the **Me 210A-2** with DB 601Aa engines and the **Me 410C-2** with DB 605B engines; these started to equip II/ZG 1 on the Eastern Front shortly after the German attack on the USSR opened but, following a number of fatal accidents when pilots lost control in shock stalls during ground attacks, the aircraft was quickly withdrawn from operational use. By the time a remedy had been found, in mid-1942 (by fitting wing slats), some 600 aircraft had been completed and the majority of these underwent modification.

In the event no more than 258 Me 210s ever reached the Luftwaffe and few of the modified aircraft equipped fully-operational ground-attack units. This was because, by 1943, interest centred on the **Me 410 Hornisse** (hornet), which was in effect a DB 603A-powered Me 210 with lengthened engine nacelles and all the stability-associated modifications found essential in the earlier aircraft. By 1943 the operational distinction between close-support and tactical bombing had become blurred in the Luftwaffe and, although the **Me 410A** equipped 5./KG 2 at Lechfeld, and 2.(F)/122 and III/ZG 1 in the central Mediterranean, only the operational sorties by the last-named unit could be described as 'close support' of the German army. Another bomber unit, I/KG 51 'Edelweiss', was equipped with Me 410As in June 1943 for night raids over the UK (and, on account of its excellent performance, proved a tough adversary even for the RAF's de Havilland Mosquito night-fighters); however, I/KG 51 switched to the tactical role at the time of the Normandy landings and became very active over the invasion area. Of the total of 1,160 Me 410s produced, not more than about 200 ever equipped ground-attack units, the remainder serving as conventional medium-level light bombers, reconnaissance aircraft and as bomber-destroyers in the air defence of the Reich.

Specification
Messerschmitt Me 410A-1
Type: two-seat fighter/fighter-bomber
Powerplant: two 1305-kW (1,750-hp) Daimler-Benz DB 603A inverted V-12 piston engines
Performance: maximum speed 638 km/h (396 mph) at 6700 m (21,980 ft) or 549 km/h (341 mph) at sea level; climb to 6700 m (21,980 ft) in 10.7 minutes; service ceiling 10000 m (32,810 ft); normal range 1480 km (920 miles)
Weights: empty 6050 kg (13,338 lb); maximum take-off 10530 kg (23,215 lb)
Dimensions: span 16.35 m (53 ft 7.75 in); length 12.41 m (40 ft 8.5 in);

height 4.28 m (14 ft 0.5 in); wing area 36.19 m² (389.6 sq ft)
Armament: two MG 151/20 20-mm cannon and two 7.92-mm (0.31-in) MG 17 machine-guns in the nose and single 13-mm (0.51-in) MG 131 heavy machine-gun in each of two remotely-controlled FDL 131 barbettes on the sides of the centre fuselage, plus a bombload of up to two 1000-kg (2,205-lb) bombs internally, or up to 10 50-kg (110-lb) bombs internally and on external racks

This Me 210A-1 of III/ZG 1 was based in Tunisia during the final stages of the battle for North Africa, during April 1943. The aircraft were used in the Zerstörer/ground attack role.

Seen during the aircraft's trials, one of the eight pre-production Me 210A-0s is seen in formation with an Me 210A-1, the nearer of the two. Seen in retrospect the craft was unsuccessful from the first.

Allied Ground Attack Aircraft

The early ground attack aircraft of the war were easy pickings for air and ground defences alike, but later designs overcame these deficiencies by strength and speed. Here we describe the main types employed by the Allies along with their development and deployment.

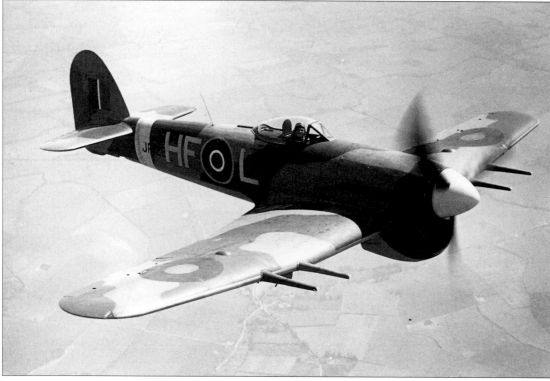

The Hawker Typhoon was a devastating asset to the advancing Allied forces. Its 76.2mm (3in) rockets made it a pioneer of today's strike aircraft, such an essential concept in modern warfare.

Continuing the 'trench fighter' concept of World War I, most fighter aircraft of the warring nations in World War II were adapted to carry weapons with which to support their ground forces, both above the battlefield itself or at the enemy's immediate rear. Although the ground support tactic had been pursued by the Luftwaffe as an inherent feature since its formation in 1934, and demonstrated by the Legion Condor during the Spanish Civil War, the RAF was slow to convert its fighters to ground attack aircraft, preferring to employ specialist light bombers in the task; and when its Fairey Battles were shown to possess neither the speed nor defensive ability to survive enemy fighters and Flak, the Hawker Hurricane eventually took over, using guns and bombs in the cross-Channel sweeps that started in 1941.

In the early stages of the war, however, the UK and her fast diminishing European Allies were thrown almost entirely on the defensive, and such campaigns were not conducive to the use of fighter aircraft in the ground attack role, but rather in disputing enemy air superiority. Only when the Allies were ready to take the initiative, at first in isolated operations, such as at Dieppe, and later in major campaigns in North Africa and ultimately throughout Europe, did the ground attack aircraft really come into its own. All manner of specialist support tasks were undertaken, including bombing, rocket-firing, smoke-laying, tactical reconnaissance, anti-tank attack, and so on. What had euphemistically been termed the 'army co-operation' by the RAF for 20 years was now deemed a major strike element of the ground offensive.

The Hawker Typhoon, a relative failure in its original role as an interceptor, was shown to be a devastating ground attack fighter, and can now be seen as the prototype of a new generation of strike aircraft, its rudimentary 76.2mm (3in) rockets presaging a new concept of artillery that would dominate the battleground of armour and entrenched or concrete defences. Indeed, the speed of land advances during the final year of the war in Europe and the Far East was directly proportional to the weight of tactical air support, whether by hordes of Soviet Shturmoviks in the Ukraine or by Hurricanes over Rangoon.

Bristol Beaufighter

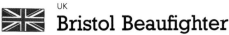

Originally designed and introduced into service as the RAF's first purpose-built twin-engine night-fighter in 1940, the **Bristol Beaufighter** was impressive from the outset as a rugged, powerful and heavily-armed aircraft. Its long-term success in this role was to some extent compromised by poor radar, however, and by the time this short-coming had been overcome the de Havilland Mosquito night-fighter, with much improved performance, had arrived. Therefore, although remaining in service as a night-fighter overseas, from the autumn of 1942 the Beaufighter started service in the strike role.

As early as March 1941 a Beaufighter had undergone trials as a torpedo bomber, and in September 1942 a **Beaufighter Mk VIC** was first armed with rocket projectiles. Two months later the first Beaufighter anti-shipping strike wing was formed at North Coates, Lincolnshire, comprising No. 143 Squadron with fighters, No. 236 Squadron with bombers (carrying two 113-kg/250-lb bombs under the wings) and No. 254 Squadron with torpedo Beaufighters. The rocket-firing Beaufighters (dubbed the Flakbeau as its task during strike sorties was to attack defending Flak ships and batteries) entered squadron service in March 1943.

The first Beaufighter strike aircraft were all Mk VIs, although specific aircraft were designated for bomb-, rocket- or torpedo-carrying. In June 1943 the first **Beaufighter TF.Mk X** aircraft entered service with No. 39 Squadron in the UK and No. 47 Squadron in North Africa; this version, with nose-mounted ASV radar, could carry combinations of all these weapons and was particularly effective against Axis shipping in the Mediterranean in 1943.

It was in South East Asia, however, that the Beaufighter earned lasting fame as a strike fighter: here it was called 'Whispering Death' by the Japanese following a series of surprise strikes on enemy depots in the Burmese jungle. Early operations involved strikes against Japanese coastal shipping sailing along the Burma coast, but in due course, in the face of persistent attacks by the Beaufighters and other Allied aircraft, this traffic dwindled, leaving the Beaufighter free to engage land targets with cannon, rockets and bombs, a task they continued to perform right up to the end of the war.

Specification
Bristol Beaufighter TF.Mk X
Type: two-seat strike fighter

The Bristol Beaufighter was built in Australia and used by the RAAF against the Japanese in the Far East theatre alongside the RAF machines. They came to be one of the most effective attack aircraft in the Far East and their metal structure was suited to the climate.

Powerplant: two 1,770-hp (1320-kW) Bristol Hercules XVII air-cooled radial piston engines
Performance: maximum speed 488 km/h (303 mph) at 395 m (1,300 ft); climb to 1525 m (5,000 ft) in 3 minutes 30 seconds; service ceiling 4570 m (15,000 ft); range 2365 km (1,470 miles)
Weights: empty 7076 kg (15,600 lb); maximum take-off 11431 kg (25,200 lb)
Dimensions: span 17.63 m (57 ft 10 in); length 12.70 m (41 ft 8 in); height 4.83 m (15 ft 10 in); wing area 46.73 m² (503 sq ft)

Armament: four 20-mm Hispano cannon in nose and one 7.7-mm (0.303-in) machine-gun in dorsal hatch, plus either one 45.7-cm (18-in) torpedo, or eight 27.2-kg (60-lb) rocket projectiles, or two 227-kg (500-lb) and two 113-kg (250-lb) bombs

A German train is blasted by an RAF Beaufighter over Norway in 1943. The Beaufighter became the prime strike aircraft early in the war before such types as the Mosquito came to the fore.

Fairey Battle

Envisaged as a replacement for the famous Hawker Hart and Hind light bombers of the early and mid-1930s, the **Fairey Battle** was selected as the cornerstone of the rapidly-expanding RAF and was intended to equip the large number of light bomber squadrons during the latter part of that decade. When the war started, however, the Battle was already obsolescent and was particularly vulnerable in the context of German *Blitzkrieg* tactics. Before the opening of the great German assault in the West on 10 May 1940, 10 Battle squadrons (Nos 12, 40, 88, 98, 103, 105, 142, 150, 218 and 226) had been sent to France to support the British Expeditionary Force, and were committed to action in the face of overwhelming enemy air superiority. Already unescorted daylight bombing operations had resulted in heavy losses (as early as 30 September 1939 four out of five No. 150 Squadron Battles had been shot down in a single raid), and, although escorts had been provided during the winter, little could be done to protect the slow bombers when the storm burst in the spring. Carrying no more than four 113-kg (250-lb) bombs at an operating speed of about 278 km/h (160 mph), the Battles were sent against key river bridges being used by enemy armoured columns advancing through Belgium. In an attack by No. 12 Squadron against the Maastricht bridges, carried out in the face of heavy Flak and fighter opposition, almost all the bombers were shot down, the RAF's first Victoria Crosses of World War II being awarded post-humously to Flying Officer D.E. Garland and Sergeant T. Gray. Four days later 71 Battles from Nos 12, 103, 105, 150 and 218 Squadrons were assembled for an attack on German pontoon bridges in the Sédan area; no fewer than 40 aircraft failed to return. The survivors of the squadrons were withdrawn from France, but several of them, based in England, continued to attack German-held ports on the Channel Coast until the threat of invasion receded. Thereafter the Battle was relegated to training and target-towing duties, many being shipped to Canada where they served with air gunnery schools.

The Battle was an anachronism and its shortcomings should have been anticipated long before the traumas of May 1940. It was, after all, powered by the same engine as the single-seat Hurricane, yet with a crew of three and 60 per cent heavier when fully-equipped, it was sent against single-seat fighters of twice its performance and expected to defend itself with only two rifle-calibre machine-guns.

Specification
Fairey Battle
Type: three-seat light bomber
Powerplant: one 1,030-hp (768-kW) Rolls-Royce Merlin II liquid-cooled V-12 piston engine
Performance: maximum speed

Fairey Battle of No. 106 Sqn as it appeared in 1938 whilst stationed at Abingdon. The Battle was extremely vulnerable to both air and ground fire due to its sluggish performance, and its combat career was cut short in 1940.

388 km/h (241 mph) at 3050 m (10,000 ft); initial climb rate 280 m (920 ft) per minute; service ceiling 7620 m (25,000 ft); range 1450 km (900 miles)
Weights: empty 3015 kg (6,647 lb); maximum take-off 4895 kg (10,792 lb)
Dimensions: span 16.46 m (54 ft 0 in); length 12.85 m (42 ft 1¾ in); height 4.72 m (15 ft 6 in); wing area 39.20 m² (422 sq ft)
Armament: one 7.7-mm (0.303-in) machine-gun in starboard wing and one 7.7-mm (0.303-in) machine-gun in rear cockpit, plus a bombload of four 113-kg (250-lb) bombs carried internally

Hawker Hurricane

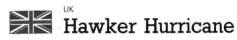

Rugged and combat-proven with flying colours in the Battle of Britain, the **Hawker Hurricane** was the natural choice of aircraft with which to carry the war back to the Germans when the RAF began to venture on to the offensive with cross-Channel attacks after the winter of 1940-1.

The **Hurricane Mk II**, with a more powerful Merlin XX engine, began appearing in the autumn of 1940, the **Hurricane Mk IIB** introducing a 12-gun wing, and the **Hurricane Mk IIC** an armament of four 20-mm cannon, the latter being regarded as a very heavy punch for a single-seater. Stemming from early tests to fit long-range tanks to enable Hurricanes to reinforce the Middle East with minimum refuelling stops, the Hurricane Mk IIB was soon equipped with wing racks to carry a pair of 113-kg (250-lb) or, later 227-kg (500-lb) bombs, and it was this version that went into action as the 'Hurribomber' with No. 607 Squadron on 30 October 1941 in 'Channel Stop' anti-shipping strikes, later being joined by Nos 175 and 402 Squadrons.

Hurricanes were particularly active in the ground-attack role in North Africa from mid-1941 and it was in this theatre that the next version, the **Hurricane Mk IID** tank-buster, made its first impact; armed with a pair of 40-mm

Vickers anti-tank guns under the wings, aircraft of No. 6 Squadron were used to excellent effect in support of the Free French forces in the Battle of Bir Hakeim in 1942. By 1943, outclassed as a pure interceptor, the Hurricane was the RAF's first single-seater to be fitted with 76.2-mm (3-in) rocket projectiles, using these weapons on operations for the first time against the Hansweert Canal lock gates in the Netherlands on 2 September 1943.

Ground-attack Hurricanes continued to operate on the European and Mediterranean fronts until 1944; in March the previous year there had appeared a new version, the **Hurricane Mk IV** in which a 'universal' wing was introduced, allowing application of bombs, anti-tank guns, rockets, smoke-laying equipment, drop tanks and other store combinations to be carried, and this ver-

sion continued in service in the Far East until the end of the Pacific war. Hurricane Mk IVs fought with outstanding success in the final advance in Burma, one of their great achievements being the destruction of 13 Japanese tanks by No. 20 Squadron in a single attack during the advance on Rangoon.

Specification
Hawker Hurricane Mk IIB
Type: single-seat fighter-bomber
Powerplant: one 1,280-hp (955-kW) Rolls-Royce Merlin XX liquid-cooled V-12 piston engine
Performance: maximum speed

The achievements of the Hurricane in the early desert war led to its being adapted to carry two 40-mm cannon under the wings for tank-busting, this version being known as the Mk IID. This example served with No. 6 Sqn in 1942.

549 km/h (341 mph) at 6555 m (21,500 ft); climb to 6095 m (20,000 ft) in 9 minutes; service ceiling 10850 m (35,600 ft); range 740 km (460 miles)
Weights: empty 2604 kg (5,740 lb); maximum take-off 3649 kg (8,044 lb)
Dimensions: span 12.19 m (40 ft 0 in); length 9.75 m (32 ft 0 in); height 4.00 m (13 ft 1½ in); wing area 23.92 m² (257.5 sq ft)
Armament: 12 7.7-mm (0.303-in) machine-guns in the wings, plus an external load of up to two 227 kg (500-lb) bombs, small bomb containers, smoke-laying equipment, six 27.2-kg (60-lb) rocket projectiles or two long-range fuel tanks

Hurricane Mk IICs saw service in the Far East as light ground attack aircraft. They carried an armament of four 20-mm cannon and could also carry small bombs. As here, long range fuel tanks helped the Hurricane reach the enemy.

Below: Ready for take-off from an improvised sand strip in the Western Desert, Hurricane Mk IIDs such as these proved of enormous help to the ground forces in suppressing Axis armour. They were cumbersome, and easy meat for German fighters, so top cover was necessary.

Supermarine Spitfire

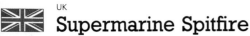

Immortalized as one of the greatest fighters of all time, the **Supermarine Spitfire** was also widely used as a fighter-bomber, although in this role it fell far short of the Hurricane, being tricky to fly with bombs attached, whether under fuselage or wings.

With the adoption of the **Spitfire Mk V** as Fighter Command's standard single-seat fighter in 1941, the **Spitfire Mk VC** became the fighter-bomber version, capable of carrying a single 227-kg (500-lb) bomb centrally under the fuselage or two 113 kg (250 lb) bombs under the wings. Most Spitfire Mk VCs featured clipped wings for better low-altitude performance, not being expected to engage enemy fighters above about 1525 m (5,000 ft).

Originally a hastily-introduced answer to the Focke-Wulf Fw 190A, the **Spitfire Mk IX** was intended to operate at medium and high altitudes but, like the Spitfire Mk V, was also built in clipped-wing form (**Spitfire L F.Mk IX**) and entered service with a total of 27 squadrons of the RAF in the UK, Middle East and Far East. With a 1,720-hp (1283-kW) Merlin 66, this version had a top speed without bombs of 650 km/h (404 mph) and could carry two 227-kg (500-lb) bombs under the wings; normal gun armament was two 20-mm and four 7.7-mm (0.303-in) guns, but the **Spitfire Mk IXE** sub-variant had the four rifle-calibre guns replaced by two 12.7-mm (0.5-in) guns.

Whereas the Spitfire Mk IX had been a hasty adaptation of the Spitfire Mk V to take the Merlin 61/66 series engine, the **Spitfire Mk VIII** was designed from the outset for this engine and included other refinements, including a retractable tailwheel; all were equipped for tropical service and therefore served mainly in the Mediterranean and Far East theatres, the majority of them equipping fighter-bomber squadrons.

The Griffon 65-powered **Spitfire Mk XIV** served as both a fighter and a fighter-bomber, entering service in mid-1944 in the UK. Among their outstanding achievements in the latter role was the heaviest single RAF fighter-bomber attack of the war when, on 24 December that year, 33 Spitfire Mk XIVs of Nos 229, 453 and 602 Squadrons, each carrying a 227-kg (500-lb) and two 113-kg (250-lb) bombs, attacked a V-2 rocket-launching site in the Netherlands.

Final fighter-bomber version of the Spitfire to see service during the war was the Packard Merlin 266-powered **Spitfire Mk XVI**, whose sub-variants were the same as for the Spitfire Mk IX, and could be fitted with four under-wing rails for 27.2-kg (60-lb) rocket projectiles in addition to an under-fuselage 227-kg (500-lb) bomb. At the end of the war in Europe fighter-bomber Spitfire Mk XVIs equipped 11 squadrons of the 2nd Tactical Air Force.

Specification
Supermarine Spitfire Mk XVI
Type: single-seat fighter-bomber
Powerplant: one 1,720-hp (1283-kW) Packard Rolls-Royce Merlin 266

No. 74 Sqn flew the Spitfire LF.Mk XVIE for only a couple of months at the end of the war on fighter-bomber sweeps through Germany. The Mk XVI had a Packard-built Merlin and could carry 113-kg (250-lb) bombs or rocket projectiles.

liquid-cooled V-12 piston engine
Performance: maximum speed 652 km/h (405 mph) at 6705 m (22,000 ft); climb to 6095 m (20,000 ft) in 6 minutes 42 seconds; service ceiling 12650 m (41,500 ft); range without external tanks 690 km (430 miles)
Weights: empty 2547 kg (5,615 lb); maximum take-off 4311 kg (9,505 lb)
Dimensions: span, clipped 9.96 m (32 ft 8 in); length 9.55 m (31 ft 4 in); height 3.85 m (12 ft 7¾ in); wing area 21.46 m² (231 sq ft)
Armament: two 20-mm and four 7.7-

Although usually used for providing top cover for the Hurricanes in Italy, these Spitfire Mk Vs of the SAAF carry 113-kg (250-lb) bombs on the centreline rack. After releasing the bombs, the aircraft could strafe targets at will.

mm (0.303-in) or two 12.7-mm (0.5-in) guns, plus one 227-kg (500-lb) and two 113-kg (250-lb) bombs, or as an alternative to the wing bombs four 27.2-kg (60-lb) rocket projectiles

---

Hawker Typhoon

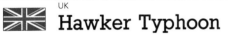

One of the last Typhoons to be built with the car-type door, this aircraft from No. 198 Sqn is seen before the application of invasion stripes in early 1944. The squadron at the time was learning to use the new rocket projectiles.

Compromised from the outset by a host of design and development difficulties, and no less by a disastrously accelerated engine development that left unsolved numerous weaknesses when it entered service, the **Hawker Typhoon** was intended to replace the Hurricane as an interceptor. However, after the anti-climactic debacle over Dieppe and its singularly disappointing performance as an interceptor, the Typhoon came to be recognized as potentially an effective ground-attack fighter and, following trials at Boscombe Down in 1942, it resumed cross-Channel operations carrying a pair of 113-kg (250-lb) bombs to supplement its four 20-mm Hispano cannon armament. Flying alongside the aged 'Hurribombers', **Typhoon Mk IB** fighter-bombers of Nos 175, 181 and 245 Squadrons continued the 'Channel Stop' operations throughout 1943, while others ventured over enemy-occupied France and the Low Countries, attacking airfields, road and rail traffic and other key targets.

Early operations had shown the **Typhoon Mk IA**, with its wing armament of 12 7.7-mm (0.303-in) Browning machine-guns, to be relatively ineffective in the ground-attack role, and this version was discontinued. Another weakness was found to lie in the joint of the tail unit to the rear fuselage, numerous early accidents being ascribed to the entire tail unit becoming detached

in flight, for which a crude remedy was effected by simply riveting numerous plates around the joint. An early operational problem lay in the Typhoon's superficial resemblance to the Focke-Wulf Fw 190, resulting in a number of aircraft being shot down by 'friendly' guns, until prominent black and white recognition stripes were painted under the Typhoon's inner wing sections.

For all these unfortunate tribulations the chunky aeroplane emerged in 1944 as one of the most powerful weapons in the Allies' armoury when the Normandy invasion was launched in June that year. With a bombload progressively increased to 907 kg (2,000 lb), the Typhoon was also used with devastating effect as a rocket-firing fighter, eliminating vital enemy coastal radar stations before the landings themselves and destroying German armoured concentrations as the Allies broke out of the beach-head. Always something of a handful to fly, the Typhoon nevertheless provided an overwhelming form of powerful, accurate and mobile artillery for the Allies as they surged through northern Europe in the last nine months of the war.

Specification
Hawker Typhoon Mk IB
Type: single-seat fighter-bomber
Powerplant: one 2,180-hp (1626-kW) Napier Sabre II liquid-cooled H-24 piston engine
Performance: maximum speed 652 km/h (405 mph) at 5485 m (18,000 ft); climb to 4570 m (15,000 ft) in 6 minutes 12 seconds; service ceiling 10365 m (34,000 ft); range with bombs

Close-up of the business end of a Typhoon Mk IB, showing the four Hispano cannon.

820 km (510 miles)
Weights: empty 3993 kg (8,800 lb); maximum take-off 6341 kg (13,980 lb)
Dimensions: span 12.67 m (41 ft 7 in); length 9.73 m (31 ft 11 in); height 4.66 m (15 ft 3½ in); wing area 25.92 m² (279 sq ft)
Armament: four wing-mounted 20-mm cannon, plus either two 454-kg (1,000-lb) bombs or eight 27.2-kg (60-lb) rocket projectiles

Bell P-39 Airacobra

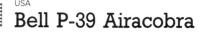

The radical **Bell P-39 Airacobra**, with midships engine and tricycle landing gear, enjoyed a disappointing career as a fighter with the American and British air forces as a result mainly of the abandonment of the turbosupercharger which had promised to bestow excellent performance at high altitude; this equipment was in any case banned from export to the UK, with the result that the Airacobra did not match up to RAF requirements for an interceptor. The upshot of this was a gradual change to the ground-attack role in American service, and disposal of very large numbers to the Soviet Union from 1942 onwards, 4,773 of the 9,558 built being supplied to that nation, mainly through Iran, but also over the Trans-Siberian railway. More than 200 Bell Airacobras were also shipped to the USSR in the North Cape convoys.

P-39s entered service with the V-VS early in 1943, the principal variant being the **P-39N** which featured a hub-firing 37-mm cannon, two nose-mounted 12.7-mm (0.5-in) and four wing-mounted 7.62-mm (0.3-in) machine-guns; a single 227-kg (500-lb) bomb could be carried under the fuselage.

In Soviet service the P-39 was used initially as a pure fighter, but gradually as the tide of fortunes changed most Soviet *polks* (fighter regiments) undertook a dual role in response to the demands of the massive ground battles that raged on the Eastern Front. Often the P-39s would be called on to carry out specific bombing tasks, after which they would revert to fighters to provide cover while subsequent bombing attacks went in. The majority of P-39 *polks* were deployed on the central and southern fronts, and numerous Soviet pilots achieved considerable success in the aircraft; Captain Grigori Rechkalov scored 44 of his 58 air victories in a P-39 with the 9th Guards Fighter Division, and Aleksandr Pokryshkin, who commanded a P-39 *eskadril* in the 216th Guards Fighter Division's 16th Polk and later became the Soviet Union's second highest scoring pilot, shot down 48 of his 59 victims while flying P-39s, many of these falling in the course of dual-role fighter/ bombing missions. For all the P-39's

The Bell P-39L Airacobra was a failure as an air combat fighter (apart from notable exceptions such as the aircraft shown here, of the Russian, Major Pokryshkin) and was used mainly in the ground attack role.

obvious success on the Eastern Front, wastage through accidents was by all accounts very high, relatively inexperienced pilots finding the aircraft tricky to handle and, with the big Allison engine located behind the cockpit, forced landings and other landing mishaps were frequently fatal. A much smaller number of the later but related **Bell P-63 Kingcobra** was also supplied to the Soviet Union, this aircraft being equipped to carry three 227-kg (500-lb) bombs.

Specification
Bell P-39N Airacobra
Type: single-seat fighter-bomber
Powerplant: one 1,200-hp (895-kW) Allison V-1710-85 liquid-cooled V-12 piston engine

Performance: maximum speed 642 km/h (399 mph) at 3355 m (11,000 ft); climb to 4570 m (15,000 ft) in 5 minutes 20 seconds; service ceiling 11735 m (38,500 ft); range 1205 km (750 miles)
Weights: empty 2562 kg (5,645 lb); maximum take-off 3720 kg (8,200 lb)
Dimensions: span 10.36 m (34 ft 0 in); length 9.19 m (30 ft 2 in); height 3.78 m (12 ft 5 in); wing area 19.79 m² (213 sq ft)
Armament: one hub-firing 37-mm cannon, two nose-mounted 12.7-mm (0.5-in) and four wing-mounted 7.62-mm (0.3-in) machine-guns, plus a single 227-kg (500-lb) bomb carried under the fuselage

---

Curtiss P-40

The Kittyhawk Mk IV was the RAF equivalent of the P-40N Warhawk, and is shown here in the markings of No. 112 Sqn in 1944.

Although firmly rooted among the first generation of monoplane fighters of the late 1930s, the famous **Curtiss P-40** family underwent progressive modernization, and as each version became outmoded by later fighters, it came to be employed as a passable fighter-bomber. Adopted as the USAAC's standard fighter and subject of heavy British purchasing in 1940, the early **P-40B**, **P-40C** and **Tomahawk** entered service in 1941, the first RAF squadron to receive the latter being No. 112 in the Middle East. The Tomahawk's performance as an interceptor was disappointing, being generally inferior to the Hurricane Mk II, and it was therefore employed mainly for ground attack, although the armament of six rifle-calibre machine-guns was far from adequate. Tomahawks (and the equivalent P-40B/Cs) were shipped to the USSR and Turkey, and were flown by American pilots in the Pacific and South East Asia. The **P-40D** represented something of a transformation, with the Allison engine installed in a shortened nose, fuselage guns removed and the radiator moved forward. Known as the **Warhawk** in American service (as were all P-40s) and **Kittyhawk** in RAF service, this and subsequent similar versions were built in very large numbers up to 1944, from mid-1942 being equipped as fighter-bombers in the USAAF, RAF and other Allied air forces to carry up to three 227-kg (500-lb) bombs under fuselage and wings; later versions could carry a 454-kg (1,000-lb) bomb under the fuselage. They were particularly active in the close-support role in North Africa after the victory at Alamein and the 'Torch' landings, and in the campaigns in Sicily, Italy and the Balkans. The Packard built Merlin was used in the American **P-40F** and **P-40L** versions, but the **P-40N** (of which 5,219 were produced) reverted to the Allison engine and this served from 1943 until the end of the war. Despite its widespread use as a fighter-bomber the P-40 was not generally appreciated as a result of its control sluggishness and lateral trim changes as speed built up in a diving attack; the latter behaviour, which gave rise to excessive yawing at the moment of bomb release, made accurate bombing extremely difficult, and P-40s were more usually employed for attacks on larger rather than smaller targets.

Specification
Curtiss P-40N Warhawk
Type: single-seat fighter-bomber
Powerplant: one 1,360-hp (1015-kW) Allison V-1710-81 liquid-cooled V-12 piston engine
Performance: maximum speed 609 km/h (378 mph) at 3200 m (10,500 ft); climb to 4570 m (15,000 ft) in 6 minutes 49 seconds; service ceiling 11580 m (38,000 ft); range on internal fuel 547 km (340 miles)
Weights: empty 2722 kg (6,000 lb); maximum take-off 5171 kg (11,400 lb)
Dimensions: span 11.38 m (37 ft 4 in);

length 10.16 m (33 ft 4 in); height 3.76 m (12 ft 4 in); wing area 21.92 m² (236 sq ft)

Armament: six wing-mounted 12.7-mm (0.5-in) machine-guns, plus one 454-kg (1,000-lb) bomb under the fuselage and two 227-kg (500-lb) bombs under the wings

Bearing the famous shark's teeth markings of No. 112 Sqn, these Tomahawks are ready for take-off at Sidi Haneish in the autumn of 1941. The difference in nose shape to the later Kittyhawk is obvious, with the chin radiator being much smaller.

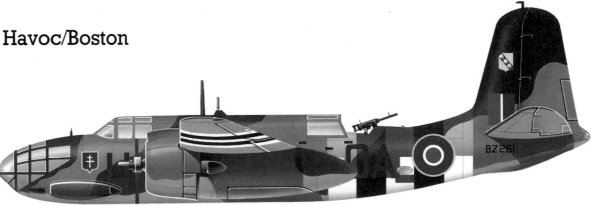

Douglas A-20 Havoc/Boston

Perpetuating a misconception of the nature of modern warfare during the late 1930s, the American 'attack' bomber was envisaged as a means of saturating fixed enemy defences in the immediate area of the ground battle, and took little account of the swift movement of armies so capably demonstrated during the German conquests of 1939-41. Moreover the **Douglas A-20**, known as the **Havoc** and **Boston** by American and British air forces respectively, was so unwieldy that it could only be employed over a battleground in the face of enemy air opposition provided it was furnished with strong fighter escort.

Nevertheless production momentum already gained by British and French orders at the beginning of the war resulted in the A-20 being available in quickly growing numbers when the United States entered the conflict. And, despite fairly heavy losses early on, the type eventually came to play an important tactical role, being used first as a 'light-medium' bomber for attacks on fixed battlefield targets, such as forward enemy landing grounds, road, rail and river bridges and vehicle parks, etc.

The RAF was the first to use the aircraft, as the Boston (after a night-fighter version, confusingly known as the Havoc, had been largely superseded in 1941) early in 1942; indeed the first combat use of the aircraft by the Americans in Europe involved RAF Bostons being flown from the UK by an American squadron in July that year.

From late in 1942 both the British and American air forces flew the Boston and A-20 on close-support duties, particularly on 'softening up' raids before assaults by ground forces. RAF Bostons in particular were much in evidence during the numerous combined operations launched across the Channel in 1942-4, and were also used to lay smoke screens to cover amphibious landings. The **A-20G** introduced a 'solid' nose and dispensed with the bomb aimer, a battery of cannon or machine-guns being substituted for true ground-attack work. In the Pacific theatre A-20s were widely used for low-level attack, using fragmentation bombs to good effect over Japanese shipping and airfields. RAF **Boston Mk IV** and **Boston Mk V** aircraft served with the 2nd Tactical Air Force and the Desert Air Force in Italy in the close-support role right up to the end of the war against Germany.

Specification
Douglas A-20G Havoc

Douglas Boston Mk IIIA of No. 342 Sqn 'Lorraine', RAF, based at Hartford Bridge (today called Blackbushe). Aircraft from this squadron were the first French-flown aircraft to arrive back in France after D-Day.

Type: three-seat attack aircraft
Powerplant: two 1,600-hp (1194-kW) Wright Cyclone R-2600-23 air-cooled radial piston engines
Performance: maximum speed 546 km/h (339 mph) at 3780 m (12,400 ft); climb to 3050 m (10,000 ft) in 7 minutes 6 seconds; service ceiling 7650 m (25,100 ft); range 1755 km (1,090 miles)
Weights: empty 7250 kg (15,984 lb); maximum take-off 12338 kg (27,200 lb)
Dimensions: span 18.69 m (61 ft 4 in); length 14.63 m (48 ft 0 in); height 5.36 m (17 ft 7 in); wing area 43.11 m² (464 sq ft)

One of the tasks for the airborne forces during the D-Day invasion was smoke-laying. These two Boston Mk IIIs are equipped with four pipes under the fuselage for providing smoke over the beach-head.

Armament: up to eight 12.7-mm (0.5-in) machine-guns in nose and two in rear dorsal position (later aircraft had electrically-operated turret), plus up to 1814 kg (4,000 lb) of bombs, comprising four 227-kg (500-lb) bombs internally and two 454-kg (1,000 lb) bombs on wing racks

---

Douglas A-26 Invader

The demarcation between the true ground-support aircraft and the so-called light bomber was conveniently defined by the American 'attack' designation; nevertheless the **Douglas A-26 Invader** leaned much closer to the latter category in that its battlefield operations were more of the set-piece strike and less of the ad hoc attack.

Although three parallel versions were originally conceived (a night-fighter, a level bomber and an attack aircraft) the last-named version was selected for initial production and eventually entered combat service as the **A-26B** with the US 9th Air Force in Europe in November 1944. This version carried six heavy machine-guns in the nose, sometimes supplemented by eight in underwing packs, and by locking the dorsal turret guns to fire forward, making a total of 16 forward-firing guns! The cabin and fuel tanks were heavily armoured to withstand ground small-arms fire, and a total of 1814 kg (4,000 lb) of bombs was carried internally.

Though obviously a very powerful weapon to unleash over the battlefield (and even more so when underwing 127-mm/5-in rocket projectiles were added to its arsenal) the Invader enjoyed only partial success as a truly tactical support aircraft in Europe, being found generally unsuitable for operations from forward airfields unless such facilities were captured wholly intact. It was for this reason, and the length of time taken to reach the front line from bases in the distant rear, that A-26 attacks were largely confined to fixed targets such as airfields and bridges, and these were more fre-

This formation of A-26s of the 386th Bomb Group en route to Germany in April 1945 contains aircraft with both glazed nose for bomb-aimer and solid nose packed with machine-guns. They also carry machine-gun packs under the wings.

quently and effectively struck by the larger resources of medium bombers available.

For the 'island-hopping' nature of the Pacific war against Japan, the USAAF employed the **A-26C** which retained a bombardier in place of the nose gun battery to facilitate bombing from medium altitude, and as such the Invader was operated almost exclusively as a conventional medium bomber.

Douglas A-26B Invader of the 552nd Bomb Squadron, 386th Bomb Group, 9th Air Force based at Beaumont-sur-Oise in April 1945. The Invader also saw valuable service over the hotly contested islands of Japan during the last few months of the war.

Specification
Douglas A-26B Invader
Type: three-seat tactical support aircraft
Powerplant: two 2,000-hp (1492-kW) Pratt & Whitney R-2800-27 air-cooled radial piston engines

Performance: maximum speed 572 km/h (355 mph) at 3660 m (12,000 ft); climb to 3050 m (10,000 ft) in 8 minutes 6 seconds; service ceiling 6735 m (22,100 ft); range 2255 km (1,400 miles)
Weights: empty 10147 kg (22,370 lb);

maximum take-off 15876 kg (35,000 lb)
Dimensions: span 21.34 m (70 ft 0 in); length 15.24 m (50 ft 0 in); height 5.64 m (18 ft 6 in); wing area 50.17 m² (540 sq ft)
Armament: six fixed forward-firing 12.7-mm (0.5-in) machine-guns in nose

and two in each of dorsal and ventral turrets, plus an internal bombload of 1814 kg (4,000 lb) and an external load of up to 907 kg (2,000 lb) of bombs, or up to 16 127-mm (5-in) rocket projectiles

---

USA
Lockheed P-38 Lightning

The **Lockheed P-38 Lightning** is, like its famous partners (the Republic P-47 and North American P-51), best remembered as a pure fighter both in the European and Pacific theatres. Yet from mid 1942 the P-38F destined for the USAAC possessed external racks for up to 907 kg (2,000 lb) of bombs. (Although the Lightning was originally ordered for the RAF, the ban on export of turbosuperchargers so compromised the aircraft's performance that it did not enter British service.)

USAAF fighter groups began flying **P-38F** aircraft in Europe and North Africa during 1942, but the aircraft proved disappointing in combat against German fighters, and it was in the last stages of the Tunisian campaign that the aircraft began to demonstrate its capabilities as a ground-support fighter, bombing and machine-gunning the Axis forces in their final withdrawal to Tunis and Bizerta.

The introduction of the much improved **P-38J** (identifiable by its 'chin' radiators) resulted in a new lease of life as an escort fighter, particularly during the 1943 daylight Boeing B-17 and Consolidated B-24 raids over Europe, but in 1944, as deliveries of P-47s and P-51s were stepped up to the UK and the Mediterranean, the P-38J and the more powerful **P-38L** version came to be used more and more in the ground-attack role, both versions being capable of lifting a pair of 726-kg (1,600-lb) bombs. The P-38L was also modified to carry 10 69.8-mm (2.75-in) rockets on 'Christmas-tree' tiers under the wings; it was also the first Allied fighter-bomber to drop napalm bombs on the Germans in the latter half of 1944.

The ability of the P-51D to escort the daylight heavy bombers all the way to Berlin rendered use of the P-38 as a long-range fighter superfluous, and the type was employed almost exclusively as a support fighter-bomber during the last six months of the war, and a new tactic emerged involving the use of a two-seater P-38 'lead ship' complete with bombardier; the aircraft would lead a formation of single-

Due to its size and performance, the P-38 Lightning proved an excellent ground attack aircraft, able to carry rockets and bombs large distances into enemy territory. This is a P-38L serving with the 97th FS, 82nd FG, USAAF.

A theatre in which the P-38 excelled was the Mediterranean. This P-38L of the 94th Fighter Group is having a bomb winched on to its wing rack somewhere in Italy. During the height of the campaign, operations continued through the night.

seaters and, using its very accurate Norden bomb sight, would control the bombing of the entire formation. A refinement of this, involving bombing-through-overcast (BTO) radar in the lead ship, was intended to enable close support to be given in conditions of bad weather over the ground battle, but in one of the only occasions it was employed with any numbers of P-38s (during the Battle of the Ardennes) heavy casualties were caused when most of the bombs dropped fell among American armoured vehicles.

Specification
Lockheed P-38L Lightning
Type: single-seat fighter-bomber
Powerplant: two 1,475-hp (1100-kW) Allison V-1710-111/113 liquid-cooled inline piston engines
Performance: maximum speed 667 km/h (414 mph) at 7620 m (25,000 ft); climb to 6095 m (20,000 ft) in

7 minutes; service ceiling 13410 m (44,000 ft); range on internal fuel 730 km (454 miles)
Weights: empty 5806 kg (12,800 lb); maximum take-off 9798 kg (21,600 lb)
Dimensions: span 15.85 m (52 ft 0 in); length 11.53 m (37 ft 10 in); height 3.00 m (9 ft 10 in); wing area 30.42 m²

(327.5 sq ft)
Armament: one 20-mm and four 12.7-mm (0.5-in) guns in the nose, plus a bombload of two 726-kg (1,600-lb) bombs, or 10 69.8-mm (2.75-in) rocket projectiles together with two 1173-litre (258-gal) drop tanks if required

The Lightning had exceptional performance for a twin-engined aircraft and the secret of this lay in the small frontal area made possible by the twin boom layout. The position of the racks for either bombs or, as here, fuel tanks is clearly visible.

Republic P-47 Thunderbolt

The big **Republic P-47 Thunderbolt** served for more than a year before being seriously considered for service as a ground-support aircraft; indeed, after considerable misgivings as to whether it would be able to match the nimble German interceptors in dog-fighting, it came to represent a vital and effective long-range escort for the American day bombers over Europe during 1943. As mass production got under way (a total of 15,579 being ultimately produced) the **P-47D-25** introduced underwing bomb racks capable of mounting a pair of 454-kg (1,000-lb) bombs, in addition to a 568-litre 125-gal drop tank under the fuselage. In due course the **P-47D-30** was capable of carrying up to 1134 kg (2,500 lb) of external ordnance, including up to 10 127-mm (5-in) rocket projectiles.

P-47D fighter-bombers first entered service with the 348th Fighter Group in Australia, whence they were flown against Japanese targets in New Guinea. They were then issued to fighter and fighter-bomber groups of the US 9th and 15th Air Forces in the UK and the Mediterranean theatre. From mid-1944, as the superlative North American P-51D assumed the lion's share of air combat and escort duties over Europe, the P-47D was assigned more and more of the close-support work over Italy and France, proving immensely strong in the punishing ground-attack role.

A total of 826 Thunderbolts was delivered to the RAF, of which the majority were equivalent to the P-47D-25 and designated **Thunderbolt Mk II**. They entered service with the RAF in India and Burma in the summer of 1944, eventually serving with Nos 5, 30, 34, 42, 60, 79, 81, 113, 123, 131, 134, 135, 146, 258, 261 and 615 Squadrons. Flying over the Burma jungle the 'cab rank' patrols that were being used to such good effect by Hawker Typhoons in Europe, these excellent fighter-bombers gave constant support to the 14th Army during its final victorious advance towards Rangoon in the last year of the war. Time and again the Thunderbolts were called down by the mobile control officers to eliminate some Japanese strongpoint with guns and bombs. The P-47 and the Typhoon were the best American and British fighter-bombers of the year.

P-47D (razorback) of the 19th Fighter Squadron, 218th Fighter Group, based on Saipan island in the Marianas during July 1944. The 'Jug' was a hardy fighter, and the fierce war fought in the Far East suited its strength and speed.

As the P-51D took over in the long-range escort role, more P-47s were released to attack duties. This example served with the 352nd Fighter Squadron, 353rd Fighter Group at Gaydon at the time of the Normandy invasion, and features the 'bubble' cockpit.

Specification
Republic P-47D-25 Thunderbolt
Type: single-seat fighter-bomber
Powerplant: one 2,000-hp (1492-kW) Pratt & Whitney R-2800-59 air-cooled radial piston engine
Performance: maximum speed 689 km/h (428 mph) at 9145 m (30,000 ft); climb to 6095 m (20,000 ft) in 9 minutes; service ceiling 12800 m (42,000 ft); range on internal fuel 765 km (475 miles)
Weights: empty 4536 kg (10,000 lb); maximum take-off 8808 kg (19,400 lb)
Dimensions: span 12.42 m (40 ft 9 in); length 11.00 m (36 ft 1 in); height 4.32 m (14 ft 2 in); wing area 27.87 m²

(300 sq ft)
Armament: eight fixed forward-firing 12.7-mm (0.5-in) machine-guns in

wings, plus two 454-kg (1,000-lb) bombs or six 69.8-mm (2.75-in) rocket projectiles under the wings

This 12th Air Force P-47 in Italy demonstrates the three main weapons of the wartime fighter-bomber, namely machine-guns, bombs and rockets. Such aircraft were the workhorses of the Allied drive up the Italian mainland.

Vultee Vengeance

Powerfully influenced by the successes achieved by the German Junkers Ju 87 dive-bomber in the early months of the war, the British in 1940 ordered several hundred **Vultee V-72** aircraft from the USA, a type that had not then been selected for the US Army Air Corps, and production lines were established at Vultee's Nashville plant and the Northrop plant at Hawthorne, California. Before the first British aircraft was delivered in 1942, however, the United States had entered the war, and further aircraft were ordered for the USAAF. The American aircraft (designated the **A-31** and **A-35**, but generally referred to as the V-72) did not match up to expectations and almost all were relegated to target-towing and other training duties from the outset.

The Vengeance saw considerably more service in the RAF, a total of 1,205 being delivered, the **Vengeance Mk I**, **Vengeance Mk II** and **Vengeance Mk III** corresponding to the American A-31, and the **Vengeance Mk IV** to the A-35. Tests with the first Vengeance Mk Is led to numerous alterations, and it was not until late 1942 that deliveries started in earnest. By that time the tactical weakness of the dive-bomber had been recognized, and it was decided not to employ the Vengeance in Europe where it would be easy prey for the excellent German fighters. Instead the type was sent to equip RAF squadrons in India and Burma where, operating under top cover provided by Hawker Hurricanes (and later by Supermarine Spitfires and Republic Thunderbolts), it would represent the

No. 45 Sqn flew the Vengeance for 15 months in the Far East, where it achieved limited success. This example is a Vengeance Mk II shown whilst based in India in 1943. The Vengeance was based on the German idea of the 'Stuka', and similarly needed fighter cover to operate with any success.

best weapon against difficult jungle targets.

The Vengeance was first in action in July 1943 in Burma, having started to replace the veteran Bristol Blenheim with the RAF; it eventually equipped four squadrons (Nos 45, 82, 84 and 110) as well as several in the Indian Air Force. As expected, however, the Vengeance proved extremely vulnerable in the presence of Japaneose fighters and so seldom ventured abroad without strong fighter escort.

The type did nevertheless prove very effective during the Arakan campaign, and in a number of successful raids destroyed a large number of Japanese vehicles and quantities of stores being assembled in the jungle.

By the last year of the war conventional fighter-bomber tactics were seen as the best means of ground support, and demands for the Vengeance diminished rapidly. By mid-1945 most had been relegated to target-towing duties.

Specification
Vultee Vengeance Mk I
Type: two-seat dive-bomber
Powerplant: one 1,700-hp (1268-kW) Wright R-2600-A5B-5 air-cooled radial piston engine
Performance: maximum speed 449 km/h (279 mph) at 4115 m (13,500 ft); climb to 4570 m (15,000 ft) in 11 minutes 18 seconds; service ceiling 6795 m (22,300 ft); range 1930 km (1200 miles)
Weights: empty 4672 kg (10,300 lb);

maximum take-off 7440 kg (16,400 lb)
Dimensions: span 14.63 m (48 ft 0 in); length 12.12 m (39 ft 9 in); height 3.91 m (12 ft 10 in); wing area 30.84 m² (332 sq ft)
Armament: four wing-mounted 7.62-mm (0.3-in) machine-guns and two 7.62-mm (0.3-in) machine-guns in the rear cockpit, plus a bombload of four 227-kg (500-lb) bombs carried internally

---

Ilyushin Il-2

The Soviet **Ilyushin Il-2** succeeded where the British Fairey Battle had failed. Immense strength and armoured protection, powerful armament and committal to combat under heavy fighter protection all combined to render the *bronirovannyi shturmovik* (armoured assault aircraft) a decisive weapon in the Soviet armoury during the final two years of the war in Europe.

Christened the 'flying tank' by the Soviet infrantrymen, and the *schwarzer Tod* (Black Death) by the men of the German army, the Il-2 originated as a two-seater but was modified to a single-seater and in this form was entering service with the V-VS at the time of Germany's invasion of the USSR on 22 June 1941. However, in those early months of almost total German air supremacy the early Il-2s emerged amidst a welter of criticism, being found to lack punch against the enemy's armoured fighting vehicles (their principal targets) and hopelessly vulnerable in the presence of enemy fighters.

The aircraft accordingly underwent rapid redesign, the great armoured 'bath' that constituted the pilot's cockpit being extended to accommodate a rear gunner with heavy-calibre machine-gun. The 1,680-hp (1253-kW) AM-38 engine was replaced by a 1,750-hp (1306-kW) AM-38F, and the two wing-mounted 20-mm ShVAK cannon gave place to high muzzle velocity 23-mm VYa guns.

The new two-seater **Il-2m3** entered service from August 1942, and thereafter gun, bomb and rocket armament underwent progressive increase as the production accelerated. By the winter of 1943-4 vast numbers of Il-2m3s were in service (some sources put the number as high as 12,000), and remained in constant use up to and beyond the end of the war in Europe. Their use in combat was almost invariably confined to attacks from extremely low level, often no more than 6 m (20 ft), the favourite tactic being to circle to the rear of enemy forces in single line-ahead stream to attack the thinly-armoured rear of German tanks. Many *shturmovik* pilots were holders of the Gold Star of Hero of the Soviet Union, and women pilots were by no means rare. The Il-2m3 proved to be extremely popular among its crews, par-

An Il-2m3 in late 1944 on the Eastern front. Soviet gunners often removed the rear cockpit canopy to give them a better field of fire.

During the winter, the Il-2s were quickly painted with a soluble white scheme over their normal camouflage. This Il-2 served over the battlefields of Stalingrad in 1943.

ticularly on account of its ability to survive battle damage, many aircraft returning to base riddled by enemy ground fire, the armoured 'bath' alone remaining unscathed. More Il-2s were built (36,183) than any other single type of aircraft.

Specification
Ilyushin Il-2m3 (late model)
Type: two-seat assault aircraft
Powerplant: one 1,770-hp (1320-kW) Mikulin Am-38F liquid-cooled inline piston engine
Performance: maximum speed 404 km/h (251 mph) at 760 m (2,500 ft); service ceiling 5945 m (19,500 ft); range 600 km (375 miles)
Weights: empty 4525 kg (9,976 lb); maximum take-off 6360 kg (14,021 lb)
Dimensions: span 14.60 m (47 ft 10¾ in); length 11.60 m (38 ft 0½ in); height 3.40 m (11 ft 1½ in); wing area 38.54 m² (414.4 sq ft)

Armament: (typical) wing-mounted armament of two 37-mm (1.46-in) and two 7.62-mm (0.3-in) guns, and one 12.7-mm (0.5-in) machine-gun in the rear cockpit, plus 200 2.5-kg (5.5-lb) PTAB hollow-charge anti-tank bombs, or eight RS-82 or RS-132 rocket projectiles

Armed with heavy cannon and rockets, and with bomb racks under the wings, the Il-2s of the V-VS flew over all the battlefields of the Eastern Front in vast numbers. This ability to absorb massive amounts of battle damage made them popular with their crews.

Lavochkin La-5 and La-7

Syemyon Lavochkin's excellent fighters, the **Lavochkin La-5** and **La-7**, were among the best Soviet fighters produced during the war, their relatively simple, mainly wooden structure assisting the production of large numbers, and their large, air-cooled radial engines making for ease of maintenance in the bleak, cold Russian winters.

Developed in turn from the LaGG-1 and LaGG-3 of 1940-1, and the LaG-5 of 1941, the La-5 passed its state acceptance trials in May 1942 and, in view of the successive disasters being suffered at the hands of the Luftwaffe, was ordered into large-scale production, more than 1,000 aircraft being completed in the first six months.

pleted in the first six months. Despite some early troubles with the M-82 radial, in a most advanced installation, the La-5 entered squadron service with the V-VS in the autumn of 1942 and first saw widespread combat during the Stalingrad campaign that started in November

that year. The La-5 was essentially a low-altitude fighter, well capable of holding its own against the Focke-Wulf Fw 190 and Messerschmitt Bf 109 below about 3700 m (12,140 ft) and it was its good performance at low level that encouraged the La-5's employment in the ground-support role; in the great Battle of Kursk at least two regiments of La-5s were flown as anti-tank aircraft with rockets and hollow-charge bombs, which were particularly effective against lightly-armoured fighting vehicles. The **La-5FN** (*forsirovannyi nyeposredstvenno*), or direct fuel-injection engine) was the most widely used sub-variant.

In mid-1944 a development of the La-5, the **La-7**, was introduced with numerous alterations, such as improved location of oil cooler intakes and changes in the cockpit outline. However, despite its improvements, production of the La-5FN was not terminated and both aircraft continued to operate side-by-side for the remainder of the war. The La-7 was seldom employed in the ground-attack role, usually being flown as top cover while the earlier aircraft attacked German army targets with the growing arsenal of assault weapons. Almost all the most famous Soviet pilots flew La-5s and La-7s, among them Colonel Generals Ivan Kojedub (who destroyed 62 German aircraft, including a jet Me 262 while flying Las) and Aleksandr Pokryshkin

(59 kills); both these pilots were three-time recipients of the Gold Star, the only airmen thus decorated.

Specification
Lavochkin La-5FN
Type: single-seat fighter-bomber
Powerplant: one 1,650-hp (1230-kW) Shvetsov M-82FN (ASh-82FN) air-cooled radial piston engine
Performance: maximum speed 647 km/h (402 mph) at 5000 m (16,405 ft); climb to 5000 m (16,405 ft) in 4 minutes 42 seconds; service ceiling 10000 m (32,810 ft); range 700 km (435 miles)
Weights: empty 2800 kg (6,173 lb); maximum take-off 3360 kg (7,408 lb)
Dimensions: span 9.80 m (32 ft 2 in); length 8.67 m (28 ft 5⅓ in); height 2.54 m (8 ft 4 in); wing area 17.59 m² (189.34 sq ft)
Armament: two 20-mm ShVAK cannon and either four 82-mm (3.23-in) RS-82 rockets or four 150-kg (331-lb) bombs; later aircraft had two 23-mm NS cannon

This Lavochkin La-5FN was presented to the V-VS by a Mongolian collective. The La-5 was a good all-round aeroplane and its low-level performance suited it well to the ground-attack role, often carrying rocket launchers.

Used in much the same roving role as the Typhoon and Thunderbolt, the La-5/7 series saw much action during the victorious advance to

Berlin, flying ahead of the Soviet tanks and attacking German positions with light bombs and rockets.

Sukhoi Su-2

Only a marginally later design than the British Fairey Battle, the Soviet **Sukhoi Su-2**, designed by Pavel Sukhoi, previously of the Tupolev design bureau, entered service with the V-VS early in 1941 but, as far as is known, was not encountered during the Winter War which ended the previous year. Derived from Sukhoi's **ANT-51** and designated **BB-1** during its early trials, the aircraft was fairly efficient by current standards once the M-87 engine had been replaced by the M-88 and then the M-88B. Tactical concepts changed swiftly during the first two years of the war, however, and the use by the Germans of large forces of single-seat fighters in support of their advancing armies came as a body blow to the Soviets in mid-1941. Despite being further improved by installation of the 1,000-hp (746-kW) M-88B radial, the Su-2 was found to be desperately vulnerable and virtually unable to defend itself with its single small-calibre machine-gun in the unwieldy manually-operated dorsal turret. Estimates suggest that about 100 were in service with the *Frontovaya Aviatsya* at the time that the German army rolled into the Soviet Union in June 1941, but that dozens were shot down by Flak and fighters in the first few disastrous weeks; moreover, such was the generally poor standard of training in the Soviet air force that the Su-2 proved almost useless as a weapon against mobile battlefield targets.

The parlous state of the Soviet aircraft industry in 1941 prevented much being done to remedy the immediate lack of suitable ground support aircraft (until production of the two-seat Il-2m3 could be stepped up) and recourse was made to further attempts to improve the Su-2 by installation of the 1,520-hp (1134-kW) M-82 radial and frequent deletion of the dorsal turret, but with little tactical benefit. Accepting that losses would remain high, the Soviets therefore simply loaded the aircraft with further bombs and rockets on the supposition that the more explosive delivered against the enemy the better the chances of some degree of success. This version, as well as the completely redesigned **Su-6**, were abandoned in favour of all-out dependence on the Il-2m3. The Su-2 probably did not survive in production beyond mid-1942.

Specification
Sukhoi Su-2 (late production)
Type: two-seat close-support aircraft
Powerplant: one 1,520-hp (1134-kW) Shvetsov M-82 air-cooled radial piston engine
Performance: maximum speed 486 km/h (302 mph) at 1525 m (5,000 ft);

service ceiling 8800 m (28,870 ft); range with bomb load 1100 km (683 miles)
Weights: empty 3273 kg (7,216 lb); maximum take-off 4700 kg (10,362 lb)
Dimensions: span 14.30 m (46 ft 11 in); length 10.46 m (34 ft 3¾ in); height 3.80 m (12 ft 6 in); wing area 29.0 m² (312.1 sq ft)
Armament: four fixed forward-firing 7.62-mm (0.3-in) machine-guns in wings and one or two in dorsal turret, plus a bombload of 400 kg (882 lb)

A Sukhoi Su-2 with the 746-kW (1000-hp) M-88B radial engine. Owing to the type's obsolescence and vulnerability, engines of increasing power were tried, but without success. When the Il-2 became generally available, the Su-2 was relegated to second-line units.

By 1942, the Su-2 was receiving such a battering from the German ground and air forces that it was quickly withdrawn to second-line units. This aircraft served with one such unit in the Sverdlovsk area in the winter of 1942.

carried internally and either bombs or rockets up to about 500 kg (1,102 lb) carried externally

Night-Fighters

World War II saw the development of night-fighting from a very imprecise, hit-or-miss art using rudimentary equipment in hastily converted aircraft, to a refined science using highly developed tactics in purpose-built aircraft equipped with sophisticated radar and weapons.

When World War II started in September 1939 no air force was equipped with aircraft specifically designed for the night-fighting role. Only the UK had woken up to the fact that, with the *raison d'être* of the modern air force being offensive bombing operations, such aircraft would be needed urgently; most air forces made do by using night-flying day fighters, in conjunction with ground searchlights. While the RAF was conducting experiments with rudimentary airborne radar in a handful of obsolescent Bristol Blenheims, the Bristol aircraft company was hard at work developing the Bristol Beaufighter, the world's first dedicated night-fighter to carry radar, produced entirely on their own initiative. This entered service during the Battle of Britain and first saw combat in the German night Blitz of 1940–1.

From these small beginnings came an entirely new science of aircraft interception that has continued to advance ever since: the science of locating the enemy on ground radar, guiding the fighter towards its target by means of ground controllers and, eventually, using airborne radar, closing to within range of the fighter's own weapons for the kill. Although more within the scope of the bombers' operations, the night-

Britain led the way in pioneering night-fighters to intercept enemy raiders. The Boulton Paul Defiant was an early design which was to be eclipsed by the Bristol Beaufighter and the de Havilland Mosquito in its highly effective night-fighter variant.

fighter crews had to contend with a growing, parallel science of countermeasures, as the bombers began to include equipment able to blind the ground radar and to provide warning of the approach of a night-fighter.

Although the British advanced relatively quickly with successively improved Beaufighters and de Havilland Mosquitoes (as well as discarding the outmoded Blenheims, Boulton Paul Defiants and Hawker Hurricanes), and unquestionably led the world in night-fighting techniques and

technology (until the arrival of the American-developed centimetric AI Mk X), German ingenuity produced highly efficient night-fighter adaptations of the Messerschmitt Bf 110 and Junkers Ju 88; these two aircraft, together with the excellent Heinkel He 219, provided the backbone of the Reich's night-fighter defence between 1942 and 1945. Not surprisingly, with so many RAF heavy bombers operating almost nightly over Europe during this period, there came onto the scene numerous Luftwaffe night-fighter

pilots whose individual victory scores far eclipsed any achievements of their Allied counterparts, it being fairly commonplace for German pilots to destroy four or more Avro Lancasters and Handley Page Halifaxes on a single sortie; once they had entered the great bomber stream their victory bag was limited only by their use of ammunition and fuel. Moreover, the development of the upward-firing cannon (not to mention fairly efficient airborne radar) enabled the Germans to destroy RAF bombers in such a way that the British 'didn't know what had hit them'.

Elsewhere, with concerted night operations conducted on a much lesser scale until the onset of the great American night offensive against Japan in 1944, night fighting demanded less attention to sophisticated equipment and tactics than in Europe, although these were quickly introduced when the Boeing B-29 started operations. By and large, during the first two years of the Pacific War, neither Japan nor the United States engaged in significant night bombing, and accordingly did little until 1943 to introduce specialist night-fighters, the Douglas P-70 (though widely employed) being unequivocally a makeshift adaptation of a light bomber.

Bristol Blenheim Mk IF

The **Bristol Blenheim** entered RAF service as a light bomber in 1937 and, despite great hopes for the type, it was becoming outmoded from the day it arrived, being under-armed and therefore capable of carrying no more than a puny bombload by later standards. It was a neat and compact design, however, and lent itself to further development as a bomber, the Blenheim Mk IV with lengthened nose joining the RAF in 1939. In the realization that the Blenheim Mk I would quickly be superseded, plans were put in hand to introduce it as a night-fighter for service with Fighter Command, and in December 1938 four squadrons (Nos 23, 25, 29 and 64) started taking deliveries. Most of these early aircraft were ex-Bomber Command aircraft with sealed bomb doors and bomb gear removed; their armament remained a single fixed forward-firing 7.7-mm (0.303-in) Browning gun and a Vickers 'K' gas-operated gun of the same calibre in the dorsal turret. These four regular squadrons, together with Nos 600, 601 and 604 of the Auxiliary Air Force (re-equipped in the following month) were employed principally to work up and calibrate the new CH coastal radar chain being built at top speed along the UK's south and east coasts. Early in 1939, however, there became available the first of 200 gun packs, each containing four Browning guns and manufactured by the Southern Railway's depot at

The nose transmitter and wing receiver aerials (antennas) of the early AI Mk III radar can be seen on this Blenheim Mk IF, which in 1941 was training crews at No. 54 Operational Training Unit, RAF.

Ashford, Kent, and by the outbreak of war in September 1939 most converted Blenheim Mk I (now termed **Blenheim Mk IF**) aircraft had been modified to have such a pack fitted under the fuselage nose. Meanwhile one flight from No. 25 Squadron had had its Blenheims modified with the first 'breadboard' examples of airborne interception radar, and these were undergoing faltering trials over the Thames Estuary in collaboration with the Bawdsey Manor CH coastal radar when war broke out. In due course this radar was standardized to become AI Mk III and was fitted in about two dozen Blenheims, most of the remainder being flown by the Fighter Interception Unit (FIU). Several other Blenheim night-fighter squadrons (among them Nos 68, 145, 219 and 222) were formed, but they were most-

ly short-lived. At the time of the Battle of Britain night-fighter Blenheims soldiered on in search of the small numbers of German night raiders, and on 21/22 July 1940 an aircraft of the FIU made history when it became the first employing AI radar to destroy an enemy raider (a Dornier Do 17) at night. Possessing very pedestrian capabilities, the Blenheim could scarcely catch any of the modern aircraft of 1940 and, although it achieved further victories during the German night *Blitz* of 1940-1 (indeed, formed the backbone of the UK's night defence), it was gradually phased out of service with the arrival of the powerful Bristol Beaufighter.

Specification
Blenheim Mk IF
Type: three-seat night-fighter

Powerplant: two 840-hp (626-kW) Bristol Mercury VIII nine-cylinder air-cooled radial piston engines
Performance: maximum speed 418 km/h (260 mph) at 4265 m (14,000 ft); initial climb rate 488 m (1,600 ft) per minute; service ceiling 8230 m (27,000 ft); normal range 1770 km (1,100 miles)
Weights: empty 3651 kg (8,050 lb); maximum take-off 5489 kg (12,100 lb)
Dimensions: span 17.17 m (56 ft 4 in); length 12.45 m (40 ft 10 in); height 3.00 m (9 ft 10 in); wing area 43.57 m² (469 sq ft)
Armament: four 7.7-mm (0.303-in) machine-guns in ventral tray firing forward, and one 7.7-mm (0.303-in) machine-gun in dorsal turret

---

Bristol Beaufighter

First flown in prototype form on 17 July 1939, the **Bristol Beaufighter** took over the task of night-fighter defence from the makeshift Bristol Blenheim Mk IF fighter during the German night *Blitz* of the winter of 1940-1. Powered initially by 1,400-hp (1044-kW) Bristol Hercules III sleeve-valve radials, the **Beaufighter Mk IF** was equipped with AI Mk IV radar (characterized by a 'broad-arrow' transmitter aerial on the aircraft's nose) and, having undergone initial operational trials with the Fighter Interception Unit during the latter stages of the Battle of Britain, started delivery to RAF night-fighter squadrons in September 1940. Lack of fami-

This Beaufighter Mk II served with one of the RAF's Polish squadrons, No. 307, from August 1941 until about mid-1942, when the Hercules-engined Beaufighter Mk VIF began to replace this Merlin-engined version.

liarity with AI radar resulted in few combat successes during 1940, but in the last three months of the *Blitz* the Beaufighter began taking an increasing toll of German bombers. Home

night-fighter squadrons equipped with Beaufighter Mk IFs included Nos 25, 29, 68, 141, 153, 219, 256, 600 and 604. Production was stepped up, and included 1,000 aircraft ordered from the 'shadow' factories, the 51st and subsequent aircraft being armed with six wing-mounted 7.7 mm (0.303-in) machine-guns in addition to the four belly-mounted 20-mm cannon to guard. Delays with improved Hercules radials resulted in the Rolls-Royce Merlin XX V-12 engine being selected to power the **Beaufighter Mk II**, the first production example of which was flown at Filton on 22 March 1941; the type entered Fighter Command service with No. 255 Squadron in July, followed by the Polish-manned No. 307 Squadron in August, and Nos 96 and 125 Squadrons in 1942. The **Beaufighter Mk III** (a lightened version) and the **Beaufighter Mk IV** (with Rolls-Royce Griffon engines) did not materialize as such, although a Beaufighter Mk II was experimentally flown with Griffon IIB

Three AI Mk IV-equipped Beaufighter Mk Is of No. 600 Sqn are seen here on a mission from Colerne during the winter of 1940-1.

engines. The **Beaufighter Mk V** featured a four-gun Defiant-type dorsal turret but was abandoned as this impeded the pilot's emergency exit. The **Beaufighter Mk VIF** then became standard as the RAF's principal night-fighter until the arrival of the de Havilland Mosquito Mk II, equipping as night-fighters Nos 29, 68, 96, 125, 141, 153, 219, 255, 256, 307, 600 and 604 Squadrons in the UK, and Nos 46, 89, 108, 144, 252 and 272 Squadrons in the Middle East during 1942-3. Among the home-based Beaufighter Mk VIF squadrons which moved to the Mediterranean theatre after the North African landings were Nos 255 and 600 Squadrons, and with the latter Flight Sergeant Downing and Sergeant Lyons in a Beaufighter Mk VIF shot down five Junkers Ju 52/3m transports in 10 minutes off Setif on 30 April 1943. In the Far East night-fighter Beaufighter Mk VIF's served with Nos 27, 89, 176 and 177 Squadrons, principally in the Calcutta area and over Burma. When it first arrived in service the Beaufighter was widely regarded as tricky to fly, particularly on one engine; in due course the fin area was increased and dihedral applied to the tailplane to improve lateral control, resulting in a fine night-fighter on which the RAF came to depend for two years in the mid-war period.

Specification
Beaufighter Mk VIF

Type: two-seat night-fighter
Powerplant: two 1,670-hp (1245-kW) Bristol Hercules VI or XVI air-cooled sleeve-valve radial piston engines
Performance: maximum speed 536 km/h (333 mph) at 4755 m (15,600 ft); climb to 4570 m (15,000 ft) in 7 minutes 48 seconds; service ceiling 8075 m (26,500 ft); normal range 2382 km (1,480 miles)
Weights: empty 6623 kg (14,600 lb);

This Beaufighter Mk VIF has a dihedralled tailplane, but is still fitted with original AI Mk IV radar, with a 'harpoon' arrowhead on the nose and receiver dipoles on the

maximum take-off 9798 kg (21,600 lb)
Dimensions: span 17.63 m (57 ft 10 in); length 12.70 m (41 ft 8 in); height 4.83 m (15 ft 10 in); wing area 46.73 m^2 (503 sq ft)

wings. The RAF unit is not known, but it was home-based because in the Mediterranean inlet air filters were fitted.

Armament: four 20-mm cannon in nose and six 7.7-mm (0.303-in) machine-guns in the outer wings, and one hand-held 7.7-mm (0.303-in) machine-gun in dorsal hatch

UK
Boulton Paul Defiant

An original Defiant Mk I of No. 264 Sqn (CO's aircraft), with turret fairings raised and ventral radio masts extended.

The saga of the **Boulton Paul Defiant Mk I** began with the type's short and disastrous service in RAF Fighter Command as a day fighter, entering combat at the time of the Dunkirk evacuation. By the opening of the Battle of Britain the Luftwaffe had the measure of the British two-seat turret fighter and decimated the two squadrons, Nos 141 and 264, so equipped. Hurriedly withdrawn as a day fighter at the end of August 1940, the Defiant transferred to night fighting and gained its first two night victories during the latter half of September. Indeed for many years the Defiant was credited with the highest number of victories per interception of any RAF night fighter during the night *Blitz*; only relatively recently has this distinction been correctly assigned to the Bristol Blenheim in the last four months of 1940, and to the Beaufighter in the first five months of 1941. Early operations by Defiants at night were carried out without the benefit of AI radar, the aircraft simply being day fighters flown at night in conjunction with searchlights. The first Defiant squadron formed specifically for night fighting was No. 307, staffed by Polish pilots with the RAF in September 1940, followed by Nos 255 and 256 Squadrons in November, and No. 151 Squadron in December. All these became operational in early 1941 when the first conversions to mount AI Mk VI radar became available.

No. 85 Squadron received Defiants in January 1941 but flew only three operational sorties before discarding the aircraft on receiving orders to convert to the Douglas Havoc; No. 96 Squadron, on the other hand, flew Defiants from February 1941 until June 1942, initially to provide night defen-

sive patrols over Merseyside. Only two other squadrons flew the Defiant as a night-fighter (apart from the ex-day squadrons, Nos 141 and 264), No. 125 being formed in June 1941 and No. 153 in October the same year. All remained in the UK.

The tactics employed by the Defiant night-fighter were as difficult as they were unique, as the turret guns (the only armament possessed by the aircraft) were seldom fired forward because their flash blinded the pilot. Instead the aircraft, using its AI radar, would engage in a long stern chase (for the Defiant was slow by comparison with other fighters), gradually draw alongside or beneath the enemy bomber before opening fire with its rifle-calibre guns. Quick direct hits were needed in vital parts of the target before the enemy gunners returned the fire or the German pilot took violent evasive action; by that time both Defiant crew members would have lost all night vision.

One other night duty was undertaken by night-flying Defiants when aircraft of No. 515 Squadron, specially equipped by TRE (Telecommunications Research Establishment), were used to jam enemy coastal radar from 1942 onwards.

Specification
Defiant Mk I
Type: two-seat night-fighter
Powerplant: one 1,030-hp (768-kW) Rolls-Royce Merlin III V-12 liquid-cooled piston engine
Performance: maximum speed 488 km/h (303 mph) at 5030 m (16,500 ft); initial climb rate 579 m (1,900 ft) per minute; service ceiling 9295 m (30,500 ft); range 756 km (470

miles)
Weights: empty 2722 kg (6,000 lb); maximum take-off 3788 kg (8,350 lb)
Dimensions: span 11.99 m (39 ft 4 in); length 10.77 m (35 ft 4 in); height 3.71 m (12 ft 2 in); wing area 23.225 m^2 (250 sq ft)
Armament: four 7.7-mm (0.303-in) Browning machine-guns in Boulton Paul power-operated gun turret with 600 rounds per gun

In contrast, this Defiant Mk II is seen much later in the war, serving as a night fighter with No. 151 Sqn, one of

the longest-established night fighter units in the world (that was its special task in 1917).

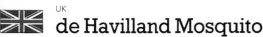

UK

de Havilland Mosquito

Although originally conceived principally as an unarmed fast light bomber, the **de Havilland Mosquito** was also envisaged both as a photo-reconnaissance aircraft and as a nightfighter, the second aircraft flown (on 15 May 1941) being in fact the nightfighter prototype. This version differed from the bomber in having strengthened wing spars, a flat windscreen, an armament of four 20-mm cannon and four 7.7-mm (0.303-in) machine guns in the nose, crew entry through a starboard side hatch, and AI Mk IV radar. With a top speed of 595 km/h (370 mph), the **Mosquito NF.Mk II** (of which 466 were produced) entered service with No. 23 (Fighter) Squadron at Ford in May 1942, followed by No. 157 Squadron in August. The next night-fighter version was the **Mosquito NF.Mk XII**, 97 of which were produced by fitting AI Mk VIII radar in Mk IIs, the four machine-guns being removed; it first joined the Polish-staffed No. 307 Squadron in December 1942; 270 **Mos-**

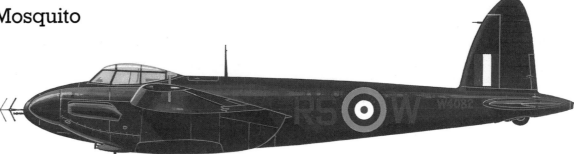

This early Mosquito Mk II is running up on the ground, despite the fact that the main access hatch to the AI Mk IV radar transmitter appears to have been removed.

quito NF.Mk XIII aircraft were similar but were newly built. One hundred Mk IIs were converted to become **Mosquito NF.Mk XVII** aircraft by installation of the American centimetric AI Mk X in a somewhat enlarged nose radome. A derivative of this version, the **Mosquito NF.Mk XIX**, of which 220 were produced from new, operated at an increased all-up weight and were powered by 1,635-hp (1219-kW) Rolls-Royce Merlin 25s, this version serving with eight RAF squadrons. A parallel design was initiated to produce a high-altitude night-fighter, the **Mosquito NF.Mk XV**, to combat the high-flying Junkers Ju 86P reconnaissance aircraft which started flying over the UK in 1942; with a span increased to 19.05 m (62 ft 6 in), armament reduced to four

W4082 was the fifth production Mosquito Mk II, delivered in January 1942. Note the exhaust flame dampers, which reduced flight performance.

rifle-calibre machine guns, and 1,710-hp (1275-kW) Merlin 76/77s, this aircraft was flown to 13260 m (43,500 ft), but was never flown in combat by the single squadron, No. 85, thus equipped. The last wartime night-fighter Mosquito was the **Mosquito NF.Mk 30**, which first equipped No. 219 Squadron at Bradwell Bay in July 1944 and went on to join a dozen other squadrons during the last year of the war. Powered by Merlin 72/73, 76/77 or 113/114 engines, this version had a top speed of 655 km/h (407 mph) and an operating ceiling of 11580 m (38,000 ft). Some 230 examples of this, the best of all Mosquito night-fighters produced during

the war, were built.

The Mosquito was undoubtedly the finest Allied night-fighter of the war, replacing almost all Bristol Beaufighter night fighters in service in northern Europe by 1944, and being employed not only for home defence but also night intruder and bomber support/night escort duties. The only enemy night-fighter capable of matching the Mosquito was the superb Heinkel He 219 (as well as the few night-fighter Me 262s), but these were so few in number as scarcely to affect the scale of night operations over the continent. The most famous of all Mosquito night-fighter pilots was Group Captain John Cunningham, who later became chief test pilot at the de Havilland company.

Specification
Mosquito NF.Mk 30
Type: two-seat night fighter/bomber support aircraft
Powerplant: two 1,710-hp (1275-kW) Rolls-Royce Merlin 76 V-12 liquid-cooled piston engines
Performance: maximum speed 655 km/h (407 mph) at 8535 m (28,000 ft); climb to 4570 m (15,000 ft) in 7 minutes 30 seconds; service ceiling 11885 m (39,000 ft); normal range 2092 km (1,300 miles)
Weights: empty 6985 kg (15,400 lb); maximum take-off 9798 kg (21,600 lb)
Dimensions: span 16.51 m (54 ft 2 in); length 12.73 m (41 ft 9 in); height 4.65 m (15 ft 3 in); wing area 40.41 m^2 (435 sq ft)
Armament: four forward-firing 20-mm Hispano cannon under nose

UK

Hawker Hurricane Mk II

From its earliest service days the **Hawker Hurricane** single-seater proved a pleasant aeroplane to fly at night (unlike the Supermarine Spitfire), and as early as the Battle of Britain Hurricanes were regularly flying night patrols to complement those of the night-fighter Bristol Blenheims. For example No. 92 (Fighter) Squadron operated a detached flight at Bibury in Gloucestershire for this work. As the daylight battle petered out in October the Hurri-

cane was increasingly flown at night and with the introduction of the more powerful **Hurricane Mk II** with progressively heavier armament (eight machine-guns in the **Hurricane Mk IIA**, 12 machine-guns in the **Hurricane Mk IIB** and four 20-mm cannon in the **Hurricane Mk IIC**), the aircraft not only performed night defensive patrols but also

became increasingly used as an intruder over German bomber bases in northern France and the Low Countries. Among the best known night fighter/intruder squadrons to fly Hurricane Mk IIs in 1941-2 were Nos 1, 3, 46, 79 and 87; to them was ascribed the destruction of 52 enemy aircraft, 16 coastal vessels, 105 road vehicles and 17 locomotives during the last six months of 1941. Without question the most successful pilot of this mid-war period was Flight Lieutenant Karel Kuttelwascher (a Czech veteran of the Battle of Britain) of No. 1 (Fighter) Squadron, who scored his first 'intruder' victory, a Junkers Ju 88, on 1 April 1942 and went on to shoot down 14 more enemy aircraft (seven Dornier Do 217s, five Heinkel He 111s, a Dornier Do 17 and another Ju 88) in the next eight weeks, for which he was

After the mauled No. 87 Sqn returned from France in June 1940 it was remustered as a night fighter unit, and in 1942 one of its aircraft was this Langley-built Hurricane Mk IIC, flown by the CO.

353

awarded two DFCs: among his victories were three He 111s shot down over St André in the space of four minutes at midnight on 4/5 May, no mean feat for a single-seater without the benefit of radar.

The specialist night intruder Hurricane differed from its day fighter counterpart only in being painted matt black overall and having small antiglare panels between the engine exhaust stubs and the pilot's windscreen. Hurricane Mk IIs provided the first night-fighter equipment in the Middle East with the arrival of No. 213 Squadron in the Canal Zone in May 1941, and in May 1943 Hurricane Mk IICs with pilot-AI radar served with No. 176 Squadron in the Calcutta area.

Finally, mention should be made of the Turbinlite squadrons which, using searchlight- and AI-equipped Douglas Havocs and Douglas Bostons to locate

enemy raiders, also flew Hurricane Mk IIBs and Mk IICs during 1942; an almost total absence of success, together with rapid development of AI radar, caused this wasteful and fruitless experiment to be abandoned in January 1943.

Specification
Hurricane Mk IIC
Type: single-seat night-fighter/intruder

The white hexagon has adorned No. 85 Sqn aircraft since 1916; since this Hurricane Mk I, No. 85 Sqn has flown most RAF night fighter types.

Powerplant: one 1,280-hp (954-kW) Rolls-Royce Merlin XX V-12 liquid-cooled piston engine
Performance: maximum speed 546 km/h (339 mph) at 6705 m (22,000 ft); climb to 6095 m (20,000 ft) in 9 minutes 6 seconds; service ceiling 10850 m (35,600 ft); normal night-fighting range 740-km (460 miles)

Weights: empty 2631 kg (5,800 lb); maximum take-off 3583 kg (7,800 lb)
Dimensions: span 12.19 m (40 ft 0 in); length 9.75 m (32 ft 0 in); height 4.00 m (13 ft 1½ in); wing area 23.92 m² (257.5 sq ft)
Armament: four wing-mounted 20-mm Hispano cannon, plus (intruder version) two 227-kg (500-lb) bombs

---

Dornier Do 17, Do 215 and Do 217

The Do 17Z-10 Kauz II was the first sensor-equipped Luftwaffe night fighter, with the Spanner sight projecting through the windscreen. R4+LK served with I/NJG 2 at Gilze-Rijen (note NJG badge on nose).

The **Dornier Do 17** came to be employed in the night fighting role not so much because it was particularly suited to the task as for its availability in growing numbers as it approached the end of its service as a front line bomber. The opening of RAF bombing attacks on Germany in May 1940 caught the Luftwaffe wrong-footed, without an organized night-fighter defence, and although such a force was quickly established using the Messerschmitt Bf 110 and Junkers Ju 88C, consideration was also given to the use of other bombers converted to the night-fighter role. A standard Dornier Do 17Z-3 was therefore fitted with the nose of a Ju 88C-2 carrying an armament of one 20-mm MG FF cannon and three 7.92-mm (0.31-in) MG 17 machine-guns. Termed the **Do 17Z-6 Kauz I** (Screech Owl I), this version was found to be unsatisfactory and was abandoned. A fresh start was made with an entirely new nose accommodating two 20-mm cannon and four 7.92-mm (0.31-in) machine-guns together with an infra-red detection equipment (*Spanner Anlage*) operating in conjunction with a Q-Rohr sighting screen. Nine such **Do 17Z-10 Kauz II** aircraft were completed, and these served for a short time late in 1940 with I/NJG 2; the infra-red equipment was found to be too sensitive for operational use, however, and no further Do 17s were converted. A similar conversion was made to the Do 215 as the **Do 215B-5**, also with two cannon and four machine-guns, this version first joining 4./NJG 2 during the spring of 1941 for intruder sorties over British bomber bases and, following a fair degree of success (18 RAF bombers were lost to intruders between April and June 1941), further examples equipped I, III and IV/NJG 1 and I and II/NJG 2 later in that year. Rather more attention was paid to producing night-fighter versions of the Do 217, the first of which, the **Do 217J-1** night intruder, entered service in the summer of 1942, fol-

lowed by the **Do 217J-2** night-fighter with Lichtenstein BC radar. These served in small numbers with NJG 1 and NJG 2, and equipped the whole of NJG 3 and III/NJG 4. The final variant, the **Do 217N**, existed in numerous forms of which one, the **Do 217N-1/U3**, often carried four 20-mm cannon in a *schräge Musik* upward-firing installation, but with a speed of around 525 km/h (326 mph) night interception was little more than speculative. Nevertheless Do 217Ns, of which some 200 are said to have been built, served with NJG 3 and NJG 4, as well as II/NJG

and II/NJG 2 in th Mediterranean theatre in 1943. However, their cost and the disruption to bomber production led to their discontinuation by the middle of that year in favour of the established Bf 110 and Ju 88.

Specification
Do 17Z-10 Kauz II
Type: three-seat night-fighter
Powerplant: two 1,000-hp (746-kW) Bramo 323P nine-cylinder air-cooled radial piston engines
Performance: maximum speed 415 km/h (258 mph) at 4000 m

(13,125 ft); initial climb rate 290 m (950 ft) per minutes; service ceiling 6650 m (21,820 ft); maximum range 1270 km (789 miles)
Weights: empty 5150 kg (11,354 lb); maximum take-off 8445 kg (18,618 lb)
Dimensions: span 18.00 m (59 ft 0½ in); length 16.00 m (52 ft 6 in); height 4.55 m (14 ft 11¼ in); wing area 55.00 m² (592 sq ft)
Armament: two 20-mm MG FF cannon and four 7.92-mm (0.31-in) MG 17 machine-guns in nose, and up to four 7.92-mm (0.31-in) MG 17 guns in lateral, dorsal and ventral positions

KD+MZ were the Dornier factory codes of the Do 217J development aircraft, seen here with the bomb bay of the Do 217J-1 but the Lichtenstein BC (FuG 202) radar of the Do 217J-2. Operational Do 217J-2s were all-black.

Focke-Wulf Fw 190A

The **Focke-Wulf Fw 190** was never strictly a night-fighter in the accepted sense of being designed or modified for night fighting yet, on account of operational circumstances forced upon the Luftwaffe, came to be employed under certain conditions very successfully in the night battle over Germany. Following the introduction of 'Window' jamming of German radar at the beginning of the Battle of Hamburg, which caused major dislocation of the *Himmelbett* (four-poster bed) defence system, a distinguished German bomber pilot, Major Hajo Herrmann, suggested employing day fighters at night, particularly when RAF jamming threatened paralysis of the radar control of night-fighters. Accordingly a special unit (codenamed *wilde Sau*, or 'wild boar' to differentiate its tactics from *zahme Sau* or 'tame boar' tactics, which embraced night-fighters operating under radar control) was formed as Jagddivision 300, under Herrmann himself; based principally in north and west Germany, the *Geschwaderstab* and II/JG 300 flew **Fw 190A-5/U2** fighters while I and III/JG 300 flew Messerschmitt Bf 109Gs at the outset. In its first major night operation, during the RAF attack on Peenemünde on 17/

This Fw 190A-6/R11 was flown by Oberleutnant Krause of 1/NJGr 10 (not NJG 10). Note the wilde Sau *badge on the cowl and the FuG 217 Neptun aerials.*

18 August 1943, JG 300 failed to make contact when bombing feints suggested that Berlin was the target. However, during the next month the *wilde Sau* tactics paid handsome dividends, and Herrmann was acclaimed a national hero, and promoted Oberstleutnant as commander of a much expanded Jagddivision 30, comprising JG 300, now commanded by Oberstleutnant Kurt Kettner, JG 301 under Helmut Weinrich at Neubiberg and JG 302 at Doberitz under Major Ewald Janssen. Henceforth *wilde Sau* tactics were employed on any moonlit night, and on any other occasion over the target where the light of the ground fires silhouetted the bombers. Winter flying conditions curtailed the operations severely, as did the wear on the

aircraft themselves, of which Fw 190A-5 and **Fw 190A-8** fighters came to outnumber the Bf 109. Among the most succesful of the *wilde Sau* pilots were Konrad Bauer (*Staffelkapitän* of 5./JG 300 with 32 night victories), Kurt Welter (JG 301 with 29 victories), Friedrich-Karl Müller (JG 300's technical officer with 23 victories) and Walter Loos (of Stab JG 300 with 22 victories); Hajo Herrmann himself destroyed nine RAF bombers in the course of 50 sorties while Iro Ilk, *Gruppenkommandeur* of III/JG 300, shot down four Avro Lancasters in one night during April 1944.

Specification
Fw 190A-8
Type: single-seat day/night fighter
Powerplant: one 1,700-hp (1268-kW)

BMW 801Dg 14-cylinder air-cooled radial piston engine with GM-1 nitrous oxide power boosting
Performance: maximum speed 655 km/h (407 mph) at 6000 m (19,685 ft); initial climb rate 720 m (2,360 ft) per minute; service ceiling 11400 m (37,400 ft); normal range 800 km (497 miles)
Weights: empty 3170 kg (6,989 lb); maximum take-off 4430 kg (9,766 lb)
Dimensions: span 34 ft 5½ in (10.50 m); length 8.80 m (28 ft 10½ in); height 3.95 m (13 ft 0 in); wing area 18.30 m² (196.98 sq ft)
Armament: two 20-mm MG 151/20 cannon in wing roots, two 30-mm MG 108 cannon in outer wings and two 13-mm (0.51-in) MG 131 heavy machine-guns on nose, all firing forward

---

Messerschmitt Bf 110

After proving something of a disappointment as a daylight 'heavy fighter' in the first year of the war (although continuing in that role to a lesser extent), the **Messerschmitt Bf 110** became numerically Germany's most important night-fighter, being selected from the outset in mid-1940 to provide the basic equipment of Josef Kammhüber's *Nachtjagdverband*,

Below: Most aerodynamically cluttered of all Bf 110 versions, the Bf 110G-4b/R3 had both SN-2 and C-1 radars, usually carried a crew of

three and, with flame dampers and drop tanks as shown, had a maximum speed of typically 465 km/h (289 mph), barely faster than a Lancaster.

Above: Though fitted with enlarged fins and DB 605A engines, the early Bf 110G models lacked flame-damped exhausts, and this Bf 110G-2 of 12/NJG 3 had no radar. It was based at Stavanger until the final collapse in May 1945.

Seen serving with the NJ Staffel Norway at the end of the war, the Bf 110G-4c/R3 was almost the last version built. By 1944 the problems with the SN-2 radar at short ranges had been overcome, and the C-1 set could be eliminated.

formed on 20 July that year. At first standard **Bf 110C-2** and **Bf 110D-1** aircraft were used, these equipping I Gruppe, Nachtjagdgeschwader 1 (previously I/ZG 1) under Hauptmann Günther Radusch, but they were soon replaced by the first dedicated night-fighter version, the **Bf 110F-4** with 1,300-hp (969-kW) Daimler-Benz DB 601E engines, this version remaining in service, alongside later types, until the last year of the war. Within a year five *Nachtjagdgruppen* had been formed, four of them flying Bf 110s. The next night-fighter derivative, the **Bf 110G** series, was the principal version, usually powered by 1,475-hp (1100-kW) DB 605B engines. The **Bf 110G-4** possessed a basic armament of two 20-mm MG 151 cannon and four 7.92-mm (0.31-in) MG 17 machine-guns, but this was varied by numerous *Rüstsatz* field kits, of which the R8 introduced the *schräge Musik* twin upward-firing cannon in 1943 (also fitted in the **Bf 110F-4/U1**); suffix letters also identified changes in radar, the **Bf 110G-4a** with FuG 212 Lichtenstein C-1 radar, the **Bf 110G-4B** with both C-1 and SN-2 radar, the **Bf 110G-4c** with SN-2 radar only, and the **Bf 110G-4d** with FuG 227 Flensburg homing radar (tuned to the British 'Monica' tail-warning radar). There

was also considerable work done with water-methanol and nitrous oxide injection in efforts to boost the performance of the Bf 110 and, although such improvements were only marginal, the aircraft remained in production almost up to the last months of the war. However, constant use of the night-fighters to assist in daylight defence against the American bomber offensive did much to prevent a much greater build-up of the night-fighter force, which nevertheless grew from 389 aircraft at the end of 1942 to 913 aircraft two years later. Only when the Messerschmitt Me 410 replaced the Bf 110

in service with the *Zerstörergeschwader* in 1944 were virtually all Bf 110Gs allocated to the *Nachtjagdverband*. Even then priority was given to the new Junkers Ju 88G and Heinkel He 219 night-fighters, so by the end of 1944 only about 150 Bf 110 night-fighters remained in service.

Specification
Bf 110G-4b/R3
Type: two-seat night-fighter
Powerplant: two 1,475-hp (1100-kW) Daimler-Benz DB 605B-1 inverted V-12 liquid-cooled piston engines
Performance: maximum speed

550 km/h (342 mph) at 7000 m (22,950 ft); climb to 5500 m (18,045 ft) in 8 minutes 6 seconds; service ceiling 8000 m (26,245 ft); maximum range 2100 km (1,305 miles)
Weights: empty 5100 kg (11,243 lb); maximum take-off 9900 kg (21,825 lb)
Dimensions: span 16.27 m (53 ft 4¾ in); length 12.65 m (41 ft 6¼ in); height 13 ft 1½ in (4.00 m); wing area 38.40 m² (413.33 sq ft)
Armament: two 30-mm MK 108 and two 20-mm MG 151/20 cannon in the nose, and two 7.92-mm (0.31-in) MG 15 machine-guns in rear cockpit (MG 81Z installation)

Messerschmitt Me 262B-1a/U1

The fast declining ability of the German night-fighter force to halt RAF Bomber Command's offensve in the latter half of 1944 (when it was resumed after the Normandy invasion) prompted Oberst Hajo Herrmann, well known for his advocacy of drastic fighting tactics and commander of

Jagddivision 30, to suggest adaptation of the **Messerschmitt Me 262** jet aircraft as a night-fighter; both he and Oberleutnant Behrens of the E-Stelle Rechlin tested an Me 262 experimentally fitted with Lichtenstein SN-2 radar and pronounced it a potentially excellent night-fighter. It was

therefore proposed to undertake conversion of **Me 262B-1a** two-seat trainers as night-fighters, installing a formidable collection of radar and radio equipment, including FuG 16ZY VHF radio, FuG 25a IFF, FuG 120a Bernadine visual read-out repeater, FuG 125, FuG 218 Neptun V search radar and FuG 350ZC Naxos radar homer; the use of an ungainly 'toasting fork' aerial array on the nose reduced the

Me 262's maximum speed from 873 km/h (542 mph) to 813 km/h (505 mph), but the ultimate production version, the **Me 262B-2a**, was intended

All the Luftwaffe aircraft which went to the USA in 1945-6 were badly repainted with incorrect markings, the Hakenkreuz and in this case the Iron Cross being pre-1938 style, too early for this Me 262B-1a/U1.

to incorporate a rear fuselage extended by 114 cm (45 in) to accommodate approximately 910 litres (200 Imp gal) of additional fuel. A pair of upward-firing 30-mm MK 108 cannon was mounted in a *schräge Musik* installation. Only one example of this version was flown before the end of the war, although a second aircraft which, equipped with centimetric AI radar in a blunt nose fairing and so dispensing with the ungainly external aerial array, was awaiting flight test when the war ended; it was expected to possess a top speed of 860 km/h (534 mph).

In terms of performance, if not equipment, these aircraft were far in advance of Allied night-fighters, and had they existed in service in significant numbers (and had Germany possessed the fuel to operate them) they must have inflicted prohibitive losses upon Bomber Command. As it was, one experimental unit, Kommando Stamp (under Major Gerhard Stamp, previously of I/JG 300, a *wilde Sau* unit) flew about 10 Me 262B-1a/U1 fighters, the unit later being redesignated Kommando Welter under Oberleutnant Kurt Welter and deployed for the night defence of Berlin in March 1945; Welter himself is said to have shot down about 20 Allied aircraft at night in Me 262s in the last eight weeks of the war, and probably remains the world's most successful night-fighter jet pilot to this day.

Specification
Me 262B-1a/U1
Type: two-seat night-fighter
Powerplant: two 900-kg (1,984-lb) thrust Junkers Jumo 109-004B-1 axial-flow turbojets
Performance: maximum speed 813 km/h (505 mph) at 6000 m (19,685 ft); climb to 6000 m (19,685 ft) in 6 minutes 54 seconds; service ceiling 10850 m (35,600 ft); normal range 1050 km (652 miles)
Weights: empty about 4585 kg (10,110 lb); maximum take-off about 6585 kg (14,515 lb)
Dimensions: span 12.48 m (40 ft 11½ in); length 11.53 (37 ft 10 in); height 3.84 m (12 ft 7 in); wing area 21.70 m² (233.6 sq ft)
Armament: four forward-firing 30-mm MK 108 cannon in fuselage nose with a total of 360 rounds

USA
Douglas P-70 Havoc

It is tempting to reason that it was on account of the USA's preoccupation with daylight bombing that the creation of a night-fighter force to counter any other nation's night bombing was regarded as superfluous. Whether such is even partly accurate or not, the fact remains that the USAAF possessed no dedicated night-fighter in service at the time of Pearl Harbor. Instead it was the British who first exploited the **Douglas A-20** as a night-fighter, converting about one hundred **Boston Mk II** light bomber variants to that role during the winter of 1940-1 by fitting an armament of eight machine-guns and AI Mk IV radar in the nose, flame-damping engine exhaust pipes and additional armour. Known as the **Havoc** in RAF service, this night-fighter first equipped No. 23 Squadron and was also involved in the lengthy Turbinlite (airborne searchlight) night fighting tactic, an almost worthless experiment that lasted about 18 months and occupied the efforts of no fewer than 10 squadrons. Another abortive RAF experiment involving Havocs was the 'Pandora' project, about 20 aircraft (eventually designated Havoc Mk III) being modified to trail the 'Long Aerial Mine' in the path of enemy bomber streams.

When eventually faced with sporadic night air attacks by the Japanese in the Western Pacific in 1942, the Americans decided to modify the A-20 as an interim night-fighter (pending the arrival of the P-61 in service), the first example originally produced for the USAAF undergoing conversion to feature a pair of 1,600-hp (1194-kW) Wright R-2600-11 radials, AI radar in a 'solid' nose and an armament of four 20-mm cannon in a pack under the fuselage. Some 39 **P-70A-1** night-fighters followed in 1943, in which the ventral guns were usually replaced by six 12.7-mm (0.5-in) guns in the nose, as well as a pair of hand-held guns in the rear cockpit; 65 conversions from A-20Gs produced the **P-70A-2**, similar to the P-70A-1 but without the rear guns. Most of these night-fighters were delivered to the squadrons of the 18th Fighter Group, commanded by Colonels Charles R. Greening and Robert A. Zaiser, which flew from Guadalcanal, supported American forces on Bougainville and flew night patrols over US bases in the Solomons. This was the only group to fly the P-70 extensively on operations. The final version was the **P-70B-2** night-fighter trainer, of which 105 were converted from A-20Gs and A-20Js to feature American SCR-720 and SCR-729 radar. These served with the 50th Fighter Group at Alachua Army Air Field, Florida, under Colonel Robert S. Quinn as a night-fighter crew training group before moving to the UK in 1944 as a fighter-bomber unit flying Republic P-47s. With the arrival of the P-61 in service in 1944, P-70As were distributed among the USAAF's new night-fighter

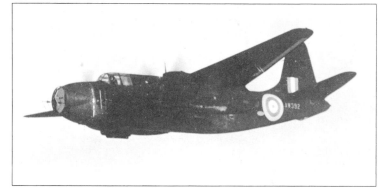

squadrons to provide operational training in AI procedures, but by the end of the year almost all had disappeared from the service's front-line inventory.

Specification
P-70A Havoc
Type: three-seat night-fighter
Powerplant: two 1,600-hp (1193-kW) Wright R-2600-11 14-cylinder air-cooled radial piston engines
Performance: maximum speed 529 km/h (329 mph) at 4265 m (14,000 ft); climb to 3660 m (12,000 ft) in 8 minutes; service ceiling 8610 m (28,250 ft); normal range 1706 km (1,060 miles)
Weights: empty 7272 kg (16,031 lb); maximum take-off 9645 kg (21,264 lb)
Dimensions: span 18.69 m (61 ft 4 in); length 14.50 m (47 ft 7 in); height 5.36 m (17 ft 7 in); wing area 43.11 m²

AW392 was the first Havoc Mk I (Turbinlite), originally supplied to the RAF on a diverted French contract in 1940 and one of the early small-tail series with Twin Wasp engines. AI Mk IV radar was fitted to aim the searchlight, no guns being carried.

(464 sq ft)
Armament: most aircraft (P-70A-2) had six 12.7-mm (0.5-in) machine-guns in nose and two others of the same calibre (hand-held) in rear cockpit

A very rare bird, the Douglas P-70B-1 was a 1943 rebuild of an A-20G attack bomber with AI Mk IV radar and forward-firing armament of six 'fifty-calibre' in packs at the sides of the fuselage. No ventral cannon were fitted.

Northrop P-61 Black Widow

Stung to action in 1940 by events in Europe where night bombing attacks were beginning to assume significant proportions, the US Army Air Corps issued a general requirement for a specialized night-fighter, and to meet this Northrop offered a large twin-boom, twin-engine, three-seat aircraft with provision for yet-to-be developed airborne interception radar and a heavy offensive armament. Two Northrop XP-61 prototypes were ordered on 11 January 1941, and production contracts totalling 573 aircraft were issued within the next 13 months. The first prototype was flown on 21 May 1942, by which time the USA had been at war for nearly six months, and it was to be a further 18 months before the first production **P-61A Black Widow** aircraft appeared, the first 37 aircraft mounting a remotely-controlled dorsal turret with four 12.7-mm (0.5-in) guns in addition to four fixed 20-mm cannon in the fuselage belly. Air flow instability aft of the turret caused its deletion from the 38th aircraft onwards, and the first deliveries were made to the 18th Fighter Group of the USAAF, then based at Guadalcanal. This unit scored its first night victory on 7 July 1944, and the type progressively replaced all the interim Douglas P-70s in service.

The P-61A was not generally considered wholly satisfactory, being plagued by unserviceability of the big R-2800-65 engines; as the situation improved, after 200 of this version had been produced, deliveries of the first of 450 **P-61B** aircraft started, also in July 1944; this version, though still officially termed a night-fighter, was as much an intruder as a true fighter, being capable of carrying up to four 726-kg (1,600-lb) bombs or four 1136-litre (300-US gal) drop tanks under the wings. Some Far East units also carried out field modifications to carry eight 12.7 cm (5-in) rocket projectiles for night use against Japanese surface vessels, but their use was limited on account of the blinding flash of the rocket motors. The final 250 P-61Bs had the dorsal turret reinstated, and the last production version was the **P-61C**, of which 41 were built with 2,800-hp (2088kW) R-2800-73 engines and a top speed of fractionally under 644 km/h (400 mph).

In Europe the Black Widow was severely criticized when tested by the RAF, but deliveries of the first P-61As

Unusual in having a completely unpainted radome over its SCR-720 radar, this early P-61A-1 was one of those delivered with the four-gun turret, and, like all three aircraft illustrated here went to the Pacific. In this case the recipient unit was the USAAF 6th NFS based on Saipan.

Almost all Widows were painted black overall, like this P-61B-15, one of the later models with the turret restored as standard. It was on the strength of one of the later units in the CPA (Central Pacific Area) in 1944, the 548th NFS. Note the 1173-litre (258-gal) drop tanks.

Almost identical to the machine above, this P-61B-1 was assigned to a unit of the US 13th Air Force, the 550th NFS operating in the New Guinea and New Britain area from Morotai in the final nine months of the Pacific war. The turret must have been fitted retroactively.

went ahead to the 422nd Night Fighter Squadron at Scorton, England, on 23 May 1944, followed by the 425th at Charmy Down, their purpose being to provide night protection for the American bases after the Normandy landing then imminent. While based in the UK the P-61s were flown with limited suc-

cess against V-1 flying bombs before being flown to the Continent, where they achieved a few night victories against the relatively small number of German aircraft which operated at night during the last eight months of the war.

Specification
P-61B Black Widow
Type: three-seat night-fighter
Powerplant: two 2,000-hp (1491-kW) Pratt & Whitney R-2800-65 18-cylinder air-cooled radial piston engines
Performance: maximum speed 589 km/h (366 mph) at 6095 m (20,000 ft); climb to 6095 m (20,000 ft) in 12 minutes; service ceiling 10090 m (33,100 ft); maximum range 4506 km (2,800 miles)
Weights: empty 9979 kg (22,000 lb); maximum take-off 13472 kg (29700 lb)
Dimensions: span 20.12 m (66 ft 0 in); length 15.11 m (49 ft 7 in); height 4.46 m (14 ft 8 in); wing area 61.69 m^2 (664 sq ft)
Armament: four 20-mm cannon in fuselage belly fixed to fire forward, plus provision to carry up to four 726-kg (1,600-lb) bombs under the wings; the last 250 aircraft were also armed with four 12.7-mm (0.5-in) machine-guns in remotely-controlled dorsal turret

One of the first P-61s to see action was this P-61A-10 of the 422nd Night Fighter Squadron based at Charmy Down, Scorton and then various advanced bases in France. Their kills were mainly flying bombs and locomotives.

Kawasaki Ki-45 Toryu

Constant development frustrations delayed introduction into service of the Imperial Japanese Army's **Kawasaki Ki-45 Toryu** (dragon killer) until August 1942, its design having been initiated five years earlier, and it was not until 1944 that the night-fighter version, the **Ki-45 KAIc**, became operational as the only army night-fighter of the war. Retaining the two 1,080-hp (805-kW) Mitsubishi Ha-102 radials of the previous Ki-45 KAIb heavy day fighter (an aircraft whose role was akin to that of the German *Zerstörer*), the Ki-45 KAIc was armed with a single forward-firing semi-automatic 37-mm Type 98 cannon in a fairing under the fuselage, two oblique/upward-firing 20-mm Ho-5 cannon in the centre fuselage, and a single hand-held machine-gun in the rear cockpit. It had been intended to fit airborne radar in the nose, and therefore no nose guns were included; however, production difficulties seriously delayed this equipment and it did not enter service, although a single aircraft flew with centimetric radar shortly before the end of the war. Production of the Ki-45 KAIc got underway at Kawasaki's Akashi plant in March 1944, the first aircraft being completed the following month. On 15 June American Boeing B-29s of XX Bomber Command launched their first raid on the Japanese homeland, and were intercepted by eight Toryus

whose pilots shot down eight of the big bombers. At that time about 40 Ki-45 KAIc fighters had been completed, and the aircraft went on to serve with the 4th Sentai at Usuki in the Oita prefecture, the 5th Sentai at Usuki and Komachi in the Aichi prefecture, the 53rd Sentai at Matsudo in the Chiba prefecture, and the 70th Sentai at Kashiwa. Toryus shared the night defence of Japan with the navy's J1N1-S and Yokosuka P1Y1-S, and were probably the most successful in action against the massive American raids in the last six months of the war; the 4th Sentai alone was credited with 150 kills, of which 26 were gained by one pilot, Captain Isamu Kashiide, all despite the lack of any AI radar. Away from the homeland Ki-45 KAIc night-fighters also served with the 45th Sentai in the Philippines and New Guinea

late in 1944, and with the 71st Dokuritsu Hiko Chutai at Singapore in August 1945. Production of the Ki-45 KAIc reached 477 aircraft before being terminated in December 1944. The type was codenamed **'Nick'** by the Allies.

Specification
Ki-45 KAIC
Type: two-seat night-fighter
Powerplant: two 1,080-hp (805-kW) Mitsubishi Ha-102 14-cylinder air-cooled radial piston engines
Performance: maximum speed 540 km/h (335 mph) at 6000 m (19,685 ft); climb to 5000 m (16,405 ft) in 7 minutes; service ceiling 10000 m (32,810 ft); normal range 2000 km (1,243 miles)

Weights: empty 4000 kg (8,818 lb); maximum take-off 5500 kg (12,125 lb)
Dimensions: span 15.02 m (49 ft 3¼ in); length 11.00 m (36 ft 1 in); height 3.70 m (12 ft 1¾ in); wing area 32.00 m² (344.44 sq ft)
Armament: one 37-mm cannon firing forward under nose, two upward-firing 20-mm cannon amidships and one 7.92-mm (0.31-in) hand-held machine-gun in dorsal position

Probably the best surviving picture of a Kawasaki Ki-45, this Ki-45 KAIc night fighter has no radar but carries a 37-mm Ho-203 cannon firing ahead and two 20-mm Ho-5 cannon firing obliquely upwards. A total of 477 was built at Akashi in late 1944.

The Kawasaki Ki-45 Toryu was the Imperial Japanese Army's only night fighter, and despite not being fitted with AI radar was probably their most effective one.

Nakajima J1N1-S Gekko

Just as specialist night-fighter design had largely been ignored by European nations before World War II, Japan's similar failing left the country without adequate night defence when the fortunes of war began their inexorable turn against her in 1943. Fortunately, however, the Imperial Japanese Navy possessed a number of excellent heavy fighters and reconnaissance aircraft, of which the **Nakajima J1N Gekko** (moonlight) had been arriving in service slowly since April 1942 with reconnaissance units in the

Western Pacific. When first encountered in action during the Solomons campaign the aircraft was mistakenly thought to be a fighter and codenamed **'Irving'** by the Allies. As night air attacks were stepped up by the Americans it was the commanding officer of the 251st Kokutai, Commander Yasuna Kozono, then based at Rabaul, New Guinea, who first suggested adaptation of the J1N as a night-fighter by installing two 20-mm cannon in the observer's cockpit, fixed to fire obliquely forward and upward at an angle of 30°,

and another pair firing forward and downward. When two Consolidated B-24s were quickly destroyed, the modifications came to the attention of the Japanese naval staff and an order was placed with Nakajima to go ahead with a dedicated night-fighter version, designed and built as such from scratch. This version, the **J1N1-S**, entered production in August 1943 and continued until December 1944, during which period a total of 420 J1Ns were produced, the great majority of them J1N1-S night-fighters. These differed from the earlier reconnaissance version in having the crew reduced from three to two, the observer's cock-

pit being eliminated and faired over; all aircraft retained the upward-firing cannon, but the downward firing guns (found difficult to aim and seldom used) were omitted from later aircraft, while a third upper gun and a forward-firing 20-mm cannon was fitted in the **J1N1-Sa**. Rudimentary centrimetric AI radar was installed in the nose and some aircraft also carried a small nose searchlight. In service with the 251st, 302nd and 322nd Kokutais, the J1N1-S night-fighters proved fairly effective against the B-24, which was not in any case well-suited to night operations, but with the appearance of the Boeing B-29 the Japanese night-fighters

Most J1N1-S night fighters were black, but this J1N1-Sa, with nose radar, was unpainted. In the rear is a P1Y1.

Nakajima NK1F Sakae 21 14-cylinder air-cooled radial piston engines
Performance: maximum speed 505 km/h (314 mph) at 5840 m (19,160 ft); climb to 5000 m (16,405 ft) in 9 minutes 36 seconds; service ceiling 9320 m (30,610 ft); normal range 2540 km (1,578 miles)
Weights: empty 4840 kg (10,670 lb); maximum take-off 8185 kg (18,045 lb)
Dimensions: span 16.98 m (55 ft 8½ in); length 12.77 m (41 ft 10¾ in); height 4.56 m (14 ft 11⅔ in); wing area 40.00 m² (430.56 sq ft)
Armament: two (sometimes three) upward-firing 20-mm Type 99 cannon, two downward-firing 20-mm cannon and (optional) one forward-firing 20-mm cannon

proved too slow and were seldom able to make more than a single firing attack. Most of them were expended during the final months of the war when, equipped to carry two 250-kg (551-lb) bombs, they were employed in *kamikaze* attacks against ground targets.

Specification
J1N1-S
Type: two-seat night-fighter
Powerplant: two 1,130-hp (843-kW)

FRANCE
Potez 631

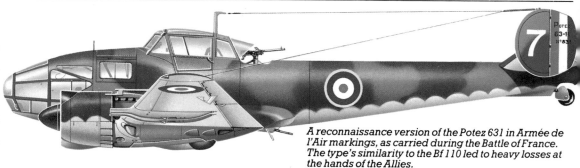

The French **Potez 631** night-fighter corresponded in many respects to the RAF's Bristol Blenheim, being very similar in size and performance (though somewhat lighter) as well as being conceived as a variation of a light bomber. The French aircraft was one of a family of design variations of the Potez 63 which had originated in a requirement issued in 1934 for a two/three-seat 'multi-purpose' aircraft. Although a night-fighter prototype had flown in March 1937 as the **Potez 631-0**, French re-equipment policies were blurred by lack of purpose (being confused by the likely form of warfare being studied by Germany), with the result that orders for development aircraft included four-general purpose two/three-seat day/night fighters, three two-seat night-fighters, one light bomber, one reconnaissance aircraft and one close-support aircraft. Relatively little importance was placed on the Potez 631 night-fighter, and it was not until June 1938 that production orders totalling 207 were confirmed.

By 1 April 1939 the Armée de l'Air had taken delivery of 88 aircraft, of which 20 were in service; in May two night-fighter units, Groupes de Chasse de Nuit GCN III/1 and II/4, and one day fighter unit, GC II/8, were equipped with about 30 aircraft; four other Potez 631s were serving at Djibouti. At the outbreak of war a total of 206 aircraft had been delivered, and the type had also joined GCN I/13 and GCN II/13, as well as seven *escadres de chasse*. Some aircraft were later transferred to the Aéronavale. When the German attack opened in the West the various Potez 631 units were in constant action both by day and night, although lack of radar prevented much success during the hours of darkness. In the first 11 days of the campaign Aéronavale's Flotille F1C shot down 12 German aircraft for the loss of eight, but the Armée de l'Air night-fighter units were ordered to assume day ground-attack duties, losing heavily to enemy flak. Moreover, losses were exceptionally heavy to Allied guns and fighters as a result of the Potez 631's superficial similarity to the German Messerschmitt Bf 110; it has been estimated that as many as 30 of the French aircraft were shot down in error. In all, Potez 631 night-fighters destroyed a total of 29 German aircraft in the Battle of France, but for a loss of 93 of their own number. Of the remainder about 110 were in the Free French Zone (Vichy France) at the time of the armistice, but their number dwindled quickly because of a chronic lack of spares, although ECN 3/13 moved to Tunisia with a small number of Potez 631s in June 1941.

A reconnaissance version of the Potez 631 in Armée de l'Air markings, as carried during the Battle of France. The type's similarity to the Bf 110 led to heavy losses at the hands of the Allies.

Specification
Potez 631
Type: two-seat night-fighter
Powerplant: two 700-hp (522-kW) Gnome-Rhône 14 air-cooled radial piston engines
Performance: maximum speed 442 km/h (275 mph) at 4500 m (14,765 ft); climb to 4000 m (13,125 ft) in 5 minutes 54 seconds; service ceiling 8800 m (28,870 ft); range 1220 km (758 miles)
Weights: empty about 2450 kg (5,401 lb); maximum take-off about 3760 kg (8,289 lb)
Dimensions: span 16.00 m (52 ft 6 in); length 11.07 m (36 ft 4 in); height 3.62 m (11 ft 10½ in); wing area 32.70 m² (351.98 sq ft)
Armament: two fixed forward-firing 20-mm cannon under fuselage and one hand-held 7.5-mm (0.295-in) machine-gun in dorsal position; some aircraft were also fitted with two 7.5-mm (0.295-in) machine-guns under each wing

Though over 300 Potez 631 night fighters had been delivered at the time of the French Armistice on 25 June 1940, at least 70 and possibly many more either had no propellers or had them removed deliberately. This one was luckier, and flew with a unit of GCN 13 in the Battle for France.

Allied and Axis Flying-Boats

During the early years of World War II, flying-boats were of crucial importance in allowing long-range maritime patrols. However, with the introduction of very long-range land-based aircraft, which had greater flexibility and which could operate from ordinary airfields, the flying-boats gradually faded from the scene.

If glamour ever attached to fighting men there was little but monotony in the work of the flying-boat crews of World War II. Few nations had paid heed to this class of military aeroplane in the years of peace beforehand, with the result that when war came recourse was widely made to the adaptation of ageing commercial aircraft and none of the belligerent powers produced a wholly new design from concept during the war years in time to reach production and service. As might be expected from the maritime nations, the USA, the UK and Japan possessed the most consistently successful aircraft from the outset: the Consolidated PBY Catalina, the Short Sunderland and the Kawasaki H8K 'Emily' boats respectively.

For the UK alone the work of RAF Coastal Command's flying-boats was vital for the nation's survival: given the existence of brutally effective submarine warfare, responsibility for airborne countermeasures and protection of the UK's vulnerable shipping lanes fell squarely on that command's aircrews and their Sunderlands and Catalinas.

Germany, on the other hand, had afforded low priority to the military flying-boat and only an adaptation of the excellent but

The Consolidated PBY Catalina was the workhorse of Allied maritime reconnaissance work and the leading type in its class. It was the 'Cat' which shadowed the German battleship *Bismarck*.

venerable Dornier Do 18 had reached service status by 1939. The radical Blohm und Voss Bv 138 had been slow in development and suffered numerous problems before finally achieving an acceptable combat status.

Both Japan and the United States produced really superlative military flying-boats, the Kawasaki H8K proving to possess a most

impressive performance; the Catalina, of which more were produced than all other flying-boats of all nations combined, came to provide the yardstick by which all maritime reconnaissance work would be measured.

Yet World War II was to sound the death knell of the big 'boat' for, even as the Catalinas and Sunderlands were ranging far

over the oceans, the very-long-range land-based aeroplane (exemplified by the Consolidated Liberator) was proving to be no less effective. Being more readily available and requiring none of the special base facilities of the flying-boat, this craft pointed a different path to the future, a path that has consigned these graceful 'boats' to the pages of history.

Saro Lerwick

UK

The twin-engine **Saro Lerwick** was an attractive and compact design intended to meet a medium-range maritime reconnaissance requirement, Specification R.1/36, but was a total failure. First flown before the end of 1938, the prototype featured twin fins and rudders but from the outset was found to be seriously lacking in lateral stability, and displayed a determination to roll and yaw in cruising flight, making the aircraft impossible to fly 'hands off', a damning indictment for a maritime patrol aircraft. In due course a single fin and rudder was fitted, but not until this was considerably enlarged was any improvement in the handling characteristics discernible. Starting with the seventh production example, wing incidence was increased and enlarged propellers fitted to the Hercules II radials, but the latter were found unsuitable for operating on rough water. Moreover, stalling tests showed the Lerwick to have vicious traits, the stall under alighting conditions being accompanied by sharp wing-drop. Nevertheless 21 examples were produced and the Lerwick was first delivered for service with No. 209 Squadron in December 1939 at Oban, but after the type had flown a small number of semi-operational patrols it was decided to abandon further efforts to rectify its problems. The last eight aircraft were powered by Hercules

IVs and the final example was completed in November 1940; one aircraft was flown by No. 240 Squadron but was lost on 20 February of that year, and some flew with No. 4 Operational Training Unit at Invergordon.

Specification
Saro Lerwick
Type: six-crew medium-range reconnaissance flying-boat
Powerplant: two 1,375-hp (1026-kW) Bristol Hercules II 14-cylinder air-cooled radials

Performance: maximum speed 348 km/h (216 mph) at 1220 m (4,000 ft); initial climb rate 268 m (880 ft) per minute; service ceiling 4265 m (14,000 ft)
Weights: normal loaded 12928 kg (28,500 lb); overload take-off 15060 kg (33,200 lb)
Dimensions: span 24.63 m (80 ft 10 in); length 19.39 m (63 ft 7½ in); height 6.10 m (20 ft 0 in); wing area 78.50 m² (845 sq ft)
Armament: one 7.7-mm (0.303-in) machine-gun in nose turret, twin 7.7-

The ill-fated Saro Lerwick, which served with only a single Coastal Command squadron, No. 209, at Oban, Pembroke Dock and Stranraer. As can be seen, the aircraft rode very low in the water and demanded considerable distance to become airborne.

mm (0.303-in) machine-guns in dorsal turret and four 7.7-mm (0.303-in) machine-guns in tail turret, plus up to 907 kg (2,000 lb) of bombs, mines or depth charges

Saro London

UK

Reflecting the design concept of British flying-boats that had originated in the 1920s, the **Saro London** twin-engine biplane was an all-metal aircraft with fabric-covered wings and tail, and a metal-skinned hull. The type served with RAF Coastal Command during the first two years of World War II. Designed to Air Ministry Specification R.24/31, the prototype first flew in 1934 with two 750-hp (559-kW) Bristol Pegasus III radials, the engines being mounted on the top wing to be well clear of spray while taking off and landing; the prototype went on to serve for periods between 1934 and 1936 with Nos 209 and 210 Squadrons at Felixstowe and Gibraltar. Production deliveries started in March 1936 with Pegasus III engines, but from the eleventh aircraft the Pegasus X was fitted and the aircraft's designation changed to **London Mk II**, this variant equipping Nos 201 and 204 Squadrons in 1936 at Calshot and Mount Batten repectively. In 1937 they joined No. 202 Squadron at Kalafrana (Malta) and No. 228 Squadron at Pembroke Dock respectively. By the outbreak of war in September 1939 Londons still equipped No. 201 Squadron, then at Sullom Voe in the Shetland Islands, and No. 202 Squadron still at Gibraltar, while No. 240 Squadron had re-equipped with Londons in July 1939 and was stationed at Invergordon. These flying-boats carried out sea patrols over the North Sea and the Mediterranean, some aircraft being fitted with a large dorsal fuel tank to increase their range. Bombs, depth charges and (occasionally) mines up to a total weight of 2,000 lb (907 kg) could be carried under the lower wing roots. Indeed, the old biplanes undertook a considerable share of the patrol work over the North Sea, keeping watch for the likely

breakout into the Atlantic by German surface and submarine raiders as well as the return to German port by blockade runners. Gradually maritime reconnaissance aircraft such as the Lockheed Hudson came to assume these responsibilities while Short Sunderland flying-boats equipped the squadrons flying over the Atlantic and Mediterranean. The Londons were replaced on No. 201 Squadron in April 1940, followed two months later by those on No. 240 Squadron. Only No. 202 Squadron continued to fly Londons at Gibraltar until June 1941.

Specification
Saro London Mk II
Type: six-crew coastal reconnaissance flying-boat
Powerplant: two 920-hp (686-kW) Bristol Pegasus X nine-cylinder air-cooled radials
Performance: maximum speed 228 km/h (142 mph) at sea level; initial climb rate 360 m (1,180 ft) per minute; service ceiling 6065 m (19,900 m); maximum range 2800 km (1,740 miles)
Weights: empty 5035 kg (11,100 lb); maximum take-off 9979 kg (22,000 lb)

Dimensions: span 24.38 m (80 ft 0 in); length 17.31 m (56 ft 9½ in); height 5.71 m (18 ft 9 in); wing area 132.38 m² (1,425 sq ft)
Armament: single hand-held 7.7-mm (0.303-in) Lewis machine-guns in open bow, midships and tail positions, plus up to 907 kg (2,000 lb) of bombs, mines or depth charges carried externally under the lower wings

Saro London flying-boats still served with Nos 201, 202 and 240 Sqns when war broke out in 1939. This example, of No. 240 Sqn, was based at Sullom Voe and Invergordon in 1939-40.

A pre-war shot of a Saro London Mk I. These big aircraft, together with the Supermarine Stranraer, marked the end of a nostalgic era.

Supermarine Walrus

One of the unsung heroes of World War II, the **Supermarine Walrus** amphibian was a private venture development of the 1922 Seagull I, and indeed first flew as the **Seagull V** on 21 June 1933. A production order by the Australian government prompted evaluation by the Royal Navy's No. 702 Catapult Flight, which in turn led to an initial contract for 12 **Walrus Mk I** aircraft being placed by the Air Ministry in 1935. Following further trials, during which a Walrus was catapulted fully-loaded from HMS *Nelson*, production orders for 204 aircraft with the 635-hp (474-kW) Pegasus II M2 radial were placed, and the little flying-boat entered Fleet Air Arm service in 1936. Early in World War II Walrus amphibians were serving aboard battleships and cruisers of the Royal Navy all over the world as components of No. 700 Squadron, as well as with Nos 701, 711, 712 and 714 Squadrons, their principal duties being over-the-horizon search for enemy shipping; they were also employed for gunnery spotting, anti-submarine and convoy protection duties. A Walrus was even catapulted from the cruiser HMS *Dorsetshire* to bomb a target in Italian Somaliland on 18 November 1940.

Undoubtedly the work for which the Walrus (affectionately known as the Shagbat) will be best remembered was air/sea rescue, serving in this role with Nos 269, 275, 276, 277, 278, 281 and 282 Squadrons at stations in the United Kingdom, and with Nos 283, 284, 292 and 294 Squadrons in the Middle East. Called out in any weather, day or night, Walrus air/sea rescue aircraft frequently alighted in enemy coastal waters to pick up ditched Allied airmen from their dinghies, sometimes putting down in minefields where rescue launches could not venture. With their curious pusher engine nacelle located between the wings (and angled off centre), the sight of a Walrus to a shot-down airman meant the difference between rescue and years in a prison camp. The Walrus was slowly replaced in service from 1944 onwards by the tractor Mercury-powered Sea Otter from the same stable, although No. 624 Squadron was re-formed at

The Supermarine Walrus served with the Royal Air Force principally in the air-sea rescue role, mainly in the UK but also abroad; although frequently required to fly close to enemy shores, they were not provided with a gun with which to offer defence.

An example of a Walrus in Fleet Air Arm markings. Although ostensibly supplied to the larger vessels of the Royal Navy for gunnery spotting duties, they were more frequently used to transport officers and despatches between ships and shore.

Grottaglie in Italy in December that year with Walrus aircraft for mine-spotting duties. A total of 740 Walrus aircraft was built, production of the Walrus Mk I with metal-clad hull being terminated at Supermarine after 287 had been completed; thereafter production was switched to Saunders-Roe who built 453 **Walrus Mk II** aircraft with wooden hulls before finally ending in January 1944.

Specification
Supermarine Walrus Mk II
Type: three/four-crew shipboard observation and air/sea rescue amphibian flying-boat
Powerplant: one 775-hp (578-kW) Bristol Pegasus VI nine-cylinder air-cooled radial
Performance: maximum speed 200 km/h (124 mph) at sea level; initial climb rate 320 m (1,050 ft) per minute; service ceiling 5640 m (18,500 ft); range 965 km (600 miles)
Weights: empty 2223 kg (4,900 lb); maximum take-off 3266 kg (7,200 lb)
Dimensions: span 13.97 m (45 ft 10 in); length 11.45 m (37 ft 7 in); height 4.65 m (15 ft 3 in); wing area 56.67 m²

(610 sq ft)
Armament: one 7.7-mm (0.303-in) machine-gun on open bow position, plus up to 227 kg (500 lb) of bombs or depth charges on underwing racks (shipboard version only)

A Walrus taxis in to be hoisted aboard its parent cruiser; the crew member perched beside the engine nacelle will attach the lifting gear to a lug in the top wing for hoisting.

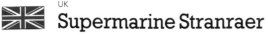

Supermarine Stranraer

Designed to the same specification, R.24/31, as the Saro London, the **Supermarine Stranraer** twin-engine biplane flying-boat survived in service slightly longer than the other, and was generally preferred by those crews who were able to compare the two types. The prototype, originally known as the **Singapore V**, was powered by Bristol Pegasus IIIM radials driving two-blade wooden propellers and first flew in mid-1935, but was immediately renamed Stranraer. It also underwent comparative trials with the London on No. 210 Squadron in October and November 1935, during which it was found to be somewhat underpowered. Production deliveries of aircraft powered by a pair of Pegasus X radials driving a three-blade Fairey Reed metal propeller started December 1936, and the type was declared operational in April the following year with No. 228 Squadron at Pembroke Dock, remaining with this squadron until April 1939. In December 1938 Stranraers joined No. 209 Squadron at Felixstowe, and later moving to Invergordon and Oban for patrols over the North Sea until supplanted by the ill-fated Lerwick the following year. No. 240 Squadron was the only other RAF Coastal Command squadron to fly the Stranraer, converting to the aircraft in June 1940 at Pembroke Dock for short-range patrol work over the Western Approaches; the Stranraers were eventually replaced by Catalina 'boats in March 1941. Although RAF Stranraers did not serve at overseas stations, a total of 40 aircraft was licence-built by Canadian-Vickers between 1939 and 1941, and served in the coastal reconnaissance/anti-submarine role with the RCAF until finally replaced by the Consolidated Canso (Catalina) during 1943.

Above: No. 240 Sqn Stranraer flying-boat K7295 based at Pembroke Dock, South Wales, in 1940 for patrols over the Western Approaches; in July that year the squadron moved to Oban and converted to Catalina boats the following March.

Right: A quartet of Stranraers of No. 209 Sqn at Felixstowe, Suffolk, in May 1939. Note the absence of camouflage (applied on the outbreak of war) and the underwing fuel tanks. Just before the war the squadron moved north to Invergordon.

Specification
Supermarine Stranraer
Type: seven-crew coastal reconnaissance flying-boat
Powerplant: two 920-hp (686-kW) Bristol Pegasus X nine-cylinder air-cooled radials
Performance: maximum speed 241 km/h (150 mph) at sea level; initial climb rate 411 m (1,350 ft) per minute; service ceiling 5640 m (18,500 ft); range 1609 km (1,000 miles)
Weights: empty 5103 kg (11,250 lb); maximum take-off 8618 kg (19,000 lb)
Dimensions: span 25.91 m (85 ft 0 in); length 16.71 m (54 ft 10 in); height 6.63 m (21 ft 9 in); wing area 135.36 m² (1,457 sq ft)
Armament: single hand-held 7.7-mm (0.303-in) machine guns in open bow, midships and tail positions, plus up to 454 kg (1,000 lb) of bombs, mines or depth charges carried on underwing racks

Short Sunderland

The graceful Short C-class 'Empire' flying-boat, ordered for Imperial Airways in 1934, marked the greatest-ever single step forward in the design of the flying-boat and, with the issue of a military specification, R.2/33, for a four-engine monoplane reconnaissance flying-boat, it was perhaps logical to adapt the new airliner to meet this requirement. The first prototype **Short Sunderland** was flown in October 1937 and was followed only eight months later by the first production **Sunderland Mk I** aircraft. By the outbreak of war four squadrons, No. 204 at Sullom Voe, No. 210 at Pembroke Dock, No. 228 returning to the UK from Egypt and No. 230 at Singapore, had been equipped with the Sunderland Mk I. The big 'boat was quickly in the news when, on 21 September 1939, two aircraft of Nos 204 and 228 Squadrons rescued the entire crew of the torpedoed merchantman *Kensington Court*. In January 1940 a U-boat scuttled itself on sighting an aircraft of No. 228 Squadron. Some 75 Sunderland Mk Is were

produced and went on to equip Nos 95, 201 and 270 Squadrons before the **Sunderland Mk II** with Pegasus XVIII radials and ASV.Mk II radar was introduced at the end of 1941, a year which saw Sunderlands carrying to safety hundreds of British troops during the evacuation of Greece and Crete. A total of 55 Sunderland Mk IIs were built by Short Bros and Blackburn, equipping Nos 119, 201, 202, 204, 228 and 230 Squadrons. The **Sunderland Mk II** introduced a new planing bottom to the hull, the less pronounced forward step giving better unstick characteristics; 407 of this version (including the **Sunderland Mk IIIA** with ASV.Mk III radar) were produced by the same two manufacturers and joined Nos 95, 119, 201, 202, 204, 228, 230, 246, 270, 330 and 343 Squadrons. Late in 1943 the final production version, the **Sunderland Mk V** with Pratt & Whitney engines and ASV.Mk VIc radar, started to appear; 143 examples of this version were produced, and by the end of the war Sunderlands equipped no fewer

than 28 RAF squadrons the world over. Very early in the war this fine aeroplane had earned the German nickname *Stachelschwein* (porcupine) on account of its ability to defend itself with its bristling machine-guns, and indeed the Sunderland gained an impressive war record, often having to engage U-boats on the surface (and sinking many of them), and being engaged by enemy fighters and other aircraft. Yet for all its spectacular achievements, the Sunderland's real contribution to the war at sea lay in the long, monotonous patrols far out over the oceans in company with the UK's shipping convoys, when the mere presence of the big 'boat was enough reason to discourage many a U-boat commander from launching an attack.

Specification
Short Sunderland Mk V
Type: 10-crew long-range maritime reconnaissance flying-boat
Powerplant: four 1,200-hp (895-kW) Pratt & Whitney R-1830-90 Twin Wasp 14-cylinder air-cooled radials
Performance: maximum speed 349 km/h (213 mph) at 1525 m (5,000 ft); climb to 3660 m (12,000 ft) in 16.0 minutes; service ceiling 5445 m (17,900 ft); normal range 4765 km (2,960 miles)
Weights: empty 16738 kg (36,900 lb); maximum take-off 27216 kg (60,000 lb)
Dimensions: span 34.36 m (112 ft 9½ in); length 26.00 m (85 ft 3½ in); height 10.52 m (34 ft 6 in); wing area 138.14 m² (1,487 sq ft)
Armament: two fixed forward-firing 7.7-mm (0.303-in) machine-guns, two 7.7-mm (0.303-in) machine-guns each in bow and dorsal turrets, and four 7.7-mm (0.303-in) in tail turret, plus a bombload of up to 2250 kg (4,960 lb) of bombs, mines or depth charges on retractable racks in hull sides

Blohm und Voss Bv 138

Originally conceived in 1934 as a very-long-range reconnaissance flying-boat, the **Blohm und Voss Ha 138 V1** prototype was first flown on 15 July 1937 as a shoulder gull-wing flying-boat with twin tail booms and three Jumo 205C engines. Directional stability and poor water handling characteristics in the prototype caused extensive redesign in the pre-production version, the **Bv 138A-0**, of which six were built with a considerably enlarged hull and an ungulled wing.

The first 25 production **Bv 138A-1** aircraft flew in April 1940, taking a limited part in the invasion of Norway, and entered general service in western France late that year. Considerable structural strengthening was found to be necessary and this was incorporated in the **Bv 138B-1**, 14 of which emerged from the production line in December, and seven more in 1941, powered by 880-hp (656-kW) Jumo 205D engines. A new turret was introduced mounting a single MG 151 20-mm cannon forward of the pilot's cockpit and another in the rear of the hull. The Bv 138Bs were very active in 1941, particularly those based in Norway after the sailing of the first North Cape convoys. Trouble had been experienced with the Bv 138B-1's engines and propellers, however, and an improved version, the **Bv 138C-1**, in which all the previous problems were eliminated, began appearing in March 1941; 227 of this version were built before production was terminated midway through 1943. In this model the centre Jumo 205D drove a four-blade propeller and provision was made for increased bombloads. The most successful exponents of the Bv 138C were probably the crews of Küstenfliegergruppe 406 based in northern Norway, this unit being responsible for much of the successful locating and shadowing of the North Cape convoys, particularly PQ 16 in April 1942. Some aircraft were equipped with FuG 200 Hohentwiel search radar for anti-shipping duties, while in the transport role the Bv 138 could carry up to 10 passengers. All versions could be fitted with two 500-kg (1,102-lb) thrust assisted take-off rockets, and a number of redundant Bv 138B-0s, redesignated **Bv 138MS**, were fitted with a large dural hoop energized by an auxiliary generator for magnetic mine clearance with the *Minensuchsgruppe*.

Specification
Blohm und Voss Bv 138C-1
Type: five-crew long-range maritime reconnaissance flying-boat
Powerplant: three 880-hp (656-kW) Junkers Jumo 205D 12-cylinder inline diesel engines
Performance: maximum speed 285 km/h (177 mph) at 3000 m (9,845 ft); normal service ceiling 5000 m (16,405 ft); maximum range 4300 km (2,672 miles)
Weights: empty 11780 kg (25,970 lb); maximum take-off 17670 kg (38,995 lb)
Dimensions: span 26.94 m (88 ft 4 in); length 19.85 m (65 ft 1½ in); height 5.90 m (19 ft 4¼ in); wing area 112.00 m² (1,205.56 sq ft)
Armament: one 20-mm MG 151 cannon each in bow and stern turrets, one 13-mm (0.51-in) MG 131 machine-gun in open position aft of central engine, and one 7.92-mm (031-in) MG 15 gun in

Wearing the customary splinter camouflage and yellow theatre bands, this Blohm und Voss Bv 138C-1 served with 3(F) Staffel, Seeaufklärungsgruppe 125, based at Constanza, Bulgaria, in April 1943 for service over the Black Sea.

Nicknamed the Flying Clog (der fliegende Holschuh) – reflected in its unit badge – this Bv 138C-1/U1 of 1.(F)/SAGr 130 was based at Trondheim, Norway, in April 1944 and sports a temporary winter camouflage.

Blohm und Voss Bv 138 three-engine flying-boats replaced Dornier Do 18s of 6/MSGr 1 (previously Küstenfliegergruppe 506), this Bv 138MS being based at Grossenbrode in the last year of the war.

hatch of starboard side of hull, plus up to four 150-kg (331-lb) depth charges or equivalent weight of bombs on six racks

The curious three-engined Blohm und Voss Bv 138C-1 suffered lengthy development problems but eventually emerged as an effective aircraft. It was chiefly employed in the Baltic and against the North Cape convoys to the Soviet Union.

Blohm und Voss Bv 222 Wiking

Largest flying-boat to achieve production status during World War II, the six-engine **Blohm und Voss Bv 222 Wiking** was designed in 1936 to provide Deutsche Lufthansa with a 24-passenger airliner for the North and South Atlantic routes, but it was not until 7 September 1940 that the first prototype **Bv 222 V1** was first flown by Flugkapitän Helmut Wasa Rodig. Flying characteristics were pronounced good and the first operation for the Luftwaffe was flown by a civilian crew between Hamburg and Kirkenes, Norway, on 10 July 1941. Usually escorted by a pair of Messerchmitt Bf 110 fighters the Bv 222 V1, with six Bramo Fafnir radials, then started flying regular supply missions across the Mediterranean for German forces in North Africa. Several narrow escapes from Allied fighters emphasized the need for some defensive armament and the second and subsequent prototypes included a number of gun positions, while the Bv 222 V1 was fitted with seven single 7.92-mm (0.31-in) and 13-mm (0.51-in) machine-guns, and under each wing a gondola mounting a pair of the latter. The **Bv 222 V3** featured gun turrets on top of the wing between the outboard engines, each with a 20-mm cannon. By March 1943 a total of seven transport prototypes had been completed, all with armament variations; all served with Lufttransportstaffel See 222 (LTS See 222) in the Mediterranean, three being lost (two shot down by fighters and one sunk after striking a buoy while landing at Athens). The remaining aircraft, the **Bv 222 V2, Bv 222 V3, Bv 222 V4** and **Bv 222 V5**, were converted for maritime reconnaissance and served with Fliegerführer Atlantik, some with FuG 200 search radar; the Bv 222 V3 and Bv 222 V5 were destroyed at their moorings at Biscarosse by Allied fighters in June 1943, and another aircraft was shot down by an Avro Lancaster over the Bay of Biscay in the following October. The Bv 222 V7 was the prototype

of the production version, the **Bv 222C**, of which five examples were completed with six 1,000-hp (746-kW) Junkers Jumo 205D or 207C diesel inlines and a total armament of three 20-mm and five 13-mm (0.51-in) guns. Of these one was shot down by a British night-fighter near Biscarosse and another was hit by strafing Mustangs at Travemünde; the Bv 222 V2 was destroyed during the Allied reoccupation of Norway; two others were sunk by their crews at the end of the war, two were flown to the USA and one was ferried to the UK after the end of hostilities.

Specification
Blohm und Voss Bv 222C-0
Type: 11/14-crew long-range reconnaissance and transport flying-boat
Powerplant: six 1,000-hp (746-kW) Junkers Jumo 207C 12-cylinder diesel inline engines
Performance: maximum speed 390 km/h (242 mph) at 5000 m (16,405 ft); initial climb rate 144 m (472 ft) per minute; service ceiling 7300 m (23,950 ft); range 6100 km (3,790 miles)
Weights: empty 30680 kg (67,367 lb); maximum take-off 50000 kg (108,026 lb)

The fifth Blohm und Voss Bv 222A-O was delivered to Lufttransportstaffel (See) 222 at Petsamo, Finland, in 1943 for transport duties over the northern sector of the Eastern Front. Note the over-wing gun turret.

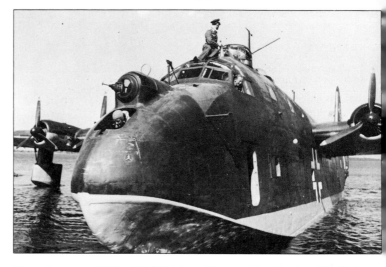

Dimensions: span 46.00 m (150 ft 11 in); length 37.00 m (121 ft 4⅔ in); height 10.90 m (35 ft 9 in); wing area 255.00 m² (2,745 sq ft)
Armament: one 13-mm (0.51-in) machine-gun in bow position, one 20-mm cannon each in forward dorsal turret and in two overwing turrets, and four 13-mm (0.51-in) machine-guns in cabin windows; in the transport role

The considerable size of the Blohm und Voss Bv 222 six-engined flying-boat is evident from this photo of what is probably one of the prototypes. The struts on top and sides of the nose are the mountings for the FuG 200 search radar antenna

the Bv 222 could carry about 92 fully-armed troops

Dornier Do 18

Culmination of a series of successful pre-war flying-boats, which had begun as the Dornier Wal (whale) in the 1920s and progressed through the transatlantic mailplanes (the *Monsun, Zyklon, Zephir, Pampero* and *Aeolus*), the **Dornier Do 18D** was the first military adaptation of this attractive aeroplane. Powered by a pair of liquid-cooled 600-hp (448-kW) Jumo 205C diesel inline engines mounted in tandem in a nacelle on the high-mounted wing, the **Do 18D-1** and **Do 18D-2** started appearing in 1938 and were operational in September that year, it becoming customary to equip the second *Staffel* on each of the Luftwaffe's Küstenfliegergruppen (coastal patrol groups) with the Do 18 (eg 2./KüFlGr 306), the others usually flying Heinkel He 59 floatplanes. Armament of these aircraft comprised a single 7.92-mm (0.31-in) machine-gun in an open bow position and another in a midships position. In 1939 a more powerful version, the **Do 18G-1** with a pair of 880-hp (656-kW) Jumo 205Ds, was introduced with a 13-mm (0.51-in) MG 131 heavy machine-gun in the open bow position and a power-operated gun turret amidships mount-

Developed from the successful commercial mail-carrying flying-boats, the Dornier Do 18D entered Luftwaffe service in 1938. The aircraft shown served on 3./Küstenfliegergruppe 406 at List, Sylt, in August 1939. Note the open bow and midships gun positions.

A Dornier Do 18G is hoisted from the water onto its servicing trolley; the nose and midships armament is clearly visible, as are the unusual tandem engine arrangement and stabilizing sponsons.

ing a single 20-mm MG 151 cannon. At the beginning of World War II Do 18Gs were equipping Küstenfliegergruppen 106, 406 and 906. Indeed it was an aircraft of 2./KüFlGr 106 that was the first German aircraft to fall to British guns on 26 September 1939; three Do 18s were shadowing British capital ships in the North Sea when they were attacked by nine Blackburn Skuas of No. 803 Squadron; one of the Dorniers was forced down and, after its crew had been taken aboard a British destroyer, it was sunk by gunfire. A total of 49 Do 18Gs was produced during 1940, but manufacture was terminated in September that year after fewer than 100 aircraft, including 70 Do 18Gs, had been completed. During the Battle of France six *Staffeln* were flying Do 18s, but in June 1940 most were withdrawn for conversion to the **Do 18H** dual-control trainer and the **Do 18N-1** air-sea rescue versions. During the Battle of Britain only 2./KüFlGr 106 was still fully operational with the Do 18, the majority of work being confined to air-

sea rescue in the English Channel. However, 3./KüFlGr 906 returned to operations and continued to fly Do 18s over the North Sea until 1942, when the Do 18s were replaced by Blohm und Voss Bv 138s.

Specification
Dornier Do 18G-1
Type: four-crew medium-range maritime reconnaissance flying-boat

The Dornier Do 18 entered service over the Mediterranean in 1941, performing air-sea rescue duties in the Malta-Sicily area. This Do 18G of 6. Seenotstaffel features the midships gun turret of the later service versions.

Powerplant: two 880-hp (656-kW) Junkers Jumo 205D 12-cylinder liquid-cooled diesel inline engines
Performance: maximum speed 266 km/h (165 mph) at 2000 m (6,560 ft); climb to 1000 m (3,280 ft) in 7 minutes 48 seconds; service ceiling 4200 m (13,800 ft); maximum range 3500 km (2,175 miles)
Weights: empty 5980 kg (13,180 lb); maximum take-off 10800 kg (23,810 lb)

Dimensions: span 23.70 m (77 ft 9¼ in); length 19.37 m (63 ft 7 in); height 5.32 m (17 ft 5½ in); wing area 98.00 m² (1,054.86 sq ft)
Armament: one 13-mm (0.51-in) MG 131 machine-gun in bow position and one 20-mm MG 151 cannon in power-operated turret amidships, plus provision for four 50-kg (110-lb) bombs

GERMANY

Dornier Do 24

Another graceful Dornier flying-boat was the **Dornier Do 24**, originally designed in 1936 to meet a Royal Netherlands naval air service requirement for a flying-boat to operate in the East Indies. The Do 24 was a large parasol-wing monoplane with three engines on the wing and with *Flossentummeln* (sponsons) for stability on the water. The first flight by a prototype Do 24, powered by three 890-hp (664-kW) Wright R-1820 Cyclone radials, was made on 3 July 1937, this aircraft being delivered to The Netherlands that year and followed by the export of 11 similar production aircraft designated **Do 24K**. Licence production by Aviolanda/de Schelde accounted for 25 further aircraft before the invasion by Germany of 10 May 1940; many of these Dutch aircraft subsequently saw service in the Pacific theatre and six eventually found their way into the Royal Australian Air Force. Meanwhile the aircraft that had been partly completed in The Netherlands were transferred to Germany, and under the designation **Do 24N-1** were completed and issued to the Luftwaffe for air-sea rescue duties. Production in The Netherlands was resumed in 1941 under German supervision, 16 maritime reconnaissance/transport derivatives (the **Do 24T-1** and **Do 24T-2**) being completed that year. In 1942 the French seaplane manufacturer, Chantiers Aéro-Maritimes de la Seine (CAMS), then of course under German control, joined the Do 24T production programme and produced 46 examples to add to 154 from The Netherlands. Some of the French-built aircraft had not been completed at the time of the German retreat from France in 1944 and these were subsequently delivered to the French navy, whose Flottille 9F Tr was formed on 5 December that year to operate them.

In Luftwaffe service the Do 24N served on three *Staffeln* of the Seenotgruppe (air-sea rescue group) at Berre, near Marseilles, and at Biscarosse. The 2. and 3./KG 200 (which flew Focke-Wulf Fw 200s on long distance maritime patrols) also flew a small number of Do 24Ns for rescue pur-

A Dornier Do 24 wearing the skull emblem of the 8. Seenotstaffel, SBK XII operating in the Black Sea area during 1942. The Do 24 was especially suitable for the air-sea rescue role due to its unrivalled rough-water capabilities.

Contrary to wartime propaganda by the Allies, the Germans were scrupulous in omitting all armament from aircraft bearing Red Cross markings, as in this Dornier Do 24 flying-boat employed in casualty evacuation and air-sea rescue.

poses, as did the small semi-autonomous ASR flights under command of the Seenotdienstführer.

Specification
Dornier Do 24T-1
Type: five/six-crew maritime reconnaissance and transport flying-boat
Powerplant: three 1,000-hp (746-kW) BMW/Bramo Fafnir 323R-2 nine-cylinder air-cooled radials
Performance: maximum speed 340 km/h (211 mph) at 2000 m (6,560 m); climb to 2000 m (6,560 ft) in 14 minutes 30 seconds; service ceiling 5900 m (19,355 ft); maximum range 4750 km (2,950 miles)
Weights: empty 9100 kg (20,062 lb); maximum take-off 18400 kg (40,564 lb)
Dimensions: span 27.00 m (87 ft 7 in); length 22.00 m (72 ft 4 in); height 5.75 m

(18 ft 10¼ in); wing area 108.00 m² (1,162.5 sq ft)
Armament: one 7.92-mm (0.31-in) MG 15 machine-gun each in bow and tail positions and one 20-mm MG 151 cannon in midships turret, plus provision to carry up to 12 50-kg (110-lb) bombs

A Dornier Do 24, probably one of the Netherlands-built Do 24N-1s which were modified for service with the Luftwaffe and served with the Seenotstaffeln on air-sea rescue duties in the Mediterranean.

Kawanishi H6K

Owing much to current American and French flying-boat design of the mid-1930s, the large four-engine **Kawanishi Type 97** parasol monoplane flying-boat, which had first flown in July 1936, was Japan's only in-service long-range reconnaissance flying-boat when that nation went to war in December 1941, much effort having been dissipated in transport conversions and deliveries to Japan's commercial operators in the Pacific. The **H6K1** initial military version entered limited service with the Imperial Japanese Navy in 1938, and was followed by 10 **H6K2** flying-boats. The first major production version, the **H6K4** was powered by four Mitsubishsi Kinsei 43 radials and armed with four 7.7-mm (0.303-in) machine-guns in bow and midships positions and a 20-mm cannon in a tail turret, and was capable of carrying two 800-kg (1,764-lb) bombs or torpedoes, a total of 66 being in service at the time of Pearl Harbor; later aircraft were powered by Kinsei 46 engines. These 'boats were widely employed, although the initial heavy defeats inflicted on the Allies in the Pacific rendered maritime reconnaissance duties subordinate to the need for air transportation of Japanese troops during the swift conquests in the East Indies and elsewhere. A number of aircraft, designated **H6K4-L**, were therefore converted for transport duties and were each able to accommodate about 18 fully-armed troops; lacking armour and self-sealing fuel tanks, however, they were extremely vulnerable to fighter attacks and, after a number had been shot down, a new version entered production as the **H6K5** in August

1942; by that time the maritime reconnaissance version had been given the reporting codename **'Mavis'** by the Allies, the transport derivative being named **'Tillie'**. Powered by either Kinsei 51 or 53 radials, the H6K5 was intended to eliminate the shortcomings of the earlier versions, but although the open bow gun position was replaced by a single-gun turret immediately aft of the pilot's cockpit, the overall armament was not increased. Only 36 H6K5s were completed by 1943, when production gave place to the greatly superior H8K. H6Ks served with the 8th, 14th, 801st, Toko and Yokohama Kokutais, and some of the H6K5s were employed as naval staff transports throughout the Pacific in 1943. Eighteen aircraft served on the quasi-commercial courier services in South East Asia, a number of them being destroyed by Allied aircraft both in the air and at their moorings.

Specification
Kawanishi H6K5
Type: nine-crew maritime reconnaissance flying-boat
Powerplant: four 1,300-hp (970-kW) Mitsubishi Kinsei 53 14-cylinder air-cooled radials
Performance: maximum speed 385 km/h (239 mph) at 6000 m (19,685 ft); climb to 5000 m (16,405 ft) in 13 minutes 24 seconds; service ceiling 9600 m (31,495 ft); maximum range 6775 km (4,210 miles)
Weights: empty 12380 kg (27,293 lb); maximum take-off 23000 kg (50,705 lb)
Dimensions: span 40.00 m (131 ft 2¾ in); length 25.63 m (84 ft 0¾ in); height 6.27 m (20 ft 6¾ in); wing area 170.00 m² (1,829.86 sq ft)
Armament: four 7.7-mm (0.303-in) machine-guns in front and midships dorsal positions and two beam blisters, and one 20-mm cannon in tail, plus a bombload of up to 2000 kg (4,409 lb) or two 800-kg (1,764-lb) torpedoes

Final production version of the graceful Kawanishi Navy Type 97 Flying Boat Model 1 was the H6K5 which, though highly vulnerable to modern Allied fighters over the Pacific, remained in service up to the end of the war.

A Kawanishi H6K5 Navy Type 97 flying-boat of the Imperial Japanese Navy; its midships gun blisters are essentially similar to those of the American Catalina PBY. Note the weapon racks under the wing struts.

Kawanishi H8K

Although only 167 examples were produced, the large **Kawanishi H8K** was the most outstanding and advanced flying-boat to achieve production status during World War II. Designed to meet a requirement issued in 1938 for a four-engine maritime reconnaissance flying-boat superior in all respects to the British Short Sunderland, the **H8K1** prototype was first flown in January 1941, but proved initially to possess very poor water handling qualities. Extensive modifications were made and after successfully completing its service trials the aircraft was ordered into production as the **Navy Type 2 Flying-Boat Model 11**, powered by four 1,530-hp (1141-kW) Mitsubishsi Kasei 11 or 12 radials. Armament of these early aircraft comprised two 20-mm cannon and four 7.7-mm (0.303-in) machine-guns. With armour protection, self-sealing fuel tanks and a maximum speed of 433 km/h (269 mph), the new flying-boat indeed represented a considerable advance over the H6K. It carried out its first operational mission in March 1942 when two aircraft of the Yokohama Kokutai set out from Wotje Atoll in the Marshalls to bomb Oahu Island (Pearl Harbor), putting down at French Frigate Shoals to refuel from a submarine; however, arriving over the American base, the Japanese crews found heavy cloud and the raid was ineffective. Nevertheless as a long-range maritime reconnaissance aircraft, the H8K1 (codenamed **'Emily'** by the Allies) with its 7200-km (4,475-mile) range heavy armament and good per-

formance proved a highly competent aircraft much respected by the Allies. The further-improved **H8K2**, with 1,850-hp (1380-kW) Kasei 22 radials and armament increased to five 20-mm cannon and four 7.7-mm (0.303-in) machine-guns, of which 112 were built between 1943 and 1945, was unquestionably the toughest opponent faced by the Allies in the Pacific. It was also equipped with ASV radar, being responsible for the sinking of at least three American submarines in the area north of the Philippines during the last 18 months of the war. Additional to the maritime reconnaissance version, 36 **H8K2-L** 'boats were built in the last two years of the war, these being equipped as naval staff and troop transports capable of accommodating either 29 staff passengers or 64 fully-armed troops. The progressively deteriorating war situation for Japan led

to a run-down in production of flying-boats during 1945 in favour of fighters for home defence, and later versions of the H8K were accordingly abandoned. Nevertheless this excellent aircraft saw considerable service, being flown by the 14th, 801st, 851st, 1001st, 1021st, Takuma, Toko, Yokohama and Yokosuka Chinjufu Kokutais.

Specification
Kawanishi H8K2
Type: 10-crew maritime reconnaissance bomber flying-boat
Powerplant: four 1,850-hp (1380-kW) Mitsubishi Kasei 22 14-cylinder air-cooled radials
Performance: maximum speed 467 km/h (290 mph) at 5000 m (16,405 ft); climb to 5000 m (16,405 ft) in 10 minutes 12 seconds; service ceiling 8760 m (28,740 ft); maximum range 7180 km (4,460 miles)

Weights: empty 18380 kg (40,521 lb); maximum take-off 32500 kg (71,650 lb)
Dimensions: span 38.00 m (14 ft 8 in); length 28.13 m (92 ft 3½ in); height 9.15 m (30 ft 0 in); wing area 160.00 m² (1,722 sq ft)
Armament: single 20-mm cannon each in bow, dorsal and tail turrets and in two beam blisters, and four hand-held 7.7-mm (0.303-in) machine-guns in beam hatches, plus a bombload of up to 2000 kg (4,409 lb) or two 800-kg (1,764-lb) torpedoes

A captured Kawanishi H8K2 which had previously been flown by the 801st Kokutai over the Pacific and was later extensively evaluated by the US Navy. The aircraft's maximum range of 4,445 miles (7200 km) was impressive by any standards.

Consolidated PB2Y Coronado

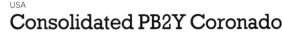

While pursuing a course of isolationism the United States had recognized during the mid-1930s the spectre of world war, the possibility of such a war being waged on the oceans bordering the North American continent encouraging interest by the US Navy in the evolution of large maritime reconnaissance bombers. On 27 July 1936 the Consolidated Aircraft Corporation was contracted to design and build such an aircraft. Designated **Consolidated XPB2Y-1**, the resulting design was a big four-engine shoulder-wing monoplane with single fin and rudder and retracting wing-tip stabilizing floats. First flown on 17 December 1937, the prototype disclosed serious directional instability in the air and much to be desired in handling on the water, and in due course the tail unit was redesigned to incorporate a pair of circular endplate fins and rudders. After trials with the US Navy six production **PB2Y-2** aircraft were ordered and entered service with US Navy Patrol Squadron VP-13 on 31 December 1940. These aircraft, lacking armour and self-sealing fuel tanks, were largely confined to trials but a new version, the **PB2Y-3**, of which 210 were produced, started delivery in 1941 with 907-kg (2,000 lb) of armour plate as well as self-sealing fuel tanks; they also featured enlarged 'zulu shield' fins and rudders that were a characteristic of the Consolidated B-24 Liberator bomber. Ten of these aircraft were transferred to the Royal Air Force whose Transport Command flew them as **Consolidated Coronado Mk I** freighters on a North Atlantic service with No. 231 Squadron. An American transport version was designated **PB2Y-3R**, 31 examples being converted to accommodate up to 45 passengers or a 7258-kg (16,000-lb) freight load. For relatively low altitude work some PB2Y-3s were re-engined with R-1830-92s for

oversea patrol work below 3050 m (10,000 ft) under the designation **PB2Y-5**, and an ambulance version which served in the Pacific as the **PB2Y-5R**. Other distinctive features of the PB2Y-3 and PB2Y-5 versions included the rearward extension of the rear hull chine to improve water stability and handling. In the event the Coronado was not widely used in the maritime reconnaissance role as preference grew for use of land-based aircraft such as the Consolidated PB4Y-1 which required no specialist training in water operation, while the excellent Consolidated PBY Catalina remained unequalled for long distance ocean reconnaissance.

Specification
Consolidated PB2Y-3
Type: 10-crew maritime reconnaissance bomber flying-boat
Powerplant: four 1,200-hp (895-kW) Pratt & Whitney R-1830-88 Twin Wasp

The Consolidated PB2Y-3 Coronado entered service late in the war with increased armament, armour and self-sealing fuel tanks; its bomb bays were located in the relatively thick wing roots.

The big Consolidated PB2Y Coronado four-engined flying-boat, seen here with ASV radome above the cockpit, featured retractable wingtip floats like those of its forebear, the Catalina.

14-cylinder air-cooled radials
Performance: maximum speed 359 km/h (223 mph) at 6095 m (20,000 ft); initial climb rate 174 m (570 ft) per minute; service ceiling 6250 m (20,500 ft); maximum range 3815 km (2,370 miles)
Weights: empty 18568 kg (40,935 lb); maximum take-off 30845 kg (68,000 lb)
Dimensions: span 35.05 m (115 ft 0 in); length 24.20 m (79 ft 3 in); height 8.38 m (27 ft 6 in); wing area 175.4 m² (1,780 sq ft)
Armament: twin 12.7-mm (0.5-in) machine-guns each in bow, dorsal and

tail turrets, and two 12.7-mm (0.5-in) guns in beam hatches, plus a bombload of up to eight 454-kg (1,000-lb) bombs internally and four 454-kg (1,000-lb) bombs or two torpedoes externally; transport version furnished to carry up to 45 passengers

---

Martin PBM Mariner

Representing a later generation of maritime patrol flying-boats than the PBY Catalina, the Martin PBM Mariner nevertheless never achieved the widespread popularity and use of its predecessor. The aircraft shown here served with US Navy Patrol Squadron VP-74 in 1942.

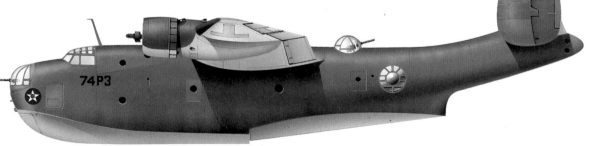

Stung to competition by the success of the PBY Catalina from Consolidated, the US Navy's other great flying boat manufacturer came up with a twin-engine shoulder-wing monoplane boat, the **Martin Model 162**, in 1937. Featuring a deep hull and twin fins and rudders, the prototype **XPBM-1** was first flown on 18 February 1939 with 1,600-hp (1194-kW) Wright Cyclone R-2600-6 radials mounted at the crank of the gull wing so that the propellers were clear of the spray. Twenty **PBM-1** aircraft had been ordered for the US Navy before the end of 1937 and these entered service with Patrol Squadron VP-74 during 1941. Further orders for 379 **PBM-3 Mariner** aircraft were placed in 1940, these and all later aircraft having the underwing stabilizing floats fixed instead of being retractable as in the earlier aircraft; the engine nacelles were also lengthened to accommodate a 907-kg (2,000-lb) load of ordnance. Variants included 50 unarmed **PBM-3R** transports with accommodation for up to 20 passengers, 274 **PBM-3C** aircraft with standardized American/British equipment and 201 PBM-3D 'boats with R-2600-22 engines, and improved armament and armour. Many of the PBM-3Cs and PBM-3Ds were equipped with ASV search radar in a large fairing over the cockpit and,

following initial experience with these aircraft, a new, specialized long-range anti-submarine version, the **PBM-3S**, appeared in 1944; 156 were built. The **PBM-5**, of which 631 were completed, was the last version of the Mariner to be produced during the war, being delivered to the US Navy from August 1944 onwards; this featured an armament of eight 12.7-mm (0.5-in) machine-guns and AN/APS-15 search radar. Five examples of the PBM-3B were delivered to the RAF under Lend-Lease and were flown as **Marine GR.Mk I** aircraft for a short period at the end of 1943 by No. 524 Squadron of Coastal Command at Oban, this squadron being formed to evaluate the aircraft in service, but it was not adopted.

Most of the PBM's service was in the Pacific theatre, and from 1943 onwards was widely deployed, being constantly engaged in searching for and shadowing elements of the declining Japanese navy, although many came to be used on air-sea rescue duties as long-range land-based aircraft gradually assumed a greater share of the maritime reconnaissance role.

Specification
Martin PBM-3D
Type: seven/nine-crew maritime reconnaissance flying-boat
Powerplant: two 1,900-hp (1417-kW) Wright R-2600-22 Cyclone 14-cylinder

air-cooled radials
Performance: maximum speed 340 km/h (211 mph) at 4875 m (16,000 ft); climb to 3050 m (10,000 ft) in 22 minutes 12 seconds; service ceiling 6035 m (19,800 ft); range 3605 km (2,240 miles)
Weights: empty 15048 kg (33,175 lb); maximum take-off 26309 kg (58,000 lb)
Dimensions: span 35.97 m (118 ft 0 in); length 24.33 m (79 ft 10 in); height 8.38 m (27 ft 6 in); wing area 130.80 m² (1,408 sq ft)
Armament: twin 12.7-mm (0.5-in) machine-guns each in bow, dorsal and tail turrets, and one 12.7-mm (0.5-in) machine-gun in each of two beam hatches, plus a bombload of up to 3629 kg (8,000 lb)

Consolidated PBY Catalina

Outstanding among parasol mono-plane flying-boats, Isaac Laddon's **Consolidated PBY** was originally ordered by the US Navy as far back as October 1933, and was first flown with a pair of 825-hp (615-kW) Pratt & Whitney R-1830-58 radials on 28 March 1935. Among its distinctive features were the stabilizing floats which, when retracted, formed the wing tips. Production orders followed quickly and the **PBY-1** entered service with more powerful R-1830-64 engines with Patrol Squadron VP-11F in October 1936. The next year the modified **PBY-2** joined the US Navy, followed by the **PBY-3** with 1,000-hp (746-kW) engines. The **PBY-4**, which appeared in 1938, featured the large midships 'blister' gun positions that were to become a well-known characteristic of the **Catalina**, as the boat came to be named. The outbreak of World War II brought orders from the UK, Australia, Canada and the Dutch East Indies for a new version, the **PBY-5** with 1,200-hp (895-kW) R-1830-92 radials, and by the date of the USA's entry into the war the US Navy possessed 16 PBY-5 squadrons, three of PBY-3s and two of PBY-4s. Following tests with a retractable tricycle wheel landing gear in last PBY-4, the final 33 US Navy PBY-5s were completed in this amphibian form, as were 761 **PBY-5A** aircraft. Following early successful use of the PBY-5 by the RAF's Coastal Command in 1941 as the **Catalina Mk I**, large orders continued to be placed for the US Navy, additional production being undertaken by Canadian Vickers and Boeing of Canada. A total of more than 500 examples eventually served with the RAF alone, while in Canadian service the PBY-5 was named the **Canso**. Another version, the **PBN-1**, was produced by the Naval Aircraft Factory with taller fin and rudder, and 138 of the 156 built were supplied to the USSR; 235 **PBY-6A** amphibians with search radar mounted over the cockpit were built, of which 112 were delivered to the US Navy, 75 to the USAAF (as the **OA-10B**) and 48 to the USSR. Production of this classic aeroplane, which ended in April 1945, included 2,398 by Consolidated and 892 by NAF and the Canadian manufacturers, plus an unknown number built in the Soviet Union under the designation **GST**. Among the Catalina's memorable achievements were the successful shadowing of the German battleship *Bismarck* which led ultimately to the warship's destruction, and the magnificent trailing of the Japanese fleets in the early stages of so many of the great naval battles in the Pacific.

Specification
Consolidated PBY-5A
Type: seven/nine-crew maritime reconnaissance flying-boat amphibian
Powerplant: two 1,200-hp (895-kW) Pratt & Whitney R-1830-92 Twin Wasp 14-cylinder air-cooled radials
Performance: maximum speed 288 km/h (179 mph) at 2135 m (7,000 ft); climb to 3050 m (10,000 ft) in 19 minutes 18 seconds; service ceiling 4480 m (14,700 ft); maximum range 4095 km (2,545 miles)
Weights: empty 9485 kg (20,910 lb); maximum take-off 16067 kg (35,420 lb)
Dimensions: span 31.70 m (104 ft 0 in); length 19.45 m (63 ft 10½ in); height 6.15 m (20 ft 2 in); wing area 130.06 m² (1,400 sq ft)

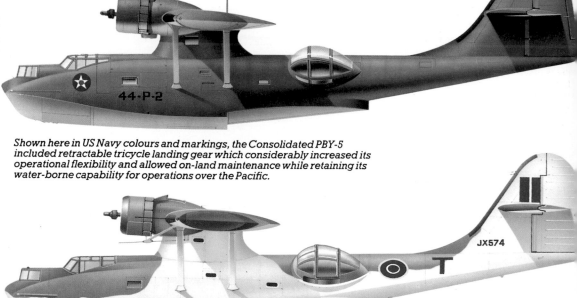

Shown here in US Navy colours and markings, the Consolidated PBY-5 included retractable tricycle landing gear which considerably increased its operational flexibility and allowed on-land maintenance while retaining its water-borne capability for operations over the Pacific.

An ASV-equipped Consolidated Catalina IVA (PBY-5A) of RAF Coastal Command. Although generally regarded as under-powered, the 'Cat' gave magnificent service with the RAF, its very long endurance bestowing a capability to cover huge areas of ocean.

Armament: two 12.7-mm (0.5-in) machine-guns in bow turret, one 12.7-mm (0.5-in) gun in each beam blister, and one 7.62-mm (0.3-in) machine-gun in ventral tunnel, plus a bombload of up to 1814 kg (4,000 lb) of bombs, mines or depth charges, or two torpedoes

Above: An early Catalina of an RAF Coastal Command training unit. The Catalina is armed with four depth charges for an operational sortie.

Below: Catalina Mk IB (PBY-5B) in RAF service. The extensive radar aerial arrays on fuselage and wings were fitted by Scottish Aviation or Saunders Roe after delivery from the American factory. Note the retractable wingtip floats.

Cant Z.501 Gabbiano

The **Cant Z.501 Gabbiano** (gull) light reconnaissance flying-boat was serving in fairly large numbers with the Regia Aeronautica when Italy entered World War II in June 1940. Designed by Filippo Zappata in the early 1930s, the prototype was first flown in 1934 at Monfalcone, Trieste, and later in that year established a new world seaplane distance record of 4120 km (2,560 miles) with a nonstop flight from Monfalcone to Massawa in Eritrea. In July the following year the Gabbiano raised the record to 4957 km (3,080 miles) by flying from Monfalcone to Berbera in Somaliland.

The Z.501 entered production in 1935 and the first deliveries were made to the maritime reconnaissance squadrons (*squadriglie da ricognizione marittima*) of the Regia Aeronautica the following year. Of all-wood construction with fabric-covered control surfaces, the Z.501 was a parasol monoplane with its single Isotta Fraschini 12-cylinder liquid-cooled inline engine with semi-annular cowling in a long nacelle on the wing above the fuselage. A curious feature was the location of an enclosed gun position with single 7.7-mm (0.303-in) Breda-SAFAT machine-gun in this nacelle; early production aircraft were also armed with single machine-guns in part-enclosed bow and midships positions; later aircraft had the bow gun removed and the observer's cockpit in the bows fully enclosed. Bomb shackles were fitted at the intersection of the wing and float struts and these were capable of carrying up to four 160-kg (353-lb) or two 250-kg (551-lb) bombs. The planing bottom of the hull was also of unusual design being of concave section.

In June 1940 202 Cant Z.501s were in service with the Regia Aeronautica, flying patrols along the Adriatic coasts as well as in the central Mediterra-

Despite its archaic appearance, the Cant Z.501 Gabbiano gave long service in the Mediterranean, the example shown here serving with the 2° Escuadrilla, Grupo No. 62, Agrupacion Espagnola (the Spanish Nationalist Air Force) at Majorca in 1939.

nean, where they performed air-sea rescue and other short-range maritime duties. More than 40 known instances are on record of encounters with Allied aircraft and many were shot down, although they were also involved in the rescue of several ditched RAF aircrews. After the armistice with Italy in September 1943 19 Cant Z.501s continued to serve in the Italian Co-Belligerent Air Force, while others went on flying with the Aviazione della RSI.

Specification
Cant Z.501 Gabbiano
Type: four/five-crew light reconnaissance flying-boat
Powerplant: one 900-hp (671-kW) Isotta Fraschini Asso XI R2C.15 12-cylinder liquid-cooled inline engine
Performance: maximum speed 275 km/h 171 mph at 2500 m (8,200 ft); climb to 4000 m (13,125 ft) in 16 minutes; service ceiling 7000 m (22,965 ft); maximum range 2400 km (1,490 miles)
Weights: empty 3850 kg (8,488 lb); maximum take-off 7050 kg (15,342 lb)
Dimensions: span 22.50 m (73 ft 9¾ in);

length 14.30 m (46 ft 11 in); height 4.40 m (14 ft 6 in); wing area 62.00 m² (667.36 sq ft)
Armament: single 7.7-mm (0.303-in) machine-gun each in of bow, engine nacelle and dorsal positions, plus a bombload of up to 640 kg (1,411 lb)

A Cant Z.501 flying-boat at its moorings at Preveza on the West Coast of Greece, during a low level attack by two RAF Beaufighters. The Z.501 was a useful maritime reconnaissance tool, not least because of its long range.

Beriev Be-2 (MBR-2)

Never seriously countenancing the possibility of being involved in all-out maritime warfare with a major nation, the Soviet Union accorded low priority to military flying-boats in the 1930s within an air force which in most respects lagged behind other nations in modern technology. Only the designs of G.M. Beriev had attracted any significant attention and these, together with his later designs, constituted almost the only flying-boats flown by the VVS-VMF during World War II.

The **MBR-2** (later redesignated **Beriev Be-2**) was first flown back in 1931 and was then considered to be modern by the current international standards. It was a small single-engine monoplane with wooden hull and strictly tailored to the needs of coastal units in the Baltic and Black Seas, though it could also be operated with skis or wheel landing gear. The outbreak of World War II triggered hurried efforts to develop a new version, the **MBR-2bis**, which was powered by an 860-hp (642-kW) AM-34 engine in place of the earlier 680-hp (507-kW) M-17 engine; increased fuel tankage raised the range from 960 km (597 miles) to 1400 km (870 miles); for the purposes of maritime reconnaissance over the confined waters of the Baltic and Black Seas, as well as the northern

Arctic seaboard, the new version was seen as an ideal interim aircraft pending the arrival in service of substantial numbers of the MDR-6 (Be-4), and in 1942 about 1,500 aircraft were delivered to the VVS-VMF. Being thus the most widely-used Soviet short-range 'boat in the first three years of the war one of its principal tasks was the sea rescue of downed airmen although, with only token defensive armament and no performance worth mention, the MBR-2 fell easy prey to the massively superior aircraft of the Luftwaffe during that period. Away from such depredations another version, designated the **MP-1**, was employed as a transport with accommodation for up

to eight passengers; a pre-war commercial example had established a number of world altitude records for women pilots, and one of these records remained intact for more than 20 years.

Specification
MBR-2bis
Type: four/five-crew short-range reconnaissance flying-boat
Powerplant: one 860-hp (642-kW) AM-34NB 12-cylinder liquid-cooled inline engine
Performance: maximum speed 248 km/h (154 mph) at 2000 m (6,560 ft); service ceiling 6000 m (19,685 ft); maximum range 1400 km (870 miles)

The Beriev MBR-2 was a short range flying-boat and had its inline engine mounted above the wings, driving a pusher propellor. This Soviet navy example carries an unusual winter camouflage scheme.

Weight: maximum take-off 4245 kg (9,359 lb)
Dimensions: span 19.00 m (62 ft 4 in); length 13.50 m (44 ft 3¾ in); wing area 55.00 m² (592 sq ft)
Armament: one hand-held 7.62-mm (0.3-in) machine-gun in open bow position and one 7.62-mm (0.3-in) gun in midships dorsal turret, plus up to 300 kg (661 lb) of bombs, mines or depth charges on underwing racks

Allied and Axis Seaplanes

Seaplanes served in a wide variety of roles in all major theatres of war. A Japanese floatplane launched from a submarine dropped the only bombs to hit the US mainland; more significantly, seaplanes reconnoitred for many German commerce raiders, including Bismarck *and* Atlantis, *and directed their long-range naval gunfire.*

A German seaplane, the Arado A 196, about to leave the ship *Prinz Eugen*. Used to mount sea patrols and intercept Allied ASW missions, they also facilitated ship-to-shore communications.

Regarded with hindsight as something of an anachronism, the float seaplane was flown with varying success by all the major powers during World War II, performing all manner of tasks from active combat to clandestine roles such as delivering agents to hostile coastlines. Of all the major warring nations, however, the UK employed this type of aircraft least and was the first to discard it, most of its usual duties being more conveniently performed by carrierborne aircraft, flying-boats or even long-range land-based aircraft. Indeed in the Royal Navy the Swordfish and Fairey Seafox seaplanes survived in service only in the traditional role of gunnery spotting with cruisers and capital ships until superseded for ever by the advent of radar relatively early in the war. It was perhaps ironic that four other seaplanes, the German Heinkel He 115, the French Latecoere 298, and the American Vought Kingfisher and Northrop N-3PB Nomad, gave more extensive service with the British forces than did the indigenous types. The great maritime powers,

the UK, the USA and Japan, all employed floatplanes aboard their capital ships, as did Germany and Italy, the use of these planes being mainly confined to limited sea patrols and ship-to-shore communications.

However, whereas all-out efforts were made by the UK and the USA to bridge the Atlantic with flying-boats and long-range land-based aircraft to counter the depredations of enemy surface raiders and submarines, the Pacific's vast expanse encouraged widespread use of floatplanes, particularly by the Japanese; indeed the only bombs dropped by aeroplanes on the USA during the war were two light bombs from a Yokosuka E14Y1 carried by a Japanese submarine to within range of the American mainland.

The US Navy was equipped with a variety of floatplanes, including the Curtiss SOC Seagull and Grumman J2F Duck biplanes and the Curtiss SO3C, SC-1 Seahawk and Vought OS2U Kingfisher monoplanes. Of all these the venerable Seagull probably enjoyed the most illustrious service career, being present in the actions at Guadalcanal, Wake, Gilbert and Marshall Islands, and also serving aboard American warships in the Atlantic and Mediterranean until 1944.

Latécoère 298

Most widely used of a dozen French floatplane types that were in service in 1939, the **Latécoère 298** saw considerable action during the Battle of France the following year. Of all-metal construction, this robust twin-float aircraft was intended for service with the seaplane carrier *Commandant Teste* and made its maiden flight on 8 May 1936, and by the beginning of World War II a total of 81 aircraft had been ordered, of which 53 had been delivered. Most aircraft (**Laté 298A** machines with fixed wings) were serving with Escadrilles T1 at Berre and T2 at Cherbourg, while about 17 **Laté 298B** and **Laté 298D** aircraft with folding wings and fixed wings respectively, were with Escadrilles HB 1 and HB 2 aboard the *Commandant Teste*. Another 65 Laté 298s were ordered on 22 November, a further *escadrille*, T3, having been formed on 15 September; T4 was to be formed on 15 January.

When the German attack in the West opened on 10 May 1940 the French navy possessed some 60 Laté 298s in front-line service; all were now shore-based as the *Commandant Teste* had been relegated to other duties, roughly half the force being based on the Channel Coast and the remainder in the Mediterranean. In the early stages of the Battle of France the Laté 298s were flown as cover for the Allied occupation of Walcheren, but were forced to evacuate Boulogne on 21 May, thereafter engaging in dive and level bombing attacks on the advancing German columns; on 23 May 18 of the seaplanes dive-bombed a number of key bridges in northern

France with 500-kg (1,102-lb) bombs, losing four aircraft to enemy fire. Losses began to mount so that by 3 June the number of serviceable Laté 298s stood at 27, and it was deemed prudent to confine their attacks to night sorties, although a daylight attack was carried out by Laté 298s of T2 against enemy columns near Abbeville on 6 June. Seven other aircraft were lost before the armistice but about 30 aircraft (including the survivors of T2) made their way to Lac d'Oubeira in Algeria.

Production was reinstated in 1942 by the Vichy government, some 30 **Laté 298F** aircraft (similar to the Laté 298D) being built. Units of the Vichy air force in North Africa continued to fly the Laté 298s throughout 1942-3, and at least two

escadrilles flew alongside the RAF in the Mediterranean until 1944 when French forces once more regained their autonomous identities.

Specification
Latécoère 298D
Type: two/three-seat torpedo-bomber and bomber floatplane
Powerplant: one 656-kW (880-hp) Hispano-Suiza 12Ycrs-1 inline piston engine
Performance: maximum speed 290 km/h (180 mph) at 2000 m (6,560 ft); climb to 1500 m (4,920 ft) in 5 minutes 42 seconds; service ceiling 6500 m (21,325 ft); range with maximum warload 800 km (497 miles)
Weights: empty 3071 kg (6,770 lb);

A Latécoère 298 of the Vichy French air force passes a German Dornier Do 24 on the Aegean coast. The most widely-used French floatplane in 1940, Laté 298s were also flown by two escadrilles of the Free French.

maximum take-off 4800 kg (10,582 lb)
Dimensions: span 15.50 m (50 ft 10.2 in); length 12.56 m (41 ft 2.5 in); height 5.23 m (17 ft 1.9 in); wing area 31.6 m² (340.15 sq ft)
Armament: two fixed forward-firing 7.5-mm (0.295-in) machine-guns in the wings and one 7.5-mm (0.295-in) trainable machine-gun in the rear cockpit, plus 500 kg (1,102 lb) of bombs or one 670-kg (1,477-lb) torpedo, or depth charge

---

Cant Z.506B Airone

Largest float seaplane to give widespread operational service during World War II (although arguably the convertible Junkers Ju 52/3mW might lay claim to this achievement), the Italian **Cant Z.506B Airone** (heron) three-engine twin-float maritime reconnaissance bomber was developed from the commercial Z.506A in 1936, production of the military aircraft starting the following year with a batch of 32 aircraft (Serie I) and differing from the earlier aircraft in featuring a long ventral gondola accommodating bomb bay, bomb-aimer's station and a rear ventral gun position; a semi-retractable gun turret was also added.

The early Z.506B aircraft were evaluated with the Aviazione Legionaria in Spain during 1939, 30 other aircraft having also been ordered by the Polish naval wing (in the event only one of the latter had arrived in Poland when the Germans invaded in September, and the remaining aircraft were taken on charge by Italy's Regia Marina). By the date of Italy's entry into the war in June 1940 the Z.506B was in full production, 95 aircraft having been completed by the parent company. Most of these were serving with the 31° and 35° Stormi Bombardamento Marittimo at Elmas and Brindisi respectively; these units were fairly heavily engaged during the campaign in Greece, although they seldom operated when likely to be opposed by RAF fighters. They participated in the capture of Corfu, Cefalonia and Zante, and attempted to shadow British naval forces after the Battle of Cape Matapan

but sheered away when faced by Fleet Air Arm Fairey Fulmar fighters. Thereafter the Airone was almost entirely withdrawn from use as a bomber and torpedo attack aircraft, the Italian navy calling for its greater use in maritime reconnaissance, air-sea rescue, convoy escort and anti-submarine patrol roles: such had been the shift in naval superiority in the Mediterranean following the debacle at Taranto and the Battle of Cape Matapan.

Development and production of the Airone continued, with small modifications being introduced with each new production batch (*serie*), of which Serie XII was the most important. A special air-sea rescue conversion was the **Z.506S** (Soccorso), this version being also used in small numbers by

the Luftwaffe. After the Italian surrender 23 Z.506B and five Z.506S aircraft were flown to Allied ports and subsequently flew with the Co-Belligerent Air Force's Raggruppamento Idro, performing transport and other second-line tasks.

Specification
Cant Z.506B Serie XII
Type: five-seat bomber and torpedo-bomber floatplane
Powerplant: three 559-kW (750-hp) Alfa-Romeo 126RC.34 radial piston engines
Performance: maximum speed 350 km/h (217 mph) at 4000 m (13,125 ft); climb to 4000 m (13,125 ft) in 20 minutes 6 seconds; service ceiling 7000 m (22,965 ft); range 2000 km

(1,243 miles)
Weights: empty 8750 kg (19,290 lb); maximum take-off 12705 kg (28,010 lb)
Dimensions: span 26.50 m (86 ft 11.3 in); length 19.24 m (63 ft 1.5 in); height 7.45 m (24 ft 5.3 in); wing area 86.26 m² (928.53 sq ft)
Armament: one 12.7-mm (0.5-in) trainable machine-gun in the dorsal position, and three 7.7-mm (0.303-in) trainable machine-guns in the two beam and one ventral positions, plus a bombload of 1200 kg (2,646 lb) or one 800-kg (1,764-lb) torpedo

The largest operational floatplane of the war was the Cant Z.506, an example of which was forced down at Mondello beach, Sicily, in November, 1943.

Arado Ar 196

Although the attractive **Arado Ar 196** twin-float seaplane was frequently encountered by Allied aircraft around the coasts of Europe during World War II, it had originally been developed to replace the Heinkel He 60 float biplane aboard Germany's larger warships whose construction was advancing apace during the late 1930s. Of all-metal structure with metal and fabric covering, the Ar 196 was by all accounts an extremely pleasant aeroplane to fly, the crew being afforded excellent fields of view. After first flights by the four prototypes in 1938 (of which one featured a single central float and small underwing outrigger floats), the first service deliveries of the **Ar 196A-1** were made in July 1939, in time to embark examples in the pocket battleships *Deutschland* and *Admiral Graf Spee* before they sailed for their war stations in August. During the following six weeks 18 Ar 196s were embarked in the battlecruisers *Scharnhorst* and *Gneisenau*, the pocket battleship *Admiral Scheer*, the heavy cruiser *Admiral Hipper* at Kiel and the light cruisers *Emden, Köln, Königsberg, Leipzig* and *Nürnberg* at Wilhelmshaven.

The *Deutschland* made constant use of her aircraft during her early foray into the Atlantic (which resulted in the sinking of nine merchantmen), as did the *Scharnhorst* and *Gneisenau* during their sortie northwards late in November, but the *Graf Spee* did not attempt to launch her aircraft during the Battle of the River Plate because of the difficulty of its recovery during the chase by the British cruisers; in any case her guns were apparently adequately served by radar. During the pursuit of the battleship *Bismarck* in May 1941, which led ultimately to her destruction, at least two Ar 196s were launched in attempts to prevent RAF Consolidated Catalinas from shadowing the warship.

In 1940 the Ar 196A entered service with Luftwaffe coastal units throughout northern Europe, and an aircraft of Küstenfliegergruppe 706 attacked and damaged the submarine HMS *Seal* in the Kattegat, leading to the boat's capture by the Germans. Although several Ar 196s were shot down by the RAF during the Battle of Britain, most losses were attributable to storms at their anchorages. In 1941-2, flown from French bases, they were used to intercept RAF Coastal Command anti-submarine patrols over the Bay of Biscay, their pilots claiming more than a dozen victories. Total production amounted to 593 aircraft.

Specification
Arado Ar 196A-3
Type: two-seat shipborne and coastal patrol floatplane
Powerplant: one 723-kW (970-hp) BMW 132K radial piston engine
Performance: maximum speed 310 km/h (193 mph) at 4000 m (13,125 ft); climb to 3000 m (9,845 ft) in 8 minutes 42 seconds; service ceiling 7020 m (23,030 ft); range 1070 km (665 miles)
Weights: empty 2335 kg (5,148 lb); maximum take-off 3303 kg (7,282 lb)
Dimensions: span 12.40 m (40 ft 8.2 in); length 11.00 m (36 ft 1.1 in); height 4.45 m (14 ft 7.2 in); wing area 28.3 m² (304.62 sq ft)
Armament: two fixed forward-firing 20-mm cannon and one fixed forward-firing 7.92-mm (0.31-in) machine-gun, and two 7.92-mm (0.31-in) trainable machine-guns in the rear cockpit, plus provision for two 50-kg (110-lb) bombs under the wings

Arado Ar 196s were embarked on several of Germany's major warships, including the 'Scharnhorst', 'Deutschland' and 'Hipper' classes. This example is embarked on the heavy cruiser Admiral Hipper.

Designed to replace the Heinkel He 60 floatplane aboard German warships, the Arado Ar 196 was pressed into service with Luftwaffe coastal units in 1940. Flying from French bases during 1941 and 1942, they intercepted ASW patrols mounted by RAF Coastal Command and claimed over a dozen victories.

Arado Ar 196A-3 cutaway drawing key

1 Spinner
2 Propeller hub
3 Starboard fuselage fixed 7.9-mm MG 17 gun port
4 Schwarz adjustable-pitch three-blade propeller
5 Cowling ring
6 Cylinder head fairings
7 BMW 132K nine-cylinder air cooled radial engine
8 Cowling panel frame
9 Quick-release catch
10 Cowling flaps
11 Engine lower bearers
12 Handholds
13 Engine accessories
14 Air louvre
15 Firewall bulkhead frame
16 Oil tank
17 Starboard MG 7 trough
18 Fuselage frame/engine support attachment
19 Engine upper bearers
20 Forward fuselage decking
21 Starboard wing skinning
22 Leading-edge rib stations
23 Starboard outer rib
24 Starboard navigation light
25 Starboard wingtip
26 Starbord aileron
27 Aileron mass balance
28 Underwing access panel
29 Aileron control linkage
30 Windscreen
31 Instrument panel
32 Forward fuselage upper frame
33 Sea rudder lever
34 Handhold
35 Sea equipment locker (inc. drag-line and anchor/heaving-line)
36 Rudder pedal assembly
37 Seat support frame
38 Entry footstep
39 Seat adjustment handwheel
40 Armrest and seat harness
41 Control column
42 Pilot's seat
43 Sliding canopy
44 Rear-view mirror
45 Aerial mast
46 (Starboard) wing fold position
47 Pilot's headrest
48 Support frame
49 Canopy aft section
50 Aft canopy lock/release
51 First-aid kit
52 Observer/gunner's sliding seat
53 Entry footstep
54 Flare cartridge stowage

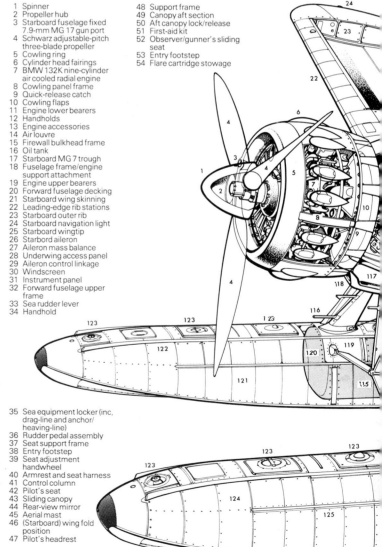

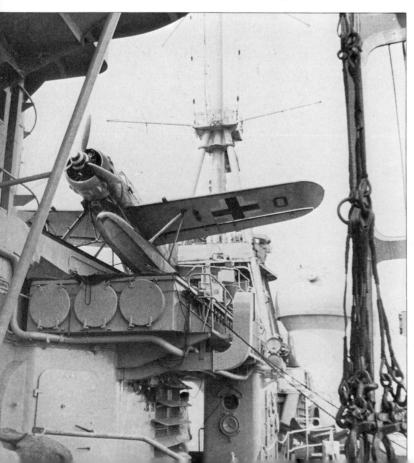

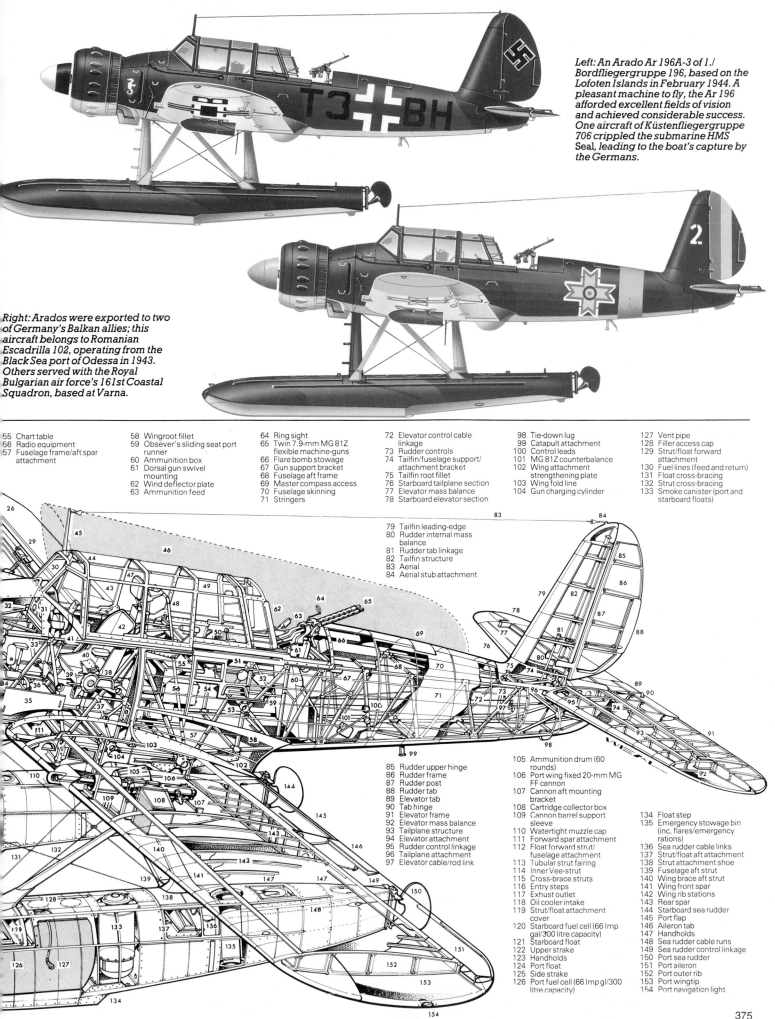

Left: An Arado Ar 196A-3 of 1./ Bordfliegergruppe 196, based on the Lofoten Islands in February 1944. A pleasant machine to fly, the Ar 196 afforded excellent fields of vision and achieved considerable success. One aircraft of Küstenfliegergruppe 706 crippled the submarine HMS Seal, leading to the boat's capture by the Germans.

Right: Arados were exported to two of Germany's Balkan allies; this aircraft belongs to Romanian Escadrilla 102, operating from the Black Sea port of Odessa in 1943. Others served with the Royal Bulgarian air force's 161st Coastal Squadron, based at Varna.

55 Chart table
56 Radio equipment
57 Fuselage frame/aft spar attachment
58 Wingroot fillet
59 Observer's sliding seat port runner
60 Ammunition box
61 Dorsal gun swivel mounting
62 Wind deflector plate
63 Ammunition feed
64 Ring sight
65 Twin 7.9-mm MG 81Z flexible machine-guns
66 Flare bomb stowage
67 Gun support bracket
68 Fuselage aft frame
69 Master compass access
70 Fuselage skinning
71 Stringers
72 Elevator control cable linkage
73 Rudder controls
74 Tailfin/fuselage support/ attachment bracket
75 Tailfin root fillet
76 Starboard tailplane section
77 Elevator mass balance
78 Starboard elevator section
98 Tie-down lug
99 Catapult attachment
100 Control leads
101 MG 81Z counterbalance
102 Wing attachment strengthening plate
103 Wing fold line
104 Gun charging cylinder
127 Vent pipe
128 Filler access cap
129 Strut/float forward attachment
130 Fuel lines (feed and return)
131 Float cross-bracing
132 Strut cross-bracing
133 Smoke canister (port and starboard floats)

79 Tailfin leading-edge
80 Rudder internal mass balance
81 Rudder tab linkage
82 Tailfin structure
83 Aerial
84 Aerial stub attachment

85 Rudder upper hinge
86 Rudder frame
87 Rudder post
88 Rudder tab
89 Elevator tab
90 Tab hinge
91 Elevator frame
92 Elevator mass balance
93 Tailplane structure
94 Elevator attachment
95 Rudder control linkage
96 Tailplane attachment
97 Elevator cable/rod link
105 Ammunition drum (60 rounds)
106 Port wing fixed 20-mm MG FF cannon
107 Cannon aft mounting bracket
108 Cartridge collector box
109 Cannon barrel support sleeve
110 Watertight muzzle cap
111 Forward spar attachment
112 Float forward strut/ fuselage attachment
113 Tubular strut fairing
114 Inner Vee-strut
115 Cross-brace struts
116 Entry steps
117 Exhaust outlet
118 Oil cooler intake
119 Strut/float attachment cover
120 Starboard fuel cell (66 Imp gal/300 litre capacity)
121 Starboard float
122 Upper strake
123 Handholds
124 Port float
125 Side strake
126 Port fuel cell (66 Imp gl/300 litre capacity)
134 Float step
135 Emergency stowage bin (inc. flares/emergency rations)
136 Sea rudder cable links
137 Strut/float aft attachment
138 Strut attachment shoe
139 Fuselage aft strut
140 Wing brace aft strut
141 Wing front spar
142 Wing rib stations
143 Rear spar
144 Starboard sea rudder
145 Port flap
146 Aileron tab
147 Handholds
148 Sea rudder cable runs
149 Sea rudder control linkage
150 Port sea rudder
151 Port aileron
152 Port outer rib
153 Port wingtip
154 Port navigation light

Fokker T.VIII-W

Designed in 1937 to replace ageing reconnaissance/torpedo-bomber biplanes in service with the Dutch Marine Luchtvaardienst (MLD), the twin-engine twin-float Fokker T.VIII-W seaplane was of mixed wood and metal construction and accommodated a three-man crew. The aircraft, initially powered by Wright Whirlwind radials, was considered to be very underpowered, but plans to introduce Bristol Mercury engines were effectively overtaken by the German invasion of the Netherlands. The T.VIII-W entered service with the MLD in 1939 and by the time of the German attack the following May 11 aircraft had been delivered (including one that had been shot down in error by the Luftwaffe). Quickly realizing the futility of flying the seaplanes in the presence of the Luftwaffe's fighters, the MLD ordered the nine serviceable aircraft to be flown to French bases on the Channel coast, one aircraft being used to fly two members of the Dutch government to the UK. Arriving in France on 12 May, the T.VIII-Ws flew a number of patrols over the Channel during the following 10 days, but such operations lacked cohesion and purpose as there remained little unified command in the rapidly dwindling air forces in northern France. Therefore,

on 22 May, the MLD ordered all surviving Dutch aircrews to fly their aircraft to the UK, a total of eight T.VIII-Ws eventually assembling at Pembroke Dock in South Wales where, on 1 June, these crews formed the nucleus of No. 320 (Dutch) Squadron of the RAF. For two months the Fokkers (carrying the British serials AV958-AV965) flew anti-shipping patrols over the Western Approaches until an increasing lack of spares forced the withdrawal of the Dutch seaplanes in favour of Avro Ansons and Lockheed Hudsons, which were flown from Carew Cheriton.

In the meantime Fokker had, at the time of the German invasion, been pro-

ducing a larger version of the aircraft, the T.VIII-W/C, for Finland; powered by Bristol Mercury XI radials, this aircraft possessed a top speed some 72 km/h (45 mph) faster than the MLD version. In all the Germans took over 20 partially-completed T.VIII-Ws and five T.VIII-W/Cs, these aircraft subsequently being completed by Fokker and entering service with the Luftwaffe on anti-shipping and air-sea rescue duties over the North Sea.

Specification
Fokker T.VIII-W
Type: three-seat reconnaissance and torpedo-bomber floatplane

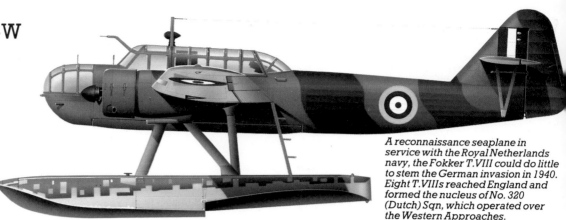

A reconnaissance seaplane in service with the Royal Netherlands navy, the Fokker T.VIII could do little to stem the German invasion in 1940. Eight T.VIIIs reached England and formed the nucleus of No. 320 (Dutch) Sqn, which operated over the Western Approaches.

Powerplant: two 336-kW (450-hp) Wright R-975-E3 Whirlwind radial piston engines
Performance: maximum speed 285 km/h (177 mph) at sea level; service ceiling 6800 m (22,310 ft); range 2100 km (1,305 miles)
Weights: empty 3100 kg (6,834 lb); maximum take-off 5000 kg (11,023 lb)
Dimensions: span 18.00 m (59 ft 0.7 in); length 13.00 m (42 ft 7.8 in); height 5.00 m (16 ft 4.9 in); wing area 44.00 m² (473.6 sq ft)
Armament: one fixed forward-firing and two trainable 7.92-mm (0.31-in) machine-guns, plus 605 kg (1,334 lb) of bombs or one torpedo

Fairey Seafox

Designed to a 1932 specification the Fairey Seafox prototype was first flown on 27 May 1936; its operational purpose was to equip Royal Navy trade-protection light cruisers which, in time of war, would patrol the world's oceans on the lookout for enemy surface raiders and blockade runners. Equipped with cross-braced twin-float alighting gear, the Seafox was unable to carry a torpedo (being some 40 per cent lighter than the Swordfish) and its role was entirely passive; its value was, however, accepted as lying in its ability to spot for the cruiser's guns if brought to action by enemy warships. The Seafox was of all-metal structure with monocoque fuselage and fabric-covered wings and tail; it was fully stressed for catapulting and the pilot was accommodated in an open cockpit, his observer being enclosed beneath a glazed canopy.

A total of 64 production Seafoxes was built (K8569-K8617 and L4519-L4533), the first being delivered to the Royal Navy on 23 April 1937; they subsequently served with Nos 702, 713, 714, 716 and 718 Catapult Flights, as well as Nos 753 and 754 Training Squadrons. The Catapult Flights embarked single or pairs of aircraft in ships of the 3rd Cruiser Squadron in the Mediterranean, the 9th Cruiser Squadron and South American Division of the South Atlantic command. At the outbreak of war 32 Seafoxes were at sea with the Royal Navy as well as light cruisers of the Royal Australian Navy and the New Zealand Division of the Royal Navy.

Fairey Seafoxes were embarked on Royal Navy cruisers of the 3rd and 9th Squadrons as well as those of the South American division of South Atlantic Command. HMS Ajax launched one of hers during the fight with KMS Graf Spee.

When the German pocket battleship *Admiral Graf Spee* was being hunted in the South Atlantic during November 1939 Seafoxes were in constant use by the British cruisers, and during the Battle of the River Plate the light cruiser HMS *Ajax* launched one of her two aircraft for gunnery spotting, although difficulty was experienced with the air-to-ship radio contact. Later the Seafox crew kept a watch on Montevideo harbour while the *Graf Spee* was seeking shelter from British warships before her scuttling. Seafoxes continued

to serve at sea until 1943, two aircraft being lost when the 'Ajax'-class cruiser HMS *Orion* was severely damaged by German air attack during the evacuation of Crete on 28 April 1941.

Specification
Fairey Seafox
Type: two-seat light fleet reconnaissance floatplane
Powerplant: one 295-kW (395-hp) Napier Rapier VI inline piston engine
Performance: maximum speed 200 km/h (124 mph) at 1785 m (5,860 ft);

climb to 1525 m (5,000 ft) in 10 minutes 24 seconds; service ceiling 3355 m (11,000 ft); range 708 km (440 miles)
Weights: empty 1726 kg (3,805 lb); maximum take-off 2459 kg (5,421 lb)
Dimensions: span 12.19 m (40 ft 0 in); length 10.81 m (35 ft 5.5 in); height 3.68 m (12 ft 1 in); wing area 40.32 m² (434 sq ft)
Armament: provision for one 7.7-mm (0.303-in) Lewis gun in the rear cockpit; some aircraft were adapted to carry underwing racks for flares or four 9-kg (20-lb) bombs

Heinkel He 59

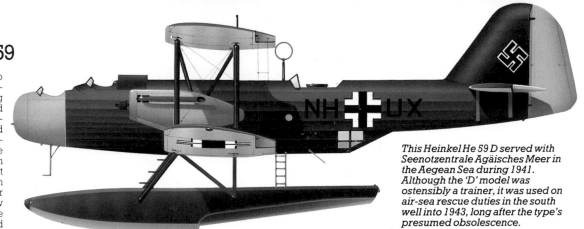

The Germans' use of float seaplanes to deliver combat troops into action is believed to have been unique during World War II, and principally involved the large **Heinkel He 59** two-float twin-engine biplane, an aircraft designed back in 1930 as a reconnaissance bomber landplane during the clandestine activities which eventually resulted in the creation of the Luftwaffe. The first floatplane example made its maiden flight in January 1932 and the first major production version, the **He 59B-2**, saw operational service in Spain with the Legion Condor as a night bomber and for coastal patrol.

By the outbreak of war about 70 He 59Bs had been completed and served with the third *Staffeln* of Küstenfliegergruppen 106, 406, 506 and 706 for coastal reconnaissance, anti-shipping patrols and minelaying (being capable of carrying two 500-kg/1,102-lb magnetic mines). They also equipped the *Seenotdienststaffeln* and the Staffel Schwilben for air-sea rescue duties over the North Sea and Baltic. Later they joined KGrzbV 108 for specialist coastal assault troop-carrying duties, and I Gruppe of KG 200 for air-sea rescue work. During the invasion of Norway most of these units were pressed into use for coastal patrol and air-sea rescue, and during the initial assault phase were occasionally employed to deliver assault parties into the fjords. During the German assault in the West on 10 May 1940 12 He 59Bs of the Staffel Schwilben transported 120 troops to the banks of the River Maas to capture the key bridge at Rotterdam, losing four aircraft to the Dutch defences.

During the Battle of Britain the He 59s of the Seenotdienstkommando were extremely active all round the coasts of the UK, ostensibly on the lookout for downed German aircrew, but when it became apparent that despite displaying prominent Red Crosses the aircraft were being used to shadow and report British convoys, orders were given to RAF pilots to shoot down enemy seaplanes; no fewer than 31 He 59s (11 of them from Seenotflugkommando 3, based at Boulogne) were lost during the Battle of Britain, with seven others badly damaged. Set against this more than 400 German airmen were recovered from the sea round the UK.

Specialist versions included the **He 59C-2** air-sea rescue aircraft, the **He 59D-1** and **He 59N** series trainers, the **He 59E-1** torpedo trainer and **He 59E-2** long-range reconnaissance aircraft. Air-sea rescue He 59s continued to serve in the Mediterranean and Ae-

Although an old, outdated design, the He 59 was pressed into a number of duties: as a trainer, minelayer, assault transport, air-sea rescue and coastal reconnaissance aircraft.

gean until mid-1943. At least one *Staffel* served on the Black Sea.

Specification
Heinkel He 59B-2
Type: four-seat maritime reconnaissance and air-sea rescue floatplane
Powerplant: two 492-kW (660-hp) BMW VI 6,0ZU V-12 piston engines
Performance: maximum speed 220 km/h (137 mph) at sea level; climb to 1000 m (3,280 ft) in 4 minutes 48

This Heinkel He 59 D served with Seenotzentrale Agäisches Meer in the Aegean Sea during 1941. Although the 'D' model was ostensibly a trainer, it was used on air-sea rescue duties in the south well into 1943, long after the type's presumed obsolescence.

seconds; service ceiling 3475 m (11,400 ft); range 1750 km (1,087 miles)
Weights: empty 5000 kg (11,023 lb); maximum take-off 9100 kg (20,062 lb)
Dimensions: span 23.70 m (77 ft 9 in); length 17.40 m (57 ft 1 in); height 7.10 m (23 ft 3.5 in); wing area 152.8m^2 (1,644.78 sq ft)
Armament: three 7.92-m (0.31-in) trainable machine-guns (one each in the bow, dorsal and ventral positions), plus a load of up to 1000 kg (2,205 lb) of bombs and/or mines or one torpedo

Heinkel He 115

Flown largely by Kriegsmarine pilots during much of the war, the **Heinkel He 115** twin-engine two-float seaplane was almost certainly the best such aircraft to serve with any air force in World War II. Designed in competition with the Blohm und Voss Ha 140, the He 115 was first flown in 1936 and two years later established eight world speed records for its class in various payload and range categories. Technically in advance of any British, French or American maritime aircraft of similar concept, the type was ordered into production, the **He 115A-1** version joining the Luftwaffe in 1938 (being followed by the He 115A-2, of which six were exported to Norway and 10 to Sweden in 1939).

In September 1939 about 60 He 115A and **He 115B** aircraft (the latter with increased fuel capacity) were serving with the *Küstenfliegergruppen*. Apart from some reconnaissance work over the Baltic during the Polish campaign, their first important task involved sealing the gaps in the minefields off the east coast of the British Isles, the first such mission being flown by 3./KüFlGr 906 on 20/21 November 1939. These activities continued for more than 18 months (and sporadically thereafter for two years), the mining units losing 33 aircraft destroyed and six aircraft severely damaged during the period of the Battle of Britain; most casualties were suffered from British coastal flak.

Before the end of the Battle of Britain the first examples of the **He 115C** series were in service with increased defensive armament while the **He 115C-2**, introduced in 1941, featured strengthened floats to allow operation from snow and ice surfaces. The **He 115C-3** and **He 115C-4** were respectively specialist minelayers and torpedo bombers, the latter being flown against the North Cape convoys. Production was halted in 1941 when operations in the USSR made more pressing demands for other aircraft. In 1943 production was resumed and 141 He 115E multipurpose aircraft were delivered to the Luftwaffe in the following year; some He 115Cs and He 115Es were armed with single forward-firing MG 151 20-mm cannon under the nose for flak-

suppression during torpedo attacks.

At the end of the Norwegian campaign three of that country's He 115A-2s and a captured He 115B-1 were flown to the UK, where they were evaluated by the RAF before being committed to clandestine operations between the UK and Norway, and in the Mediterranean for carrying agents into enemy-occupied territory in North Africa. Total production was about 500 aircraft.

Specification
Heinkel He 115C-1
Type: three-seat minelaying, torpedo-bombing and reconnaissance floatplane
Powerplant: two 716-kW (960-hp) BME 132K radial piston engines

The Heinkel 115 served the Luftwaffe in a wide variety of theatres, from the Mediterranean to the North Cape. This particular aircraft was operated by 1./KuFlGr 406 out of northern Norway in 1942.

Performance: maximum speed 300 km/h (186 mph) at 1000 m (3,280 ft); climb to 1000 m (3,280 ft) in 5 minutes 6 seconds; range 2800 km (1,740 miles)
Weights: empty 6870 kg (15,146 lb); maximum take-off 10680 kg (23,545 lb)
Dimensions: span 22.28 m (73 ft 1.2 in); length 17.30 m (56 ft 9.1 in); height 6.59 m (21 ft 7.5 in); wing area 86.7 m^2 (933.26 sq ft)
Armament: one 7.92-mm (0.31-in) trainable machine-gun and one 15-mm fixed cannon in the nose, one 7.92-mm (0.31-in) fixed rearward-firing machine-gun in each engine nacelle, and one 7.92-mm (0.31-in) trainable machine-gun in the rear cockpit, plus a load of 1250 kg (2,756 lb) of bombs and/or mines, or one 500-kg (1,102-lb) torpedo

Aichi E13A

Numerically the most important of all Japanese float seaplanes during World War II, the **Aichi E13A** monoplane (of which 1,418 were produced) originated in a naval staff specification issued to Aichi, Kawanishi and Nakajima in 1937 for a three-seat reconnaissance seaplane to replace the six-year-old Kawanishi E7K2 float biplane. A prototype was completed late in 1938 and after competitive trials with the Kawanishi E13K in December 1940 was ordered into production as the **Navy Type 0 Reconnaissance Seaplane Model 1**. Early aircraft were embarked in Japanese cruisers and seaplane tenders the following year and, carrying a single 250-kg (551-lb) bomb apiece, flew a series of raids on the Hankow-Canton railway. Soon afterwards **E13A1** floatplanes accompanied the Japanese 8th Cruiser Division for reconnaissance patrols during the strike against Pearl Harbor in December 1941.

Thereafter, as production switched to Kyushu Hikoki KK at Zasshonokuma and accelerated, the seaplanes (codenamed **'Jake'** by the Allies) were embarked in the battleships and cruisers of the *Kantais* (fleets), including the battleship *Haruna* and cruisers *Chikuma* and *Tone* of Vice Admiral Nagumo's Carrier Striking Force at the Battle of Midway. Because of mechanical problems with the ships' catapults there were delays in launching one of the four E13A1s to search for the American carriers at dawn on the crucial 4 June 1942, depriving the Japanese of the vital initiative during the early stages of the assault on Midway. Furthermore the *Chikuma*'s E13A1 was forced to return early when it suffered engine trouble, further reducing the all-important search area. One of the other 'Jake' pilots, from the cruiser *Tone*, eventually sighted the American fleet but at first failed to report the presence of carriers, causing a further 30-minute delay in arming the strike aircraft awaiting orders to launch from

An Aichi E13A 'Jake' of the Imperial Japanese Navy is seen in the early wartime colour scheme that would have been worn at sea aboard the fleet's cruisers and battleships.

Japanese carriers. As it was, when the Americans launched their first strike, the pilots found the decks of the carriers *Akakgi*, *Kaga*, *Soryu* and *Hiryu* clogged with aircraft which should have been attacking the American fleet.

In all, it is estimated that by mid-1943 more than 250 E13A1s were at sea aboard Japanese ships, though their use was severely curtailed whenever American fighters were in evidence. Nevertheless they continued to serve right up to the end of the war, many of them being ultimately used in suicide attacks on the huge American invasion fleets closing on the Japanese homeland.

Specification
Aichi E13A1a
Type: three-seat reconnaissance floatplane
Powerplant: one 790-kW (1,060-hp) Mitsubishi Kinsei 43 radial piston engine
Performance: maximum speed 377 km/h (234 mph) at 2180 m (7,155 ft); climb to 3000 m (9,845 ft) in 6 minutes 5 seconds; service ceiling 8730 m (28,640 ft); range 2089 km (1,298 miles)
Weights: empty 2642 kg (5,825 lb); maximum take-off 4000 kg (8,818 lb)
Dimensions: span 14.50 m (47 ft 6.9 in);

length 11.30 m (37 ft 0.9 in); height 7.40 m (24 ft 3.3 in); wing area 36.0 m² (387.5 sq ft)
Armament: one 7.7-mm (0.303-in) trainable machine-gun in the rear cockpit, plus 250 kg (551 lb) of bombs and/or depth charges

At a Japanese seaplane base somewhere in the Pacific the crew of an E13A leave their cockpits. With a range of nearly 2100 km (1,300 miles), sorties could, and often did, mean up to 15 hours at a time in the cockpit for the three-man crew.

Kawanishi N1K Kyofu

Anticipation of a need for single-seat float-equipped interceptor seaplanes prompted the Japanese navy to initiate a development programme for such aircraft in 1940, the Nakajima A6M2-N floatplane adaptation of the famous Mitsubishi A6M2 Zero being intended as a stopgap until a purpose-designed aircraft could be introduced. This was to be the highly-imaginative and attractive **Kawanishi N1K Kyofu** (mighty wind), whose design was started in September of that year. Featuring a central float and twin wing-mounted stabilizing floats, the new prototype retained the same gun armament as the A6M2 but was powered by a 1089-kW (1,460-hp) Kasei 14 radial engine driving two-blade contraprops in an attempt to counter the torque-induced swing on take-off. The wing-mounted floats were originally intended to be retractable but design problems led to these being fixed before the aircraft's first flight. Persistent trouble with the contraprop gearbox resulted in a change to the Kasei 13 engine driving a single three-blade propeller from the second prototype onwards.

First flown on 6 May 1942, the **N1K1**

went on to trials with the navy, whose pilots were enthusiastic about the performance, although expressing misgivings over the tricky take-off characteristics. In the air, with its combat flaps, the Kyofu handled beautifully and possessed excellent manoeuvrability. At a time (the end of 1942) when the Zero naval fighter had effectively won air superiority for the Japanese in the Pacific, the N1K1 was ordered into production, but the delivery rate was slow to accelerate and fortunes changed rapidly during 1943. Thus in December of that year, with only 15 aircraft being completed each month and Japanese offensive initiative dwindling, it was decided to end production of the aircraft, and in March 1944 the last of 89 Kyofus was delivered to the service.

Codenamed **'Rex'** by the Allies, the N1K1 was first deployed for the defence of Balikpapan in Borneo, whose recovery by the Allies was regarded as no longer pressing as American forces surged closer to the Japanese homeland, while the Japanese then lacked the carriers with which to protect their isolated garrisons. In the final weeks of the war N1K1s flew alongside

the 'Rufes' of the Otsu Kokutai from Lake Biwa in defence of central Honshu against the increasing American raids on Japan. It was ironic that so promising was the N1K1 that the Japanese had reversed the process of adaptation, and with it produced the N1K2-J 'George' landplane fighter, certainly one of the best Japanese aircraft to see combat during the war.

Specification
Kawanishi N1K1
Type: single-seat interceptor fighter floatplane
Powerplant: one 1089-kW (1,460-hp) Mitsubishi MK4C Kasei 13 radial piston engine
Performance: maximum speed 489 km/h (304 mph) at 5700 m (18,700 ft); climb to 5000 m (16,405 ft) in

5 minutes 30 seconds; service ceiling 10600 m (34,775 ft); range 1050 km (652 miles)
Weights: empty 2752 kg (6,067 lb); maximum take-off 3712 kg (8,184 lb)
Dimensions: span 12.00 m (39 ft 4.4 in); length 10.59 m (34 ft 8.9 in); height 4.75 m (15 ft 7 in); wing area 23.5 m² (252.96 sq ft)
Armament: two fixed forward-firing 20-mm cannon and two fixed forward-firing 7.7-mm (0.303-in) machine-guns, plus two 30-kg (66-lb) bombs under the wings

Designed as a fighter to support offensive operations far from land-based air cover, the Kyofu was a fine machine overtaken by events in the Pacific which saw its planned role made superfluous.

Mitsubishi F1M

Roughly equivalent to the American Curtiss SOC Seagull observation float biplane, the smaller **Mitsubishi F1M** was of more compact and neater design, its development starting about two years later in 1934. First flown in June 1936, the **F1M1** embodied all the efforts of its designers to achieve an exceptionally clean aerodynamic shape, including low-drag float mountings, single interplane struts and all-metal construction, only the control surfaces being fabric-covered. The early aircraft displayed poor water handling and a lack of in-flight directional stability, however, but after fairly extensive alterations the production **F1M2** emerged as a thoroughly efficient aircraft, acceptable in all respects.

Initial production by Mitsubishi, which got under way in 1938, amounted to 524 aircraft before it was transferred to the 21st Naval Air Arsenal (Dai-Nijuichi Kaigun Kokusho) at Sasebo, where a further 590 were built. In due course the F1M2 equipped all but one of the K-Maru (6,900-ton) and S-Maru (7,200/8,300-ton) classes of converted merchant seaplane tenders, as well as numerous battleships and cruisers of the Imperial Japanese Navy. Codenamed **'Pete'** by the Allies, F1M2s were present at the Battle of Midway, two aircraft being launched from the battleship *Kirishima* (but being lost when the Japanese scuttled the sorely-crippled ship at the end of the Battle of the Solomons). The giant superbattleships *Musashi* and *Yamato* each carried several 'Petes' to spot for their 460-mm (18.1-in) main gun armament at the time of the Marianas bat-

tles, but none was used in earnest; instead the *Musashi* succumbed to American bombs and torpedoes in the Sibuyan Sea; the *Yamato*, bent on a suicide mission to Okinawa, followed her to the bottom on 7 April 1945.

Nevertheless 'Pete' seaplanes were widely used throughout the Pacific war, accompanying every seaborne landing by Japanese forces, providing gunnery spotting during preliminary bombardment by supporting warships and subsequently serving as covering fighters (and even dive-bombers) once the assault forces were ashore. It was also flown on convoy escort duties with the many supply convoys sailed by the Japanese during the mid-war period. In the last stages of the war, the

type was committed to the unequal task of defending the Japanese homeland from the devastating American raids, serving alongside 'Rex' and 'Rufe' seaplane fighters with the Otsu Kokutai in 1945.

Specification
Mitsubishi F1M2
Type: two-seat observation floatplane
Powerplant: one 611-kW (820-hp) Mitsubishi Hikari 1 radial piston engine
Performance: maximum speed 370 km/h (230 mph) at 3440 m (11,285 ft); climb to 5000 m (16,405 ft) in 9 minutes 36 seconds; service ceiling 9440 m (30,970 ft); range 740 km (460 miles)

Unlike the reconnaissance types carried by major Japanese surface units, the Mitsubishi F1M 'Pete' was an observation aircraft, designed for such tasks as gunfire direction, but was rarely used for that purpose.

Weights: empty 1928 kg (4,251 lb); maximum take-off 2550 kg (5,622 lb)
Dimensions: span 11.00 m (36 ft 1.1 in); length 9.50 m (31 ft 2 in); height 4.00 m (13 ft 1.5 in); wing area 29.54 m² (317.97 sq ft)
Armament: two fixed forward-firing 7.7-mm (0.303-in) machine-guns and one 7.7-mm (0.303-in) trainable machine-gun in the rear cockpit, plus two 60-kg (132-lb) bombs under the wings

---

Nakajima A6M2-N

Japan was the only nation to produce and deliver into service float-equipped single-seat interceptor fighter seaplanes (the British Spitfire float adaptation did not progress beyond the experimental stage). When in 1940 the Japanese navy initiated the design of a new interceptor seaplane (the Kawanishi N1K1 Kyofu, or 'Rex'), the need was also expressed for a stopgap aircraft and the Nakajima company was instructed in February 1941 to develop a float-equipped version of the excellent Mitsubishi A6M2 Zero naval interceptor. As evidence of Japan's long-standing plans for territorial expansion through the Pacific, it had been recognized that in the inevitable 'island-hopping' war there would be few ready-made air bases from which to provide air cover during the occupation of the smaller islands, and that the construction of runways would be impractical. Although equipped with almost a dozen aircraft-carriers, the Japanese would be unable to use them in support of every single island invasion.

After removing the wheel landing gear and fairing over the wheel wells of a standard A6M2, Nakajima mounted a large float under the fuselage by means of a forward-raked central pylon and a pair of V-struts below the cockpit; two cantilever stabilizing floats were also mounted under the wings. The standard Zero gun armament was retained, and the first prototype was flown on 7 December 1941, the day on which the Japanese navy

attacked Pearl Harbor.

Entering production as the **Nakajima A6M2-N** and codenamed **'Rufe'** by the Allies, the new fighter still displayed a creditable performance, being first issued to the Yokohama Kokutai and deployed to Tulagi in the Solomons where the Japanese had first landed during the Battle of the Coral Sea. However, almost all the 'Rufes' were destroyed in a strike on the seaplane base by 15 Grumman F4Fs from USS *Wasp* on 7 August 1942. Better success attended the 'Rufes' which fought in the later Aleutian campaign, but losses soared as soon as American fighter strength could be built up. During the final year of the war, when American heavy bombers and naval aircraft opened their great attacks on the Japanese homeland, 'Rufes' of the Otsu Kokutai, based on Lake Biwa, were thrown into the battle as interceptors in defence of Central Honshu but suffered very heavy losses. Total production of 'Rufe' amounted to 327 before being halted in September 1943.

Specification
Nakajima A6M2-N
Type: single-seat interceptor fighter floatplane
Powerplant: one 708-kW (950-hp) Nakajima NK1C Sakae 12 radial piston engine
Performance: maximum speed 435 km/h (270 mph) at 5000 m (16,405 ft); climb to 3000 m (9,845 ft) in 3 minute 54 seconds; service ceiling

10000 m (32,810 ft); range 1781 km (1,107 miles)
Weights: empty 1912 kg (4,215 lb); maximum take-off 2880 kg (6,349 lb)
Dimensions: span 12.00 m (39 ft 4.6 in); length 10.10 m (33 ft 1.6 in); height 4.30 m (14 ft 1.3 in); wing area 22.44 m² (241.54 sq ft)
Armament: two fixed forward-firing 20-mm cannon and two fixed forward-

firing 7.7-mm (0.303-in) machine-guns, plus provision for two 60-kg (132-lb) bombs under the wings

Until the purpose-designed N1K could be produced, the Japanese navy acquired a stopgap floatplane fighter in the Nakajima adaptation of Mitsubishi's famed A6M 'Zero'.

Curtiss SOC Seagull

USA

At the climax of its Service life the **Curtiss SOC Seagull** scout-observation seaplane in 1940 was serving aboard every battleship, cruiser and carrier in the US Navy, as well as a destroyer, a seaplane carrier and two gunboats, with a US Marine Corps squadron and at a US Coast Guard station. It had entered production in 1935 having beaten the Douglas XO2D-1 and Vought XO5U-1 in competition, and on 12 November that year the first operational **SOC-1** was assigned to the light cruiser USS *Marblehead*. Subsequent versions were the **SOC-2**, **SOC-3** and **SOC-4** (the **SOC-2A** and **SOC-3A** being fitted with arrester gear) and the **SON-1** produced by the Naval Aircraft Factory.

Featuring interchangeable wheel and float alighting gear (in the latter configuration it was fitted with single central float and outrigged wing floats), the SOC replaced Vought O2Us and O3Us, and was used to spot for the fleet's big guns, increasing the accuracy of the main gun armament of the US Navy's battleships. Each such battleship embarked three or four SOCs, the heavy cruisers four and the light cruisers two. Flagships usually carried an additional Seagull for use by the force commander. Production contracts, totalling 304 aircraft for the US Navy (plus three for the US Coast Guard), had been placed by the end of 1938; within two years 279 were in service, including 83 aboard the battleship divisions of the Battle Fleet and

63 with the cruiser divisions of the Scouting Force; there were also 30 SOCs with the Atlantic Squadron and 15 with Carrier Divisions One and Two in the Pacific.

During the Japanese attack on Pearl Harbor nine embarked SOCs and 13 ashore were listed as destroyed, and although no SOC was directly involved in the great Battle of Midway about 20 Seagulls undertook scouting sorties before the Solomon campaign, flying with Task Force 61. They were still extremely active in 1943, particularly in the Wake, Marshalls and Gilberts campaigns. Although by 1943 most of the 150-odd aircraft still surviving in service were usually equipped with wheel landing gear aboard American escort carriers, some cruisers still continued to carry the floatplanes, and these were present at the American landings in North Africa in November that year. The Curtiss SO-3C Seamew monoplane had been introduced to replace the SOC in 1942, but this later machine proved disappointing and, although a greater number was produced, it was the old Seagull that remained in US Navy service longer, surviving up to the end of 1944.

Specification
Curtiss SOC-1 Seagull
Type: two-seat scout and observation floatplane
Powerplant: one 447-kW (600-hp) Pratt & Whitney R-1340-18 Wasp radial piston engine

Performance: maximum speed 253 km/h (157 mph) at sea level; climb to 1525 m (5,000 ft) in 5 minutes 54 seconds; service ceiling 4540 m (14,900 ft); range 1535 km (954 miles)
Weights: empty 1591 kg (3,508 lb); maximum take-off 2466 kg (5,437 lb)
Dimensions: span 10.97 m (36 ft 0 in); length 9.65 m (31 ft 8 in); height 4.29 m (14 ft 1 in); wing area 32.33 m² (348 sq ft)
Armament: one fixed forward-firing

A Curtiss SOC Seagull stands ready for launch on the catapult aboard the battleship USS West Virginia. *In 1940 this scout-observation seaplane was shipped aboard every battleship, cruiser and carrier in the US Navy.*

7.62-mm (0.3-in) machine-gun and one 7.62-mm (0.3-in) trainable machine-gun in the rear cockpit, plus two 45-kg (100-lb) bombs under the wings

---

Curtiss SC-1 Seahawk

USA

The Curtiss SC-1 Seahawk monoplane was unique among American scout seaplanes of World war II in being a relatively high performance single-seater with an almost fighter-like speed. It was almost the last of a long line of aircraft in the scout-observation category built by Curtiss to serve aboard American battleships and cruisers. Like its immediate predecessor, it featured a single large central float with stabilizing wing-tip floats, these being replaceable by fixed wheel landing gear for shore base operation.

Subject of Curtiss design proposals, the SC-1 Seahawk was accepted by US Navy letter of intent on 30 October 1942 and prototypes were ordered on 31 March 1943. The first of two **SC-1** aircraft made its first flight on 16 February 1944, by which time production orders for 500 SC-1s had been placed. Production deliveries started in the late summer that year, the aircraft being completed with wheel landing gear for delivery to shore depots; the Edo float assemblies, being purchased separately, were fitted to the aircraft according to fleet requirements; the first aircraft were shipped aboard transports to Australia late in 1944 for delivery to warships of the US 7th Fleet. The first aircraft was embarked in USS *Guam* on 22 October.

The Seahawk saw little operational service other than constant air-sea rescue patrols, this despite the provision of a somewhat cramped bunk in the rear fuselage limiting such rescues to single ditched airmen. In the relatively straightforward recovery of Borneo, however, which was regarded as something of a sideshow at the end of

The Seahawk was a high-performance single-seater ordered by the US Navy in 1942, and entering service in 1944 aboard USS Guam. *In the event it saw little combat and was mainly used for air-sea rescue patrols.*

the war with Japan and which was opposed by only small numbers of Japanese aircraft, a few Seahawks with the 7th Fleet were used for gunnery control during the preliminary bombardment before the seaborne landings. Some aircraft were said to have been used in the 'attack' category, the Seahawk being capable of carrying a pair of 45-kg (100-lb) bombs in a bay in the central float; for anti-submarine work the aircraft would mount an ASH radar set in a pod under the starboard wing and a 113-kg (250-lb) bomb under the port wing.

Total production of the Seahawk, before VJ-Day brought cancellation of outstanding orders, was 566 aircraft; nine examples of an improved two-seat version, the **SC-2**, were delivered to the US Navy in 1946.

Specification
Curtiss SC-1 Seahawk
Type: single-seat shipborne scout and air-sea rescue floatplane
Powerplant: one 1007-kW (1,350-hp) Wright R-1820-62 Cyclone radial piston engine
Performance: maximum speed 504 km/h (313 mph) at 8715 m (28,600 ft); climb to 3050 m (10,000 ft) in 4 minutes 6 seconds; service ceiling 11370 m (37,300 ft); range 1016 km (625 miles)
Weights: empty 2867 kg (6,320 lb); maximum take-off 4082 kg (9,000 lb)

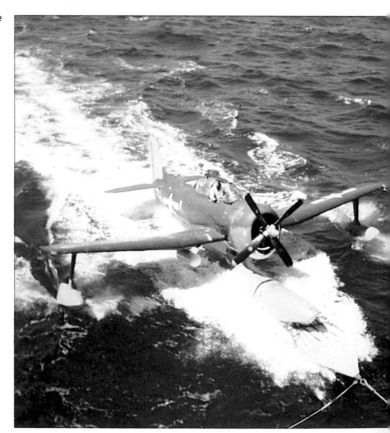

Dimensions: span 12.50 m (41 ft 0 in); length 11.09 m (36 ft 4.5 in); height 5.49 m (18 ft 0 in); wing area 26.01 m² (280 sq ft)

Armament: two fixed forward-firing 12.7-mm (0.5-in) machine-guns, plus two 113- and two 45-kg (250- and 100-lb) bombs

Vought OS2U Kingfisher

Displaying many of the traditional features of the American naval observation and scouting biplanes of the 1930s (radial engine, deep spacious cockpit, large 'glasshouse' over the rear cockpit and central main float), the **Vought OS2U** monoplane was the first military aircraft to employ spot welding in its primary structure.

Ordered in prototype form in 1937, the first **XOS2U-1** made its maiden flight on 20 July of the following year, initial service deliveries being made in August 1940. The first aircraft to serve aboard an American battleship was embarked in USS *Colorado*. Of the 54 **OS2U-1** floatplanes completed in that year the majority was distributed between the Pearl Harbor Battle Force, Alameda NAS Battle Force and the Pensacola naval air station.

Progressively improved **OS2U-2** and **OS2U-3** aircraft were delivered up to 1942, the latter being the most widely used version with increased fuel capacity and improved armour protection for the crew; a total of 1,306 was produced (including 300 **OS2N-1** aircraft built by the Naval Aircraft Factory at Philadelphia). Apart from ships of the US Navy, the type equipped the Inshore Patrol Squadrons (which became exclusively equipped with the type), and OS2U-3s also served at Pensacola and Jacksonville naval air stations; their operational tasks included scouting for the fleet, gunnery spotting, anti-submarine patrol, ship-to-shore communciations and rescue of ditched airmen, of whom Captain Eddie Rickenbacker (forced down in the South Pacific) was the most famous. The interchangeable float/wheel landing gear enabled them to operate from shore bases when necessary. There were even occasions when OS2U floatplanes were flown into action as dive-bombers.

The OS2U-3 was selected by the British Purchasing Mission in 1941, and 100 aircraft (FN650-FN749) entered service with the Fleet Air Arm as the **Kingfisher Mk I**. Some of these joined No. 703 Squadron and, equipped with floats, served aboard British armed merchant cruisers for sea patrol during operations to combat German blockade runners. Most aircraft were delivered direct to the Middle East and West Africa, where they found limited

Below: Over 1,300 Kingfishers were manufactured and became the exclusive equipment of the Inshore Patrol Squadrons, as well as serving with the fleet in various roles.

A Vought Kingfisher Mk I of No. 107 Squadron, Royal Australian Air Force, in 1942. Kingfishers also served with the Fleet Air Arm aboard armed merchant cruisers. In the US Navy most Kingfishers were catapulted from the fantails of battleships and cruisers.

use for coastal patrol and air-sea rescue. Fourteen aircraft were also used as trainers in Jamaica; 20 others intended for British use were in fact delivered to the US Navy.

Specification
Vought OS2U-3
Type: two-seat shipborne observation and scout floatplane
Powerplant: one 336-kW (450-hp) Pratt & Whitney R-985-AN-2 or -8 Wasp Junior radial piston engine
Performance: maximum speed 264 km/h (164 mph) at 1675 m (5,500 ft); climb to 1525 m (5,000 ft) in 12 minutes 6 seconds; service ceiling 3960 m (13,000 ft); range 1851 km (1,150 miles)
Weights: empty 1870 kg (4,123 lb); maximum take-off 2722 kg (6,000 lb)
Dimensions: span 10.95 m (35 ft 11 in); length 10.24 m (33 ft 7.25 in); height 4.60 m (15 ft 1 in); wing area 24.34 m² (262 sq ft)

A Kingfisher catapults from USS Texas in the Mediterranean, 1944. Texas was the first US battleship to launch aircraft after being fitted with a flying-off platform while serving with the British Grand Fleet in 1918.

Armament: one fixed forward-firing 7.62-mm (0.3-in) machine-gun and one 7.62-mm (0.3-in) machine-gun in the rear cockpit, plus 295 kg (650 lb) of bombs

Grumman J2F Duck

The **Grumman J2F** was an attractive float biplane embodying a wheel landing gear that retracted into the sides on the central float, an ingenious arrangement successfully developed by Grumman in 1930 and incorporated in the JF-1 utility amphibian which served aboard the carrier USS *Lexington* with VS-3 from 1934 onwards. A development of this, which it closely resembled, was the slightly larger J2F, popularly known as the **Duck**, which was first flown on 25 June 1935. Some 89 **J2F-1** aircraft were supplied to the US Navy. As well as accommodating a crew of two under a long canopy the aircraft could carry two additional crew members or passengers side-by-side within the large fairing that joined the central float to the fuselage. These aircraft also served aboard American carriers immediately before the war (being equipped with arrester gear), and were followed by 30 **J2F-2** aircraft, of which nine **J2F-2A** variants with two 7.62-mm (0.3-in) machine-guns and light bomb racks were produced for the US Marine Corps Squadron VMS-3 serving at St Thomas in the Virgin Islands.

Further minor changes resulted in 20 **J2F-3** aircraft (with Wright R-1820-36 engines) and 32 **J2F-4** aircraft (with -30 engines) being produced, but the increasing risk of war prompted the US Navy to order 144 **J2F-5** machines from Grumman at the end of 1940, powered by -50 engines. These aircraft undertook a multitude of 'utility' tasks with the US Navy, including communications with off-shore vessels, target-towing, air-sea rescue, ambulance and non-operational reconnaissance work. Several aircraft served with the US Coast Guard, and one was evaluated by the USAAF as the **OA-12** in the observation role.

Increasing pressure on the Grumman plant at Bethpage, New York, for production of Wildcat fighters caused production of the Duck (as the **J2F-5** was now officially known) to be transferred to Columbia Aircraft's Valley Stream factory when a new order for 330 **J2F-6** aircraft was placed immediately after Pearl Harbor. These, powered by 671 kW (900-hp) -54 engines, brought the total Duck production to 653, the last being completed in 1945. Most aircraft served at shore stations during the latter part of the war, their arrester gear being removed or omitted. They were also employed on anti-submarine patrol work, equipped to carry two 147-kg (325-lb) depth bombs.

Specification
Grumman J2F-5 Duck
Type: three-seat utility amphibious floatplane
Powerplant: one 634-kW (850-hp) Wright R-1920-50 Cyclone radial piston engine
Performance: maximum speed

This J2F-3 Duck was the personal transport of a Rear Admiral, the all-over blue being reserved for flag officers. The stars of his rank were attached to the rear of the cockpit.

303 km/h (188 mph) at 3960 m (13,000 ft); climb to 3050 m (10,000 ft) in 10 minutes 12 seconds; service ceiling 7955 m (26,100 ft); range 1255 km (780 miles)
Weights: empty 1950 kg (4,300 lb); maximum take-off 3044 kg (6,711 lb)
Dimensions: span 11.89 m (39 ft 0 in); length 10.36 m (34 ft 0 in); height 3.76 m (12 ft 4 in) with wheels retracted; wing area 38.0 m² (409 sq ft)
Armament: one 7.62-mm (0.3-in)

The main external distinguishing feature of the Grumman J2F compared with the original JF series was the later aircraft's lack of a strut linking the ailerons on the upper and lower wings. The retractable landing gear was a particularly neat feature.

trainable machine-gun in the rear cockpit, and up to 295 kg (650 lb) of bombs and/or depth charges under the wings

Northrop N-3PB Nomad

The company headed by John K. Northrop had been successful in securing US Army contracts for its A-17 attack bombers in the mid-1930s but at the time of its merger with the Douglas Aircraft Company business was beginning to fall away. Among the few projects then being pursued was a twin-float seaplane whose design owed much to the earlier wheel-equipped attack bombers. Believing that such an aircraft would be required by the US Navy, Northrop persisted with its design. This was shown to members of a Norwegian Purchasing Commission which visited the USA early in 1940, seeking to obtain a patrol/attack seaplane for coastal work to discourage the use of Norwegian waters by German shipping. Twenty-four such **Northrop N-3PB** aircraft were ordered straight from the drawing board.

Before these aircraft could be delivered Norway fell to the Germans in April/June 1940. Production went ahead, however, at the request of the UK and, as a number of Norwegian aircrew had succeeded in escaping the German invasion, it was decided to form a squadron manned by volunteers in Iceland to serve alongside the RAF. Accordingly No. 330 Squadron was formed at Reykjavik on 25 April 1941; a month later the Norwegian freighter *Fjordheim* arrived from Canada bringing 18 dismantled N-

3PBs. These were disembarked and assembled in a seaplane hangar at Reykjavik, the first aircraft being air tested on 2 June. Employed for convoy escort and anti-submarine patrols, and named **Nomad**, the floatplanes were flown from Reykjavik, Akureyri and Bordheyri, and remained with the squadron for well over a year being joined later by Consolidated Catalina flying-boats. Most of the early North Cape convoys, which were sailed from Iceland to the North Russian ports during 1941-2, were provided with escort patrols by Nomads for the first 240 km (150 miles) of their voyages. In July 1942 two prowling Focke-Wulf Fw 200s long-range reconnaissance aircraft were intercepted by the seaplanes and chased away.

Despite their sterling service the Nomads were not wholly suited to the demands of service in the far north, and the long range and better sea-going qualities of the flying-boat caused their withdrawal from service in January 1943. (The N-3PB Nomad should not be confused with the Northrop 8-A5 Nomad which, surplus to American needs as the A-17A, was supplied under Lend-Lease, principally to South Africa.)

Specification
Northrop N-3PB Nomad
Type: three-seat patrol and bomber

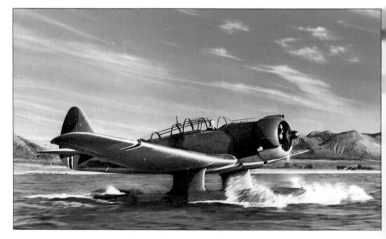

floatplane
Powerplant: one 820-kW (1,100-hp) Wright GR-1820-G205A radial piston engine
Performance: maximum speed 414 km/h (257 mph) at sea level; climb to 4570 m (15,000 ft) in 14 minutes 24 seconds; service ceiling 7315 m (24,000 ft); range 1609 km (1,000 miles)
Weights: empty 2808 kg (6,190 lb); maximum take-off 4808 kg (10,600 lb)
Dimensions: span 14.91 m (48 ft 11 in); length 10.97 m (36 ft 0 in); height 3.66 m (12 ft 0 in); wing area 34.93 m² (376 sq ft)

The first flying tests of the Northrop N-3PB patrol bomber took place at Lake Elsinor, California. The aircraft were in Norwegian colours, but had not been delivered when the German invasion took place.

Armament: four fixed forward-firing 12.7-mm (0.5-in) machine-guns, one 7.62-mm (0.3-in) trainable machine-gun in the dorsal position, and one 7.62-mm (0.3-in) trainable machine-gun in the ventral position, plus four 227-kg (500-lb) bombs

Anti-Shipping Aircraft

Attacks against shipping around the war-zone coasts, and the incessant vigil against submarines, kept many aircraft busy throughout the war. These ranged from fighters to heavy bombers, all playing their part in denying the enemy freedom of the seas.

Of all the nations drawn into World War II during 1939 and 1940 none had a more pressing need for anti-shipping aircraft than the UK for, as a sea-girt power, her lifelines were critically vulnerable to attack from surface raider, submarine and aircraft alike. Yet all responsibility for defence against this threat was, as it had been for centuries, vested almost exclusively in the British Royal Navy. Lip service had been paid to the RAF with the provision of such aircraft as the Avro Anson, while the Lockheed Hudson began arriving from America in 1939 to provide relatively long-range reconnaissance/attack muscle for Coastal Command.

As in so many of the wartime air forces, the emergence of the maritime strike role after the outbreak of hostilities brought about the demand for adaptation of obsolescent aircraft (fighters, bombers and even transports) to meet the operational requirements. The parameters of the requirements themselves were so broad (the equation involving long-range navigation accuracy over featureless oceans, precision of attack equipment and a wide assortment of weapons which included cannon, depth charges, bombs, rockets and torpedoes)

The mighty Consolidated B-24 Liberator had a long-range capability which made her an ideal choice for adaptation to an ocean patrol and long-distance attack role, the latter in which she excelled against Japanese cargo shipping.

that no single aircraft could be considered ideal. Moreover, beyond the scope of this section were the other important anti-shipping aircraft, the minelayers.

It may be said that premeditated anti-shipping operations, as distinct from long-range anti-submarine attacks which were usually the result of chance sightings during tedious ocean patrols, were confined largely to the 'narrow seas' around Europe, from the North Cape of Norway to the Mediterranean, although the US and Japanese air forces also

engaged in anti-shipping operations in the Pacific, particularly during the latter part of the war, as did the RAF in the Bay of Bengal.

Ignoring the relatively fruitless efforts by Bristol Blenheims and Avro Ansons in the early months, the RAF began to achieve worthwhile successes when such aircraft as the Vickers Wellington, Bristol Beaufort and Bristol Beaufighter arrived at Coastal Command, while in the Axis air forces the Dornier Do 217 and Junkers Ju 88 proved fairly effec-

tive, particularly in operations against the Allied North Cape convoys, in which the Heinkel He 111 also participated. In the Savoia-Marchetti S.M.789 the Italians also possessed an excellent torpedo bomber which was flown to good effect against British shipping in the Mediterranean.

The Americans, however, were caught largely unprepared for anti-shipping tasks and so relied heavily on adaptation of the Boeing B-17 and Consolidated B-24, the latter's very long range suiting it admirably for ocean patrol and long-distance attack. Likewise the Japanese, despite embarking on their far-flung Pacific campaign, had assumed that carrierborne attack bombers would embrace the majority of maritime strike operations. Such was the nature of the organization of the Imperial Japanese Navy, however, that from the first days of the Pacific war considerable dependence was placed on land-based anti-shipping bombers, and it was the Mitsubishi G3M that participated in the successful attack on the British capital ships HMS *Prince of Wales* and HMS *Repulse*, one of the war's most successful air strikes against major warships at sea.

UK
Avro Anson

Anachronistic relic of pre-war RAF expansion, the **Avro Anson** was originally the result of a coastal reconnaissance aircraft requirement, and was developed from a six-seat commercial aircraft. It first flew on 24 March 1935 and, powered by Cheetah engines, the **Anson Mk I** entered service with No. 48 Squadron in March 1936, and was the first RAF aircraft with a retractable landing gear, albeit manually operated. The Anson subsequently served with 12 squadrons of Coastal Command up to the beginning of the war, when the first Lockheed Hudsons were just beginning to arrive from America. Nevertheless Ansons were retained on short-range coastal reconnaissance duties in diminishing numbers until 1942, occasionally having brushes with the enemy. By the beginning of the war, however, the Anson was already in use as an aircrew trainer for navigators, wireless operators and air gunners, and it was for this long and priceless service that the 'faithful Annie' is best remembered. Jacobs- and Wright-powered **Anson Mk III** and **Anson Mk IV** aircraft were shipped to Canada to equip the growing numbers of flying schools under the Commonwealth Air Training Scheme. Canadian manufacturers also producing the **Anson Mks II, V** and **VI**. Light transport conversions from the Anson Mk I resulted in the **Anson Mks X, XI** and **XII**, some of which were employed as air ambulances; the **Anson Mk XI** was powered by Cheetah XIX engines driving Fairey-Reed metal propellers, and the **Anson Mk XII** had Cheetah XVs driving constant-speed Rotol propellers. Production, which continued after the war with the **Anson**

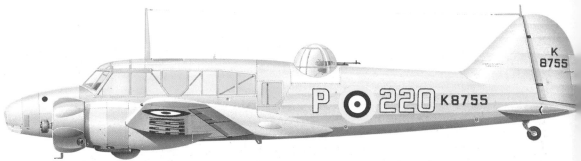

Avro Anson GR.Mk I of No. 220 Sqn, Coastal Command, in the overall silver pre-war paint scheme.

Mks **19, 20, 21** and **22**, reached a total of 11,020 aircraft, including 2,822 built in Canada.

Specification
Avro Anson Mk I
Type: three-seat general-reconnaissance aircraft
Powerplant: two 350-hp (261- kW) Armstrong Siddeley Cheetah IX radial piston engines

Performance: maximum speed 303 km/h (188 mph) at 2134 m (7,000 ft); initial climb rate 219 m (720 ft) per minute; service ceiling 5791 m (19,000 ft); range 1271 km (790 miles)
Weights: empty 2438 kg (5,375 lb); maximum take-off 3629 kg (8,000 lb)
Dimensions: span 17.22 m (56 ft 6 in); length 12.88 m (42 ft 3 in); height 3.99 m (13 ft 1in); wing area 43.01 m^2 (463.0 sq ft)
Armament: one fixed forward-firing

Ever on the alert, an Anson of No. 48 Sqn keeps watch on a convoy out of Liverpool. At the outbreak of war, the Anson formed the bulk of Coastal Command's fleet. No. 48 Sqn was based at Hooton Park to protect the Western Approaches.

7.7-mm (0.303-in) machine-gun in nose and one 7.7-mm machine-gun in dorsal turret, plus provision to carry up to 163 kg (360 lb) of bombs

---

UK
Bristol Beaufighter

To a large extent responsible for the defence against the German Blitz of 1940-1 as the RAF's first purpose-built night-fighter, the **Bristol Beaufighter** remained in service as such almost to the end of the war. Such was its performance, however, that in 1941 it also came to be developed, first as an intruder and, as a natural follow-on, a specialist anti-shipping strike aircraft. It was moreover no stranger to RAF Coastal Command, the **Beaufighter Mk IC** having been specially prepared as a long-range maritime fighter with additional navigation and radio equipment. The **Beaufighter Mk VIC** with 1,650-hp (1230.4-kW) Hercules VI or XVI radials featured for the first time an additional dorsal machine-gun to provide token defence against enemy fighters which Coastal Command squadrons frequently encountered over the Bay of Biscay.

As early as March 1941 a Beaufighter Mk I underwent trials with a torpedo, and in September the following year another aircraft was fitted with 76.2-mm (3-in) rocket projectiles. Two months later the first Beaufighter Strike Wing was formed at North Coates, Lincolnshire, comprising No. 143 Squadron (Beaufighter fighters), No. 236

Towards the end of the war, the unguided rocket became the major anti-shipping weapon, especially against the small targets often encountered in the Channel. These were usually ripple-fired.

Bristol Beaufighter TF.Mk X of No. 455 Sqn armed with eight underwing, unguided rockets.

Beaufighters were particularly accurate against shipping, proving to be a steady platform during the diving attack. As well as serving in home waters, the Beaufighter had great success against Japanese shipping.

Squadron (Beaufighter bombers with a pair of 113- or 227-kg/250- or 500-lb bombs) and No. 254 Squadron ('Torbeau' torpedo-carrying Beaufighters). By the spring of 1943 the wing was in frequent action against German supply ships sailing between enemy-held ports in the North Sea. In May that year rocket-firing Beaufighter Mk VICs entered service, their principal task being to attack escorting *Flak* ships while the torpedo aircraft and bombers went for the enemy merchantmen.

As the Beaufighter was gradually replaced in service as a night-fighter its importance as a maritime strike aircraft grew. The **Beaufighter TF.Mk X** was introduced with ASV (air-to-surface vessel) radar and carried universal racks which enabled combinations of bombs, rockets and torpedo to be carried. Strike Beaufighters served with a total of 11 home-based Coastal Command squadrons, and seven in the Middle East. The aircraft reached the Far East in January 1943 and soon afterwards began to re-equip five strike squadrons (Nos 22, 27, 177, 211 and 217), proving deadly when flown against Japanese shipping being sailed along the Burma coast.

Specification
Bristol Beaufighter TF.Mk X
Type: two-seat torpedo-strike fighter
Powerplant: two 1,770-hp (1319.9-kW) Bristol Hercules XVII 14-cylinder air-cooled radial piston engines
Performance: maximum speed 488 km/h (303 mph) at 396 m (1,300 ft); climb to 1524 m (5,000 ft) in 3.5 minutes; service ceiling 4572 m (15,000 ft); normal range 2366 km (1,470 miles)
Weights: empty 7076 kg (15,600 lb); maximum take-off 11431 kg (25,200 lb)

Beaufighter attack! Trailing vortices from its wingtips, this 'Beau' is pulling out from its strike against a German ship. Further aircraft behind it succeed in turning the water white.

Dimensions: span 17.63 m (57 ft 10 in); length 12.70 m (41 ft 8 in); height 4.82 m (15 ft 10 in); wing area 46.73 m² (503 sq ft)
Armament: four 20-mm Hispano cannon in nose and one 7.7-m (0.303-in) machine-gun in dorsal position, plus either eight 76.2 mm (3-in) rocket projectiles and two 227-kg (500 lb) bombs or a single 748-kg (1,650-lb) or 965-kg (2,127-lb) torpedo

---

 UK
Bristol Beaufort

Until superseded by the torpedo-carrying Beaufighter, the **Bristol Beaufort** was the RAF's standard torpedo-bomber from 1940 to 1943, replacing the aged Vickers Vildebeest biplane. First flown on 15 October 1938, the **Beaufort Mk I**, of which early versions were powered by 1,010-hp (753.2-kW) Bristol Taurus II radials (later replaced by Taurus VIs), joined No. 22 Squadron in December 1939 and carried out their first minelaying sortie on 15-16 August 1940. Beauforts also dropped the RAF's first 907-kg (2,000-lb) bomb on 7 May. Total production of the Beaufort Mk I was 965, and this version was followed by the **Beaufort Mk II** with American Pratt & Whitney Twin Wasp radials, production continuing until 1943, by which time 415 had been produced. The final Beaufort Mk IIs were completed as trainers with the two-gun dorsal turret deleted. Beauforts equipped six Coastal Command squadrons in the United Kingdom and four in the Middle East, their most famous operations being carried out against the German warships

Scharnhorst and *Gneisenau* on 6 April 1941 in Brest harbour (which earned a posthumous VC for Flying Officer K. Campbell of No. 22 Squadron), and during the warships' escape up the English Channel early in 1942. Beauforts were also very active while based on Malta, attacking Axis shipping being sailed to North Africa. The **Beaufort Mks V-IX** were built in Australia for the RAAF in the Far East, production totalling 700.

Specification
Bristol Beaufort Mk I
Type: four-seat torpedo-bomber

Bristol Beaufort Mk I of No. 22 Sqn, Coastal Command. No. 22 Sqn was the first in service with this torpedo-bomber. Despite early problems, it went on to provide useful service.

Powerplant: two 1,130-hp (842.6-kW) Bristol Taurus VI radial piston engines
Performance: maximum speed 426 km/h (265 mph) at 1829 m (6,000 ft); service ceiling 5029 m (16,500 ft); range 2575 km (1,600 miles)
Weights: empty 5942 kg (13,100 lb); maximum take-off 9629 kg (21,228 lb)
Dimensions: span 17.62 m (57 ft 10 in); length 13.49 m (44 ft 3 in); height 4.34 m (14 ft 3 in); wing area 46.73 m² (503.0 sq ft)
Armament: two 7.7-mm (0.303-in) machine-guns in nose and dorsal turret

(some aircraft had a rear-firing machine-gun under the nose and two in beam-firing positions), plus a bombload up to 907 kg (2,000 lb) or one 728-kg (1,605-lb) 457-mm (18-in) torpedo

No. 217 Sqn flew its Beauforts from Malta, and these were responsible for many of the problems faced by Axis shipping in the Mediterranean. Only one torpedo could be carried, but the aircraft possessed bombing and minelaying capability.

de Havilland Mosquito

In much the same manner that the Beaufighter came to be introduced into RAF Coastal Command as an anti-shipping strike fighter, so the classic **de Havilland Mosquito** achieved considerable success in this role, being used principally with rocket projectiles and bombs. A torpedo-carrying version was under development at the end of the war.

It was not until the Mosquito had been successfully developed as a fighter-bomber (effectively combining its night-fighter cannon armament with its ability to carry bombs internally) that the **Mosquito FB.Mk VI** was selected for service with Coastal Command, trials being undertaken at Boscombe Down with an aircraft fitted with eight 76.2-mm (3-in) rocket projectiles under the wings. In addition to a nose armament of four 20-mm and four 7.7-mm (0.303-in) guns, the Mosquito FB.Mk VI could also carry a pair of short-finned 227-kg (500-lb) bombs in the rear of the bomb bay; alterna-

tively, later aircraft were strengthened to carry a further pair of 227-kg (500-lb) weapons under the wings in place of the rockets.

Following the success of the Beaufighter anti-shipping strike wings in 1943, a Mosquito Strike Wing was formed at Banff in Scotland before the end of that year, No. 333 (Norwegian) Squadron being the first to receive Mosquito FB.Mk VIs in November. No. 248 Squadron followed in the next month, and No. 235 in June 1944. Employed almost exclusively against enemy shipping off the Norwegian coast, the Norwegian pilots of No. 333 Squadron usually flew as pathfinders for the wing, leading Mosquito formations along the winding fjords in search of German vessels.

Of greater interest than true operational value was the **Mosquito FB.Mk XVIII** anti-shipping strike aircraft, armed with a single 57-mm Molins gun in the nose. A converted Mosquito FB.Mk VI thus armed made its first

flight on 25 August 1943, after which 27 production aircraft were built and entered service with No. 248 Squadron at Banff in January 1944. Detachments were sent south for patrols over the English Channel and on 25 March a Mosquito FB.Mk XVIII pilot attacked and claimed to have sunk an enemy submarine off the French coast. Weighing over 907 kg (2,000 lb), the Molins gun was not considered a success as its recoil constantly caused local structural damage in the Mosquito's nose. No. 248 Squadron retained its aircraft until February 1945, after which the survivors were handed over to No. 254 Squadron at North Coates for the remainder of the war.

Specification
de Havilland Mosquito FB.Mk VI
Type: two-seat anti-shipping strike fighter
Powerplant: two 1,230-hp (917.2-kW) Rolls-Royce Merlin XXI 12-cylinder liquid-cooled inline piston engines

Performance: maximum speed 612 km/h (380 mph) at 3962 m (13,000 ft); climb to 4572 m (15,000 ft) in 7.0 minutes; service ceiling 10972 m (36,000 ft); normal range 2092 km (1,300 miles)
Weights: empty 6486 kg (14,300 lb); maximum take-off 10115 kg (22,300 lb)
Dimensions: span 16.51 m (54 ft 2 in); length 12.34 m (40 ft 6 in); height 4.63 m (15 ft 3 in); wing area 40.41 m² (435 sq ft)
Armament: four 20-mm and four 7.7-mm (0.303-in) guns in the nose, plus either two 227-kg (500-lb) bombs and eight 76.2-mm (3-inch) rocket projectiles or up to four 227-kg (500-lb) bombs

As effective as the Beaufighter, the de Havilland Mosquito was also used in low-level rocket and strafing attacks against shipping. No. 143 Sqn flew its FB.Mk VIs from Banff in Scotland against shipping off Norway.

Vickers Wellington and Warwick

The famous **Vickers Wellington** bomber enjoyed a long and valuable career with RAF Coastal Command in a number of roles, not least in the maritime general reconnaissance role, a term that euphemistically embraced anti-shipping duties. Apart from a small number of Wellingtons equipped for mine-exploding in 1940, Coastal Command's first aircraft specifically prepared for maritime work were **Wellington Mk VIII** machines de-

veloped in 1941 for use with the Leigh Light for illuminating surfaced U-boats, particularly in the Bay of Biscay; the first such aircraft were delivered to No. 221 Squadron in the Mediterranean in January 1942, however. ASV radar came to be fitted in some Mk VIIIs (which were in effect conversions of the Wellington Mk IC bomber), but the **Wellington GR.Mk XI** employed the improved airframe of the Wellington Mk X and was capable of carrying a

wide range of anti-submarine weapons including two 190.5-kg (420-lb) depth charges or a single 457-mm (18-in) torpedo. The **Wellington GR.Mk XII** was also equipped with a Leigh Light, which retracted into an aperture in the midships fuselage structure. The **Wellington GR.Mk XIII**, intended for daylight use only, omitted the Leigh light but carried two 457-mm (18-in) torpedoes in addition to ASV Mk III radar, while the **Wellington**

GR.Mk XIV could carry depth charges or bombs, and featured Leigh Light and ASV Mk III for night operations. Anti-shipping Wellingtons remained in service for the remainder of the war serving on a total of 21 squadrons at home, in the Mediterranean and Middle and Far East.

A bomber development was the **Vickers Warwick** which, overtaken by technological progress, never survived to serve as such; instead it, like

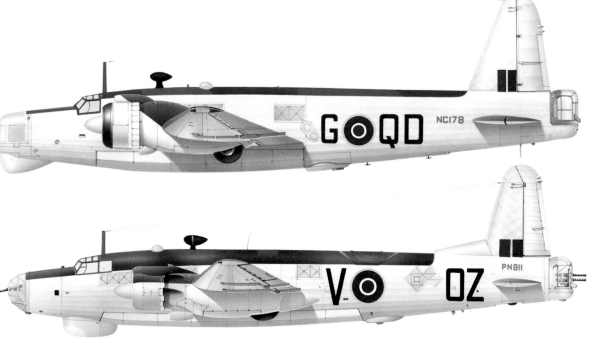

The Vickers Wellington GR.Mk XIV was the final version of this able aircraft used by Coastal Command. This example is a Mk XIV issued to No. 304 (Polish) Squadron in 1944.

the Wellington, came to be developed for maritime duties. However, although it gave considerable service with Coastal Command in the air-sea rescue role from 1943 onwards, lengthy delays in development (and shortage of Centaurus engines) prevented the **Warwick GR.Mk V**, with Leigh Light and ASV, from entering service with No. 179 Squadron until November 1944; this squadron flew anti-submarine patrols over the Bay of Biscay and the Western Approaches during the last three months of the war.

Specification
Vickers Wellington GR.Mk XIII
Type: six/seven-seat anti-shipping/submarine aircraft
Powerplant: two 1,735-hp (1293.8-kW) Bristol Hercules XVII air-cooled radial piston engines
Performance: maximum speed 406 km/h (252 mph) at 1219 m (4,000 ft); climb to 1219 m (4,000 ft) in 6.9 minutes; service ceiling 4877 m (16,000 ft); normal range 2816 kg (1,750 miles)
Weights: empty 9974 kg (21,988 lb); maximum take-off 14107 kg (31,100 lb)
Dimensions: span 26.26 m (86 ft 2 in); length 19.68 m (64 ft 7 in); height 5.38 m (17 ft 8 in); wing area 78.04 m² (840 sq ft)
Armament: two 7.7-mm (0.303-in) machine-guns in nose turret and four in tail turret, and some aircraft mounted two machine-guns in fuselage beam positions, plus an offensive load of either bombs and depth charges up to 2041 kg (4,500 lb) or two 457-mm (18-in) torpedoes

Transmitting and receiving aerials for the ASV Mk II radar adorn this Wellington on routine patrol over the Mediterranean. This radar enabled the aircraft to detect small objects projecting above the surface, such as submarine conning towers.

The Warwick GR.Mk V did not enter service until late 1944. It carried ASV radar and a Leigh light and was used over the Bay of Biscay on anti-submarine patrols. This aircraft served with No. 179 Sqn.

USA
Boeing B-17 Fortress

America's enforced entry into World War II undoubtedly caught her air forces unprepared for maritime operations, and the sudden appearance of long-range U-boats off her eastern seaboard and in the Caribbean caused some 122 aged Douglas B-18Bs to be deployed on anti-submarine patrols along the coasts of the USA. Meanwhile, however, the **Boeing B-17D Fortress**, which had supplanted the B-18 in service with the USAAC's heavy bombardment groups in 1941, had already pioneered anti-shipping operations by this aircraft with an attack against Japanese vessels on 10 December 1941. This was the first occasion on which American aircrews flew an offensive mission. No specialist B-17 version was produced for the anti-shipping role with the American air forces, the machines that were later employed in maritime operations being standard **B-17E** and **B-17F** aircraft.

Fortresses were supplied to the RAF in fairly large numbers, however,

and after a period of inauspicious service as bombers the survivors of a batch of 20 **B-17C (Fortress Mk I)** aircraft were pressed into service with Nos 206 and 220 Squadrons of Coastal Command for maritime reconnaissance duties over the Western Approaches. Starting in mid-1942 about 150 of the improved B-17E were delivered to Coastal Command as the **Fortress Mk II** and **Fortress Mk IIA**, serving with Nos 59, 86, 206 and 220 Squadrons, operating from Benbecula, Chivenor, Thorney Island, the Azores and Iceland.

Although possessing shorter range than the B-24 Liberator, the Fortress

contributed considerably to the patrol efforts demanded by the frequent sailing of wartime convoys, particularly at the height of the great U-boat campaign in the Atlantic. RAF Fortresses were employed on anti-shipping strike missions, their weapons being almost entirely confined to depth charges.

Specification
Boeing Fortress Mk II
Type: eight-seat maritime reconnaissance aircraft
Powerplant: four 894.8-kW (1,200-hp) Wright Cyclone GR-1820-65 air-cooled radial piston engines
Performance: maximum speed 480 km/h (298 mph) at 6096 m (20,000 ft); climb to 1524 m (5,000 ft) in

7.5 minutes; service ceiling 10363 m (34,000 ft); normal range 1835 km (1,140 miles)
Weights: empty 12542 kg (27,650 lb); maximum take-off 24041 kg (53,000 lb)
Dimensions: span 31.62 m (103 ft 9 in); length 22.50 m (73 ft 10 in); height 5.84 m (19 ft 2 in); wing area 131.92 m² (1,420 sq ft)
Armament: total of 10 12.7-mm (0.5-in) machine-guns in nose, dorsal, ventral, tail and beam positions, plus a normal bombload of up to 2722 kg (6,000 lb) of bombs and/or depth charges

Boeing Fortress Mk IIA (B-17E) of No. 220 Sqn flying from the Azores on long-range anti-submarine patrols over the Atlantic.

Consolidated B-24 Liberator

With its long-range performance the **Consolidated B-24 Liberator**, when introduced into service in the maritime reconnaissance role, did more than any other aircraft to turn the tide in the Allies' favour in the long Battle of the Atlantic, effectively 'closing the gap' between the patrol areas of east- and west-based aircraft and thereby denying German U-boats (and surface vessels) a vast tract of ocean in which they had been wholly safe from air attack.

First to use the B-24 in the maritime role, was the RAF whose first **Liberator Mk I** aircraft reached the UK during March 1941 and joined No. 120 Squadron at Nutts Corner, Northern Ireland, in June of that year. These were joined by the **Liberator Mk II** (equivalent to the **B-24C**) in December 1941, and later by the **Liberator Mk III** (**B-24D**), these three versions equipping a total of 16 RAF squadrons. Subsequent deliveries to Coastal Command included the **Liberator Mk IV** (**B-24E**), **Liberator GR.Mk V** (**B-24G**), **Liberator GR.Mk VI** (**B-24G** and **B-24H**) and **Liberator GR.Mk VIII**. With well over 1,000 Liberators flying with RAF maritime reconnaissance squadron in almost every war theatre, it was to be expected that their achievements should be unsurpassed in the war's ocean struggle. For example, in November 1942 the Liberators of No. 224 Squadron in the Bay of Biscay sank two U-boats which were manoeuvring to attack the troop convoys sailing for the 'Torch' landings, attacks that would otherwise have caused enormous casualties among the troops. In March 1945 Liberators of five RAF squadrons sank seven U-boats in six days. Like other RAF maritime patrol aircraft Liberators were widely equipped with the Leigh Light, and other aircraft were armed with rocket projectiles and batteries of cannon for use against submarines.

In US Navy service the Liberator served as the **PB4Y-1**, 977 such aircraft being delivered. A developed version, the **PB4Y-2 Privateer**, entered service with at least one squadron, VP-24, some PB4Y-2Bs being armed with

Consolidated Liberator Mk I of No. 120 Sqn flying from Nutt's Corner in 1941. It carries a four-cannon pack under the fuselage for strafing.

Liberator GR.Mk V of No. 224 Sqn in November 1942. This was the RAF version of the B-24G, and introduced greater range and armament over its predecessor.

an ASM-N-2 Bat anti-shipping glide bomb under each wing. Total Privateer production amounted to 736 aircraft.

Specification
Consolidated PBY-1 Liberator
Type: 10-seat maritime patrol bomber
Powerplant: four 1,200-hp (894.8-kW) Pratt & Whitney R-1830-43 or -65 air-cooled radial piston engines
Performance: maximum speed 449 km/h (279 mph) at 8077 m (26,500 ft); climb to 1219 m (4,000 ft) in

PB4Y-1 Liberator of VPB-110, US Navy based in Devon, during the winter of 1944. Such US units provided a much-needed back-up to the Coastal Command squadrons.

7.8 minutes; service ceiling 9693 m (31,800 ft); normal patrol range 4764 km (2,960 miles)
Weights: empty 16761 kg (36,950 lb); maximum take-off 27216 kg (60,000 lb)
Dimensions: span 33.53 m (110 ft 0 in); length 20.50 m (67 ft 3 in); height 5.46 m (17 ft 11 in); wing area 97.36 m² (1,048 sq ft)
Armament: eight 12.7-mm (0.5-in) machine-guns in nose, dorsal and tail

turrets and waist hatches amidships, plus up to 5806 kg (12,800 lb) of bombs, mines or depth charges

Arriving in service late in the war, the Consolidated PB4Y-2 Privateer was developed from the Liberator, the main difference being the single fin. These mainly saw action in the Far East and continued in use for many years after the war's end.

Dornier Do 217

After the departure eastwards of the bulk of Germany's light bombing force from western Europe in May 1941, the principal bomber unit remaining in the Netherlands was Kampfgeschwader 2. This unit by itself was inadequate to sustain a prolonged bombing campaign against the UK, but was nevertheless re-equipped with a new version of the Do 17, the **Dornier Do 217**. At about the same time the specialist anti-shipping unit in the West, KG 40, received its first Do 217s, II/KG 2 receiving **Do 217E-1** aircraft in August 1941. Although these aircraft were fundamentally standard bombers, concessions were soon forthcoming to suit the aircraft to the anti-shipping role with the issue of *Rüstsätze* (conversion kits); among these were the R-10 and R-15 kits to enable the Do 217E to mount anti-shipping weapons, later to include the Henschel Hs 293A guided missiles; the **Do 217E-5** was designed from the outset to accommodate these weapons. Other anti-shipping variants were the **Do 217K-2** equipped to deliver two Fritz X rocket-propelled missiles, and the **Do 217K-3** capable of carrying either Hs 293As or Fritz Xs. Sub-variants of the **Do 217M** were also produced for the anti-shipping role.

In mid-1943 II and III/KG 100 were withdrawn from the Eastern Front and re-equipped with Do 217E-5s and Do 217K-2s respectively, the former unit moving to Cognac with Hs 293As and the latter to Marseilles with the Fritz X. The first success in action was gained on 27 August when Hs 293As sank the Canadian destroyer HMCS *Athabaskan* and the corvette HMS *Egret* in the Bay of Biscay. In the Mediterranean III/KG 100 sank the Italian battleship *Roma* and damaged the *Italia* with Fritz Xs on 9 September; shortly afterwards Major Bernhard Jope (the pilot who, in a Fw 200, had fatally damaged the *Empress of Britain* back in October 1940) discharged a Fritz X against HMS *Warspite*, putting the battleship out of

Dornier Do 217E-2 of 9.Staffel, Kampfgeschwader 40 based at Bordeaux-Mérignac in 1942. The badge on the nose shows a winged bomb over Britain.

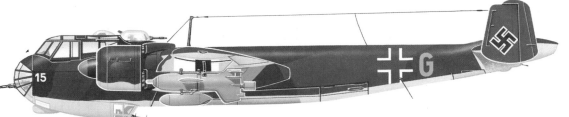

Dornier Do 217E-5 of KG 40. This aircraft is carrying two of the Henschel Hs 293A stand-off guided anti-ship missiles, which were used with some degree of success in the Mediterranean.

action. In terms of Allied shipping sunk or severely crippled, the Do 217 was unquestionably the most effective of all German anti-shipping aircraft when armed with these guided weapons.

Specification
Dornier Do 217E-5
Type: four-seat anti-shipping bomber
Powerplant: two 1,580-hp (1178.2-kW) BMW 801C 14-cylinder air-cooled radial piston engines
Performance: maximum speed 515 km/h (320 mph) at 5200 m (17,060 ft); climb to 925 m (3,035 ft) in 4.45 minutes; service ceiling 9000 m (29,528 ft); normal range 2300 km (1,429 miles)
Weights: empty 8855 kg (19,522 lb); maximum take-off 16465 kg (36,299 lb)

Another KG 40 Do 217 is loaded with bombs. The camouflage is typical of German maritime paint schemes, with disruptive wave patterns applied over the standard paint.

Dimensions: span 19.00 m (62 ft 4 in); length 18.20 m (59 ft 8.5 in); height 5.02 m (16 ft 6 in); wing area 57.00 m² (613.54 sq ft)
Armament: one fixed 15-mm (0.59-in) gun in the nose, one 13-mm (0.51-in) gun in a dorsal turret, one 13-mm (0.51-in) gun in ventral position, and three

trainable 7.92-mm (0.31-in) guns in nose and beam positions (the Do 217E-5/R19 also carried four 7.92-mm/0.31-in) guns in the extreme tail), plus an offensive load of two 1045-kg (2,304-lb) Hs 293A remotely-controlled weapons, with 295-kg (650-lb) warheads, carried under the wings

Heinkel He 111

Combat experience gained by the Luftwaffe during the first 18 months of the war suggested that in anti-shipping attacks the bomb was a relatively wasteful and inaccurate weapon, except when delivered by fighter-bombers and dive-bombers, a conclusion amply borne out as the defensive armament on British ships was progressively increased. Thus it was that early in 1941 the Luftwaffe chose to place greater emphasis on the torpedo (notwithstanding considerable difficulties then being experienced in the German navy with their arming pistols) and, following trials and aircrew training at Grossenbrode in the Baltic and Grosseto in Italy, the **Heinkel He 111H-6**, carrying two 765-kg (1,687-lb) LT F5b torpedoes under the wing roots, was first delivered to I/KG 26 at Grosseto early in 1942. By June that year the whole *Geschwader* had been re-equipped and had moved to Banak and Bardufoss in northern Norway for operations against the Allied North Cape convoys. Until the inclusion of British escort carriers in these convoys, the German torpedo bombers (which also numbered some He 115 floatplanes) achieved outstanding success. Nevertheless, even when con-

fronted by fighters over the convoy PQ.18, the He 111s of KG 26, led by Major Werner Klümper, sank eight Allied ships.

Increasingly bad weather and fighter opposition led to diminishing success in the Arctic, and in November 1942 KG 26 was redeployed to the Mediterranean. New torpedo variants were introduced, including the **He 111H-15** which featured FuG 200 anti-shipping search radar and increased gun armament. *Rüstsätz* conversion kits were also introduced to modify bomber variants to the torpedo role, but the **He 111H-12** variant, which underwent trials with two underwing Henschel Hs 293A anti-shipping weapons in conjunction with FuG 203b Kehl III guidance system, failed to achieve operational status.

Specification
Heinkel He 111H-6
Type: six-seat torpedo bomber
Powerplant: two 1,400-hp (1044-kW) Junkers Jumo 211F-1 12-cylinder liquid-cooled Vee piston engines
Performance: maximum speed 435 km/h (270 mph) at 6000 m (19,685 ft); climb to 2000 m (6,562 ft) in 8.5 minutes; service ceiling 8500 m

(27,887 ft); normal range 1900 km (1,181 miles)
Weights: empty 8690 kg (19,158 lb); maximum take-off 14000 kg (30,864 lb)
Dimensions: span 22.60 m (74 ft 1.75 in); length 16.45 m (53 ft 11.5 in); height 4.00 m (13 ft 1.75 in); wing area 86.50 m² (931.07 sq ft)
Armament: six 7.92-mm (0.31-in) machine-guns in nose, dorsal, beam and ventral positions, one 20-mm cannon in the extreme nose, and

(some aircraft) a remotely-fired 7.92-mm (0.31-in) gun in the extreme tail, plus an offensive load of either two 1000-kg (2,205-lb) bombs or two 765-kg (1,687-lb) LT F5b torpedoes carried on external PVC racks

A pair of LT F5b practice torpedoes are loaded on to the underfuselage racks of a Heinkel He 111H-6. The H-6 was also used for trials with guided missiles and glide-bombs.

Focke-Wulf Fw 200 Condor

Famous as a pre-war airliner with a number of formidable long-distance flights and records to its credit, the four-engine **Focke-Wulf Fw 200 Condor** was dsigned by Kurt Tank in 1936, and underwent military adaptation into a fairly potent anti-shipping aircraft with the Luftwaffe. Ten pre-production **Fw-200C-0** maritime reconnaissance aircraft were delivered to the Luftwaffe in September 1939, some of them serving with I/KG 40 in 1940. The five-crew production **Fw 200C-1** was powered by four 830-hp (618.9-kW) BMW 132H engines, was armed with a 20-mm gun in the nose and three 7.92-mm (0.31-in) guns in other positions and could carry four 250-kg (551-lb) bombs. Apart from long-range maritime patrols over the Atlantic, the Fw 200C-1s also undertook extensive minelaying in British waters during 1940, each carrying two 1000-kg (2,205-lb) mines. Numerous sub-variants of the C-series appeared, of which the **Fw 200C-3** with 1,000-hp (745.7-kW) Bramo 323R-2 radials was the most important. Later in the war the **Fw 200C-6** and **Fw 200C-8** were produced in an effort to enhance the Condor's operational potential by adaptation to carry two Henschel Hs 293 missiles in conjunction with FuG 203b missile control radio.

Rugged operating conditions highlighted the Fw 200's numerous structural weaknesses and there were numerous accidents in service, and for a short time in the mid-war years Fw 20s were employed as military trans-

Based at Bordeaux-Mérignac in late 1940, this Fw 200C of 1./KG 40 carries the badge associated with many pre-war record-breaking flights by civil Condors.

The Fw 200C-6 featured FuG 200 Hohentwiel radar and the ability to carry the Hs 293A guided missile. Two missiles could be carried under the outboard engine nacelles.

ports, 18 aircraft being flown by Kampfgruppe zur besonderen Verwendung 200 in support of the beleaguered German forces at Stalingrad. Other Condors were used by Hitler and Himmler as personal transports. Focke-Wulf Fw 200 production for the Luftwaffe amounted to 252 aircraft between 1940 and 1944.

Specification
Focke-Wulf Fw 200C-3/U4
Type: seven-seat long-range maritime reconnaissance bomber

Powerplant: four 1,000-hp (745.7-kW) BMW-Bramo 323R-2 radial piston engines
Performance: maximum speed 360 km/h (224 mph) at 4700 m (15,420 ft); service ceiling 6000 m (19,685 ft); range 3560 km (2,211 miles)
Weights: empty 17000 kg (37,478 lb); maximum take-off 22700 kg (50,044 lb)
Dimensions: span 32.84 m (107 ft 9.5 in); length 23.85 m (76 ft 11.5 in); height 6.30 m (20 ft 8 in); wing area 118.00 m² (1,290.0 sq ft)
Armament: one 7.92-mm (0.31-in) gun

in forward dorsal turret, one 13-mm (0.51-in) gun in rear dorsal position, two 13-mm (0.51-in) guns in beam positions, one 20-mm gun in forward position of ventral gondola and one 7.92-mm (0.31-in) gun in aft ventral position, plus a maximum bomb load of 2100 kg (4,630 lb).

Junkers Ju 88 and Ju 188

Junkers Ju 188D-2 of 1./FAGr 124 based at Kirkenes in Norway. Note the disruptive wave camouflage for maritime operations.

Just as the Heinkel He 111 corresponded roughly to the RAF's Vickers Wellington in the maritime role, so the **Junkers Ju 88** was a contemporary of and superficially equivalent to Coastal Command's Bristol Beaufighter. However, whereas the latter was conceived from the outset as a fighter, the Ju 88 was fundamentally a bomber which came to serve as a night-fighter and intruder.

Ju 88s flew anti-shipping missions with specialist *Kampfgeschwader*, notably KG 30, as early as the Norwegian campaign of April 1940, although the aircraft themselves were standard **Ju 88A** bombers. And it was KG 30's Ju 88s that were flown with such devastating success against British shipping during the Greek campaign of 1941. In an attack by 7./KG 30 on the approaches to Piraeus harbour Hauptmann Hajo Herrmann's bombs struck the freighter *Clan Frazer* which was loaded with explosives and blew up, destroying 10 other ships. Soon afterwards KG 30 was assembled in northern Norway for attacks against the North Cape (PQ) convoys being sailed between Iceland and Soviet ports.

Although no version of the Ju 88 was developed specifically for the anti-shipping strike role, the extensively redesigned **Junkers Ju 188**, which began making real progress before the end of 1942, appeared in several versions as a torpedo bomber. The first, the **Ju 188E-2**, could carry two 800-kg (1,764-lb) torpedoes under the wings and some aircraft also carried FuG 200 sea-search radar. This version and another, the **Ju 188A-3** with water methanol boosted engines, served in

small numbers with the anti-shipping unit III/KG 26 towards the end of 1944.

The Ju 188 was a popular aircraft with its crew but, following the switch of priorities by the Germans in favour of fighters in the latter half of 1944, production of the bomber and torpedo bomber versions was halted, although they remained in fast-diminishing service until the end of the war.

Specification
Junkers Ju 188E-2
Type: four-seat torpedo bomber
Powerplant: two 1,700-hp (1267.7-kW) BMW 801D air-cooled radial piston engines
Performance: maximum speed 500 km/h (311 mph) at 6000 m (19,685 ft); climb to 6000 m (19,685 ft) in 17.6 minutes; service ceiling 9300 m

(30,512 ft); normal range 1950 km (1,212 miles)
Weights: empty 9860 kg (21,737 lb); maximum take-off 14470 kg (31,898 lb)
Dimensions: span 22.00 m (72 ft 2 in); length 14.90 m (48 ft 0.5 in); height 4.44 m (14 ft 6.8 in); wing area 56.00 m²

(602.78 sq ft)
Armament: gun armament (commonly) of two 13-mm (0.51-in) machine-guns in nose and dorsal positions, plus an offensive load of up to 3000 kg (6,614 lb) or two 800-kg (1,764-lb) LT lb torpedoes carried under the wings.

The superlative Ju 88 was effective in many roles, and anti-shipping was no exception. This aircraft bears 10 ship kills from the Mediterranean, denoted by the fuselage theatre band.

Junkers Ju 290

Developed directly from the Ju 90 commercial and military transport, the four-engine **Junkers Ju 290** was intended to replace the Focke-Wulf Fw 200 Condor which by 1942 was proving slow and vulnerable when confronted by RAF aircraft over the 'narrow seas' around Europe. Developments of the Ju 290 nevertheless embraced considerable work to suit it for the transport role, and it was not until early 1943 that the **Ju 290A-1** underwent extensive modification as a maritime reconnaissance aircraft, including the installation of marine radio, FuG 200 Hohentwiel sea search radar and a second dorsal HDL 151 gun turret mounting an MG 151/20 cannon.

At the same time a long-range reconnaissance group, Fernaufklärungs-gruppe 5, was formed and during the late summer of 1943 three of the new Ju 290A-2s were delivered to its 1.Staffel, which became operational at Mont de Marsan in France on 15 October of that year. Five **Ju 290A-3** aircraft with more powerful BMW 801D engines followed, as did five **Ju 290A-4** aircraft with improved dorsal turrets. In November a second *Staffel* was acti-

vated and, with a range of over 6100 km (3,790 miles) the Ju 290s ranged far out over the Atlantic, relaying convoy sightings to U-boats. Eleven **Ju 290A-5** aircraft with increased armour protection and 20-mm cannon in place of the earlier beam machine-guns were delivered to FAGr 5 early in 1944, as were about a dozen of the **Ju 290A-7** variant; the latter was a true anti-shipping strike aircraft capable of carrying either three Henschel Hs 293 or Fritz X weapons under fuselage and wings. It also featured a new nose section combining a nose gun position with 20-mm cannon with the FuG 200 aerial array. Only three **Ju 290A-9** aircraft were completed with reduced armament and increased fuel capacity which bestowed a maximum range of 8000 km (4,971 miles).

Fernaufklärungsgruppe (FAGr) 5 was the only operator of the Junkers Ju 290 maritime versions and used these from Mont de Marsan in France. The A-7 variant could carry up to three of the Hs 293A missiles.

As the Battle of the Atlantic swung irrevocably in favour of the Allies with the loss by the Germans of French bases in August 1944, FAGr 5 was withdrawn eastwards and began operating as a transport unit, some of the Ju 290s even being flown nonstop to Manchuria carrying special supplies to the Japanese and returning with raw materials vital to Germany.

Specification
Junkers Ju 290A-5
Type: nine-seat maritime reconnaissance aircraft
Powerplant: four 1,700-hp (1267.7-kW) BMW 801D air-cooled radial piston engines
Performance: maximum speed

440 km/h (273 mph) at 6000 m (19,685 ft); climb to 1000 m (3,281 ft) in 4.2 minutes; service ceiling 6000 m (19,685 ft); maximum range 6150 km (3,822 miles)
Weights: empty about 27700 kg (61,067 lb); maximum take-off 45000 kg (99,206 lb)
Dimensions: span 42.00 m (137 ft 9.5 in); length 28.64 m (93 ft 11.5 in); height 6.83 m (22 ft 4.75 in); wing area 204.00 m² (2,195.9 sq ft)
Armament: six MG 151/20 20-mm cannon in ventral gondola, two dorsal turrets, a tail position and two beam hatches, and one 13-mm (0.51-in) machine-gun in the ventral gondola; bombs were not normally carried

---

Savoia-Marchetti S.M.79

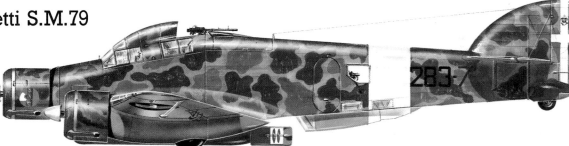

Developed from an eight-seat commercial airliner of 1934, the three-engine **Savoia-Marchetti S.M.79 Sparviero** entered service as a conventional medium bomber with the Regia Aeronautica in 1937, and served operationally with the Aviacion del Tercio alongside the Nationalist forces during the Spanish Civil War. Also in 1937 the S.M.79 embarked on trials at Gorizia as a torpedo bomber, being equipped to launch a single 450-mm (17.7-in) naval torpedo from an offset rack under the fuselage. The following year trials with paired torpedoes led to the adoption of the **S.M.79-II** aircraft as standard torpedo bomber equipment. Following Italy's entry into the war in June 1940, when Sparvieri (sparrowhawks) equipped 14 *stormi* based in Italy, Sicily, Sardinia and Libya, the aircraft was constantly in action in the anti-shipping role, its first action being an attack by 19 S.M.79s of the 9° and 46° Stormi on French shipping off the Riviera coast on 13/14 June.

During the invasion of Crete S.M.79s of the 92° Gruppo and the 281ª Squadriglia were active against Allied shipping in the Aegean, after which most aircraft were redeployed to Libya for operations against British naval forces and convoys in the Central Mediterranean as well as the naval base at Malta. Among the ships of the Royal Navy sunk by S.M.79s in the Mediterranean were the destroyers HMS *Husky*, HMS *Jaguar*, HMS *Legion*, and HMS *Southwall*, while the battleship HMS *Malaya* and the carriers HMS *Indomitable* and HMS *Victorious* were all struck by torpedoes launched by the Italian torpedo bombers; the majority of these ships were hit during the attacks on the Operation 'Pedestal' convoy which sailed with 14 merchant ships and

The S.M.79 was a fine torpedo-bomber which scored many hits against Allied shipping in the Mediterranean. It was fast for its size, and this enabled it to become one of the best Italian aircraft.

heavy escort for the relief of Malta. Among the famous Italian pilots of the Sparviero were men such as Capitani Buscaglia, Cimicchi, di Bella and Melley. An improved version was the **S.M.79-III** without the ventral gondola but with a forward-firing 20-mm cannon.

Despite the obvious value of the S.M.79 to the Axis forces in the Mediterranean, the aircraft (like so many Italian aircraft) suffered from poor servicing facilities, and it was unusual for even as much as half the available strength of Sparvieri to be fit for operations at any given time. Nevertheless the S.M.79 was acknowledged

Operating in the Mediterranean in 1942, this Savoia-Marchetti S.M.79 served with the 283ª Squadriglia, 130° Gruppo Autonoma. One torpedo is carried beneath the fuselage.

as being among the best torpedo aircraft to serve in the Mediterranean theatre during World War II.

Specification
Savoia-Marchetti S.M.79-II
Type: five-seat torpedo bomber
Powerplant: three 1,000-hp (745.7-kW) Piaggio P.XI RC 40 air-cooled radial piston engines
Performance: maximum speed 435 km/h (270 mph) at 3650 m (11,975 ft); service ceiling 7000 m (22,966 ft); normal range 2000 km (1,243 miles)

Weights: empty 7600 kg (16,755 lb); maximum take-off 11300 kg (24,912 lb)
Dimensions: span 21.20 m (69 ft 6.66 in); length 16.20 m (53 ft 1.75 in); height 4.10 m (13 ft 1.5 in); wing area 61.7 m² (664.14 sq ft)
Armament: three 12.7-mm (0.5-in) Breda-SAFAT machine-guns in two dorsal positions and one ventral position, and one 7.7-mm (0.303-in) Lewis gun on a sliding mount in the rear fuselage to provide beam defence plus two 450-mm (17.7-in) torpedoes or 1250 kg (2,756 lb) of bombs.

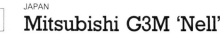

Mitsubishi G3M 'Nell'

As far back as 1935, in response to Japanese naval requirement for a land-based twin-engine reconnaissance aircraft, Mitsubishi flew the first **Ka-15** prototype, an aircraft which possessed a design potential that allowed development as a long-range medium bomber. Accordingly, following successful flight trials, the aircraft entered production in June 1936 as the **Navy Type 96 Attack Bomber Model 11 (Mitsubishi G3M1)**. The initial version, of which 34 were produced, was powered by 910-hp (678.6-kW) Kinsei 3 radials and possessed a maximum speed of 360 km/h (224 mph) at 1975 m (6,480 ft). As the improved Kinsei 41 and 42 engine became available in 1937 a new version, the **G3M2**, started production and, with a total of 581 built by mid-1941, was the principal variant. With a top speed now increased to 374 km/h (232 mph), a bombload of up to 800 kg (1,764 lb) carried externally and a defensive armament of three 7.7-mm (0.303-in) machine-guns, the G3M2 possessed a maximum range of 4380 km (2,722 miles). A yet further improved version, of which production was undertaken by Nakajima during 1941-3, was the **G3M3** with 1,300-hp (969.4-kW) Kinsei 51 radials and a top speed of 415 km/h (258 mph) at 6000 m (19,685 ft).

Mitsubishi G3M2s were first flown in action by the Japanese navy's Kanoya Kokutai in August 1937 in raids on Hangchow and Kwangteh in China. By 1940 four *kokutais* in China were equipped with a total of about 130 G3M2s, a number that grew to 204 by the date of Pearl Harbor with the deployment of forces against Wake Island, the Philippines and the Marianas. And it was a force of 60 G3M2s of the Genzan and Mihoro Kokutais (with 26 Mitsubishi G4M1s of the Kanoya Kokutai) which, flying from bases in Indo-China, found and sank the British warships HMS *Prince of Wales* and HMS *Repulse* as they steamed without fighter protection off the Malayan coast on 10 December 1941. The type was known to the Allies as the 'Nell'.

Mitsubishi G3M2 of the Genzan Kokutai flying from Saigon, Indo-China, in December 1941. This aircraft participated in the sinking of HMS Prince of Wales *and* Repulse.

Specification
Mitsubishi G3M2 Model 22
Type: five/seven-seat medium/torpedo bomber
Powerplant: two 1,075-hp (801.6-kW) Mitsubishi Kinsei 45 14-cylinder air-cooled radial piston engines
Performance: maximum speed 374 km/h (232 mph) at 4200 m (13780 ft); climb to 3000 m (9,843 ft) in 8.34 minutes; service ceiling 9130 m (29,954 ft); maximum range 4380 km (2,722 miles)
Weights: empty 4965 kg (10,946 lb); maximum take-off 8010 kg (17,659 lb)
Dimensions: span 25.00 m (82 ft 0.25 in); length 16.45 m (53 ft 11.66 in); height 3.685 m (12 ft 1.1 in); wing area 75.0 m² (807.32 sq ft)
Armament: three 7.7-mm (0.303-in) Type 92 machine-guns in a retractable dorsal turret and two lateral blisters, and one 20-mm Type 99 cannon in a second dorsal turret, plus one 800-kg (1,764-lb) torpedo or equivalent bomb load carried externally

A formation of Mitsubishi G3Ms cross the Japanese coast during a training exercise. This aircraft was widely used, especially in the early days of the war, on all kinds of maritime operations, including torpedo dropping, bombing and patrol. Its successor, the same company's G4M, was employed alongside the G3M on similar missions.

Mitsubishi Ki-67 'Peggy'

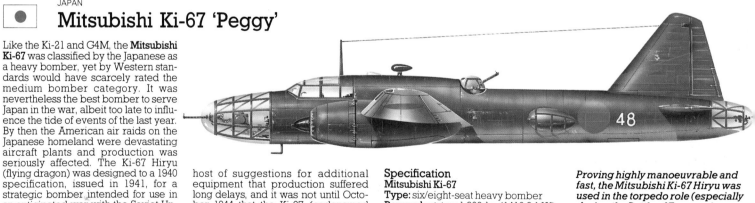

Like the Ki-21 and G4M, the **Mitsubishi Ki-67** was classified by the Japanese as a heavy bomber, yet by Western standards would have scarcely rated the medium bomber category. It was nevertheless the best bomber to serve Japan in the war, albeit too late to influence the tide of events of the last year. By then the American air raids on the Japanese homeland were devastating aircraft plants and production was seriously affected. The Ki-67 Hiryu (flying dragon) was designed to a 1940 specification, issued in 1941, for a strategic bomber intended for use in an anticipated war with the Soviet Union on the Siberia-Manchukuo border. By departing from established Japanese practice and including armour protection and self-sealing fuel tanks, design of the prototype Ki-67 was protracted, and it was not until 27 December 1942 that the first aircraft flew; it proved to be highly manoeuvrable and pleasant to fly, and possessed a top speed of 538 km/h (334 mph). In the same month it was decided to adapt some Ki-67s as torpedo-bombers. The army put forward such a

host of suggestions for additional equipment that production suffered long delays, and it was not until October 1944 that the Ki-67 (codenamed 'Peggy' by the Allies) was first flown in combat by the 7th and 98th Sentais, and by the navy's 762nd Kokutai in the torpedo role during the battle off Formosa. Thereafter modifications were held to a minimum as production was afforded the highest priority; but by then American raids (and a devastating earthquake in December 1944) severely disrupted production, and no more than 698 Ki-67s were produced, some of them being flown in *kamikaze* strikes in the last months of the war.

Specification
Mitsubishi Ki-67
Type: six/eight-seat heavy bomber
Powerplant: two 1,900-hp (1416.8-kW) Mitsubishi Ha-104 radial piston engines
Performance: maximum speed 537 km/h (334 mph) at 6090 m (19,980 ft); climb to 6000 m (19,685 ft) in 14.5 minutes; service ceiling 9470 m (31,070 ft); range 2800 km (1,740 miles)
Weights: empty 8649 kg (19,068 lb); normal loaded 13765 kg (30,347 lb)
Dimensions: span 22.50 m (73 ft 9.75 in); length 18.70 m (61 ft 4.25 in); height 7.70 m (25 ft 3.2 in); wing area 65.85 m² (708.8 sq ft)

Proving highly manoeuvrable and fast, the Mitsubishi Ki-67 Hiryu was used in the torpedo role (especially during the Battle of Formosa). Production of this effective aircraft was severely restricted following American bombing raids and an earthquake.

Armament: single trainable 12.7-mm (0.5-in) Type 1 machine-guns in nose, two beam positions and tail, and one 20-mm Ho-5 cannon in dorsal turret, plus a bombload of 800 kg (1,764 lb) or one 1070-kg (2,359 lb) torpedo, or 2900-kg (6,393-lb) of bombs for *kamikaze* mission

Carrier Aircraft

Carrierborne airpower reached such a peak in World War II that several battles which took place over the Pacific were fought solely with carrierborne aircraft. Elsewhere the carriers were protecting convoys, fighting submarines and covering beach assaults.

The overwhelming importance of carrierborne air power to warfare at sea was only dimly foreseen in the years which led up to World War II. Historically, it had been the battleship and the naval gunnery which had dominated the oceans ever since the days of the Spanish Armada right up to the Battle of Jutland. In addition, battleships considerably outnumbered carriers in navies throughout the world.

Nevertheless, the 1930s saw the evolution of the methods and tactics that were to dominate the Pacific War and which were also to contribute greatly to the successful conclusion of the war in the Atlantic. It was the US Navy that was eventually to become the master of carrier warfare; however, both the Royal Navy and the Imperial Japanese navy were able to make significant contributions.

The demands made by this new form of warfare were considerable, especially upon the aircraft used and upon the young pilots who flew them. The 'controlled crash' of a carrier landing demanded strong nerves and a strong aircraft. If the sea itself was anything other than calm (which unfortunately it so often was), the motion of the waves would cause the deck to pitch and roll alarm-

The US Navy led the field in carrier warfare. These Grumman TBF Avengers and F-6F Hellcats are on the deck of USS *Monterey* in the Pacific theatre.

ingly, making landings rather tricky.

In general, purpose-designed carrier aircraft had inferior performance when compared to their land-based contemporaries – although this did not prevent the Fairey Swordfish from amassing a war record which was second to none – while conversions of landplanes, such as the

Supermarine Spitfire produced performance – at the expense of durability Instead, it was left to the Japanese to show that the carrier aircraft, in the shape of the Mitsubishi A6M Zero, could outfly and outfight its land-based opponents.

It was, however, the swarm of big, beefy US Navy aircraft, which were based upon the navy's

massive American carrier force, that was to prove decisive in the Pacific. Led by the Grumman F6F Hellcat and the Vought F4U Corsair, US and Allied naval aircraft in their thousands ranged the skies over Japan during the final months of the war, in a display of naval air power undreamed of only five years before.

JAPAN
Aichi D3A 'Val'

Although thought to be obsolescent when Japan entered the war, the **Aichi D3A** with fixed spatted landing gear was the first Japanese aircraft to drop bombs on American targets when aircraft of this type took part in the great raid on Pearl Harbor on 7 December 1941. Designed to a 1936 carrier-based dive-bomber requirement, the prototype was flown in January 1938 with a 529.4-kW (710-hp) Nakajima Hikari 1 radial. Production **D3A1** aircraft had slightly smaller wings and were powered by the 745.7-kW (1,000-hp) Mitsubishi Kinsei 43 radial. A dorsal fin extension considerably improved the aircraft's manoeuvrability, although the armament of only two forward-firing 7.7-mm (0.303-in) machine-guns, with another of the same calibre in the rear cockpit, was undeniably puny. After limited land-based operations in China and Indo-China, D3As were flown in all major carrier actions during the first 10 months of the war and sank more Allied naval vessels than any other Axis aircraft. Among British casualties in D3A1 attacks were HMS *Hermes* (the world's first carrier to be sunk by carrier aircraft), and the cruisers *Cornwall* and *Dorsetshire*. Heavy losses among D3A1s during and after the Battle of the Coral Sea, however, forced withdrawal by most of the survivors to land bases. In 1942 the **D3A2** was introduced with increased fuel capacity and more powerful engine, but by 1944 the aircraft were hopelessly outclassed by American fighters; a

small number was subsequently employed in *kamikaze* attacks. Production amounted to 476 D3A1s and 1,016 D3A2. The Allied reporting name was 'Val'.

Specification
Aichi D3A2
Type: two-seat carrierborne dive-bomber
Powerplant: one 969.4-kW (1,300-hp) Mitsubishi Kinsei 54 radial piston engine
Performance: maximum speed 430 km/h (267 mph) at 6200 m (20,341 ft); climb to 3000 m (9,843 ft) in 5.76 minutes; service ceiling 10500 m (34,449 ft); range 1352 km (840 miles)
Weights: empty 2570 kg (5,666 lb); maximum take-off 3800 kg (8,378 lb)
Dimensions: span 14.38 m (47 ft 2.1 in);

length 10.20 m (33 ft 5.6 in); height 3.85 m (12 ft 7.6 in); wing area 34.90 m^2 (375.7 sq ft)
Armament: two forward-firing 7.7-mm (0.303-in) Type 97 machine-guns in the

Aichi D3A1 of the Yokosuka Kokutai in 1940. 'Vals' were among the most accurate of dive-bombers owing to the steep dive employed.

The D3A was the standard dive-bomber of the Japanese air groups during the early years of the campaign. Its most notable

successes were the attacks on Pearl Harbor and the sinking of the British carrier HMS Hermes. *This is the better-looking D3A2.*

nose and one trainable 7.7-mm (0.303-in) Type 92 gun in the rear cockpit, plus one 250-kg (551-lb) bomb under the fuselage and two 60-kg (132-lb) bombs under the wings

JAPAN
Mitsubishi A6M 'Zeke'

The famous **Mitsubishi A6M**, popularly known as the 'Zero', was the first carrierborne fighter in the world capable of outperforming any contemporary land-based fighter it was likely to confront. Because of inept Allied intelligence it was able to achieve immediate air superiority over the East Indies and South East Asia from the day Japan entered the war. Designed under the leadership of Jiro Horikoshi in 1937 as a replacement for the neat but obsolescent A5M, the prototype **A6M1** was first flown on 1 April 1939 with a 581.6-kW (780-hp) Mitsubishi Zuisei 13 radial; production **A6M2** fighters with two wing-mounted 20-mm guns and two nose-mounted 7.7-mm (0.303-in) guns were fitted with the 708.4-kW (950-hp) Nakajima Sakae 12 radial, and it was with this version that the Japanese navy escorted the raiding force sent against Pearl Harbor, and gained air superiority over Malaya, the Philippines and Burma. In the spring of 1942 the **A6M3** with two-stage supercharged Sakae 21 entered service, later aircraft having their folding wing tips removed. The Battle of Midway represented the Zero's combat zenith; thereafter the agile Japanese fighter found itself ever more outclassed by the American F6F Hellcat and P-38 Lightning. To counter the new American fighters the **A6M5** was rushed to front-line units; this version, with Sakae 21 engine and improved exhaust system, possessed a top speed of 565 km/h (351 mph), more A6M5s (and subvariants) being produced than any other Japanese aircraft. It was five A6M5s of the Shikishima *kamikaze* unit that sank the carrier *St Lo* and damaged three others on 25 October 1944.

Other versions were the **A6M6** with water-methanol boosted Sakae 31 engine and the **A6M7** fighter/dive-bomber. Total production of all A6Ms was 10,937. (The reporting name 'Zeke' was given to the A6M, and 'Rufe' to a float version, the **A6M2-N**.)

Specification
Mitsubishi A6M5b 'Zeke'
Type: single-seat carrierborne fighter
Powerplant: one 820.3-kW (1,100-hp) Nakajima NK2F Sakae 21 radial piston engine
Performance: maximum speed 565 km/h (351 mph) at 6000 m (19,685 ft); climb to 6000 m (19,685 ft) in 7.0 minutes; service ceiling 11740 m (38,517 ft); range 1143 km (710 miles)

Weights: empty 1876 kg (4,136 lb); normal loaded 2733 kg (6,025 lb)
Dimensions: span 11.00 m (36 ft 1.1 in);

length 9.12 m (29 ft 11.1 in); height 3.51 m (11 ft 6.2 in); wing area 21.30 m^2 (229.28 sq ft)

Mitsubishi A6M2 of the fighter complement aboard Hiryu *during the attack on Pearl Harbor in December 1941.*

Feared by all Allied pilots before the arrival of the Hellcat in Pacific waters, the A6M featured astonishing manoeuvrability and good endurance, especially when equipped with an underfuselage fuel tank, as here. These A6M2s are on a long-range fighter patrol.

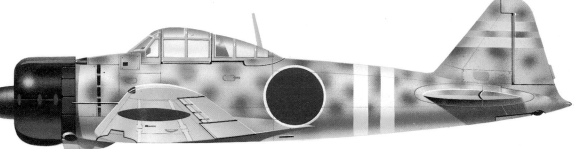

Armament: one 7.7-mm (0.303-in) Type 97 and one 13.2-mm (0.52-in) Type 3 machine-gun in nose, and two wing-mounted 20-mm type 99 cannon, plus underwing provision for two 60- or 250-kg (132- or 551-lb) bombs

Mitsubishi A6M2 of the 6th Kokutai based at Rabaul, New Britain, in November 1942.

Nakajima B5N 'Kate'

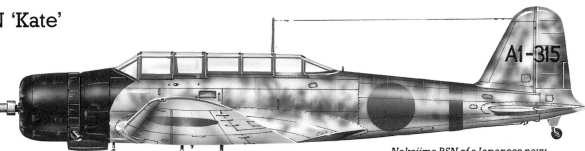

Nakajima B5N of a Japanese navy unit. This type was responsible for many successful attacks on Allied shipping in the Pacific theatre.

Designed to a 1935 requirement, and already in service for four years when Japan entered the war, the **Nakajima B5N** was in 1941 without question the best carrierborne torpedo-bomber in the world. Powered by a Nakajima Hikari radial engine, the low-wing three-crew monoplane with inwards-retracting wide-track landing gear was exceptionally clean, and first flew in January 1937. The following year production **B5N1** aircraft were embarking in Japan's carriers and shore-based units were deployed in China. In 1939 the improved **B5N2** appeared with a more powerful Sakae 11 engine in a smaller cowling, although armament and bombload were unchanged, and this version remained in production until 1943. When Japan attacked the USA the B5N2 had wholly replaced the B5N1 with operational units, and 144 B5N2s were involved in the fateful attack on Pearl Harbor; within the next 12 months aircraft of this type sank the American carriers USS *Hornet*, *Lexington* and *Yorktown*. Given the reporting name **'Kate'** by the Allies, the B5N certainly earned the respect of the Americans, and in all the major carrier battles of the Pacific War attracted the undivided attention of defending fighters. With its puny defensive armament of a single machine-gun and laden with a large bomb or torpedo, however, the B5N began to suffer very heavily, and although the type was fully committed during the Solomons campaign the

survivors were withdrawn from combat after the Philippine battles of 1944. Thereafter, on account of their excellent range, they were assigned to anti-submarine and maritime reconnaissance duties in areas beyond the range of Allied fighters. Production of all B5Ns reached 1,149.

Specification
Nakajima B5N2 'Kate'
Type: three-crew carrierborne torpedo-bomber
Powerplant: one 745.7-kW (1,000hp) Nakajima NK1B Sakae 11 radial piston engine
Performance: maximum speed 378 km/h (235 mph) at 3600 m (11,811 ft); climb to 3000 m (9,843 ft) in 7.7 minutes; service ceiling 8260 m (27,100 ft); range 1990 km (1,237 miles)

These two B5Ns are seen flying over the mighty 70,000-ton battleship Yamato (the largest ever). The underfuselage shackles for the torpedo (or bombs) are visible.

Weights: empty 2279 kg (5,024 lb); maximum take-off 4100 kg (9,039 lb)
Dimensions: span 15.52 m (50 ft 11 in); length 10.30 m (33 ft 9.5 in); height 3.70 m (12 ft 1.7 in); wing area 37.70 m² (405.8 sq ft
Armament: one 7.7-mm (0.303-in) Type

92 trainable machine-gun in rear cockpit, plus one 800-kg (1,764-lb) torpedo or an equivalent weight of bombs

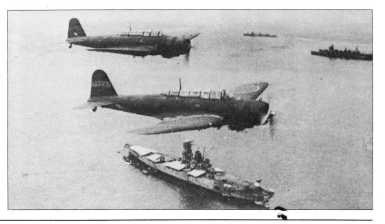

Nakajima B6N 'Jill'

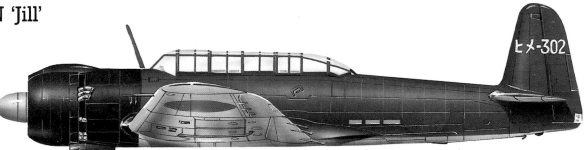

Nakajima B6N2 Tenzan of the Imperial Japanese Navy. This type was designed to supersede the B5N and saw intensive use during the latter part of the war.

At a time when the triumphs of the B5N were still almost three years in the future, the Japanese navy issued a specification for a replacement, recognizing that only limited overall design improvement of the B5N could be achieved in the B5N2. Accordingly design went ahead in 1939 of the **Nakajima B6N** and, despite the navy's preference for the Mitsubishi Kasei radial, a Nakajima Mamoru was selected for the prototype which flew early in 1941. Superficially the **B6N Tenzan** (heavenly mountain) resembled the earlier aircraft, but the much increased power and torque of the big engine and four-blade propeller was found to impose considerable directional stability problems, demanding that the vertical tail surfaces be offset to one side. Flight trials dragged on, and were further delayed by troubles during carrier acceptance tests; then Nakajima was ordered to stop production of the Mamoru engine, so modifications had to be introduced to suit installation of the Kasei. In due course **B6N1** aircraft (of which only 133 were

built) were embarked in the carriers *Shokaku*, *Taiho*, *Hiyo*, *Junyo* and *Zuikaku*, and took part in the great Battle of the Philippine Sea of June 1943, many being lost when the three first-named carriers were sunk. In that month production started of the slightly improved **B6N2** (of which 1,133 were produced before the end of the war), but the heavy losses among Japanese carriers resulted in the **'Jill'** being largely deployed ashore, particularly after the Battle of Leyte Gulf. Thereafter many B5Ns were consigned to the *kamikaze* role.

Specification
Nakajima B6N2 'Jill'
Type: three-crew carrierborne torpedo bomber
Powerplant: one 1379.5-kW (1,850-hp) Mitsubishi MK4T Kasei 25 radial piston engine
Performance: maximum speed 481 km/h (299 mph) at 4900 m (16,076 ft); climb to 5000 m (16,404 ft) in 10.4 minutes; service ceiling 9040 m (29,659 ft); range 1746 km (1,085 miles)
Weights: empty 3010 kg (6,636 lb); maximum take-off 5650 kg (12,456 lb)
Dimensions: span 14.89 m (48 ft

10.2 in); length 10.87 m (35 ft 8 in); height 3.80 m (12 ft 5.6 in); wing area 37.20 m² (400.43 sq ft)
Armament: one trainable 13-mm (0.51-in) Type 2 machine-gun in rear cockpit and one 7.7-mm (0.303-in) Type 97 machine-gun in ventral tunnel position, plus one 800-kg (1,764-lb) torpedo or an equivalent weight of bombs

Yokosuka D4Y 'Judy'

Well-proportioned and purposeful in appearance, the **Yokosuka D4Y** possessed an excellent performance and owed much of its concept to the German He 118, for whose manufacturing rights Japan negotiated in 1938. Designed as a fast carrier-based attack bomber and powered by an imported Daimler-Benz DB 600G engine, the **D4Y1** was first flown in December 1941; **D4Y1-C** reconnaissance aircraft were ordered into production at Aichi's Nagoya plant, the first of 660 aircraft being completed in the late spring of 1942. The first service aircraft were lost when the *Soryu* was sunk at Midway. Named **Suisei** (comet) in service and codenamed **'Judy'** by the Allies, many D4Y1s were completed as dive-bombers, and 174 Suiseis of the 1st, 2nd and 3rd Koku Sentais were embarked in nine carriers before the Battle of the Philippine Sea. However, they were intercepted by American carriers, and suffered heavy casualties without achieving any success. A new version with 1044-kW (1,400-hp) Aichi Atsuta 32 engine appeared in 1944 as

the **D4Y2** but, in the interests of preserving high performance, nothing was done to introduce armour protection for crew or fuel tanks, and the sole improvement in gun armament was the inclusion of a 13.2-mm (0.52-in) trainable gun (replacing the previous 7.92-mm/0.31-in gun) in the rear cockpit. This version suffered heavily in the battle for the Philippines. Problems of reliability with the Atsuta (DB 601) engine led to adoption of a Kinsei 62 radial in the **D4Y3**, and this engine was retained in the **D4Y4** which was developed in 1945 as a single-seat suicide dive-bomber. A total of 2,033 production D4Ys was completed.

Yokosuka D4Y3 of the Imperial Japanese Navy. This version introduced the Mitsubishi MK8P Kinsei 62 radial engine, which avoided the reliability problems of the earlier Aichi Atsuta engine.

Specification
Yokosuka D4Y3 'Judy'
Type: two-seat carrierborne dive-bomber
Powerplant: one 1163.3-kW (1,560-hp) Mitsubishi MK8P Kinsei 62 radial piston engine
Performance: maximum speed 575 km/h (357 mph) at 6050 m (19,849 ft); climb to 3000 m (9,843 ft) 4.55 minutes; service ceiling 10500 m (34,449 ft); range 1520 km (944 miles)

Weights: empty 2501 kg (5,514 lb); maximum take-off 4657 kg (10.267 lb)
Dimensions: span 11.50 m (37 ft 8.75 in); length 10.22 m (33 ft 6.4 in); height 3.74 m (12 ft 3.2 in); wing area 23.60 m² (254.04 sq ft)
Armament: two fixed forward-firing 7.7-mm (0.303-in) Type 97 machine-guns in nose and one 13.1-mm (0.5-in) Type 2 trainable gun in rear cockpit, plus a maximum bombload of 560 kg (1,235 lb)

Curtiss SB2C Helldiver

Last of a long line of Curtiss aircraft to carry the name **Helldiver** (the earlier aircraft being inter-war biplanes), the **Curtiss SB2C** was first flown as the **XSB2C-1** on 18 December 1940. Production **SB2C-1** aircraft featured an enlarged fin and rudder assembly, increased fuel capacity and four 12.7-mm (0.5-in) guns in the wings. The **SB2C-1C** carried an armament of two 20-mm guns in the wings. The **SB2C-3** appeared in 1944 with more powerful engine, and the **SB2C-4** had provision to carry eight 127-mm (5-in) rockets or 454 kg (1,000 lb) of bombs under the wings (in addition to the 454-kg/1,000-lb internal bombload); the **SB2C-4** carried radar in a small pod under the wing, and the **SB2C-5** had increased fuel. Production amounted to 7,199 of all aircraft, including 300 by Fairchild in Canada, 984 by the Canadian Car and Foundry, and 900 produced for the USAAF as the **A-25A** (most of which were taken over by the US Marine Corps and redesignated **SB2C-1A**). Helldivers first went into action on 11 November 1943 with a raid by VB-17 on Rabaul. During 1944 they gradually replaced the Douglas SBD Dauntless, and were in constant action against the Japanese. Some 26 Canadian-built aircraft were supplied to the UK.

Specification
Curtiss SB2C-4 Helldiver
Type: two-seat scout-bomber
Powerplant: one 1416.8-kW (1,900-hp) Wright R-2600-20 radial piston engine

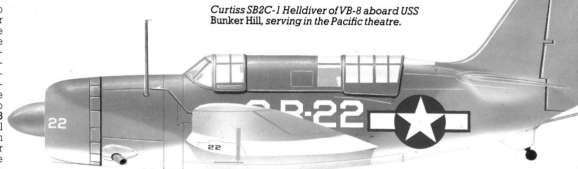

Curtiss SB2C-1 Helldiver of VB-8 aboard USS Bunker Hill, serving in the Pacific theatre.

Right: These two SB2C-1C Helldivers from VB-1 are on patrol in 1944. The Helldiver was not liked by pilots or ground crew and was referred to by many derogatory nicknames, the most common of which was 'The Beast'. Despite its reputation, the type put in much service in the thick of the battle against Japan.

Performance: maximum speed 475 km/h (295 mph) at 5090 m (16,700 ft); initial climb rate 549 m (1,800 ft) per minute; service ceiling 8870 m (29,100 ft); range 1875 km (1,165 miles)
Weights: empty 4784 kg (10,547 lb); maximum take-off 7537 kg (16,616 lb)
Dimensions: span 15.16 m (49 ft 9 in); length 11.18 m (36 ft 8 in); height 4.01 m (13 ft 2 in); wing area 39.20 m² (422.0 sq ft)

Armament: two fixed forward-firing 20-mm guns in the wings and two 7.62-mm (0.3-in) trainable guns in the rear cockpit, plus a bombload of 454 kg (1,000 lb) under the wings and 454 kg (1,000 lb) internally

---

Vought F4U Corsair

Vought F4U-1A Corsair of No. 17 Sqn, Royal New Zealand Air Force, based on Guadalcanal island in the Solomon group during August 1944.

Distinctive yet not unattractive with its inverted gull wing, the **Vought F4U Corsair** was unquestionably the best shipborne fighter of the war, and gained an 11:1 kill:loss ratio in the Pacific. Designed by Rex B. Beisel, the **XF4U-1** was flown on 29 May 1940, the first production **F4U-1** fighters being delivered to VF-12 in October 1942, although most of the early aircraft went to the US Marine Corps. It was a land-

based US Marine squadron, VMF-124, that first flew the Corsair into action, on 13 February 1943 over Bougainville. Additional production lines were set up by Brewster and Goodyear, these companies producing the **F3A-1** and **FG-1** respectively. To improve the pilot's field of view, later aircraft introduced a raised cockpit, and the **F4U-1C** had a four 20-mm cannon armament. The **F4U-1D**, **FG-1D** and **F3A-1D** were powered by water-injection boosted R-2800-8W engines, and could carry two 454-kg (1,000-lb) bombs or eight 127-mm (5-in) rockets under the wings. Late in the war a night-fighter version, the **XF4U-2**, saw limited service with VFN-75 and VFN-101. Wartime production of the Corsair (which continued until 1952 with later versions) reached 4,120 F4U-1s, 735 F3A-1s and 3,808 FG-1s; of these 2,012 were supplied to the UK's Fleet Air Arm and 370 to New Zealand. Indeed, it was the Royal Navy's **Corsair Mk II** aircraft of No. 1834 Squadron that were the first Corsairs to operate from a carrier when, on 3 April 1944, they took part in operations against the *Tirpitz*.

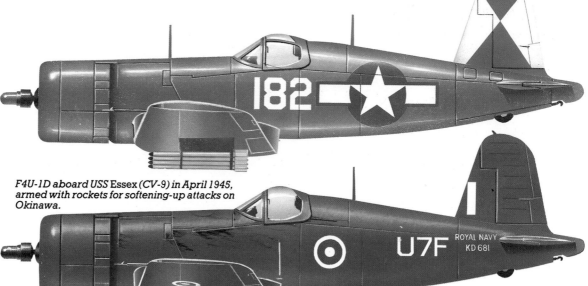

F4U-1D aboard USS Essex *(CV-9) in April 1945, armed with rockets for softening-up attacks on Okinawa.*

Goodyear-built Corsair Mk IV (FG-1D) serving with No. 1850 Sqn, Fleet Air Arm, HMS Vengeance, *whilst on Pacific duty in 1945.*

Specification
Vought F4U-1 Corsair
Type: single-seat shipboard fighter
Powerplant: one 1491.4-kW (2,000-hp) Pratt & Whitney R-2800-8 radial piston engine
Performance: maximum speed 671 km/h (417 mph) at 6066 m (19,900 ft); initial climb rate 881 m (2,890 ft) per minute; service ceiling 11247 m (36,900 ft); range 1633 km (1,015 miles)
Weights: empty 4074 kg (8,982 lb); maximum take-off 6350 kg (14,000 lb)
Dimensions: span 12.50 m (41 ft 0 in); length 10.17 m (33 ft 4.5 in); height 4.90 m (16 ft 1 in); wing area 29.17 m^2 (314.0 sq ft)
Armament: six forward-firing 12.7-mm (0.5-in) machine-guns in the wings

The finest naval fighter produced in the war, Vought's distinctive Corsair was also an excellent ground-attack platform with bombs and rockets.

Douglas SBD Dauntless

Developed directly from the **Northrop BT-1** (the Northrop Corporation became a division of Douglas), the prototype of the **Douglas SBD Dauntless** two-seat carrierborne dive bomber was in fact a much modified production BT-1. Production orders for 57 **SBD-1** and 87 **SBD-2** aircraft were placed in April 1939, the former being delivered to US Marine Corps bombing and scout-bombing squadrons, and the latter to US Navy scout and bombing squadrons. The **SBD-3**, with two additional 12.7-mm (0.5-in) guns in the nose, self-sealing tanks and R-1820-52 engine, appeared in March 1941, and by the time of Pearl Harbor in December that year 584 SBD-3s had been delivered. Some 780 **SBD-4** aircraft (with 24-volt electrical system but otherwise as the SBD-3 and produced at El Segundo, California) were built in 1942; photo-reconnaissance modifications (the **SBD-1P**, **SBD-2P** and **SBD-3P**) were also produced during 1941-2. A new Douglas plant at Tulsa, Oklahoma, built 2,409 **SBD-5** aircraft with 894.8-kW (1,200-hp) R-1820-60 engines, follow-

ing these with 451 **SBD-6** aircraft with -66 engines. The USAAF took delivery of 168 SBD-3A, 170 SBD-4A and 615 SBD-5A aircraft as the **A-24**, **A-24A** and **A-24B** respectively, bringing the total Douglas production to 5,936 SBDs. They were unquestionably one of the USA's most important weapons in the Pacific war, and sank a greater tonnage of Japanese shipping than any other aircraft, as well as playing a key part in the great battles of Midway, the Coral Sea and the Solomons.

Specification
Douglas SBD-5 Dauntless
Type: two-crew carrierborne scout/dive-bomber
Powerplant: one 894.8-kW (1,200-hp) Wright R-1820-60 radial piston engine
Performance: maximum speed 394 km/h (245 mph) at 4816 m (15,800 ft); initial climb rate 363 m (1,190 ft) per minute; service ceiling 7407 m (24,300 ft); range 1770 km (1,100 miles)
Weights: empty 3028 kg (6,675 lb);

maximum take-off 4924 kg (10,855 lb)
Dimensions: span 12.65 m (41 ft 6.25 in); length 10.06 m (33 ft 0 in); height 3.94 m (12 ft 11 in); wing area 30.19 m^2 (325.0 sq ft)
Armament: two fixed forward-firing 12.7-mm (0.5-in) machine-guns and two trainable 7.62-mm (0.3-in) guns in rear cockpit, plus a bombload of one 726-kg (1,600-lb) bomb under the fuselage and two 147-kg (325-lb) bombs under the wings

Douglas SBD-4 Dauntless of VMSB-243, 1st Marine Air Wing, USMC, based on Munda, New Georgia island (Solomons) in August 1943.

Grumman F4F Wildcat

When first flown on 2 September 1937, the **Grumman XF4F-2** single-seat naval fighter prototype proved to be only 16 km/h (10 mph) faster than the Brewster F2A-1, and only when a two-stage supercharged XR-1830-76 was fitted was the true potential of the design recognized, and a speed of 537 km/h (333.5 mph) was recorded during US Navy trials with the **XF4F-3**. Some 54 production **F4F-3** fighters were ordered in August 1939, 22 of which had been delivered by the end of 1940. These aircraft (Grumman's first monoplanes for the US Navy and later named **Wildcat**) served with VF-4 and VF-7, and were followed by 95 **F4F-3A** aircraft with single-stage super-charged R-1830-90 engines. The Wildcat was ordered by France in 1939 but the entire batch of 81 aircraft was transferred to the UK, with whose Royal Navy they served as the **Martlet**, being first flown in combat during 1940. US Navy and US Marine Corps F4Fs were heavily engaged during the early months of the war with the Japanese, numerous aircraft being destroyed on the ground, but also scoring a number of outstanding victories. The **F4F-4**, with manually-folding wings (of which 1,169 were produced), was delivered during 1942, and an unarmed long-range recon-naissance version of this, the **F4F-7**, had a range of over 5633 km (3,500 miles). The F4F-4 was also built by General Motors as the **FM-1**, and a more powerful version, the **FM-2**, for operation from escort carriers. FM-1s and 2s were supplied to the UK as the **Wildcat Mk V** and **Wildcat Mk VI** (the name Martlet having been dropped). F4F-4s were heavily committed in the battles of the Coral Sea and Midway. Total production of the Wildcat (excluding prototypes) was 7,885, including 5,237 FM-1s and FM-2s by General Motors, and 1,100 for the UK.

Specification
Grumman F4F-4 Wildcat
Type: single-seat shipboard fighter
Powerplant: one 894.8-kW (1,200-hp) Pratt & Whitney R-1830-86 radial piston engine
Performance: maximum speed

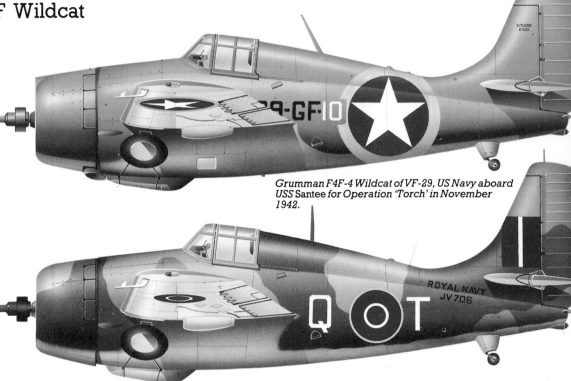

Grumman F4F-4 Wildcat of VF-29, US Navy aboard USS Santee for Operation 'Torch' in November 1942.

General Motors (Grumman) Wildcat Mk VI (FM-2) of No. 835 Sqn, Fleet Air Arm, aboard HMS Nairana in August 1944.

Although slow and unmanoeuvrable when compared with the Mitsubishi A6M, the Grumman F4F was the best that the US Navy could field in the early days of the war. Flown by highly trained and brave pilots, the Wildcat held its own until more modern aircraft arrived in service.

512 km/h (318 mph) at 5913 m (19,400 ft); initial climb rate 594 m (1,950 ft) per minute; service ceiling 10638 m (34,900 ft); range 1239 km (770 miles)
Weights: empty 2624 kg (5,785 lb); maximum take-off 3607 kg (7,952 lb)
Dimensions: span 11.58 m (38 ft 0 in); length 8.76 m (28 ft 9 in); height 3.61 m (11 ft 10 in); wing area 24.15 m² (260.0 sq ft)
Armament: six forward-firing 12.7-mm

(0.5-in) machine guns; FM-2 had four guns and provision to carry two 113-kg

(250-lb) bombs or six 127-mm (5-in) rockets

Grumman F6F Hellcat

One of America's best wartime ship-board fighters, and ably partnering the F4U Corsair, the **Grumman F6F Hellcat** was the logical development of the F4F Wildcat, and was first flown as the **XF6F-3** on 26 June 1942; this was given an uprated engine and flew again five weeks later. Deliveries to VF-9 aboard USS *Essex* started early in 1943; night-fighter versions were the **F6F-3E** and **F6F-3N** with radar in a wing pod. In 1944 the **F6F-5** appeared with provision for 907 kg (2,000 lb) of bombs and two 20-mm cannon sometimes replacing the inboard wing 12.7-mm (0.5-in) guns: the radar-equipped night-fighter version was the **F6F-5N**; production totalled 6,435 F6F-5Ns, while 252 F6F-3s and 930 F6F-5s served with the British Fleet Air Arm as the **Hellcat Mk I** and **Hellcat Mk II** respectively. Production of all F6Fs amounted to 12,275, and official figures credited the US Navy and Marine Corps aircraft with the destruction of 5,156 enemy aircraft in air combat, about 75 per cent of all

Grumman Hellcat Mk II of No. 800 Sqn, Fleet Air Arm, flying from HMS Emperor off the coast of Malaya in September 1945. The Fleet Air Arm adopted US-style midnight blue in the Far East and some aircraft sported white bars each side of the national insignia.

the US Navy's air combat victories in the war. The Hellcat's greatest single victory was in that largest of all carrier operations, the Battle of the Philippine Sea, in which 15 American carriers

embarked 480 F6F fighters (plus 222 dive-bombers and 199 torpedo-bombers); by the end of a week's fighting Task Force 58 had destroyed more than 400 Japanese aircraft and

sunk three carriers. Hellcats were still serving with the US Navy several years after the war.

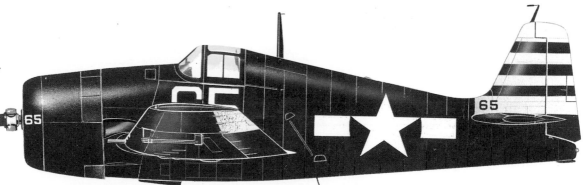

Grumman F6F-6 Hellcat of VF-12, US Navy aboard USS Randolph operating in Japanese waters in early 1945.

Specification

Grumman F6F-5 Hellcat

Type: single-seat shipboard fighter
Powerplant: one 1491.4-kW (2,000-hp) Pratt & Whitney R-2800-10W radial piston engine
Performance: maximum speed 612 km/h (380 mph) at 7132 m (23,400 ft); initial climb rate 908 m (2,980 ft) per minute; service ceiling 11369 m (37,300 ft); range 1521 km (945 miles)
Weights: empty 4190 kg (9,238 lb); maximum take-off 6991 kg (15,413 lb)
Dimensions: span 13.05 m (42 ft 10 in); length 10.24 m (33 ft 7 in); height 3.99 m (13 ft 1 in); wing area 31.03 m^2 (334.0 sq ft)
Armament: six 12.7-mm (0.5-in) machine-guns in wings, or two 20-mm cannon and four 12.7-mm (0.5-in) guns in wings, plus provision for two 454-kg (1,000-lb) bombs

The Hellcat finally enabled the Americans to defeat the Mitsubishi A6M. This VD-5 aircraft was used in the photo-reconnaissance role.

 USA

Grumman TBF Avenger

Destined to become one of the best shipborne torpedo-bombers of the war, the **Grumman TBF-Avenger** first saw combat during the great Battle of Midway. The **XTBF-1** prototype was first flown on 1 August 1941 after an order for 286 aircraft had already been placed. The first **TBF-1** aircraft appeared in January 1942 and VT-8 ('Torpedo-Eight') received its first aircraft during the following May. On 4 June six of VT-8's aircraft were launched at the height of the Battle of Midway, but only one returned – and this with one dead gunner and the other wounded. Despite this inauspicious start, production was accelerating as General Motors undertook production in addition to Grumman, producing the **TBM-1** version. Sub-variants included the **TBF-1C** with two 20-mm cannon in the wings, the **TBF-1B** which was supplied to the UK under Lend-Lease, the **TBF-1D** and **TBF-1E** with ASV radar, and the **TBF-1L** with a searchlight in the bomb bay. Production of the TBF-1 and TBM-1, as well as sub-variants, were 2,290 and 2,882 respectively. General Motors (Eastern Divison) went on to produce 4,664 **TBM-3** aircraft with R-2600-20 engines, and the sub-variants corresponded with those of the TBF-1s. The UK received 395 TBF-1Bs and 526 TBM-3Bs, and New Zealand 63. The **TBM-3P** camera-equipped aircraft and the **TBM-3H** with search radar were the final wartime versions, although the Avenger went on to serve with the US Navy until 1954.

Specification

Grumman (General Motors) TBM-3E Avenger

Type: three-crew carrierborne torpedo-bomber
Powerplant: one 1416.8-kW (1,900-hp) Wright R-2600-20 radial piston engine
Performance: maximum speed

Grumman TBF Avenger of the US Navy. Armament of the dorsal turret was one 0.5-calibre machine-gun.

444 km/h (276 mph) at 5029 m (16,500 ft); initial climb rate 628 m (2,060 ft) per minute; service ceiling 9174 m (30,100 ft); range 1625 km (1,010 miles)
Weights: empty 4783 kg (10,545 lb); maximum take-off 8117 kg (17,895 lb)
Dimensions: span 16.51 m (54 ft 2 in);

length 12.48 m (40 ft 11.5 in); height 4.70 m (15 ft 5 in); wing area 45.52 m^2 (490.0 sq ft)
Armament: two fixed forward-firing 12.7-mm (0.5-in) guns, one 12.7-mm (0.5-in) gun in dorsal turret and one 7.62-mm (0.3-in) gun in ventral position, plus an offensive load of up to

907 kg (2,000 lb) of bombs, or one torpedo, in weapons bay

Avengers replaced the hopelessly outclassed Devastator on the torpedo squadrons from 1942 onwards. These Avengers are seen on a practice torpedo run.

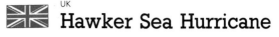

UK
Hawker Sea Hurricane

Based on the RAF's Hurricane, the **Hawker Sea Hurricane** was introduced to provide modern fighter protection for convoys of merchant ships. Over 800 were delivered, the majority of them being conversions of Hurricanes, including many which had seen operational service. A number were modifications of newly delivered Canadian-built aircraft.

The first version to appear was the **Sea Hurricane Mk IA** fitted with catapult spools so that they could be flown from specially fitted merchant ships in the event of the appearance of an enemy aircraft. This was followed by the **Sea Hurricane Mk IB**, which in addition to the spools had deck arrester gear to enable it to be used for carrier operations. The **Sea Hurricane Mk IC**, of which only a few were produced, had four wing-mounted 20-mm cannon in place of the machine-guns of the earlier versions. Re-engined with the Rolls-Royce Merlin XX it became the **Sea Hurricane Mk IIB** when fitted with machine-guns, and the **Sea Hurricane Mk IIC** with cannon. Canadian-built aircraft also used these designations, irrespective of their original mark numbers.

Sea Hurricanes first entered operational service in February 1941 with No. 804 Squadron for deployment from catapult-armed merchantmen, or CAM-ships as they were generally known. The first carrier squadron to equip was No. 880 Squadron in March 1941, seeing action in July from HMS *Furious* during a raid on the Arctic port of Petsamo. The following month an aircraft of No. 804 Squadron catapulted from HMS *Maplin* accounted for a Focke-Wulf Condor. The disadvantage of this method of operation was

that unless the pilot could reach land he had no choice but to ditch his aircraft. The CAM-ship task and aircraft were later passed on to the RAF's Merchant Ship Fighter Unit at Speke. When the first escort carriers came into service with the Royal Navy, Sea Hurricanes were attached to several of them, seeing service in the Arctic and the Mediterranean until being replaced in 1943 by Seafires and Wildcats.

Specification
Hawker Sea Hurricane Mk IIC
Type: carrierborne fighter
Powerplant: one 954.5-kW (1,280-hp) Rolls-Royce Merlin XX V-12 piston engine
Performance: maximum speed 505 km/h (314 mph) at 5944 m (19,500 ft); service ceiling 10516 m (34,500 ft); range 1207 km (750 miles)
Weights: empty 2617 kg (5,770 lb); maximum take-off 3511 kg (7,740 lb)

Dimensions: span 12.20 m (40 ft 0 in); length 9.83 m (32 ft 3 in); height 4.00 m (13 ft 1.5 in); wing area 23.92 m² (257.5 sq ft)
Armament: four 20-mm cannon

After the failure of such types as the Sea Gladiator and Fulmar to provide adequate fighter protection, the Hurricane was hastily adapted for carrier decks. The result was a fine fighter which saw much action.

UK
Supermarine Seafire

Following the success of the Sea Hurricane adaptation, a Spitfire VB was fitted with a 'V' arrester hook and satisfactory trials were carried out in HMS *Illustrious* towards the end of 1941. A number of these aircraft with 'B' type wings were similarly modified and named **Supermarine Seafire Mk IB**. In May 1942 the **Seafire Mk IIC** began to come off the production line, fitted with the 'C' type Spitfire wing with provision for four 20-mm cannon, and having a reinforced fuselage, catapult spools and rocket-assisted take-off gear (RATOG). A low-altitude version was the **Seafire L.Mk IIC**, and a few were fitted with cameras for photographic reconnaissance work, being designated **Seafire LR.Mk IIC**. A manually-operated folding wing was introduced on the **Seafire F.Mk III**, and as with the earlier mark there was a **Seafire L.Mk III** variant for low-altitude work, a few being modified as the **Seafire LR.MK III** for photo-reconnaissance duties.

In 1945 the Griffon-engined Seafire **F.Mk XV** appeared, with a sting-type arrester hook, being followed by the **Seafire F.Mk XVII** with a clear-view bubble hood, cutaway rear fuselage and increased fuel capacity. The **Seafire FR.Mk XVII** reconnaissance variant had two cameras. Based on the Spitfire F.Mk 21, the **Seafire F.Mk 45** had a later Griffon fitted with either a five-blade propeller or two three-blade counter-rotating propellers. The clear-view bubble hood and cutaway

rear fuselage were fitted to the **Seafire F.Mk 46**, a reconnaissance version being the **Seafire FR.Mk 46**. The final version, the **Seafire F.Mk 47**, and the **Seafire FR.Mk 47** variant, had power-folding wings and other changes.

The Seafire participated successfully in the North African landings in November 1942, and later at Salerno and the south of France. Its principle failing was highlighted at Salerno, where lack of windspeed over the carrier decks led to numerous collapsed landing gears. Several squadrons were active in the Pacific, and after the

war the Griffon-engined versions remained in service until 1954, many with reserve squadrons.

Specification
Supermarine Seafire F.Mk III
Type: carrierborne fighter
Powerplant: one 1096-kW (1,470-hp) Rolls-Royce Merlin 45, 50 or 55 V-12 piston engine
Performance: maximum speed 566 km/h (352 mph) at 3734 m (12,250 ft); service ceiling 10302 m (33,800 ft); range 748 km (465 miles) on internal fuel

Weights: empty 2449 kg (5,400 lb); maximum take-off 3175 kg (7,000 lb)
Dimensions: span 11.23 m (36 ft 10 in); length 9.12 m (29 ft 11 in); height 3.48 m (11 ft 5 in); wing area 22.48 m² (242.0 sq ft)
Armament: two 20-mm cannon and four 7.7-mm (0.303-in) machine-guns, plus provision for one 227-kg (500-lb) bomb or two 113-kg (250-lb) bombs

Seafires were potent fighters with high performance for a deck-launched aircraft but suffered a great deal from weak undercarriages and relatively high landing speed.

Fairey Albacore

Wholly eclipsed by the Swordfish, which it was intended to replace, the **Fairey Albacore** was in essence a cleaned-up version of the celebrated 'Stringbag' with an enclosed cabin to improve the operational efficiency of the crew and a Bristol Taurus radial to provide higher performance despite considerably greater weights. First flown in December 1938, the initial prototype was fitted with a wheel landing gear, while the second had twin floats. The Albacore, which was inevitably called the 'Applecore' in service, differed from the Swordfish in being used operationally only on the wheeled type of landing gear. The type entered service with the Royal Navy's Fleet Air Arm in 1940, and production amounted to 798 aircraft. The Albacore was first flown in action during attacks on Boulogne in September 1940. Most Albacores were land-based throughout their careers, but the type's brief moment of glory arrived when the Albacores from the carrier HMS *Formidable* severely damaged the Italian battleship *Vittorio Veneto* during the Battle of Cape Matapan in March 1941. After this time the Albacore was occasionally used for bombing in the Western Desert, usually at night to prevent the depredations of Axis fighters, and the type played an important part in the operations leading up to the Battle of Alamein in October 1942. In carrier operations the Albacore saw service in the North Atlan-

Fairey Albacore of the Fleet Air Arm. It was not as well liked as its predecessor, the Swordfish, despite its enclosed cockpit.

Right: Inevitably called the 'Applecore', the Albacore gave good if undistinguished service, especially in North Africa and the Mediterranean. This aircraft is seen dropping a practice 457-mm (18-in) torpedo.

tic, Arctic, Mediterranean and Indian oceans; and the type was also used with some success as a support aircraft during seaborne invasions, notably those of Sicily, Italy and northern France, the last in the hands of Royal Canadian Air Force squadrons.

Specification
Fairey Albacore
Type: three-crew naval torpedo-bomber
Powerplant: one 794.2-kW (1,065-hp) Bristol Taurus II radial piston engine
Performance: maximum speed 259 km/h (161 mph) at 2134 m (7,000 ft); climb to 1829 m (6,000 ft) in 8.0 minutes; service ceiling 6309 m (20,700 ft); range 1320 km (820 miles)
Weights: empty 3266 kg (7,200 lb); maximum take-off 5715 kg (12,600 lb)
Dimensions: span 15.24 m (50 ft 0 in); length 12.13 m (39 ft 9.5 in); height 4.65 m (15 ft 3 in); wing area 57.88 m² (623.0 sq ft)
Armament: one forward-firing 7.7-mm (0.303in) Vickers machine-gun and two 7.7-mm (0.303-in) Vickers 'K' machine-guns in the rear cockpit, plus one 457-mm (18-in) torpedo or up to 907 kg (2,000 lb) of bombs

---

Fairey Barracuda

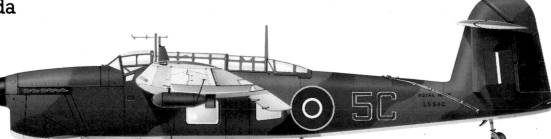

Intended to replace the Albacore, itself a replacement for the Swordfish, the **Fairey Barracuda** was an altogether more advanced aircraft conceptually, and was designed as a high-performance monoplane to meet a 1937 requirement. The intended powerplant was the Rolls-Royce Exe, and the programme was delayed substantially when this engine was abandoned and the structure had to be revised to accommodate a Merlin engine from the same manufacturer. Thus the Barracuda prototype did not fly until 7 December 1940, and it was immediately apparent that the performance of the heavy Barracuda would be limited by the power available: the 939.6-kW (1,260-hp) Merlin XXX in the **Barracuda Mk I** and the 1222.9-kW (1,640-hp) Merlin 32 for the **Barracuda Mk II** and **Barracuda Mk III**. At a time when production priorities were afforded mostly to the RAF, deliveries of the Barracuda to the Fleet Air Arm were slow to start, and it was January 1943 before Barracuda Mk Is began to enter service with the Fleet Air Arm. The Barracuda Mk I was little more than a service-test type, only 23 being built. The two main wartime models were thus the Barracuda Mk II with ASV Mk IIN radar (1,635 built by Fairey, Blackburn, Boulton Paul and Westland) and the Barracuda Mk III torpedo-reconnaissance version with ASV Mk X radar (912 built by the parent company). The Barracuda saw only limited service in home waters, the highpoint of its career being a highly successful strike on the German battleship *Tirpitz* in April 1944; but in the Pacific campaigns of 1944 and 1945 the Barracuda was one of the more prominent British aircraft.

Fairey Barracuda Mk II of the Fleet Air Arm, complete with anti-submarine radar and underwing depth bombs.

Specification
Fairey Barracuda Mk II
Type: three-crew shipborne torpedo- and dive-bomber
Powerplant: one 1222.9-kW (1,640-hp) Rolls-Royce Merlin 32 V-12 piston engine
Performance: maximum speed 367 km/h (228 mph) at 533 m (1,750 ft); climb to 1524 m (5,000 ft) in 6.0 minutes; service ceiling 5060 m (16,600 ft); range 1851 km (1,150 miles)
Weights: empty 4241 kg (9,350 lb); maximum take-off 6396 kg (14,100 lb)
Dimensions: span 14.99 m (49 ft 2 in); length 12.12 m (39 ft 9 in); height 4.60 m (15 ft 1 in); wing area 34.09 m² (367.0 sq ft)
Armament: two 7.7-mm (0.303-in) Vickers 'K' machine-guns in the rear cockpit, plus one 735-kg (1,620-lb) torpedo, or four 204-kg (450-lb) depth charges, or six 113-kg (250-lb) bombs

Altogether more advanced than the Albacore, the Barracuda was delayed by difficulties with engine-mounting. When it did reach service in January 1943, the aircraft acquitted itself well, especially during the attacks on Tirpitz.

Fairey Firefly

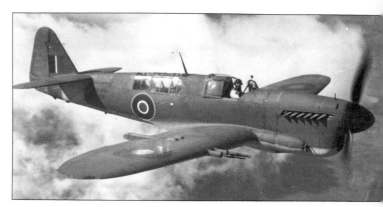

Numbered amongst the most successful aircraft ever used by the Fleet Air Arm, the **Fairey Firefly** served in its various versions for nearly 15 years, a total of 1,702 being produced before production ceased in 1956. The prototype took the air on 22 December 1941, and the first production **Firefly F.Mk I** entered service in March 1943. Later production Mk Is were fitted with ASH radar, in which form they became **Firefly FR.Mk I** reconnaissance fighters. A number of aircraft were produced as **Firefly NF.Mk I** nightfighters equipped with a different radio for night flying, and with shrouded exhausts. Another nightfighter version, the **Firefly NF.MK II**, had AI.Mk X radar mounted on each wing, whilst the **Firefly F.Mk IA** was a modification of the Mk I brought up to FR.Mk I standard by the addition of ASH radar. A trial modification fitted with a Griffon 61 and a nose radiator was designated **Firefly F.Mk 3**, but this was superseded by the **Firefly FR.Mk 4** reconnaissance fighter with a Griffon 74. This went into service in 1946, but from 1948 it gave way to variants of the **Firefly Mk 5** with improved equipment, the surviving FR.Mk 4s being

converted to **Firefly TT.Mk 4** target tugs. Then followed the **Firefly AS.Mk 6** anti-submarine reconnaissance and strike aircraft, the final version to enter first-line service, of which 152 were delivered as such, including some converted from Mk 5s on the production line, in addition to many other Mk 5s converted after seeing service. Other versions of the Firefly included trainers and target drones, the last to appear being the **Firefly U.Mk 9** drone in 1956.

The Firefly was an immediate success on entering service, participating in attacks on the German battleship *Tirpitz* as well as taking part in numerous Norwegian raids. It was equally successful in the Pacific, making raids against Japanese occupied islands early in 1945, and against the Japanese mainland shortly before VJ-day. In the post-war years several squadrons took an active part in the Korean War, and one squadron later carried out attacks against Malayan bandits.

Specification
Fairey Firefly F.Mk I
Type: two-seat carrierborne fighter
Powerplant: one 1294-kW (1,735-hp)

Rolls-Royce Griffon IIB V-12 piston engine
Performance: maximum speed 509 km/h (316 mph) at 4267 m (14,000 ft); service ceiling 8534 m (28,000 ft); range 2092 km (1,300 miles)
Weights: empty 4423 kg (9,750 lb); maximum take-off 6359 kg (14,020 lb)
Dimensions: span 13.56 m (44 ft 6 in); length 11.46 m (37 ft 7 in); height 4.14 m (13 ft 7 in); wing area 30.47 m² (328.0 sq ft)

Fairey Firefly Mk Is reached squadron service in October 1943, and were soon active against such targets as the Tirpitz. A transfer to the Far East saw more action for the aircraft, but, as with the Fulmar, it was hampered by its size and two-man crew.

Armament: four 20-mm cannon, plus eight 27.2-kg (60-lb) rockets or two 454 (1,000-lb) bombs

Fairey Fulmar

The first true shipborne monoplane fighter for the Fleet Air Arm, the eight-gun **Fairey Fulmar** tends to be overlooked in the part it played in the first three years of the war, until replaced by deck-operating adaptations of the Hurricane and Spitfire, and by the Martlet. Developed from the Fairey P.4/34 light bomber prototypes which flew in 1937, the Fulmar fleet fighter prototype was flown on 4 January 1940, with production aircraft being completed soon after. Early trials showed the aircraft to have a disappointing performance, although it was recognized as being a fairly large aeroplane with the same engine as the Hurricane single-seater. In 1942, after 127 production **Fulmar Mk 1** fighters had been completed, the **Fulmar Mk II** appeared with 939.6-kW (1,260-hp) Merlin XXX, an engine which raised the top speed to 438 km/h (272 mph). Fulmar Mk Is of No. 808 Squadron of the Fleet Air Arm were listed in RAF Fighter Command's order of battle during the Battle of Britain, although they were not engaged in combat. By November 1940, however, Fulmars were in action from HMS *Illustrious* at the time of the Battle of Taranto, and soon afterwards from *Ark Royal* defending the vital convoys sailing to Malta. At the Battle of Cape Matapan Fulmars from *Formidable* escorted the Albacores and Swordfish which torpedoed the Italian battleship *Vittorio*

Fairey Fulmar Mk I in standard early war Fleet Air Arm finish.

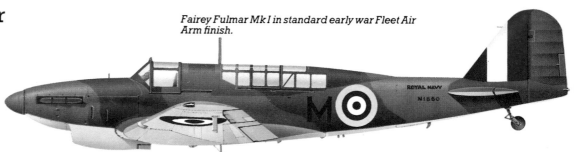

Right: Although powered by the same Merlin engine as the Hurricane and Spitfire, the Fulmar was considerably larger and carried an extra crew member. It was not the equal of the best enemy fighters, but gave a good account of itself.

Veneto. Early in 1942, as Japanese naval forces sailed into the Indian Ocean to threaten Ceylon, two squadrons of Fulmars were based there as part of Colombo's air defences; when confronted for the first time by the much superior carrierbased Mitsubishi A6M fighters the Fulmars were utterly outclassed and almost all were shot down or damaged. A total of 450 Fulmar Mk IIs was built, and some served as nightfighters.

Specification
Fairey Fulmar Mk II
Type: two-seat carrierborne fighter

Powerplant: one 939.6-kW (1,260-hp) Rolls-Royce Merlin XXX V-12 piston engine
Performance: maximum speed 438 km/h (272 mph) at 5029 m (16,500 ft); initial climb rate 402 m (1,320 ft) per minute; service ceiling 8291 m (27,200 ft); range 1255 km (780 miles)
Weights: empty 3349 kg (7,384 lb);

maximum take-off 4627 kg (10,200 lb)
Dimensions: span 14.14 m (46 ft 4.5 in); length 12.24 m (40 ft 2 in); height 3.25 m (10 ft 8 in); wing area 31.77 m² (342.0 sq ft)
Armament: eight 7.7-mm (0.303-in) machine-guns in wings, and a few aircraft also had a single trainable 7.7-mm (0.303-in) machine-gun in the rear cockpit

Fairey Swordfish

Of all aircraft regarded as anachronisms the **Fairey Swordfish** torpedo-bomber must be the supreme example, for even back in the 1930s it appeared archaic and cumbersome. Stemming from an earlier design whose prototype had crashed, the first prototype Swordfish (the **TSR.II**) first flew on 17 April 1934 and the production **Swordfish Mk I** was prepared to

Specification S.38/34 with slightly swept-back top wing; construction was all-metal with fabric covering. By the outbreak of war in 1939 a total of 689 aircraft had been delivered or were on

A Fairey Swordfish Mk II is 'struck down' following an anti-submarine patrol.

Fairey Swordfish Mk I of No. 820 Sqn serving aboard HMS Ark Royal in 1939. This aircraft is carrying the standard 457-mm (18-in) torpedo.

Throughout the later months of the war, Swordfish were used on general attacks against German shipping in the North Sea. These were often small vessels and their light defences proved inadequate against the tough Swordfish. Rockets were the favoured weapon for these strikes.

Fairey Swordfish Mk II of No. 811 Sqn aboard HMS Biter in 1944, complete with invasion stripes.

order, serving with both wheel and float landing gear aboard Royal Navy carriers, battleships, battle-cruisers and cruisers in the torpedo-spotter reconnaissance role. Among the memorable events in which the old 'Stringbag'

Seemingly an anachronism in World War II, the Swordfish remained unmatched by any other British naval aircraft in terms of battle honours. At the heart of this was the aircraft's immense sturdiness and basic good design. This typically well-worn example is carrying a practice bomb.

participated was the action at Taranto on 11 November 1940, when Swordfish aircraft from HMS *Illustrious* severely damaged three Italian battleships; the crippling of the *Bismarck* in the Atlantic; and the suicidal attack on the German warships, *Scharnhorst, Gneisenau* and *Prinz Eugen* during their famous escape up the English Channel in February 1942. Production of the Swordfish was undertaken largely by Blackburn, the **Swordfish Mk II** being introduced with a strengthened lower wing to allow eight rocket projectiles to be mounted, the **Swordfish Mk III**

with ASV radar between the landing legs, and the **Swordfish Mk IV** conversion of the Mk II with a rudimentary enclosed cabin. Production ended on 18 August 1944, by which time a total of 2,396 Swordfish had been completed.

Specification
Fairey Swordfish Mk II
Type: three-crew torpedo/anti-submarine aircraft
Powerplant: one 559.3-kW (750-hp) Bristol Pegasus XXX radial piston engine
Performance: maximum speed

222 km/h (138 mph) at sea level; initial climb rate 372 m (1,220 ft) per minute; service ceiling 5867 m (19,250 ft); range 879 km (546 miles)
Weights: empty 2132 kg (4,700 lb); maximum take-off 3406 kg (7,510 lb)
Dimensions: span 12.87 m (45 ft 6 in); length 10.87 m (35 ft 8 in); height 3.76 m (12 ft 4 in); wing area 56.39 m² (607.0 sq ft)
Armament: one fixed forward-firing 7.7-mm (0.303-in) machine-gun and one trainable 7.7-mm (0.303-in) gun in rear cockpit, plus an offensive load of one 457-mm (18-in) torpedo or eight 27.2-kg (60-lb) rocket projectiles

Transport and Assault Aircraft

Military transport aircraft were to make a significant breakthrough during World War II by developing the ability to deliver manpower and weapons direct to the battlefield from the air: this was the ultimate expression of mobile warfare.

Douglas C-47 Dakotas and Waco CG-4 Hadrian gliders lining an airstrip in March 1945; both were essential tools for delivering forces direct to the battlefield.

'We ought to have a corps of at least 5000 parachute troops.'

Thus wrote Winston Churchill to his chief of staff on 22 June 1940. This message was, in effect, to give birth to the British airborne division.

It has long been the dream of military men to have the means and the capability to transport large numbers of soldiers by air around the war zone, and at least one Napoleonic print exists showing this being achieved across the English Channel, each man under an individual balloon! However, it was the Soviet Union and not Britain which was to give the dream substance, for it was during the summer manoeuvres of 1936 that a demonstration troop of 1200 Soviet soldiers complete with 150 machine-guns served to impress the world.

Even so, Nazi Germany was quick to imitate such a manoeuvre and it was her paratroops and a new method of transporting armed men, by means of towed gliders, that first saw both methods of transport used in action during the opening months of World War II. The lessons learned from this experience were soon being applied by the Germans to the altogether larger action in Crete.

Up until this time, transport aircraft had been used only as aerial troop carriers. However, following on from the advances initiated by the Soviet Union and Germany, a third method of transportation now awaited these aircraft: that of air-landing operations in which soldiers were disembarked directly under fire on to enemy territory. All three methods were used on a scale hitherto only imagined when the UK, the USA and their allies invaded the continent of Europe in 1944, moving by air not only men and arms, but also heavy equipment and vehicles, some (like the human cargoes) even being deposited by parachute.

Although made as perfect as possible, the susceptibility to error of these schemes was brought sharply home by the Arnheim operation, while the aerial movement of armies had spawned a whole range of ancillary systems, such as the reclaiming of gliders by the snatch method. After almost 200 years the dream had become a reality.

Curtiss C-46 Commando

In common with its more prolific contemporary, the Douglas C-47, the **Curtiss C-46 Commando** was initially developed for the civil market, in the shape of the **CW-20** prototype which first flew on 26 March 1940 on the power of two 1193.1-kW (1,600-hp) Wright Cyclone 586-C14-BA2 engines. The aircraft featured a twin-finned tail unit but this was soon changed to a large single unit. In September 1940 a large order was placed for a militarized version which was to be designated C-46 and powered by the Pratt & Whitney Double Wasp.

Quickly following the C-46 was the main production version, the **C-46A**, which featured double cargo doors and a hydraulic winch. This allowed the crew to load the aircraft without ground assistance. Other main versions were the **C-46D** with revised nose and doors for paratroop operations, and the **C-46F** which introduced more powerful engines and blunted wing tips. The **C-46E** sported a stepped windscreen.

In service the C-46 proved reliable and able to carry much greater loads than the C-47, and the large-diameter cabin allowed awkward items to be carried. The cabin floor was strengthened to allow the airlift of light vehicles and artillery.

The C-46 entered service in mid-1942 and was used initially on local duties. Its operations were soon extended to cover the South Atlantic routes supplying the Allied troops in

Seen here flying above the Himalayas (the famous 'hump' between India and China), the Curtiss C-46 Commando was capable of carrying 50 troops, compared with about 28 by the C-47.

North Africa but it was in Europe and the Far East that the aircraft was used extensively, its most famous route being over the 'Hump' between India and China. This consisted of mountainous passes and treacherous makeshift airfields, the cargoes often consisting of ammunition and fuel. The C-46 was used in most of the 'trucking' operations during the last two years of the Pacific war in the hands of the US Army Air Force and the US Marine Corps (designated **R5C-1**), and the end of hostilities in the Far East spelt the end of production for this hard-working beast of burden. A total

of 3,180 C-46s was built, and many of these continued in US service throughout Korea until the early days of the Vietnam conflict. A handful continue in small-scale civil freighting today.

Specification
Curtiss C-46 Commando
Type: paratroop and general transport
Powerplant: two 1491.4-kW (2,000-hp) Pratt & Whitney R-2800-43 18-cylinder air-cooled radial piston engines
Performance: maximum speed 425 km/h (264 mph) at 3962 m (13,000 ft); service ceiling 8412 m (27,600 ft); range 3701 km (2,300 miles)

On account of its better performance at altitude than the C-47/53 Skytrain, the Curtiss C-46 Commando was extensively used by the USAAF in the Pacific theatre and for the supply of war matériel from India to China over the 'hump'. Here Indian troops embark in a C-46A.

Weights: empty 13374 kg (29,485 lb); maximum take-off 21773 kg (48,000 lb)
Dimensions: span 32.92 m (108 ft 0 in); length 23.27 m (76 ft 4 in); height 6.71 m (22 ft 0 in); wing area 126.16 m² (1,358 sq ft)
Armament: none

USA

Douglas C-47 Skytrain

Probably the best known transport aeroplane of all time, whether as an airliner or military transport, the **Douglas C-47 Skytrain** evolved from the DC-3 airliner which introduced new levels of speed and comfort to travel during the late 1930s. First flown as a commercial aircraft on 17 December 1935, the C-47 was not ordered by the US Army Air Corps until 1940, the airline interior giving way to bucket seats along the cabin sides, and Pratt & Whitney R-1830 radials replacing the DC-3's Wright Cyclones. Some 93 C-47s were built before production switched to the **C-47A** with 24-volt in place of 12-volt electrical system; a total of 4,931 C-47As was built. High-altitude superchargers and R-1830-90 engines were introduced in 3,241 **C-47B** aircraft (including 133 **TC-47B** trainers) intended for use in South East Asia. Many other variations were produced under separate designations, of which the **C-53 Skytrooper** was the most important, being in effect an airline standard aircraft for military purposes. Wartime military production of the C-47

Developed from the DC-2 and DC-3 airliners, the C-47 was the most important transport in the Allied inventory by the time of the invasion of France.

reached 10,048, plus an estimated 2,700 produced in the Soviet Union as the **Lisunov Li-2**. It was also produced in Japan as the L2D. In the USAAF the C-47 became the standard transport and glider tug in service from 1942 onwards, being flown in large numbers in every airborne forces operation during the war; furthermore, some 1,895 Dakotas served with 25 RAF squadrons, the **Dakota Mk I** corresponding to the C-47, the **Dakota Mk II** to the C-53, the **Dakota Mk III** to the C-47A and the **Dakota Mk IV** to the

C-47B. As late as 1961 the USAF still had over 1,000 C-47s on its inventory, and the type was also used by the US Navy as the **R4D** in several variants.

Specification
Douglas C-47 Skytrain (Dakota Mk I)
Type: three-crew 27-troop military transport
Powerplant: two 894.8-kW (1,200-hp) Pratt & Whitney R-1830-92 14-cylinder radial piston engines

Performance: maximum speed 370 km/h (230 mph) at 2591 m (8,500 ft); climb to 3048 m (10,000 ft) in 9.6 minutes; service ceiling 7315 m (24,000 ft); range 2575 km (1,600 miles)
Weights: empty 8255 kg (18,200 lb); maximum take-off 11793 kg (26,000 lb)
Dimensions: span 29.11 m (95 ft 6 in); length 19.43 m (63 ft 9 in); height 5.18 m (17 ft 0 in); wing area 91.69 m² (987.0 sq ft)
Armament: none

Above: The C-47/Dakota gained affection borne of familiarity among Allied troops the world over, affectionately dubbed 'Old Bucket Seats' and 'Gooney Bird'. Shown here is a USAAF aircraft in South East Asia that survived a suicide ramming by a Japanese fighter.

A sight typical of any one of a score of airfields in Britain occupied by the C-47s and C-53s of the US IX Troop Carrier Command in 1943-4. At peak strength the command in Britain fielded 52 squadrons in 13 groups, with almost 900 C-47s/53s. This picture was taken early in 1944.

A C-47B Skytrain, the version developed specifically for flights over the 'hump' to China. In the opinion of General Dwight D. Eisenhower the C-47 joined the bazooka, jeep and atomic bomb as the Allied weapons that contributed most to the victory in World War II.

Consolidated C-87 Liberator

Whilst it is most widely remembered as one of the most important bombers to see wartime service, the Consolidated B-24 Liberator also saw extensive use as a transport. Initial deliveries were to the British airline BOAC in March 1941; designated LB-30A, the first six aircraft were later transferred to RAF Ferry Command, along with aircraft subsequently delivered from the USA.

By June 1941, the US Air Corps Ferrying Command was receiving B-24A transports, these being similar in configuration to the LB-30As, and going on to see extensive wartime service around the world.

From those initial models, plans were put in hand to produce a dedicated transport variant, this taking shape in 1942 as the C-87, a development of the B-24D; 287 were ordered by the USAAC.

Apart from use by the US Army and US Navy (**RY**), this **Consolidated C-87** version of the Liberator was also used by the RAF which flew its **Liberator C.Mk VII** transports for air trooping on an extensive scale. The purpose of this new mobility was at first the necessity of moving men to India for operations against the Japanese and the repatriation of time-expired troops; six RAF Liberators were earmarked for the work in company with Short Stirlings and Douglas Dakotas, there being two each of these latter types.

With room for 38 men and stores, the capacious ex-bomber was the subject for several experiments into the new art of mass-transportation of troops, so that two were the subject of trials after

the war to compare the advantages of matting (on which the men could lie) with those of conventional seats. But the design was not without its problems, such as a weak nose wheel, so swift had been the C-87's development.

Specification
Consolidated C-87 Liberator
Type: air trooping and cargo transport
Powerplant: four 894.8-kW (1,200-hp) Pratt & Whitney Twin Wasp R-1830-43 14-cylinder air-cooled radial piston engines
Performance: maximum speed 435.5 km/h (270 mph) at 6096 m (20,000 ft), service ceiling 9754 m (32,000 ft); range 3685 km (2,290 miles)
Weights: empty 16783 kg (37,000 lb); maximum take-off 28123 kg (62,000 lb)
Dimensions: span 33.53 m (110 ft 0 in); length 20.45 m (67 ft 1 in); height 5.46 m (17 ft 11 in); wing area 97.55 m² (1,050 sq ft)
Armament: none

Both the USAAF and RAF flew the B-24 Liberator as VIP transports. The aircraft depicted here, an LB-30B diverted from an RAF order to an early USAAF contract, was a VIP transport based at Bolling Field, Washington, in the autumn of 1941. The prominent American flag marking was applied to emphasize America's neutrality at that time.

Utilizing the aircraft's long range, RAF Transport Command used various versions of the Consolidated Liberator, converted for trooping and staff transport. Flying the command's routes between the UK, the Middle East and the Far East, these makeshift transports served with the RAF's Nos 46 and 229 Groups.

Waco CG-4A Hadrian

The only US glider to see combat service, the **Waco CG-4** (known to the British as the **Hadrian** and to the Americans as the **Haig**) was constructed from steel tube and wood (covered with fabric) with a large hinged nose to allow the loading and unloading of light vehicles, although the type could also be used for the transport of 15 fully armed troops who travelled seated on benches along the fuselage walls.

Developed from the smaller **XCG-3**, which seated only nine, the CG-4A, or 'Jayhawk' as it was nicknamed, was produced in large numbers at several plants, Beech, Boeing, Cessna and Ford all being involved, while the sub-assemblies were the products of often quite small cabinet-making firms.

Hadrians were first used in an operation by British and American airborne forces, when they were employed in the preliminary assaults of 1943 which led to the capture of Sicily during that summer. A second claim to history was made in July of the same year when a British-operated Douglas Dakota towed one in stages from Montreal to England in a total flying time of 28 hours over the distance of 5633 km (3,500 miles). A load of vaccines for the USSR formed the cargo.

A number of experiments were carried out to investigate the possibility of producing a powered version, and to his end different engines (including the Franklin four-cylinder horizontally-opposed type) were tried out, a pair of engines being fitted to the wing struts. None of these **PG** variants entered full production.

Two years of CG-4 production saw a total of 12,393 delivered, and several thousand of the type were in use in 1944 and 1945, not only for the D-Day landings, but also for the Rhine crossing. Later, a vast number was taken to the Far East as a preliminary to the planned invasion of Japan; had these been used, it seems likely that some would have been towed in side-by-side pairs in the manner reported by observers of the D-Day assault. An improved version built in limited numbers was the **CG-15A**, with span reduced to 18.95 m (62 ft 2 in), a revised nose and cantilever landing gear.

Specification
Waco CG-4A
Type: troop and supply glider
Performance: maximum towing speed 201 km/h (125 mph)
Weights: empty 1719 kg (3,790 lb); maximum take-off 4082 kg (9,000 lb)
Dimensions: span 25.50 m (83 ft 8 in); length 14.73 m (48 ft 3.75 in); height

Smaller and lighter than the British Horsa glider, the American Waco Hadrian could carry 15 troops, a standard Jeep or a 75-mm howitzer and crew. Towed by C-46s and C-47s, Hadrians took part in landings in Sicily, Burma, Normandy, Holland and in the Rhine crossing. A total of 12,393 was delivered.

3.85 m (12 ft 7.5 in); wing area 83.61 m² (900 sq ft)
Armament: none

407

GERMANY
DFS 230

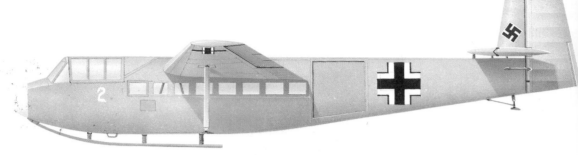

What was to become Nazi Germany's chief troop glider for a substantial part of the war years was designed before 1937, when the **DFS 230** was demonstrated to senior officers who were impressed by the quick deployment of its eight-man load when the glider landed, having cast off from a Junkers Ju 52/3m at 1000m (3,280 ft). Thus a production contract quickly followed, a small glider command being formed in the next year.

The **DFS 230A-1** initial production model made history on 10 May 1940 when the fort of Eben-Emael on the strategic perimeter of the Albert Canal in Belgium was captured in the early hours of the morning with little resistance after a gliderborne party of assault engineers had landed on its roof. This was the first time in history that gliders had been used in action and the sortie was sufficient to prove that troops delivered to a target in this way had distinct advantages over paratroops; both types shared the common factor of a silent approach, but all the gliderborne troops were concentrated at a single point and wasted no time in linking up.

However, the major action in which the DFS 230 was deployed was certainly that carried out exactly a year later when Crete was invaded, the numbers involved being indicated by the fact that the lead group alone was made up of 53 of these aircraft. On the other hand, the losses sustained were such that an operation of this type was never again attempted.

One reason for the enormous waste of life and matériel had been the small capacity of the DFS, and reports current at the time spoke of trains of up to

Above: First assault glider used by any air force was the DFS 230A, of which this example was allocated to I Gruppe, Luftlandgeschwader 1 for the invasion of Crete in 1941. Though small in size, the DFS 230A could carry 10 troops and 275 kg (606 lb) of military equipment.

six gliders being towed by a single Junkers Ju 52/3m, although the usual number was two or three. The DFS 230B-1 was similar to the DFS 230A-1 but for a braking parachute and provision for defensive armament.

DFS gliders were also used in North Africa, but probably the most interesting operation in which they were involved was the rescue of the imprisoned Mussolini from the Rifugio Hotel, Abruzzi by a party dropped from 12 DFS **230C-1** gliders (each with three braking rockets in the nose), the Italian dictator then being flown out in a Fieseler Storch. A later version, the **DFS 230F-1**, had a capacity of 15 men but it was not produced in numbers.

Specification
DFS 230A-1
Type: troop glider

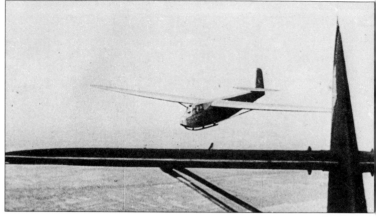

Performance: maximum towing speed 210 km/h (130 mph)
Weights: empty 860 kg (1,896 lb); maximum take-off 2100 kg (4,630 lb)
Dimensions: span 20.87 (68 ft 5.7 in); length 11.24 m (36 ft 10.5 in); height 2.74 m (8 ft 11.9 in); wing area 41.3 m² (444.56 sq ft)

The German eight-man DFS 230A glider featured in the first-ever assault by glider-borne troops when 41 of these aircraft carried some 300 members of Sturm-Abteilung Koch into action against Fort Eben-Emael and other key targets in Belgium on 10 May 1940. The DFS 230A also participated in the costly invasion of Crete.

GERMANY
Gotha Go 242 and Go 244

Capable of carrying either 21 troops and their equipment or a military vehicle, the **Gotha Go 242** with its capacious central pod and twin booms offered obvious advantages over the small DFS 230 in that its capacity was something like three times greater.

Early models of both the freighter (**Go 242A-1**) and troop (**Go 242A-2**) versions appeared with rather crude landing gears but 1942, the year when the first examples were entering service, saw the introduction of a more refined landing gear with sprung oleo legs at each side (**Go 242B-2**). Additionally, the Gotha was the subject of trials of various rocket units to assist take-off, and was developed as the **Go 242B-2** and **Go 242B-3** paratroop versions with a large loading door at the rear, while the **Go 242C** version had a hull and floats so that landings on water were possible.

Some 1,500 Go 242 were delivered, the first operational use of these being made in the Middle East, but of this total 133 were converted to **Go 244** standard.

This was a powered glider version with tricycle landing gear and two engines mounted on forward extensions of the tail booms, the first examples of this type being delivered to operational units in Crete and Greece in March 1942. Some also formed the equipment of transport *Geschwader* in the Middle East and southern USSR, but on the former front they proved vulnerable to anti-aircraft fire and were withdrawn,

being replaced by Junkers Ju 52/3m or Messerschmitt Me 323 transports.

Although the engines of most Go 244s were of French origin, some captured Soviet engines were tried, and plans were submitted for nose-mounted single-engine versions powered by the Argus As 10C or Junkers Jumo 211. Other developments included a pair designated **Go 245** which would have had Argus pulsejets mounted under the wings and a conventional fuselage.

Specification
Gotha 244B
Type: transport
Powerplant: two 850.1-kW (1,140-hp) Gnome-Rhône 14N 14-cylinder air-cooled radial piston engines
Performance: maximum speed 290 km/h (180 mph) at 3000 m (9,843 ft); service ceiling 7500 m (24,607 ft);

range 740 km (460 miles)
Weights: empty 5100 kg (11,244 lb); maximum take-off 7800 kg (17,196 lb)
Dimensions: span 24.50 m (80 ft 4.6 in); length 15.80 m (51 ft 10 in); height

The Gotha Go 244B was a powered version of the Go 242 glider, the example shown carrying the insignia of 4. Staffel, KGrzbV 106, early in 1943 in the Mediterranean theatre. The aircraft saw limited service in the Balkans and among the Aegean islands

Capable of lifting a standard Kübelwagen or 21 fully-armed troops, the Gotha Go 242 was Germany's most-used glider, more than 1,500 being produced. Seldom –

4.70 m (15 ft 5 in); wing area 64.4 m² (693.2 sq ft)
Armament: four manually-operated 7.92-mm (0.312-in) MG34 machine-guns

if ever – used for assault, the Go 242 was, however, employed on the Eastern Front, the Balkans, Sicily and the Western Desert in support of the Wehrmacht in the field.

Heinkel He 111H and He 111Z

Originally built as a bomber and used as a civil transport, the Siegfried and Walter Günther **Heinkel He 111** design is better known as a bomber, so it is something of a surprise to learn that with the development of the special transport matters had come full circle.

The designation of this variant was **He 111H-20/R1**, which was built from the outset as a paratroop transport with accommodation for 16 men, and as such had a ventral jump hatch and external racks for two 800-kg (1,764-lb) supply containers. Similar to this type was the **He 111H-20/R2**, the glider tug version, although it was also capable of employment as a freighter. Armament included an electrically-operated dorsal turret with a 13-mm (0.51-in) MG131 machine-gun.

The suffix of these designations indicated that the necessary changes were carried out by means of *Rüstsätze*, or standard equipment sets, and this is also true of the earlier **He 111H-16/R2**, which was fitted with boom-type glider-towing gear in the rear of the fuselage. Other conversions were the **He 111H-11/R2** glider tug, and the **He 111H-23** for eight paratroops.

Yet probably the strangest version of the basic He 111 design was that which became known as the **He 111Z-1**, consisting of two He 111H airframes joined by a special centre section containing a fifth Jumo liquid-cooled

motor, so that a span of 35.20 m (115 ft 5.8 in) resulted, as did a loaded weight of 28500 kg (62,832 lb). The task for this model was to tow the huge Messerschmitt Me 321 glider, or even three Gotha Go 242s, although the maximum speed possible when this was done was a mere 225 km/h (140 mph).

Historically the Heinkel transport is of interest in that the type was responsible for one of the last paratroop operations of the war. This took place when aircraft of TGr 30 based at Grossostheim dropped men behind the Allied lines in 1944 during the battle of the Ardennes.

Specification
Heinkel He 111H-16/R
Type: glider tug and paratroop transport
Powerplant: two 1006.7-kW (1,350-hp) Junkers Jumo 211F-2 12-cylinder liquid-cooled piston engines
Performance: maximum speed 400 km/h (249 mph) at 6000 m (19,685 ft); service ceiling 6700 m (21,982 ft); range 1950 km (1,212 miles)
Weights: empty 8680 kg (19,136 lb); maximum take-off 14000 kg (30,865 lb)
Dimensions: span 22.60 m (74 ft 1.8 in); length 17.50 m (57 ft 5 in); height 4.40 m (14 ft 5.2 in); wing area 87.6 m²

One of the war's strangest expedients was the Heinkel He 111Z (Zwilling, or Twin), consisting of two He 111s joined with a new centre wing section and a fifth engine. The Z-1 glider-tug saw limited service behind the Eastern Front, capable of towing the huge Me 321 or three Go 242 gliders.

(942.9 sq ft)
Armament: one 13-mm (0.51-in) MG131 in electrically-operated dorsal turret, and one 20-mm MG FF cannon in nose

---

Messerschmitt Me 321 and Me 323

Making its first flight in March 1941 behind a Junkers Ju 90 tug, the **Messerschmitt Me 321** (a massive welded steel and wood glider with mixed ply and fabric covering) had surprisingly only one pilot on board, a man of sufficient stature to use the controls by physical means alone since there was no power assistance, although later three crew members became the accepted complement.

Designed to transport a company of soldiers, or an anti-aircraft gun, or a tracked vehicle or the equivalent weight of freight, the **Me 321A** initial version was supported on the ground by a multi-wheel bogie at each side, although in the later **Me 321B** a more conventional type with two large-diameter wheels was adopted. Even with a tow provided by means of three Messerschmitt Bf 110s or one Heinkel He 111Z, there was often insufficient power to lift the huge glider off the ground, so auxiliary rockets were provided. Trials were also made with pulsejets to increase range after release from the tow.

This problem led to the evolution of the similar **Me 323D** 'powered glider' series with six piston engines and a suitably-strengthened airframe, although the prototype was fitted with only four motors. Structurally similar to the earlier design, all the powered variants retained the clamshell doors in the nose and reverted to the bogie landing gear, and in this form the type was capable of providing transport for a minimum of 130 troops and a crew which was now increased to five on the **Me 323D-6** variant which appeared in December 1942. The additional members were a pair of engineers to look after the problem of engine synchronization, while in the later **Me 323E-1** version with engines of increased

power this number was augmented by a further pair of men to operate an extra two gun turrets.

Production was planned to continue into 1945, but it in fact ceased in the spring of the previous year when less than 200 examples had been delivered of the powered type, a design which (like its predecessor) was understandably unpopular with those who had to fly it and which proved devastatingly vulnerable to fighter interception.

Specification
Messerschmitt Me 323D-6
Type: heavy transport
Powerplant: six 850.1-kW (1,140-hp) Gnome-Rhône 14N 14-cylinder air-cooled radial piston engines
Performance: maximum speed 285 km/h (177 mph) at sea level; range 1100 km (684 miles)
Weights: empty 27330 kg (60,252 lb); maximum take-off 43000 kg (94,799 lb)
Dimensions: span 55.00 m (180 ft 5.4 in); length 28.15 m (92 ft 4.3 in); height 8.30 m (27 ft 2.8 in); wing area 300 m² (3,229.3 sq ft)
Armament: varied, but frequently consisted of a maximum of 10 7.92-mm (0.312-in) MG34 or 42 machine-guns aimed through the sides of the fuselage, and five of similar calibre in the nose and upper fuselage

The six-engine Me 323 transport normally carried up to about 120 troops, though in emergencies about 200 could be crammed in. The aircraft here was an Me 323E with a defensive armament of six machine-guns and two 20-mm cannon.

Born of desperation, the huge six-engine Messerschmitt Me 323 transport was never intended for front-line service, being employed for movement of supplies and

reinforcements behind the Eastern Front. When indeed they were used to support the doomed Axis forces in Tunisia in 1943 they were decimated by Allied fighters over the sea.

Savoia-Marchetti S.M.81 Pipistrello

After Italy's surrender to the Allies in September 1943, elements of the Italian air force continued to serve alongside the Luftwaffe. This Savoia-Marchetti S.M.81 of the Gruppo Trasporti 'Terraciano', Republica Sociale Italiana, carried Luftwaffe markings on the Eastern Front in 1944.

Like the larger Junkers Ju 52/3m which it resembled, the **Savoia-Marchetti S.M.81 Pipistrello** (bat) had originally been designed as a bomber, the work of Alessandro Marchetti, and as such had seen service in both the Spanish and Abyssinian wars; also like the German design it had its root in civil aviation, being based on the **S.M.73**, which also had a fixed landing gear arrangement.

Dating as it did from 1935, the S.M.81 was already suffering a degree of obsolescence when Italy entered World War II, so that despite the robust mixed construction which proved capable of absorbing much battle damage, it was rapidly replaced as a bomber by the S.M.79, production having ceased in March 1938 after 534 had been delivered; the 304 which remained on the strength of the Regia Aeronautica were converted to troop carriers (18 men) after withdrawal from front-line *squadriglie*.

In this capacity, the S.M.81 was relegated to service on the African and Eastern fronts, where it proved sufficiently useful for production to be resumed in 1943 of the version which by then had been designated **S.M.81/T**. However, the coming of the armistice with the Allies in September 1943 meant that only about 80 of these additional aircraft were built, and only four remained in the south by this time

although no less than two complete transport units were still equipped with the type in the 'Saló' Republic of Italy (Fascist-controlled northern Italy). An interesting historical fact is that one transport model of the S.M.81 was later used as the personal transport of Mussolini, a specimen that received the inappropriate name *Taratuga* (tortoise).

A variety of different radial motors was fitted, including the 484.7-kW (650-hp) or 507.1-kW (680-hp) Alfa Romeo 125 RC.35 or 126 RC.34 respectively, the 484.7-kW (650-hp) Gnome-Rhône 14K or the 499.6-kW (670-hp) Piaggio P.X RC.35.

Specification
Savoia-Marchetti S.M.81/T
Type: troop transport
Powerplant: three 499.6-kW (670-hp) Piaggio P.X RC.35 9-cylinder air-cooled radial piston engines
Performance: maximum speed 340 km/h (211 mph) at 1000 m (3,281 ft); service ceiling 7000 m (22,966 m); range 2000 km (1,243 miles)

Weights: empty 5800 kg (12,787 lb); maximum take-off 10500 kg (23,149 lb)
Dimensions: span 24.00 m (78 ft 8.9 in); length 17.80 m (58 ft 4.8 in); height 4.45 m (14 ft 7.2 in); wing area 92.80 m² (998.9 sq ft)
Armament: five 7.7-mm (0.303-in) Breda-SAFAT machine-guns

The Italian Savoia-Marchetti S.M.81 'Pipistrello' served both as a bomber and a troop transport. In the latter role aircraft of the 37°Stormo took part in the 1939 invasion of Albania; dubbed Lumace *('slugs') on account of their very low speed, they also took part in the Axis evacuation of Tunisia in 1943.*

Airspeed Horsa

It was December 1940 when the design staff of the Airspeed Company at London Colney received Specification X.26/40 calling for a type capable of taking 25 soldiers with their equipment in a glider with a wing span greater than that of a Wellington bomber. About 11 months later one of a pair of **Airspeed Horsa** prototypes was towed off from Fairey's Great West Aerodrome, later incorporated into London Airport, by an Armstrong Whitworth Whitley. Simultaneously, five more were being put together at Portsmouth to facilitate trial loading of military vehicles.

Two types of glider were evolved, the **Horsa Mk I** with a hinged door-ramp on the port side and towed by a 'Y' tow rope, and the **Horsa Mk II** with a single cable and a hinged nose to facilitate the loading of light guns etc.

Being made almost entirely of wood, the Horsa could be manufactured quite simply by the furniture industry, the well-known firm of Harris Lebus producing the majority, although the Austin Motor Company produced a quantity. The parent firm was responsible for a mere 700, the only Horsas built, assembled and tested on a single site. The overall total was 3,633.

One of the first uses of the Horsa was when 30 were towed in daylight to North Africa from the UK, and of this total only three were lost, one alone

apparently to enemy action. A short time later the type received its baptism of fire during the invasion of Sicily: of 137 Waco Hadrian and Horsa gliders despatched, only 12 reached their correct landing zones, and 10 of these were Horsas. About a year later Horsas were in use during the D-Day invasion, and were employed in subsequent actions, including that at Arnhem when about 600 were operated.

On occasions such as these 20 men per aircraft were carried. The Horsa's

capacity being greater than that of the Hadrian, many Horsas went for use by US forces, although these continued to be towed into action by British tugs. Wheels, although able to be jettisoned, were largely retained in action.

Specification
Airspeed Horsa Mk II
Type: troop and general transport glider
Performance: maximum towing speed 161 km/h (100 mph)

Runway scene in Britain in 1944 as Stirling Mk IVs start their take-offs with Horsa gliders in tow – resplendent in their black and white 'invasion stripes'. The Horsa Mk II had a hinged nose for ease of loading.

Weights: empty 3402 kg (7,500 lb); maximum take-off 6917 kg (15,250 lb)
Dimensions: span 26.82 m (88 ft 0 in); length 20.42 m (67 ft 0 in); height 6.40 m (21 ft 0 in); wing area 106.65 m² (1,148 sq ft)

Armstrong Whitworth Albemarle

Originally a Bristol design for a reconnaissance bomber with Taurus motors, the **Armstrong Whitworth Albemarle** was transferred from its parent organization. When the prototype first flew on 20 March 1940 it was something of a pioneer in that not only did it incorporate composite steel and wood construction, which would have facilitated wide sub-contracting, but it also boasted a tricycle landing gear, an arrangement not hitherto used in the UK on a production design.

Delivery of the first examples was slow, not beginning until October 1941, the first 42 **Albemarle Mk I** aircraft alone being completed as bombers and subsequently converted, the remaining 558 Albemarles being produced as special transports and glider tugs. Manufacture was entirely sub-contracted outside the aircraft industry, final assembly being undertaken at a plant set up at Gloucester by Hawker Siddeley with the name of A.W. Hawksley Ltd.

Before December 1944 when production ceased, a total of 247 had been delivered as tugs (**Albemarle Mk V** and **Albemarle Mk VI** for the most part), the first RAF squadron to receive the type being No. 295 in January 1943. It fell to another squadron, No. 297, to use the type first in action, when in July 1943 they towed gliders at the invasion of Sicily in company with those of No. 296.

An example of the special transport role of the **Albemarle Mk II** and Albemarle Mk VI took place during the D-Day landings in June 1944: on this occasion six Albemarles acted as pathfinders dropping men of the 22nd Independent Parachute Company. However, the type acted chiefly as a

glider tug, four Albemarle squadrons taking Airspeed Horsas to France, while in September two squadrons from No. 38 Group took the gliders of the 1st Airborne Division to Arnhem. But probably the most abiding memory of the type is the pall of smoke in which they taxied on return, caused by the overheating engines having to supply high power at low speed.

Specification
Armstrong Whitworth Albemarle Mk II
Type: glider-tug and special transport
Powerplant: two 1185.7-kW (1,590-hp) Bristol Hercules XI 14-cylinder radial air-cooled piston engines
Performance: maximum speed 412 km/h (256 mph) at 3200 m (10,500 ft); service ceiling 5486 m (18,000 ft); range 2173 km (1,350 miles)
Weights: empty 10251 kg (22,600 lb); maximum take-off 16556 kg (36,500 lb)
Dimensions: span 23.47 m (77 ft 0 in); length 18.26 m (59 ft 11 in); height 4.75 m (15 ft 7 in); wing area 74.65 m² (803.6 sq ft)
Armament: two 7.7-mm (0.303-in) manually-operated Vickers 'K' machine-guns

This Armstrong Whitworth Albemarle Mk V of No. 297 Squadron was employed in the invasion of Sicily in July 1943. A generally unpopular aircraft among both aircrew and passengers, it was unusual among British-designed wartime aircraft in being fitted with a tricycle landing gear.

The Albemarle, of largely wooden construction, having failed to find favour as a bomber, entered service as a transport with No. 295 Squadron, RAF, in January 1943 and, as a glider tug towing Horsas, took part in the landings in Sicily, Normandy and Arnhem.

Armstrong Whitworth Whitley

The first glider-tug and paratroop trainer had been an **Armstrong Whitworth Whitley Mk II** used by No. 1 Parachute Training School at Ringway in the summer of 1940. The drops were made from a platform in place of the rear turret, although exit was later made via the ventral turret aperture, and the aircraft made a strange sight with its landing gear lowered to reduce speed on practice runs.

Initial use of the type in airborne action was when **Whitley Mk V** aircraft were used in the first British paratroop action, the abortive operation 'Colossus' of 10 February 1941 when an attempt was made to destroy the viaducts at Tragino, Campagna, which would have cut the supply of all water to southern Italy.

The second paratroop action involving the Whitley was that led by Wing Commander P.C. Pickering against Nazi radar installations at Bruneval on the night of 27/28 February 1942, the aircraft in this case being found by No. 51 Squadron.

Used only for training was the Whitley glider-tug. For this use the aircraft

had their rear turrets removed, leaving the position open, and Whitleys in this configuration were a common sight over the Oxfordshire countryside and elsewhere, the former being those which operated with Airspeed Horsas from Brize Norton with No. 21 Heavy Glider Conversion Unit.

In June 1943 the last Whitley from a total of 1,814 was delivered by the parent company, 1,466 being of the Whitley Mk V model distinguished by a 38.1-cm (15-in) increase to the fuselage length and straight leading edges to the fins.

However, not all airborne versions were used for their intended role, it being on record that the summer of 1943 saw some tugs pressed into service to drop leaflets over the Low Countries after a flight from Thruxton!

Specification
Armstrong Whitworth Whitley Mk V
Type: glider-tug trainer and paratroop transport
Powerplant: two 853.8-kW (1,145-hp) Rolls-Royce Merlin X 12-cylinder Vee

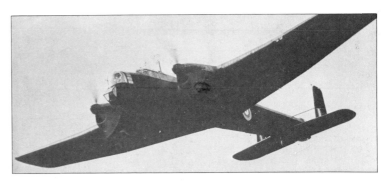

The venerable Whitley, veteran of early wartime bombing missions, was employed from 1941 as a troop transport. In Operation 'Biting', the

liquid-cooled piston engines
Performance: maximum speed 357 km/h (222 mph) at 5182 m (17,000 ft); service ceiling 5364 m (17,600 ft); range 2655 km (1,650 miles)
Weights: empty 8768 kg (19,330 lb); maximum take-off 15195 kg (33,500 lb)

airborne landing at Bruneval on 27 February 1942, 12 Whitleys from Thruxton dropped 119 paratroops round the German radar station.

Dimensions: span 25.60 m (84 ft 0 in); length 21.49 m (70 ft 6 in); height 4.57 m (15 ft 0 in); wing 114.45 m² (1,232 sq ft)
Armament: (as bomber) four 7.7-mm (0.303-in) Browning machine-guns in a power operated rear turret, and one 7.7-mm machine-gun in a nose turret

Although Whitleys were not used operationally as glider tugs, many were converted to tow Horsas with No. 21 Heavy Glider Conversion Unit at Brize Norton in 1943.

General Aircraft Hamilcar

The **General Aircraft Hamilcar** was the largest and heaviest glider used by the RAF, and the first capable of accommodating a 7-ton tank. A total of 412 of the **Hamilcar Mk I** was built after the first flight of the prototype on 27 March 1942, all the tests being completed within three weeks. This may in part have been due to the previous construction of a half-scale model for tests at one-eighth of the loaded weight.

To facilitate the loading and rapid unloading of heavy equipment, the nose was hinged, this enabling vehicles to be driven straight out immediately on landing. This feature proved invaluable at the first use of the type in support of the 6th Airborne Division in Normandy at the beginning of June 1944, when tugs were supplied by units flying the Handley Page Halifax, 70 being used in the first action.

With an eye to re-use on the return journey as well as improving take-off from indifferent airfields, the powered **Hamilcar Mk X** was evolved primarily for the proposed invasion of Japan. The powerplant for this variant consisted of two 719.6-kW (965-hp) Bristol Mercury 31 radials with simplified controls including a single-lever engine operation, no cooling gills, fixed-pitch wooden propellers, and hydraulic hand-pumps to restore the 'sinking undercarriage' (designed to ease loading) to its original position. Single-point towing was used for the Hamilcar Mk X instead of the bifurcated system of the pure glider Hamilcar Mk I. The type was quite capable of being used alternatively as a solo aeroplane with a loaded weight not exceeding 14742 kg (32,500 lb). Maximum speed and range were 233 km/h (145 mph) and 1135 km (705 miles) respectively.

It is interesting to note the fact that the military load of the Hamilcar Mk I

consisted of some 50 per cent of the all-up weight compared with 30 per cent in the Hamilcar Mk X.

Specification
General Aircraft Hamilcar Mk I
Type: transport glider

Performance: maximum towing speed 241 km/h (150 mph)
Weights: empty 8845 kg (19,500 lb); maximum take-off 16783 kg (37,000 lb)
Dimensions: span 33.53 m (110 ft 0 in); length 20.73 m (68 ft 0 in); height 6.17 m (20 ft 3 in); wing area 154.03 m² (1,658 sq ft)

Seen beneath the wing of a Halifax is a line-up of British Hamilcar assault heavy gliders at the time of the Normandy landings. The only Allied aircraft capable of delivering a light tank into battle, the Hamilcar could carry a Tetrarch or Locust.

General Aircraft Hotspur

Toward the end of 1940 a British specification was issued for an assault glider capable of flying 161 km (100 miles) from its point of release at 6096 m (20,000 ft), and the **General Aircraft Hotspur Mk I** was the result. In fact it could glide only 134 km (83 miles), but this was quite an achievement since the original demand, that this be done with a load of seven fully equipped troops and a pilot, was really too stringent.

The Hotspur Mk I had a span of 18.90 m (62 ft 0 in) and was distinguishable from the later models by having cabin portholes. Despite the fact that 23 examples were built, the type was not accepted for widespread operational use, being developed instead into the **Hotspur Mk II** training glider whose simple wooden construction lent itself admirably to large-scale subcontracted manufacture.

Although never used for its intended purpose, the Hotspur was nevertheless built in numbers and performed useful service at glider schools where dual instruction was carried out following a period on single-engine powered aircraft at an EFTS.

Apart from the reduced span, the Hotspur Mk II differed in some detail from the earlier Hotspur Mk I, which had proved difficult to handle on the ground. The changes included the adoption of inset ailerons, revised sea-

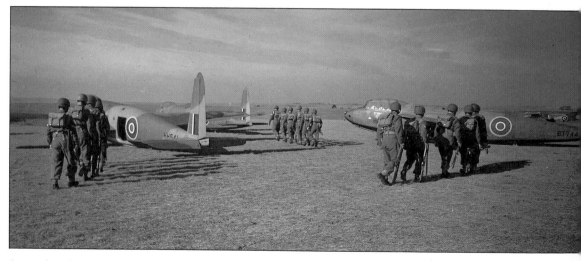

ting and a deeper cockpit canopy, although it retained the jettisonable landing gear legs (and the central skid on which the type was designed to land after the wheels had been dropped, although this facility was seldom used).

The monocoque structure of the glider naturally lent itself to quite a high degree of adaptation, and a further variant was the **Twin Hotspur**, consisting of two fuselages with outer wing panels joined by a common centre section and tailplane; although a prototype was built in 1942 this version did not go into production.

Specification
General Aircraft Hotspur Mk II
Type: training glider
Performance: maximum towing speed 145 km/h (90 mph)
Weights: empty 753 kg (1,661 lb); maximum take-off 1632 kg (3,598 lb)

The Hotspur was a familiar sight throughout Britain during the war years. Capable of being towed by redundant biplanes, most members of the British airborne forces and their pilots were introduced to gliders in these all-wooden craft.

Dimensions: span 13.99 m (45 ft 10.75 in); length 12.11 m (39 ft 8.75 in); height 3.30 m (10 ft 10 in); wing area 25.27 m² (272 sq ft)

Handley Page Halifax

Another bomber used for both glider-towing and the dropping of paratroops was the **Handley Page Halifax**, of which the **Halifax A.Mk III, Halifax A.Mk V** and **Halifax A.Mk VII** were commonly used throughout Europe for this work. Indeed, the Halifax was the only type capable of towing the giant General Aircraft Hamilcar glider when the latter was loaded with its light tank, while the final version, the paratroop-carrying **Halifax A.Mk 9** produced after the war, was able to take 16 men with their associated equipment.

The first experimental flights of an airborne forces' Halifax with a Hamilcar glider took place in February 1942 at Newmarket, although the first operational sortie, which was carried out nine months later on the night of 19/20 November, was conducted with two Airspeed Horsas. This was Operation 'Freshman', which took men to attack the German-run heavy water plant in southern Norway. Halifaxes also towed two Horsas apiece to North Africa for the invasion of Sicily, Operation 'Husky' launched on 10 July 1943.

Operation 'Elaborate' mounted over a period between August and October 1943 was intended to bring reinforcements to this theatre, and 10 Halifaxes plus Armstrong Whitworth Albemarles were used to take 25 Horsas. Unfortunately five of the gliders fell into the sea on the Portreath to Sale leg of the journey, either due to bad weather or enemy action, while three force-landed in Portugal, together with their Halifax tugs; another had to put down in the sea, where it was lost.

Other operations with which the Halifax is associated were, of course, that at Arnhem and the final crossing of

the Rhine. In the latter the German forces were on the defensive on 24 March 1945, when 440 tugs were involved with an equal number of gliders, both Hamilcars and Horsas, all the troops in the former having emplaned at Woodbridge. Almost half of this force of tugs was made up of Halifaxes, there being an equal number of Short Stirlings and only a small number of Douglas Dakotas.

Specification
Handley Page Halifax A.Mk III
Type: glider tug and paratroop transport
Powerplant: four 1204.3-kW (1,615-hp) Bristol Hercules XVI 14-cylinder air-cooled radial piston engines
Performance: maximum speed 454 km/h (282 mph) at 4115 m (13,500 ft); service ceiling 6096 m (20,000 ft); range 1733 km (1,077 miles)
Weights: empty 14969 kg (33,000 lb); maximum take-off 24675 kg (54,400 lb)
Dimensions: span 30.12 m (98 ft 10 in); length 21.82 m (71 ft 7 in); height 6.32 m (20 ft 9 in) wing area 116.13 m² (1,250 sq ft)
Armament: one Vickers 'K' 7.7-mm (0.303-in) manually-operated machine-gun in nose, four 7.7-mm Browning machine-guns in power-operated Boulton Paul dorsal turret, and four guns of similar calibre in tail turret (if fitted)

The powerful Handley Page Halifax was the only type used for glider towing which could handle the massive General Aircraft Hamilcar glider when fully loaded. It was also used for clandestine missions over Europe.

The Halifax, apart from giving excellent service as a heavy bomber, proved adaptable as a glider-tug and transport during the war, equipping a total of 13 RAF squadrons. The Mk VIII version, shown here with a large ventral freight pannier, entered service with three squadrons shortly after the war's end.

Short Stirling

From the beginning of 1944 the main role of the **Short Stirling**, designed as a bomber, was that of glider tug and transport operating with No. 38 Group, Transport Command. The prototype of the **Stirling Mk IV**, a converted Stirling Mk III, had first flown in 1943, and although the powerplant was unchanged, considerable alteration had taken place in the armament with the nose and dorsal turrets deleted (the former being replaced by a transparent fairing), and glider towing gear was installed in the rear fuselage, which retained the defensive turret in this position.

The capacious fuselage meant that the troop-carrying version was capable of taking either 40 fully-equipped soldiers or half that number of paratroops, but the first use of the Stirling in its new role was towing Airspeed Horsa gliders into action when the continent of Europe was invaded on 6 June 1944, the aircraft being drawn from Nos 190 and 622 Squadrons at Fairford and Nos 196 and 299 Squadrons at Keevil. The type also participated in

the historic action at Arnhem and in the final assault across the river Rhine in March 1945.

Production was dispersed among a number of contractors, the largest number (236) coming from Short & Harland at Belfast; the Austin Motor Company was responsible for 198, and the remainder being produced by the company's Rochester works. In all 577 Stirling Mk IVs were delivered, although not all had originated in this form, a number being converted Stirling Mk IIIs.

Another task performed by this version of the Stirling was the paradropping of supplies to parachute troops in forward areas, as well as the delivery of food and ammunition to Resistance workers on the continent. The type was also used to ferry petrol, a capacity load consisting of 2841.25 litres (625 Imp gal) in 139 cans.

Specification
Short Stirling Mk IV
Type: glider tug and general transport
Powerplant: four 1230.4-kW (1,650-hp)

Bristol Hercules XVI 14-cylinder air-cooled radial piston engines
Performance: maximum speed 451 km/h (280 mph) at 3200 m (10,500 ft); service ceiling 5182 m (17,000 ft); range 4828 km (3,000 miles)
Weights; empty 19595 kg (43,200 lb); maximum take-off 31751 kg (70,000 lb)

Dimensions: span 30.20 m (99 ft 1 in); length 26.59 m (87 ft 3 in); height 6.93 m (22 ft 9 in); wing area 135.63 m² (1,460 sq ft)
Armament: four 7.7-mm (0.303-in) Browning machine-guns in power-operated tail turret

Above: Formerly heavy bombers, Short Stirling glider tugs were employed in all the major airborne operations over Northern Europe in 1944-5. The Stirling Mk IV, seen here taking off with a Horsa glider at Harwell, Oxfordshire, belonged to No. 295 squadron.

Converted to carry 40 troops, the Stirling Mk V transport entered service with No. 46 Squadron, RAF Transport Command, in February 1945 but was too late to see combat.

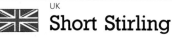

Air-to-Ground Weapons

After World War I it was believed that air power would make all other machines of war obsolete. World War II quickly exposed the limitations of air power: daylight bombing could be prevented by aggressive fighter aircraft, and night bombing was wildly inaccurate. But by 1943 new weapons and tactics had been developed.

An 'Upkeep' or bouncing-bomb equipped Avro Lancaster of the RAF's 617 Squadron. This bomb was a specially designed dam-busting mine.

The art of dropping explosives from an aircraft at great height is almost as old as aviation itself. For example, it has been recorded that in 1911 Giulio Gavotti dropped a quartet of picric acid bombs of 1.8kg (4lb) on Turkish troops in the Libyan desert. Seven years later the art of 'launching' air-to-ground weapons had progressed a little bit futher than this crude (but no doubt reasonably effective) experiment, and was beginning to develop into a science. This progress was as a direct result of the design of such specialist machines as the Sopwith Salamander.

Such new developments meant new tactics. That new targets would have to include armoured vehicles had already become clear during the 'dress rehearsal' of World War II that was the Spanish Civil War. Soon after this, refinements, such as the Dinort extension rods (added on to the noses of the SC 50 bombs delivered by that supreme exponent of the early ground attack, the Junkers Ju 87) were to become a commonplace means of ensuring a maximum blast effect over a wide area of ground.

Although heavier guns were soon in great demand as the thickness of armour on 'hard-skinned' vehicles began to increase, it was really the re-invention of the rocket as a weapon that was to move the science forward.

In addition, taking on a less hit-and-miss aspect was the manner of dropping conventional free-fall bombs. The early methods of bombing merely entailed destroying everything with huge quantities of high explosive released over a target. This rather wasteful method later gave place to what became known as controlled 'carpet bombing'. It also gave place to the system which was to prove the comparative crudity of earlier methods, namely that of opening up buildings by blowing the roofs off with high explosive and then destroying the unprotected structures with a rain of incendiary bombs. Over and above all these advances, some thoughts were given to increasing the psychological effect of ground attack by adding screamers to bomb fins to augment the normal 'whistle', and 'Jericho trumpets' on the legs of diving Stukas.

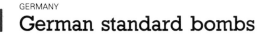

German standard bombs

Three categories of standard bomb were in use by the Luftwaffe, all in the general-purpose group designated according to their nature and weight. First of these was the high explosive **SC** (*Sprengbombe Cylindrisch*), a thin-walled type for normal free-fall use; then there was the semi-armour piercing **SD** (*Sprengbombe Dickwändig*), a thick-walled type; and finally there was the armour-piercing **PC** (*Panzersprengbombe Cylindrisch*) with extra thick walls.

Of these, among the most commonly used were the **SC 250** type, the second part of the designation indicating the weight of the explosive in kilogrammes (551 lb), and eight of these or 32 of the **SC 50** or **SD 50** (10 lb) type would make up a typical load for a Heinkel He 111 bomber, and be deposited on target mixed with incendiaries.

Many of these bombs rapidly acquired names so that while the latest of the GP bombs (the **SD 1700**) for some reason had none, the **SD 1400** became 'Fritz', the slightly smaller **SD 1000** being 'Esau'. Strangely, there was none for the common **SD 500** of which there were two types, one with strengthening bands and trunnion bolts on a differently shaped case. At the other end of the scale the **SC 1000** was 'Herman' and the **SC 1800** was 'Satan'.

Carried either on external or inter-

Below: A Junkers Ju 88A-5 prepares for take-off, carrying a pair of SC 250 bombs underneath the wings inboard of the engine nacelles. Lacking capacious bomb bays, many German bombers carried the majority of their ordnance on external mountings.

nal racks, German bombs were suspended from single 'H' or 'T' lugs (or less commonly a ring bolt), and were colour-coded with a stripe between the quadrants of the tail cone (or the entire cone in the case of small bombs such as the SC 50 etc.) denoting their classification: SC was yellow, SD red and PC blue.

Electrically-charged impact fuses were fitted with charging plungers above the main fuse body with its tumbler switch. Below this lay the flash pellet, Penthrite wax and picric acid to complete the whole, although variations were incorporated such as the Type 17 clockwork delayed action devices or the Type 50 with a trembler switch fuse acting as a booby trap, or the infamous Z.U.S.40 set beneath the normal fuse in such a way that the extraction of one, made 'safe', activated the other concealed beneath it.

Right: A Heinkel He 111 could carry up to 32 of the SC 50 (110-lb) bombs seen here, although it was common practice to mix a number of incendiaries into the bombload.

The SC 2000 was among the heaviest of air-to-ground weapons used by the Luftwaffe. The number after the letter designation was supposed to be the weight of the weapon in kilograms but it actually weighed 1953 kg (4,306 lb).

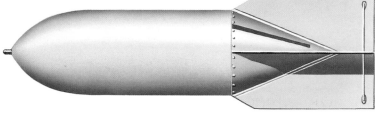

SD 250s were thicker-walled than the SC series to give them limited armour-piercing capability at the cost of a slight reduction in payload.

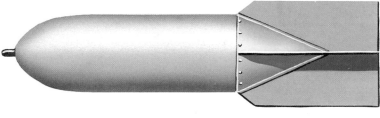

Specification
SC 2000
Type: high explosive bomb
Weights: 1953.2 kg (4,306 lb)
Dimensions: length 3.44 m (11 ft 3.4 in); diameter 0.661 m (2 ft 2 in)
Filling: Tinalin

Above: This 1800-kg (3,968-lb) German bomb was found at Barce, an air base in Libya, in 1942. The 1800 kg bomb was one of the biggest in general use by the Luftwaffe, and was generally carried by Heinkel He 111s.

Allied forces found these German bombs scattered from a wrecked ammunition train near Taranto. Most of the bombs appear to be of the SC 250 type, which had stiffening stays between the fins, whereas some larger bombs had annular rings.

GERMANY

Ruhrstahl/Kramer X-1 (Fritz X)

The agreed surrender of the Italian fleet to the Allies on 9 September 1943 saw the battleships *Italia* (damaged) and the *Roma* (sunk) as the targets of a new type of air-launched weapon, the **Ruhrstahl/Kramer X-1** (or **Fritz X**). This was a free-fall bomb that could be guided towards its target after release from an altitude of about 6000 m (19,685 ft); by the time it had reached its target perhaps 2.4 km (1.5 miles) distant it had gained a velocity approaching that of sound.

Control was by means of electro-magnetically operated spoilers activated in sympathy with radio signals from the aircraft (frequently a Dornier Do 217) that, after releasing the bomb, had its motors throttled back and was taken to a higher altitude so that it was over the target at the moment of impact, the observer having kept track of the missile with the aid of a conventional Lotfe 7 bombsight. Wire-link control using transmission lines some 8 km (4.97 miles) long was later discarded as an economy measure.

Tests were begun in Germany during 1942, later being moved to Italy. Here pneumatic power was experimentally substituted for the electro-magnetic actuation of the spoilers, but variations in temperature created problems so the concept was dropped.

The Allied assault on Italy meant that the Fritz X was pressed into increased use: the cruiser USS *Savannah* was successfully attacked, as were some naval transports, while in the confusion created by a night attack two British cruisers came into collision. Seven days later the battleship HMS *Warspite* was hit by these armour-piercers, so that a tow to Malta was necessary.

About 66 of the bombs were produced each month, far short of the target figure, and about half of these were used during tests conducted during 1943 and into the following year.

But the real end to the Fritz X programme was brought about not by production difficulties but by the high loss rate among the bombers equipped to deliver the missile: because of the need for relatively slow speed over the target area, the launch aircraft became particularly vulnerable.

Specification
X-1
Type: free-fall guided bomb
Powerplant: none
Performance: maximum speed 1035 km/h (643 mph)

This is all that remained of the 45,000-ton battleship Roma after two X-1 glide bombs struck her as she steamed to Malta to surrender to the Allies. The first bomb passed through the ship and detonated underneath; the second penetrated the forward magazine, which blew her in half.

Weights: round 1570 kg (3,461 lb); explosive 320 kg (705.5 lb)
Dimensions: span (over fins) 1.352 m (4 ft 5.2 in); length 3.262 m (10 ft 8.4 in); fuselage diameter 0.562 m (1 ft 10.1 in)

GERMANY

German unguided missiles

Although ground attack was one of the major roles of the Luftwaffe, this task was generally carried out with conventional aircraft armament, plus either normal free-fall bombs up to the 250-kg (551-lb) capacity, or those of specialist design including the small SD 2 fragmentation ('butterfly') bomb, which was first used on the opening day of the German assault on the Soviet Union. It was, however, this same country that was to influence the Luftwaffe's introduction of rockets as air-to-ground weapons.

The slow advent of these weapons

was in part due to the lack of results seemingly achieved by the Soviet 82-mm (3.23-in) rockets, and the importance of such unguided weapons seemed to be further devalued by experience of German field trials. These had taken place during 1942 when Jagdgeschwader 54 had been temporarily equipped for operational tests against targets crossing Lake Ladoga to supply Leningrad. The missiles employed were adapted army-type 210-mm (8.27-in) rockets on launchers under the wings of Messerschmitt Bf 109Fs. Unfortunately these rockets

proved almost impossible to aim since their low velocity after release resulted in a sudden drop in their trajectory.

However, although these were discarded, two years later some Focke-Wulf Fw 190s were fitted with an improved rocket variant in October 1944, the first to be fitted to these aircraft. These were **Panzerschreck** missiles of 88-mm (3.46-in) calibre, the design source being originally the infantry 'bazooka'. Each aircraft was fitted to take six of these weapons, and in December the new **Panzerblitz Pb 1** mis-

sile (also of 88-mm calibre) was introduced: this packed something like twice the punch of the Panzerschreck, but neither was used on any scale.

Specification
Panzerblitz Pb 1
Type: air-to-ground aircraft-launched rocket
Weight: 6.9 kg (15.21 lb)
Dimensions: length 0.70 m (2 ft 3.6 in); diameter 8.8 cm (3.46 in)

Henschel Hs 293

The beginnings of what was to evolve into the **Henschel Hs 293** were laid as early as 1939, and a test model taking the form of a glider was constructed the following year, the ultimate intention being to develop a missile that could be used against shipping under remote control from a launching aircraft.

Although a suitable rocket motor was still not available, development went ahead using a standard SC 500 bomb fitted with wings and tail unit, although no rudder was incorporated, and as time progressed the programme saw the fitting of the first version with a propulsive unit, this taking the form of a liquid rocket (using T-stoff and Z-stoff propellants) slung under the main body. An 18-channel radio system ensured control.

It was anticipated that the missile would be carried into action under a parent aircraft, from which warm air was channelled to prevent the missile from freezing up at the high altitude at which it was released, but at 1400 m (4,595 ft) a maximum of 3 km (5 miles) could be anticipated. Once released the Hs 293 dropped some 90 m (295 ft) before the rocket developed maximum thrust, and the parent aircraft continued to fly a set course parallel with the target, while permitting the bomb-aimer to keep the missile in sight and guide it with the aid of a small control box on which was mounted a miniature control column, keeping in sight the red guidance flare in the tail, the actual flight path being a series of arcs as corrections were received.

The main disadvantage of the Hs 293A was that the launching aircraft had to maintain a steady, level course and evasive action to escape AA fire was impossible. An improved Hs 293D with a television aiming system was planned, but the war ended before it could be constructed.

However, icing was a problem never really overcome and as a consequence further propulsion units were developed. But these were never taken beyond the experimental stage.

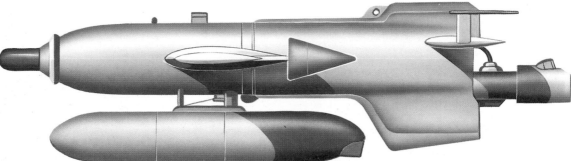

The Henschel Hs 293A stand-off guided bomb was dropped from the carrier aircraft on a parallel course to the target on the port side, and radio-guided to the target. A flare in the rear of the bomb gave visible evidence of the missile's position to the aimer.

Specification
Hs 293
Type: rocket-propelled anti-ship missile
Powerplant: one 600-kg (1,323-lb) thrust Walter 109-507B rocket
Performance: maximum speed 900 km/h (559 mph)
Weights: round 1045 kg (2,304 lb); explosive 295 kg (650 lb)
Dimensions: span 3.14 m (10 ft 3.6 in); length 3.58 m (11 ft 9 in); fuselage diameter 0.48 m (1 ft 6.9 in); wing area 1.92 m² (20.67 sq ft)

Above: This Henschel Hs 293 has had its rocket propulsion unit removed to show the internal equipment. The flare unit for visual location of the missile in flight can be seen at the back of the weapon.

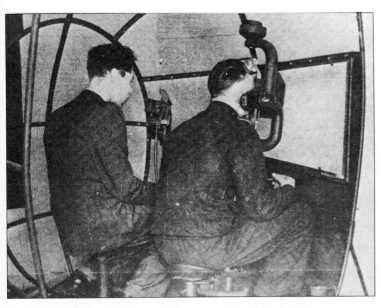

Crew members learn to control the Henschel Hs 293 guided bomb in a simulator. The guidance operators always sat on the starboard (right) side of the cabin, and therefore it was always necessary to attack a target from the port side and in the same movement direction.

A Henschel Hs 293A stand-off guided bomb. This example was found near Paris in 1944 by Allied forces. The flat disc around the nose of the bomb prevented deep penetration before exploding.

About 50 slightly smaller **Ohka Model 22** aircraft (with a reduced 600-kg/1,323-lb warhead and a gas turbine engine, and designed to be carried by Yokosuka P1Y1 Ginga bombers) proved a failure as they were underpowered, and the jet-powered **Ohka Model 33** (with the original-capacity warhead and designed to be transported by the Nakajima G8N1 Renzan bomber) was not completed by the end of the war. The jet-powered **Ohka Model 43A** and **Ohka Model 43B** (the former with folding and the latter with fixed wings) remained no more than projects; an interesting feature of the Model 43B was the facility for the pilot to jettison the wingtips during the final dive to increase impact speed.

Specification
Ohka Model 11
Type: rocket-propelled suicide

The Ohka Model 11 piloted flying bomb's shallow dive speed was boosted by three solid fuel rockets. The Ohka Model 22 was a longer-ranged version powered by a Tsu-II gas-turbine engine.

explosive missile
Powerplant: three Type 4 Mk 1 Model 20 solid-propellant rockets providing a combined thrust of 800 kg (1,764 lb)
Performance: maximum speed 649 km/h (403 mph) at 3500 m (11,485 ft); dive velocity 927 km/h (576 mph); range 37 km (23 miles)
Weights: maximum take-off 2140 kg (4,718 lb); explosive 1200 kg (2,646 lb)
Dimensions: span 5.12 m (16 ft 9.6 in); length 6.066 m (19 ft 10.8 in); height 1.16 m (3 ft 9.7 in); wing area 6.0 m² (64.59 sq ft)

Japanese standard bombs

Ranging from comparatively simple bomb containers capable of taking 30 bombs weighing 0.735 kg (1.6 lb), each albeit for anti-aircraft work, via the larger ones capable of scattering no less than 76 such bomblets to the 800-kg (1,763.7-lb) general-purpose high explosive naval bomb, Japan possessed a good range of air-to-ground missiles in World War II. Smallest of these was the 15-kg (33.07-lb) anti-personnel type with a 10.16-cm (4-in) diameter body measuring only 64 cm (25.2 in) in length.

In the majority of Japanese bombs, fuses were carried in the nose, and it was only on the introduction of the 50-kg (110.23-lb) HE bomb that both nose and tail fuses were employed, although this combination is usually associated with the 250-kg (551.15-lb) high explosive bomb, of which there were two variants.

Construction of Japanese bombs followed conventional lines with plain fins lacking a ring, and prominently-riveted sheet metal was frequently employed. Forged steel was, however, used for the body of the 800-kg (1,763.7-lb) armour-piercing bomb, an impressive naval weapon with a pair of B-2(b) tail fuses. Filling was Trinitro Anisol with an aluminium plug in the forward end of the cavity, deep in the steel body, to prevent the filling taking too great a shock on striking the target; the single-piece machined-steel body had eight recesses in the nose for the fixing of windshields if the bomb was adapted as a projectile.

The most widely used Japanese general-purpose bomb was the naval 250-kg type and its army equivalent. There were two versions of the naval weapon, the later model being slightly larger with thicker walls and having a continuous welded/spot-welded nose, although the tail cone was still fastened by rivets. The army favoured screwed steel bodies and nose, with a welded tail cone.

The Japanese armoury included a contemporary of the German 'oil bomb', used by the navy. This contained a central thermite core surrounded by a mixture of kerosene, petrol and alchohol-soap; alternatively rubber pie-shaped pellets impregnated with iron and aluminium were packed round the explosive in its central tube to act as a bursting and scattering charge.

Specification
250-kg GP
Type: high explosive general-purpose bomb
Weight: 250 kg (551.15 lb)
Dimensions: length 1.937 m (6 ft 4.3 in); diameter 30.0 cm (11.8 in)
Filling: preformed picric

Above: The Type 99 no. 80 750-kg GP bomb was one of the largest bombs regularly employed by the Japanese.

Left: The Japanese Type 2 no. 25 Mk 111 250-kg bomb had twisted fins to spin-stabilize the bomb and to activate the fuses by centrifugal force.

Below: Japanese armourers unload bombs, probably of 50-kg GP type, from a truck. Judging from the flying gear being worn, the photograph suggests that the flying crew members also acted as armourers and loaded their own bombs into their aircraft.

The Type 97 no. 6 59-kg bomb was a general-purpose weapon carried by a variety of Japanese aircraft, from heavy bombers to fighters.

British standard bombs

Although there existed in 1918 not only the 816.5-kg (1,800-lb) GP high-explosive bomb used principally by No. 207 Squadron RAF, together with the 1496.9-kg (3,300-lb) HE bomb intended to be delivered by the Handley Page V/1500, these were comparatively crude weapons. The art of bomb design was concentrated on the lighter types, so that at the outbreak of World War II offensive loads consisted in the main of bombs weighing 113.4 kg (250 lb) or 226.8 kg (500 lb).

Certainly there was still scope for the use of smaller free-fall bombs, and these particularly came into their own with the advent of the Hawker 'Hurri-bomber' equipped to take four 22.68-kg (50-lb) bombs under each wing.

Nevertheless, British bombs did present some variations of shape, and while the ones carried by fighters soon assumed near-conical noses with flattened fronts, the majority were of conventional appearance with 'egg-like' contours until the introduction of the 'thousand-pounder', the 453.6-kg type designed for the external racks of the Hawker Typhoon, all illustrations of the advancing state of the art in refining the shape of bombs for the RAF.

A degree of agreement was certain-

Left: The 54-kg (120-lb) GP HE bomb was one of a series of new, improved bombs of better aerodynamic shape than those used since World War I. This weapon replaced the old 50-kg (112-lb) GP bomb.

Right: The 227-kg (500-lb) MC, Mk III HE bomb was much more effective than the earlier 500-lb GP bomb, due to a higher filling-to-overall-weight ratio. The cropped annular vane permitted four of these bombs to be carried by the Mosquito bomber. It did not affect stability.

ly evident concerning the design of that vital part of a bomb, the tail, and almost throughout the design of British standard bombs, the assembly here consisted of four sheet fins with a broad ring containing their trailing edges. These facts were in part dictated by the British practice of stowing bombs horizontally, the resultant release being the most aerodynamic that could be achieved, since a bomb dropping away from an aeroplane of the time inevitably spun or otherwise

became unstable when struck by the slipstream; it was the tail that finally straightened its flight as the forward momentum imparted by the launch aircraft was lost and the downward path commenced in an arc towards the target as gravity exerted a pull. All these factors were common to the standard bombs of the day which were all of pre-1940 design and included the largely-forgotten HE type of 54 kg (120 lb); there were different versions of all types, some of these variants

being readily identified from their casing that might have strengthening bands as on some '500-pounders'.

Specification
Mk 1 to Mk 3 GP
Type: general-purpose high explosive bomb
Weight: 119.4 kg (263 lb)
Dimensions: length 1.37 m (4 ft 6 in); diameter 0.26 m (10.3 in)
Filling: TNT or Amatol 80/20

The bombs of the RAF. From the top: 9979-kg (22,000-lb) MC; 5443-kg (12,000-lb) HC; nose of 5443-kg (12,000-lb) MC; 3629-kg (8,000-lb) HC; 1814-kg (4,000-lb) HC; (right) 862-kg (1,900-lb) GP; 907-kg (2,000-lb) AP; (front) 454-kg (1,000-lb) and 227-kg (500-lb) GPs. The small bomb is 18 kg (40-lb).

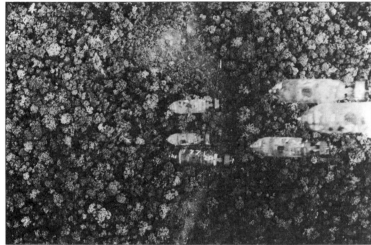

454-kg (1,000-lb) MC bombs drop from an RAF bomber into the jungle of Burma. Earlier RAF bombs had long annular tail vanes, but by cropping the vanes of 227-kg (500-lb) bombs the bomb bay of Mosquitoes could accommodate four instead of two of these weapons.

Airfields have always presented a challenge to the bomber, proving very difficult to knock out. Lacking today's specialist weapons, the RAF had to rely on accuracy and delayed action bombs to frustrate repair work. Here, a stick of bombs impacts on a Japanese airfield in Burma.

A 227-kg (500-lb) Mk III MC bomb is loaded on the wing rack of a Hawker Typhoon. The pistol and detonator has not yet been installed in the nose of the bomb; the armed bomb had pistols and detonators in both nose and tail.

British heavy bombs

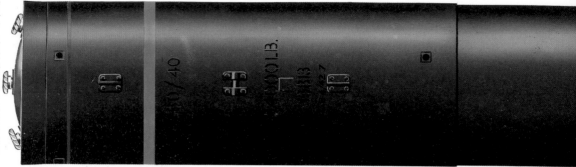

The largest of the British war-time bombs was the well-known 'Grand Slam', a 9979-kg (22,000-lb) missile designed chiefly for deep penetration, equipped with aerodynamically shaped fins to impart an assisting twist to its fall. Forty-one of these monsters were dropped by specially-modified Avro Lancasters in 1945, the first on 14 March when Lancaster B.Mk 1 (Special) PD112 of No. 617 Squadron, with Squadron-Leader C.C. Calder at the controls, demolished two spans of the Bielefeld Viaduct with one of these weapons only a single day after the first test-drop had been made.

British heavy bombs of 5443-kg (12,000-lb) capacity were of two types, the most sophisticated being the 'Tallboy' designed for deep penetration, and of which no less than 854 were dropped by Avro Lancasters following the first attack with them on the night of 8/9 June 1944.

While the 'Tallboy' was of conventional streamlined shape, the other 5443-kg missile was a departure from common practice in that it was cylindrical and was in fact formed from three 1814-kg (4,000-lb) 'Cookies' bolted together (the sections being clearly visible) with an annular-ringed six-fin tail attached. This was the General-Purpose 'Factory Buster', also much used in 1944, but in fact first used during a raid on the Dortmund-Ems Canal during the hours of darkness of 15/16 September in the previous year.

'Big, beautiful' bombs were pioneered by the 907-kg (2,000-lb) version first used during the night attack on the Emden shipyards on 31 March/1 April 1941. However, a comparison of weight alone is deceptive, since the explosive power of the later bomb was greater than that of the fillings used at the beginning of the war, when a 907-kg 'heavy' certainly existed in armour-piercing form for attacks on shipping, although the version of a mere 227-kg (500-lb) weapon was the accepted 'big bomb' in the RAF.

The ordinary 'Cookie' had made its operational debut over Wilhelmshaven on 8 July 1942, observers at the time reporting that 'whole houses took to the air', thus gaining for the weapon the name of 'Block Buster' in the UK, although the Germans knew the type as *Bezirkbomben*. The existence of these was, however, not announced until some time after their first use, not in fact until September, and it was not

Above: The 1814-kg (4,000-lb) HC Mk III HE bomb had three pistols and detonators in the nose. In the centre of the bomb there was a continuous tube with exploders linked into the central detonator. These bombs had a very high explosive filling to overall weight ratio.

Right: A 1814-kg (4,000-lb) HC Mk I high-explosive bomb is wheeled up to a Wellington B.Mk III. This was an early version with a single pistol and detonator in the nose. This example is painted in the yellow-buff shade originally used on high-explosive bombs.

for a further two years that the general public was to know the name of the man who had taken such a prominent part in the development of British wartime bombs, Air Commodore Patrick Huskinson, who had himself been blinded during a raid by the Luftwaffe in 1941.

Specification
GP 'Factory Buster'
Type: general-purpose high explosive bomb
Weight: 5443 kg (12,000 lb)
Dimensions: length 5.33 m (17 ft 6 in); diameter 1.02 m (3 ft 4 in)
Filling: 2358.7 kg (5,200 lb) of Torpex 'cemented' within a 25.4-mm (1-in) jacket of TNT

A typical scene on any Lancaster base during later years of World War II: a 3629-kg (8,000-lb) HC blast bomb is brought up by tractor for loading into the capacious bomb bay of a Lancaster. The Lancaster, Manchester and Halifax could carry these bombs internally.

British 25-lb rocket

British rockets employed a solid propellant inside a cast iron tube and mounted a variety of warheads and fuses. Their bodies were a length of 7.62-cm (3-in) diameter cast pipe fitted with a set of flat plate fins to constitute a cruciform tail, and a pair of lugs by means of which it was slung from the aircraft's launching rail. On one end was screwed the 11.34-kg (25-lb) armour-piercing warhead. A solid-propellant filling was packed into the length of pipe that made up the greater part of the missile, which was electrically fired in such a way that, although exhausting from the open end, burning was initiated from the front, a system necessary in order to ensure that the balance of the rocket was not dis-

Three versions of the 11.34-kg (25-lb) warhead existed, two armour-piercing and one semi-armour-piercing. The AP shell no. 1, Mk I shown was used at dive angle of 15 degrees or over, while the AP shell no. 2, Mk I was used under 15 degrees. The SAP shown was for training only.

turbed as the charge was consumed. Concrete heads were employed for practice.

Experimental work took up the greater part of 1942, and included tests mounted under the wings of the new Hawker Typhoon, but it was the Hawker Hurricane that was to fly the rocket into action for the first time when aircraft of No. 184 Squadron made Fighter Command's first operational strike. Unfortunately the long rails necessary for launching exacted a serious penalty from the aircraft's performance, and except from a very steep dive the missiles were difficult to aim because of their sharp trajectory drop, aiming being by means of the standard Mk IIG reflector gunsight, which was not real-

ly equal to the demands made on it.

This British innovation was disliked by pilots because of its effect on performance, and there was a sharp temptation to expend them on the first available target, whatever it was, regardless of what warhead was being carried.

Specification
Type: air-to-ground aircraft-launched armour-piercing rocket
Warhead weight: 11.34 kg (25 lb)
Dimensions: length 1.69 m (5 ft 6.5 in); diameter 8.89 cm (3.5 in)

British 60-lb rocket

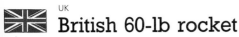

With a similar basic concept to the 11.34-kg (25-lb) armour-piercing projectile, the rocket with a 27.22-kg (60-lb) high explosive head became standard after 1943, while later in the war fragmentation missiles of similar weights were introduced.

By this time a method of delivery designed to ensure maximum destruction of the target had been perfected. This called for the aircraft formation, now usually Typhoons, to make an approach at between 1829 m (6,000 ft) and 3048 m (10,000 ft), and from this the leader would make the first dive at about 40° to mark the target, he being followed at a similar angle at 644 km/h (400 mph) or at 30° when a lower speed of some 612 km/h (380 mph) was indicated. At an altitude of not more than 152 m (500 ft) and a distance of 500 m (550 yards) from the target the complete salvo, said to have a striking power equivalent to the broadside from a destroyer's guns, might be fired before the pilot pulled up sharply and took himself out of the radius of action, there being about five seconds before the shrapnel from the exploding rockets constituted a real danger to the aircraft that had launched them. Unfortunately it is on record that some 25 per cent of the rockets failed to detonate, particularly in the earlier days, and there was a definite tendency to undershoot and the trajectory drop to be inaccurately estimated.

Before the end of the war, zero-length rocket rails were introduced which affected the aircraft's performance less markedly. Some of these revised the position of the missiles so that

The 76.2-mm (3-in) rocket was used by the Royal Air Force for attacking a variety of targets, including ships, tanks, strongpoints, submarines and troop concentrations. A number of warheads were evolved for different types of target; the most-used was the 27.22-kg (60-lb) HE head shown here.

a load of four weapons under each wing was no longer carried side by side but instead, on the Mk 7 installation, fitted in two vertical pairs. A variation of this was to be found on the Mk 6 fitted to the Bristol Beaufighter, which grouped the four round a central fairing from which they could be jettisoned.

Developments of the basic 27.22-kg rocket included the 81.65-kg (180-lb) projectile with its three tubes of propellant, and the 'Admonitor' with seven motors inside a large diameter casing fitted with six fins, and having a 113.4-kg (250-lb) warhead.

Specification
Type: air-to-ground aircraft-launched high explosive rocket
Warhead weight: 27.22 kg (60 lb)
Dimensions: length 1.88 m (6 ft 2 in); diameter 15.24 cm (6 in)

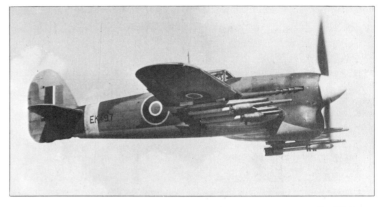

A Hawker Typhoon Mk IB, with the old 'car door' type canopy, carries 76.2-mm (3-in) rockets. The shells attached are the 27.22-kg (60-lb) SAP type. Other types used were the 27.22-kg (60-lb) 'F' fragmentation shell, 11.34-kg (25-lb) AP and 25-lb SAP shells, and concrete practice versions of these shells.

76.2-mm (3-in) rockets speed towards locomotives waiting in a siding, fired from a South African Air Force Beaufighter. The 27.22-kg (60-lb) shell was effective for penetrating locomotive boilers, but the 11.34-kg (25-lb) AP shell was specified for use against merchant ships and submarines.

For use against 'soft' targets the 27-kg (60-lb) HE Type F shell was developed. This was a thick-walled shell, which exploded into small high-velocity fragments. Pilots using this weapon were warned not to use it under 550 m (600 yards) because of flying fragments.

Left: Debris flies high in the air after a rocket strike by an SAAF Bristol Beaufighter against locomotives waiting in a siding. This locomotive target was in Yugoslavia during the German occupation of that country.

Above: Four rockets are launched from a Hawker Typhoon at a German barge on the Wester Schelde. These are 76.2-mm (3-in) aircraft rockets with 27.22-kg (60-lb) semi-armour-piercing shells. Heat from the rocket motor ignited the thermal initiator.

American bombs

Observers in 1945 were in the habit of making comparison between what they called the 'superior aerodynamic shape' of British bombs and the more standardized lines of those dropped by the Luftwaffe. Be this as it may, the United States probably displayed the greatest variety of profiles among its free-fall bombs. Almost German in their appearance were the 907-kg (2,000-lb) **AN-M66** GPs used by the US Army and Navy; this type proved its value against ammunition dumps, railway junctions, airfields and factory sites, while a modified version of the AN-M66 could be fitted with an AN-Mk 230 hydrostatic fuse, enabling it to be employed against heavily armed surface vessels, as well as submarines. Either Amatol or TNT were the fillings used for this type.

The 454-kg (1,000-lb) general-purpose bomb resembled the larger version, but probably less closely than it did the 227-kg (500-lb) bomb with its squat construction and a semi-braced tail with sheet fins, which was really the typical United States weapon of World War II. Employed once more by both the US Army and Navy, these were used against similar targets to the larger versions, their nose fuses being in the main of AN-M103 pattern, although the AN-M125 long-delay time fuse could be substituted if the target justified such a change.

A feature of United States bombs, some of which were equipped with lugs permitting British-style single-point suspension, was that they carried an external arming wire. This ran fore and aft of the lifting lug position, where it was formed into an eye. From this point it was led through the twin suspension eyes to the nose and tail fuses. The weight of the released bomb tugged this wire free as it left the rack and thus armed the missile in a crude but effective safety system.

Both the **Mk 1** and **Mk 4** 'thousand-pounders' were declared obsolete in 1944, although they continued in service as long as bases held any in store, so that they remained in use until the end of the fighting in one theatre or another. These, in common with the majority of American bombs for general-purpose use, had a tail formed by four vanes welded to the tail cone which was fastened to the body by screws. A box form resulted from webs connecting the fins, and the whole was strut-braced internally.

At the opposite end of the scale of United States bombs mention must be made of the obsolete armour-piercing types forming the 'M' series. Of these the heaviest was the 408-kg (900-lb) **M6**, which like the rest of the group were converted artillery projectiles.

Specification
AN-M81
Type: high explosive fragmentation bomb
Weights: 117.9 kg (260 lb)
Dimensions: length 1.092 m (3 ft 7 in); diameter 0.203 m (8 in)

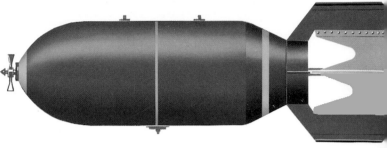

The 454-kg (1,000-lb) armour-piercing bomb used by the USAAF was a thick-cased weapon with an explosive filling to weight ratio of only 14 per cent.

A typical general purpose bomb in use with US forces was the 227-kg (500-lb) weapon shown. It had an explosive filling to weight ratio of 51 per cent brought about by the use of a thin case. The bomb had two fuses, one in the nose and the other in the tail.

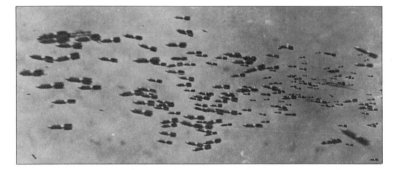

This shower of bombs descends from B-17s during an 8th Air Force raid on Germany in January 1945. Despite enormous advances in aiming techniques and navigational aids, errors still occurred and sometimes it was not only the wrong city that was bombed, but the wrong country.

The familiar pictures of Hiroshima have tended to obscure the fact that US conventional raids on Japan often caused greater destruction; this is Hammamatsu after a visit from the B-29 Superfortresses. Japanese cities proved horribly vulnerable to incendiary munitions.

Armourers ride on two 454-kg (1,000-lb) GP bombs being brought up for loading into Boeing B-17E day bombers of the United States Army Air Corps. The front bomb still has the transit plug fitted in the nose; this would have been replaced by the fuse and arming vane.

In the Pacific war the aircraft made little use of guided weapons, relying on torpedoes and accurate bombing. Here a Japanese escort takes a direct hit from a bomb dropped by a B-25 during an attack on a convoy off Leyte.

American heavy bombs

Rapidly becoming known by the generic title of 'concrete-piercers', United States bombs designed for attacks against reinforced targets of concrete or steel construction were, although formidable, never to rival the British 'heavies' in power and size.

Largest was the 725.7-kg (1,600-lb) armour-piercing **AN-Mk 1** fitted with a single tail fuse, the AN-Mk 228 with a 0.08-second delay. Filled with pressed 'Explosive D' or TNT, the AN-Mk 1 was formed from a single piece of steel, forged and machined, with a pointed nose, parallel sides and slight boat tailing leading to a male-type base plate. To this was fitted the normal box type tail assembly while the body was equipped with side trunnions between the two suspension lugs on the upper segment, with British single point below.

Similar to this type in detail was the **AN-Mk 33**, 272 kg (600 lb) lighter but capable of being used against similar targets, which might also include battleships and cruisers. These smaller bombs were later modified (as were the Mk 1s) for suspension by means of screw-in lugs secured by bolts, thus replacing those of the welded type fitted to bands set in grooves in the casing.

A second type of 454-kg (1,000-lb) American bomb, intended for use against land targets of concrete or

The US 1814-kg (4,000-lb) light case bomb was used for large-scale demolition of targets such as factories. It had an explosive filling to weight ratio of 80 per cent.

steel construction, was the SAP (semi-armour-piercing) type. This was capable of having an alternative fitting of either AN-M102A2 or AN-M103 fuses in the tail and nose respectively so that fragmentation could be achieved on suitable targets. These weapons were of single-piece cast or spun construction with streamlined, semi-pointed noses in which a threaded opening received a fuse-seat liner and steel plug, which could be exchanged for an instantaneous fuse if required.

A modified version of the generally similar **AN-M58** weighing only 227 kg (500 lb) was produced by the removal of 4.31 kg (9.5 lb) of the Amatol filling and replacing it with 14.29 kg (31.5 lb) of steel to improve penetration. They were then re-designated **AN-M58A1**.

Specification
AN-Mk 1
Type: armour-piercing high explosive bomb
Weight: 721.2 kg (1,590 lb)
Dimensions: length 2.11 m (6 ft 11 in)
Filling: compressed explosive 'D' or cast TNT

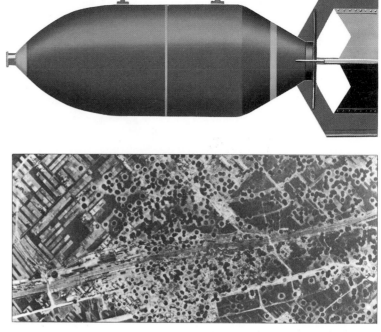

A good example of the high concentration of bombing obtained by US day bombers: the target in this case was Marifu railyard, two miles south of Otaka, Japan, which was bombed by Boeing B-29s of the 21st Bombardment Group during August 1945.

Soviet rockets

The Soviet Union may well be able to claim that it pioneered the introduction of the rocket as a modern aerial weapon, but this was when they were envisaged as air-to-air weapons, tested first in 1937, the idea being that all fighters would be equipped to carry a battery of six to eight rockets on underwing launchers. They were to receive the designations **RS-75** and **RS-82**, the numerical suffix referring to their diameters, 75 mm (2.95 in) and 82 mm (3.23 in) respectively.

A ground-attack version was developed during the following year, and this was larger and of increased diameter. This **RS-132** was intended for fitting to bombers.

Meanwhile the RS-75 was used for the first time over Mongolia, during the Nomonhan Incident against Japanese aircraft, but although some successes were claimed, the RS-75 and RS-82 missiles ceased to be mentioned in reports after the opening months of the war against Germany, although their development was to make an important contribution in another field.

This took the form of a specialized ground-attack rocket, the **RBS-82**, that was introduced in 1941. It was from this that a new variant was produced with an improved velocity and increased propellant capacity as the armour-piercing **ROFS-132**, while much the same time saw the introduction of a version intended for use against con-

crete defensive positions, the **BETAB-150DS**.

It is perhaps not fully realized that one of the contributions to the acclaim heaped on the Ilyushin Il-2 aircraft as the war progressed was the type's effective use of 82-mm rockets, which were deployed with success against targets such as soft-skinned transport and troop concentrations, particularly if the latter were caught unprepared in the open.

Introduced at a later date were the RS-132 variants: similar to the ROFS-132, these could be fitted with two types of head, the solid version being intended for building demolition, while that with a hollow-charge head was directed against armour.

Specification
RS-82
Type: air-to-ground aircraft-launched rocket
Weight: 24.9 kg (55 lb)
Dimensions: length 0.864 m (2 ft 10 in); diameter 82 mm (3.23 in)

The Soviet Union's rocket weapons for airborne use were produced in three sizes, RS-75, RS-82 and RS-132, the numerals denoting the diameter in millimetres. The RS-132 shown has an explosive head for piercing strongpoints. Il-2s used these bombs and 37-mm cannon to great effect.

The 100-kg (220-lb) high-explosive bomb was a standard weapon used by Ilyushin Il-2s for ground attack work. The famous heavily-armoured attack aircraft could carry six of these bombs.

The Soviet Union commenced production of airborne rocket weapons in 1937, the first being the RS-75, a 750-mm diameter rocket. At first this was used for air-to-air combat, but later these weapons were used for ground attack. The rocket shown is equipped with a fragmentation head.

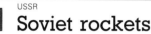

A MiG-3 of the 12th Fighter Regiment in 1942 carries RS-82 rocket weapons under the wings. This 82-mm rocket could be used as an air-to-air or air-to-ground weapon. Firings of rockets of 75, 82 and 132-mm diameter began in the USSR in 1933, and the RS-75 was first produced in 1937.

Light Aircraft

Light aircraft were used for all manner of tasks in World War II, from everyday missions like artillery spotting and general liaison duties to clandestine flights behind the lines, carrying agents. Aircraft like the Lysander and the ubiquitous Fieseler Storch performed valuable work throughout the war.

A British Taylorcraft Auster artillery observation plane. It played a vital part in the war effort, being used for spotting and co-ordinating purposes.

The use of light aircraft by the warring nations of World War II for operational purposes (as distinct from training tasks) was widespread and covered a host of duties. The reasons why they were used so extensively are equally diverse, ranging from ready availability of the aircraft, via low-cost production, operation and performance suitable

for a specific task, to simplicity of training and flying.

In general terms the category which was termed 'light aircraft' may be said to include those aircraft whose normal loaded weight was below about 2750kg (6060lb), although in most instances the true light aircraft of World War II actually took off at a third of this weight. At one end of

the scale the UK's Westland Lysander was a relatively large aeroplane but qualified for inclusion in the category on account of its outstanding agility, short field performance and slow-speed capability, attributes which should all have rendered it ideal for that nebulous duty undertaken by the RAF during the first half of the war: army co-operation.

When it was discovered that the British Westland Lysander (and the German Henschel Hs 126) actually fell short of the requirements which the true ground support role demanded (for the harsh battle conditions of the Blitzkrieg could never have been countenanced), the whole gamut of air operations over the battlefield had to change: the true army co-operation duties (in particular artillery observation) were undertaken by genuine light-planes (such as the Austers and 'Grasshoppers') while ground support moved up the scale to embrace the capabilities of the high-performance fighter-bomber.

For duties that involved covert operations, such as the transport of secret agents, the rescue of airmen who had been shot down in enemy territory and in other duties involving the use of remote or confined sites, the lightplane was the obvious solution to use. Of all the aircraft employed in these tasks none better than the Fieseler Storch was ever produced: its great agility became and then remained forever legendary, even after the helicopter had become an accepted component of arsenals all around the world.

British Taylorcraft Auster series

In 1936 the Taylorcraft Aviation Company was formed in the USA to design and manufacture lightplanes for private use. Most successful of the prewar aircraft to emanate from this company were designated Models B, C, and D, and in November 1938 Taylorcraft Aeroplanes (England) Ltd was established at Thurmaston, Leicestershire, to build these aircraft under licence.

Six American-built Model As were imported into the UK, followed by one Model B. Of braced high-wing monoplane configuration, with a fabric-covered wing of composite wood and metal construction, the aircraft featured a fuselage and tail unit both of welded steel tube with fabric covering. Accommodation within the enclosed cabin was for two persons, seated side by side, and landing gear was of basic non-retractable tailwheel type, with main unit shock-absorption by rubber bungee. Powerplant of the imported Model As consisted of one 30-kW (40-hp) Continental A-40 flat-four engine.

The British-built equivalent to the Model A was designated the **British Taylorcraft Model C**, but this was soon redesignated **Plus C**, reflecting the improved performance resulting from installation of a 41-kW (55-hp) Lycoming O-145-A2 engine.

Other than provision of split trailing-edge flaps to improve short-field performance, the aircraft of the Plus-C derived **British Taylorcraft Auster** series were to change little throughout the war. During this time more than 1,600 were built for service use, the **Auster Mk I** entering service with No. 654 Squadron in August 1942.

At the height of their utilization, Austers equipped Nos 652, 653, 657, 658, 659, 660, 661, 662, 664 and 665 Squadrons of the 2nd Tactical Air Force, and Nos 651, 654, 655, 656, 663, 666, 671, 672 and 673 Squadrons of the Desert Air Force. They were used also in small numbers by associated Canadian and Dutch squadrons. Their initial deployment in an operational role was during

The Auster AOP.6 was the last development of the wartime Taylorcraft design. With a more powerful de Havilland engine and a larger propeller (making longer wheel struts necessary) it was actually a poorer performer in many respects than its predecessors.

the invasion of Algeria, and they were to prove an indispensible tool in the Sicilian and Italian campaigns. Just three weeks after D-Day, these unarmed lightplanes were in the forefront of the action as the Allied armies advanced into France.

Specification
British Taylorcraft Auster
Type: light liaison/observation aircraft
Powerplant: (Auster Mk V) one 97-kW (130-hp) Lycoming O-290-3 flat-four piston engine
Performance: maximum speed 209 km/h (130 mph) at sea level; cruising speed 180 km/h (112 mph);

normal range 402 km (250 miles)
Weights: empty 499 kg (1,100 lb); maximum take-off 839 kg (1,850 lb)
Dimensions: span 10.97 m (36 ft 0 in); length 6.83 m (22 ft 5 in); height 2.44 m (8 ft 0 in); wing area 15.51 m² (167.0 sq ft)
Armament: none

Unglamorous and unglamorized artillery observation aircraft played a decisive part in the war; the main British types were the five British Taylorcraft Austers. This is the Mk III, which had a de Havilland Gypsy Major engine.

Westland Lysander

First flown in prototype form during June 1936, the **Westland Lysander** was a two-seat high-wing monoplane army co-operation aircraft with excellent STOL capabilities. The first production series was the **Lysander Mk I**, and aircraft of this version entered service in late 1938 with No. 16 Squadron, based at Old Sarum. Lysanders went on to equip some 30 RAF squadrons, and these served in Europe, the Middle East and the Far East. The type was built in three marks, these being distinguished mainly by the different powerplants used. The Lysander Mk I featured the 664-kW (890-hp) Bristol

Mercury XII radial; the **Lysander Mk II**, which was built in the UK by Westland and in Canada by the National Steel Car Corporation, had the 708-kW (950-hp) Bristol Perseus XII radial; and the **Lysander Mk III**, which was also built in the UK and Canada, used the 649-kW (870-hp) Mercury XX or Mercury XXX radial.

The Lysander operated in its intended role for only a short time in the war, European operations confirming that such large and relatively slow aircraft were deathtraps in the presence of determined opposition, both ground and air. However, the type went on to a

notably successful second career in air-sea rescue, radar calibration and, perhaps most significantly, agent dropping and recovery in occupied Europe. Total production was 1,368 aircraft.

Specification
Westland Lysander Mk I
Type: two-seat army co-operation aircraft and short-range tactical reconnaissance aircraft
Powerplant: one (664-kW) 890-hp Bristol Mercury XII radial piston engine
Performance: maximum speed

369 km/h (229 mph) at 3050 m (10,000 ft); climb to 3050 m (10,000 ft) in 5.5 minutes; service ceiling 7925 m (26,000 ft); range 966 km (600 miles)
Weights: empty 1844 kg (4,065 lb); normal loaded 2685 kg (5,920 lb)
Dimensions: span 15.24 m (50 ft 0 in); length 9.30 m (30 ft 6 in); height 3.51 m (11 ft 6 in); wing area 24.15 m² (260.0 sq ft)
Armament: two forward-firing 7.7-mm (0.303-in) machine-guns in wheel fairings and two 7.7-mm (0.303-in) machine-guns in the rear cockpit, plus provision for eight 9.07-kg (20-lb) bombs on stub winglets

Letov Š 328

The Czech Letov company began in 1932 the design of a general-purpose biplane for service with the Finnish air force. An equal-span single-bay biplane with fixed tailwheel landing gear and conventional braced tail unit, this **Letov Š 328** had accommodation for a pilot and observer/gunner in separate open cockpits in tandem. The **Š 328 F** prototype for Finland was completed during 1933, its powerplant a 433-kW (580-hp) Bristol Pegasus IIM-2 radial engine. Armament comprised two 7.7-mm (0.303-in) forward-firing machine-guns in the upper wing, and two more weapons of the same calibre on a flexible mounting in the rear cockpit. Although no production aircraft were ordered by Finland, political changes and growing tension in Europe caused the Czech air ministry to order the type into production during 1934 for use by its own air force in the role of a bomber/reconnaissance aircraft. A total of 445 was built under the designation Š 328, and most of these were impressed for service with the Luftwaffe or the new Slovak air force when Bohemia-Moravia was occupied by German forces in March 1939, but a small number were later supplied to Bulgaria. When production ended a total of 470 had been built, and included 13 examples of a night-fighter variant designated **Š 328 N** which was armed with four fixed forward-firing and two trainably-mounted machine-guns. Letov had plans to produced developed versions, one **Š 428** prototype resulting from the conversion of an Š 328 production aircraft by replacing the standard powerplant with a 485-kW (650-hp) Avia Vr-36 (licence-built Hispano-Suiza 12Nbr) and with armament of four forward-firing machine-guns.

Slovak Š 328 aircraft took part in the

campaign against Poland in 1940 and were operating on the Eastern Front in 1941, but by 1944 there came a reversal of loyalties, many Slovak pilots defecting to the USSR in their Š 328s to take part in operations against the German forces on Soviet territory.

This Letov Š 328 was one of three flown by Slovak patriots during the Nationalist uprising of August 1944. The aircraft operated out of Tri Duby airfield in the foothills of the Carpathians, largely on reconnaissance duties against Slovakia's erstwhile masters, the Germans.

Specification
Letov Š 328
Type: two-seat bomber/reconnaissance aircraft
Powerplant: one 474-kW (635-hp) Walter-built Bristol Pegasus IIM-2 radial piston engine
Performance: maximum speed 280 km/h (174 mph) at 1800 m (5,905 ft); service ceiling 7200 m (23,620 ft); range 700 km (435 miles)
Weights: 1680 kg (3,704 lb); maximum take-off 2675 kg (5,897 lb)
Dimensions: 13.70 m (44 ft 11.4 in); length 10.40 m (34 ft 1.4 in); height 3.40 m (11 ft 1.9 in); wing area 67.10 m² (722.28 sq ft)
Armament: four 7.7-mm (0.303-in) machine-guns, two in upper wing and two on flexible mount in rear cockpit, plus up to 500 kg (1,102 lb) of bombs

Widely used on the Eastern Front by Slovak and Luftwaffe pilots, the Š 328 was operated in the battlefield reconnaissance and light bomber roles as well as night harassment missions in 1943.

Repülögpégyàr Levente

In October 1940 Repülögpégyàr flew the prototype of a parasol-wing two-seat primary trainer which it designated **Repülögpégyàr Levente I**. This was modified subsequently to serve as the prototype of an improved **Levente II** which entered service with the Hungarian air force during 1943. By then, Hungary had allied itself with Germany and had participated in the invasion of the USSR. The result was that the 100 Levente IIs built to serve with the air force as primary trainers were, in fact, deployed with operational squadrons where they were used in communications/liaison roles until the end of the war.

Specification
Repülögpégyàr Levente II
Type: two-seat liaison/training aircraft
Powerplant: one licence-built 78-kW (105-hp) Hirth HM 504A-2 inverted inline piston engine
Performance: maximum speed 180 km/h (112 mph); cruising speed 160 km/h (99 mph); service ceiling 4500 m (14,765 ft); range 650 km (404 miles)
Weights: 470 kg (1,036 lb); maximum take-off 750 kg (1,653 lb)
Dimensions: span 9.45 m (31 ft 0 in); length 6.08 m (19 ft 11.4 in); height 2.53 m (8 ft 3.6 in); wing area 13.50 m² (145.32 sq ft)
Armament: none

The Levente II was used on the Eastern Front as a communications and liaison aircraft by the Hungarian air force. It was powered by a licence-built Hirth 4-cylinder engine, giving a maximum speed of 180 km/h (112 mph).

Mitsubishi Ki-15

In July 1935 the Imperial Japanese Army drew up its specification for a new two-seat reconnaissance aircraft, and Mitsubishi responded with a cantilever low-wing monoplane, the **Mitsubishi Ki-15**. Service testing was completed without difficulty and the type was ordered into production under the official designation **Army Type 97 Command Reconnaissance Plane Model 1**. In May 1937, a year after the first flight, delivery of production aircraft to the army began.

Just before that, however, military observers in the west should have gained some premonition of Japan's growing capability in aircraft design when the second (civil) prototype was used to establish a new record flight time between Japan and England.

The army's **Ki-15-I** had been received in time to make a significant impact at the beginning of the war with China, the type's high speed giving it freedom of the skies until China introduced the Soviet Polikarpov I-16. However, plans had already been made to upgrade performance of the KI-15-I, this being achieved by installing the 671-kW (900-hp), smaller-diameter Mitsubishi Ha-26-I engine, its incorporation providing an opportunity to overcome what had been the major shortcoming of the type, a poor forward field of view past the large-dia-

meter Nakajima engine. The improved version entered production for the army in September 1939 as the **Ki-15-II**, but before that the Japanese navy, impressed by the performance of this aircraft, ordered 20 examples of the Ki-15-II under the official designation **Navy Type 98 Reconnaissance Plane Model 1**, Mitsubishi designation **C5M1**. The navy acquired subsequently 30 **C5M2** aircraft that were generally similar except for installation of the more powerful 708-kW (950-hp) Nakajima Sakae (prosperity) 12 engine. When production ended almost 500 of all versions had been built, the majority being in first-line service when the

Pacific war started. Given the Allied codename **'Babs'**, the type was relegated to second-line roles in early 1943, but many survived to be used in *kamikaze* attacks at the war's end.

Specification
Mitsubishi Ki-15-I
Type: two-seat reconnaissance aircraft
Powerplant: one 477-kW (640-hp) Nakajima Ha-8 radial piston engine
Performance: maximum speed 480 km/h (298 mph) at 4000 m (13,125 ft); cruising speed 320 km/h (199 mph) at 5000 m (16,405 ft); service ceiling 11400 m (37,400 ft); range 2400 km (1,491 miles)

A Navy version of the Ki-15-II designated C5M, featured the small-diameter Ha-26-I engine. For its time the 'Babs', as it came to be called by the Allies, had an excellent performance, superior to some contemporary fighters.

Weights: empty 1400 kg (3,086 lb); maximum take-off 2300 kg (5,071 lb)
Dimensions: span 12.00 m (39 ft 4.4 in); length 8.70 m (28 ft 6.5 in); height 3.35 m (11 ft 0 in); wing area 20.36 m² (219.16 sq ft)
Armament: all versions had one 7.7-mm (0.303-in) machine-gun on a trainable mount in the rear cockpit

---

Tachikawa Ki-36/Ki-55

The Chinese People's Liberation Army operated Tachikawa Ki-55 advanced trainers in the years following 1945. Large numbers had been supplied to the Japanese puppet regime of Manchukuo, and these fell into the hands of the Communists (with the considerable assistance of the invading Russians).

First flown in prototype form on 20 April 1938, the **Tachikawa Ki-36** was a cantilever low-wing monoplane of all-metal basic structure, covered by a mix of light alloy and fabric. Landing gear was of fixed tailwheel type, the main units enclosed in speed fairings, and power was provided by a 336-kW (450-hp) Hitachi Ha-13 radial engine. The two-man crew was enclosed by a long 'greenhouse' canopy and both men had good fields of view, that of the observer being improved by clear-view panels in the floor. The type was ordered into production in November 1938 as the **Army Type 98 Direct Co-Operation Plane**. Generally similar to the prototypes, the type was armed with two 7.7-mm (0.303-in) machine-guns and introduced the more powerful Hitachi Ha-13a engine. When construction ended in January 1944, a total of 1,334 had been built by Tachikawa (862) and Kawasaki (472).

The handling characteristics and reliability of the Ki-36 made the army realize that it was ideal for use as an advanced trainer, resulting in development of the **Ki-55**, intended specifically for this role and having armament reduced to a single forward-firing machine-gun. Following the testing of a prototype in September 1939, the army ordered this aircraft as the **Army Type 99 Advanced Trainer**; when production was terminated in December 1943 a total of 1,389 had been built by Tachikawa (1,078) and Kawasaki (311).

Both versions were allocated the Allied codename **'Ida'**, and the Ki-36 was first deployed with considerable success in China. However, when confronted by Allied fighters at the beginning of the Pacific War it was found to be too vulnerable, being redeployed in China where it was less likely to be confronted by such aircraft. It was also

considered suitable for *kamikaze* use in the closing stages of the war, being modified to carry internally a bomb of up to 500 kg (1,102 lb).

Specification
Tachikawa Ki-36
Type:
Powerplant: one 380-kW (510-hp) Hitachi Ha-13a radial piston engine
Performance: maximum speed 348 km/h (216 mph) at 1800 m (5,905 ft); cruising speed 235 km/h (146 mph); service ceiling 8150 m (26,740 ft); range 1235 km (767 miles)
Weights: empty 1247 kg (2,749 lb); maximum take-off 1660 kg (3,660 lb)
Dimensions: span 11.80 m (38 ft 8.6 in); length 8.00 m (25 ft 3 in); height 3.64 m (11 ft 11.3 in); wing area 20.00 m² (215.29 sq ft)
Armament: two 7.7-mm (0.303-in) machine-guns (one forward-firing and one on a trainable mounting in the rear cockpit), plus an external bombload of up to 150 kg (331 lb)

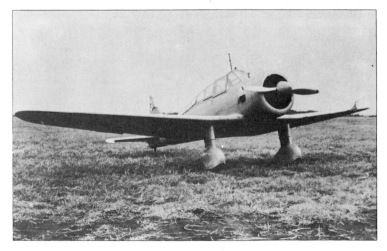

The Type 98 Chokusetsu-Kyodoki (Direct Co-operation Plane) was built by Tachikawa under the designation Ki-36. Trainer versions were designated Ki-55 and were used for kamikaze attacks late in the war.

Henschel Hs 126

In 1935 Henschel developed the parasol-wing Henschel Hs 122 short-range reconnaissance aircraft as a replacement for the Heinkel He 45 and He 46, but although a few of the 492-kW (660-hp) Siemens SAM 22B-engined aircraft were built, the Hs 122 was not adopted for Luftwaffe use. From it, however, Henschel's chief designer Friedrich Nicolaus derived the **Henschel Hs 126** which incorporated a new wing, cantilever main landing gear and a canopy over the pilot's cockpit, the observer's position being left open. During 1937 Henschel built 10 pre-production **Hs 126A-0** aircraft based on the third prototype, and some were used for operational evaluation by the Luftwaffe's Lehrgruppe reconnaissance unit in the spring of 1938. Initial production version was the **Hs 126A-1**, generally similar to the pre-production aircraft but powered by the 656-kW (880-hp) BMW 132dc radial engine. Armament comprised one forward-firing 7.92-mm (0.31-in) MG 17 machine-gun, plus one similar weapon on a trainable mounting in the rear cockpit, and five 10-kg (22-lb) bombs or a single 50-kg (110-lb) bomb could be carried on an underfuselage rack. A hand-held Rb 12.5/9×7 camera in the rear cockpit was supplemented by a Zeiss instrument in a rear-fuselage bay. Six of this version were used by the Legion Condor in Spain during 1938, being trans-

ferred later to the Spanish air force, and 16 were delivered to the Greek air force. An improved but similar **He 126B-1** was introduced during the summer of 1939, this incorporating FuG 17 radio equipment and either the Bramo 323A-1 or 671-kW (900-hp) 323A-2.

Production aircraft were built in Berlin, at Schönefeld and Johannisthal, from 1938 and entered operational service first with AufklGr. 35. By the outbreak of World War II the re-equipment of He 45- and He 46-equipped reconnaissance units with the Hs 126 was well under way. The type was withdrawn progressively from front-

line service during 1942 on replacement by the Focke-Wulf Fw 189. Just over 600 aircraft were built.

Specification
Henschel Hs 126B-1
Type: two-seat short-range reconnaissance aircraft
Powerplant: one 634-kw (850-hp) Bramo 323A-1 radial piston engine
Performance: maximum speed 310 km/h (193 mph) at sea level; service ceiling 8300 m (27,230 ft); maximum range 720 km (447 miles)
Weights: empty 2030 kg (4,475 lb); maximum take-off 3090 kg (6,812 lb)

A Henschel Hs 126B-1 of the tactical Aufklärungsstaffel 3.(H)/21 as it appeared on the Don front in January 1943. Stalingrad was about to fall, and the initiative in the East was at last to swing decisively in favour of the Soviet army and air force.

Dimensions: span 14.50 m (47 ft 6.9 in); length 10.85 m (35 ft 7.2 in); height 3.75 m (12 ft 3.6 in); wing area 31.60 m² (340.15 sq ft)
Armament: two 7.92-mm (0.31-in) MG 17 machine-guns, plus one 50-kg (110-lb) or five 10-kg (22-lb) bombs

An early Hs 126 in pre-war markings displays the distinctive parasol wing. A contemporary of the Lysander, the Henschel was initially more successful because it operated under a protective umbrella of Messerschmitt Bf 109 fighters and in conditions of near-total air superiority.

Fieseler Fi 156 Storch

Best-known of all the Fieseler designs because of its extensive use during World War II, the **Fieseler Fi 156 Storch** (stork) was a remarkable STOL (short take-off and landing) aircraft that was first flown during the early months of 1936. A braced high-wing monoplane of mixed construction, with a conventional braced tail unit and fixed tailskid landing gear with long stroke main units, the Fi 156 was powered by an Argus inverted-Vee piston engine, and its extensively glazed cabin provided an excellent view for its three-man crew. As with the Fi 97, the key to the success of this aircraft was its wing incorporating the company's high-lift devices. The capability of this aircraft more than exceeded its STOL expectations, for with little more than a

light breeze blowing it needed a take-off run of only about 60 m (200 ft) and could land in about one-third of that distance.

Service tests confirmed that Germany's armed forces had acquired a 'go-anywhere' aircraft, and for the remainder of World War II the Storch was found virtually everywhere German forces operated, production of all variants totalling 2,549 aircraft. The designation **Fi 156C-1** applied to a variant intended to be deployed in liaison and staff transport roles, and the **Fi 156C-2** was basically a two-crew reconnaissance version carrying a single camera; some late examples of the Fi 156C-2 were, however, equipped to carry one stretcher for casualty evacuation. The **Fi 156C-3** was the first to be equipped

for multi-purpose use, the majority of the type being powered by the improved Argus As 10P engine, which was also standard in the generally similar **Fi 156C-5** which had provision to carry an underfuselage camera or jettisonable fuel tank.

Because of their capability, Fi 156s were used in some remarkable exploits. Best known are the rescue of Benito Mussolini from imprisonment in a hotel amid the Apennine mountains, on 12 September 1943, and the flight made by Hanna Reitsch into the ruins of Berlin on 26 April 1945, carrying Generaloberst Ritter von Greim to be appointed by Adolf Hitler as his new commander of the Luftwaffe.

Specification
Fieseler Fi 156C-2
Type: two-seat army co-operation/reconnaissance aircraft
Powerplant: one 179-kW (240-hp) Argus As 10C-3 inverted-Vee piston engine
Performance: maximum speed 170 km/h (109 mph) at sea level; economical cruising speed 130 km/h (81 mph); service ceiling 4600 m (15,090 ft); range 385 km (239 miles)
Weights: empty 930 kg (2,050 lb); maximum take-off 1325 kg (2,921 lb)
Dimensions: span 14.25 m (46 ft 9 in); length 9.90 m (32 ft 5.8 in); 3.05 m (10 ft 0 in); wing area 26.00 m² (279.87 sq ft)
Armament: one rear-firing 7.92-mm (0.31-in) machine-gun on a trainable mount

Focke-Wulf Fw 189 Uhu

In February 1937 the Reichsluftfahrtministerium issued a specification for a short-range reconnaissance aircraft. Focke-Wulf responded with the **Focke-Wulf Fw 189 Uhu** (eagle owl), an all metal stressed-skin low-wing monoplane that had an extensively glazed fuselage pod, and twin booms carrying the tail surfaces. The crew nacelle provided accommodation for pilot, navigator/radio operator and engineer/gunner, and power for the prototype was supplied by two 321-kW (430-hp) Argus As 410 engines. Construction of this aircraft began in April 1937, and designer Tank performed the first flight in July 1938. It was a dual-control trainer version which gained the first order in the summer of 1939. These **Fw 189B** aircraft preceded the **Fw 189A** into manufacture and service, some being used as conversion trainers by 9.(H)/LG 2 during the spring and summer of 1940. In a similar manner the construction of 10 **Fw 189A-0** pre-production aircraft began in 1940, some of them being delivered to 9.(H)/LG 2 for operational trials, and being followed by the initial production **Fw 189A-1**. Further developments of this version included the **Fw 189A-1/Trop** which carried desert survival equipment, and the **Fw 189A-1/U2** and **Fw 189A-1/U3** which were equipped as personal transports for the use of Generalfeldmarschall Kesselring and General Jeschonnek respectively. The remaining Fw 189A variants included the **Fw 189A-2** introduced in 1942, which had the trainably mounted MG 15 machine-guns replaced by twin 7.92-mm (0.31-in) MG 81Zs; the **Fw 189A-3** two-seat dual-control trainer which was built in limited numbers; and the light ground-attack **Fw 189A-4** which was armed with two 20-mm MG 151/20 cannon and two 7.92-mm (0.31-in) machine-guns in the wing roots, and had armour protection for the underside of the fuselage, engines and fuel tanks.

Total production of the Fw 189 then amounted to 864 aircraft including prototypes, built not only by Heinkel but also by Aero in Prague from 1940 to 1943, and by SNCASO at Bordeaux-Mérignac until 1944.

Fw 189s were supplied in small

Fw 189A-1s lined up fresh from the factory, awaiting armament. Very tough machines, they handled superbly and some reportedly returned minus one tail boom as a result of ramming attacks by Soviet aircraft.

numbers to the Slovakian and Hungarian air forces operating on the Eastern Front, in which theatre the type was deployed most extensively by the Luftwaffe, but at least one *Staffel* used the type operationally in North Africa.

Specification
Focke-Wulf Fw 189A-1
Type: two-seat short-range reconnaissance aircraft
Powerplant: two 347-kW (465-hp) Argus As 410A-1 inverted-Vee piston engines
Performance: maximum speed 335 km/h (208 mph); cruising speed 315 km/h (196 mph); service ceiling 7000 m (22,965 ft); range 670 km (416 miles)
Weights: empty 2805 kg (6,184 lb; maximum take-off 3950 kg (8,708 lb)
Dimensions: span 18.40 m (60 ft 4.4 m); length 12.03 m (39 ft 5.6 in); height 3.10 m (10 ft 2 in); wing area 38.00 m² (409.04 sq ft)

A Focke-Wulf Fw 189A-1 Uhu (owl) of Aufklärungsstaffel 1.(H)/32 based at Kemi, Finland, in the summer of 1942. The later years of the war were to see the Fw 189 as the Wehrmacht's primary tactical 'eye in the sky', particularly on the Eastern Front.

A Focke-Wulf Fw 189A-2 of the Hungarian 3/1 Short Range Reconnaissance Squadron based at Zamocz, Poland, in March 1944. The A-2 model differed from the A-1 solely in having twin MG 81s in the dorsal and tailcone positions.

Armament: two trainable 7.92-mm (0.31-in) MG 15 machine-guns and two fixed 7.92-mm (0.31-in) MG 17 machine-guns, plus four 50-kg (110-lb) bombs

Stinson L-1 Vigilant

The two-seat light observation aircraft had been an essential adjunct to US Army operations, the concept dating back to World War I. In the years between then and the late 1930s, observation aircraft had, of course, been developed to offer much improved performance, some with high-lift devices which made it possible for them to operate into and out of quite small unprepared areas.

When, in 1940, the US Army Air Corps realized the need to reinforce its aircraft in this category, specifications were circulated and resulted in several contracts. Stinson was

awarded a contract for 142 of its design, a braced high-wing monoplane, with an all-metal basic structure, part metal- and part fabric-covered, designated **Stinson O-49**. To provide low-speed and high-lift performance, the whole of the wing leading edge was provided with automatically-operated slats, and the entire trailing edge was

A Stinson O-49F casualty evacuation plane fitted with twin Edo amphibious floats comes in to land. It was re-designated as the L-1 in 1942, when the 'observation' classification was changed to 'liaison'.

429

occupied by wide-span (almost two-thirds) slotted flaps and large slotted ailerons which drooped 26° when the flaps were fully down. The non-retractable tailwheel landing gear was designed specially for operation from unprepared strips. The powerplant consisted of a 213-kW (285-hp) Lycoming R-680-9 radial engine with a two-blade constant-speed propeller. An enclosed cabin seated two in tandem, and the pilot and observer had an excellent field of view all around, above and below.

A second contract covered the construction of 182 **O-49A** aircraft, which differed by having a slightly longer fuselage and minor equipment changes. Designation changes in 1942 resulted in the O-49 and O-49A becoming the **L-1** and **L-1A** respectively. Both versions were supplied to the RAF under Lend-Lease, and these were given the British name **Vigilant**.

No further production of new Vigilant aircraft followed, for the type was superseded by the more effective lightweight Grasshopper family. Nevertheless, Vigilants saw quite wide use in both the European and Pacific theatres, the RAF operating many of its aircraft for artillery liaison in Italy, Sicily and Tunisia.

Specification
Stinson L-1A
Type: two-seat light liaison/observation aircraft
Powerplant: one 220-kW (295-hp) Lycoming R-680-9 radial piston engine
Performance: maximum speed 196 km/h (122 mph); service ceiling 3900 m (12,800 ft); range 451 km (280 miles)
Weights: empty 1211 kg (2,670 lb); maximum take-off 1542 kg (3,400 lb)
Dimensions: span 15.52 m (50 ft 11 in); length 10.44 m (34 ft 3 in); height 3.10 m (10 ft 2 in); wing area 30.56 m² (329 sq ft)
Armament: none

A United States Army Air Force L-1F is seen in Burma. Converted from a standard L-1A, it is metallic silver except for the top surfaces, which have been sprayed olive drab.

Taylorcraft L-2 Grasshopper

In 1941 the US Army conducted an operational evaluation with four of each of three types of two-seat light aircraft for use in the artillery spotting and liaison roles, the three types being the **Taylorcraft YO-57**, the Aeronca YO-58 and the Piper YO-59; all were known as Grasshoppers. The successful use of the aircraft during the US Army's manoeuvres, operating directly with ground forces, resulted in increased production contracts for all three, although the Piper design was to be the most prolific.

The first four Taylorcraft YO-57s were standard civil Taylorcraft Model Ds, powered by the 48-kW (65-hp) Continental YO-170-3 flat-four engine, and were followed by 70 basically-similar O-57 aircraft. However, the need to provide an all-round view resulted in modifications to the cabin and rear fuselage and the introduction of trailing-edge cut-outs at the wing roots. Other alterations to fit the aircraft for its specialized tasks included an observer's seat which could be turned around to face the rear, and the installation of radio. In this form the type was designated **O-57A** and 336 were manufactured.

A further 140 were built under the designation **L-2A**, US Army aircraft of this class having been reclassified, from observation to liaison in 1942. The YO-57s and O-57s were reclassified **L-2** and the YO-57As were redesignated **L-2A**. Some 490 aircraft with special equipment, built for service with the field artillery, were designated **L-2B** and the final variant, with a production run of 900, was the **L-2M**, identified by the fully cowled engine and the fitting of wing spoilers.

Taylorcraft were involved in the training programme of military glider pilots, involving 43 impressed civil machines which were used to provide an initial powered flying course.

The company also developed a light training glider version which was known as the **Taylorcraft ST-100** and given the designation **TG-6**. The front fuselage was extended and a 'glasshouse' canopy fitted, the landing gear simplified and a skid added under the nose; the lengthened nose necessitated increased fin area. Production totalled 253, including three for US Navy trials.

Specification
Taylorcraft L-2A
Type: two-seat liaison aircraft/training glider
Powerplant: one 48-kW (65-hp) Continental O-170-3 flat-four piston engine
Performance: maximum speed 142 km/h (88 mph); service ceiling 3050 m (10,000 ft); range 370 km (230 miles)
Weights: empty 397 kg (875 lb); maximum take-off 590 kg (1,300 lb)
Dimensions: span 10.79 m (35 ft 5 in); length 6.93 m (22 ft 9 in); height 2.44 m (8 ft 0 in); wing area 16.81 m² (181 sq ft)
Armament: none

A Taylorcraft L-2A liaison aircraft is seen in 1942. This was a fully militarized version of the civilian Taylorcraft Model D, with improved rear vision and trailing edge cut-outs at the wing roots. The design was the progenitor of the British Auster.

Aeronca L-3 Grasshopper

The name Aeronca Aircraft Corporation had been adopted in 1941 by the company established in late 1928 as the Aeronautical Corporation of America. One of its most successful products was the **Aeronca Model 65** highwing monoplane, developed to meet commercial requirements for a reliable dual-control tandem two-seat trainer. The four of these aircraft supplied initially to the USAAC became designated **YO-58**, and these were followed by 50 **O-58**, 20 **O-58A** and 335 **O-58B** aircraft, serving with the USAAF (established on 20 June 1941). In the following year the O (Observation) designation was changed to L (Liaison), and the O-58, O-58A and O-58B designations became respectively **L-3, L-3A** and **L-3B Grasshopper**. An additional 540 aircraft were delivered as L-3Bs and 490 **L-3C** aircraft were manufactured before production ended in 1944. The designations **L-3D/ -3E/-3F/-3G/-3H/-3J** were applied to civil Model 65s with varying powerplant installations and impressed into military service when the United States became involved in World War II.

Most L-3s were generally similar, with small changes in equipment representing the variation from one to another. All shared the welded steel-tube fuselage/tail unit with fabric covering, and wings with spruce spars, light alloy ribs and metal frame ailerons, all fabric-covered. Landing gear was of non-retractable tailwheel type, with the main units divided and incorporating oleo-spring shock-absorbers in the side vees.

With the requirement for a trainer suitable for glider pilots, Aeronca de-

An Aeronca L-3C is seen during the last months of the war. Together with the Taylorcraft and Piper models of the Grasshopper, the L-3C was powered by a 65-hp 0-170-3 Continental piston engine.

veloped an unpowered version of the Model 65. This retained the wings, tail unit and aft fuselage of the L-3, but introduced a new front fuselage providing a third seat forward for an instructor, the original tandem seats being used by two pupils: all three occupants had similar flying controls and instruments. A total of 250 of these training gliders was supplied to the USAAF under the designation **TG-5**, and three supplied to the US Navy for

An Aeronca L-3B of a US Army Air Force liaison/observation unit is seen in a late war colour scheme. The various L-3 models differed only in equipment fit, with A, B and C models being externally very similar. Over 1,400 L-3s had been delivered by 1944.

evaluation were identified as **LNR**. Production of Aeronca liaison aircraft continued after the war, with planes supplied to the USAF under the designation **L-16**.

Specification
Aeronca L-3
Type: two-seat light liaison and observation monoplane
Powerplant: one 48-kW (65-hp) Continental O-170 flat-four piston

engine
Performance: maximum speed 140 km/h (87 mph); cruising speed 74 km/h (46 mph); service ceiling 3050 m (10,000 ft); range 322 km (200 miles)
Weights: empty 379 kg (835 lb); maximum take-off 590 kg (1,300 lb)
Dimensions: span 10.67 m (35 ft 0 in); length 6.40 m (21 ft 0 in); height 2.34 m (7 ft 8 in); wing area 14.68 m² (158 sq ft)
Armament: none

Piper L-4 Grasshopper

Evaluated for the role of artillery spotting and front-line liaison, four examples of the **Piper Cub Model J-3C-65** were acquired for this purpose by the US Army Air Corps in mid-1941. These were allocated the designation **YO-59** and, almost simultaneously, 40 additional examples were ordered as **O-59** aircraft.

Experience on manoeuvres made it possible to procure a new version more specifically tailored to the US Army's requirements. This, designated **O-59A**, was of braced high-wing monoplane configuration and was of composite construction comprising wooden spars, light alloy ribs and fabric covering. The fuselage and braced tail unit had basic structures of welded steel tube and were fabric-covered. Landing gear was of the fixed tailwheel type, and the powerplant of the O-59A comprised a 48-kW (65-hp) Continental O-170-3 flat-four engine. Primary requirement of the O-59A specification was improved accommodation for pilot and observer, which was achieved with a modified enclosure for the tandem cockpits to provide better all-round visibility. The

The original designation of the wartime military Cub was O-59, but these early aircraft were subsequently identified in the 'liaison' category as L-4s when the redesignation of 'observation' aircraft was carried out in 1942. This L-4H is painted in standard Army drab. The wire and cork fuel indicator is clearly visible.

type was later redesignated **L-4A**.

In 1942 Piper was requested to develop a training glider from the basic L-4 design, this involving the removal of the powerplant and landing gear. In its modified form it had a simple cross-axle landing gear with hydraulic brakes, and the powerplant was replaced by a new front fuselage to accommodate an instructor, and he

and both pupils were provided with full flying controls. A total of 250 was built for the USAAF under the designation **TG-8**, plus three for evaluation by the US Navy which designated them **XLNP-1**.

Apart from the three XLNP-1s which the US Navy acquired for evaluation, this service also procured 230 **NE-1** aircraft basically similar to the US

Army's L-4s, and these were used as primary trainers. Twenty similar aircraft procured at a later date were designated **NE-2**, and 100 examples of the **Piper J-5C Cub** which were acquired for ambulance use (carrying one stretcher) were originally **HE-1**. When, in 1943, the letter H was allocated to identify helicopters, the HE-1s were redesignated **AE-1**.

Specification
Piper L-4
Type: two-seat lightweight liaison aircraft
Powerplant: one 48-kW (65-hp) Continental O-170-3 flat-four piston engine
Performance: maximum speed 137 km/h (85 mph); cruising speed 121 km/h (75 mph); service ceiling 2835 m (9,300 ft); range 306 km (190 miles)
Weights: empty 331 kg (730 lb); maximum take-off 553 kg (1,220 lb)
Dimensions: span 10.74 m (35 ft 3 in); length 6.71 m (22 ft 0 in); height 2.03 m (6 ft 8 in); wing area 16.63 m² (179 sq ft)
Armament: none

The Piper Cub was built in improved versions up until 1981, and has been used by a great many air forces. The Israeli air force, operators of this late-model Super Cub, have been using the type since its creation in the late 1940s.

 USA
Stinson L-5 Sentinel

The **Stinson** (part of Vultee) **105 Voyager** was an attractive three-seat civil lightplane, and in 1941 the US Army acquired six of these civil aircraft which it evaluated for use in a light liaison role. Successful testing resulted in an initial order of 1941 for 275 aircraft to be powered by the Lycoming O-435-1 flat-four engine. The following order covered 1,456 similar aircraft, under the designation **L-5**.

Construction of the L-5s was changed from that of the original Voyager design following a decision to reserve alloy materials for the construction of combat aircraft. Instead of the mixed construction which had been used for the wing and tail unit of the Voyager, those of the L-5 were all-wood, but retained the welded steel-tube fuselage structure. Other changes included rearrangement of the enclosed cabin to seat two in tandem, a reduction in height of the rear fuselage to provide an improved rearward view, and the provision of clear transparent panels in the roof. The original wing design had included leading-edge slots and slotted trailing-edge flaps, and these were retained. The main units of the non-retractable tailwheel type landing gear were modified so that the stroke of the oleo-spring shock-absorbers was almost doubled.

The L-5C, of which 200 were built, had provision for the installation of a K-20 reconnaissance camera. In addition to the aircraft procured directly by the US Army, eight commercial Voyagers were commandeered in 1941 and designated **AT-19A** (later **L-9A**), and 12 others as **AT-19B** (**L-9B**).

Used extensively by the USAAF throughout World War II, especially in the Pacific theatre, many L-5s were still in use to provide valuable service during the Korean War. The RAF was allocated 100 of these aircraft under Lend-Lease, and these were used widely in Burma for liaison spotting and air ambulance duties under the name **Sentinel**. The US Marine Corps acquired a total of 306 L-5s of differing versions, but all were designated **OY-1**, the Y signifying origin from Consolidated after a merger with Vultee in early 1943. The US Marine Corps deployed its Sentinels for similar missions to those of the RAF and USAAF in support of its operations in the Pacific.

Specification
Stinson L-5
Type: two-seat light liaison aircraft
Powerplant: one 138-kW (185-hp) Lycoming O-435-1 flat-four piston engine
Performance: maximum speed 209 km/h (130 mph); service ceiling 4815 m (15,800 ft); range 676 km (420 miles)
Weights: empty 703 kg (1,550 lb); maximum take-off 916 kg (2,020 lb)
Dimensions: span 10.36 m (34 ft 0 in); length 7.34 m (24 ft 1 in); height 2.41 m (7 ft 11 in); wing area 14.40 m² (155 sq ft)
Armament: none

Above: Two of the 100 Stinson Sentinels supplied under Lend-Lease to the RAF in Burma fly over the paddy fields. They were used for artillery spotting, air ambulance and general liaison duties.

Developed from the Stinson 105 Voyager, the L-5 Sentinel was used extensively by the USAAF, especially in the Pacific. This example is from the 163rd Liaison Squadron, based on Okinawa in the middle of 1945.

Polikarpov U-2

Occupying a unique position in Soviet aviation history, the **Polikarpov U-2** primary trainer biplane had an inauspicious start. The **U-2TPK** prototype, which appeared in early 1927, had been built to achieve economy in repair and maintenance, the wings comprising four identical thick-section interchangeable rectangular panels with square tips. Similarly, a common control surface was used for ailerons, elevators and rudder. The result was a biplane with very poor flight characteristics. It had thus to be redesigned, appearing as a neat, manoeuvrable biplane having staggered single-bay wing with rounded tips, conventional cross-axle landing gear, and tandem open cockpits for instructor and pupil. Powered by a 75-kW (100-hp) radial engine, the new prototype made its first flight on 7 January 1928. An immediate success, it was placed in quantity production, deliveries starting in 1928, and by the time of the German invasion of the Soviet Union in mid-1941 over 13,000 had been completed.

Though its principle role was primary training, the U-2 was soon modified as a light passenger transport, air ambulance and agricultural aircraft. Production continued on a massive scale during World War II, and the U-2 took on an even wider range of duties, including liaison, light attack, night nuisance raider and propaganda aircraft complete with microphone and loudspeaker.

After Polikarpov's death, on 30 July 1944, the U-2 was redesignated **Po-2** in his honour, and post-war it continued in production in the USSR for several years. Trainer and ambulance variants were built on a large scale in Poland from 1948 to 1953. Po-2s served with many Soviet allies and a small number still remain in flying condition in the USSR and several other countries. The total built is credibly reported to be in excess of 40,000.

Specification
Polikarpov U-2VS
Type: trainer and multi-purpose aircraft
Powerplant: one 75-kW (100-hp) M-11 radial piston engine
Performance: maximum speed 156 km/h (97 mph); service ceiling 4000 m (13,125 ft); range 400 km (249 miles)
Weights: empty equipped 635 kg (1,400 lb); maximum take-off 890 kg (1,962 lb)
Dimensions: span 11.40 m (37 ft 4.8 in); length 8.17 m (26 ft 9.78 in); height 3.10 m (10 ft 2 in); wing area 33.15 m² (356.84 sq ft)
Armament: none

Built on a large scale in Poland as the CSS-13, the Polikarpov U-2 (known as the Po-2 after the designer's death in 1944) was used in a wide array of both civil and military roles, and has probably been built in greater numbers and in more variants than any other aircraft in history.

A Soviet built U-2 supplied to the Polish forces at the end of World War II, preserved at a Polish museum. Over 100 regiments, each of 42 aircraft, operated the 'Kuburuznile' ('Corn Cutter') at the height of the war.

Meridionali Ro.37bis

Meridionali, then named Officine Ferroviarie Meridionali, first became involved in the Italian aircraft industry in 1923, beginning manufacturing activities two years later by licence-construction of Fokker designs. Subsequently, after two years under the name Romeo, the title Industrie Meccaniche e Aeronautiche Meridionali (IMAM) was adopted in 1936.

In 1934 the company had started design and production of a two-seat fighter/reconnaissance biplane under the designation **Romeo Ro.37**. This was an unequal-span single-bay biplane of mixed wood and metal construction. Its design included fixed tailwheel landing gear, all three wheels being provided with speed fairings; a braced tail unit incorporating a variable-incidence tailplane; and accommodation for two in tandem enclosed cockpits. Power was provided by a 522-kW (700-hp) Fiat A.30RA Vee engine. An improved **Ro.37bis** was developed subsequently, and this introduced an optional radial powerplant comprising either the Piaggio P.IX or P.X supercharged engine. Both models proved popular for their day, with production of the Ro.37 and Ro.37bis exceeding 160 and 475 respectively, and export orders were received from Afghanistan, Hungary and from countries in Central and South America.

Ro.37 and Ro.37bis aircraft were involved in the Spanish Civil War from October 1936 and were used extensively by the Regia Aeronautica during Mussolini's invasion of Abyssinia between October 1935 and May 1936 and during the Italian occupation of that country until 1941. Some 275 Ro.37bis aircraft were in service with the Regia Aeronautica when Italy became involved in World War II, and these saw first-line service in the East and North African campaigns and in the Balkans. After withdrawal from first-line service they found a variety of uses, but all had been retired before Italy's armistice with the Allies on 8 September 1943.

Specification
Meridionali Ro.37bis
Type: two-seat fighter/reconnaissance aircraft
Powerplant: one 418-kW (560-hp) Piaggio P.IX RC.40 radial piston engine
Performance: maximum speed 330 km/h (205 mph) at 5000 m (16,405 ft); cruising speed 250 km/h (155 mph); service ceiling 7200 m (23,620 ft); maximum range 1120 km (696 miles)
Weights: empty 1585 kg (3,494 lb); maximum take-off 2420 kg (5,335 lb)
Dimensions: span 11.08 m (36 ft 4.2 in); length 8.56 m (28 ft 1 in); height 3.15 m (10 ft 4 in); wing area 31.35 m² (337.46 sq ft)
Armament: two fixed forward-firing 7.7-mm (0.303-in) machine-guns and one gun of same calibre on trainable mount in rear cockpit, plus up to 180 kg (397 lb) of bombs on underfuselage racks

The Meridionali Ro.37 saw its heyday during the Spanish Civil War. A few soldiered on into World War II, this example being captured during the battle for Monte Corvino near Salerno in 1943.

Axis Submarines

The struggle for supremacy above and beneath the swirling waters of the North Atlantic was the most important battle fought by the submarine forces of the Axis navies. However, Axis submarines ranged the sealanes from the Atlantic through the Indian Ocean to the South Pacific.

U47, a Type VIIB U-boat under the command of ace commander Gunther Prien, returning to port. Germany built some 1100 U-boats of which well over half were lost in action.

During World War II the common factor that permitted the USA to wage war in both Europe and the Pacific simultaneously, and which allowed the UK to exist at all, was merchant shipping. Losses of warships could cause problems, but losses of merchantmen were potentially disastrous. If the loss rate had exceeded the construction rate

for a significant period, the Allies' capacity to wage war would have slowed, to the point of eventual capitulation.

As World War I had adequately proved to the Germans that submarines were the best vehicles for this form of warfare, it seems extraordinary that more resources were not put into their construction in the late 1930s. Those

available caused damage enough, but greater numbers and a higher construction rate from the outset would have swamped the ability to cope of current Allied defences.

Throughout the conflict, the Germans strove to improve both the technical quality of their boats and the methods by which they could best be employed, a

natural energy that contrasted strangely with that of their Axis partners. Both Italy and Japan had sizeable submarine fleets and, as each joined the war at later dates, they had adequate time to learn at first hand the problems of submarine warfare before actually committing themselves.

Italy, however, found her boats to be deficient in quality and their crews both poorly trained and, in many cases, suffering from the same lack of motivation and conviction that affected her surface fleet.

Japan, on the other hand, had no lack of motivation but was stricken with an inflexibility of purpose that worked to the American advantage. War waged against merchant shipping was viewed as 'defensive' so, despite in most cases being manifestly unsuitable for the purpose, Japanese submarines were employed almost exclusively against warships. The twin facts that American lines of communication vulnerably straddled two oceans and that American submarines were throttling Japan by blockade went unnoticed.

There was no lack of sacrifice. In pursuing their various objectives, the Axis partners lost more than 950 boats in action and many more from other causes.

JAPAN
'RO-100' and 'RO-35' classes

Small- to medium-sized boats in the IJN were designated 'RO', equivalent to the Western 'B'. In the case of the **'RO-100' class**, the term **'Kaisho'** or **Type KS** was also used, denoting 'small'. They were designed originally as limited-endurance boats for use in the waters off the Japanese home islands, and for this reason operational depth could be reduced to only 75 m (245 ft). The function of the boats was, however, extended to protection of the numerous islands that were acquired to defend the outer perimeter of the new empire. As these were often surrounded by deep water, the 'RO-100' boats started at a disadvantage. Once submerged, the boats' small sonar profile did not compensate for their poor performance and all 18 of the class were sunk, significantly only two by aircraft. That one was sunk off eastern India says much for the endurance of its crew. No less than five of the class were des-

troyed by the American destroyer-escort USS *England* on various dates.

The design was a diminutive of, but very different from, the earlier 'RO-33'. In size and potential it equated roughly with the British U-class. They were unsuitable for attacking the warships that were designated their prime targets yet, whilst they could have operated effectively against mercantile targets, the Japanese submarine command showed the lack of imagination and flexibility that was characteristic throughout the war and which was primarily responsible for its poor showing.

The class of 18 was ordered pre-war

but were being completed up to 1944. Nine further projected units were cancelled.

The parallel RO type, the **'RO-35' class** ('Kaichu' or **Type K6**) was larger and comprised the last medium-sized boats built by the IJN. Of the 18 completed only one survived the war, having been used defensively despite their superior potential. Between them, the combined 'RO-35' and 'RI-100' classes are credited with four minor warships and six merchantmen sunk, a catastrophically poor rate of exchange that led also to the cancellation of 60 further 'RO-35s'.

Directly comparable in performance and size to the British 'U-class' boats, the 'RO-100s' should have been equally successful, but were to prove less able to cope with operational limitations.

Specification
'RO-100' class
Type: coastal submarine
Displacement: 601 tons surfaced and 782 tons submerged
Dimensions: length 60.90 m (199 ft 10 in); beam 6.10 m (20 ft 0 in); draught 3.50 m (11 ft 6 in)
Propulsion: surfaced diesels delivering 1,100 bhp (820 kW) and submerged electric motors delivering 760 hp (570 kW) to two shafts
Speed: surfaced 14 kts and submerged 8 kts
Range: surfaced 6500 km (4,040 miles) at 12 kts and submerged 110 km (68 miles) at 3 kts
Armament: one 76-mm (3-in) gun (often removed), and four 533-mm (21-in) torpedo tubes (all forward) with eight torpedoes
Complement: 38

JAPAN
'I-15' class

An 'I' prefix, equivalent to the Western 'A', denoted a larger submarine designed for fleet or cruising work. These two functions were tending to merge, for the 'fleet' concept was a hangover from earlier British ideas of using large boats with a good surface performance to act closely as an element of the surface fleet, a concept that was not successful at that time. The **'I-15' class** was, therefore, derived from twin sources. First of these was the 'Type KD' fleet submarine of the mid-1930s, capable of a 23-kt surface speed and a range suitable for a return trip across the Pacific. The other was the 'Junsen', or cruiser submarine, of a slightly later date, which incorporated one or two floatplanes in a pressure-tight hangar forming part of the superstructure. It would seem that the idea of these aircraft was to increase the boat's scouting capability rather than for offensive purposes.

Really the first variant **'Type B1'** of three, the 'I-15' group was 20 strong, with the hangar a low, streamlined structure protruding (usually forward) from the tower. The freeboard was high to improve aircraft handling in a seaway, and was made higher by a sloping catapult track; a folding crane was also incorporated for recovery purposes. A 140-mm (5.5-in) gun was set on a substantial bandstand. In practice, the aircraft and its equipment proved more trouble than they were

worth, and several boats had such provision removed in favour of a second gun to suit them better for the attack role. As such, the boats were among the more successful of Japanese classes, being credited with the sinking of eight warships (including the carrier USS *Wasp* by *I-19*) and 59 merchantmen of about 400,000 gross registered tons.

Despite these successes, the losses of the 'I-15' boats were catastrophically high, as a result mainly of their poor submerged performance and of the fact that only three full salvoes of torpedoes were carried; only one boat of 20 survived to surrender. A couple of the class, along with others from the very

similar **'Type B2'** and **'Type B3'** variants, were modified to carry *Kaiten* (suicide midget submarines). The 'Type B2' was the **'I-40' class** (six completed) and the 'Type B3' was the **'I-54' class** (three completed).

Specification
'I-15' class
Type: ocean-going submarine
Displacement: 2,590 tons surfaced and 3,655 tons submerged
Dimensions: length 108.60 m (356 ft 4 in); beam 9.30 m (30 ft 6 in); draught 5.10 m (16 ft 9 in)
Propulsion: surfaced diesels delivering 12,400 bhp (9245 kW) and submerged electric motors delivering

This picture portrays the high surface speed of the Japanese Type B1 ('I-15') class. To improve targeting in the commerce-raiding role, a 'Glen' floatplane was carried.

2,000 hp (1490 kW) to two shafts
Speed: surfaced 23.5 kts and submerged 8 kts
Range: surfaced 26000 km (16,155 miles) at 16 kts and submerged 185 km (115 miles) at 3 kts
Armament: one 140-mm (5.5-in) gun, two 25-mm AA guns, one Yokosuka E14Y1 aircraft, and six 533-mm (21-in) torpedo tubes (all forward) with 17 torpedoes
Complement: 100

In terms of naval architectural problems, the 'I-15' class boats were a clean and satisfactory solution to putting aircraft into submarines. The reasons for doing so were, however, questionable.

'Ha-201' class

Technically the most interesting of Japan's many submarine designs, the little **'Ha-201' class** boats, complemented by the 78-m (255.9-ft) 'I-201' class boats, were the equivalent of the German Types XXIII and XXI respectively. With the Americans pressing ever closer to the home islands, the Japanese seem in 1943 at last to have grasped the fact that they had the wrong types of submarine to tackle their chosen prime targets, warships. Their strategy would best have been served by concentrating their existing boats, as did the Americans, on mercantile targets but, persevering to the end, the Japanese developed the 'Ha 201' class or **Type STS** as a fast, manoeuvrable design to protect the home islands against warships. Like similar German boats, however, they arrived too late to be of use, their enemy already having achieved absolute superiority.

Using experimental data derived from the prewar experiments with the 43-m (141-ft) evaluation boat, *No. 71*,

the Japanese planned the rapid production of 90 boats. Even with extensive prefabrication and the use of five separate yards, they managed to complete only about 10, none of which managed an offensive patrol, though 28 more were in an advanced state of construction at the surrender.

The prefix 'Ha' corresponds to 'C', denoting a small boat. The exterior was kept as clean of protruberances as possible, though there was rather a lot of forward casing. The boats were capable of 'grouping-up' for limited bursts of high submerged speed, necessary as they had only two torpedo tubes and attacks needed to be carried out from close range to guarantee success. Interestingly, they were propelled by a

single, centreline propeller, set abaft a cruciform control surface assembly, remarkably similar to modern arrangements. They possessed only limited endurance and their crew of 22 could be supported for about 15 days. A type of snort was fitted to allow prolonged periods of submersion, necessary for them to survive at a time when American air power was virtually unchallenged. Together with advanced German submarine types, they yielded the Americans much valuable post-war data to apply to their 'Guppy' programmes.

Specification
'Ha-201' class
Type: coastal submarine

Displacement: 377 tons surfaced and 440 tons submerged
Dimensions: length 53.00 m (173 ft 11 in); beam 4.00 m (13 ft 1 in); draught 3.40 m (11 ft 2 in)
Propulsion: surfaced diesel delivering 400 bhp (298 kW) and submerged electric motor delivering 1,250 hp (930 kW) to one shaft
Speed: surfaced 10.5 kts and submerged 13 kts
Range: surfaced 5600 km (3,480 miles) at 10.5 kts and submerged 185 km (115 miles) at 2 kts
Armament: one 7.7-mm (0.303-in) machine-gun, and two 533-mm (21-in) torpedo tubes (both forward) with four torpedoes
Complement: 22

Like the German Type XXIIIs, the 'Ha-201' class boats were small, fast and handy. They were also too late to be of use, in spite of prefabricated construction. Larger than their German equivalents, they had superior endurance.

Type II

In 1935 Germany repudiated the treaty by which she was prevented from operating submarines, forcing an Anglo-German agreement which allowed direct construction up to a ceiling of total tonnage equivalent to 45 per cent of that operated by the British. A major task for the submarine supremo, Karl Dönitz, was to break this figure down into numbers and types of boat that would fulfil a wartime strategy. One requirement identified was that of a coastal submarine roughly equivalent to the later UB series that operated successfully in UK waters during World War I. During the fallow years of the treaty, German design expertise was maintained through work for export, and the prototype for the **Type IIA** can thus be found in the *Vesikko*, itself based on an amalgam of data from the UBII and the later UF. This boat was built in Finland in 1933 to German design.

The Type IIAs went quickly into production following the go-ahead, and proved to be handy and manoeuvrable, being able to crash-dive in 25 seconds. Their profile and lively surface characteristics earned them the nickname of 'canoes'. Though the small displacement of the Type IIA favoured larger numbers in a restricted ceiling, the design was very limited on endurance, requiring progressive 'stretch-

ing' through the **Type IIB, Type IIC** and **Type IID** sub-types: the Type IIB had greater bunkerage and radius, the Type IIC was modelled on the Type IIB with more powerful engines, and the Type IID had saddle tanks.

The design encompassed a single hull with a trim tank at each end of the pressure hull and an internal 'rapid-dive' tank amidships. As only three torpedo tubes and limited reloads were carried, a load of mines was an alternative rather than an addition.

With the emphasis of the sea war moving deep-sea, construction of the

Type IIs ceased in 1941, the boats thereafter being used much for training and trials purposes, including early experimentation with snort gear. In total, there were built six Type IIAs, 20 Type IIBs, eight type IICs and 16 Type IIDs.

Specification
Type IID
Type: coastal submarine
Displacement: 314 tons surfaced and 364 tons submerged
Dimensions: length 43.95 m (144 ft 2 in); beam 4.87 m (16 ft 0 in); draught 3.90 m (12 ft 9 in)
Propulsion: surfaced diesels delivering 700 bhp (522 kW) and

The small size of the German Type IIB is emphasized by the scale of the crew in the tower. Seen here in prewar livery, U-9 was sunk by bombing in 1944 in the Black Sea.

submerged electric motors delivering 410 hp (306 kW) to two shafts
Speed: surfaced 13 kts and submerged 7.5 kts
Range: surfaced 6500 km (4,040 miles) at 12 kts and submerged 105 km (65 miles) at 4 kts
Armament: one (later four) 20-mm AA guns and three 533-mm (21-in) torpedo tubes (all forward) with six torpedoes
Complement: 25

Type II coastal boats lacked the endurance necessary for much of the war at sea, and were not built after 1941. Shown here is the U-3, an early command of the ace Schepke.

Type VII

Like that of the Type II, the design of the **Type VII** seagoing boat had export origins in a Finnish-built series of 1930-1 (the 'Vetehinen' class) and, beyond that, in the UB III of 1918. To permit the greatest number of hulls to be built within the ceiling tonnage agreed, size was severely limited in the 10 **Type VIIA** boats (626/745 tons). With performance and offensive capacity optimized, conditions aboard were somewhat spartan even with internal space saved by mounting the after tube in the casing (where it could be reloaded only with difficulty and then on the surface) and by the stowage of spare torpedoes and part of the bunker capacity externally (where they were vulnerable to depth charging). The **Type VIIB** and **Type VIIC** were, therefore, stretched to increase internal volume to rectify some of the shortcomings and to allow more powerful diesels to be fitted, a significant factor in surface operations. This modified boat was highly successful, nearly 700 units being built in various sub-variants until the war's end. Later improvements included greater operational depths, reinforced towers, enhanced AA armament and snorts, all features reflecting developing Allied anti-submarine procedures. Significantly, most lacked a deck gun as surface operations became impossible.

While mines configured to the standard 533-mm (21-in) torpedo tube could be laid by all German submarines, these weapons could not guarantee a sinking as opposed to disablement. To lay the largest moored mines, therefore, six Type VIIs were stretched by the addition of an extra 10-m (32.8-ft) section amidships containing five vertical free-flooding tubes, each containing three complete mine assemblies. These tubes protruded upward to 01 level into an extended tower. The class was known as the **Type VIID**. A further four boats, the **Type VIIF** sub-class, were similarly lengthened, with the additional space given over to spare torpedoes for transfer to extend the operational duration of other boats. Up to 25 torpedoes could be carried but transfer operations with both boats temporarily immobilized on the surface became increasingly uopular and were abandoned. The **Type VIIE**, a study in improved propulsion, never progressed beyond the drawing board.

Specification
Type VIIC
Type: sea-going submarine
Displacement: 769 tons surfaced and 871 tons submerged
Dimensions: length 66.50 m (218 ft 2 in); beam 6.20 m (20 ft 4 in). draught 4.75 m (15 ft 7 in)
Propulsion: surfaced diesels delivering 2,800 bhp (2089 kW) and submerged electric motors delivering 750 hp (559 kW) to two shafts
Speed: surfaced 17.5 kts and submerged 7.5 kts
Range: surfaced 15750 km (9,785 miles) at 10 kts and submerged 150 km (93 miles) at 4 kts
Armament: one 88-mm (3.465-in) gun, one 37-mm AA gun, two (later eight) 20-mm AA guns, and five 533-mm (21-in) torpedo tubes (four forward and one aft) with 14 torpedoes
Complement: 44

Above: A Type VIIC boat, probably U-402, is re-launched after maintenance, her broad keelson allowing her to sit on the cradle with little auxiliary support. Note the blisters of the external ballast tanks and the skeg aft spreading braces to keep wires clear of the twin rudders.

Below: A clutch of Type VIIA boats of the Second Flotilla alongside at Kiel prewar. The tender is the converted minesweeper Fuchs. U-27 on the left of the picture was an early loss, sunk by British destroyers off Scotland.

Below: Belonging to the best-known German submarine flotilla, the 7th (Stier), U-52 is a Type VIIB which survived until the war's last days. Larger than the 'A' variant, the 'B' lacks the odd hump aft, the after torpedo tubes having been relocated within the hull.

Type IX

GERMANY

The **Type IX** class was designed for ocean warfare. Loosely based on the far smaller **Type II**, it differed fundamentally in having a double hull. This feature increased useful internal volume by enabling fuel and ballast tanks to be sited externally. In turn, the extra hull improved survivability by cushioning the inner (pressure) hull from explosive shock and gave the boats greatly improved seakindliness on the surface. Habitability was improved for operations of longer duration and the number of torpedoes carried, at 22, was about 50 per cent more than those of a Type VIIC. The deck gun was increased in calibre from 88 to 105 mm (3.465 to 4.13 in).

To give an idea of how designs developed during the course of the war, the **Type IXA** and Type VIIA variants were, respectively, 76.5 and 64.5 m (251 and 211.6 ft) long, while the final **Type IXD** and Type VIIF marks, were 87.5 and 77.6 m (287.07 and 254.6 ft) long.

The major objective with the Type IX variants was to improve range rather than offensive capability. Thus the eight Type IXA boats could achieve 19500 km (12,120 miles) on the surface at 10 kts yet, even before September 1939, were being complemented by the first of 14 **Type IXB** boats capable of 22250 km (13,825 miles). These were followed by the largest group, the **Type IXC** and slightly modified **Type IXC-40**, 149 boats with bunkers for 25000 km (15,535 miles).

From the opening of hostilities, the Type IXs worked the western and southern Atlantic and, on the entry into the war of the United States, were supplemented by Type VIICs for the 'Happy Time', ravaging shipping down the USA's eastern seaboard to the Caribbean before a proper convoy system had been instituted.

As early as 1940, the **Type IXD** was on the board, with an extra 10.8-m (35.4-ft) section worked in. Two examples of the **Type IXD1** were built, with

no armament, but capable of stowing over 250 tons of fuel for the topping-up of other boats. The 29 **Type IXD2s** boats were operational boats with the phenomenal range of 58400 km (36,290 miles), enabling them to work the Indian Ocean and even reach Japan. Some included a small, single-seat towed gyro kite to increase their visual search radius. The Type IXD2 was further refined to the **Type IXD2-42**, but only one of this variant was ever completed. Advanced diesels in the Type IXD1s gave a 21-kt surface speed, but were found unreliable and not repeated.

Specification
Type IXC
Type: ocean-going submarine
Displacement: 1,120 tons surfaced and 1,232 tons submerged
Dimensions: length 76.70 m (251 ft 8 in); beam 6.75 m (22 ft 2 in); draught 4.70 m (15 ft 5 in)
Propulsion: surfaced diesels delivering 4,400 hp (3281 kW) and submerged electric motors delivering 1,000 hp (746 kW) to two shafts
Speed: surfaced 18.2 kts and submerged 7.5 kts
Range: surfaced 25000 km (15,535 miles) at 10 kts and submerged 115 km

Already wearing the 'Old Glory', a surrendered Type IX U-boat wallows in a quiet sea off the American coast, in May 1945, watched by a DE and a blimp. This example was a 'D' variant, longer than earlier versions.

(71.5 miles) at 4 kts
Armament: one 105-mm (4.13-in) gun, one 37-mm AA gun, one 20-mm AA gun, and six 533-mm (21-in) torpedo tubes (four forward and two aft) with 22 torpedoes
Complement: 48

With each variant operating ever further afield, the Type IX was a most successful design. Shown is the 'B' variant U-106, which was particularly successful in the North Atlantic, off the American eastern seaboard, in the Caribbean and off West Africa. She also torpedoed the battleship Malaya.

Type X and Type XI

GERMANY

Of the five main types of U-boat identified by pre-war staff requirements, the patrol submarines of short-, medium- and long-endurance capabilities became the Type II, Type VII and Type IX respectively. The others were a 'small' minelayer and a long-range cruiser submarine; with modifications, these became the **Type X** and **Type XI**.

Only three type XIs were ever built, these being very large boats with a length of 115 m (377.3 ft) and a surface displacement of 3140 tons. Essentially submersible surface raiders, they had a useful surface speed of 23 kts, and a superstructure that included stowage for a small scout seaplane and paired 127-mm (5-in) guns at each end.

Though the large cruiser submarine had enjoyed some success during

World War I, its mode of operation rapidly became impossible in World War II and the type was discontinued. Indeed, the boats' most noteworthy achievement seems to have been *U-601*'s initial sighting of the British convoy JW 55B in the Norwegian Sea on Christmas Day 1943. Her contact report was responsible for the sailing of the *Scharnhorst*, bent on interception. She, in turn, was met by the Royal Navy and sunk the following day.

The **Type XA** was, in fact, a very large minelayer design, a 2,500-tonner incorporating multiple vertical minestowage shafts of the type used successfully in the Type VIIDs. Possibly considered vulnerable because of its size, the Type XA never progressed beyond the drawing board, being superseded by the **Type XB**. These eight

boats were smaller, with a circular-section pressure hull flanked by a slab-sided outer hull of generous proportions. On the centre-line forward, six mine storages projected from keel to the top of a hump in the casing, each accommodating three mine assemblies. On each side, in the space between the hulls, were fitted 12 shorter stowages, each containing two mines. The total load was, therefore, 66 large mines. Built to avoid action as far as possible, the type XBs had only two torpedo tubes, squeezed in right aft. They proved to be better employed in resupply rather than minelaying.

Specification
Type XB
Type: minelaying submarine
Displacement: 1,763 tons surfaced and

2,177 tons submerged
Dimensions: length 89.80 m (294 ft 7 in); beam 9.20 m (30 ft 2 in); draught 4.11 m (13 ft 6 in)
Propulsion: surfaced diesels delivering 4,200 bhp (3131 kW) and submerged electric motors delivering 1,100 hp (820 kW) to two shafts
Speed: surfaced 16.5 kts and submerged 7 kts
Range: surfaced 34400 km (21,375 miles) at 10 kts and submerged 175 km 109 miles) at 4 kts
Armament: one 105-mm (4.13-in) gun (later removed), one 37-mm AA gun, one (later four) 20-mm AA guns, two 533-mm (21-in) torpedo tubes (both aft) with 15 torpedoes, and 66 mines
Complement: 52

Planned at a time when the larger cruiser submarine idea was still in vogue, only three Type XI were built, due to changing priorities. With a length of 115 m (377 ft), the four boats (U-112/-115) would have had a range of 25430 km (15,800 miles) at 12 kts. Their armament included four 127-mm guns and an autogyro was carried.

GERMANY

Type XVII

A combination of anti-submarine aircraft and radar gradually made it impossible for U-boats to use their high surface speed as a basis for attack and, to ensure their survival as a viable attack platform, submarines had to be optimized for submerged performance. Only a machinery system independent of surface air in combination with a cleaned-up, high-speed hull would suffice, and the **Type XVII** marked this fundamental and transitional step forward.

The key to the concept was the Walter closed-cycle propulsion system that relied on the near-explosive decomposition of concentrated hydrogen peroxide in the presence of a catalyst. The reaction produced a high-temperature mix of steam and free oxygen into which fuel oil was injected and fired, resulting in high-pressure gases that were made to drive a conventional turbine. A weakness of the principle was that almost any impurity could act as a catalyst to initiate the process at a disastrously early stage.

Two prototype boats proved the machinery feasible, and the system was pressed into service in the Type XVIIs. A drawback was the extreme thirst of the system, dictating a small boat with a single propeller. For cruise purposes, this was driven by a conventional diesel/electric combination, with the Walter coupled up only to force or decline an engagement.

Externally, the hull was cleaned-up, with no guns and a minimum of proturberances. It was of figure-eight section, formed of two overlapping circular pressure hulls of unequal diameter. In practice, the length to beam ratio was too high, resulting in an unnecessarily high drag. This meant that the **Type XVIIA** never realized its theoretical top speed of 25 kts possible with two turbines on a common shaft. So only four such boats were built, the

modified **Type XVIIB** (three completed) having only one turbine. Space was available for only two torpedo tubes, but with one reload for each, a deficiency offset by the increasing lethality of the weapon.

A projected **Type XVIIK** would have abandoned the volatile Walter for conventional diesels aspirated with pure oxygen stored aboard.

Specification
Type XVIIB
Type: coastal submarine
Displacement: 312 tons surfaced and 357 tons submerged
Dimensions: length 41.50 m (136 ft 2 in); beam 3.40 m (11 ft 2 in); draught 4.25 m (14 ft 0 in)

Propulsion: surfaced diesel delivering 210 bhp (157 kW) and submerged Walter closed-cycle engine delivering 2,500 hp (1865 kW) or electric motor delivering 77 hp (57 kW) to one shaft
Speed: surfaced 9 kts and submerged 21.5 kts on Walter engine or 5 kts on electric motor
Range: surfaced 5550 km (3,450 miles) at 9 kts and submerged 210 km (130.5 miles) on Walter engine or 75 km (46.6 miles) on electric motor
Armament: two 533-mm (21-in) torpedo tubes (both forward) with four torpedoes
Complement: 19

One of the nearly complete Type XVII Walter turbine boats is transferred by a 350-ton floating crane through the shattered Kiel yard of Howaldtswerke. Advanced features include a hydrodynamically clean hull and a single propeller set in cruciform control surfaces. Note the sonar dome forward.

Few in numbers but rich in variants, the Type XVII U-boat was not a success, trying to press the Walter turbine into service before its time. Planned to run to a dozen boats (U-1081/1092), the 'G' variant was halted before any were complete. It was designed for an ultimate submerged speed of 25 kts.

Type XXI

One of the most influential designs in the history of the submarine, the **Type XXI** was to set standards until the introduction of the nuclear boat a decade later. Though both closed-cycle turbines and diesels had been introduced, both still needed development, so a stopgap high-power electric boat was produced, using mostly established technology. With the lower pressure hull packed with high power-density cells, the Type XXIs could, for the first time, develop more power submerged than surfaced. Their main propulsion motors were supplemented by low power units for silent manoeuvring.

Like that in the Type XVII, the pressure hull of the Type XXI was of 'double-bubble' cross section, though externally framed. It was prefabricated in eight sections at a variety of sites, being brought together for final assembly at the shipyard. The external framing increased volume and facilitated the addition of a hydrodynamically clean outer skin. Construction was all-welded to a target of three boats per week in an ambitious programme to produce an eventual 1,500 units (U-2500 to U-4000). Most other submarine programmes were curtailed or cancelled to this end.

The Type XXIs were designed to spend their full patrol time submerged, so the snort was used mainly to run diesels for battery recharge. Habitability was greatly improved, with air-conditioning and air-regeneration apparatus.

The only guns were paired automatic weapons set into the forward and after profiles of the elongated fin. A combination of active and passive sonars was used to provide a full torpedo-firing solution without recourse to the periscope. Two proposed but unbuilt variants, the **Type XXIB** and **Type XXIC**, would have increased the number of torpedo tubes from six to 12 and 18 respectively by the insertion of extra sections into the hull. Fortunately

Above: Lack of paint on both tower and stemhead are clues to the high speeds attained by this Type XXI. The hull is faired into an almost elliptical cross-section, leaving little deck, and the forward hydroplanes fold back into slots to reduce drag.

Left: The Blohm und Voss slips in May 1945 give an idea of the level to which series production of submarines had progressed. These Type XXI boats are being assembled from hull sections prefabricated at many inland sites and transported to Hamburg by water.

for the Allies, the Type XXI never became fully operational. Several were sunk, all by aircraft and in home waters.

Specification
Type XXIA
Type: ocean-going submarine
Displacement: 1,621 tons surfaced and 1,819 tons submerged
Dimensions: length 76.70 m (251 ft 8 in); beam 6.62 m (21 ft 9 in); draught 6.20 m (20 ft 4 in)
Propulsion: surfaced diesels delivering 4,000 bhp (2985 kW) and

Optimized for submerged performance, the profile of the Type XXI contrasts with those of earlier submarines. No deck gun is needed, but chin sonar and sonar mast are prominent. The first to commission, U-2511, was Norwegian-based, but, beyond a 'dummy' attack on a cruiser, had no luck.

submerged electric motors delivering 5,000 hp (3730 kW) or electric motors delivering 226 hp (169 kW) to two shafts
Speed: surfaced 15.5 kts and submerged 16 kts on main electric motor or 3.5 kts on creeping electric motors
Range: surfaced 28800 km (17,895 miles) and submerged 525 km (325 miles) at 6 kts
Armament: four 30-mm or 20-mm AA guns, and six 533-mm (21-in) torpedo tubes (all forward) with 23 torpedoes
Complement: 57

Type XXIII

Rather than search the Atlantic for convoys it may, in retrospect, have been more rewarding for the German submarine arm to develop tactics to tackle them at their known points of arrival and departure, despite the likely concentrations of escorts. A suitable vehicle would have been the **Type XXIII**, small and agile for shallow water operations and, like its larger cousin the Type XXI, packed with high-capacity battery cells for maximum underwater speed. Its hull had the 'double-bubble' cross section over the forward half but was internally framed and prefabricated in four sections. A departure was the near abandonment of outer casing except in the transitional zones and this, together

The very small size of the German Type XXIII is apparent from this view of U-2326 alongside a Dundee quay in May 1945. Few fittings protrude to spoil the flow over the very clean hull and tower. Only two bow torpedo tubes were fitted.

with a very low reserve buoyancy (the difference between surfaced and submerged displacements was only 24 tons) allowed for rapid crash-dive, times of less than 10 seconds being recorded. Even smaller than the Type XVII Walter boats, the Type XXIIIs also had a single shaft but a propeller proportionately larger in diameter for greater propulsive efficiency.

Though the boat was designed to operate submerged, its silhouette on the surface was very small, being little more than the slim tower with the attached low casing that enclosed the

snort induction and engine exhaust arrangements. No guns were carried and, oddly, only two torpedo tubes. With no space inboard for orthodox loading, the boat needed to be trimmed by the stern to expose the bow caps. As no spares could be carried an extra tube or four tubes forward would have been a bonus. As it was, attacks had to be carried out positively, from close range and with very fast or very stealthy disengagements. That this was possible was shown by the last U-boat attack in European waters, which occurred on 7 May 1945 well inside the Firth of Forth, when the *U-2336* sank two British merchantmen of an escorted convoy. One torpedo was used on each, fired on the strength of passive sonar bearings from ranges of less than 500 m (545 yards). By this time 62 type XXIIIs had entered service and their only losses had been to aircraft; it was fortunate for the Allies that the enemy's training and dedication no longer matched his technology.

Specification
Type XXIII
Type: coastal submarine
Displacement: 232 tons surfaced and 256 tons submerged
Dimensions: length 34.10 m (112 ft 0 in); beam 3.00 m (9 ft 10 in); draught 3.75 m (12 ft 3 in)
Propulsion: surfaced diesel delivering 580 bhp (433 kW) and submerged electric motor delivering 600 hp (447 kW) or electric motor delivering 35 hp (26 kW) to one shaft
Speed: surfaced 10 kts and submerged 12.5 kts on main electric motor or 2 kts on creeping electric motor
Range: surfaced 2500 km (1,555 miles) and submerged 325 km (202 miles) at 4 kts
Armament: two 533-mm (21-in) torpedo tubes (both forward) with two torpedoes
Complement: 14

From the tower aft the Type XXIII was all machinery. The forward quarter was all torpedo room and, except for a miniscule control room, the crew was squeezed above the banks of high-capacity battery cells. Note the single screw and unusual control surfaces.

'Sirena', 'Perla', 'Adua' and 'Acciaio' classes

Dating from a period of great expansion for the Italian navy's submarine arm, the 12 **'Sirena' class** submarines were known also as the **'600' class** boats. This figure was indicative of their standard surface displacement and, though the final design exceeded it by a considerable margin, they proved very handy boats for the constricted conditions of the Mediterranean. Their detail design was greatly influenced by that of the preceding 'Argonauta' class, but, as they were laid down before the latter's entry into service, they did not benefit from working experience. Simple and robust, they were heavily used and suffered accordingly, only one surviving beyond the armistice of September 1943.

Ten almost identical derivatives, the **'Perla' class**, followed on. Two of these, *Iride* and *Onice*, served somewhat controversially under Spanish Nationalist colours during the Spanish Civil War. During World War II, the *Iride*, together with the *Ambra*, were converted to carry SLC human torpedoes. The latter boat had already distinguished herself when, two days after the Battle of Cape Matapan, she had sunk the British cruiser HMS *Bonaventure*. Once converted, she went on to attack the harbour at Algiers in December 1942, heavily damaging four ships totalling 20,000 gross registered tons.

Yet another virtual repeat class had followed in the 17 **'Adua' class** boats, launched 1936-8. Two of these also were converted to carry SLCs and one of these the *Scirè,* was particularly successful. She attacked Gibraltar on no less than four occasions, the raid of September 1941 accounting for two ships, including the auxiliary tanker *Denbydale*. Her greatest coup, however, was in December 1941 when her three SLCs put the battleships HMS *Queen Elizabeth* and HMS *Valiant*, together with a tanker, on the bottom of Alexandria harbour. She was finally sunk by the anti-submarine trawler *Islay* outside Haifa in August 1942.

The final expression of the '600' type was in the enlarged 13-boat **Acciaio class** of 1941-2.

Specification
'Sirena' class
Type: sea-going submarine
Displacement: between 679 and 701

The Italian submarine Perla at Beirut after capture in 1942. The shadow accentuates the unusual tumblehome of the casing.

tons surfaced and between 842 and 860 tons submerged
Dimensions: length 60.18 m (197 ft 6 in); beam 6.45 m (21 ft 2 in); draught 4.70 m (15 ft 5 in)
Propulsion: surfaced diesels delivering 1,200 bhp (895 kW) and submerged electric motors delivering 800 hp (597 kW) to two shafts

Speed: surfaced 14 kts and submerged 8 kts
Range: surfaced 9000 km (5,590 miles) at 8 kts and submerged 135 km (84 miles) at 4 kts
Armament: one 100-mm (3.9-in) gun, two (later four) 13.2-mm (0.52-in) machine-guns, and six 533-mm (21-in) torpedo tubes (four forward and two aft) with 12 torpedoes
Complement: 45

Above: Handy-sized 'Mediterranean' boats, the 17-strong 'Adua' class were named after places in Italian North Africa. Boats of the class were modified to SLC carriers.

Below: A more powerful 'Adna'/ 'Perla' with reduced tower, Acciaio was lead boat of a class of 13. She was sunk by HM Submarine Unruly on 13 July 1943.

ITALY
'Cagni' class

It is not clear how the Italian navy, with minimal commitments outside the Mediterranean, could justify investment in submarines for ocean warfare. Italy's merchant marine, while of reasonable size, could not be protected on a worldwide basis by Italy's surface fleet, which was geared to short-endurance, high-speed undertakings, so coherent operations in the defence of trade were out of the question, even against the rival neighbour France. Despite this, the four **'Cagni' class** submarines were all laid down in September and October 1939 on the outbreak of hostilities between Germany and the Anglo-French alliance. As these submarines were aimed specifically at long-range commerce raiding, one can only speculate that Italy, as yet uninvolved, saw involvement against the maritime powers as only a matter of time.

The 'Cagnis' were the largest attack boats yet built for the Italian navy and, interestingly, were armed with small 450-mm (17.7-in) torpedoes. Though these were longer than the standard 450-mm (17.7-in) weapons, enabling them to carry a warhead of 200 kg (441 lb) in place of the more usual 110 kg (243 lb), this payload was still considerably less than the 270 kg (595 lb) of the larger 533-mm (21-in) torpedoes. As the torpedoes were for use primarily against 'soft' targets, however, this was judged acceptable, together with their lack of range. The bonus for this compromise was the ability to carry 36 torpedoes, the eight tubes forward and six aft permitting large spreads to enhance chances of success. An unusual feature was that torpedoes could be transferred from one end of the boat to the other. Two large deck guns were also carried to conserve torpedoes.

Unfortunately for Italian plans, the Mediterranean sea war required the keeping open of the vital North Africa supply route. Following heavy surface losses, the navy pressed large submarines into this service. In completing 15 trips, three of the four boats in the class were sunk in only three months. Only the name boat *Ammiraglio Cagni* worked as designed, but unsuccessfully, sinking less than 10,000 gross registered tons in two long patrols.

Specification
'Cagni' class
Type: ocean-going submarine

Displacement: 1,680 tons surfaced and 2,170 tons submerged
Dimensions: length 87.90 m (288 ft 5 in); beam 7.76 m (25 ft 6 in); draught 5.72 m (18 ft 9 in)
Propulsion: surfaced diesels delivering 4,370 bhp (3260 kW) and submerged electric motors delivering 1,800 hp (1345 kW) to two shafts
Speed: surfaced 17 kts and submerged 8.5 kts
Range: surfaced 20000 km (12,425 miles) at 12 kts and submerged 200 km (124 miles) at 3.5 kts

Ammiraglio Cagni returns from sea with a damaged after casing. The heavy armament of two 100-mm and four 13.2-mm guns can be seen, also the generally bulky appearance typical of most Italian ocean-going boats.

Armament: two 100-mm (3.9-in) guns, four 13.2-mm (0.52-in) machine-guns, and 14 450-mm (17.7-in) torpedo tubes (eight forward and six aft) with 36 torpedoes
Complement: 82

Nameship and sole survivor of her class, Cagni is seen here with a modified and rather Germanic-style tower, reducing her radar profile.

ITALY
'Archimede' class

The four **'Archimede' class** submarines were enlargements of the preceding 'Settembrini' design with ballasting rearranged to improve bunker capacity. An extra gun was also fitted, in keeping with the boats' 'ocean' role. All were launched in 1934 and, as part of their covert support of the Nationalist cause during the Spanish Civil War, the Italians transferred two to Spanish colours. These were the *Archimede* and the *Torricelli* and, to 'conceal' their transfer, two of the follow-on 'Brins' assumed their names. The three classes of boat formed a closely-related group, used extensively in colonial work.

That part of the Italian navy stationed in the Red Sea in June 1940 was cut off from the homeland and severely handled by the British as a threat astride the route from the Suez Canal eastward. The *Galilei* sank a Norwegian tanker less than a week after the outbreak of hostilities and announced her position further only two days later by stopping a neutral for examination. On the following day she was intercepted by the British anti-submarine trawler *Moonstone*, which inflicted damage that caused the boat to be filled with noxious fumes. Unable to dive, she fought it out on the surface. Far larger, faster and more heavily armed than her opponent she should have been successful had not the *Moonstone* shot up every gun's crew that emerged topside. With most of its officers dead, the demoralized crew surrendered. Captured, the boat assumed the British pennant P711 until her eventual disposal in 1946.

Galilei's replacement *Torricelli* was also apprehended by British forces. Forced to the surface near Perim Island, she engaged in a gun action with three 'K' class destroyers and a sloop. She was, inevitably, sunk but not before she had hit both the sloop and the destroyer HMS *Khartoum*. The hit on

the latter was on one of the banks of torpedo tubes and, apparently, caused a compressed air explosion followed by the detonation of a torpedo warhead. The ship was destroyed.

Specification
'Archimede' class
Type: sea-going submarine
Displacement: 985 tons surfaced and 1,259 tons submerged
Dimensions: length 70.50 m (231 ft 4 in); beam 6.83 m (22 ft 5 in); draught 4.10 m (13 ft 6 in)
Propulsion: surfaced diesels

delivering 3,000 bhp (2235 kW) and submerged electric motors delivering 1,300 hp (970 kW) to two shafts
Speed: surfaced 17 kts and submerged 8 kts
Range: surfaced 19000 km (11,805 miles) at 8 kts and submerged 195 km (121 miles) at 3 kts
Armament: two 100-mm (3.9-in) guns, two 13.2-mm (0.52-in) machine-guns, and eight 533-mm (21-in) torpedo tubes (four forward and four aft) with 16 torpedoes
Complement: 55

The 'Archimede' class submarine Galilei is seen about to be taken in tow by the British destroyer Kandahar. Noxious gases filled the boat and caused her surrender.

Allied Submarines

While not achieving the notoriety of the German 'wolf packs', Allied submarine forces still made significant contributions to the war effort. In Europe they were active from Norway to the Mediterranean, and in the Far East the collapse of the Japanese economy at the end of the war was largely due to the US submarine blockade.

Submarines sighted in the Atlantic during World War II were, very likely, those of the Germans, for the area was largely devoid of targets for Allied boats. The British, reinforced by such submarines as were able to escape their various countries' rapid collapse, concentrated their efforts in European waters, where the Axis forces were forced to risk surface movement. Thus, submarine attack was used effectively in the Norwegian campaign, against U-boats that were in transit, and also in the long struggle in the Mediterranean. The shortage of boats, as in everything else in World War II, obliged the British initially to a virtual denuding of the Far East of larger submarines for use in constricted waters where they proved to be both unsatisfactory and vulnerable. When, eventually, the Far East itself was engulfed in war, the British submarine presence was only minimal, many of the diverted boats having already been lost. It was only when the Mediterranean sea war effectively came to an end following the surrender of enemy forces in North Africa that the Royal Navy was able to redeploy its improved 'T' class boats to the eastern theatre, where the submarine

USS *Swordfish* being launched in 1941. The US Navy used its submarines to good effect in a blockade of Japan, and *Swordfish* sank the first of more than 1000 Japanese merchant ships.

war against Japan was already dominated by the Americans.

The position of the American submarine arm vis-a-vis the Japanese mercantile marine was analogous to the relationship between the Germans and the British at this time. Both maritime-based empires depended upon their seaborne trade; it stood to reason that if this area could be throttled the empire would inevitably collapse. Because the British were experienced they were also prepared. As a result they were to survive the onslaught (albeit narrowly). The Japanese, however, laid themselves wide open and were totally blinkered to the truth of their own shortcomings. The typical skipper of an American submarine time and again proved himself to be determined, adaptable and highly innovative, devising original and bold attack techniques. His fleet organization gave him full backing with temporary advanced bases and tenders used to the full to follow the war's advance, shortening transit times and maximizing time on patrol.

FRANCE
'Saphir' class

Like the Royal Navy, the French had a six-strong class of minelaying submarines, the **'Saphir' class** of 1925-9. These were much smaller than the British boats, being geared to Mediterranean operations. Again, as a mine capable of being launched through a standard torpedo tube had not been developed, the hull design was dominated by the mine stowage. The design for this had been produced by the well-known submarine builder, Normand, but was based on that of the British 'E' class minelayers of 1914-8: 16 vertical chutes were built into the space between the widely-separated double hulls, in four groups of four, and each chute could accommodate two mines, though a weakness of the arrangement was that these were of special manufacture. The British had abandoned the system in favour of laying over the stern with the mines stowed within the upper casing.

Four stretched versions, continuing the 'jewel' names as the **'Emeraude' class**, were scheduled to follow in 1937-8. Lengthened by nearly 7 m (22.97 ft), they would have carried 25 per cent more mines, but only the nameship was ever laid down and she was destroyed on the slip at the occupation.

Of the 'Saphirs', three (*Nautilus, Saphir* and *Turquoise*) were taken by the enemy at Bizerta and one (*Le Diamant*) was scuttled at Toulon. The *Rubis* and *Perle* operated for the duration of the war (the latter was sunk in error by British aircraft in July 1944) under the Free French flag. The *Rubis* began operating with the British Home Fleet in April 1940, laying mines in Norwegian waters. Between then and

the end of 1944 she carried out no less than 22 successful minelaying operations, most to interrupt the enemy's coast-hugging mercantile routes. The total of 15 ships known to have been destroyed on her mines included several Scandinavians carrying German ore cargoes, a minesweeper and four small anti-submarine vessels. She also torpedoed and sank one more, a Finn.

Specification
'Saphir' class
Displacement: 761 tons surfaced and 925 tons submerged
Dimensions: length 65.90 m (216.21 ft); beam 7.12 m (23.36 ft); draught 4.30 m (14.11 ft)

Propulsion: two diesels delivering 969.4 kW (1,300 bhp) and two electric motors delivering 820.3 kW (1,100 hp) to two shafts
Speed: 12 kts surfaced and 9 kts submerged
Endurance: 12970 km (8,059 miles) at 7.5 kts surfaced and 148 km (92 miles) at 4 kts submerged
Armament: one 75-mm (2.95-in) gun, three 550-mm (21.65-in) torpedo tubes (two bow and one stern), two 400-mm (15.75-in) torpedo tubes in a trainable mounting, and 32 mines
Complement: 42

The most successful minelaying submarine of the war, Rubis was responsible in her 22 minelaying patrols for the sinking of at least 15 vessels. These included five warships as well as vessels running iron ore in coastal convoys to Germany.

FRANCE
'Surcouf' class

Most of the major maritime nations at sometime or other experimented with the idea of the cruiser submarine. All were larger than usual, with an exceptional surface armament and good endurance. Some carried an aircraft to increase their effective search radius. The only design to combine, reasonably successfully, all these features in one hull was the *Surcouf*. Ordered under the 1926 programme as the first in a class of three, she was destined to be the only unit of the **'Surcouf' class**, and the largest submarine in the world in terms of displacement, though shorter than both the American 'Narwhal' and the Japanese 'A' boats.

At the time of the Washington Treaty the British *M1* to *M3* had 304.8-mm (12-in) guns and, to prevent further escalation in this direction (though even these were overlarge and totally unwieldy) the treaty limited future submarines to 203.2-mm (8-in) weapons. Only the French ever fitted the latter, and these to the *Surcouf*, paired in a complex pressure-tight turret. This structure was faired into a pressure-tight 'hangar' abaft it and containing a specially-designed Besson M.B.411 floatplane. This had to be taken out and the wings attached before it could be lowered into the water, a time-consuming and highly risky business which, while acceptable in 1926, was certainly not in 1939-45. Only the French could ever have specified the

torpedo tube fit. This comprised four 550-mm (21.65-in) tubes set in an orthodox bow arrangement, with six reloads; one quadruple 550-mm trainable mounting in the casing threequarters aft; and a quadruple 400-mm (15.75-in) trainable mounting in the casing right aft, with four reloads.

The suggested mode of operation of submarines such as these was always rather woolly and the *Surcouf*, like the rest of her kind, was never to find a proper role. Seized in Plymouth in July 1940, she was operated by a Free French crew on several Atlantic pat-

rols. In December 1941 she participated with three French corvettes in the seizure of the Vichy islands of St Pierre and Miquelon, in the St Lawrence estuary. In February 1942 she sank in the Caribbean after a collision.

Specification
'Surcouf' class
Displacement: 3,270 tons surfaced and 4,250 tons submerged
Dimensions: length 110.00 m (360.89 ft); beam 9.00 m (29.53 ft); draught 9.07 m (29.76 ft)
Propulsion: two diesels delivering

5667.3 kW (7,600 bhp) and two electric motors delivering 2535.4 kW (3,400 hp) to two shafts
Speed: 18 kts surfaced and 8.5 kts submerged
Endurance: 18531 km (11,515 miles) at 10 kts surfaced and 111 km (69 miles) at 5 kts submerged
Armament: two 203.2-mm (8-in) guns, two 37-mm guns, eight 550-mm (21.65-in) torpedo tubes (four bow and four in a trainable mounting), and four 400-mm (15.75-in) torpedo tubes (in a trainable mounting aft)
Complement: 118

Surcouf, seen here in the Clyde estuary, was a product of the inter-war concept of the 'cruiser submarine', espoused by many navies. She was the closest of all such designs to being a success, without ever having the chance to be employed against enemy merchant shipping.

USA
Old 'S' class

Like the 'O' and 'R' classes, the World War I-designed 'S' class (or 'Sugar') boats were well represented in the US Navy in December 1941, when the USA found itself in World War II. Sixty-four of these boats were still available, though many had for years been involved only in training. All suffered from having been designed at a time when the submarine was still regarded by the US Navy as a weapon for use in the defence of home territory. None, therefore, had adequate endurance for the Pacific operations that, with Japan as an ally in 1914-8, had not been foreseeable.

The 'O' and 'R' boats were fitted with 457-mm (18-in) torpedo tubes and had poor endurance, and the general specification for the improved 'S' class had

been put out to competition. At this time, US submarine practice was dominated by the companies owned by Holland and Lake; each tendered, together with the Portsmouth Navy Yard. Three prototypes were built to the designs, the S2 by Lake being thought unsatisfactory. In total, 25 Holland-designed boats, known as the 'S' class Group 1, were launched between 1918 and 1922, followed by six of an improved version known as the 'S' class Group 3. The 15 'S' class Group 2 boats were to the naval design (some built by Lake's yard), and these were followed by four improved 'S' class Group 4 boats. Though all had about the same speed, armament and complement, they varied greatly in size and, somewhat, in endurance. All

were of double-hulled design, one carried a seaplane for an experimental period, and four were fitted with an extra tube aft.

Six were transferred to the Royal Navy early in the war, one then being passed on to the Poles. As the *Jastrzab* she was sunk in error by the British in the course of a convoy action in 1942; by tragic irony, one of the escorts concerned was also ex-American, the 'four-piper' HMS *St Albans*. Most of the American 'S' class boats in the Far East had been replaced by newer boats by late 1943, but some had success. Before the Savo Island action, for instance, Mikawa's approach was sighted and reported by the *S38*, and the *S44* exacted a toll of the victors by sending

the *Kako* to the bottom. In October 1943 this old veteran's luck ran out and she was sunk near the Kamchatka peninsula.

Specification
Old 'S' class (first group)
Displacement: 854 tons surfaced and 1,065 tons submerged
Dimensions: length 66.83 m (219.25 ft); beam 6.30 m (20.67 ft); draught 4.72 m (15.5 ft)
Propulsion: two diesels delivering 894.8 kW (1,200 bhp) and two electric motors delivering 1118.6 kW (1,500 hp) to two shafts
Speed: 14.5 kts surfaced and 11 kts submerged
Endurance: 9270 km (5,760 miles) at 10 kts surfaced
Armament: one 101.6- or 76.2-mm (4- or 3-in) gun and four or five 533-mm (21-in) torpedo tubes (all bow or four bow and one stern) for 12 torpedoes
Complement: 42

S28 as she appeared in 1943. One of the Holland-designed boats, she, along with her sisters, saw action early in the war, and at that time was not devoid of success. While most of the class was replaced by 1943, S28 was lost in 1944.

USA
'Narwhal' class

The two **'Narwhal' class** units USS *Narwhal* and *Nautilus* must be classed as a group with the USS *Argonaut* that immediately preceded them. The large German transport submarines that worked the eastern US seaboard during World War I made a great impression on an oceanically-minded navy, and the early 1920s saw designs produced for a minelayer (*V-4*, later *Argonaut*) and two cruiser submarines *Narwhal* (**V-5**) and *Nautilus* (**V-6**). They were all large, even the latter boats (3.20 m/10.5 ft the shorter) being of greater length than the monstrous French *Surcouf*. As a minelayer, the *V-4* could load 60 mines, which were laid through two tubes exiting beneath the counter.

Forward of the after bulkhead of the engine room the 'Narwhals' were nearly identical, mounting four torpedo tubes aft in place of the mine stowage, a smaller demand on space that accounted for their shorter length. To match the boat's endurance, torpedo stowage was on a grand scale, upwards of 36 being carried both within the hull and the casing topside. To stretch them even further, two 152.4-mm (6-in) deck guns were mounted, the largest in any American submarine. Scouting for targets was the task for a small seaplane, the plans for which were, however, dropped.

All were considered slow by US standards but, though all were due to be re-engined, only the *Nautilus* was so modified by the outbreak of war. The latter was fitted also with two extra tubes in the after casing and the other two gained four, all in the amidships casing, two firing forward and two aft.

Despite the US fleet's shortage of submarines in 1942, these three boats were considered too slow and vulnerable for combat patrols and were modified in various degrees for clandestine operations, running personnel and supplies. The *Nautilus* had facilities for refuelling long-range seaplanes, an echo of Japanese practice, but was never so used during hostilities. All operated particularly between their west Australian bases and the Philippines. The *Nautilus* finished off the stricken Japanese carrier *Soryu* after Midway, and landed personnel on an unoccupied island near Tarawa to build a secret airstrip. Other raids were carried out on Makin Island and Attu in the Aleutians. The *Argonaut* was lost in 1943.

Specification
'Narwhal' class (as built)
Displacement: 2,730 tons surfaced and 3,900 tons submerged
Dimensions: length 112.95 m

(370.58 ft); beam 10.13 m (33.25 ft); draught 4.80 m (15.75 ft)
Propulsion: combination drive with four diesels delivering 4026.8 kW (5,400 bhp) and two electric motors delivering 1894.1 kW (2,540 hp) to two shafts
Speed: 17 kts surfaced and 8 kts submerged
Endurance: 33354 km (20,725 miles) at 10 kts surfaced and 93 km (58 miles) at 5 kts submerged
Armament: two single 152.4-mm (6-in)

Narwhal and her sisters were the largest submarines in US service until the arrival of the nuclear submarines of the 1950s. In a scene from the happier pre-war days, Narwhal is seen towing a seaplane with engine trouble back to Pearl Harbor.

guns and six 533-mm (21-in) torpedo tubes (four bow and two stern) later increased to 10 tubes for 40 torpedoes
Complement: 89

USS Nautilus in pre-war trim. The two 'Narwhals' were thought to be too slow for fleet submarine work during the war, and were often used for clandestine operations, although it was Nautilus that finished off the stricken Soryu after Midway.

New 'S' class

Known as the **New 'S' class** because the early units confusingly took pendants of the Old 'S' class boats still in service, 16 boats were built in two very similar groups. Their design was based closely upon that of the preceding 1,320-ton 'P' class, but differed particularly in having a deeper stern to accommodate an increase in the after torpedo tube complement from two to four. The 'P' and 'S' class boats were the first all-welded submarines in the US Navy and, though techniques were still being developed, the workmanship was sound, as evinced by the survival of the USS *Salmon* (SS 182), lead boat of the **New 'S' class Group 1**, which was severely depth charged in October 1944 by four Japanese escorts after torpedoing a tanker off Kyushu. The combination of concussion and the effects of overpressures through being driven far below design depth left the hull dished between frames, but the boat made it home. Irreparable, she was eventually scrapped. The double hull of the American boats was a protective feature, provided that the ballast and fuel tanks within retained an ullage space over the liquid contents.

Composite propulsion systems were fitted in some, arrangements whereby the two forward diesels drove generators directly and the two after units were geared to the shafts, the gearing being shared also by two propulsion motors on each shaft. Though complex, the arrangement proved satisfactory.

Twelve reload torpedoes were located within the pressure hull and four more in external stowage in the casing, an arrangement vulnerable to the effects of depth charge attack. Two mines could be carried for each internal torpedo and laid through the tubes. Originally a 76.2-mm (3-in) gun was fitted, but this was changed to a 101.6-mm (4-in) weapon in the majority of boats. Wartime modifications saw the bulky 'sails' cut down to a profile similar to that of later classes.

The **New 'S' class Group 2** included the USS *Squalus* (SS 192), which foundered through an induction valve failure while on trials in May 1939. Salvaged and refitted, she survived the war as the USS *Sailfish*. The USS *Swordfish* (SS 193) was credited with the first Japanese merchantman sunk, a week after the outbreak of war.

Specification
New 'S' class ('Salmon' group)
Displacement: 1,440 tons surfaced and 2,200 tons submerged

Dimensions: length 93.88 m (308.0 ft); beam 7.98 m (26.17 ft); draught 4.34 m (14.25 ft)
Propulsion: composite drive with four diesels delivering 4101.4 kW (5,500 bhp) and four electric motors delivering 1983.6 kW (2,660 hp) to two shafts
Speed: 21 kts surfaced and 9 kts submerged
Endurance: 18532 km (11,515 miles) at 10 kts surfaced and 158 km (98 miles) at 5 kts submerged
Armament: one 76.2-mm (3-in) gun

The launch of USS Swordfish, *on 1 April 1941. Few of those present could have foreseen that in nine months, within a week of Pearl Harbor,* Swordfish *would sink the first of 1,113 Japanese merchant ships to fall victim to the US submarine fleet.*

(later upgraded to one 101.6-mm/4-in gun in most units) and eight 533-mm (21-in) torpedo tubes (four bow and four stern) for 24 (later 20) torpedoes
Complement: 75

'Gato' class

From the New 'S' class design the Americans developed the **'T' class** submarine, a dozen of which were launched in barely 13 months, mostly in 1940. They differed primarily in receiving two extra tubes forward (10 in all) and later substituting a specially-modified 127-mm (5-in) deck gun for the earlier 101.6-mm (4-in) gun, or 76.2-mm (3-in) gun in some cases. This gradual evolutionary process was successful and produced at the right time a submarine with acceptable characteristics for the Pacific war. What was needed was a long endurance and self-sufficiency. Because of the distances involved, patrols were much longer than those in the European theatre and more boats were needed to maintain numbers on station.

Thus the **'Gato' class** was an improved 'T' and went into volume production, the first of class, the USS *Drum* (SS 228), being completed shortly before hostilities commenced. Officially capable of operating down to 91 m (300 ft) they often went deeper. The earlier boats had a large, solid looking sail, similar to those of pre-war designs. These were soon reduced as boats came in for repair but, although the structure could be lowered the very high standards ('shears') demanded by the long periscopes remained a lofty feature. Operating on the surface more than would have been possible in European waters, they began also to accumulate varied outfits of

automatic weapons, regular and non-regular, the structures gaining various platforms to support them. Even extra main-calibre deck guns appeared, all in the cause of making the 24 torpedoes aboard last longer.

After 73 boats the hull was secretly improved by the adoption of HT steels and advanced sections, increasing their official limit to 122-m (400-ft) depths. No less than 256 of these were ordered and known as the **'Balao' class**, but only 122 were actually completed, a further 10 unfinished hulls being scrapped.

The combined group formed the backbone of the US Navy's wartime submarine strength, achieved much and suffered 29 losses. Post-war, with the example of German developments, many were modernized under the GUPPY programmes, remaining the greater part of the fleet's underwater arm until introduction of the nuclear boats. Many 'went foreign', some still serving.

Specification
'Gato' class
Displacement: 1,525 tons surfaced and 2,415 tons submerged
Dimensions: length 95.02 m (311.75 ft); beam 8.31 m (27.25 ft); draught 4.65 m (15.25 ft)

A 'Gato' class boat of late 1942. By this time production was approaching three per month from three separate yards, and operational experience was being incorporated through the adoption of a smaller sail and more weapons for surface work.

USS Darter *aground on Bombay shoal during the battle of Leyte Gulf. After the triumph of the previous day when she torpedoed and sank the cruiser* Atago *(flagship of Admiral Kurita), as well as damaging the cruiser* Takao, *she was badly damaged and finally scuttled on 24 October.*

Propulsion: four diesels delivering 4026.8 kW (5,400 bhp) and four electric motors delivering 2043.2 kW (2,740 hp) to two shafts
Speed: 20 kts surfaced and 8.5 kts submerged
Endurance: 21316 km (13,245 miles) at 10 kts surfaced and 175 km (109 miles) at 5 kts submerged
Armament: one 127-mm (5-in) gun and 10 533-mm (21-in) torpedo tubes (six bow and four stern) for 24 torpedoes
Complement: 80

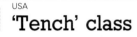
USA

'Tench' class

The **'Tench' class** marked the ultimate refinement in the basic design whose ancestry could be traced back to the 'P' class. Externally they were virtually identical with the 'Balaos', and so closely related was the design that some of the later Balao contracts were converted to 'Tenches'. Though 25 boats had been completed by the end of hostilities, most were still working up in home waters; not a dozen, therefore, managed to see operational duty and none of these was lost. Total production was 33 boats between 1944 and 1946, with another 101 cancelled or scrapped incomplete.

Differences, though not obvious, were important. The first concerned machinery. In the 'Balao' class the four diesels each ran a direct-coupled generator, which served both to charge batteries and power the electric propulsion motors when surfaced. Each shaft had two motors, coupled to it via reduction gearing. Both the high-speed motors and the reduction gear were noisy (to the extent where it was fortunate that Japanese ASW techniques and equipment were so backward). Reduction gears were also expensive, temperamental, easy to damage and, traditionally, a slow delivery item in the USA (as was the turbo-electric propulsion in battleships). It made sense, therefore, to develop a large and slow-turning motor that could be direct-coupled. Two of these larger units, with no associated gear housings, could be accommodated without the earlier awkward crank in the hull, but illustrates some of the problems facing submarine designers.

Fuel and ballast tanks were better organized, firstly to obviate the need to lead the vents of the ballast tanks through the pressure hull (where they constituted a flooding hazard) and, secondly, the better to compensate for the considerable change in weight and trim as stores were consumed during a long patrol. Even a further four torpedo reloads were squeezed in, and this, combined with radar and efficient mechanical fire-control computers, put the 'Tenches' far ahead of the opposition. In order to improve on the average, but slow, diving times of 55-60 seconds, the casings were pierced with many more lightening holes.

Specification
'Tench' class
Displacement: 1,570 tons surfaced and 2,415 tons submerged
Dimensions: length 95.0 m (311.67 ft); beam 8.31 m (27.25 ft); draught 4.65 m (15.25 ft)
Propulsion: four diesels delivering 4026.8 kW (5,400 bhp) and two electric motors delivering 2043.2 kW

(2,740 hp) to two shafts
Speed: 20 kts surfaced and 9 kts submerged
Endurance: 21316 km (13,245 miles) at 10 kts surfaced and 204 km (127 miles) at 4 kts
Armament: one or two 127-mm (5-in) guns and 10 533-mm (21-in) torpedo tubes (six bow and four stern) for 28 torpedoes

USS Pickerel, *one of the later war-built fleet submarines, caught during one of the most dramatic methods of surfacing. Transferred to Italy in 1972 after extensive updating, she served under the name* Gianfranco Gazzana Priaroggia *until 1981.*

Complement: 81

447

'O', 'P' and 'R' classes

The 'O' class (later 'Oberon' class) was developed as a replacement for the ocean-going 'L' class of World War I design. They were categorized as overseas patrol submarines, and it is of interest to note that, even as early as the concept stage in 1922, there was a requirement for long range with an eye to possible future operations against Japan (an ally during 1914-8). The lead boat, HMS *Oberon*, was laid down by Chatham Dockyard in 1924 and was closely followed by two sisters, HMS *Otway* and *Oxley*. Six bow and two stern tubes were fitted, with a reload for each. These, together with extensive bunker spaces, made for a large hull which proved distinctly unhandy, with speed reduced by a plethora of external fittings. Even after much fairing and attention they barely achieved their designed surface speed, and failed altogether to reach

the required speed submerged.

The hull was fitted with saddle tanks, which contained most of the ballast capacity. Some could double as extra fuel tanks but were unpopular as they inevitably emitted telltale oil traces through leaky rivet heads. As with the 'L' class boats, a 101.6-mm (4-in) gun was fitted in the tower to allow it to be worked in heavy seas.

Because of the limitations with the 'Oberons', an improved **'Odin' class** was evolved: longer to accommodate more powerful machinery and beamier to improve stability in the surfaced condition. Completed in 1928-9, these boats were HMS *Odin*, *Olympus*, *Orpheus*, *Osiris*, *Oswald* and *Otus*. Though still plagued by weeping oil, their outsides were marked by a great clean-up of general clutter. An interesting idea, fortunately not pursued, was to install auxiliary accom-

modation in the upper casing to ease the confines of the crew on extended patrols. The **'Parthian'** and **'Rainbow' classes** were essentially 'Odin' repeats; six of each were ordered, differing only in detail. Two 'Rainbows' were ultimately cancelled, and the units completed in 1929-30 were HMS *Parthian*, *Perseus*, *Phoenix*, *Poseidon*, *Proteus*, *Pandora*, *Rainbow*, *Regent*, *Regulus* and *Rover*.

Most of the 'O' class boats were in the Far East in September 1939 but one of those in home waters, the *Oxley*, had the melancholy record of being the first British submarine lost when torpedoed in error by another British submarine, HMS *Triton*. Of the joint class total of 18, 12 were lost, most by the end of 1940 and many in the Mediterranean, for whose confines they were totally unsuited.

Specification
'Odin' class
Displacement: 1,781 tons surfaced and 2,038 tons submerged
Dimensions: length 86.41 m (283.5 ft); beam 9.12 m (29.92 ft); draught 4.17 m (13.67 ft)
Propulsion: two diesels delivering 3281.1 kW (4,400 bhp) and two electric motors delivering 984.3 kW (1,320 hp) to two shafts
Speed: 17.5 kts surfaced and 9 kts submerged
Endurance: 21123 km (13,125 miles) at 8 kts surfaced and 97 km (60 miles) at 4 kts submerged
Armament: one 101.6-mm (4-in) gun and eight 533-mm (21-in) torpedo tubes (six bow and two stern)
Complement: 53

HMS Odin *as she appeared at the start of the war. Completed in the late 1920s, the 'O' class were large vessels designed to operate down to 90 m (300 ft). Odin was sunk in 1940 by Italian destroyers.*

'Porpoise' class

Based on the recently-completed 'Parthians', the **'Porpoise' class** submarines were purpose-built minelayers. German practice tended to near-vertical mine shutes located within the envelope of the pressure hull, but the British preferred external stowage, despite risk of damage from overpressures or depth-charging. 'E' and 'L' class minelayers had had stowages in the saddle tanks on each side but, in the experimental conversion of the *M3* in 1927, tracks were laid atop the hull over the greater part of her length and inside the free-flooding space contained within an extra-deep casing. An endless-chain mechanism fed the mines through doors right aft as the submarine moved slowly ahead. This system was basically that incorporated in the 'Porpoises'; in the name ship it extended over about three-quarters of her length, but was longer in the remainder. All this gear added about 54 tons of topweight, making the boats very tender when first surfaced with a full load in a heavy sea. Extra

lightening holes improved both draining and flooding time, allowing the boats also to dive more quickly. Launched between 1932 and 1938, the boats were HMS *Porpoise*, *Grampus*, *Narwhale*, *Rorqual*, *Cachalot* and *Seal*. Three other units were cancelled.

Being weight-critical the class took rather small diesel engines, resulting in a modest surface speed. To avoid detection from fuel leaks all bunkers were internal, it being found necessary to extend the pressure hull downwards like a box keelson to meet the saddle tanks. This oddly-shaped and weaker cross-section undoubtedly contributed to the designed depth being limited to 91 m (300 ft) com-

pared with the 152 m (500 ft) of the 'Parthians'.

The main function of the 'Porpoises' was, officially at least, superseded by the development of a mine capable of being laid through a conventional torpedo tube. But despite this the class was still to lay some 2,600 mines operationally. They proved invaluable during the height of the siege of Malta when, in concert with the available 'O' class boats, they moved in personnel and supplies. The *Seal*, after damaging herself by mine in the Kattegat and unable to dive, had to surrender to two Arado floatplanes. Repaired, she was recommissioned as the *UB-A* but not used operationally. Only the *Rorqual* survived World War II.

Specification
'Porpoise' class
Displacement: 1,768 tons surfaced and 2,053 tons submerged
Dimensions: length 88.09 m (289.0 ft); beam 9.09 m (29.83 ft); draught 4.88 m (16.0 ft)
Propulsion: two diesels delivering 2460.8 kW (3,300 bhp) and two electric motors delivering 1215.5 kW (1,630 hp) to two shafts
Speed: 15.5 kts surfaced and 9 kts submerged
Endurance: 21308 km (13,240 miles) at 8 kts surfaced and 122 km (76 miles) at 4 kts submerged
Armament: one 101.6 mm (4-in) gun, six 533-mm (21-in) torpedo tubes (all bow) for 12 torpedoes, and 50 mines
Complement: 59

Similar to the 'Parthian' class from which it was derived, Porpoise could lay some 50 mines. She was sunk by Japanese aircraft in January 1945.

'Thames' class

With the steam-driven 'K' class boats and the experimental *X1*, the Royal Navy had attempted to produce submarines with characteristics appropriate for operations with the surface fleet. Unfortunately, the 'K' boats were disastrously problem-prone and the *X1* remained a one-off. The requirement still existed, therefore, for a boat to fill the role while avoiding the weaknesses of the 'O' class. Adhering to the limitations of the Geneva Conference it was decided to build 20 boats, each of the maximum allowable surface displacement of 1,800 tons, with the combined functions of fleet work and long-range patrols. In the event, with the surface fleet becoming faster, policy was changed and only three of the class were completed between 1932 and 1934 as the **'Thames' class** units HMS **Thames**, **Severn** and **Clyde**. The boats were only 1.83 m (6 ft) shorter overall than the monstrous 'K' class boats and were actually beamier overall, despite a narrower pressure hull. In cross-section the hull was carried downward at the keel to meet the line of the outer hull. Little oil fuel was carried inboard, most of it being stowed in spaces above the main ballast tanks. Weepage was apt to be into the main hull through started rivet-heads.

Only now were diesels available of the size and power to match the 'K' class legend speed of 23.5 kts. Engine design was by the Admiralty, and turned out to be lighter than forecast. This was fortunate as the boats were highly weight-critical. For their extended patrols, for instance, 41 tons of fresh and distilled water were carried, some two per cent of surface displacement. General submarine policy of substituting 101.6-mm (4-in) for 119.4-

mm (4.7-in) guns saved some 6 tons, while a further 8 tons was gained by burning fuel of a lower specific gravity.

In the Norwegian campaign of 1940, the *Thames* was lost on a mine, while the *Clyde* succeeded in damaging the *Gneisenau* by torpedo. The *Clyde* ran an invaluable 1,200 tons of supplies to a beleaguered Malta and sank several enemy merchantmen while working out of Gibraltar. The *Severn* was active for a time in the little-known Levant operations.

Specification
'Thames' class
Displacement: 2,165 tons surfaced and 2,680 tons submerged
Dimensions: length 105.16 m (345.0 ft); beam 8.61 m (28.25 ft); draught 4.78 m (15.67 ft)
Propulsion: two diesels delivering 7457.0 kW (10,000 bhp) and two electric motors delivering 1864.25 kW (2,500 hp) to two shafts
Speed: 22.5 kts surfaced and 10.5 kts submerged
Endurance: 18532 km (11,515 miles) at

The 'Thames' class submarine HMS Clyde is seen acting as escort while the tanker Dingledale *refuels the 'Dido' class cruiser* Hermione. *These large boats were very capable and about 20 had been planned in the early 1930s.*

8 kts surfaced and 219 km (136 miles) at 4 kts submerged
Armament: one 101.6-mm (4-in) gun and six 533-mm (21-in) torpedo tubes (all bow) for 12 torpedoes
Complement: 61

'S' class

Though its origins went back to 1928, the **'S' class** was highly successful during the war and, with 62 completions, was the Royal Navy's most prolific class. Ostensibly 'H' class replacements, the performance of the 'S' class boats was required to be enhanced to allow operation in the Baltic and Mediterranean. A tight, 600-ton surfaced displacement target was set to produce a small submarine which, nevertheless, was required to be able to transit 805 km (500 miles) to and from its patrol area, where it was expected to remain up to 10 days. Any increase in the 805-km (500-mile) range meant having to find space for very much larger radio equipment. The specification was later to be altered drastically, calling for 1930-km (1,200-mile) passages at not less than 9 kts and eight days on station.

Initially, a class of four (**'Swordfish' type**) was built; launched between 1931 and 1933 by Chatham Dockyard, these displaced 640 tons despite every effort at weight control. The design was really too tight and was relaxed to 670 tons for the eight lengthened **'Shark' type** boats of 1934-7. Though it was planned to terminate the class at 12, war saw the design stretched further and constructed in series.

To save on topweight a 76.2-in (3-in) gun was fitted but, with the extra hull length, a further torpedo tube was worked-in aft on some boats. Others traded both of these for a single 101.6-

mm (4-in) gun. With only 12 or 13 torpedoes aboard, the gun was a useful means of disposing of 'soft' targets which, while not warranting the expenditure of a torpedo, were often reluctant to sink. Earlier boats had fuel tanks within the pressure hull, but later units supplemented these with external capacity, which allowed them to work even in the Far East.

Interestingly, eight units were lost from the original 12, the same number as were lost from the following 50. All of the first group losses occurred before February 1941, while the first hull of succeeding groups was not launched until October 1941. Submarine operations in European waters during the early months of the war were clearly hazardous.

HMS Storm *returns to the UK in 1945. During her Far East commission, she sank 20 Japanese supply vessels – 19 by gunfire – together with a destroyer and four escorts. On her most successful patrol she sank 11 vessels, nine on a single day. Note that torpedoes were reserved for warships, gunfire sufficing to despatch cargo ships.*

Specification

'S' class (later boats)
Displacement: 860 tons surfaced and 990 tons submerged
Dimensions: length 66.14 m (217.0 ft); beam 7.16 m (23.5 ft); draught 3.20 m (10.5 ft)
Propulsion: two diesels delivering 1416.8 kW (1,900 bhp) and two electric motors delivering 969.4 kW (1,300 hp) to two shafts
Speed: 15 kts surfaced and 9 kts submerged
Endurance: 13897 km (8,635 miles) at 10 kts surfaced

HMS Sibyl enters Algiers harbour in May 1943. Originally intended for operations in the Mediterranean and Baltic, 'S' class boats also found themselves in the East Indies. Sixty-two were produced, making them the largest class in the Royal Navy.

Armament: one 101.6-mm (4-in) gun and six 533-mm (21-in) torpedo tubes, or one 76.2-mm (3-in) gun and seven 533-mm torpedo tubes
Complement: 44

 UK

'T' class

Instantly recognizable as a result of their oddly cranked profiles, the **'T' class** boats were the Royal Navy's standard wartime patrol submarines. Between HMS *Triton* and *Tabard*, launched in October 1937 and November 1945 respectively, the class reached a respectable 54 in number. With the 'Thames' class abandoned for the reasons discussed and a replacement required for the unsatisfactory 'O' class, the 'T' class design needed not only to rectify shortcomings but also to conform to the treaty agreements that bedevilled interwar planning. The London Naval Treaty limited total (rather than individual) displacement so, to obtain maximum numbers of boats, a 1,000-ton target was set. Into this a 42-day endurance was to be packed. That the final result was only some 9 per cent heavy, while being highly reliable, was a credit to the design team.

Because of their limiting parameters, the 'T' class boats could ship only small-sized diesels and their surface speed was thus modest. In contrast they carried a large punch, the six forward tubes within the pressure hull being augmented by a pair in the bulged bow casing and a further pair in the casing, one on each side of the tower. Thus, a 10-torpedo forward salvo could be fired, albeit at the cost of a highly individual profile.

This arrangement applied to all 22 boats built before World War II, later units having the amidships tubes taken farther aft and reversed, and a single tube added in the casing right aft. War-built boats also had their bows altered to set the external tubes higher, and some external ballast tanks converted to bunker space. Oil fuel capacity was almost doubled and the endurance of the boat became more than that of her crew and their supplies.

Fourteen of the pre-war boats were lost, mainly in the Mediterranean. Those from the wartime programmes were completed largely after the end of the Mediterranean war and only one was lost at sea. Post-war many were sold, while others were stretched and streamlined, serving alongside their successors, the 'A' class, until the late 1960s. Four units were cancelled and another only projected.

Below: HMS Tigris seen alongside a depot ship just before her final patrol. She was one of the original 'T' class boats, launched in October 1939, but she was lost in March 1943, probably to mines. Note the external tubes at the bow and amidships, and the unusual hull profile.

Above: HMS Tally-ho in transit to the Far East. Such passages of the Bitter Lakes of the Suez canal had become more common in January 1945, with any German naval threat extinct and resources gradually being released for service against the Japanese.

Specification

'T' class
Displacement: 1,325 tons surfaced and 1,570 tons submerged
Dimensions: length 83.82 m (275.0 ft); beam 8.10 m (26.58 ft); draught 4.50 m (14.75 ft)
Propulsion: two diesels delivering 1864.25 kW (2,500 bhp) and two electric motors delivering 1081.3 kW (1,450 hp) to two shafts
Speed: 15.25 kts surfaced and 9 kts submerged
Endurance: 20382 km (12,665 miles) at 10 kts surfaced
Armament: one 101.6-mm (4-in) gun and 10 or 11 533-mm (21-in) torpedo tubes (in first group 10 bow and in second group eight bow and three stern)
Complement: 56 (first group) or 61 (second group)

Below: The 'T' class 1940 designs were slow but of long endurance, although because of their limited size they were not capable of supporting their crews for such a length of time.

'U' and 'V' classes

For a simple, unsophisticated type, the 'U' class proved remarkably successful. Seen in Mediterranean colours, and with the original bow form, it was boats like this, out of Malta, that put a stranglehold on Rommel and his army.

A successful type, the single-hulled **'U' class** boats were designed originally as unarmed targets to replace the elderly 'H' class boats, and were little larger. Three were laid down as such but, as the Royal Navy did not possess a modern 'coastal' submarine, it seemed advantageous to modify the bow to take torpedo tubes from the outset. The after hull had a sharp taper and the casing ended short of the stern, so all armament was set forward, four tubes in the pressure hull and, surprisingly (though a reflection on the doubtful accuracy of the torpedo salvoes of the day), the bow casing was also bulged to take two more. This was not a good feature as the restricted height of the design meant a shallow periscope depth, and the oversize bow casing made it both difficult to maintain constant depth and also caused a distinctive 'pressure hump' in the water above. With the outbreak of war a further group of 12 boats was ordered, 1.6 m (5.25 ft) longer to improve the lines and ease the cramped internals; most of these had only four tubes. Thirty-four more boats of this type followed, with improved lines and increased bunker space. Though extremely handy, the 'U' class boats were rather limited in diving depth and had a low surface speed.

Again, therefore, the design was updated. This time an extra midbody section was inserted to house uprated machinery, and the hull was redesigned to permit submergence to 91 m (300 ft) rather than the 60 m (200 ft) of the earlier boats, and to facilitate all-welded construction in modules that would produce faster building times. This later type was known as the **'V' class**, of which 33 were ordered but only 21 completed. It is a noteworthy fact that, except for two early units built in Chatham Dockyard, all 81 boats were built in the two Vickers Armstrong yards at Barrow and on Tyneside.

The 'U' and 'V' classes were particularly suited to the shallow and confined waters of the North Sea and Mediterranean but, though successful, they suffered 19 losses. After the end of the Mediterranean war they had little use and many were either transferred or reverted to a training role.

Specification
'V' class
Displacement: 670 tons surfaced and 740 tons submerged
Dimensions: length 62.79 m (206.0 ft); beam 4.88 m (16.0 ft); draught 4.72 m (15.5 ft)
Propulsion: two diesels delivering 596.6 kW (800 bhp) and two electric motors delivering 566.7 kW (760 hp) to two shafts
Speed: 12.5 kts surfaced and 9 kts submerged
Endurance: 8715 km (5,415 miles) at 10 kts surfaced and 113 km (70 miles) at 7 kts submerged
Armament: one 76.2-mm (3-in) gun and four 533-mm (21-in) torpedo tubes (all bow) for eight torpedoes
Complement: 37

The 'V' class represented an improved and updated 'U' design permitting deeper diving and quieter underwater operations. All survived the war, unlike the preceding version, and many served post-war with Europan navies.

HMS Utmost alongside a depot ship (either Forth or Maidstone) and the 'S' class boat Seawolf. Utmost had recently returned from a Mediterranean commission, during which she torpedoed the heavy cruiser Trieste, causing severe damage as well as sinking several supply vessels and also undertaking other clandestine operations.

HMS Uproar shows the small size of these boats. In a short-range war, such as in the North Sea or the Mediterranean, endurance is much less important than manoeuvrability, and the 'U' class proved very handy, in spite of having been designed as a training boat.

British Aircraft Carriers

With a limited number of ships but with worldwide responsibilities, the Royal Navy deployed and operated its carriers in a very different way to the Americans. Yet despite their lack of numbers and mediocre aircraft, British carriers made a vital contribution to the victory at sea.

HMS *Victorious* fought in every major theatre of operations during World War II, even surviving two *kamikaze* attacks by the Japanese.

Though the British pioneered aviation at sea and at the end of World War I were well ahead of everybody in the field, they lost their way badly between the wars, squandering their great initial advantage. Probably the most contentious issue of the time was RAF control of the Fleet Air Arm for the two decades from 1918 to 1938, with interservice problems doing nothing for the spirit of the service. Second was the deteriorating performance of FAA aircraft in comparison with foreign equivalents: this problem was as much naval as RAF in origin but meant that, initially at least, the Royal Navy's aircraft were almost invariably outclassed in combat. Lastly, there were the ships themselves. The UK's naval appropriations between the wars resulted in the first of the third-generation carriers coming forward too late for working experience to be gained before the emergency programmes began. Thus, the Royal Navy entered the war with too few flightdecks, while those that were coming forward were, it could be argued, over-protected. With massive vertical armouring, their aircraft capacity was drastically reduced and construction times lengthened. Late in the war, it was quite convincingly shown that the later fleet carriers, with the same horizontal but much reduced vertical protection, survived kamikaze strikes as well as their heavier sisters, while enjoying the benefits of an enhanced aircraft capacity.

The Royal Navy fought a different type of war to the Americans and Japanese. Instead of the latters' vast trials of strength in a comparatively limited theatre, there were worldwide responsibilities in the defence of trade and vital outposts, together with long and patient operations against unwillingly disturbed fleets-in-being that could not be ignored. These functions, together with the value placed on each carrier, engendered a defensive approach. Only with the formation of the British Pacific Fleet could the Royal Navy permit itself the luxury of hazarding major units by going on the offensive. For the first time, four and five fleet carriers worked together, the irony being that they were fighting a war already won by a US fleet that overshadowed their efforts in every way. Yet a similar force working in European waters, even only a couple of years previously, would have rewritten maritime history.

HMS *Furious*

The several guises of HMS *Furious* represented the transitional stages between what might be termed 'air-capable' ships and the true aircraft-carrier. As the third of Admiral Fisher's 'tin-clad' light battle-cruisers (laid down in 1915), she was launched in August 1916 but delayed in completion to allow her to ship the navy's largest gun, a 457-mm (18-in) weapon, in single mounts at each end. Although virtually complete in March 1917, she then had her forward gun removed in favour of a sloping flying-off deck some 69.5 m (228 ft) in length. A hangar beneath this deck accommodated up to 10 aircraft (some seaplanes and some wheeled). Completed thus in July 1917 she rapidly showed the limitations of carrying aircraft that could not (officially at least) be recovered after a flight. In November 1917, therefore, her after gun mounting made way for a 86.6-m (284-ft) flying-on deck over a second hangar. Much of her superstructure still remained, however, and the high speeds at which she steamed to create the necessary wind-over-deck resulted in severe turbulence, causing an unacceptable accident rate among would-be landers-on. Relegated again to flying-off only, the *Furious* still had the distinction of mounting the first real carrier-based air strike when, on 19 July 1918, seven of her Sopwith Camels destroyed two Zeppelins and their sheds at Tondern. A through-deck was obviously required, as on the new *Argus*, and she was thus modified between 1921 and 1925. Even following this, she was still of interim design, having no island. Not until her final pre-war refit did she acquire a vestigial superstructure, topped-off by a diminutive mast that supported a distinctive homing beacon.

Despite her age and infirmities, the *Furious* saw service in Atlantic hunting groups and convoy escorts, the Norwegian campaign, aircraft-ferrying to both Malta and West Africa, and the North African landings. Her last flying was against the *Tirpitz*, immured in a Norwegian fjord, before she went into reserve during September 1944. She was scrapped in 1948.

Specification
HMS *Furious*
Type: fleet aircraft-carrier
Displacement: 22,500 tons standard and 28,500 tons full load
Dimensions: length 239.5 m (785.75 ft); beam 27.4 m (90 ft); draught 7.3 m (24 ft)
Propulsion: 4-shaft geared steam turbines delivering 90,000 shp (67113 kW)
Speed: 31.5 kts
Armour: belt 51-76 mm (2-3-in); hangar deck 38 mm (1.5 in)
Armament: six twin 102-mm (4-in) AA, three octuple 2-pdr AA, and several smaller-calibre guns
Aircraft: 33
Complement: 750 excluding aircrew

Above: Landing on HMS Furious's forward deck was very dangerous; Squadron Commander Dunning was killed when his Sopwith Pup overshot. In November 1917 the after 18-in gun was removed in favour of a flying-on deck.

Right: The first ship to launch an air strike, HMS Furious was originally designed for Admiral Fisher's plan to attack Germany's Baltic coast during World War I.

Right: HMS Furious in April 1927. The superstructure was removed in 1921 as it created serious turbulence problems. Further alterations took place in the 1930s, cross-deck arrester gear was fitted and the AA gun arrangement changed.

Below: In her World War II guise HMS Furious looked radically different from the ship that attacked the Zeppelin sheds in 1918. By the time she took part in Operation 'Torch', the Allied landings in North Africa, she carried 33 aircraft.

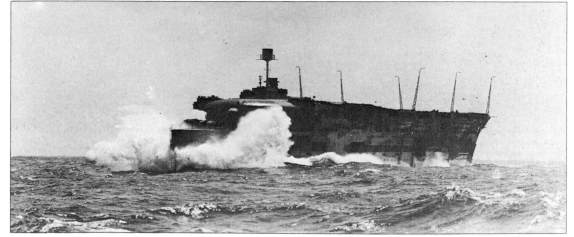

Below: The World War II camouflage does not conceal HMS Furious's battlecruiser origins. The island was not added until 1939.

HMS *Argus*

Proposals had been made before World War I for an aircraft-carrier with a straight-through flightdeck capable of handling the launch and recovery of wheeled aircraft, but the Royal Navy had to 'make do' with improvised seaplane carriers, and it was not until 1916 that the proposer, the Beardmore commercial yard, was given the contract to complete a half-finished Italian liner as a prototype carrier. The ship, the *Conte Rosso*, had been laid down in 1914 and had suitable dimensions plus the high freeboard necessary for the job. No superstructure was planned to interrupt the flightdeck which, like those of all pioneering carriers, was pointed at the forward end. A single hangar was provided and the necessary small charthouse was made retractable into the flightdeck. As full of character as she was devoid of grace, HMS *Argus* was understandably known as 'The Flatiron'.

Her name (Argus was all-vigilant, with 100 eyes) suggests that she was seen by planners as being strongly reconnaissance-orientated, particularly with the recent memory of Jutland, a victory lost for want of good intelligence. She was wanted for the end of 1917 but was launched only in December of that year, and eventually commissioned only weeks before the Armistice of November 1918, carrying a squadron of the unpopular Sopwith Cuckoo torpedo aircraft.

In the late 1920s the *Argus* was bulged to improve stability as much as to enhance survivability and, after the completion of the larger fleet carriers, acted as a training and target aircraft-carrier. Small and slow by World War II standards, she gave valuable service ferrying fighter aircraft to Gibraltar, Malta and Takoradi (for onward staged flights to Egypt). Lack of carriers saw her also in operational roles from time to time, notably on an Arctic convoy and at the North African landings. From mid-1943 she was used only for training in home waters, being paid off in 1944. She was scrapped in 1947.

HMS Argus *off the North African coast, November 1942. The Royal Navy's first flush-decked carrier started life as an Italian liner. She was extensively used as a trials ship in the years after World War I, proving the validity of the straight-through flightdeck design.*

Specification
HMS *Argus*
Type: training, aircraft-ferry and second-line aircraft-carrier
Displacement: 14,000 tons standard and 15,750 tons full load
Dimensions: length 172.2 m (565 ft); beam 20.7 m (68 ft); draught 7.3 m (24 ft)
Propulsion: 4-shaft geared steam turbines delivering 21,000 shp (15660 kW)
Speed: 20.5 kts
Armour: none
Armament: six 102-mm (4-in) AA, and several smaller-calibre guns
Aircraft: about 20
Complement: 370 excluding aircrew

Handicapped by her lack of speed, HMS Argus *was removed from front line service during the 1930s. She nevertheless had to act as a replacement carrier for Force H after Ark Royal was sunk.*

HMS *Eagle*

Before World War I, Chile ordered two stretched 'Iron Duke' class battleships from Armstrong's Elswick yard. Only one of these, the *Almirante Latorre*, was well advanced by August 1914; compulsorily purchased by the Admiralty, she was completed in 1915 as HMS *Canada*. Work on her unlaunched sister, the *Almirante Cochrane* (laid down in 1913) ceased with hostilities but she was taken in hand, post-Jutland, for completion as an aircraft-carrier. Like the *Hermes* she was far too late for the war, being launched in June 1918 and commissioning for extended trials in 1920. Several versions of the pioneering island superstructure were tried after initial experiments on the *Argus*. This kept her in dockyard hands for a great portion of the period between 1920 and 1923, when the *Hermes* was commissioned. The final version of the island was long and low, topped-off by two funnel casings with the same thick and thin proportions as the ship's erstwhile sister. Her more ample battleship proportions made her considerably slower than the large cruiser conversions, but she had better stability. Despite the fact that she introduced the two-level hangar, she still had only modest aircraft capacity.

Much of the *Eagle*'s pre-World War II service was in the Far East, but the carrier moved into the Indian Ocean in September 1939, thence to the Mediterranean to replace the *Glorious*. Following air strikes against Italian shipping at Tobruk she was badly shaken by bombing during the action off Calabria, suffering damage that eventually caused her to miss the

HMS Eagle *flew Spitfires to Malta during March 1942 and was sunk in August during Operation 'Pedestal'.*

HMS Eagle *spent the bulk of her service career on the China station, returning to the Mediterranean in spring 1940.*

Taranto raid. Before she could refit in the UK, she saw further action in the Red Sea and the South Atlantic. Arriving back in the Mediterranean early in 1942, she was later involved in the famous August convoy (Operation 'Pedestal') when 41 warships fought through just five out of 14 merchantmen to lift the Malta siege. The *Eagle* was a major casualty, sunk by four torpedoes from *U-73* on 11 August 1942.

Specification
HMS Eagle
Type: fleet aircraft-carrier
Displacement: 22,600 tons standard and 26,500 tons full load
Dimensions: length 203.3 m (667 ft); beam 32.1 m (105.25 ft); draught 7.3 m (24 ft)
Propulsion: 4-shaft geared steam turbines delivering 50,000 shp (37285 kW)
Speed: 24 kts
Armour: belt 102-178 mm (4-7 in); flightdeck 25 mm (1 in); hangar deck 102 mm (4 in), shields 25 mm (1 in)
Armament: nine 152-mm (6-in), four

102-mm (4-in) AA, and eight 2-pdr AA guns
Aircraft: 21
Complement: 750 excluding aircrew

HMS Eagle *photographed from a 'Queen Elizabeth' class battleship, probably HMS Malaya, in the Mediterranean, March 1942. During*

that month Eagle *made three sorties to Malta, flying off a total of 31 Spitfire Mk Vs.*

HMS *Hermes*

The *Argus* concept was obviously considered sound for early in 1918, before her completion, the keel was laid down for HMS *Hermes*. Though she was designed for the job, it was obviously not with the benefit of operational experience. Lacking a precedent, her designers made her too small, prompting the Japanese to repeat the error with their pioneer *Hosho*, laid down in the following year. With the end of World War I, construction was leisurely, the ship being launched in September 1919 and with completion delayed until 1923. As a result she entered service after the much larger but converted HMS *Eagle*, which had meanwhile proved the idea of the island superstructure. Like that of the *Eagle*, *Hermes*' island seemed disproportionately large, with a massive battleship-style tripod and fighting top, bearing rangefinders for the unusual armament of six 140-mm (5.5-in) guns: early carriers were expected to be able to repel light surface attack, the potential of their aircraft not having been fully evaluated. A light armour belt was also worked in. An improvement on the *Argus* was a doubling of installed power to give a speed increase of over 4 kts.

A distinctive feature on the after flightdeck was a low hump, designed to decelerate incoming aircraft. This was also copied by the Japanese, but neither fleet found it a success and abandoned it.

Though obsolete by World War II, the *Hermes* made an extremely valuable contribution in lower-threat areas. This found her hunting for raiders in the Atlantic, undertaking spotting and reconnaissance missions in operations against the Vichy French in West Africa and the Italians in the Red Sea, giving shore support during the suppression of the Iraqi rebellion of

HMS Hermes *served in the Far East for most of her career. This photograph clearly shows her unusually large island superstructure. Purpose-built, she carried almost as many aircraft as* Eagle, *a ship of twice her displacement.*

1941 and escorting Indian ocean convoys. She was sunk in April 1942 off Ceylon during the Japanese carrier raids, but had adequately demonstrated the value of even a small flightdeck in areas where no other aviation support existed.

Specification
HMS Hermes
Type: second-line light aircraft-carrier
Displacement: 10,850 tons standard and 12,950 tons full load
Dimensions: length 182.3 m (598 ft); beam 21.4 m (70.25 ft); draught 6.9 m (22.6 ft)
Propulsion: 2-shaft geared steam turbines delivering 40,000 shp (29828 kW)
Speed: 25 kts
Armour: belt 51-76 mm (2-3 in); hangar deck 25 mm (1 in) shields 25 mm (1 in)
Armament: six 140-mm (5.5-in), and three 102-mm (4-in) AA guns
Aircraft: about 20
Complement: 660 excluding aircrew

The first British carrier actually designed as such, HMS Hermes *was built along the lines of a light cruiser. She carried six 140-mm (5.5-in) guns, as it was not believed that aircraft alone could repel enemy surface attack.*

Above: HMS Hermes *sinks off Ceylon (Sri Lanka) after a Japanese carrier aircraft attack in April 1942. Symptomatic of British handling of the war in the Far East at this time, she had no aircraft aboard and no means of signalling for help if attacked.*

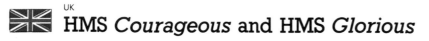

HMS *Courageous* and HMS *Glorious*

Known, for political reasons, as large light cruisers, Jackie Fisher's famous trio of light battle-cruisers were supposed to be the largest units of a 600-strong, shallow-draught armada constructed to realize his vision of landing an army on the Baltic coast of Germany, only 130 km (80 miles) from Berlin. The plan died with Fisher's departure from the Admiralty in 1915 but his strange ships were completed as a legacy. Ready for sea in 1917, the first two were HMS *Courageous* and HMS *Glorious* (laid down in 1915, and launched in February and April 1916), but were found to be virtually unemployable in the active fleet, unprotected and, with only four of their great 381-mm (15-in) guns, slow to get on to the target. On the only occasion when they saw serious action, against conventional light cruisers, they suffered more damage than they inflicted.

Under the terms of the Washington Treaty, the two ships were eligible for conversion into aircraft-carriers. Rebuilding of both started in 1924, the *Courageous* completing in 1928 and the *Glorious* in 1930. *Furious* (with no island) had had her uptakes led well aft, detracting from her hangar space, but these later conversions had the benefit of developments on the *Hermes* and *Eagle*, their combined funnel and bridge structure boosting their air complement considerably. The *Courageous* and *Glorious* had similar forward flightdecks, which terminated about 20 per cent of the ship's length back from the bows. The hangar deck was extended forward at forecastle level, allowing fighters to take off from the lower level in favourable circumstances. Both ships were extensively bulged to improve stability.

The *Courageous* was the Royal Navy's first major casualty of World War II, being sunk only a fortnight after hostilities commenced. Her loss brought the *Glorious* back from the Mediterranean as a replacement and she, too, was lost only nine months later during the evacuation of Norway.

HMS Courageous *and* Glorious, *like* Furious, *were light battlecruisers intended for Admiral Fisher's ill-conceived Baltic strategy. This is* Glorious *on her sea trials in 1917. Her speed was an impressive 31 knots but her lack of armour made her unfit for serious combat.*

Specification
'Courageous' class
Type: fleet aircraft-carrier
Displacement: 22,500 tons standard and 26,500 tons full load
Dimensions: length 239.5 m (785.75 ft); beam 27.6 m (90.5 ft); draught 7.3 m (24 ft)
Propulsion: 4-shaft geared steam turbines delivering 90,000 shp (67113 kW)
Speed: 31 kts
Armour: belt 38-76 mm (1.5-3 in); hangar deck 25-76 mm (1-3 in)
Armament: 16 120-mm (4.7-in) AA guns
Aircraft: about 45
Complement: 1,215 including aircrew

HMS Glorious *could be distinguished from her sister by her longer flight deck aft. Her aircraft gave sterling service over Norway in 1940, but she was caught and sunk during the withdrawal by the German battlecruisers* Scharnhorst *and* Gneisenau.

HMS Courageous *and* Glorious *carried a balanced airgroup of 16 Flycatchers, 16 III F spotter/ reconnaissance aircraft and 16 Ripon torpedo bombers.*

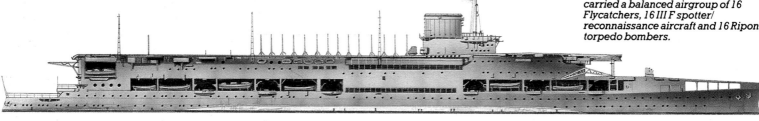

HMS *Ark Royal*

Completed in 1938, HMS **Ark Royal** was the Royal Navy's first 'modern' carrier. A combination of meagre naval budgets and the lowly status of the Fleet Air Arm meant that she was the first carrier to join the fleet since the remodelled *Glorious* back in 1930. Plenty of time had thus been available to plan her, resulting in a thoroughly workmanlike and influential design laid down in 1935 and launched in April 1937. Though much of a size and displacement as the *Glorious*, she appeared much larger, having two levels of hangars with adequate headroom. Three elevators were incorporated but they were small and, had the ship enjoyed a longer career, would

have required replacement to cater for the rapidly increasing size of aircraft. She had two catapults ('accelerators') from the outset.

The *Ark Royal*'s most innovatory feature was her strength, the ship introducing armoured flight and hangar decks, with the hangar walls an integral part of the main hull girder. Despite the space-consuming aspects of this configuration, she could stow a far greater number of aircraft than the *Glorious*. Capable of 31 kts, she was also as fast as the earlier ships.

Though the earlier conversions had 16 medium-calibre guns, these were poorly sited, mainly with a view to defence against surface attack. The *Ark*

Royal carried eight twin-barrelled destroyer-type mountings, with high elevations conferring a true dual-purpose capability and sited four on each beam at the flightdeck edges to give good firing arcs. Designers were, at last, alive to the dangers of air attack and a comprehensive fit of smaller automatic weapons was also incorporated. Though aircraft were, indeed, to prove the main hazard to both American and Japanese carriers, the Royal Navy was pitted primarily against fleets without carriers, so suffering most of its carrier casualties, the *Ark Royal* included on 14 November 1941, from submarine attack.

Specification
HMS *Ark Royal*
Type: fleet aircraft-carrier
Displacement: 22,000 tons standard and 26,700 tons full load
Dimensions: length 243.8 m (800 ft); beam 28.9 m (94.75 ft); draught 6.9 m (22.66 ft)
Propulsion: 3-shaft geared steam turbines delivering 102,000 shp (76061 kW)
Speed: 31 kts
Armour: belt 114 mm (4.5 in); deck 64 mm (2.5 in)
Armament: eight twin 114 mm (4.5-in) AA, six octuple 2-pdr AA, and eight quadruple 12.7-mm (0.5-in) AA guns
Aircraft: about 65
Complement: 1,575 including aircrew

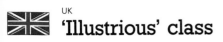
'Illustrious' class

The *Ark Royal* was very much a prototype, combining speed with capacity and new standards of protection. Though late coming, she had hardly been launched when a new **'Illustrious' class** of four aircraft-carriers was laid down in 1937 to respond to the already increasing likelihood of war. Operational experience was, therefore, not a part of the later concept, which took the scale of the *Ark Royal*'s belt and horizontal protection, and added a 114-mm (4.5-in) hangar well. Thus the whole of the vulnerable aircraft accommodation became an armoured box, but so much weight high in the ship limited the protection to only one hangar and, though HMS *Illustrious*, HMS *Victorious* and HMS *Formidable* (all launched in 1939) were not significantly smaller than the *Ark Royal*, they carried far fewer aircraft. There must have been second thoughts on reducing the ships' primary arm so drastically, for HMS *Indomitable*, launched in 1940 as last of the four, and the two 'Implacable' class ships that followed, reverted to lighter protection and an extra half-length hangar.

The immense strength of the ships stood them in good stead, for their war turned out to be one of air, rather than submarine attack. Soon after Taranto, the *Illustrious* survived punishment from dive-bombing that would have sunk any other carrier afloat, a performance echoed by the *Formidable* after Matapan. In the Pacific War most of them withstood one or even two *kamikaze* strikes without having to leave station. But all these immense blows were absorbed mainly by the ships' horizontal protection and it would seem in retrospect that the vertical armour was bought at an excessive price in operational efficiency even though, in the Pacific, the class worked with something like 60 per cent over its designed aircraft complement. When the Americans copied the armoured deck concept, it was not at the cost of capacity, so carrier sizes began their inevitable escalation. The ships were scrapped in 1956, 1969, 1955 and 1953 respectively.

Specification
'Illustrious' class
Type: fleet aircraft-carrier
Displacement: 23,000 tons standard and 25,500 tons full load
Dimensions: length 229.7 m (753.5 ft); beam 29.2 m (95.75 ft); draught 7.3 m (24 ft)
Propulsion: 3-shaft geared steam turbines delivering 110,000 shp (82027 kW)
Speed: 31 kts
Armour: belt and hangar wall 114 mm (4.5 in) except *Indomitable* 38 mm (1.5 in); deck 76 mm (3 in)
Armament: eight twin 114-mm (4.5-in) DP, six octuple 2-pdr AA, and eight 20-mm AA guns
Aircraft: about 45 except *Indomitable* about 65
Complement: 1,400 including aircrew

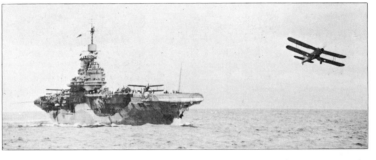

Above: HMS Formidable, *seen here from HMS* Warspite, *fought for most of the war in the Mediterranean. An attack by her aircraft on the Italian fleet on 28 March 1941 damaged the battleship* Vittorio Veneto *and crippled the cruiser* Pola, *which was subsequently sunk.*

Left: Joining the fleet in August 1940, HMS Illustrious *steamed straight to the Mediterranean, where her airgroup sank two Italian destroyers and raided North Africa.*

Despite having rather lighter protection than her sisterships, HMS Indomitable *absorbed a great deal of punishment, surviving two hits from 500 kg (1,100 lb) bombs during Operation 'Pedestal', a torpedo hit off Sicily in 1943 and several kamikaze attacks in the Far East.*

Below: The 'Illustrious' class were probably the toughest carriers afloat in World War II, but although their thick armour enabled them to withstand some heavy blows it was only achieved by a large reduction in aircraft strength.

'Implacable' class
UK

Completed some 30 months after the four 'Illustrious' class ships, the two 'Implacable' class aircraft-carriers were more closely related to the prototype *Ark Royal*, with the hangar walls slimmed down to only 38 mm (1.5 in). This allowed a better weight distribution for the ships' increased displacement, including the all-important lower hangar. The ships were slightly longer but appeared much bulkier than their half-sisters, their larger hull containing also a fourth set of machinery. This gave them the extra speed that enabled them to pace an American 'Essex' class unit in the Pacific war, although they were considerably smaller in terms of both size and capacity.

Though both were laid down in 1939, HMS *Implacable* and HMS *Indefatigable* were launched in 1942 and 1944 respectively, but their completion went back because of higher shipyard priorities. When they were most needed, they were still on the stocks, underlining the truth that the navy fights a war largely with what it has available at the beginning. Once finally completed in 1944 they were active for a comparatively short period. In March 1944, while still a new ship, the *Indefatigable* achieved a 'first' in the first-ever deck landing by a twin-engine aircraft, a de Havilland Mosquito. Before heading east to join the rapidly-expanding British Pacific Fleet, she participated in some of the

many carrier strikes against the *Tirpitz*, holed-up in Norwegian waters. Though damaging the target sufficiently to keep her almost permanently under repair, the aircraft of the time were the ship's weakest link until they were replaced. Once in the BPF, the ships were engaged in a war already won, in which the British participation was not welcomed in all quarters. Postwar, they were employed mainly in the training role and were scrapped in 1955 and 1956 after hardly a decade of service, being thought not worth the vast expense of a rebuilding along the lines of the *Victorious*.

Specification
'Implacable' class
Type: fleet aircraft-carrier
Displacement: 26,000 tons standard and 31,100 tons full load
Dimensions: length 233.4 m (765.75 ft); beam 29.2 m (95.75 ft); draught 7.9 m (26 ft)
Propulsion: 4-shaft geared steam turbines delivering 110,000 shp (82027 kW)
Speed: 32.5 kts
Armour: belt 114 mm (4.5-in); hangar wall 38 mm (1.5 in); deck 76 mm (3 in)
Armament: eight twin 114-mm (4.5-in) DP, six octuple 2-pdr AA and about 38 20-mm AA guns
Aircraft: about 70
Complement: 1,800 including aircrew

HMS Implacable *was faster and carried many more aircraft than the* 'Illustrious' *class. She is seen (above)* returning to Sydney in 1945 and (below) on her way through the Suez Canal to join the Pacific Fleet.

HMS *Unicorn*
UK

With commendable foresight, considering the quantity of tonnage then being ordered, the 1938 Naval Estimates allowed for the construction of one of a new type of ship, to be employed on the maintenance of the aircraft of a Fleet Air Arm that was obviously due for expansion. She was to be the aviation equivalent of a submarine or destroyer depot ship in providing major forward repair facilities for jobs beyond the capabilities of the average carrier. Though described as an 'aircraft maintenance carrier', it would appear that acting as a carrier was part of her specification, an option taken up due to the wartime shortage of flightdecks. Like the *Ark Royal*, HMS *Unicorn* was given two hangars and a flightdeck increased in length by an ungainly overhang aft. She possessed great freeboard with only moderate length, giving an oddly foreshortened aspect.

The *Unicorn* was laid down in 1939, launched in 1941 and completed in 1943, in time to join the CVEs of Force V, tasked to provide the fighter cover for both fleet and forces ashore in the first 24 hours following the landings at Salerno. In the event, it was nearly four days before the capture of an airfield ashore could relieve the force of the

responsibility, during which time the combination of the CVEs' low speed and small decks while operating in near windless conditions, wrote off over 40 fragile Supermarine Seafire fighters in deck accidents alone. The *Unicorn*'s 6-kt speed advantage and larger deck prevented even more losses.

By early 1944 the *Unicorn* was in the Far East, still doubling as operational carrier pending the delayed arrival of the *Victorious*. Laid up for several years after the war, she was reactivated for the Korean War, finding at last her true vocation at a time when shore air support was almost all carrier-based. The *Unicorn* shuttled with replacement aircraft to and from Singapore, her space frequently being used as short-term trooping accommodation. She was scrapped in 1959.

Specification
HMS *Unicorn*
Type: maintenance carrier and secondary light fleet aircraft-carrier
Displacement: 14,750 tons standard
Dimensions: length 195.1 m (640 ft); beam 27.4 m (90 ft); draught 5.8 m (19 ft)
Propulsion: 2-shaft geared steam turbines delivering 40,000 shp (29828 kW)

Speed: 24 kts
Armour: none
Armament: four twin 114-mm (4.5-in) DP, three quadruple 2-pdr AA, and 12 20-mm AA guns
Aircraft: 35 when used as a light fleet carrier
Complement: 1,050

Designed as an 'aircraft maintenance carrier', wartime shortage of carriers led to HMS Unicorn *being pressed into front line service. As part of Force V,* Unicorn *helped provide fighter support for the Salerno landings in 1943 and saw action off Okinawa the next year.*

Equipped with a double hangar like Ark Royal, Unicorn *had a shortened hull, giving her a rather cumbersome appearance. In reserve from 1946 to 1949, she was recommissioned as a transport carrier for the Korean war, ferrying aircraft and serving as a troopship.*

CAM ships

UK

With the European coast from the North Cape to the Spanish border under enemy control by mid-1940, long-range German aircraft began to prove a serious menace to British convoys. The latter, beyond the range of their own air-support and with the escort carrier still in the future, the aircraft vectoring in marauding U-boats and, increasingly boldly, attacking stragglers. In 1940, aircraft alone accounted for 192 Allied ships of 580,000 gross registered tons, a total passed in the first four months of 1941. A somewhat desperate measure to counter these pests was the **Catapult-Armed Merchantman** or **CAM ship**, a series of which were converted while the CVEs were building. Initially, three merchantmen and the old seaplane carrier HMS *Pegasus* were each fitted with a catapult upon which was mounted an early Hawker Hurricane or Fairey Fulmar fighter. This group, termed **Fighter Catapult Ships**, proved the idea and a 50-ship programme was initiated, using merchantmen of various sizes. All wore the red ensign, carried cargo and had civilian crews but, spanning the forecastle and No. 1 hatch, was the ungainly catapult structure fixed axially and facing forward. Pilots, drawn from the RAF's Merchant Ship Fighter

Unit, would sit for hours, strapped in the cockpit, awaiting the sighting of a 'snooper'. Once launched, they were committed to catching the enemy and returning on a limited amount of fuel. There was no landing-on; if friendly land were close enough (a rare event) the pilot would try to reach it but, more usually, he had to return to the convoy (often getting shot at) and 'ditch' alongside a likely ship, hoping to be rescued quickly before death arrived from exposure or drowning. It demanded a special sort of bravery.

Once contact was made, the enemy usually fell easily to the high-performance eight-gun fighters. The first recorded kill was by a Hurricane from the FCS *Maplin* early in August 1941, shortly before the CVE HMS *Audacity*'s epic maiden run and, by the end of the year, some six successes had been achieved.

The first CAM ship was the *Empire Rainbow*. The *Empire Lawrence* formed part of the contentious USSR-bound convoy PQ16 in mid-1942. Her aircraft downed one Heinkel He 111 torpedo bomber and damaged another, returning to find her ship sunk. During PQ18, the *Empire Morn's* Hurricane, during its brief flight, destroyed one aircraft, broke up the attacks of others and succeeded in

making Soviet soil.

The CAMs served briefly before being supplemented and then displaced by MACs and CVEs, but their gallant contribution at a desperate time deserves to be fully recognized.

No specification is possible for this widely disparate group of ships.

Once launched from a CAM ship there was no way of landing; after hopefully destroying the intruder, the pilot had to bale out over the convoy knowing that unless he was quickly rescued he would die in the icy water.

Britain's chronic shortage of aircraft carriers in the early years of the war left the Atlantic convoys very vulnerable to long-range German aircraft. A desperate solution was the CAM ship, a merchantman with a fighter plane on a forward catapult.

HMS *Audacity*

UK

Though contingency plans existed pre-war to convert merchant ships to auxiliary aircraft carriers, the production of the first such ship seems, in retrospect, to have been leisurely considering the urgency of the situation. The hull selected for conversion was that of the fire-damaged *Hannover*, an almost new Hamburg-Amerika cargo liner seized by the Royal Navy off San Domingo in February 1940. She commissioned as HMS *Audacity* in June 1941 with the functions of carrying fighters to curb the menace of the long-range German maritime aircraft and, if possible, Fairey Swordfish to provide a measure of anti-submarine protection. Her facilities were basic, a 140-m (460-ft) flightdeck being laid from the raised forecastle over a lowered bridge structure to a built-up poop. There were just two arrester wires and a barrier; no elevator was fitted because there was no hangar: the six aircraft were stowed and serviced on deck, flight operations involving much manual rearrangement. Because of a shortage of Hawker Sea Hurricanes, she took Grumman F4F-3 Wildcats to sea for the first time in the Royal Navy. Contrasting with the spartan aviation

arrangements, *Audacity* retained much of her original accommodation.

September 1941 saw the little carrier's first trip, with the UK-Gibraltar convoy OG41. Heavy attacks from both submarine and aircraft sank six ships but greater losses were prevented by the *Audacity*'s aircraft, which caused several U-boats to dive and lose contact. They also shot down a Focke-Wulf Fw 200C and chased off other intruders.

The *Audacity* returned with the next convoy, HG76, in mid-December 1941. During a four-day nonstop battle the enemy lost five submarines for two

merchantmen. With radar direction, the carrier had downed two more snoopers and spoiled the attacks of various U-boats. On 21 December she herself fell victim to three submarine torpedoes but had proved the value of the escort carrier.

The first escort carrier, HMS Audacity's handful of fighters could mean the difference between life or death for a convoy. With convoy OG41 her airgroup destroyed a Focke-Wulf Fw 200C and chased off several U-boats.

Specification
HMS Audacity
Type: escort aircraft-carrier
Displacement: 5,540 tons standard
Dimensions: length 144.7 m (474.75 ft); beam 17.1 m (56 ft); draught 8.3 m (27.25 ft)
Propulsion: 2-shaft diesels delivering

4,750 bhp (3542 kW)
Speed: 15 kts
Armour: none
Armament: one 102-mm (4-in) and some smaller guns
Aircraft: six
Complement: not known

MAC ships

Lead orders for escort carriers (CVEs) were placed in early 1942, but urgent measures were required to close the mid-Atlantic gap during their building. One such was the CAM ship, the other the **MAC (Merchant Aircraft Carrier)**, an ingenious solution later copied by the Japanese. The Ministry of War Transport was, understandably, reluctant to release good-class cargo tonnage for conversion to dedicated CVEs, but the MAC retained the greater part of its cargo capacity while having a flight deck topside. Breakbulkers required hatches and cargo-handling gear to function, but grain carriers required only small apertures to their holds, through which the hoses for loading and discharging grain could be inserted. This arrangement was fully compatible with fitting a flightdeck. Like the CAMs, the MACs sailed under the red ensign, only their flight personnel being Royal Navy. Similarly, they were integrated more with the convoy than its escort, though requiring more manoeuvring space. Appropriately carrying Empire 'Mac' names (particularly so as they came from Scottish yards), the first six were all converted from incomplete ships, with 129 by 19 m (423 by 62 ft) flight-decks and a diminutive hangar aft capable of accommodating four Fairey Swordfish aircraft.

From the point of view of cargo requirements and dimensions, tankers were also very suitable candidates for conversion, but the Admiralty had grave doubts of the fire risk. Anglo-Saxon Petroleum (now Shell) resolved the problem on their behalf, resulting in nine of their tankers being converted (though retaining their familiar Shell names) and four more liquid-cargo Empire 'Macs' being launched for the job. The main difference between the wet and dry cargo carriers lay in the lack of a hangar on the tankers, the aircraft remaining topside in all weathers. Despite the urgency of the programme, it was April 1943 before the first MAC entered service. They were exceedingly fortunate ships, all 19 surviving the war to be reconverted.

The dry-cargo 'Empire Mac' class ships were the *Empire Macalpine, Empire Macandrew, Empire Maccallum, Empire Macdermott, Empire Mackendrick* and *Empire Macrae*. The equivalent tanker 'Empire Mac' class comprised the *Empire Maccabe, Empire Maccoll, Empire Mackay* and *Empire Macmahon*. Finally, the units of the 'Shell' class were the *Acavus, Adula, Alexia, Amastra, Ancylus, Gadila, Macoma, Miralda* and *Rapana*.

Specification
'Empire Mac' dry class
Type: merchant aircraft-carrier
Displacement: 7,930 to 8,250 gross tons
Dimensions: length between 135.6 and 139.9 m (445 and 459 ft); beam between 17.1 and 17.7 m (56 and 58 ft); draught 7.5 m (24.66 ft)
Propulsion: 1-shaft diesel delivering 3,300 bhp (2461 kW)
Speed: 12.5 kts
Armour: none
Armament: one 102-mm (4-in), two 40-mm AA and some smaller guns
Aircraft: four
Complement: 110

Specification
'Empire Mac' tanker class
Type: merchant aircraft-carrier
Displacement: 8,850 to 9,250 gross tons
Dimensions: length 146.7 to 148 m (481.3 to 485.5 ft); beam 18.0 to 18.8 m (59 to 61.66 ft); draught 8.0 to 8.4 m (26.25 to 27.5 ft)

Propulsion: 1-shaft diesel delivering 3,300 bhp (2461 kW)
Speed: 11.5 kts
Armour: none
Armament: one 102-mm (4-in) and some smaller guns
Aircraft: four
Complement: 110

Specification
'Shell' class
Type: merchant aircraft-carrier
Displacement: 8,000 gross tons
Dimensions: length 146.5 to 147 m (480.66 to 482.25 ft); beam 18.0 m (59 ft); draught 8.4 m (27.66 ft)
Propulsion: 1-shaft diesel delivering 3,750 bhp (2796 kW)
Speed: 13 kts
Armour: none
Armament: one 102-mm (4-in) and some smaller guns
Aircraft: four
Complement: 105

MAC ships were merchant vessels only partially converted into aircraft carriers; a flight deck was fitted, but they could still carry cargo. Their aircraft protected convoys in the 'Atlantic Gap', the area in mid-Atlantic out of range of Allied shore-based aircraft.

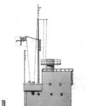

British-built escort carriers

Few escort carriers were produced by British yards, which worked on more specialized ships, leaving series production to the Americans. There was, understandably, also reluctance to release good-quality mercantile tonnage for conversion at a time of severe shortage. As a result, only five British-built CVEs saw service, HMS *Vindex* and the roughly-similar HMS *Nairana*, the smaller HMS *Activity*, the larger HMS *Campania* and the ex-passenger liner HMS *Pretoria Castle*. Unlike their American counterparts, built from similar hulls, they were all different, tending to have longer but narrower flightdecks. In addition the hangar was served by only one elevator, which made for much manhandling of aircraft. They were more solidly built than the American CVEs, with steel-sided hangars and steel flightdecks. On average, they stowed 15 to 18 aircraft, in the approximate ratio of two Fairey Swordfish to one fighter (Hawker Sea Hurricane, Grumman Wildcat or Fairey Fulmar). The *Activity* stowed fewer, and the larger *Pretoria Castle* spent most of her operational career in the training role. The four smaller ships were converted from twin-screw diesel cargo liners of the Blue Funnel and Port Lines, which could be reconverted post-war.

Short of spare merchant tonnage, Britain built few escort carriers, but ships like HMS Vindex, seen here in 1944, proved very successful working with submarine hunting groups.

The British CVEs ran extensively with convoys to and from Gibraltar. Working in pairs, they became potent anti-submarine ships. Their Swordfish were equipped with search radar and they themselves with Asdic (sonar), which allowed co-operation with dedicated hunter-killer groups, a luxury possible only after all the convoys were adequately escorted. Later in the war they were used on the Arctic convoy route, the significance of their contribution being recognized by their wearing the flag of the senior naval officer. They were less successful in the severe northern conditions, their lack of length making them extremely lively in pitch, which restricted flight operations.

Specification
HMS *Activity*
Type: escort aircraft-carrier
Displacement: 11,800 tons standard
Dimensions: length 156.2 m (512.5 ft); beam 20.3 m (66.66 ft); draught 6.7 m (22 ft)

Propulsion: 2-shaft diesels delivering 12,000 bhp (8948 kW)
Speed: 18 kts
Armour: none
Armament: two 102-mm (4-in) AA and 10 twin 20-mm AA guns
Aircraft: 15
Complement: 700

Specification
HMS *Pretoria Castle*
Type: escort aircraft-carrier
Displacement: 17,400 tons standard
Dimensions: length 181.1 m (594 ft); beam 23.3 m (76.6 ft); draught 8.8 m (28.75 ft)

Propulsion: 2-shaft diesels delivering 11,400 bhp (8501 kW)
Speed: 16 kts
Armour: none
Armament: two twin 102-mm (4-in) AA, four quadruple 2-pdr AA, and 10 twin 20-mm AA guns
Aircraft: 15
Complement: not known

HMS Nairana is seen here in her 1943 colour scheme.

American-built escort carriers

Like the British, the Americans had pre-war ideas on the conversion of mercantile hulls to auxiliary carriers. Early in 1941, two C3 hulls were thus earmarked and the first was rebuilt in only three months, commissioning as the USS *Long Island* (AVG.1) within days of the British *Audacity*. In concept, the American ship was well ahead, having both hangar and elevator, though making poor use of available space. Such early AVGs had a hangar occupying only the after quarter or so of the underdeck space, a similar volume ahead of it being devoted to accommodation (which should have gone below in the original cargo spaces in the hull proper). Below the forward half of the flightdeck the space was open, the overheads being supported on frame structures. What they did have was a catapult (known as an 'accelerator') and the popular bunk beds and cafeteria messing.

The *Long Island*'s first sister was not completed until November 1941, and was transferred to the British as HMS *Archer* (BAVG.1), being joined later by three more '**Archer**' class ships. As the programme got into its stride the Royal Navy received eight of the '**Attacker**' class and 26 of the very similar '**Ruler**' class. Both had full-length hangars, the later class having improved stowage factors. Following early experience, the British required higher standards of fuel and fire protection than the Americans, promoting a measure of criticism of 'gold-plating'. Early American ships were diesel-driven, later units having steam plant; both types experienced a fair share of machinery problems.

With limited capacity for flexibility, CVEs tended to be fitted out for roles either in convoy escort or in assault support, their organization and aircraft complement being tailored to suit. Once available in larger numbers they were often integrated directly with AS groups. They often worked in larger groups (five at Salerno and nine for the South of France landings), but some saw no action, being engaged on aircraft ferrying. All that were still fit were converted back to mercantile roles after the war.

The 'Archer' class comprised five ships, namely HMS **Archer**, HMS **Avenger**, HMS **Biter**, HMS **Charger** and HMS **Dasher**, though the *Charger* was retained by the US Navy as CVE.30 for the training of British aircrews in American waters. The 'Attacker' class was larger, and was made up of HMS **Attacker**, HMS **Battler**, HMS **Chaser**, HMS **Fencer**, HMS **Pursuer**, HMS **Stalker**, HMS **Striker** and HMS **Trailer**. Finally there was the 'Ruler' class, which was made up of HMS **Patroller**, HMS **Puncher**, HMS **Ravager**, HMS **Reaper**, HMS **Searcher**, HMS **Slinger**, HMS **Smiter**, HMS **Speaker**, HMS **Tracker**, HMS **Trouncer**, HMS **Trumpeter**, HMS **Ameer**, HMS **Arbiter**, HMS **Atheling**, HMS **Begum**, HMS **Emperor**, HMS **Empress**, HMS **Khedive**, HMS **Nabob**, HMS **Premier**, HMS **Queen**, HMS **Rajah**, HMS **Ranee**, HMS **Ruler**, HMS **Shah** and HMS **Thane**.

Specification
'Archer' class
Type: escort aircraft-carrier

Britain received eight 'Attacker' class and 26 'Ruler' class escort carriers from the USA. They were used both for convoy escort and anti-submarine warfare as well as providing air support during several of the Mediterranean amphibious assaults.

HMS Avenger and Biter, pictured here in heavy seas, were both 'Archer' class escort carriers.

Displacement: 8,250 tons standard except *Archer* 9,000 tons standard
Dimensions: length 150.0 m (492.25 ft); beam 20.2 m (66.25 ft); draught 7.1 m (23.25 ft)
Propulsion: 1-shaft diesel delivering 8,500 bhp (6,338 kW) except *Archer* 1-shaft diesel delivering 9,000 bhp (6711 kW)
Speed: 16.5 kts except *Archer* 17 kts
Armour: none
Armament: three 102-mm (4-in) AA, and 15 20-mm AA guns
Aircraft: 15
Complement: 555

Specification
'Attacker' class
Type: escort aircraft-carrier
Displacement: 11,400 tons standard
Dimensions: length 150.0 m (492.25 ft); beam 21.2 m (69.5 ft); draught 7.3 m (24 ft)
Propulsion: 1-shaft geared steam turbine delivering 9,350 shp (6972 kW)
Speed: 17 kts
Armour: none

Armament: two 102-mm (4-in) AA, four twin 40-mm AA, and 15 20-mm AA guns
Aircraft: 18
Complement: 645

Specification
'Ruler' class
Type: escort aircraft-carrier
Displacement: 11,400 tons standard
Dimensions: length 150.0 m (492.25 ft); beam 21.2 m (69.5 ft); draught 7.7 m (25.25 ft)
Propulsion: 1-shaft geared steam turbine delivering 9,350 shp (6972 kW)
Speed: 17 kts
Armour: none
Armament: two 102-mm (4-in) AA, eight twin 40-mm AA, and 20 20-mm AA guns
Aircraft: 22
Complement: 645

HMS *Perseus* and HMS *Pioneer*

Far Eastern operations had to be conducted far from established bases and maintenance facilities. High attrition rates in aircraft would demand 'repair by replacement' to keep the front-line carriers fully operational, CVEs being used extensively in the exchange process. Lightly damaged aircraft or routine maintenance tasks could be carried out on the fleet carrier herself but lack of space and time demanded that anything more complex be shipped out for repair and, by the very nature of things, the repair facilities had to be afloat. With the only specialist maintenance carrier *Unicorn* used permanently in an operational role, two of the new light fleet carriers of the 'Colossus' class were earmarked as replacements. Though lacking the extra hangar, they were marginally faster but looked 'unfinished' with few of the deck-edge fixtures sported by the operational carriers.

Both HMS *Perseus* and HMS *Pioneer* were completed by the end of the war, but only the *Pioneer* succeeded in getting to an operational theatre, with the 11th ACS, arriving in the Far East just in time for the Japanese surrender. Paradoxically, earlier in the war when they could have been of use, they would (like the *Unicorn*) almost certainly have been pressed into an operational role, leaving CVEs to be used as auxiliaries, while in peace too few active flightdecks were maintained to warrant their existence. With little post-war application, the *Pioneer* was scrapped as early as 1954 (earlier intentions of conversions to passenger liners were not pursued due probably to a combination of cost and a diminishing demand for these ships by a public acquiring a taste for air travel). The *Perseus* was nearly recommissioned for the Suez affair of 1956, but then scrapped in 1958.

Specification
HMS *Perseus* and HMS *Pioneer*
Type: maintenance aircraft-carrier

Displacement: 13,300 tons standard
Dimensions: length 211.8 m (695 ft); beam 24.4 m (80 ft); draught 5.6 m (18.4 ft)
Propulsion: 2-shaft geared steam turbines delivering 42,000 shp (31319 kW)
Speed: 25 kts
Armour: minimal
Armament: three quadruple 2-pdr AA and 10 20-mm AA guns
Aircraft: none
Complement: not known

HMS Perseus and Pioneer were 'Colossus' class carriers, completed as maintenance ships unable to operate in a combat role. Too late to serve in the wartime fleet, they were among the first British carriers to be scrapped.

Japanese Aircraft Carriers

The six months following 7 December 1941 saw the Imperial Japanese Navy wage one of the most astonishing campaigns in naval history. From the attack on Pearl Harbor to the defeat at Midway, it was carrier power that proved decisive, and the transformation of war at sea was irrevocable.

Japanese aircraft carrier *Zuiho* under aerial attack off Cape Engano by planes from USS *Enterprise* during the decisive action at Leyte Gulf in October 1944.

Unlike her Axis partners, Japan was a true maritime power that well understood the potential of aviation at sea. Launching a war of her own choosing in the Pacific, she had not succeeded in significantly outbuilding the Americans in aircraft-carriers but had the advantage that the 11 she had in service in 1941 did not have to be split between two oceans. The grouping of the six best units into Nagumo's 1st Air Fleet showed bold innovation, a gamble that paid off by exploiting the old principle of the Schwerpunkt: overwhelming force where it mattered.

In the initial phase of the Pacific war, the Allied fleets were caught ill-prepared and for a while the Japanese seemed unstoppable, but inevitably as their boundaries expanded and their commitments grew, the Japanese had to break up the hard-worked cohesive carrier units. At the same time the Americans, stung to war, prepared their challenge. The Coral Sea demonstrated that the enemy could be checked but Midway was a total triumph for American intelligence, organization and strategy.

After Midway, the good days were clearly over for the Japanese. Despite a long period of balance, the advantage slowly changed sides. The 2nd Battle of the Solomon Sea, riposted at Santa Cruz, saw the pendulum at mid-swing. The Saipan amphibious operation forced the Japanese to act in strength against a powerful American defence; the Philippine Sea battle, as it was known, cost the Japanese carriers their main strength, namely the last of their trained aircrews.

Shortly after this, at Leyte Gulf, came Armageddon, with virtually the whole of the surviving fleet engaged in a final, one-way, do-or-die mission to destroy the spearhead of the American advance. Short of fuel, aircrew, aircraft and ammunition, the remnants of the Japanese carrier force had no use other than to act as a lure at a crucial point in the action. They succeeded brilliantly, but in vain, for the Americans were too many.

In the short term, the bold uses to which the Japanese put naval air power proved decisive but, once the war was allowed to drag on, the old tag was once again proved right: 'a good big 'un will always beat a good little 'un.'

JAPAN
Hosho

The first carrier built for the Imperial Japanese Navy, like so many others, was a conversion. The naval oiler *Hiryu*, laid down late in 1919, was taken over in 1921 and emerged as the carrier *Hosho* at the end of the following year. The design owed much to a British technical mission, which had broad details of the new British carrier *Hermes* and the details of the Sopwith Cuckoo torpedo-bomber. The original triple-expansion steam engines were replaced by destroyer-type turbines to give a speed of 25 knots and, as in the USS *Langley*, smoke was vented

Hosho, converted from an oiler, was commissioned as a carrier in 1922 following the visit of a British technical mission. Originally equipped with an island navigating bridge, within a year she was flush decked, and provided the Imperial Japanese Navy with valuable early experience in carrier operations.

through triple folding funnels, which hinged downwards when flying was in progress.

The ship was the first to have an 'island' navigating bridge, but this proved so unpopular with the pilots that it was removed in 1923. The *Hosho* proved very small and lacked sufficient margin of stability to be able to carry her full armament and complement of aircraft. By the outbreak of World War II her air group had shrunk from 21 to 12 aircraft, and all the original guns had been replaced by light anti-aircraft weapons. However, the *Hosho* provided invaluable experience for the conversion of *Akagi* and *Kaga*, as well as design of *Ryujo*, the first Japanese carrier built as such from the keel up. She also saw considerable action off the China coast in the late 1930s and ferried aircraft during the Sino-Japanese War.

Despite her drawbacks the elderly training carrier served with Carrier Division 3 from December 1941, alongside the *Zuiho*, but after four months in the Palau Islands she was returned to training duties in Japan. Then she became operational again for the Midway campaign, carrying 11 Nakajima B5N 'Kate' bombers to provide reconnaissance for Admiral Yamamoto's battleships.

Finally withdrawn in June 1942, the *Hosho* thereafter led a charmed life. Although damaged by grounding in 1944 and hit twice by American bombs at Kure she was still afloat when the war ended. She had been finally laid up in April 1945 for lack of aircrew to man her aircraft, and was thus one of the few Japanese carriers still in existence on VJ-Day. She was to have a second lease of life, however, for she was recommissioned as a transport to

repatriate Japanese servicemen from all over the Far East. She continued in this job until August 1946, but was finally scrapped in 1947 after nearly 25 years of service.

Specification
Hosho
Displacement: 7,470 tons standard, 10,000 tons full load
Dimensions: length 168.1 m (551 ft 6 in); overall; beam 18.0 m (59 ft 0 in); draught 6.2 m (20 ft 4 in)
Machinery: 2-shaft geared steam turbines delivering 30,000 shp (22370 kW)
Speed: 25 knots
Armour: uncertain
Armament: (1941) eight twin 25-mm AA guns
Aircraft: (1942) 11 'Kate' torpedo-bombers
Complement: 550 officers and men

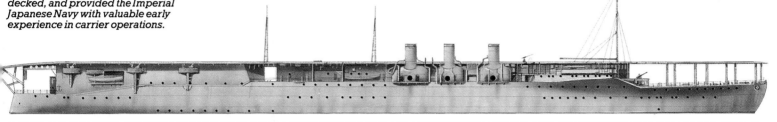

JAPAN
Akagi

The outcome of the Washington Naval Disarmament Treaty left the Imperial Japanese Navy with several incomplete capital ships destined for the scrapyard. As the Americans and British had declared their intention of converting similar hulls into carriers, and in the light of successful experience with the *Hosho*, the naval staff decided to press ahead with two similar carrier conversions Two battle-cruisers, to be known as *Akagi* and *Amagi*, were chosen; these were projected as 40,000-ton ships capable of 30 knots. Work started in 1923 but the hull of the *Amagi* was badly damaged during the great Tokyo earthquake in September, and she was scrapped.

The *Akagi* was completed in March 1927, a flush-decked ship with two funnels at the starboard edge of the flight deck, a triple flight deck forward, and 10 200-mm (7.9-in) guns, six of them in old-fashioned casemates low down aft.

Ten years later she was completely rebuilt, with a small island superstructure on the port side, and a full-length flight deck. It was hoped that the portside island would simplify operations when operating in company with other carriers (allowing her aircraft to be marshalled separately) but it caused far more landing accidents than a starboard island.

With her half-sister *Kaga* she formed Carrier Division 1 and as Vice Admiral Nagumo's flagship led the attack on Pearl Harbor. She then led the other carriers on a brilliant series of raids through the East Indies and Indian Ocean, the force sinking the British carrier *Hermes*, driving the Allies out of Java and Sumatra and even getting as far as Darwin in northern Australia.

At the Battle of Midway on 4 June 1942 *Akagi*'s air group attacked Midway itself, and she suffered slight damage when a shore-based torpedo-

bomber bounced off the deck early in the morning. At 10.22 she was attacked by aircraft from the USS *Enterprise*, which hit her twice with bombs. A 1,000-lb (454-kg) bomb burst in the hangar and started a fire among torpedo-warheads which spread to aviation fuel spilling from fractured lines; a second bomb (of 500 lb/227 kg) also started a fire among aircraft parked on the flight deck. Within 30 minutes the fire was out of control and Nagumo had shifted his flag to a light cruiser. The *Akagi* was abandoned but burned for another 9 hours or more. After vain efforts to board her the order was given to a destroyer to torpedo her.

Specification
Akagi
Displacement: (1941) 36,500 tons standard, 42,000 tons full load
Dimensions: length 260.6 m (855 ft 0 in) overall; beam 31.3 m (102 ft 8 in);

draught 8.6 m (28 ft 3 in)
Machinery: 4-shaft geared steam turbines delivering 133,000 shp (99180 kW)
Speed: 31 knots
Armour: uncertain
Armament: six 200-mm (7.9-in), six twin 120-mm (4.7-in) AA, and 14 twin 25-mm AA guns
Aircraft: (June 1942) 21 Mitsubishi A6M Zero fighters, 21 Aichi D3A 'Val' dive-bombers and 21 Nakajima B5N 'Kate' torpedo-bombers
Complement: 1,340 officers and men

Akagi at sea, a few months prior to Pearl Harbor. The left-hand island is noteworthy, as she was designed to operate in tandem with Kaga. With an operational aircraft complement of 70 or more, Akagi was a considerable advance on Hosho.

Kaga

The Japanese battleship **Kaga** was laid down in 1918 and launched in November 1921, but as a result of the Washington Naval Disarmament Treaty of 1922 was scheduled to be scrapped. In September 1923, however, the Tokyo earthquake caused severe damage to the battle-cruiser Amagi, which was about to start her conversion to an aircraft-carrier, and the hull of the slightly smaller Kaga was substituted. The 4½-year conversion produced a carrier similar to the original Akagi conversion, with a flush deck and two short 'flying-off' decks forward. But unlike Akagi she had her smoke-ducts trunked on the starboard side. She was not an unqualified success, and was not operational until two years of trials had been conducted, and only four years after that, in 1934, she was taken in hand for modernization.

In her new guise she was considerably better, with more aircraft (90 instead of 60) and a small 'island' superstructure. However, unlike Western carriers, she still had a large downward-angled funnel below the edge of the flight deck. As displacement had gone up by 9,000 tons (standard) more powerful machinery had to be installed, with endurance to match, and many of the original faults were eliminated.

The Kaga was one of the six carriers which attacked Pearl Harbor on 7 De-cember 1941, and she launched 27 Nakajima B5N 'Kate' torpedo-bombers, followed by 18 Mitsubishi A6M Zeros and 26 Aichi D3A 'Val' dive-bombers. She and the Akagi (Carrier Division 1) then took part in the devastating series of strikes in the East Indies, South Pacific and Indian Ocean which destroyed Allied military power in the first half of 1942.

At Midway on 4 June 1942, two hours after beating off American attacks successfully, Kaga was hit by four bombs from Douglas SBD Dauntless dive-bombers from the USS Enterprise, and near-missed by five more. Blast fractured fuel lines, feeding fuel to the fires already started among the aircraft waiting, fully armed and fuelled. With-

in 30 minutes the 38,000-ton carrier had to be abandoned, though she continued to burn for another 9 hours. At dusk the flames reached a magazine, and she blew up and sank quickly. Over 800 men went down with her, many trapped by the fires and others killed by the blast of the original explosions.

Specification
Kaga
Displacement: (1941) 38,200 tons standard, 43,650 tons full load
Dimensions: length 247.6 m (812 ft 4 in) overall; beam 32.5 m (106 ft 7 in) over flight deck; draught 9.5 m (31 ft 2 in)
Machinery: 4-shaft geared steam turbines delivering 127,400 shp

Kaga in wartime configuration; a maximum of 90 aircraft could be carried, but 81 was a more normal complement. Kaga was sunk by Douglas SBD Dauntlesses from USS Enterprise.

(95020 kW)
Speed: 28⅓ knots
Armour: uncertain
Armament: 10 200-mm (7.9-in), 16 127-mm (5-in) AA and eight twin 25-mm AA guns
Aircraft: 90 fighters, dive-bombers and torpedo-bombers
Complement: 2,016 officers and men

Kaga was completed in 1928 with a flush deck and two short 'flying off' decks forward of each hangar. These were not a success, and a 1934 refit eliminated them.

Ryujo

Under the Washington Treaty Japan was limited to 80,000 tons of carriers, but as the treaty exempted vessels under 10,000 tons the naval staff thought that it was worth trying to build an extra carrier inside the limit. The initial design was for an 8,000-ton ship carrying 24 aircraft, but the staff then insisted on adding a second hangar to double the aircraft capacity. This pushed the standard displacement 150 tons over the limit, but nothing was said to Japan's fellow-signatories – the first significant cheating by Japan, but not the last. Even with the illicit extra tonnage the new carrier, called Ryujo, was top-heavy when she was completed in 1933. She was twice rebuilt, with bulges added, some guns removed and the forecastle raised, but the true displacement was now nearer 12,000 tons.

As may be imagined, the Ryujo was not popular in the fleet. Quite apart from her topweight problems, her flight deck was too small and she carried too few aircraft to be effective; she took longer than other carriers to launch and recover aircraft, because of congestion on the deck. However, the experience was put to use in designing the Hiryu and Shokaku classes.

The Ryujo was not part of the main carrier force which attacked Pearl Harbor, but supported the amphibious landings in the Philippines. In April

1942 she attacked Allied merchant shipping and two months later she joined in operations against the Aleutian Islands, but her only major action was the Battle of the Eastern Solomons. The Ryujo was chosen to spearhead an operation to reinforce the defenders of Guadalcanal, and with an escort of a heavy cruiser and two destroyers, was to lure the Americans away from the main force. It worked well, for at 09.05 on 24 August 1942 she was spotted from the air, but other search planes also located the Shokaku and Zuikaku. Ryujo was heavily attacked by aircraft from the Enterprise and Saratoga in the afternoon. In a brilliant attack dive-bombers and five torpedo-bombers smothered the carrier, scoring an esti-

mated 10 bomb hits and two torpedo hits and escaping without casualties. Japanese records say that only one torpedo hit the carrier, but that was enough to set her on fire from end to end. Her rudder was also jammed, and the doomed ship was unable to steam or steer. Only 300 survivors left the ship, including Captain Kato, and she sank about four hours later.

Specification
Ryujo
Displacement: 10,600 tons standard, 14,000 tons full load
Dimensions: length 180.0 m (590 ft 6 in) overall; beam 20.8 m (68 ft 3 in); draught 7.1 m (23 ft 4 in)

An attempt to build as much as possible into limited tonnage, Ryujo was not a popular ship. The double hangar made her top heavy, her flight deck was too small, and she carried too few aircraft to be an effective fleet carrier.

Machinery: 2-shaft geared steam turbines delivering 65,000 shp (48470 kW)
Speed: 29 knots
Armour: uncertain
Armament: four twin 127-mm (5-in) AA and 12 twin 25-mm AA guns
Aircraft: 24 Mitsubishi A6M Zero fighters and 12 bombers
Complement: 924 officers and men

Shokaku

Japan's withdrawal from the international treaties limiting the size of warships at the end of 1936 enabled her constructors at last to design carriers that suited requirements. Under the 1937 Reinforcement Programme two more carriers were to be built, basically similar to the *Hiryu* but large enough to accommodate all that was required.

In the 'Shokaku' class all the earlier faults were remedied. Two catapults were provided, and a much larger hangar enabled aircraft capacity to be increased from 63 to 75. Even with a considerable increase in power (the most powerful machinery ever fitted in a Japanese warship) the two ships could achieve a range of nearly 10,000 miles (16000 km) as they carried 5,000 tons of fuel. Equally important, they were well armoured and carried a much heavier anti-aircraft armament than their predecessors. In most re-

Probably the best carriers extant at the time of their introduction, the 'Shokakus' had a strong anti-aircraft armament, but suffered from the common Japanese vulnerability of the fuel systems. Indeed, a fuel explosion following torpedo damage sank Shokaku in June 1944.

spects they were the best carriers in the world, being surpassed only by the later 'Essex' class, but like all Japanese carriers they suffered from vulnerable fuel systems. Not only were the fuel lines to the hangars and flight deck liable to be ruptured by explosions some distance away, but the fuel storage tanks were inadequately protected against shock.

Shokaku was begun at the end of 1937 and went to sea in August 1941, just two months before Pearl Harbor. Although she took part in the attack her aircrews were too inexperienced to do more than bomb the airfields on Oahu. With her sister *Zuikaku* she formed Carrier Division 5, and after their work-up early in 1942 they operated off Ceylon and New Guinea.

During the Battle of the Coral Sea *Shokaku* was damaged by a strike from the *Yorktown*; although she caught fire she was saved with some difficulty, and had to return to Japan for repairs. The worst casualties were, however, the loss of 86 aircraft and most of their aircrews, so that neither carrier could take part in the Battle of Midway. On 14 July they joined the new Carrier Division 1, with the light carrier *Zuiho*. In the Battle of the East-

ern Solomons they damaged the *Enterprise* but again lost precious aircrew and aircraft. On 26 October the *Shokaku* was severely damaged by a dive-bomber strike from the *Hornet*.

During the Battle of the Philippine Sea on 19 June 1944 she was hit by three torpedoes from the submarine USS *Cavalla*, and an explosion from ruptured aviation fuel tanks subsequently sank her.

Specification
Shokaku
Displacement: 25,675 tons standard, 32,000 tons full load
Dimensions: length 257.5 m (844 ft 9 in) overall; beam 26.0 m (85 ft 4 in); draught 8.9 m (29 ft 2 in)
Machinery: 4-shaft geared steam

Shokaku on acceptance trials in August 1941. In Shokaku, the majority of faults of Hiryu and Soryu were rectified, although the aircraft capacity was similar. Speed remained above 34 knots, and protection was increased dramatically.

turbines delivering 160,000 shp (119310 kW)
Speed: 34.2 knots
Armour: belt 215 mm (8½ in); deck 170 mm (6¾ in)
Armament: eight twin 127-mm (5-in) dual-purpose and 12 triple 25-mm AA guns
Aircraft: 27 fighters, 27 dive-bombers and 18 torpedo-bombers
Complement: 1,660 officers and men

Zuikaku

Zuikaku, the second ship of the 'Shokaku' class, was laid down in May 1938 and entered service in September 1941. She joined her sister in Carrier Division 5, and for the next three years the two were inseparable. The inexperience of CarDiv 5's aircrews prevented the ships from having anything more than a supporting role during the Pearl Harbor attack, but they were fully worked up by the time CarDiv 5 began its destructive raids on the British in Ceylon. They then left the main carrier force and went to Truk, from where they covered the invasion of Port Moresby on 1 May 1942.

In the ensuing Battle of the Coral Sea CarDiv 5 scored a tactical victory by sinking the *Lexington*, in exchange for the light carrier *Shoho*. The Japanese carriers wasted their efforts on sinking a destroyer and a fleet oiler, which they misidentified as a cruiser and a carrier. A strike of 24 Nakajima B5N 'Kate' and 36 Aichi D3A 'Val' bombers failed to penetrate the US carriers' screen, but on 8 May a similar strike failed to find the *Zuikaku* in a rain squall. Although *Zuikaku* was undamaged her highly trained aircrew had suffered serious attrition, and she had to return to Japan with her damaged sister to retrain her air group. As a result CarDiv 5 missed the Battle of Midway, and in the month after Midway they were incorporated into a new CarDiv 1. In the following month they left for the Solomons to challenge American power in Guadalcanal, but so severe was the shortage that neither

carrier had her full complement of aircraft embarked.

In the Battle of the Eastern Solomons on 24 August *Zuikaku* damaged the *Enterprise* but at the price of heavy losses. She escaped from the slaughter of the Philippine Sea Battle in June 1944 but as part of the reconstituted CarDiv 3 she was part of the forlorn hope which tried to lure the American fast carriers away from Leyte Gulf. They sailed on 20 October, and four days later *Zuikaku* launched her last air strike against the enemy. All were shot down, and next day the American pilots took their revenge by sinking all four Japanese carriers, in the Battle of Cape Engano. The *Zuikaku* was made the chief target, some 80 aircraft

attacking her from all sides with bombs and torpedoes. She took an early hit from a torpedo and started to list heavily. A second wave of more than 100 aircraft attacked and hit with an estimated seven torpedoes and four bombs. No ship could withstand such damage, and she soon rolled over and sank.

Specification
Zuikaku
Displacement: 25,675 tons standard, 32,000 tons full load
Dimensions: length 257.5 m (844 ft 9 in) overall; beam 26.0 m (85 ft 4 in); draught 8.9 m (29 ft 2 in)
Machinery: 4-shaft geared steam turbines delivering 160,000 shp

(119310 kW)
Speed: 34.2 knots
Armour: belt 215 mm (8½ in); deck 170 mm (6¾ in)
Armament: eight twin 127-mm (5-in) dual-purpose and 12 triple 25-mm AA guns
Aircraft: 27 fighters, 27 dive-bombers and 18 torpedo-bombers
Complement: 1,660 officers and men

Zuikaku lasted some four months longer than her sister, but was finally lost off Cape Engano during the Battle of Leyte Gulf. As the ship sank, crew members found positions to salute the naval ensign as it was lowered.

Zuiho

In a desperate attempt to remedy the shortage of aircraft-carriers, the Japanese naval staff decided that certain large fleet auxiliaries such as submarine tenders should be designed for rapid conversion to carriers in wartime. One such class was the 'Tsurigizaki' class of high-speed oilers, which were ordered under the 1934 Second Reinforcement Programme; their hulls were specially strengthened. The design was then altered to submarine tenders, and the lead-ship entered service in that role early in 1939. Her sister ship *Takasaki*, however, was not completed, and was laid up in the shipyard for nearly four years. Work on her conversion to a carrier started in January 1940, under the new name *Zuiho*.

Apart from the replacement of the unreliable diesels with geared steam turbines, as much of the original hull was retained as possible. A single hangar was provided, accommodating a maximum of 30 aircraft, with two centreline lifts; there were two catapults but no island superstructure. To retain the high speed and endurance all planned armouring was deleted. The conversion was carried out in a year, and the *Zuiho* joined the Combined

Fleet in January 1941. With the old *Hosho* (Carrier Division 3) she was sent to the Palaus in the late autumn of that year and took part in the attack on the Philippines. She then returned to Japan for repairs before taking part in the conquest of the East Indies in the spring.

Luckily for the carrier, she was with the Support Force at Midway, and escaped the destruction of the main carrier force. In the Battle of the Santa Cruz Islands she was part of Admiral Nagumo's Carrier Strike Force. At 07.40 on 25 October 1942 a dive-bomber from the USS *Enterprise* made a surprise attack out of low cloud, dropping its bomb in the centre of the flight deck. With a 50-ft (15-m) crater in her flight deck the *Zuiho* could no longer operate aircraft, and so after launching her aircraft the *Zuiho* returned to base.

In February 1944 *Zuiho* rejoined Carrier Division 3, and she took part in the Battle of the Philippine Sea, when her aircraft scored a hit on the battleship *South Dakota*. In the fighting around Leyte Gulf she was one of the doomed carriers which attempted to decoy the Americans: in the Battle of

Cape Engano she was hit by two bombs on the flight deck and was near-missed six times. In spite of a serious fire and flooding she was under way for another 6 hours, as the other carriers were picked off. Finally it was her turn, and three waves of attackers finished her off.

Zuiho *off Tateyama a year before Pearl Harbor. Part of the support force at Midway, she escaped destruction and went on to serve in the Solomons and the Philippine Sea before meeting her fate off Cape Engano at Leyte Gulf.*

Specification
Zuiho
Displacement: 11,262 tons standard, 14,200 tons full load
Dimensions: length 204.8 m (672 ft 0 in) overall; beam 18.2 m (59 ft 8 in); draught 6.6 m (21 ft 8 in)
Machinery: 2-shaft geared steam turbines delivering 52,000 shp (38770 kW)
Speed: 28.2 knots
Armour: none
Armament: four twin 127-mm (5-in) dual-purpose and four twin 25-mm AA guns
Aircraft: 30
Complement: 785 officers and men

Originally diesel-powered submarine support ships, Zuiho *and her sister* Shoho *were fitted with steam turbines during conversion. With single hangars, aircraft capacity was 30.*

Shoho

The submarine tender *Tsurigizaki* had been serving with the Combined Fleet in 1939-1940, but as soon as the conversion of her sister *Takasaki* into a carrier was completed in December 1940 she was taken in hand, re-emerging in January 1942 as the light carrier *Shoho*. *Shoho* did not see any action until the spring of 1942, when she covered the Port Moresby invasion, in the Support Force commanded by Rear-Admiral Aritomo Goto. It was this move by the Japanese which led to the Battle of the

Coral Sea, the first carrier-versus-carrier battle in history.

The *Shoho* was heading for Port Moresby on 6 May 1942 when at 10.30 she was sighted 60 miles (100 km) south of Bougainville by four Boeing B-17 bombers. The four aircraft attempted a high-level bombing attack on the carrier, but caused negligible damage. The two sides were largely ignorant of each other's whereabouts. In a desperate attempt to find the American carriers, Takagi flew off

reconnaissance planes for a dawn sweep on the next day. At 07.30 they reported a carrier and a cruiser, and the *Shokaku* and *Zuikaku* immediately flew off a large strike. Unfortunately the 'task force' turned out to be the US Navy oiler *Neosho* and her escorting destroyer, the USS *Sims*. It was a fatal error, for while the Japanese were sinking these ships they missed the chance of finding Task Force 17, and left the Americans time to discover the *Shoho*'s carrier group.

The luckless *Shoho* had been ordered to launch all available aircraft for an attack on the American carriers, and when at 09.50 the *Lexington*'s

Shoho *entered service in January 1942, but unlike* Zuiho *her operational career was extremely brief.* Shoho *had the unhappy distinction of being Japan's first aircraft carrier loss, sunk by aircraft from USS* Yorktown *on 7 May 1942 in the Coral Sea.*

strike spotted her turning into wind they encountered no resistance. The first strike scored no hits, but a near-miss blew five aircraft off her deck. At 10.25 a second strike arrived, from the *Yorktown* this time. This strike scored two devastating hits with 1,000-lb (454-kg) bombs on the flight deck, in spite of a curtain of anti-aircraft fire from the *Shoho*'s escorts. The carrier reeled under the blows, and as she began to lose speed more bombs and torpedoes found their mark. According to Japanese records as many as 11 more bombs and seven torpedoes hit, and *Shoho* burst into flames.

Only six minutes after the last American plane had departed the order was given to abandon ship, and at 10.35 the burning carrier rolled over and sank. Only 255 men out of an estimated total of 800 on board were saved. The Japanese had lost their first aircraft-carrier.

Specification
Shoho
Displacement: 11,262 tons standard, 14,200 tons full load
Dimensions: length 204.8 m (672 ft 0 in) overall; beam 18.2 m (59 ft 8 in); draught 6.6 m (21 ft 8 in)
Machinery: 2-shaft geared steam turbines delivering 52,000 shp (38770 kW)
Speed: 28.2 knots
Armour: none
Armament: four twin 127-mm (5-in) dual-purpose and four twin 25-mm AA guns
Aircraft: 30
Complement: 785 officers and men

'Junyo' class aircraft-carriers

Like the trio of 'Taiyo' class ships that preceded them, the *Junyo* and her sister *Hiyo* of the 'Junyo' class were useful conversions from Nippon Yusen Kaisha liners that had been designed from the outset with this procedure in mind. Where the earlier ships had undergone rebuilding at a late stage, the larger 'Taiyo' class ships were taken in hand before launching, both being in the water by June 1941, over five months before the Pacific War began, and completed in mid-1942.

As they had been designed as passenger liners, they had considerable freeboard and could accommodate two hangars, albeit of restricted headroom. They also had respectably-sized flight decks, measuring 210.2 m by 27.3 m (689.6 ft by 89.6 ft), and two centreline elevators, but suffered badly from the combination of their low mercantile speed and lack of catapults.

The two ships were the first Japanese carriers to incorporate a funnel as part of the island, though it was of strange aspect, canted outward at a sharp angle. Except for the never-completed Italian *Aquila*, this pair of carriers were the largest ever converted from mercantile hulls.

Junyo's 53 aircraft could have had a decisive effect at Midway but the ship was engaged in the rather fruitless Aleutians diversion. At Santa Cruz in October 1942 her aircraft damaged the battleship USS *South Dakota* and a cruiser, playing also a significant role in the sinking of the carrier USS *Hornet*. The two sisters operated together as Kakuta's Carrier Division Two but, at the battle of the Philippine Sea, where Ozawa took on the vastly superior force of Mitscher's TF 58, the partnership was broken, the *Junyo* being heavily damaged by bombing and *Hiyo* sunk after blowing up. The *Hiyo* had been struck by two torpedoes and was probably lost from the detonation of a build-up of vapour from leaking Avgas tanks.

The *Junyo*, newly repaired, was torpedoed in December 1944 and, though she was not sunk, she never re-entered service, surviving to be one of the very few Japanese naval ships of any size to fall eventually into American hands.

Specification
'Junyo' class
Displacement: 24,500 tons standard and 26,950 tons full load
Dimensions: length 219.2 m (719 ft 2 in); beam 26.7 m (87 ft 7 in); draught 8.2 m (26 ft 11 in)
Propulsion: geared steam turbines delivering 56,000 shp (41760 kW) to two shafts

Seen at Sasebo after the surrender of Japan, Junyo *displays the unusual funnel of the class. Converted from passenger liners, the two 'Junyo' class carriers were the first in Japanese service to feature a funnel on the island.*

Speed: 25 knots
Armament: 12 127-mm (5-in) DP and 24 25-mm AA guns
Aircraft: 53
Armour: none
Complement: about 1,220

While their capacious liner hulls had room for two hangars, the 'Junyo' class vessels suffered from a lack of speed, and without catapults aircraft operations were hampered. Both were at the Battle of the Philippine Sea, Junyo *being damaged and* Hiyo *sinking.*

JAPAN
Taiho

In many ways technically the most advanced of the Japanese carriers, the *Taiho* was unique. In 1939 Japanese intelligence learned that the British 'Illustrious' class carriers would have armoured decks, and so a new type of armoured carrier was planned under the Fourth Reinforcement Programme. The appalling carnage of Midway lent even more emphasis to the need for armoured flight decks, and two units more were ordered in 1942.

The Japanese design differed considerably from the British 'box-hangar' concept, for only the flight deck was protected by 75-mm (3-in) armour, and then only between the lifts. There

Probably the most advanced of all Japanese carriers, Taiho had an armoured flight deck, enclosed bow and the latest in AA defences (including an air warning radar for the first time). Taiho was lost just before the Battle of the Philippine Sea.

were two hangars, the lower hangar being protected by 35 mm (1.3 in) armour as well. Waterline armour was also provided but on a more lavish scale, 150 mm (5.9 in) abreast of the magazines and 55 mm (2.2 in) over the machinery. All this armour involved a colossal topweight penalty, and to preserve stability the designers were forced to allow one less deck above the waterline, in comparison with the 'Shokaku' class. This meant that the lower hangar deck was just above the waterline, and the bottom of the lift-wells was below the waterline.

The opportunity was taken to use the latest defensive guns: a new high-velocity 100-mm (3.9-in) Type 98 twin mounting. For the first time an air-warning radar was included. It had been hoped to operate 84 aircraft, but only 75 could be spared by the time the ship was ready: the aircraft were available, but not sufficient aircrew.

The new carrier, to be called *Taiho*,

was laid down in July 1941 and went to sea in March 1944. Immediately she joined Carrier Division 1, and was sent with the *Shokaku* and *Zuikaku* to Singapore. As soon as her air group was trained CarDiv 1 was sent to Tawi Tawi in the southern Philippines to join the First Mobile Fleet. On 19 June, during the Battle of the Philippine Sea, the *Taiho* had just launched her aircraft when the American submarine *Albacore* fired a spread of six 21-in (533-mm) torpedoes, one of which hit. Although her fuel tanks were ruptured, the *Taiho* lost only a little speed, and preparations were made to plank over the jammed forward lift, to permit flying operations to continue. But deadly gasoline vapour was spreading throughout the ship, and about 5 hours after the torpedo hits, some mischance (probably the switch on an electric pump) sparked off a colossal explosion. The armoured flight deck was split down the middle, the sides of the

hangar were blown out, and it seems that holes were blown through the keel. About 90 minutes later the remains of the *Taiho* sank, taking with her all but 500 of her crew.

Specification
Taiho
Displacement: 29,300 tons standard, 37,270 tons full load
Dimensions: length 260.5 m (854 ft 8 in); beam 27.7 m (90 ft 10 in); draught 9.6 m (31 ft 6 in)
Machinery: 4-shaft geared steam turbines delivering 180,000 shp (134225 kW)
Speed: 33⅓ knots
Armour: see text
Armament: six twin 100-mm (3.9-in) AA and 15 triple 25-mm AA guns
Aircraft: 30 Yokosuka D4Y 'Judy' dive-bombers, 27 Mitsubishi A6M Zero fighters and 18 Nakajima B6N 'Jill' torpedo-bombers
Complement: 2,150 officers and men

JAPAN
'Unryu' class aircraft-carriers

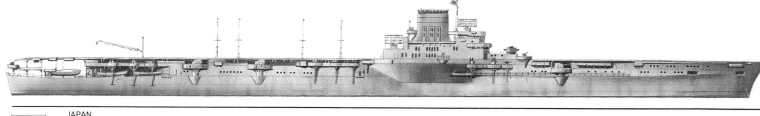

Like the Americans, the Japanese recognized that series production of a standard design was the only way of commissioning adequate numbers of good quality carriers in time to be of any use. To this end the basic 'Hiryu' design was modified and simplified, orders being placed at a variety of shipyards under the 1941-2 War Programme. Seventeen units of this **'Unryu' class** were planned initially but, even though construction of some had started before Midway, the catastrophe of this battle convinced the Japanese that shorter-term solutions needed to be found in a variety of conversions. These seem to have enjoyed higher priorities in the cause of haste, and the 'Unryu' class programme slowed badly, eventually halting through lack of materials. In the event, only three were ever completed and three more launched. The three completed were the **Amagi** (August 1944), the *Katsuragi* (October 1944) and *Unryu* (August 1944); the three others launched were the *Aso, Ikoma* and *Kasagi*. The main differences between the 'Unryu' and the 'Hiryu' designs was an elevator less and an altered layout of main armament in the former. Though of about the same length, the 'Unryo' class ships gained stability through a greater beam yet, for some reason unknown, had a smaller aircraft capacity. For their size,

they were well protected over vitals. Like all larger 'regular' Japanese carriers, the 'Unryu' class units had a good turn of speed, having the same machinery as later heavy cruiser classes. With shortages biting, however, two of those launched had to take a couple of sets each of destroyer machinery. Despite a one-third reduction in power, the speed penalty was only a couple of knots. The *Amagi* was lost to air attack in Kure during July 1945, the *Katsuragi* survived and was surrendered (for scrapping in 1947) and the *Unryu* was sunk in December 1944 by a US submarine.

The 'Unryu' class were to have been a standard design, produced in quantity. Although 17 were planned, only three of the modified, simplified

'Hiryu' design were built, with only Unryu being completed in time to get some war service.

Specification
'Unryu' class
Displacement: 17,250 tons standard and 22,550 tons full load
Dimensions: length 227.2 m (745 ft 5 in); beam 22.0 m (72 ft 2 in); draught 7.8 m (25 ft 7 in); flight deck dimensions 216.9 m (711 ft 7 in) by 27.0 m (88 ft 7 in)
Propulsion: geared steam turbines delivering 152,000 shp (113345 kW) in *Unryu* and 104,000 shp (77555 kW) in *Aso* and *Katsuragi* to four shafts
Speed: 34 kts for *Unryu* and 32 kts for *Aso* and *Katsuragi*

Unryu at sea in 1944. She was not destined to serve long, being sunk in December 1944 in the East China Sea. Two torpedoes from the American submarine USS Redfish sufficed to send her to the bottom.

Armament: 12 127-mm (5-in) DP and between 51 and 89 25-mm AA guns
Aircraft: 64
Armour: belt 25-150 mm (1-5.9 in); deck 55 mm (2.17 in)
Complement: 1,450

JAPAN
'Shinano' class aircraft-carrier

The catastrophic loss of four carriers at Midway, solely from the attentions of aircraft from US carriers, convinced the Japanese not only that carriers were more useful than battleships, but also that they needed to increase their numbers as a matter of great urgency. Most of their ambitious programme of conversions date from this point, none of them more impressive than the *Shinano*. Created from the incomplete third 'Yamato' class battleship, this giant displaced nearly 72,000 tons full load, a figure not eclipsed until the advent of the US post-war supercarriers. The hull was already fitted with a 200-mm (7.87-in) armoured deck and vertical protection of the same order, and the ship's great beam (increased further by bulging) allowed for a flight deck

of 80-mm (3.15-in) thickness over most of its area.

Despite the ship's size, her flight deck was over 1 m (3.3 ft) shorter than that of the *Taiho* of less than half the displacement, although it was far wider. Viewed probably as too slow to act as an attack carrier, *Shinano* was not even fitted with catapults and, although originally slated to have a small air group of 18 aircraft, she was completed to carry a still-undersized complement of 47. Her considerable stowage was looked upon mainly as a repair and re-supply facility for the front-line carriers.

Like the *Taiho*, the *Shinano* had an integral funnel and island, but lacked the smaller ship's British-style 'hurricane bow'. Her shortcomings were, in

the event, of only academic interest. Not quite complete in time for the Japanese fleet's self-immolation at Leyte Gulf in October 1944, she transferred from Yokosuka to Kure for final fitting-out. On the way she was hit by a full spread of six torpedoes from an American submarine: her watertight subdivision still incomplete, she foundered from virtually uncontrolled flooding on 29 November.

Specification
'Shinano' class
Displacement: 64,000 tons standard and 71,900 tons full load
Dimensions: length 265.8 m (872 ft); beam 36.3 m (119 ft); draught 10.3 m (33 ft 10 in); flightdeck 255.9 (839 ft 7 in) by 40.1 m (131 ft 7 in)

Propulsion: geared steam turbines delivering 150,000 shp (111855 kW) to four shafts
Speed: 27 kts
Armour: belt 205 mm (8.07 in); flight deck 80 mm (3.15 in); hangar deck 200 mm (7.87 in)
Armament: 16 127-mm (5-in) DP and 145 25-mm AA guns, and 12 28-barrel AA rocket-launchers
Aircraft: 18 (later 47)
Complement: 2,400

By far the largest carrier of the war, Shinano was to have been the third 'Yamato' class battleship. Her small aircraft capacity and slow speed pointed to her eventual role as repair and resupply vessel to front-line carriers, a role she was destined never to fulfil.

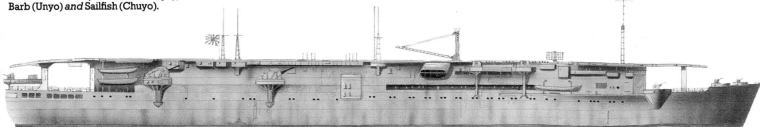

JAPAN
'Taiyo' class escort carrier

Carriers were required by the Japanese for other than fleet purposes. Firstly, and with increasing urgency, for the defence of trade. This was a function that had been badly neglected prewar due to a lack of hard experience and the belief that the war that they would promote would be a short one. Secondly, for the training of large numbers of aircrew for carrier operations, a task for which first-line units could not be spared. Thirdly, for the ferrying of aircraft, a task made essential by the sheer size of the newly-acquired empire, which had airfields thousands of miles from the homeland itself.

Like Western fleets, the Japanese navy rebuilt good-class mercantile tonnage into auxiliary carriers, particularly NYK ships, which had government-subsidized features built into them. The *Taiyo* was the first such example, converted from the *Kasuga Maru* in 1941 as the lead ship of the 'Taiyo' class, before the outbreak of the Pacific war. After a few months of evaluation, the similar *Yawata Maru* and *Nitta Maru* were rebuilt into the *Unyo* and *Chuyo* respectively. Though

The three 'Taiyo' class vessels were largely used for aircraft transport and training. Their heavy AA armament was to no avail, all three succumbing to submarine attacks from USS Rasher (which sank Taiyo), Barb (Unyo) and Sailfish (Chuyo).

of a larger size than Western escort carriers, none of them was equipped with arrester gear or catapults which, combined with their low speed, made aircraft launch and recovery difficult. All were lost to submarine torpedo attack within a space of 10 months between December 1943 and September 1944 having spent their lives engaged in auxiliary tasks.

Probably for reasons of availability, the first of the class, the *Taiyo*, was armed with 120-mm (4.7-in) guns,

probably spare weapons from older destroyers.

Specification
'Taiyo' class
Displacement: 17,850 tons standard
Dimensions: length 180.1 m (590 ft 11 in); beam 22.5 m (73 ft 10 in); draught 8.0 m (26 ft 3 in); flight deck 171.9 m (564 ft) by 23.5 m (77 ft 1 in)
Machinery: geared steam turbines delivering 25,200 shp (18790 kW) to two shafts

Like the British and American fleets, Japan's need for escort carriers was met by converting merchant hulls. Kaiyo, seen here in late 1943, was similar to the 'Taiyo' class conversions.

Armament: eight 127-mm (5-in) DP (except Taiyo, see text) and eight (later 22) 25-mm AA guns
Aircraft: 27
Armour: none
Complement: 800

469

American Aircraft Carriers

The Pacific War was to a large extent the war of the aircraft carrier; from Pearl Harbor to Okinawa, it was the effective use of the carrier forces which proved decisive. For the first time, battles were fought with hundreds of miles of ocean between the combatants.

An early shot showing a biplane Corsair flying over USS *Saratoga* in 1929. With her sister USS *Lexington*, she played a major role in developing the concept of the fast carrier task force.

From the moment Japanese carrier aircraft struck at the US Pacific Fleet on 7 December 1941, a new era in naval warfare was born. Although naval air power had already proved its ability to strike at an enemy fleet in its own harbours, Pearl Harbor was the dawn of carrier warfare across the broad oceans, in a way that pre-war theorists had never imagined.

The reason for this lay in the fact that the battleships with which aircraft carriers had been meant to fight were now sunk or disabled. For at least six months the US Pacific Fleet could only take the offensive with its carriers, and so the concept of the fast carrier task force was created, using the carriers' dive-bombers and torpedo-bombers as long-range substitutes for the 406mm (16in) gun. Because the tactics and the aircraft were comparatively primitive, the first attempts by the US Navy to carry the war to the Japanese were barely effective, and there was little that could be done to stop the Japanese carriers from overrunning the Philippines and the Dutch East Indies.

The first pitched battle, in the Coral Sea, was fought in May 1942 to stop the Japanese from gaining a foothold in Port Moresby, New Guinea. It cost the Americans one of their biggest carriers, the USS *Lexington*, but the amphibious operation was called off after the small carrier *Shoho* was sunk. What distinguished the battle was that opposing fleets never saw each other: it was the first carrier-versus-carrier battle.

A rash attempt by the Japanese to capture Midway Island brought on the next battle in June 1942, but superior American intelligence and much improved tactics made the Battle of Midway decisive. The Japanese lost their four front-line carriers in quick succession, and with them the best-trained aircrews in the world. In the months that followed the Japanese squandered the lives of their carrier aircrews faster than they could be replaced. Thus, when the Allies took the offensive by landing in the Solomons, the Battles of the Eastern Solomons and the Santa Cruz islands thinned the ranks of Japanese naval pilots to a fatal degree. In contrast the US Navy replaced lost pilots with thousands of new aircrew and a generation of more powerful aircraft.

In June 1944 the US assault on the Marianas brought on another great carrier battle, the Philippine Sea. The 'Great Marianas Turkey Shoot' saw the slaughter of hundreds of semi-skilled pilots, and when four months later the remnants of the Imperial Navy were flung into the Battle of Leyte Gulf there were hardly any pilots left for the carriers. From October 1944 the survivors of the once-mighty force were sunk at their moorings in Japan, unable to move because of the total lack of fuel.

USS *Langley*

The potential of naval aviation was so clearly seen at the end of World War I that the US Navy wanted to press ahead with the construction of aircraft carriers. But to gain practical experience before building new ships it was essential to carry out experiments, and the quickest and cheapest way was to convert an existing ship.

The big fleet collier *Jupiter* (AC.3) was taken in hand in March 1920. A month later she was renamed USS *Langley* (CV.1) and started trials in July 1922. The ship which emerged was flush-decked, with two hinged funnels on the port side. The former coal holds had been converted to workshops, accommodation and storerooms, while the former upper deck was now the hangar. The biggest drawback to the *Langley* was her low speed, for the 5335-kW (7,150-shp) turbo-electric machinery was badly underpowered. In service the *Langley* could only make 14 knots, which was some 7 knots below the speed of the battle fleet. However in spite of this handicap she served with the fleet, and for five years she played the role which was to be taken over so successfully by the *Lexington* and *Saratoga* from 1928 onwards.

Although originally designed to operate 24 aircraft, her capacious hangar allowed a maximum of 33 to be accommodated. She did not stop operating aircraft until 1936, when she was converted to a seaplane carrier and redesignated AV.3. After a short refit she reappeared in April 1937 with a short flight deck, as the forward part had been removed.

One most important contributions made to naval aviation by the *Langley* was to test various systems of arrester

gear. When she was first commissioned she had a British system of longitudinal wires, which were intended to engage hooks in the landing gear of the aircraft, and prevent it from slewing from side to side. However, the US Navy added a back-up system of transverse wires, whose retarding action was achieved by hanging sand-filled shellcases on the ends. This system (refined into a proper hydraulic arrester system) ultimately proved better, and is the basis of all modern carrier landings. Another innovation was a pair of flush-mounted pneumatic catapults on the flight deck; intended for seaplanes, they later proved that they could speed up the launching of con-

ventional aircraft, and like the arrester gear, this procedure is still standard today.

The veteran 'Covered Wagon' spent her short war service as a humble aircraft transport. On 27 February 1942 a group of Japanese naval bombers operating from Bali caught her en route for Tjilatjap in Java, and sank her with five bombs.

Specification
USS *Langley* (CV.1)
Displacement: 11,050 tons standard, 14,700 tons full load
Dimensions: length 165.3 m (542 ft 4 in) overall; beam 19.96 m (65 ft 6 in); draught 7.32 m (24 ft 0 in)

The old Langley, *with the forward part of her flight deck removed, served as a seaplane carrier from 1936. In her short wartime career, the first US aircraft carrier humbly acted as an aircraft transport until sunk by Japanese bombers in February 1942.*

Machinery: 1-shaft steam turbo-electric delivering 5335 kW (7,150 shp)
Speed: 14 knots
Armour: none
Armament: four 127-mm (5-in) guns
Aircraft: (1923) 30 fighters
Complement: 410 officers and enlisted men

USS *Lexington*

Under the Washington Treaty the US Navy was allowed to convert two incomplete 33,000-ton battle-cruisers into aircraft-carriers. The ships chosen were the *Lexington* and *Saratoga*, and the opportunity was taken to incorporate many ideas from a cancelled carrier design of 1919. When completed in 1925 the USS *Lexington* (CV.2) was a remarkable ship, with a massive 'island' superstructure on the starboard side, flanked by two twin 203-mm (8-in) gun turrets forward and two aft.

At the time of Pearl Harbor the ship was delivering aircraft to the US Marines on Midway Island, and so escaped the disaster. She was hurriedly refitted, losing her cumbersome 203-mm (8-in) guns and four 127-mm (5-in) guns, although she received a few single 20-mm Oerlikon guns to supplement her meagre close-range anti-aircraft armament.

The *Lexington*'s first operation was an abortive attempt to relieve Wake Island immediately after Pearl Harbor, but at the end of January 1942 she provided distant cover for a raid on the

Marshall Islands and thereafter saw limited action in the South West Pacific. Not until she was joined by the newer carrier *Yorktown* in March 1942 did the *Lexington* really begin to flex her muscles.

After a short refit at Pearl Harbor the ship returned to the Coral Sea, where the Japanese carriers were supporting an attack on Port Moresby, New Guinea. On 8 May her Douglas SBD Dauntless dive-bombers attacked the *Shokaku* and *Zuikaku*, but without scoring any hits. Unfortunately while this attack was in progress a Japanese counter-strike succeeded in hitting the *Lexington* with two torpedoes on the port side, and the ship also suffered two bomb hits and several near misses. The 'whip' of the 270.7-m (888-ft)

hull from the explosions ruptured the aviation gasoline tanks, so that even after the fires had been extinguished the lethal vapour continued to seep through the ship. About an hour after the attack a chance spark ignited this vapour, and the ship began to suffer a series of devastating internal explosions. Six hours after the first hit the order was given to abandon ship, and after escorting destroyers had rescued as many of her crewmen as possible the blazing wreck was torpedoed. Surprisingly only 216 lives out of 2,951 were lost.

In her short war career the *Lexington* had failed to inflict severe damage on the enemy, largely as a result of the inexperience of her air group and because of faulty tactical US Navy doctrine, and the loss of a big carrier was a heavy price to pay for the Coral Sea victory.

Specification
USS *Lexington* (CV.2)
Displacement: 36,000 tons standard, 47,700 tons full load
Dimensions: length 270.66 m (888 ft 0 in) overall; beam 39.62 m (130 ft 0 in) over flight deck; draught 9.75 m (32 ft 0 in)
Machinery: 4-shaft steam turbo-electric delivering 156660 kW (210,000 shp)
Speed: 34 knots
Armour: belt 152 mm (6 in); flight deck 25 mm (1 in); main deck 51 mm (2 in); lower deck 25–76 mm (1–3 in); turrets 38–76 mm (1½–3 in); barbettes 152 mm (6 in)
Armament: (in 1942) eight 127-mm (5-in) AA, 30 20-mm AA and six quadruple 27.94-mm (1.1-in) AA guns
Aircraft: (1942) 22 fighters, 36 dive-bombers and 12 torpedo-bombers
Complement: 2,951 officers and enlisted men

To encase the uptakes from 16 boilers, the Lexington *and* Saratoga *were each given a massive funnel. Both ships had their 8-inch guns removed at the outbreak of World War II, and* Saratoga *was considerably altered in appearance by 1945.*

USS *Saratoga*

Like her sister *Lexington*, the USS *Saratoga* (CV.3) was launched in 1925 after three years of conversion from an incomplete battle-cruiser hull. Like her sister she played a major role in developing the concept of the fast carrier task force, and from 1928 the two ships took part in the annual 'Fleet Problem' or war game of the Pacific Fleet.

At the time of Pearl Harbor the 'Sara' was back at San Diego on the US west coast undergoing a short refit, but she sailed shortly afterwards and took part with her sister 'Lex' in an abortive attempt to relieve Wake Island. During her refit the four twin 203-mm (8-in) turrets were removed, and in their place she received four twin 127-mm (5-in) dual-purpose mountings. She was torpedoed by a Japanese submarine off Hawaii, on 11 January 1942, and needed four months of repairs.

The 'Sara' was used to ferry fresh aircraft out to the Central Pacific, and so missed the Battle of Midway, but she was a welcome reinforcement by 8 June, the day after the sinking of the *Yorktown*. Her fighters and dive-bombers were given the task of softening up the defences of Guadalcanal on 7 August 1942 before the big amphibious landing by the US Marines. The Japanese responded vigorously to this challenge, and by 20 August a powerful carrier task force was nearing the Eastern Solomons.

The *Saratoga*, *Enterprise* and *Wasp* were heavily engaged in the Battle of the Eastern Solomons, but the 'Sara' escaped lightly. Not until 31 August did she sustain damage, when she was torpedoed by the submarine *I-68* just after dawn. The carrier was not badly damaged by the hit, in spite of having one boiler room flooded and another partly flooded, but an electrical failure soon put her machinery out of action. Two hours later she got back limited

power, and reached Pearl Harbor six days later; repairs took six weeks to complete.

In 1943-4 the *Saratoga* took part in the great 'island-hopping' drive across the Pacific, and in 1944 was detached to the East Indies, where she cooperated with the British and Free French in attacking Japanese positions in Java and Sumatra. On 21 February 1945 she was hit by a *kamikaze* while supporting the landings on Iwo Jima. By now she was showing her age, and although repaired was restricted to training duties at Pearl Harbor.

On 25 July 1946 the stripped hull of the *Saratoga* was sunk in Bikini Atoll during a series of nuclear tests.

Specification
USS *Saratoga* (CV.3)
Displacement: 36,000 tons standard, 47,700 tons full load
Dimensions: length 270.66 m (888 ft 0 in) overall; beam 32.2 m (105 ft 6 in) hull; draught 9.75 m (32 ft 0 in)
Machinery: 4-shaft steam turbo-electric delivering 156660 kW (210,000 shp)
Speed: 34 knots
Armour: belt 152 mm (6 in); flight deck 25 mm (1 in); main deck 51 mm (2 in); lower deck 25–76 mm (1–3); barbettes 152 mm (6 in)
Armament: (in 1945) eight twin 127-mm (5-in) dual-purpose, 24 quadruple 40-mm Bofors AA, two twin 40-mm AA and 16 20-mm AA guns
Aircraft: (1945) 57 fighters and 18 torpedo-bombers
Complement: (1945) 3,373 officers and enlisted men

The USS Saratoga *(CV.3) in March 1932 with a large part of her air group at the forward end of the flight deck. She and her sister 'fought' each other in annual manoeuvres.*

'Sara' in September 1944, painted in Camouflage Measure 32/11A. Twin 5-inch and light AA guns have replaced the 8-inch guns. Despite her age she was still the biggest US carrier, if not the most capacious.

USS *Yorktown*

The USS *Yorktown* (CV.5) was the lead-ship of a new class of aircraft-carrier authorized out of President Roosevelt's Public Works Administration, the Federal unemployment relief agency. She and her sister *Enterprise* (CV.6) were authorized in 1933, and were followed by the *Hornet* (CV.8) five years later.

The design was a development of that of the *Ranger*, with an 'open' hangar rather than the 'closed' type of the *Lexington* and *Saratoga*, to allow up to 80 aircraft to be carried. This arrangement proved highly successful, and formed the basis for the even more successful 'Essex' class.

The ship was commissioned in September 1937, and was hurriedly

transferred to the Pacific after Pearl Harbor. Under Rear Admiral Frank J. Fletcher she was sent to the South West Pacific in the spring of 1942 and took part in the Battle of the Coral Sea. Her Air Group 5, comprising 20 Grumman F4F Wildcat fighters, 38 Douglas SBD Dauntless dive-bombers and 13 Douglas TBD Devastator torpedo-bombers, played a major role in the battle, sinking the light carrier *Shoho* in a brilliant attack lasting only 10 minutes. On the next day, 8 May, her dive-bombers inflicted damage on the carrier *Zuikaku*, but in return a force of Nakajima B5N 'Kate' torpedo-bombers and Aichi D3A 'Val' dive-bombers penetrated a dense screen of fighters and gunfire to score a devastating hit

on the flight deck.

The bomb went through three decks before exploding, and numerous fires were started. The damage control parties brought the fires under control, and the ship was able to return to Pearl Harbor for repairs.

Working around the clock, the repair teams were able to get *Yorktown* back in action in only four days, just in time for the Battle of Midway in June 1942. At a crucial point in the battle *Yorktown*'s dive-bombers took part in the attack on the Japanese carriers, and her aircraft were the only ones able to mount a search for the surviving Japanese carrier *Hiryu*. Even after the *Yorktown* was hit by three 250-kg (551-lb) bombs she was able to operate her aircraft, and it was not until she was hit by two torpedoes that she was fully out of action.

The *Yorktown* might have survived even this heavy damage, for by first light on 6 June salvage parties had put out the fires and had started to pump out flooded compartments. But the submarine *I-168* put two more torpedoes into her, and early next morning she capsized and sank.

Specification
USS *Yorktown* (CV.8)
Displacement: 19,800 tons standard, 27,500 tons full load
Dimensions: length 246.7 m (809 ft 6 in) overall; beam 25.3 m (83 ft 0 in); draught 8.53 m (28 ft)
Machinery: 4-shaft geared steam turbines delivering 89520 kW (120,000 shp)
Speed: 33 knots
Armour: belt 102 mm (4 in); main deck 76 mm (3 in); lower deck 25-76 mm (1-3 in)
Armament: (1942) eight 127-mm (0.5-in) AA, four quadruple 27.94-mm (1.1-in) AA and 16 12.7-mm (0.5-in) machine-guns
Aircraft: (1942) 20 fighters, 38 dive-bombers and 13 torpedo-bombers
Complement: 2,919 officers and enlisted men

The Yorktown *(CV.5) and her sisters were prototypes for the successful 'Essex' class. Much smaller than the 'Lexingtons', they could actually carry more aircraft.*

USS *Enterprise*

Easily the most distinguished carrier of the Pacific War, the 'Big E' played a major role in the US Navy's victory and epitomized the new type of warfare.

The USS *Enterprise* (CV.6) was the second of the 'Yorktown' class, and joined the Pacific Fleet in 1938. Fortunately she and the other two carriers of the Pacific Fleet were away from Pearl Harbor on 7 December 1941 when the Japanese attacked. When they returned to Oahu they were immediately put into the front line, for the battle fleet no longer existed. Three days afterwards the *Enterprise*'s aircraft sank the submarine *I-170*, the first Japanese submarine to be destroyed.

The *Enterprise* escorted her sister *Hornet* on the Tokyo Raid in April 1942 but did not embark B-25 bombers as her aircraft were to be used to sink the Japanese early warning picket line. Neither carrier was back in time for the Battle of the Coral Sea in the following month, but they joined the *Yorktown* in time for Midway in June. Here the Douglas SBD Dauntlesses from the *Enterprise* sank the carriers *Kaga* and *Akagi*, and *Yorktown*'s Dauntlesses flying off *Enterprise*'s deck joined the group which sank the *Hiryu*. Two days later the *Enterprise*'s dive-bombers sank the heavy cruiser *Mikuma* and damaged the cruiser *Mogami* and two destroyers.

The *Enterprise* covered the Guadalcanal landings in August 1942, and her aircraft shot down 17 Japanese aircraft in two days. During the Battle of the Eastern Solomons on 24 August she was hit by three bombs, and returned to Pearl Harbor for two months' repairs. In the Battle of Santa Cruz on 26 October she once again took three hits, but was still able to operate her aircraft, and as she was now the only US carrier left she had to remain in the forward area. On 13 November her Grumman TBF Avenger torpedo-

bombers finished off the damaged battleship *Hiei*, and next day devastated a troop convoy of 11 ships with no fewer than 26 bomb and six torpedo hits.

Enterprise was finally given lengthy repairs in the United States and did not return to the Pacific until mid-1943. On 25 November 1943 one of her Avengers achieved the world's first night 'kill' at sea. She took part in the massive strike on Truk in February 1944, and in the famous 'Marianas Turkey Shoot' during the Battle of the Philippine Sea the following June. She continued in action into 1945, surviving two *kamikaze* attacks. A third *kamikaze* strike on 14 May finally brought her career to an end, for she had to return to the United States for major repairs.

As the holder of 19 Battle Stars the 'Big E' was a candidate for preservation as a memorial, but efforts to save her came to nothing and in 1958 she was sold for scrap, releasing her name for the first nuclear carrier.

Specification
USS *Enterprise* (CV.6)
Displacement: 19,800 tons standard, 25,500 tons full load
Dimensions: length 246.74 m (809 ft 6 in; beam 34.75 m (114 ft 0 in) over flight deck; draught 8.84 m (29 ft 0 in)
Machinery: 4-shaft geared steam turbines delivering 89520 kW (120,000 shp)
Speed: 33 knots
Armour: belt 102 mm (4 in); main deck 76 mm (3 in); lower deck 25–76 mm (1–3 in)
Armament: (1942) eight 127-mm (5-in) AA, four quadruple 27.94-mm (1.1-in) AA and 16 12.7 mm (0.5-in) machine-guns
Aircraft: (1942) 27 fighters, 37 dive-bombers and 15 torpedo-bombers
Complement: 2,919 officers and enlisted men

Right: The USS Enterprise *(CV.6) with aircraft ranged on the after part of the flight deck. No flying operations are in progress; the crewmen are clearly relaxing on deck.*

Below: Hellcats spotted on the port and starboard catapults. Although aircraft could take off in the ordinary way, catapulting them speeded up the launch of a large strike and enabled more of the flight deck to be used.

USS *Hornet*

Although she was the third member of the 'Yorktown' class, the USS *Hornet* (CV.8) was authorized some years after her sisters. She commissioned on 20 October 1940, seven weeks before Pearl Harbor. After a shakedown cruise with her air group in the Caribbean in January 1942 the ship embarked the first twin-engine North American B-25 bombers for the famous Doolittle Raid on Tokyo. After two months of intensive trials and training the Hornet left for the Pacific on 2 April, carrying 16 B-25 Mitchell bombers.

The raid on 18 April took the Japanese completely by surprise, and most of the bombers reached China safely. The *Hornet*'s next assignment was the Battle of Midway, on 4-6 June 1942. Although her air group lost all its Douglas TBD Devastator torpedo-bombers and five Grumman TBF Avengers in an unsuccessful strike, and failed to hit the Japanese carrier *Hiryu* in a second strike, on the last day of the battle it made amends by sinking the damaged heavy cruiser *Mikuma* and inflicting severe damage on her sister *Mogami*.

The *Hornet* was ferrying US Marine Corps fighters at the time of the Guadalcanal landings in August 1942, but after landing her aircraft she joined the *Wasp* and *Saratoga* in the covering

force. Although withdrawn to Espiritu Santo to avoid being sunk by submarines, she sortied early in October to attack Japanese targets, and on 25 October met the Japanese carriers once more, in the Battle of Santa Cruz.

On 26 October, after the two sides had located one another, the two American carriers launched an air strike (a total of 158 aircraft), while the four Japanese carriers launched most of their 207 aircraft. But while the *Hornet*'s torpedo-bombers and dive-bombers were on their way, 27 Japanese strike aircraft broke through the fighter screen and scored six bomb and two torpedo hits on the *Hornet*. Although heroic efforts were made to extinguish the fires and get the carrier under way, four hours later another Japanese strike scored a torpedo hit and two more bomb hits. By now the American destroyers screening the *Hornet* were dangerously exposed, with the Japanese searching for them in the darkness. The decision was taken to scuttle the *Hornet*, but to the Americans' dismay several torpedoes failed to detonate, and a total of 430 127-mm (5-in) shells fired at the carrier's waterline had no appreciable effect. The waterlogged hulk was abandoned, but the Japanese found it impossible to tow her, and finally two Japanese destroyers gave the *Hornet* her death-blow in the early hours of 27 October.

Specification
USS *Hornet* (CV.8)
Displacement: 19,000 tons standard, 29,100 tons full load
Dimensions: length 252.2 m (827 ft 5 in overall; beam 34.8 m (114 ft 2 in) over flight deck; draught 8.84 m (29 ft 0 in)
Machinery: 4-shaft geared steam turbines delivering 89520 kW (120,000 shp)
Speed: 33 knots
Armour: belt 64–102 mm (2½–4in); main deck 76 mm (3 in); lower deck 25–76 mm (1–3 in)
Armament: (1942) eight 127 mm (5-in) AA, four quadruple 27.94-mm (1.1-in) AA, 30 20-mm AA and nine 12.7-mm (0.5-in) machine-guns
Aircraft: (1942) 36 fighters, 36 dive-bombers and 15 torpedo-bombers
Complement: 2,919 officers and enlisted men

The new carrier Hornet *(CV.8) on trials in 1941. She was commissioned seven weeks before Pearl Harbor and left for the Pacific in March 1942.*

USS *Wasp*

Under the terms of the Washington Naval Treaty the US Navy was restricted to 135,000 tons of aircraft-carriers, and so could only build a further 14,700 tons of carriers after the completion of *Lexington, Saratoga, Ranger, Yorktown* and *Enterprise*. Thus in 1935 an improved version of the *Ranger* was ordered, also with modest speed and light armour but big aircraft capacity. The opportunity was taken to eradicate the worst faults of the *Ranger*, and the new carrier was given a proper island superstructure and better compartmentation.

The USS *Wasp* (CV.7) was commissioned in April 1941, and from the autumn of that year was in the Atlantic on training duties. Late in March 1942 she went to the Mediterranean to ferry RAF Spitfires to Malta. At the beginning of July she left San Diego for the Pacific and took part in the Guadalcanal landings, where her aircraft flew more than 300 sorties. She missed the Battle of the Eastern Solomons as she had been detached to refuel, and she returned to Noumea to take on board a consignment of fighter aircraft for the US Marines on Guadalcanal.

Early in the afternoon of 15 September 1942 the *Wasp* flew off her fighters, but shortly afterwards she was hit by three torpedoes fired by the Japanese submarine *I-19*. Two of the torpedoes struck her on the port side near the aviation gasoline tanks, while the third

struck higher up and damaged the refuelling system, which had already been ruptured.

The ship was very quickly gutted by fire and explosions, which proved impossible to contain as the torpedo detonations had also ruptured the fire mains. In less than an hour the order to abandon ship was given, and she continued to burn for another 3½ hours; finally the destroyer *Lansdowne* was ordered to sink her, and four torpedoes were fired.

The *Wasp* proved the least battle-worthy of all American carriers, and her loss provided important lessons for the future. A board of enquiry showed that the majority of the damage was caused by the third torpedo-hit, for the first two hits had left the machinery and auxiliary power undamaged. However, the shock of the explosions and the 'whip' of the hull had knocked out electrical switchboards and the damage control organization. Thereafter a series of subsidiary explosions of bombs, torpedoes, ammunition and aircraft fuel tanks wrecked the ship.

The Wasp *(CV.7) at Pearl Harbor on 8 August 1942, a month before she was sunk.*

Specification
USS Wasp (CV.7)
Displacement: 14,700 tons standard, 20,500 tons full load
Dimensions: length 225.93 m (741 ft 3 in) overall; beam 24.61 m (80 ft 9 in); draught 8.53 m (28 ft 0 in)
Machinery: 2-shaft geared steam turbines delivering 55950 kW (75,000 shp)
Speed: 29½ knots
Armour: belt 102 mm (4 in); main and lower decks 38 mm (1½ in)
Armament: (1942) eight 127-mm (5-in) AA, four quadruple 27.94-mm (1.1-in) AA and 30 20-mm AA guns
Aircraft: (1942) 29 fighters, 36 dive-bombers and 15 torpedo-bombers
Complement: 2,367 officers and enlisted men

Port profile of the Wasp. *Her tall funnel made her unique among US carriers.*

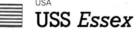

USS *Essex*

The 'Essex' class can claim to be the most cost-effective and successful aircraft-carriers ever built. The specification, issued in June 1939, was for an improved 'Yorktown' class, but with displacement increased by 7,000 tons to provide stronger defensive armament, thicker armour, more power and above all, more aviation fuel. With more than 6,300 tons of oil fuel the endurance was 27360 km (17,000 miles) at 20 knots, while 690 tons of gasoline and 220 tons of ammunition pushed up the number of sorties which could be flown. Above all, the same number of aircraft could be carried, although in practice many more could be carried; the nominal strength was 82 but by 1945 108 of the latest aircraft could be embarked.

Eleven of the class were ordered in 1940 and a further 13 were built during World War II. Building times were extremely short; USS *Essex* (CV.9) was built in 20 months, and the wartime average was cut to 17½ months.

The lead-ship of her class, the *Essex* reached the Pacific in May 1943, by which time the worst was over, but she saw considerable heavy fighting with

the Fast Carrier Task Force, with the *Enterprise* and *Saratoga* and the light fleet carriers of the 'Independence' class. In the spring of 1944 the *Essex* was withdrawn for a short refit, but returned to join Task Group 12.1 for the raid on the Marcus Islands. Later she formed part of the famous Task Group 38.3 in Task Force 38. On 25 November 1944, while supporting the Leyte Gulf landings, she was hit on the port side by a *kamikaze*, suffering 15 dead and 44 wounded, and had to be withdrawn for repairs. However, she was back in action after only three weeks.

In 1945 the *Essex* returned to TF 38, and took part in the attacks on Lingayen, Formosa, Sakishima Gunto and Okinawa. With TF 58 she took part in the final assault on Japan, and was one of the enormous fleet mustered in Tokyo Bay for the Japanese surrender in August 1945. On her return the battered carrier received her first full repairs and was put into reserve.

In retrospect, the 'Essex' design proved ideal for the Pacific. It was seaworthy and had the endurance needed to cover the enormous distances involved, not only for itself but for its aircraft. Despite its 'open' hangars, the class proved surprisingly rugged, and during the first 14 months

in action only three units of the class were damaged by enemy action; apart from the *Franklin* (CV.13) all returned to active service after sustaining severe battle damage.

Specification
USS Essex (CV.9)
Displacement: 27,100 tons standard, 33,000 tons full load
Dimensions: length 267.21 m (876 ft 8 in) overall; beam 45.0 m (147 ft 8 in) over flight deck; draught 8.69 m (28 ft 6 in)
Machinery: 4-shaft geared steam turbines delivering 111900 kW (150,000 shp)

Speed: 33 knots
Armour: belt 64–102 mm (2½–4 in); flight deck 38 mm (1½ in); hangar deck 76 mm (3 in); main deck 38 mm (1½ in); turrets and barbettes 38 mm (1½ in)
Armament: (1943) 12 127-mm (5-in) AA, 11 quadruple 40-mm bofors AA, and 44 20-mm AA guns
Aircraft: (1943) 6 fighters, 36 dive-bombers and 18 torpedo-bombers
Complement: 3,240 officers and enlisted men

USS Essex *being fitted out at Pearl Harbor in 1942.*

USS *Franklin*

The fifth unit of the 'Essex' class was authorized in 1940 but was not started until a year after Pearl Harbor as there were no slipways of the right length available. However, her builders, Newport News Shipbuilding Company, made up for the delay by completing her in less than 14 months.

The USS *Franklin* (CV.13) was commissioned at the end of January 1944 and joined Task Group 58.2 exactly six months later for an attack on the Bonin Islands. From then on she was constantly in action: during an attack on Formosa and the Ryukyus in October she was hit by a bomber which crashed on deck, and two days later her deck-edge lift was hit by a bomb which killed three men.

During the Battle of Surigao Strait on 24 October 1944 the *Franklin's* aircraft sank a destroyer, and then attacked the giant battleship *Musashi* in the Sibuyan Sea. On the next day, during the Battle of Cape Engano, they crip-

pled the light carrier *Chiyoda* and finished off the *Zuikaku*. The *Franklin's* run of good luck ended on 30 October. While defending the Leyte Gulf landing area she and the light carrier were attacked by five *kamikaze* aircraft which had broken through the fighter screen: she lost 56 dead and 60 wounded, while 33 aircraft were destroyed by the fire which followed. She had to return to Bremerton Navy Yard for major repairs, and did not return to active service until February 1945.

As part of TF 58 the *Franklin* attacked Kyushu in the Japanese home islands on 18 March. On the next day two Yokosuka D4Y 'Judy' bombers made a daring low-level attack, and hit the *Franklin* with two 250-kg (551-lb) bombs just as she was preparing her

The Franklin *(CV.13) was gutted by fire after being hit by bombs off Kyushu on 19 March 1945, but still got home.*

second strike. At first the damage did not seem serious for the bombs had not penetrated below the hangar deck, but as the aircraft caught fire their bombs and rockets, as well as the spare ordnance in the hangar, started to explode. Toxic smoke was drawn through the ship's ventilation system, with the result that many of the 724 dead were suffocated (another 265 were wounded). The ship lay dead in the water for three hours as the engine rooms and boiler rooms could not be manned.

Finally the fires were put out and on the next day the *Franklin* was able to get up steam once again. She limped back to Pearl Harbor and then across the Pacific to New York Navy Yard for lengthy repairs. She did not reappear until after the end of the war, and never returned to full commission, being laid up permanently in reserve in February 1947.

Specification
USS *Franklin* (CV.13)
Displacement: 27,100 tons standard, 36,500 tons full load
Dimensions: length 267.21 m (867 ft 8 in); beam 45.0 m (147 ft 8 in) over flight deck; draught 9.40 m (30 ft 10 in)
Machinery: 4-shaft geared steam turbines delivering 111900 kW (150,000 shp)
Speed: 33 knots
Armour: belt 64–102 mm (2½–3 in); flight deck 38 mm (1½ in); hangar deck 76 mm (3 in); main deck 38 mm (1½ in); turrets and barbettes 38 mm (1½ in)
Aircraft: (1945) 74 fighters, 15 dive-bombers and 30 torpedo-bombers.
Complement: 3,240 officers and enlisted men

Although cleaned up, the Franklin *still shows her battle scars on her return to the USA. She was never recommissioned.*

USS *Princeton*

To meet the acute shortage of carriers after Pearl Harbor the US Navy decided to complete nine 'Cleveland' class light cruisers as carriers. The *Amsterdam* (CL.59), *Tallahassee* (CL.61), *New Haven* (CL.76), *Huntington* (CL.77), *Dayton* (CL.78), *Fargo* (CL.85), *Wilmington* (CL.79), *Buffalo* (CL.99) and *Newark* (CL.100) thus became the USS *Independence* (CVL.22), *Princeton* (CVL.23), *Belleau Wood* (CVL.24), *Cowpens* (CVL.25), *Monterey* (CVL.26), *Langley* (CVL.27), *Cabot* (CVL.28), *Bataan* (CVL.29) and *San Jacinto* (CVL.30). Although it was an ingenious conversion, the results were disappointing, for the small hangar (65.5 m/215 ft by 17.7 m/58 ft) could accommodate fewer aircraft than that of the 'Sangamon' class CVEs, 33 instead of the 45 planned. However, this

'Independence' class had the speed to keep up with the fast carriers, and that fact kept its members in the front line.

The USS *Princeton* was commissioned late in February 1943, just over a month after the lead-ship *Independence*. She arrived at Pearl Harbor in August 1943 and began exercising with the new *Essex* and *Yorktown*. They launched their first strike on 1 September against Marcus Island. Five weeks later she and two sisters joined in a successful raid on Wake Island.

During the Battle of Leyte Gulf the *Princeton* was part of Task Group 38.3, in the main Fast Carrier Group. On the morning of 24 October 1944 a lone Yokosuka D4Y 'Judy' bomber came out of cloud cover and dropped two 250-kg (551-lb) bombs on the flight deck of

the *Princeton*. The bombs passed through three decks before exploding, and the blast started fierce fires in the hangar. Six armed Avengers caught fire, and their torpedoes exploded, adding to the carnage. At 10.10, about half an hour after the attack, other ships were ordered alongside to take off all but essential firefighters and damage control personnel.

The light cruisers *Birmingham* and *Reno* lay alongside, pumping water and providing power for pumps, and all the while ships and friendly aircraft fought off Japanese air attacks. At 14.45 it appeared that all fires were out, but at 15.23 the *Princeton* blew up in a huge explosion. The blast swept the crowded decks of the *Birmingham*, killing 229 men and wounding another 420; the carrier herself had over 100 men killed and 190 injured. Surprisingly the shattered hulk of the *Princeton* was still afloat, but wrecked beyond any hope of salvage. At 16.00 she was abandoned and the cruiser *Reno* was ordered to sink her with two torpe-

does, after the destroyer *Irwin* had missed her with four.

Specification
USS *Princeton* (CVL.23)
Displacement: 11,000 tons standard, 14,300 tons full load
Dimensions: length 189.74 m (622 ft 6 in) overall; beam 33.3 m (109 ft 3 in) over flight deck; draught 7.92 m (26 ft 0 in)
Machinery: 4-shaft geared steam turbines delivering 74600 kW (100,000 shp)
Speed: 31½ knots
Armour: belt 38-127 mm (1½-5-in); main deck 76 mm (3 in); lower deck 51 mm (2 in)
Armament: (1943) two 127-mm (5-in) AA, two quadruple 40-mm Bofors AA, nine twin 40-mm Bofors AA and 12 20-mm AA guns
Aircraft: (1943) 24 Grumman F4F Wildcat fighters and nine Grumman TBF Avenger torpedo-bombers
Complement: 1,569 officers and enlisted men

The Princeton *(CVL.23) was converted on the stocks from the hull of the light cruiser* Tallahassee. *Although cramped, the CVLs were fast and could keep up with the Fast Carrier Groups. Later they operated night fighters.*

USS *Bogue*

The urgent need for air cover for convoys in the Battle of the Atlantic was met by converting mercantile hulls into small aircraft-carriers. In the summer of 1941 both the British and the Americans converted merchantmen into the first experimental 'escort carriers' or CVEs, and when these proved their worth orders went out for the first production class of 21 CVEs from US shipyards. Of these 11 went straight to the Royal Navy as the 'Attacker' class, while the remainder became the US Navy's 'Bogue' class. Being conversions of partially completed hulls, the 'Bogue' class was a great improvement on the prototypes, and had a full-length hangar, with two centreline lifts. The USS *Bogue* (CVE.9) and her sisters *Card* (CVE.11) and *Core* (CVE.13) even had two catapults. They carried 28 aircraft, and the *Bogue* was launched in January 1942.

With a good outfit of air-warning radar and more space than the destroyers and frigates, the escort carriers made good flagships for 'hunter-killer' or anti-submarine support groups, which were being established in the autumn of 1942. The *Bogue* and her

support group sank no fewer than 13 U-boats, while planes from her sisters *Card*, *Core*, *Block Island* and *Croatan* helped to sink another 20.

The USS *Bogue* joined the Atlantic Fleet in February 1943 as the Battle of the Atlantic reached crisis point. On her fourth crossing of the Atlantic her aircraft sank their first U-boat; two more followed on her next trip. On the seventh cruise, late in July 1943, her aircraft sank one U-Boat, and one of her escorting destroyers sank another.

The worst point of the battle was now over, and the tide had turned against the U-boats. The hunter-killer groups could not take the offensive against U-boats farther out in the Atlantic, and in November-December 1943 the *Bogue* and her group accounted for three U-boats. After a short break early in 1944 to ferry aircraft to the UK she returned to submarine-hunting, and in March helped to sink *U-575*. Three more U-boats were sunk by September 1944, when the *Bogue* returned to the United States for a period on training duties. Her last hunter-killer mission in April 1945 accounted for the last of 13 U-Boats, *U-546*, when

she was operating as part of Captain G. J. Dufek's Second Barrier Force.

In the closing months of the war the *Bogue* was sent to the Pacific, ferrying aircraft and stores to outlying garrisons, but with the collapse of Japan she was re-assigned to the 'Magic Carpet' operations, ferrying PoWs and servicemen back to the United States.

Specification
USS *Bogue* (CVE.9)
Displacement: 11,000 tons standard,

Port profile of the 'Bogue' class, showing the ex-mercantile hull clearly. Despite their austere design they were a great success, particularly in anti-submarine warfare in the Atlantic.

The escort carrier Bogue *(CVE.9) with Grumman Avenger TBFs on her wooden flight deck.*

15,400 tons full load
Dimensions: length 151.1 m (495 ft 8 in) overall; beam 34.0 m (111 ft 6 in) over flight deck; draught 7.92 m (26 ft 0 in)
Machinery: 1-shaft geared steam turbine delivering 6340 kW (8,500 shp)
Speed: 18 knots
Armour: none
Armament: two 127-mm (5-in) AA, four twin 40-mm Bofors AA and 12 20-mm AA guns
Aircraft: (1943) 12 Grumman F4F Wildcat fighters and 12 Grumman TBF Avenger torpedo-bombers
Complement: 890 officers and enlisted men

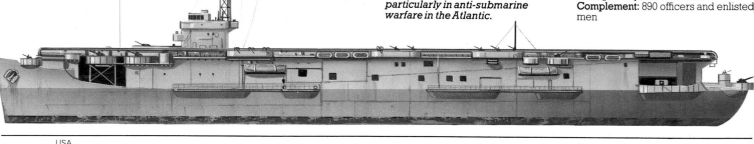

USS *Sangamon*

The conversion of escort carriers was given top priority in 1942, but the rate at which these useful utility carriers could be brought into service was limited by the number of hulls available. Four newly-built US Navy oilers, the *Sangamon* (AO.28), *Santee* (AO.29), *Chenango* (AO.31) and *Suwannee* (AO.33), were taken out of commission in January 1942, reclassified as AVGs (Aircraft Escort Vessels) and were immediately stripped of superstructures and fittings for a conversion lasting six to eight months.

Despite being an adaptation, the 'Sangamon' class was more successful than the earlier escort carriers, being larger and faster. Designed as tankers, they had their machinery right aft, and thus the small smoke-ducts caused

less interference with flying operations. Provision was made for two catapults, although the second unit was not installed until 1944, and a number of large openings in the sides provided good ventilation for the hangar.

The *Santee* (AVG.29, later CVE.29) was the first to be commissioned, on 24 August 1942, followed a day later by the USS *Sangamon* (CVE.26); the *Suwannee* (CVE.27) was commissioned on 24 September, five days after the *Chenango* (CVE.28). The acute shortage of carriers in late 1942 and early 1943, combined with their good turn of speed and aircraft capacity meant that these new carriers were used with the main fleet more than other CVEs, and frequently operated together. All four supported the land-

ings in North Africa in October and November 1942, and then transferred to the Pacific, where they operated with CarDiv 22 in the South Pacific. The *Santee* returned to the Atlantic in March 1943, operating south of the Azores and off the coast of Brazil with a hunter-killer group, but rejoined her sisters in the Pacific in February 1944, as the great 'island-hopping' drive across the Pacific got under way.

All four took part in the Battle of Leyte Gulf, forming 'Taffy One' (under Rear Admiral Thomas L. Sprague) as part of Task Group 77.4. On 25 October the *Santee* was badly damaged by a *kamikaze* attack, and shortly afterwards by a torpedo hit from the submarine *I-56*, but managed to survive. Then a *kamikaze* hit the *Suwannee*, having missed the *Sangamon*. In spite of these hits all three were operational by the spring of 1945. The *Sangamon* was badly damaged by a *kamikaze* hit off Okinawa on 4 May 1945, and lost 11 dead, 21 seriously wounded and 25 missing, but like her sisters, proved

rugged enough to be returned to service.

Specification
USS *Sangamon* (CVE.26)
Displacement: 10,500 tons standard, 23,875 tons full load
Dimensions: length 168.71 m (553 ft 6 in) overall; beam 34.82 m (114 ft 3 in) over flight deck; draught 9.32 m (30 ft 7 in)
Machinery: 2-shaft geared steam turbines delivering 10070 kW (13,500 shp)
Speed: 18 knots
Armour: none
Armament: two 127-mm (5-in) AA, two quadruple 40-mm Bofors AA, seven twin 40-mm Bofors AA and 21 20-mm AA guns
Aircraft: (1942) 12 Grumman F4F Wildcat fighters, nine Douglas SBD Dauntless dive-bombers and nine Grumman TBF Avenger torpedo-bombers
Complement: 1,100 officers and enlisted men

The Sangamon's *port profile shows her tanker origin, with the original well deck marked by large openings in the sides. Being fast and capacious, they were the most successful of all the CVE conversions.*

USS *St Lô*

The success of the converted CVEs led to a fresh design being prepared 'from the keel up', using a mercantile design as a basis but tailoring it to meet CVE needs, rather than adapting a hull on the slipway. These adaptations were more concerned with ease of construction than any radical improvement in operational capability. In all, 50 units of the 'Casablanca' class (CVE.55-104) were authorized late in 1942. Although the flight deck was short (500 ft/152.4 m by 108 ft/32.9 m), two lifts and a catapult were provided, and as there were two propeller shafts there was greater manoeuvrability than with one shaft. To speed up manufacture, triple-expansion steam machinery was chosen, but in other respects the 'Casablanca' design took the best of the 'Sangamon', 'Bogue' and 'Prince William' classes, and was a considerable success.

The USS *St Lô* (CVE.63) was laid down as the *Chapin Bay* (AVG.63) at Henry Kaiser's Vancouver shipyard in January 1943, but in April she was renamed *Midway* in honour of the recent battle, and entered service under that name in October 1943. The name was then allocated to a much bigger carrier, as it was considered too important for such a minor warship, and on 15 September 1944 CVE.63 became the USS *St Lô*. The little carrier had already made two ferry trips out to the Pacific

and had supported the amphibious landings in Saipan, Eniwetok, Tinian and Morotai. In October 1944 she formed part of 'Taffy Three', part of the vast armada which fought the Battle of Leyte Gulf. 'Taffy Three', the most northern group of escort carriers covering the amphibious landing, had already suffered a gruelling bombardmen from Japanese surface warships for the best part of 3 hours during the morning of 25 October 1944. After a lull of about 1 hour the *kamikazes* made a low-level attack, five Zeros coming in at low level before climbing rapidly to 1525 m (5,000 ft) and then diving straight onto the flight deck. One of a pair attacking the *Fanshaw Bay* suddenly switched to the *St Lô*, striking her flight deck aft. The two bombs slung underneath the Zero set off gasoline, bombs and ammunition in the hangar, and wrecked the ship.

The *kamikaze* hit at 10.53, and five minutes later a huge explosion devastated the carrier. She sank about 1 hour later, with 100 dead and many injured, the first American ship sunk by *kamikaze* attack.

Specification
USS *St Lô* (CVE.63)
Displacement: 7,800 tons standard, 10,400 tons full load
Dimensions: length 156.13 m (512 ft 3 in) overall; beam 39.92 m (108 ft 0 in) over flight deck; draught 6.86 m (22 ft 6 in)
Machinery: 2-shaft vertical triple-expansion delivering 6715 kW (9,000 ihp)
Speed: 19 knots
Armour: none

The new escort carrier Midway *(CVE.63), which was subsequently renamed* St Lô *to release the name for a bigger carrier.*

Armament: one 127-mm (5-in) AA, eight twin 40-mm Bofors AA and 20 20-mm AA guns
Aircraft: (October 1944) 17 Grumman F4F Wildcat fighters and 12 Grumman TBF Avenger torpedo-bombers
Complement: 860 officers and enlisted men

Below: The port profile of the 'Casablanca' class; these ships were an improved version of the Bogue *design, tailored for faster construction.*

Bottom: The St Lô *blows up after being set on fire by Japanese gunfire during the battle off Samar in October 1944.*

Allied and Axis Battleships

Gunpower has dominated fighting at sea since the days of Sir Francis Drake. While the armoured colossi of 1939 bore no resemblance to Nelson's Victory, they served the same purpose: to destroy the enemy with their guns. World War II, however, was to see great changes in the role of the battleship.

HMS *Howe* a, Royal Navy battleship of the King George V class, on a visit to Auckland Harbour, New Zealand.

When World War II broke out in September 1939 it was widely assumed that the battleship was still the most powerful warship available to both the Allied and Axis powers. However, by 1945 the place of the battleship had been taken by the aircraft carrier. Air power had proved itself to be capable of overwhelming defensive gunpower, and the air attack on Pearl Harbor, coupled with the loss of the British *Prince of Wales* and the *Repulse* to air attack, signalled the end of the reign of the battleship.

Nevertheless, the battleship continued to play a useful role right up to the end of World War II. Battleships were an integral part of the fast carrier task forces, providing not only defensive anti-aircraft fire but also invaluable gunfire in support of amphibious landings. Thus it was not so much that battleships had become useless but rather that the bombs and torpedoes of carrier strike aircraft could do a great deal more damage at a much greater distance. The vulnerability of the carrier was just as great, but its offensive potential made the aircraft carrier a weapon that was worth defending.

In the early years of World War II, when shore-based aircraft were often unavailable, battleships' guns were generally the only way of stopping enemy heavy ships. In May 1941 Germany's *Bismarck* could only be stopped by other battleships, even if Allied carrier aircraft played a vital role in slowing her down. Similarly, in October 1944 it was the US Navy's old battleships at Surigao Strait that were the only sure way of stopping the Japanese battleships: destroyers and motor torpedo boats did their best but just did not have the necessary stopping power.

As the full danger of air attack began to be taken more seriously, all battleships were to receive extra anti-aircraft batteries. However, the only way in which to guarantee immunity was to provide air cover. For example, in the course of World War II, six battleships were sunk by air attack (bombs and torpedoes), and only two by submarine torpedoes at sea. Another 12 ships were sunk in harbour, either by high-level bombing or by special assault units.

HMS *Renown*

The battle-cruiser HMS **Renown** was a veteran of World War I but, unlike her sister *Repulse*, underwent full modernization. She emerged from Portsmouth Dockyard on 2 September 1939, just in time for the outbreak of war.

During her three-year refit she had been almost totally rebuilt, with new machinery and boilers (saving 2,800 tons of weight), new superstructure and bridgework, and additional armour. The three gun turrets were taken out and modified to give the 381-mm (15-in) guns 30° elevation, and an entirely new anti-aircraft armament was provided: 10 twin 114-mm (4.5-in) gun mountings, three 8-barrelled pom-poms and four quadruple 12.7-mm (0.5-in) machine-guns. The weight saved on machinery was used to strengthen deck armour, particularly by adding 102-mm (4-in) armour over the magazines and 51-mm (2-in) armour over the machinery. She was also given a cross-deck catapult and a large hangar capable of accommodating two Walrus amphibian aircraft.

The new role for the ship was to act as a fast escort for aircraft-carriers, and

when the *Renown* joined the Home Fleet she was teamed with the new carrier HMS *Ark Royal* in a partnership which continued for a long time. After hunting for KMS *Graf Spee* in the South Atlantic in November 1939 she returned to the Home Fleet as flagship of Vice Admiral Whitworth, and took part in the Norwegian campaign.

Early on the morning of 9 April 1940 the *Renown* was steaming about 130 km (80 miles) west of the Lofoten Islands in company with nine destroyers when she sighted the German battle-cruisers KMS *Scharnhorst* and KMS *Gneisenau*. The British ship had the advantage of the light and at 04.17 scored a hit on *Gneisenau*'s main fire-control position. The German ships turned away and escaped under cover of snow squalls, but not before the *Renown* had scored two more hits. She was hit by two or three 280-mm (11-in) shells but suffered only slight damage.

In August the *Renown* went to Gibraltar as part of Force 'H' with the *Ark Royal*, but returned to home waters in October 1941. After covering the North African landings she took Winston

Churchill to Canada and was then sent to the Eastern Fleet, which was operating in the East Indies. On her return in March 1945 the *Renown* was laid up in reserve, and was sold for scrapping in 1948. Her career had spanned over 30 years, and she had served in every major theatre of the naval war.

Specification
HMS *Renown*
Displacement: 30,750 tons standard, 36,080 tons full load

The old battle cruiser HMS Renown *was completely rebuilt for service in World War II as a fast carrier escort. She served in the Atlantic, Mediterranean and Far East.*

Dimensions: length 242.0 m (794 ft) overall; beam 27.4 m (90 ft); draught 14.4 m (30 ft 6 in)
Machinery: 4-shaft geared steam turbines delivering 108,000 shp (80536 kW)
Speed: 29½ kts
Armour: belt 229 mm (9 in); decks 51-102 mm (2-4 in); turrets and barbettes 178-229 mm (7-9 in)
Armament: (1944) six 381-in (15-in), 20 114-mm (4.5-in) DP, 28 2-pdr pom-pom and 64 20-mm AA guns, and eight 533-mm (21-in) torpedo tubes
Aircraft: two Supermarine Walrus amphibians
Complement: 1,200 officers and men

HMS Renown *as she was in July 1942, prior to the removal of her Walrus aircraft and with extra AA armament. World War II saw a constant increment in the numbers of AA weapons carried by capital ships.*

HMS *Nelson*

At the outbreak of the war HMS **Nelson** and her sister HMS *Rodney* were the most modern British battleships in service. They had been completed in 1927, and were the only capital ships allowed to be built for the Royal Navy under the Washington Treaty. As such they were severely constrained by the need to keep within a standard displacement of 35,000 tons while at the same time carrying 406-mm (16-in) guns and heavy protection.

The designers adopted many unusual expedients to meet the specifications, including an 'all-or-nothing' scheme of armouring and the concentration of all three 406-mm (16-in) turrets forward of the bridge, and all 152-mm (6-in) guns aft. Another important innovation, not revealed until long after

World War II, was the provision of 'water protection' or liquid-loaded vertical bulkheads below the waterline. With an additional 2,800 tons of water held in these compartments, any torpedo explosion would dissipate its effect over a large area of the bulkhead. Although the standard displacement of the two ships averaged 1,300 tons below the treaty limit, this was achieved by not flooding the vertical compartments in peacetime.

The *Nelson* was very badly damaged by a magnetic mine while entering Loch Ewe in December 1939, and was under repair until August 1940. In September 1941 she left the Home Fleet to join Force 'H' for a Malta convoy operation. On 27 September she was hit forward by an Italian aircraft

torpedo but reached Gibraltar safely. The *Nelson* provided covering fire for the amphibious landings in North Africa, Sicily and Italy, and the armistice between Italy and the Allies was signed on board in Grand Harbour,

The awesome sight of a salvo from the 406-mm (16-in) guns of HMS Nelson, *steaming at full speed.*

Below: HMS Nelson, *shown serving in the Indian ocean in June 1942. Although slow, Nelson and Rodney were the most powerful battleships in the Royal Navy.*

Malta, on 29 September 1943.

The ship sailed to the United States for an overhaul in September 1944, and five months later she sailed for the East Indies as flagship of the Eastern Fleet. On her return at the end of 1945 she replaced her sister *Rodney* as flagship of the Home Fleet at Scapa Flow. Having been recently modernized she remained in commission and in 1946 joined the Training Squadron at Portland for two years. With her sister she was laid up in the Firth of Forth in 1948 and used as a target for aerial bombing before being scrapped. She and her sister were greatly under-rated, and in 1939 they were certainly among the most powerful battleships afloat, with many more advanced features than contemporary designs in other navies.

Specification
HMS *Nelson*
Displacement: 33,313 tons standard, 38,400 tons full load
Dimensions: length 216.4 m (710 ft) overall; beam 32.3 m (106 ft); draught 8.5 m (28 ft)
Machinery: 2-shaft geared steam turbines of 45,000 shp (33556 kW)
Speed: 23 kts
Armour: belt 330-356 mm (13-14 in); decks 95-159 mm (3.75-6.25 in); turrets and barbettes 381-406 mm (15-16 in)
Armament: nine 406-mm (16-in), 12 152-mm (6-in), six 120-mm (4.7-in) AA, 16 2-pdr pom-pom and eight 12.7-mm (0.5 in) AA guns, and two 622-mm (24.5-in) torpedo tubes
Aircraft: none
Complement: 1,314 officers and men

HMS Rodney *and her sister ship* Nelson *were unusual in having all* three 406-mm (16-in) turrets grouped forward.

HMS *Prince of Wales*

The second ship of the 'King George V' class, HMS *Prince of Wales* was laid down in January 1937, launched in May 1939 and completed at the end of March 1941. She was still working up to operational efficiency on 23 May when she was ordered to leave Scapa Flow, with the flagship HMS *Hood*, to engage the German battleship KMS *Bismarck*.

The *Prince of Wales* was still suffering from teething troubles: one of her 356-mm (14-in) turrets could only fire one shell, the turrets were all subject to minor breakdowns, and the new Type 284 gunnery radar was not working. To make matters worse the inexperienced crew of 'Y' quadruple 356-mm (14-in) turret made an error in loading drill which jammed the turret. When the flagship *Hood* blew up, the *Prince of Wales* was thus badly placed to withstand the fire of two undamaged German ships. In spite of this she acquitted herself well. The Type 281 air-warning set was used to provide ranges to the guns, enabling her to get 'straddles' on the *Bismarck* resulting in two or three underwater hits. One of these hits caused serious contamination of the oil fuel and another reduced the *Bismarck's* speed by 2 kts, so it can be fairly said that the *Prince of Wales* initiated the chain of events which brought the *Bismarck* to her doom.

Although hit seven times the *Prince of Wales* suffered comparatively little damage as only three of the shells detonated. The most serious damage was caused by a ricochet on the compass platform, which killed or wounded all but the captain.

In August 1941 the 'PoW' carried Winston Churchill across the Atlantic to the Atlantic Charter meeting with President Roosevelt in Newfoundland. She hoisted the flag of Sir Tom Phillips, C-in-C Eastern Fleet in October, and

left for Singapore on 25 October, in company with HMS *Repulse*. Force 'Z', as the two ships were designated, arrived at Singapore on 2 December, but eight days later they were sunk by Japanese torpedo-bombers. The *Prince of Wales* was crippled by a single torpedo which struck the port side abreast of the aftermost 133-mm (5.25-in) gun turret. The port outer propeller shaft was badly distorted, and because it was not rapidly disconnected it continued to revolve, making an enormous hole in the after bulkheads. Then the shock-effect of near-

misses from bombs put five of the eight dynamos out of action, robbing the ship of pumping and power for the anti-aircraft guns. Out of control, she was unable to avoid another four torpedoes. She finally sank an hour and twenty minutes after the first attack, with the loss of Admiral Phillips and Captain Leach.

Specification
HMS *Prince of Wales*
Displacement: 38,000 tons standard, 43,350 tons full load

The doomed Prince of Wales *arriving at Singapore on 2 December 1941. She would be sunk only eight days later by Japanese aircraft off the coast of Malaya.*

Dimensions: length 227.0 m (745 ft); beam 31.4 m (103 ft); draught 8.5 m (28 ft) mean
Machinery: 4-shaft geared steam turbines delivering 110,000 shp (82027 kW)
Speed: 28 kts
Armour: belt 356-281 mm (14-15 in); decks 127-152 mm (5-6 in); turrets and barbettes 305 mm (12 in)
Armament: 10 356-mm (14-in), 16 133-mm (5.25-in) DP, 32 2-pdr pom-pom, and 16 12.7-mm (0.5 in) AA guns
Aircraft: two Supermarine Walrus amphibians
Complement: 1,422 officers and men

The 'King George V' class reflected the impact of air power on British battleship design, with the first combined high angle/low angle secondary armament and the first integral aircraft and catapult.

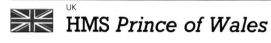

KMS *Scharnhorst*

KMS *Scharnhorst* was planned as the *Ersatz Elsass*, fourth of a class of six planned 'pocket battleships'. By 1933, however, the weaknesses of the 'pocket battleship' or *Panzerschiffe* were so obvious that Hitler gave the German navy permission to expand the design to 26,000 tons as a reply to the French *Dunkerque*.

It was hoped to arm the ship with three twin 380-mm (15-in) turrets, but to save time three triple 280-mm (11-in) turrets were used. The design was nominally of 26,000 tons, but had reached 32,000 tons; to conceal the size of the new battle-cruiser the Kriegsmarine continued to quote the lower figure.

For most of her active life the *Scharnhorst* operated with her sister KMS *Gneisenau*, and both ships made forays into the North Atlantic in 1940-1. The *Scharnhorst* was badly damaged by a torpedo fired by the destroyer HMS *Acasta* while attacking the carrier HMS *Glorious* in June 1940.

Although the two ships posed a considerable threat to the British while lying at Brest in 1941 and the repeated raids by the Royal Air Force were far too inaccurate to do any serious damage, Hitler felt the two units were too exposed, and ordered them to return. Operation 'Cerberus', the daylight dash through the English Channel in February 1942, was probably the Kriegsmarine's greatest success, for it took the British completely by surprise, the two battle-cruisers and the heavy cruiser *Prinze Eugen* slipping past ineffectual air and sea attacks. Apart from slight damage to *Scharnhorst* from a magnetic mine during the final phase it had been a humiliation for the British and proof that audacity pays.

After repairs lasting until August 1942 the ship was sent to Norway in March 1943. She took part in the raid on Spitzbergen in September but otherwise lay in a remote fjord until December 1943, when Admiral Dönitz ordered her to sea for an attack on a British convoy.

Scharnhorst had a more eventful war career than most Kriegsmarine capital ships, yet this scene would have been a rare event for her crew, confined to harbour as she was for so long.

It was a badly planned operation, and the *Scharnhorst* failed in her attempt to brush aside the destroyers and cruisers escorting the convoy. Incompetent reconnaissance by the Luftwaffe left her with no idea that the battleship HMS *Duke of York* was closing fast, and she was taken by surprise when 356-mm (14-in) shells started to hit her. She disengaged but the British and Norwegian destroyers slowed her down with torpedoes, allowing the *Duke of York* to pound her again. She was finally sunk by torpedoes from HMS *Sheffield* and HMS *Jamaica* and went down with the loss of all but 46 of 1,840 men on board.

Specification
KMS *Scharnhorst*
Displacement: 32,000 tons standard, 38,900 tons full load
Dimensions: length 234.9 m (770 ft 8 in) overall; beam 30.0 m (98 ft 5 in); draught 9.1 m (29 ft 10 in) deep
Machinery: 3-shaft geared steam turbines delivering 160,000 shp (119312 kW)
Speed: 32 kts
Armour: belt 330 mm (13 in); decks 50-110 mm (2-4.25 in); turrets 355 mm (14 in)
Armament: nine 280-mm (11-in), 12 150-mm (5.9-in), 14 105-mm (4.1-in) AA and 16 37-mm AA guns, and six 533-mm (21-in) torpedo tubes
Aircraft: two Arado floatplanes
Complement: 1,840 officers and men

Although rated by the British as battle cruisers, the Scharnhorst *and her sister* Gneisenau *were built as fast but lightly armed battleships.*

Below: Scharnhorst *and her sister ship were designed to accept 380-mm (15-in) guns, but wartime conditions prevented this.*

KMS *Bismarck*

The first full-scale battleships built for Germany's new Kriegsmarine after Hitler abrogated the Versailles Treaty were two 35,000-ton ships. As with the battle-cruisers, the design followed closely the final designs of the previous war, but with considerably higher installed power. The first of this pair was launched and christened KMS *Bismarck* on 14 February 1939. She was in fact 6,000 tons heavier than the international treaty limits allowed, but much of the extra tonnage went into additional fuel stowage.

The *Bismarck* was commissioned in August 1940 but underwent a further eight months of training in the Baltic before she was considered ready for a breakout into the Atlantic. In May 1941 she and the heavy cruiser *Prinz Eugen* left the Baltic bound for Bergen, but their passage had been detected by pro-British Swedes and the Admiralty

had been alerted by analysis of radio traffic. As a result the heavy cruiser HMS *Suffolk* was already on station in the Denmark Strait on 23 May, and detected the two German ships on radar.

On the next morning the British Battle-Cruiser Squadron tried to intercept the German ships, but the German ships got the range quickly. *Prinz Eugen's* shells started a fire aboard HMS *Hood*, and shortly afterwards she blew up, while the *Bismarck* hit HMS *Prince of Wales* in the bridge. The British ship was then ordered to break off the action and to retire, leaving the German ships to continue their foray into the Atlantic.

Examination soon showed that a large quantity of fuel had been contaminated by underwater damage, and Admiral Lütjens decided to head for Brest. That night Fairey Swordfish torpedo-bombers from HMS *Victo-

rious* attacked with torpedoes, but the single hit inflicted only minor damage. For a while the *Bismarck* eluded her pursuers, but after unwisely transmitting a long radio signal she was detected on 26 May, and that night more Swordfish from HMS *Ark Royal* hit her with two torpedoes, wrecking her steering gear. Further attacks by destroyers followed, although without success, but the *Bismarck* was doomed, unable to manoeuvre and steaming at only 5 kts. On the next morning HMS *King George V* and HMS *Rodney* came over the northern horizon, opening fire at 08.47. The British fire was deadly, and by 09.20 the *Bismarck* was silenced. During that time she had scored only one 'straddle' on the *Rodney* and hit her with a few splinters. In the final stages the range came down to only 3660 m (4,000 yards), and the *Bismarck* was battered into a water-

logged wreck. She was finally torpedoed by the cruiser HMS *Dorsetshire* and sank at 10.40.

Specification
KMS *Bismarck*
Displacement: 41,676 tons standard, 50,153 tons full load
Dimensions: length 251.0 m (823 ft 6 in) overall; beam 36.0 m (118 ft); draught 9.3 m (30 ft 7 in) mean
Machinery: 3-shaft geared steam turbines delivering 138,000 shp (102907 kW)
Speed: 29 kts
Armour: belt 320 mm (12.6 in); decks 50-120 mm (2-4.7 in); turrets and barbettes 230-355 mm (9-14 in)
Armament: eight 380-mm (15-in), 12 150-mm (5.9-in), 16 105-mm (4.1-in) AA, 16 37-mm AA and 12 20-mm AA guns
Aircraft: two Arado floatplanes
Complement: 2,192 officers and men

KMS *Tirpitz*

KMS *Tirpitz* was laid down in October 1936 as *Schlachtschiff G*, launched on 1 April 1939 and started sea trials in late February 1941. She was in most respects identical to her sister *Bismarck* but incorporated minor improvements, notably the addition of two sets of quadruple torpedo-tubes and improved aircraft-handling arrangements.

After a lengthy work-up in the Baltic the *Tirpitz* was ready for operational service towards the end of September 1941, and her first operation was a cruise in the Gulf of Finland to prevent any breakout by the Soviet Baltic Fleet. She was then sent to Trondheim in Norway to disrupt Allied convoys to Murmansk, but on her first sortie she failed to find the convoy and narrowly escaped damage from Fairey Albacore torpedo-bombers from HMS *Victorious* on 9 March. Her next move was much more successful, but inadvertent, for shift of berth led the British to think that she was putting to sea. As a result the convoy PQ-17 was ordered to scatter, allowing U-boats and bombers to sink 24 merchant ships.

Although the *Tirpitz* never made another sortie her presence could not be ignored, and the Royal Navy was forced to keep two capital ships and a fleet carrier in home waters in case the *Tirpitz* should break out. The first of a long series of attempts to neutralize her was an attack by 'Chariot' human torpedoes in October 1942, but this achieved nothing as the Chariots were lost by accident. In September 1943 the *Tirpitz* put to sea once more, but only to bombard Spitzbergen. Late that month two British X-craft or midget submarines penetrated the defences of Altenfjord and laid 2-ton charges under the *Tirpitz* keel, causing extensive shock damage to the 380-mm (15-in) turrets and the main machinery. Repairs lasted until the spring of 1944 but just as the battleship was getting under way on 3 April she was attacked by 40 Fairey Barracuda dive-bombers from British carriers. This Fleet Air Arm attack inflicted serious damage, but two later attacks in July and August did very little damage, for the steep sides of the fjord made accurate bombing almost impossible. Finally, on 15 September, RAF Avro Lancasters managed to hit the *Tirpitz* with 5443-kg (12,000-lb) bombs, causing severe damage. The *Tirpitz* then had to be moved south to Trondheim

Above: Seen sailing in coastal waters, Tirpitz *(or possibly a 'Hipper' class cruiser – the designs were intentionally very similar) was a constant threat to Allied convoys bound for Murmansk. Considerable Royal Navy resources had to be tied down on the chance that the powerful battleship might make a strike.*

Right: The Tirpitz *in Kaafjord in March 1944, seen from an RAF aircraft 3,000 feet up.*

Below: When completed the Tirpitz *differed only in minor details from her sister* Bismarck, *but more AA guns were added later.*

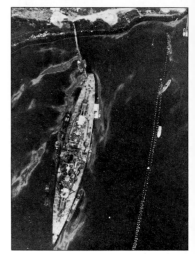

for repairs, where two more attacks by Lancasters achieved her destruction. On 12 November she was hit by three 5443-kg (12,000-lb) 'Tallboy' bombs and capsized with the loss of 1,000 crewmen.

Specification
KMS *Tirpitz*
Displacement: 42,900 tons standard, 52,600 tons full load
Dimensions: length 250.5 m (821 ft 10 in) overall; beam 36.0 m (118 ft 1 in); draught 11.0 m (36 ft 1 in) maximum
Machinery: 3-shaft geared steam turbines delivering 138,000 shp (102907 kW)
Speed: 29 kts
Armour: belt 320 mm (12.6 in); decks 50-120 mm (2-4.7 in); turrets and barbettes 230-355 mm (9-14 in)
Armament: eight 380-mm (15-in), 12 150-mm (5.9-in), 16 105-mm (4.1-in) AA, 16 37-mm AA and 70 20-mm AA guns, and eight 533-mm (21-in) torpedo tubes
Aircraft: four Arado floatplanes
Complement: 2,530 officers and men

USS *Arizona*

The USS *Arizona* (BB.39) was laid down in March 1914, launched in June 1915 and commissioned in October 1916. She crossed the Atlantic to serve with the 6th Squadron as part of the British Grand Fleet in the last days of World War I, and then helped to repatriate American soldiers from France. In 1929-31 she was modernized, and on 7 December 1941 was part of the Pacific Fleet, lying in 'Battleship Row' in Pearl Harbor.

Her peacetime service had been humdrum. After a short trip to the Mediterranean in April-July 1919 she returned to the East coast, and then transferred to the Pacific Fleet in 1921 for a period of eight years. In 1929 she returned to Norfolk to start her mod-

ernization, and on recommissioning took President Hoover on a cruise to the West Indies before passing through the Panama Canal on her way back to the Pacific Fleet. There she remained for the rest of her life.

The first wave of Japanese aircraft to reach Pearl Harbor on 7 December had no difficulty in identifying their targets, for 'Battleship Row' contained seven ships: USS *Oklahoma*, USS *West Virginia* and the repair ship USS *Vestal* in the outer line, and USS *Maryland*, USS *Tennessee*, the *Arizona* and USS *Nevada* in the inner line. A torpedo and an estimated eight bombs hit the *Arizona*, setting her on fire and starting a massive flooding. The bomb which did most damage was a 725-kg (1,600-

lb) weapon which struck at 08.10, penetrated the armoured deck and detonated in the forward magazine. The ship blew up and sank at her

The USS Arizona *in September 1939. During modernization her 'basket' masts had been replaced by massive tripods.*

moorings, trapping and killing a total of 1,104 of her crew, including Rear Admiral Kidd and Captain van Valkenburgh.

Salvage teams tried to raise the hull, but it was damaged beyond repair. Subsequently two of the *Arizona*'s triple 356-mm (14-in) turrets were recovered and the guns were installed in coast defence positions on land. The hull of the *Arizona* was later declared a national shrine commemorating the men and ships lost in the attack. Today a concrete memorial has been built over the *Arizona*'s remains, and an oil slick shows that oil is still leaking slowly from her fuel tanks.

The sister of the *Arizona*, USS *Pennsylvania* (BB.38) was in dry dock at the time and suffered only superficial damage from a single bomb hit. After repairs and modernization she rejoined the Pacific Fleet and saw action across the Pacific, through to the Japanese surrender in August 1945.

Right at the end of the war she was damaged by an aircraft torpedo but survived and was used as a target in the Bikini nuclear tests in 1946.

Specification
USS *Arizona* (BB.39)
Displacement: 32,600 tons standard, 36,500 tons full load
Dimensions: length 185.32 m (608 ft); beam 29.56 m (97 ft); draught 8.76 m (28 ft 9 in)
Machinery: 4-shaft geared steam turbines delivering 33,500 shp (24980 kW)
Speed: 21 kts
Armour: belt 356 mm (14 in); deck 203 mm (8 in); turrets 229-457 mm (9-18 in)
Armament: 12 356-mm (14-in), 12 127-mm (5-in), 12 127-mm (5-in) AA and eight 12.7-mm (0.5-in) AA guns
Aircraft: three floatplanes
Complement: 2,290 officers and men

The Arizona's tripod masts sags slowly to port after the detonation of the forward 356-mm (14-in) magazine had wrecked the ship.

Below: The Arizona and Pennsylvania were among the world's most powerful battleships when new. Both were modernized in the late 1920s.

USS *Washington*

When the 15-year 'holiday' in battleship construction came to an end in 1937, the US Navy had plans to lay down two modern capital ships as soon as possible. The 35,000-ton limit was still in force, but the 1936 London Naval Treaty had reduced gun calibre from 406 to 356 mm (16 to 14 in). The specification which emerged was very similar to the original design of HMS *King George V*, with three quadruple 356-mm (14-in) mountings and a speed of 28 kts. However, unlike the British the Americans could afford to wait, and when the Japanese refused to ratify the 1936 treaty the USN announced that it would exercise its right to go back to 406-mm (16-in) guns. On the dimensions it was only possible to have three triple mountings, and nothing could be

The Washington *and* North Carolina *were the first US battleships built since the Washington Treaty in 1922, and were intended to have 356-mm (14-in) guns but were built with 406-mm (16-in) triple turrets.*

done to increase protection, which had been planned to withstand 356-mm (14-in) shellfire.

USS *Washington* (BB.56) was the second of the two 'North Carolina' class; she was laid down in June 1938 and commissioned in May 1941. She went to the Home Fleet for a while in 1942, and on 1 May was damaged by the explosion of HMS *Punjabi*'s depth charges after the destroyer had been rammed by HMS *King George V* just ahead of her. By September that year she was back in the Pacific, with Task Force 17 in the Solomons.

On the night of 14/15 November the *Washington* and USS *South Dakota* were stalking a Japanese task force attempting to bombard Henderson Field, but just before the US ships

could open fire the blast of a 127-mm (5-in) gun knocked out the *South Dakota*'s electrical system. Fortunately the *Washington* had not yet switched on her searchlights, and remained undetected while the Japanese concentrated their fire on the *South Dakota*.

From a range of about 7315 m (8,000 yards) the *Washington* closed the range to 1830 m (2,000 yards) before opening fire; in seven minutes she fired 75 406-in (16-in) and hundreds of 127-mm (5-in) shells, crippling the *Kirishima* with nine 406-mm (16-in) hits. Her intervention saved the *South Dakota* from serious damage and not only sank the *Kirishima* but badly damaged two heavy cruisers as well and saved Henderson Field from bombardment.

On 1 February 1944 the *Washington* was badly damaged in a collision with the *Indiana*, but she was repaired in time for the Battle of the Philippine Sea in June 1944 and the final onslaught on Okinawa and the Japanese Home Islands. She was decommissioned in June 1947 and was stricken in 1960.

Specification
USS *Washington* (BB.56)
Displacement: 36,900 tons standard, 44,800 tons full load
Dimensions: length 222.12 m (728 ft 9 in) overall; beam 33.0 m (108 ft 3 in); draught 10.82 m (35 ft 6 in)
Machinery: 4-shaft geared steam turbines delivering 121,000 shp (90230 kW)
Speed: 27 kts
Armour: belt 165-305 mm (6.5-12 in); decks 38-140 mm (1.5-5.5 in); turrets 178-406 mm (7-16 in)
Armament: nine 406-mm (16-in), 20 127-mm (5-in) DP, 16 28-mm (1.1-in) AA and 12 12.7-mm (0.5-in) AA guns
Aircraft: three Vought Kingfisher floatplanes
Complement: 1,880 officers and men

USS *South Dakota*

The need for a class of battleships powerful enough to resist 406-mm (16-in) shellfire without infringing the 35,000-ton treaty limit was clear in 1937. To achieve this, however, was another matter, and the US Navy's designers were forced to make several compromises. Shortening the waterline length saved weight, but to support the additional weight of armour there had to be an increase in beam.

This caused more drag, and to maintain a speed of 28 kts more power was needed, but in the shorter hull there was now less space for machinery. The problems were solved eventually by considerable attention paid to redesign of machinery, and as a result the 'South Dakota' class proved to be cost-effective. The short hull was manoeuvrable, and protection against shellfire, bombs and torpedoes was as

good as any contemporary built to the same nominal limitations. In fact, like the British 'King George V' class, the 'South Dakota' class worked out at 38,000 tons, an 8.5 per cent difference, considerably lower than those of French, German or Italian designs.

The lead-ship USS *South Dakota* (BB.57) was laid down in July 1939, launched in June 1941 and commissioned in March 1942. She went

straight to the Pacific after her shakedown cruise, but damaged herself by running aground. Repairs were completed in time for the Battle of Santa Cruz, and on 26 October 1942 she claimed to have shot down 26 Japanese aircraft. This phenomenal performance can be explained by the fact that she was the first ship to use the new proximity-fused 127-mm (5-in) shells.

The next engagement was the Battle

of Guadalcanal on the night of 14/15 November 1942, but this time the *South Dakota* was less successful. While approaching the Japanese battle line in company with USS *Washington* she inadvertently blew the ring main and put her entire electrical supply out of action. With no radar, fire control, lighting or navigation aids she blundered towards the Japanese and got within 4570 m (5,000 yards), at which range she was soon hit by a number of shells. She was hit by one 356-mm (14-in), 18 203-mm (8-in), six 152-mm (6-in) and one 127-mm (5-in) shells, plus one of unknown calibre, suffering extensive splinter damage which killed 38 men and wounded 60.

In 1943 the *South Dakota* joined the Home Fleet with her sister USS *Alabama*, but she returned to the Pacific later in that year. With her three sisters she took part in all the major amphibious operations which culminated in the surrender of Japan in August 1945. She was decommissioned in 1947 and stricken in 1962.

Specification
USS *South Dakota* (BB.57)
Displacement: 38,000 tons standard, 44,374 tons full load
Dimensions: length 207.3 m (680 ft) overall; beam 33.0 m (108 ft 3 in); draught 11.1 m (36 ft 3 in) maximum
Machinery: 4-shaft geared steam turbines delivering 130,000 shp (96940 kW)
Speed: 28 kts
Armour: belt 311 m (12.25 in); decks 38-127 mm (1.5-5 in); turrets 457 mm (18 in)
Armament: nine 406-mm (16-in), 16 127-mm (5-in) DP, 40 40-mm AA and 40 20-mm AA guns
Aircraft: three Vought Kingfisher floatplanes
Complement: 2,354

The USS South Dakota *with escorting destroyer, in the South Pacific in August 1943.*

Below: The South Dakota *design was shorter than that of the* Washington *to permit heavier protection against a 406-mm (16-in) shellfire.*

USA

USS *Iowa*

Early in 1937 the US Navy started work on the design of 45,000-ton battleships as a contingency against any Japanese refusal to continue the international treaty limits on displacement. In January 1938 emphasis switched from ships with heavy armament and protection but modest speed (12 406-mm/16-in guns, 27 knots) to fast designs, capable of 30 kts or more. The new 'Essex' class carriers were taking shape on the drawing board at this time, and there was a need to provide them with battleship escorts of similar performance.

The 'Iowa' class which resulted sacrificed gunpower (only nine 406-mm/16-in guns) and protection (310-mm/12.2-in belt armour) to permit the speed to be increased to 33 kts. Although intelligence sources suspected that the new Japanese battleships would have 457-mm (18-in) guns, it was hoped that the 'Iowa' class would not have to fight them as carrier aircraft would keep the Japanese giants outside gun-range. The 'Iowas' were primarily intended to keep heavy cruisers, rather than battleships, at bay, and as such they came close to the original concept of the battlecruiser, although never rated as such.

The *Iowa* (BB.61) was laid down in June 1940, launched in August 1942 and commissioned in February 1943. In August of that year she escorted convoys from Newfoundland and then took President Roosevelt to North Africa, before being sent to the Pacific to join the 5th Fleet. She took part in the Marshall Islands landing, and suffered slight damage from Japanese artillery. At Leyte she was part of Vice Admiral William Halsey's Fast Carrier Force, and took part in the Okinawa landing; in July 1945 she bombarded targets on Hokkaido and Honshu, and was part of the enormous force anchored in Tokyo

Bay for the Japanese surrender.

The *Iowa* was mothballed in 1949 but reactivated in 1951 for service in the Korean War. She carried out a large number of shore bombardments but was decommissioned once more in 1953. It was widely thought that she would be scrapped, but in 1981 she was towed to New Orleans to begin reactivation. In her new configuration she will carry a large number of Harpoon anti-ship missiles and Tomahawk cruise missiles to enable her to function as the main unit of a Surface Action Group (SAG). Her 406-in (16-in) guns

are to be retained to provide gunfire support.

Specification
USS *Iowa* (BB.61)
Displacement: 48,500 tons standard, 57,450 tons full load
Dimensions: length 270.43 m (887 ft 3 in) overall; beam 32.97 m (108 ft 2 in); draught 11.58 m (38 ft)
Machinery: 4-shaft geared steam turbines delivering 212,000 shp (158088 kW)
Speed: 33 kts
Armour: belt 310 mm (12.2 in); decks

USS Iowa *refuels from an oiler in the Pacific. Although comparatively lightly armoured, its high speed and endurance gave this class great fighting power.*

38-120 mm (1.5-4.7 in); turrets 457 mm (18 in)
Armament: nine 406-mm (16 in), 20 127-mm (5-in) DP, 60 40-mm AA and 60 20-mm AA guns
Aircraft: three Vought Kingfisher floatplanes
Complement: 1,921 officers and men

IJN *Kirishima*

IJN *Kirishima* was the third of four 'Kongo' class battlecruisers built for the Imperial Japanese Navy between 1912 and 1915. Launched in December 1913, the *Kirishima* was completed in April 1915.

In common with her sisters *Kirishima* was modernized twice, in 1927-31 and 1934-40. The second modernization transformed her into a fast battleship for escorting carriers, with speed raised from 26 to 30 kts by doubling the horsepower, and with heavier anti-aircraft armament. The original three funnels had been reduced to two in the first reconstruction, and the second gave her a typical 'pagoda' foremast.

When war broke out in December 1941 all four were serving with the 3rd Battle Division, and *Kirishima* and *Hiei* accompanied the force which attacked Pearl Harbor. In June 1942 the *Kirishima* suffered slight damage from air attacks during the Battle of Midway.

With her sister *Hiei* she attacked US forces on Guadalcanal on the night of 12/13 November 1942. The two fast battleships engaged a force of American cruisers, sinking USS *Atlanta*, damaging USS *San Francisco*, *Juneau*, *Helena* and *Portland* and sinking the destroyers USS *Barton* and *Laffey* in a confused melée at short range.

Two nights later the Japanese tried again to get a troop convoy through to Guadalcanal and to bombard Henderson Field but ran into an American force. This time the battleships USS *South Dakota* and USS *Washington* were in support, both modern ships

with radar, but superior night-fighting techniques enabled the Japanese to plan an ambush in which the American destroyers came off worse. When the light cruiser *Nagara* turned her searchlights on the *South Dakota*, the *Kirishima* immediately opened fire with her 356-mm (14-in) battery, but in the confusion the Japanese lookouts failed to spot the *Washington*, closing from 7300 m (8,000 yards). Five minutes after midnight her deadly 406-mm (16-in) salvoes began to burst around the *Kirishima*, which was quickly overwhelmed by an estimated total of nine 406-mm (16-in) and 40 127-mm (5-in) hits. Seven minutes later she

was ablaze, unable to steer and taking on water fast from underwater damage.

Admiral Kondo ordered the destroyers IJN *Asagumo*, IJN *Teruzuki*, and IJN *Samidare* to take off survivors but no attempt was made to save the ship. *Kirishima*'s sea cocks were opened and she sank at 03.23, about 11 km (7 miles) north west of Savo Island.

Specification
IJN *Kirishima* (after second reconstruction)
Displacement: 31,980 tons standard, 36,600 tons full load

The Japanese Kirishima, *built as a battle cruiser in 1915, was rebuilt as a fast battleship in the 1930s.*

Dimensions: length 222.0 m (728 ft 6 in) overall; beam 31.0 m (102 ft 4 in); draught 9.7 m (31 ft 9 in)
Machinery: 4-shaft geared steam turbines delivering 136,000 shp (101415 kW)
Speed: 30½ kts
Armour: belt 76-203 mm (3-8 in); deck 121 mm (4.75 in); turrets 280 mm (11 in)
Armament: eight 356-mm (14-in), 14 152-mm (6-in), eight 127-mm (5-in) AA, and 20 25-mm (1-in) AA guns
Aircraft: three floatplanes
Complement: 1,437 officers and men

The horsepower of the Kirishima *and her three sisters was doubled during reconstruction to add five knots to their speed.*

IJN *Yamato*

The Imperial Japanese Navy, pursuing a goal of quality to offset the numerical advantage of the US Navy, started work in 1934 on a design of battleship to outclass any possible opponent. The ships were to be faster, better armoured and have longer-range guns, but the only way in which these qualities could be achieved would be to breach the existing international treaty limits of 35,000 tons and 406-mm (16-in) guns.

The design evolved to meet the requirement displaced 64,000 tons and was armed with nine 460-mm (18.1-in) guns capable of hitting the target at 48 km (30 miles). The protection was on an equally massive scale, with 410-mm (16.14-in) belt armour and 650-mm (25.6-in) face plates on the turrets. To get the ships built without alarming the Americans and British required total

secrecy, the theory being that if Japan refused to ratify the next naval treaty in 1936 and had the ships ready by 1940 (when all tonnage limits expired) nobody could accuse the Japanese of cheating. It was also assumed that if the new ships were longer and wider than the locks of the Panama Canal the US Navy would be unable to build battleships of equivalent power, and would be unable to oppose the Japanese Fleet in the Pacific without the enormous expense (and delay) of widening the Panama Canal.

Two ships, IJN *Yamato* and IJN *Musashi*, were ordered under the 3rd Reinforcement Programme of 1937. *Yamato* was laid down in November 1937, launched in August 1940 and completed in December 1941, just over a week after Pearl Harbor. She was Admiral Yamamoto's flagship at

the Battle of Midway, but turned back before getting within gun-range of the American carriers. *Yamato* was torpedoed by the USS *Skate* in February 1944 but repairs were completed in time for her to take part in the Battle of the Philippine Sea in June 1944, in Vanguard Force of the 1st Mobile Fleet.

The *Yamato*, *Musashi* and *Nagato* formed the main strength of Vice-Admiral Kurita's Force 'A' in the Battle of Leyte Gulf, and *Yamato* fired her 460-mm (18.1-in) guns for the first and last time at surface targets when she engaged American light forces. However, poor visibility prevented her from using her monster guns to good effect. Her last sortie was a suicide mission from the Home Islands to Okinawa, but long before she could achieve anything she was sunk on 7 April 1945 by massive air strikes.

Specification
IJN *Yamato*
Displacement: 64,000 tons standard, 69,988 tons full load
Dimensions: length 263.0 m (863 ft) overall; beam 38.9 m (127 ft 9 in); draught 10.45 m (34 ft 3 in)
Machinery: 4-shaft geared steam turbines delivering 150,000 shp (111895 kW)
Speed: 27 kts
Armour: belt 100-410 mm (3.94-16.14 in); bulkheads 300-350 mm (11.8-13.78 in); decks 200-230 mm (7.87-9.06 in); barbettes 380-560 mm (14.96-22.05 in); turrets 190-650 mm (7.48-25.6 in); conning tower 75-500 mm (2.95-19.7 in)
Armament: nine 460-mm (18.1-in), 12 155-mm (6.1-in) DP, 12 127-mm (5-in) AA, 24 25-mm AA and four 13-mm (0.52-in) AA guns
Aircraft: six floatplanes
Complement: 2,500 officers and men

The 64,000-ton Yamato *had the heaviest armour and her 460-mm (18.1-in) guns were the most powerful ever fitted to a battleship.*

Richelieu

To maintain its position relative to other major navies, the French navy authorized two 35,000-ton battleships in 1935, to be named **Richelieu** and *Jean Bart*. They were basically enlarged editions of the 26,000-ton battlecruisers *Dunkerque* and *Strasbourg*, also with high speed and two quadruple turrets forward, but much heavier armament and protection.

The design which emerged was unique, with two large quadruple turrets well forward and widely spaced, and an ugly backward-angled funnel forming part of the after superstructure. They were, however, powerful and well-protected ships and their only drawback was low endurance, a result of being intended to operate primarily in the Mediterranean.

The *Richelieu* bore a charmed life, for she was running her trials at Brest when France fell in June 1940, but managed to escape to North Africa. She went to Dakar, and escaped without damage when a British motor launch

tried to drop four depth charges under her stern. Early on the morning of 8 July she was attacked by six Fairey Swordfish torpedo bombers from HMS *Hermes*. One 457-mm (18-in) torpedo struck the *Richelieu's* stern, and flooding caused her to settle on the bottom of the harbour. However, her 380-mm (15-in) guns were still functioning, and accurate salvoes helped to defeat an attack by British and Free French forces in September despite the fact that the ship was unable to steam, and that three of her guns were unable to fire.

As soon as her refit was completed the ship sailed to the UK via Toulon, and joined the Home Fleet at Scapa Flow, covering convoys to Murmansk and working up to full efficiency. In March 1944 she left the Home Fleet and was sent to Trincomalee to serve with the Eastern Fleet. She saw no great battles but took part in a number of bombardments and came under air attack on several occasions. Apart

from a short refit at Casablanca from October 1944 to January 1945 she remained in the East Indies until October 1945, when she sailed for Indo-China.

The incomplete Richelieu *escaped from Brest to Dakar in June 1940, where she was damaged by a British attack.*

Specification
Richelieu
Displacement: 41,000 tons standard, 47,500 tons full load
Dimensions: length 247.9 m (813 ft 4 in) overall; beam 33.0 m (108 ft 3 in); draught 9.7 m (31 ft 10 in)
Machinery: 4-shaft geared steam turbines delivering 150,000 shp (111855 kw)
Speed: 30 kts
Armour: belt 343 mm (13.5 in); decks 50-170 mm (2-6.75 in); turrets 170-445 mm (6.75-17.5 in)
Armament: eight 380-mm (15-in), nine 152-mm (6-in) DP, 12 100-mm (3.9-in) AA, 16 37-mm AA and eight 13.2-mm (0.52-in) AA guns
Aircraft: three Loire-Nieuport floatplanes
Complement: 1,550 officers and men

The 'Richelieu' class, like the British 'Nelson', grouped the main armament forward to concentrate the armour belt, but, being larger ships, could carry a heavier secondary armament.

Vittorio Veneto

With her sister *Littorio*, the **Vittorio Veneto** formed the spearhead of the Italian navy at the outbreak of World War II, having been completed in April and May 1940 respectively. Both formed the 9th Division at Taranto, where it was hoped they would deter the British Mediterranean Fleet by virtue of their high speed and heavy armament.

Both ships put to sea several times in response to British operations, but they missed the Battle of Calabria on 9 July 1940. The *Vittorio Veneto* was lucky not to be damaged during the Fleet air raid on Taranto in November 1940, but she was the direct cause of the next disaster which overtook the Italian navy, the Battle of Matapan. On 28 March 1941 while taking part in a sweep against the British convoys evacuating troops from Greece to Alexandria and Crete, the *Vittorio Veneto* was hit by a torpedo dropped by one of HMS *Formidable's* Fairey Albacores. The 457-mm (18-in) torpedo hit abaft 'Y' turret on the port side at 15.21. Serious flooding followed and power was lost on the port outer propeller shaft, but she could still steam, and limped away to the north west.

More British attacks followed at dusk, missing the battleship but hitting one of her escorting cruisers, the *Pola*. The engineers and damage control parties worked hard to stem the flooding, and by 20.34 the *Vittorio Veneto's* speed had increased to 19 kts, and she

was able to make her way back to Taranto for repairs, leaving the *Pola* and two sisters to be destroyed by the British Mediterranean fleet during the night.

In December 1941 the *Vittorio Veneto* was hit by a torpedo from the British submarine HMS *Urge*, and needed another three months in dock. She joined the *Littorio* for an operation against a British convoy in mid-June 1942, but the Italians were losing the initiative, and thereafter she spent most of her time in La Spezia as Taranto was under constant air attack. On 5 June 1943 she was damaged by Allied bombers, and the following September she joined the melancholy line which steamed to Malta to surrender to the British.

The *Vittorio Veneto* was interned at Alexandria while the Allies debated the future of all Italian warships. There was talk of 'tropicalizing' the three 'Littorio' class battleships as fast carrier escorts for the Pacific but they lacked endurance, and although they re-

turned to Italy in 1946 they were not permitted to be incorporated into the post-war Italian Navy, being sold for scrap in 1951.

Specification
Vittorio Veneto
Displacement: 41,700 tons standard, 45,460 tons full load
Dimensions: 237.8 m (780 ft) overall; beam 32.9 m (108 ft); draught 10.5 m (34 ft 5 in)
Machinery: 4-shaft geared steam turbines delivering 128,000 shp (95450 kW)
Speed: 30 kts
Armour: belt 60-345 mm (2.4-13.6 in); decks 165 mm (6.4 in); turrets and barbettes 200-280 mm (7.9-11 in)
Armament: nine 381-mm (15-in), 12 152-mm (6-in), 12 90-mm (3.5-in) AA, 20 37-mm AA and 16 20-mm AA guns
Aircraft: three floatplanes
Complement: 1,872 officers and men

The Italian Littorio *turning at speed on one of her rare trips to sea. Although well armed and fast, she and her sisters were short on endurance.*

The Vittorio Veneto *saw more action than any other Italian battleship, being hit twice by torpedoes and once by bombs.*

Allied and Axis Cruisers

With duties that varied from commerce protection to convoy raiding, and from offensive operations to fleet reconnaissance, the World War II cruiser inherited the mantle of the frigate of Nelson's day. Fast, well-armed vessels ranged the oceans in the service of all the major combatants, and proved extremely effective.

Though World War II could not be won for the Allies at sea, nevertheless the war could certainly have been lost there. Fortunately, there were many maritime arenas in which to fight, and the cruiser proved its value in each.

British trade, via merchant shipping, was as vulnerable as ever to attack from the Axis powers. Indeed, the Germans re-used a tactic that had proved successful a quarter-century earlier, when they had used cruisers to harry the merchant ships that the British had deployed cruisers to protect. Both the German and Japanese fleets employed cruisers effectively in small-scale, surprise assaults, and they often went to the extent of using them as transports. The Italians tried the same tactic, but it only suffered as the desperate measure that it was.

To the British, as an island-nation, the protection of their country's supply routes was clearly of paramount importance. The Atlantic convoys were largely the concern of smaller escorts, which were fighting an anti-submarine war, but the Mediterranean and, to a lesser extent, the Arctic routes were dominated by enemy air power.

USS *Biloxi* of the Cleveland class firing her 152.4mm (6in) guns, of which she had 12 in four triple turrets. Twenty-six Cleveland class entered service during the war.

This threat to the Allies meant that close escort by cruisers was required – especially by cruisers that were equipped with adequate modern AA armament and direction.

Cruisers were occasionally operated by the British in offensive squadrons. During these operations they often played vital roles, for instance, in the sinking of tactically important ships, such as the *Admiral Graf Spee*, *Bismarck* and *Scharnhorst*. For large-scale 'fleet' use, however, one needs to look at the Pacific War where the Americans were able to take on, and eventually to prevail over, an enemy on his chosen ground. This was quite a feat.

The Japanese had probably the best cruisers of that era. Their crews were superbly trained and the boats themselves superbly handled, and used very imaginatively as well. The Americans profited by their early reverses to improve both ship design and tactics; besides having excellent material, they developed the will to win, the most important weapon of all.

'La Galissonnière' class light cruiser

Contemporary with the penultimate pair of Italian 'Condottieri', the French **'La Galissonnière'** class design had a distinct edge. By adopting a triple 152-mm (6-in) turret, the designers managed an excellent balance on the low standard displacement of 7,600 tons. Three mountings conferred a one-gun advantage over their rivals while economizing on overall weight, length of hull and area to be protected. Thus vertical protection of up to 120 mm (4.62 in) could be worked in, together with a 50-mm (1.97-in) protective deck. Where the Italians could dispose of 120,000 shp (89485 kW) the French had only 84,000 shp (62640 kW), yet their effective speeds in a seaway were little different at 33 to 34 kts. Interestingly, the French hulls incorporated wide transom sterns; these are today virtually universal in warship design, reducing resistance through the suppression of the stern wave.

Six ships of the type were built, but they fared badly with the changing fortunes of the French state. Following the 1940 capitulation, the loyalties of French Senegal were not known to the British, who mounted an operation against Dakar: the *Gloire*, together with the *Montcalm* and *Georges Leygues*, sailed from Toulon to assist. Suffering from machinery problems the *Gloire* went into Casablanca but the other two reached Dakar. This port, though effectively neutralized,

passed to Allied control only when the Axis finally occupied Vichy France, the three cruisers coming over to the Allied cause. With the occupation, the remaining French fleet, still inactive at Toulon, was scuttled, including the three remaining ships of the class. Of these, two were salvaged by the Italians only to be sunk finally by Allied bombing in 1943. The *Gloire* was present at Anzio, and the *Montcalm* at Normandy.

Specification
'La Galissonnière' class
Ships in class (launched): *La*

Galissonnière (1933), *Jean de Vienne* (1935), *Marseillaise* (1935), *Gloire* (1935), *Montcalm* (1935) and *Georges Leygues* (1936)
Displacement: 7,600 tons standard and 9,120 tons full load
Dimensions: length 179.0 m (586 ft 3 in); beam 17.5 m (57 ft 4 in); draught 5.3 m (17 ft 5 in)
Propulsion: Rateau-Bretagne or Parsons geared turbines delivering 84,000 shp (63640 kW) to two shafts
Speed: 35.7 kts
Armour: belt 75-120 mm (3-4.7 in); deck 50 mm (2 in); turrets 75-130 mm (3-5.1 in)

An example of the most successful of pre-war French cruiser designs, the bizarrely camouflaged Gloire is shown after her 1943 refit in the USA, with much increased AA armament and equipped with radar. Two of her sister ships received similar treatment.

Armament: nine 152-mm (6-in), eight 90-mm (3.5-in) DP and eight 13.2-mm (0.52-in) AA guns, plus four 550-mm (21.7-in) torpedo tubes
Aircraft: two floatplanes
Complement: 540

'Zara' class heavy cruiser

Latent Franco-Italian naval rivalry broke out anew after the Washington Treaty, the two French 'Duquesne' class cruisers being immediately trumped by the Italian 'Trento' class with superior protection. The latter were not even completed before the French embarked on the four 'Suffren' class cruisers, whose survivability was improved a little at the cost of some speed. As it then took Italy three years to reply, predictably, with the four **'Zara' class** cruisers, it would seem that the French design was acquired and thoroughly digested beforehand. In any case, the Italian units were excellent ships, with reduced power on only two shafts but with a high level of protection, whose weight took the ships beyond treaty limits.

Three of the class formed the 1st Cruiser Division at the Battle of Calabria, only a month after the outbreak of the Mediterranean war. The action proved an anti-climax, the Italian fleet disengaging immediately the flagship had been hit.

The next significant action was also their last when, near the end of March

1941, a complex set of Italian fleet movements was undertaken with the object of intercepting a British convoy near Crete. The British, aware of what was afoot, cleared the area and set a trap for the Italians but the latter, as nervous and fleet as any antelope, smelled danger and made for home. Anxious to bring the Italian battleship to account, the British used carrier air strikes to slow it sufficiently to allow their heavy ships to close. Only the 1st Division's *Pola* was thus stopped, however, her two running mates *Zara* and *Fiume* with two destroyers then staying to assist. Admiral Cunningham's battleships fell on them and despatched them with close-range 381-mm (15-in) salvoes at what became known as the night Battle of Matapan. With the American 'Astoria' and British 'Cressy' classes the 'Zara' class thus has the melancholy record of losing three of its type in one engagement.

Specification
'Zara' class
Ships in class (launched): *Zara* (1930),

Fiume (1930), *Gorizia* (1930) and *Pola* (1931)
Displacement: 11,500-11,900 tons standard and 14,200-14,600 tons full load
Dimensions: length 182.7 m (599 ft 5 in); beam 20.6 m (67 ft 7 in); draught 5.9 m (19 ft 4 in)
Propulsion: Parsons geared turbines delivering 108,000 shp (80535 kW) to two shafts
Speed: 32 kts
Armour: belt 100-150 mm (3.9-5.9 in); deck 70 mm (2.75 in); turrets 120-140 mm (4.7-5.5 in); barbettes 140-150 mm (5.5-5.9 in)
Armament: eight 203-mm (8-in), 16 100-mm (3.9-in) DP and eight 37-mm AA guns
Aircraft: two floatplanes
Complement: 830

Right: 'Zara' class cruisers on patrol in the Mediterranean. Built in the early 1930s in response to the new French vessels then entering service, the 'Zara' class were fine, well-balanced ships, somewhat larger than the size set down in the Washington Treaty.

In contrast to the preceding 'Trento' class, the 'Zara' class sacrificed high speed in the interests of much improved protection. Zara and two of her three sisters met their end at the hands of the British Mediterranean fleet off Cape Matapan in March 1941.

'Condottieri' class cruiser

Though the Italians built many fine cruisers, lack of an offensive policy in war led to few of them being really tested in action. The 12 **'Condottieri' class** ships formed the backbone of their light cruiser strength, a quartet and four pairs constituting a logical development sequence over a five-year period. The *Garibaldi* and her sister were the ultimate pair and were very close to the 10,000-ton limit.

As a yardstick for the **'Giussano' class**, the four-strong first group of 'Condottieri', laid down in 1928, the French 'Duguay-Trouins' class was completed less than two years previously. Both classes carried four twin turrets and, though the Italian ships were rather faster, neither type was more than minimally protected. An immediate response in the French 'La Galissonniere' class was paralleled by the remaining 'Condottieri' over the same period. With the French ships incorporating a measure of protection, the Italians successively increased power and dimensions to maintain speed while improving survivability in the **'Bande Nere', 'Diaz', 'Montecuccoli'** and **'Aosta' classes**. The last pair comprised the **'Garibaldi' class** whose beam, draught and displacement were increased significantly to allow two extra guns (in triple A and Y turrets) and a further upgrading of protection. A fundamental shift in policy was the acceptance of a lower speed but this was acceptable as still representing a margin over the equivalent French ships.

The *Garibaldi*'s war was involved mainly in the distant cover for the various convoys to North Africa. In July 1941 she was torpedoed and heavily damaged by the submarine HMS *Upholder*.

Both sisters survived to be incorporated into the post-war fleet, the *Garibaldi* lasting until the 1970s converted to a prototype guided-missile cruiser with Terrier surface-to-air missiles.

Specification
'Condottieri' class (Group 5)
Ships in class (launched): Group 1 *Alberto di Giussano* (1930), *Giovanni delle Bande Nere* (1930), *Alberico da Barbiano* (1930) and *Bartolomeo Colleoni* (1930); Group 2 *Armando Diaz* (1930) and *Luigi Cadorna* (1930); Group 3 *Raimondo Montecuccoli* (1931) and *Muzio Attendolo* (1933);

Group 4 *Emanuele Filiberto Duca d'Aosta* (1932) and *Eugenio di Savoia* (1933); and Group 5 *Luigi di Savoia Duca degli Abruzzi* (1933) and *Giuseppe Garibaldi* (1933)
Displacement: 9,195 tons standard and 11,260 tons full load
Dimensions: length 187.0 m (612 ft 5 in); beam 18.9 m (61 ft 11 in); draught 5.2 m (17 ft)
Machinery: Parsons geared turbines delivering 102,000 shp (76060 kW) to two shafts
Speed: 33.5 kts
Armour: belts 130 mm (5.1 in); deck 40 mm (1.6 in); turrets 135 mm (5.3 in)

Backbone of the Italian light cruiser force, the five groups of 'Condottieri' class cruisers were built over a five-year period in the 1920s and early 1930s. Giuseppe Garibaldi was one of the last two to be built, surviving wartime damage to serve the Italian navy into the 1970s.

Armament: 10 152-mm (6-in), eight 100-mm (3.9-in) AA, eight 37-mm AA and 10 20-mm AA guns, plus six 533-mm (21-in) torpedo tubes
Aircraft: two floatplanes
Complement: 900

The final 'Condottieri' class vessels were increased in size and accepted a reduced performance in the interests of protection. The Luigi di Savoia Duca degli Abruzzi, seen here in 1942 pattern-dazzle camouflage, also survived the war, and served until 1961.

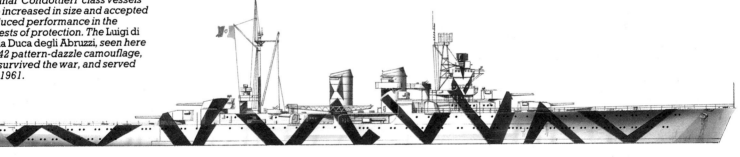

'Capitani Romani' class light cruiser

The British concept of the small cruiser as used in World War I was followed by the Japanese in the 1920s but, thereafter, development lapsed for a decade until the French embarked on the 'Mogador' class. These looked like, and were, super destroyers but which, on a deep displacement of barely 4,000 tons, could outgun a 'Dido' class cruiser. With about 92,000 shp (68605 KW) they could also make 40 kts. The Italians, stung to urgency, produced the **'Capitani Romani' class**, laying down no less than 12 keels in the space of six months. As a result of Italy's varying fortunes of war, however, only four were completed.

Less than 5 m (16 ft 5 in) longer than the 'Mogador' class ships, the 'Capitani Romani' class vessels looked like small cruisers, their extra beam allowing space for machinery developing an astonishing maximum of 125,000 shp (93210 kW), equivalent to that of a 'Salem' class heavy cruiser of four times the displacement. At this power the Italian ships were good for 43 kts and, while they were virtually unprotected, they also shipped a very respectable main battery. In addition, eight torpedo tubes were fitted and mines could be carried, though probably in lieu of other topweight.

Their Roman names were splendidly euphoric, belying the headache that they could have caused any convoy escort commander not blessed with air support. As it was, four were demolished on the ways, five more being sunk through various agencies whilst

fitting out. Three were completed in 1942-3, and one other was eventually salvaged and fitted out, the four being the *Attilio Regolo*, *Pompeo Magno*, *Giulio Germanico* and *Scipione Africano*.

One pair served post-war with each of the French and Italian fleets. Of the Italians, the *San Giorgio* (ex-*Giulio Germanico*) served, albeit re-engined, until very recently. None of the four mounted its original armament, supply considerations dictating American 127-mm (5-in) L/38s in the Italian ships and ex-German 105-mm (4.1-in) weapons in the French units.

Specification
'Capitani Romani' class
Ships in class (launched): *Attilio*

Regolo (1940), *Pompeo Magno* (1941), *Giulio Germanico* (1941) and *Scipione Africano* (1941)
Displacement: 3,750 tons standard and 5,400 tons full load
Dimensions: length 142.2 m (466 ft 6 in); beam 14.4 m (47 ft 3 in); draught 4.1 m (13 ft 5 in)
Propulsion: geared turbines delivering 110,000 shp (82025 kW) to two shafts
Speed: 40+ kts
Armour: not known
Armament: eight 135-mm (5.3-in), eight 37-mm AA and eight 20-mm AA guns, plus eight 533-mm (21-in) torpedo tubes
Aircraft: none
Complement: 425

'Deutschland' class 'pocket battleship'

Until 1934 Germany was bound by the Treaty of Versailles, under whose terms no warship exceeding 10,000 tons could be built. To extract the maximum potency within this general limitation, the designers had to balance finely the conflicting requirements of speed, armament and protection. Long endurance was required to conduct an extensive *guerre de course* against France and the UK and the three **'Deutschland' class** ships were given the quite novel machinery of eight diesels driving two shafts, allowing for flexible and highly economical propulsion.

Electric welding saved 15 per cent on weight as compared with riveting, allowing for extra weight to be allocated to both armament and protection. Despite the overt weight-saving, however, the ships all exceeded their stated displacements. When constructed, they continued the concept of the armoured cruiser, being faster than any battleship and more powerful than any cruiser. Like armoured cruisers, they were vulnerable to battlecruisers.

Until 1940, the ships were officially classified as *Panzerschiffe* (armoured ships), but were popularly known to the Allies as 'pocket battleships'. After the destruction of the *Admiral Graf Spee*, subsequent to the River Plate action, the surviving pair were recategorized as heavy cruisers. The *Admiral Scheer* had a brief but successful career as a raider, gaining particular notoriety with her sinking of the armed merchant cruiser *Jervis Bay*. The *Deutschland* herself was politically renamed *Lützow* after the *Admiral Graf Spee* affair and, until early 1942,

spent much time in dock after being torpedoed on two separate occasions. Her major action was the tactical defeat off North Cape on 30/31 December 1942. Both ships were finally sunk by British bombing in the closing days of the European war.

Specification
'Deutschland' class (*Admiral Graf Spee*)
Ships in class (launched): *Deutschland* (1931), *Admiral Scheer* (1933) and *Admiral Graf Spee* (1934)

Displacement: 12,100 tons standard and 16,200 tons full load
Dimensions: length 186.0 m (610 ft 3 in); beam 21.3 m (69 ft 11 in); draught 5.8 m (19 ft)
Propulsion: eight MAN diesels delivering 56,000 shp (41760 kW) to two shafts
Speed: 28.5 kts
Armour: belt 80 mm (3.1 in); deck 45 mm (1.8 in); turrets 85-140 mm (3.3-5.5 in); barbettes 100 mm (3.9 in)
Armament: six 280-mm (11-in), eight 150-mm (5.9-in), six 105-mm (4.1-in)

Designed as very heavily armed commerce raiders, the German 'pocket battleships' utilized diesel propulsion and electric welded hulls (to save weight) in the quest for long endurance. Graf Spee, weathering a storm, displays the flat funnel cap and vertical bow of pre-war days.

AA, eight 37-mm AA and 10 20-mm AA guns, plus eight 533-mm (21-in) torpedo tubes
Aircraft: two floatplanes
Complement: 1,150

Lützow (formerly Deutschland) as she appeared in 1945. The curved bow was fitted in 1940, and the tall funnel cap in 1941. She was scuttled in May 1945 after being damaged beyond repair by near misses from RAF 'Tallboy' 5443-kg (12,000-lb) bombs.

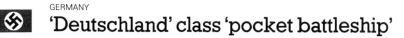

'Hipper' class heavy cruiser

When heavy cruisers were finally built by Germany in the late 1930s, they were of orthodox design, showing no influence from the 'Deutschland' class *Panzerschiff*. The nameship of the **'Hipper' class**, the *Admiral Hipper*, was launched in February 1937 after the various treaties had lapsed and she was, as a result, comparable in displacement with the big Japanese cruisers. By shipping only an eight-gun main battery, however, the Germans had more scope for improved protection. The *Admiral Hipper* was the best known of the class, being active in the Norwegian campaign of 1940, during which she was rammed and damaged by an intended victim, the British destroyer HMS *Glowworm*. In late 1940 and early 1941, she had a successful period as a raider before moving again to Norway, where her presence was partly responsible for the PQ.17 disaster in July 1942. On the last day of the

year, in company with the 'pocket battleship' *Lützow* and a destroyer force, she unsuccessfully attacked the JW.51B convoy off North Cape. The outclassed British destroyer escort kept the Germans at arm's length for three hours until relieved by a cruiser force, Hitler's reaction at this rather inept operation being an order to decommission all heavy units. The *Hipper* thus survived to be taken in 1945. Also captured was the *Prinz Eugen*, best known for her being in company with the *Bismarck* in May 1941, and later accompanying the battle-

Continued on page 806

After Prinz Eugen was ceded to the US Navy in 1945, it was found that the high pressure steam machinery was a constant source of trouble. She was expended as an atom bomb target two weeks after this photograph was taken.

cruisers *Scharnhorst* and *Gneisenau* in their celebrated dash up the English Channel. She was expended at the Pacific A-bomb trials after the war. The *Blücher*, a brand new ship, went down in April 1940 with a heavy loss of life when overwhelmed by Norwegian shore defences while heading up Oslofjord carrying an invasion force. *Lützow* (II) was sold to the Soviets in 1940 and the *Seydlitz* was never completed.

Specification
'Hipper' class (*Prinz Eugen*)
Ships in class (launched): *Admiral Hipper* (1937), *Blücher* (1937) and *Prinz Eugen* (1938)

Displacement: 14,475 tons standard and 18,400 tons full load
Dimensions: length 210.4 m (690 ft 4 in); beam 21.9 m (71 ft 10 in); draught 7.9 m (25 ft 10 in)
Propulsion: Brown Boveri geared turbines delivering 132,000 shp (98430 kW) to three shafts
Speed: 33.4 kts
Armour: belt 70-80 mm (2.75-3.1 in); deck 12-50 mm (0.5-2 in); turrets 70-105 mm (2.75-4.1 in)
Armament: eight 203-mm (8-in), 12 105-mm (4.1-in) DP, 12 37-mm AA and 24 20-mm AA guns, plus 12 533-mm (21-in) torpedo tubes
Aircraft: two floatpanes
Complement: 1,450

Prinz Eugen at Brest in May 1941. After accompanying the battleship Bismarck into the Atlantic and participating in the sinking of HMS Hood, Prinz Eugen made independently for safety, thereby avoiding the fate of her mighty partner.

Supposedly built to the Washington Treaty limit of 10,000 tons, the 'Hipper' class varied in standard tonnage from 14,000 to 17,000 tons and could approach 20,000 tons when deeply loaded. Prinz Eugen is seen here as she was at Bergen in April 1941. The dazzle stripes were later painted over.

UK
'County' class heavy cruiser

It was because of the new British 'Hawkins' class ships (nearly 10,000 tons displacement and armed with 190.5-mm (7.5-in guns) that the Washington Treaty limits on cruisers were set as they were. In keeping with the remainder of the signatories, who built up to these limits, the British produced the **'A'** or **'County' class**. Their designers eschewed, however, the current competitions for optimal armament or speed, producing instead a compromise well-suited to duties on imperial trade routes. Even so they were well-armed, had an adequate turn of speed, and were reasonably protected. They were notable for their considerable freeboard and three funnels, instantly recognizable anywhere. Excellent endurance and good standards of habitability made them both effective and popular. The London Treaty came into force before the construction programme was complete and some five planned units were cancelled.

Though built in three separate groups as the **'Kent' class** (seven ships), **'London' class** (four ships) and **'Norfolk' class** (two ships), the 'County' class ships were originally very similar, but modernization during the 1930s produced variations. On four the after superstructure was greatly enlarged as an aircraft hangar, two of them being cut down a deck aft to compensate as the hull had a reputation for hard rolling. HMS *London* (only) emerged in 1941 from a rebuilding that left her looking like an enlarged 'Fiji'

class cruiser with improved AA armament, the war preventing further such exercises.

In surface action, the ships proved generally effective but fell victim to air attack as readily as any other of their vintage. Their main contribution to the war at sea lay in the unspectacular but vital tasks of convoy protection and operations against raiders. Losses were HMAS *Canberra*, HMS *Dorsetshire* and HMS *Cornwall*.

Specification
'County' class ('London' sub-class)
Ships in class (launched): *Berwick* (1926), *Cornwall* (1926), *Cumberland* (1926), *Kent* (1926), *Suffolk* (1926), *Australia* (1927), *Canberra* (1927), *Devonshire* (1927), *London* (1927), *Shropshire* (1928), *Sussex* (1928), *Dorsetshire* (1929) and *Norfolk* (1928)
Displacement: 9,8250 tons standard and 14,000 tons full load
Dimensions: length 193.3 m (633 ft) beam 20.2 m (66 ft); draught 6.6 m (21 ft 6 in)
Propulsion: Parsons or Brown Curtis geared turbines delivering 80,000 shp (59655 kW) to four shafts
Speed: 32 kts
Armour: belt 76-127 mm (3-5 in); deck 38-102 mm (1.5-4 in); turrets 38-51 mm (1.5-2 in); barbettes 25 mm (1 in)
Armament: eight 203-mm (8-in), eight 102-mm (4-in) AA and eight or 16 2-pdr AA guns, plus eight 533-mm (21-in) torpedo tubes
Aircraft: one or three flying-boats
Complement: 660

The 'County' class cruiser HMS Devonshire draws alongside HMS Mauritius in the Indian Ocean. The two ships are about to effect a transfer of either stores or personnel, with a line being passed from one ship to the other by means of a small rocket.

Below: HMS Norfolk as she appeared in 1943. The 'County' class heavy cruisers were a compromise designed to operate effectively in the protection of long trade routes. They had excellent endurance and were popular with their crews.

'Arethusa' class light cruiser

At the time of the London Treaty of 1930, the UK was building the first 152-mm (6-in) cruisers designed since World War I. Ostensibly replacements for the little 'C' and 'D' class cruisers, these were the five eight-gun 'Leander' class ships designed around a twin-gun mounting tried experimentally on HMS *Enterprise*. A three-ship derivative, the **'Amphion' class**, differed mainly in having widely spaced funnels through the improved layout of machinery spaces.

Once ratified, the treaty imposed limits on the total replacement 152-mm (6-in) tonnage that the British were permitted to build, and the Admiralty experimented with a cut-down six-gunned version known as the **'Arethusa' class**. In tonnage terms, four could be built for three 'Leander' class ships, but they were considered too small and only four were built.

Despite their lack of size, the 'Arethusa' class cruisers found their ideal slot in the Mediterranean war. Best known were HMS *Aurora* and HMS *Penelope* which, while forming the core of Force K working out of Malta in 1941, destroyed convoyed Italian shipping at a rate which caused the Axis armies in North Africa acute supply problems. Both were damaged on the night when Force K was very nearly destroyed in a minefield. The *Penelope*, repaired, went on to see the most hard-fought of the Malta convoys, including Admiral Vian's superb defence at 2nd Battle of Sirte in March 1942. Docked again in Malta, she was so riddled with splinters as to earn the soubriquet 'HMS Pepperpot'. Together again with the *Aurora* in Force Q the *Penelope* saw the end of Axis ambitions in North Africa, going on to the Sicilian and Salerno landings. Bombed and damaged in the Aegean, she saw her last action at Anzio, being sunk by a submarine's torpedo whilst returning to Naples in February 1944. Also sunk in the war was HMS *Galatea*.

Built within Washington Treaty limits, the six-gun 'Arethusa' class cruisers were considered too small, but gave fine service in the Mediterranean. Here an 'Arethusa' class vessel is photographed from HMS King George V, possibly while hunting the Bismarck in May 1941.

Specification
'Arethusa' class
Ships in class (launched): *Arethusa* (1934), *Galatea* (1934), *Penelope* (1935) and *Aurora* (1936)
Displacement: 5,250 tons standard
Dimensions: length 154.2 m (506 ft); beam 15.5 m (51 ft); draught 4.2 m (13 ft 9 in)
Propulsion: geared turbines delivering 64,000 shp (47725 kW) to four shafts
Speed: 32.25 kts
Armour: belt 51 mm (2 in); deck 51 mm (2 in); turrets 25 mm (1 in); conning tower 25 mm (1 in)
Armament: six 152-mm (6-in), eight 102-mm (4-in) AA, and eight 2-pdr AA guns, plus six 533-mm (21-in) torpedo tubes
Aircraft: one flying-boat (not in *Aurora*)
Complement: 470

Below: Three generations of light cruiser are seen heading to join the naval bombardment of Normandy in June 1944. Beyond HMS Arethusa can be seen HMS Danae, dating from 1918, and HMS Mauritius, completed in 1941.

'Town' class heavy cruiser

The eight **'Southampton'** or **'Town' class** cruisers represented the end of British involvement with treaty obligations. With their 'Brooklyn' class the Americans had matched the Japanese 'Mogami' class, and the Admiralty felt obliged to respond with a powerful 152-mm (6-in) cruiser aimed at fleet work rather than commerce protection, as was the case with the 'Leander' class and its successors. Launched during 1936-7 the class was completed for the outbreak of war. Though designed on a smaller scale than the clas-ses that had brought about their build-ing, these ships carried 12 reliable guns in a new-pattern triple turret, and could maintain more than 32 kts in a seaway. They were used mainly in the European theatre, where they were more than adequate; though three were lost in the Mediterranean, none was sunk through conventional surface action.

For the ship's size and scale of pro-tection the main battery was a little ambitious, and the last three units of the 'Southampton' class proper (HMS

Above: HMS Sheffield, a Type I 'Town' class 152-mm (6-in) cruiser, is seen on convoy escort duty. The 'Town' class was designed to match the Japanese 'Mogami' class, and represented Britain's final abandonment of treaty obligations.

HMS Southampton depicted just prior to her loss in January 1941. The triple 152-mm (6-in) gunned turrets represented a significant increase in firepower over the immediately preceding 'Leander' and 'Arethusa' classes.

Liverpool, HMS *Manchester* and HMS *Gloucester*) having an increased beam. Later modernizations saw the removal of X turret and the enhancement of the AA armament.

In 1938 two examples of an improved version were launched. While carrying the same armament as their predecessors HMS *Belfast* and HMS *Edinburgh* were larger, better protected and had more powerful machinery. All of the 'Town' class ships were well built, giving in some cases over 30 years of useful service. Indeed the *Belfast* is still afloat as the sole remaining example of a long line of British cruisers.

Developed from the 'Town' class was the 'Fiji' or 'Crown Colony' class (11 ships) and its first derivative, the **Swiftsure' class** (six ships). Smaller but slightly faster, these were emergency programme ships and, while effective in service, their inferior construction was reflected in their shorter life-spans.

Specification
'Town' class (Type III)
Ships in class (launched): Type I or

Developed from the 'Town' class, the 'Crown Colony' class cruisers such as HMS Kenya took wartime lessons into account while being built. Shorter but slightly faster than their predecessors, they had much improved secondary ammunition supply.

'Southampton' class *Newcastle* (1936), *Southampton* (1936), *Birmingham* (1936), *Glasgow* (1936) and *Sheffield* (1936); Type II or 'Liverpool' class *Liverpool* (1937), *Manchester* (1937) and *Gloucester* (1937); and Type III or 'Belfast' class *Belfast* (1938) and *Edinburgh* (1938)
Displacement: 10,550 tons standard and 13,175 tons full load
Dimensions: length 187.0 m (613 ft); beam 19.3 m (63 ft 3 in); draught 5.3 m (17 ft 6 in)
Propulsion: Parsons geared turbines delivering 82,500 shp (61520 kW) to four shafts
Speed: 32 kts
Armour: belt 114 mm (4.5 in); deck 51 mm (2 in); turrets 25-63.5 mm (1-2.5 in); conning tower 102 mm 94 in)

Armament: 12 152-mm (6-in), eight 102-mm (4-in) AA, and eight or 16 2-pdr guns, plus six 533-mm (21-in) torpedo tubes
Aircraft: three flying-boats
Complement: 850

'Dido' class light cruiser

An increasing awareness of the threat from aerial attack was apparent in the warship design programmes just before World War II. Besides, for instance, rebuilding some of its older cruisers as AA ships, the Royal Navy acquired the 16-strong **'Dido' class** in two groups for close defence work. Only a little larger than the 'Arethusa' class cruisers, the original 11 ships had a lean, elegant appearance, beautifully proportioned. They had no secondary armament, the main battery being 10 133-mm (5.25-in) guns in the twin mountings developed as a secondary weapon for the 'King George V' class battleships. These were light enough to permit three superimposed mountings forward, though in later years the proliferation of tophamper resulted in the landing of the upper, or Q mounting.

The last five ships, labelled **'Improved Dido' class** ships, had eight-gun fits from the start, with shorter vertical funnels and sturdier masts. These modifications did nothing for their looks but the ships certainly served much farther afield, even for Arctic convoy escort, whereas the earlier ships were used mainly in the Mediterranean. In the latter theatre they were superb and, though HMS *Spartan* of the later group was sunk by glider bomb attack off Anzio, none was destroyed by direct air attack.

It could not be claimed that the 133-mm (5.25-in) weapon was the ideal dual-purpose gun, for it was rather on the light side for surface engagements against the protected ships of the day yet too heavy for effective use against aircraft, with too slow a rate of fire and reaction. In the post-war fleet the 'Dido' class ships proved of little more use to the Royal Navy than the equivalent 'Atlanta' class, did to the US Navy, and most of them had been scrapped by the end of the 1950s. Wartime losses were HMS *Charybdis*, HMS *Hermione*, HMS *Bonaventure*, HMS *Naiad* and HMS *Spartan*.

Specification
'Dido' class (Type II)
Ships in class (launched): Type I *Dido* (1939), *Euryalus* (1939), *Naiad* (1939), *Phoebe* (1939), *Sirius* (1940), *Bonaventure* (1939), *Hermione* (1939), *Charybdis* (1940), *Cleopatra* (1940), *Scylla* (1940) and *Argonaut* (1941); Type II *Bellona* (1942), *Black Prince* (1942), *Diadem* (1942), *Royalist* (1942) and *Spartan* (1942)
Displacement: 5,770 tons standard and 6,970 tons full load
Dimensions: length 156.3 m (512 ft); beam 15.4 m (50 ft 6 in); draught 5.3 m (17 ft 3 in)
Propulsion: Parsons geared turbines delivering 64,000 shp (47725 kW) to four shafts

Speed: 32.25 kts
Armour: belt 76 mm (3 in); deck 35 mm (1 in); turrets 25-38 mm (1-1.5 in); barbettes 13-19 mm (0.5-0.75 in); conning tower 25 mm (1 in)
Armament: eight 133-mm (5.25-in) DP, eight or 12 2-pdr AA, and 12 20-mm AA guns, plus six 533-mm (21-in) torpedo tubes **Complement:** 535

HMS Dido on fire support duty off Gaeta during the drive up the Italian peninsula. The dual purpose 113-mm (5.25-in) turrets were originally designed as secondary armament for the 'King George V' class battleships

HMS Naiad is depicted in an unusual colour scheme dating from June 1940. The guns at their maximum elevation of 70° give a clue as to the AA function of the 'Dido' class cruisers.

'Mogami' class heavy cruiser

Unlike her earlier naval model, the UK, Japan took to the 203-mm (8-in) cruiser enthusiastically, her only light cruisers being her 140-mm (5.5-in) gunned scouts such as the 'Sendai' class. But because of the restrictions of the 1930 London Treaty, however, four large 155-mm (6.1-in) gunned ships were built as the 'Mogami' class, this in turn stimulating the Americans to build the 'Brooklyn' class, each class having a 15-tun main battery. To achieve the high designed speed of 37 kts, the Japanese ships were very slender and proved to be dangerously vulnerable. They were, therefore, bulged externally in 1937. Less than two years later, all treaties having lapsed, they were again modified, their triple 155-mm (6.1-in) turrets being exchanged for

twin 203-mm (8-in) turrets and the bulge being increased in size. Their speed was now barely 34 kts, the same as that of the 'Brooklyn' class but with 50 per cent extra power.

During World War II the class formed the coherent 7th Cruiser Squadron under the redoubtable Rear Admiral Kurita, and was continuously active. The *Mogami*, in company with the *Mikuma*, was instrumental in the destruction of the USS *Houston* and HMAS *Perth* after the Java Sea battle. Later, as part of the diversionary force involved in the Midway action, the two

cruisers collided heavily before being attacked by carrier aircraft; the *Mikuma* was sunk but *Mogami*, with 300 dead, survived to fight another day.

In November 1943 the *Mogami*, together with a large force of the Japanese fleet, was caught unawares by air attack at Rabaul. Hit heavily, blazing and down by the bows from flooded magazines, she again just made it. She then survived the Battle of the Philippine Sea only to meet her end at the night action in the Surigao Strait. Battered by gunfire, she collided with the *Nachi* but, typically, went in again. Shattered but afloat, she was attacked next day by aircraft. Her surviving crew removed, she was then sunk by a Japanese torpedo. The other two units were also lost in the war.

Specification
'Mogami' class cruiser
Ships in class (launched): *Mogami* (1934), *Mikuma* (1934), *Suzuya* (1934) and *Kumano* (1936)
Displacement: 12,400 tons standard
Dimensions: length 203.9 m (669 ft); beam 20.2 m (66 ft 3 in); draught 5.8 m (19 ft)
Propulsion: geared turbines delivering 150,000 shp (111855 kW) to four shafts
Armour: belt 100 mm (3.9 in); deck 35 mm (1.5 in); turrets 25 mm (1 in)
Armament: 10 203-mm (8-in), eight 127-mm (5-in) DP and eight 25-mm AA guns, plus 12 610-mm (24-in) torpedo tubes
Aircraft: three floatplanes
Complement: 850

The lapse of the various naval treaties in the late 1930s saw Japan replace the triple 152-mm (6-in) turrets on the 'Mogami' class with twin 203-mm (8-in) mounts. Depicted just before the Battle of Midway, Mogami was to be severely damaged several times before finally succumbing in October 1944.

'Myoko' class heavy cruiser

While showing a distinct family relationship with the preceding 'Aoba' class, the four 'Myoko' class cruisers were some 10 per cent longer and introduced the fearsomely massive aspect characteristic of the next decade of Japanese cruiser construction. Proportionately more 'beamy' than earlier classes, the 'Myoko' class ships mounted 10 203-mm (8-in) guns and still had improved protection worked in. Like most of their kind, they looked strange to Western eyes but were powerfully built and extraordinarily difficult to sink. Immediately before the outbreak of World War II, their torpedo armament was increased to 16 610-mm (24-in) tubes in keeping with the aggressive tactical doctrine that

was to pay such handsome dividends. Their topweight reserves must thereby have been pushed to the limit, however, for when AA armament was urgently enhanced later in the war, some had the torpedo armament reduced again.

Like most of the hard worked Japanese cruiser classes, the 'Myoko' class ships were all lost (the *Myoko* being surrendered in a totally unserviceable state). Unusually, two of the four were sunk by the Royal Navy, the *Ashigara* being sunk by submarine torpedo in the Bangka Strait and the *Haguro* falling to a classically-executed night destroyer attack. The *Haguro* had been a particularly doughty opponent at the Java Sea, Sun-

da Strait and the action off Samar. She had survived Midway, Empress Augusta Bay and the 2nd Solomon Sea actions. It was, therefore, particularly gratifying for the renascent British Pacific Fleet to intercept her as she passed through the Malacca Strait in May 1945 en route to evacuate the garrison of the Andamans. Five destroyers of the 26th Flotilla attacked in divisions so that, in avoiding the torpedoes of the first, the *Haguro* ran foul of those of the second.

Specification
'Myoko' class
Ships in class (launched): *Myoko* (1927), *Nachi* (1927), *Haguro* (1928) and *Ashigara* (1928)

Displacement: 13,380 tons standard
Dimensions: length 201.7 m (661 ft 9 in) waterline; beam 20.7 m (68 ft); draught 6.3 m (20 ft 9 in)
Propulsion: geared turbines delivering 130,000 shp (96940 kW) to four shafts
Speed: 33.5 kts
Armour: belt 100 mm (3.9 in); deck 65-125 mm (2.5-5 in); turrets 40 mm (1.5 in)
Armament: 10 203-mm (8-in), eight 127-mm (5-in) DP and eight 25-mm AA guns, plus 16 610-mm (21-in) torpedo tubes
Aircraft: three floatplanes
Complement: 780

Myoko (1944, after major refit) cutaway drawing key

1 Balanced rudder
2 Propeller
3 Shaft
4 Support
5 Oil-fired boilers
6 Boiler rooms
7 Smoke-emitting installation room
8 Rice and wheat store
9 Crew's quarters
10 Officers' quarters
11 Lower flat
12 Refrigerator room
13 203-mm (8-in) 50-calibre guns
14 Turret
15 Sighting hood
16 Rangefinder
17 Barbette
18 Turntable
19 Switch room
20 Stores
21 Shell room
22 Ammunition hoist
23 Torpedo-handling room
24 Torpedo tubes
25 Catapult
26 Keel
27 Armour belt
28 Aft boiler room
29 Forward boiler room
30 Aft control
31 Aft lookout position
32 Entrance to hangar
33 Tripod mainmast
34 Aft funnel
35 Two funnels trunked into one
36 Funnel casing

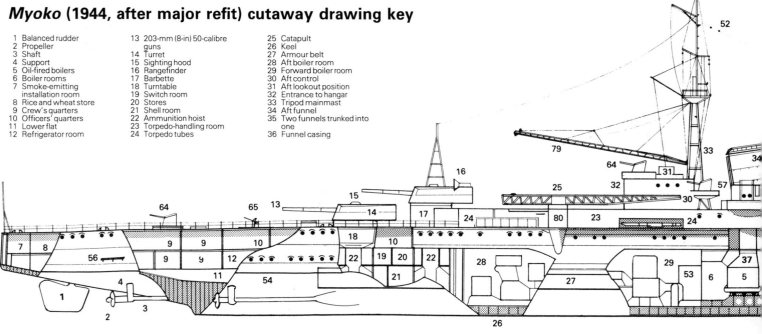

'Northampton' class cruiser

The USA's first two Washington Treaty cruisers were the two **'Pensacola' class** heavy cruisers of 1929. Both had very active lives in World War II, but their design was not particularly successful, being cramped and having an extremely low freeboard. Their 10-gun 203-mm (8-in) armament (set, unusually, in mixed twin and triple turrets) was overambitious to the point where the ships were extremely tender. Even before their completion an improved design, the **'Northampton' class**, was well advanced. These not only regrouped the main battery into a homogeneous nine guns set in three triple turrets, but had a hull 4.4 m (14 ft 6 in) greater in length plus a raised forecastle to improve seaworthiness.

Of the class of six ships, the USS *Houston* was lost in March 1942 in the aftermath of the Java Sea debacle. The USS *Chicago* survived the shambles of the Savo Island battle in August 1942 with most of her bows removed by a Japanese torpedo. Guadalcanal still claimed her, however, for after repairs she returned shortly afterward to cover a replenishment trip to the island. Near Rennell Island she was sunk by air-dropped torpedoes. The USS *Northampton* also went down in the area, only a couple of miles from Savo, in the dreadful night action of Tassafaronga. An American force of five cruisers and six destroyers fell foul of the so-called 'Tokyo Express'. The latter were surprised, but acted with great resolution and speed, using their specialized night-fighting training to good advantage. Despite being encumbered with embarked troops and stores, they split into subdivisions and launched a devastating torpedo attack.

Four of the five American cruisers were hit, although only the *Northampton* was a total loss. The surviving trio of the class, known as the **'Chester' class**, lasted until 1960.

Specification
'Northampton' class
Ships in class (launched):
Northampton (1929), *Chester* (1929), *Louisville* (1930), *Chicago* (1930), *Houston* (1929) and *Augusta* (1930)
Displacement: 9,050-9,300 tons standard and 12,350 tons full load
Dimensions: length 183.0 m (600 ft

3 in); beam 20.1 m (66 ft); draught 4.95 m (16 ft 3 in)
Propulsion: Parsons geared turbines delivering 107,000 shp (79790 kW) to four shafts
Speed: 32.5 kts
Armour: belt 76 mm (3 in); deck 51 mm (2 in); turrets 38-64 mm (1.5-2.5 in); barbettes 38 mm (1.5 in); conning tower 203 mm (8 in)
Armament: nine 203-mm (8-in), eight 127-mm (5-in) AA, two 3-pdr, and eight 12.7-mm (0.5-in) AA guns
Aircraft: four floatplanes
Complement: 1,200

An improvement on the preceding 'Pensacola' class, the Northamptons were found to be dangerously vulnerable to Japanese 203-mm (8-in) shells even at long ranges. USS Northampton *is depicted as she was in mid-1942, before her final campaign around Guadalcanal.*

Haguro in 1944. The four ships in the class were largely responsible for Allied losses in the Java Sea in 1942, but all had been lost or put out of action by overwhelming Allied power in 1944 and 1945.

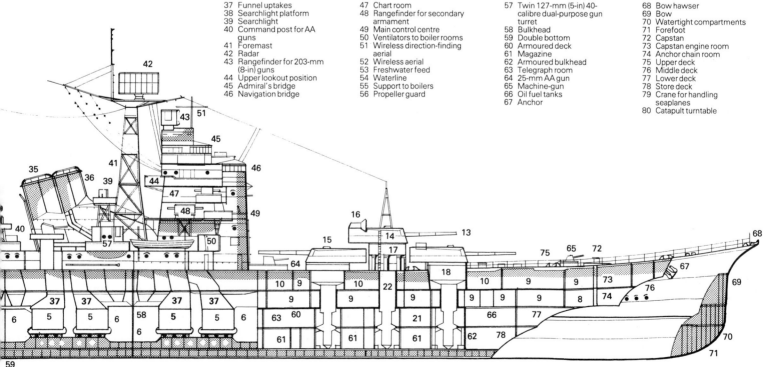

37 Funnel uptakes	47 Chart room	57 Twin 127-mm (5-in) 40-	68 Bow hawser
38 Searchlight platform	48 Rangefinder for secondary	calibre dual-purpose gun	69 Bow
39 Searchlight	armament	turret	70 Watertight compartments
40 Command post for AA	49 Main control centre	58 Bulkhead	71 Forefoot
guns	50 Ventilators to boiler rooms	59 Double bottom	72 Capstan
41 Foremast	51 Wireless direction-finding	60 Armoured deck	73 Capstan engine room
42 Radar	aerial	61 Magazine	74 Anchor chain room
43 Rangefinder for 203-mm	52 Wireless aerial	62 Armoured bulkhead	75 Upper deck
(8-in) guns	53 Freshwater feed	63 Telegraph room	76 Middle deck
44 Upper lookout position	54 Waterline	64 25-mm AA gun	77 Lower deck
45 Admiral's bridge	55 Support to boilers	65 Machine-gun	78 Store deck
46 Navigation bridge	56 Propeller guard	66 Oil fuel tanks	79 Crane for handling
		67 Anchor	seaplanes
			80 Catapult turntable

59

'Cleveland' class cruiser

Stimulated by the Japanese 152-mm (6-in) 'Mogami' class, the Americans built the nine 15-gun **'Brooklyn' class** cruisers during the 1930s. For the war programmes, however, a more practical 12-gun layout was adopted, with enhanced secondary and AA batteries. While obviously derivatives of the 'Brooklyn' class, these new **'Cleveland' class** cruisers were beamier on about the same length, and were better protected. The name ship was laid down in July 1940 and five years later the class stood at 26 units, with a further nine hulls converted to fast light carriers (CVL) of the 'Independence' class. Three more were cancelled and a fourth completed as a guided-missile cruiser, making a total of 39, the largest cruiser programme ever.

As with the heavy cruisers, layout was improved by development of a single-funnelled version, the **'Fargo' class.** Only two of these were completed because of the war's end and the introduction of a fully automatic 6-in gun mounting. As a result of the extra bulk of its loading gear, this weapon was accommodated in a new twin mounting and, with its higher rate of fire fewer barrels per ship could have been expected. Even so, the US Navy still demanded 12 guns and the resultant six-turret ships, the **'Worcester' class** needed to be 21.7 m (69 ft 3 in)

longer, with 20 per cent greater power.

Like all guns of its generation, the automatic 152-mm (6-in) weapon arrived too late to avoid being overtaken by the guided missile. Only two 'Worcester' class ships were completed, being rebuilt aft as interim CLGs with the long-range Talos surface-to-air missile. These survived until recently, largely because their unfashionably spacious accommodation made them popular as peacetime flagships. No 'Cleveland' class ships were lost in World War II.

Specification
'Cleveland' class

Ships in class (launched): *Cleveland* (1941), *Columbia* (1941), *Montpelier* (1941), *Denver* (1942), *Santa Fe* (1942), *Birmingham* (1942), *Mobile* (1942), *Vincennes* (1943), *Pasadena* (1943), *Springfield* (1944), *Topeka* (1944), *Biloxi* (1943), *Houston* (1943), *Providence* (1944), *Manchester* (1946), *Vicksburg* (1943), *Duluth* (1944), *Miami* (1942), *Astoria* (1943), *Oklahoma City* (1944), *Little Rock* (1944), *Galveston* (1945), *Amsterdam* (1944), *Portsmouth* (1944), *Wilkes-Barre* (1943), *Atlanta* (1944), *Dayton* (1944), *Baltimore* (1942), *Boston* (1942), *Canberra* (1943), *Quincy* (1943), *Pittsburg* (1944), *St Paul* (1944), *Columbia* (1944), *Helena* (1945),

Bremerton (1944), *Fall River* (1944), *Macon* (1944), *Toledo* (1945), *Los Angeles* (1944) and *Chicago* (1944)
Displacement: 10,000 tons standard and 13,775 tons full load
Dimensions: length 185.9 m (610 ft); beam 20.3 m (66 ft 6 in); draught 7.6 m (25 ft)
Propulsion: General Electric geared turbines delivering 100,000 shp (74570 kW) to four shafts
Speed: 33 kts
Armour: belt 38-127 mm (1.5-5 in); deck 76 mm (3 in); turrets 76-127 mm

(3-5 in); barbettes 127 mm (5 in); conning tower 165 mm (6.5 in)
Armament: 12 152-mm (6-in), 12 127-mm (5-in) DP, eight (first two) or 24 (eight ships) or 28 (others) 40-mm AA, and between 10 and 21 20-mm AA guns
Aircraft: four floatplanes
Complement: 1,425

Twenty-six 'Cleveland' class vessels entered service during World War II. USS Biloxi was commissioned in August 1943 and broken up in 1962.

Developed from the 'Brooklyn' class but with a wider hull, the 'Cleveland' class carried 12 152-mm (6-in) guns in four triple turrets. The two-tone scheme depicted is typical of postwar colour schemes.

'Salem' class heavy cruiser

Though completed too late to take part in World War II, the **'Salem' class** cruisers are very much ships of that war and proved to be the final word in conventional cruiser development. Their design stemmed directly from the preceding **'Oregon City' class** which was itself a tidied-up **'Baltimore' class.** Both latter classes shared a common 205.7-m (675-ft) hull, the 'Oregon City' class adopting a single-funnelled layout and more compact superstructure to improve firing arcs.

Though all shared the typically American fit of three triple 203-mm (8-in) turrets with three twin 127-mm (5-in) gunhouses disposed symmetrically at each end of the superstructure, these ships represented a transition

step in AA warfare, up to 52 40-mm guns in the 'Baltimore' class ships giving way to 20 76-mm (3-in) guns in the later 'Oregon City' class. The 'Salem' class featured 24 76-mm (3-in) guns from the outset, weapons large enough to not only disable a suicide aircraft but disintegrate it. The great innovation of the 'Salem' class, however, was the adoption of a fully-automatic main battery, the ships' greater dimensions reflecting the extra bulk and magazine space required.

Amply-proportioned hulls permitted adequate protection for all these classes, the 'Salem' class particularly so. Interestingly, these close-associated groups, the complete American heavy cruiser war programme, all stemmed from a single prototype, the USS *Wichita*, a 203-mm (8-in) version of the 'Brooklyn' class completed in 1939.

Last used in Vietnam, all three 'Salem' class cruisers are still in the reserve fleet, their conventional armament a valuable asset. With enhanced munitions their potential is still very good, and they have a life expectancy limited only by their material condition. No ships from any of these classes was lost in World War II.

Specification
'Salem' class
Ships in class (launched): *Des Moines* (1946), *Newport News* (1947) and

Salem (1947)
Displacement: 17,000 tons standard and 21,500 tons full load
Dimensions: length 218.4 m (716 ft 6 in); beam 23.3 m (76 ft 6 in); draught 6.7 m (22 ft)
Propulsion: General Electric geared turbines delivering 120,000 shp (89485 kW) to four shafts
Speed: 33 kts
Armour: belt 152-203 mm (6-8 in); deck 76 mm (3 in); turrets 152-mm (6 in); barbettes 152 mm (6 in); conning tower 203 mm (8 in)
Armament: nine 203-mm (8-in), 12 127-mm (5-in) DP, 24 76-mm (3-in) DP, and 12 20-mm AA guns
Aircraft: four floatplanes
Complement: 1,860

The ultimate in World War II cruiser design, USS Salem, Des Moines and Newport News displaced more than 20,000 tons at full load, and were equipped with fully automatic main 203-mm (8-in) batteries. None saw action during the war, but were in use off the coast of Vietnam.

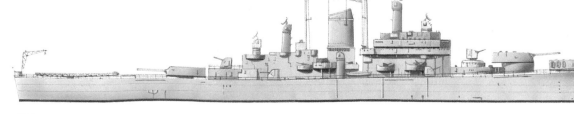

Axis Destroyers

Destroyers were the most active surface units of the Axis fleets. The Japanese had the finest destroyers in the world; these won a series of dramatic victories across the Pacific. In European waters, German destroyers preyed on the Soviet convoys while in the Mediterranean the Italians revealed a talent for anti-submarine warfare.

All three of the major Axis fleets started World War II with considerable destroyer forces but found, just as the British did, that the attrition rate was high, particularly when the ships were used for duties other than those for which they had been designed. This occurred most of the time.

German ships tended to be overambitious, as the result of the twin requirements of meeting (officially at least) treaty limitations on displacement, while not appearing inferior on paper to the French ships seen as the inevitable enemy. British equivalents may have appeared more modest, but they could always fight their armament in a seaway, something that none of the larger German ships could boast. Following their losses in Norway, the German destroyer forces made little further impact on the naval war.

The Japanese used their many ships both in their designed fleet context and in other independent roles, largely in support of the army. Their supreme achievement was in the vicious six-month dispute for Guadalcanal. Not only did the destroyers make contention possible at all but, in doing so, made the island a catalyst, enabling them to take the

Italian torpedo boat, or light destroyer, *Libra* of the Alcione class of vessels, which were brought into service in 1938 and lasted until the 1960s.

war to the American fleet. That the policy of attrition against so powerful and numerous an enemy was flawed from the outset was a top-level strategic blunder and in no way detracted from the toughness and resource of the Japanese destroyer skippers.

Though never sacrificing their main weapon, the 610mm (24in) torpedo, the Japanese ships shed much of their main battery firepower in order to accommodate extra AA armament and to give space for troops, equipment and supplies. A similar role fell to many Italian destroyers, which also could just make the return trip to their beleaguered comrades in North Africa within the hours of darkness. Their contribution was useful but, again, losses

were high because (as the British involved in the Tobruk siege discovered) ships were of necessity predictable in their timetable. Nevertheless it was preferable to sharing the big ships' usual routine of swinging around the buoy. Most successful of the Italians were the 'torpedo boats', which proved adept at anti-submarine warfare.

'Minekaze' class

The 'Kamikaze' class destroyers, follow-ons to the 'Minekazes', represented something of a departure for the Japanese navy, which had hitherto followed Royal Navy designs, although the choice of 120-mm (4.72-in) guns as main armament reflected British policy.

At the end of World War I the Japanese had the concept of first- and second-class destroyers, the one being a scaled-up version of the other. Before this the Japanese navy had either bought British ships or copied them closely, but with the 21 **'Momi' class** and 15 **'Minekaze' class** second- and first-class destroyers they produced something a little more original, following an earlier German lead in providing a well between the short forecastle and the bridge structure. Destroyers of the time were quite short overall and, still without the benefit of a superimposed gun on a deckhouse forward,

were prone to bury their noses in a short head sea. At best this made life difficult for the bridge personnel, and at worst there was danger of the structure being flattened or swept clean. The forward well acted as a natural break and, as it moved things aft, also provided space for one set of torpedo tubes. The 'Minekazes', all launched between 1919 and 1922, were the *Akikaze, Hakaze, Hokaze, Minekaze, Namikaze, Nokaze, Numakaze, Okikaze, Sawakaze, Shiokaze, Tachikaze, Yakaze* and *Yukaze*.

The classes introduced the 533-mm (21-in) torpedo tube to Japanese des-

troyers, twins in the 'Momis' and triples in the 'Minekazes' (and in the nine similar **'Kamikaze' class** follow-ons). Both types carried their 120-mm (4.72-in) guns (the calibre itself reflecting earlier British influence) high on deckhouses and forecastle, enabling them to be fought in poor conditions when the weather deck was likely to be swept by loose water.

By World War II standards the 'Minekazes' were both small and old and, with the shortage of escorts being quickly and dramatically exploited by American submarines, most of the class shed half their main-calibre guns,

minesweeping gear and all but a pair of torpedo tubes to mount depth-charge throwers and ammunition, together with an ever-increasing number of light AA guns.

Four units, after the fashion of some older British destroyers, had a very thorough conversion to convoy escorts with some boiler capacity sacrificed for extra bunker space. One, the *Sawakaze*, was reportedly fitted with an ahead-firing nine-barrelled AS rocket-launcher. Nine of the class themselves fell victim to submarine attack, the nameship being sunk by the USS *Pogy* in the East China Sea early in 1944 at a time when destroyers were made priority torpedo targets.

Above: The venerable 'Minekazes' were launched between 1919 and 1922 but served throughout the war. Many had their original weapon fit altered to include depth-charge throwers and light anti-aircraft guns, as the enemy was no longer likely to be another destroyer.

Specification
'Minekaze' class
Displacement: 1,215 tons standard and 1,650 tons full load
Dimensions: length 102.5 m (336.3 ft); beam 9.0 m (29.5 ft); draught 2.89 m (9.5 ft)
Propulsion: two sets of geared steam turbines delivering 28709 kW (38,500 shp) to two shafts
Speed: 39 kts
Endurance: 6670 km (4,145 miles) at 14 kts
Armament: four single 120-mm (4.72-in) guns, two machine-guns, two triple 533-mm (21-in) torpedo tube mountings and up to 20 mines
Complement: 148

Below: This is a 'Minekaze' as she appeared in late 1944 after being converted to carry Kaiten suicide torpedo craft. This desperate expedient failed to achieve success on a scale to rival that of the kamikaze aircraft, which had begun to launch their attacks earlier in the year.

'Fubuki' class

At the time of their construction, the 20 **'Fubuki' class** destroyers (launched in 1927-31) were among the trend-setters of the destroyer world. They had been preceded by the 12 **'Mutsuki' class** destroyers, which had further refined the 'Kamikazes' with their strong Anglo-German influences. Only then did the Japanese designers go fully their own way and produce a type of destroyer so advanced that it was still formidable 15 years later at the end of World War II, besides influencing all the classes that followed it. Firstly a significant increase in size was accepted to accommodate more top-

weight. The awkward forward well was discontinued in favour of a more conventional continuous forecastle, the freeboard of which was increased, and the bridgework was both strengthened and raised to reduce water impact damage. In the preceding class

The 'Fubuki' class revolutionized destroyer design by substantially increasing the size of the vessel. This reduced the vulnerability to heavy seas and enabled them to carry a formidable armament of six 127-mm (5-in) guns and nine 610-mm (24-in) torpedo tubes.

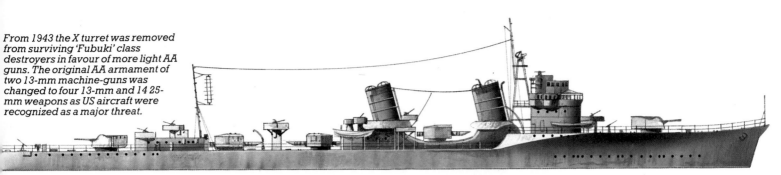
From 1943 the X turret was removed from surviving 'Fubuki' class destroyers in favour of more light AA guns. The original AA armament of two 13-mm machine-guns was changed to four 13-mm and 14 25-mm weapons as US aircraft were recognized as a major threat.

the 610-mm (24-in) torpedo had been introduced and the 'Fubukis' carried three triple mountings, with stowage for nine spare torpedoes. This early commitment to the torpedo was obviously, yet Allied forces were constantly surprised by the bold and ready manner in which the Japanese were prepared to use them in World War II.

A further innovation was the uprating of the main calibre guns to 127 mm (5 in) and mounting these in fully enclosed twin gunhouses, one forward and two aft to lower their combined centre of gravity. In those units launched from 1929 the elevation of the main battery was increased to 70°, an angle unmatched in their day to give a dual-purpose capacity that was little short of visionary.

This splendid class was also of high power, the 37285 kW (50,000 shp) being good for 38 kts. Unfortunately,

Ushio was the only one of the 20 'Fubuki' class to survive the war. Seen here just after her 1936 refit, she was the last 'Fubuki' to be launched, and her 127-mm (5-in) guns had their elevation increased from 40 to 75 degrees: a remarkably innovative feature.

this was bought at the expense of hull strength, and a degree of tenderness. Service during the 1930s highlighted these failings, and the ships were heavily strengthened and given extra ballast. This added another 400 tons to the displacement, slowing them by 4 kts. Further topweight was saved later by not carrying spare torpedoes and landing the superfiring after mountings in favour of a very necessary enhancement to the AA defences. The class served widely in all theatres,

only one unit surviving the war. The ships were the *Akebono, Amagiri, Asagiri, Ayanami, Fubuki, Hatsuyuki, Isonami, Miyuki, Murakumo, Oboro, Sagiri, Sazanami, Shikinami, Shinonome, Shirakumo, Shirayuki, Uranami, Ushio, Usugumo* and *Yugiri.*

Specification
'Fubuki' class (as built)
Displacement: 2,090 tons standard
Dimensions: length 118.35 m (388.3 ft); beam 10.36 m (34.0 ft); draught 3.2 m (10.5 ft)
Propulsion: two sets of geared steam turbines delivering 37285 kW (50,000 shp) to two shafts
Speed: 37 kts
Endurance: 8700 km (5,406 miles) at 15 kts
Armament: three twin 127-mm (5-in) guns, two machine-guns, three triple 610-mm (24-in) torpedo tube mountings with nine reloads, and up to 18 mines
Complement: 197

'Tomodzura' and 'Ootori' classes

While it may demonstrate the ingenuity of the naval architect, warship design rarely profits from attempting an ambitious fit on a limited displacement, yet this is just what the interwar treaties brought about. The Japanese had operated a class of first-class torpedo boat (or coastal destroyer) up to the mid-1920s, but had not repeated the type until the four-ship **'Tomodzura' class**, ordered in 1931 to top-up the Japanese tonnage entitled under the London Treaty. The value of such small craft is evident when it is remembered that Japanese interests looked not only eastward over the Pacific but also at the mainland Orient across the shallow and unrestricted Sea of Japan. At 650-ton standard displacement, these ships carried a very ambitious armament of a single and a twin 127-mm (5-in) gunhouse and two pairs of 533-mm (21-in) torpedo tubes, all on a fine hull able to achieve 30 kts on a modest 8203 kW (11,000 shp). The weakness of this maritime conjuring was made rudely evident when the nameship capsized in heavy weather in 1943. As the hulk did not founder it was recovered, heavily modified (as were the remainder of the class) and recommissioned.

The lesson was timely as regards the whole fleet but particularly so in the case of the follow-on **'Ootori' class** boats, then about to be ordered. Surprisingly, though the latter were en-

larged their slender proportions hardly changed, the length:beam ratio still being nearly 11:1. As a comparison, the 'Ootoris' were longer than either a British Type II 'Hunt; (86.1 m/282.5 ft) or an American DE (88.1 m/289 ft), yet the beams of the latter were 9.6 m (31.5 ft) and 10.7 m (35 ft) respectively. At the same time the Japanese had eventually to accept a greatly reduced armament of two 120-mm (4.72-in) guns and only one pair of tubes. The price of a destroyer's speed was, indeed, high.

Although eight of the 16 units projected were cancelled, those completed (the *Hato, Hayabusa, Hiyodori, Kari, Kasasagi, Kiji, Ootori* and *Sagi,* all launched in 1935-7) were reportedly good AS ships, though both the *Sagi* and *Hiyodori* were sunk separately by the American submarine USS *Gunnel* on the same patrol. The nameship was sunk off Saipan in June 1944 with no less than 13 other ships when a convoy was totally overwhelmed by American carrierborne aircraft.

Specification
'Ootori' class (as built)
Displacement: 840 tons standard and 1,050 tons full load
Dimensions: length 88.35 m (289.9 ft); beam 8.2 m (26.9 ft); draught 2.84 m (9.3 ft)
Propulsion: two sets of geared steam turbines delivering 14168 kW (19,000 shp) to two shafts
Speed: 30 kts
Endurance: 7400 km (4,598 miles) at 14 kts
Armament: three single 120-mm (4.72-in) and one 40-mm AA guns, and one triple 533-mm (21-in) torpedo tube mounting
Complement: 112

Chitori, second ship of the 'Tomodzura' class, is seen here off Maizuru in 1934, the year the nameship capsized while on running trials due to the designers' attempt to cram an excessive armament on to a vessel of modest displacement.

'Akatsuki' and 'Kagero' classes

It is worthy of note that in the 'Fubukis' the Japanese had destroyers of a specification superior to that of the British 'J' class, yet a full decade earlier. This sudden leap in capability was bound to bring problems, as succeeding classes demonstrated. The four **'Akatsuki' class** ships of 1931-3 kept the same arrangement on a slightly shorter hull but reduced the forward funnel to a thick pipe to save topweight, with lightweight masting and a reduction in depth charges. The *Hibiki* of this group was the first all-welded Japanese destroyer. In the six **'Hatsuhara' class** ships that followed, length was again cut, along with one 127-mm (5-in) gun and a set of torpedo tubes with reloads; installed power and speed were also reduced as designers wrestled with London Treaty restrictions. They were largely repeated with the 10 **'Shiratsuyu' class** ships, which again experienced a reduction in length, yet succeeded in increasing the torpedo armament to eight 610-mm (24-in) torpedoes with the usual set of reload weapons. The 10 **'Asashio' class** ships of 1937 were late enough to bypass lip service to treaties and returned to a size and armament almost identical with the 'Fubukis' of nearly a decade before. That this basic design was still relevant was underscored by recognizing it as the basis of the necessary expansion in destroyers on the lead-up to war. Thus 18 more destroyers, nearly identical, but proportionately beamier and known as the **'Kagero' class**, were put into the water between 1938 and 1941.

Their main characteristics were little different from those of the 'Fubukis', with superimposed twin gunhouses aft and one forward, the latter separated from the blockhouse of a bridge by a distinctive gap, which allowed very wide arcs. Both sets of torpedo tubes could be reloaded rapidly from low stowages flanking the forward funnel and in the after deckhouse. A 20-ship repeat class, the **'Yugumo' class**, followed in 1941-3.

The 'Kageros' themselves were heavily involved, only one ship surviv-

Above: Shiranuki *leaves the Uraga shipyard in Tokyo after her commissioning ceremony in 1939. Very similar to the 'Asashio' class, the 'Kageros' were excellent fleet destroyers. One of their number, the Hamakaze, became the first Japanese destroyer to receive radar in 1943.*

Right: Shiranuki *in less happier circumstances, berthed in Maizuru dock after narrowly surviving a torpedo hit from a US submarine off the Aleutians. The Japanese destroyer fleet was designed for surface action and had to be hastily modified for AA and ASW operations.*

ing the war. The *Natsushio* was one of the very early losses when sunk by the veteran American submarine USS *S37* during the operation to take Makassar. Two more, the *Arashi* and *Hagikaze*, were sunk by a total of five torpedo hits when the 'Tokyo Express' had the tables turned on it at Vella Lavella in August 1943. The other 'Kageros' were the *Amatsukaze, Hamakaze, Hatsukaze, Hayashio, Isokaze, Kagero,* *Kuroshio, Maikaze, Nowake, Oyashio, Shiranuki, Tanikaze, Tokitsukaze, Urakaze* and *Yukikaze*.

Specification
'Kagero' class (as built)
Displacement: 2,035 tons standard and 2,490 tons full load
Dimensions: length 118.45 m (388.6 ft); beam 10.8 m (35.4 ft); draught 3.76 m (12.3 ft)

Propulsion: two sets of geared steam turbines delivering 38776 kW (52,000 shp) to two shafts
Speed: 35 kts
Endurance: 9250 km (5,748 miles) at 15 kts
Armament: three twin 127-mm (5-in) and two twin 25-mm AA guns, and two quadruple 610-mm (24-in) torpedo tube mountings
Complement: 240

Above: Arashi *creates an impressive wake at nearly 35 kts. Just after midnight on 7 August 1943, she and three other destroyers were intercepted by six US destroyers while on a resupply mission, and in a furious action lasting just 30 minutes she and two of her companions were torpedoed and sunk.*

Above: Kiyoshimo *cruises peacefully off Uraga in May 1944, seven months before meeting her end at the hands of US PT boats and aircraft. Similar to the 'Kageros', the 'Yugumo' class featured an improved bridge and increased main battery elevation.*

Below: Hibiki *was Japan's first welded warship, and was the only 'Akatsuki' class destroyer to survive the war. Her X turret was replaced with more light AA weapons in 1942, and she ended the war carrying 28 25-mm cannon.*

JAPAN
'Akitsuki' class

By far the largest destroyers built in series by the Japanese, the **'Akitsuki' class** ships were conceived originally as AA escorts comparable with the British 'Dido' and US 'Atlanta' cruiser classes and, by comparison, offered a cheaper solution to the problem. The choice of a 100-mm (3.94-in) gun was probably better than that of the 133.4-mm (5.25-in) and 127-mm (5-in) weapons of the Western ships, whose rate of fire was considerably lower, though the lively hull of a destroyer must have made them less effective than cruisers when firing at aircraft. They were the only eight-gun destroyers in the Japanese fleet, and it would seem that the quadruple torpedo tube mounting was something of a late addition. Though they had the basis of an effective design, the Japanese too had underestimated the devastating effect of a determined air attack and only four light automatic guns of the standard 25-mm calibre were originally shipped. War experience encouraged the addition of more at virtually any opportunity, so that, by the end of the war, those still afloat (six were sunk) could dispose of up to 50 such weapons. Launched between 1941 and 1944, the ships of the class were the *Akitsuki, Fuyutsuki, Hanatsuki, Harutsuki, Hatsutsuki, Natsusuki, Niitsuki, Shimotsuki, Suzutsuki, Terutsuki, Wakatsuki* and *Yoitsuki*.

The most distinctive feature of the class was the complex casing of the single stack; extensive trunking enabled the funnel to be sited far enough abaft the bridge both to cut the smoke problem and greatly improve visibility, while placing it sufficiently far forward to permit extra AA platforms to

'Akitsuki' class destroyers could easily be distinguished by their single funnel. Sited well abaft the bridge, it allowed greater visibility and less smoke difficulty while allowing more AA weapons to be shipped in the space where their contemporaries had a second stack.

be installed where the after stack would normally have been.

A feature of preceding classes had been their extremely light masts, but the 'Akitsukis' were among the first to have their masts strengthened for the support of the considerable bulk of the Type 22 surveillance radar antenna. The size of the hull, combined with a comparatively light gun armament and few torpedoes, allowed more generous topweight margins than was customary with Japanese destroyers, one result being a large depth-charge capacity. Nearly 40 more hulls to two improved designs were planned but never completed.

Specification
'Akitsuki' class (as built)
Displacement: 2,700 tons standard and 3,700 tons full load
Dimensions: length 134.12 m (440.0 ft); beam 11.6 m (38.1 ft); draught 4.11 m (13.5 ft)
Propulsion: two sets of geared steam turbines delivering 38776 kW (52,000 shp) to two shafts

Speed: 33 kts
Endurance: 14825 km (9,212 miles) at 18 kts
Armament: four twin 100-mm (3.94-in) and two twin 25-mm AA guns, and one quadruple 610-mm (24-in) torpedo tube mounting
Complement: 285

Above: 'Akitsuki' class destroyers were built as fast AA escorts to operate with the carrier groups, the choice of eight 100-mm (3.94-in) guns being more appropriate to the task than the bigger weapons fitted to US or Royal Navy AA vessels.

Carrying only a light gun armament and four torpedo tubes, the 'Akitsukis' could accommodate a substantial depth-charge capacity. Their large hulls soon bristled with light AA weapons, 40 to 50 25-mm guns being fitted to the units that were still operational in 1945.

JAPAN
'Matsu' class

Japan's commitment to a short war was nowhere more evident than in her lack of plans for rapid fleet expansion. Convoy escorts were virtually non-existent (as, indeed, were plans for the convoy system itself) and pre-war fleet destroyers, that were being lost and disabled at an alarming rate, were being replaced by ships of equal quality. Though the notion was laudable, there simply was neither the time nor the capacity to produce such ships, and a

Japanese destroyer losses rapidly outpaced shipyard production, and in common with her enemies Japan resorted to the construction of a utility class of escort destroyer. Nevertheless, the 'Matsu' class were better armed and more comfortable vessels than their Allied equivalents.

utility design had rapidly to be developed. In profile this, the **'Matsu' class**, looked large by virtue of the two spindly and widely spaced funnels, but it was the smallest both in terms of size and displacement to be built since World War I. The correct scale was given by the gun mountings, which appeared overlarge. These were simple in the extreme, a single handworked 127-mm (5-in) weapon in a shield forward and a twin in a open structure aft. Installed power was little more than one-third that of the fleet destroyers, but the 'Matsus' could still manage about 28 kts, more than adequate for convoy work. A respectable two dozen 25-mm automatic AA weapons were carried, though many of these were single-barrelled mountings, sited in very exposed positions along the edges of the hull. Right amidships was a quadruple 610-mm (24-in) torpedo tube bank; a new-pattern sextuple unit had been planned but not completed. In a ship of this capacity and speed the tubes were mainly of defensive value but still had the splinter-proof house from which this important weapon could be worked in some comfort. This, and the enclosed bridge, contrasted with the spartan appointments on British ships where, at the time, it seemed little appreciated that a comfortable crew actually performed better, without the

tendency to 'go soft'.

Only 17 of the planned 28 'Matsus' were so completed in 1944-5, by which time the design had been even further simplified into the **'Tachibana' class** variant, of which 23 were laid down but many were not completed. Ninety further units never proceeded beyond the planning stage. By virtue of their being completed late in the war and engaged on second-line duties, an unusual number survived, losses amounting to 11.

Specification
'Matsu' class
Displacement: 1,260 tons standard and 1,530 tons full load
Dimensions: length 100.0 m (328.1 ft); beam 9.35 m (30.7 ft); draught 3.27 m (10.7 ft)
Propulsion: two sets of geared steam turbines delivering 14168 kW (19,000 shp) to two shafts
Speed: 27.5 kts
Endurance: 8350 km (5,188 miles) at 16 kts
Armament: one twin and one single

Designed for rapid production, the 'Matsu' class's turbines provided only about a third of the power of a fleet destroyer's machinery, but they were capable of a respectable 28 kts. The 'Matsu' class had their two sets of machinery arranged in separate units for better damage control.

127-mm (5-in) plus four triple and 12 single 25-mm AA guns, and one quadruple 610-mm (24-in) torpedo tube mounting
Complement: not known

ITALY
'Generale' class

Like the Germans, the Italians operated a large force of light destroyers alongside their main fleet units. Both navies referred to these as torpedo boats, a term which sometimes confuses the British reader, who may think of them in terms of MTBs. The nearest thing to such ships in the Royal Navy were the 'Hunt' classes which were more robust but slower; equivalent to the older enemy boats were the few Admiralty 'S' class units still serving.

The six **'Generale' class** ships were the last of four very similar 73-m (239.5-ft) classes which commenced with the eight-strong **'Pilo' class** of 1914-5. These were narrow-gutted three-stackers, typical destroyers of their time, which were downgraded to torpedo boat status between the wars as larger ships commissioned. For their size they were quite ambitiously armed, with five single 102-mm (4-in) guns and two twin 440-mm (17.3-in) torpedo tube mountings. The gun layout was hardly satisfactory, with one mounting on the raised forecastle, two sided amidships and two on the quarterdeck, no more than three being effective on either beam. The four **'Sirtori' class** ships squeezed in an extra gun on an already tight topweight reserve. These dated from 1916-7 and were followed by the eight **'La Masa' class** ships of 1917-9, which had their armament reduced to only four guns. In 1919-20 came four **'Palestro' class** ships, slightly larger at 82 m (269 ft) to accommodate a near 50 per cent increase in power. Though these were to have a follow-on in the **'Curtatone' class** of 1922-3, these two groups were separated by one last 73-m (239.5-ft) class, the 'Generali', all six of which were launched in 1921-2 by the single yard of Odero, at Sestri Ponente. The ships were the *Generale Antonio*

Cantore, Generale Antonio Cascino, Generale Antonio Chinotto, Generale Carlo Montanari, Generale Achille Papa and *Generale Marcello Prestinari*. Of similar size to the earlier ships, they carried only three guns, a complement to which most were eventually reduced by wartime demands. None of these small and elderly ships was employed in front-line operations, but all nevertheless became war casualties. Three were mined, one of them the *Chinotto*, sinking in a field laid by the British submarine HMS *Rorqual* during a particularly fruitful patrol. These mines, off western Sicily, also claimed two merchantmen, while the submarine also sank another and an Italian submarine by torpedo

Specification
'Generale' class (as built)
Displacement: 635 tons standard and 890 tons full load
Dimensions: length 73.5 m (241.1 ft); beam 7.33 m (24.0 ft); draught 2.5 m (8.2 ft)
Propulsion: two sets of steam turbines delivering 11186 kW (15,000 shp) to two shafts

Speed: 30 kts
Armament: three single 102-mm (4-in) and two 76-mm (3-in) AA guns, two twin 450-mm (17.72-in) torpedo tube mountings and up to 18 mines
Complement: 105

The Italian navy, like the German navy, classified its light destroyers as 'torpedo boats'. Eight-hundred-ton vessels mounting three 102-mm (4-in) guns, a pair of 450-mm (17.7-in) torpedoes and up to 18 mines, the versatile 'Generale' class were built in the early 1920s.

'Turbine' class

Turbine, in the scheme she adopted at Piraeus in 1942, was taken over by the Germans after the Italian surrender and was destroyed by American aircraft off Salamis in 1944. Turbine herself topped 39 kts on trials, but the best sea speed of the class was nearer 33 kts.

Dating from 1927-8, the eight **'Turbine' class** destroyers (*Aquilone, Borea, Espero, Euro, Nembo, Ostro, Turbine* and *Zeffiro*) were nearly identical with the quartet of **'Sauro' class** units that immediately preceded them, the major difference being an extra 3 m (9.84 ft) or so in length to accommodate an approximate 11 per cent increase in power. A feature of both types was the massive armoured 'pillbox' of a conning tower that topped-off the enclosed bridge. They were the last Italian destroyers to have the low velocity 45-calibre 120-mm (4.72-in) guns, all those following having a 50-calibre weapon. They were, however, the first to mount a second director for the after guns; this was sited between the torpedo tube groups but was probably set too low to be of very much use.

The four 'Sauro' class ships were destroyed as part of the hopelessly isolated Red Sea squadron, while no less than six of the 'Turbine' class were sunk in 1940. Each of the class, in common with most Italian destroyers, could carry over 50 mines, and four of them thoroughly mined the waters off Tobruk. The Axis garrison there was to prove as much a problem to support as later it did for the British, and the *Espero* became the first casualty as early as 28 June 1940 when caught by the Australian cruiser HMAS *Sydney*, the ship that went on to sink the cruiser *Bartolomeo Colleoni* off Cape Spada only three weeks later. 'Stringbags'

from the carrier HMS *Eagle* disposed of the *Zeffiro* and a freighter, and heavily damaged the *Euro* in Tobruk harbour during early July, repeating the exercise barely a fortnight later when they sank the *Ostro* and *Nembo* together with a freighter in the adjacent Gulf of Bomba. It was these same aircraft, working from a shore base near Port Sudan, that were to sink two of the 'Sauros' in the Red Sea in the following April. Carrier-based air attack accounted for another pair on the night of 16/17 September when HMS *Illustrious* blitzed Benghazi. The *Euro* was sunk by German bombers after the Italian capitulation, while the *Turbine* herself, captured by the Germans, was finally sunk by American

aircraft in September 1944.

Specification
'Turbine' class
Displacement: 1,090 tons standard and 1,700 tons full load
Dimensions: length 92.65 m (304.0 ft); beam 9.2 m (30.2 ft); draught 2.9 m (9.5 ft)
Propulsion: two sets of geared steam turbines delivering 29828 kW (40,000 shp)
Speed: 36 kts
Armament: two twin 120-mm (4.72-in) and two single 40-mm AA guns, two triple 533-mm (21-in) torpedo tube mountings and up to 52 mines
Complement: 180

'Navigatore' class

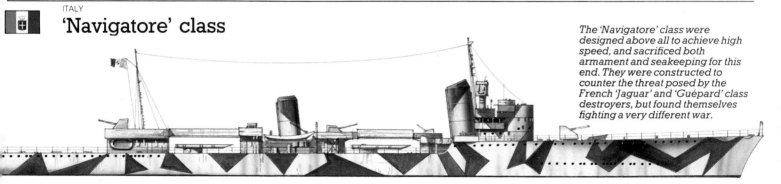

The 'Navigatore' class were designed above all to achieve high speed, and sacrificed both armament and seakeeping for this end. They were constructed to counter the threat posed by the French 'Jaguar' and 'Guépard' class destroyers, but found themselves fighting a very different war.

Some four years after the completion of the 'Leone' class scouts, the Italians produced between 1928 and 1930 (launch dates) another oversized class in the 12 **'Navigatore' class** destroyers, namely the *Alvise da Mosto, Antonio da Noli, Antonio Pigafetta, Antoniotto Usodimare, Emanuelle Pessagno, Giovanni da Verazzano, Lanzerotto Malocello, Leone Pancaldo, Luca Tarigo, Nicoloso da Recco, Nicolo Zeno* and *Ugolino Vivaldi*. They were, in fact, of slightly smaller dimensions but of greater displacement. Much of this was accounted for by machinery producing a maximum of nearly 44742 kW (60,000 shp) and a third twin 120-mm (4.72-in) gun mounting between the two groups of torpedo tubes. Though large for their day, the gradually increasing scale of destroyers in general meant that the ships' size

and displacement was equalled by those of the second group of 'Soldati' a decade later. The 'Navigatori' were produced at a time when high speed was an obsession with the Italians. Parallel with their construction was that of the first group of 'Condottiere' class cruisers; often running without armament and stores, these were forced to the point where they produced trial speeds of better than 42 kts. Only the 'Navigatori' were large enough to have a hope of matching such performance in a seaway and to prove this possible, at least theoretically, their machinery was overrun briefly on trials to return better than 44 kts. They were extremely lightly built and their seakeeping left something to be desired, though it was improved later by increasing their freeboard. Another futile gesture toward weight-saving was the original

provision of torpedo tubes of only 440-mm (17.3-in) calibre.

Their fates were a reflection of the confusion of loyalties suffered by the Italians during the war. Eleven of the 12 were sunk: six of these losses were from direct action by the British and another by mine; two were sunk in action with the Germans; one was scuttled; and the last was sunk in error by an Italian submarine. The *Pancaldo* was an early loss, sunk by aircraft from HMS *Eagle* outside Augusta after returning from the Battle of Calabria. She was later salvaged and recommissioned, only to be sunk again (and finally) by aircraft off Cape Bon in April 1943 while running supplies to the remnants of the army in North Africa. Another, the *Pigafetta*, was also sunk twice, being scuttled at Fiume at the Italian surrender, but refloated and put

back into service by the Germans, only to be destroyed by British air attack on Trieste in February 1945.

Specification
'Navigatore' class
Displacement: 1,945 tons standard and 2,580 tons full load
Dimensions: length 107.75 m (353.5 ft); beam 10.2 m (33.5 ft); draught 3.5 m (11.5 ft)
Propulsion: two sets of geared steam turbines delivering 37285 kW (50,000 shp) to two shafts
Speed: 38 kts
Armament: three twin 120-mm (4.72-in) and three single 37-mm AA guns, two twin or triple 533-mm (21-in) torpedo tube mountings and up to 54 mines
Complement: 225

'Soldato' class

The extensive **'Soldato' class** was the ultimate development of a sequence that began with the four-ship **'Dardo' class** of 1930-2. They used deck space very effectively by successfully trunking all boiler uptakes into one substantial funnel casing. Four 120-mm (4.72-

in) guns were carried but, unlike the British disposition, these were sited in two twin mountings, one on the forecastle deck and one on the same level atop a house set well aft, saving both deckspace and topweight. Slightly smaller than their British counterparts,

the Italian ships were more highly powered, being deficient only in their torpedo complement, weapons that the Italians never valued very highly. Their distinctive profile became very much associated with the Italian fleet and was repeated in the largely similar

'Folgore' class quartet built in parallel. A feature was a separate director for each pair of guns, allowing two targets to be engaged effectively and simultaneously.

It was to improve seaworthiness and fighting qualities that the four **'Maes-**

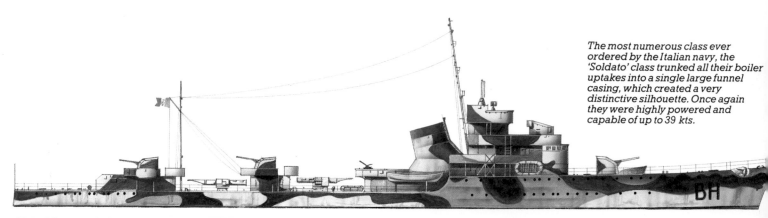

The most numerous class ever ordered by the Italian navy, the 'Soldato' class trunked all their boiler uptakes into a single large funnel casing, which created a very distinctive silhouette. Once again they were highly powered and capable of up to 39 kts.

Right: Like many Italian destroyers, the 'Soldato' class emphasized speed at the expense of armament and strength, and the Lanciere, seen here, foundered in the storm after the battle of Sirte, not because of British action but simply because her light design betrayed her.

trale' class ships of 1934 were lengthened by nearly 10 m (32.8 ft), with a proportionate increase in beam; in other respects they and the four 'Oriani' class ships of 1936 were essentially repeats, the latter having slightly increased power.

With war in Europe looming the Italian navy expanded, a 12-ship repeat 'Oriani' order being shared between four yards. All were launched 1937-8 as the first group of 'Soldati', and were the *Alpino, Artigliere, Ascari, Aviere, Bersagliere, Camicia Nera, Carabiniere, Corazziere, Fuciliere, Geniere, Granatiere* and *Lanciere*. Four of these introduced the first major change by taking a fifth 120-mm gun in a single mounting between the torpedo tube groups. The arrangement was kept in all but one of a further series of seven, only five of which were completed.

The *Lanciere*, of the first group, and the 'Maestrale' class *Scirocco* foundered in the gale through which the 2nd Battle of Sirte was fought; they had suffered no action damage and their loss was a reflection on the generally overlight scantlings used in Italian design. Four of the first group and three of the second survived the war. Of these the three were ceded to France and two of the others to the Soviet Union.

Specification
'Soldato' class (first series)
Displacement: 1,830 tons standard and 2,460 tons full load
Dimensions: length 106.75 m (350.2 ft); beam 10.15 m (33.3 ft); draught 3.6 m (11.8 ft)
Propulsion: two sets of geared steam turbines delivering 35794 kW (48,000 shp) to two shafts)
Speed: 39 kts
Armament: four or five 120-mm (4.72-

in) and one 37-mm AA guns, two triple 533-mm (21-in) torpedo tube mountings and up to 48 mines
Complement: 219

Scirocco, fourth ship of the similar 'Maestrale' class, also went down in the storm that overwhelmed Lanciere. Despite this terrible vulnerability to heavy seas, the 'Maestrales' were judged an adequate design and were the basis for the 'Soldato' class.

ITALY

'Ariete' class

With the 32 **'Spica' class** torpedo boats launched in 1936-8, the Italians were able to adopt a single-funnel arrangement, the more efficient hull being driven at the same speed as the preceding 'Curtatoni' for less power. Their profile was remarkably similar to that of the contemporary 'Oriani' class fleet destroyers, the major difference being the much bulkier funnel casing of the

latter, necessary because of extensive trunking from two separate boiler spaces. They also lacked the funnel cap of the torpedo boats. With the 'Spicas' the 100-mm (3.94-in) gun was introduced; only three were carried and they were essentially for use against ships, having an elevation of only 45° and a rate of fire of about eight rounds per minute. Surprisingly, considering

their category, they adhered to only four of the small 450-mm (17.72-in) tubes and these were largely wasted by initially siding them as singles, only two tubes thus bearing on either broadside. Centreline twin mountings were later substituted.

The **'Ariete' class** design was only that of an improved 'Spica', whose extra beam demanded about 15 per cent

more installed power but allowed greater topweight. This was used by two extra torpedo tubes (these were never uprated to the far more useful 533-mm/21-in), an increase in mine capacity from 20 to 28, or an equivalent increase in depth charge capacity. The Italians used their torpedo boats extensively and effectively for minelaying.

Ariete was the only vessel of the class to serve with the Italian navy, the others being seized by the Germans in September 1943. The 'Arietes' were improved 'Spica' class boats intended primarily to protect convoys from a surface threat. The 'Spicas' themselves became very active minelayers during the war.

Not until 1942-3 were the 'Arieti' laid down, the fleet having by then the benefit of combat experience. Over 40 units were planned in an extended programme but, though spread among three yards, only 16 (namely the *Alabarda, Ariete, Arturo, Auriga, Balestra, Daga, Dragone, Eridano, Fionda, Gladio, Lancia, Pugnale, Rigel, Spa-* *da, Spica* and *Stella Polare*) were actually laid down. Of these only the nameship was actually delivered to the Italian fleet, a month before the armistice. The remainder, in various stages of completion, fell into German hands, only 13 of them actually seeing service at sea. Only two (*Ariete* and *Balestra*) survived to serve post-war, both under the Yugoslav flag.

Specification
'Ariete' class
Displacement: 800 tons standard and 1,125 tons full load
Dimensions: length 82.25 m (269.8 ft); beam 8.6 m (28.2 ft); draught 2.8 m (9.2 ft)
Propulsion: two sets of geared steam turbines delivering 16405 kW (22,000 shp) to two shafts
Speed: 31 kts
Armament: two single 100-mm (3.94-in) and two single 37-mm AA guns, two triple 450-mm (17.72-in) torpedo tube mountings and up to 28 mines
Complement: 155

GERMANY
'Type 34' or 'Maass' class

When the keels of the first **'Type 34' class** destroyers were laid in late 1934 for launch between 1937 and 1939, the Germans had had virtually no experience in the production of true destroyers since the end of World War I. This lack of continuity was to result in the incorporation of much that was untried, particularly with respect to boilers and machinery, and the ships thus gained a reputation for unreliability. Despite this, they were of conventional layout and more than a little influenced by contemporary British fleet destroyers. Advantage was conferred by extra length, though this was offset by a poorly-designed forward end which, lacking sufficient freeboard and flare, left them very wet ships in any sea. A new 127-mm (5-in) calibre was selected rather than the better-tried 105-mm (4.13-in) size in order to match the weight of standard French projectiles. The new gun proved a reliable weapon but was not dual purpose. Five were carried (three singles aft and two singles forward), each group being capable of separate control with its own rangefinder.

Two quadruple banks of 533-mm (21-in) torpedo tubes were shipped. Like the Japanese, the Germans believed in the weapons, trained in them and used them to good effect when allowed. Four reloads could be carried. The ships were also tracked along both sides of the upper deck to give capacity for 60 mines.

In all, there were 22 named destroyers of fairly homogeneous design but, of these, only the first four were 'Type 34s'. Officially, the next 16 were **'Type 34A' class** ships and the remainder **'Type 36' class** units. There were few differences externally and these went across type boundaries as did the several small changes in hull length, though it is noteworthy that the final group of four featured a hull some 6 m (19.7 ft) longer than that of the original quartet. This increase partly met the type's poor endurance figures, which were due to the fact that their stability range did not allow running at below

The 'Type 34' or 'Maass' class were the first German destroyers to be built since World War I. Of conventional layout, their only major problem was lack of freeboard, which had disagreeable consequences in heavy seas.

Below: The 'Type 34A' class were again armed with new 127-mm (5-in) guns rather than the trusted 105-mm (4.1-in) weapons in order to match the broadside of contemporary French vessels. Some of the later units were lengthened to improve stability.

Leberecht Maass is seen in a disruptive camouflage pattern which included a false bow wave and wash Soon after completion she had her hull strengthened by additional plating and her bow extended slightly. The ship had the misfortune to run into a minefield laid by Heinkel He 111 bombers in the North Sea.

30 per cent bunker capacity.

It was the misfortune of the group to lose 10 of its number at Narvik, mainly through poor leadership. Another five were lost later in the war. During the first couple of months of the war, these ships had contributed greatly to the mining campaign off the east coast that cost the British dear. The ships in the class were the *Leberecht Maass (Z1)*, *Georg Thiele (Z2)*, *Max Schultz (Z3)*, *Richard Beitzen (Z4)*, *Paul Jacobi (Z5)*, *Theodor Riedel (Z6)*, *Hermann Schömann (Z7)*, *Bruno Heinemann (Z8)*, *Wolfgang Zenker (Z9)*, *Hans Lody (Z10)*, *Bernd von Arnim (Z11)*, *Erich Giese (Z12)*, *Erich Köllner (Z13)*, *Friedrich Ihn (Z14)*, *Erich Steinbrinck (Z15)*, *Friedrich Eckoldt (Z16)*, *Diether von Röder (Z17)*, *Hans Lüdemann (Z18)*, *Hermann Küne (Z19)*, *Karl Galster (Z20)*, *Wilhelm Heidkamp (Z21)* and *Anton Schmitt (Z22)*.

Specification
'Type 34' class (as built)
Displacement: 2,230 tons standard and 3,160 tons full load
Dimensions: length 119.0 m (390.4 ft); beam 11.3 m (37.1 ft); draught 3.8 m (12.5 ft)
Propulsion: two seats of geared steam turbines delivering 52199 kW (70,000 shp) to two shafts
Speed: 38 kts
Endurance: 8150 km (5,064 miles) at 19 kts
Armament: five single 127-mm (5-in), two twin 37-mm AA and six single 20-mm AA guns, two quadruple 533-mm (21-in) torpedo tube mountings, and up to 60 mines
Complement: 315

Karl Galster shows off her clipper bow, which was fitted to all subsequent German destroyers. Her machinery was theoretically capable of 40 kts, but wartime shortages of material made maintenance increasingly difficult.

Below: Karl Galster was the fourth of six units of the 'Type 36' destroyers, which were slightly modified 'Type 34s'. All five of her sister ships were sunk at Narvik, but Z20 survived the war and ended her days in Soviet service in the Baltic, renamed the Protshnyi. She was broken up in the 1950s.

'Type 36A' or 'Z23' classss

The **'Type 36A' class** destroyers were war-built and launched in 1940-2, and while the fleet would have preferred a ship enlarged from the 'Type 34' and capable of long-range operation, it received another stretch of the original design with the major difference of an increase in main battery calibre to 150 mm (5.91 in). This had 60 per cent greater weight of shot and a better range, but was difficult and slow for handworking. The weight of the two forward superimposed guns was to be cut by substituting a twin turret, but this was long in development and trouble-prone when it finally entered service, and most of the class started their lives with only one single mounting forward which, if it did nothing for their fighting potential, certainly improved their seakeeping. Those that were retrofitted with the twin turret experienced severe green water effects forward in heavy weather. A problem with the earlier class, poor manoeuvrability, was met by a redesign of the area of the cut-up and the provision of twin

The 'Type 36A' class were enlarged Type 36s, designed to carry 150-mm (5.9-in) guns, although the planned double turret was not always available and single turrets had to do. The larger guns failed to live up to expectation, the heavier shell proving slow to hand-load.

rudders but, overall, the 'Type 36A' did not appeal to a seaman.

The initial order for the 'Type 36A' comprised *Z23* to *Z30*; seven more, *Z31* to *Z34* and *Z37* to *Z39* (to a slightly modified design) were later added. These ships, though unnamed, were popularly known as the **'Narvik' class**, the name originating with the Germans themselves, their Norwegian-based units adopting something of the earlier ships that had been destroyed there in April 1940.

Perhaps surprisingly, only six of the 15 'Type 36As' were lost during the war. Two of the survivors gave the French fleet over a decade of post-war use while another, the *Z38*, was actual-

Laid down between November 1938 and April 1940, the 'Type 36A' vessels were essentially enlarged 'Type 36' ships, more manoeuvrable than their predecessors but still mediocre sea-boats. Those destroyers that eventually received the planned twin gun turret in the 'A' position found their performance further reduced.

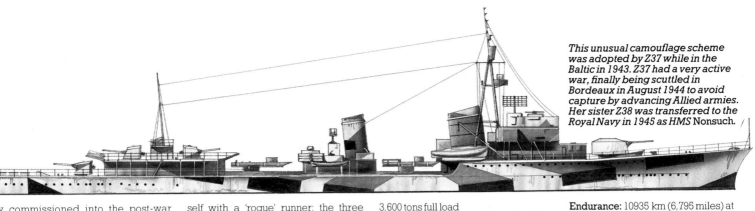

ly commissioned into the post-war Royal Navy as HMS *Nonsuch* for machinery evaluation and 'special trials'. The *Z26* was lost in March 1942 during the destroyer attack on convoy PQ13; it was in launching a salvo of torpedoes to finish off this ship that the British cruiser HMS *Trinidad* hit her-

self with a 'rogue' runner: the three German ships involved had already launched about 20 torpedoes in a fruitless attempt to secure the same result!

Specification
'Type 36A' class
Displacement: 2,600 tons standard and

3,600 tons full load
Dimensions: length 127.0 m (416.67 ft); beam 12.0 m (39.4 ft); draught 3.9 m (12.8 ft)
Propulsion: two sets of geared steam turbines delivering 52199 kW (70,000 shp) to two shafts
Speed: 36 kts

Endurance: 10935 km (6,795 miles) at 19 kts
Armament: three single and one twin 150-mm (5.9-in), two twin 37-mm AA and five single 20-mm AA guns, two quadruple 533-mm (21-in) torpedo tube mountings and up to 60 mines
Complement: 321

Z25 cruises purposefully off the Norwegian coast before her conversion to 'Barbara' standard, which gave her an impressive AA capacity of 12 37-mm (1.45-in) and 18 20-mm (0.78-in) automatic weapons. Transferred to the French navy, she served as the Hoche until 1956.

Z39 was taken over by the Royal Navy in 1945, but transferred to the USA. Whereas many of her contemporaries ended up scuttled in the Skagerrak loaded with poison gas shells, Z39 was finally handed to France and cannibalized for the ex-German destroyers in French service.

GERMANY

'Type 36B' or 'Z35' class

Early experience with their 150-mm (5.91-in) gunned destroyers convinced the German naval planners of their mistake, and seven ships (*Z35*, *Z36* and *Z43* to *Z47*) of the same basic hull and machinery were redesigned around the earlier 127-mm (5-in) single mountings. These ships were known as the **'Type 36B' class** but, confusingly, the last two of the group were again re-labelled the **'Type 36C' class** when yet another proposed design would have introduced a new twin 127-mm turret and uprated machinery performance. The confusion of types and pennant number sequences about this time were symptomatic of ambitious naval plans running foul of day-to-day priorities in meeting an overextended range of construction and repair demands. In short, the system could not cope, and

the *Z43* was the last destroyer actually completed for German service. This was in March 1944 but it was of only academic importance as, by this stage of the war, ocean operations had effectively ceased for the surface fleet, which existed largely in the relative safety of the Baltic.

The three units actually completed (*Z35*, *Z36* and *Z43*) had a main battery disposition identical with that of the earlier 'Type 34s', but were given a greatly enhanced AA outfit. By virtue of the lower topweight of the 127-mm armament it was possible to ship two twin 37-mm, and three quadruple and three single 20-mm guns, the generosity of which scale reflected the aerial threat at this stage in the war. As all German destroyers could lay mines, the possible increase in capacity to 76

was important.

The minelaying capacity of all three was being utilized on the night of 11/12 December 1944 when, accompanied by a pair of torpedo boats, they were due to lay a field west of the Estonian port of Reval. A combination of faulty navigation and a desire to 'press on' despite darkness and very poor weather conditions found the group straying into an earlier field. Both the *Z35* and *Z36* were blown up with their full loads and their complete crews. The *Z43* survived to support the northern flank of the retreating German armies in the last desperate weeks of early 1945. Finally, damaged by ground mines and bombing, she was scuttled in the Geltinger Bucht.

Specification
'Type 36B' class
Displacement: 2,525 tons standard and 3,505 tons full load
Dimensions: length 127.0 m (416.67 ft); beam 12.0 m (39.4 ft); draught 3.52 m (11.55 ft)
Propulsion: two sets of geared steam turbines delivering 52199 kW (70,000 shp) to two shafts
Speed: 36 kts
Endurance: 11120 km (6,910 miles) at 19 kts
Armament: five single 127-mm (5-in), two twin 37-mm AA, and three quadruple and three single 20-mm AA guns, two quadruple 533-mm (21-in) torpedo tube mountings and up to 76 mines
Complement: 321

GERMANY

'SP1' or 'Z40' class

The Germans seemed concerned at the potential firepower of the big French destroyers and, perceiving a requirement for ships of their own capable of a degree of independent action, initiated the **Spähkreuzer** (scout cruiser) or **SP** concept. At the beginning of World War II, however the planned number of destroyers was trimmed in view of other priorities. Of the five stricken from the 'Type 36A' programme three (*Z40* to *Z42*) were

reinstated early in 1941 as an enlarged trio, which were to be followed by another with hull number unspecified. The design passed through several phases before losing favour and being recast into the so-called **'Zerstörer 1941'**, construction being suspended in 1942 and the incomplete hulls being scrapped in 1943.

With range a problem in earlier destroyers, the SPs would have had better endurance conferred by a three-shaft

layout, with steam turbines on the wing shafts and cruising-diesel drive on a centreline shaft. They would have been nearly 10 m (32.8 ft) longer than the comparable 'Capitani Romani' of the Italian fleet and, while lacking the latters' speed, would have been still more truly destroyers in concept. Their extra size would have made for steadier gun platforms and justified the 150-mm (5.91-in) main battery. Final innovations were the uprated torpedo

tube battery and mine stowage.

Beyond the SPs the Germans worked on a couple of all-diesel designs. The multi-diesel layout was a popular concept with their designers since the proven reliability and economy of those in the Panzerschiffe. Lighter distillate fuels were more readily available in Germany by synthesis than heavy bunker oils, which had to be imported. The **'Type 42' class** embraced initially only one prototype,

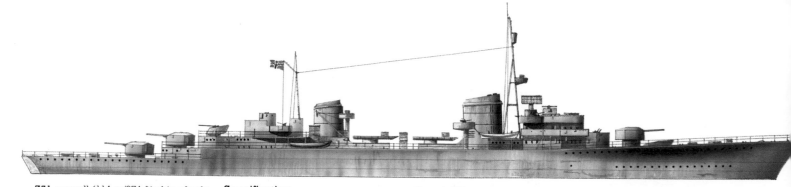

Z51, a small (114-m/374-ft) ship of only 2,050 tons standard displacement and a four 127-mm (5-in) gun armament. Lack of supply caused the six-diesel/three-shaft layout to be truncated to a four-diesel/single-shaft arrangement. Her value was never known as she was wrecked by bombing while fitting out in 1945. Plans for larger diesel destroyers never reached the metal-cutting stage.

Specification
'SP1' class
Displacement: 4,540 tons standard
Dimensions: length 152.0 m (498.7 ft); beam 14.6 m (47.9 ft); draught 4.6 m (15.1 ft)
Propulsion: two sets of geared steam turbines delivering 57792 kW (77,500 shp) to the two wing shafts and one diesel delivering 10813 kW (14,500 bhp) to one centreline shaft

Speed: 36 kts on steam power
Endurance: 22250 km (13,826 miles) at 19 kts
Armament: three twin 150-mm (5.91-in), four twin 37-mm AA and three quadruple 20-mm AA guns, two quintuple 533-mm (21-in) torpedo tube mountings, and up to 140 mines
Complement: not known

Z40 according to the final plan: Z40 to Z42 were Type 36A class destroyers, cancelled but reinstated in 1941 as an enlarged threesome known as 'Zerstörer 1941'. Their larger hulls would have made a steady platform for the 150-mm (5.9-in) guns. Torpedo armament was also increased.

'T22' or 'Elbing' class

In both world wars the German navy operated so-called 'torpedo boats' which were diminutive destroyer-type ships which, spared the need to operate as units of the main fleet, could be considerably smaller while being capable of carrying the same scale of torpedoes or mines. All wore flag superior 'T' as opposed to the 'Z' of destroyers. Despite their stature they were capable of giving a good account of themselves.

During the 1920s, among the new German fleet's first ships, were built the dozen **'Albatros'** and **'Iltis' class** units. These carried not only their torpedoes but three of the still-potent 105-mm (4.13-in) guns, and proved most versatile in war. These were followed by 21 numbered ships of the **'Type 35'** and **'Type 37' classes**. Here the planners had got it wrong, shrinking the size of the craft and their armament until the ships exhibited all the weaknesses of the smaller 'S' boats while having few of their virtues. The near-common design was characterized by a single heavily-trunked funnel that served both boiler rooms.

These unpopular ships were followed by a very different vessel in the **'Type 39' class**, in which a 15-ship group (*T22* to *T36*) was built by the experienced Schichau yard at Elbing, the town giving the ships their popular name, the **'Elbing' class**. They re-adopted the two-funnelled layout and, despite their lack of raised forecastle, were imposing enough often to be mistaken for fleet destroyers. With an extra 17 m (55.8 ft) of length they could accommodate four single 105-mm guns along the centreline as well as the usual two triple banks of torpedo tubes. The ships were launched in 1942-4.

Like most of the torpedo boats, the 'Elbings' were used widely in French waters. They tangled several times with Plymouth-based 'Tribals' off the Breton coast. The *T27* and *T29* were

both thus sunk in April 1944, though the *T24* levelled the score by torpedoing and sinking HMCS *Athabaskan*. Two more, the *T25* and *T26*, had already been sunk in the extraordinary daylight action of December 1943 when a mix of 11 German ships, hampered by heavy seas, were savaged by two British cruisers in the Bay of Biscay.

Specification
'T22' class
Displacement: 1,295 tons standard and 1,755 tons full load
Dimensions: length 102.0 m (334.6 ft); beam 10.0 m (32.8 ft); draught 2.6 m (8.5 ft)
Propulsion: two sets of geared steam turbines delivering 23862 kW (32,000 shp) to two shafts
Speed: 33.5 kts

Endurance: 9300 km (5,789 miles) at 19 kts
Armament: four single 105-mm (4.13-in), two twin 37-mm AA and six single 20-mm AA guns, two triple 533-mm (21-in) torpedo tube mountings and up to 50 mines
Complement: 198

Albatros was among the first units built for the navy by the Weimar Republic, and her design reflected German experience in the 1914-8 war. Armed with six 500-mm (19.6-in) torpedoes and three 105-mm (4.1-in) guns, the class served as 'maids of all work' and all six were casualties.

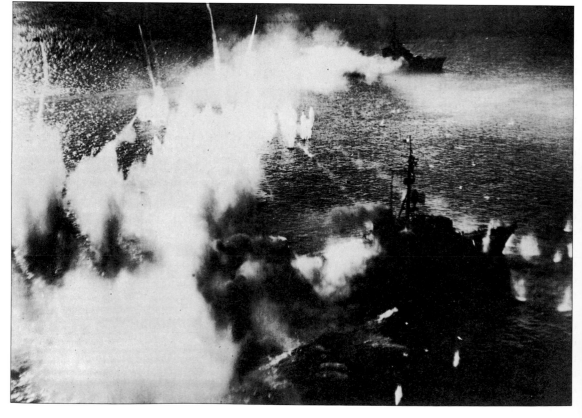

Smoke pours from the side of T24 (foreground) as she reels from a rocket salvo fired from RAF Beaufighters at the mouth of the Gironde, August 1944. T24 sank; her companion, the destroyer Z24, managed to reach her berth but capsized shortly afterwards.

Escort Vessels

Of all the combatants in World War II, it was Britain and Japan who were most dependent upon a seaborne lifeline, and it was those nations to whom a threat to their merchant fleets was mortal. Obviously, means had to be established to protect the trade routes.

Before World War I, theory had it that merchant shipping could run safely in defended maritime corridors. However, this proved a costly fallacy. Following countless attacks, all merchant shipping had to be accompanied by escorted convoys – but not before millions of tons of merchant shipping had been lost. With such a hard lesson learned, the British now had the basis of a useful escort fleet at the beginning of World War II.

Initially, the numbers of these escort vessels were quite inadequate and the designs were limited in both capability and endurance. Nevertheless, the organization existed whereby these vessels could be expanded and improved rapidly. British convoys, in particular, had to face a variety of threats (high speed E-boat attacks on coastal routes, organized U-boat group assault in the Atlantic, and combined aircraft and surface attack on the Arctic and Mediterranean movements, to name but a few) and different escorts were required for each.

With too few anti-submarine (AS) ships and with very little experience in a theatre of war, the escort forces were at first on the defensive. More and larger ships enabled the close escorts

The North Atlantic convoys were the lifeline for beleagured Britain. Here, *Enchantress* undertakes escort duty for merchantmen in 1942.

to be strengthened and enhanced in capability. Science improved both equipment and techniques. The formation of roving support groups and the rapid development of aircraft support allowed, firstly, for threatened convoys to have their escort groups reinforced rapidly and decisively and, secondly, for the taking of the offensive against the U-boat by actually

operating close astride its main route to and from its bases.

The aerial threat could never be met by direct attack and defeat of the aircraft themselves, only by land offensives which removed the aircraft bases or by satisfactory outcomes to campaigns that obviated the need to run the convoys themselves.

Interestingly, the discredited early British arguments against

convoys and, therefore, the need for 'defensive' escort ships in an essentially 'offensive' fleet, were actually taken on board and carried on by both the Americans and Japanese fleets, neither of whom had had the benefit of bitter first-hand experience. Because both powers had neglected to learn from the lesson of the British they paid dearly for their unpreparedness.

'Wolf' and 'Möwe' classes

Inasmuch as the Germans recognized that their mercantile marine would cease to function normally at the outbreak of war, they had little need of escorts in the same sense as the British. Nevertheless, the blockade of the German coast by submarine and mine entailed the covering of warships while the quite considerable volume of coastal traffic, (e.g. the iron ore trade from Scandinavia) needed protection without the tying down of major fleet units.

The six 'Möwe' class (officially 'Typ 23') ships were the first flotilla craft built by the 'new' German navy; they were strictly torpedo boats and, despite their modest size, carried two triple mountings. Though this class of ship was not designed to undertake fleet duties, the lack of any alternative at that time probably accounted for their comparatively high speed. Three boilers were required in the slim hull, necessitating two widely-spread funnels, which made them look larger than they actually were. They carried

three old, but effective 105-mm (4.13-in) guns which, together with the ambitious torpedo fit, brought up the topweight allowance to the extent that (unusually for the German navy) mines could not be carried in addition. While the 'Möwes' were still building, a second group of six, the slightly-enlarged 'Wolf' class (Typ 24) ships were ordered. Though of the same calibre, their main armament was of an improved pattern.

The ships were heavily involved in near-coastal waters during the war, gradually acquiring more light automatic weapons, some at the expense of a set of torpedo tubes. Following these two classes, subsequent development went for larger torpedo boats and

smaller S-boats. Neither of these types was viewed as an ideal escort, leaving the way clear for introduction of the specialist Geleitboote. All 12 became war casualties, no less than eight being sunk in the English Channel. Of these the *Iltis* and *Seeadler* were sunk in the Dover Strait during the night of 12/13 May 1942, torpedoed by British MTBs while covering the passage of the raider *Stier*.

Specification
'Wolf' class (as completed)
Displacement: 933 tons standard and 1,320 tons full load
Dimensions: length 93.0 m (305.1 ft); beam 8.7 m (28.5 ft); draught 2.8 m (9.2 ft)
Propulsion: two sets of geared steam turbines delivering 17151 kW (23,000 shp) to two shafts
Speed: 33 kts
Endurance: 5750 km (3,575 miles) at 17 kts
Armament: three single 105-mm (4.13-in) or 127-mm (5-in) and four single 20-mm AA guns, and two triple 533-mm (21-in) torpedo tube mountings
Complement: 129

Initially classified as destroyers, the 'Typ 23' torpedo boats saw considerable action in the North Sea and Channel. Armed primarily for surface action, they were the first flotilla craft built for the Weimar navy.

Geleitboote F1-F10

This group of 10 Geleitboote was completed by three yards in 1935-6 and, though officially termed 'escorts', they had a peacetime role in training in the Baltic and in general offshore duties. Again their wartime role was aimed at seeing larger warships through offshore barriers, for which they were given almost destroyer-like proportions and a high speed, with main parameters that had no equivalent in the Royal Navy. Handsome little ships, they looked rather more weatherly than larger German destroyers with plenty of freeboard forward and the angular bridge structure continued to the ship's sides by screens. Though the freeboard aft was low, the after 105-mm (4.13-in) gun was set on a deckhouse at the same height as that on the forecastle. They carried a good outfit of boats for their peacetime duties, these being handled by booms rather than davits. As they spent much time at low speeds they were equipped with anti-rolling tanks, not the passive, tuned variety but fitted with transfer pumps.

Their qualities must have left something to be desired for before the war, while still new ships, *F1* to *F4* and *F6* were lengthened and given raked bows. *F2* and *F4* were disarmed for use as auxiliaries but *F1*, *F3* and *F6* had the forecastle deck continued right aft to give a continuous high freeboard and much more accommodation. They were also named *Jagd*, *Hai* and *Königin Luise* respectively, the last name of which suggested an unlisted minelaying capacity, though they acted as command ships for minesweeper squadrons. As a result of their humble and largely non-involved status, the tide of war dealt kindly with them, only four being sunk.

An interesting series of 24 enlarged Geleitboote (*G1* to *G24*) was planned to follow on from both German and Dutch yards, but just *G1* was laid down,

only to be destroyed on the stocks in an air attack in 1943. Like the 'F' series, they would have had a modest speed and no torpedo tubes, but had an enhanced surface armament, a capacity of 50 mines and, almost unbelievably for the date, a helicopter.

Specification
'Geleitboote' class (as built)
Displacement: 712 tons standard and 833 tons full load
Dimensions: length 76.0 m (249.3 ft); beam 8.8 m (28.9 ft); draught 2.5 m (8.2 ft)
Propulsion: two sets of geared steam turbines delivering 10440 kW (14,000 shp) to two shafts
Speed: 28 kts
Endurance: 2780 km (1,725 miles) at 20 kts
Armament: two single 105-mm (4.13-in), two twin 37-mm AA and four single 20-mm AA guns
Complement: 121

Above: In spite of their pleasant lines, the 'F' class of fleet escort were never really satisfactory. It may be that the class was largely an experiment in the building and operation of the new high-pressure steam turbine machinery.

Below: F2 as she appeared in 1938. The advanced propulsion machinery gave much trouble, and in spite of their destroyer-like lines the Geleitboote were poor sea boats. Most were lengthened forward and had a raked stem in consequence.

ITALY
'Spica' class

Like its German counterpart the Italian navy favoured the construction of diminutive destroyer-type escorts, usually described as 'torpedo boats'. Though a long series of related classes had been completed by the mid-1920s, the type had lapsed for a decade before being resumed with the 32-strong **'Spica' class**, laid down between 1934 and 1937. The design was influenced by that of the 'Maestrale' class destroyers then completing but, though superficially similar in overall profile, their single funnel lacked the massive trunking of that of the larger ships, serving as it did only one boiler room. The main armament consisted of 100-mm (3.94-in) guns of a new pattern with a respectable 16-km (10-mile) range. As these came only in single mountings, three were carried in the usual layout of one forward and two superimposed aft. Despite the fact that previous torpedo boats had been fitted with 533-mm (21-in) torpedo tubes, the

'Spicas' reverted to the earlier 450-mm (17.72-in) weapons of far inferior hitting power and range. For some odd reason these were initially single, sided mountings only, later exchanged for the more logical twin centreline type. As with most Italian ships they could lay mines but were also fitted for high-speed minesweeping, with conspicuous paravanes and associated gear right aft. Under the wartime construction programme a group of 42 improved 'Spicas' was also planned. Of these, known as the **'Ariete' class**, only 16 were laid down, the majority of them being completed by the Germans after the Italian capitulation.

Of the 32 'Spicas', 23 became war casualties and a pair were sold, perhaps oddly, to the Swedish navy.

The *Airone* and *Ariel* were sunk together in October 1940 when, with others, they unwisely attacked a British cruiser force covering an early Malta convoy. Of the latter, HMS *Ajax* was instrumental in their sinking, damaging also the destroyers *Artigliere* and *Aviere*, the former of which was eventually lost while in tow. A year later another pair, the **Aldebaran** and **Altair**, were lost in a minefield laid by the British submarine HMS *Rorqual* in the Gulf of Athens.

Specification
'Spica' class
Displacement: 795 tons standard and 1,020 tons full load
Dimensions: length 83.5 m (273.95 ft); beam 8.1 m (26.57 ft); draught 2.55 m (8.37 ft)
Propulsion: two sets of geared steam turbines delivering 14168 kW (19,000 shp) to two shafts
Speed: 34 kts
Armament: three single 100-mm (3.94-in), four twin and two single 20-mm AA, and two single 13.2-mm (0.52-in) AA guns, four single or two twin 450-mm (17.7-in) torpedo tubes, and up to 20 mines
Complement: 116

Resembling reduced versions of the contemporary 'Freccia' class fleet destroyers, the 'Spica' class was designed for the torpedo-boat role, but in fact became anti-submarine escorts.

ITALY
'Gabbiano' class

With British submarines playing havoc on the vital supply route to North Africa, the Italians embarked in 1942 on an ambitious programme of **'Gabbiano' class** corvette construction. This type of ship was new to the Italian fleet and, in British terms, may be said to equate to the 'Flowers' where the 'Spicas' equated to 'Hunts'. There the resemblance ended, however, for where the British ships were stubby and robust, the Italian ships were slightly longer but very much narrower in the beam. Not having to face North Atlantic winters they were able to place speed higher in their priorities. Even so, their seakeeping qualities were adequate, with a long forecastle of high freeboard that early 'Flower' skippers would have envied.

The great contrast was in propulsion. The British ships with their whaler origins had a pronounced trim by the stern to give adequate submergence for the single large-diameter screw, driven by a steam reciprocating engine. On the other hand the Italians, with a good industrial base for small diesel and petrol engines, favoured the former of these. Twin-shaft propulsion was adopted to take advantage of established marques of engine, at the same time achieving redundancy, improving manoeuvrability and, with smaller-diameter propellers, allowing a full 1 m (3.3 ft) less draught, an important factor in the shallow and increasingly mine-ridden Mediterranean. The price was more complex construction and extremely noisy ships with the diesels effectively secured to the hull framing and the

necessarily high-speed propellers a source of cavitation. This was recognized as a necessary drawback in the interests of volume production and, very interestingly for the date, each shaft could be turned by a low-power electric motor for stalking submarines. This permitted not only silent manoeuvring but also an improved performance from the ships' own indifferent sonar. The 60-ship class (of which

only 42 were completed after launching in 1942-3) defeated the usual Italian lettered pendant system, the ships taking numbers. Few were completed in time to be used in earnest by the Italians; many were taken by the Germans, who did. War losses amounted to 20.

Specification
'Gabbiano' class
Displacement: 670 tons standard and 740 tons full load

The diesel-powered 'Gabbiano' class were unusual in being fitted with an electric motor for silent stalking of submarines, for which they were armed with up to 10 depth-charge throwers.

Name-ship of a class intended to include some 60 vessels, Gabbiano displayed the typically fine lines of Italian marine design. Unlike their British counterparts, these corvettes did not have to be able to withstand winter in the North Atlantic.

Dimensions: length 64.4 m (211.29 ft); beam 8.7 m (28.54 ft); draught 2.53 m (8.3 ft)
Propulsion: two diesels and two electric motors delivering 3207 kW (4,300 bhp) and 112 kW (150 hp) to two shafts
Speed: 18 kts
Armament: one 100-mm (3.94-in) and seven single 20-mm AA guns, and (on some) two 450-mm (17.7-in) torpedo tubes
Complement: 108

 'Isles' class

The UK's large fishing fleet in 1939 provided the Royal Navy with a ready source of ships and trained crews, not only for the obvious purposes of the Auxiliary Patrol, minesweeping and harbour defence but also, in the case of the large distant water trawlers, of convoy escorts at a time when these were in short supply. The speed of such vessels was limited but both endurance and seakeeping were adequate, and they were commonly employed on the Arctic convoy route in the early days.

From its experience in 1914-8 the Admiralty had forewarning of its needs and had already formulated plans for trawler construction at yards that were familiar with them and which were, in many cases, too small for the building of regular escorts. The 27 ships of the 'Hill', 'Military' and 'Fish' classes were all produced by one yard and had the very pretty lines of the distant water trawler. Half a dozen 'Lakes' from Smith's Dock were still almost pure whale-catchers. Most, however, were of a design developed from the prototype HMS *Basset*, completed by Robb's in 1936. This ship, though having an obvious trawler-type hull, had in addition a high raised forecastle and the bridge and funnel sited well amidships, leaving a short well deck forward, a long superstructure and a usable quarterdeck. With minor modifications, particularly in the height of the bridge structure, the type went into volume production, first as the **'Tree', 'Shakespeare'** and **'Dance' classes**, then as the **'Isles' class**, which became the best-known group. Altogether, these four groups comprised 218 trawlers. The 'Isles' class numbered 168 units built between 1940 and 1945 (130 in the UK, 22 in India and 16 in Canada).

Though many were equipped for anti-submarine work, their sonars were not generally very effective and few had radar. With only 11 or 12 kts speed, dropping depth charges on a shallow target could be an advantage, while the pursuit of a submarine on the surface was clearly impossible, the submarine having a greatly superior speed in addition to out-gunning the average trawler's 12-pdr. The object was to force a submarine down, where it would lose touch with a convoy. Many of these 'rugged coal-burners' were sold out to commercial owners after the war to make good their grievous losses, though their layout was unsatisfactory for trawling until modified. Twelve 'Isles' were lost in the war.

HMS Shillay *is seen in February 1945. Though the trawler hull gave the type good seakeeping and endurance, it could never be said to have had a sparkling performance. They were easily built, however, and in quantity (a total of 168 in four related classes).*

Specification
'Isles' class (as designed)
Displacement: 545 tons standard
Dimensions: length 44.2 m (145.0 ft); beam 8.4 m (27.5 ft); draught 3.2 m (10.5 ft)
Propulsion: one triple-expansion steam engine delivering 634 kW (850 ihp) to one shaft
Speed: 12 kts
Armament: one 12-pdr, and three single 20-mm AA guns, and depth charges
Complement: 40

'Flower' class escort cutaway drawing key

1. Waterline
2. Ramp
3. Rudder
4. Single screw
5. Depth charge racks
6. Davit
7. Lifeline cable reel
8. Jack staff
9. Steering gear compartment/minesweeping store
10. Stores/lobby
11. Solid bulwarks
12. Aft galley
13. Engine room skylight
14. Stored depth charges along deck
15. PO mess
16. Aft peak
17. Engineer's stores
18. Single shaft
19. Engine room
20. Triple expansion 1700-kW (2,880-hp) engine
21. Reduction gear
22. 2-pdr pom-pom
23. Pom-pom platform
24. Platform support
25. Guncrew shelter and ready ammunition
26. Snowflake locker
27. Handrail
28. Ladder
29. Wireless aerial
30. Funnel casing
31. Ventilator
32. Boiler casing
33. Carly raft
34. No. 1 boiler room
35. No. 2 boiler room
36. Admiralty drum boiler
37. Oil fuel in wing tanks
38. Double bottom
39. Funnel uptake
40. Bulkhead
41. Fresh water tank
42. Galley
43. Foremast
44. Lookout
45. Access ladder
46. Office for Type 271 radar
47. Searchlight
48. Twin 20-mm machine-guns
49. Bridge
50. Compass house
51. Asdic hut
52. Chart house
53. Ready use locker for 4-in ammunition
54. 4-in Mk 10 gun
55. Gun shield
56. Breakwater
57. Depression rail
58. Semtex walkway on port side
59. Wooden fore deck
60. Anchor windlass
61. Handrail
62. Side plating
63. Stores/lobby/spirit store
64. Wardroom
65. Cabins/stokers' mess
66. Oil fuel tank
67. Reserve feed water tank
68. Asdic compartment
69. Fresh water tank
70. Magazine
71. RF wireless
72. Crew sleeping area
73. Crew area
74. Stores/lamps etc
75. Paint store
76. Chain locker
77. Anchor
78. 16-ft dinghy

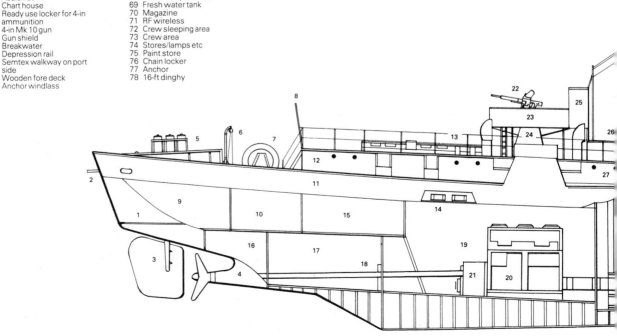

'Flower' class

Possibly because of their homely names or their rather unwarlike appearance, the units of the **'Flower' class** (145 built in the UK and 113 in Canada for launch in 1940-2) came to be regarded by the British as the archetypal escort ship. Though they made their reputation in the early days of the Battle of the Atlantic, they were not really suited to the job, the type being developed primarily as a coastal escort fitted for minesweeping. This, however, would seem to be at variance with the fact that the design was based on that of a commercial whale-catcher, a hullform meant to survive the worst of the weather in the forbidding Southern Ocean. It was the rapid escalation of the North Atlantic convoy war and a general shortage of escorts that forced these little ships into ocean work. They were superb seaboats but, being so short, were horribly lively and wet in the deep ocean, exhausting the best of crews within days, though refuelling at sea kept them out for longer. It was the limitations that convinced the Admiralty that the larger frigate was the answer.

The 'Flowers' were business-like ships whose ancestry could be seen in the hull, with its pronounced sheer, strong flare and cutaway forefoot. Early units had a short forecastle with the single mast stepped forward of a mercantile-style bridge structure, but most of these were subsequently modified to the layout of the later **Modified Flower' class** ships (included in the totals above). These had the forecastle

extended aft to the funnel, increasing accommodation and improving seaworthiness, particularly with respect to reducing wetness in the waist.

Machinery was purposely kept simple for mass production and operation by rapidly-trained personnel, the four-cylinder triple expansion engine taking steam from two Admiralty cylindrical single-ended boilers. The ships were, at that time, rare in the Royal Navy in being single-screw types.

All had an old pattern 101.6-mm (4-in) gun on a 'band stand' forward, but the original inadequate AA outfit of machine-guns rapidly gave way to a 2-pdr pom-pom and as many 20-mm Oerlikons as could be 'come by'. Later ships, incorporating all modifications, certainly looked more 'pusser' and many, surprisingly, went on to serve in a mercantile role after the war. Also built in Canada, they served under a variety of Allied flags, including that of the USA when its need was greatest in 1942. Total wartime losses were 31.

Specification
'Flower' class (original specification)
Displacement: 940 tons standard and 1,160 tons full load
Dimensions: length 62.5 m (205.1 ft); beam 10.1 m (33.1 ft); draught 3.5 m (11.5 ft)
Propulsion: 4-cylinder triple-expansion steam engine delivering 2051 kW (2,750 ihp) to one shaft
Speed: 16 kts
Endurance: 6400 km (3,975 miles) at 12 kts
Armament: one 101.6-mm (4-in) gun, one 2-pdr or one quadruple 12.7-mm (0.5-in) AA gun, and depth charges
Complement: 85 maximum

HMS Myositis at sea displays the battered appearance that constant Atlantic exposure made inevitable. Based upon a commercial whaler hull, the 'Flower' class filled the gap in British escort capacity early in the war, until replaced by new frigates.

HMS Lotus is seen before her 1942 transfer to France as the Commandante d'Estienne d'Orves. She is fitted with minesweeping gear, which was to be a secondary task after the designed role as a coastal escort. Only the severe shortage of ocean escorts saw the class employed in the North Atlantic.

'Black Swan' class

The powerful little ships of the 'Black Swan' class (13 built) had little in common with the remainder of the Royal Navy's sloops, most of which were later regarded as ocean minesweepers or simply patrol ships. Earlier units were certainly fitted with minesweeping gear, though under what circumstances such expensive and useful ships were expected to go looking for mines is not clear; at the same time the space and topweight margin consumed by this gear detracted considerably from the design's anti-submarine capacity. It was only with the 'Modified Black Swan' class (24 built) that this equipment was finally landed, enabling the ships to become extremely efficient dedicated submarine hunters.

The origins of the 'Black Swans' went back to HMS *Enchantress*, which had been launched in 1934. Though capable of minesweeping, the ship had a gun armament comparable with that of a fleet destroyer. The third of the class, HMS *Bittern*, differed in being completed in 1938 with three of the new high angle 101.6-mm (4-in) mountings and a prototype fin stabilizer system. This arrangement was so promising that the three follow-on 'Egret' class units, on very little increase in dimensions, were completed with four such

Fine submarine hunters, the modified 'Black Swan' class were at their most effective in the Battle of the Atlantic. This is HMS Amethyst, seen in her wartime colours. Some years later she was to be at the heart of the 'Yangtse Incident', suffering damage during the Chinese civil war.

mountings, which was definitely over-ambitious. The 'Black Swans', very similar in appearance, were slightly larger with a useful quadruple 2-pdr in the Y position, from which it was later removed to improve quarterdeck layout, and as the close range armament elsewhere was beefed-up by the improving availability of 20-mm and 40-mm weapons.

The first impression of the apearance of the 'Black Swans' was the mass of superstructure, which was probably in accord with the desire to produce an easy roll to improve them as AA gun platforms. Oddly, they did not fare too well against aircraft, four being sunk by bombing out of a total of five lost. The reason was probably that, unlike the similarly-armed 'Hunts', they were slow and less nimble. They were, therefore, little used in the Mediterranean, making their name in ocean warfare with later units being able to ship

over 100 depth charges and a Hedgehog split to flank B mounting. Most, logically, were sent to the Far East in 1945. Best known ships of the class were Walker's HMS *Starling* and HMS *Amethyst* of the 1948 'Yangtse Incident'.

Specification
'Black Swan' class
Displacement: 1,300 tons standard
Dimensions: length 91.3 m (299.5 ft); beam 11.43 m (37.5 ft); draught 2.59 m (8.5 ft)
Propulsion: two sets of geared steam turbines delivering 2685 kW (3,600 shp) to two shafts
Speed: 19.5 kts
Endurance: 14825 km (9,215 miles) at 12 kts
Armament: three twin 101.6 mm (4-in) DP, one quadruple 2-pdr AA and six twin 20-mm AA guns, and depth charges
Complement: 180

'Hunt' class

Aware of the shortage of escorts even in 1938, the Admiralty designed what was termed a Fast Escort Vessel (FEV) to give convoys both AA and anti-submarine coverage without tying down the precious (and, as it turned out, inadequate) fleet destroyers. Rather shortsightedly, there was perceived the need for speed (in order to prosecute sonar contacts and rejoin smartly) but not endurance. This was seen to be the province of the true escort vessels (which had to refer to the few 'Black Swans' rather than the 'Flowers' or 'Bangors'). To improve them as gun platforms the 'Hunt' class ships, as they were known, were fitted initially with active stabilizers as standard, but the power demands of these and their poor control systems made them so unpopular that later ships had extra bunker space instead, which considerably improved their very poor endurance.

Though their category was simplified to 'destroyer' before they entered service, the 'Hunts' really equated to the 'torpedo boats' of the German and Italian fleets, except that the majority carried no torpedo tubes. This was because the specification for six HA 101.6-mm (4-in) guns and two/four torpedo tubes was too ambitious on the target displacement; combined with a basic error in the design calculations the first of the class, HMS *Atherstone*, was found deficient in stability. Those building, therefore, sacrificed their tubes and exchanged X mounting for a quadruple 2-pdr, together with a further large number of minor weight-saving measures. These became known as the 'Hunt Type I'

class and were 19 strong. Hulls at an earlier stage of construction were split longitudinally and an extra 0.76 m (2.5 ft) of beam incorporated. These were able to accommodate the specified third 101.6-mm mounting and became the 36 'Hunt Type II' class units but, because of their extra fullness, they were rather slower. On the same dimensions a third variant, the 28 'Hunt Type III' class units, was produced with only two gun mountings, but with the valuable addition of a twin torpedo tube mounting. War experience showed the guns to be more useful, the Hunts being prominent in the Mediterranean and in the defence of the British east and south coasts. In all, 19 were lost. Significantly only three were to aircraft and of these one was stationary at the time and another was sunk by a glider bomb.

Specification
'Hunt Type III' class
Displacement: 1,015 tons standard and 1,090 tons full load
Dimensions: length 85.7 m (281.25 ft); beam 9.6 m (31.5 ft); draught 2.36 m (7.75 ft)
Propulsion: two sets of geared steam turbines delivering 14168 kW (19,000 shp) to two shafts
Speed: 25 kts
Endurance: 4635 km (2,880 miles) at 20 kts
Armament: two twin 101.6-mm (4-in)

DP, one quadruple (and in some vessels one single) 2-pdr AA, and one twin and up to four single 20-mm AA guns, two 533-mm (21-in) torpedo tubes, and depth charges
Complement: 170

The 'Hunt Type I' class destroyer HMS Southdown lies at her mooring in an east coast port. These small but relatively powerfully armed vessels did not have the range to operate in the Atlantic, but their armament made them more suitable for use in the Mediterranean and the North Sea.

'Hunt Type IIIs' differed from the 'Type II' mainly by the addition of twin torpedo tubes in place of X turret, providing a more balanced weapon fit. The 'Type IIIs' were the last of more than 80 'Hunts' built, 19 being lost before 1945. Many went to serve other navies in the years following the war.

'Castle' class

The last of the 'Flowers' were launched in early 1942 and, considering that their limitations for North Atlantic operations had already begat the true frigate, it may well be assumed that the corvette had reached the end of its development. There were, however, a number of smaller yards engaged in the 'Flower' programme which could not physically cope with the larger frigates. To keep them usefully occupied a large corvette, of length about midway between the 'Flower' and 'River', was designed, again by Smith's Dock, the home of the 'Flowers'. Named after British castles, the new **'Castle' class** ships embodied all the lessons learned with their forebears, while contriving to look remarkably like them. The hull was, again, of sweet line, although designed for series production with a large proportion of welded seams. This showed itself as minor cranks in the sheerstrake, the bow and stern sections being of constant sheer angle rather than the earlier continuous curve. The broad flat transom made for ease of construction and plenty of room aft. Some 44 units were launched in 1943-4, and another 38 were cancelled.

The 'Castles' boasted the same large and spacious bridge as the frigates, together with a substantial lattice mast to elevate the considerable mass of the early radars, made possible with the larger hull. Their great advance was in the inclusion of the Squid anti-submarine mortar, a weapon too heavy

for retrofitting into either the 'Flowers' or the 'Rivers'. This was sited at 01 level, forward of the bridge, with a new-pattern 101.6-mm (4-in) gun on a bandstand ahead of it. The squid's advantage was that it could lay a pattern of three heavy bombs around a submerged target up to 500 m (550 yards) ahead while the contact was still in the ship's sonar beam. As the ships retained the single well-tried steam reciprocating engine, the performance of the 'Castle' class did not match that of the frigates and they found their main employment not as close convoy escorts, but in homogeneously-composed escort groups which were being formed in larger numbers toward the end of the war. All were based on the UK with the exception of a dozen transferred to the Royal Canadian Navy and one to the Norwegians.

Specification
'Castle' class
Displacement: 1,060 tons standard
Dimensions: length 76.8 m (252.0 ft); beam 11.2 m (36.75 ft); draught 3.05 m (10.0 ft)
Propulsion: one 4-cylinder triple-expansion steam engine delivering 2200 kW (2,950 ihp) to one shaft
Speed: 16.5 kts
Endurance: 6,910 km (4,295 miles) at 15 kts

Armament: one 101.6-mm (4-in) DP, and two twin and six single 20-mm AA guns, one Squid, and depth charges
Complement: 120

HMS Hedingham Castle *displays her family relationship to the 'Flower' class, but the extra 15 m (50 ft) made a great difference in habitability on the Atlantic run. The major offensive improvement came with the fitting of the heavy 'Squid' system of anti-submarine mortars.*

One consequence of fitting the triple Squid launcher between the gun and the bridge was a reduction in the numbers of conventional depth charges carried. Where a 'Flower' might be armed with 72 charges, the normal depth charge fit of a 'Castle' was only 15.

'Bangor', 'Bathurst' and 'Algerine' classes

'Escort' is an all-embracing word and mention should be made of the contribution of the 'minesweeping sloops' and 'fleet minesweepers', both types of which performed valuable service in either role. Somewhat confusingly, there were still serving 26 coal-burning 'Hunts'; of 1917-9 vintage, twin-screw ships with limited sea-keeping ability due to their lack of forecastle. During the 1930s there were built the 'Grimsby' class (with sweep capacity but more truly sloops) and the extensive 'Halcyon' class (ocean minesweepers with a corvette's speed and firepower but viewed as expensive). For series production at the war's outbreak, therefore, the 'Halcyon' was scaled down to produce the **'Bangor' class**. These doughty little 650-ton ships were extremely cramped, their size being governed primarily by the space necessary for the crew. Propulsion was by diesel, steam turbine or steam reciprocating machinery, and 113 ships were built in the UK, Canada, India and even Hong Kong. A further 60 were built in Australia to a modified design known as the **'Bathurst' class**. It will be appreciated that the 'Bangors' were in reality a series of variants.

HMIS *Bengal*, an Indian-flag unit of the 'Bathursts', was escorting the Royal Dutch/Shell tanker *Ondina* in the Indian Ocean in November 1942 when attacked by two Japanese surface raiders. The Allied ships had a 12-pdr and

a 101.6-mm (4-in) gun between them, yet not only succeeded in fighting off their adversaries with 152.4-mm (6-in) guns but actually sank one of them, the *Ilokoku Maru*.

With the need to add the massive generators and electrical sweep gear for magnetic mines to the 'Bangors', already quite cramped with conventional sweeps, an improved 'Halcyon' was produced in the **'Algerine' class**. These smart little ships had adequate space, a good armament and all accommodation thoughtfully sited above the main deck. A total of 101 'Algerines' was built (53 in Canada and

48 in the UK). A dozen were retained by the Royal Canadian Navy with no minesweeping gear but fitted as full anti-submarine escorts, for which they not only shipped a Hedgehog mortar but carried 90 depth charges as well. War losses amounted to seven.

Specification
'Algerine' class (as minesweeper)
Displacement: 850 tons standard and 970 tons full load
Dimensions: length 70.1 m (230.0 ft); beam 10.8 m (35.5 ft); draught 2.9 m (9.5 ft)
Propulsion: two sets of geared steam

turbines or two sets of triple-expansion steam engines delivering 1491 kW (2,000 hp) to two shafts
Speed: 16.5 kts
Armament: one 101.6-mm (4-in) DP and between four and eight 20-mm AA guns, and more than 90 depth charges
Complement: 105

HMS Rowena *was one of the 'Algerine' class fitted with vertical triple expansion engines, only 29 out of 101 units had the planned turbines. Although used as an escort, the class was really for ocean minesweeping.*

'River' class

With the limitations of the 'Flowers' readily apparent, the Admiralty rapidly produced a design for a larger 'twin-screw corvette' which became known as the **'River' class**. (The term 'frigate' was not officially reintroduced until 1942). Overall they were about 28.30 m (93 ft) longer than the later 'Flowers' and this made a very great difference in seakeeping, bunker capacity, installed power and armament. Between 1942 and 1944 some 57 were launched in the UK, 70 in Canada and 11 in Australia.

The hull had the raised forecastle extended well aft, with a low quarter-deck for the depth-charge gear and the minesweeping equipment with which too many useful escorts were cluttered at that time. They were the first ships to be fitted as standard with the Hedgehog anti-submarine spigot mortar which, with new sonar gear, made for a more rapid and accurate attack. The Hedgehog was originally sited well forward and was thus extremely exposed, but later units had the weapon split into two 12-bomb throwers which were sited one deck higher, winged out abaft the forward 101.6-mm (4-in) gun. Longer endurance demanded a larger depth-charge capacity, and up to 200 could be carried, compared with a maximum of 70 on the 'Flowers'.

Though not developed from a mercantile hull form the 'Rivers' were built to mercantile standards, which speeded construction. They featured a flat transom, which not only obviated much of the complex curvature of traditionally-shaped sterns but also actually improved the hull hydrodynamics. It is noteworthy that over half the 'Rivers' were Canadian-built (with more ships coming from Australia) and it is probably all too easily overlooked how magnificent a contribution the Canadian yards and the Royal Canadian Navy made to victory in the Atlantic. Most Canadian-built units had a

HMS Helmsdale *was a 'River' class frigate, and as such was a great improvement on previous escort designs. Unlike most 'Rivers', she had her prominent Hedgehog ASW mortar system replaced by the much heavier and effective Squid triple barrelled ASW charge launcher.*

twin 101.6-mm mounting forward and a single 12-pdr aft. They also had their full outfit of 14 20-mm weapons, which British-built ships rarely achieved. The machinery was simply that of the 'Flowers' doubled, though drawing steam from more efficient water-tube boilers. Four ships only were built with steam turbines, which were not generally adopted as a result of shortages of components. The 'Rivers' were highly successful, but most of the survivors (seven were sunk in the war) had been scrapped by the mid-1950s. Further 'Rivers', to a slightly modified design, were built by the Americans as the **'PF' type**; of these 21 served in the Royal Navy as the **'Colony' class**.

Specification
'River' class (original specification)
Displacement: 1,370 tons standard
Dimensions: length 91.9 m (301.5 ft); beam 11.12 m (36.5 ft); draught 3.91 m (12.83 ft)
Propulsion: two sets of 4-cylinder triple-expansion steam engines delivering 4101 kW (5,500 ihp) to two shafts
Speed: 20 kts
Endurance: 12970 km (8,060 miles) at 12 kts
Armament: two single 101.6-mm (4-in) guns, two single 2-pdr and 20-mm AA guns (later replaced by 10 20-mm AA guns), one Hedgehog, and depth charges
Complement: 107

A typically battered Atlantic escort, HMS Spey *steams up the line of a convoy during February 1944, when this particular 'River' class frigate sank the Type VIIC U-boats U-406 (on 18 February) and U-386 (on 19 February).*

Designed as ocean-going escorts with a range of 12970 km (8,060 miles), the 'Rivers' were at first fitted with almost totally superfluous minesweeping gear. Once this was eliminated from the design, oil storage rose from 440 tons to 646 tons, with a consequent improvement in endurance.

'Loch' and 'Bay' classes

The **'Bay' class** began to appear late in 1944 as a direct consequence of the course of the war, and in 1945 the last of 19 was launched. In the Atlantic the dour struggle against the U-boat had been successful (though was not yet done) and planning began to be directed more at building up the British Pacific Fleet in order to make a real contribution in the defeat of Japan, before reclaiming the UK's lost imperial possessions in the East.

In the Atlantic war the Canadian yards had been concentrating on production of 'Modified Rivers', to which they were most suited, while in the UK production since the commencement of 1944 had been of the **'Loch' class**, of which 31 were completed as escorts. This bore all the marks of its 'River' class ancestry in appearance and machinery, but had important differences. For the first time all corners had been cut to allow the introduction of modular construction, the shipbuilder assembling hull components from a

variety of sources. The structure had been greatly strengthened to allow the installation of a pair of triple-barrelled Squid anti-submarine mortars forward of the bridge. The spacious quarter-deck was now devoted not so much to depth charges and their caparison (whose functions the Squid had largely superseded) but to the trappings of a more scientific war, largely the towed Foxer gear, for defeating the menace of the acoustic torpedo with its affinity for frigate propellers. A major difference from the recognition point of view was the substantial lattice mast for the all-important radars. The 'Lochs' proved deadly against the U-boat but,

HMS Loch Tarbert *comes alongside after a voyage with a fo'c'sle party ready to pass a line ashore. Improved versions of the 'River' designs, the 'Loch' class had a pair of triple-barrelled Squid ASW mortars as main anti-submarine weaponry.*

though they soldiered on after the war until the 1960s, their speed would have been totally inadequate to meet the threat of such as the 'Type XXI' U-boats. These fortunately arrived too late, but during the early 1950s stimulated the prototype fast frigate in the 'Type 15' destroyer conversions.

In contrast, the Pacific war was predominantly AA in nature, and the 19 units of the **'Bay'** class completed in 1944-5 were no more than 'Lochs' with their forward 101.6-mm (4-in) and after quadruple 2-pdr guns replaced by two twin HA 101.6-mm mountings, with a proper director atop the bridge. The heavy Squids, now non-essential, were replaced by the less effective Hedgehog, allowing also the substitution of

two twin 40-mm mountings for some of the original 20-mm weapons.

Specification
'Bay' class
Displacement: 1,580 tons standard
Dimensions: length 93.6 m (307.25 ft); beam 11.73 m (38.5 ft); draught 2.9 m (9.5 ft)
Propulsion: two sets of 4-cylinder triple expansion steam engines delivering 4101 kW (5,500 ihp) to two shafts
Speed: 19.5 kts
Endurance: 17605 km (10,940 miles)
Armament: two twin 101.6-mm (4-in) DP, two twin 40-mm AA and two twin 20-mm AA guns, one Hedgehog, and depth charges
Complement: 157

The 'Bay' class frigates were versions of the 'Loch' class optimized for Pacific operations, where escorts were more likely to be attacked from the air. The heavy Squid system was landed in favour of the lighter but less effective Hedgehog, and AA armament was improved.

DE type

The Americans, like the Japanese, had seen little need of defensive ships such as escorts before the war and, in its early days had little beyond their totally unsuitable and veteran flush-deckers. It was the Royal Navy, desperately seeking to meet the submarine threat, that produced a specification for an Atlantic escort, followed by orders for no less than 300 being placed in the USA between November 1941 and January 1942. Termed by the Americans destroyer escorts (**DE type**, a new category), they also met the sudden need at home, and the organization was put in hand to build over 1,000 of them, though the earliest still arrived too late to prevent the backyard holocaust known to the U-boat men as the 'Happy Time'.

The DEs were built after the fashion of American fleet destroyers, having a long flush deck with a prominent sheer line in place of the more commodious long forecastle decks preferred by the British. Far more emphasis was placed on gun armament, with superimposed 76.2-mm (3-in) guns forward, a single aft and numerous guntubs with a mixture of close-range weaponry, mostly single 20-mm guns. Hedgehog was sited forward and, by RN standards, the after deck was cramped, though by the use of double-depth, sided stowage racks the British units (78 **'Captain'** class) managed to stow upwards of 200 depth charges.

Although 'only' 565 DEs were eventually completed, their construction rate was phenomenal, no less than 425 being commissioned in the 12 months between April 1943 and April 1944 alone. Bethlehem actually completed the USS *Underhill* (DE 682) in under two months! The US Navy was very much a 'steam-turbine' navy, but production on this scale was impossible so the ships fell into several classes, depending on whether they were diesel (85 **'Edsall'** class units) diesel-electric (97 **'Evarts'** and 76 **'Bostwick'** class units) or turbo-electrically (152 **'Buckley'**, 74 **'John C. Butler'** and 81 **'Rudderow'** class units) driven. Most of those incorporating diesels were low powered as the bulk of existing diesel output was at

that time earmarked for landing craft. As anti-submarine ships the DEs were very effective, while many went on after the war to be converted into fast transports (APD) or radar-pickets (DER).

Specification
'Buckley' class
Displacement: 1,400 tons standard and 1,720 tons full load
Dimensions: length 93.27 m (306.0 ft); beam 11.27 m (37.0 ft); draught 2.89 m (9.5 ft)
Propulsion: two sets of geared steam turbines and two propulsion motors delivering 8948 kW (12,000 shp) to two shafts
Speed: 24 kts
Armament: three single 76.2-mm (3-in) DP, six single 40-mm AA, and two twin and four single 20-mm AA guns, three 533-mm (21-in) torpedo tubes, one Hedgehog, and depth charges
Complement: 220

USS Harmon, a turbine-powered destroyer escort launched in July 1943, was named after a Navy Cross winner killed in the sea battle off Guadalcanal. The Harmon established a record, being delivered to the navy only 92 days after the keel was laid. Later vessels were built in even shorter times.

Above: This is one of the earliest of more than 565 DEs built for the US Navy. The six classes delivered were variations on a theme, with differing propulsion systems.

Below: Apart from the choice of main armament, most DEs carried similar weaponry. Depth charges were handled by eight DC throwers and two DC racks.

213

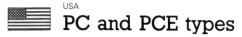
PC and PCE types

Given the immense length of the Atlantic and Pacific coasts together with further major transCarribbean routes, particularly to the Venezuelan oil terminals and the Panama Canal, the US Navy had a major problem in protecting its coastal traffic, the pattern and volume of which was very different to that of the UK. The vulnerability of the shipping on the eastern seaboard was ruthlessly exposed by the German U-boat campaign of 1942, but had been anticipated to the extent that three prototype 53.26 m (174 ft 9 in) Patrol Craft (**PC type**) had been completed before the USA's entry into the war. These were slim-gutted diesel craft which, though relatively well armed, were

Unlike the smaller PC classes, the PCEs were adapted from a minesweeper design as an interim coastal escort until the construction of more PCs.

restricted by their size to inshore work. Needing to expand the escort fleet rapidly and with the PC design to hand, it is understandable that a massive construction programme was rapidly instituted. In fact, over 350 of these craft were built using resources that, in retrospect, would better have been diverted to the production of larger and more versatile anti-submarine ships. Not until mid-1943, therefore, was the **PCE type** introduced which, while only 3 m (10 ft) longer, was also a full 10 ft beamier. Unlike the PCs, with their characteristically American flush deck with pronounced sheer, the PCEs followed British frigate practice in their freeboard and long forecastle. Early units were funnelless, their diesels exhausting through the shell,

but later examples had a thin stovepipe and the last a diminutive stack with a curved cap. Construction amounted to 78 units.

Their armament was better than that of many British frigates, a 76.2-mm (3-in) gun and a full Hedgehog forward, two/three single 40-mm and up to five 20-mm AA guns, with depth charges

aft. Fifteen crossed the Atlantic for service with the Royal Navy. Known as the **'Kil' class** they served primarily off Gibraltar and Sierra Leone. One, HMS *Kilmarnock*, participated in the only U-boat sinking credited to the class, that of the *U-731* off Tangier in May 1944.

Specification
'PCE' class
Displacement: 795 tons standard and 850 tons full load
Dimensions: length 56.24 m (184.5 ft); beam 10.05 m (33.0 ft); draught 2.89 m (9.5 ft)
Propulsion: two diesel engines delivering 1417 kW (1,900 bhp) to two shafts
Speed: 16 kts
Armament: one 76.2 mm (3-in) DP, two or three single 40-mm AA, and four single 20-mm AA guns, one Hedgehog, and depth charges
Complement: 100

'Elan' class

At the outbreak of war the French fleet was poorly served for escorts in the accepted sense of the word, those available being designed primarily for colonial service. For effective anti-submarine work during the war, therefore, the Free French navy relied on frigates, corvettes and DEs transferred from the Royal Navy or the US Navy.

The 13-strong **'Elan' class** had been completed in 1939-40 as corvette-type vessels with minesweeping capability. Their 78 by 8.48 m (255.9 by 27.8 ft) hull dimensions, compared with the 62.50 by 10.10 m (205 by 33.1 ft) of the British-built 'Flowers' that served under the same flag, characterize the greatly different approach, with strong emphasis on speed. Despite their fine lines, however, their low-power twin-shaft diesel machinery could drive them at only 20 kts, but their excellent official endurance figures emphasize the economy of diesel propulsion. The first group were decidedly odd in appearance, with a distinctively low foredeck. What was in the designer's mind is hard to say but acute wetness must well have been anticipated as the bridge was perched atop a solid house. No armament was mounted forward and the impact of green seas on the front of the house can only be imagined. An interesting detail was the rounded sheerstrake, extending the length of the hull, possibly better to accommodate the anticipated stresses generated in the hull when labouring in heavy seas. Two 100-mm (3.94-in)

guns could be carried though only one was usually fitted, on the after house.

Where ships are concerned it is often said that 'if it looks right, it is right'. The converse apparently holds good, for a follow-on series of nine **'Chamois' class** ships, whose entry into service was disrupted by the war, virtually repeated the design but incorporated a raised forecastle and looked altogether more workmanlike. Their careers were typically complex with, for instance, *l'Impetueuse* being scuttled by the French at Toulon, only to be salvaged by the Italians and then, at their capitulation, being taken in turn by the Germans who, finally, scuttled her again at Marseilles. Another three units were war losses.

Specification
'Elan' class (as built)
Displacement: 630 tons standard and 740 tons full load
Dimensions: length 78.0 m (255.9 ft); beam 8.5 m (27.9 ft); draught 2.4 m (7.9 ft)
Propulsion: two diesels delivering 2982 kW (4,000 bhp) to two shafts
Speed: 20 kts
Endurance: 16675 km (10,360 miles) at 14 kts
Armament: two 100-mm (3.94-in) guns, and two twin and four single 13.2-mm (0.52-in) machine-guns
Complement: not known

The early 'Elan' class vessels were notable for their unusual appearance; with no armament on their distinctive low foredeck and the rounded sheerstrake continuing the length of the hull, from some angles the Elans bore a resemblance to a top-heavy submarine.

The twin 100-mm (3.94-in) guns originally fitted to the French vessels were replaced in British service by British 4-in (102-mm) weapons. The minesweeping capability was never used, but two DCTs and a DC rack were fitted. Typically, after the surrender of France the class found itself in use by both sides.

Coastal Craft

Putting to sea in some of the fastest and most dashing warships of the time, the coastal naval forces saw much fierce fighting in locations as diverse as the North Sea and the 'Slot' in the Solomon Islands. Young, inexperienced crews took their fragile and inflammable craft into action, and often paid the highest price for their courage.

It is in the nature of things that in times of peace 'blue water' fleets tend to devote their limited resources to meeting the problems of ocean warfare; coastal warfare may or may not be required in some unspecified emergency in the future and, lacking urgency, inevitably lacked funds. Therefore, it is hardly surprising to discover that between the wars, British expertise was kept alive mainly through the dedication of private firms who were prepared to risk casting both their efforts and funds into the bottomless well of official disinterest. This was doubly fortunate, for the USA had similarly underinvested and owed much to Scott-Paine's British Power Boat Company for the eventual success of the PT boat.

Smaller fleets, however, with limited objectives and even more limited funds, tend to look harder at promisingly cost-effective solutions to countering possible hostile sea-powers. The submarine, the raider and mine warfare are three such solutions, and the high-speed coastal craft is a fourth, if geography permits. Germany, therefore, put much effort and ingenuity during the 1930s into producing the S-boat, one of her major successes of World War II. This success was

A US Navy PT boat intended for use in coastal waters, where its speed was put to good effect provided it had sufficient firepower – normally torpedoes and cannon.

mainly because due to the fact that there had been sufficient time for its development. Taken out of context, the effect of the S-boat on World War II was not great in a material sense but, measured in psychological and disruptive terms, it was a major nuisance, requiring a large expenditure of scarce war effort to counter.

Likewise, the geography of the central Mediterranean favoured the Italian use of such craft. The Italians had seen major successes from these craft in World War I and had every intention of keeping abreast of any new developments. Like the Germans they evolved reliable, high-speed machinery which stood them in good stead.

Finally, it was radar-controlled gunfire from would-be targets by night and air power by day that constrained the torpedo-boat's potential. With the comparatively recent introduction of the surface-to-surface missile the wheel has once again turned, putting a large measure of advantage back with the cheap, high-speed minor warship, the midget with the big clout.

Soviet coastal craft

There were strong influences working on the post-revolutionary Soviet navy to develop a powerful and effective force of coastal craft. The fleet itself had been relegated to the status of a means of guaranteeing the seaward flanks of the primary service, the army. These seaward flanks were all of shallow and sheltered water, and distances involved were small. Further, the successful attacks by British CMBs in 1919 had shown the potential of even a few such boats in the right hands, and a couple of unserviceable and damaged Thornycroft 55-footers were available as exemplars. From these beginnings the Soviets had produced by 1928 a reasonably successful 18-m (59.06-ft) craft known as an **S4**. The indifferent Soviet technology of the time

required the incorporation of American petrol engines, but the reliability of these and the sound hull shape made for a very high trials speed, approaching 50 kts, though considerably diminished by a load of two 457-mm (18-in) torpedoes or anything but calm conditions. About 60 S4s were built, giving the Soviets considerable experience.

The Tsarist navy had been known for its innovation and readiness to adopt ideas, and this policy continued with the purchase of technology in hull design and machinery from France, Germany and Italy as available. With this as a baseline the Soviets produced a 19-m (62.3-ft) **G5** type, which was still heavily influenced by the British CMB in having a stepped hull and two

troughs aft for the stern launching of torpedoes that had been increased in size to 533 mm (21 in). For this craft the Soviets built a successful petrol engine that was tolerably reliable and capable of being upgraded. The fault with the G5 was its early use of aluminium alloy for both shell and frames, so that it was plagued with corrosion problems. For this reason, the follow-on 21.6-m (70.9-ft) **D3** craft were wooden-built, differing further in having side-launching gear for their torpedoes. Numerous G5 and D3 types served during the war, supplemented by over 200 boats from the USA and UK. Also produced in large numbers were armoured craft of many types, comparatively slow but armed with guns and cannon in tank turrets. They proved

formidable craft both offshore and up rivers.

Specification
G5 type (late production)
Displacement: 16 tons
Dimensions: length 19.1 m (62.66 ft); beam 3.4 m (11.15 ft); draught 1.0 m (3.28 ft)
Propulsion: two petrol engines delivering 1491 kW (2,000 bhp) to two shafts
Speed: 48 kts
Endurance: about 370 km (230 miles) at 48 kts
Armament: two 533-mm (21-in) torpedoes, and two 12.7-mm (0.5-in) machine-guns
Complement: 7

The extremely fast G5 torpedo boat was ultimately derived from a series of designs by a team under the leadership of the noted aircraft designer A.N. Tupolev. Nearly 300 were built, with 73 being lost during the war, and dozens remained in commission after 1945.

Japanese coastal craft

Like the majority of major fleets, the Japanese navy had largely ignored coastal craft between the world wars. As a type it did not fit into ocean warfare and, though the acquisition of a many-islanded empire was accepted strategy, prolonged supply problems in the face of an actively hostile fleet were not. Even as a redeployment of their submarine forces to assault the US Navy's fleet train would have seriously affected that navy's ability to operate, so would a powerful force of Japanese coastal craft have been able both to assist in the garrison supply task and to dispute the American's aim to disrupt it.

With their overrunning of China and Far East imperial possessions, the Japanese acquired a variety of foreign costal craft in various states of repair (Dutch, British, German and Italian), all

of which influenced subsequent designs. All were driven by petrol engines, but the Japanese had no capacity to build either these or small high-speed marine diesels in any quantity. Though engines were copied, they were low-powered and always in desperately short supply; as multi-engined layouts were thus out of the question, boats themselves had to be small to attain any speed. The largest Japanese MTBs were, therefore, of only about 18 m (59.06 ft) overall length. All were of hard-chine design to get over the low power problem and this, combined with their lack of

length, gave them a poor performance in anything but sheltered waters. Designs were in both wood and steel and were such as to permit construction by undertakings unskilled in boatbuilding. And though aero engines were tried as prime movers, they proved unsatisfactory in a marine environment.

Most numerous of the many Japanese varieties were the 15-m (49.2-ft), single-screwed 49-strong **Type 14** and the 18-m (59.06-ft) twin-screwed **Type 38**. Although the smaller boat could make 33 kts in good conditions, the larger was good for only

27.5 kts and, like others, could be armed as an MGB rather than with two 457-mm (18-in) torpedoes. A 32.4-m (106.3-ft) Lürssen type was also copied as the **Type 51**, but these proved a disappointment and the 18-boat programme was never completed.

Specification
Type 14
Displacement: 15 tons
Dimensions: length 15.0 m (49.2 ft); beam 3.66 m (12.0 ft); beam 0.85 m (2.8 ft)
Propulsion: one petrol engine delivering 686 kW (920 bhp) to one shaft
Speed: 33 kts
Endurance: not known
Armament: two 457-mm (18-in) torpedoes, and one 25-mm cannon
Complement: 7

Apart from their small torpedo craft, the Imperial Japanese Navy operated a limited number of Type 51 boats. These, based on the German S-boat concept, were much larger than was usual in a Japanese design, and were intended as division boats for their smaller sisters. Armament could include eight depth charges as well as the usual 457-mm (18-in) torpedoes.

LS and KM

Paralleling the carriage of small torpedo craft by major units in the Victorian era, the pre-war German navy investigated two possibilities of stowage for a small *Schnellboot*. Two 12.5-m (41-ft) **LS** type prototypes were built in the late 1930s, light enough to be handled by heavy deck gear yet able to carry two 457-mm (18-in) torpedoes. Only one of these, built of light alloy, met the weight limit and was put into service as *LS2* (LS for *Leicht Schnellboot*). The torpedo gear was not standard in the German navy and was not available in time, so the boat was modified to lay three mines through apertures in the broad transom. Though this reduced the direct usefulness of the craft, she was shipped as an auxiliary aboard the raider *Komet*. The boat was a failure as the aero engines fitted in place of the planned diesels (also not available) failed with vibration and transmission problems.

LS3 and *LS4* both received their designed pair of Daimler-Benz diesels, an interesting feature being that a gearbox was added to increase engine speed by 50 per cent to drive the propellers at a supercavitating 3,300 rpm. Of these two craft the former was a minelayer attached to the raider *Kormoran*, and the latter (the first torpedo-fitted boat) was attached to the raider *Michel*.

Official policy regarding the use of these interesting little craft, which were armed also with a 15-mm or 20-mm gun in an aircraft turret, seemed to be lacking. Of the remaining eight that were completed, most went overland to the Aegean to be used, ineffectually, for AS duties, carrying 11 depth charges but no sonar. In practice, they acted as high-speed inter-island vedettes.

Another innovative little craft was the 16-m (52.5-ft) **KM** type coastal minelayer (KM for *Küstenminenleger*). Equipped with twin 410-kW (550-hp) aero engine drive, these 36 craft had sufficient speed to reach the British coast with four mines and return during dark hours, having placed them far more accurately than aircraft. They proved too small for the job and were expended in theatres with sheltered waters.

Specification
LS type (as designed)
Displacement: 11.5 tons
Dimensions: length 12.5 m (41.0 ft); beam 3.3 m (10.83 ft); draught 0.76 m (2.5 ft)
Speed: 42.5 kts
Endurance: 555 km (345 miles) at 30 kts

LS4 was fitted with an aircraft gun turret and two 533-mm torpedoes. Named 'Esau', it was carried by the German commerce raider Michel,which sailed from Flushing in March 1942 and met its end at the hands of the American submarine USS Tarpon off Yokohama in 1943.

Armament: two 450-mm (17.7-in) torpedoes, and one 20-mm cannon
Complement: 9

R-Boot

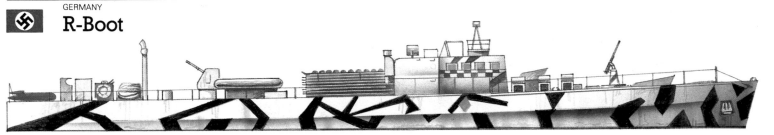

Raumen is the German verb 'to clear' or 'to remove', hence the **Raumboot** or **R-boat** type of coastal minesweeper. These craft were of such a useful size, however, that they also did duty as minelayers and, suitably rearmed, as escorts to convoys, in which guise they were involved in frequent brushes with British craft.

The original group, *R1-16*, was constructed in the early 1930s. Like the S-boats, they were built of wood on metal framing with round bilges. They were, however, of only 60-ton displacement and 26-m (85.3-ft) length. Propulsion was by twin-screw diesels for a modest 17 kts although one unit, *R8*, was fitted with Voith Schnider cycloidal propellers, which made for great manoeuvrability at the cost of some speed. This experiment was deemed successful, and over 100 R-boats were eventually so fitted.

From *R17* onwards dimensions were very similar to those of the S-boats, though with extra beam, and increased draught by virtue of their greater displacement. Even with progressively improved diesels, the average R-boat never much exceeded 20 kts and, when not actually involved

Above: The German R-boats were pressed into service as minelayers and convoy escorts. Although they received increasingly powerful diesels they could rarely manage much more than half the maximum speed of an S-boat.

in the minesweeping for which the type had been designed, was employed defensively. The exceptions were the dozen so-called **GR-Boote** (G for *Geleit*, or escort), *R301-312*, built to a stretched 41-m (134.5-ft) design displacing 175 tons. They had triple-screw propulsion for 24 kts and were fitted with a pair of torpedoes. Though used in something like the role for which the British employed MGBs, their firepower was little enhanced, and 88 more projected craft were cancelled.

Their construction did suggest the need for a true multi-purpose escort for the many coastal convoys that the Germans ran around North European waters. The result was the hybrid, steel-built **MZ-Boot** design (Mz for *Mehrzweck*, or multi-purpose) which, while having a heavy surface armament including two 88-mm (3.46-in)

An R-boat is shown off the Norwegian coast, where the Germans ran so many convoys that they constructed a purpose-built convoy escort based on the R-boat design. By 1944 R-boats bristled with guns, carrying a 37-mm (1.45-in) cannon and up to six 20-mm mounts. Many were fitted with Voith Schneider propellers, which increased manoeuvrability at the expense of some speed.

guns and two torpedo tubes, were of only single-shaft propulsion. Only *Mz1* was ever completed, not proving sufficiently satisfactory to warrant further priority being given for completion of the remaining 11.

Specification
R-boat 140-ton type
Displacement: 140 tons standard
Dimensions: length 40.0 m (131.23 ft); beam 5.6 m (18.37 ft); draught 1.45 m (4.75 ft)
Propulsion: two diesels delivering 1901 kW (2,550 bhp) to two shafts
Speed: 20.5 kts
Endurance: 2040 km (1,268 miles) at 15 kts
Armament: one 37-mm cannon and up to six 20-mm cannon
Complement: 38

The R-boats were originally 60-ton craft armed with a couple of 20-mm cannon plus depth charges or mines, as appropriate. From R17 on they grew to S-boat size, and mounted an increased armament – necessary on the vital Norwegian iron ore route.

S-Boot

Known to the British for some ill-defined reason as an **E-boat**, the German *Schnellboot*, or **S-Boot**, differed greatly from its Royal Navy counterparts. From its origins in a Lürssen civil design of the early 1930s, the S-boat was built of wood on alloy frames and had a round-bilged hull form which, while possessing a lower maximum speed than the hard-chined British equivalents, was very much more seakindly. In the event, the S-boat was able to sustain its maximum speed in sea states that forced the British to throttle back to avoid excessive pounding.

Diesel drive was specified from the outset, though the prototype *S1* of 1930 and the follow-on *S2-S5* of 1931-2 had to take petrol engines while Daimler-Benz and MAN developed a suitable unit. Only with the *S6-13* of 1934-5 did the three-shaft diesel layout become established. These craft were 32.4 m (106.3 ft) in length and powered for 35 kts. This speed was considered insufficient, so in the next group the seven-cylinder diesels were exchanged for 11-cylinder units, improving speed but necessitating an increase in length to 34.7 m (113.8 ft), which remained remarkably constant until 1945, in stark contrast to the variety of boats under the British flag.

Because of their greater length the S-boats carried their two torpedo tubes forward of the wheelhouse, giving space for two skid-mounted reloads abaft them. It was then a small design step from *S26* onwards to raise the forecastle by 1 m (3.28 ft), so enclosing the tubes and leaving a forward gun-pit between them and, importantly, raising the freeboard to give the craft an enviable dryness.

Always quieter than British equivalents, the S-boats also had a profile that was hard to spot without radar. Gun armament had continually to be increased to match that of their opponents, the extra weight being offset to a great extent by improved weight-saving techniques in hull construction and engines of higher power. Protection was improved by the adoption of the armoured 'Kalotte' type bridge. By 1945 speeds had been pushed (by extremely unreliable engines) to a maximum 42 kts and, while no longer, the *S700* type introduced two extra, aft-facing torpedo tubes. Over 200 S-boats were built, of which about half survived the war.

Specification
'S 26' class
Displacement: 93 tons standard and 115 tons full load
Dimensions: length 34.95 m (114.67 ft); beam 5.1 m (16.73 ft); draught 1.4 m (4.6 ft)
Propulsion: three diesels delivering 4474 kW (6,000 bhp) to three shafts
Speed: 39.5 kts
Endurance: 1390 km (864 miles) at 35 kts
Armament: two 533-m (21-in) torpedo tubes with four torpedoes, and two 20-mm cannon
Complement: up to 21

S1, the prototype S-boat, here seen in the Kiel canal, had to make do with a petrol engine while a diesel unit was perfected. The round-bilged hull enabled the S-boats to maintain high speeds even in a rough sea.

The 100-ton S81 works up to her full speed of 39 kts. Note the difference made by raising the forecastle 1 m (3.28 ft), enclosing the torpedo tubes and leaving space for a forward 20-mm (0.78-in) gun-pit. The low profile of the S-boats was a considerable advantage in the nocturnal melées along the Channel coast.

British Power Boats 60-ft types

As a result mainly of lack of funds, the British did not develop the CMB concept further until 1935, when British Power Boats interested the Admiralty in an 18.3-m (60-ft) boat developed as a private venture. It was wooden-hulled with, initially, aluminium decking and, in contrast to the CMB, was hard-chined without a step. Two 457-mm (18-in) torpedoes were carried; though launched over the stern as in earlier boats, the arrangement was different. The torpedoes protruded through ports in the transom and had their outboard halves supported on lattice outriggers that could be hinged back on deck when not required. The engine room crew had to work with the business ends of the torpedoes supported on overhead runways over the wing shafts. Launching involved running the torpedoes up, removing their restraints and suddenly accelerating the boat. With the torpedoes having to adjust in the disturbed water of the boat's wake, aiming was somewhat haphazard.

A strong paper defence was afforded by no less than eight Lewis guns but these, being arranged in two quadruple mountings set in pits at the extreme ends of the boat, proved un-satisfactory. The hull design, though slower than that of the CMB, proved more seakindly if, like all of its kind,

It was discovered very soon that the BPB armament of quad Lewis guns at bow and stern was inadequate, and that a larger design would be necessary to handle the increased weaponry.

prone to pounding in a head sea. The **BPB 60-footer** proved seaworthy and capable of staging as far as Malta; the first type to be termed a motor torpedo boat, it rekindled interest on the part of the Admiralty.

Eighteen were built in the initial batches between 1936 and 1939 (**MTB1-12** and **MTB14-19**), BPB then producing a two-engined version whose torpedoes were exchanged for depth charges. Known as **MA/SB** ('Masby') craft, they found little em-ployment in their initial form and most were later refitted as early **MGB** types to support MTBs in their operations. For this they carried, usually, a single 2-pdr and four 12.7-mm (0.5-in) machine-guns, but many armament variations existed. Interestingly, depth charges were still often carried: set shallow, these could be used to deter pursuit or, hair-raisingly, to drop alongside a target.

Specification
BPB 60-ft type
Displacement: 22 tons
Dimensions: length 18.36 m (60.25 ft); beam 4.1 m (13.4 ft); draught 0.86 m (2.83 ft)
Propulsion: three petrol engines delivering 1342 kW (1,800 hp) to three shafts
Speed: 33 kts
Endurance: 652 km (405 miles) at 33 kts

British power boats were instrumental in the revival of Royal Navy interest in coastal craft in the 1930s. Their designs sold abroad, these 70-ft MGBs originally being built as stretched MA/SBs for the French until taken over and completed for the Royal Navy.

Armament: two 457-mm (18-in) torpedoes, and eight 7.7-mm (0.303-in) machine-guns
Complement: 9

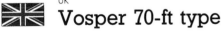

Vosper 70-ft type

The successful **Vosper 70-ft** type ori-ginated in the single 20.7-m (68-ft) boat built by Vosper as a private venture in 1935-6 and eventually commissioned by the navy as *MTB 102*. Built com-pletely in wood, she was driven by three Isotta-Fraschini petrol engines with a maximum output of 2573 kW (3,450 bhp). These drove the boat at a maximum speed of nearly 44 kts in calm water, and were chosen as no British-built equivalent existed. Like all such engines they were extremely noisy, so a low-power Ford engine was also available to clutch into the wing shafts for a low-speed, but silent, approach. Centreline torpedo tubes were originally included, one forward and one aft. But the navy did not like them and developed the sided arrangement adopted thereafter. *MTB 102* was notable also for being the first

MTB 376, a US-built Vosper design, supplied under Lend-Lease, leaves harbour at Livorno. Both Royal and US Navies were involved in operations between Genoa and La Spezia from May 1944, and achieved considerable success harrying German supply convoys.

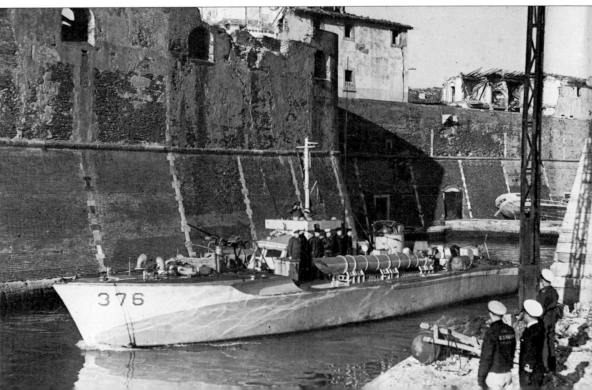

376

Royal Navy vessel fitted with the later universal 20-mm Oerlikon cannon.

Despite a further strong challenge by BPB with an alternative 21.34-m (70-ft) private-venture boat, the Admiralty chose the Vosper design as being the stronger in heavy seas. (Actually keeping these fast wooden hulls together in poor conditions was a problem that was never satisfactorily solved.) Four Vosper and two similar Thornycroft boats were ordered in 1938 and provided the basis for the war programme, with little design change except a nominal increase in length to improve seakeeping and cater for the growing load of topweight. Alternative engines were a problem; a few converted Merlins were coaxed from the Air Ministry but many boats had to take low-powered Hall-Scotts until the powerful American Packard became available. Oerlikons were virtually unobtainable, and the alternative 7.7-mm (0.303-in) machine-guns proved of little use against E-boats running as MGBs. Eventually 12.7-mm (0.5-in) machine-guns and 6-pdr guns were fitted which, with radar, made for an efficient night-fighting boat. Stronger but lighter hulls, together with uprated engines, meant that boats were carrying a 70-per cent increased equipment load by 1944 with little speed penalty. Orders for 193 boats were met between 1939 and 1945 with the exception of a few late boats which were cancelled.

Specification
Vosper 72.5-ft type
Displacement: 36 to 49 tons
Dimensions: length 22.1 m (72.5 ft); beam 5.94 m (19.5 ft); draught 1.68 m (5.5 ft)
Propulsion: three petrol engines delivering 2983 kW (4,000 bhp) to three shafts

Speed: 40 kts
Endurance: 463 km (288 miles) at 40 kts
Armament: two 533-mm (21-in) torpedoes, and various combinations of 6-pdr gun, 20-mm cannon, and 12.7-mm (0.5-in) and 7.7-mm (0.303-in) machine-guns
Complement: 12 or 13

MTB 80 was one of the first of Vosper's 72.2-footers. The class was to give excellent service when fitted with 6 pdrs and 20-mm cannon, but the original armament of two 12.7-mm (0.5-in) and four 7.7-mm (0.303-in) MGs was not adequate (as was unfortunately proven when MTB 80 was lost in 1941).

 UK
Fairmile 'D' type

Practical pre-war experience demonstrated that MTBs would probably find difficulty in penetrating a determined escort to reach a target, particularly if that escort was of 'E-boats'. What was required was a more heavily armed, but still fast craft to occupy the latter's attentions, to defend the MTBs and allow them to concentrate on the main objectives. A further requirement was the need to defend convoys against E-boats in the absence of a destroyer escort. As already related, a few of the available BPB 'Masby' boats were rearmed to serve temporarily but, for the long term, the **Fairmile 'D' type** and the steam gunboat were developed.

Half as long again as the average MTB, the 'D' type was of unique form in having flattish vee sections aft merging into a round-bilge form forward, the transition taking the form of a pronounced hard knuckle that acted usefully as a spray deflector. This compromise hull and the extra length allowed them to operate in more severe sea states without the usual heavy pounding. The wide transom permitted quadruple shaft propulsion but,

where this decreased the draught as a result of smaller-diameter propellers, it was due more to the power of available engines than design requirements. Early craft had direct drive but gearboxes were later introduced, improving both efficiency and speed. Hard driving exposed the weaknesses of mass-producing an all-wood craft of this size, and repairs and strengthening were frequent. Some 200 'D' Type craft were produced between 1942 and 1944.

Armaments, official and otherwise, varied considerably, the boats serving as MGBs (90-ton displacement), MTBs (95-ton displacement) or combination MGM/MTBs (105-ton displacement). In the last role the armament was formidable, with four 457-mm (18-in) torpedo tubes, two 6-pdr guns, and four 12.7-mm (0.5-in) and four 7.7-mm (0.303-in) machine-guns. The speed, inevitably, was reduced to about 29 kts. A short-barrelled 114.3-in (4.5-in) gun was fitted forward on some.

Because of their size (and endurance when fitted with auxiliary tanks) Shetland-based 'D' types were able to work the Norwegian coast and, operating out of Malta and Bône, to add to the

misery heaped on the Afrika Korps' supply convoys. Against the low-profile E-boats, they possessed the great advantage of radar.

Fairmile 'D' MTB 1944 cutaway drawing key

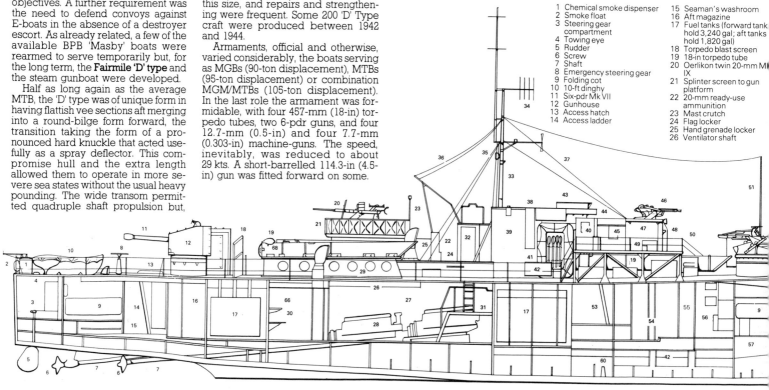

1 Chemical smoke dispenser
2 Smoke float
3 Steering gear compartment
4 Towing eye
5 Rudder
6 Screw
7 Shaft
8 Emergency steering gear
9 Folding cot
10 10-ft dinghy
11 Six-pdr Mk VII
12 Gunhouse
13 Access hatch
14 Access ladder
15 Seaman's washroom
16 Aft magazine
17 Fuel tanks (forward tank hold 3,240 gal; aft tanks hold 1,820 gal)
18 Torpedo blast screen
19 18-in torpedo tube
20 Oerlikon twin 20-mm Mk IX
21 Splinter screen to gun platform
22 20-mm ready-use ammunition
23 Mast crutch
24 Flag locker
25 Hand grenade locker
26 Ventilator shaft

Fairmile 'A' and 'C' types

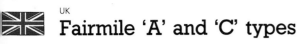

So well associated with the construction of coastal craft did the name of Fairmile become that it is, perhaps, suprising to discover that it began operations as late as 1939. It convinced the Admiralty of the need for a motor launch (ML) along the lines of those that served during World War I. These had been built in the USA and, mainly through lack of length, were not totally satisfactory in service. Fairmile proposed to increase length substantially from 22.85-24.37 m (75-80 ft) to 33.53 m (110 ft) and to gear up to an extended programme by prefabrication. Thus, in place of a yard framing up a boat, planking it and fitting it out in the traditional (and slow) manner a variety of wood-working companies, not necessarily connected with boat building, would be involved in the series construction of component parts. These, made from standard jigs, would then be assembled rapidly in the actual waterside yard, even the planking being supplied in ready-to-assemble numbered sets.

To test the system, the Admiralty ordered 12 **Fairmile 'A' type** craft, numbered *ML100-111*. They were, indeed, produced rapidly in 1940, but the design itself was found to be less than ideal. It had been developed for general inshore patrol and auxiliary duties, an asdic (sonar) set and 12 depth charges being carried as standard. In practice, the design's hard-chine form tended to pound in a sea-

way and throw spray. More seriously, the bunker capacity for the three Hall Scott petrol engines was far too small. For the long wartime production runs, therefore, a new design known as the Fairmile 'B' type was produced.

The initial 12 'A' type boats were later converted into inshore mine-layers, with a capacity of up to nine mines each. During the invasion scare of 1940, motor gun boats (MGBs) were needed urgently and the 'A' type jigs were used to construct 24, known as the **Fairmile 'C' type.** These had super-

charged engines and better laid out topsides, MTB-style, with an enhanced armament of two 2-pdr guns and two twin 12.7-mm (0.5-in) machine-guns.

Specification
Fairmile 'A' type
Displacement: 58 tons
Dimensions: length 33.53 m (110.0 ft); beam 5.31 m (17.42 ft); draught 1.83 m (6.0 ft)
Propulsion: three petrol engines delivering 1342 kW (1,800 bhp) to three shafts

A Fairmile 'C' MGB with the original armament of two 2-pdrs and two pairs of 12.7-mm (0.5-in) MGs makes her way at close to her maximum speed of 25 kts. Slower but larger than standard MGBs, the Fairmiles were also up-gunned, with up to six 20-mm cannon being shipped.

Speed: 22 kts
Endurance: not known
Armament: one 3-pdr gun, and two 7.7-mm (0.303-in) machine-guns
Complement: 16

Specification
Fairmile 'D' type
Displacement: 90 tons
Dimensions: length 33.53 m (110.0 ft); beam 6.4 m (21.0 ft); draught 1.58 m (5.17 ft)
Propulsion: four petrol engines delivering 3728 kW (5,000 bhp) to four shafts
Speed: 29 kts

Endurance: not known
Armament: two single 6-pdr guns, one twin 20-mm cannon, two twin 12.7-mm (0.5-in) machine-guns, and (optional) four 457-mm (18-in) torpedoes
Complement: up to 30

Below: Considerably larger than preceding MTB types, the Fairmile 'D' was of similar dimensions to its main opponent, the S-boat.

Bottom: A Fairmile 'D' enters harbour at Algiers during the North African campaign, when the big boats were much used in harassing Rommel's supply routes to Tunis. Being such capable boats they were used where the fighting was thickest, which explains the loss of nearly 40 of the class in action.

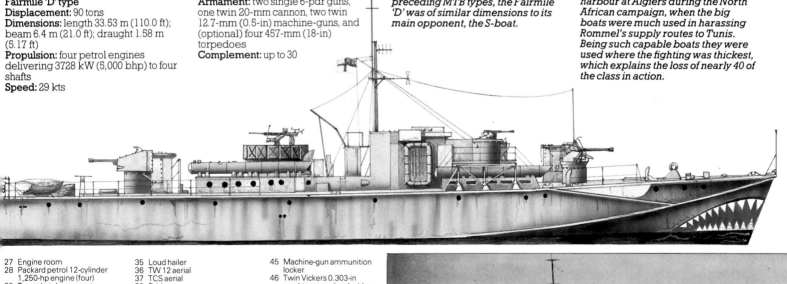

27 Engine room
28 Packard petrol 12-cylinder 1,250-hp engine (four)
29 Torpedo tube support frame
30 Work benches
31 Platform
32 Compass platform
33 Mast
34 Radar Type 291 or 242
35 Loud hailer
36 TW 12 aerial
37 TCS aerial
38 Bridge
39 Wheel house
40 Radar office
41 Pattern 23 liferaft
42 Fresh water tank (five)
43 Windscreen
44 Wind deflector
45 Machine-gun ammunition locker
46 Twin Vickers 0.303-in machine-guns (each side of bridge)
47 Power mounting
48 2-in rocket flares
49 Catwalk
50 Oilskin locker
51 Mast aerial
52 Open six-pdr Mk VII
53 Wardroom
54 Outer hull frames to hard chine hull
55 Lobby
56 CO's cabin
57 Forward magazine/shell room
58 Recessed scoop in hull
59 Type 715A hydrophone
60 Pitometer log
61 Stem eye
62 Crew's WC
63 Forepeak
64 Waterline
65 Electric heater
66 Aft machine stores
67 Anchor windlass
68 Explosion chamber to torpedo tube

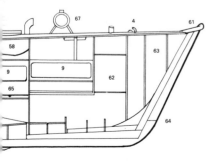

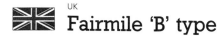

Fairmile 'B' type

One of the most versatile types of warship ever to see service, the **Fairmile 'B" type** motor launch (ML) was also one of the most numerous, some 670 being built in all between 1940 and 1944. The lines, in contrast with those of the 'A' type, were of a seakindly round-bilge form and were of Admiralty design, being turned over to Fairmile for the preparation of constructional drawings to suit a mass production programme. A large number of yards were involved in the construction, ranging in the UK from Sheerness Royal Naval Dockyard to Southampton Steam Joinery, and all over the Commonwealth from Vancouver Shipyard to the Anglo-American Nile Tourist Company at Cairo.

The initial requirement was for a triple-screwed craft, but the Hall Scott petrol engines specified were in short supply and only two were ever fitted, incurring a speed penalty of 4 to 5 kts. Their legend armament was a 3-pdr gun, two 7.7-mm (0.303-in) Lewis guns and a dozen depth charges (supported by an asdic set) but in practice they took a bewildering variety of fits. Torpedo tubes were removed from the Lease-Lend flush-deck destroyers and fitted to some, making them the world's only 20-kt MTBs, a measure of the desperate stop gaps adopted in 1940. They served as gunboats, air-sea rescue boats, AS patrol boats, inshore magnetic and acoustic minesweepers, smokelayers, hospital boats and convoy escorts, for which duty they sailed

on their own bottoms to the West Indies, West Africa and the Mediterranean. Hulls were supplied with standard fittings to allow rapid change of armament or the shipping of auxiliary fuel tanks.

Probably the best-known involvement of MLs in an operation was that of 16 in the raid on St Nazaire in March 1942, the situation of the port inside a well-defended estuary demanding shoal-draught vessels. In fighting their way both in and out, landing and recovering the commandos they carried, 12 were destroyed, some needing to be scuttled during the retirement for damage received.

Specification
Fairmile 'B' type
Displacement: 67 to 85 tons
Dimensions: length 34.14 m (112.0 ft); beam 5.56 m (18.25 ft); draught 1.52 m (5.0 ft)
Propulsion: two petrol engines delivering 895 kW (1,200 bhp) to two shafts
Speed: 20 kts
Endurance: 1112 km (691 miles) at 20 kts
Armament: (as designed) one 3-pdr gun, two 7.7-mm (0.303-in) machine-guns, and depth charges
Complement: 16

It was perhaps inevitable that such a versatile class built in some numbers would see considerable variation in weapon fit.

Above: ML 136 is seen on patrol off the Scottish coast early in her career. Armed with a Hotchkiss 3-pdr forward and two twin Lewis guns abaft the funnel, the class had room for more weaponry, and indeed six of the usual fit of 12 depth charges can be seen at the stern.

Harbour Defence Motor Launch

Far removed from the 'mile-a-minute navy' image of the coastal forces, so beloved of the popular press, was the **Harbour Defence Motor Launch (HDML)**, really a smaller 12-kt version of the Fairmile 'B' type. It was a general-purpose utility craft whose defined employment demanded only modest performance and endurance; should such craft be required for foreign service they were to be shipped as deck cargo. War, as ever, changed all that.

It was widely assumed before World War II that the immediate approaches to ports would, somehow, be infested with submarines and it was in ASW that the craft was generally planned to be used. They were equipped with a small asdic (sonar) set and eight depth charges, though the combination of little or no live practice allied to immense enthusiasm, shallow water and low speed suggests that the HDML would have been at greater hazard than a U-boat!

For the low propulsive powers required, small diesels did exist from British manufacturers, and a boat's maximum speed varied according to which type she had fitted. The HDMLs were double-planked on bent frames,

which required a higher level of craftsmanship in construction than did the Fairmiles. Some had to make do with inferior timber as a result of shortages, and were consequently short-lived. Despite their greater complexity they were built widely, not only in the UK but also in the USA and all over the Commonwealth. Pendants ran from 1001 to 1600 but it is by no means certain that all of these were actually issued. They were lovely craft to handle, seakindly and responsive with their double rudders. Employed in large numbers in every theatre, they travelled on their own bottoms as far afield as Iceland. One flotilla, required for use in the West Indies, was fitted with temporary sailing rig to assist fuel economy on the long transatlantic leg; though sailing was demonstrably feasible, the craft were re-allocated to the North African landing forces. They worked also as inshore minesweepers, despatch boats and (radar-fitted) as navigation markers for major amphibious operations.

Specification
Harbour Defence Motor Launch
Displacement: 54 tons

Dimensions: length 21.95 m (72.0 ft); beam 4.82 m (15.83 ft); draught 1.68 m (5.5 ft)
Propulsion: two diesels delivering 239 kW (320 bhp) to two shafts
Speed: 12 kts
Endurance: not known
Armament: one 3-pdr gun, one 20-mm cannon, and two 7.7-mm (0.303-in)

HDML 1383 leaves Harwich harbour past HMS Curzon (formerly the US destroyer escort DE-84). This example is armed with a 20-mm Oerlikon fore and aft and twin Lewis guns on each side of the bridge.

machine-guns
Complement: 10

Steam Gun Boat

UK

Developed in parallel with the Fairmile 'D's type was the **Steam Gun Boat (SGB)**, a type which at over 44-m (144.4-ft) length was viewed as virtual 'Queen Marys' by the coastal forces. The first of class commenced trials in November 1941, some three months ahead of the first 'D' type. The concept existed at all only as a typically British solution to a problem that should not have existed in the first place, i.e. the lack of a suitable indigenous small diesel engine. Steam plant had the advantage of quietness but, even with the most compact twin-screw plant drawing steam from a single boiler, it demanded a large hull which while having the disadvantage of being a larger target was a positive factor for seakeeping, in which the E-boat was acknowledged to be excellent.

Wooden hulls of this size were not feasible for mass production and steel was used. Unfortunately this meant that both hulls and machinery were now beyond the scope of the small yards engaged in the rapid expansion of the coastal forces, and the SGB thus competed for berths in yards hard put to produce urgently required convoy escorts. Of the 60 planned, therefore, it is not surprising that only nine were ordered, and of these but seven completed, in 1941-2.

In practice the steam plant proved complex and vulnerable, with initial troubles concentrated on insufficient energy being delivered by the boiler and heavily-cavitating propellers. Even when these problems were cured, fuel consumption remained heavy, with the added disadvantage that where a petrol-engined boat could start from cold and get away immediately, an SGB had to remain in steam, using a considerable amount of fuel and man hours in the process.

In action, however, the E-boat commanders respected the SGBs only a little less than destroyers, as they could pounce unexpectedly and hold their speed in a seaway. They proved excessively vulnerable to action damage in the machinery spaces, and the necessary addition of 18-mm (0.7-in) protective plate added much weight. More armament and crew increased displacement further and service speed was eventually reduced to only 30 kts.

Specification
Steam Gun Boat
Displacement: 165 tons
Dimensions: length 44.42 m (145.75 ft); beam 6.1 m (20.0 ft); draught 1.68 m (5.5 ft)
Propulsion: two sets of geared steam turbines delivering 5965 kW (8,000 shp) to two shafts
Speed: 35 kts
Endurance: not known
Armament: (final arrangement) one 76.2-mm (3-in) gun, two single 6-pdr guns, and two twin 20-mm cannon
Complement: 27

Veritable battleships of the coastal forces, the Steam Gun Boats were fast and heavily-armed vessels, although vulnerable to damage in the machinery rooms. Nonetheless, they were warily respected by their opponents across the North Sea.

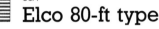

Elco 80-ft type

USA

During World War I the Electric Boat Company (Elco) had built a large number of small craft for the US Navy, but had lost design continuity with the navy's post-war lack of interest. When an official competition was announced in the late 1930s, therefore, Elco acquired from the British Power Boat Company a state-of-the-art European boat in a 21.34-m (70-ft) private venture, armed with four 457-mm (18-in) torpedoes. Elco succeeded in getting the US Navy not only to purchase the boat but also to order 23 more based on the design, 12 of them fitted with depth charges rather than torpedoes. The PT versions began to enter service in November 1940. They were viewed as experimental and, though satisfactory, it was recommended that further boats incorporate standard Packard petrol engines and 533-mm (21-in) torpedo tubes. This necessitated an increase in length to 23.47 m (77 ft). Five were thus constructed for the competition in 1941, and the 70-footers were transferred to the UK under Lend-Lease terms.

In the play-off the Elco boats did well, returning high speeds with good manoeuvrability. On the other hand, they slammed worse than the others and suffered minor structural failures that required design modification. Extra length was also recommended for improved seaworthiness and habitability; as the specification put the maximum at 25 m (82 ft), Elco went to 24.38 m (80-ft). By then the USA was at war and Elco had already constructed four squadrons of 77-footers which still carried the non-preferred 457-mm (18-in) torpedoes. All told, 358 Elco 80-footers were constructed, the three Packard engines giving them an edge in speed over their similarly-powered Higgins running mates. Of the two, the Elco was the preferred design but suffered as a result of its extra reserve displacement, resulting from its

length, being bought up by additional equipment. This was partially offset by the Packard engine being progressively uprated in power.

Specification
Elco 80-ft type
Displacement: 38 tons
Dimensions: length 24.38 m (80.0 ft); beam 6.32 m (20.75 ft); draught 1.52 m (5.0 ft)

A 1944 experiment saw an Elco boat painted in this startling dazzle scheme.

Elco PT Boats were expanded versions of the original Hall-Scott design, with room for four torpedoes and a wide variety of guns.

Propulsion: three petrol engines delivering 3020 kW (4,050 bhp) to three shafts
Speed: 40 kts
Endurance: not known
Armament: (typical) four 533-mm (21-in) torpedoes, one 40-mm gun, one 20-mm cannon, and four 12.7-mm (0.5-in) machine-guns
Complement: 14

Higgins 78-ft type

The **Higgins 78-ft** type had its origins in a series of trials held by the US Navy in 1941 to determine the boat best suited to its purposes from a series of contenders. Higgins entered a 25.15-m (82.5-ft) private-venture boat derived from an earlier Sparkman and Stevens design. Six boats of various types were exhaustively evaluated in a range of conditions. From this experience a short list of three was selected for mass production against a light specification. One of these was the Higgins, which was to be 'suitably reduced in size to carry such ordnance loads as are required by our Navy'.

Those boats chosen were of hard-chine wooden construction and propelled by three Packard petrol engines, which had emerged as the most reliable and economical for the job. Each would carry four 533-mm (21-in) torpedoes and four 12.7-mm (0.5-in) machine-guns. Fully laden they would be capable of 40 kts for one hour. From virtually nothing the Americans created, in a space of three years, the nucleus of a powerful force of PT boats. Two dozen (two squadrons) of Higgins' boats, now 23.77 m (78 ft) in length, were initially ordered, but these did not start to enter service until the second half of 1942 and, of these, six were transferred to the British and four to the Soviets. Eventually over 200 were constructed which, with the Elco 24.38-m (80-ft) type, were to be the US Navy's standard choices. The third type successful in the pre-war play-off, the Huckins 23.77-m (78-ft) type, was used in the training role.

Service speed, always heavily dependent upon weather conditions, de-teriorated further as more and more armament and equipment were added. To assist matters a new light-weight torpedo was developed. This had a heavier warhead and a higher speed, but only a short range. It could be launched by dropping gear, obviating the need for torpedo tubes. Gun armament varied considerably and unofficially. Most later craft had a 40-mm weapon aft, a 20-mm cannon forward and up to five 12.7-mm (0.5-in) machine-guns. Some landed their torpedoes in favour of more guns for use in an MGB role against the Japanese.

Specification
Higgins 78-ft type
Displacement: 35 tons
Dimensions: length 23.77 m (78.0 ft); beam 6.32 m (20.75 ft); draught 1.52 m (5.0 ft)
Propulsion: three petrol engines delivering 3356 kW (4,500 bhp) to three shafts
Speed: 41 kts
Endurance: 555 km (345 miles) at 41 kts
Armament: four 533-mm (21-in) torpedoes, one 40-mm gun, and two 20-mm cannon
Complement: 17

The Higgins boats (along with the Elco design) bore the brunt of the US PT boat war. At 78 ft (23.77 m), it was also large enough to carry four torpedoes although some were landed later in the war in favour of more guns.

While the activities of the PT boats in the Solomons and the Philippines are well known, it should be remembered that they contributed to campaigns as far apart as those of the Adriatic or (as seen here) around the Aleutians in the Northern Pacific.

Initially the secondary armament on PTBs was limited to 12.7-mm (0.5-in) MGs, but before long heavier weapons, such as stern-mounted 20-mm cannon, began to be fitted.

Assault Ships

The ability of the Allies to wage successful amphibious warfare contributed in no small measure to the eventual downfall of the Axis powers. Development was fast, when it became clear that Allied success would require a cross-Channel assault, and the very nature of the Pacific war demanded mastery of the new form of battle.

Although in the late 1930s war in Europe was viewed by the services as only a matter of time, its likely form was difficult to predict, so available rearmament resources were expanded in generally conventional directions. The total subjugation by the Axis powers of Europe, and later the Far East, changed the situation completely. Both areas would need to be reconquered through the carriage by Allies of vast forces over very considerable distances. Established ports, even if they were available, would be either heavily defended or destroyed. Obviously it became increasingly desirable to put everything 'over the beach' in order to retain the initiative.

Only the most basic consideration had been paid officially to landing craft before the war but from the time of Dunkirk onwards the British developed ideas rapidly, passing them to the Americans for implementation under the Lend-Lease agreement. By the time that the USA became embroiled in the war, in December 1941, it had already accumulated much experience upon which to build.

The vast armada of amphibious warfare vessels that was ultimately produced was, for the most part, built to standards that

A Landing Craft Tank (LCT) putting vehicles ashore in Normandy. The Allies developed a vast armada of these amphibious warfare vessels.

were totally unacceptable before the war, but which held together and displayed a high degree of innovation. The vessels fell into several major groups:

(a) ships for carrying the infantry themselves, the Landing Ships, Infantry or LSIs, which differed from ordinary troop ships in also carrying their own assault landing craft;

(b) ships, mainly Landing Ships, Dock or LSDs, for carrying smaller craft in numbers, these craft being of insufficient size in which to make protracted sea crossings;

(c) landing craft, which were smaller than landing ships, for putting vehicles, equipment and personnel directly on the beach, where categories (a) and

(b) needed to anchor offshore; and

(d) miscellaneous vessels, which covered a range as diverse as the vital Headquarters Ships to the humble, but equally vital, Landing Barge, Kitchen.

This motley armada of 'floating bootboxes' did not, of itself, win the war, but the war could not have been won without it.

Landing Ship, Headquarters (LSH) and Amphibious Force Flagship (AGC)

Amphibious operations are exceedingly complex and, despite meticulous planning and allowance for apparently adequate contingencies, everything that can go wrong will try to go wrong. Headquarters ships were devised to lie off the beach and control operations until a proper HQ could be set up ashore, after which they could probably stay on as long as there was any requirement for naval support. Early practice was to employ a major warship in the role, but suitably equipped ships were rare, never had sufficient accommodation and were liable to be called out to do some fighting. Not until 1942 were dedicated ships introduced: medium-sized merchantmen (with plenty of space for conversion) were selected, and these were instantly recognizable by the variety of communications antennas that were added (and, it was rumoured, by the wine bottles floating around them). These ships handled a tremendous volume of signal traffic, the embarked staff being able to make rapid decisions on the spot to counter any problem as it arose. On occasion the **Landing Ship, Headquarters (LSH)** even acted as an aircraft-direction ship, a complex-enough task in itself and usually undertaken by a specialist **Landing Ship, Fighter Direction (LSF)**, with which it worked closely. For major landings, more than one LSH might be required and, in any case, a replacement was a wise precaution, particularly when the enemy recognized their importance and singled them out for attention.

HMS *Bulolo* was a typical British conversion, starting as an armed merchant cruiser before doing a spell as an LSI. As an LSH she saw service at Algiers, in the Levant, at Anzio and, finally, at Normandy, where she was damaged by bombing. Other large British conversions were HMS *Hilary, Largs* and *Lothian*. The American equivalent was the **Amphibious Force Flagship (AGC)**, converted C2 and C3 hulls, the former going to 17 units. For smaller operations the British modified eight assorted frigates and gunboats, the Americans preferring the more suitable long-endurance coastguard cutters which are available for regular naval use in time of war.

Specification
HMS *Bulolo*
Displacement: 9,110 tons standard

Dimensions: length 125.7 m (412.5 ft); beam 17.8 m (58.25 ft); draught 6.6 m (21.7 ft)
Propulsion: two diesels delivering 4698 kW (6,300 bhp) to two shafts
Performance: maximum speed 15 kts
Armament: two twin 102-mm (4-in) AA, five single 40-mm AA and 14 single 20-mm AA guns
Capacity: as an LSI(L) six LCP(L)s and 258 troops
Complement: 264

HMS Hilary, *built in 1931 as a cargo-liner, spent the first part of the war as an ocean boarding vessel. She was converted into a headquarters ship in 1943, being fitted with the complex communication systems required to control an amphibious landing.*

Formerly a liner, the USS Ancon *was taken over in 1942 as a transport, but soon became an amphibious force flagship with the US Navy. She was used as an HQ ship at the Sicily landings, Salerno, Normandy and Okinawa, and was present at the Japanese surrender at Tokyo Bay.*

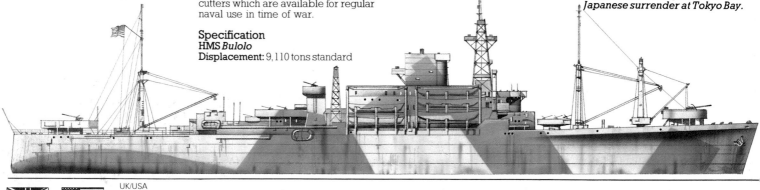

Landing Ship, Infantry (Large) (LSI(L))/Transport (AP)

The **Landing Ship, Infantry (Large)** or **LSI(L)** was used for the delivery of troops over distances too great for their embarkation and support in landing craft. Many were little more than basic conversions of passenger or cargo/passenger liners, but others were rebuilt for more specific purposes. Such were the trio of Glen Line ships (**Glenearn, Glengyle** and **Glenroy**) converted in 1941 following initial service as stores carriers and commando ships. These were new and powerful ships built for the Blue Funnel/Glen/Shire services in the Far East, and the conversion involved much subdivision of the cargo spaces into accommodation for upwards of 1,300 personnel. Sleeping was in the traditional hammock, but mess spaces, latrines, wash places, and general stowage had to be created, together with space for such heavy equipment as had also to be put ashore. Extra sets of davits were installed for the stowage of 12 LCAs, and two heavier LCMs were also carried on deck, handled by the ship's derricks. The ships were well armed, commensurate with their high value, originally with eight 2-pdr pompoms but later with six 102-mm (4-in) AA guns, four 2-pdr guns and up to eight 20-mm Oerlikons. Despite heavy involvement, for instance in Crete, Syria, Malta and Dieppe, none of the three was lost. There were three further sisters; of these *Breconshire* of the Shire Line became briefly famous in her runs to Malta at the height of the siege until she was finally sunk. *Glengarry* was a fourth Glen ship, building in Denmark

The Empire Arquebus, *built in the USA under the massive US maritime commission programme and supplied under Lend-Lease. It was similar in many respects to the US Navy's 'General' and 'Admiral' classes, and like them was used as an infantry transport.*

when the Germans invaded. She was converted to the auxiliary cruiser *Meersburg* and also survived the war. Last was the Blue Funneler *Telemachus*, converted to the escort carrier HMS *Activity*.

AP was the general category for American troop transports, modified to **APA** for the more specialist **Attack Transport** category. Most were basic conversions but notable classes designed to purpose were the 11,500-ton 'Generals' and 12,700-ton 'Admirals' with steam turbine or turbo-electric propulsion for about 20 kts. They went on to give very useful service after World War II.

Specification
'Glen' class
Displacement: 9,800 tons gross
Dimensions: length 155.7 m (511 ft); beam 20.3 m (66.7 ft); draught 8.5 m (27.75 ft)
Propulsion: two diesels delivering 8948 kW (12,000 bhp) to two shafts
Performance: maximum speed 18 kts; range 22250 km (13,825 miles) at 14 kts
Armament: three twin 102-mm (4-in) AA four single or twin 2-pdr AA, and eight to 12 single 20-mm AA guns
Capacity: two LCMs, 12 LCAs, 232 landing craft crew and 1,087 troops
Complement: 291

Below: Llangibby Castle *was typical of the many mercantile vessels fitted as infantry landing ships for the major European landing operations from 1942 to 1944. Most only took part in one such landing, and were then returned to trade.*

Above: Requisitioned and commissioned in 1939, HMS Glenearn *and her sisters could each carry over 1,000 troops. Their heavy armament made them amongst the most battleworthy of all British LSIs.*

UK/USA
Landing Ship, Infantry (Medium) (LSI(M))/High-Speed Transport (APD)

Cross-channel packets, though short-legged, were fast and showed great potential for conversion in World War I. So it was in World War II, with the bonus that the German invasion of the Low Countries provided many fine Belgian and Dutch ships in addition to British and French vessels. *Queen Emma (Koningen Emma)* and *Princess Beatrix (Prinses Beatrix)* had been completed by Dutch yards only months before hostilities and, being motorships, had the advantage of small machinery spaces and great economy. They were converted for small-scale assault as **Landing Ship, Infantry (Medium)** or **LSI(M)**, their large accommodation areas being ideal for some 600 complement: crew, landing craft crews and army personnel. The troops were put ashore by six LCAs, stowed under davits. Two LCMs were also davit-carried but the machinery's 39-ton capacity limited their use, the craft having to be pre-loaded with vehicles by crane. Both ships, together with several smaller ex-Belgian vessels, carried the bulk of the force on the Dieppe raid, all returning safely.

Not strictly similar in designed function but often used as such were the American **APD**, or **High-Speed Transport** ships. The first group comprised 32 very-similar flushdecked destroyers (the venerable 'four-pipers'). By stripping out the forward machinery spaces, accommodation was created for about 150 troops, though 200 could be carried over short hauls.

Even with only half power remaining, they were still good for 23 kts. Topside, the two forward funnels and all torpedo tubes were landed and four LCP(R) added in davits. These 11-m (36-ft) craft could each land up to 36 troops. Each weighed about 6 tonnes in davits, and must have posed a stability problem to such narrow-gutted ships. These destroyer conversions were followed by nearly 10 rebuildings of destroyer escorts (DE) with very similar size and speed. These carried four LCVPs, nested in pairs under two distinctive gantry davits. Up to 150 troops, four carts, four 75-mm (2.95-in) pack howitzers and up to 255 m³ (9,000 cu ft) of stores, ammunition and fuel could be carried, the ships being equipped with a pair of cargo booms (derricks) for their handling. The APD proved extremely useful in the island war of the western Pacific and, having retained her surface armament, was comparatively independent.

Specification
'Queen Emma' class
Displacement: 4,140 tons gross
Dimensions: length 115.8 m (380 ft); beam 14.4 m (47.25 ft); draught 4.6 m (15 ft)

Propulsion: two diesels delivering 9694 kW (13,000 bhp) to two shafts
Performance: maximum speed 22 kts; range 12979 km (8,065 miles) at 13 kts
Armament: two single 76-mm (3-in) AA, two single 2-pdr AA and six single 20-mm AA guns
Capacity: two LCMs, six LCAs, 60 landing craft crew and 372 troops
Complement: 167

HMS Princess Beatrix, *in common with most other Channel packets, was relatively fast but short-ranged. This was no real handicap on operations to the coast of Europe, and with her sister and several smaller ex-Belgian ferries she took part in the Dieppe raid.*

The long and varied careers of the US Navy's flush-decked four-stackers saw a number converted to fast transports for use in the island-hopping campaigns of the Pacific War. Eight were lost, but only one of the 94 succeeding converted destroyer-escorts went down.

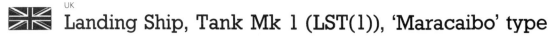

Landing Ship, Tank Mk 1 (LST(1)), 'Maracaibo' type

As early as 1940 Winston Churchill's energetic mind was turned to matters offensive and he perceived the need for a vessel able to put armour and vehicles ashore 'over beaches' and 'anywhere in the world'. Ultimately ships could be designed and built for this revolutionary purpose but, at the time, only conversions were feasible to prove the concept. The problem was a nice one, for a beach of a gradient kind enough for the operation would have shallow approaches. This required a ship large enough both for ocean passage and to accommodate the designed load, yet of shallow enough draught to put her bows ashore. Even then it was likely that a considerable width of water would still exist between herself and the beach, so a bow door together with ramps of considerable length were needed.

The ships identified for conversion were the *Bachaquero*, *Misoa* and *Tasajera*, launched in 1937-8 and used in British operations to shuttle oil from Venezuela's shallow Lake Maracaibo and, therefore, designed with a mean draught of only 3 m (9.8 ft). Their original design was that of a turret-decker, the weather decks at the side flanking a deep centreline trunk. As the ships' length:beam ratio was only about 6:1, they had plenty of deck space once the side decks were plated over. The drawback was that

the resultant tank deck was well above the waterline, making even more acute the design of the bow ramp. In the event, the already bluff bows were modified with a flat rectangular door which hinged from its lower edge. This allowed a two-stage ramp to be run down an internal slope, under the control of several winches. The first 21.6-m (71-ft) long stage supported a 16.5-m (54-ft) extension. While these permitted the dry landing of a 30-ton tank, they were very greedy of internal space. The 'Maracaibos' can claim to be the first LSTs and though far from ideal, particularly in terms of speed, these **Landing Ship, Tank Mk 1** or **LST(1)** vessels demonstrated the practicality of working on and off a beach in a controlled manner, the value of good subdivision and the need for well-distributed ballast space. Interestingly, even the eventual 'last word' in LSTs never claimed to be able to work more than 17 per cent of the world's beaches, with the American LCAC air cushion landing craft of 1985 not extending this beyond a reported 70 per cent.

Specification
LST(1), 'Maracaibo' type
Displacement: 4,890 tons gross
Dimensions: length 116.5 m (382.5 ft); beam 19.5 m (64 ft); draught 4.6 m (15 ft); beaching draught 1.3 m (4.25 ft)

forward
Propulsion: two sets of reciprocating steam engines delivering 2237 kW (3,000 ihp) to two shafts
Performance: maximum speed 11 kts; range 12045 km (7,845 miles) at 10 kts
Armament: two 102-mm (4-in) smoke mortars, and four single 2-pdr AA and six single 20-mm AA guns

The very first tank landing ship was HMS Bachaquero, *a converted 'Maracaibo' type tanker. She is seen in Alexandria in March 1943.*

Capacity: two LCMs, 20 25-ton tanks and 207 supernumeries
Complement: 98
(NB: the *Tasajera* was slightly smaller)

Landing Ship, Tank Mk 1 (LST(1)), 'Boxer' type

The 'Maracaibo' LST conversions were never viewed as more than useful prototype exercises and their 10-kt speed was widely criticized as insufficient for possible sea passages to a distant assault area. Although a higher speed directly conflicted as a design requirement with the needs for shallow draught, bow doors and large capacity, the first purpose-built LSTs, the trio of **Landing Ship, Tank Mk 1 'Boxer' type** for the Royal Navy, were capable of 17 kts. As it turned out, this speed was unrealistically high but the specification, it should be remembered, had been formulated without the benefit of any previous experience, the whole concept being novel. A bow door and ramp were regarded as essential and, as a ship-type bow was necessary, a pair of vertically-hinged doors was adopted (a 'first' for Harland & Wolff and later used on many post-war vehicular ferries) behind which a set of transverse watertight doors was placed instead of a conventional bulkhead. Thirteen 40-ton or 20 25-ton tanks could be stowed on the tank deck, which also formed the freeboard deck, close above the waterline and avoiding any hoisting or negotiation of steep ramps. Much space on this deck was lost, firstly because of the large inboard-stowing ramp that was required to span a distance of about 30 m (100 ft) to the shore and, secondly, through a deliberate reduction in area to reduce free-surface effects in the event of flooding. The resulting side subdivision allowed steam plant to be fitted, thus providing the relatively high power required. This machinery was placed amidships, with the uptakes and funnel offset to starboard to allow clear passage below. On the weather deck up to 27 loaded 3-ton lorries could be stowed

HMS Boxer, *seen soon after her completion in early 1943, was the first vessel designed from the outset as an LST. A complex design, the three completed ships were beaten into service by the LST(2).*

via a vehicle lift from the tank deck. A hatch was provided abaft the superstructure, serviced by a 40-ton crane, to offload vehicles in the event of damage to the bow door. The complexity of the 'Boxers' (*Boxer*, *Bruizer* and *Thruster*) meant that the first was not ready until early in 1943, by which time the better features had been incorporated in the far superior LST(2s). The speed and endurance of the 'Boxers' thus saw them suitable for conversion to LSFs, with four tall masts covered in antennae for the purpose of aircraft direction.

Specification
LST(1), 'Boxer' type
Displacement: 3,615 tons standard and 5,410 tons full load
Dimensions: length 121.9 m (400 ft); beam 14.9 m (49 ft); draught 1.7/4.4 m (5.5/14.5 ft)
Propulsion: two sets of geared steam turbines delivering 5220 kW (7,000 shp) to two shafts
Performance: maximum speed 17 kts; range 14830 km (9,215 miles) at 14 kts
Armament: two 102-mm (4-in) smoke mortars, and four single 2-pdr AA and eight single 20-mm AA guns
Capacity: 20 medium or 13 heavy tanks, 27 loaded lorries and 193 troops
Complement: 169

By the time of the invasion of Normandy, the three 'Boxers' had been converted to LSF (Landing Ship Fighter-direction).

Landing Ship, Tank Mk 2 (LST(2))

Even while the three LST(1)s were still in the early stages of construction, before Pearl Harbor and the USA's entry into the war, it was realized that a great number of large landing craft would ultimately be required for the assault that would have to precede the reconquest of Europe. Only construction in the USA under Lend-Lease terms could produce these numbers, but the resulting ships would need to be capable of crossing the Atlantic. The conception of the **Landing Ship, Tank Mk 2** or LST(2), despite frequent US claims to the contrary, was British and was worked out in detail by a British mission in Washington in the winter of 1941-2, the first order being placed in February 1942.

The major differences from the LST(1) were the adoption of an engines-aft layout, a smaller length:beam ratio and an acceptance of a 10-kt maximum speed. A suitable locomotive-type diesel was available in the USA. Two of these developed sufficient power while having only a limited height, enabling the tank deck to be continued over the machinery space, and thus run the full useful length of the ship. By adopting a bluff, beamy form, the loaded draught was considerably reduced; for sea passages the ship could be ballasted down and, for beaching, trimmed by the stern to give a very small forward draught. This, in turn, enabled the vessel to ground much closer to the tideline and only a short ramp was fitted inside the vertically-hinged bow doors. On beaches with the minimum declivity of 1 in 50 this still meant a lot of water for vehicles to traverse, and research was started into their waterproofing. Only with the adoption in 1943 of sectioned pontoons for the rapid construction of ship-to-shore causeways was the problem really solved.

A spacious upper deck, encumbered only with the exhaust vents from the tank deck, was served both by hatch and elevator (or ramp in later versions). It could be used for stowage of lighter vehicles or, if required, an LCT(5) or LCT(6). Heavy gravity davits could accommodate up to six LCVPs for use as lifeboats or general utility craft. The double-skin hull flanking the tank deck gave accommodation to up to 163 army personnel.

The LST(2) became the standard assault ship and played an indispensable role in all theatres, 1,077 of these ships being built between 1942 and 1945.

Specification
LST(2)
Displacement: 1,490 tons standard and 2,160 tons full load
Dimensions: length 100 m (328 ft); beam 15.2 m (50 ft); draught 0.9/2.9 m (3.1/9.5 ft)
Propulsion: two diesels delivering 1341 kW (1,800 bhp) to two shafts
Performance: maximum speed 10.5 kts; range 11120 km (6,910 miles) at 9 kts
Armament: one 127-mm (5-in) or 76-mm (3-in) DP guns, which was usually omitted when the full secondary battery of two twin and four single 40-mm AA and six to 12 single 20-mm AA guns was carried
Capacity: two LCVPs, 18 heavy tanks, 27 lorries or one LCT(5), and 163 troops
Complement: 211

Above: LST 216 after conversion to fighter-director. Offices built into the tank deck included those for communications, fighter control and radar plotting, as well as workshops and stores.

Below: Unloading equipment from LST(2)s at the Allied beach-head at Anzio. Such scenes were to become common in every maritime theatre of the war, with the ubiquitous LST continually coming and going.

Landing Ship, Tank Mk 3 (LST(3))

So well did the LST(2) suit the needs of the Americans that the UK had difficulty in being allocated suitable numbers from the construction programme that it had itself initiated. Eighty were needed, and it was decided to improvise on the LST(2) design, with 45 to be built in the UK and the remainder in Canada. There were two major problems.

Firstly, the locomotive diesels used by the Americans were fully committed and, as no alternative existed for the British, they had to specify the simple steam reciprocating engines used in the frigate programme. As amphibious warfare ships were now commanding a priority as high (or even higher) than frigates, this caused little headache, but the machinery and its boilers were bulky and heavy, both intruding into the tank deck space and causing the ship to ground by the stern rather than the bows on beaches of minimum declivity.

The second problem lay in construction techniques for as British and Canadian yards had, as yet, no experience in large-scale welding, riveting was necessary. Even though a hard chine was adopted to simplify construction, the **Landing Ship, Tank Mk 3** or **LST(3)** took longer to build, and the resulting low-efficiency hull was disappointingly slow. Though significantly longer to accommodate the steam machinery and disposing of over three times the power, the LCT(3) was only 3 kts faster than the diesel-driven American LST(2)s. No camber was included on the weather deck; this was a counter-productive shortcut as loose water was very loathe to disperse.

With their deeper draught, the LST(3)s tended to ground farther from the dry beach and a double-section bow ramp was incorporated as part-compensation, although floating causeway sections were again a successful answer. The LST(3)s were very well built, having LCAs under their gravity davits and the capacity to stow up to seven LCM(7)s on the upper deck. These were offloaded via a 30-ton SWL derrick set on a portside king-post forward of the bridge. A 15-ton derrick was stepped on the other post. Though a few of the programme were eventually cancelled, the 44 British and 28 Canadian ships completed gave 20 years and more of post-war service.

Specification
LST(3)
Displacement: 2,255 tons standard and 3,065 tons full load
Dimensions: length 105.4 m (345.75 ft); beam 16.5 m (54 ft); draught 1.4/3.5 m (4.5/11.5 ft)
Propulsion: two sets of reciprocating steam engines delivering 4101 kW (5,500 ihp) to two shafts
Performance: maximum speed 13.5 kts; range 14822 km (9,210 miles) at 11 kts
Armament: two twin 40-mm AA and six single 20-mm AA guns
Capacity: five LCAs, 15 heavy or 27 medium tanks, 14 lorries and 168 troops
Complement: 104

Landing Ship, Dock (LSD)

So many examples of the **Landing Ship, Dock (LSD)** and its derivatives have been constructed by the Americans during the last 40 years that one could be forgiven for assuming that the concept stemmed from the US Navy. In fact the draft was prepared in the UK as a carrier for the largest LCTs then envisaged. This was September 1941, when the sea-going LST had not yet been developed. The LCT was not regarded as sea-going yet, loaded, was far too heavy to be handled by the likes of the LSS or LSG, hence the idea of floating them in and out of a self-propelled floating dock. The draft was put to the Americans for completion and execution under the terms of Lend-Lease. Seven were requested but, in the event, the Americans completed another 20 to their own account. The 27 ships were launched between 1942 and 1946.

They were designed around a pontoon deck (or dockfloor) large enough to stow two LCTs. This was enclosed by the dock walls and a full-width stern gate pivoted at the lower edge. From the forward end of the dock well the craft was an orthodox ship. All were steam-propelled, the first eight having Uniflow reciprocating engines and the last seven conventional steam turbines. The latter were preferred as all machinery and boilers were sited below the pontoon deck and height was limited. Uptakes and funnels were sided to avoid impeding the clear dock space. A later addition was temporary decking spanning the dock for the stowage of motor vehicles and stores, which could be trans-shipped by crane.

In the event, the LSDs proved excessively stable and the sides below the deep waterline were flared-in, reducing also the amount of ballast necessary to trim the ship down. Though an apparently enormous volume was available for ballast space, it was scarcely adequate in practice. Flooding down usually took 1½ hours and pumping dry took 2½ hours, even at a pumping rate of 69650 litres (18,400 US gal) per minute. Initially dividing gates were provided on the pontoon deck, but the expected surge (or 'bath water effect') did not materialize. The LSD concept also provided the basis for today's RoRo cargo vessel.

Specification
LSD
Displacement: 4,270 tons standard and 7,950 tons full load
Dimensions: length 139.5 m (457.75 ft); beam 22.0 m (72.25 ft); draught 5.3 m (17.5 ft)
Propulsion: (LSD1-8) two sets of reciprocating steam engines delivering 8203 kW (11,000 ihp) to two shafts, or (others) two sets of geared steam turbines delivering 5593 kW (7,500 shp) to two shafts
Performance: maximum speed (LSD1-8) 17 kts or (others) 15.5 kts; range 14830 km (9,215 miles) at 15 kts
Armament: one 127-mm (5-in) or (British ships) 76-mm (3-in) DP, and six twin 40-mm AA or 16 single 20-mm AA guns
Capacity: two LCT(3)s or LCT(4)s, or three LCT(5)s, or 36 LCMs, landing craft crew (varying with landing craft carried) and 263 troops
Complement: 254

The Landing Ship, Dock was planned as a carrier for the largest LCTs, which in 1941 were still not sea-going. They had a pontoon deck big enough for two LCTs; here trucks are transferred from the LSD deck to a waiting LCT.

USS Belle Grove was the second vessel of the first class of US LSDs, and had Skinner Uniflow reciprocating engines which were replaced by steam turbines in subsequent classes. The wartime LSDs provided the basis for the Ro-Ro ships of today.

Landing Craft, Tank Mks 1 to 3 (LCT (1-3))

Landing craft, as opposed to landing ships, were not designed for extensive sea passages, their more limited performance being deliberately aimed at different operations. Little work had been done before World War II with respect to putting wheeled and tracked vehicles over a beach, simply because no application was then seen for it: Dunkirk and Churchill changed all that. With no previous experience as a basis, it was decided that a suitably-dimensioned craft could be built around the carriage of three 40-ton tanks, the largest then contemplated, being able to offload them in under 1 m (3.3 ft) of water on a 1 in 35 beach. **Landing Craft, Tank Mk 1** or **LCT(1)** that resulted was the first of its type anywhere and, despite its wayward course-keeping, proved remarkably sound. The reinforced tank deck was over and between heavily compartmented double skins which accommodated ballast and trim tanks, together with bunkers and stowage. Cargo was screened by high coamings on the inboard edges of the side decks; it was normally open to the sky, obviating the exhaust ventilation problems experienced by the larger ships, but could be covered with light tarpaulins spread over hatch beams. The single-element bow ramp was not particularly watertight and was backed by a pair of low watertight doors. Propulsion had to be by two of the readily available Hall-Scott petrol engines used on coastal craft but, nevertheless, achieved the required 10 kts. Most LCT(1)s were built (during 1940-1) in four sections, which could be broken down for shipment to distant parts.

Thirty LCT(1)s were built before the type was superseded by the **Landing Craft, Tank Mk 2** or **LCT(2)**. With only small increases in dimensions, these could accommodate two rows of smaller tanks and increase endurance from 1665 to 5000 km (1,035 to 3,110 miles).

After Dunkirk a requirement was issued for a craft able to land three 40-ton tanks in a metre of water on a beach with up to 2.8 per cent slope. The LCT(2)s seen above displaced 460 tons loaded and could carry up to seven 20-ton tanks.

Three engines were fitted, petrol or diesel as available. For the first time the design lent itself to construction by general steel fabricators, relieving the load on shipyards. To increase capacity yet further, a fifth midbody section was then inserted to create the **Landing Craft, Tank Mk 3** or **LCT(3)** with a length of 58.52 m (192 ft). These could carry five heavy or 11 medium tanks for very little extra draught and, despite reversion to twin-screw propulsion, were only marginally slower.

Specification
LCT(1)
Displacement: 226 tons light and 372 tons loaded

LCT(3)s were essentially LCT(2)s with a 9.75-m (32-ft) section added amidships, enabling them to accommodate up to five 40-ton or 11 30-ton tanks. Later units were fitted with petrol engines giving a maximum speed of 10 kts.

Dimensions: length 46.3 m (152 ft); beam 8.8 m (29 ft); draught 0.9/1.75 m (3/5.75 ft)
Propulsion: two petrol engines delivering 746 kW (1,000 hp) to two shafts
Performance: maximum speed 10 kts; range 1666 km (1,035 miles) at 10 kts
Armament: two single 2-pdr pompoms
Capacity: three heavy or six medium tanks
Complement: 12

Below: Only 30 LCT(1)s were constructed before the three-shaft LCT(2)s were introduced. Beside and underneath the tank deck, the double skin of the vessel was heavily compartmented into ballast and trim tanks plus bunkers and stowage.

Landing Craft, Tank Mk 4 (LCT(4))

While the LCT(1), (2) and (3) were admirable in concept, they were too deep-draughted to use on French beaches, which were found to have far shallower gradients than had been suspected. At the same time, larger numbers of craft were seen as necessary, each having greater capacity. In October 1941, therefore, a new version, the **Landing Craft, Tank Mk 4** or **LCT(4)** was put into production. Again, no shipyard was involved and, to achieve the lightest possible draught, scantlings were extremely flimsy and would never have met peacetime standards. Compared with the LCT(3), the new design was a little shorter but considerably beamier; propelled by the same diesel machinery it was, therefore, considerably slower. The tank deck was sized to accommodate six heavy tanks in two rows of three, or nine medium tanks in three rows. Deadweight tonnage was about 300 and, in the loaded condition, the craft could beach successfully on a 1 in 150 slope, putting wading vehicles down in the specified depth of only 76 cm (30 in) of water.

To simplify production, the 865 planned craft were initially specified without armament, but this was very soon added once they were completed. The side coamings were comparatively shallow so that the stowage space could not be covered, as in the earlier types and, more importantly, it lacked sufficient longitudinal stiffness. With the first craft entering service in the autumn of 1942, it was already realized that they would eventually be required to operate in the Far East, where sea passages would be expected of them. Extra stiffening was, therefore, incorporated by bringing the shell plating up to the height of the coaming, effectively creating a box section of maximum depth, using heavier plate where appropriate. These measures did nothing for their draught figures

but did enable them to proceed to the Indian Ocean on their own bottoms. Some were converted to **Landing Craft, Flak Mk 4** or **LCF(4)** by the addition of four 2-pdr pompoms and eight 20-mm Oerlikons, or **Landing Craft, Gun Mk 4** or **LCG(4)** with two 119-mm (4.7-in) guns from old destroyers and up to a dozen 20-mm weapons.

Specification
LCT(4)
Displacement: 200 tons light and 586 tons loaded (or 611 tons when stiffened)
Dimensions: length 57.1 m (187.25 ft); beam 11.8 m (38.7 ft); draught 1.1/1.4 m (3.5/4.7 ft)
Propulsion: two diesels delivering 686 kW (920 bhp) to two shafts
Performance: maximum speed 9 kts; range 2035 km (1,265 miles) at 8 kts
Armament: up to two single 20-mm AA guns
Capacity: six heavy or nine medium tanks
Complement: 12

Above: LCT(4)s were developed because the earlier LCTs were of too deep a draught for the French beaches on which the Allies intended to land.

Below: Compared to the LCT(3)s the LCT(4)s were beamier and a little shorter. Their shallow draught enabled them to beach on a 1 in 150 slope, putting vehicles ashore in less than a metre of water.

Landing Craft, Tank Mks 5 to 8 (LCT 5-8))

As World War II proceeded, it became apparent that the draught problem would inhibit the use of LSTs in some instances and the British proposed a short, beamy, drive-through craft (another new concept) that could either ferry the LSTs' vehicles ashore (a slow process for a landing) or act as a temporary bridge to link the large vessel to the beach. The result was the

Landing Craft, Tank Mk 5 or **LCT(5)**, which could either be transported in sections to a desired theatre and assembled afloat, or actually transported complete on an LST's upper deck and launched by simply sliding all 134 tons of it over the side. She was a slow short-haul craft and nearly 500 were built in the USA with a conventional layout before the **Landing Craft, Tank Mk 6** or **LCT(6)** was introduced on much the same dimensions but finally with the bridge on the starboard side to permit the earlier-proposed drive-through operation. Triple-screw propulsion suited the diesels available and improved the craft's handling somewhat.

Some LCT(5) and (6) vessels supplied to the British were subsequently lengthened by about 12 m (39.4 ft). At about this same time in 1943 the Americans designed their first large craft

from scratch, designated the **Landing Craft, Tank Mk 7** or **LCT(7)** for a time but then, as a blend of LCT and LST, known as an **LSM (Landing Ship, Medium)**. Though larger than an LCT(3), it had finer lines and a ship-type bow with vertically-hinged doors to be capable of ocean passages at 12 kts. As a result, its capacity was a reduced three heavy or five medium tanks and its draught increased. The LSM had a characteristically high tower of a bridge, set amidships on the starboard side, and enclosed accommodation for over 50 troops.

The LSM was not suitable for use by the British who, nevertheless, used the basic idea for their final **Landing Craft, Tank Mk 8** or **LCT Mk 8**. At 68.6 m (225 ft) this was limited to eight medium tanks. The production of LCT(8)s with their four-diesel, two-shaft drive and improved facilities could be undertaken only because of the relaxing of supply problems near the war's end.

Specification
LCT(7) or LSM
Displacement: 513 tons light and 900 tons full load
Dimensions: length 62.0 m (203.5 ft); beam 10.4 m (34 ft); draught 1.0/2.1 m (3.4/6.9 ft)
Propulsion: two diesels delivering 2088 kW (2,800 bhp) to two shafts
Performance: maximum speed 13 kts; range 6486 km (4,030 miles) at 11 kts
Armament: two single 40-mm AA and six single 20-mm AA guns
Capacity: three heavy or five medium tanks, and 54 troops
Complement: 52

A short, beamy, drive-through craft, the LCT(6) series was designed to ferry vehicles ashore from an LST if her draught was too great for the beach or to make an improvised bridge for the same purpose.

Landing Craft, Infantry Large and Small (LCI(L) and (S))

First described as a **Giant Raiding Craft**, the **Landing Craft, Infantry (Large)** or **LCI(L)** was a relatively fast craft designed around the carriage of 210 troops on sea crossings of up to 48-hour duration. The type was first mooted in 1942 for general raiding around the coast of occupied Europe and, as the troops needed to get ashore rapidly, a gangway (or 'brow') was included on either bow. Once lowered, these were required to put the troops down in water shallow enough to wade ashore. In turn, this demanded such a shallow beaching draught forward as to necessitate steel, rather than wood construction. For this reason, the LCI(L) was American-built to British requirements. From **LCI(L) 351** onwards, a centreline bow ramp operating through bow doors was adopted (though not universally), more protective for the troops but more vulnerable mechanically. As it did not carry vehicular cargo, the LCI(L) was

comparatively finely built, with a ship-type bow.

The propulsion system was typically a product of war ingenuity, with eight General Motor diesel truck engines driving the twin shafts through rubber friction rollers. Numbers up to LCI(L) 1139 were allocated, though few over 900 were completed as designed. Over 300 further hulls were completed

for special roles, notably over 160 armed as inshore fire support craft. Though known as **Landing Craft, Infantry (Gun)** or **LCI(G)**, i.e. gunboat, many of these had 127-mm (5-in) rocket-launchers or mortars.

Complementing the LCI(L) in its raiding role was the **Landing Craft, Infantry (Small)** or **LCI(S)** though neither type is believed ever to have been used as intended. As only half the number of troops was carried, the originally-planned wood construction was adopted, the design being the responsibility of Fairmile, which mass-produced them after the manner in which they built so many coastal forces craft. The double-diagonally laid plywood of much of the craft's external surfaces was overhung with 6.4-mm (0.25-in) HT steel plate for added protection, but troops below still incurred many casualties on approach to land-

ings where they were finally used. No less than four brows were arranged forward, together with a (typically British) stowage for 12 bicycles. Propulsion was by a pair of the well-tried Hall-Scott petrol engines, and the craft were capable of 15 kts when these were turbocharged.

Specification
LCI(L)
Displacement: 246 tons light and 384 tons full load
Dimensions: length 48.9 m (160.3 ft); beam 7.2 m (23.5 ft); draught 0.9/1.6 m (2.9/5.25 ft)
Propulsion: two diesels delivering 1730 kW (2,320 bhp) to two shafts
Performance: maximum speed 14 kts; range 14822 km (9,210 miles) at 12 kts
Armament: five single 20-mm AA guns
Capacity: 210 troops
Complement: 29

Above: A US LCI Mk 3. Fast by landing craft standards, these vessels stemmed from a 1942 requirement for a raiding craft able to land 200 infantrymen. Built in the USA to British requirements, the shallow beaching draught forward necessitated steel, not wood, construction.

Below: The Landing Craft, Infantry (Large) or LCI(L) could accommodate up to 210 troops, and from LCI(L) 351 onwards they featured a centreline bow ramp operating through bow doors.

Landing Craft, Mechanized Mks 1 to 7 (LCM (1-7))

Motor Landing Craft (MLC) had been the subject of experiments in various guises by the British as far back as 1926, but the true progenitor of the species was *MLC10*, completed in 1929. She was a 12.8-m (42-ft) craft capable of beaching with a 12-ton tank. An interesting feature contributing to her low draught was water-jet propulsion, although the low efficiency of units at this time resulted in a speed of barely 5 kts. Developed from this modest prototype, Thornycroft completed in early 1940 the first **Landing Craft, Mechanized Mk 1** or **LCM(1)**, slightly longer and able to carry a single 14-ton tank. Screw propulsion was used, and this increased speed by 50 per cent. Well described by its designer as a 'powered pontoon with bulwarks', this little craft could be hoisted under heavy davits even when loaded. Trials were not even complete when Dunkirk

stimulated an order for two dozen more. Eventually about 500 LCM(1)s were constructed, largely by railway workshops.

While these activities were in progress, the US Marine Corps had its own specification prepared for a similar type of craft. This was based on the hull of an up-river, shallow-draught tug and became known as the **LCM(2)**. The craft were very close to the British craft in both layout and performance, even to the unloved petrol engine propulsion. About 150 were built before an improved 15.24-m (50-ft) version was produced at the suggestion of the Brit-

Thornycroft completed the first LCM in 1940, describing it as a 'powered pontoon with bulwarks'. Able to carry a 14-ton light tank, it could be hoisted under davits even when loaded.

ish, increasing its capacity from a single 16-ton tank to one of 30 tons. An immediate success, the **LCM(3)** ran to over 8,600 craft, built from 1942 to 1945. Two distinct types, the '**Bureau**' and the '**Higgins**', were built by the Americans to the same specification.

The **LCM(4)** and **LCM(6)** were essentially the same craft, an LCM(3) with an extra 1.83-m (6-ft) section added amidships for extra capacity, and some 2,700 were built. The **LCM(5)** was stillborn, but the British-built **LCM(7)**, which first appeared late in 1944, was really a further-enlarged LCM(3) aimed primarily at operations

The US LCM(2)s were based on the design of shallow-draught up-river tugs. This LCM(2) is being used by men of the 30th Infantry Division during the Rhine crossings in March 1945.

in the Far East. Its length was over 18.3 m (60 ft), but it had the size for versatility, being used also in a wide variety of (chiefly unofficial) gunboat guises for fire-support purposes.

Specification
LCM(3)
Displacement: 23 tons light and 52 tons full load
Dimensions: length 15.2 m (50 ft); beam 4.3 m (14.1 ft); draught 1.0/1.3 m (3.25/4.25 ft)
Propulsion: two diesels delivering 164/336 kW (220/450 bhp) to two shafts
Performance: average speed about 8.5 kts; range 1577 km (980 miles) at 6 kts
Armament: one twin 12.7-mm (0.5-in) machine-gun
Capacity: one medium tank or 60 troops
Complement: 4

Landing Craft, Flak (LCF) and Landing Craft, Support (LCS)

Not all landing craft were used for the carriage of men or machinery: a goodly number were converted to auxiliary, if unorthodox, warships. Some, the **Landing Craft, Flak** or **LCF** type, were produced to give AA protection where sufficient regular navy back-up was likely to be lacking, while the **Landing Craft, Support** or **LCS** was able to go right inshore to render direct support to personnel actually on the beach, particularly in the awkward gap between the main 'softening-up' barrage lifting or rolling forward and the assault troops actually touching down and getting off the beach.

Two prototype LCFs were produced from LCT(2) hulls in late 1941. The first was a 'Rolls-Royce' with two twin 102-mm (4-in) HA mountings and three 20-mm guns. Besides the work involved, which was considerable, these mountings were already in great demand for a wide range of escort ships, the LCT structure was inherently flimsy and, last but not least, the low-sited director in combination with ship motion made for poor accuracy. More realistically, the LCT(2) took eight single 2-pdr pompoms and four 20-mm guns. Such mountings were more easily come by and could not only hose out a reassuringly large volume of fire against aircraft, but could also work devastatingly against any enemy personnel foolish enough to break cover ashore. Thus the final LCF forms were based on the **LCF(2)**, with the **LCF(3)** and **LCF(4)** being built on LCT(3) and LCT(4) hulls respectively, with the bow ramp permanently secured and a false deck added over the cargo well.

Above: The LCSs were designed for the close support of troops on the beach. This is an LCS(L)2 fitted with the turret of the obsolete Valentine tank, two 20-mm cannon and a 4-in smoke mortar.

Below: LCF Mk 3s were LCT(3)s converted to anti-aircraft gun platforms carrying up to eight single pom-poms and four 20-mm cannon (first batch), or four pom-poms and eight 20-mm guns (second batch).

A further refinement was the LCS which carried, either singly or in combination, a medium-calibre weapon for tackling enemy armoured vehicles, or mortars to engage enemy infantry who, all too frequently, were dug-in behind the rise that backed the beach, virtually safe from close range low-trajectory fire. LCS(S)s were actually converted from the fairly fast but wooden-hulled LCI(S) which, rather

The LCS(M)2s were built to provide close support for the LCAs during the approach to the beach. They carried a pair of 4-in (100-mm) machine-guns and a smoke mortar.

quirkily, were equipped with British armoured tank turrets containing a 6-pdr gun or, in the American case, with heavy and light machine-guns, and racks for light rockets.

Specification
LCF(3)
Displacement: 420 tons light and 515 tons full load
Dimensions: length 58.1 m (190.75 ft); beam 9.4 m (31 ft); draught 1.1/2.1 m (1.75/7 ft)
Propulsion: two diesels delivering 746 kW (1,000 bhp) to two shafts
Performance: maximum speed 9.5 kts; range 2688 km (1,670 miles) at 8.5 kts

A Landing Craft, Flak displays an impressive selection of automatic weapons: visible are 2-pdr pom-pom single mounts, and much smaller 20-mm (0.78-in) cannon.

Armament: eight single 2-pdr pompoms and four single 20-mm AA guns
Complement: 68

🇬🇧 UK Landing Craft, Assault (LCA)

'Like floating bootboxes pretending to be motorboats, mere square shells for carrying troops' is a description of a **Landing Craft, Assault (LCA)** by one who spent the war in landing craft. The LCA was one of the smallest of the practical, mass-produced craft arising from a specification written by the British Landing Craft Committee in 1938, calling for a craft which, with a loaded weight of under 10 tons, should be capable of being slung under a liner's davits. It should be able to carry an army platoon fully equipped and land the men in less than 0.5 m (19.7 in) of water. Two prototypes were built, one of aluminium alloy and one of wood with protective plating. These (originally called **Assault Landing Craft**) gave experience for the final design, whose wooden construction allowed them to be built by a wide variety of concerns.

Troops along both sides sat covered from the worst of the elements, but a centreline row had to tolerate both wetness and the inevitable sea sickness. In any sea the LCA could make little way and passage times could be protracted when a friendly tow was not available. The low, protected steering position was sited forward and on the starboard side, immediately abaft two-element armoured doors which kept out the water from the leaky bow ramp, while protecting the troops within from end-on fire during the approach to the beach.

An interesting variant was the **LCA(HR)**, the suffix standing, for Hedgerow, four rows of six mortars which laid their bombs in lanes across the beach to explode any buried mines. The craft were little modified for the function and life could be quite exciting for their crews. Equivalent American designs were the 11.05-m

LCAs assemble for an inspection by HM The King. In any sea the LCA could make little progress, and a tow was always preferred. In ideal conditions they could make 7 kts.

(36.25-ft) **LCV** and **LCVP (Landing Craft, Vehicle** and **Landing Craft, Vehicle/Personnel).**

Specification
LCA
Displacement: 10 tons light and 13 tons full load
Dimensions: length 12.6 m (41.5 ft); beam 3.0 m (10 ft); draught 0.5/0.7 m (1.75/2.25 ft)
Propulsion: two petrol engines delivering 97 kW (130 bhp) to two shafts
Performance: maximum speed 7 kts; range 95-150 km (59-93 miles) depending on sea conditions
Armament: two or three machine-guns
Capacity: 35 troops with 363 kg (800 lb) of equipment
Crew: 4

A Royal Marine LCA disgorges its troops during the crossing of the river Maas. Specifications for these 10-ton mass-produced craft dated from the deliberations of the 1938 Landing Craft Committee.

Landing Craft, Gun (LCG) and Landing Craft, Tank (Rocket) (LCT(R))

UK

Support firepower during landings was anticipated as being in short supply so, profiting from the successful LCF conversions, 23 LCT(3)s were fitted with two single 119-mm (4.7-in) guns and recategorized **Landing Craft, Gun (Large)** or **LCG(L)**. They had ex-destroyer mountings, the latter ships having been rearmed for anti-submarine work. The guns were sited at the same level on a new upper deck with deep bulwarks, and the after weapon had only limited arcs on the beam. Range-finding was rudimentary but the craft needed to operate at some distance from the beach, firstly to gain some falling trajectory for their guns and secondly to stay out of range of enemy weapons (particularly mortars) as their ammunition stowage was considered vulnerable.

They served well in Europe, so 10 LCT(4)s were also converted. These craft were flimsier but had extra beam, making for a steadier platform. They had a simple director, with their larger guns mounted superimposed and with full blast shielding. Light armouring was also added. Unfortunately only one was completed in time for the Far Eastern war.

The **Landing Craft, Gun (Medium)** or **LCG(M)** was designed to go right in and was protected for the purpose, while carrying two army 25- or 17-pdr guns in single armoured turrets. They were considered proof against medium-calibre return fire (in fact, they were not) and were meant to engage targets on the run in, and then to flood down to reduce freeboard as far as possible and, by sitting on the bottom, shoot accurately while gaining extra protection from their submergence. Their hulls were one-offs, with a ship bow and a low initial freeboard. Their metacentric heights gave them legendary roll angles and they manoeuvred poorly.

A most spectacular modification to LCTs was to the **Landing Craft, Tank (Rocket)** or **LCT(R)**. Both LCT(2)s and LCT(3)s were used, the whole forward end looking like a vast milk crate for the launch of 792 or 1,064 127-mm (5-in) rockets. Fixed in elevation and bearing, the weapons were launched from precisely 2-mile (3.2-km) range in 24 salvoes. Ideally the bombs came down at 10-yard intervals, laying a carpet of about 17 tons of explosive over an area of 685 by 145 m (750 by 160 yards) of

Converted from LCT(3)s or LCT(4)s, the Landing Craft, Gun (Large) or LCG(L) was designed to provide close-in fire support to an amphibious landing, and was armed with two single 4.7-in (119-mm) guns.

the enemy defences. One set of reloads was carried and, this fired, the craft disposed of her launchers and did duty as a ferry.

Specification
LCG(L) Mk 3
Displacement: 495 tons full load
Dimensions: length 58.5 m (192 ft); beam 9.4 m (31 ft); draught 1.1/1.8 m (3.5/6 ft)
Propulsion: two diesels delivering 746 kW (1,000 bhp) to two shafts
Performance: maximum speed 10 kts; range 2688 km (1,670 miles) at 8.5 kts
Armament: two single 119-mm (4.7-in) and one or two twin 20-mm AA guns
Complement: 47

Right: The LCG(M) was specially designed to engage enemy pillboxes, so it carried two turrets with either 17-pdr anti-tank or (as here) 25-pdr guns.

Below: The most spectacular of all the landing craft conversions, the LCT(R) was able to launch 5-in (127-mm) rockets over a two-mile range.

Above: The LCT(R) Mk 3 could carry over a thousand rockets, which were released in 24 salvoes. Anyone in the target area (measuring some 685 m by 145 m/750 by 160 yards) would be unlikely to feel happy as 17 tons of explosive burst around him!

Below: The LCG(L) Mk 4 usually had its turrets manned by Royal Marines, and proved most successful. It was more elaborate than its Mk 3 predecessor, with more 20-mm mountings, a modified bow form and the after 4.7-in (119-mm) gun made superfiring.

Glossary of Weapons

Tanks

American
Light Tank M1
Light Tank M2
Light Tank M3
Light Tank M5 General Stuart
Light Tank M22 Locust
Light Tank M24 Chaffee
Medium Tank M2
Medium Tank M3 General Grant
Medium Tank M4 General Sherman
Medium/Heavy Tank M26
 Pershing

British
Black Prince Infantry Tank (A43)
Cavalier Cruiser Tank (A24)
Centaur Cruiser Tank (A27L)
Centurion Cruiser Tank (A41)
Churchill Infantry Tank (A22)
Comet Cruiser Tank (A34)
Covenanter Cruiser Tank (A13)
Cromwell Cruiser Tank (A27M)
Crusader Cruiser Tank (A15)
General Grant Medium Tank
 (US M3)
General Lee Medium Tank (US M3)
General Stuart (Honey) Light Tank
 (US M2)
General Stuart Light Tank (US M5)
Harry Hopkins (Light Tank Mk VIII)
Light Tank Mk VI
Matilda I Infantry Tank (A11)
Matilda II Infantry Tank (A12)
Sherman Firefly Medium Tank
 (US M4, modified)
Tetrarch (Light Tank Mk VII)
Tortoise Heavy Tank (A39)
Valentine Infantry Tank
Valiant Infantry Tank (A38)

French
Char B-1 Medium Tank
Hotchkiss H-35 Char Léger Light
 Tank
Renault R-35 Char Léger Light Tank
Renault AMC-35 Automitrailleuse
 de Combat Light Tank
Renault AMR-35 Automitrailleuse
 de Reconnaissance Light Tank
Somua S-35 Medium Tank

German
PzKpfw I (SdKfz 101) Light Tank
PzKpfw II (SdKfz 121) Light Tank
PzKpfw III (SdKfz 141) Medium
 Tank
PzKpfw IV (SdKfz 161) Medium
 Tank
PzKpfw V Panther (SdKfz 171)
 Heavy Medium Tank
PzKpfw VI Tiger (SdKfz 181)
 Heavy Tank
PzKpfw VI Tiger II (SdKfz 182)
 Heavy Tank
PzKpfw 38(t) (TNHP) Light Tank
PzKpfw NbFzA/B Heavy Tank

Italian
L.3/33 Light Tank
L.3/35 Light Tank
L.6/40 Light Tank
M.11/39 Medium Tank
M.13/40 Medium Tank
M.14/41 Medium Tank
M.15/42 Medium Tank
P.26/40 Heavy Medium Tank

Japanese
Type 95 (Ha-Go) Light Tank
Type 98 (Ke-Ni) Light Tank
Type 5 (Ke-Ho) Light Tank
Type 89 (Otsu) Medium Tank
Type 97 (Chi-Ha) Medium Tank
Type 1 (Chi-He) Medium Tank
Type 3 (Chi-Nu) Medium Tank
Type 4 (Chi-To) Medium Tank
Type 5 (Chi-Ri) Medium Tank
Type 94 Tankette
Type 97 (Te-Ke) Tankette

Russian
BT-5 Fast Medium Tank
BT-7 Fast Medium Tank
T-26 Light Tank
T-28 Heavy Tank
T-32 Heavy Tank
T-35 Heavy Tank
T-34/76 Medium Tank
T-34/85 Medium Tank
T-60 Light Tank
T-70 Light Tank
T-100/SMK Heavy Tank
KV (Klimenti Voroshilov) series
 Heavy Tanks
IS (Iosef Stalin) series Heavy Tanks

Others
AC-1 Sentinel (Aus) Cruiser Tank
Grizzly (Can) Medium Tank
Ram Mk I (Can) Medium Tank
Ram Mk II (Can) Medium Tank
LT-35 (Cz) Light Tank
TNHP (Cz) Light Tank
TK.3 (Pol) Light Tank
7TP (Pol) Light Tank
10TP (Pol) Medium Tank

Tank Destroyers

American
3in Gun Motor Carriage M10, -M18
 Hellcat
90mm Gun Motor Carriage M36

British
Achilles (M10)
Archer

German
Jagdpanzer IV (SdKfz 162)
Jagdtiger (Panzerjäger Tiger Ausf. B)
Marder II (SdKfz 131)
Nashorn/Hornisse (SdKfz 164)
Panzerjäger I
Panzerjäger 38(t) (Marder III)
Panzerjäger 38(t) (Hetzer)
Panzerjäger Panther (SdKfz 173)
 (Jagdpanther)
Panzerjäger Tiger (SdKfz 184)
 (Elefant/Ferdinand)
Sturmgeschjätz III (SdKfz 172)

Italy
Semovente L.40, -M.41

Special-Purpose Tanks (see also Flame Weapons)

American
M3 Grant/M4 Sherman (Beach)
 Armored Recovery Vehicle
 (M31/M32)

M3 Grant/M4 Sherman Mine-
 Clearing Flails (Crab)
M3 Grant/M4 Sherman Mine-
 Clearing Ploughs
M3 Grant/M4 Sherman Mine-
 Clearing Rollers
M3 Grant/M4 Sherman
 Searchlight Tanks
M4 Sherman Tankdozer
M6 Gun Tractor
M30 Cargo Carrier
M33/M34/M35 Prime Movers

British
Churchill ARK Bridging Tank
Churchill Armoured Recovery
 Vehicle
Churchill Armoured Vehicle-
 Launched Bridge (AVLB)
Churchill Armoured Vehicle, Royal
 Engineers (AVRE)
Churchill Mine-Clearing Rollers
Grant Canal Defence Light Tanks
Grant Mine-Clearing Flail (Scorpion)
Matilda Canal Defence Light Tanks
Matilda Mine-Clearing Flail
 (Baron/Scorpion)
Ram Kangeroo APC
Sherman Kangeroo APC
Sherman Mine-Clearing Flail (Crab)
Valentine ARK ('Burmark')
Valentine Mine-Clearing Flail
 (Scorpion)

German
Bergepanther (SdKfz179)
Munitionspanzer IV
Panzerbefehlswagen (PzBefWg) I
 (SdKfz265)
Panzerbefehlswagen III (SdKfz266)
Panzerbefehlswagen Panther
 (SdKfz267)
Panzerbefehlswagen Tiger
 (SdKfz268)
Panzerbeobachtungswagen III
 (SdKfz143)

Amphibious Vehicles

American
DUKW
LVT 2
LVT 3
LVT 4
M29C Weasel
Medium Tank M4 Sherman w/M19
 Device

British
Sherman Duplex Drive (DD)
 Medium Tank
Terrapin
Valentine DD Infantry Tank

German
Land-Wasser Schlepper
Schwimmwagen
 (Schwimmfahiger Gelandeng
 Typ 168)

Japan
Amphibious Tank Type 2 (Ka-Mi)

Russia
T-37 Amphibious Light Tank
T-38 Amphibious Light Tank
T-40 Amphibious Light Tank

Halftrack Vehicles

American
M3
M9
M14

French
Citröen-Kégresse series

German
Klienes Kettenrad (SdKfz 2)
Leichter Zugkraftwagen 1t
 (SdKfz 10)
Maultier
Leichter Zugkraftwagen 3t
 (SdKfz 11)
Mittlerer Zugkraftwagen 5t
 (SdKfz 6)
Mittlerer Zugkraftwagen 8t
 (SdKfz 7)
Schwerer Zugkraftwagen 12t
 (SdKfz 8)
Schwerer Zugkraftwagen 18t
 (SdKfz 9)
Schwerer Wehrmachtsschlepper
Leichter Schätzenpanzerwagen
 (SdKfz 250)
Mittlerer Schätzenpanzerwagen
 (SdKfz 251)

Russian
Vezdekhods Model B
Vezdekhods Model BM
Vezdekhods Model VZ
Ya-SP
Zis-33
Zis-42

Armoured Cars

American
Armoured Car M6 Staghound
Armoured Car T18 Boarhound
Armoured Car T19
Armoured Car M38
Light Armoured Car M8 Greyhound
Marmon-Herrington Armoured Car
Scout Car M3/M3A1 (White)

British
AEC Armoured Car
Coventry Armoured Car
Crossley Armoured Car (obs)
Daimler Armoured Car
Daimler Scout Car (Dingo)
Humber Armoured Car

French
Panhard Type 178

German
Leichter Panzerspähwagen
 (SdKfz 222)
Schwerer Panzerspähwagen
 (6-Rad) (SdKfz 231)
Schwerer Panzerspähwagen
 (8-Rad) (SdKfz 231)

Italian
Autoblindo 40
Autoblindo 41

Russian
BA-10

Others
Ford Lynx (Can)

GM Fox (Can)
GM C15TA (Can)
CAPLAD (Can)

Passenger Cars & Light Vehicles

American
Willys 'Jeep'

German
Auto Union/Horch Typ 830 (Kfz 11)
Daimler-Benz G5
Kübelwagen (Volkswagen Typ 62)
Mercedes-Benz 320/340 (Kfz 15)
Stöver 40 (Kfz 2)

Self-Propelled Guns

American
75mm Gun Motor Carriage M3
105mm Howitzer Motor Carriage
 M7 ('Priest'), -M37
155mm Gun Motor Carrige M12
155mm Gun Motor Carriage M40
155mm Howitzer Motor Carriage
 M41
8in Howitzer Motor Carriage M43
240mm Gun Motor Carriage T92

British
Alecto
Bishop (Carrier, Valentine, 25-pdr
 Gun, Mk I)

German
Bison (SdKfz 138) (sIG 33 15cm)
Brummbär
Geschützenwagen I (sIG 33 auf
 PzKpfw I, 15cm)
Geschützenwagen II (SdKfz 121)
 (sIG 33 auf PzKpfw II, 15cm)
Grille (sIG 33 auf PzKpfw 38(t),
 15cm)
Heuschrecke IVB
Hummel (SdKfz 165) (sFH 18 auf
 PzKpfw IV, 15cm)
Karl (Mörser Gerät 040, 60cm)
Karl (Mörser Gerät 041, 54cm)
Sturmgeschätz IV (7.5cm)
Sturmgeschätz 40 (7.5cm)
Sturmmörser (Sturmtiger) (38cm)
Wespe (SdKfz 124) (leFH 18 auf
 PzKpfw II, 10.5cm)

Italian
Semovente 90
Semovente 149

Japanese
Type 38 (Ho-Ro), 150mm

Russian
ISU-122
ISU-152
SU-76
SU-85

Heavy Artillery

American
4.7in Gun M1917
4.5in Gun M1
155mm Gun M1
8in Gun M1
8in Howitzer M1
240mm Howitzer M1918

240mm Howitzer M1
'Little David' (Bomb Testing Device T1)

British
4.5in Gun Mk2
5in (60pdr) Gun Mk1/Mk2
5.5in Gun Mk 3
7.2in Howitzer Mk1
7.2in Howitzer Mk 6

French
155mm Gun Modèle 1917 CGPF
155mm Gun Mle 32
155mm Howitzer Mle 1917
155mm Howitzer Mle 29

German
10.5cm Kanone 18
10.5cm schwere K 18/40
15cm K 18
15cm K 39
15cm schwere Feld Haubitze 13
15cm sFH 18
15cm sFH 36
17cm K 18
21cm K 38
21cm K 39
21cm Mörser 18
24cm K 3/K 4
24cm Haubitze 39
35.5cm H M1

Italian
Canone da 149/40 Modello 35 (Gun)
Obice de 210/22 M35 (Howitzer)

Japanese
150mm Gun, Model 89
150mm Howitzer, Model 96

Russian
122mm Gun, M31/37
152mm Gun, M09/30
152mm Gun, M10/30
152mm Gun, M10/34
152mm Gun, BR-2, M1935
152mm Howitzer, M-10, M1938
152mm Howitzer, D-1, M1943
152mm Gun/Howitzer, ML-20, M1937
203mm Howitzer, L-25 (B-4), M1931
210mm Gun, M39/40, M1940
305mm Howitzer, BR-18, M1940

Others
15cm FH, M38 (Austria)
150mm Howitzer vz37 (Cz)
220mm Howitzer M.28 (Cz)

Field Artillery

American
75mm Gun M2A2
105mm Howitzer M1
105mm Howitzer M2A1
105mm Howitzer M3A1

British
25pdr Mk 2 (Ordnance, QF, 25-pdr Mk II)
25pdr Short, Mk 1

French
75mm Gun Modèle 1897
75mm Mle 32 (Mountain Gun)
105mm Gun Mle 13TR (L 13S)
105mm Gun Mle 36
105mm Canon Court Mle 35 (Howitzer)

German
7.5cm FeldKanone 15nA
7.5cm Leicht FK18
7.5cm FK38
7.5cm FK7M85
7.5cm GebergsKanone15

(Mountain Gun)
7.5cm Geb.G36 (Mountain Gun)
7.5cm Infanteriegeschätz L/13
7.5cm IG18
7.5cm IG37
7.5cm IG42
10.5cm LeichtFeldhaubitz18
10.5cm leFH18M
10.5cm leFH18/40
10.5cm leFH42
10.5cm leFH43
10.5cm Geb.H40 (Mountain Gun)
15cm Schwere IG33

Italian
Cannone da 75/27 Modello 06/11
Cannone da 75/32 M37
Cannone da 105/40 M42
Obice da 75/18 M34 (Mountain Gun)
Obice da 75/18 M35
Obice da 105/28

Japanese
75mm Field Gun Type 38 (Improved)
75mm Field Gun Type 90
75mm Field Gun Type 95
105mm Gun Type 14
105mm Gun Type 92
105mm Howitzer Type 91

Russian
76.2mm Field Gun, M00, M02, M02/30
76.2mm Regimental Gun, M27
76.2mm Divisional Gun, M33
76.2mm Divisional Gun, F-22, M1936
76.2mm Divisional Gun, USV, M1939
76.2mm Gun, M41
76.2mm Gun, ZIS-3, M1942
85mm Divisional Gun, D-44, M1944
85mm Divisional Gun, D-48, M1945
107mm Gun, M10/30
122mm Howitzer, M10/30
122mm Howitzer, M38

Others
75mm Field Gun, vz35 (Cz)
76.5mm Field Gun, vz30 (Cz)
76.5mm Field Gun, vz39 (Cz)
80mm Field Gun, vz30 (Cz)
100mm Field Gun, vz 35 (Cz)
100mm Field Howitzer, vz30/34 (Cz)
100mm Field Howitzer, H3 (Cz)

Heavy Anti-Aircraft Artillery

American
3in M1917A
3in M3
3in M4
90mm M1
105mm M3
120mm M1

British
3in 20cwt Mk 1 (Ordnance, QF, 3in, 20cwt)
3.7in Mk 1 (Ordnance, QF, 3.7in, Mk I)
3.7in Mk 6 (Ordnance, QF, 3.7in, Mk VI)
4.5in Mk 2 (Ordnance, QF, 4.5in, Mk II)
5.25in Mk 2 (Ordnance, QF, 5.25in, Mk II)

French
75mm Modèle 17/34
75mm Mle 32, -33, -36

German
7.5cm FliegerabwehrKanone38
8.8cm FlaK18, -36, -37
8.8cm FlaK41
10.5cm FlaK38, -39
12.8cm FlaK40

Italian
Cannone da 75/46 Contraerea Modello 34/35
Cannone da 75/50 CA M38
Cannone da 90/53 CA M38
Cannone da 102/35 CA M38

Japanese
Type 88 75mm
Type 4 75mm
Type 99 80mm
Type 3 120mm

Russian
76.2mm M31
76.2mm M38
85mm M39, -M44

Others
75mm Kan. PP Let vz32 (Cz)
76mm Kan. PP Let vz28 (Cz)
83mm Kan. PL vz22 (Cz)
75mm L/52 Bofors (Swe)
80mm L/50 Bofors (Swe)

Light Anti-Aircraft Artillery

American
Multiple Gun Motor Carriage M16 (SP)
37mm Antiaircraft Gun M1
40mm Antiaircraft Gun M1

British
20mm Polsten Mk 1
2-pdr Mk 8
6-pdr 6cwt Mk 1
Crusader AA Tank

French
25mm Hotchkiss Modèle 38, -39, -40
37mm Schneider Mle 1930

German
2cm FliegerabwehrKanone30
2cm FlaK38/FlaKvierling 38
3.7cm FlaK18, -36, -37
3.7cm FlaK43/FlaKzwilling 43
5cm FlaK41

Italian
Cannone-Mitragliera da 20/77 (Scotti)
Cannone-Mitragliera da 20/65 Modello 1935 (Breda)
Cannone Contraerea da 37/54 M1925 (Breda)

Japanese
Type 98 Machine Cannon 20mm
Type 91 40mm

Russian
37mm Gun M39

Others
Skink (SP) (Can)
40mm Bofors (Swe)

Rocket Artillery

American
4.5in Rocket, High Explosive, M8
4.5in Rocket, High Explosive, M16
7.2in Rocket, High Explosive, M17

British
2in Rocket, Mounting Mk 2 ('Pillar Box')

3in Rocket, Projector No 2, No 4, No 6
Lilo
Mattress/Land Mattress

German
15cm Wurfgranate41
21cm Wgr.42
28- & 32cm Wurfkörper41

Japanese
200mm Rocket, Launcher Type 4
447mm Rocket

Russian
82mm M8 (Launchers BM-8-24 & BM-8-48) (Katyusha)
132mm M13 (Launcher BM-13-16)
300mm M30/M31 (Launcher BM-30-12 & BM-31-12) (Rama)

Anti-Tank Guns

American
37mm Antitank Gun M3
57mm Antitank Gun M1
3in Antitank Gun M5
90mm Antitank Gun T8/M3

British
2pdr (ordnance, QF, 2pdr)
6pdr (Ordnance, QF, 6pdr)
17pdr (Ordnance, QF, 17pdr)

French
Canon Léger de 25 Antichar Modèle 1934 (Hotchkiss)
Canon Léger de 25 Antichar M1937
Canon de 47 Antichar M1937 (Puteaux)

German
3.7cm PanzerabwehrKanone36
4.2cm Leicht PaK41 (Taper-Bore)
5cm PaK38
7.5cm PaK40
7.5cm PaK41 (Taper-Bore)
7.5cm PaK97/38
8cm PanzerabwehrWerfer 600 (PanzerwerfKanone 8H63)
8.8cm PaK43
12.8cm PaK44

Italian
Canone Anticarro da 47/32 Modello 1935/37 (Böhler)

Japanese
Type 1 47mm

Russian
45mm M1932
45mm M1937
45mm M 1942
57mm ZIS-2 (M1943)
100mm BS-3 (M1944)

Infantry Support Weapons

American
37mm Gun M3A1
57mm Recoilless Rifle M18
60mm Mortar M2
60mm Mortar M19
75mm Pack Howitzer M1A1
75mm Recoilless Rifle M20
81mm Mortar M1

British
2in Mortar (Ordnance, Smooth Bore, Muzzle Loading, 2in Mortar, MkI-MkVIII)
6pdr 7cwt Gun Mk 1
3in Mortar (MkI & MkII)

95mm (3.7in) Infantry Howitzer Mk2
4.2in Mortar

French
Mortier Brandt de 81mm Modèle 27/31

German
5cm Leicht Granatwerfer 36
8cm Schwere GrW 34
7.5cm Leicht Infanteriegeschätz 18
15cm Schwere IG 33

Italy
Cannone da 45/5 Modello 1935 'Brixa'
Cannone da 81mm M 1935

Japan
Type 89 50mm Mortar
Type 92 70mm Battalion Gun

Russian
50mm PM 38/39/40
107mm PHSM 38
120mm HM 38

Infantry Anti-Tank Weapons

American
2.36in Rocket Launcher M1/M1A1 ('Bazooka')
Grenade M9

British
Boys Rifle (Rifle, Anti-tank, 0.55in)
Grenade, Rifle, No 68
Grenade, No 74 ('Sticky Bomb')
PIAT (Projectile, Infantry, Anti-Tank)

German
7.92mm Panzerbüchse 38/39 (Anti-Tank Rifle)
2cm PzB S18-1000/785(s) (Anti-Tank Rifle)
8.8cm Raketenpanzerbüchse 43/54 ('Ofenrohr' or 'Panzerschreck')
8.8cm Raketenwerfer 43 ('Püppchen')
Gewehr Panzergranaten (Rifle Grenades)
Klein Panzerfaust 30
Panzerfaust 30/60/100
Panzerwurfkörper (Pistol Grenade)
Panzerwurfmine

Japanese
Type 97 20mm Anti-Tank Rifle

Russian
14.5mm PTRD M1941
14.5mm PTRS M1941

Others
20mm Lahti Modell 39 (Fin)
7.92mm Karabin WZ/35 'Maroscezk' (Pol)

Rifles

American
Carbine, .30 M1/M2/M3
Rifle, Calibre .30 M1903 ('Springfield')
Rifle, Calibre .30 M1917 ('Enfield')
Rifle, Calibre .30 M1 'Garand'
Rifle, Calibre .30 M1941 (Johnson)

British
Rifle, .303in, Short, Magazine, Lee-Enfield (SMLE) Mk III
Rifle, .303in, Lee-Enfield No 4 Mk I
Rifle, .303in, Lee-Enfield, No 5 ('Jungle Carbine')

De Lisle Carbine (.45SAA) (silenced)

French
Berthier Fusil d'Infanterie Modèle 1907/15, M34 (8mm)
Lebel Mle 1886/93 (8mm)
MAS36 (7.5mm)

German
Gewehr 98 (7.92mm)
Karabiner 98k (7.92mm)
Gewehr 41(W) (Gew41(W)) (7.92mm)
Fallschirmjägergewehr 42 (FG42) (7.92mm)
Maschinenkarabiner 42(H) (MKb42(H)) (7.92mm)
MKb42(W) (7.92mm pist.)
Gew/Kar 43 (7.92mm)
Maschinenpistole 43/44 (MP43/44) (Sturmgewehr 44) (7.92mm pist.)
Veruchs-Gerät/Volkssturm-Gewehr 1-5 (7.92mm pist.)

Italian
6.5mm Fucile Modello 91 (Mannlicher-Carcano)
7.35mm Fucile Modello 38 (Mannlicher-Carcano)

Japanese
6.5mm Arisaka Meiji 38
7.7mm Rifle Type 99
7.7mm Parachutist's Rifle Type 2

Russian
7.62mm Mosin-Nagant M1891/30
7.62mm Model 1938
7.62mm AVS/AVS36 (Simonov)
7.62mm SVT38 (Tokarev)
7.62mm AVT40 (Tokarev)

Others
ZH29 (7.92mm) (Cz)
ZK420 (7.92mm) (Cz)

Pistols

American
Pistol, Automatic, Caliber .45in, M1911
Revolver, Caliber .45in, M1917 (Smith & Wesson)
Revolver, Caliber .45in, M1917 (Colt 'N ew Service)
Pistol, Caliber .45in, M1942 'Liberator'

British
Revolver, Enfield, No 2 Mk I (.38in)
Revolver, Smith & Wesson .38in
Revolver, Webley, Mk 4 (.38in)

French
Lebel Revolver, Modèle 1892 (8mm)
MAB P-15 (9mm Parabellum)
SFAC M1928 (Le Français) (9mm Browning)
MAC M1935A/M1935S (7.65mm Long)

German
P08 (Luger) (9mm Parabellum)
P38 (Walther) 9mm Parabellum) (9mm Parabellum)
PP/PPK (Walther) (7.65mm)
Sauer-Selbstladepistole Modell 38H (Sauer) (7.65mm)
Selbstladepistole Modell HSc (Mauser) (7.65mm)

Italy
Bodeo Revolver, Modello 1889 (10.35mm)
Glisenti M1910 (9mm Glisenti)
Berreta M1934 (9mm Short)

Japanese
9mm Revolver Type 26
Pistol Type 04 (Nambu) (8mm)
Pistol Type 14 (Nambu) (8mm)
Pistol Type 94 (8mm)

Russian
Nagant Revolver, M1895 (7.62mm)
Tokarev TT, M1933 (7.62mm)

Others
Browning Modèle 1910 (.32in ACP or 9mm Short) (Bel)
Browning GP35/HP (9mm Parabellum) (Bel)
Radom/Pistole Model 35/VIS-35 (9mm Parabellum) (Pol)
Steyr Modell 1912 (9mm Parabellum) (Austria)

Machine-Guns

America
Automatic Rifle, Caliber .30 M1918/M1922 (BAR)
Machine Gun, Caliber .30 M1919
Machine Gun, Caliber .50 M1921/M2

Britain
Gun, Machine, Besa, 7.92mm, Marks 1–3
Gun, Machine, Besa, 15mm, Mark 1
Gun, Machine, Besal/Faulkener, .303
Gun, Machine, Bren, .303, Marks 1–4
Gun, Machine, Hotchkiss, .303, Mark 1
Gun, Machine, Lewis, .303, Marks 1–3
Gun, Machine, Vickers, .303, Marks 1–7 (Type C)
Gun, Machine, Vickers, .303, (Type K/'VGO')
Gun, Machine, Vickers-Berthier, .303, Marks 1–3

French
Fusil Mitrailleur Modèle 1924/1929/1931 (7.5mm)

German
Maschinengewehr 08 (Maxim) (7.92mm)
MG34 (7.92mm)
MG42 (7.92mm)

Italian
Mitragliatrice Sistema Revelli, Modello 14 (6.5mm)
Breda M30 (6.5mm)
Breda RM M31 (13.2mm)
Breda M37 (8mm)
FIAT/Revelli M35 (8mm)
Scotti M28 (7.7mm/.303in British)

Japanese
Type 11 6.5mm
Type 96 6.5mm
Type 97 7.7mm
Type 99 7.7mm

Russian
Maxim M1910 (7.62mm)
DP/DT M1928 (7.62mm)
ShKAS KM33/KM35/KM36/KM41 (7.62mm)
ShVAK/KPV (12.7mm/20mm)
DShK M1938 (12.7mm)
SG43 (7.62mm)
DPM (7.62mm)

Others
Let Maskingevaer Madsen (8mm) (Den)
Schwarzlose Modell 07/12 (8mm) (Austria)
ZB26 (7.92mm) (Cz)

ZB30 (7.92mm) (Cz)
ZB53 (vz37) (7.92mm) (Cz)

Sub-Machine Guns

American
Sub-machine-gun Caliber .45 M1928/M1/M1A1 (Thompson)
Reising Model 50/Model 55 (.45 ACP)
UD M42 (9mm Parabellum/.45 ACP)
US Sub-machine-gun Caliber .45 M3/M3A1

British
Machine Carbine, 9mm, Lanchester
Machine Carbine, 9mm, Sten, Marks 1–6
Machine Carbine, 9mm, V42
Machine Carbine, 9mm, Welgun

French
Pistole Mitrailleur MAS Modèle 38 (7.65mm Long)

German
Maschinenpistole 28/II (9mm Parabellum)
MP34 (9mm Parabellum)
MP38 (9mm Parabellum)
MP40 (9mm Parabellum)
MP3008 (9mm Parabellum) (Sten copy)
MPE (9mm Parabellum)
MPE44 (9mm Parabellum)
Solothurn S1-100 (9mm Parabellum)

Italian
Pistola Mitragliatrice Berreta Modello 38 (9mm Parabellum)
Berreta M 38/42FNAB M 43 (9mm Parabellum)

Japanese
Type 100 8mm

Russian
PPD M1934/38 (7.62mm)
PPD40 M1940 (7.62mm)
PPSh41 M1941 (7.62mm)
PPS43 M1943 (7.62mm)

Others
Machine Carbine, 9mm, Austen (Aus)
Machine Carbine, 9mm, Owen (Aus)
ZK383 (9mm Parabellum) (Cz)
M39M (9mm Parabellum) (Hun)
M/26 & M/31 'Suomi' (7.63mm Mauser/9mm Parabellum) (Fin)
M/44 (9mm Parabellum) (Fin)

Flame Weapons

American
Portable Flame-Thrower M1/M1A1
Portable Flame-Thrower M2-2
M3-4-3 (M4 tank-mounted)
M5-4 (M4 tank-mounted)
Sherman Crocodile

British
Adder (tank-mounted)
Crocodile (tank-towed)
Harvey
Flame-Thrower, Portable, No 2, Mark I and II (Lifebuoy)
Salamander (tank-mounted)
Wasp (Universal Carrier-mounted)
Wasp II (APC-mounted)

German
Flammenwerfer 35
Flammenwerfer 41
Abwehrflammenwerfer 42
Flammpanzer I (PzKpfw I)
Flammpanzer II (PzKpfw II)

Flammpanzer III (PzKpfw III)
Flammpanzer 38(t) (PzKpfw 38(t))
Mittlerer Flampanzerwagen (SdKfz 251)

Italian
Lanciafiamme Modello 35
Lanciafiamme M40
Lanciafiamme L3 (L3 Light Tank-mounted)

Japanese
Portable Flamethrower Type 93/Type 100

Russian
ROKS-2
ROKS-3
ATO-41/42 (tank-mounted)

Fighter Aircraft

American
Bell P-39 Airacobra
Bell P-63 Kingcobra
Curtiss P-36
Curtiss P-40 Warhawk
Lockheed P-38 Lightning
North American P-51 Mustang
Republic P-43 Lancer
Republic P-47 Thunderbolt
Seversky P-35

British
Blackburn Roc
Blackburn Skua
Bolton-Paul Defiant
Gloster Gauntlet
Gloster Gladiator
Hawker Fury
Hawker Hurricane
Hawker Tempest
Hawker Typhoon
Supermarine Spitfire

French
Arsenal VG 33
Bloch B 152
Caudron C 714
Dewoitine D 371
Dewoitine 520
Morane-Saulnier MS 406

Germany
Focke-Wulf Fw.190
Messerschmitt Bf.109
Messerschmitt Bf.110

Italian
Ambrosini SAI 207
Caproni-Reggiane Re 2000
Caproni-Reggiane Re 2001 Ariete
Caproni-Reggiane Re 2005 Saggitario
FIAT CR 42 Falco
FIAT G 50 Freccia
FIAT G 55 Centauro
Macchi MC 200 Saetta
Macchi MC 202 Folgore
Macchi MC 205 Veltro
Meridionali Ro 57

Japanese
Kawanishi N1K1-J Shiden ('George')
Kawasaki Ki-61 Hien ('Tony')
Kawasaki Ki-100
Kawasaki Ki-102 ('Randy')
Mitsubishi A6M Zero-Sen ('Zeke')
Mitsubishi J2M Raiden ('Jack')
Nakajima Ki-27 ('Abdul'/'Nate')
Nakajima Ki-43 Hayabusa ('Jim'/'Oscar')
Nakajima Ki-44 Shoki ('Tojo')
Nakajima Ki-84 Hayate ('Frank')

Russian
Lavochkin LaGG-3

Lavochkin La-5/La-7
Lavochkin La-9/La-11
Mikoyan-Gurevich MiG-1/MiG-3
Mikoyan-Gurevich MiG-5
Mikoyan-Gurevich MiG-7
Polikarpov I-15
Polikarpov I-16
Polikarpov I-153
Rogozarski IK-3
Yakovlev Yak-1
Yakovlev Yak-3
Yakovlev Yak-7
Yakovlev Yak-9

Others
Avia B.534 (Cz)
Commonwealth CA-12 Boomerang (Aus)
Fokker D XXI (Hol)
IAR 80 (Rom)
Ikarus IK-2 (Yug)
PZL P.24 (Pol)
VL Myrsky II (Fin)

Heavy Bombers

American
Boeing B-17 Flying Fortress
Boeing B-29 Superfortress
Consolidated B-24 Liberator

British
Armstrong-Whitworth AW 38 Whitley
Avro 679 Manchester
Avro 683 Lancaster
Avro 694 Lincoln
Handley-Page HP 57 Halifax
Short S 29 Stirling
Vickers Type 271 Wellington

French
Bloch 162
Farman F-221/F-222

German
Heinkel He.177 Greif

Italian
Piaggio P.108

Japanese
Mitsubishi G4M ('Betty')
Nakajima G8N Renzan ('Rita')

Russian
Petlyakov Pe-8
Tupolev ANT-6 (TB-3)

Light- & Medium Bombers

American
Douglas B-18 Bolo
Martin B-26 Marauder
North American B-25 Mitchell

British
Bristol Type 142 Blenheim
de Havilland DH 98 Mosquito
Fairey Battle
Handley-Page HP 52 Hampden
Handley-Page HP 53 Hereford
Vickers Type 287 Wellesley

French
Amiot 143
Amiot 354
Bloch 174
Lioré et Olivier LeO 451

German
Dornier Do. 17
Dornier Do. 217
Heinkel He. 111
Junkers Ju. 86
Junkers Ju. 88

Junkers Ju. 188
'Mistel' composite aircraft

Italian
CRDA CANT Z.1007 Airone
FIAT BR. 20 Cicogna
Savoia-Marchetti S.M. 79 Sparviero
Savoia-Marchetti S.M. 81 Pipistrello
Savoia-Marchetti S.M. 82 Canguru
Savoia-Marchetti S.M. 84

Japanese
Kawasaki Ki-32 ('Mary')
Kawasaki Ki-48 ('Lily')
Mitsubishi G3M ('Nell')
Mitsubishi Ki-21 ('Sally')
Mitsubishi Ki-67 Hiryu ('Peggy')
Nakajima Ki-49 Donryu ('Helen')
Yokosuka P1Y Ginga ('Francis')

Russian
Ilyushin DB-3
Ilyushin Il-4
Petlyakov Pe-2
Tupolev SB-2
Tupolev Tu-2
Yakovlev Yak-2/Yak-4

Jet/Rocket Aircraft

American
Bell P-59 Airacomet
Lockheed P-80 Shooting Star
Ryan FR-1 (composite radial/
    turbojet)

British
de Havilland Vampire F. Mk 1
Gloster Meteor F. Mk I/Mk III

German
Arado Ar. 234
Bachem Ba. 349 Natter
Feisler Fi. 103R
Gotha Go. 229
Heinkel He. 162 Salamander
Heinkel He. 178
Heinkel He. 280
Henschel Hs. 132
Junkers Ju. 287
Messerschmitt Me. 163 Komet
Messerschmitt Me. 262

Japanese
Nakajima Kikka
Yokosuka MXY7 Ohka

Russian
Berez-Isa BI

Ground Attack Aircraft

American
Douglas A-20 Boston/Havoc
Douglas A-26 Invader
Lockheed A-28 Hudson
Martin A-30 Baltimore
Vultee A-31/A-35 (V-72) Vengeance

British
Bristol Type 156 Beaufighter TF
Bristol Type 164 Brigand
Hawker Hurricane
    ('Hurribomber')
Hawker Tempest FB
Hawker Typhoon
Supermarine Spitfire Mk XIV, -XVI
Westland Whirlwind Mk 1A

French
Breguet Bre. 690-series

German
Focke-Wulf Fw. 190B-5/UB
Henschel Hs. 123

Henschel Hs. 129
Junkers Ju. 87 Stuka
Junkers Ju. 88P
Messerschmitt Me. 210/410
    Zerstörer

Italian
Breda Ba. 65
Breda Ba. 88
Caproni Bergamaschi Ca. 300-
    series

Japanese
Aichi D3A1 ('Val')
Mitsubishi Ki-30 ('Ann')
Mitsubishi Ki-51 ('Sonia')
Kawasaki Ki-45 Toryu ('Nick')

Russian
Ilyushin Il-2 Shturmovik
Sukhoi Su-2

Night-Fighters

American
Douglas P-70 Havoc
Northrop P-61 Black Widow

British
Bristol Type 142 Blenheim Mk 1F
Bristol Type 156 Beaufighter Mk
    IF/Mk VIF
de Havilland Mosquito NF Mk
    II–Mk XV, Mk 30

French
Potez 631

German
Dornier Do. 17/Do. 215/Do. 217
Heinkel He. 219
Messerschmitt Bf. 110
Messerschmitt Me. 262B

Japanese
Kawasaki Ki-45 Toryu ('Nick')
Nakajima J1N1 Gekko ('Irving')

Flying-Boats

American
Boeing C-98
Consolidated PBY Catalina
Consolidated PB2Y Coronado
Grumman G-21 Goose
Martin PBM Mariner

British
Saunders-Roe (Saro) A.27
    London
Saro S.36 Lerwick
Short Sunderland
Supermarine Sea Otter
Supermarine Stranraer
Supermarine Walrus

French
Breguet Bre. 521 Bizerte
Latécoère Laté. 523

German
Blohm u. Voss Bv. 138
Blohm u. Voss Bv. 222 Wiking
Dornier Do. 18
Dornier Do. 24

Italian
CRDA CANT Z.501 Gabbiano

Japanese
Kawanishi H6K ('Mavis')
Kawanishi H8K ('Emily')

Russian
Beriev MBR-2
Beriev KOR-2
Chetverikov MDR-6

Floatplanes/ Seaplanes

American
Curtiss SOC Seagull
Curtiss SC-1 Seahawk
Grumman J2F Duck
Northrop N-3PB Nomad
Vought OS2U Kingfisher

British
Fairey Seafox

French
Latécoère 298

German
Arado Ar. 196
Arado Ar. 231
Heinkel He. 59
Heinkel He. 115

Italian
CRDA CANT Z.506 Airone

Japanese
Aichi E13A ('Jake')
Aichi E16A Zuiun ('Paul')
Kawanishi N1K1 Kyofu ('Rex')
Mistubishi F1M ('Pete')
Nakajima A6M2-N ('Rufe')

Russian
Beriev KOR-1

Others
Fokker T.VIII-W (Hol)

Anti-Shipping Aircraft

American
Boeing B-17 Flying Fortress
Consolidated B-25 Liberator
Lockheed A-28 Hudson

British
Armstrong-Whitworth Whitley
Avro Anson
Bristol Type 142 Blenheim
Bristol Type 152 Beaufort
Bristol Type 156 Beaufighter Mk
    IC/Mk VIC
de Havilland DH 68 Mosquito FB
    Mk VI/Mk VIII
Vickers Wellington/Warwick

German
Dornier Do. 217
Focke-Wulf Fw. 200 Condor
Heinkel He. 111
Junkers Ju. 88/Ju. 188
Junkers Ju. 290

Italian
Savoia-Marchetti SM 79

Japanese
Mitsubishi G3M ('Nell')
Mitsubishi Ki-67 ('Peggy')

Carrier Aircraft

American
Curtiss SB2C Helldiver
Douglas SBD Dauntless
Grumman F4F Wildcat
Grumman F6F Hellcat
Grumman TBF Avenger
Vought F4U Corsair

British
Fairey Albacore
Fairey Barracuda
Fairey Firefly
Fairey Fulmar
Fairey Swordfish

Hawker Sea Hurricane
Supermarine Seafire

Japanese
Aichi D3N ('Val')
Mitsubishi A5M ('C laude')
Mitsubishi A6M ('Zeke')
Mitsubishi J2M ('Jack')
Nakajima B5N ('Kate')
Nakajima B6N ('Jill')
Yokosuka D4Y ('Judy')

Shipping
*(All headings refer to classes of
ship, though of course, a class
may have consisted of only one
example. 'British' includes Royal
Australian Navy and Royal
Canadian Navy.)*

Submarines

American
Argonaut
Balao
Barracuda
Cachalot
Dolphin
Gato
Mackerel/Marlin
Narwhal
O-class
Perch
Porpoise
R-class
S-class
Salmon
Sargo/Sea Dragon
Shark
T-class
Tambor
Tench

British
A-class
Grampus
Oberon
Odin
Oxley
P611-class
Parthian
Porpoise
Rainbow
S-class
Shark
Swordfish
T-class
Thames
Triton
U-class
Undine
X craft

French
Ariane
Argonaute
Aurore
Circé
Diane
Minerve
Orion
Requin
Redoutable
Saphir
Surcouf

German
Type IA
Type IIA
Type IIB
Type IIC
Type IID
Type VIIA
Type VIIB
Type VIIC
Type VIIC/41
Type VIIC/42

Type VIID
Type VIIF
Type IXA
Type IXB
Type IXC
Type IXC/40
Type IXD-1
Type IXD-2 & IXD/42
Type XB
Type XIV
Type XVIIB
Type XVIIG
Type XXI
Type XXIII
Type Wa201
Type Wk202

Italian
Acciaio
Adua
Archimede
Argo
Argonauta
Balilla
Bandiera
Bragadin
Brin
CA Type 1, -Type 2
Cagni
Calvi
CB
CC
Ettore Fieramosca
Flutto Type 1
Flutto Type 2
Foca
Glauco
Liuzzi
Mameli
Marcello
Marconi
Perla
Pietro Micca
Pisani
Romolo
Settembrini
Sirena
Squalo

Japanese
A1
A2
AM
B1
B2
B3
C1
C2
C3
D1
D2
J1
J1M
J2
J3
K5
K6
KD1
KD2
KD3a
KD3b
KD4
KD5
KD6a
KD6b
KD7
KRS
KS
L4
SH
SS
ST
STH
STO
STS
Yu1
Yu1001

midget submarines:
- A Type
- B/C Type
- D Type (Koryu Type)
- Kairyu Type
- Kaiten Type (human torpedoes)

Russian
Kalev
Ronis
Series I
Series II
Series III
Series IV
Series V
Series VI
Series X
Series XI
Series XII
Series XIII
Series XIV
Series XV
Series XVI

Others
Capitan O'Brien (Chile)
Daphne (Den)
Havmanden (Den)
Kalev (Estonia)
Saukko (Fin)
Vetehinen (Fin)
Vesikko (Fin)
Katsonis (Gr)
Proteus (Gr)
KXI-class (Hol)
KXIV-class (Hol)
O9-class
O12-class (Hol)
O16-class (Hol)
O19-class (Hol)
O21-class (Hol)
R-class (Peru)
Orzel (Pol)
Wilk (Pol)
Delfinul (Rom)
Marsuinul (Rom)
Requinul (Rom)
C-class (Sp)
D-class (Sp)
Delfinen (Swe)
Draken (Swe)
Neptun (Swe)
Sjöljonet (Swe)
U1-class (Swe)
Valen (Swe)
Sinsamudar (Thai)
AY-class (Tr)
Batiray (Tr)
Birindci Inönü (Tr)
Dumlupynar (Tr)
Gur (Tr)
Oruc Reis (Tr)
Sakarya (Tr)

Aircraft Carriers

American
Bogue
Casablanca
Commencement Bay
Essex
Independence
Langley
Lexington
Long Island
Midway
Ranger
Sangamon
Wasp
Yorktown

British
Activity
Ameer
Archer
Ark Royal
Attacker
Audacity
Avenger
Campania
Colossus
Courageous
Furious
Illustrious
Implacable
Indomitable
Pretoria Castle
Vindex

French
Béarn
Commandant Teste (seaplane tender)
Dixmunde (ex-HMS Biter)
Joffre (not completed)

German
Graf Zepplin (not completed)

Italian
Aquila (Conversion not completed)
Sparviero (Conversion not completed)

Japanese
Akagi
Chitose
Hiryu
Hosho
Ibuki
Junyo
Kaga
Kaiyo
Ryuho
Ryujo
Shinano
Shinyo
Shokaku
Soryu
Taiho
Taiyo
Unryu
Zuibo

Battleships

American
California
Iowa
Maryland
Nevada
New Mexico
North Carolina
Pennsylvania
South Dakota
Texas
Wyoming

British
Nelson
Lion
King George V
Queen Elizabeth
Royal Sovereign
Vanguard

French
Bretagne
Dunkerque
Richelieu

German
Bismarck
Scharnhorst

Italian
Andrea Doria
Cavour
Littorio

Japanese
Fuso
Ise
Kaga
Nagato
Yamato

Cruisers

American
Alaska
Atlanta
Baltimore
Brooklyn
Cleveland
New Orleans
Northampton
Pensacola
Portland
Wichita

British
Abdiel (Cruiser/minelayer)
Adventure (Cruiser/minelayer)
Arethusa
Bellona
Dido
Edinburgh
Exeter
Fiji
Gloucester
Kent
Leander
London
Norfolk
Perth
Southampton
Surrey
Swiftsure
York

French
Algérie
Duguay Trouin
Duquesnes
Emile Bertin
La Galissonnière
Jeanne d'Arc
Pluton
Suffren

German
Deutschland
Emden
Hipper
K-class
Leipzig
Nürnberg

Italian
Abruzzi
Bolzano
Cadorna
Capitani Romani
Costanzo Ciano
Duca d'Aosta
Giussano
MontecuccoliTrento
Zara

Japanese
Agano
Aoba
Furutaka
Katori
Mogami
Nachi
Oyodo
Sendai
Takao
Tone
Yubari

Russian
Profintern
Kirov
Krasnyi Kavkaz
Maxim Gorkiy

Others
De Ruyter (Hol)
Tromp (Hol)
Provincien (Hol)
Alfonso (Sp)
Canarias (Sp)
Gotland (Swe)
Tre Kronor (Swe)

Destroyers

American
Allen M Sumner
Bagley
Benham
Benson/Gleaves
Clemson (many transferred to Britain, 1940)
Farragut
Fletcher
Gearing
Gridley
Mahan
Porter
Sims
Somers
Wickes (many transferred to Britain, 1940)

British
A-class/B-class
Amazon
Ambuscade
Battle
C-class/D-class
E-class/F-class
G-class/H-class/I-class
J-class/K-class/N-class
L-class/M-class
O-class/P-class
Q-class/R-class
Tribal
S-class/T-class/U-class/V-class/W-class
Z-class/Ca-class
Ch-class/Co-class/Cr-class

French
Aigle
Bourrasque
Chacal
L'Adroit
Le Fantasque
Le Hardi
Mogador
Guépard
Vauquelin

German
1934 Type
1936 Type
1940/41 Type
1942 Type

Italian
Folgore
Freccia
Maestrale
Navigatori
Oriani
Sauro
Sella
Soldati
Turbine

Japanese
Akatsuki
Akitsuki
Asahio
Fubuki
Hatsuharu
Kagero
Mitsuki
Shimakaze
Shiratsuyu
Yugumo

Russian
Gnevnyi
Kiev (Flotilla Leaders)
Leningrad (Flotilla Leaders)
Ognevoi
Opytnyi
Storozhevoi
Tashkent (Flotilla Leaders)

Others
Vasilefs Georgios (Gr)
Ydra (Gr)
Tjerk Hiddes (Hol)
Van Galen (Hol)
Van Ghent (Hol)
Aalesund (Nor)
Grom (Pol)
Wicher (Pol)
Douro (Port)
Alava (Sp)
Churruca (Sp)
Ehrensköld (Swe)
Göteborg (Swe)
Mode (Swe)
Öland (Swe)
Psilander (Swe)
Klas Horn (Swe)
Romulus (Swe)
Visby (Swe)

Escorts

American
DET-class/FMR-class
GMT-class
TE-class
TEV-class/WGT-class

patrol frigates:
- Asheville/Tacoma

British
Hunt (Types 1-4)

frigates:
- Bay
- Captain (ex-US GMT & TE class)
- Loch
- River/Modified River

sloops:
- Bittern/Modified Bittern
- Black Swan/Modified Black Swan
- Bridgewater
- Egret
- Grimsby
- Hastings
- Hindustan
- Indus
- Shoreham

corvettes:
- Castle
- Flower/Modified Flower

patrol vessels:
- Kil-class
- Kingfisher
- Shearwater

German
F-class

Italian
Ariete
Ciclone
Pegaso
Spica

Japanese
Etorofu
Matsu
Mikura
Shimushu
Tachibana
Type D
Ukuru

Russian
ET1-class